MW01620359

MARC APPLETON

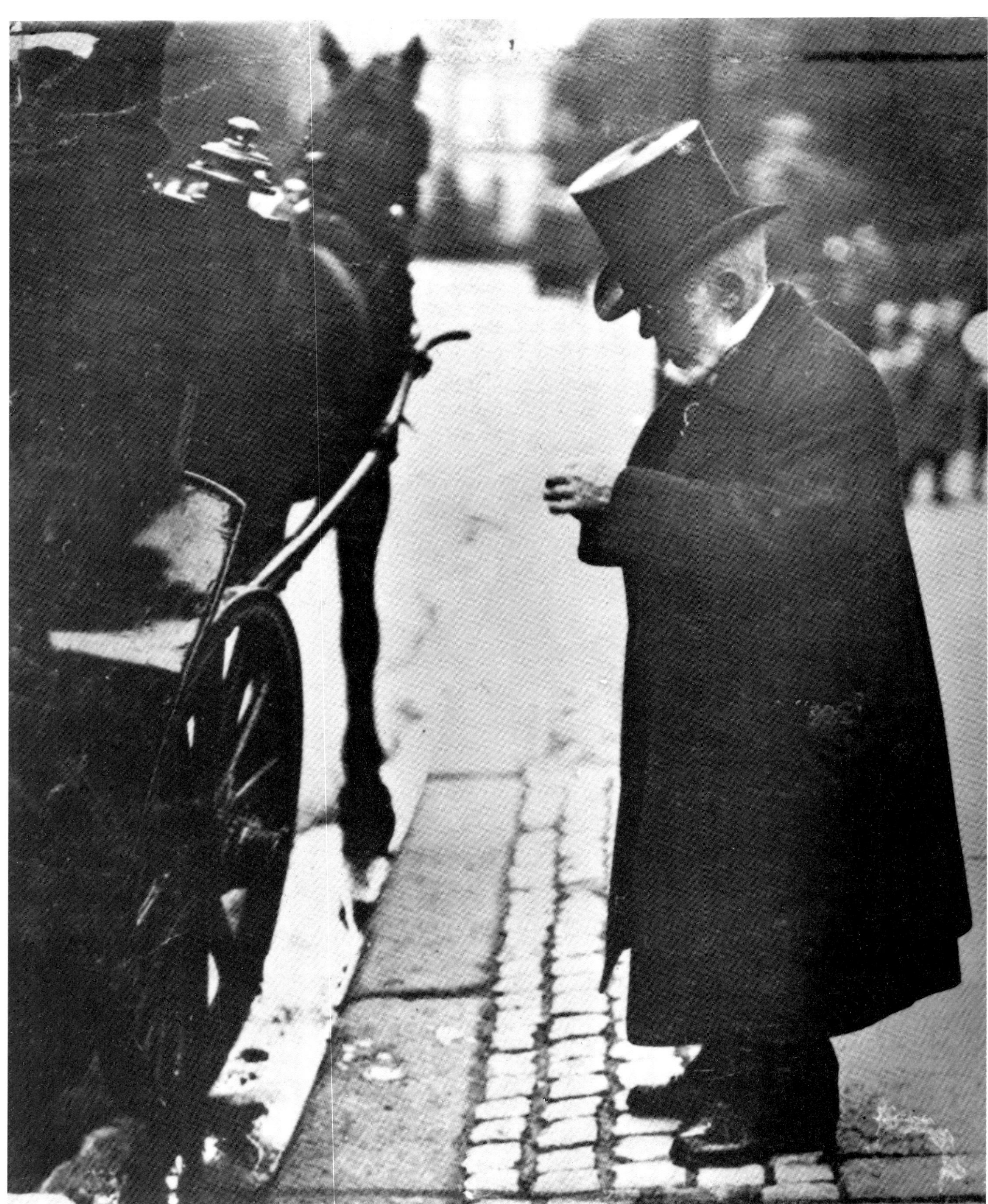

ADOLPH MENZEL
1815-1905

Between Romanticism and Impressionism

Edited by
Claude Keisch
Marie Ursula Riemann-Reyher

YALE UNIVERSITY PRESS
NEW HAVEN & LONDON
in association with
NATIONAL GALLERY OF ART, WASHINGTON

This exhibition was organised by the National Gallery of Art, Washington, the Stiftung Preussischer Kulturbesitz, Berlin, and the Réunion des Musées Nationaux/Musée d'Orsay, Paris

The exhibition is supported by an indemnity from the Federal Council on the Arts and the Humanities

Musée d'Orsay, Paris
15 April–28 July 1996

National Gallery of Art, Washington
15 September 1996–5 January 1997

Alte Nationalgalerie, Berlin
7 February–11 May 1997

Translated by Michael Cunningham, Judith Hayward, Simon Knight and Elizabeth MacDonald for First Edition Translations Ltd., Cambridge, England

Printed in Germany

Library of Congress Catalog Card Number 96-60916
ISBN 0-300-06954-5

A catalogue record for this book is available from the British Library

Frontispiece: Menzel paying a cab driver, 1903, anonymous photograph.

Curators of the exhibition

Claude Keisch
Curator at the Alte Nationalgalerie, Berlin

Marie Ursula Riemann-Reyher
Curator at the Kupferstichkabinett, Berlin

Henri Loyrette
Director of the Musée d'Orsay

Philip Conisbee
Curator at the National Gallery of Art, Washington

We would like to thank everybody who contributed to this exhibition, and especially:

Arturo Cuéllar, Benno Griebert, Heinrich Merz, Peter and Barbara Nathan, Lothar Schmidt, Alexander von Berswordt-Wallrabe

and all those people who wished to remain anonymous.

We would also like to thank those in charge of the following collections:

Austria

Vienna	Graphische Sammlung, Albertina
	Österreichische Galerie

United States of America

Pittsburgh	The Carnegie Museum of Art
San Francisco	The Fine Arts Museum of San Francisco

France

Strasbourg	Musée d'Art moderne et contemporain

Hungary

Budapest	Szépmüveszeti Muzeum

Poland

Poznan	Muzeum Narodowe w Poznaniu
Warsaw	Muzeum Narodowe w Warszawie

Federal Republic of Germany

Berlin	Staatliche Museen zu Berlin, Nationalgalerie
	Staatliche Museen zu Berlin, Kupferstichkabinett, Sammlung der Zeichnungen und Druckgraphik
Cologne	Wallraf-Richartz-Museum
Dresden	Staatliche Kunstsammlungen, Gemäldegalerie Neue Meister
Düsseldorf	Kunstmuseum Düsseldorf im Ehrenhof
Essen	Museum Folkwang
Frankfurt-am-Main	Kunsthandel Peter Fichter
	Städelsches Kunstinstitut
Hamburg	Hamburger Kunsthalle
Hechingen	Burg Hohenzollern
Karlsruhe	Staatliche Kunsthalle
Leipzig	Museum der bildenden Künste
Mainz	Landesmuseum Mainz
Munich	Bayerische Staatsgemäldesammlungen, Neue Pinakothek
Potsdam	Stiftung Preussische Schlösser und Gärten, Berlin-Brandenburg
Regensburg	Museum Ostdeutsche Galerie Regensburg

Czech Republic

Liberec	Oblastní Galerie

Russia

Moscow	Pushkin State Museum of Fine Arts

Switzerland

Winterthur	Museum Stiftung Oskar Reinhart Winterthur
Zurich	Kunsthaus Zürich

The members of the exhibition committee thank everybody who made a contribution, and in particular, Juliette Armand, Carole Robardey, Massimo Quendolo; the picture restorers Eveline Alex, Renate Fricke, Hans-Joachim Gronau and Roland Enge; Alexandra Le Faou for the Réunion des musées nationaux, and Inge Bodesohn-Vogel assisted by Brigitte Mirche, and Peter Dreesen assisted by Matias Möller, of the DuMont publishing house, who put tremendous hard work and energy into producing the catalogue; Peter-Klaus Schuster, who gave them constant advice and support; Christina Grummt, Andreas Heese, Anne Schmedding who helped them to prepare data sheets and the bibliography; Kathy Kerpan, Sabine Schlenker who prepared the index; Andrea Bärnreuther, Thomas Friedrich, Karin Schröder, Anne Schmedding who were responsible for iconographic research; Babette Warncke who helped to make the Menzel map of Berlin; plus many others who gave their assistance, information or ideas, and in particular: Helmut Börsch-Supan, Christian Bührle, Werner Busch, Claudia Czok, Cornelia Dörr, Susanne von Falckenhausen, Jörn Grabowski, Doris Grunchec, Thomas Habeck, Christoph Heilmann, Heike Höcherl, Christine Kühn, Ulf Küster, Gisold Lammel, Helmut R. Leppien, Franziska Lesák, Mario-Andreas von Lüttichau, Karl-Heinz Mehnert, Stefan Pucks, Gottfried Riemann, Eckhard Schaar, Annette Schlagenhauff, Werner Schmidt, Britta Schmidts, Bernd Schultz, Elke Schulze, Bernd Töpfer, Elisabeth Vogl, Joachim von Wartenberg, Annette Wellhausen, Angelika Wesenberg.

At the National Gallery of Art, we would like to thank Anne Bigley Robertson, Kate Haw, and Faya Causey.

Foreword

In France and the United States, Menzel's name and work were better known a hundred years ago than they are today. A few exhibitions, some articles (in France) and a handful of purchases by art lovers were quite enough to establish his reputation. He was then bundled aside by a movement that swallowed up the glories of the nineteenth century at the beginning of the twentieth, and he all but vanished from international view. Few of his works hang in museums, and his critical fortunes in Germany have not helped him to be rehabilitated abroad. He was unable to charm the public either as the Prussian bard, as he had been seen by some of his supporters, or as the German champion taking an illusory route towards Impressionism.

We now want to view Menzel afresh, and to highlight his true qualities. We therefore need to grasp the diversity of his work spread over seven decades, as well as the contradictory elements that are scattered here and there but which are nonetheless of intrinsic significance. In a monograph such as this, it is no longer acceptable to mimic past generations of art lovers and critics who were selective in their preferences, and so ignored whole chapters of his work. We have to comprehend the whole structure of Menzel's output, and understand its internal unity.

It would be pointless to revisit the 1905 exhibition that was organized in Berlin immediately after his death. The catalogue contained almost 7000 items, and anyway it is doubtful whether we could really make much of such an exercise today. It is much more instructive to consider his most important works. However brilliant they may have been, the Menzel exhibitions that have taken place since 1945 have been affected by the atmosphere bequeathed by World War II and later cemented by the Cold War. For instance, there were two parallel exhibitions held in Berlin in 1955. The one in Dahlem, which was directed by Irmgard Wirth, drew on West German collections, while, on Museum Island, Werner Schmidt was able to show a wide range of drawings; in those days, the USSR and even China were immensely enthusiastic about Menzel's drawings. Exhibitions of paintings and drawings were organized subsequently in Berlin, Kiel and Hamburg, and the Georg Schäfer Collection lent its many acquisitions; moreover, the huge stocks of drawings on Museum Island were the basis for further exhibitions in Vienna and Copenhagen and for a travelling exhibition in the United States.

Outside Germany, however, much less was known about Menzel's paintings. It is true that important works were seen at a number of exhibitions; these included Werner Hofmann's *Peinture allemande à l'époque du romantisme* (1976–77) and the *Symboles et réalités* (1984) exhibition, both in Paris, and in America *German Masters of the 19th Century* (1981), organized by Charles H. Moffett in collaboration with Stephan Waetzoldt in New York and Ontario. They accounted, however, for a very small number of works. The situation today is much more satisfactory, thanks to the revival of the great Menzel Collection in Berlin. The paintings in the Nationalgalerie and the huge collection of drawings in the Kupferstichkabinett now constitute a superb source of the artist's work.

This exhibition could never have taken place without the organizing skills and enthusiasm, going back many years, of Charles H. Moffett, then Curator of the National Gallery, who then joined forces with Françoise Cachin, then Director of the Musée d'Orsay, with a view to establishing a cooperative venture with Berlin and introducing Menzel to their respective publics. The energy and enthusiasm of Philip Conisbee, Curator of the National Gallery of Art, ensured that the project was brought to fruition in Washington. The plan received a boost, or so it seemed at the time, from the imminent decision to carry out a major works programme at the Nationalgalerie. The programme was wide-ranging, and forced the collection out of its home for some years; as a result, major loans became a possibility. The Kupferstichkabinett was involved in preparations for the exhibition from the outset. Other collections in Germany, Austria, Poland, Russia, Switzerland, the Czech Republic and the United States also gave the project their full support and contributed important works. Our only regret was that another project prevented the Georg Schäfer Collection in Euerbach from coming in with us. Credit for seeing the project through to its conclusion goes to Claude Keisch and Marie Ursula Riemann-Reyher; we owe them our very special thanks. Lastly, we acknowledge that the different sections of the exhibition vary for practical or other reasons related to preservation, or else because of a deliberate wish to emphasize a given aspect of Menzel's work; however, we very much hope that the exhibition will stimulate surprise and wonder at a unique, and in a way subversive, contribution to art of the nineteenth century, a period that still has many secrets waiting to be discovered.

Henri Loyrette
Musée d'Orsay
Paris

Earl A. Powell III
National Gallery of Art,
Washington

Alexander Dückers
Kupferstichkabinett,
Staatliche Museen zu Berlin

Dieter Honisch
Peter-Klaus Schuster
Nationalgalerie,
Staatliche Museen zu Berlin

Contents

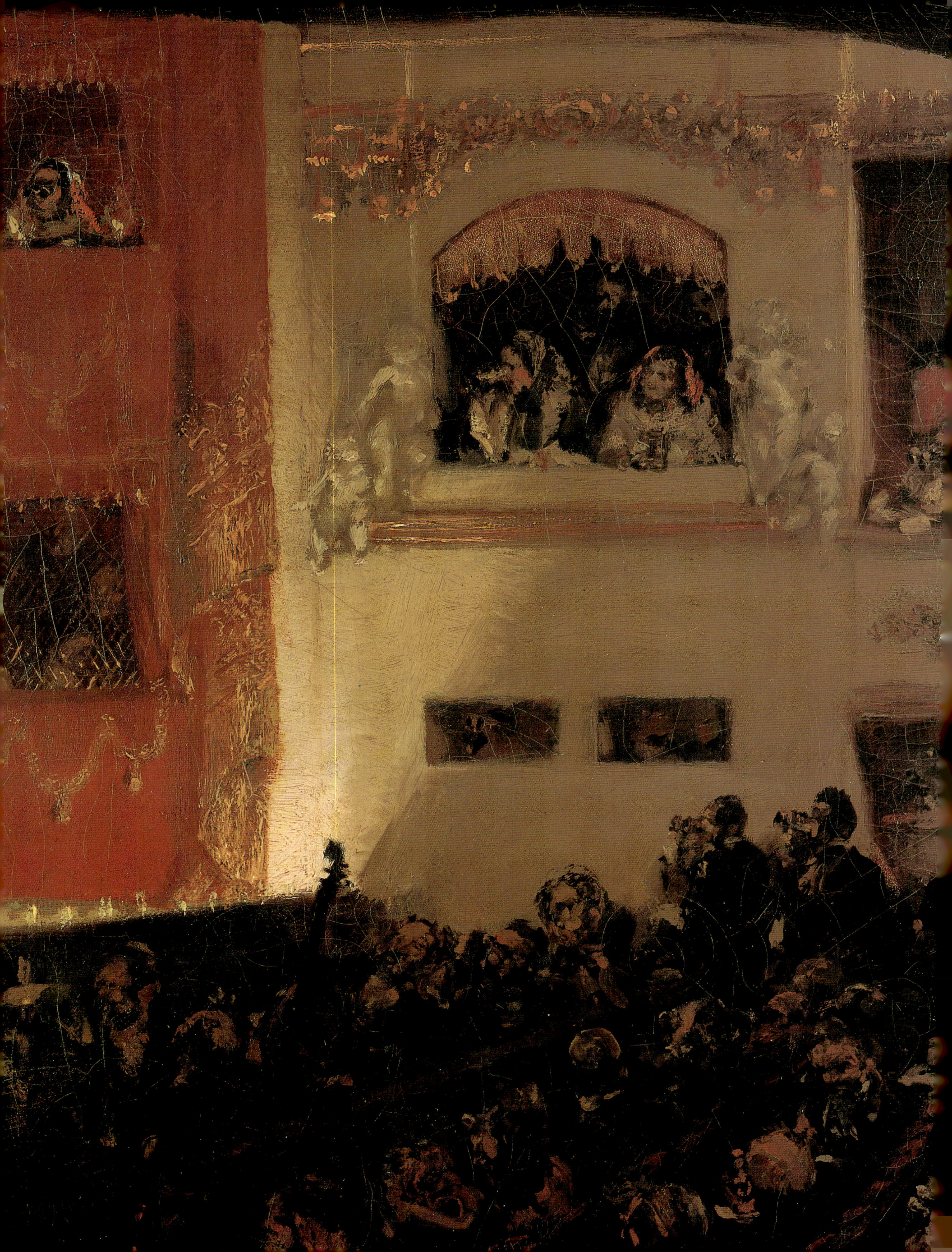

Menzel seen from America

Philip Conisbee

'The homes of the few rich people who are interested in art, or at least believe they must feign such an interest if they are to be regarded as "cultured", contain French works almost exclusively . . . The French are in fashion, and for the average American, Paris is the Mecca of the fine arts'[1]. Frederick C. Rieloff, the German consul in Saint Louis, was reporting back to his ambassador Theodor von Holleben in June 1902, a time when discussions were under way about how – and indeed whether – modern German art should be represented at the upcoming world's fair, the Louisiana Purchase Exposition, to be held in Saint Louis in 1904. The picture the consul painted of American taste was an accurate one. The heyday of American interest in contemporary German art was already long over. From the 1840s to the 1860s, many an American artist had gone to Munich or Düsseldorf to study; the Düsseldorf Gallery in New York exhibited the work of modern German artists from 1849 until its closure and the dispersal of its collections in 1866. Still in the 1870s some masterpieces of contemporary German painting, by Hans Thoma and Wilhelm Leibl, for example, entered American collections[2]. But these same decades from the 1850s to the 1870s saw the rise and eventual domination of Paris as the formative force in modern art and American taste: from Boston, New York, Philadelphia, and Chicago, artists and collectors flocked to Paris, while on their return trips they would have found French art dealers as their travelling companions aboard ship. In the minds of German officials in Berlin, such an international exhibition as that planned for Saint Louis had more to do with the bottom line of commerce, than with the cerebral realm of culture. But even in purely commercial terms Consul Rieloff was aware of the financial significance of the now well-established American taste for the painterly realism of the Barbizon school, and the more recently developed vogue for the light and colourful pleinairism of the Impressionists (Monet, through his skilful agent Paul Durand-Ruel, had been enjoying considerable American patronage for over a decade). To counter this identification of advanced yet fashionably palatable modern art with all that was French, Rieloff recommended the inclusion in the German pavilion at Saint Louis of works by the controversial young modernist painters known as the Berlin Secessionists, which included such figures as Max Liebermann, Max Slevogt and Lovis Corinth. These were painters who worked in a brushy style and depicted contemporary subject-matter, allying them, loosely speaking, with Impressionism.

The cultural politics surrounding the German contribution to the fine arts at the Saint Louis International Exposition has been expertly analysed elsewhere by Peter Paret[3]. Here it is sufficient to note that in the final event the consul's advice counted for nothing and the painters and sculptors chosen by the selection committee of the conservative-minded artists' organization in Berlin, the Kunstgenossenschaft, were on the whole a mediocre group of academics and realists. One of the few exceptions was Adolph Menzel. But most of these painters have long since been relegated to storage rooms, although occasionally a brave or foolish curator will bring one out in the forlorn hope of rehabilitating a nonetheless deservedly moth-eaten local reputation[4].

Before sending several works to Saint Louis in 1904, Menzel had exhibited in the United States already, at the 1893 World's Fair in Chicago (including cat. 203 in the present exhibition). But his was hardly a household name in America, even in artistic circles. In fact it is only quite recently that Menzel's work has attracted more than purely academic interest in the United States: he was represented in the exhibition German Masters of the 19th Century in New York in 1981, and by a travelling exhibition of his drawings, from East Berlin as it was at the time, in 1990–1[5]. Menzel has been the focus of considerable academic attention in the last decade or so, although as much for his complex and ambivalent relationship with the political world of Wilhelmine Prussia, as for the qualities of his art. He was an extraordinarily prolific draughtsman, and partly because of the availability of his characteristic and easily recognizable drawings, he is popular with a small but dedicated band of drawing dealers and collectors in this country and in Europe. Thus it is probably accurate to say that Menzel's name means little more to many an American museum visitor than those of the forgotten academic mediocrities with whom he shared the German pavilion at Saint Louis over ninety years ago. But we hope that this will change

Fig. 1. *The Théâtre du Gymnase* (cat. 80), 1856, oil, Berlin, Nationalgalerie, detail

when the exhibition is mounted in Washington, and its catalogue becomes available as the only book in English on this great artist. Menzel's lack of reputation abroad always comes as a shock to colleagues and friends in Germany, where he is rightly considered their greatest painter of the second half of the nineteenth century. However, it is sad but true that Menzel is not well known outside his native land. The focus of much of his art is on Berlin and Prussia, which may have isolated him from wider critical attention, and there are no major examples of his painting to be seen outside German-speaking countries: only two paintings in this exhibition come from American institutions (cat. 91, 126).

The greatest single concentration of Menzel's works is in the museums of Berlin, above all in the happily now reunited collections of the Nationalgalerie and its Kupferstichkabinett. In a sense this exhibition is a celebration of that reunification, although we should also acknowledge the generous loans from elsewhere. But when the exhibition is over, it will still only be by visiting Berlin that one will be able to form a satisfying impression of Menzel's art. These factors, combined with the nationalistic prejudices engendered by the tragic history of Germany from shortly after Menzel's day and into our own era (and we should not neglect the passions that can still be aroused by the Franco-Prussian War of 1870!), have not encouraged the international recognition that his art deserves.

In 1904 Menzel was eighty-nine years old, with less than a year to live. Covered with honours, above all at home but also in Britain and France – where, since his eightieth birthday in 1895, he had been a corresponding member respectively of the Royal Academy in London and of the Académie des Beaux-Arts in Paris – he was venerated as something of a living old master. A few works by Menzel had been exhibited in Paris in 1855, 1867, 1878, and in 1889, while in 1885 a modest retrospective was held there. In London it was not until 1903 that he had his own exhibition, at the French Gallery in Pall Mall. In the Berlin of Emperor William II at the turn of the nineteenth and twentieth centuries, Menzel's bourgeois realism was still regarded in official circles as the best of modern German art: his *Departure of King William I for the Army* (cat. 134), painted in 1871, was presumably selected for exhibition in Saint Louis because it presented a patriotic image of the former king and a relatively benign one of Prussian military ambition; its irony, so subtly analysed by Claude Keisch in this catalogue, was not apparent. *The Iron Rolling Mill* (cat. 160), a rare representation of the industrial world of the nineteenth century in the Saint Louis exhibition, had a definite air of modernity in its subject-matter: but it also had something of the safe status of a classic, with its heroic workers in a modern history painting, and executed as it was some thirty years before, in 1875.

Fig. 2. Edgar Degas, *Two Caricatures (Napoleon III and Bismarck?)*, pencil, Paris, Bibliothèque Nationale (notebook 31, 1878/9, p. 84)

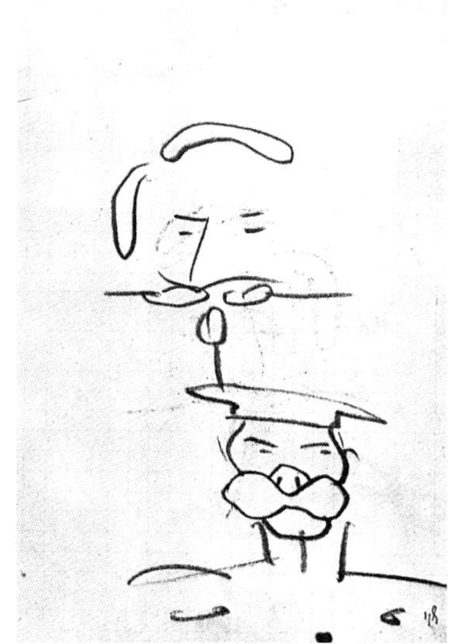

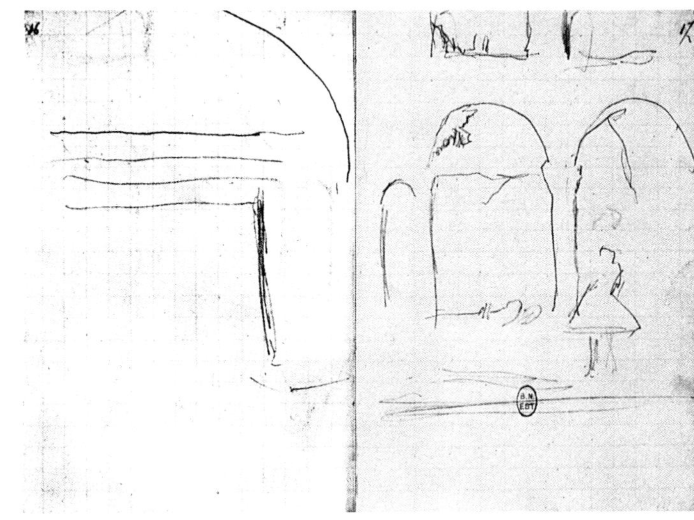

Fig. 3. Edgar Degas, *Sketch of the Ballet Robert le Diable*, pencil, Paris, Bibliothèque Nationale (notebook 1868–75).

It was most likely this last-mentioned heroic image of the modern world that stimulated what turned out, alas, to be a missed opportunity for Menzel and for the United States. He had been invited to cross the Atlantic in 1883, to undertake a monumental picture of industrial progress in North America: a grand, ceremonial painting of the opening of the Northern Pacific Railroad. The circumstances of this commission and Menzel's decision not to accept it have been thoroughly studied by Claude Keisch elsewhere, and need not be dwelt upon in detail

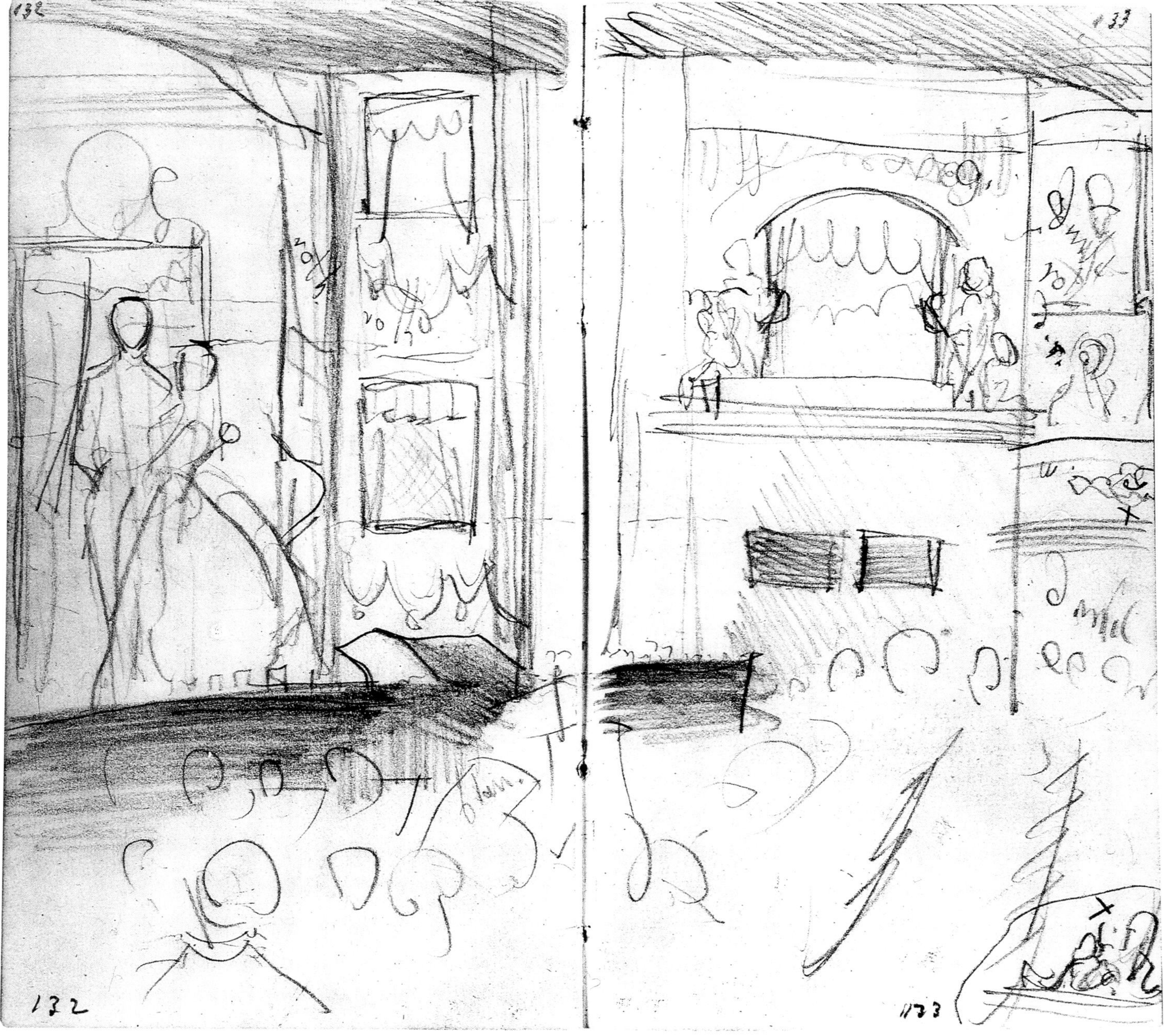

Fig. 4. *Sketch for The Théâtre du Gymnase*, 1855, pencil, Berlin, Kupferstichkabinett (sketchbook 14, pp. 132–3)

here[6]. Menzel can hardly have been chosen for any reputation as an artist in the United States, but rather because the railroad was promoted by an entrepreneur of German descent and had attracted German investors: to them, Menzel was a name to reckon with. We can imagine the scene as Menzel might have painted it: giant, snorting engines, spouting smoke and steam; a grandstand, decked with United States, German and British flags; crowds of morning-coated and crinolined folk, Americans and invited European investors, waving top hats and fluttering handkerchiefs; below them a mêlée of workers, many of them Chinese and others black, and a few colourful native Americans to add an exotic note of the Wild West; all of them shouting a loud huzzah, as the last spike, presented by Chief Iron Bull, is hammered in; and all set against the spectacular backdrop of the Rocky Mountains, with an overarching blue sky, flecked with white clouds.

It was as a modern history painter that Menzel was best known in his day – in works such as the two

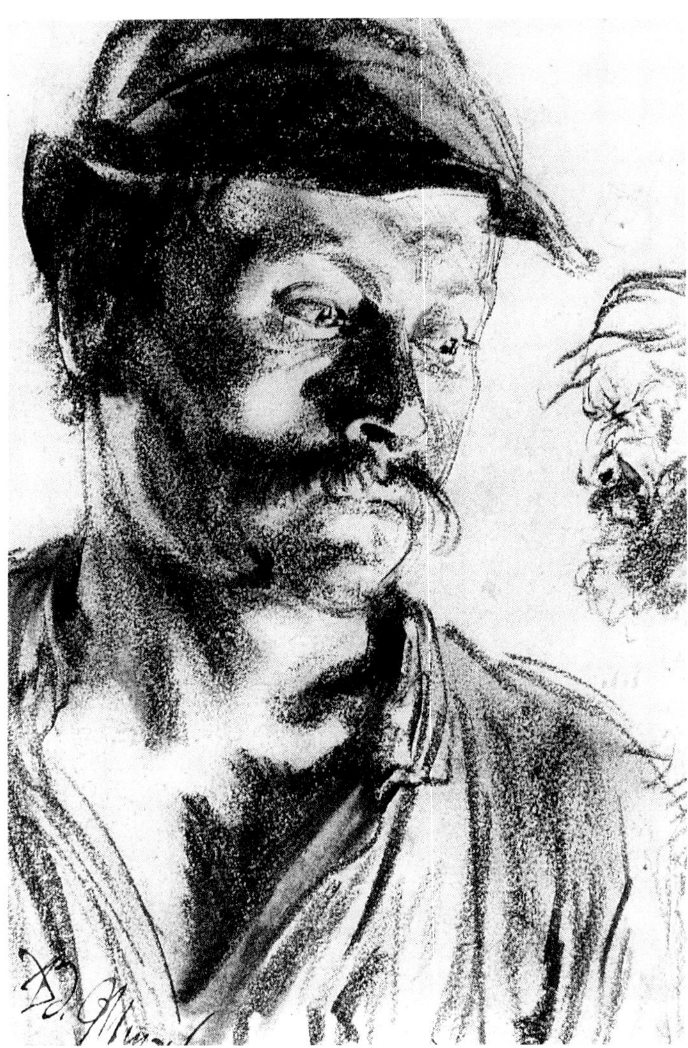

Fig 5. *Head of a Workman*, 1875, pencil, private collection

mentioned above, which were to be sent to Saint Louis in 1904, or in his mural-scale *The Coronation of William I* of 1862 (Potsdam, Neues Palais; fig. 121), for example. Earlier in his career, in the 1850s, Menzel had undertaken on his own initiative a series of paintings devoted to the life of the eighteenth-century Prussian monarch Frederick II. They are Menzel's personal brand of Romantic history painting, evoking a past he idealized and rendered with extraordinary conviction, based as they are on meticulous historical study. Menzel's historicism extended to a careful scrutiny of the works of Frederick's favourite French painter, Antoine Watteau, whose style is cunningly assimilated into Menzel's own in scenes such as *The Flute Concert of Frederick the Great at Sanssouci* (cat. 56). The Frederick cycle was not a critical or commercial success, however, because Menzel's nostalgia for the social and political ideals of Enlightenment Prussia had little contemporary resonance, and because the scrupulous historicism of his style did not conform to the dominant Nazarene idealism of Peter Cornelius and Julius Schnorr von Carolsfeld. Menzel therefore turned his attention more towards the Berlin of his own day.

It is for his modernism, brilliantly discussed by Peter-Klaus Schuster in his essay for this catalogue, that Menzel is most admired in our day. Most visitors to the exhibition in Washington will continue to associate Menzel's modernism – those aspects of his work which are most accessible to a late twentieth-century audience – with the modernist tradition which for us emanates from late nineteenth-century French art. This has every historical justification, not least because Menzel had ardent admirers among the French avant-garde: Edgar Degas was among them, for example, and probably met Menzel through their mutual friend Alfred Stevens on one of Menzel's visits to Paris in 1867 and 1868. Henri Loyrette, in his prefatory remarks to the French edition of this catalogue, has pointed out the parallels in the two artists' interest in the theatre[7]. Menzel's painting *The Théâtre du Gymnase* (fig. 1; cat. 80) – with its vivid sense of actuality conveyed by its oblique and somewhat cropped viewpoint, its lively handling, and equal attention to audience, orchestra pit, and stage – makes one think of the French theatrical and opera scenes of Daumier and Degas. Both Menzel and Degas made rapid sketchbook notations for future paintings, and Menzel's sketch made at the Théâtre du Gymnase in Paris in 1855 (fig. 4), indicating the architecture, audience and performers, along with a few colour notes, vividly captures the essence of the scene. Such a drawing is comparable with Degas' minimal notations for the ballet *Robert le Diable* (fig. 3), made just a few years later. In general both artists had a passion for drawing, and were comparably penetrating, amusing, or even cruel in their observations, always curious, sometimes prying, never banal. Perhaps Degas' finest and most flattering compliment was to purchase a drawing of a worker by Menzel (fig. 5), a vivid study for *The Iron Rolling Mill*, which he acquired at the sale of his late friend Edmond Duranty's estate in January 1881. Here, Duranty and Degas as collectors already reflect the modern preference for Menzel's drawings and oil sketches, over the more elaborate finished works. Degas paid his own painterly homage to the German by making a free – and, one has to say, much more sketchy and 'impressionist' – copy (cat. 168) of Menzel's *Supper at the Ball* (cat. 167). Menzel the observer of court life in Berlin may at first sight seem to have less modern aesthetic appeal than Degas the interpreter of Menzel. But look again at Menzel's *Supper at the Ball*: not only is it a beautifully orchestrated crowd scene and a painterly *tour-de-force*, but also ironical, witty and wry in its penetrating analysis of such a social gathering.

The critic Duranty had been a great champion of the Impressionists, notably in his celebrated essay 'The New Painting' (1876), wherein he defined in the clearest terms their Baudelairean ambitions as painters of modern urban life[8]. The moment of Duranty's untimely death at the end of 1880 fell between the publication of the two parts of a brilliant appreciation of Menzel's art in the *Gazette des Beaux-Arts*. This was the first extended critical evaluation of Menzel's art in any language, and it was bold of the French writer to sing the praises of the German artist so soon after the Franco-Prussian War and the terrible seige of Paris in 1870, a memory that still festered in the mind of many a Frenchman. At first it may seem surprising that Duranty admired the artist he described as 'a little man with glasses, with an intense look, talking little, making rapid sketches and enjoying a drink of champagne'[9]. This is certainly the same rather unappealing figure we notice lurking in the wings, quietly observing, in one of Anton von Werner's depictions of the rituals of court life (fig. 6). However, often echoing his own pages in praise of the modernity of the young Impressionists a few years before, Duranty singled out for admiration Menzel's singular powers of observation, his uncompromising quest for truth, his infallibility in grasping the essence of nature, and his powerful ability to evoke the past in his historical works, based on the voracious gathering of empirical data. Above all Duranty admired the draughtsman in Menzel (and we have seen that the critic owned a marvellous drawing), recognizing his incredible facility, but not accusing him, as some had done, of a rather mechanical approach. Duranty saw that 'he goes right to nature, wherever it is; it lures him everywhere'[10]. Yet for all that Menzel searched out nature and drew it indefatigably; he always infused it with the breath of life. Even when Menzel drew suits of armour, which he saw being removed from a dusty guard room in the royal palace in Berlin in order to create studio space for him to paint the huge *Coronation of William I* in 1862: 'He had an exactitude and an extraordinary precision in drawing all those things from the past, he measured a braid or a button with a compass if he needed to. In this way, M. Menzel has acquired such an intimate knowledge that he can give life to this previously inanimate debris. He put living men into those uniforms and empty suits of armour; those breast-plates or those sleeves, which just now hung tarnished, flat, and shapeless, those gaping and caved-in visors, those armlets with stiff joints, all take on his movements, his gestures, his lustre, his spirit, as if in response to the spell of a magician'[11]. For the meticulous artist, looking around is never a sterile waste of time, because the 'intoxication with the expressive detail' is united with the 'intoxication of light, in all its play, all its effects, according to all its sources'.

On this same fine page of Duranty's prose occurs the famous phrase, difficult to translate satisfactorily into English, but happily used for a subtitle to the Parisian showing of the present exhibition: 'He sees the world, past or present, as it is, without ever distorting it, or altering it, rendering it full of life by gesture, movement, expression, implacable exactitude. While he is perfectly well, he is neurotic about the truth [il a "*la névrose du vrai*"]. You feel a nervous shock in his works, the frisson he experiences before nature'[12].

We can sense this relentless, penetrating, passionate regard throughout Menzel's drawings in this exhibition: even in his drawings of the trivia of everyday life, such as an unmade bed (cat. 17), a plate of oysters (cat. 143), clouds (cat. 171), rain running down a street (cat. 192), shadows on a wall (cat. 197), or a study of a bicycle (cat. 198). This aesthetic elevation of the ordinary into the stuff of art is a strong aspect of Menzel's appeal in our time.

Another of Menzel's contemporary admirers was Jules Laforgue, himself one of the creators of our modern sensibility that finds poetry in the banal and the commonplace, and who expressed it in his own demotic,

Fig. 6. Anton von Werner, *Crown Prince Frederick William at a Court Ball in 1878*, 1895, oil, Berlin, Nationalgalerie

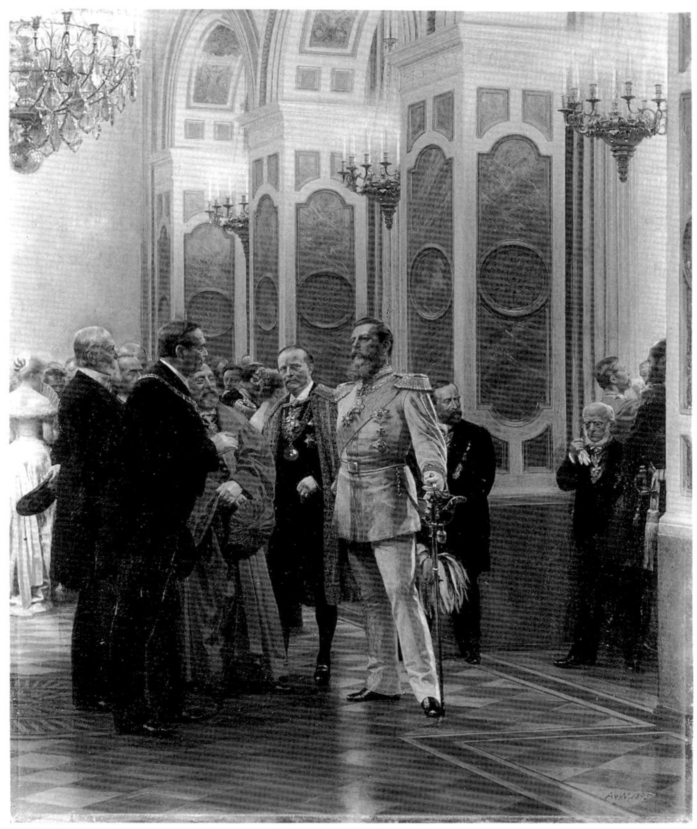

at one time shockingly slangy, poetic language. Laforgue inherited from Baudelaire, one of his literary mentors, the conviction that the modern artist should be committed to the uncompromising observation of the life of his own time; so he had no trouble in identifying – nor in identifying *with* – this modernist aspect of Menzel's work. Laforgue became acquainted with the art of Menzel while holding a court appointment as French reader to the Empress Augusta in Berlin from 1881 to 1886. The critical notices Laforgue sent to the *Gazette des Beaux-Arts* in 1884 and the *Chronique des arts et de la curiosité* in 1886 on the occasions of two exhibitions of Menzel's work in Berlin, make interesting counterparts to his contemporaneous book (published in full only posthumously, however), *Berlin, la cour et la ville*[13], which is full of fascinating and often Menzel-like observations and vignettes of life in Berlin and in court circles during the 1880s. Laforgue called Menzel 'the greatest painter in Germany', and, like Duranty, admired especially his merciless, penetrating powers of observation: 'A myopic eye, perfectly healthy and sober, perceiving life neither tender nor moved, but at all times insisting on presenting it as he feels it, patiently, through simple honesty, without pompous ado; an ironic eye, retrenched in its misanthropy behind its glasses . . . an eye with redoubtable powers of penetration, of an irresistible artist, of acute clairvoyance'[14].

A year after the modest presentation of Menzel's art at the Saint Louis exhibition, and a few months after his death in 1905, the Nationalgalerie in Berlin mounted an enormous memorial exhibition, with a monumental catalogue by its director, Hugo von Tschudi. The memorial catalogue included almost seven thousand works (!), paintings, pastels, gouaches, and above all drawings, the great bulk of them from the artist's estate, which the Nationalgalerie succeeded in acquiring in the following year. It was Tschudi, above all, himself one of the first directors of a German museum to collect and promote the modern French art of the Impressionists and Post-Impressionists, who saw in Menzel's art an affinity with and an anticipation of their aesthetic. Tschudi's modernist approach to Menzel focused on the artist's private, unexhibited works: those scenes of bourgeois life in Berlin, and above all of the life of the artist's own family circle and friends, *intimiste* in feeling and often quite sketchily handled, that have the most affinity with and indeed seem to anticipate by a decade or two the early Impressionism of Monet, or even to look forward to the Nabi interiors of Vuillard in the 1890s. Similarly, Tschudi admired the informal landscapes Menzel painted in and around Berlin in the 1840s and 1850s, and which can be read as links in the chain of a modern tradition of naturalistic, understated and unhieratic landscape painting. Menzel first encountered such things in some modest works by John Constable (see fig. 72), which he was able to admire in an exhibition in Berlin in 1839. Does it stretch the notion of this tradition too much to connect it with Tschudi's prescient acquisition for the Nationalgalerie as early as 1897 of Cézanne's *Mill on the Couleuvre at Pontoise*? This discovery of the early, private works of Menzel, revealing him in Tschudi's estimation to be a precursor of modern – that is to say in Tschudi's day 'Impressionist' – art is the justification of our subtitle for the Washington presentation of this exhibition: 'Between Romanticism and Impressionism'. Not unlike the polarities of Menzel's art suggested by Françoise Forster-Hahn in her essay for this catalogue, it brackets Menzel's art between the Romantic historicism of his Frederick cycle – whose own beauties we hope the exhibition will convincingly reveal – and what we still recognize as the first stirrings of modern art.

1. Quoted in Paret, 1980, p. 123.
2. See for example German works with American provenances acquired by Oscar Reinhart after the First World war, such as Hans Thoma's *The Artist's Mother in an Attic Room*, 1871, or Wilhelm Leibl's *Village Politicians*, 1877, in exhib. cat. Berlin, 1993, nos. 93, 99; this exhibition was also presented in Los Angeles and New York, 1992–3, with an English edition of the catalogue. American collecting of German art in the nineteenth century is virtually unstudied, as is the relationship between German and American art in the same period.
3. See Paret, 1980, ch. 4, 'German Impressionism and the conflict over art at Saint Louis', pp. 92–155.
4. Among the 218 German painters who exhibited at Saint Louis in 1904, barely more than a dozen are remembered today; perhaps the best remembered are Anselm Feuerbach, Wilhelm Leibl and Hans von Marées.
5. See exhib. cat. New York, 1981 and New York, 1990. Several masterpieces by Menzel were also included in the travelling exhibition of selections from the Oskar Reinhart Foundation, Winterthur, presented in Los Angeles and New York, 1992–3: see exhib. cat. Berlin, 1993. nos. 64–72.
6. Claude Keisch, 'Menzel and America: a missed encounter, an unpainted picture', in exhib. cat. New York, 1990, p. 33–9.
7. My comments on Menzel and Degas are freely adapted from Henri Loyrette's prefatory essay, 'Menzel à Paris' in the French edition of this catalogue, pp. 13–18, with his permission.
8. See Duranty's essay 'La Nouvelle Peinture, à propos du groupe d'artistes qui expose dans les galeries Durand-Ruel', Paris, 1876, reprd. in exhib. cat. Washington/San Francisco, 1986, pp. 477-80.
9. Duranty, 1880 II, p.123; Duranty is recalling a description of Menzel by the painter Edouard Brandon (a friend of Degas), who met Menzel at a ball in Berlin.
10. Duranty, 1880 I, p. 206.
11. Duranty, 1880 I, p. 214.
12. Duranty, 1880 II, p. 110.
13. Jules Laforgue, *Berlin, la cour at la ville*, Paris, 1922, and later eds.; for a modern German ed., see Laforgue, 1990.
14. Laforgue, 1886, p. 82.

Fig. 7. Menzel in the street, 1905, anonymous photograph

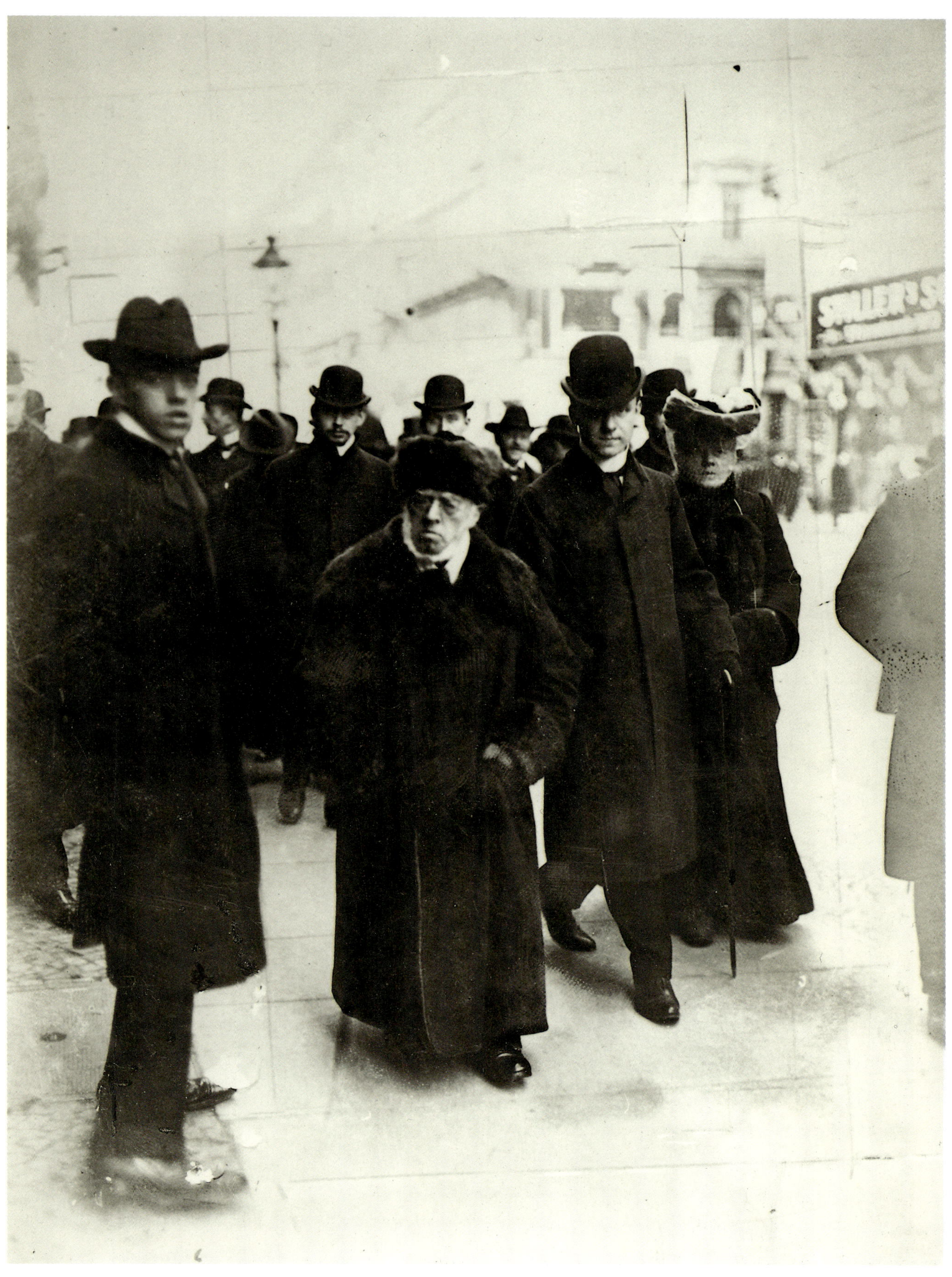

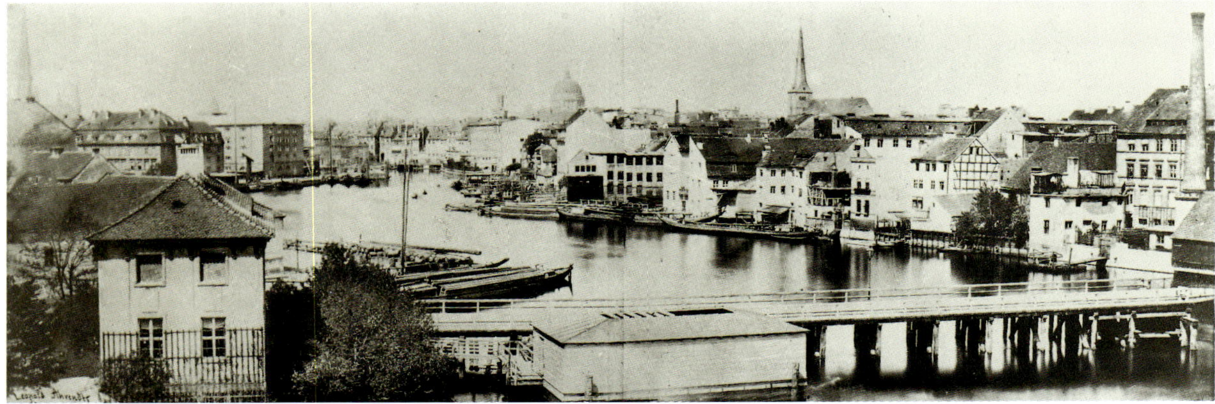

Fig. 8. View of the Waisenbrücke, looking towards the centre of old Berlin, 1885, photograph by Leopold Ahrends

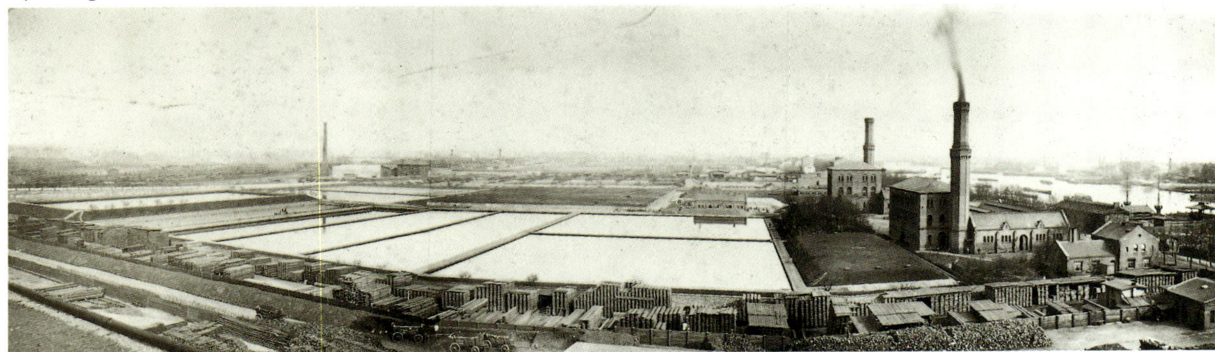

Fig. 9. The municipal waterworks near the Oberbaumbrücke, *c.* 1875, anonymous photograph

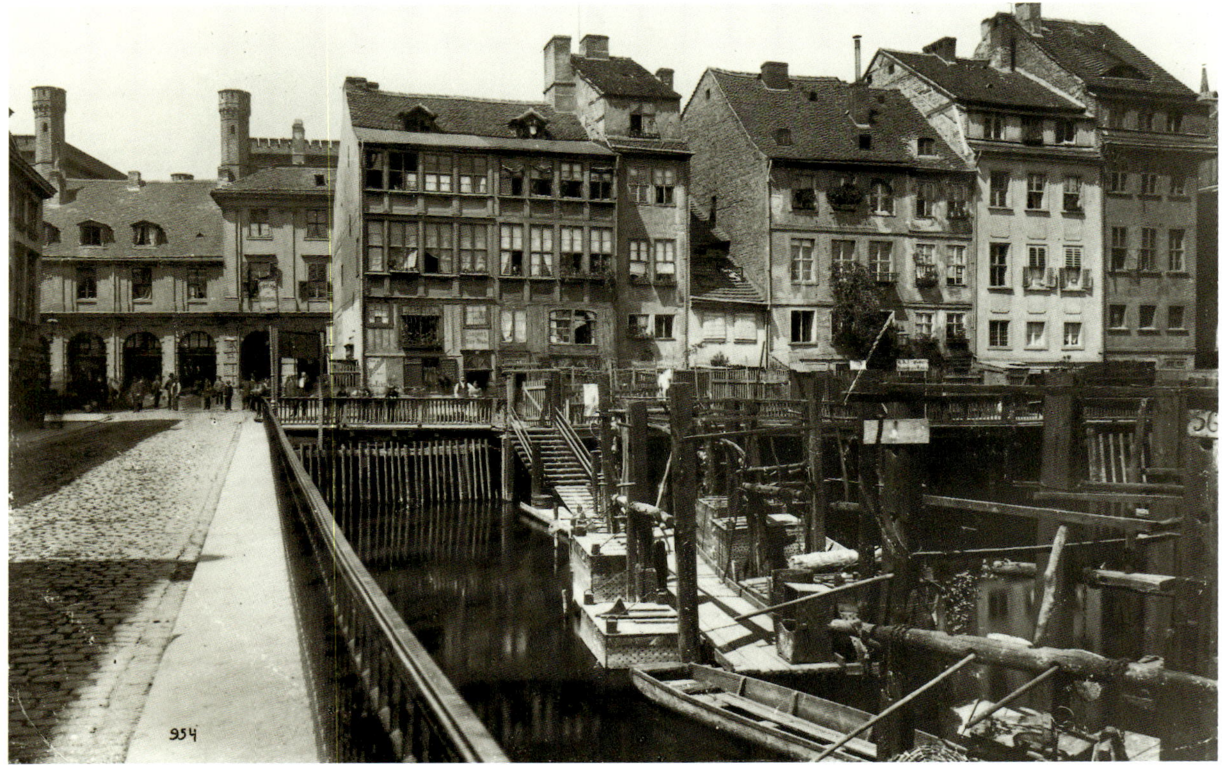

Fig. 10. The Mühlendamm and the Fischerbrücke, *c.* 1890, photograph by F. Albert Schwartz

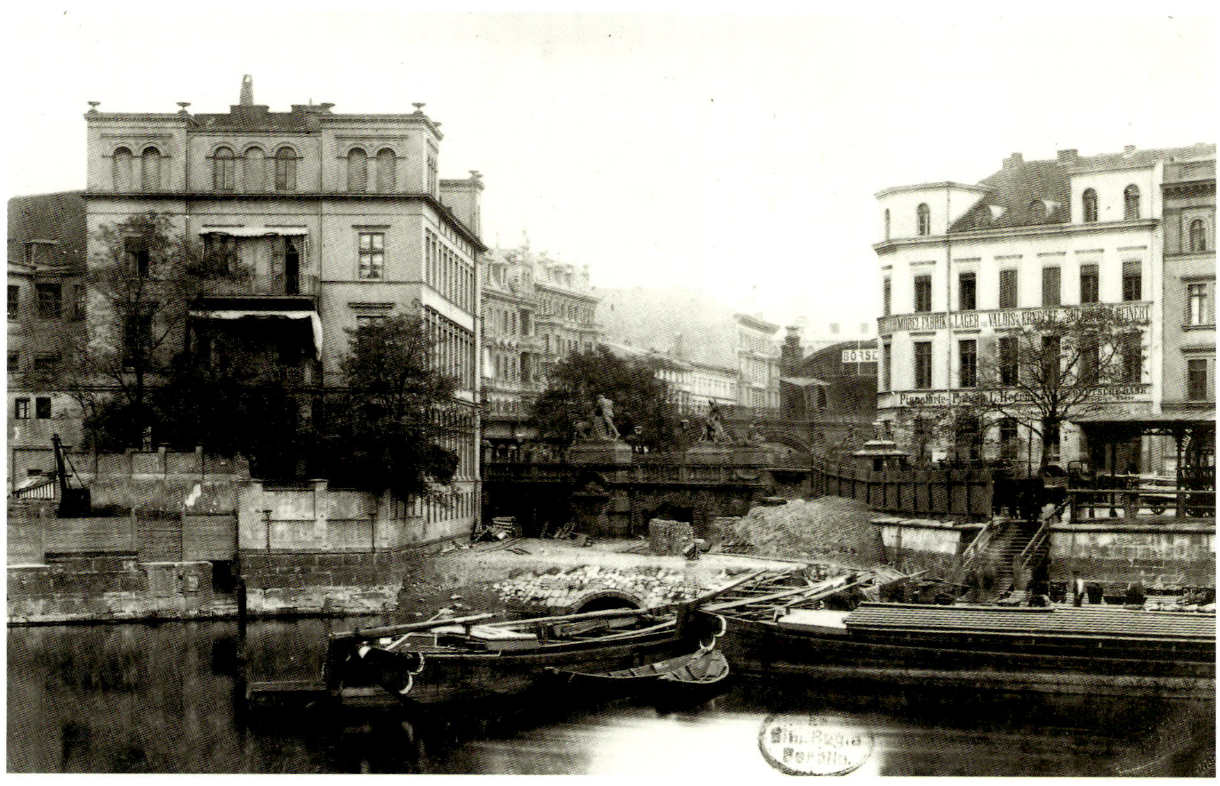

Fig. 11. The Festungsgraben discharging into the Spree opposite the Museum Island before the construction of the municipal railway, 1876-7, anonymous photograph

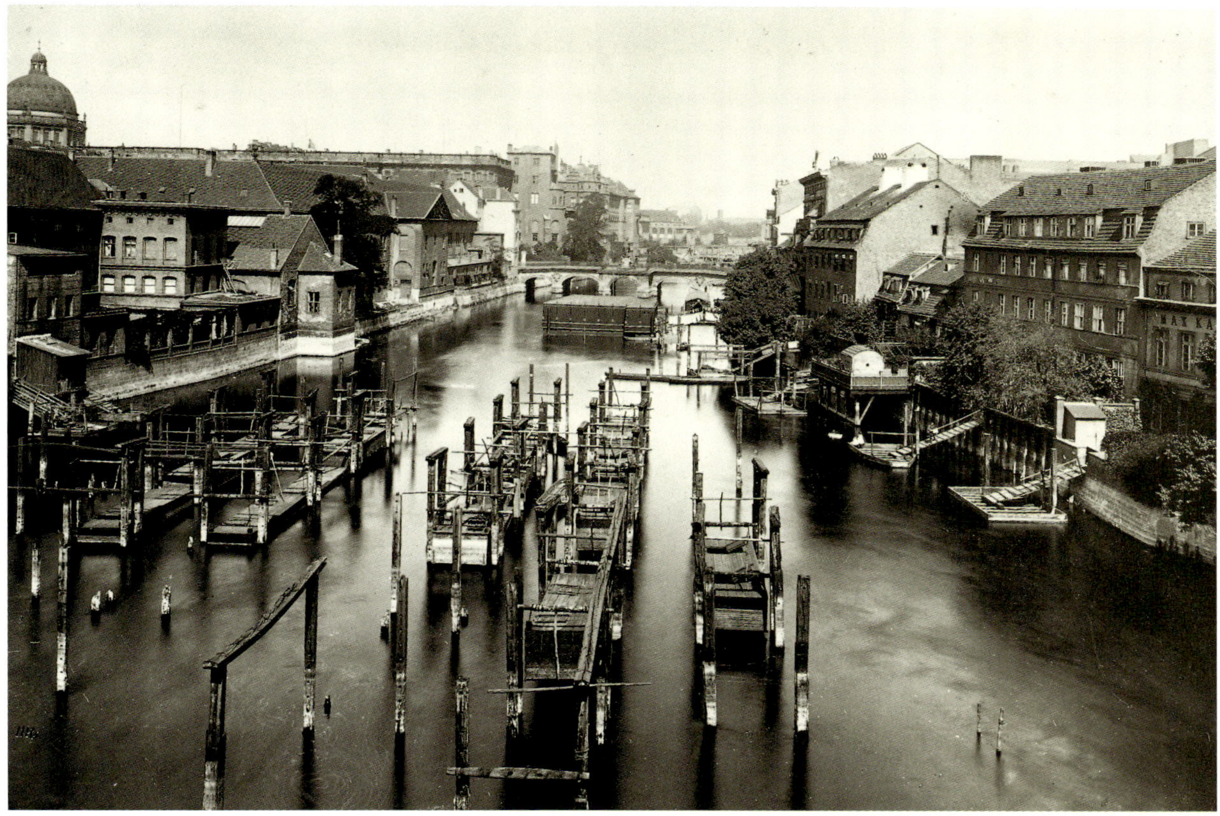

Fig. 12. View of the Mühlendamm looking towards the Kurfürstenbrücke and the royal palace, 1888, photograph by F.

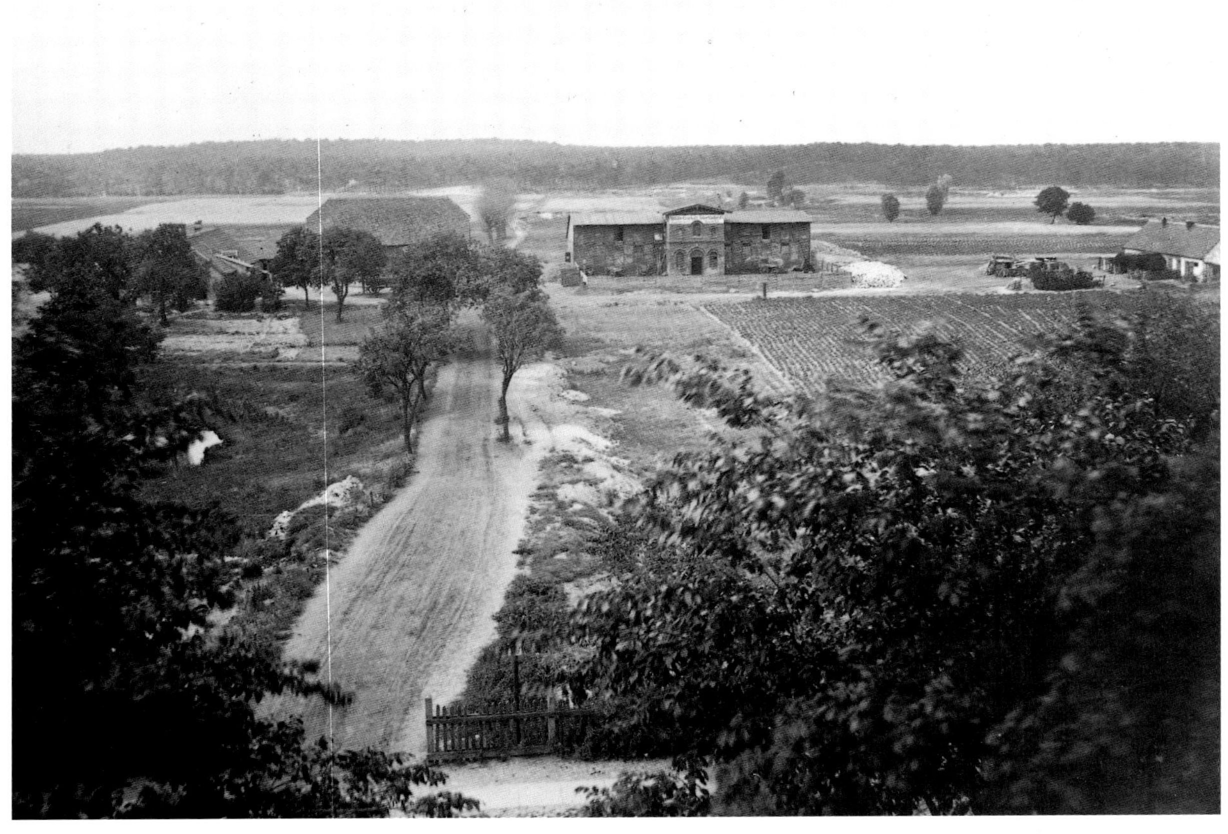

Fig. 13. The Müllerstrasse, still outside the city limits, 1893, photograph by Georg Bartels

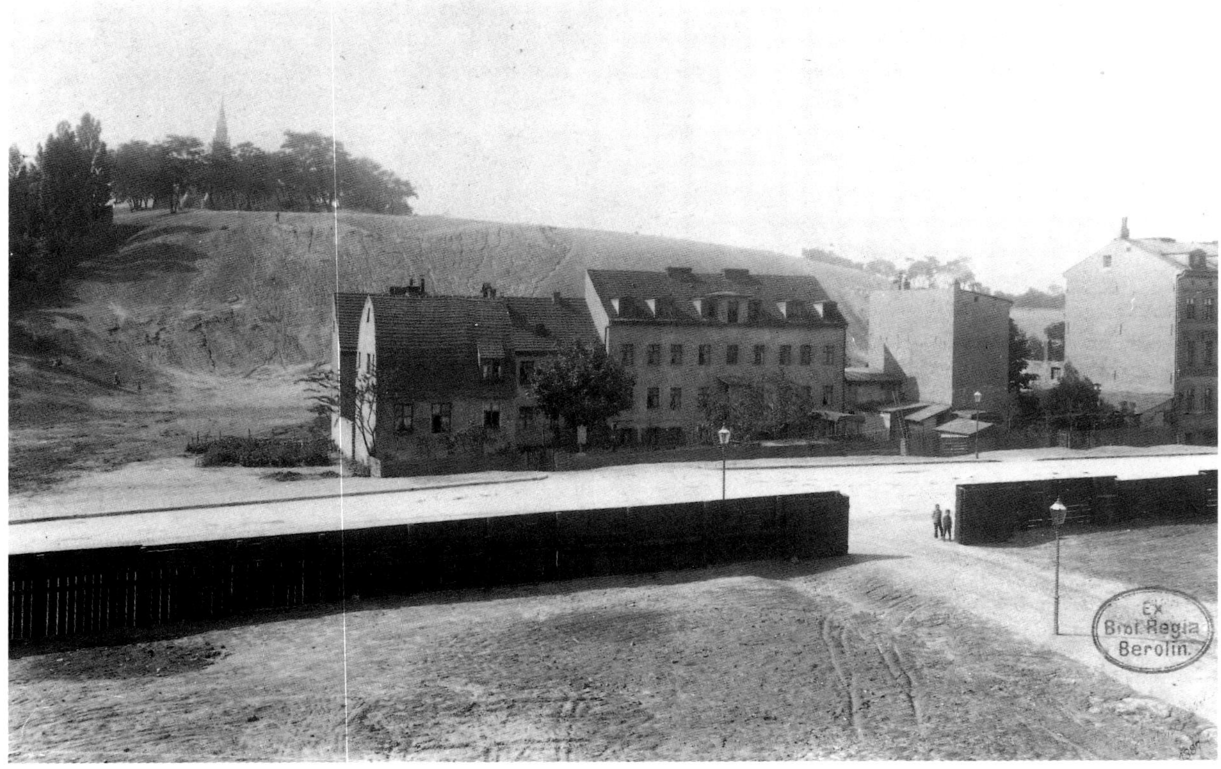

Fig. 14. View of the Kreuzberg, *c.* 1865, photograph by F. Albert Schwartz

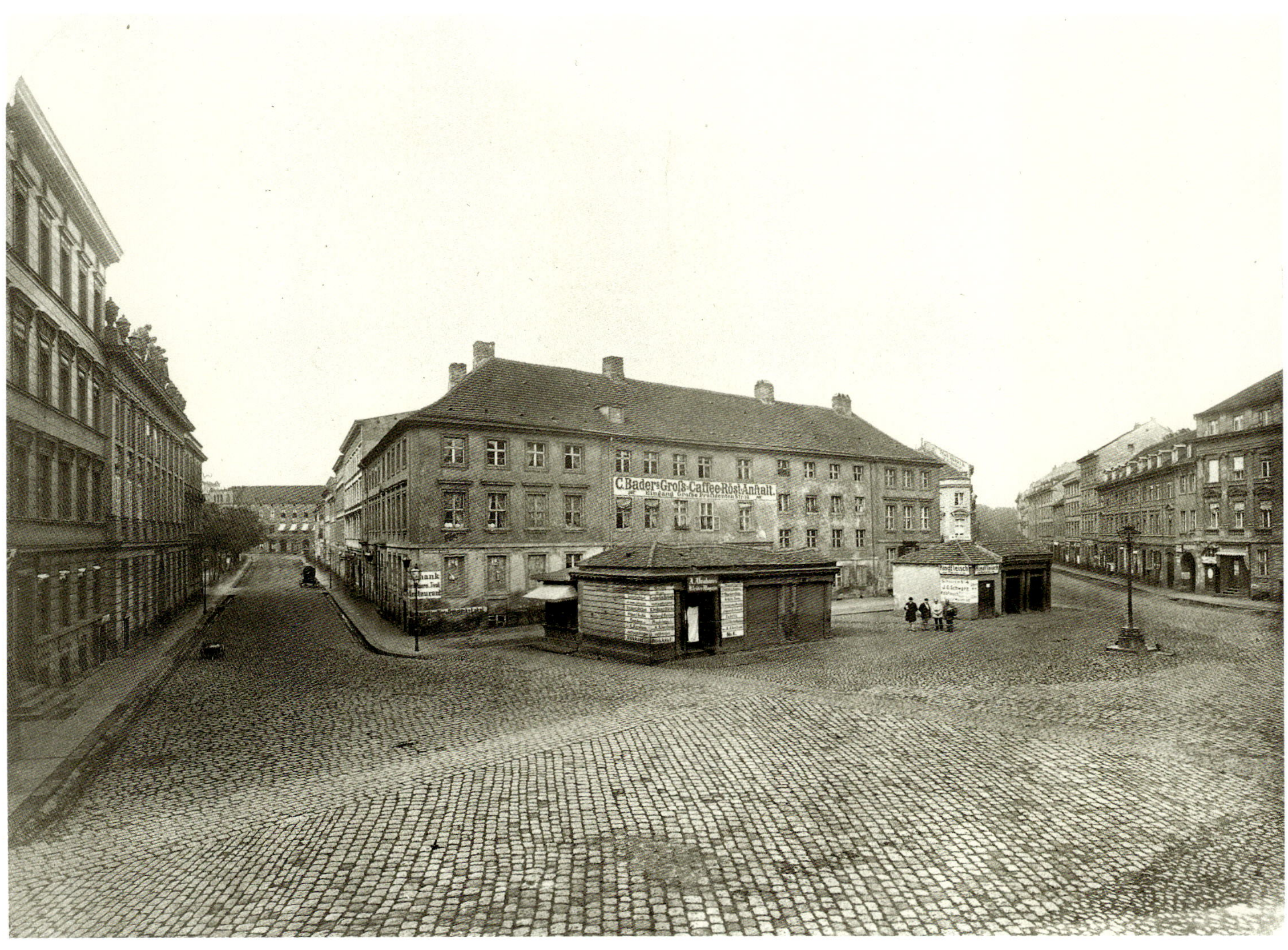

Fig. 15. Hackescher Markt square, *c.* 1870–80, anonymous photograph

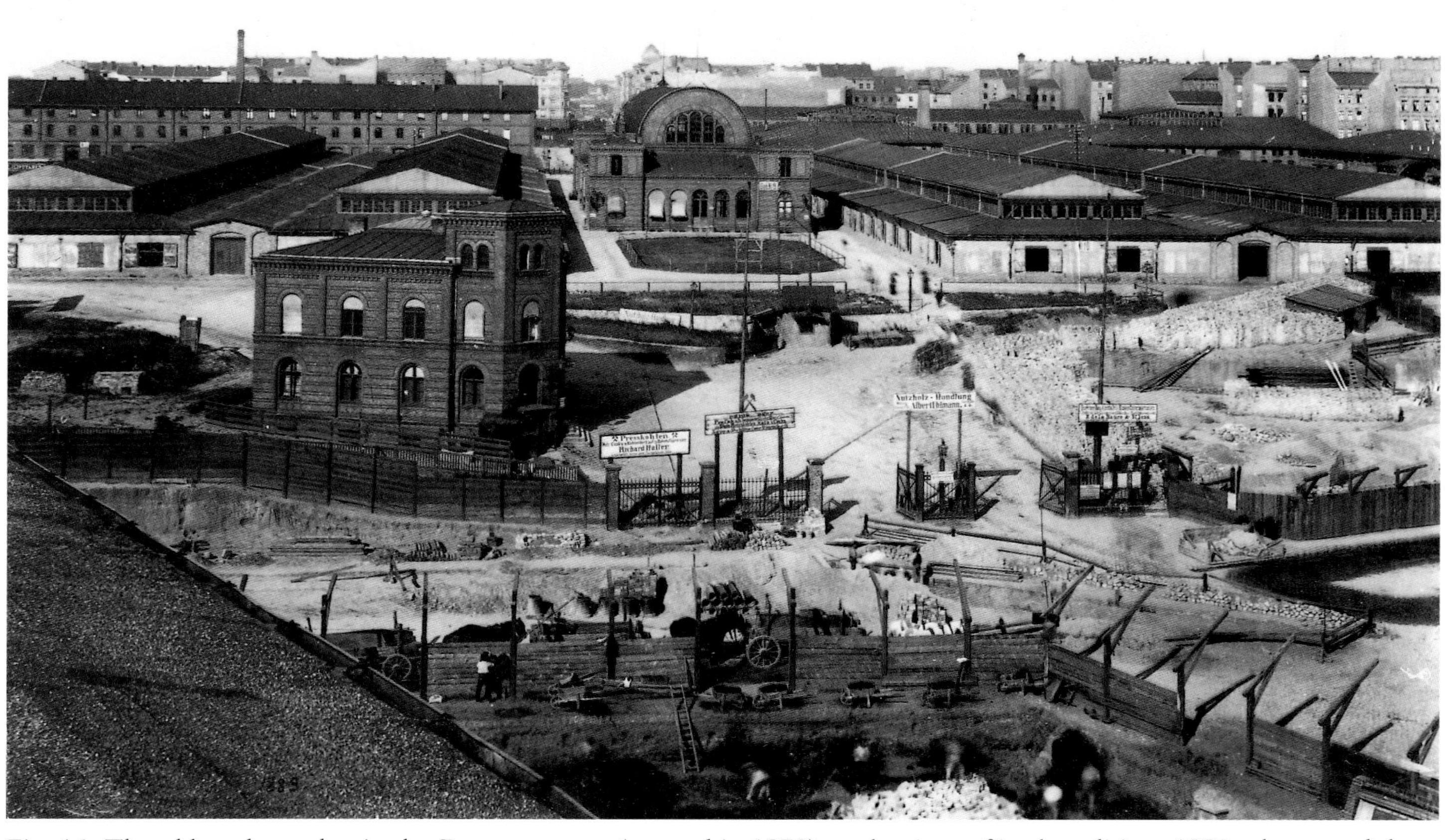

Fig. 16. The old cattle market in the Brunnenstrasse (opened in 1870), at the time of its demolition, 1880, photograph by F. Albert Schwartz

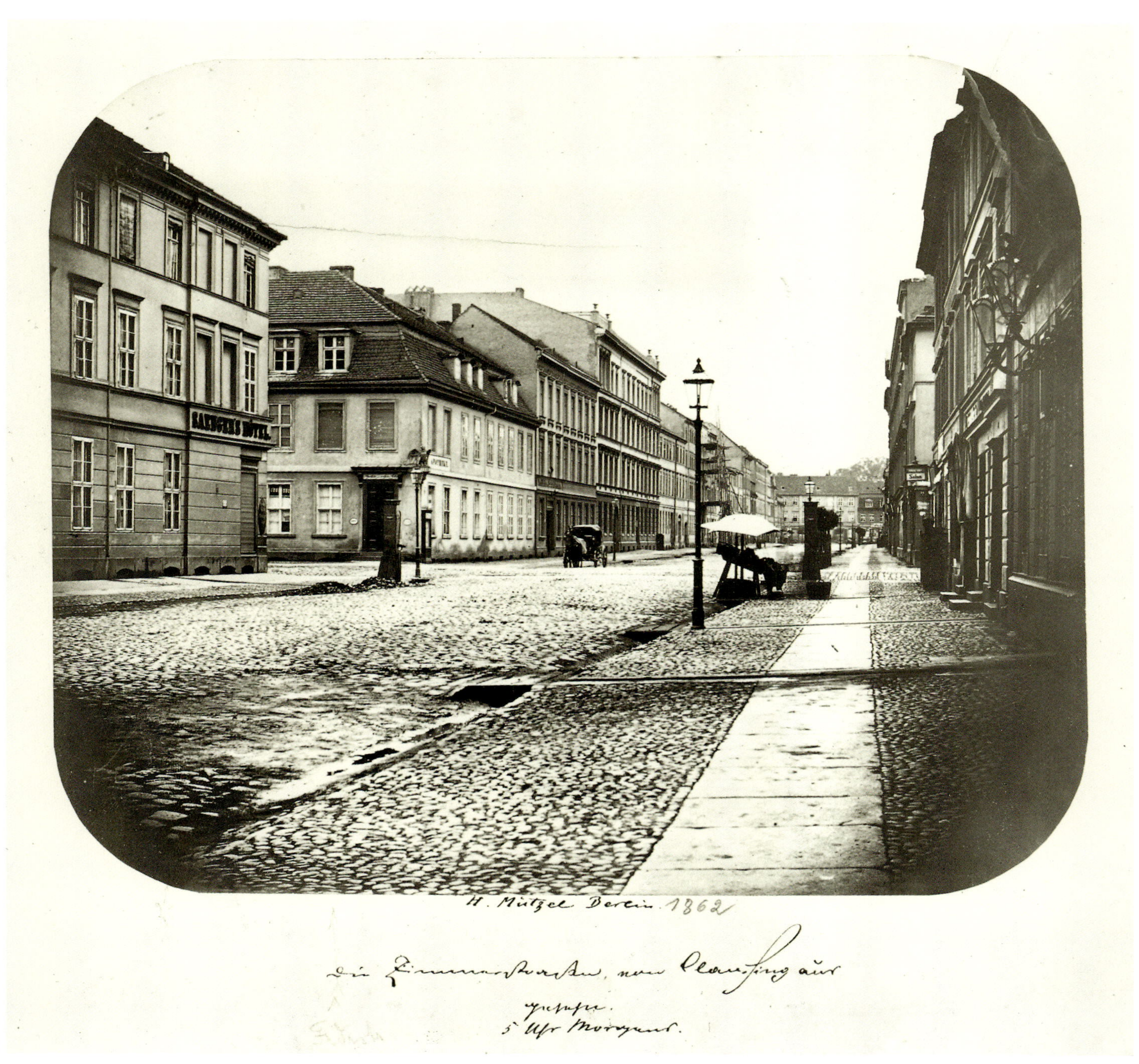

Fig. 17. The Zimmerstrasse, where Menzel lived in the early 1840s, photographed in 1862 by H. Mützel

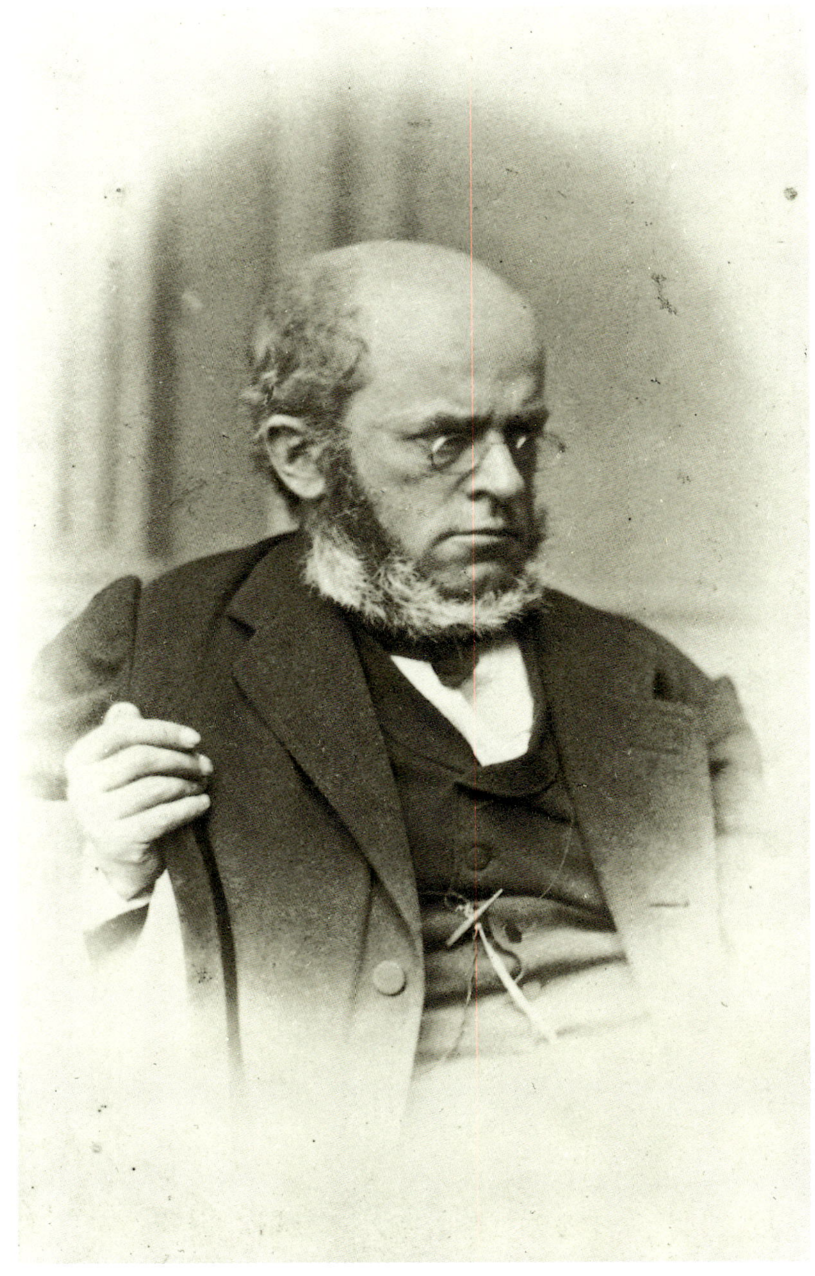

Fig. 18. Adolph Menzel, *c.* 1865, anonymous photograph

Fig. 19. Adolph Menzel, *c.* 1855, anonymous photograph

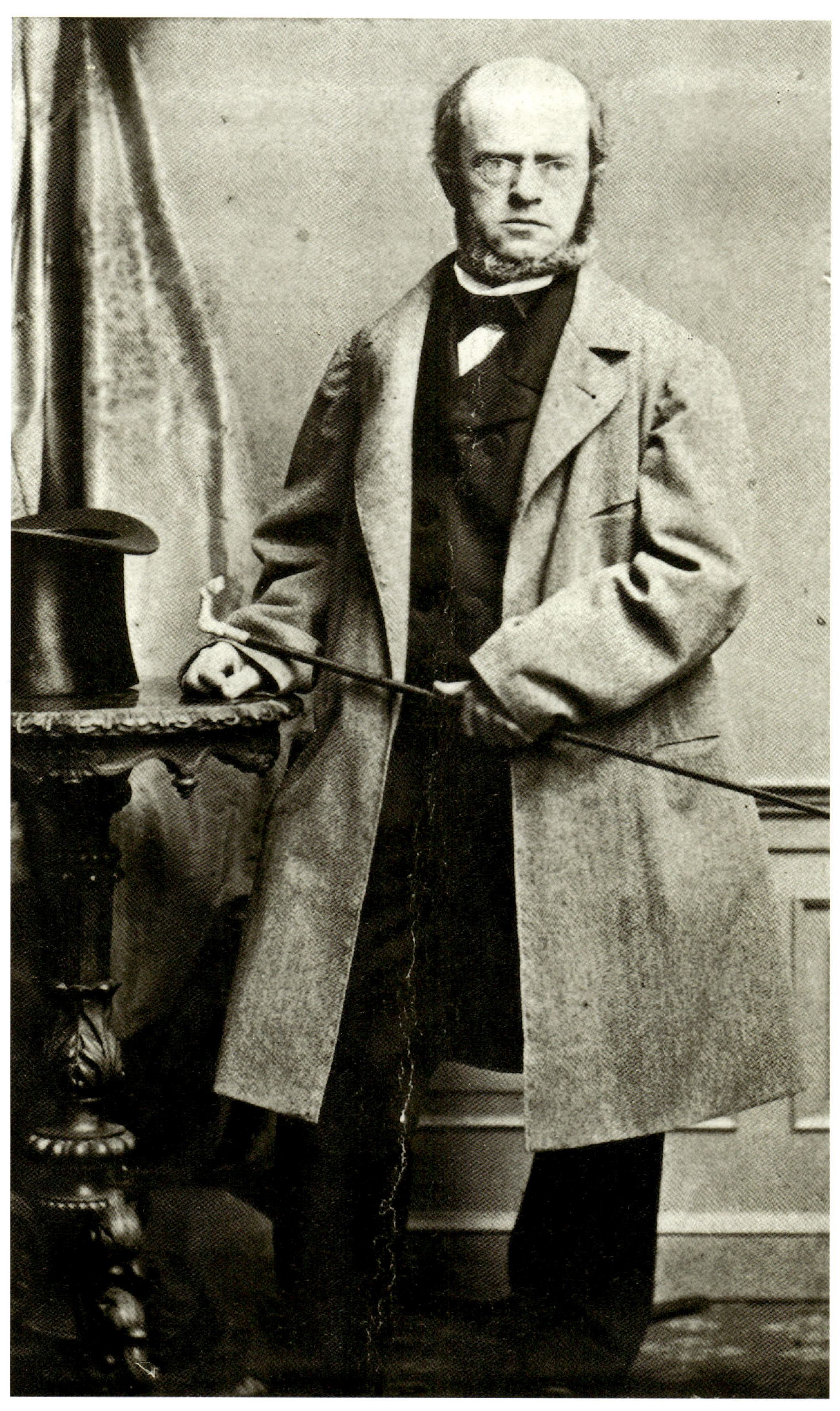

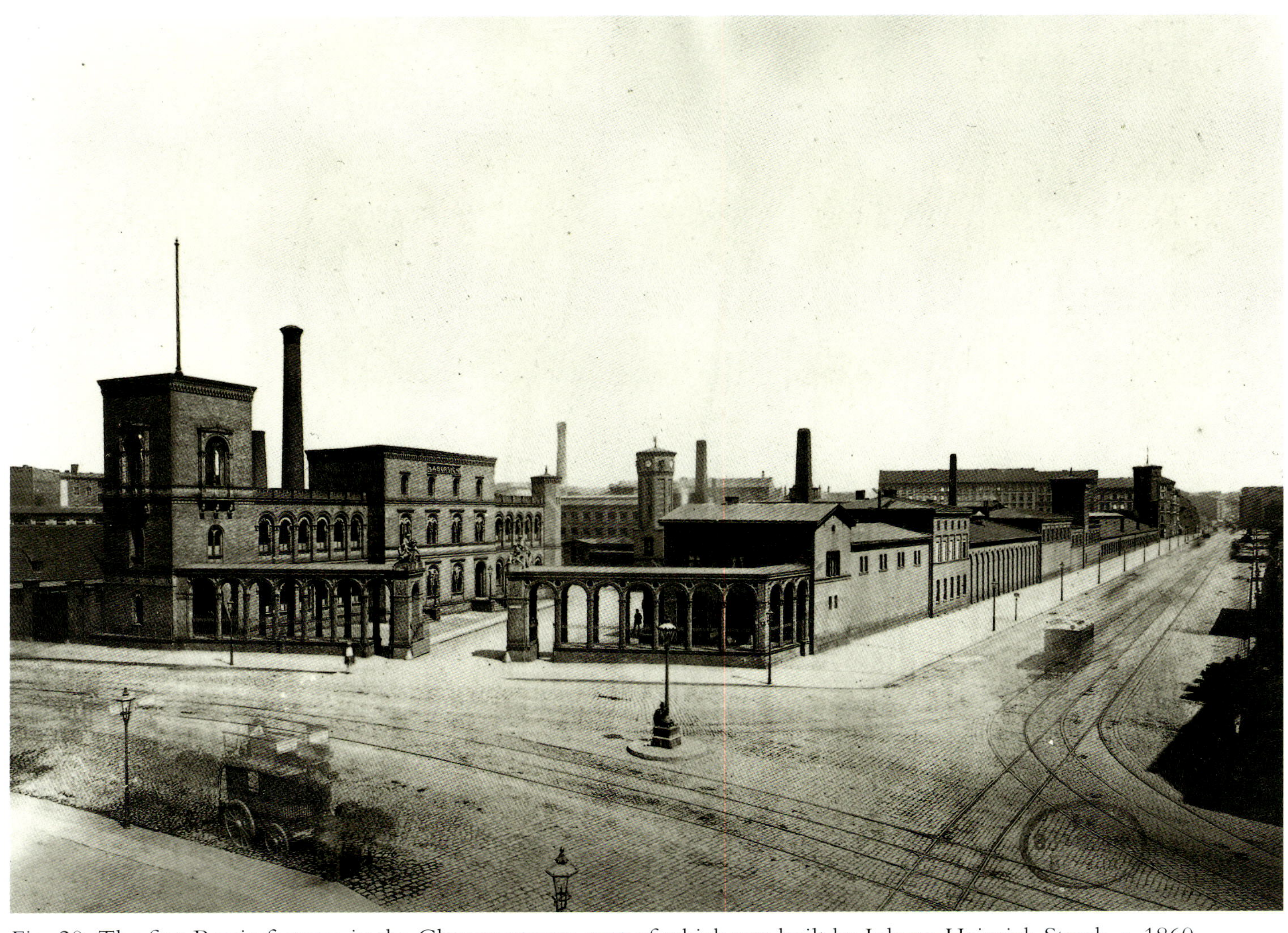

Fig. 20. The first Borsig factory, in the Chausseestrasse, part of which was built by Johann Heinrich Strack, *c.* 1860, photograph by F. Albert Schwartz

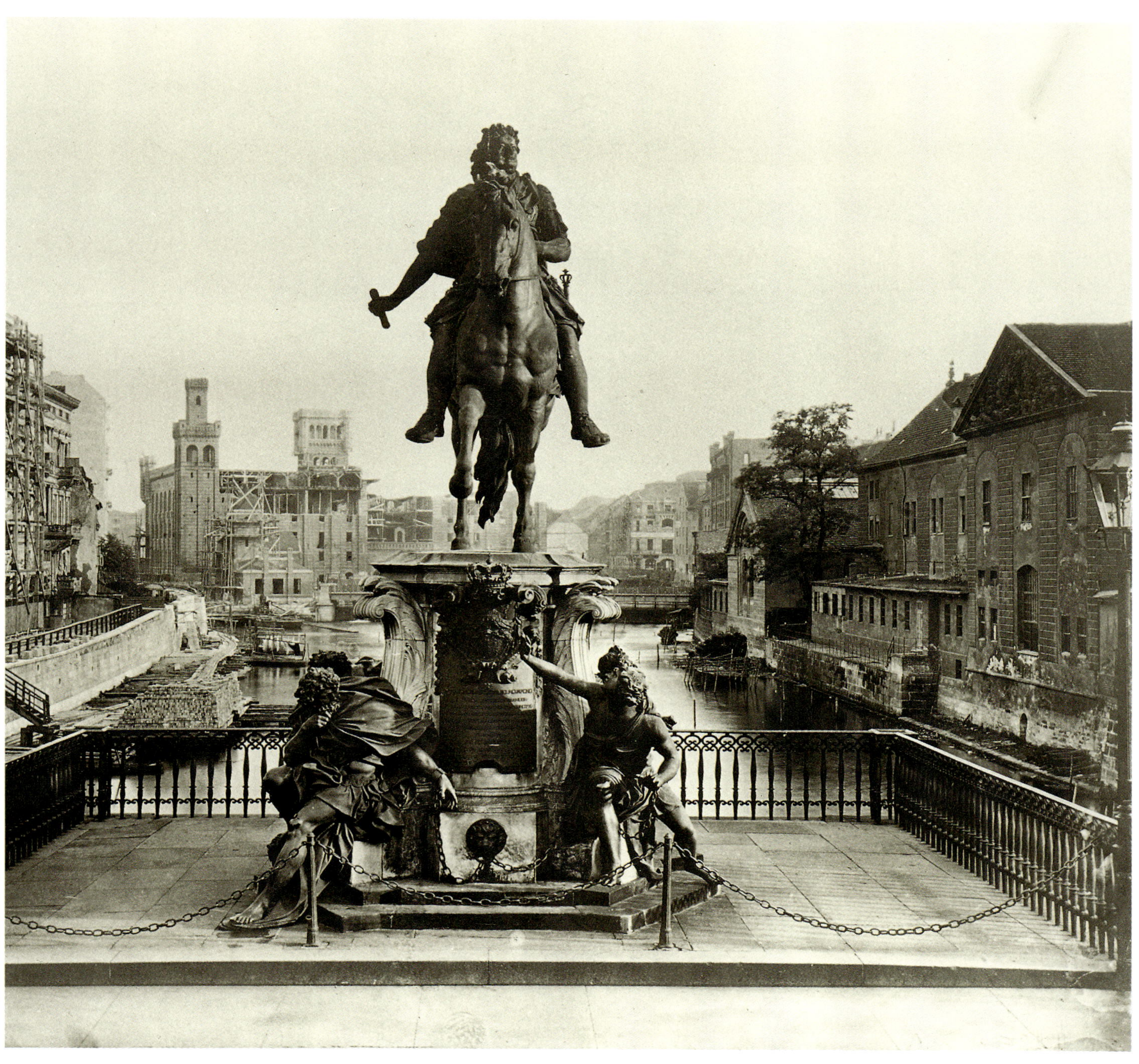

Fig. 21. The statue of Prince-Elector Frederick William (the 'Great Elector') by Andreas Schlüter, with the Royal Mills in the background, *c.* 1892, anonymous photograph

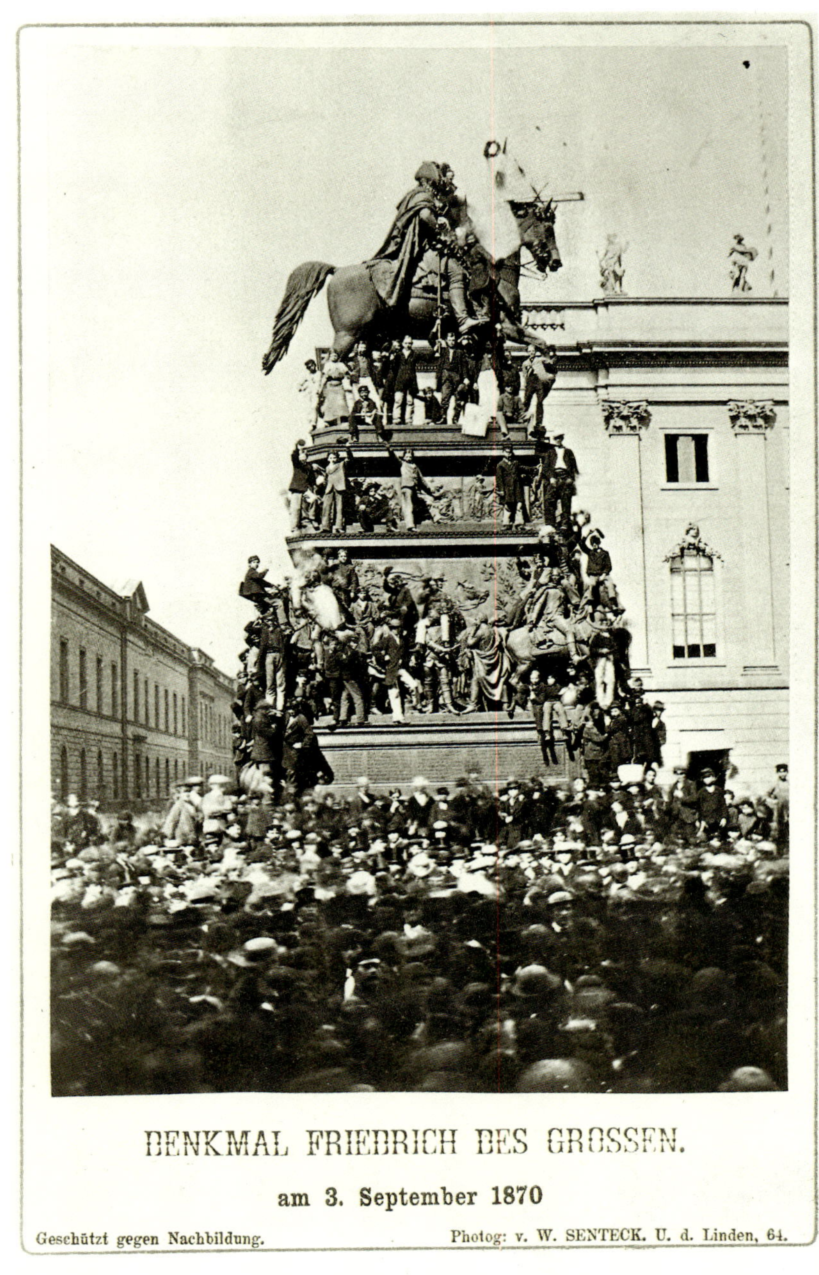

Fig. 22. Crowds surrounding the monument to Frederick the Great to hear news of the French capitulation, 3 September 1870, photograph by W. Senteck

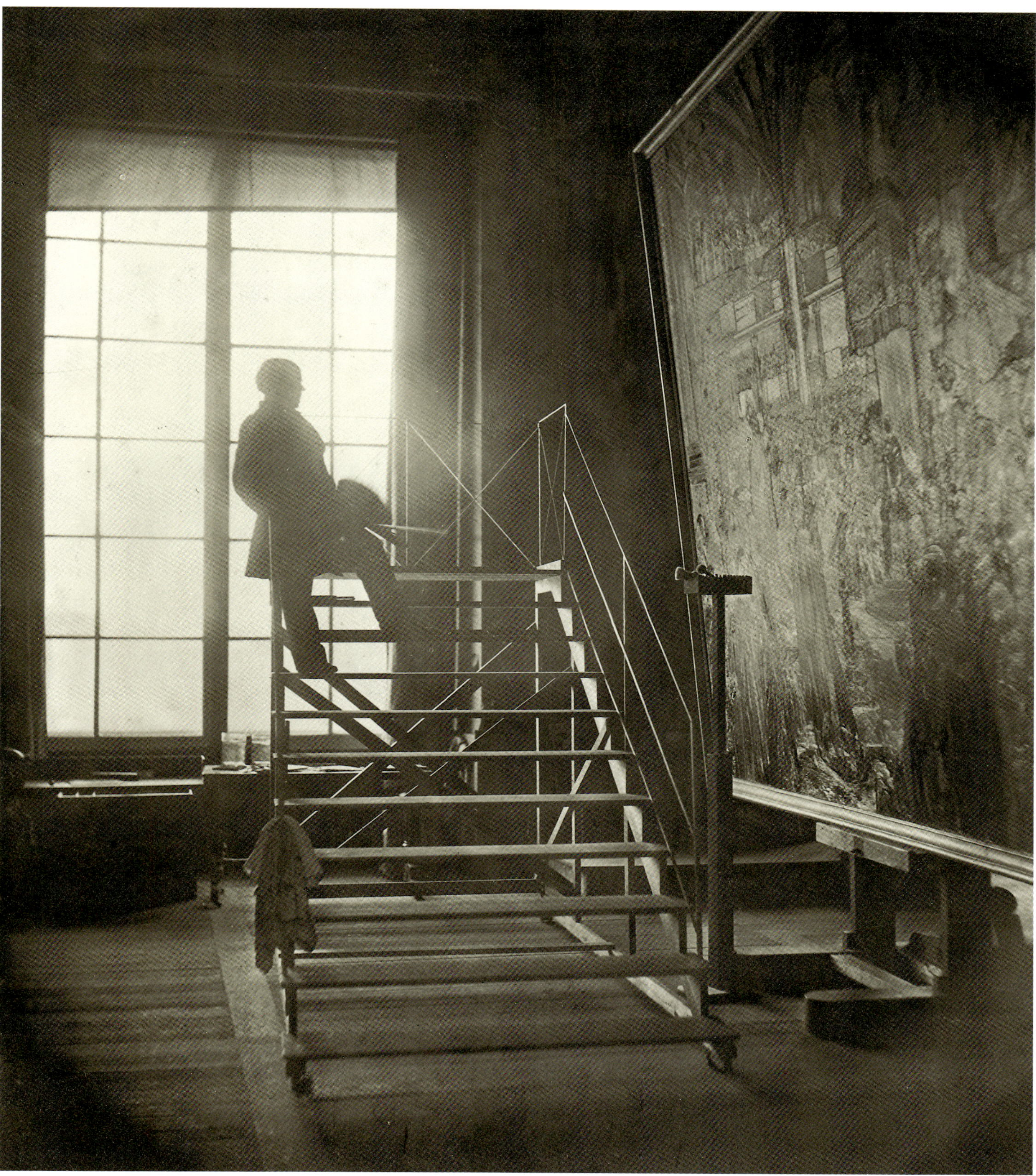

Fig 23. Menzel examining his painting of *The Coronation* (with the main features already brushed in), 1862, anonymous photograph

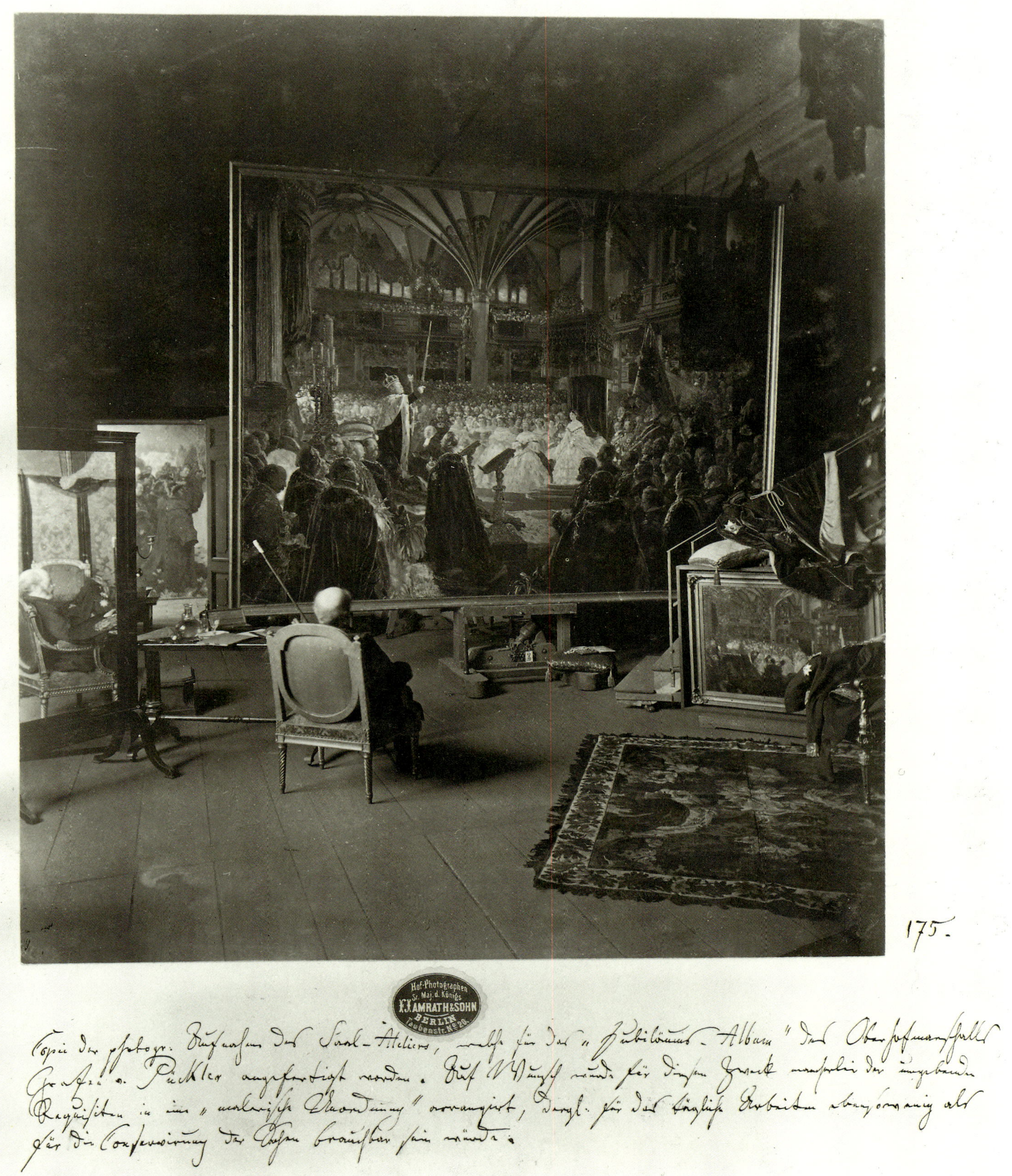

Fig 24. Menzel surveying his finished painting, *The Coronation*, 1865, anonymous photograph. Written underneath: 'Copy of the photograph of the artist's studio, taken for the *Jubilee Album* prepared by the court major-domo, Count von Pückler. For the occasion, he requested some of the studio accessories to be arranged in "picturesque disorder" – hardly conducive to the artist's daily labours or the preservation of the artefacts concerned.'

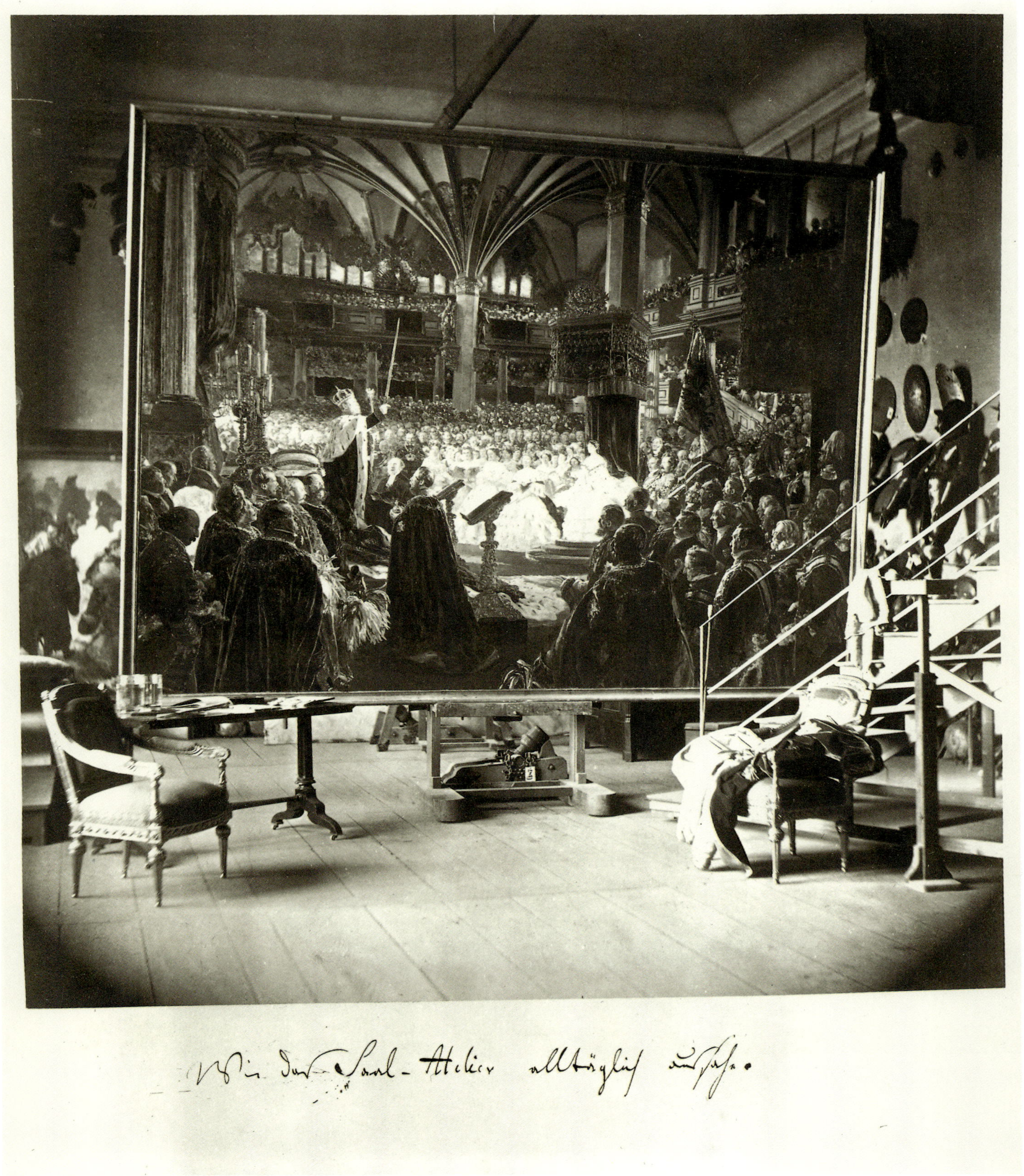

Fig. 25. 'The artist's studio in its normal state', 1865, anonymous photograph

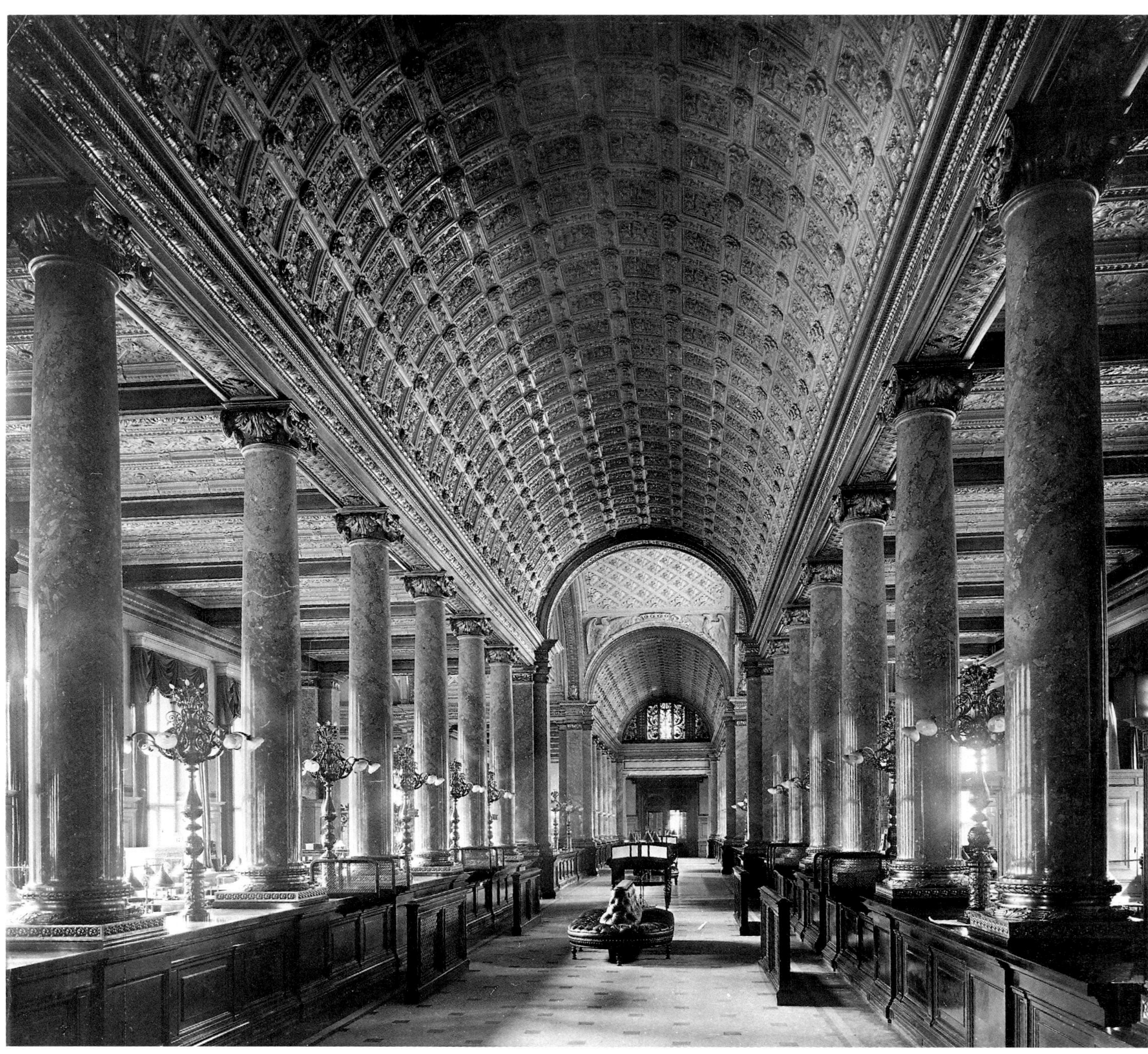

Fig. 26. The Reichsbank, which had been enlarged in 1894, *c.* 1900, anonymous photograph

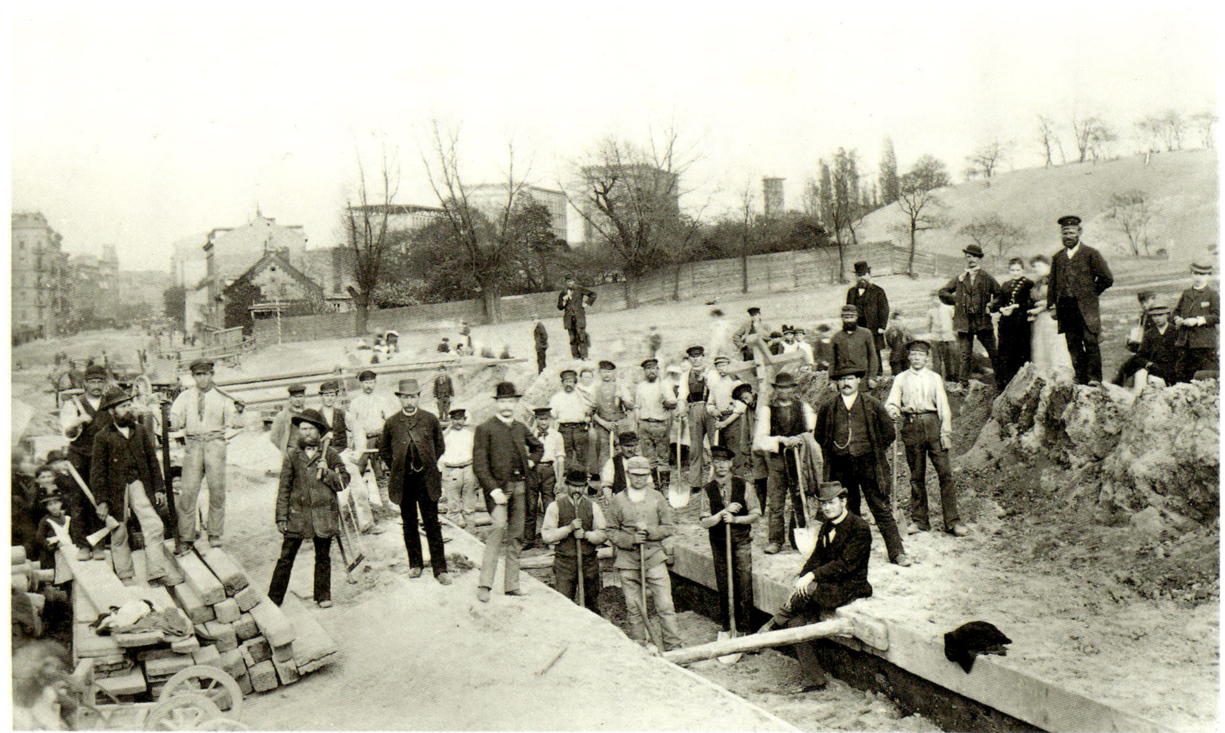

Fig. 27. Digging sewers in the Kreuzbergstrasse, 1886, photograph by Georg Bartels

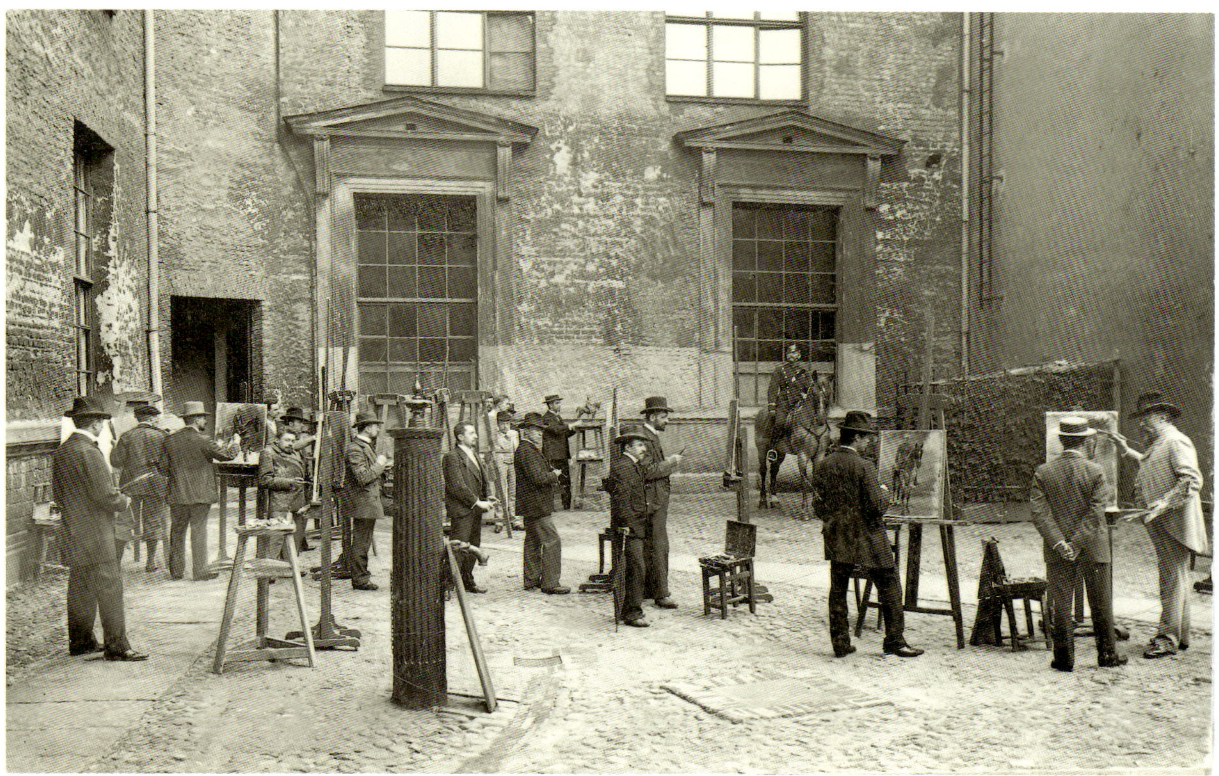

Fig. 28. Paul Meyerheim's painting class in the courtyard of the Berlin Academy, *c.* 1880, anonymous photograph

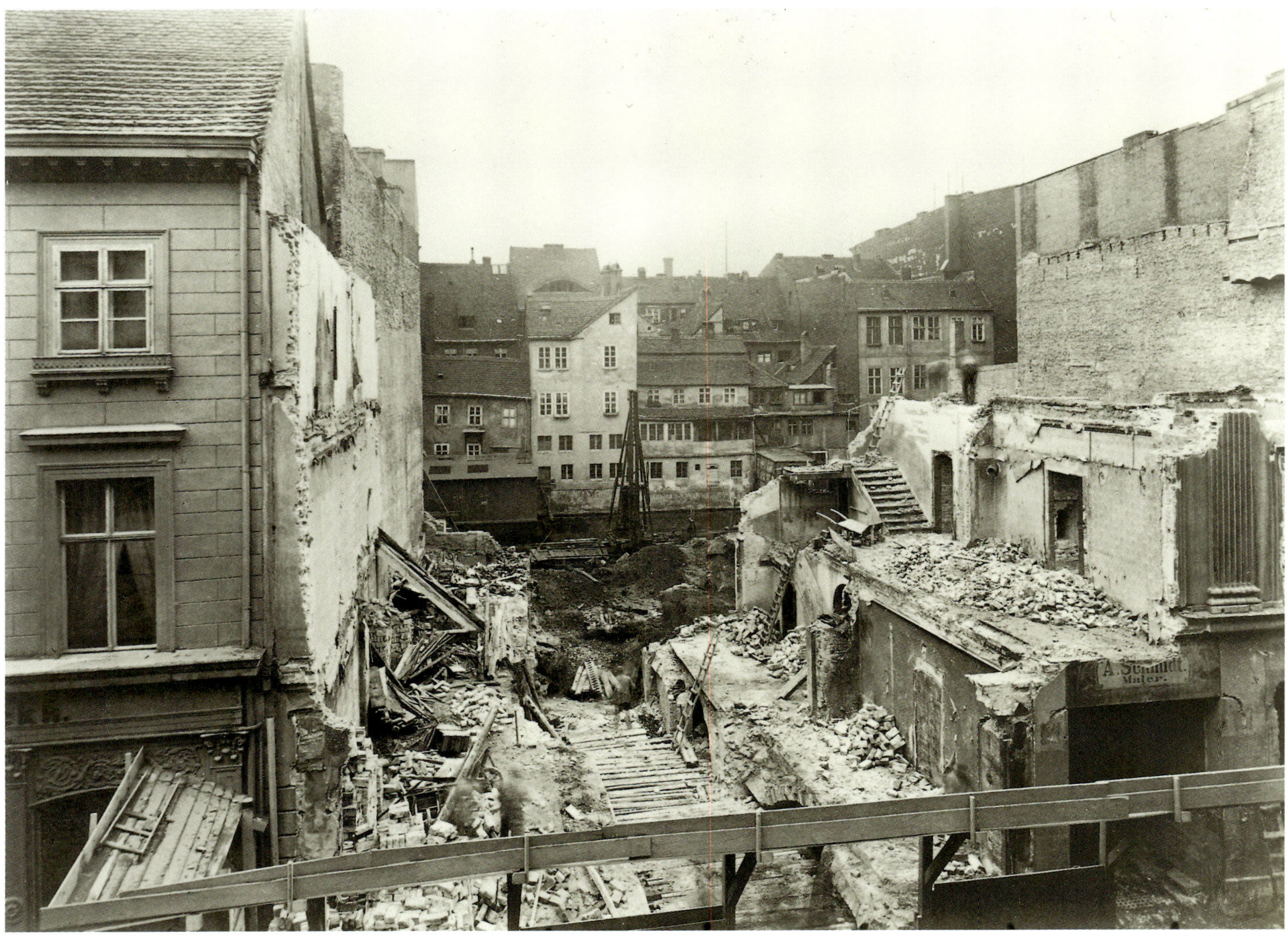

Fig. 29. Demolished house near the lock, 1897, photograph by Georg Bartels

Fig. 30. The Nationalgalerie, *c.* 1900, anonymous photograph

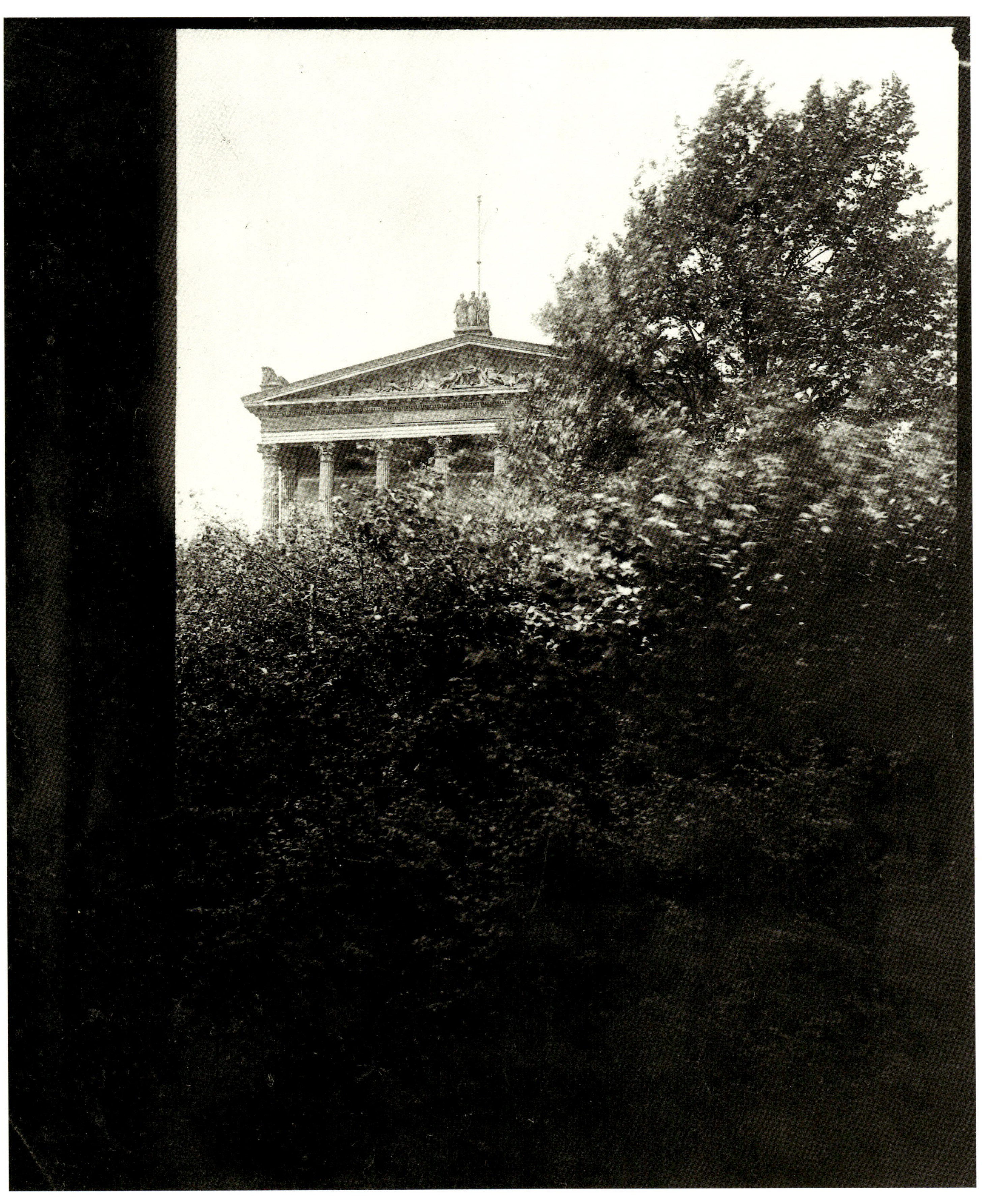

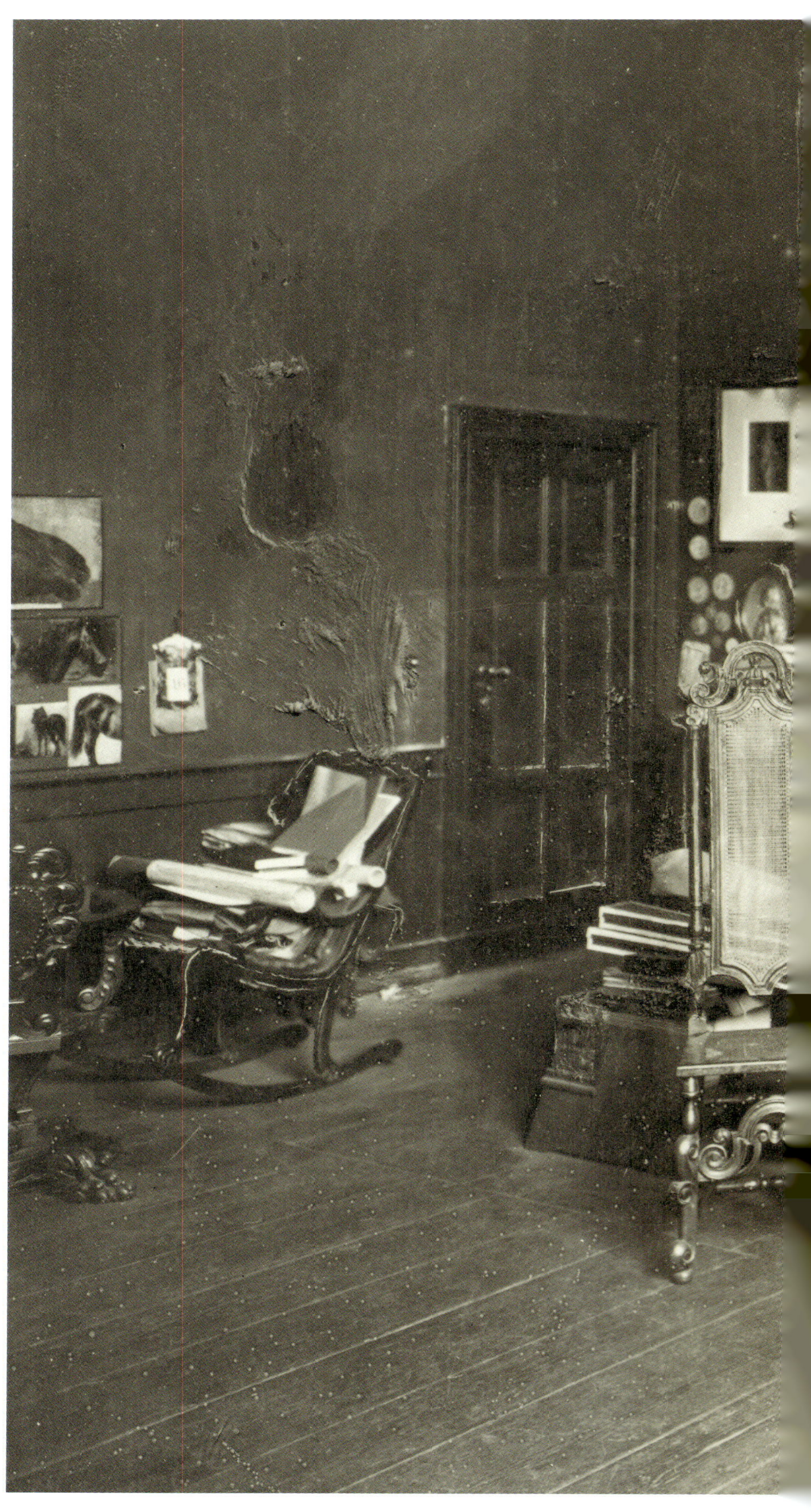

Fig. 31. Menzel in his studio, before 1899, photograph by Zander & Labisch

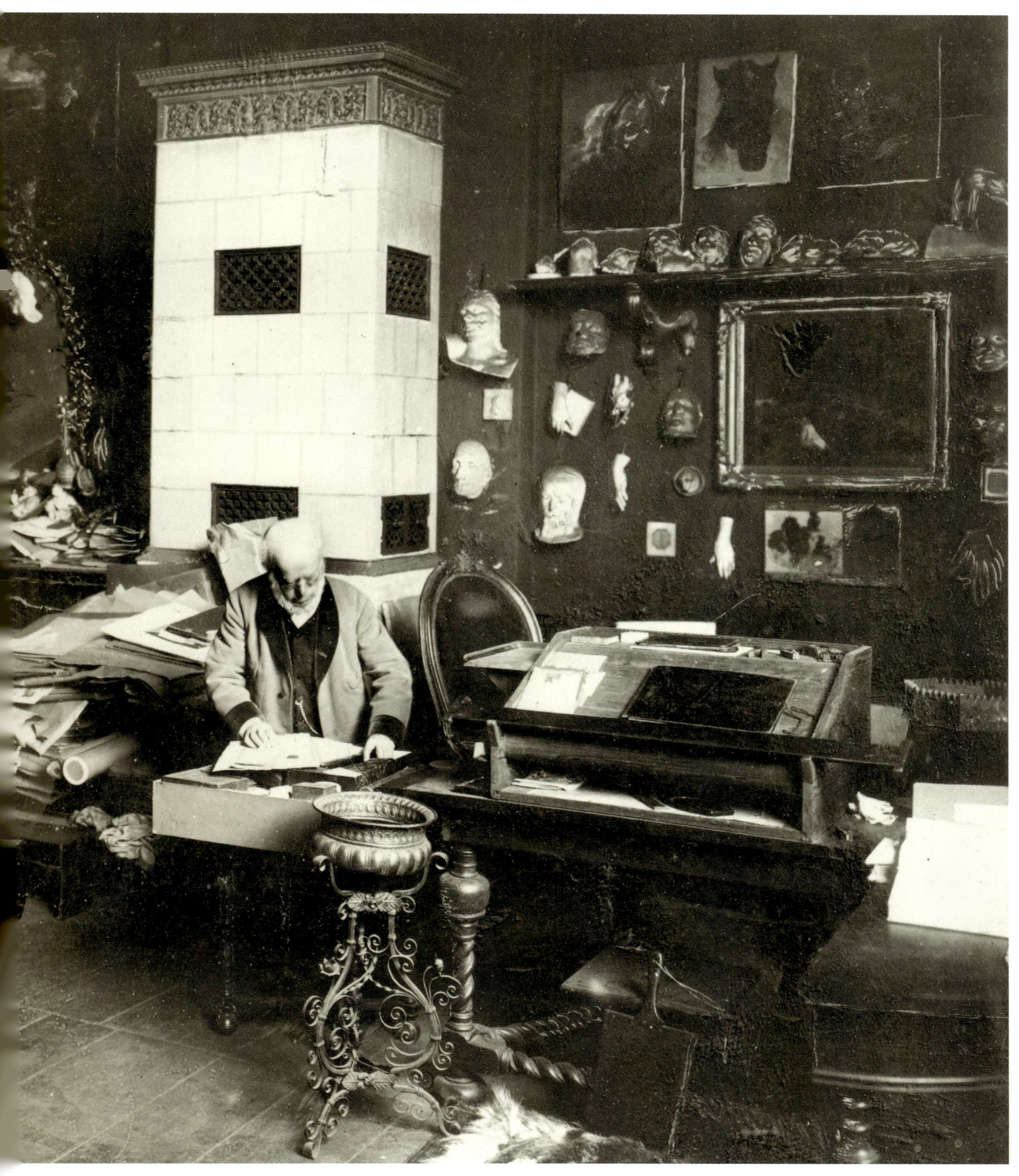

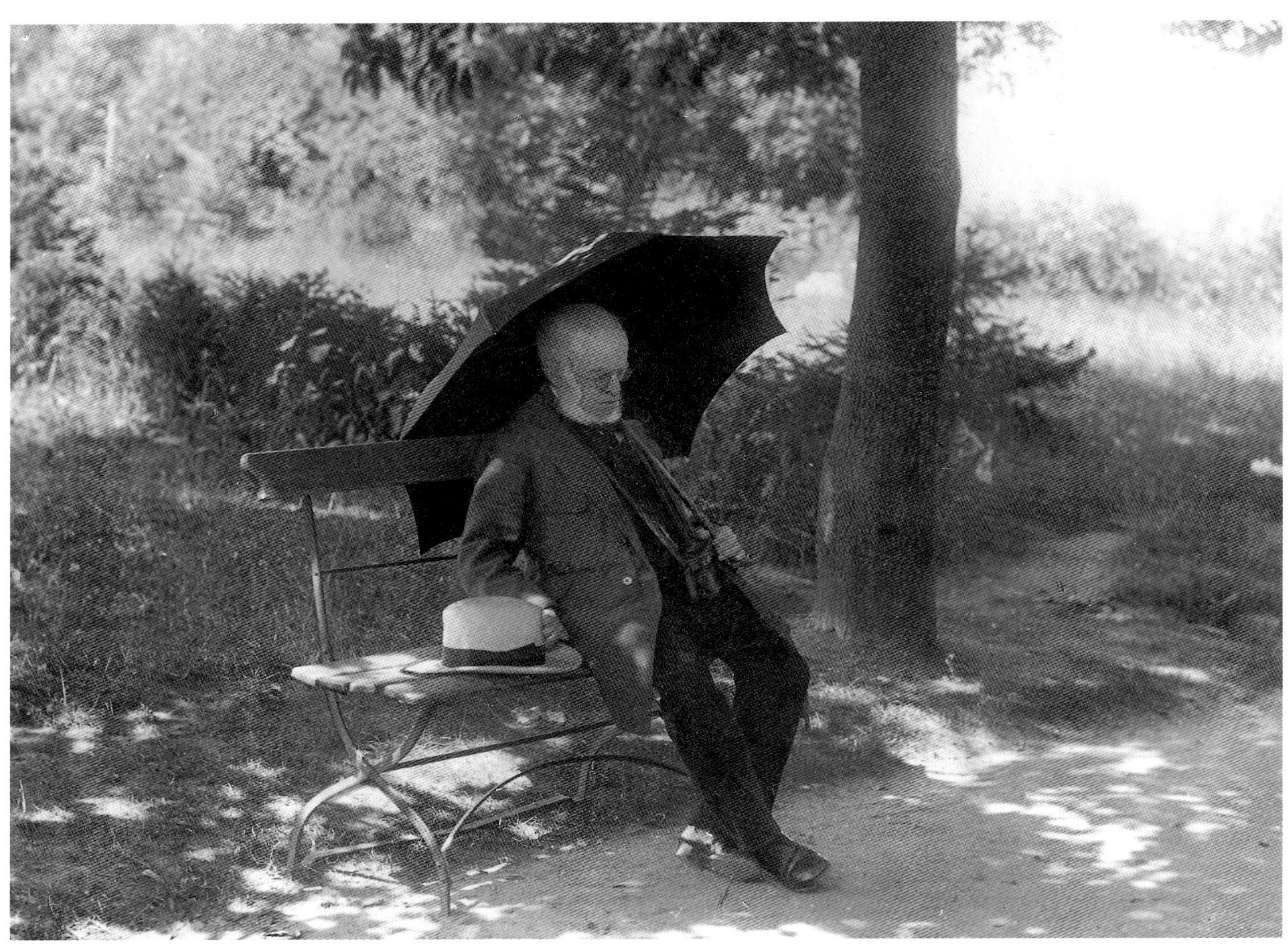

Fig. 32. Menzel in the park at Kissingen, 1904, photograph by Fritz Schuhmann

Fig. 33. Menzel travelling, *c.* 1895, anonymous photograph

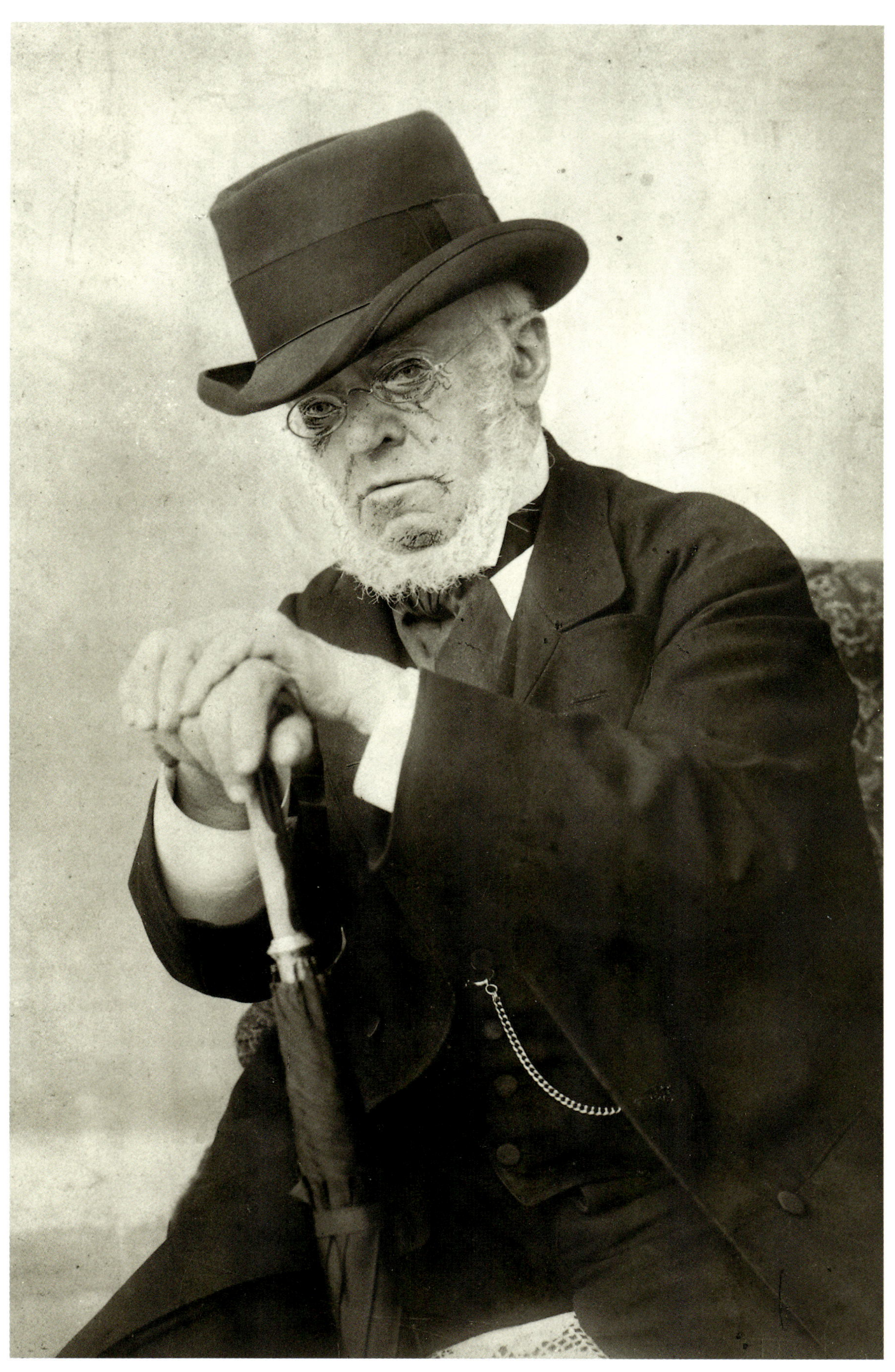

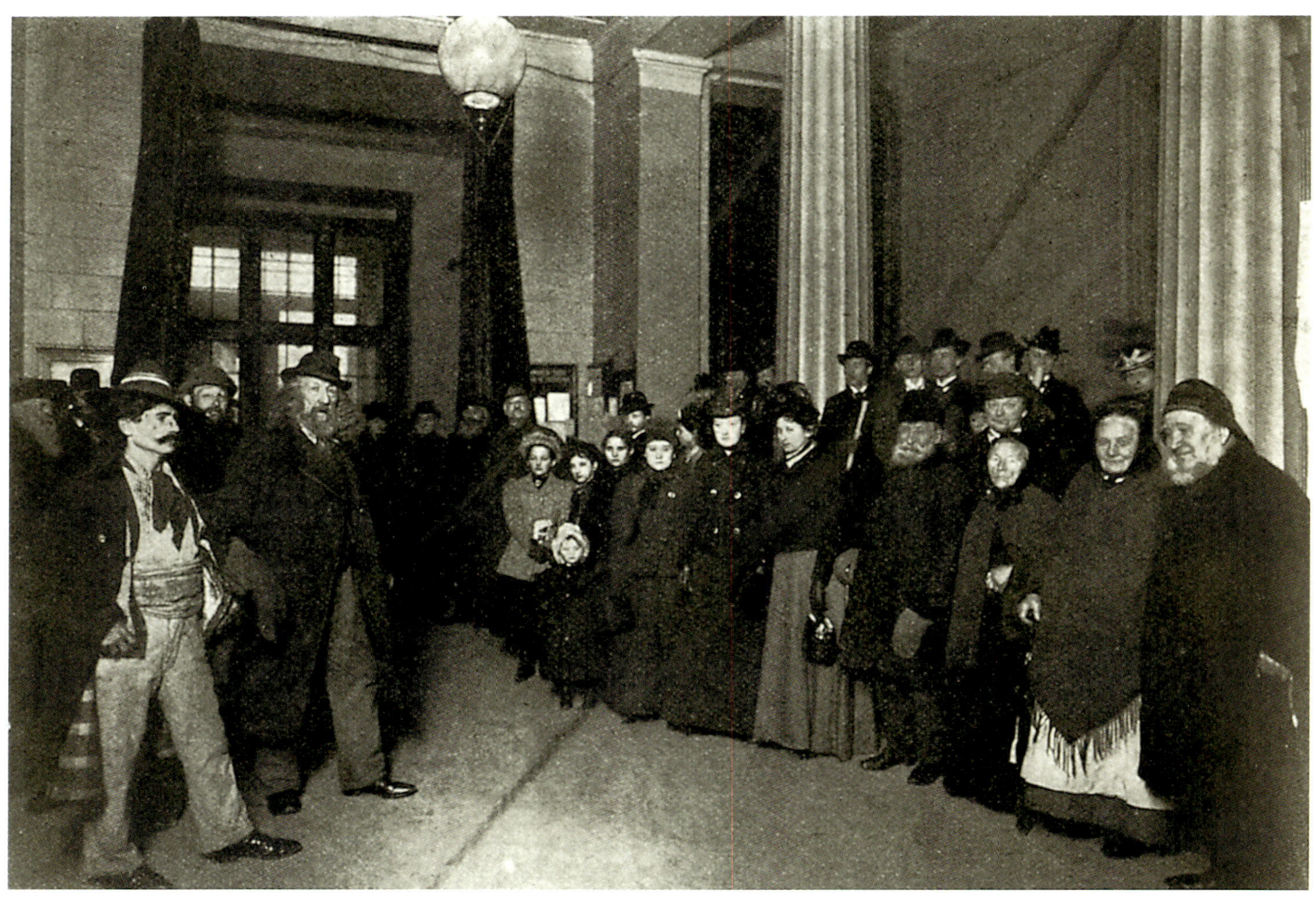

Fig. 34. Models waiting to be hired at the Academy of Arts, photograph published in the *Berliner Illustrierte Zeitung* IX, 1900, p. 182

Fig. 35. Menzel drawing, 1904, photograph by Jacob Hilsdorf

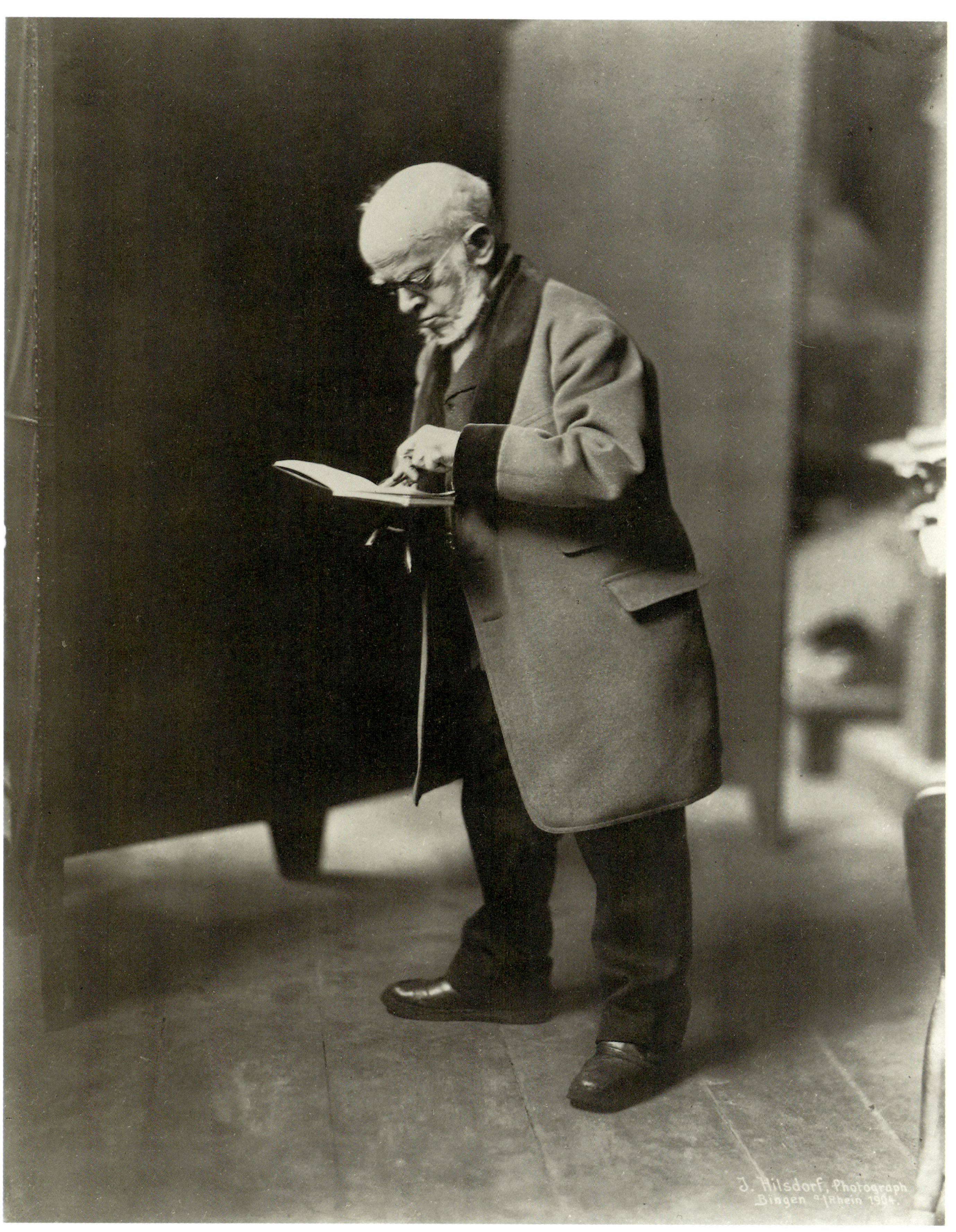
J. Hilsdorf, Photograph
Bingen a/Rhein 1904.

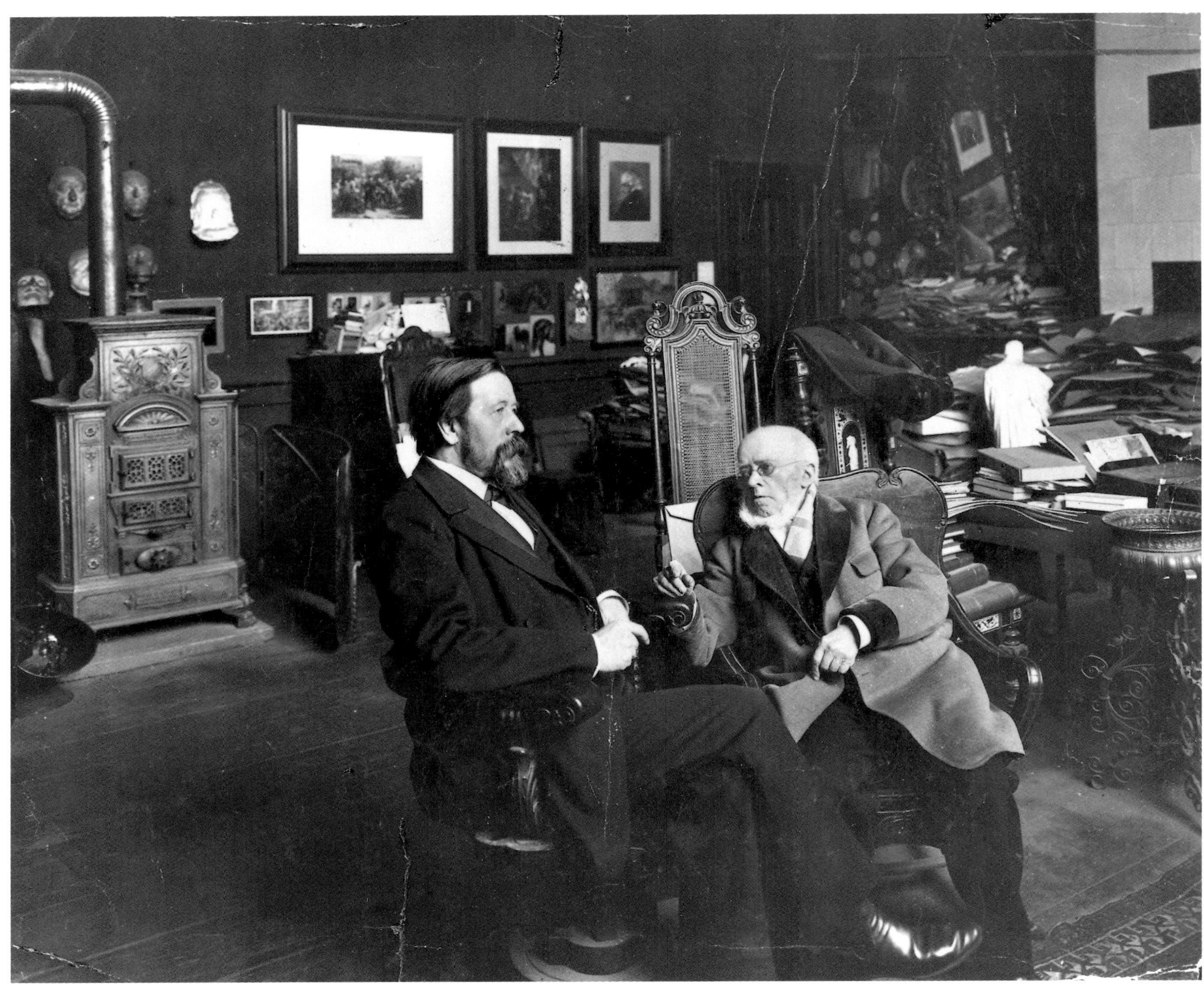

Fig. 36. Menzel in his studio with Anton von Werner, *c.* 1895, anonymous photograph

Fig. 37. Adolph Menzel, before 1899, photograph probably taken by Zander & Labisch

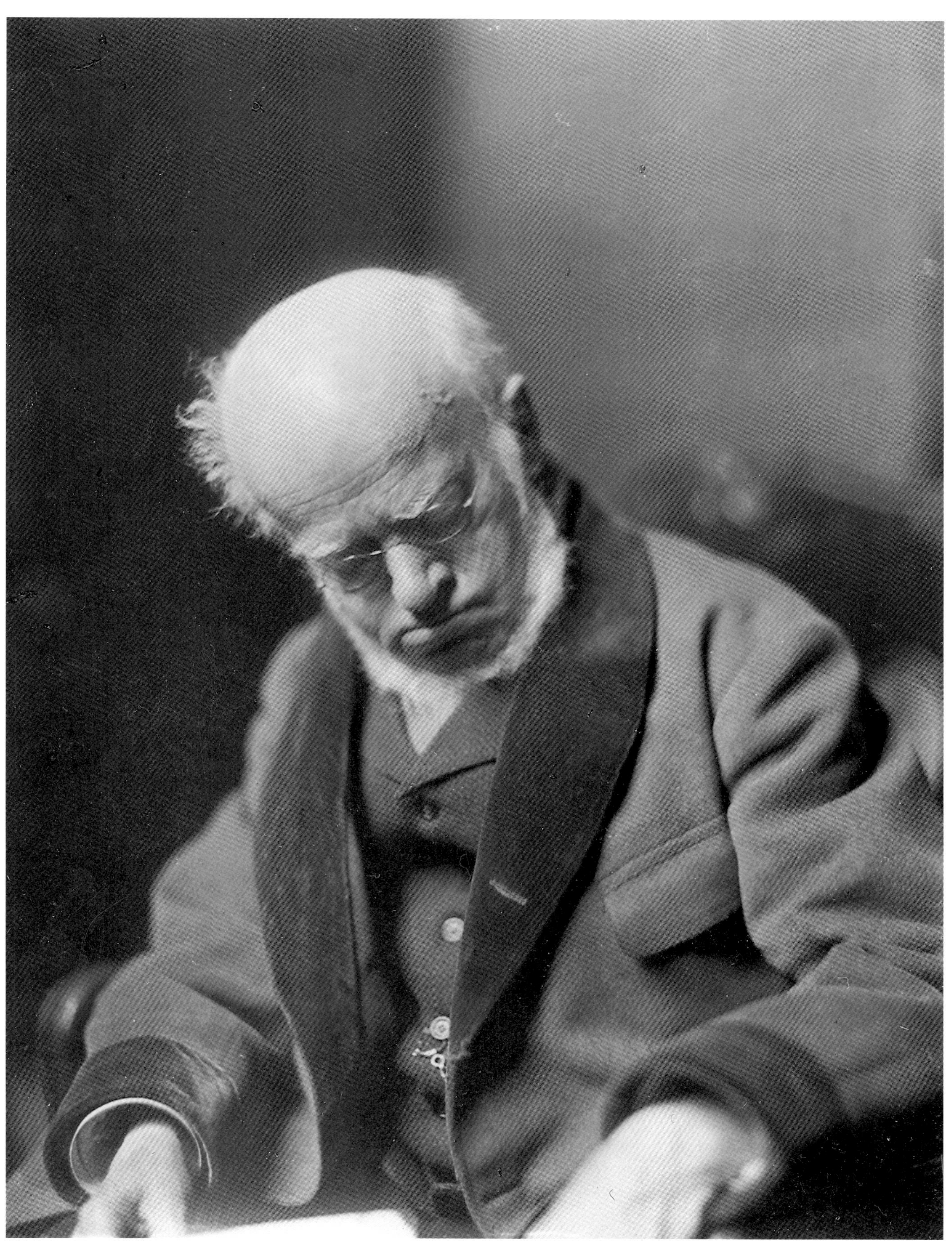

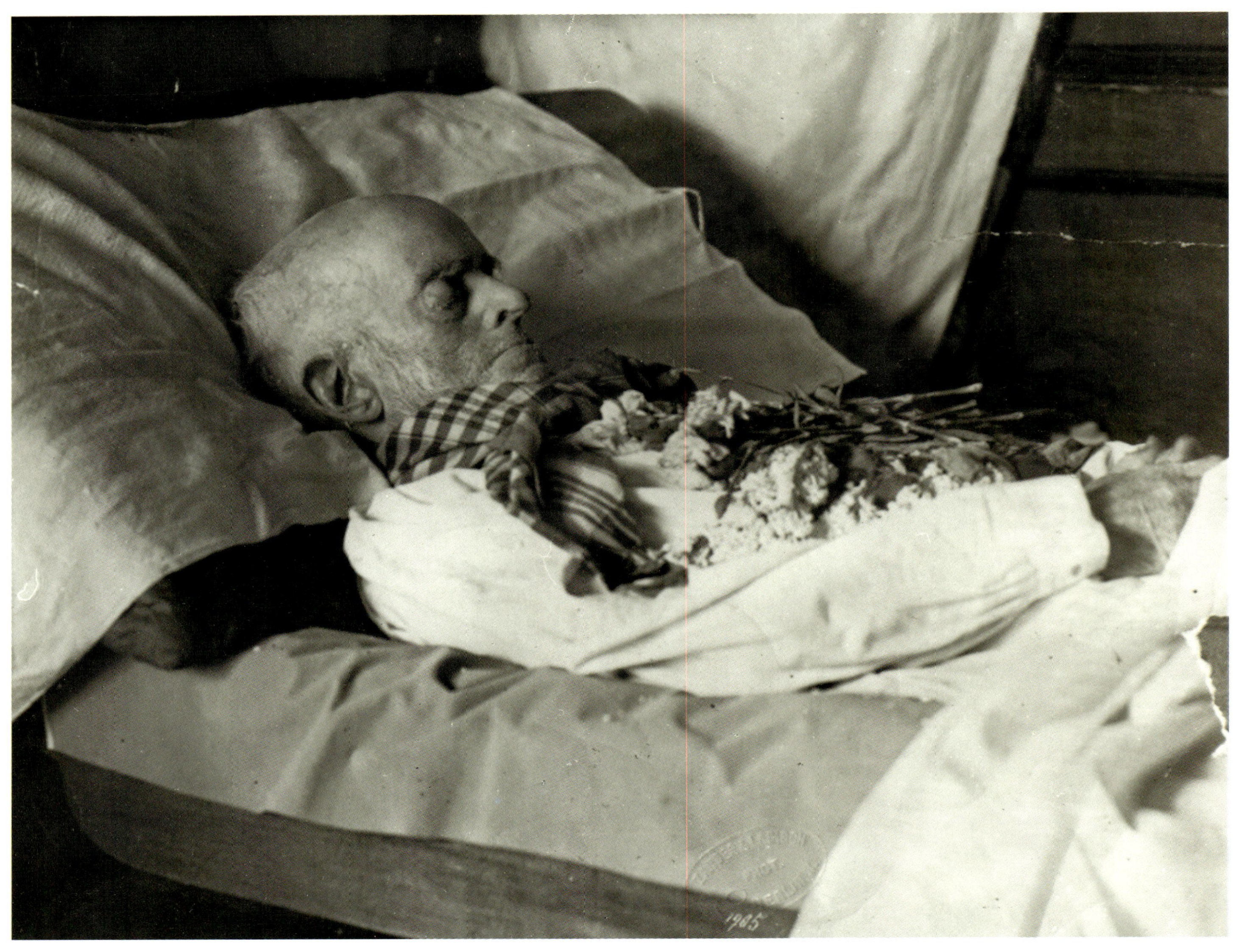

Fig. 38. Menzel on his deathbed, 1905, anonymous photograph

Fig. 39. The house built on the site of Menzel's last dwelling (with commemorative plaque), itself destroyed in 1945, anonymous photograph

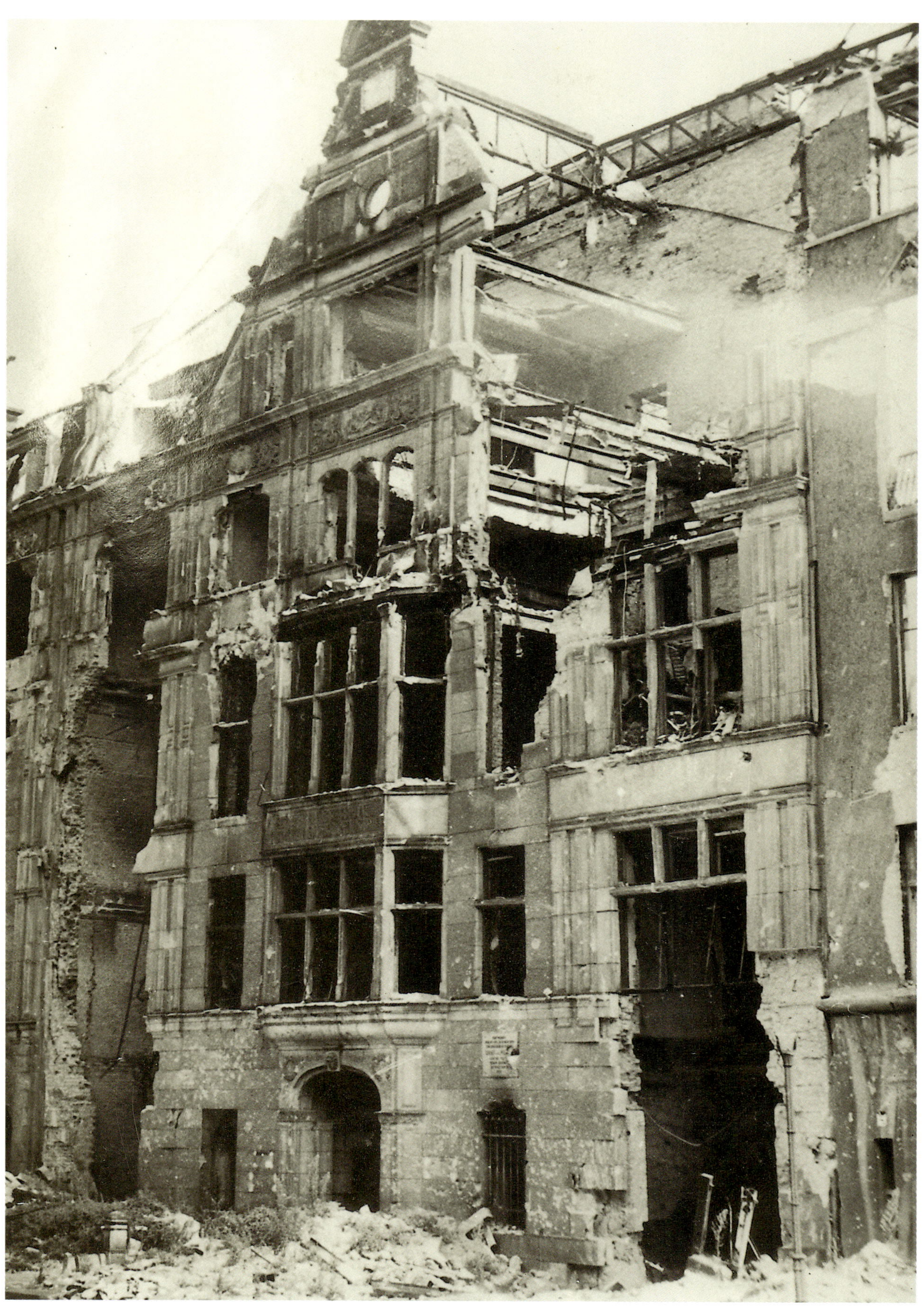

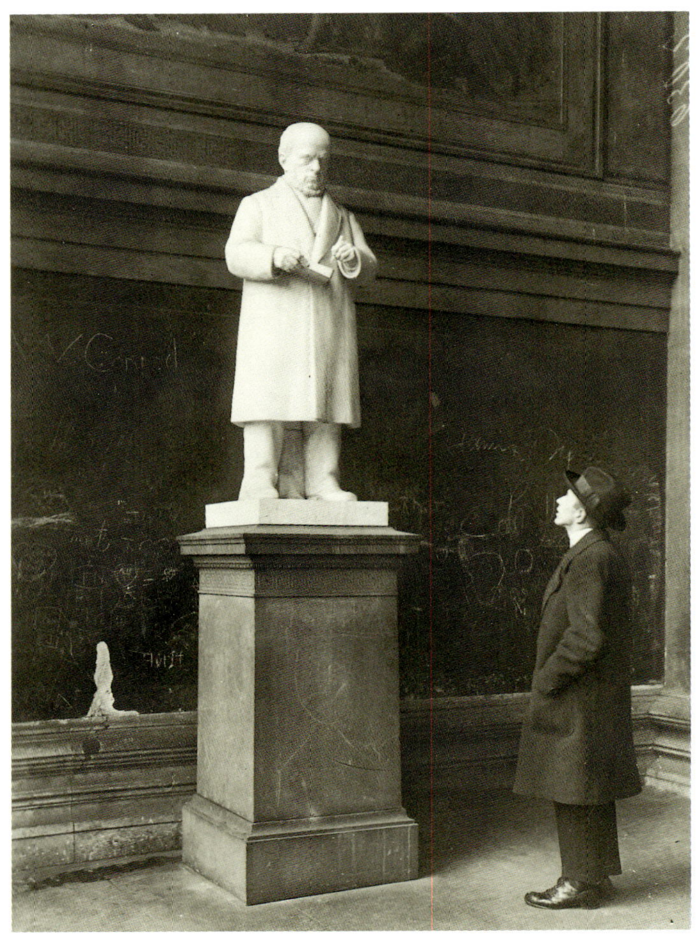

Fig. 40. Menzel's statue in the colonnade of the Altes Museum, 1930, anonymous photograph

Biography

Marie Ursula Riemann-Reyher

1815
Adolph Friedrich Erdmann Menzel born in Breslau on 8 December. His father, Carl Erdmann Menzel, is headmaster of a school; his mother, Charlotte Emilie Okrusch, the daughter of an art teacher.

1818
Menzel's father resigns his teaching post to set up a lithography workshop.

1823
Birth of Menzel's sister Emilie, on 25 July.

1826
Birth of Menzel's brother Richard, on 8 November.

1828
A chalk drawing by Menzel of a tigress suckling her young, inspired by Rubens, is shown at an exhibition of 'objets d'art, manufactured articles and natural items' held at Breslau's former Exchange building.

1829
Menzel's father prints the illustrations to Kutzen's *History of the Prussian State*. Adolph, now fourteen, draws eight lithographs for the second part of the work. Two drawings by Menzel – *The Discovery of Lucius Cecilius Metellus' Conspiracy* and *A Portrait from Nature* – are shown at an exhibition organized by the Schlesische Vaterländische Gesellschaft (Silesian Patriotic Society) in Breslau.

1830
In April, the Menzel family moves to Berlin. Adolph's talent as a draughtsman is already apparent and his father hopes he will get a better training in the capital. Menzel works in his father's lithography business and postpones his enrolment at the Academy.

1831–2
Menzel's first commission: *The Life of Luther, a Picture Book for Young People*, published by Sachse & Co. of Berlin (part 3). Menzel makes chalk drawings for seven of the thirteen lithographs.

1832
Menzel's father dies on 5 January. Aged sixteen, Menzel takes over the lithography business to provide for the rest of the family.

1833
From Easter until the autumn, Menzel sporadically attends the drawing class from plaster cast models at the Academy. Disappointed, he decides to abandon formal training and teach himself. At evening drawing sessions at the Academy, he meets the wallpaper manufacturer Carl Heinrich Arnold. They soon become firm friends. At the Arnold family home, Menzel meets many Berlin artists –Schinkel, Rauch, Drake, the painters Eduard Magnus and Eduard Meyerheim – and becomes friends with the archaeologist Adolf Schöll.
That autumn, he receives his first major commission from the publisher Louis Sachse: a series of eleven illustrations (pen lithographs, published 1833, dated 1834) for *Künstlers Erdenwallen* (The Artist's Earthly Pilgrimage) by Goethe.

1834
The illustrations for the *Artist's Earthly Pilgrimage* are praised by Johann Gottfried Schadow, director of the Berlin Academy, in the *Allgemeine Preussische Staatszeitung*.
On 22 February, Menzel becomes a member of the Jüngerer Berliner Kunstverein, an association of young Berlin artists. Between 1834 and 1836, he draws twelve chalk lithographs to illustrate *Memorable Events in the History of Brandenburg and Prussia* (published by Sachse & Co.).

1835
Menzel's friend and patron, the wallpaper manufacturer Carl Heinrich Arnold, moves with his family to Kassel. Menzel draws and prints the lithographs for the cover of the third volume of *History of Modern Art in Germany* by Count Athanasius Raczynski (published in 1841) and illustrates the margins of a musical score by Prince Anton von Radziwill based on Goethe's *Faust*.

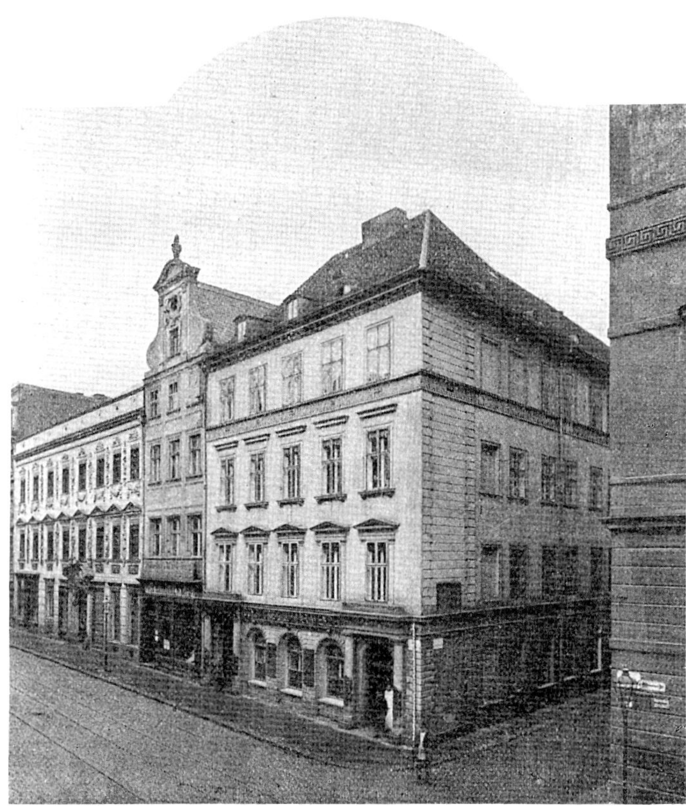

Fig. 41. The house in Breslau where Adolf Menzel was born, anonymous photograph

1836
Menzel meets the Potsdam regiment's medical officer, Dr Wilhelm Puhlmann, a member of the board of the local Art Society. The close friendship between them is to last until Puhlmann's death in 1882. Menzel designs a membership card (a pen lithograph in the form of a share certificate) for the Society. He also draws thirty lithographs for Emilie Feige's *Nursery Companion for Well-behaved Little Boys and Girls* (published by George Gropius). Menzel studies the seventeenth- and eighteenth-century Venetian, Dutch and French painters in the Berlin collections, and the work of Dürer. His first oil painting, *The Game of Chess* (cat. 1) he himself considers 'half-kneaded, half-moulded'. He also tries his hand at watercolours, but comes to prefer the opaqueness of gouache.

1837
His pen lithograph illustrating *The Lord's Prayer* (published by Sachse & Co.) demonstrates his ambitious, interpretive skills.
The Enemy Arrives (oil, present location unknown).
He writes to Arnold: '. . . this year, I have been almost constantly busy painting.'

1838
Pen lithograph for a bricklayer's certificate of qualification (Sachse & Co.) and for the diploma commemorating the fiftieth anniversary of Schadow's membership of the Berlin Academy.
The Family Council (oil, present location unknown).
The Toilette (oil, present location unknown).
Portrait of a Woman (oil, Nationalgalerie, Berlin, until 1945, since lost).
Interior of Berlin's Abbey Church (gouache, Kupferstichkabinett, Berlin).
The Organ of Berlin's Abbey Church (watercolour, present location unknown).

1839
Sixteen wood engravings for *The Amazing Story of Peter Schlemihl* by Adalbert von Chamisso. After the death of the poet, this new edition is edited by Julius Eduard Hitzig (published by J. L. Schrag, Nuremberg). Menzel completes his first commission for a painting, *Day of the Hearing* (cat. 2).
At this stage in his career, Menzel is prevented from experimenting further with painting by the many commissions he receives for illustrations. Until 1842, he is engaged on the four hundred wood engravings for Franz Kugler's *Geschichte Friedrichs des Grossen* (History of Frederick the Great), commissioned by the publisher Weber of Leipzig. As well as making an in-depth study of the time of Frederick the Great, Menzel perfects the technique of wood engraving. Not satisfied with the Parisian wood engravers assigned to execute the wood engravings, he gradually builds up a team of competent engravers in Leipzig and Berlin.
Two paintings by John Constable (died 1837) exhibited at the Hôtel de Russie in Berlin are allegedly the inspiration for Menzel's so-called 'pre-Impressionist' landscapes and interiors of the 1840s, which were not seen by the general public until almost the time of Menzel's death.
On 3 October, the Menzel family moves from 39 Wilhelmstrasse to 4 Zimmerstrasse.

1840
The first of the twenty instalments of the *History of Frederick the Great* (completed in 1842) appears on 25 February. On 26 and 28 March, a critique by Schadow of the illustrations to Kugler's book, and a defence by Menzel, are published respectively in the *Vossische Zeitung* and the *Spenersche Zeitung*.
On 22 June, Menzel travels to Leipzig for the Gutenberg celebrations, and from 1 to 12 July visits Dresden for study purposes. The baroque buildings he is interested in are still

partly in ruins since their destruction in the Seven Years War. In appreciating the beauty of this style of architecture, Menzel is decades ahead of art critics generally.
Menzel is present at the autumn manoeuvres in Potsdam.

1841
From 12 September, Menzel spends a fortnight with the Arnold family in Kassel.

1842
Menzel begins his *Armeewerk*: 436 pen lithographs for *The Army of Frederick the Great and its Uniforms* (three volumes, published by Sachse & Co., completed in 1857).

1843
Menzel begins the two hundred illustrations for *Werke Friedrichs des Grossen* (The Works of Frederick the Great; completed in 1849). Commissioned by Frederick William IV, king since 1840, this project establishes contact with the court and the king's intermediary, Ignaz von Olfers, director general of the Royal Museums.
The Interruption (cat. 19). finished in 1846, is one of Menzel's first oil paintings for many years.
Menzel is greatly impressed by paintings by the Belgians Bièvfe and Gallait, exhibited in the rotunda of the Berlin Museum, but his enthusiasm soon cools.
First etchings, including *The Sleeping Seamstress.*

1844
Menzel makes regular visits to the Kupferstichkabinett to study Dutch etchings particularly those of Rembrandt.
Experiments in Etching (title pages and six sheets) published by Sachse & Co., Berlin, Paris, London.
He visits relatives in Silesia (at Jauer and Striegau) and stops at Breslau and Frankfurt an der Oder.

1845
At the end of March, the Menzel family moves to 18 Schöneberger Strasse. Friendly relations are established with the family of Dr Carl Anton Maercker, who lives in the same building.
Friederike, the daughter of Menzel's friend Arnold, visits the Menzel family. Menzel feels great affection for her. He paints her portrait and *Balcony Room* (cat. 18).

1846
Death of Menzel's mother, on 8 October.
From early October to late December, the family receive Carl Johann Arnold, son of Menzel's friend, who becomes Menzel's pupil.
Portrait of the Artist's Brother Richard (oil, Georg Schäfer Collection, Euerbach).

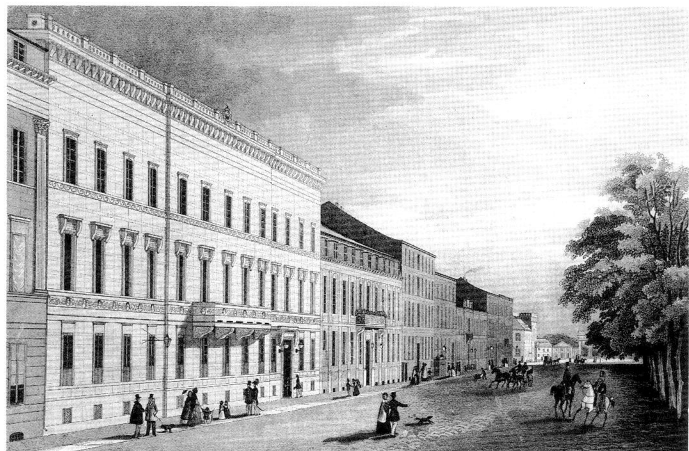

Fig. 42. Hôtel de Russie, Berlin, *c.* 1830, lithograph

Storm over the Tempelhofer Berg (cat. 21).
Building Site with Willows (cat. 22).
View over Prince Albert's Palace Park (cat. 23).
Chalk drawing of *Carl Arnold* at the age of seventeen, finished in 1847 (cat. 39).

1847
The entire Menzel family moves to 43 Ritterstrasse.
An Evening Together (cat. 28).
Portrait of Mrs Maercker (cat. 29).
At the Kreuzberg, near Berlin (cat. 31).
Back Yards in the Snow, Berlin (cat. 32).
The Berlin–Potsdam Railway, first German painting of a train (cat. 35).
The Artist's Bedroom in Ritterstrasse (cat. 34).
Sermon in the former Abbey Church, Berlin (oil, Gemäldegalerie Neue Meister, Dresden).
Living Room with the Artist's Sister (cat. 36).
Gustav Adolph Greets his Wife outside Hanau Castle (cat. 37).
On 11 August, Menzel goes to stay with the Arnolds at Kassel, travelling via Eisenach (where he visits the Wartburg). Thanks to Arnold, he receives a commission from the Hesse Art Society for a history painting to mark the sixth centenary of the house of Hesse. He has long aspired to do a painting of this kind. After four days at Marburg, for study purposes, Menzel draws the cartoon for *The Infant Henry, future Landgrave of Hesse, entering Marburg with his Mother, 1247* in charcoal, then in black chalk, finishing the work on 19 March 1848 (Kulturhistorisches Museum, Magdeburg, until 1945, now lost). However, it is not as well received as he had hoped, and Menzel is keenly disappointed.

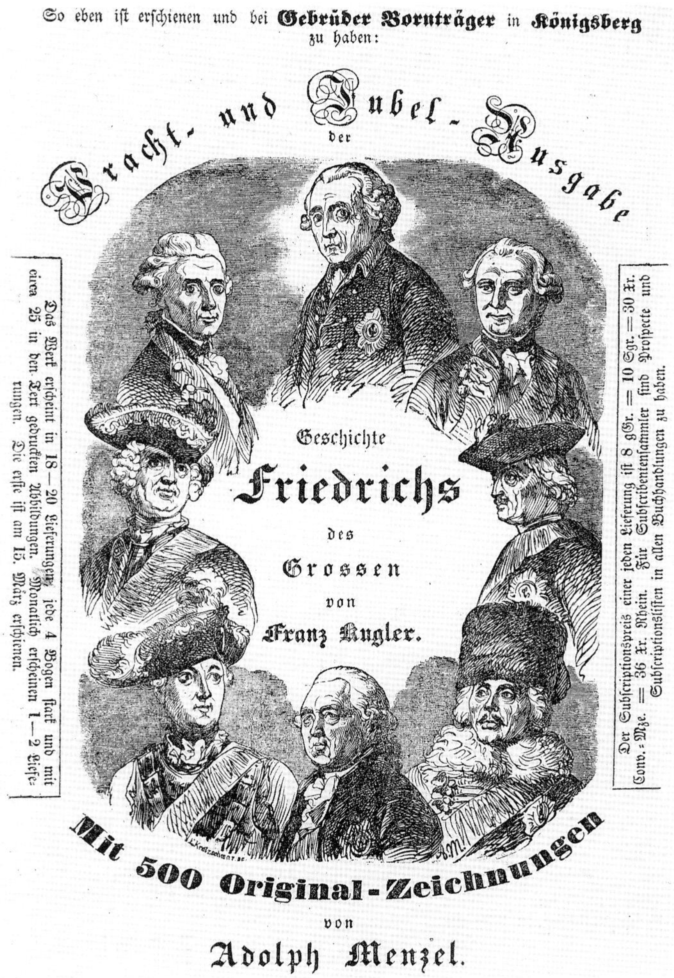

Fig. 43. Notice advertising Franz Kugler's *History of Frederick the Great*, illustrated by Menzel, 1839, wood engraving

1848

On 21 March 1848, just a few days after the street fighting, Menzel returns to Berlin. The next day, he sees the bodies of the citizens killed in the insurrection (about three hundred) laid in state in front of the German Church in the Gendarmenmarkt. Disturbed by the sight, Menzel begins the painting *Lying in State of the March Dead*, which remains unfinished (oil, Hamburger Kunsthalle, Hamburg) and has been interpreted as a striking symbol of the liberal bourgeoisie's lost hopes of a social revolution.

He paints oil studies of the heads of horses slaughtered at the abattoir (cat. 43, 44), a number of small pictures of his immediate surroundings: *Gardens of the Ministry of Justice* (oil, Bremen Kunsthalle, Bremen until 1945; now lost), *Stairway Landing in Nocturnal Lighting* (cat. 42), and some portraits: *Portrait of Clara Ilgner (later to become Mrs Schmidt von Knobelsdorf)* (cat. 46), *Carl Heinrich Arnold* (oil, Nationalgalerie, Berlin), *Richard Seated at Table* (*cf.* cat. 41, footnote 7).

1849

Menzel executes three pastels from memory: *Electors* (cat. 50, 51).

He takes an interest in paintings from the time of Frederick II. He paints *The Petition* (cat. 52), hoping that this work will become 'the seed which produces a long ear of corn' (16 January, writing to Carl Heinrich Arnold). He begins *The Flute Concert of Frederick the Great at Sanssouci*, taking it up again in 1851 and completing the work in 1852 (cat. 56), and *The Round Table of Frederick II at Sanssouci*, finished in 1850 (oil, Nationalgalerie, Berlin, until 1945, since lost).

1850

Friederike Arnold marries.

In August, Menzel travels to the Harz mountains via Dresden, Meissen, Halberstadt, the castle of Falkenstein, the Baumannhöhle near Rübeland and Goslar. He paints a number of male portraits in watercolour and gouache: *Commandant von Leithold* (Kupferstichkabinett, Berlin), *General von Prittwitz* (present location unknown), *Dr Puhlmann* (Kupferstichkabinett, Berlin), *General von Bieler* (present location unknown), *Doctor Karl Eitner* (Kupferstichkabinett, Berlin), and in pastel: *The Writer Heinrich Smidt* (Hamburger Kunsthalle, Hamburg). Menzel does not feel his vocation is as a portraitist, but continues to take an interest in facial features. He begins painting the *Night Attack at Hochkirch*, finished in 1856. He receives a commission for a series of wood engravings: *The Time of King Frederick. Heroes of War and Peace* (begun for Weber of Leipzig, published in 1856 by Duncker of Berlin).

The Zwinger at Dresden (oil, Hamburger Kunsthalle, Hamburg).

Congratulatory Address by the Berlin City Council to Prince Frederick William on his Majority (cat. 53).

On 20 October, Menzel becomes a member of the literary circle 'Tunnel über der Spree'. Members include the art historian Franz Kugler, and other well-known Berliners: poets, writers, academics, lawyers and officers. Each member is known by a pseudonym; Menzel takes the pseudonym 'Rubens'.

1851

Menzel travels to the Baltic via Pasewalk, Stralsund and the island of Rügen, returning via Stettin.

His *Experiments on Stone with Paintbrush and Scraper* (Title Page and Six Sheets) is published by Meder of Berlin. A self-portrait, *The Antiquary*, is intended for inclusion in

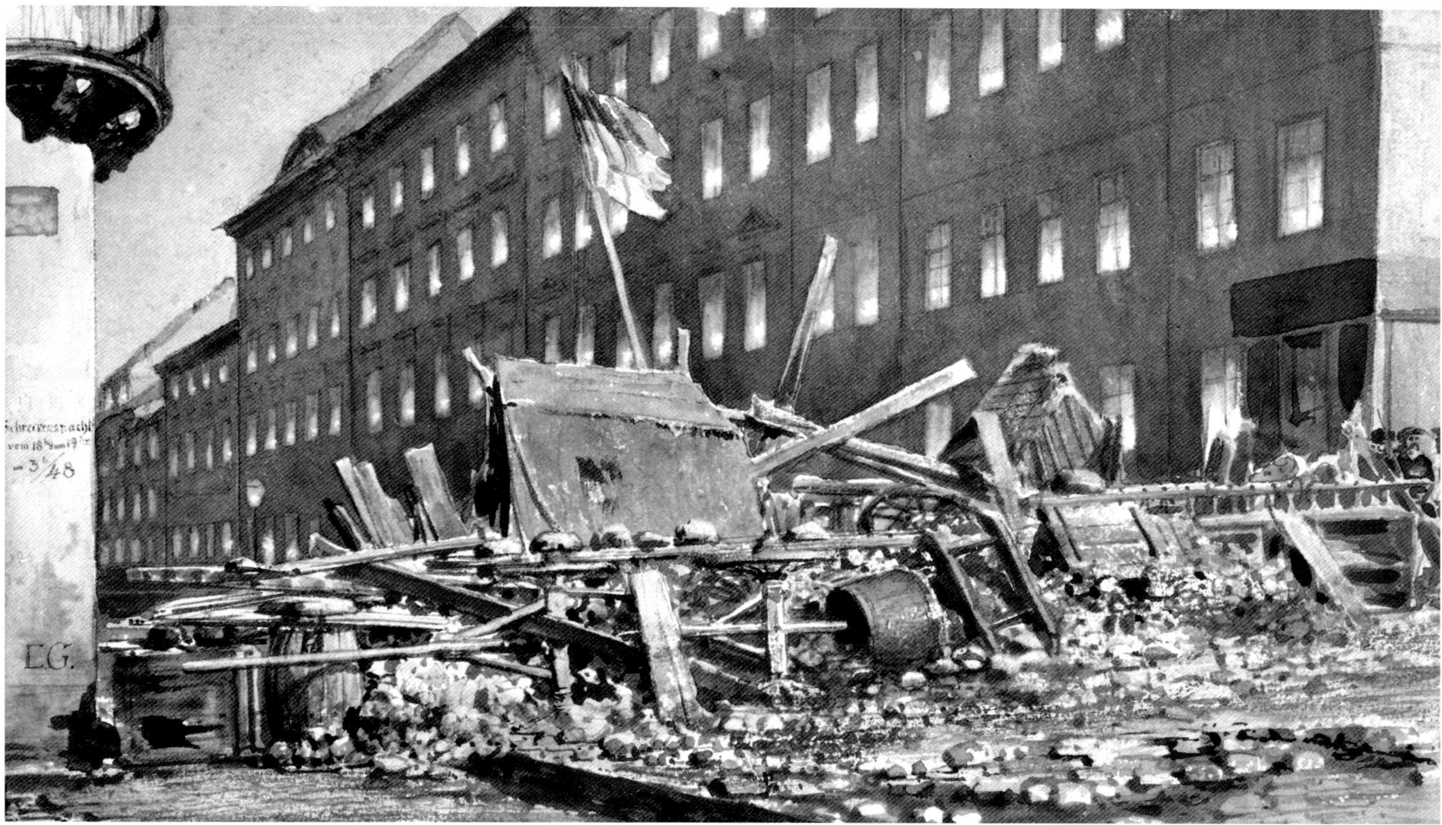

Fig. 44. Eduard Gärtner, *The Barricade on the Breite Strasse*, 1848, watercolour, Berlin, Stadtmuseum

the continuation of the series.
Elderly Jew (The Rabbi of Baghdad) (oil, reworked in 1882, private collection).
In the Boudoir (oil, Hamburger Kunsthalle, Hamburg).
In a Railway Carriage (after a Night's Journey) (watercolour and gouache, present location unknown).
Jesus among the Doctors of the Law, panel for the Academy's Christmas exhibition (present locaton unknown), and a pastel study for it (Hamburger Kunsthalle, Hamburg).

1852
During the summer, Menzel executes a lithographic version of *Jesus among the Doctors of the Law*, using a scraper. He paints two pictures for the art dealer Goupil of Paris: *Frederick the Great and the Dancer Barbarina* (cat. 63) and *Frederick the Great and General Fouqué* (cat. 64).
Studio Wall (cat. 65).
From early August to late October, he goes on his first long summer study trip with his sister: Bamberg, Nuremberg, Munich (Nymphenburg), and into Austria via the Alps: Salzburg (Hellbrunn), the Salzkammergut, Berchtesgaden, Traunstein. They sail the Danube from Donauwörth to Vienna, via Regensburg, Passau, Linz and Klosterneuburg, and returning via Prague.
In December, some members of the 'Tunnel über der Spree' literary circle set up a smaller group, the 'Rütli'. Every Saturday, at coffee time, they meet at one of the members' homes to discuss art and literature. Some of the first 'Rütlians', besides Menzel, are the writers Paul Heyse, Theodor Fontane and Theodor Storm, the art historians Franz Kugler and Friedrich Eggers, appeal court counsel Wilhelm von Merckel, provincial high school inspector Karl Bormann and officer Bernhard von Lepel.
Menzel strikes up a friendship with Fritz Werner, who occasionally produces reproductive prints of Menzel's paintings.

1853
Menzel is elected member of the Royal Academy of Arts.
Trip to Halberstadt and Brunswick.
In the Old-New Synagogue in Prague (oil, Wallraf-Richartz Museum, Cologne).
In Front of St Michael's Church in Munich (gouache, Albertina, Vienna).

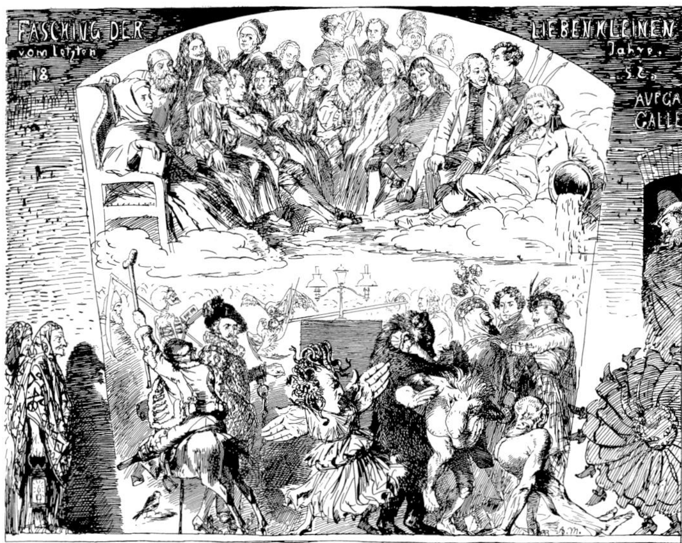

Fig. 45. Souvenir of the carnival celebration of the 'Tunnel Society', 1852, pen lithograph

1854
Frederick William IV commissions a commemorative album for his sister, the Empress Alexandra of Russia: ten gouaches for the 25th anniversary of the 'White Rose Festival' held in Potsdam on 13 July 1829 (Hermitage Museum, St Petersburg).
Frederick the Great on his Travels (oil, Nationalgalerie, Berlin).

1855
Fulfilling a commission from the Silesian Society of Arts, Menzel paints the *Homage of the Silesian Estates to Frederick II in 1741* (oil, Nationalgalerie, Berlin).
A Place for the Great Raphael! (gouache, Germanisches Nationalmuseum, Nuremberg).
As part of the restoration of the Marienburg, Menzel is commissioned to paint two *Grand Masters of the Teutonic Order* for the great refectory (*cf.* cat. 20).
On 1 August, he leaves with his sister for the Marienburg, where he paints the grand masters using a stereochrome technique. He visits the great bridge over the Vistula at Dirschau, then makes his way to Cologne without stopping in Berlin. An excursion in the Rhineland takes in the Lorelei, the Rheinfels ruins, Sankt Goar, Bingen, Heidelberg, the Black Forest and Strasbourg.
In September, he spends a fortnight in Paris for the Universal Exhibition, where international art is on show for the first time at the Palais de l'Industrie. Menzel's *Round Table* is also on display. He visits Courbet's 'Pavillon du Réalisme'. The English Pre-Raphaelites are also exhibiting their works on the continent for the first time.
The Marienburg (watercolour, Kupferstichkabinett, Berlin).
The Rheinfels Ruins (watercolour, Kupferstichkabinett, Berlin).
Moonlight on the Friedrichsgracht in Old Berlin (cat. 76).

1856
The Théâtre du Gymnase (cat. 80).
Menzel finishes and exhibits his painting of the *Night Attack at Hochkirch* at the Berlin Akademie der Künste (Academy of Arts), to widespread acclaim.
He is appointed professor at the Royal Academy of Arts, Berlin.
Journey to Neisse and Lissa in Silesia in preparation for two commissions to paint subjects relating to Frederick the Great. In March, Menzel writes to Fritz Werner: 'I am off [to Neisse and Lissa] and am recording those local scenes which have remained unchanged. . .'

1857
Gold medal from the Berlin Academy of Arts for the painting *Night Attack at Hochkirch*. He finishes the *Meeting between King Frederick II and the Emperor Joseph II in 1769 in the Bishop's Palace at Neisse* (oil, Nationalgalerie, Berlin); Menzel had been commissioned to paint this work in 1855 by the Verbindung für historische Kunst (an association founded in 1854 to encourage history painting).
Summer journey to Thuringia: Weissenfels, Griesheim bei Stadtilm, Paulinzella, the castle of Schwarzburg. Return via Dresden and Moritzburg.

Fig. 46. August Kaselowsky (?), *Menzel and his Artist Friends at the Mielentz Café in Berlin*, 1851, pencil and wash, Stockholm, Nationalmuseum

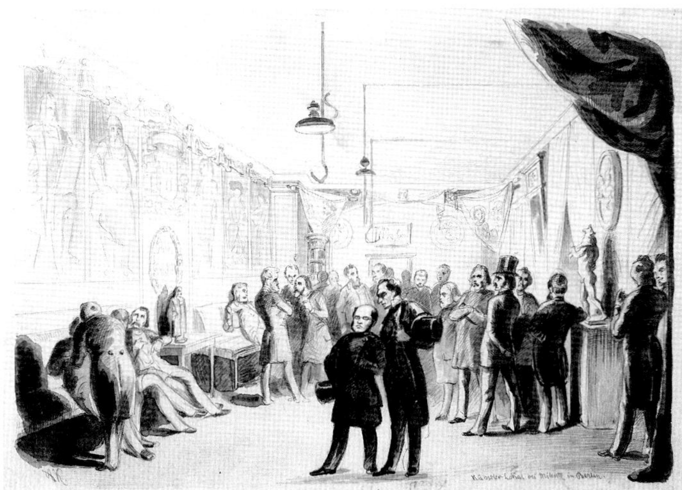

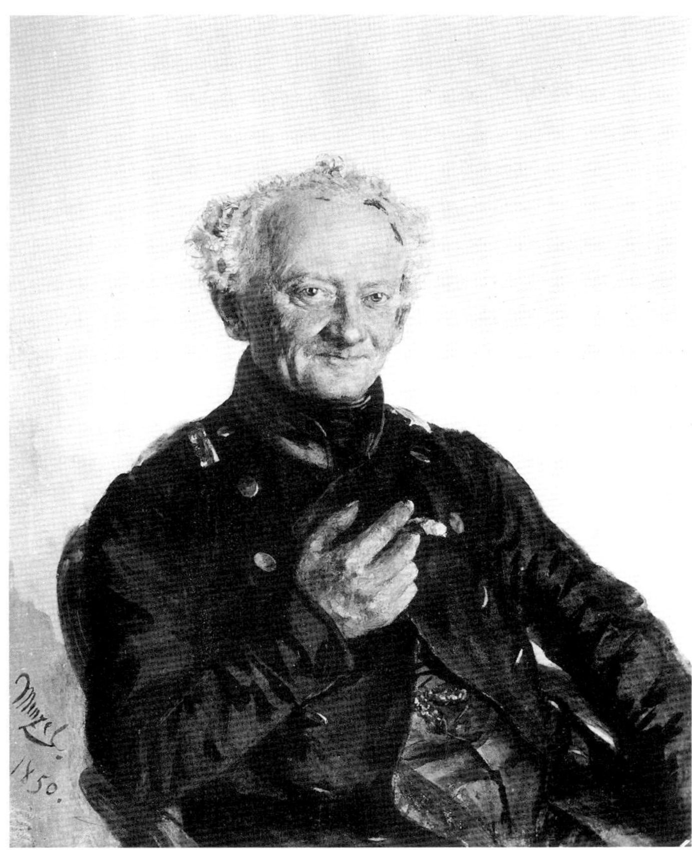

Fig. 47. *Dr Wilhelm Puhlmann*, 1850, watercolour and gouache, Berlin, Kupferstichkabinett (Nr. 1713)

1858

He leaves *Bonsoir, Messieurs! (Frederick the Great at Lissa)*, begun in 1856, unfinished (cat. 82).

Blücher and Wellington after the Battle of Waterloo, a wedding present from the court to the future Emperor Frederick III (oil, Neue Pinakothek, Munich).

After the Torchlight Procession on the Dönhoffplatz (cat. 85).

1859

On 10 May, Menzel's sister marries the royal music director and composer Hermann Krigar. The Menzels continue to live in the same building.

Summer journey to Altenburg, Bamberg, Kulmbach and Rosenheim. In September, Menzel visits the Tyrol, Kufstein, Fügen in Zillertal and Innsbruck.

Country Theatre at Kufstein (oil, Hamburger Kunsthalle).

Students' Torchlight Procession (cat. 86).

Chodowiecki drawing on the Jannowitzbrücke (oil, Georg Schäfer Collection, Euerbach).

Menzel begins the last great work in the Frederick cycle, *Frederick the Great's Address to his Generals before the Battle of Leuthen* (unfinished, cat.90). Concerning this picture, he writes to Adolf Schöll on 1 July 1859: 'Where business is concerned, I have once again taken on a big commitment, may God allow me to bring it to completion. The subject is the speech old Fritz addressed to his men before the battle of Leuthen. What I have to do is paint a moral effect . . ..'

Until 1862, Menzel did a number of gouaches for the Berlin collector and commercial consultant Kahlbaum. In some of these, he transformed the main theme of 'Frederick' into more intimate historical depictions of the time when Frederick was crown prince: *Boat Trip at Rheinsberg* (gouache, private collection), *Crown Prince Frederick Pays a Visit to the Painter Pesne on his Scaffolding at Rheinsberg*; cat. 93), *Court Ball at Rheinsberg* (gouache, Georg Schäfer Collection, Euerbach).

1860

Early October, journey to Rheinsberg, then to Neuruppin and Wustrau (Zieten castle).

At the end of the year, move to 22 Marienstrasse, next door to his brother and the Krigar family.

Twelve wood engravings for Berthold Auerbach's *Der Blitzschlosser von Wittenberg* (in the *Auerbachs Volkskalendar*, 1861).

Robing before Mass in the Sacristy of the Servite Convent in Innsbruck (gouache, present location unknown).

The End of the Evening (cat. 91)

Two Builders at Work (cat. 92).

1861

From mid-July to mid-August, illness leads Menzel to visit the spa at Bad Freienwalde in the March of Brandenburg.

Exhibition at the Berlin Künstlerhaus, including *The Théâtre du Gymnase*.

In September, journey to Antwerp (to the Congress of Artists, where Courbet gives his speech on realism). Menzel writes to Fritz Werner in Düsseldorf on 11 July 1861 that he cannot attend the Cologne exhibition because he is taking the cure, 'but I could make it to the Cours in Belgium for a time . . .'. He travels via Magdeburg to visit Brunswick, Düsseldorf, Antwerp, Ghent, Bruges, Ostend and Brussels, and returns via Cologne.

On 12 October, Menzel is informed by minister Bethmann-Hollweg that he has received a royal commission to paint a faithful representation of the *Coronation of William I at Königsberg* (oil, Stiftung Preussische Schlösser und Gärten, Potsdam). Fritz Werner accompanies him to the coronation ceremonies on 18 October, to assist him in his studies of the settings and colours. Over the next four years Menzel sketches the portraits of those present. The Guard Room in Berlin Royal Palace is made available to him as a studio. The picture is finished on 15 December 1865. From the time of this commission, Menzel is invited to court festivities. Representations of contemporary society are henceforward one of the main themes of his work.

1862
On 6 April, he begins his painting of *The Coronation* in the Guard Room.
At the Opera (cat. 100).
Market in Winter (cat. 101).

1863
Exhibition of Menzel's works on the time of Frederick II at the Academy, starting on 15 February (to mark the centenary of the Peace of Hubertusburg).
View from a Window of the Royal Palace in Berlin (cat. 102)
For his sister's two children, Menzel begins his *Children's Album* (cat. 105–14): forty-four gouaches, on which he worked for twenty years and partly revised in 1883.

1864
On 23 July, Menzel's brother Richard marries Elise Preuss. He had studied to be a photographer but, for health reasons, had been living on his property at Oderbruch since 1860. After his marriage, with Menzel's financial help, he acquired the Gustav Schauer photographic studio and returned to Berlin. In the summer, Menzel undertakes a journey in the Elbsandsteingebirge, southern Saxony and Bohemia.

1865
Moves, with the Krigar family, to 24 Luisenstrasse.
The Russian writer Ivan Turgenev visits Menzel.
Visit to Kösen, with the Krigars, for treatment and rest. There, on 14 July, he learns of the death of his brother. Menzel returns to Kösen in August.
On 25 August he enters his name in the visitors' book at Goethe's house in Weimar.
He visits the Rudelsburg at Saaleck, then Banz monastery and Würzburg.
Young Bathers in the Saale at Kösen (gouache, private collection).

1866
In July, Menzel visits the battlefields of the Austro-Prussian War. Leaving on 16 July, he travels via Görlitz, Reichenbach, Turnau, Königinhof and Horzice. On 24 July, arrives in Prague, because rail travel has been interrupted in the war zone. On his way to Pardubitz, he sees the battle fields of Königgrätz and Sadowa-Chlum,

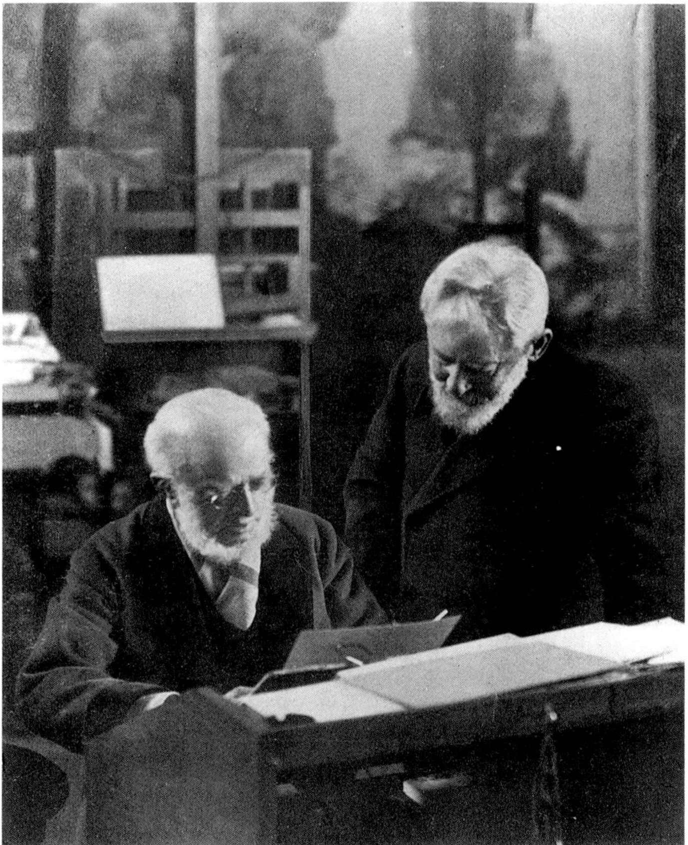
Fig. 48. The critic Ludwig Pietsch at Menzel's studio, *c.* 1895, anonymous photograph

scene of the decisive engagement in Prussia's favour on 3 July. At Königinhof, where military hospitals have been set up, he draws wounded and dying soldiers and corpses. 'I, too, was motivated by a sense of duty – he writes – which would not leave me until I had at least gone to experience the smell of war! . . .' And: 'Now I also know where Schlüter gets his Zeughaus masks from.'
In August, Menzel is at Kassel with his sister-in-law and a photographer, to advise her on setting up a 'gallery of artists' (a series of photographs of pictures in the gallery). The first volume is published by Schauer in December, including a large-format photograph of his *Coronation* picture. Menzel paints *Fantasies from the Arms Room* (cat. 117–19), watercolours and gouaches based on weapons and suits of armour kept in the Guard Room he used as a workshop.
Commemorative Diploma from the Municipality of Berlin to King William I, to mark the Entry of his Troops (gouache, present location unknown).
Interior of the Old-New Synagogue in Prague (gouache,

Georg Schäfer Collection, Euerbach).

1867
Ball Scene (gouache, Neue Pinakothek, Munich).
View from a Window in the Marienstrasse (gouache, Stiftung Oskar Reinhart Museum, Winterthur).
View of a Courtyard (gouache, Nationalgalerie, Berlin).
Guess Who? (Blind Man's Buff) (gouache, present location unknown).
From late May till early August, Menzel is in Paris for the Universal Exhibition, with the painter Paul Meyerheim and his sister-in-law Elise. He is invited to the Palais de l'Industrie with Meissonier and Meyerheim, receiving the second-place medal for his painting *Night Attack at Hochkirch*, which is on show there. He and the painter Ludwig Knaus are awarded the cross of the Légion d'honneur (29 June).
He goes to the Louvre with Knaus and several times visits the Poissy home of Meissonier, whom he first met in Berlin in 1862. He gets to know the Belgian painter Alfred Stevens, and the painters Louis Ricard and Jean Léon Gérôme. He visits the Courbet exhibition and also, probably, the Manet pavilion.
At the Louvre (cat. 122).
Afternoon in the Tuileries Gardens (cat. 123)
The American Restaurant at the Universal Exhibition in Paris (oil, present location unknown).

1868
From 9 June to 4 July, Menzel visits Paris, where his *Coronation* and two small genre paintings – *Guess Who?* and *Shall I Open It?* (gouaches, present locations unknown) were exhibited at the Salon.
Menzel visits and sketches the tomb of Heinrich Heine.
Return via Cologne, Hannover, Brunswick and Bad Harzburg.
Borussia, for a charity sale in favour of needy Silesians (cat. 124).
Sermon in the Beechwood at Kösen, based on studies done during his 1865 visit (cat. 125).
Menzel is made an honorary member of the Austrian Academy of Arts.

1869
Meissonier in his Studio at Poissy (cat. 126); a photographic reproduction of a study of Meissonier, seated at his easel, had already been published in 1867 by Schauer. Since 1866, Menzel's sister-in-law had been planning a 'Menzel Album', which appeared with an introduction by Ludwig Pietsch.
Weekday in Paris, Menzel's first large-scale street scene (cat. 127).
Old Elephant at the Jardin des Plantes (gouache, present location unknown).
Summer journey to Cologne, Trier, Koblenz, Boppard, Sankt Goar, Heidelberg, Darmstadt, Mainz and Munich, where, at the International Art Exhibition, Menzel has another opportunity to view Courbet's *The Stone-Breakers*, first seen in Paris in 1855.
Chiorstalls in Mainz Cathedral, gouache (cat. 128).
Excursion to Neuzelle an der Oder.
Diploma for the Fiftieth Anniversary of the Heckmann Factory, featuring two realistic depictions of industrial production at the Heckmann foundry (cat. 129).

1870
Menzel is awarded the 'Order of Merit' instituted by Frederick II in 1740 (to which Frederick William IV had added a section for the Arts and Sciences in 1842).
The Viennese Society of Artists exhibits watercolours and gouaches by Menzel.
Henry VIII Dancing with Anne Boleyn (monochrome gouache, Georg Schäfer Collection, Euerbach), reproduced as a photograph in autumn 1870 in Grote's *Shakespeare Gallery* in Berlin.
In November, the Menzel-Krigar family moves to 7 Potsdamer Strasse.

1871
French Prisoners of War (cat. 130–131).
Departure of King William I for the Army, 31 July 1870 (cat. 134).
Moltke and *Bismarck*, two paintings to decorate the Academy building on Unter den Linden in celebration of the Prussian victory over the French (oils, Stiftung Preussische Schlösser und Gärten, Potsdam).
Diplomas from the City of Berlin for Moltke and Bismarck (gouaches, the present location of the former is unknown; the latter can be seen at the Bismarck Museum, Friedrichsruh).
Lull during the Ball (oil, Munich, Neue Pinakothek, Euerbach).
Summer journey to Bamberg, Nuremberg, Heilbronn, Munich, Salzburg, Berchtesgaden, Linz Melk Abbey and Vienna.
Menzel visits the Holbein exhibition in Dresden.
The Esterhazy Vault in Vienna (oil, present location unknown).
Interior and Altar of St Peter's Church, Salzburg (gouache, present location unknown).
Bilse Concert (cat.135).

1872
Recollection of the Luxembourg Gardens (cat. 136).

Summer journey to Kissingen, Regensburg, Salzburg, Hofgastein, Werfen, Sankt Johann, Zell am See, Fügen in Zillertal, Innsbruck.
Interior of St James's Church, Innsbruck, with the Tomb of Archduke Maximilian III (gouache, private collection).
Menzel is made an honorary member of the Munich Academy of Arts.
Visit to Königshütte in Upper Silesia to prepare for his painting *The Iron Rolling Mill* (cat. 160), finished in 1875. This is the first major German painting representing a factory with the emphasis on men rather than machines.
In October, *Studio Wall* (cat. 137); at the centre of this allegorical composition is the death mask of Friedrich Eggers, who had died in August.
Max Liebermann's *Goose Pluckers*, exhibited at the Academy, attracts Menzel's attention and marks the beginning of their friendship.

1873
The Prussian government buys the works owned by the Friends of the Arts in Prussia for the future Nationalgalerie in Berlin, including the oil painting of *The Round Table*.
Summer journey: Sankt Gilgen am Wolfgangsee, Hofgastein, Vienna (for the Universal Exhibition), returning via Eger and Prague.
Indian Café at the Universal Exhibition in Vienna (gouache, private collection).
Inside the Rustic 'White Pigeon' Inn at Hofgastein (gouache, Georg Schäfer Collection, Euerbach).
High Altar in the Damenstiftskirche, Munich (gouache, Georg Schäfer Collection, Euerbach).

1874
Beer-Garden at Kissingen (watercolour and gouache, private collection).
Hofgastein (gouache, Nationalgalerie, Berlin, until 1945, since lost).
Summer journey: Regensburg, Linz, Hüttau, Gmunden, Gosau, Salzburg, Hofgastein, Vienna, Klosterneuburg, returning via Munich, Eger and Dresden.

1875
The Iron Rolling Mill, recently completed by Menzel, is immediately purchased by the Berlin Nationalgalerie, together with *The Flute Concert*.
The Menzel-Krigar family moves to the Sigismundstrasse, near the Tiergarten, in the 'old western part' of Berlin (Menzel's last residence and studio).
Menzel is elected to the senate of the Academy, with Gustav Richter and Reinhold Begas.
Summer journey via Banz Abbey to Bayreuth, where he draws Richard Wagner during a rehearsal (7 and 8 August). Menzel travels on to Garmisch, Ettal Abbey and Innsbruck.
Bricklayers on a Building Site (gouache, cat.162).
Interior of the Convent Church at Ettal (gouache, present location unknown).
Planning a Journey (cat. 163).

1876
Summer journey through Southern Germany and Switzerland: Wurzburg, Stuttgart, Rottweil, Constance, Lindau, Lucerne, Interlaken, Zurich, Sonthofen, Oberstdorf in Allgäu, Munich and Bayreuth, where he attends a performance of *The Ring of the Nibelungen* to inaugurate the Festival theatre. Return via Leipzig.
In October, visit to Holland – Amsterdam, Utrecht, Rotterdam, The Hague – to do studies for wood engravings illustrating a centenary edition of Kleist's *The Broken Pitcher*. This is published in 1877, with thirty illustrations and four photographs of monochrome gouaches, by Hofmann & Co. in Berlin.
By the Fireside (cat. 166).

1877
Summer journey to Regensburg and Mondsee in the Salzkammergut.

1878
The Iron Rolling Mill, The Round Table and *The Flute Concert* are sent to Paris for the Universal Exhibition. The imperial government's decision to send one hundred and sixty works to the Exhibition is made at the last minute. (Even after the Franco-Prussian War, Menzel, together with Leibl, continued to send works to Paris, although some State bodies put pressure on artists to discourage them from exhibiting).
Supper at the Ball (cat. 167).
Frederick II at the Tomb of the Great Elector (monochrome oil, present location unknown).
Four wood engravings on the theme of Frederick the Great for Johannes Scherr's cultural history *Germania* (published by Spemann of Stuttgart).
Academy of Arts Diploma for Emperor William I after the Attempt on his Life (gouache, present location unknown).

1879
The Circle of Emperor William I (oil, Georg Schäfer Collection, Euerbach).
Summer journey to Hofgastein, Salzburg and Bernried

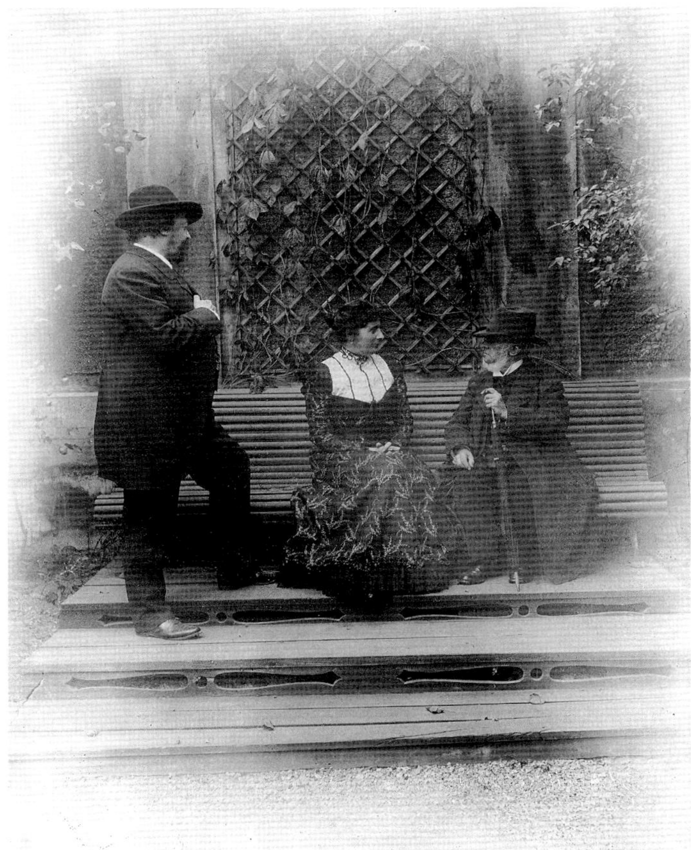

Fig. 49. Menzel visiting the poet Paul Heyse and his wife, *c.* 1890, anonymous photograph

on the Starnberg See.
Ironworks at Hofgastein (gouache, Nationalgalerie, Berlin, until 1945, now lost).
The Oyster Eater (brush and ink wash, present location unknown).

1880
Corpus Christi Procession at Hofgastein (cat. 174).
Summer journey to the Dresden and the Elbsandsteingebirge (Herrnkretschen).
Hermann Pächter, owner of the art dealership, R. Wagner, takes charge of marketing Menzel's works, an arrangement that is to continue for the rest of his life. Menzel has known Pächter since the mid-1870s. (Louis Friedrich Sachse, with whom Menzel had been connected for many years, went bankrupt after the 1873 crisis and his valuable collection was sold at auction in 1878).
Menzel writes the obituary of his brother-in-law Hermann Krigar.

1881
Knife-grinder's Workshop in the Hofgastein Smithy (cat. 175).
Sermon in the Parish Church in Innsbruck (cat. 176).
Spinet Player (gouache, present location unknown).
Summer journey to Frankfurt am Main, Baden-Baden, Fribourg in Breisgau, Villingen, Switzerland, the South Tyrol and Northern Italy (Lucerne, Interlaken, Geneva, Sankt Gallen, Fribourg, Bressanone, Bolzano, Gries, Merano, Brescia, Como, Verona, returning via Innsbruck, Munich and Nuremberg).

1882
Sketches for a dinner service made by the royal porcelain factory in Berlin to celebrate the silver wedding of the emperor and empress (watercolour and gouache). Summer journey to Vienna, Berchtesgaden, Munich, Chiavenna, Brescia, Como and Verona. In October, the Nationalgalerie acquires many works by Menzel from the estate of his late friend, Dr Wilhelm Puhlmann.

1883
Menzel is appointed vice-chancellor of the arts and sciences section of the 'Order of Merit'.
Summer journey to Regensburg, Heilbronn, Augsburg, Imst, Garmisch, Zugspitze and Verona, returning via Dresden.
Munich Beer-Garden (gouache, Georg Schäfer Collection, Euerbach).
Menzel turns down a commission from the Northern Pacific Railroad Company for a painting to mark the inauguration of their railway.

1884
Marketplace in Verona (Piazza d'Erbe) (cat. 179), begun after his first visit to Verona, is shown at the Berlin Society of Artists.
At Easter, the Nationalgalerie puts on an exhibition devoted to Menzel, to mark fifty years' activity as an artist.
The German Society of Arts in Düsseldorf makes Menzel an honorary member.
Summer journey to Kissingen, Kreuzberg, Hammelburg, Bodenlaube Ruins, Rothenburg, Würzburg, Garmisch, Berchtesgaden, Maria Plain near Salzburg and Munich.
Camel Driver at Partenkirchen (cat. 180).
At the Warm Kettle at Kissingen (gouache, present location unknown).
The Aura Ruins at Kissingen (gouache, present location unknown).

1885
26 April to 15 June, Menzel exhibition at the Pavillon de

la Ville, Paris.
Menzel exhibition at the Austrian Society of Arts, Vienna.
Summer journey to Kissingen, Interlaken, Berne, Lucerne, Schaffhausen, Rorschach, Baden-Baden and Dresden.
Lady Walking by a Fountain in the Kissingen Spa Garden (cat. 184).
Ash Wednesday Morning (gouache, Nationalgalerie, Berlin, until 1945, now lost).
Japanese Painter (cat. 183).
Altar Decoration (gouache, present location unknown).
Contribution (gouache, Kupferstichkabinett, Berlin).
To mark his seventieth birthday, the Academy shows almost all the works by Menzel to be found in Berlin, and some from his personal collection. *Studio Wall*, painted in 1872, is exhibited for the first time.
Menzel is awarded an honorary doctorate by the University of Berlin, made an honorary citizen of his native Breslau, and an honorary member of the Academy of Arts of St Petersburg.
The Berlin Society of Arts lays on a banquet, and Theodor Fontane composes a poem in Menzel's honour.

1886
Menzel is appointed chancellor of the arts and sciences section of the 'Order of Merit'.
Summer journey to Dresden, Merseburg, Friedricksroda, Meiningen and Kissingen.
Market Scene in Verona (gouache, Kupferstichkabinett, Berlin).
Menzel begins a cycle of three small historical genre paintings in gouache: *Absent-minded as Can Be* (private collection), *The Letter* (The Metropolitan Museum of Art, New York) and *Coming out of Church*, finished in 1887 (cat. 188).
Coffee Time at Kissingen (gouache, private collection).
Intervention (gouache, present location unknown).
Concert Audience (gouache, private collection).

1887
Summer journey to Altenburg, Munich, Salzburg, Berchtesgaden and Marienbad.
Japanese Dressmaker (On the Japanese Stand) (gouache, Georg Schäfer Collection, Euerbach).
Honorary Citizen's Diploma from Hamburg City Council to G.C. Schwabe (cat. 187).
Academy of Arts Honorary Diploma awarded to Minister of State Gossler (gouache, present location unknown).

1888
On 3 March, inauguration of the International Exhibition in Vienna (without the participation of France). Menzel exhibits *Corpus Christi Procession at Hofgastein* and a series of watercolours. He is awarded the gold medal by the Austrian government.
Summer journey: Kissingen, Bamberg, Pommersfelden, Munich, Sterzing, Dresden, Merseburg.
In the White Room (oil, Georg Schäfer Collection, Euerbach).
Prague Synagogue (gouache, Georg Schäfer Collection, Euerbach).
Beati Possidentes (gouache, Georg Schäfer Collection, Euerbach).
In the Peterskeller, Salzburg (water colour, present location unknown).

1889
Menzel takes part in the Universal Exhibition in Paris (marking the centenary of the French Revolution). The pro-government newspaper *Berliner Politische Nachrichten* writes: 'For most people, it is shocking that a group of German artists should exhibit their works at the Paris Exhibition . . .' Discovering that Menzel was of their number, it continues: 'it is barely credible to find such names as Liebermann, Kühl, Achenbach, Leibl, Uhde and other Munich painters among the exhibitors.'
Summer journey to Kissingen. In September, Munich Fürstenfeld Abbey, Salzburg, the Tegernsee, Regensburg and Leipzig.
In October, the Nationalgalerie purchases from Pächter 1305 drawings (*Fridericiana*), seven oil studies for history paintings, the *Children's Album*, seven sketches for the royal silver wedding dinner service, and a charcoal study *Frederick William I Visits a Village School* (1858, Kupferstichkabinett, Berlin).
After the Court Festival (oil, Muzeum Naradowe, Posnan).

Fig. 50. Hans Herrmann, *The Jury of the 1890 Berlin Academy Exhibition*, 1890, gouache, Berlin, Stadtmuseum

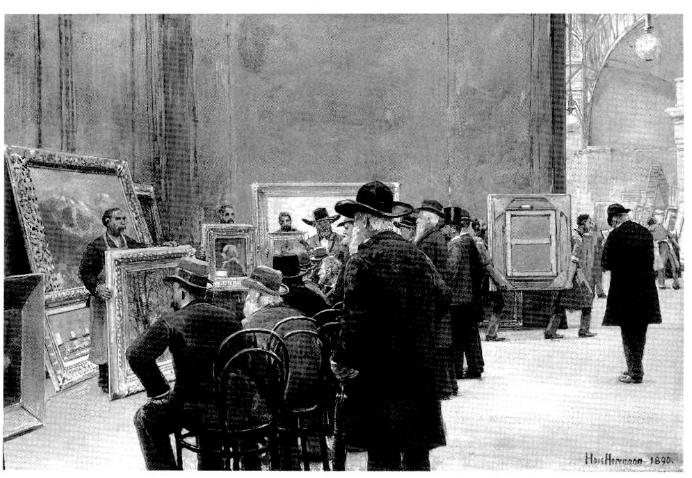

Learning Italian, engraving for the Berliner Verein für Original'Radierung (association of painters and engravers), volume IV (Menzel had been a member of the executive committee since its foundation in 1885).

1890
Lunch (gouache, present location unknown)
At the Church Door (gouache, private collection).
Summer journey: Wurzburg, Veitshöchheim, Kissingen, Munich.
Walk to the Mineral Water Fountain at Kissingen (gouache, present location unknown)
Friendship with Johannes Brahms.

1891
Summer journey: Fulda, Weimar, Eisenach.
The 3rd annual Munich Exhibition includes a special exhibition on Menzel (together with Lenbach, Böcklin, Kaulbach and Marées).
Open-air Café at Kissingen (gouache, present location unknown). *cf.* cat. 198.

1892
In May, the Berlin Academy exhibition follows the example of Munich and includes special exhibitions of the work of various artists, including Menzel.
Summer journey: Munich, Salzburg, Regensburg, Wurzburg and Kissingen.
Quiet Corner (cat. 201) and *Outing in a Dinghy* (cat. 202), Menzel's last oil paintings.
Journey through the Beauty of Nature (gouache, private collection).

1893
Menzel paints *Breakfast Buffet Given by a High-Class Bakery at Kissingen* (cat. 203) for the Universal Exhibition in Chicago.
Summer journey: Dresden, Karlsbad, Salzburg, Wiesbaden, Kassel, Kissingen. Menzel also visits Bremen and Hamburg.

1894
In March, *Studio Wall* (1872) and other works are exhibited at the Hamburg Art Exhibition.
In June, Ernst Arnold organizes an exhibition of works by Menzel in Dresden, including drawings of Dresden's baroque architecture never before shown.
Early Morning at the Café (cat. 208).
Summer journey: Kissingen, Münnerstadt, Salzburg, Sankt Gilgen, Ischl, Regensburg, Karlsbad.

1895
In June, first celebrations to mark Menzel's eightieth birthday: the court in Potsdam holds a period ball in eighteenth-century dress and puts on a tableau vivant of the famous *Flute Concert*.
Summer journey: Kissingen, Wurzburg, Weimar.
In July, Menzel exhibits *Studio Wall* (1872) at the 1st international exhibition (Biennale) in Venice.
In December, large-scale exhibition to mark Menzel's birthday: the Nationalgalerie exhibits prints, the Academy of Arts paintings, including a first public showing of the *Lying in State of the March Dead*.
Menzel is appointed 'Wirklicher Geheimer Rat mit dem Prädikat Excellenz' and honorary citizen of Berlin. He is made a member of the Académie des Beaux-Arts in Paris and of the Royal Academy in London. For his eightieth birthday, the Berlin Academy has a medal featuring his likeness struck (by Reinhold Begas).
End of the Party (etching) for the Berliner Kunstverein für Original-Radierung, volume X, Menzel's last graphic work.

1896
A Menzel exhibition, organized in Vienna by two private collectors, Paul Kuh and Max Strauss, is highly successful.
Menzel exhibition at the Hamburg Kunsthalle.
Summer journey to Kissingen.
Visits to Hamburg and Lübeck.

1897
Summer journey: Ruine Bodenlaube near Kissingen and Bamberg.
In August, he visits the painter Rudolf Alt in Vienna.
The Marienburg, gouache (a reworking of his watercolour of 1855).

1898
Summer journey to Kissingen and Salzburg.
Menzel is made a knight of the Order of the Black Eagle (the highest Prussian order, raising him to the ranks of the aristocracy).
Menzel steps down from the senate of the Berlin Academy and is made an honorary member.
The Berlin Society of Artists holds a celebration in Menzel's honour.

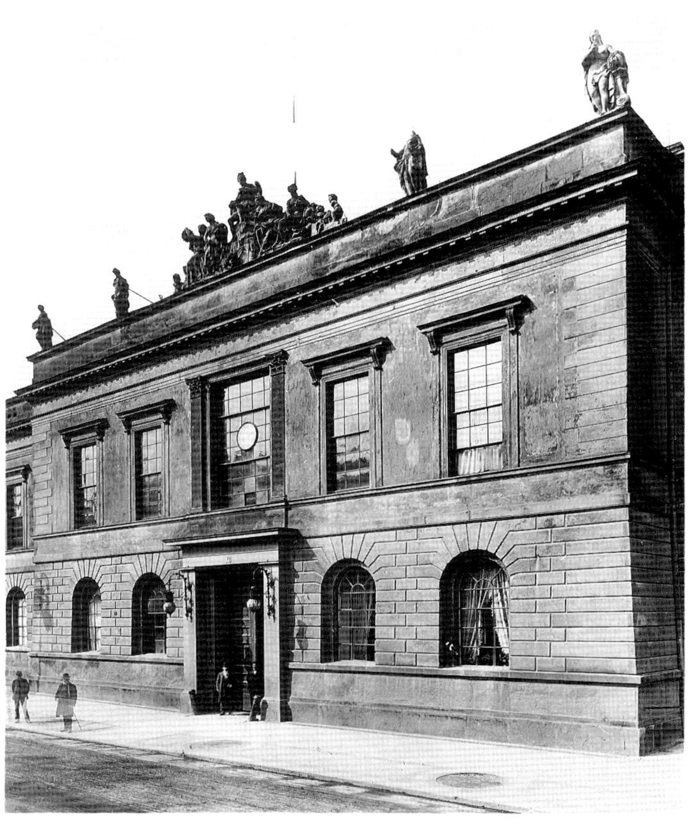

Fig. 51. The Berlin Academy of Arts, *c.* 1880, photograph

1899
Menzel is made an foreign member of the Belgian Academy of Arts. The Nationalgalerie in Berlin acquires *The Berlin-Potsdam Railway*, painted in 1847.

1900
Visit to the Ironworks (gouache, Kupferstichkabinett, Berlin).
Summer journey to Kissingen.
Two gouaches and two drawings by Menzel are shown at the Paris Universal Exhibition, where he is awarded the medal of honour for his etchings.
Menzel speaks out publicly against the *Lex Heinze* (one effect of which would have been to restrict artistic freedom).

1901
Summer journey to Würzburg, Munich and Salzburg.
The New Cockerel (gouache, present location unknown).
End of the Reconciliation Festival (gouache, Georg Schäfer Collection, Euerbach).

1902
In October, Max Klinger's *Beethoven*, defended by many artists, with Menzel prominent among them, is exhibited in Berlin.

1903
Hugo von Tschudi purchases the 1845 *Balcony Room* for the Nationalgalerie. In April, the Association of Berlin Artists exhibits two of Menzel's early oil paintings never seen publicly before – *The Kreuzberg, near Berlin*, 1847 and *First Mass*, post 1852 – together with early drawings, watercolours and gouaches. The 1856 *The Théâtre du Gymnase* is shown for the first time at the autumn exhibition of the Künstlerhaus in Berlin. For the first time, critics express the view that Menzel's early works are of

Fig. 53. Adolph Menzel, *c.* 1895, photograph

Fig. 52. *Allegory for the Bicentenary of the Royal Academy of Arts*, 1896, brush, pen, India ink with white highlights, Berlin, Academy of Arts

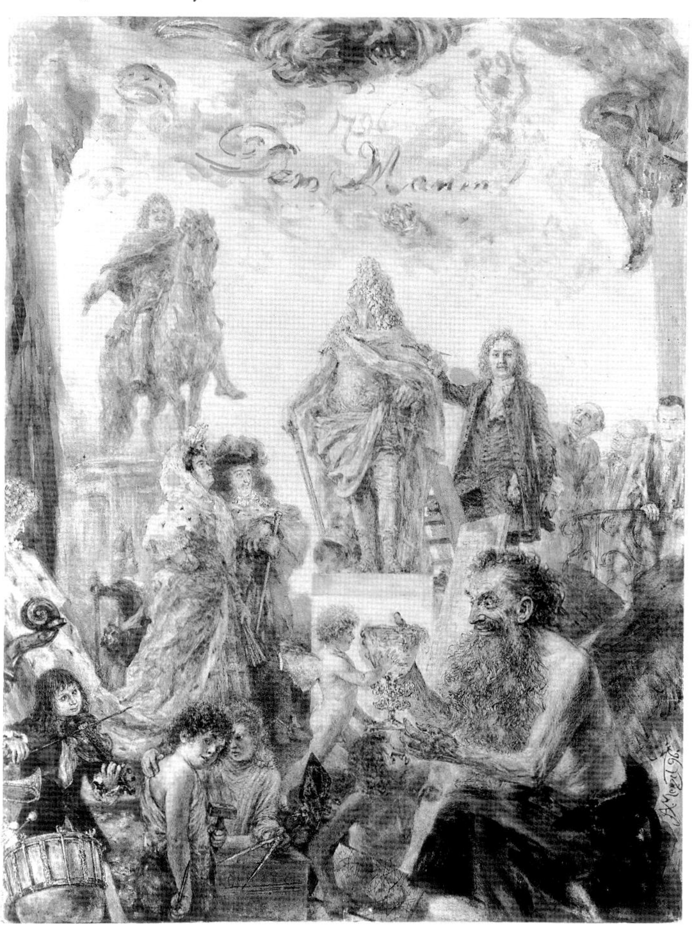

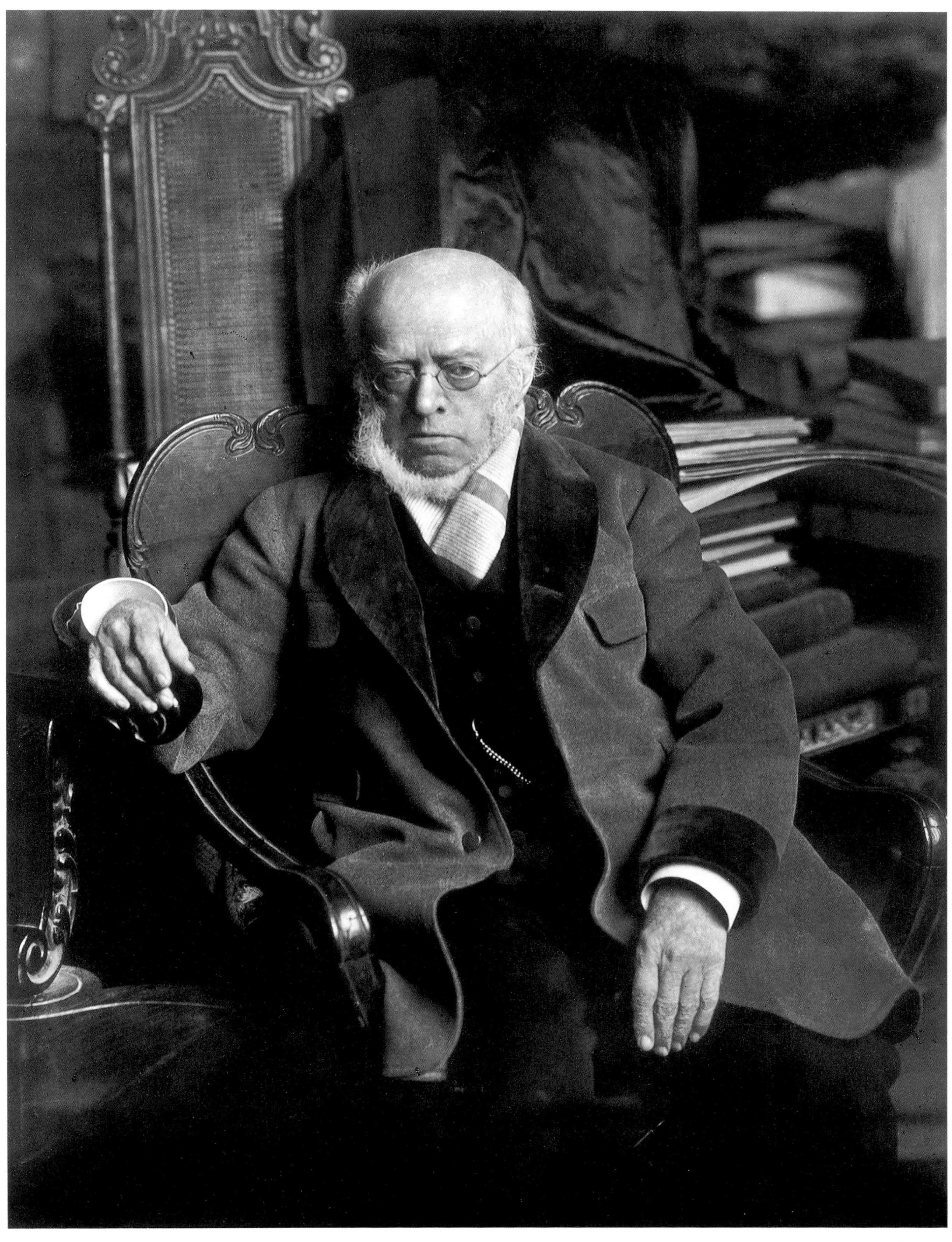

greater interest than those of his later years. In April, celebration of the fiftieth anniversary of Menzel's membership of the Royal Academy of Arts. He is appointed to the special rank of honorary senator.
Frederick the Great on Horseback (Huis Doorn, Doorn), watercolour for the musical programme of the festival to mark the one hundred and fiftieth anniversary, on 29 May, of the Döberitz training grounds.
In June, the Menzel exhibition at the French Gallery in Pall Mall, London, attracts widespread attention.
Summer journey to Karlsbad.

1904
Summer journey to Kissingen.
Menzel restricts himself to drawing in pencil.

1905
On 9 February, Menzel dies in Berlin.
On 13 February, his funeral is held in the rotunda of the Altes Museum, followed by his burial at the Dreifaltigkeits cemetery.
On 19 February, Joseph Joachim puts on a commemorative concert at the Academy of Vocal Music. His quartet plays one of Menzel's favourite pieces, the Cavatina from Beethoven's quartet in B flat.
On 6 March, the Berlin Academy of Arts stages a memorial event.
On 28 March, the Nationalgalerie opens a large-scale retrospective exhibition. After long negotiations with Menzel's sister, the Nationalgalerie acquires Menzel's own estate in 1906.

Berlin in Menzel's time

Peter Paret

The move of Menzel's parents to Berlin in 1830, a decisive event in the artist's life, was part of the great demographic flood that overwhelmed and transformed the city in the nineteenth century. For much of its earlier history, Berlin possessed little more than regional significance. It was an outpost in an underdeveloped part of Germany, with a frontier town's mix of energy, brashness and cultural isolation. Berlin's provincial character was still pronounced in the reign of Frederick the Great, but now overlaid with a screen of sophistication, which owed much to the king's intense engagement in the style even more than with the ideas of the French Enlightenment, the influx of Huguenot émigrés and Jews, and the beginnings of a public for literature and the arts. The emergence in segments of the military and bureaucratic élites of a sense for the potential of State power added a particular, unusual note to the town's social atmosphere as well as to its architecture. But the setting in which these forces appeared was still circumscribed. At the end of the Napoleonic era, less than 200,000 people – counting the large garrison – lived in Berlin. Thirty years later, on the eve of the Revolution of 1848, the city's population had more than doubled, and after another twenty-five years doubled again. At Menzel's death in 1905, the city had more than two million inhabitants, and well above three million, counting the suburbs that were soon to be incorporated into 'Greater Berlin'.

Other European cities were also expanding rapidly, even if their rate of growth could not match that of Berlin. Between 1800 and 1900, the populations of London, Paris and Vienna each increased more than six times. But these ancient capitals, firmly rooted in complex societies with rich physical and cultural resources, retained their own identities to a far greater extent. In Paris, Baron Haussmann's avenues, the new workers' districts, and the railways levelled much in their path, but the city of Louis XIV and of the first Napoleon was not eradicated. 'Berlin in Menzel's time' on the other hand, reinvented itself more than once – not only in size, but also in function and character, as it grew from the 'seat of a court', in Friedrich Engels' derisive phrase, to a commercial and industrial centre and the capital of the newest world power[1].

Berliners could, nevertheless, witness and experience changes of great magnitude over decades without being affected by each of the new developments, or even fully recognizing them. Menzel is a case in point. He sketched and painted the city's expansion, buildings going up in the gardens behind old palaces, orchards and open fields beyond the city gates giving way to apartment houses and machine shops. But we should not assume that he was familiar with every new district – whether bourgeois or the tightly clustered workers' tenements that came with industrialization from mid-century on – nor with the social and political life that filled the new streets. For most of the seventy-five years that he lived in Berlin, he rented apartments and studios in the same general area, at the edge of the city's historic core, between the north–south axis of the Friedrichstrasse and the green expanse of the Tiergarten. Gradually the plain two- and three-storey houses of the eighteenth century were demolished and replaced by larger and higher structures, with 'Renaissance' or 'Baroque' façades, but also with running water and connected to a modern sewage system. A new phase in the city's history was beginning. But men and women changed less than the houses in which they lived. And just as Menzel and many others preserved their customary mode of existence as Berlin spread into the countryside, so the city's political and social conditions enabled or compelled the artists and writers among them to pursue careers in a professional environment that, although increasing in size and complexity, changed little in its essentials from the 1830s to the early years of the new empire, nearly two generations later.

Looking back in middle age to the Berlin of the 1830s, Theodor Fontane described the city before its elevation to imperial grandeur as 'a large village, richly endowed with administrative offices and military barracks'[2]. Since the Prussian monarchy possessed no truly representative political institutions, the public sphere of the capital and its professional and cultural life were dominated by the royal court, the ministries and the military establishment. The municipal government had little authority. Much of urban life – from public safety to town planning – was in the hands of the State. The king appointed the mayor; he also appointed the members of the royal academies, the faculty of the university – already the largest in Germany – the staffs of the royal theatre and opera house, of the museums, and of a host of other civic agencies. The city's professional men and its business community functioned largely within a framework laid out and controlled by others.

Berlin was also a community of artisans – especially numerous in the textile and clothing industries – and by the 1840s was gaining a reputation as a producer of engines and machine tools. With entrepreneurial growth and the expansion of service industries and distribution networks, the professional and commercial middle classes increased in size and importance; yet they remained a thin and in some respects feeble social layer between the city's ruling groups and the great majority of the population. They possessed neither economic self-sufficiency and political power nor the high degree of interaction with the country's élite that characterized the middle classes in London and Paris. Nor could they provide a strong market for the arts. Even more than in Western Europe, writers, musicians, painters and sculptors were dependent on the State. Menzel's commission from the firm of J.J. Weber to illustrate Franz Kugler's *Geschichte Friedrichs des Grossen* (History of Frederick the Great) with 376 wood engravings was still something out of the ordinary in 1839 – and it might be noted that it was a firm from Saxony, not Berlin, that financed this unusually large project. Many other artists looked to prizes, travel grants, pensions, and other forms of government support to establish and maintain themselves. Official patronage and influence reached deep into every corner of the city's commercial and industrial life, and few institutions existed to mediate between the private individual and the official world.

In London, clubs enabled men above a certain social level but of varied status to mingle in an atmosphere of temporary social equality. Nothing exactly like it could be found in Berlin. It illustrates the hierarchical separation of Berlin society that the integrative and at the same time exclusionary function of the London club was in Berlin divided between two very different types of institutions: certain coffee houses, inelegantly called 'reading cafés', where for the price of a drink one could read German and foreign newspapers and discuss the issues of the day, and the clubs and casinos of regiments stationed in the capital, status-conscious establishments that emphasized rather than ameliorated class distinctions. At the beginning of the century, private salons had done something to bridge the gap between different social circles. In the 1830s and 1840s they survived in such newer versions as the 'at homes' of Clara Kugler, the wife of Menzel's collaborator, the art historian and cultural

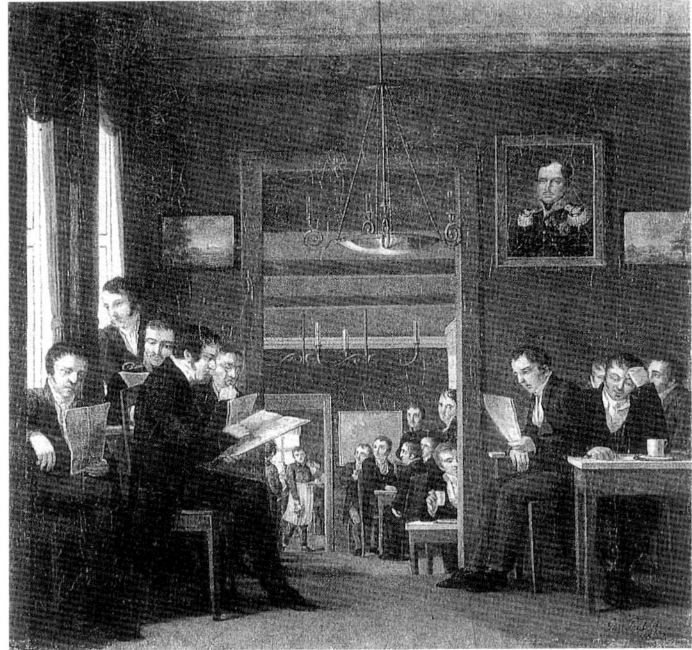

Fig. 54. Gustav Taubert, *Everyone reads Everything*, 1832, oil, Berlin, Stadtmuseum

Fig. 55. The new Stock Exchange in Berlin under construction, *c.* 1860, photograph by Leopold Ahrendts

bureaucrat Franz Kugler, who regularly brought together nobles and bourgeois, academics, artists, writers, officials, officers, Jews, gentiles. But the salons reached out only to the few; they remained expressions of a cultural élite, as did such small private reading and discussion groups as *The Tunnel over the River Spree* or *The Rütli* – both of which Menzel joined – whose members, coming from many segments of society, practised one or other of the arts or at least provided an appreciative, critical audience. Some of the early professional groups were larger, for instance the Association of Berlin Artists, the Association of Younger Berlin Artists and, particularly, the Association of Friends of the Arts in Prussia, which supported artists and furthered an interest in the arts among the public. In 1843 the Friends of the Arts had 2459 members, ranging from the highest aristocracy to painters just starting with barely a foothold on middle-class status[3]. Despite the presence of a few major talents – Schinkel, above all – the city was not an important centre of the arts – least of all, of painting; but it was the arts rather than politics –and the arts probably as much as business – that helped to open up society in Berlin before the Revolution of 1848, if only in a qualified, restricted way.

For generations, life in Berlin had been shaped by the interaction of its energetic, competitive population with an autocratic government that insisted on pronounced

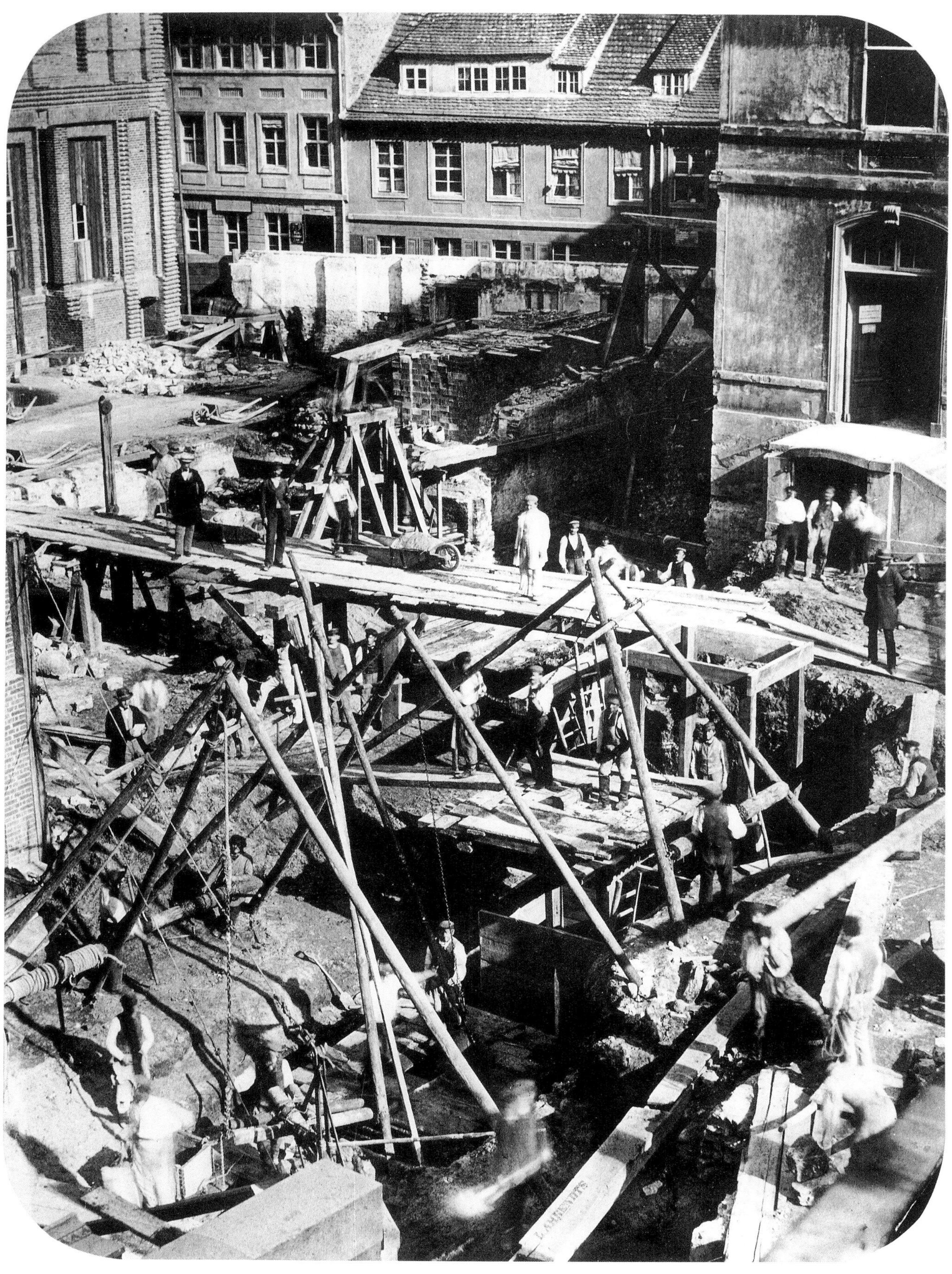

class distinctions. Differences in interest and outlook separated the privileged from those without power, but also divided the élites themselves. By the 1830s, the momentum of social and administrative reforms, first introduced over conservative opposition after the lost war of 1806, had faded; but the Prussian bureaucracy retained a sense of mission and the conviction that it had a clearer understanding than the royal court of the needs of the State and society. On a more subdued plane, the debate over modernization continued. It was stimulated by accelerating economic growth, but the bureaucracy's ultimate subjection to royal authority and inertia paralleled the helplessness of the general population. The French Revolution of 1830, the Belgian fight for independence, and the Polish uprising against Russia all fed the belief that conditions in Prussia, too, must change, and expectations were raised further with the accession to the throne of Frederick William IV, who was said to have liberal sympathies. When it became apparent that the new king opposed serious innovation, the sense of frustration and the ironic and self-ironic detachment that marked Berlin life at the time were strengthened.

An expression of this mood was the emergence of a specific Berlin wit – at least people began to think that there was such a thing, and took it seriously. Not unlike urban humour everywhere, it was driven by a sharp recognition of the local realities; it cut across social differences, penetrated protective layers of convention and pretence, and turned the speaker from a victim of conditions in the capital into their ironic observer and interpreter. A late echo was the comment of the painter Max Liebermann as he watched the torch parade of Hitler's followers through the Brandenburg Gate on the evening of 30 January 1933: 'Impossible to eat as much as one must throw up.' But humour only pointed up the stilted, unsatisfactory quality of life in Berlin, which Fontane ascribed to the insufficient scope given to the Berliners' energy and ability. Further, Berlin's remoteness, its rapid growth in 'the sandy wastes of the Mark Brandenburg', limited its inhabitants' horizon: 'they are good people, but narrow' though this was changing[4]. Other observers were more critical. Shortly before Frederick William IV appointed him royal master of music, Felix Mendelssohn complained to a friend of 'the Berlin duality: the vast pretensions, the tiny achievements; the perfect criticisms, the miserable performers; the liberal ideas, the royal servants crowding the streets'. In 1844 he wrote to the painter Carl Friedrich Lessing: 'For my taste there is too much outside glitter and too little inner vitality in the local character, and at the same time the general dissatisfaction is so great that arguing and criticizing are the only things people engage in with real energy'[5]. Jacob Burckhardt, who studied and worked in 'odious Berlin' for several years, described the city as large and dull, and in 1846 gave it as his overall impression that the city was 'repulsive, ugly, vile, mean to the point of malevolence, and with all this fortunately ridiculous'. But he praised the theatre and the museums, and liked many of the people. 'I hate the city', he wrote in the first days of 1848, 'still, one could live very well here'[6].

In March 1848, widespread economic misery and middle-class political frustrations, intensified by the unrest and revolutions breaking out in many parts of Europe, led to demonstrations and eventually street fighting in Berlin. In two days and a night about three hundred civilians and a much smaller number of soldiers were killed. Frederick William and his advisors were unable to master the crisis, the garrison withdrew from the city, and for a time royal authority in Berlin collapsed. But, as in every revolution from Paris to Vienna that year, differences in interest and outlook soon divided the apparent victors.

The new political situation in Berlin was dominated by conflicts and negotiations between the Crown and moderates, who sought a constitutional monarchy with ministers responsible to a legislative assembly. More radical groups remained a vocal minority . When they tried to recover the revolutionary impetus of the March Days by launching mass demonstrations and arming the man in the street, the new civic guards, among them an artists' corps of some 700–800 men, joined the police and units of the regular army to impose order by force. Efforts to radicalize the all-German parliament meeting in Frankfurt also failed; but the parliament was weakened by the inability of the moderates and the left to work together. At the end of October the counter-revolution triumphed in Vienna after a week of severe fighting, which was followed by summary executions of political enemies, and the conservative forces in Prussia, which had remained in control of most of the country, prepared to subdue the capital. On 10 November, 13,000 soldiers marched through the Brandenburg Gate, martial law was proclaimed, and the Prussian National Assembly, then meeting in Berlin, was dissolved. On 5 December, Frederick William issued a constitution for Prussia. He had refused to do so before the Revolution, but the document that he now imposed on the country gave away very little of the Crown's power.

The new constitution, which remained in effect in Prussia until 1918, exempted the army from parliamentary control. Other branches of the executive retained a large measure of immunity, and the introduction of the three-class franchise, which imposed a property qualification, and determined the weight of each man's vote by the amount of taxes he paid, further protected the status quo. The authority of local government was reduced even more. Mayors were now elected, but the Crown retained the right of confirmation, and the chief of police, a government appointee, was given new responsibilities that went far beyond fighting crime and maintaining public order. For the next decades, the Polizeipräsident wielded more power in Berlin than the mayor. Even when the municipal administration and its relationship to the Prussian government were modernized in 1881 and again in 1900, the police chief and other government officials continued to run large parts of the city's life.

The capital had been made politically impotent. Conservatives welcomed the taming of 'red Berlin'; others reacted with resignation and eventually with protest. After the first shock of the Revolution and its failure had worn off, Berlin began to vote for liberal candidates in local and Prussian elections. The three-class franchise, which benefited landowners and their allies in rural Prussian areas, gave professional and commercial interests an advantage in the cities. The practical consequence of their votes was limited, but the results indicate the position of the majority of Berliners who met the property qualifications of the franchise. From the early 1850s to the Franco-Prussian war and beyond, the Prussian capital, through its liberal majorities, expressed views on domestic policy that were opposed to those of the king and his ministers.

Not a few liberals suppressed their disappointment at being politically marginalized, and enthusiastically greeted the military victories over Denmark, Austria and France, and the achievement of one of the goals of 1848, the unification of Germany. But much frustration and bitterness remained. The impact this had on the cultural life of the city is in question. What is certain, however, is that, whatever the reason, despite the increase in wealth and a larger educated public, and the great intellectual resources of the university and the proliferating research institutes, Berlin was not yet a centre of the arts. Music and the theatre were showing promise, but literature and – except for Menzel – painting were still at a level that, measured by European standards, could only be regarded as respectably mediocre. In most matters that counted, the social and economic situation of the writer and artist had changed little since the Revolution, and in some respects had become worse. If more opportunities now existed, there was also more competition; a proletariat of writers and artists, who struggled, often unsuccessfully, to earn a living, was one of the by-products of the city's expansion. Unchanged above all were the dominant role of the State and court, and the patriarchal manner in which the king and new emperor, William I, continued to dispense patronage and make decisions that affected individual careers and even the form and content of particular works of art.

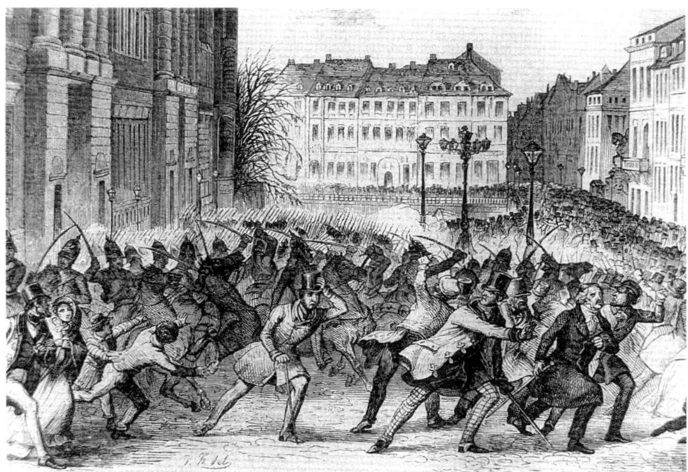

Fig. 56. *The unarmed populace attacked by the cavalry in fron of the royal palace in Berlin, 18 March, 1848*, illustration in the *Leipziger Illustrierte Zeitung*, 8 April 1848.

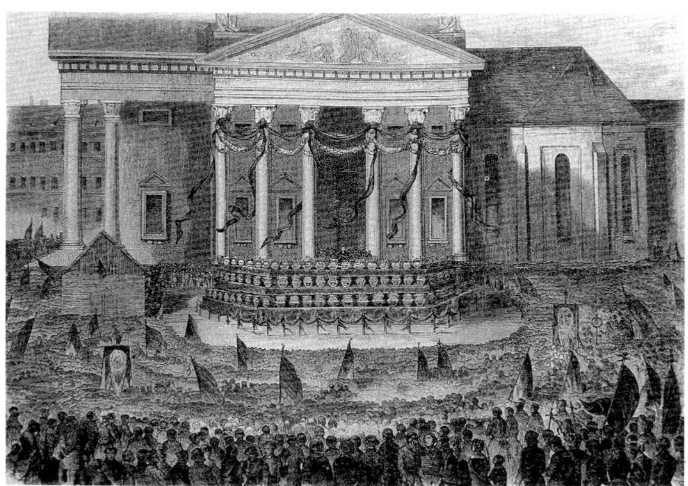

Fig. 57. *Lying in state of the March dead*, illustration in the *Leipziger Illustrierte Zeitung*, 15 April 1848.

An episode in 1876, which caused a brief sensation in the cultural world of Berlin, illustrates the ties that continued to link culture and State patronage, and the personal involvement of the monarch, even in matters of secondary importance. Menzel's friend Theodor Fontane, who had not yet published his first novel but was known throughout Germany as a poet, journalist and critic, applied for the position of first permanent

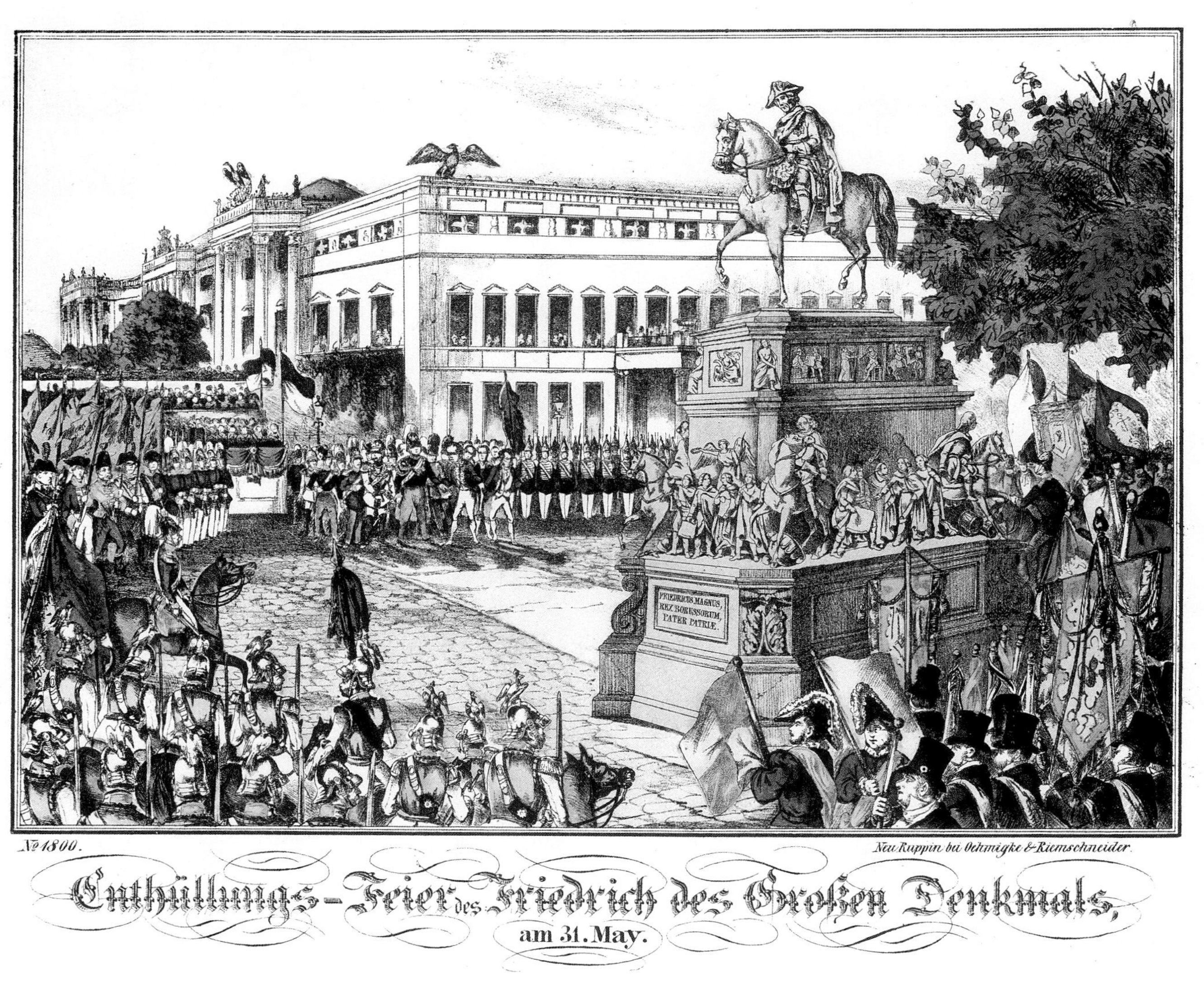

Fig. 58. *Inauguration of the Monument to Frederick II by Christian Daniel Rauch, 31 March 1851*, lithograph by Neuruppin

secretary at the Royal Academy of Arts. A civil service appointment would give him the economic security that, despite his prolific output, he had not achieved in the literary marketplace. The final decision on the appointment was the emperor's, who knew enough about Fontane and his writings to doubt that he was the right man for the post, but allowed himself to be persuaded. Within two months Fontane realized that he could not tolerate life as a bureaucrat, and in a frank letter to William I asked for permission to resign. For Fontane this step was the ultimate declaration of independence, and its impact on his life and writings can hardly be overestimated. But his original temptation to turn to the State for support, as he had several times before, and the role William I played in dispensing patronage, tells us much about the continuing centrality of the State as well as of the monarch in the small cultural world of Berlin. Even the professional situation of someone like Menzel, who never sought a position in the cultural bureaucracy, was affected by appointments and honours that society valued and only the State could award.

In the 1880s this world began to change. The old conditions did not disappear, but new elements enlarged and gradually transformed the environment for literary and artistic production in Berlin during the last twenty years of Menzel's life.

Unification of the country had not resolved the many antagonisms in German society and politics. They were intensified by recurring economic difficulties after the crash of 1873 and the continuing social and psychological dislocations brought about by industrialization, by Bismarck's conflict with political Catholicism, and by his treatment of left liberals and socialists as enemies of the State. Political antisemitism, which made its appearance in the 1880s, further signalled the growing tendency of the far right – whether of the Junker or the populist variety – to turn political differences into ideological wars.

Berlin was now the capital of both Prussia and Germany, and the contradictions of the empire were revealed with particular clarity at its centre. The new Reichstag, elected by universal male suffrage, met side by side with the Prussian parliament, based on a severely restricted franchise. The Reichstag was powerless to interfere with the control of the executive over the empire's foreign policy and armed forces, but it possessed substantial influence over large areas of domestic legislation, provided a forum for debate on all public issues – including such matters as censorship and State patronage of the arts – and became the centre for the expanding political culture of national parties and of an assertive national press. To the irritation of the imperial court and the Prussian government, Berlin continued to vote liberal. Until 1881 each of the city's six electoral districts returned liberals to the Reichstag. As liberalism gradually lost strength throughout the country, they were replaced by socialists, beginning in 1882, when, in the face of Bismarck's antisocialist legislation, Berlin elected two socialist representatives. By 1902, the city's delegation consisted of five socialists and one liberal. As a sign of his annoyance at the disloyalty of his capital, William II in 1898 refused for some months to confirm the election of a left-liberal mayor, whose self-assured response, 'I can wait', became for the time a popular phrase.

Berlin's increasing political and economic importance – it was now the empire's largest city and, with Hamburg, its wealthiest – was accompanied by a gradual expansion of its cultural life. In the fine arts, exhibitions became more frequent and interesting, new galleries opened, the reorganized annual salon – from 1892 jointly sponsored by the State and the Association of Berlin Artists – further stimulated the art market and introduced foreign artists – mainly those working in conventional styles – to a broader public. After the accession in 1888 of William II, whose genuine interest in painting and sculpture was stimulated both by their aesthetic quality and their possible political significance, government policy towards the arts assumed a new, more activist character.

William II not only rewarded artists whose work he thought supported the status quo with purchases, honours and commissions – among them such large projects as the rows of monuments, glorifying the history of his family, on the borders of a new avenue near the eastern end of the Tiergarten – he publicly criticized others whose style or subject-matter he regarded as alien to accepted values, and did his best to deny them support. The machinery of State patronage was now too large and complex to be controlled by any one person, but the emperor's influence reached far, and in some areas he possessed ultimate authority. Purchases for the Nationalgalerie were subject to his approval, for instance, and he controlled the medals of the annual salon. Although his image as emperor of *all* the Germans might have benefited, it was not to be expected that a man of his convictions would honour an artist like Käthe Kollwitz – on the advice of the Prussian minister of culture he rejected the jury's recommendation that she be

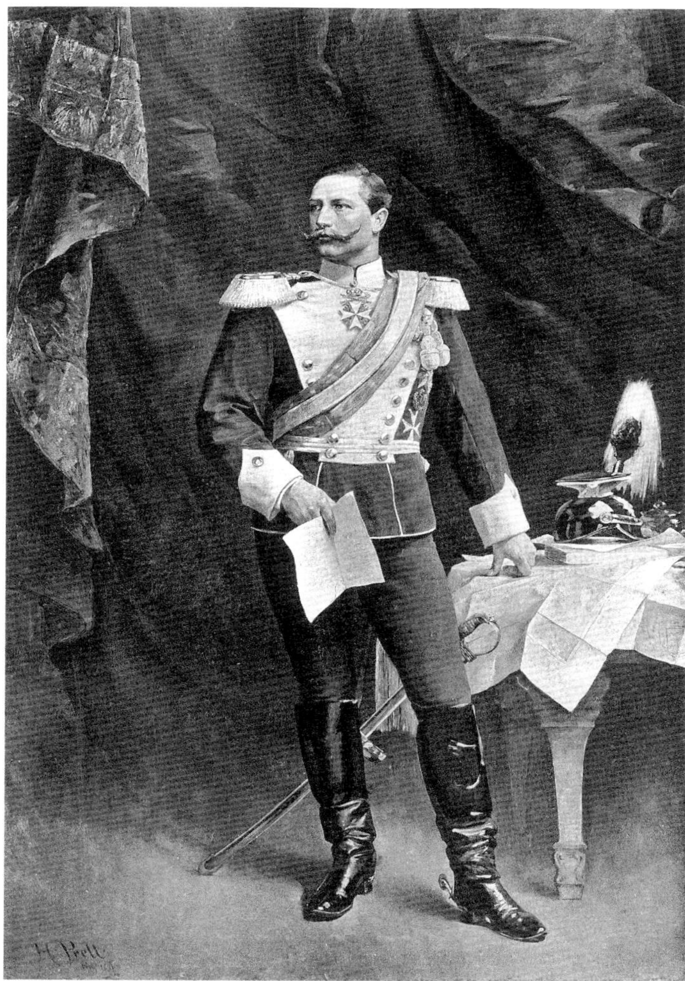

Fig. 59. Hermann Prell, *Portrait of William II*, 1891, oil, location unknown

awarded a medal in the salon of 1898. But by loudly scolding artists whose work contained no hint of social criticism, merely for their disturbingly avant-garde style, he renounced all appearance of impartiality. His crude, often offensive pronouncements strengthened the tendency of groups on the right to declare any departure from the conventional as alien and subversive, and to judge arts by the standards of a nationalism that was both aggressive and felt itself to be victimized by the modern world. In this view, society was divided between those who were loyal to Germanic culture and others who were misled or its enemies. Not that liberals and socialists were necessarily enamoured of Impressionism, let alone other forms of modernism, but in the debates on art in the Reichstag and the press they showed greater tolerance, or expressed doubt that art merited serious political attention.

It was only a question of time before modernist artists reacted against the disadvantages under which they worked. The first clear signal of change came in 1892 when eleven members of the Association of Berlin Artists set their work apart from the many hundreds of entries to the annual salon by organizing their own group shows. That same year, Edvard Munch was invited to exhibit in the Association's gallery. The show opened in November, and proved an outrage to many. At a special meeting, the Association decided by a vote of 120 to 103 to close the show and to replace the members of the exhibition committee who had brought Munch to Berlin. It indicates how closely the official and unofficial meshed, that three members of the Association, professors at the teaching institute attached to the Royal Academy of Arts, were compelled to resign their posts when they protested against the decision. But this did not end the matter. The 'Eleven' found a private gallery at which Munch could show his rejected paintings and graphics and, until the group disbanded in 1897 it continued to promote the cause of modern art within and outside the Association. In belated recognition of the national reputation of its leading member, the salon that year singled out Max Liebermann for special distinction, and the emperor did not block the award of a gold medal, nor Liebermann's election to the Academy. In the following year, however, the jury rejected a painting by another well-known modernist, Walter Leistikow, and, after futile negotiations, several dozen members resigned from the Association, and with some other artists formed a rival group, the Berlin Secession, with Liebermann as president.

It was a decisive step. The situation of artists in Berlin, never totally dominated but always strongly influenced by the State, was opened to new forces. Soon, court and

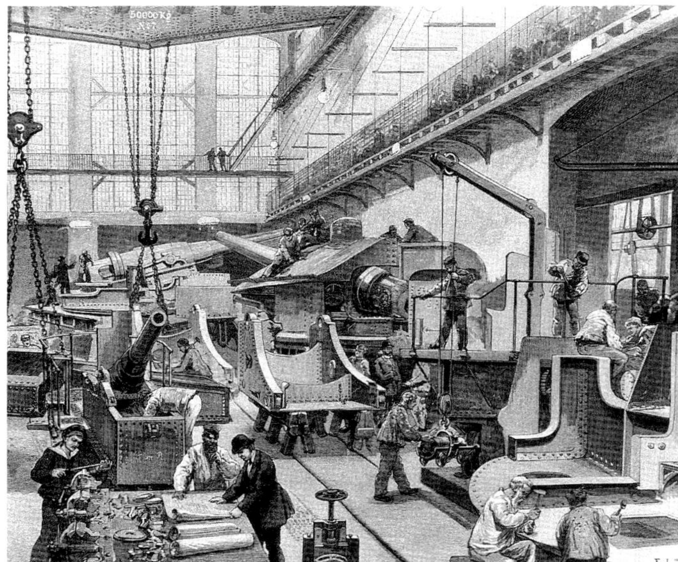

Fig. 60. *Krupp Factory*, illustration from the *Illustrierte Zeitung*, 8 November 1885

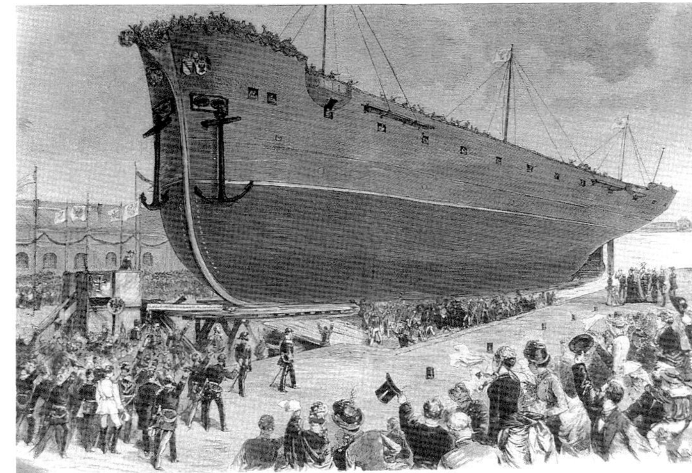

Fig. 61. *Launch of a Cruiser-Frigate*, illustration in the *Illustrierte Zeitung*, 19 September 1885

State patronage coexisted with a vigorous rival world of private groups and galleries. In the past, an individual artist might have ignored the values asserted by the emperor; now these were challenged by an organization with its own gallery and means of publicity, and with ties to like-minded groups throughout Germany and Europe. The critical and commercial success of its first exhibitions turned the Secession into a magnet for modern artists and supporters of modern art throughout Central Europe, and helped make Berlin for a time the intellectual centre of modern art in Germany, and the country's most important art market. The emperor warned art against 'descending into the gutter'; an early poster of the Secession shows a rose in the gutter being picked up by the genius of Art.

For its first exhibition in May 1899, the Secession asked collectors for the loan of several paintings and graphics by Menzel. The presence of his work in the show would demonstrate the group's indebtedness to earlier achievements of German art. It also asked for, and received, Menzel's agreement. But, two days before the opening, a Berlin newspaper published a letter in which Menzel declared that he had not known that his pictures would be in the exhibition. When shown his written consent, Menzel sent a second letter to the press, stating that he had given his agreement 'while momentarily distracted'. The exhibition committee then withdrew the pictures, although it was too late to correct the catalogue[8]. The incident remains somewhat unclear. Menzel may not have immediately realized that exhibiting with the breakaway group could seem a political statement; perhaps he was told that the Secession was exploiting his reputation; he was certainly irritated by the public clamour that erupted over the hanging of a few of his pictures in an exhibition. But it is unlikely that he paid much attention to the founding of the Secession or knew what the group stood for; now in his eighties, he might have felt indifferent to artists' quarrels and detached from the new phase in the history of art in Berlin that had begun.

How and how strongly Berlin affected Menzel during the seventy-five years he lived in the city are questions that cannot be fully answered. Decades of unrelenting work in an environment subject to great and repeated change would be difficult to analyse even if more details

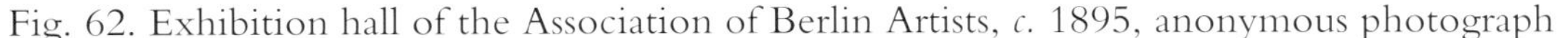

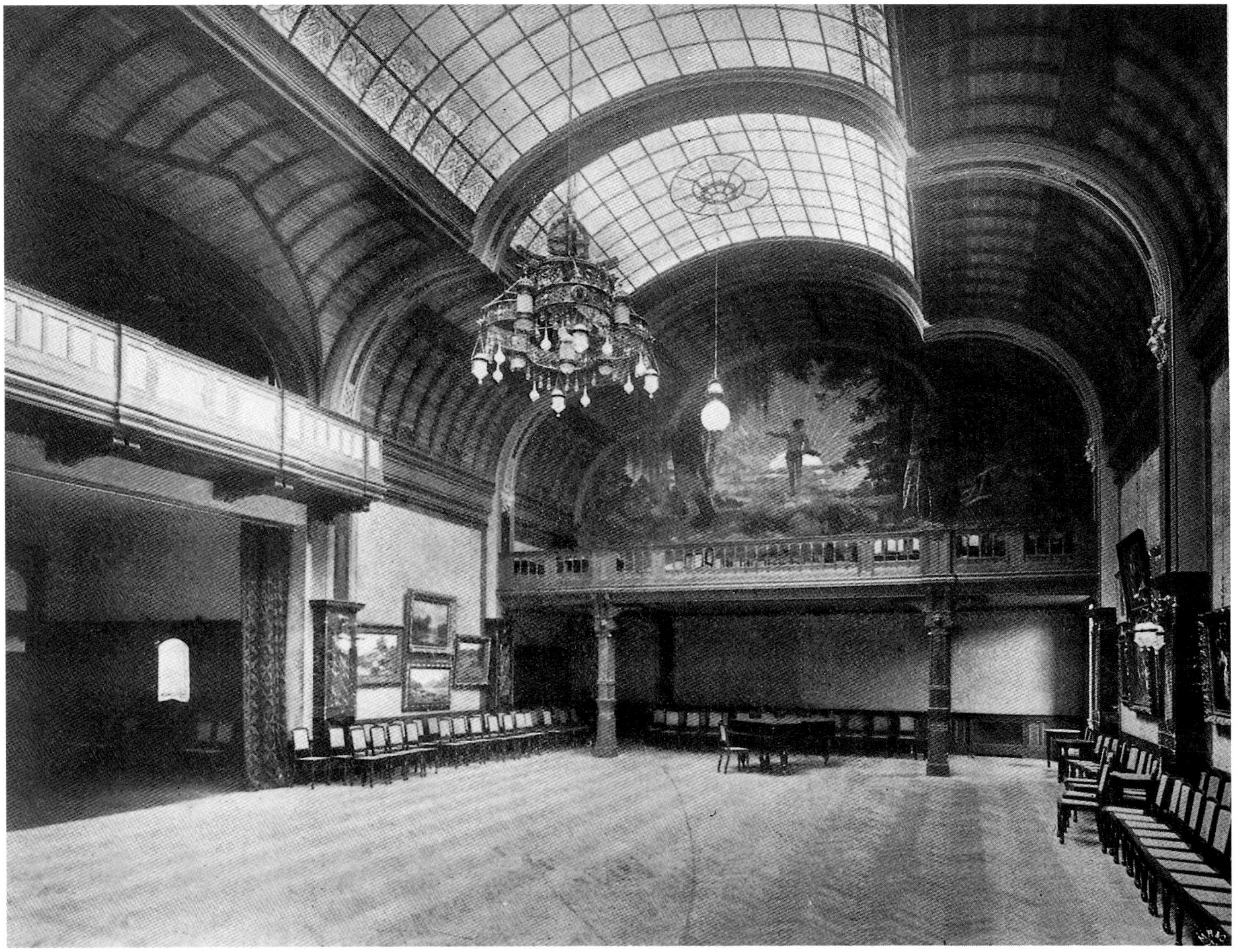

Fig. 62. Exhibition hall of the Association of Berlin Artists, *c.* 1895, anonymous photograph

of Menzel's life and work were known. But some significant elements stand out in his relationship with Berlin, and it may be useful, in conclusion, to mention three or four.

Menzel developed as a painter in a thin artistic culture. He observed and learned from a number of proficient artists, but Berlin did not stimulate him as the Rhineland or Munich might have, to say nothing of Western Europe. He may always have possessed autodidactic tendencies; if so, they were fostered in Berlin.

Success did not come easily, and even after he was well established others were regarded as Menzel's equal or superior. Only gradually was he recognized as Berlin's leading artist. After that he was not challenged for decades – a condition that implies isolation, which may or may not be beneficial. But it is worth asking what happens to an artist who, year in, year out, is undisputed master in his world? Whether Menzel's relative creative isolation had a bearing on the limited impact of his work outside Germany is another question.

As a young man, Menzel acquired the characteristic values of the educated Berlin bourgeoisie before 1848. A broad appreciation of German idealism and of the literature of German Classicism and Romanticism blended with a sense of the Prussian State as something more than a dynastic construct – an autonomous historical force, which was accepted and obeyed even as the monarch and his policies might be criticized. Menzel not only interpreted the growth of the city – a theme he shared with many artists of his time – for long periods of his life he also investigated the history of the State that had grown around its Berlin core, from the sparse, disciplined monarchy of the eighteenth century to the showy, blustering empire of William II. Menzel's intermittent concentration on political themes particular to northern Germany is a major element of his oeuvre, but it may have further limited his international reputation.

It can be no more than a subjective judgement to conclude that Menzel might have benefited from a more sophisticated and open atmosphere – as might have Berlin! Still, Menzel made use of whatever opportunities presented themselves, and created a world in which he worked and prospered after his fashion. He did not lack for inspiration in Berlin, even if other cities might have been more forthcoming socially and culturally. But context is not everything. For an understanding of the artist it is important to know something about his environment but, in the end, a talent such as Menzel's is not only influenced by the conditions in which it exists. In ways large and small, it also rises above them.

1. Friedrich Engels, 'The *Zeitungs-Halle* on the Rhine Province', *Neue Rheinische Zeitung*, no. 87, 27 August, 1848.
2. Theodor Fontane, 'Berliner Ton', written between 1876 and 1882, in *Sämtliche Werke*, eds. Kurt Schreiner and Herman Kunisch, vol. XVIII, Munich 1972, p. 464.
3. Joachim Grossman, *Künstler, Hof and Bürgertum*, Berlin, 1994, p. 96.
4. Theodor Fontane, 'Die Märker und die Berliner', 1889, in *Sämtliche Werke*, vol. XIX, Munich, 1969, p. 742.
5. Letter to Karl Klingsman, July 15, 1841; and letter to Karl Friedrich Lessing, November 14, 1844, in Rudolf Elvers, 'Uber das Berlinische Zwitterwesen: Felix Mendelssohn Batholdy in Briefen über Berlin', *Die Mendelssohns in Berlin*, exhib. cat. Bonn, Düsseldorf, Berlin, 1983, pp. 37–8, 42.
6. Letter to Eduard Schauenburg, December 5, 1846, and letter to Andreas Heusler-Ryhiner, January 19, 1848, in Jacob Burckhardt, *Briefe*, ed. Max Burckhardt, vol. III, Basle, 1955, pp. 41, 94.
7. Michael Erbe, 'Berlin im Kaiserreich (1871–1918)', in *Geschichte Berlins*, ed. Wolfgang Ribbe, vol. II, Munich, 1987, p. 762. I am indebted to this informative study.
8. Peter Paret, *The Berlin Secession*, Cambridge, Mass., 1980, p. 84, n. 83. See also Menzel's letters to Paul Meyerheim, May 4 and May ?, 1899 in *Adolph von Menzels Briefe*, ed. Hans Wolff, Berlin, 1914, pp. 234–5.

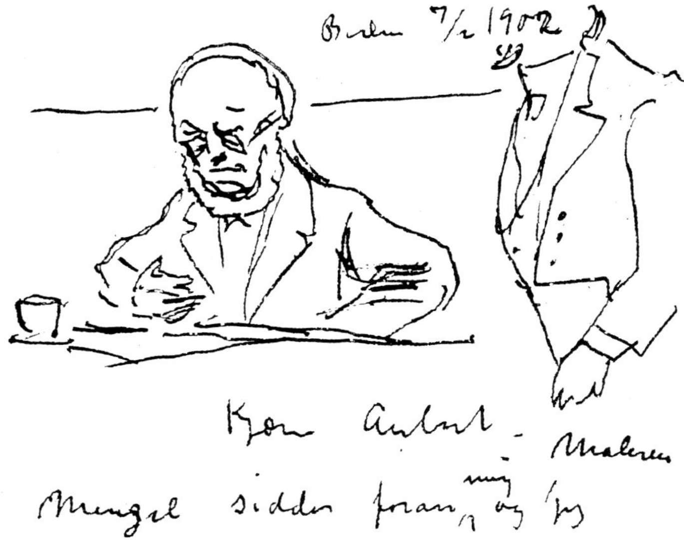

Fig. 64. Edvard Munch, *Menzel in the Café*, drawing in a letter to Andreas Aubert, 7 February 1902, Oslo, Universitetsbiblioteket

Fig. 63. Thomas Theodor Heine, poster for the exhibition for the Deutcher Künstlerbund (German Society of Artists) at the Berlin Secession, 1905, lithograph

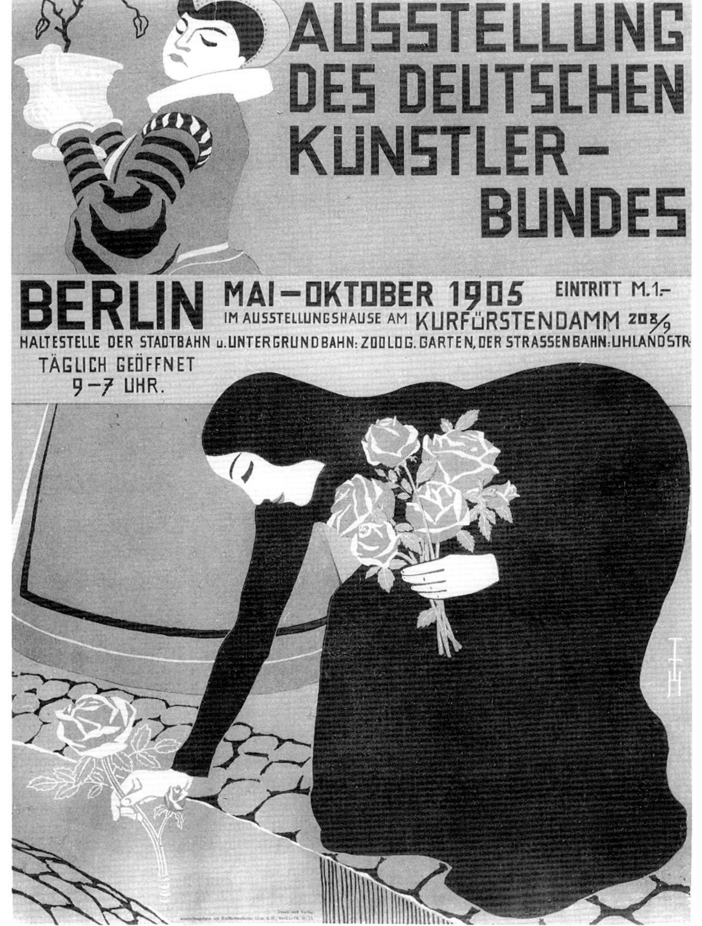

Menzel Junctures Disjunctures

Claude Keisch

Viewed within the labyrinth that is the nineteenth century, Menzel's artistic development is marked by the unpredictable. One needs only to lose him from sight for an instant and he reappears where we least expect him. A master of allegory and the arabesque in his early career, was he to become a practitioner of a belated Classicism, or a Symbolist? Can one assert that the creator of *Balcony Room* introduced Impressionism to Germany? Hardly. As the author of a cycle of paintings chronicling the life of Frederick the Great, with which he reformed the genre of history painting, did he grab at the opportunity to become official court painter once the German empire had been proclaimed in 1871? On the contrary, he shied away from official commissions altogether. Or, as an artist, who by the end of his life was lauded by art critics and public alike, had received numerous distinctions including the highest civilian order – the Order of the Black Eagle – from the Kaiser, how did he come to terms with his fame? By producing ever smaller, ever more intimate paintings depicting a world in disarray, a world that depicted the banality of bourgeois life. In the end his tireless curiosity for individual details, for exacting and (seemingly) objective truthfulness, resulted in a nebulous uncertainty visible in his late drawings.

1.

One may well wonder whether Menzel was not himself responsible for the critical appraisal afforded him. It is today difficult to comprehend the astonishment and unanimous critical success that greeted his early work at the 1905 retrospective, though two much more modest exhibitions at the Verein Berliner Künstler (Association of Berlin Artists) in 1903 can be seen to have prepared the way for this; works shown here (*cf.* cat. 31, 73, 80) had begun to redress his image as a conservative painter of Prussian themes and subjects. Acquired in the same year by the Nationalgalerie Berlin was his *Balcony Room* (cat. 18); his *Berlin–Potsdam Railway* (cat. 35) had entered this collection several years earlier, in 1899. Going back slightly further in time, the disquieting second version of the *Studio Wall* (cat. 137) had been purchased by the Kunsthalle in Hamburg in 1896, having been exhibited on a number of occasions prior to this date. And what should one make of the fact that Menzel, always so concerned about completeness and perfection, allowed unfinished works to be sold in the 1890s? *Bonsoir, Messieurs* (cat. 82) and *Lying in State of the March Dead* (fig. 65), for example, were purchased by a private collector in Zurich before entering the Kunsthalle Hamburg in 1902. The latter had also been exhibited in Berlin in 1895[1] and even reproduced as a double-page illustration in a folio art journal of 1896[2].

The key to such enigmas might be found in an exhibition of Menzel's work held in the autumn of 1861, shortly before he began work on the official commission to document the coronation of William I. He selected twelve canvases, along with drawings and watercolours – *The Théâtre du Gymnase* (cat. 80), one or more studies of horses (probably cat. 43) and other 'private' works[3] – for inclusion in this exhibition. Already in 1861 the claim was made that behind this painter of 'public' images, there stood in the shadows the creator of a universe of intriguing 'studies' which were exhibited rarely and then only due to the pressure exerted by a few friends[4]. The division of Menzel's work into two distinct parts had begun. Had the exhibition been more successful, this perception may not have remained intact until today. As this was not the case[5], it seems that the young Ludwig Pietsch wrote his long, laudatory article on Menzel entirely in vain. Only a few years later the official, more nationalist appraisal of Menzel's work – initiated by Bruno Meyer[6], and in turn supported by Adolf Rosenberg and others – became entrenched. The other part of Menzel's work sank into obscurity. Not even a trace of the painter who had created the *Balcony Room* was visible in Max Jordan's monumental three-volume monograph on the artist, published between 1885 and 1890 and extravagantly illustrated with plates. A remarkable work in that it was dealing with a living artist, Jordan's monograph was completed with the assistance of the artist himself, though it was only after Menzel's death that the author appended a few of the less conventional works to a second edition of the publication[7]. It seems, however, that, immediately after the first edition appeared, Menzel attempted to modify the image the monograph had created, here and there showing less conventional works, while simultaneously accepting official honours and accolades from critics without raising an objection. Such was the case when the lavish praise of the eminent Munich critic, Friedrich Pecht, compared Menzel with Rembrandt, concluding that the former's art was 'infinitely richer' because Prussia's 'role in world history' had been greater than Holland's[8]. For some, his acceptance of such honours and praise was distressing. The author of the naturalist drama *Die Schlesischen Weber* (The Weavers), Gerhart Hauptmann, accused Menzel of having betrayed 'the God within himself: Every real genius should have a bit of Jesus Christ in him. Imagine him receiving the Order of the Black Eagle: what horrible blasphemy!'[9]

The great achievements of Menzel the draughtsman were viewed with unanimous praise, albeit that his diligence, conscientiousness and his keenness of observation were and remain too often the focus of comment. From a similarly one-sided viewpoint, Menzel's early works were deemed marvels of colour and light. There is no doubt that the contradictions within Menzel's work have all too often been reduced to an opposition between early and late periods, a legacy of Julius Meier-Graefe's praise for the 'young Menzel' in an effort to legitimize the 'Impressionist' path of modern art.

Menzel's art abounds in ambiguities and contradictions, discouraging clear definition. Those who try, however, to divide Menzel's oeuvre – preferring the chronicler of Frederick the Great over the 'young Menzel', or vice versa, the keen observer over the poet, or the pure painter over the creator of finely crafted allegories – are often unable to reconcile myriad aspects present within a single work. Meier-Graefe's at times harsh assessment of Menzel led him to conclude, 'that in the 1840s and 1850s on one and the same day Menzel could be found in worlds as different as those of the monumental heroicism of Anton von Werner and the Impressionism of Manet'[10]. And only when one notes that he was at work on *The Flute Concert* (cat. 56) when *Night in the Forest* (cat. 58) was completed, or that the delicate intimacy of *The Artist's Room in Ritterstrasse* (cat. 60) stands alongside the classicizing objectivity of the

Fig. 65. *Lying in State of the March Dead*, 1848, oil, Hamburg, Kunsthalle

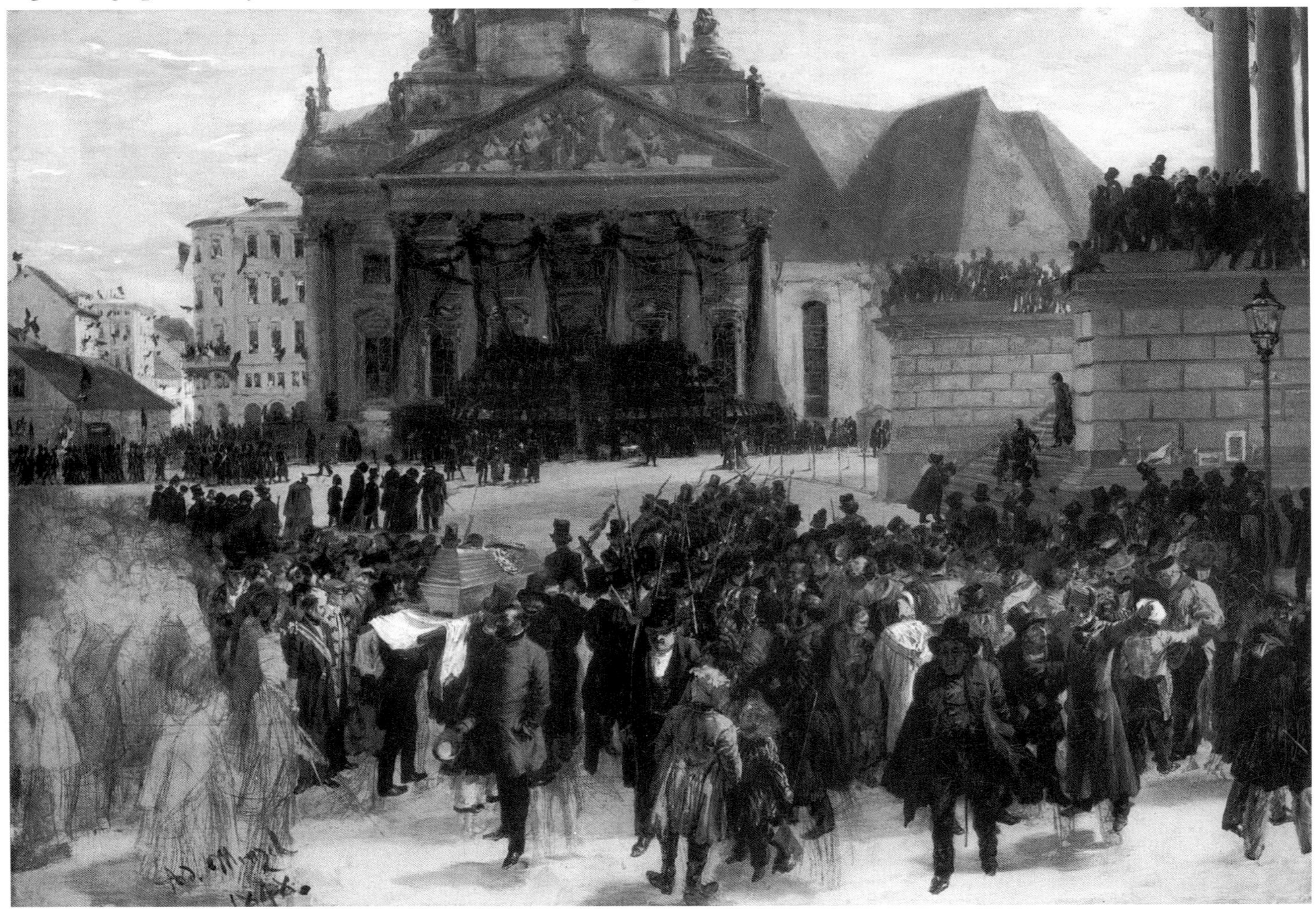

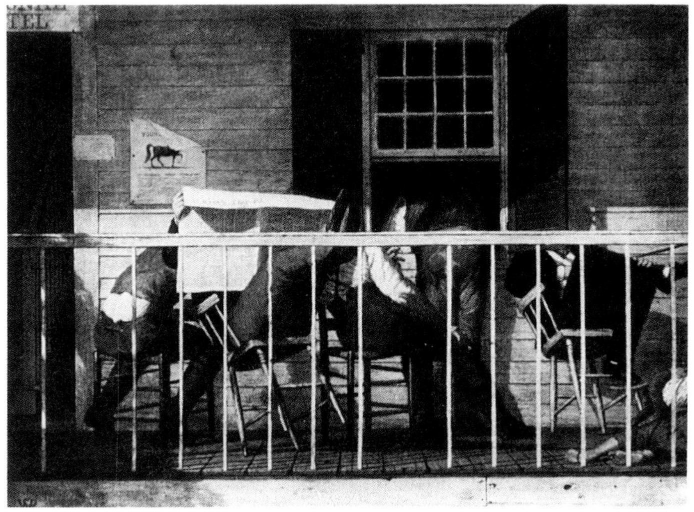

Fig. 66. Enoch Wood Perry, *The True American*, *c.* 1860, oil, New York, The Metropolitan Museum of Art

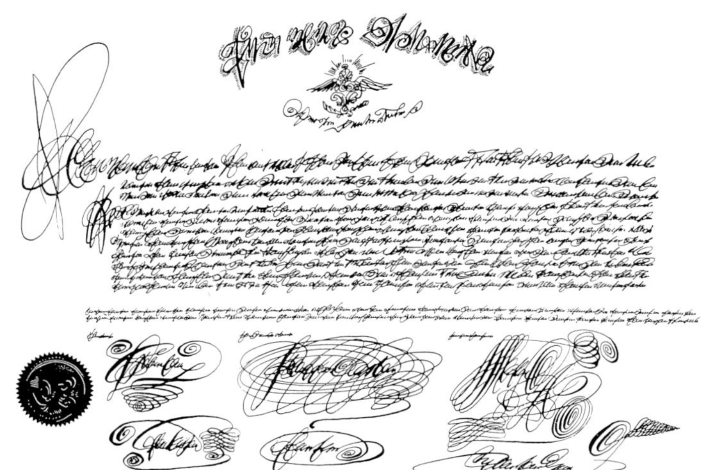

Fig. 67. Saul Steinberg, *Facsimile*, *c.* 1950, pen and ink, private collection

drawing depicting the Menzel family around the piano (cat. 61), both dating from 1851, that the inner tensions and breadth of his output can begin to be assessed. The same tensions are visible just as strongly a quarter of a century on, when one compares the crude realism of the *Artist's Foot* (cat. 165) and the narrative historicism of *By the Fireside* (cat. 166). What Werner Hofmann has described as 'bifocality' (see his chapter in this publication) can be found within individual works as well as in comparisons between Menzel's works.

2.

In the year preceding Menzel's subjective, intimate scenes and forays into *pleinairisme*, his major work was illustrating Franz Kugler's *History of Frederick the Great*. His wood engravings for this text reveal the subject-matter, the motifs and the particular way of seeing, from which his later works derive to a large extent. At times Menzel focuses intensely on the protagonists, involving the viewer in their private emotions and conversations; at times he keeps the viewer so firmly at a distance that the scene dissolves into an atmospheric rendering. Individual scenes therefore develop out of the flowing continuum of time and space. In this way, the traditionally accepted hierarchy of events and protagonists is challenged and the boundaries between history and everyday life become blurred. Occasionally the artist elects to pick a moment when all the actors have left the stage, leaving only a landscape, an ahistorical space (fig. 70). Such techniques were used by contemporaries of Menzel whose illustrations he knew: for example Raffet's wood engravings for de Norvins' *History of Napoleon*. Yet Menzel develops the technique into a system for viewing and, furthermore, transfers use of this technique to painting. He does exactly this in *View of Back Yards* (cat. 33), in which he clears the foreground of the canvas entirely: when our eye alights on the principal motif, as defined by traditional norms, it disappears.

If the illustrations to Kugler's text are a training ground for Menzel's new way of seeing – what a contrast there is, after all, between the paintings that precede and follow them – nevertheless they are accompanied by constant sketching. Although many of the sketches cannot be exactly dated, their place within this significant period of development can be confirmed by comparison, not least with the drawings contained in his many bound sketchbooks. With considerable resolve the step from drawing to painting – even if under the guise of the 'study' – is made.

In the search for precursors to Menzel's artistic development, Berlin's particularly strong tradition of Realism – as exemplified by artists like Daniel Chodowiecki and Gottfried Schadow – must be taken into account, a debt Menzel himself acknowledged. Schadow, who served as director of the Berlin Academy of Art for over thirty years, had defended the 'prosaic' in his famous debates with Goethe in 1801–3[11]. Goethe's key accusation, that now 'Poetry has been replaced by history, character and the ideal by the portrait, symbol by allegory, landscape by perspective, Humanism by patriotism. . .'[12] accurately describes the predilections of Menzel. Therefore it is not surprising that Schadow was the first to praise the young artist and, reciprocally, the mature Menzel composed many allegorical homages to Gottfried Schadow (fig. 52). Parallel to these influences on Menzel ran those of the landscape painter Carl Blechen, whose fundamental Romanticism fed on natural light and a preference for the transitory which he captured in sketches in oil. In poor health by 1835, Blechen possibly encountered Menzel at the Association of Berlin Artists, though there is no evidence of a closer relationship between the artists. Blechen's work was well known in the Berlin art world, not least because the art dealer Louis Sachse, an early promoter of Menzel's work, served as an intermediary. His colour, his *facture*, his particular means of rendering a landscape, as well as his occasional poeticizing of the incidental, certainly made an impression on the young Menzel. A large and important painting of 1828 by Blechen depicting a settlement of Semnones (native inhabitants of the March of Brandenburg), set within their severe sand and pine landscape[13], constitutes a provisional farewell to the Classical tradition of landscape, as well as to traditional history painting.

Blechen's contemporaries described his art as 'ingenious', yet problematic. One critic in particular spoke of (Romantic) irony in the work of Blechen, using such

Fig. 68. *Head of a Leaning Man*, pencil, Berlin, Kupferstichkabinett (N 3726)

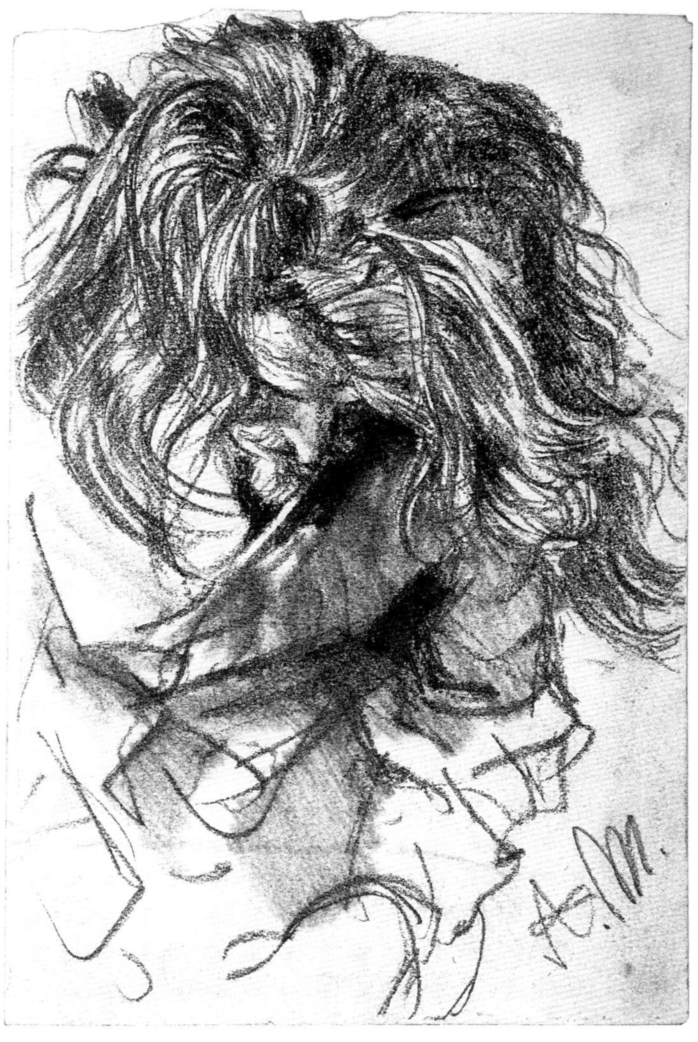

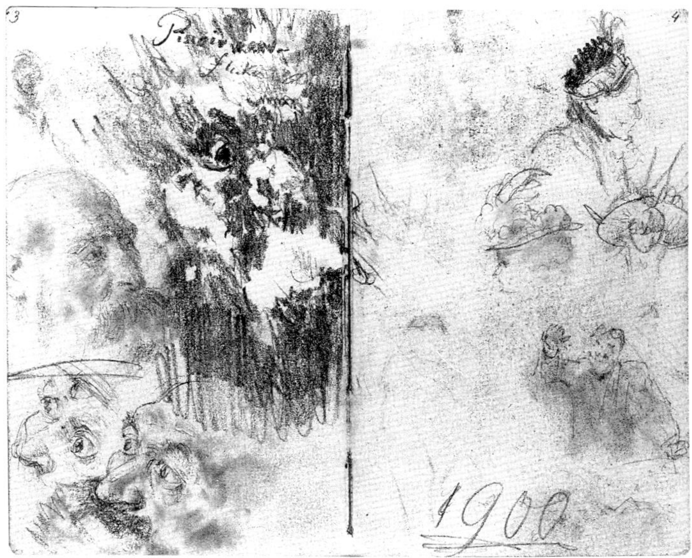

Fig. 69. 'Marks on a Urinal Wall', 1900, pencil, Berlin, Kupferstichkabinett (sketchbook no. 73, pp. 3–4)

overblown language that his text was read, until only recently, as a severely negative assessment of the oeuvre[14]. The author of the essay, however, was the young philosopher Adolf Schöll, with whom Menzel struck up a friendship two or three years later, a friendship that remained intact even after Schöll left Berlin in 1842[15]. With his unconventional theoretical views, Schöll no doubt exerted an important influence on Menzel.

Equipped thus, the young artist discovered the work of John Constable. In 1900, the promoters of the work of the early Menzel made a connection with Constable's work, speculation subsequently confirmed by the artist himself who, forty years earlier had seen two canvases by the English landscapist which had been exhibited in Berlin in 1839[16]. One contemporary reviewer described the paintings exhibited in so detailed a fashion[17] that at least one of the two landscapes can now be identified (fig. 72). *Child's Hill*, a painting first exhibited in 1825, matches the description of the reviewer: a broad plain stretches to the horizon, at which Harrow is visible; a forest crosses the picture plane in the middle distance; one sees an approaching horse-drawn cart, a number of cows and a donkey in the right foreground[18]. Less daring than other compositions by the artist, this painting nevertheless belies Constable's reverence for eighteenth-century Dutch landscape painting. Its format clearly approaches that of several works Menzel was to paint some years later; he was clearly encouraged in his development by the ordinariness of Constable's landscape, which disrupts the compositional integrity of the Classical landscape tradition.

Surely Menzel was inspired by the unstable structure

of a painting such as Constable's. This, in fact, becomes the core of Menzel's art, and separates him from his contemporaries. Although he shared an interest in the rendering in colour of natural light effects, the raising of humble subject-matter to importance – for example, back yards and intimate interiors – the manipulation of the fragmentary, and the blurring of boundaries between study and finished work, with a handful of artists in the 1820s and 1830s from Corot to the Danish artists of the 'golden age' (for example, Kobke), and even with a number of Berlin artists, in each of these cases such innovations take place within a clear and static pictorial organization. In a very provocative manner Menzel rejects this vehemently and, in doing so, leaves any Biedermeier considerations far behind.

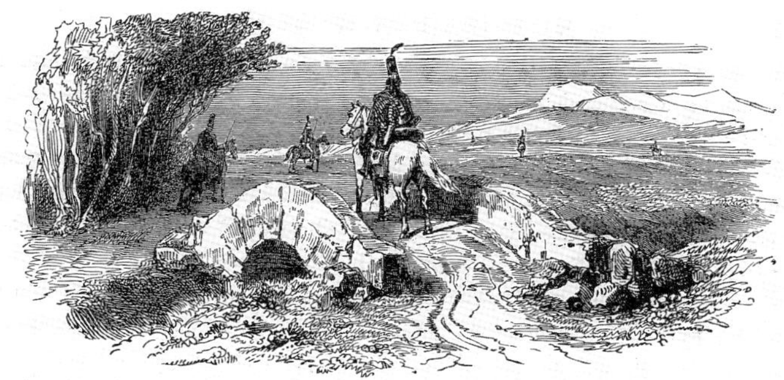

Fig. 71. Auguste Raffet, illustration from *History of Napoleon*, Norvins, 1839

3.

The year 1844 was a turning point in Menzel's artistic career. It was in this year that he began to paint *nach der Natur* (*sur le motif*[19]), enthusiastically telling friends about his progress and aware that he was taking a decisive step in his art[20]. *Balcony Room* of 1845 (cat. 18) has long been deemed an astonishing work without precedent in Menzel's oeuvre. But now that we can securely date three paintings to 1844 (cat. 11–13), our astonishment is even greater. How can one explain *Rear Courtyard and House*? How does one explain the selection of subject-matter, really an anti-subject? And how can one explain the complete dissolution of motifs in the distance?

From the beginning, and certainly not for the last time in the above-mentioned painting, Menzel questioned the very principle of mimesis. Occasionally in particular passages he abandons imitation outright, almost as if he had lost it in stages along the way. Colour – limited to the brown wash of the underpainting or, in the case of *Rear Courtyard and House*, to a blackish-grey – no longer defines forms or describes the local colour of the scene, but rather becomes a material substance which can be spread over the canvas, scraped away or otherwise treated as a prefigurative substance. The process of painting fundamentally calls itself into question here.

Fig. 70. *Landscape*, 1839–42, engraving on wood illustrating *History of Frederick the Great* (Bock, 1923, no. 734)

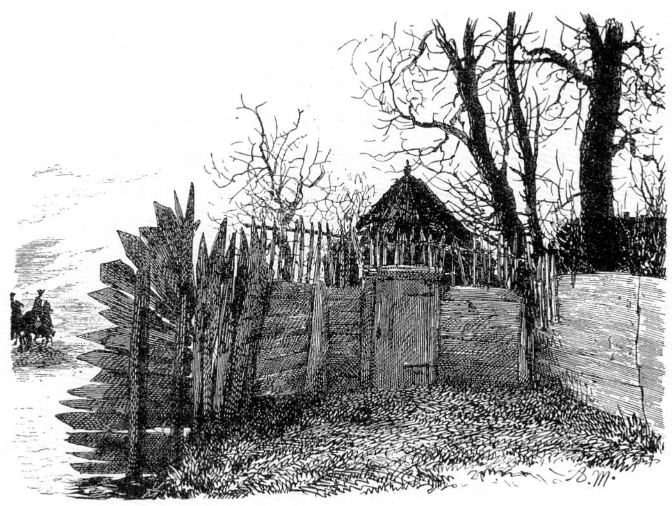

The writings of Françoise Forster-Hahn and Werner Hofmann have rescued the artist from the assessment that the fragmentariness of his paintings signalled only inconsequential arbitrariness on his part, instead identifying the fragment as an important component of modernity[21]. Although both scholars focus mainly on subject-matter and composition, fragmentation is also evident in the manner of application of the paint itself, which he used in its raw and elementary state. And just as he never tires of disrupting the rules of order in depicting objects or in reflecting aspects of society (cat. 13, 15, 15, 65, 179, 193), he also depicts the lack of order, the chaos of the natural world, as in renderings of a man's head with a wildly dishevelled mane of hair (fig. 68) or in spotty saltpetre flecks on the wall of a *pissoir* (fig. 69). In the same vein, Flaubert, a similarly talented craftsman only six years Menzel's junior, allegedly achieved the 'coloration' for his *Madame Bovary*: 'I wanted to do nothing more than depict a shade, the musty shade of woodlice'[22]. In painting of this period, the phenomenon remained singular.

The painting of this period only rarely exhibits such prefigurative amorphousness. In the case of Turner, when motifs disappear, what remains is the suggestion of fog, clouds, or storms, that is, there remains a subject. Turner, like Delacroix, too, retains the presence of baroque ornamentation, as does Victor Hugo in a

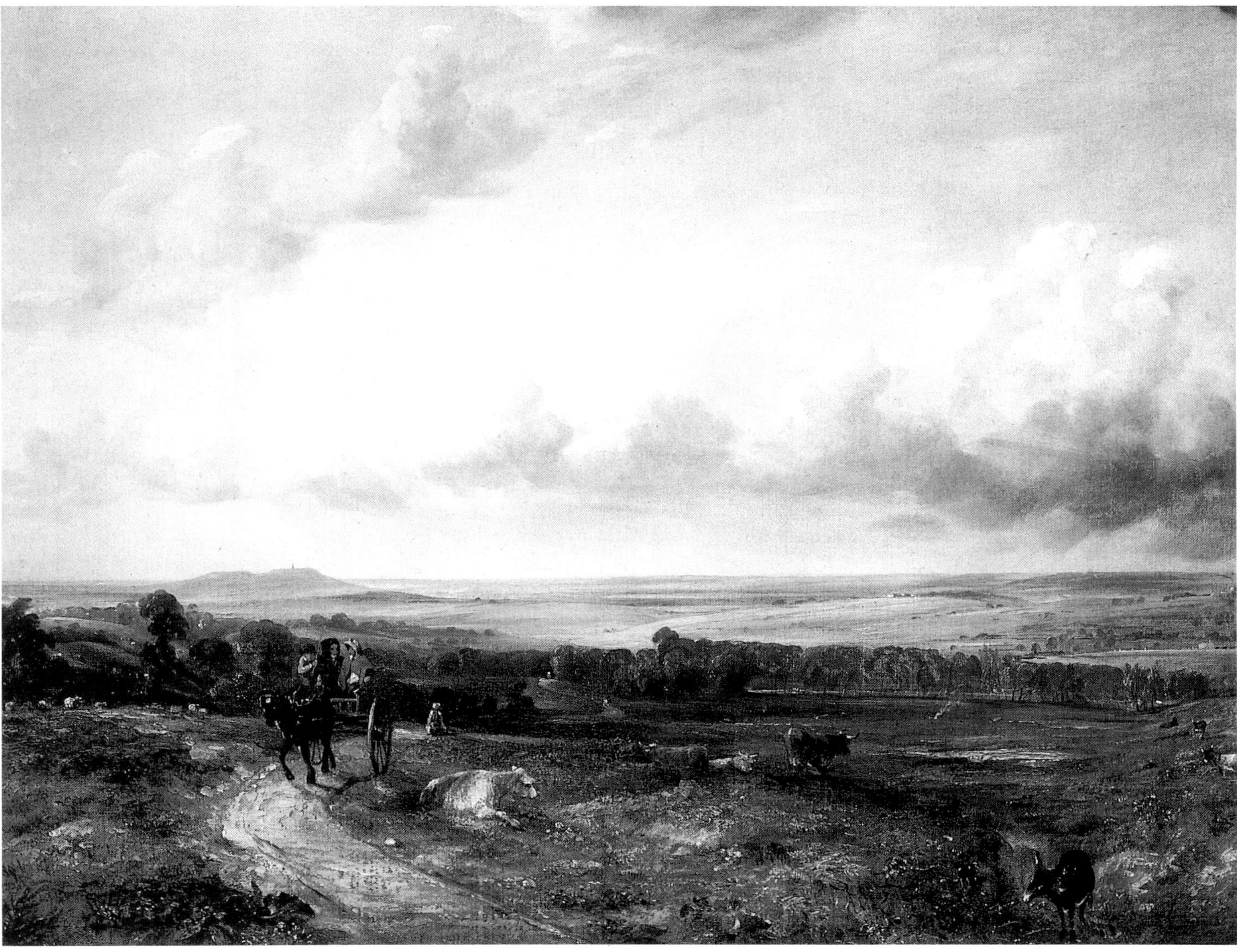

Fig. 72. John Constable, *Child's Hill*, 1824–5, oil, private collection

slightly different manner in his splotch-like abstractions. Out of spots of colour or ink – rather than out of the dynamic of the paintbrush – develop the *Kleksographien* ('splotchographies' *cf.* commentary to cat. 58), true precursors of the Rorschach Test, and of great interest to some of Menzel's German contemporaries (fig. 76). Though their creators demonstrate a need to quickly get from amorphousness to figuration and spots are interpreted by added lines, or at the very least an attempt was made to conform to a standard of beauty, in the case of the Rorschach Test via creating symmetry by folding the paper, Menzel was different, uniting a formal asceticism with a subversive lack of timidity. (One might perhaps say that he was a forerunner of today's 'bad painting' in terms of his approach to his material.) Fifty years after Menzel one finds similar qualities in the young Edvard Munch – for whom, incidentally Menzel did not speak up when, in 1892 Anton von Werner forced the closing of an exhibition of the Norwegian artist's painting at the Association of Berlin Artists – or also in the work of Gustave Moreau. What for Menzel remained an occasional impulse, and affected only small portions of his canvases, became for Munch a guiding principle his art.

In the late 1850s the ability of Menzel's gaze to revel in uncertainty, in the veiled, diminishes, though, in his very final canvas, cut in two by the artist (cat. 201, 202), hesitation and uncertainty are manifest. This, however, becomes a frequent quality in the late drawings. In these drawings the search for truthfulness is obstructed by doubt. Figures appear in threes or fours, which normally implies a perspectival distance from the subject at hand, though Menzel chooses to view these groupings myopically. We see nothing but heads and shoulders whose outlines become indistinct in a less than well-defined space (cat. 215, 218). In this manner Menzel strives for accuracy of perception in describing a social setting. His path seems momentarily to cross with the Naturalism of the 1880s and 1890s. But only by comparing such works with similar motifs in the work of the Düsseldorf painter Gerhard Janssen (fig. 75), for example, do we see how quickly Menzel's path diverges from its momentary juncture with Naturalism.

4.

In recent years, much attention has been focused on the liberties that Menzel the painter took with the rules of perspective then taught in the Academies. The rules of perspective defined the relationship between the eye of an imaginary viewer and a fictive pictorial space – and arranged the objects within this space accordingly – which Menzel replaces with a system of spatial contradictions. The art historian Werner Busch has discerned Menzel's use of perspectival devices which force the eye to glide across the painting (*cf.* cat. 18, 34). Space and time begin to dissolve into one another. We are tempted to ask to what extent was Menzel aware that he was breaking away from centuries-old, firmly held convictions? We know that Menzel was not inept, and where necessary he put the rules of linear perspective to use (cat. 173), even masterfully handling exaggerated foreshortenings (cat. 25, 93). One might ask the same about Turner, who taught perspective at the Royal Academy in London.On one occasion at least, another instructor in perspective, the Danish artist Christoffer Wilhelm Eckersberg, flagrantly broke the rules. His altar painting for the church at Frederiksberg, a depiction of the Last Supper (fig. 73) emphatically places itself in the linear perspective tradition modelled on Leonardo's famous fresco. But note the contradictory perspective with which the empty stool of Judas is rendered. Two worlds collide here, from which many took a religious meaning[23]. Such conscious manipulation of perspective is also apparent in Menzel's work, though without similar overtones.

Fig. 73. Christoffer Wilhelm Eckersberg, reredos of the church at Fredericksberg, 1839–40, oil

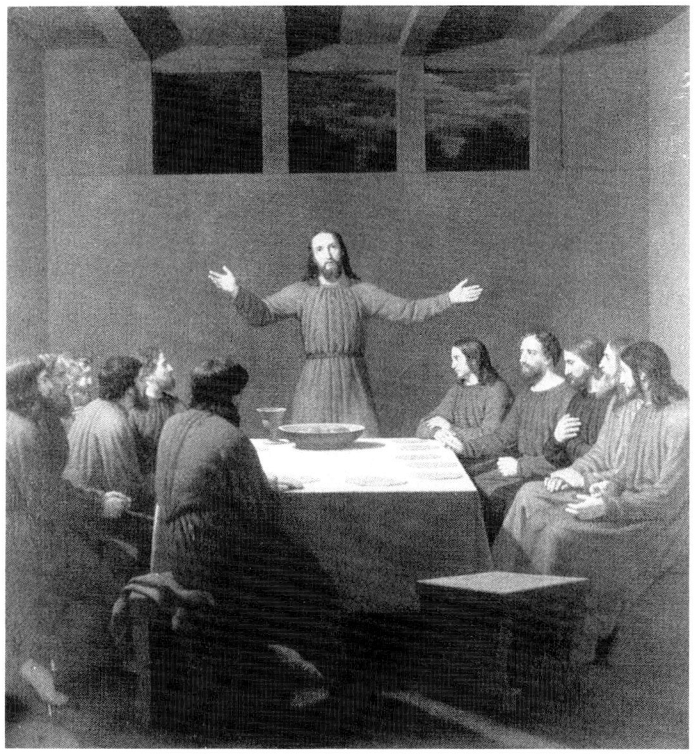

At the time when Menzel began his process of 'deconstructing' academic rules, Berlin was the site of intense philosophical discussion spurred on by the 'Young Hegelians' – among them for a time the young Karl Marx – who were concerned with moving Hegel's philosophy into the political realm. In the same year that Menzel painted *Balcony Room*, a curious book written by one of them, Max Stirner[24], *Der Einzige und sein Eigentum* – a work repudiated by Stirner's friends and subject to Prussian censorship – was published. Although it probably went unnoticed by the young Menzel, the book proclaimed in animated language the absolute rights of the individual, subservient to neither God nor society. Although it is questionable to link Menzel's art to Stirner's beliefs, it remains interesting that such a cult of subjectivity and amoralism prevailed in Berlin during Menzel's formative years. One of the book's final chapters, 'My self-enjoyment', rejects any and all duties imposed by external authorities. Here one is reminded of the unsuccessful musician in Franz Grillparzer's novel, *Der arme Spielmann*, a man who in the end plays only one note on his violin, finding it completely entrancing, or perhaps also of Menzel's handling of paint in which colour no longer defines objective forms?

Into the tumult of philosophical debate in Berlin in the period of the *Vormärz* entered also the voice of the Königsberg professor Karl Rosenkranz. He had long been working on a book that finally appeared in 1853, with the intentionally paradoxical title *Esthetik des Hässlichen* (The Aesthetics of the Ugly), found by Gottfried Keller to be 'nonsensical and romantic'. Rosenkranz derived the ugly – defined 'anti-beauty', which reached its logical conclusion in the satanic, but which was also able to be reconciled with the comical on one level – from the oppositional structure inherent in the Hegelian system and announced 'I trace the cosmos of the ugly from its first chaotic nebulousness, from amorphousness and asymmetry to the limitless diversities of disorganization which negate the beautiful through

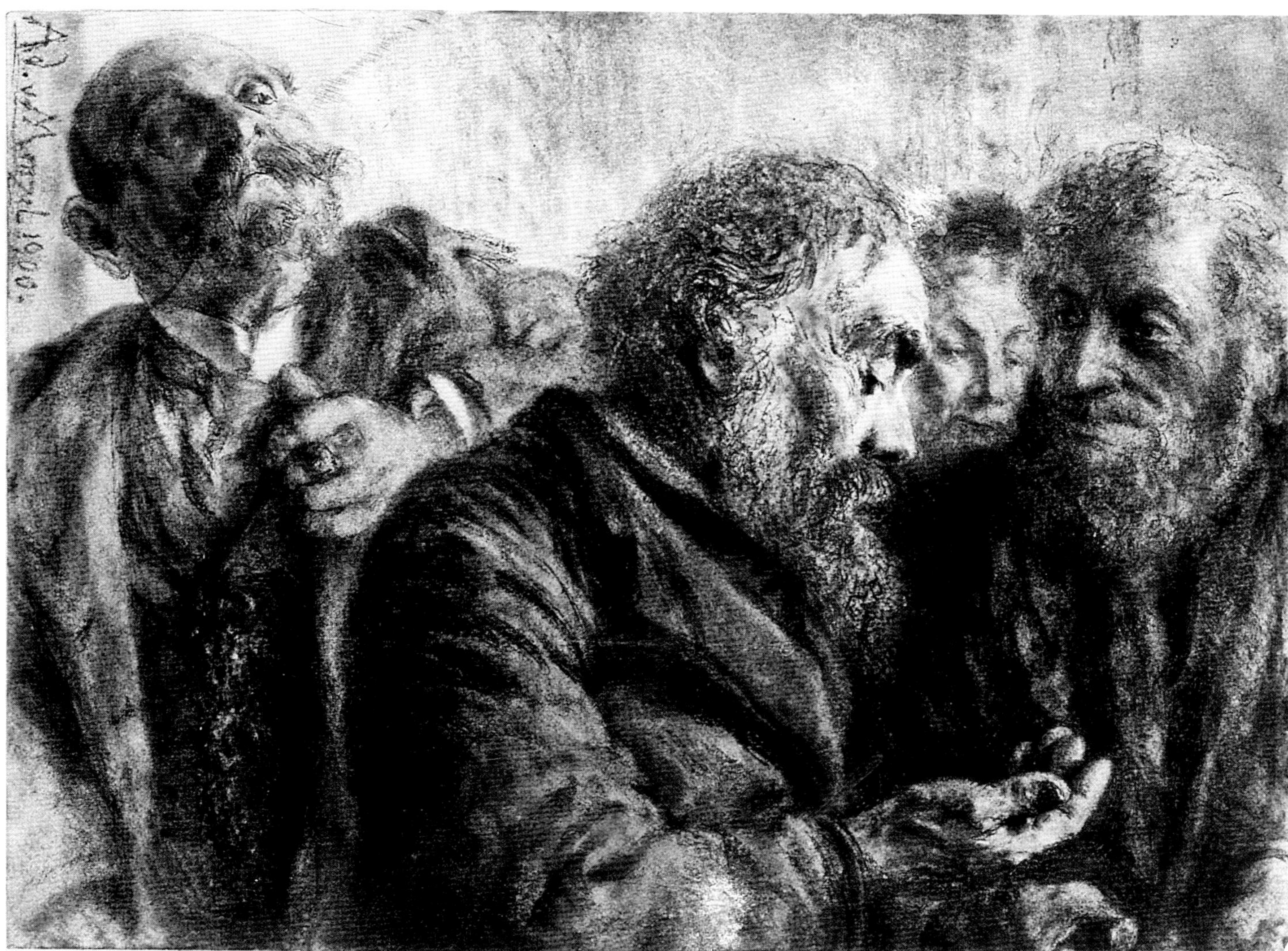

Fig. 74 *Four Characters*, 1900, pencil, Berlin, Kupferstichkabinett (N 1737)

caricature. Formlessness, incorrectness and deformation are staged in the development of each metamorphosis'[25]. Amorphousness, asymmetry, diversity and disorganization are terms which Rosenkranz sets within a context of assembled contemporary commentary, often formulated with reference to France, and the development of the modern city. A sidelong glance at Menzel is also possible here[26]. It is as if Rosenkranz had perused Menzel's drawings when he evoked the 'confusion' of 'asymmetry': 'We cannot cross the street without constantly collecting material for humorous observations. It is as if we were viewing a wagon piled high with furniture: sofas, tables, kitchen utensils, beds and paintings all in such close proximity to one another that the objects themselves would be astounded'[27] (*cf.* cat 14).

5.

Menzel's art is clearly a reflection of its times. His awareness of the symptoms of disintegration: the disintegration of accepted hierarchies, values or social structures. His need to record facts can be seen as a counterweight that acts to reassure himself of reality. His need for constant confirmation by the outside world – in the form of historical biographies, or in the study of clothing details, zoo animals, or the wrinkled features of a cabinet minister – was at the origins of his curiosity; everything was inspected, reinspected and thereby verified. The encyclopedic range of his memory, and of images collected in his sketchbooks, is made even more remarkable when it is noted that few of the elements he so assiduously gathered make an appearance in the finished paintings. In his reconstructions of historical events or subjects he strove for truth of detail, once going so far as to open the seam of one of Frederick the Great's uniforms to check its original colour[28]. In a letter to an acquaintance he explained that 'pedantry and an interest in minutiae' are

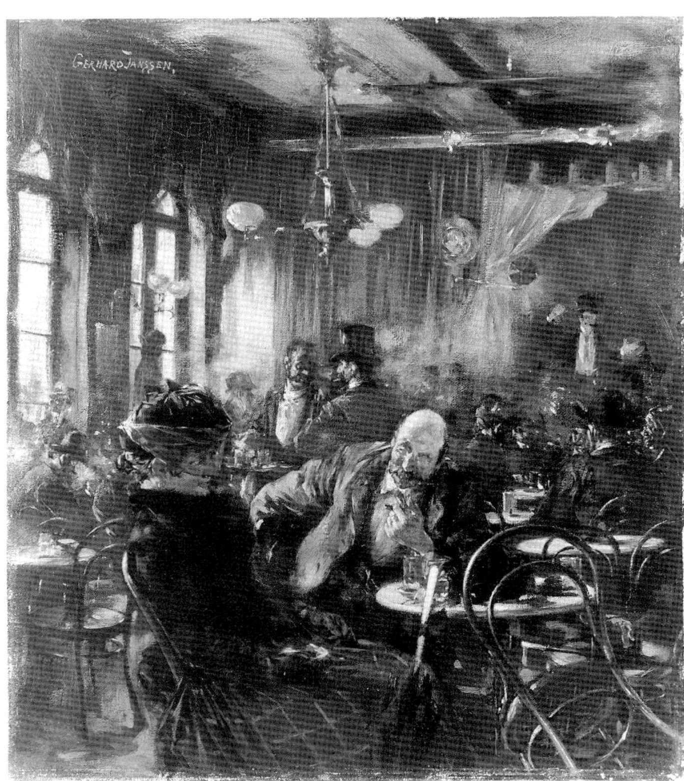

Fig. 75. Gerhard Janssen, *The Old Beer-Hall in Düsseldorf*, *c.* 1890, oil, Düsseldorf, Kunstmuseum

the traits of the historian, 'simply lots of questions for Clio. . .'[29] By contrast, in contemporary scenes where anyone would be able to make comparisons, particularly in topographical or site-specific works where 'truthfulness' to detail could be verified as such, he took great licence (*cf.* cat. 127, 167). His much-acclaimed 'authenticity' is often, therefore, a result of the viewer's first impressions, a crafted 'Truth-Fullness' of behaviours or situations. In a now-famous phrase, the French critic Duranty selects the ambiguous, multivalent word 'névrose' to describe Menzel's realism[30]: obsession, neurosis, mania? The Tantalus of the Real; Menzel wrestles with a reality that threatens to evade his reach, and then, once within his grasp, he finds that it crumbles away. In the end, the eagerness with which he collected scattered facts was matched only by the arrogance that allowed him to omit them in the final work.

Fig. 76. Julius Muhr, *The Lion Approaches*, *c.* 1847–50, drawing on a coffee stain, Berlin, Kupferstichkabinett

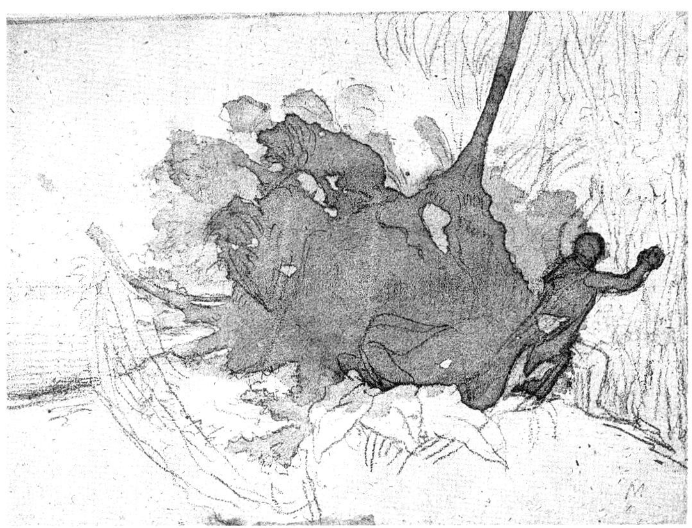

A constant in Menzel's work remains the obstruction of perception. Exaggerated foreshortenings, truncated motifs, intersections and oppositions between pictorial elements are recorded even in the earliest sketchbooks. One suspects that these constant obstacles to perception, the visual obstructions themselves, become for him a major theme.

This remained the case. Menzel is close to Degas in this respect, an artist whose artistic process was often comparable. Intentional ambiguities and disjunctures are present in the work of both, but also in the work of others. With a single-mindedness of purpose the American Enoch Wood Perry, who had studied art in Düsseldorf and Paris, confronts the issue (fig. 66) In a painting dating from the 1860s Perry depicts a row of men seated on a terrace. Each and every head (including the head of a horse depicted on a poster) is obscured from view, in complete opposition to the *trompe-l'oeil* precision with which the painting is itself rendered. A century later, a similar delusional reality is evoked by Saul Steinberg in an ink drawing in which the physical characteristics of a handwritten letter are mimicked, though the letter remains entirely illegible (fig. 67). This sense of masking reality signals a futility of lived experience that goes to the core of 'modernity'.

6.

Menzel's attentiveness and enthusiasm for contemporary life took a variety of sometimes richly surprising forms. Since a great deal has been written about his choice of modern subject-matter, it is not necessary to address this aspect here. Much more significant, and deserving of increased attention, is his attitude to the medium of photography. Although it was viewed by many of his artist contemporaries as a competitive threat to their chosen profession, Menzel was an enthusiastic witness to its introduction in Berlin. In the same year that Daguerre received his patent for the process in Paris, the art dealer and close friend of Menzel Louis Sachse brought this

Fig. 77. *Bust of a Man*, 1865, test of a negative painted by Menzel on a glass plate, location unknown

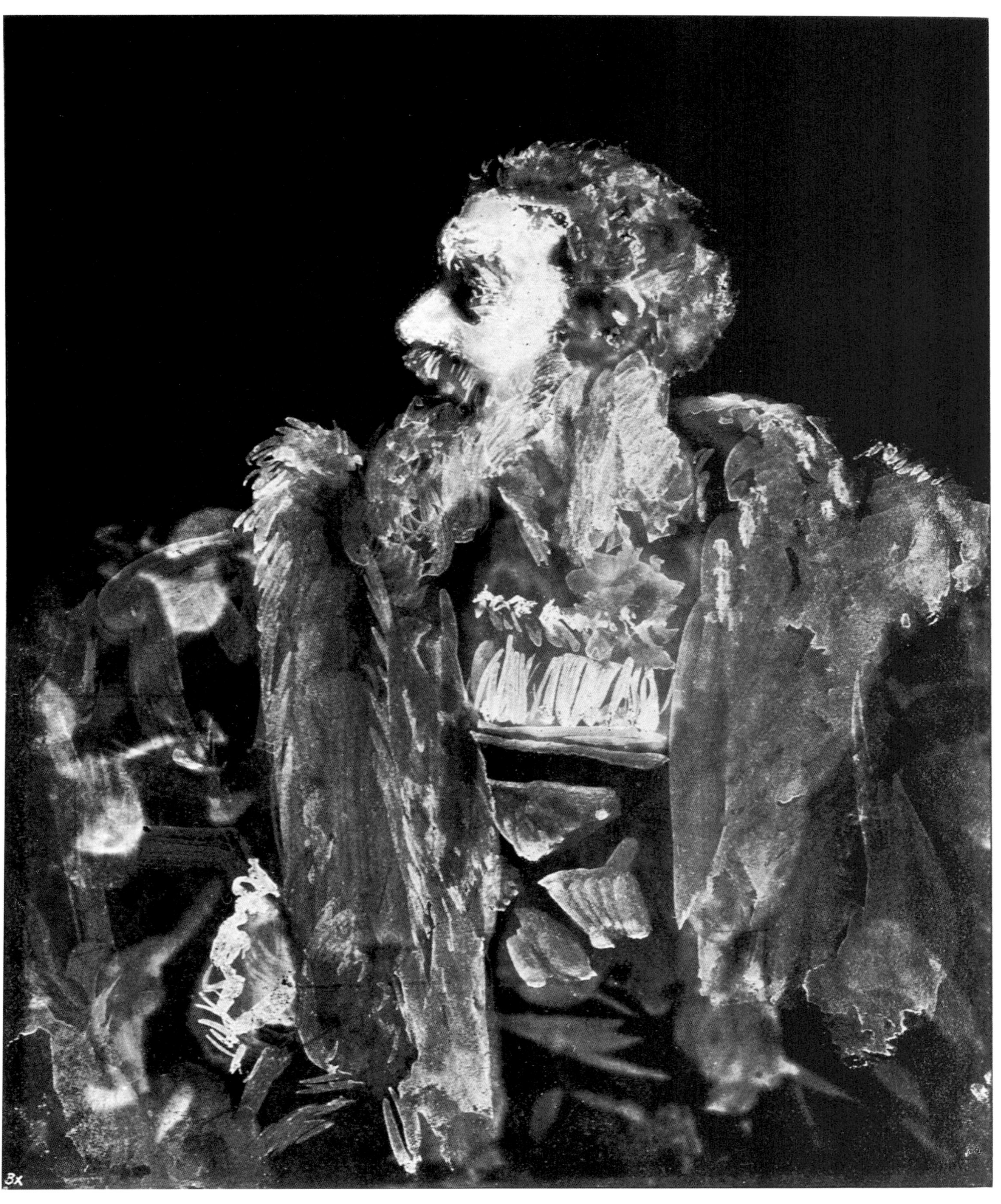

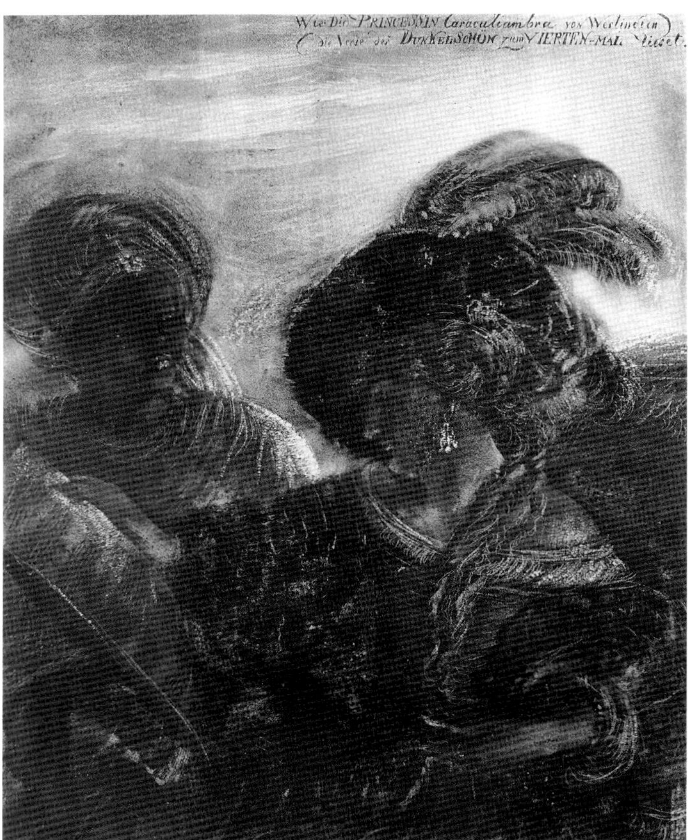

Fig. 78. *Princess Caraculiambra* (after Cervantes), *c.* 1855, paper blackened with soot and scratching, location unknown

technology to Berlin. Years later Menzel assisted his brother Richard in acquiring an important Berlin photographic institute.

In 1867, Menzel was approached by a journal devoted to scientific and artistic photography to draft a defence of the merits of the photographic process[31]. For Menzel, use of this new technology was in no way a replacement for studies from nature, nor a threat to art. Among well-known contemporaries of Menzel, complete rejection of the use of photography in the reproduction of art works was common. The academic Herman Grimm, a Berlin professor, preferred to hold up engraved reproductions in his art history lectures, rather than embrace the new technology by showing early lantern slides using a diascope. Far from lending support to such a conservative stance, Menzel even participated in his brother's business venture by supervising photographic reproduction of works in the Kassel Gallery. Early on he also began to document his own works with the assistance of photography (*cf.* cat. 20) and even allowed his drawings to be published by the process of photographic reproduction (fig. 198). In 1868 an *Album Menzel* was published with photographic reproductions of works by Menzel, accompanied by a long preface by Ludwig Pietsch, though the edition seems to have been so small that, to date, not a single copy has been located[32]. Several years later the ever-faithful Pietsch informed the readers of his newspaper of photographic reproductions of Menzel's work that had been produced in the interim[33]. At the time the inaccuracy of the photographic plates used – they did not react uniformly to convey the relationships of light and shade in the original artwork – required the negatives to be retouched. It is not difficult to imagine Menzel eagerly entering the darkroom to do the retouching himself.

Thus versed in the relationship of negative to positive, Menzel set out in 1865 to paint directly on to a glass paint with a brush dipped in carmine red paint, inverting the dark values of the images to create, in fact, a negative. What merits attention, however, is that the artist who depicts the contemporary world by traditional artistic means here chooses to lavish modern techniques on romanticized, historical subject-matter. (One is tempted to see here a similarity to the incongruities manifest, for example, in Ludwig II of Bavaria's baroque stagings of extravagant fairytales using electric light to heighten dramatic effect.) In the case of the Menzel negative, the artist captures the figure of a bearded nobleman in Renaissance costume (fig. 77), a motif that also appears in gouaches of the period. Several copies of the plate were reproduced, though all were unfortunately lost, as was the negative once in the possession of Menzel's dealer, Hermann Pächter[34]. At least an old journal illustration has survived, which allows us to confirm that Menzel's ambitions in his use of these 'clichés-verre', experiments in line rather than tone, were even greater than those of Corot. The method Menzel used was a variation on the mezzotint technique, in which a prepared, uniformly black copperplate is scraped away to produce an image derived from shades of grey (fig. 78[35]). Once again, Menzel's tendency is to damage the surface on which he works in order to create an image.

When Menzel's path crossed that of photography, he was less concerned with the precision of the reproduction, than with exploring the possibilities of inverting black and white. If his paintings can be said to reflect an interest in photography, particularly so in the late work, it is because this new technology was able to accord importance to each instant and each object indiscriminately.

7.

Also relative and limited is the relationship between international Naturalism and Menzel's paintings of big city life, crowds and genre subjects from the late 1860s to the early 1890s (cat. 123, 203). Certainly there are a

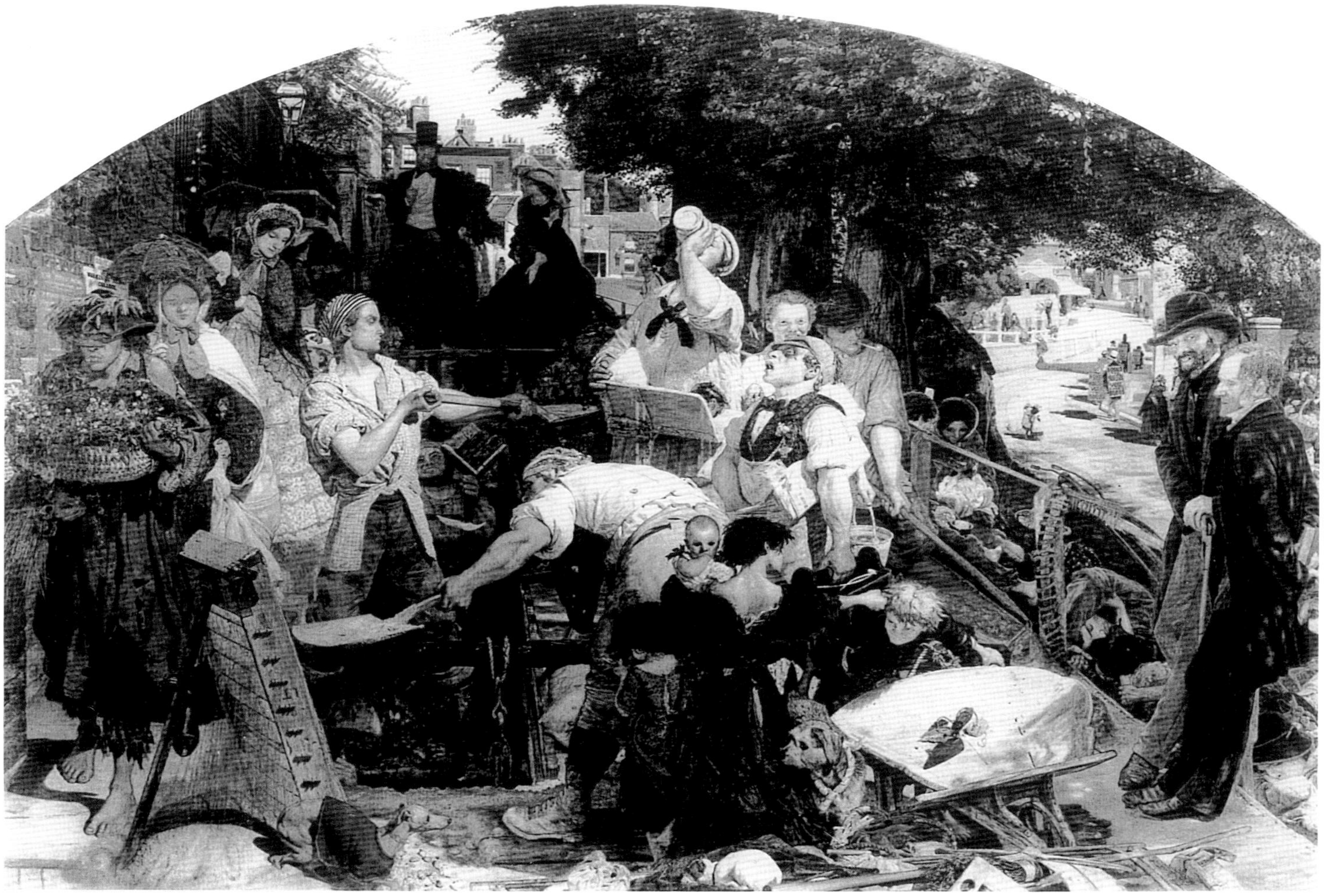

Fig. 79. Ford Madox Brown, *Work*, 1852–63, oil, Manchester, City Art Gallery

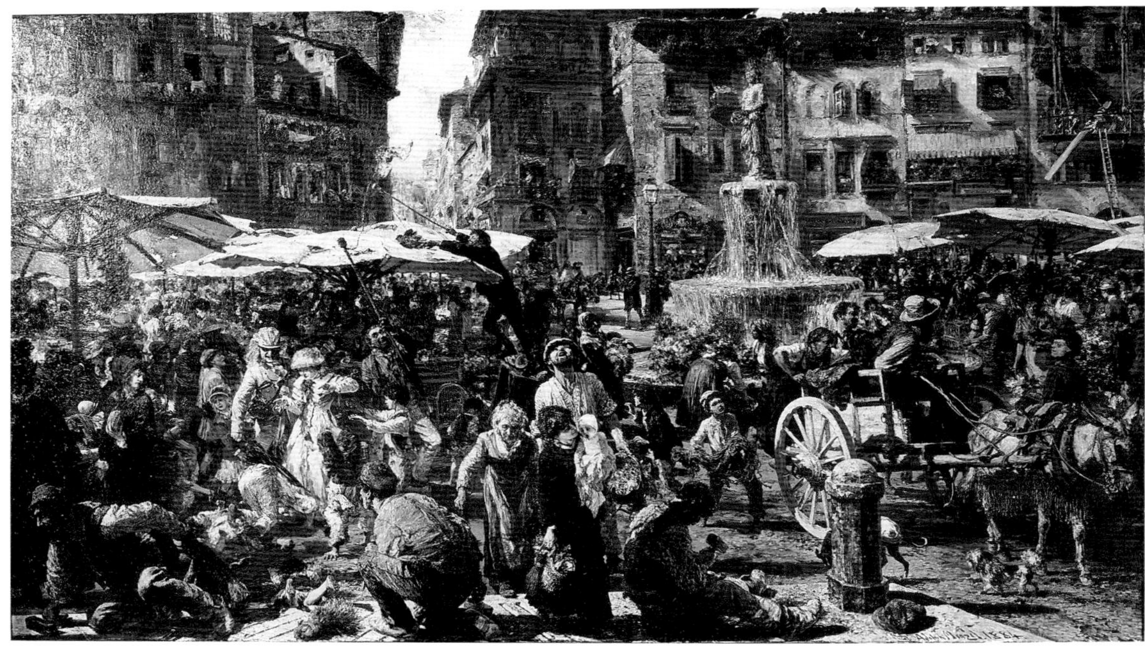

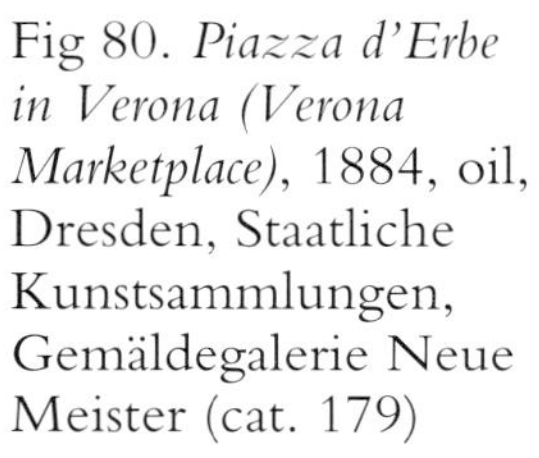

Fig 80. *Piazza d'Erbe in Verona (Verona Marketplace)*, 1884, oil, Dresden, Staatliche Kunstsammlungen, Gemäldegalerie Neue Meister (cat. 179)

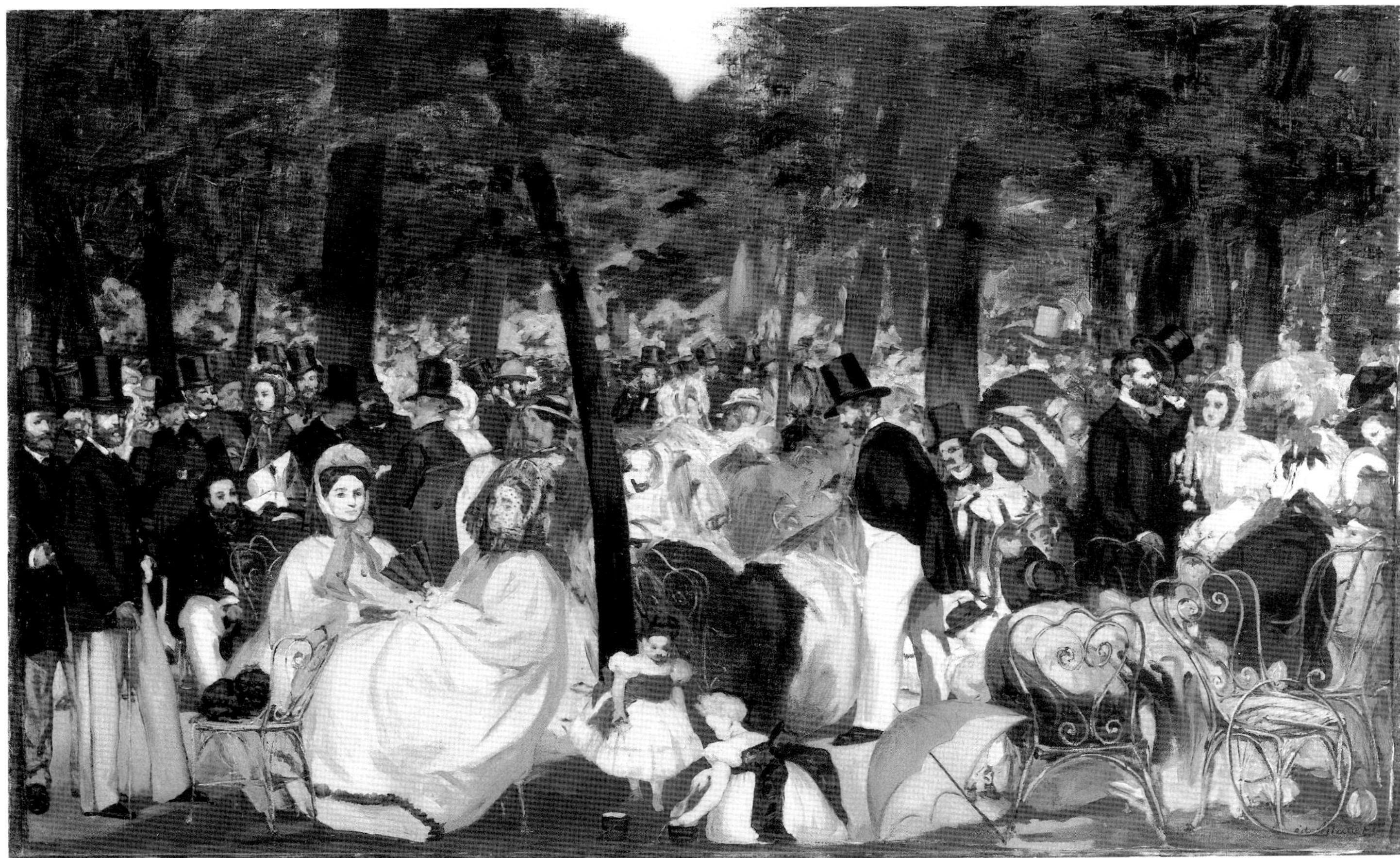

Fig. 81. Manet, *Music in the Tuileries*, 1862, oil, London, National Gallery

number of common motifs: a predilection for harsh and dusty sunlight also makes is way into paintings by Italian and Spanish contemporaries, not to mention into some rare, but important, images of contemporary life issued from the English Pre-Raphaelite circle in the middle of the century. A comparison of Ford Madox Brown's *Work* (fig. 79 and *Piazza d'Erbe in Verona* (cat. 179; fig. 80), completed several decades apart, is instructive in identifying what sets Menzel apart from other Naturalist painters. It is entirely possible that Menzel was influenced by Madox Brown's painting[36]. There are marked similarities in structure – the alignment of figures along the foreground plane, the sharp perspectival recession into the distance, the contrast between the lower and the bourgeois classes – and in motif – the figure of a mother and child in the foreground at direct centre, a male figure with tossed-back head directly behind the mother, who serves as a measure for the scale of all remaining figures, and construction workers – between the two paintings. More important, however, is the equal weight given to figures and objects depicted in both these paintings. No motif is repressed in favour of another, or even in favour of the overall composition, that is, nothing is of secondary significance. The intensity of interest accorded to

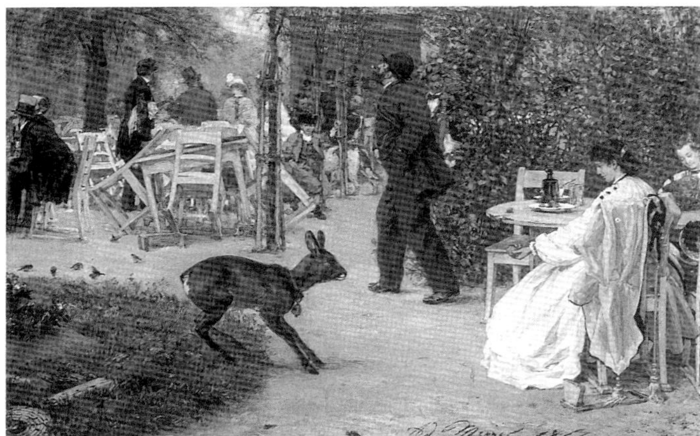

Fig. 82. *The Moritzhof Inn*, 1864, gouache, Berlin, Kupferstichkabinett (cat. 108)

each detail is, in both paintings, a result of the lack of narrative structure to events depicted. In contrast to the Menzel, *Work*, however, is at least partially structured by the presence of the two men at the right of the painting who observe the action in front of them; they serve the same function as the two philosophers in Thomas

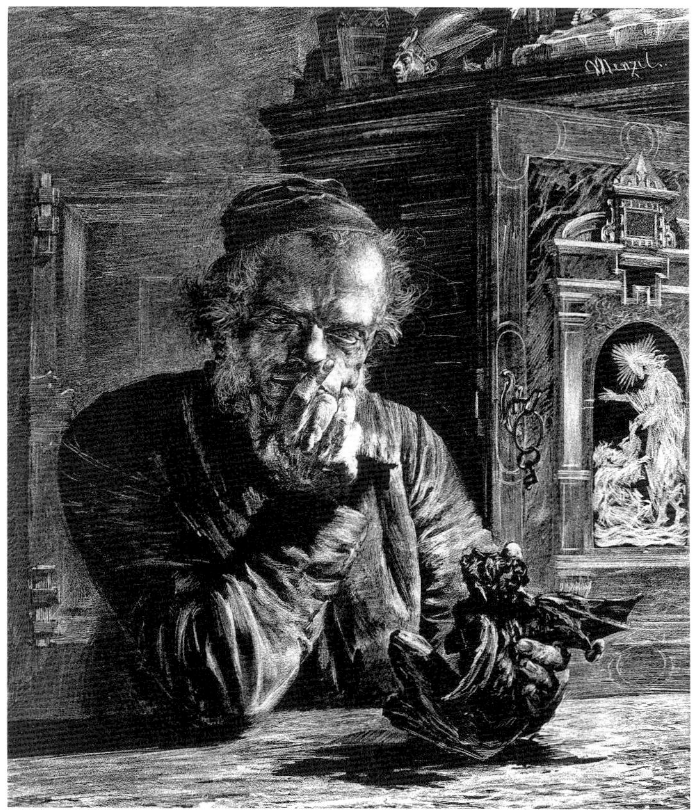

Fig. 83. *The Antiquary*, *c.* 1852, lithograph (Bock, 1923, no. 405)

Couture's *Romans in the Era of Decadence*. Menzel, by contrast, does not distance the viewer by the use of a similar technique.

A comparison between Menzel and the watercolours of the Viennese artist Rudolf von Alt can also be highly instructive, since Alt was a direct contemporary of Menzel, with a lifespan as long as Menzel's (both died in 1905) and only seven years Menzel's junior. It is very unfortunate that a much-awaited comparative exhibition of the two artists, planned by Walter Koschatzky for the Albertina in Vienna has never taken place. The exhibition would have made evident that their paths crossed in their study of light, and in their use of a mosaic-like technique to build up compositions. Von Alt, however, was never able fully to renounce his Biedermeier heritage, with its tendency toward firm, perspectival organization, as Menzel succeeded in doing.

Since the time of Tschudi, the question of Menzel's relationship to the Impressionists has been asked with great interest, although in recent times the connections have been viewed as increasingly tenuous. The recent scholarly trend to highlight differences between members of the Impressionist circle further complicates the question of Menzel's relationship to the group[37]. It remains, let it be said, of only anecdotal interest that Menzel commented negatively on an exhibition of Impressionist pictures shown in Berlin in 1883, though his criticism was picked up immediately in the French press[38]. Although one wishes to refrain from misleading conclusions, it is perhaps more informative to compare Manet's *Music in the Tuileries* (fig. 81) with *The 'Moritzhof' Inn* (cat. 108; fig. 82), also dating from the early 1860s, rather than with Menzel's painting of the Tuileries, as is frequently done[39]. Their different sizes – one executed as a large-scale oil painting, the other as a small gouache – should not hinder such comparison, but should be viewed as symptomatic of the preferences of each artist. The comparison reveals Manet, in fact, to be the Classicist and the promoter of symmetry, whereas Menzel is shown to be an artist who not only explodes our temporal understanding of events, but positions his figures in an essentially disorganized framework. Even the chairs in the Manet create an elegant, balanced still life; in the Menzel they form an unruly, chaotic mass. Furthermore, in Menzel's gouache there is very little that

Fig. 84. James Ensor, *Self-portrait with Masks*, 1899, oil, private collection

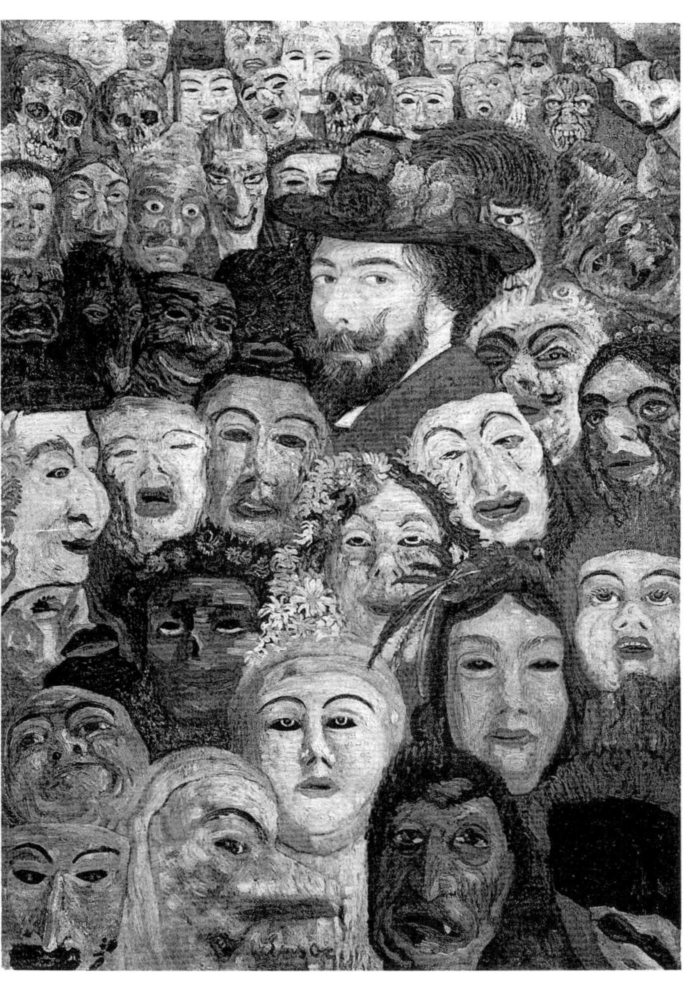

recalls the ordered chromatic layout of Manet's painting, where colour is not bound to exact description. Perhaps most importantly, the two works differ in their overall structures. Menzel's tendency towards the encyclopedic is redolent of an older painting tradition. Here too, as we can see, paths cross only briefly.

8.

In the lithograph *The Antiquary* (fig. 83) the forty-year-old artist, deep in thoughtful melancholy, surrounded by the artistic wonders of his trade and holding a bronze statuette of a harpy in his hand, sees himself as if reflected in a mirror. He is held captive in the world of the *Studio Wall*, a world in which living objects are petrified, paralysed like the harpy, a world in which faces transform into masks. Here the artist communes with the spectres of his century. The torso of Venus encircled by death masks – a sculptural simulation of the torso of a living woman – has again been moulded and shaped by the intervention of the painter. Are we not in the world of James Ensor (fig. 84), who, costumed as Rubens, peers out from the flower-adorned hat of madness, enclosed within a tragi-comic carnival whose actors confront us boldly with their gazes? The problematic that truly defines Menzel's overall work can be pinpointed in the heightened relationship between objective and subjective, major tenets of his work, as inseparable as they are contradictory.

Recollections of a similar nature may have animated the thoughts of a blind story-teller in Buenos Aires or Babylon: 'A man sets himself the task of drawing the world. Over the course of years he fills a room with pictures of provinces, kingdoms, mountains, bays, ships, islands, fishes, dwellings, tools, stars, horses and people. Shortly before he dies, he recognizes in this carefully crafted labyrinth lines the features of his own face'[40].

1. Berlin, 1895 A, no. 50.
2. *Moderne Kunst in Meisterholzschnitten*, 10, 1895–6.
3. Cat. 73, 85. *Cf.* Pietsch, 1861 A and B; Schasler, 1861.
4. Pietsch, 1861 A.
5. Pietsch, (1905) 1992, p. 331.
6. *Cf.* Françoise Forster-Hahn in this catalogue.
7. Jordan, 1905 A, p. 102 *et seq.*
8. Friedrich Pecht: Weihnachts-Bücherschau, II. In: *Die Kunst für Alle*, 3, 1887–8.
9. Hauptmann, 1985, p. 243 *et seq.*
10. Meier-Graefe, 1906, p. 263.
11. Frank, 1994–5.
12. After the publication of *Künstlers Erdenwallen* (The Artist's Earthly Pilgrimage). Schadow was, however, critical of illustrations for *History of Frederick the Great.*
13. Canvas, 126 × 200cm; formerly in the Nationalgalerie, Berlin; disappeared in 1945.
14. This new positive interpretation is convincingly argued by Heino R. Möller, *Carl Blechen. Romantische Malerei und Ironie*, Weimar 1995, p. 67 *et seq.*; *cf.* Adolf Schöll, *Über das Leben der Kunst in der Zeit aus Veranlassung der Berliner Kunstausstellung im Herbst 1832 (Fortsetzung)*. In: *Museum, Blätter für bildende Kunst*, 1833, p. 42 *et seq.*
15. For the decade-long correspondence see Deetjen, 1934.
16. Said in confidence to Tschudi. *Cf.* Tschudi, 1905 B, p. 233 (p. 23).
17. It was discovered and reproduced by Kern, 1915–16.
18. I am grateful to Andrea Bärnreuther for encouraging me to research these paintings.
19. Letter to Carl Heinrich Arnold, 23 April 1844. Wolff, 1914, p. 80.
20. Letter to Carl Heinrich Arnold, 23 April 1844, Wolff, 1914, p. 80.
21. Forster-Hahn, 1977; Hofmann (1977), 1982.
22. Edmond and Jules de Goncourt, *Journal. Mémoires de la vie littéraire*, vol 1, 1851–61, Paris, 1887, p. 366 *et seq.*
23. Erik Fischer, *Exkurs. Zwei Analysen der Arbeitsmethode Eckersbergs*. Exhib. cat. Zeichnungen aus Dänemark, Staatliche Museen zu Berlin, Nationalgalerie, 1989, pp. 11–17.
24. Actually Johann Kaspar Schmidt. The book was published in 1845.
25. Karl Rosenkrantz, *Esthetik des Hässlichen*, new ed., Leipzig, 1990, p.5
26. In 1848 Rosenkranz was a council member of the liberal cabinet of Rudolf von Auerswald, in which he was initially due to be minister of culture.
27. Rosenkranz, 1990, p. 71.
28. Letter to Friedrich Pecht, 25 October 1859. Kirstein, 1919, p. 104.
29. Letter to Honrath, 6 August 1890. Stargardt Sale, no. 478, October 1948, no. 88.
30. 'Il a la névrose du vrai.' Werner Hofmann recalled this phrase in a 1984 essay, *cf.* Paris, 1984–5. It has also been used as the Paris subtitle for this exhibition.
31. *Cf.* Anon., 1895 A, p. 285 (cites vol. 3, 1867, p. 265).
32. The Album's status is deceptive, too. Firstly, Weinhold, 1959, no. 877 contains some contorted clues; secondly, the allegorical gouache, a reproduction of which appeared on the title page and was reworked later, was published in the exhib. cat. Hamburg, 1982 (no. 203) but its original purpose was not examined.
33. Pietsch, *Schlesische Zeitung*, February 2 and 23, 1877.
34. Anon., 1895 A, p. 286; Anon., 1895 B, facing p. 288. I am grateful to Christine Kühn for putting me on the track of this forgotten work.
35. *Princess Caraculiambra* (after Cervantes), probably *c.* 1855. Liebermann/Kern, 1921, pl. 36. A miniature executed using a different technique, but similar because it included scratching, is in a private collection in Zurich.
36. Menzel's friend, the writer Theodor Fontane, had already written an essay in defence of the Pre-Raphaelites in 1857, and it is possible that Menzel could have received a photograph of this painting at a later date through him.
37. Thomas W. Gaehtgens deals with this issue at greater length elsewhere in this catalogue (p. 113 *et seq.*).
38. *Le Figaro*, 31 October 1883.
39. *Cf.* commentary on cat. 123.
40. Jorge Luis Borges, *El Hacedor* (The Creator), epilogue.

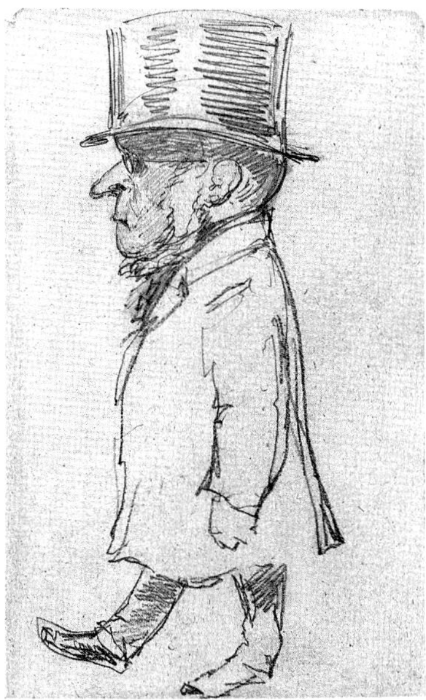

Fig. 85. Caricature of Adolph Menzel, *c.* 1870, from an album in the archives of the Association of Berlin Artists

Menzel's universality

Werner Hofmann

1.

In praising Delacroix for his universality, Baudelaire was using a criterion that had ceased to carry much conviction in the mid-nineteenth century, when pioneering qualities were the benchmark by which an artist was judged[1]. Universality was suspect, suggesting a complex ubiquity, infiltrating every area but evading clear decision-making. It was therefore a subject of controversy, in contradiction to the clear, uncompromising creed expressed in the maxim 'one must belong to one's time'[2]. This demand, stated by Deschamps in 1828, came to be seen as a moral imperative, giving contemporaneity all the aura of an article of faith. At the same time, painters and draughtsmen set fixed limits to the representation of their perceptions. From these alone the artist was to derive the subject-matter of his works, the raw material that transformed the spontaneous act of painting into a vivid event. This was the doctrine that led to Impressionism, an exclusive approach that sacrificed everything beyond the scope of immediate visual experience – history, allegory, any representation of ideas, and indeed any kind of genre painting with anecdotal embellishment – in short, any pictorial component revealing a didactic intention.

This battle of ideas was fought with particular vehemence in France and Germany, where it also coincided with the struggle between patriotism and a cosmopolitan view of the world. Whoever spoke out against French Impressionism could count on the approval of those for whom Paris embodied all that was evil in civilization. On the other hand, the man who took his stand on 'French painting' would use his progressive standpoint to preach to the German painters who remained unconvinced. This is what Meier-Graefe was doing when he settled old scores with Böcklin and pointed out Menzel's deficiencies[3]. In bestowing clear but narrow praise on Menzel's fleeting 'impressionism' – the works he painted in the 1840s but which were not publicly exhibited until after his death – he constructed the image of a man who indeed had the 'stuff of a very great artist', but who was unable to realize his potential because of his weaknesses and vices (allegory to name but one). Finally, Meier-Graefe went so far as to consider what was important in Menzel as 'a foreign body' attaching to 'the uniformity of the bulk of his work, whose sole virtue is its virtuosity'[4]. If he is to be believed, the real and authentic Menzel is the one who got lost on the way.

I do not wish to become involved in this kind of 'splitting' exercise, but rather to turn the tables and quote a remark whereby Meier-Graefe unwittingly weakens his argument that Menzel is two painters in one. What he scornfully refers to as Menzel's 'lithographic ornamentation' was, in his opinion, 'the perennial worm in his art'. And the critic unearths this tendency everywhere: 'The ornamental designs for the frontispiece of *Künstlers Erdenwallen* (The Artist's Earthly Pilgrimage) by Goethe, for the *Lord's Prayer* and other works dating from the 1830s accompany Menzel through all the periods of his career. The forms change, but the spirit remains the same'[5]. Leaving aside the final sentence, this observation can be put to good use, provided one makes a distinction and recognizes the arabesque as *one* basic figure which is in conflict with other formal impulses. Menzel's universality derives from this dialectic.

This tension can be illustrated by a comparison. In 1843–4, Menzel etched *The Schafgraben* (fig. 86) and an illustration for the poem *The Willow* by Anastasius Grün (fig. 87)[6]. The Schafgraben was on the edge of the town, a combination of urban colonization and as yet unspoilt countryside – one of those ambiguous situations that never failed to capture Menzel's attention and which distinguish him from 'naïf' landscape artists, Constable excepted. The contrast between the two areas is intensified if we set the house behind the bridge against the willow growing in the right-hand foreground. At the same time, the contorted bodily energy of the tree trunk assumes a spatial intensity: as it twists, it penetrates the surrounding space, gathering into a unity the features of the broken ground around it. The convexity produced seems to take up a defensive position against the square bulk of the buildings. The massive bridge – or dam? – cuts into this organic landscape, just like the Berlin–Potsdam railway line (1847; cat. 42). The two boys at the bow of the barge are also involved in this potential conflict, in particular the one who is standing and making energetic gestures. Disturbance is imminent, a prelude to the disorder we always find in Menzel's urban landscapes.

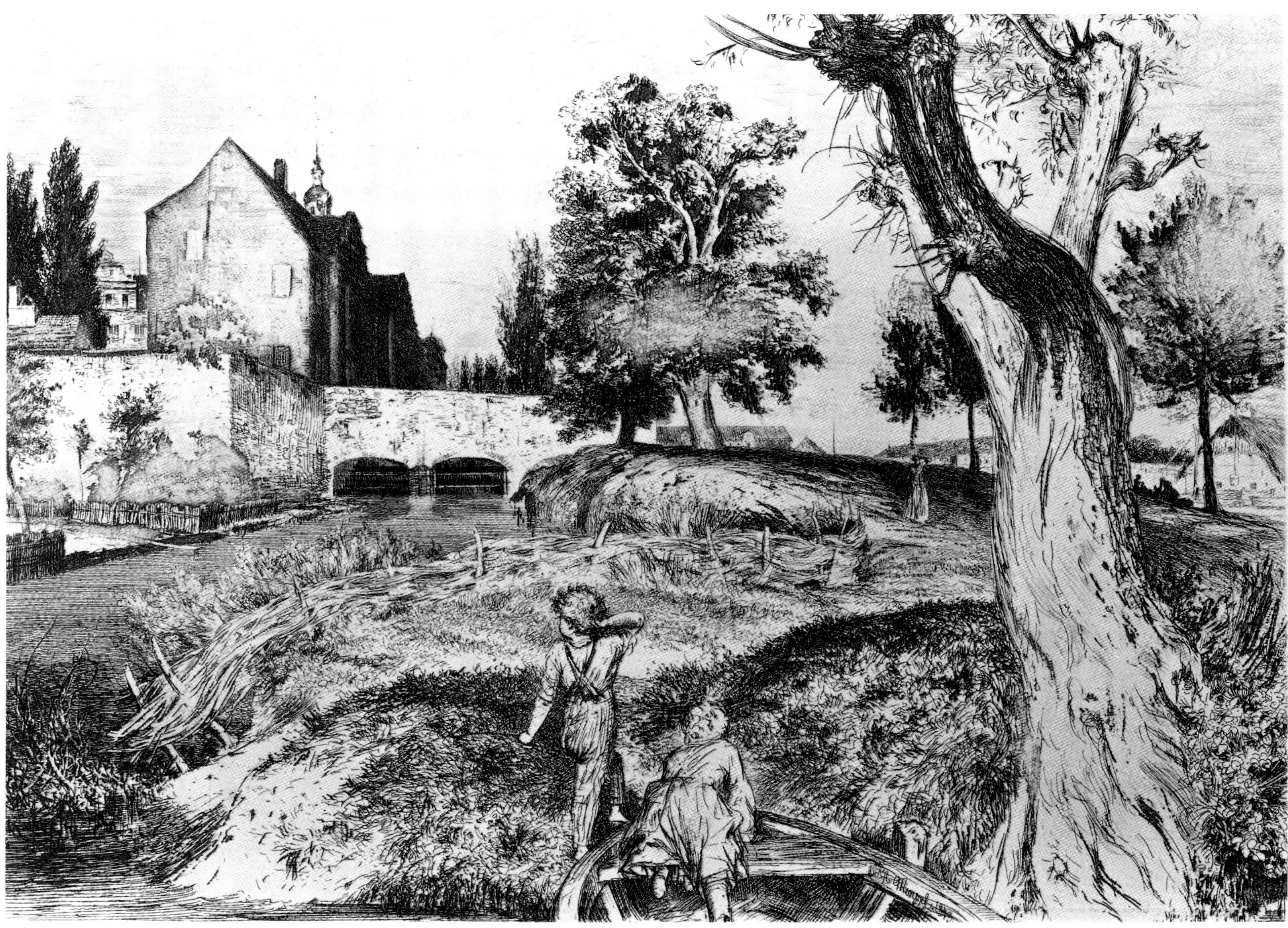

Fig. 86. *The Schafgraben*, 1843–4, etching

In the illustration to the poem, Menzel has tamed the Laocoön-like writhings of the tree. Its gnarled growth extends into harmonious branches and ramifications, whose arabesque forms are reminiscent of illuminated manuscripts. King Arthur, overcome with jealousy, squats in the branches to observe Lancelot flirting with Guinevere. It is not so much the illustration as the poem, the beginning of which it printed on the right, that informs us of the situation. The adultery is treated in a formal manner and so loses the character of surprise that we savour in Ingres' *Paolo et Francesca.* The arabesque of the willow tree is responsible for this effect. Whereas, in *The Schafgraben*, it represents prosaic energy, here the tree plays a double role: the trunk is solid prose, its ramifications the poetry whose sinuous elegance accords with symmetry. Taken as a whole, the tree represents a metamorphosis, giving the page of the book a rhythmical organization and enlivening its surface. The linear arabesque motif covers a large area, whereas in *The Schafgraben* the divergent spatial axes in some cases overlap, in others get in one another's way or fail to meet, thereby emphasizing the fragmentary and random character of the scene. Is it the work of an eye-witness who draws up their report with nothing added or omitted? A comparison with the first proof of the engraving gives a clue to the freedom with which Menzel treated his subject. In the original version, the end wall of the house has a balcony which disrupts its smooth surface; Menzel subsequently erased it to emphasize the massive appearance of the building. Considering that he often composed his 'slices of life' from a number of sketches and separate studies, effectively indulging in collage – and research has come up with plenty of examples[7] – it would not be surprising to discover that *The Schafgraben*, too, was a composite landscape. The two children are undoubtedly additions to the scene. Conceived as an element of raw nature, the willow embodies aggressive power; transformed into an ornamental figure, it orders and stabilizes formal relationships. On the one hand, it perturbs natural events; on the other, it has the opposite effect, harmonizing the conflicts between human beings. Put more simply: Menzel the observer seeks out and emphasizes dissonances; Menzel the inventor does away with them.

2.

No study has yet been made of the morphology of the 'lithographic ornamentation' decried by Meier-Graefe in the light of nineteenth-century developments seen as a whole. With the arabesque, it belongs among the transitory functions that the formal awareness of the 'Romantics' endowed with arbitrary and playful combinations. It involved an interweaving of abstraction and imitation of nature. Understood as a 'form of complex reflection'[8], the practice was extended to both asymmetrical margins and various axial arrangements. It made use of the interplay between frame and picture, and multiple fields within a picture, techniques that had not been exploited for centuries. In this morphology, we might also detect traces of the unbridled formal imagination we refer to as baroque: margins reminiscent of vaulting and *rocaille*, multiple-field compositions evocative of the ceilings of church and palace. But this does not imply any formal dependence. Even Menzel's evident pleasure in reproducing baroque buildings and their interiors offers ready explanation for his arabesques; on the contrary, they are rather the consequence of his visual need for complicated formal developments, which stimulate the attentive eye[9].

On the other hand, some works may have been instrumental in providing a definite stimulus: Dürer's drawings for Maximilian's prayer book, reproduced lithographically by Strixner (1808), which were soon well known; Runge's *The Four Seasons* (1805); Cornelius's title pages for *Faust* (1815) and *The Nibelungen* (1817); and finally Neureuther's *Vignettes for the Ballads and Romances of Goethe*, first published in 1829, and the same artist's multiple-field reportage exalting the July Revolution in Paris – four lithographs which (to Goethe's great displeasure) the enthusiastic artist dedicated to the French nation (1831)[10].

The margin, which seems improvised, transposes the freedoms of the *capriccio* into an interlacing of lines which, rather than conforming to the conventions of illusionism, brings together various items or fragments of reality in a 'fabric of relationships' (Busch). It is done in such a way, however, that this fabric seems capable of

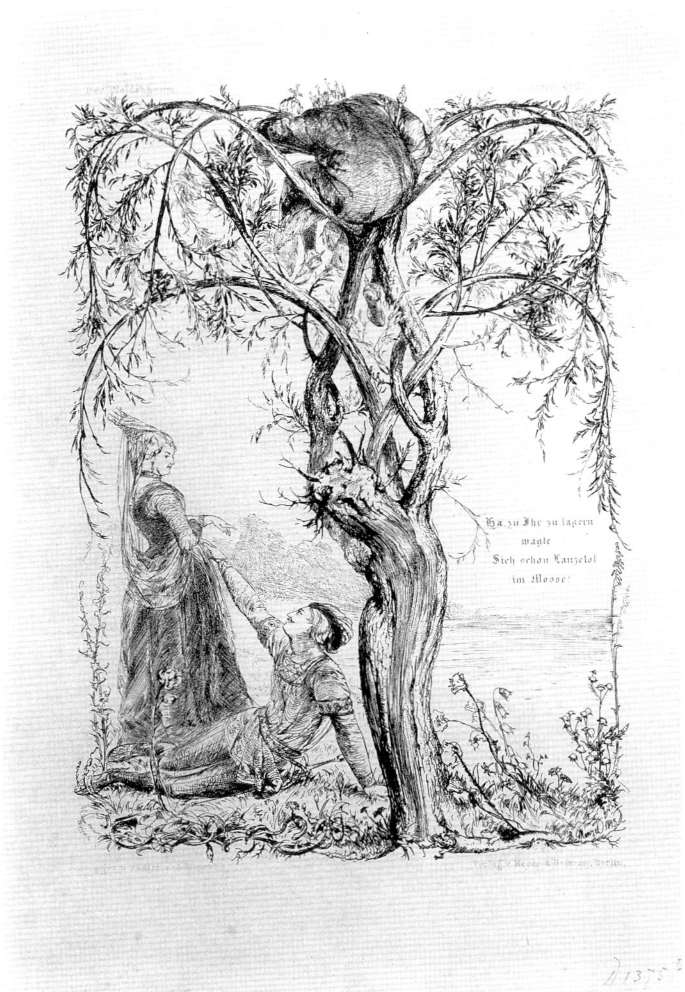

Fig. 87. Illustration to Anastasius Grün's poem *The Willow Tree*. 1834, etching

being dispersed and reproduced over large areas. The same strategy is evident in multiple-field pictures divided up by arabesques deriving from a central axis. Menzel's title page for *Künstlers Erdenwallen* (1834; fig. 88)[11] represents an intermediate stage: a continuous arabesque surrounding a central block of text. What Busch calls a 'form of complex reflection' here serves as a illusion-stripping analysis of the obstacles and encumbrances that beset the artist. The grandiose title is thus treated with irony. The critical allusions are set so cleverly in the tangles of lines that they do not immediately draw the eye. The general geometrical arrangement in fact suggests the opposite: apotheosis rather than doubt or discord.

It is true that Runge, in the layers of meaning in his arabesques, had already expressed a tension between the conventionality and originality of his symbols (Busch tried to explain this in terms of the problem of his 'double existence, barely reconcilable'[12], as both artist and the

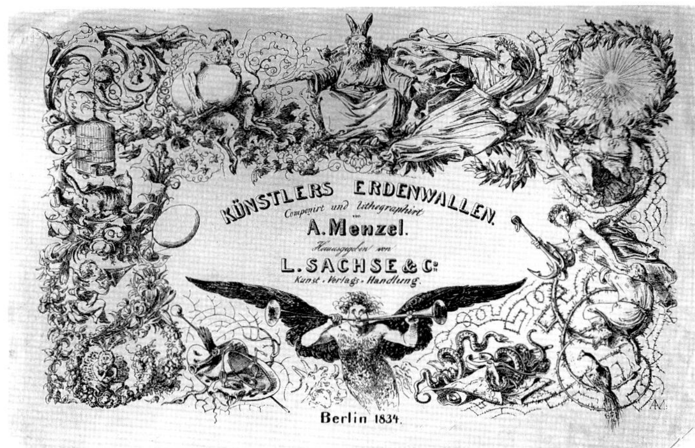

Fig. 88. Title page of *Künstlers Erdenwallen* (The Artist's Earthly Pilgrimage), 1833, pen lithograph

son of a merchant). But it was Menzel who first exploited the familiar arabesque to both juxtapose and oppose contradictory meanings. He thus achieved dialectic infiltrations, under the cover of labyrinths of lines which efface infelicities and give an illusion of harmony. Menzel himself admitted to the changes of tensions and divergences in content when, in a commentary on *The Lord's Prayer* (1837; fig. 89), he reduced the various episodes to the common denominator of a harmonious 'overall form' capable of defusing conflicts. What is significant is that he advised the spectator to adopt two viewpoints, close-up and distant: 'The backgrounds to the scenes represent: primrose and passion flower entwined to form an arabesque, seen from a distance; the whole consists of three parts, the central form: choir of angels, Christ as keystone of the vault and the apostles, simplicity . . . blessing the cross-shaped form: Hallowed be Thy name. . . (the anchor), Thy kingdom come . . . .'[13] Enshrined in this curvilinear delight to the eye, we find examples of good works: missionary practices, the lapsed being punished, converts and heretics – a most contradictory catalogue, which shows the teachings and ambitions of the Christian religion in terms of the antagonism between ideal and reality, the same theme as treated by Menzel in *Künstlers Erdenwallen*.

Stated in general terms: the individual episodes are juxtaposed in an iconic structure which avoids collisions and transforms chronological succession into simultaneous coexistence. The onlooker cannot therefore grasp the events and episodes linearly, but must first extract them as isolated elements and then reconnect them by a process of selection and combination.

Is not this complex, polyphonic 'compartmentalization' in fact the exact opposite of 'slices of life' which can be grasped, according to a basic precept, at a *single* glance? The polyfocality of the multiple-field picture would therefore appear to be opposed to the monofocality of the eye-witness account, constituting a deliberate diversity of viewpoints intended to a communicate ambiguity[14]. This article will later demonstrate that this supposed antagonism does not in fact exist.

3.

Until now, we have seen Menzel engaged in transforming the multiplicity of his content into a higher unity by using arabesques, so that a *single* denominator of *form* gathers together several denominators of *meaning*. In this strategy, a contrary impulse, the discovery of dissonances, was not considered. I would now like to show that Menzel was able to modify his viewpoint when it suited him to abandon dissimulation. He would then bring about an obvious collision by juxtaposing or interweaving different layers of reality. Ornament and arabesque were then no longer used to defuse conflicts, but to expose false harmonies. For the hundredth

Fig. 90. Vignette for the play *Der Zerbrochene Krug* (The Broken Pitcher) with portrait of the author Heinrich von Kleist and the initial letter E, wood engraving, 1877

Fig. 89. *The Lord's Prayer. Sunday Worship*, 1837, pen lithograph

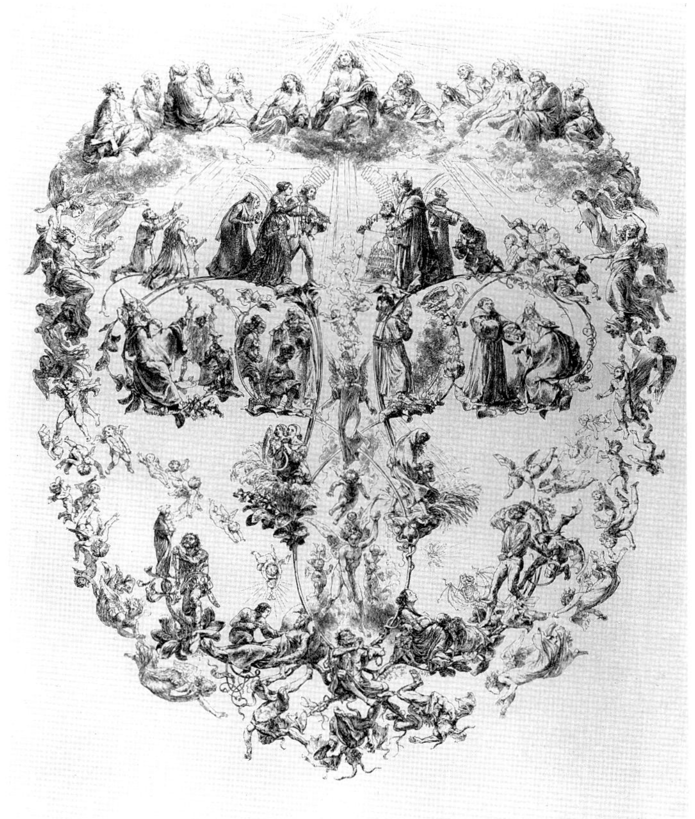

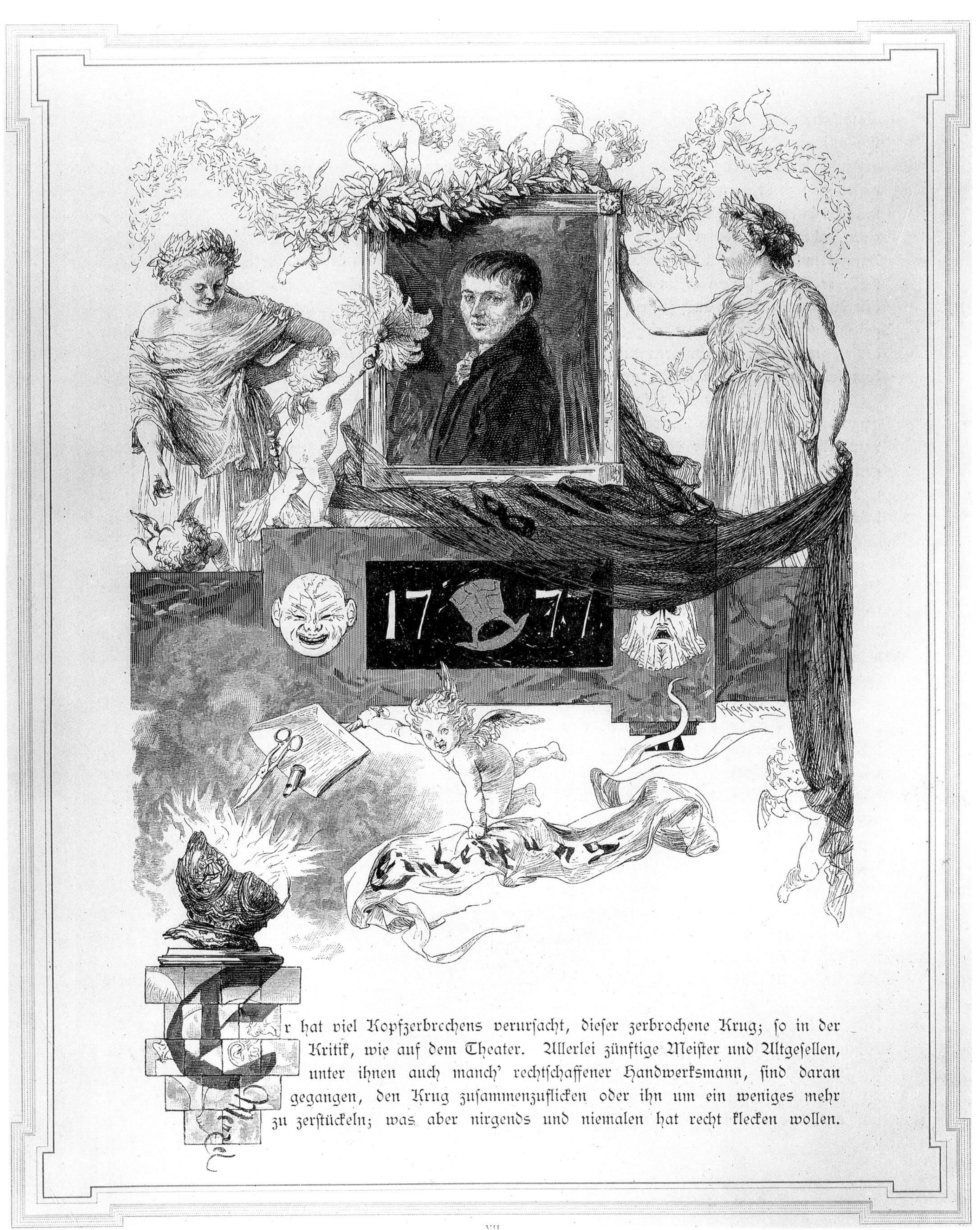

Er hat viel Kopfzerbrechens verursacht, dieser zerbrochene Krug; so in der Kritik, wie auf dem Theater. Allerlei zünftige Meister und Altgesellen, unter ihnen auch manch' rechtschaffener Handwerksmann, sind daran gegangen, den Krug zusammenzuflicken oder ihn um ein weniges mehr zu zerstückeln; was aber nirgends und niemalen hat recht klecken wollen.

VII

anniversary, in 1877, of Heinrich von Kleist's birth, Menzel illustrated Kleist's play *Der zerbrochener Krug* (The Broken Pitcher). The introductory vignette shows the artist in two different lights (fig. 90). As with the willow tree in the illustration to Grün's poem, poetry is transformed into a kind of prose or, more exactly, the apotheosis of the artist is turned into a bitter aphorism. Two kindly muses are busy about a portrait crowned with laurel. The scene below them is set off-centre, moving towards the left-hand margin. (Symmetry gives the impression of consolidating values; asymmetry gives a critical, sceptical view of them.) A cupid is depicted throwing a pair of scissors and a mysterious object – a case, a piece of the latch which features in the play? (or possibly a broken whistle?) – into the fire burning in a broken vase, which could also be taken for an urn. More clearly than the other drawings relating to Kleist's play, this concentration of symbols gives a coded clue to the 'moral' of the story: truth does not come intact, but in broken, fragmentary form. The tiles on which the vase is balanced point to the same thing. They in fact feature a 'surprise portrait'[15] (Ingeborg Becker) of Menzel himself. His profile is cut up into nine segments, which, however, 'do not fit perfectly together'. The initial E introducing the printed text conceals these discordances. The fragmented profile consists only of *membra disjecta*. There are all the constituent elements of a portrait, but they will not fit together in a formal whole. Just as he could not (or would not) reduce the world to a common denominator, the artist hidden in the tile enigma is not himself a whole, but one of the 'fragments of a great confession'. Although this expression applies equally well to Kleist and Menzel, its author is in fact Goethe[16], and he was no doubt wise enough to conceal this verdict on his work behind the image of a well-rounded personality. The 'fragments' on the tiles contradict the clarity of the official portrait of the poet honoured in the top half of the drawing. In the same way, Menzel, in the 'split' self-portrait (fig. 136) he did at roughly the same time, affirms the truth of the fragment as against the apparent truth of the whole head (cat. 177). Menzel denied Kleist the unanimous posthumous acclaim due to a Prussian court poet by giving his own portrait an enigmatic twist to protect the artist from his public and those disposed to give him uncritical praise. Again, as in the arabesques of his youth, he strove against the lie of a fine outward appearance. Already in *Künstlers Erdenwallen*, he had transposed Goethe's lament over the fate of the painter – a short piece published in 1788 – to take account of the 'mercantile pressure' of bourgeois society. Not long after, he destroyed the façade of the Christian gospel in his allegory of the *Five Senses* (1835) and *The Lord's Prayer* (1837).

A draughtsman wanting to unmask the unitary positions (messages) of works of art and break them down into their constituent elements finds in the syntax of the arabesque a wide range of possibilities. Compared with this vagabond and allusive polyfocality, the pure restitution of sense impressions seems somewhat dull – a monofocal one-way street. If such were the case, it would indeed not be possible to speak of Menzel's universality; we would have to admit the rightness of Meier-Graefe's verdict. However, polyfocal vision is also a characteristic of Menzel the observer, so that the sense impressions he selects – and the choice he makes is of the essence! – are in fact ambiguous, with no addition of any kind. Menzel the observer gets hold of a truth that has already broken down or fallen into decay, where isolation and confrontation rule. This is plain from his urban landscapes, street scenes and 'genre scenes'. The two studio wall paintings housed in Berlin and Hamburg (figs. 91 and 92) are also germane to this argument. Regarding the former, which dates from 1852, Meier-Graefe made a remark which shows that he appreciated its value: 'In this picture, painting alone is at stake'[17]. But the critic's prejudice is again evident in his statement: he could only admire a painting if he could find no 'narrative' dimension to it. And it is in similar terms that he praised the Hamburg painting. It was the formal unity of the two studio wall pictures that decided the issue: for Meier-Graefe, both were harmonious, living and organic.

I opposed this concept in 1977, in an article whose arguments can easily be carried over into this present study[18]. Whereas I then stressed the 'conglomerate aspect' and the 'fragmentary character of dead objects', I now perceive in these works a decision on the part of Menzel in favour of one of the two perspectives that determined his artistic perception (and consequently the choice of his subjects). The studio wall paintings belong to the tradition of studio interiors showing painters and their accessories. That the plaster heads could be thematized as independent still lifes presupposes a freedom of approach, which is again the consequence of the isolation that occurs when the painter is no longer convinced by the harmony of genre painting but, as it were, takes a look behind the scene and falls back on the simple presence of the constituents. In Menzel's particular case this was when the artist withdraws from his chosen subject, the idealizing, unifying scaffolding of line. We know, from the tiles bearing his self-portrait, what remains when the ornamentation of the arabesque is no longer permitted to embellish. The same disparity is produced on his studio walls.

As well as cultural references – we recognize the torso of the Venus de Milo and, below it, the profile of Dante

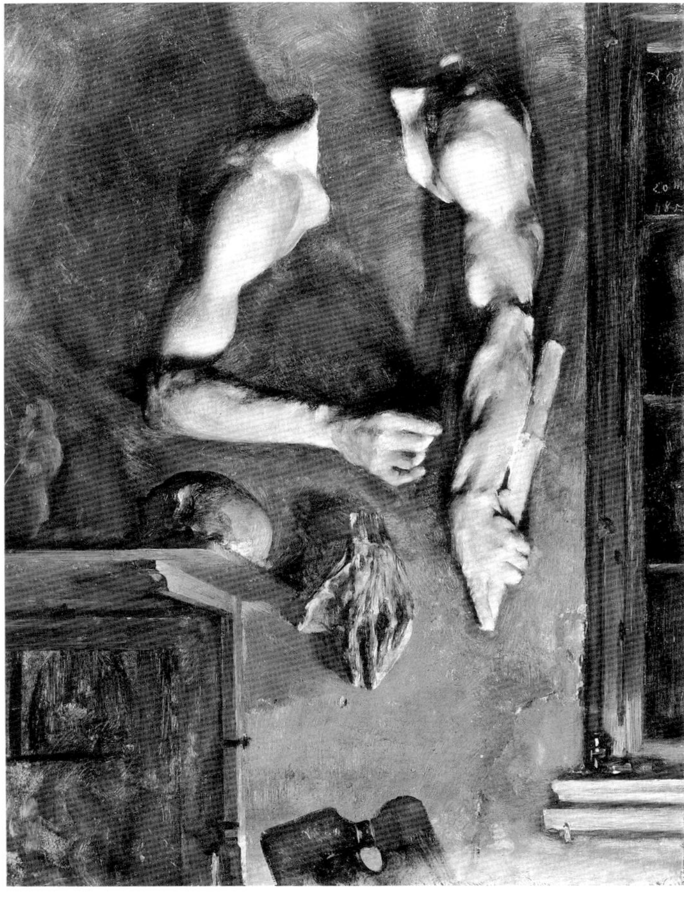

Fig. 91. *Studio Wall* (cat.65), 1852, Nationalgalerie, Berlin

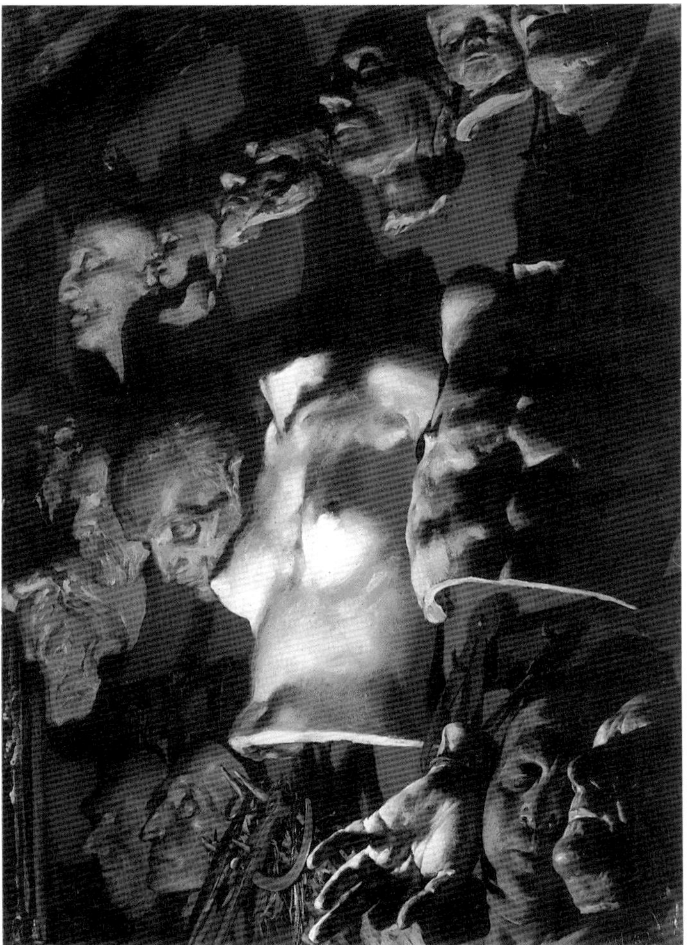

Fig. 92. *Studio Wall* (cat.137), 1872, Hamburger Kunsthalle, Hamburg

– the Hamburg picture also contains anonymous human heads and that of an animal. It would appear that Menzel deliberately blurred the dividing line between fame and anonymity. This does not mean that he used the juxtaposition of physiognomical samples solely as a pretext for pictorial lighting effects, as Meier-Graefe liked to think, but that he perceived truth as pluralist, disparate and ambiguous – not as a self-contained whole but, like the self-portrait on the tiles, a mixture of different levels. He was also responding in this way to the large-scale works representing circles of artists painted by Barry (*Elysium and Tartarus*, 1777–84) Ingres (*The Apotheosis of Homer*, 1827), Delaroche (*Ecole des Beaux-Arts, Paris*, 1835) and Overbeck (*The Triumph of Religion in the Arts*, begun in 1833). These compositions, containing large numbers of figures, bore witness to a Classical/Christian background on which solemn idealization was supposed to confer an eternal value. The distinguished rhetoric of these assemblies of great men seeks to deny the motto 'one must belong to one's time'. Menzel seems to oppose to this exclusive attitude a sentiment expressed by Goethe as a young man: 'One must love art, not its subject-matter'. He thus frees art from the tutelage of ideal models and forces the artist into direct observation of reality. Whereas the arrangers of assemblies of great men set great store by immortal values, Menzel chose banal motifs for his Hamburg *Studio Wall* and countered their pseudo-sacred aura with a juxtaposition of inert accessories thrown together at random, his brush alone infusing them with vivid life. This life, however, does not guarantee a one-way, monofocal unity of the kind imagined by Meier-Graefe. It also contains a second layer of critical importance: an allusion to the global idealism that the realist Menzel considered lost and which for him no longer had a guiding role to play.

4.

Menzel adopted a critical stance to the art scene of his time, which he saw as everywhere tainted by commercialism. This is borne out not only by his works on the theme of art and artists, as we have seen, but also by his own statements[19]. For him, artistic truth was the result of conflicts between the artist and his public. In the face of the frightening distance that seemed to separate society and the posturings of contemporary bohemians, whom the middle classes considered a group of buffoons, Menzel staked his all on his work ethic, on the diligence of hand and eye, for which he was criticized more than once[20]. Seeing himself as a diligent, reliable worker, he was bound to feel a benevolent affinity with the class that was developing more and more into a compact social reality. He saw in the manual worker something of himself: both his ceaseless activity and his marginality.

But Menzel also approached the theme of labour from several points of view, and I am not referring here to the oft-repeated contrast between the work he produced for the fiftieth anniversary of the Heckmann factory (1869; fig. 94) and *The Iron Rolling Mill* (1875, cat. 160)[21]. The exaggeratedly allegorical multiple-field picture and the 'slice of life' must both be interpreted on several levels. The *Iron Rolling Mill*, for instance, is not an account of facts compiled by addition, not a snapshot legitimized by chance, but a gigantic collective body – Max Jordan entitled it *Modern Cyclopes* – to which the individual workers, as members, all belong, even though they are not all performing the central task, but also eating, drinking, washing or gazing into space. Within this collective anatomy, each member has his own space, his 'cell', considered as a part of the total event. In reconciling the whole with the parts, Menzel was working in the realm of bifocality characteristic of his arabesques. Of course, in this case we shall look in vain for the linear framework which, in other works, supports the individual episodes. The framework of this collective body is not a matter of surface effect and symmetrical ornamentation, but arouses spatial energies which traverse the picture plane and the space behind it with equal intensity. This corporeal dynamic must be ascribed to the fascinating unison of the painting, from which even the many vanishing points cannot detract. The only foreign body, and a discreet one, in the background on the left, is the mill's manager, who seems quite unaware of the work going on. The spatial axes converge in his vicinity, but without giving him any special emphasis. He remains accessory. The picture as a whole contains many studies of detail which Menzel, not to be outdone by the physical commitment of the workers, executed *in situ*. A number of these details, noted rapidly but accurately by Menzel the observer, if taken on their own, have the status of significant fragments, on a par with the vignettes and epigrams of Menzel the inventor. This scrupulously documented reproduction of a collective industrial process does not simulate a fictitious unity, but presents us, in its specific aspects, with a global picture: the theme of 'labour' as an anonymous activity on several levels and with a new social content.

In 1858, Eugen Napoleon Neureuther painted a multiple-field picture, one of the most ambitious of its kind, devoted to the Klett machine shop and foundry (fig. 93). What is happening in the compartments of this imaginary shop window has been appropriately described by Siegfried Salzmann as a 'multiple allegory': 'The items of a universal allegory are presented on a stage consisting of a number of compartments, rather like a doll's house, in such a way as to "enshrine" the complexity of industrial reality.' Regardless of the wealth of detail with which the technical activities are depicted, its general message is clear: here we have an apotheosis of technical progress, with no darker side to it. Conceived as an allegory of 'labour', Neureuther's composition is to *The Iron Rolling Mill* what the allegories of art representing gatherings of great men are to the Hamburg *Studio Wall* picture: unreservedly positive and redolent of harmony.

Before beginning work on *The Iron Rolling Mill*, Menzel had already tackled industrial labour in the commemorative diploma he produced for the fiftieth anniversary of the Heckmann works (fig. 94). For this project, he used the mixtures of reality that had already proved their worth. He produced a multiple-field arrangement, in the central axis of which is a gilded niche with a medallion portrait of the factory owner. In front of the niche stands a winged allegorical figure which has been interpreted as a personification of Fortune. In the two lateral fields of the canvas are depicted: on the left, workers standing in front of the furnace; on the right, the foundry[22]. These realistic scenes are framed by decorative architectural fragments with six male caryatids. The entire composition is crowned by wrought-iron ornamentation interspersed with cupids and garlands of flowers.

This whole apparatus of forms would amount to a glorification of labour and of the factory owner, were it not for a few false notes. We find them in the gestures and features of the six figures supporting the entablature, which Marie Ursula Riemann-Reyher has fittingly referred to as 'worker herms', forming 'the pillars of the allegorized façade of the factory'[23]. However, some of these martial figures are visibly fulfilling their task unwillingly, thus revealing their state of enslavement. One has a pipe in his mouth, another is trying to free himself from a coil of metal wire which holds him captive. Here Menzel is again working from two viewpoints, which the spectator is required to reconcile. What, at first sight, may be interpreted as a glorification

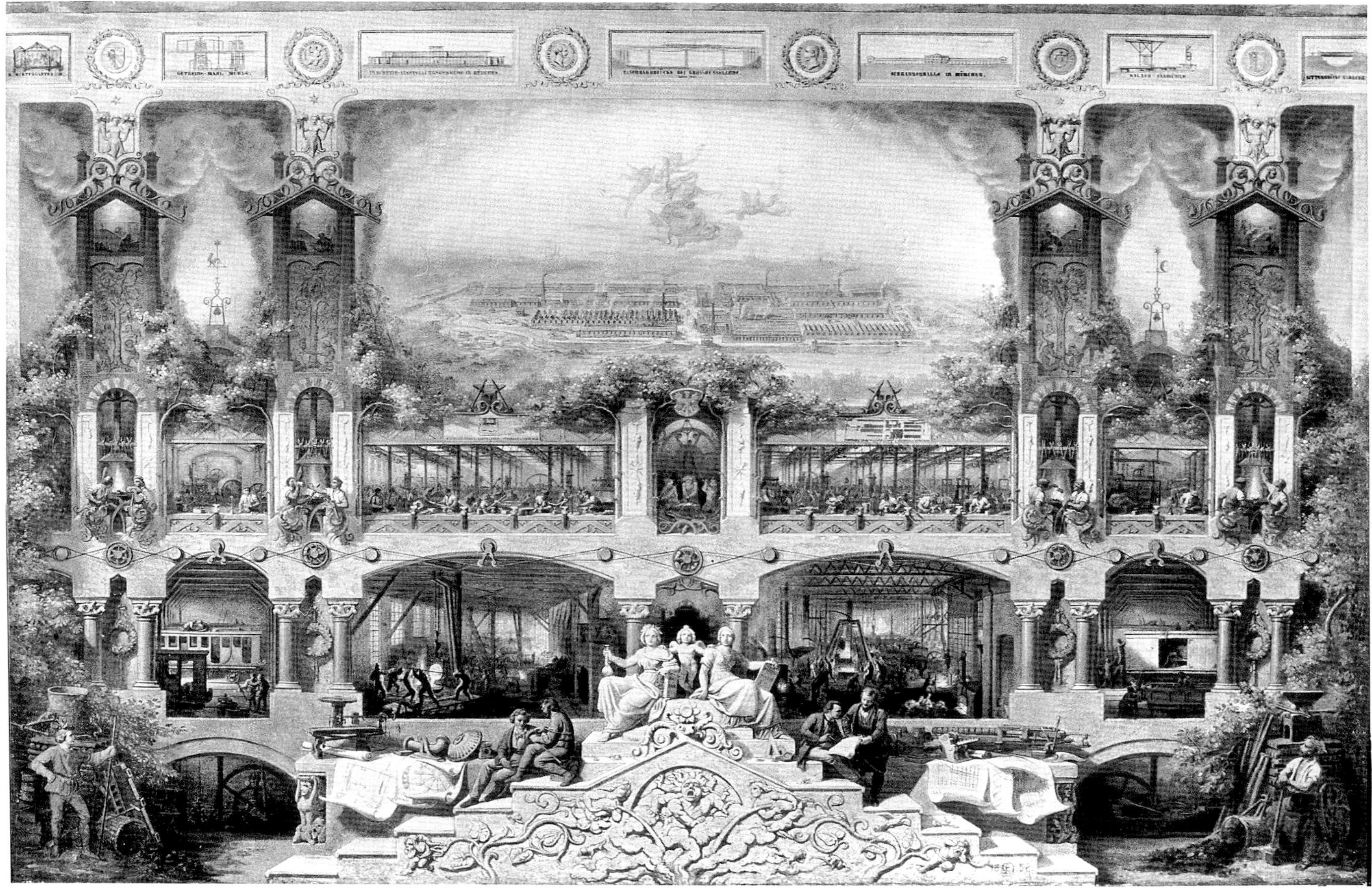

Fig. 93. Eugen Napoleon Neureuther, *Kett & Co. Machine Shop and Foundry*, 1858, oil, MAN-Archiv, Nuremberg

of manual labour and a consensus between worker and industrialist, is in fact a denunciation of this modern message. In the 'conventional' anniversary allegory, Menzel's critical distance is more forcibly expressed than in *The Iron Rolling Mill*. This is due to its polyfocality because, again, as in his arabesques, the painter is presenting both thesis and antithesis. At first sight, neither of these two portrayals of factory life has a critical axe to grind. Under the mythical disguise and mask of pseudo-baroque well-being (said to echo the herms of the Zwinger in Dresden), the rebel caryatids, so reminiscent of Alberich[24], reveal the enslavement of the factory worker, who, to paraphrase the penultimate sentence of the *Communist Manifesto*, has nothing to lose but his chains. Riemann-Reyher has recognized in the picture's slogan 'A thousand years are a single day – but fifty years a half century' an 'updated' formulation of the fourth verse of the ninetieth Psalm, but has not pursued this line of enquiry further. The exact quotation is: 'For a thousand years in Thy sight are but as yesterday when it is past, or as a watch in the night.' A never-ending night watch – could this be a description of shift work, in which there is no distinction between day and night?

5.

Menzel was constantly criticized for his profusion of detail. The formal processes analysed here suggest another view of the matter. Menzel did not treat sense data simply by making an inventory of them, but applied to them a systole–diastole (i.e. heartbeat rhythm) dynamic. Sometimes he opted for compression, sometimes for dilation, mastering the art of summarizing as well as that of being disconcertingly expansive. The linear arabesque is at the centre of these alternate movements: it regulates the interplay of large and small forms, the supremacy of the whole and the autonomy of its parts. Its evident balancing function weakens, though does not disappear completely, when Menzel decides on a radical omission or when, making a U-turn, he sets out to capture events with many figures in all their breadth and density. Isolating the emblematic or narrative 'cells' woven into the fabric of the arabesques reveals vignettes and visual epigrams which, sometimes, touch the enigma of the picture. Many examples of the systole movement can be found in Menzel's occasional engravings, and even more so in his illustrations and tailpieces, which bear witness to his sharp wit and economy of means. Here, a door handle tells an anecdote or a sleeping cupid ask questions of German literature; there, field glasses and a sword lying under a shield summarize the events of the years 1774–8. Symbols of this kind take the sting out of the battles of history. To prevent these conflicts and the misery they engender from falling into oblivion, Menzel exchanged the spirit of the inventor for the disenchanted eye of the observer and drew a woman trying to extricate herself from the ruins of a shattered town. This brings us to the Menzel who, in 1866, visited the battlefields of the Austro-Prussian War. What he saw there he had already sensed in the works he devoted to the Seven Years' War (figs 95 and 96). Duranty rightly pointed out this reciprocity: 'We can feel or understand nothing of the past except through the frame and spectacle of what is all around us. Mr Menzel was able to restore the lost life of earlier centuries, because he had studied, experienced and savoured modern life in great depth'[25].

Just as Menzel the painter of aphorisms had no counterpart among his German or European contemporaries, so his diastolic mode of working was equally out of key with the painting of his times. It is enough to compare his *Afternoon in the Tuileries Gardens* (1867; cat. 123) and *Souvenir of the Luxembourg Gardens* (1872; cat. 136) with Manet's *Concert in the Tuileries* (1860-2; fig. 91), or Menzel's *Supper at the Ball* (1878) with Degas's paraphrase of it[26] (cat. 167–168). The French aspired to achieve a dense, balanced fabric of colours and, in Manet's case, the immobility of still life – no place there for an ornamental framework. Menzel can be assimilated to no static common denominator: he leaves his figures, still or moving, in separate compartments, gathering them up in dynamic and undulating spatial and corporeal curves, maintaining the balance between systole and diastole modes. We have seen him proceed in similar manner in *The Iron Rolling Mill*: the overall collective action gives way to solitude, even to lonely meditation. Here, as in his views of streets and squares, Menzel detects solitude in the midst of the crowd.

Menzel's characters have as many qualities as his art has facets. Unlike almost any other nineteenth-century observer-inventor, he was able to express himself by pendulum swings, to opt for continuity or its dissolution, to house his own disintegration in one and the same form (the arabesque). His contemporaries therefore felt bound to break him down into several persons. Thus, in 1895, Fontane spoke of a certain Menzel beside whom 'another Menzel' was making his way[27]. I propose to re-establish Menzel as a *single* entity, albeit equipped with a penetrating bifocal eye. This is the hallmark of his universality.

Fig 94. *Diploma for the Fiftieth Anniversary of the Heckmann Factory* (cat.129), 1869, gouache, Kupferstichkabinett, Berlin, detail

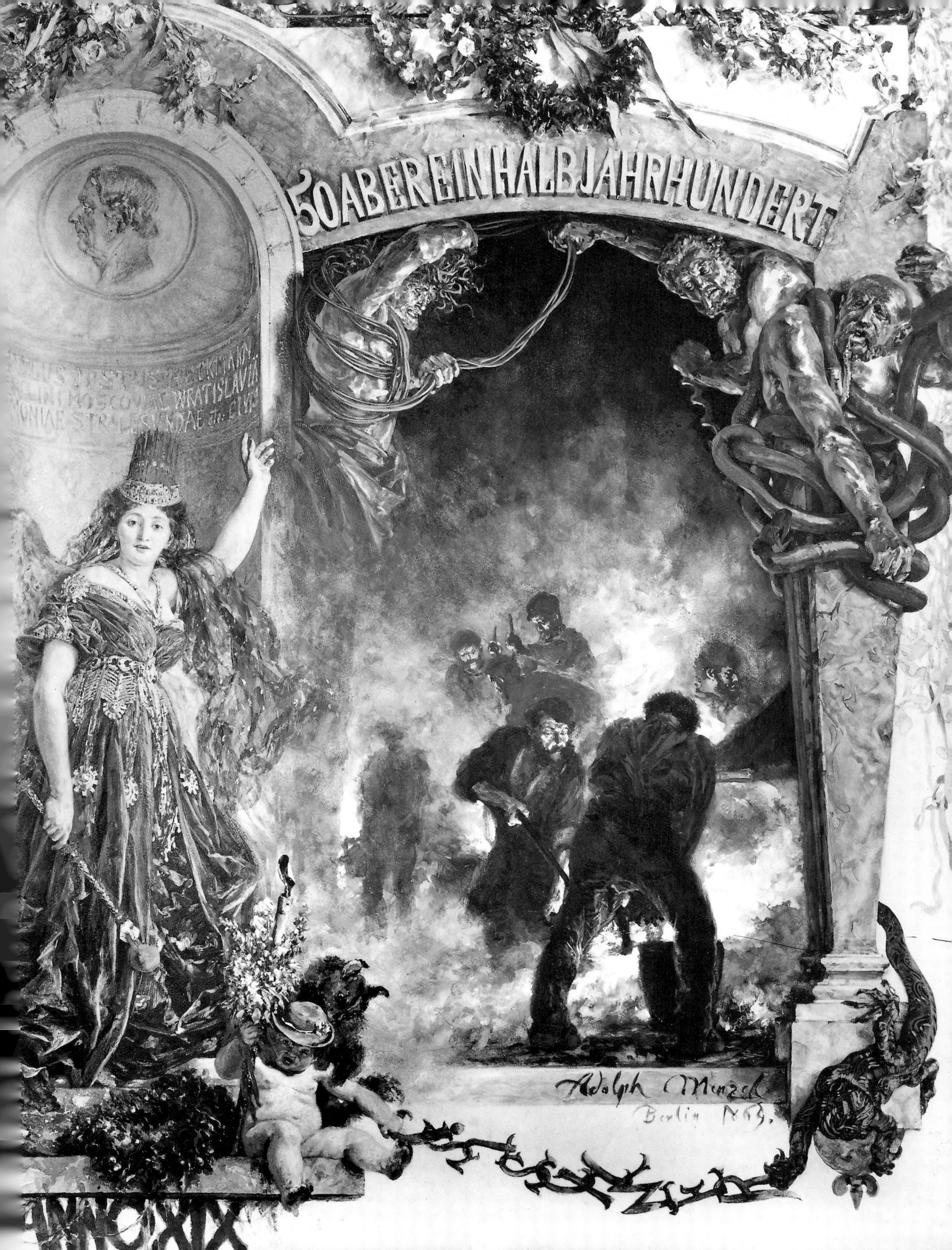

50 ABER EIN HALB JAHRHUNDERT
Adolph Menzel
Berlin 1869.

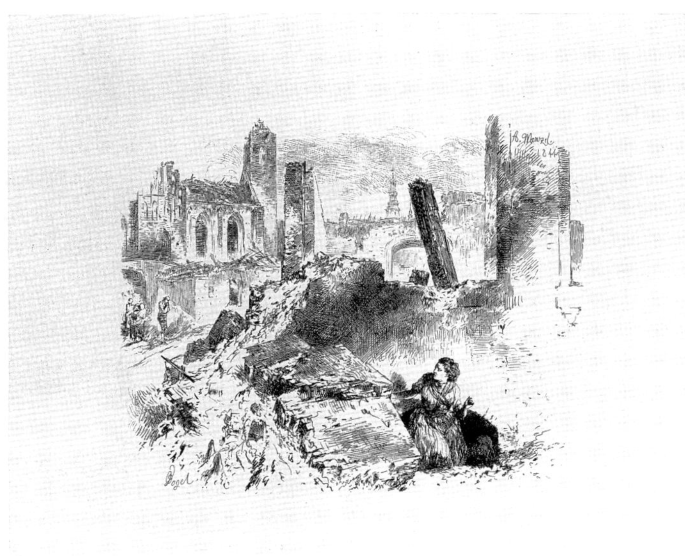

Fig. 95. *Works of Frederick the Great: the Ruins of a Town after Bombardment*, 1844, wood engraving

Fig. 96. *History of Frederick the Great: Wounded Austrian Prisoners Lying on Straw, Prague*, 1841, wood engraving

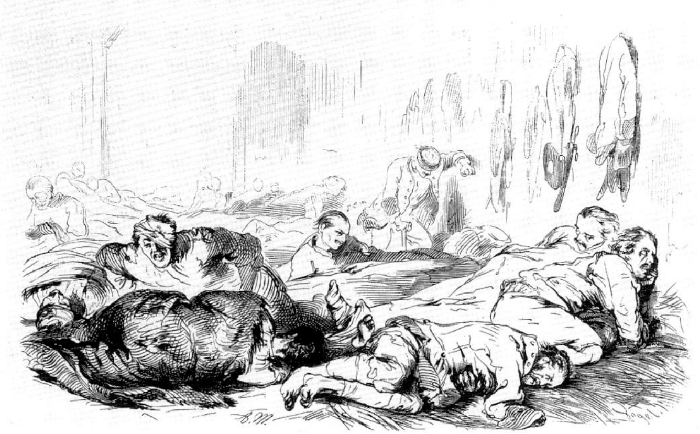

1. In the section of the 1846 Salon devoted to Delacroix.
2. Boas, 1941, p. 52 *et seq.*.
3. Meier-Graefe, 1906.
4. *Ibid.*, p. 266.
5. *Ibid.*, p. 4.
6. *Cf.* Berlin exhibition catalogue, 1984, n. 229, n. 229.2 and n. 319.1.
7. *Cf.* the research carried out by Françoise Forster-Hahn, in particular: Forster-Hahn, 1980, p.27 ff.
8. Busch, 1985, p.73.
9. The expression is borrowed from Wilhelm Pinder (Pinder, 1940, p. 63).
10. Busch, 1985, p.56 *et seq.*; Klemm, 1995, p. 62–3.
11. Hofmann, 1977, p. 124 *et seq.*.
12. Busch, 1985, p. 49.
13. Quoted from the Berlin exhibition catalogue, 1984, n. 221.
14. As regards bifocality: Busch, 1985, p.280 ('Menzel integrates two visions') and Hofmann, 1995.
15. Berlin exhib. cat., 1984, n. 335.2.
16. *Dichtung und Wahrheit*, II, 7.
17. Meier-Graefe, 1906, p. 125.
18. Hofmann, 1982, p. 31 *et seq*
19. Hofmann, 1995, figs 507, 526, 541.
20. Having to contend with some animosity, it appears that Menzel considered living in exile in Paris: Beta, (1898) 1992, p. 15.
21. Meier-Graefe, 1906, p. 230, p. 259 *et seq.*
22. Riemann-Reyher, 1976.
23. *Ibid.*
24. For the comparison between Menzel and Wagner: Jensen, 1982, p. 41.
25. Duranty, 1880, I, p. 214.
26. Lemoisne, 1946–9, n. 190.
27. Fontane, 1982, p. 544.

Adolph Menzel: readings between nationalism and modernity

Françoise Forster-Hahn

Menzel became who he was. The tensions in his work are only the reflection of his own inner conflict'[1], When Max Liebermann characterized Menzel's long and productive career in an essay of 1921, he sought to sketch an overview of the artist's oeuvre, connecting works by the young Menzel with the history paintings dating from the middle of his life as with his later works. In charting this biographical map, Liebermann attempted to establish a delicate balance between sharply contrasting phenomena in order to bridge the 'gap' in Menzel's oeuvre which critics had begun to construct at least from 1905: namely, the sharp disjuncture between works by the young 'impressionist' Menzel and those of 'the painter of Frederick the Great'. At least from the time of the comprehensive retrospective exhibition of 1905[2] and the so-called Jahrhundert Austellung of 1906[3], Menzel was celebrated as a precursor of modern art, with critics playing off the paintings of his early years against those from the middle and late phases of his career. Reviewers criticized in particular the artist's myopic fixation on precision in the copious rendering of minute detail, a practice – as Liebermann also emphasized – that disrupted the coherence and harmony of the images. Liebermann tried to explain the discrepancy between the readings of those 'who valued only the young Menzel',[4] and those who primarily praised Menzel the 'patriotic' artist of Prussian history by pointing to biographical circumstances – especially his dwarf-like physical appearance – and to the cultural-historical context in which the artist moved. In the end, however, Liebermann applies the idealistic and romantic model of 'genius' along with that of 'artistic truth'[5], dual paradigms he believed would resolve the attendant ambivalence and inherent tension in Menzel's oeuvre.

No German artist of the nineteenth century has been the subject of so many revisions and contradictory interpretations as Menzel. Not only is this ambivalence in critical reception grounded in Menzel's own life and work; it was determined in equal measure by the course of German history of the last 150 years, in so far as every shift in the critical reading of the work intersects with the pivotal moments in that history. As the long and circuitous path leading to the founding of a German nation parallels the rise of the modern movement in art, so are Menzel's life and work inseparably interwoven with this historical process. The contradictory readings of his work and persona manifested themselves poignantly in the public spectacle of his funeral: just as advocates of the avant-garde discovered in Menzel a precursor of modernity, Emperor William II stages a spectacular state funeral for him, because Menzel was for him 'the most distinguished of German artists . . . not of course the Menzel who anticipated in his street scenes, landscapes and interiors what the younger generation strove for, no, the posthumous Apelles of old Fritz'[6]. The emperor, notorious for his resistance to modern art, arranged for the dead artist 'to be carried from the rotunda of the Museum to his grave by soldiers in the uniforms of Frederick the Great's time'[7] (fig. 97), while the director of the Nationalgalerie, Hugo von Tschudi, presented 'a selection of the exquisite early works'[8] in a large retrospective exhibition in the Nationalgalerie for which the walls of the museum had been clad in modern hangings. Through this display strategy, Tschudi effectively positioned Menzel in the history of modern art (fig. 112).

The shifts and ruptures in the critical assessment of Menzel have been determined by political history and the presence of the artist and his work in the public sphere, as well as by the history and reception of modern

Fig. 97. Menzel's funeral procession in front of the Altes Museum, 1905, photograph

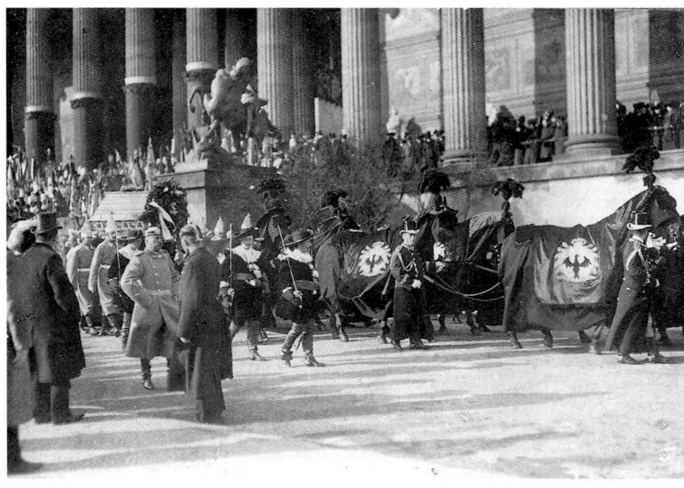

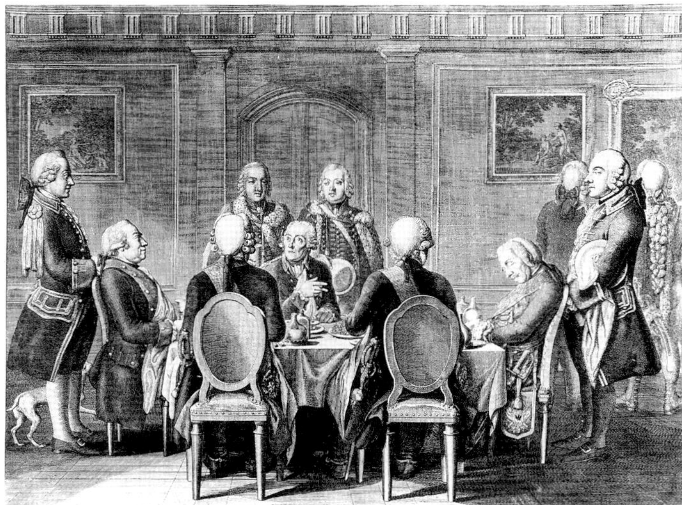

Fig. 98. Daniel Chodowiecki, *Zieten Sleeping at the Table of Frederick II*, 1800, etching

art. Menzel's own works, however, his drawings, graphics and paintings, are not the passive objects of this historical process: they are active participants in it in so far as they inscribed themselves as images into the memory of their audience. During the course of these critical reinterpretations, wherein one reading replaced another, three intersections of history and reception mark the interpretation of Menzel's work most pointedly: the years leading up to the Revolution of 1848, followed by the period of Restoration; 1871 and the founding years of the young empire; and 1905, the year of Menzel's death, which historically coincides with the period of escalating hostility among European powers[9], and art historically with the appearance of the *Brücke*, the moment when the modern movement shifted its locus from the periphery to a more central position.

The interaction of political tendencies, the artist's work and its public resonance was already volatile at the beginning of Menzel's career in the 1840s. *Geschichte Friedrichs des Grossen* (History of Frederick the Great) mapped out by Menzel for Franz Kugler's book[10] was rooted in the ideology of the liberal bourgeoisie which saw in the Prussian king a precursor of bourgeois emancipation: 'The enlightened words paved the way for the realization of the fact; religious freedom prepared the ground for bourgeois freedom; freedom of the press for philosophical research led to its application to political questions . . .'[11]

Menzel represented this liberal bourgeois interpretation of the historical figure of Frederick II in scenes that Kugler compared to the newly invented medium of photography. In order to define the novelty of Menzel's

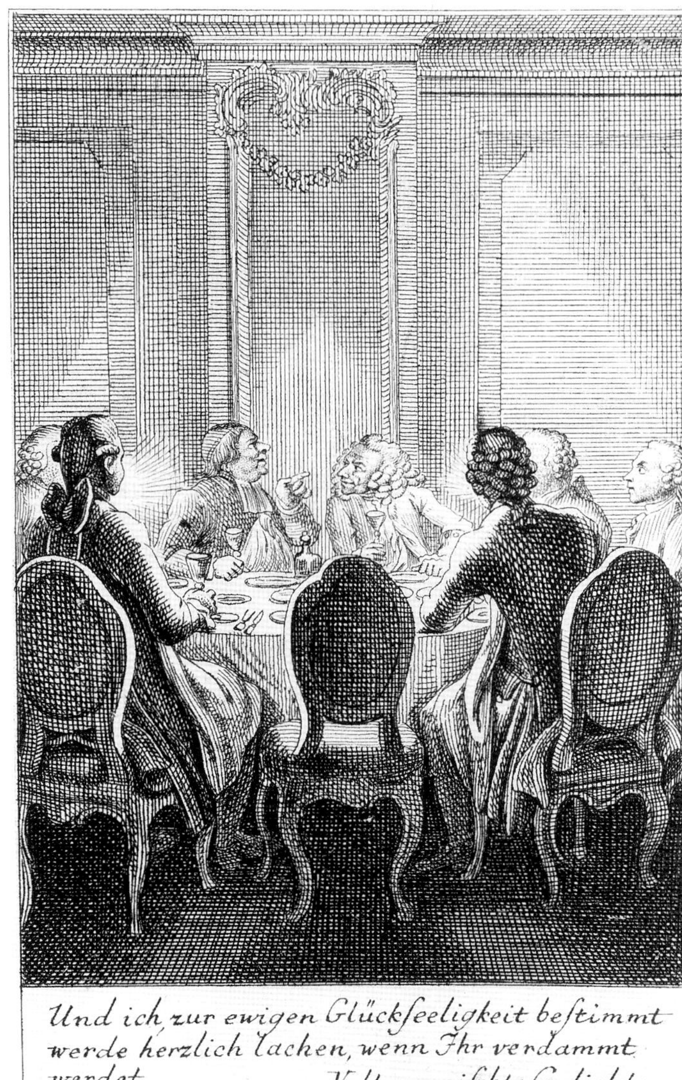

Fig. 99. Daniel Berger, after Daniel Chodowiecki, *Voltaire at Table*, engraving

exceptional pictorial strategies, only a few years after the book's first publication Kugler singled out the 'daguerrotypical reality'[12] in Menzel's images, which sharply broke with the idealism of academic history painting. The most conspicuous among Menzel's pictorial innovations were his choice of scenes to illustrate and his so-called historical 'authenticity'[13]. Menzel represented the king not only in official but also in private life; he pictured not only military victories but also military defeats; he depicted the horrors and brutality of war as well as Frederick II's reforms. Most striking, though, was Menzel's break with traditional rules of historical representation: the fragmentation and asymmetry of the compositions and the transitory nature of the historical

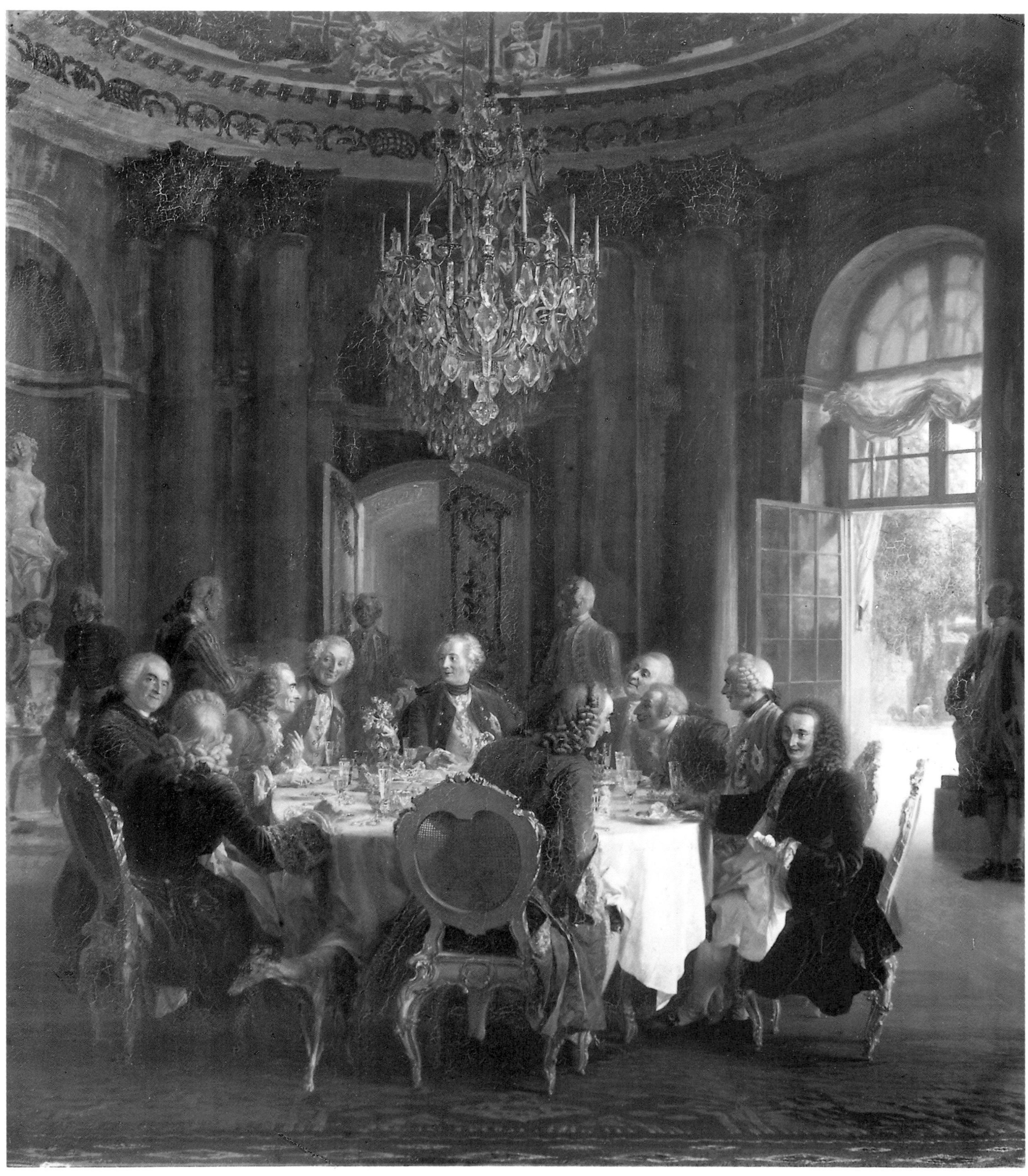

Fig. 100. *The Round Table of Frederick II at Sanssouci*, 1850, oil, formerly Berlin, Nationalgalerie, lost in the Second World War

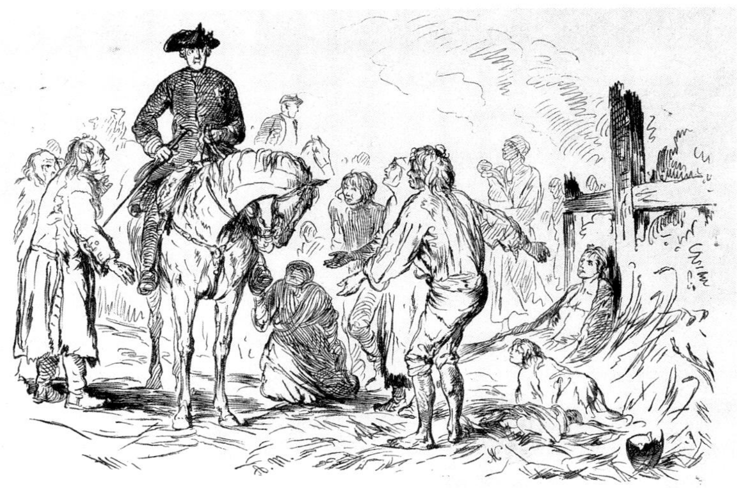

Fig. 101. *Frederick and the Inhabitants of Küstrin, Devastated by Fire* (B 668)

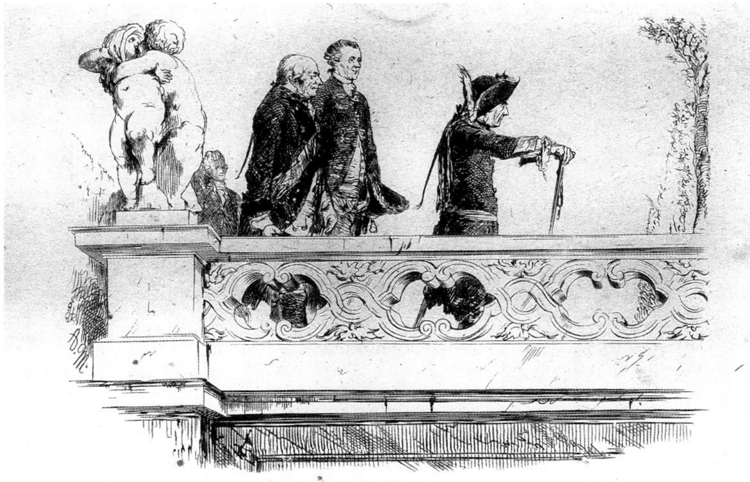

Fig. 102. *Frederick on the Terrace of the Picture Gallery at Sanssouci* (B 806)

Fig. 103. *Frederick in the Picture Gallery at Sanssouci* (B 800)

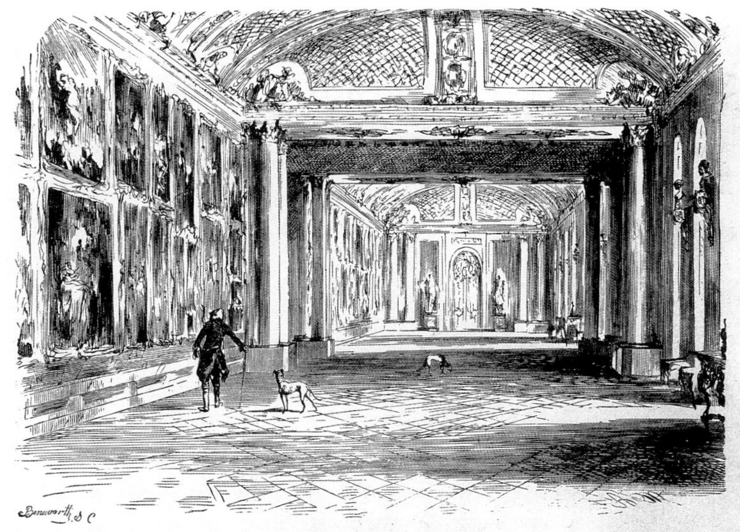

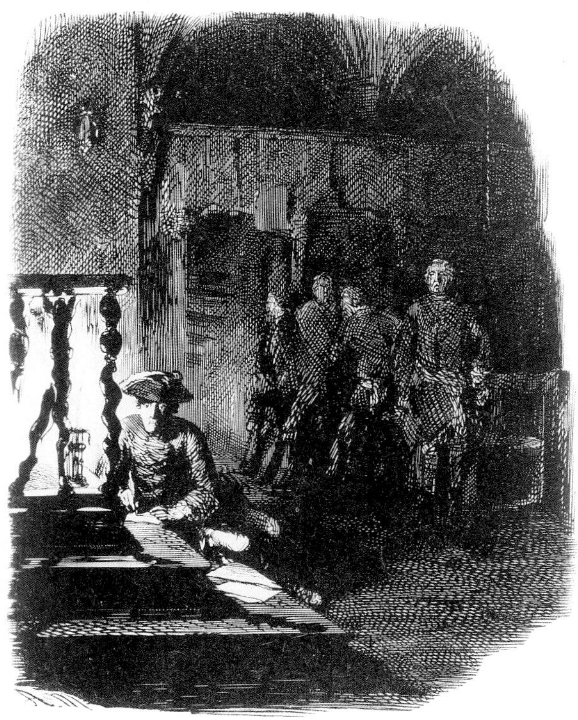

Fig. 104. *Frederick the Great after the Battle of Torgau, Sending Written Orders from a Village Church* (B 721)

Fig. 105. *The King on his Deathbed* (B 810 I)

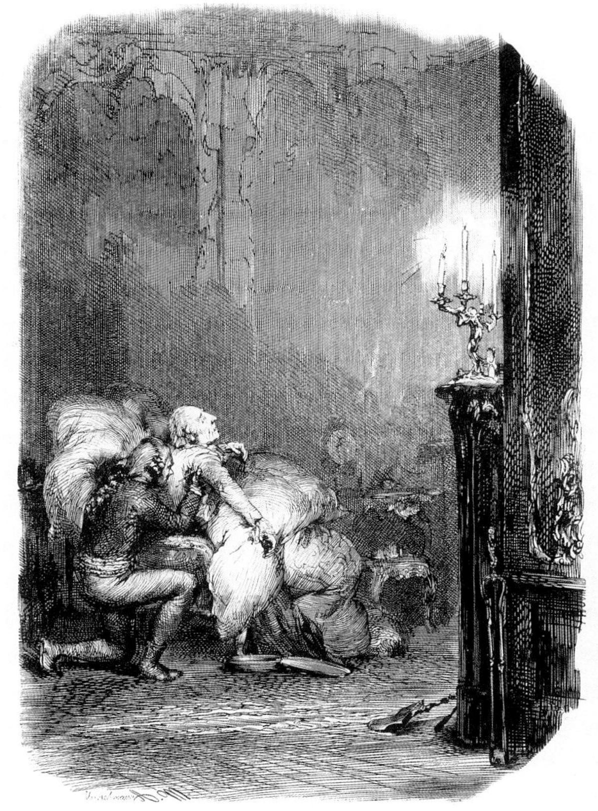

Illustrations for *History of Frederick the Great*, 1839–42, wood engravings

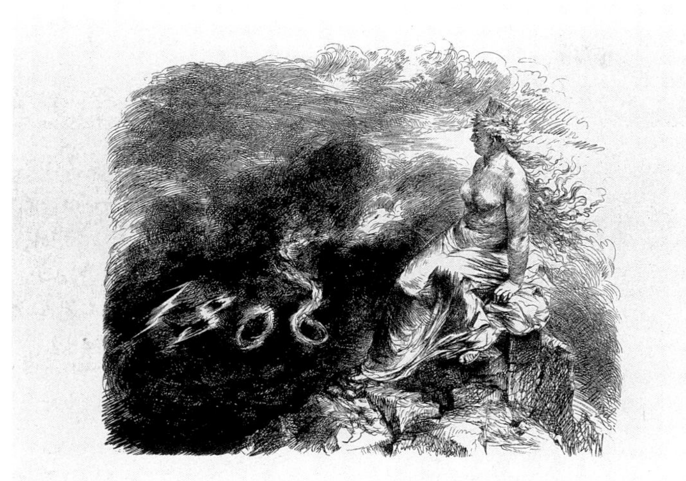

Fig. 106. *Germania Contemplates the Tragic Year 1806* (B 900)

Fig. 107. *Messenger on Horseback* (B 850)

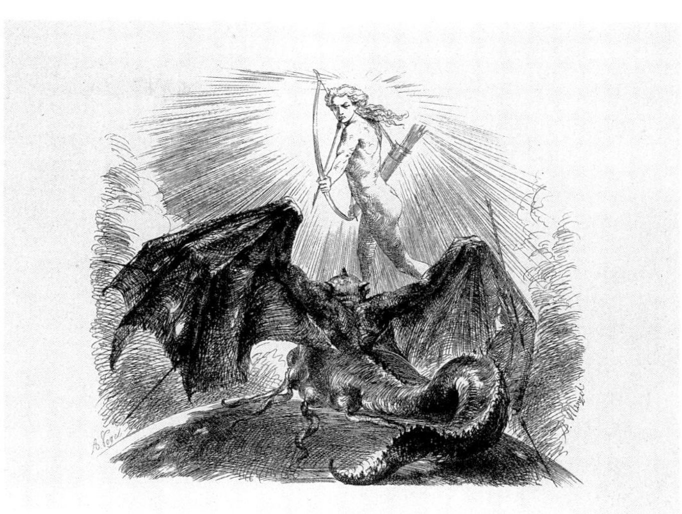

Fig. 109. *Apollo and the Dragon Stupidity* (B 997)

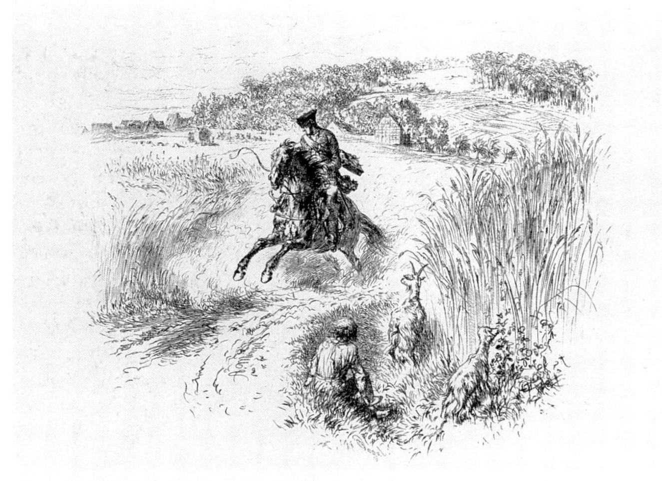

Fig. 108. *'The Palladium' Satire: the Duke of Lorraine Lost in Dreams* (B 930)

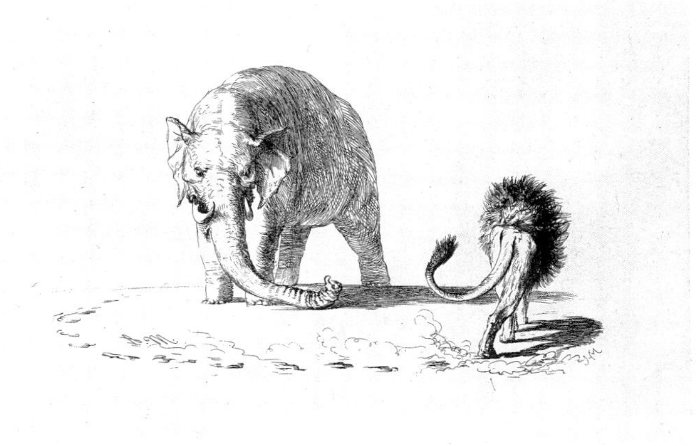

Fig. 110. *The Prussian Lion Prowls round the Austrian Elephant* (B 1015)

Fig. 111. *Family of Masons Taking a Meal in front of a New Building* (B 919)

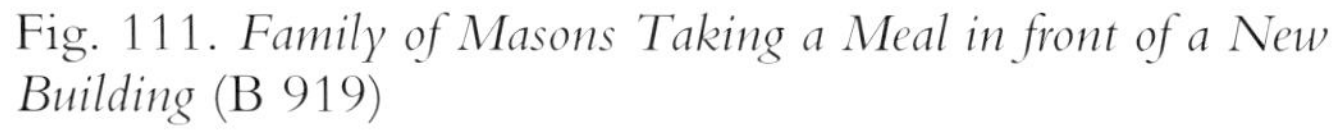

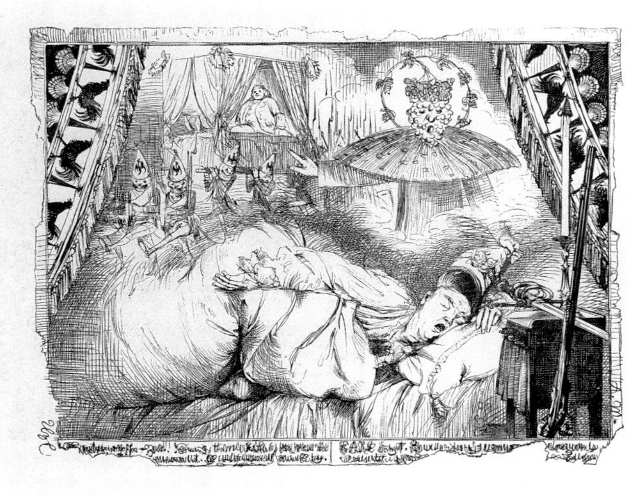

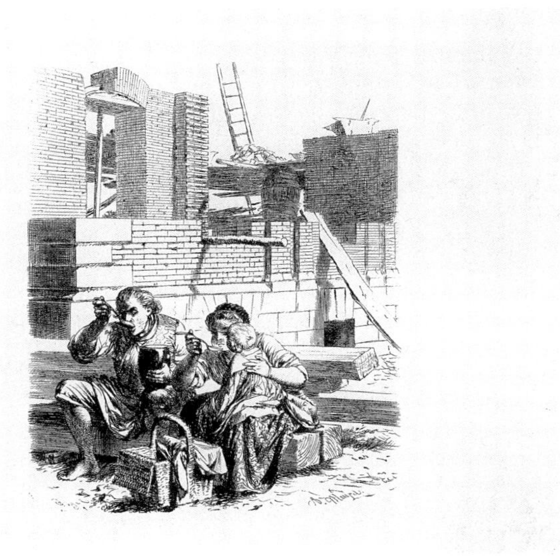

ILLUSTRATIONS FOR *WORKS OF FREDERICK THE GREAT*, 1843–49, WOOD ENGRAVINGS

moments he captured indeed endow the small black-and-white wood engravings with the characteristics of the photographic snapshot. Kugler's comparison with the daguerrotype described the core of Menzel's innovative mode of representation long before the technical advances in photography enabled the camera to produce snapshots. Menzel's mode of depicting history, rooted in the popular tradition of anecdotal imagery, was consonant with the conception of a '*Volksbuch*' (popular book) and congenial to the public that was its audience (figs 101–11).

When Menzel produced his history paintings during the 1850s, all of which were developed from the small book illustrations, he translated the pictorial strategies he had first explored in his drawings into large-scale canvases. It was therefore not surprising that the paintings, especially *The Round Table of Frederick II at Sanssouci* (fig. 100) and *The Flute Concert of Frederick the Great at Sanssouci*, were immediately degraded into the category of historical genre paintings when he first exhibited them in 1850 and 1852. Clearly, they did not meet established aesthetic standards: Menzel had neither represented '. . . the great world-historical moments of general human development . . .' nor had he pictured the king in heroic moments and with the requisite idealization. Thus, Max Schasler, who had defined the criteria of history painting in 1856, could only conclude 'that Menzel's paintings belong more to the category of historical genre rather than to that of history painting proper. Most particularly, the two most exquisite among them, *The Round Table* and *The Flute Concert*, in their choice of motif already evince the specific character of genre painting . . .'[14]. Instead of conventional abstraction and timeless idealization, Menzel had captured the spontaneity and particular essence of the historical moment, thus inventing an image of the king and Prussian history that critics in 1850 were unable to reconcile with the ideas of 'that higher characterization'[15].

Kugler and Menzel's *History of Frederick the Great* did not become a commercial success: King Frederick William IV rejected the purchase of *The Round Table*, and the history paintings were bought almost exclusively by private collectors. After completing his first and only royal commission, *The Coronation of King William I in Königsberg* (1865; cat. 94–9), which had been a long and arduous task, Menzel left the realm of history painting and turned to the representation of his own time, signalling a shift that was most likely inspired and encouraged by his impressions of Paris. During the course of his life, Menzel visited the French capital three times: twice on the occasions of the Universal Exhibitions of 1855 and 1867, and also at the time of the Salon of 1868.

When Berlin's Nationalgalerie was inaugurated on 21 March 1876, the birthday of Emperor William I, a representative selection of Menzel's works constituted the inaugural exhibition. Already before its official opening, the new museum had purchased paintings by Menzel, such as *The Round Table* in 1873, and *The Flute Concert* and *The Iron Rolling Mill* in 1875. While the canvasses of the 1840s remained in Menzel's studio, that is, in the artist's own private sphere, the history paintings moved from private collections into the public arena of the Nationalgalerie. In this prominent space they were hung in immediate proximity to the monumental battle scenes celebrating the victories of Königgrätz and Sedan, those wars that had led to the founding of the empire in 1871[16]. The version of German history that the Nationalgalerie narrated in the displays of its galleries assumed a critical function in the revision of Menzel's paintings of Frederick II and of his own role as an artist. His history paintings were now seen as a celebration of the Prussian king who had paved the way for Prussian hegemony. This new national reading was energetically advanced from the 1870s onwards. Articles, catalogues and exhibitions proclaimed Menzel 'the painter of Frederick the Great', while Menzel himself was transformed with advancing age into a legendary Berlin figure who inspired myriad anecdote, such that fiction and reality were effectively and inextricably woven together: 'He belonged to the image of the city, as it were. This dwarf-like man with his enormous head and sarcastic countenance, he was pointed out to tourists as a curiosity . . .; and when news of Menzel's death broke, one had the feeling as if the Brandenburg Gate or another monument of the city had collapsed'[17].

Just as Bruno Meyer celebrated Menzel as the painter of Prussian history in an article written on the occasion of the artist's sixtieth birthday[18], the representation and display of German history in the Nationalgalerie seamlessly integrated Menzel's images of Frederick the Great into the official historical chronology. Displaced from their original context in the liberal-bourgeois ideology of the 1840s and moved into proximity with the theatrical battle scenes, the paintings of Frederick II could assume their new historical role. As contemporary historiography elevated Frederick II to the status of proponent of Prussian hegemony and the champion of the new nation, the critical discourse of art simultaneously invented the artist 'imbued with the same spirit that created and elevated the Prussian state . . .'[19] The young empire fashioned a new national identity by establishing a historical chronology that led directly from Frederick II over the victories of Königgratz and Sedan to the founding of the Reich in Versailles. The stage was set for

Menzel to become the painter who (apparently) had already envisioned this construction of national history *avant la date* in his wood engravings and paintings.

Because the reciprocity between history and art, artist and audience, production and consumption are ongoing and dynamic processes, images not only represent and reflect history, they also invent history more concretely than do words. Especially when they are 'staged' for exhibition, images imprint themselves with a force of their own into the collective consciousness. Menzel, who reacted to his elevation to national artist *par excellence*[20] with a combination of acquiescence, ambivalence and increasing alienation[21], did not live to experience his incarnation as a precursor of modernity. The spectacle of the state funeral that William II had staged for the painter of Frederick the Great was followed by the most comprehensive exhibition of his work to date, organized by the director of the Nationalgalerie, Hugo von Tschudi. Although the Nationalgalerie had already purchased some of Menzel's early paintings prior to the retrospective, *The Berlin–Potsdam Railway* (cat. 35) in 1899 and *Balcony Room* (cat. 18) in 1903, the exhibition of 1905 brought together for the first time a larger group of the early canvasses and the gouaches of the *Children's Album* (cat. 105–14). It was the presentation of these works that introduced Menzel as a 'modern' artist to a wide audience.

The 1905 exhibition, described as a 'signal event', surprised the audience not only in terms of the sheer quantity of objects assembled (5720 items) but also in terms of Tschudi's exhibition strategies. The paintings of the 1840s, most of them shown here publicly for the first time, were all hung in one gallery[22]. This large retrospective was in a sense a rehearsal of display techniques that Tschudi and Peter Behrens would apply a year later for the Jahrhundert-Ausstellung (Centenary Exhibition). The so-called Cornelius galleries were transformed into a tranquil and homogenous exhibition space by the built-in display walls and uniform veiling of the galleries. All the walls of the main floor were covered with linen and then painted[23], so that the dramatic interplay of objects and display strategies – the paintings of the 1840s in an entirely modern ambience – radically shifted Menzel's position in the history of art.

Already in 1902, when Tschudi argued for the purchase of Menzel's *Balcony Room*, he had emphasized that the painting 'was of extraordinary freshness and originality in its painterly mode, and also for art historical reasons of greatest interest because of its early date: 1845'[24]. This reading was immediately confirmed when Hans Rosenhagen reviewed the new acquisitions of Berlin's Nationalgalerie: 'Menzel has never been more modern than when he painted this picture[25].' This 'discovery' of Menzel the modernist was engraved in the public mind and codified in the history of art through Tschudi's and Meier-Graefe's writings. Though applying different methodological approaches, they both pointed to 'the young Menzel' in the titles of their publications[26]. The Jahrhundert-Ausstellung of 1906 effectively reconfirmed the reading of Menzel and his work as 'modern' by selecting and emphasizing certain paintings and by stressing this interpretation in the accompanying publications. Thus, the monumental exhibition that 'rehabilitated' German art of the nineteenth century from a modernist perspective[27] also staged Menzel as a precursor of modern art. Menzel's early paintings were hung effectively in a group on light-coloured art nouveau wall hangings designed by Peter Behrens, which essentially masked the historical character of the Nationalgalerie[28]. It was this artfully designed environment that 'made him [Menzel] appear to be a precursor of much later tendencies[29]. Richard Hamann even used the term 'impressionist' for the early paintings in order to locate Menzel's position on the art historical map[30].

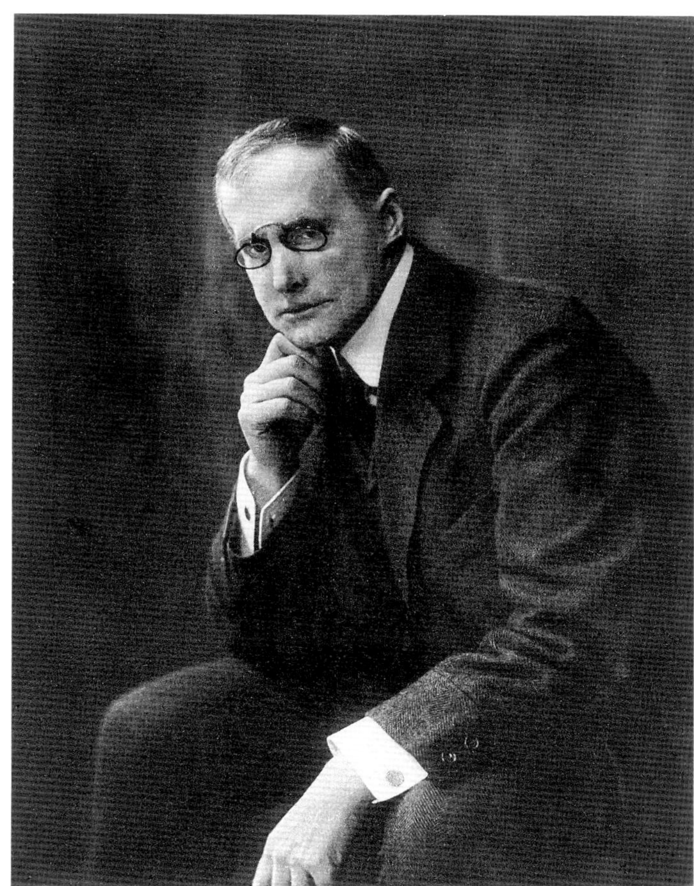

Fig. 112. Hugo von Tschudi, *c.* 1895, anonymous photograph

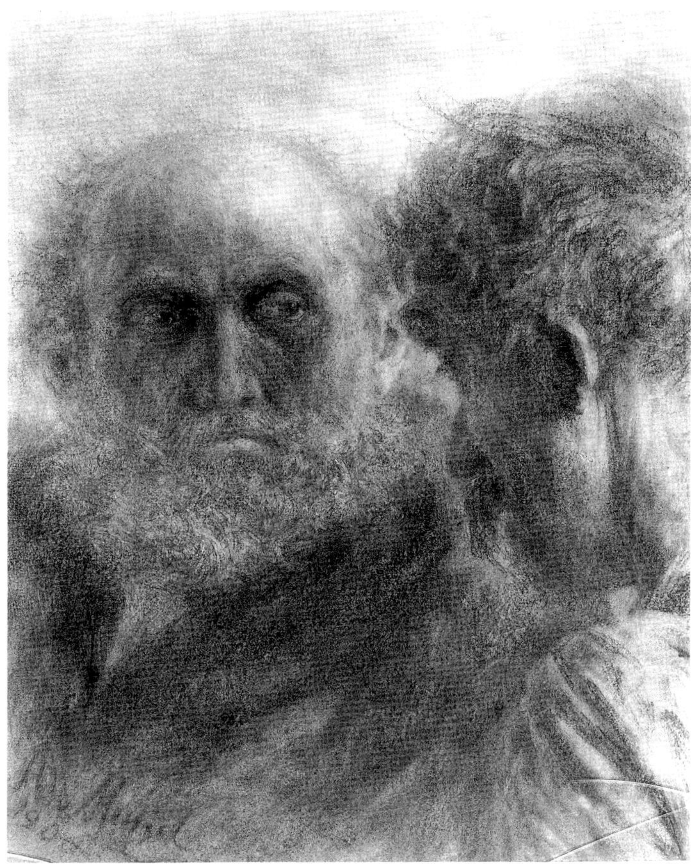

Fig. 113. *Two Elderly Men in Conversation*, 1904, pencil, Berlin, Kupferstichkabinett (N4455)

Around 1905, when the controversy concerning modern art – especially in Berlin – was determined in equal measure by political and aesthetic arguments, the polemics of the discourse were driven to extremes by Francophobia and antisemitism[31]. With Menzel's 'discovery' as a precursor of Impressionism, the history of modernism could be grounded convincingly in the German tradition: the painter of Frederick the Great was far 'advanced' as an 'impressionist' who had 'anticipated everything that contemporary France then had to offer'[32]. Thus, the conflict between German nationalistic ideology and French modernism could be resolved elegantly: German history and the history of modern art seemed reconciled in the oeuvre of Menzel.

We can only speculate about Menzel's personal assessment of Impressionism, for his often-quoted sarcastic judgements contradict his own late drawings (fig. 118). The legendary fame of his late years hardly masked the ambivalence that shaped his long life and comprehensive oeuvre. How could the artist have adjusted to a society that treated him – the dwarf – like a Berlin curiosity, a local monument?

The conflict of his late years, suspending him between conformity and alienation, re-enacted the experience of disjuncture that had marked his younger years. While he first built his reputation beyond the boundaries of Berlin during the 1840s as an illustrator of Prussian history using the graphic arts, the most public of all media, he simultaneously explored the new terrain of oil painting in the private sphere of his studio. Both of his working procedures, the critical interpretation and representation of history from a present-day perspective and the invention of modern pictorial strategies for scenes of his contemporary environment, seemed to coalesce in the *Lying in State of the March Dead* (fig. 65). But after an ambitious beginning, this conjunction abruptly collapsed: the unfinished painting became a veritable symbol of the aborted Revolution of 1848[33].

Later, during the 1850s, when critics were unable to reconcile the 'unhierarchical' images of Frederick II with the elevated status of history painting within the hierarchy of the visual arts, Menzel turned to the depiction of his own time. The images of his contemporary milieu were, however, incessantly criticized despite the artist's growing reputation. They were marked, as Liebermann defined it, by their 'contrast between the analytical and the synthetic'; their satirical elements and their lack of beauty disfigured any harmony, and the artists's obsessive fixation on detail ruptured the coherence and balance of pictorial composition. The world that Menzel drew and painted was deeply disturbed.

Two late self-portraits reflect the impossibility of synthesis between self and world: a small private drawing in Menzel's sketchbook of 1876–7, and a formal self-portrait in the dark tones of the carpenter's pencil. Seen together, these two works expose a precarious self-understanding wherein the public role masks the private – extremely fragmented, soul-searching – one. In 1895, ten years before his death, Menzel envisaged his studio after his death in a drawing entitled *End of the Party* (fig. 114), which is now lost[34]. The stillness of the desolate, empty room is suddenly disrupted by a small wooden model elephant hastily fleeing the scene, which is marked by the traces of a long and vigorous working routine. Employing strategies of the absurd and comical – the animation of an inert object – Menzel ironically questions his own philosophy of 'authenticity'. Only the *invention* of history could construct – at least on the level of historical narrative – the *semblance* of synthesis. However, the ambivalence that attended Menzel's own life and its intersection with the turning points of modern German history produced several and different histories. At the beginning of the twentieth century, these ruptures and revisions served to reconcile the

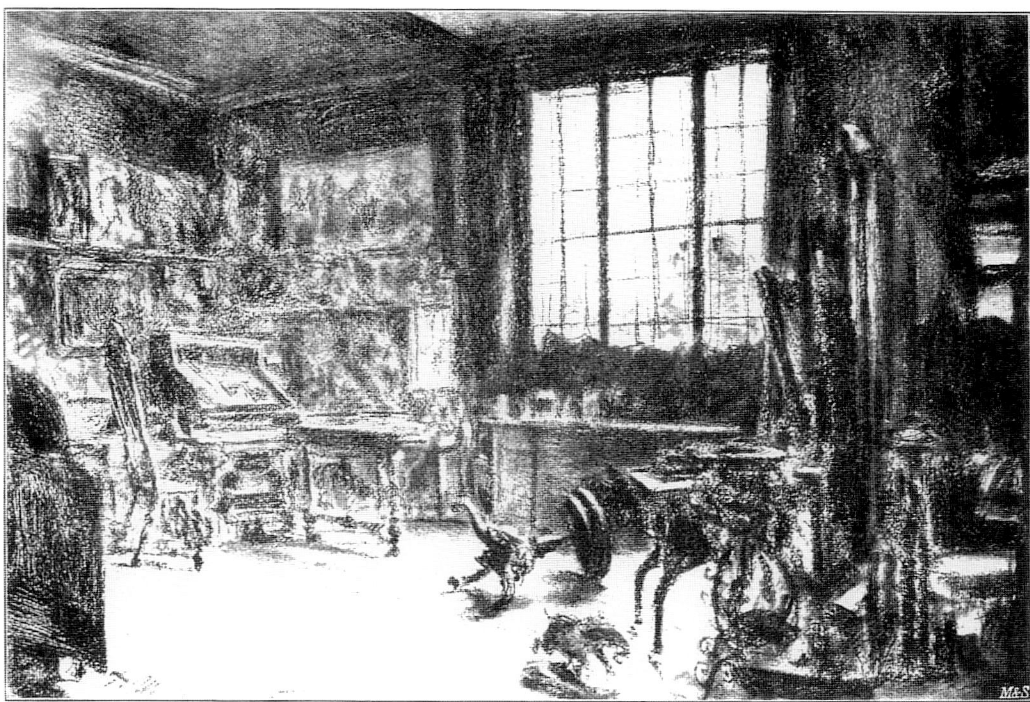

Fig. 114. *End of the Party*, 1895, pencil, location unknown

extreme positions of nationalism and the avant-garde. By attributing the role of precursor of 'Impressionism' to the 'painter of Frederick the Great', the history of modern art could be resolutely anchored in the German tradition.

I gratefully acknowledge the research and editorial assistance provided by Karen Lang and Denise Bratton.

1. Liebermann, 1978/1983, p. 142–3. Liebermann's essay 'Menzel' first appeared in the introduction to *Adolph Menzel. 50 Zeichnungen, Pastelle und Aquarelle aus dem Besitz der Nationalgalerie* (Berlin, 1921).
2. Berlin, 1905.
3. Berlin, 1906.
4. Liebermann, 1983, p. 136.
5. Liebermann, 1983, p. 146. Here Liebermann cites a sentence of Goethe's: '"Das Höchste, was man vom Genie verlangen darf, ist Wahrheit."' Diese Forderung Goethes hat Menzel wie selten ein Künstler erfüllt.'
6. Muther, 1914, 2:198.
7. Muther, 1914, 2:198. For an account of the funeral, which was covered by all the daily newspapers, *cf.* Max Jordan in his obituary, 'Adolf Menzel, in *Die Kunst. Monatshefte für freie und angewandte Kunst*, XI, 1905, 271. See also G. (Walter Gensel?), 'Menzels Begräbnis', *Kunstchronik*, n.s. XVI (24 February 1904–5, p. 254.
8. Tschudi's formulation draws upon the Jahrhundert-Ausstellung of 1906. Its presentation of Menzel immediately followed the retrospective. *Cf.* Berlin, 1906, xxiv.
9. In his review of Donald Kagan's *On the Origins of War and the Preservation of Peace*, New York, 1995, Gordon Craig emphasizes that 'Europe by 1907 was divided into two armed camps, an uneasy balance that was always trembling on the verge of collapse', *The New York Review of Books*, XLII, 20 Apr. 1995, p. 6. On the discussion of nationalism, *cf.* Anderson, 1983 and Hobsbawm, 1990.
10. *Geschichte Friedrichs des Grossen. Geschrieben von Franz Kugler. Gezeichnet von Adolph Menzel*, Leipzig, 1840. For a detailed analysis of the illustrations and history paintings, *cf.* Forster-Hahn, 1977, p. 242–61.
11. Rotteck/Welcker, 1847, emphasis on the original.
12. Kugler, 1854, 3:664–5; first published in 'Berliner Briefe', *Kunstblatt*, 36, (1848).
13. Wolff, 1914, intro. Oskar Bie, p. 27. In connection with a description of his sketches for Kugler's book, Menzel writes 'das damaliche Kostüm ist ein unendliches Feld, und da ich mir erst die Gelegenheit verschafft habe so will ich sie auch aus dem Grunde benutsen, meinen Arbeiten hierbei die grösstmöglichste Authenticität zu geben, . . .'.
14. Schasler, 1856, p. 116.
15. Schasler, 1858, p. 143–6. And 'Das gegenwärtige Bild [*The Flute Concert*] ist mehr, so zu sagen, der Reflex eines Historienbildes oder der Keim zu einem solchen.'
16. For an interpretation of the history of the Nationalgalerie and of the role played by its exhibition politics, *cf.* Forster-Hahn, 1996. On revisions in the reception of Menzel, *cf.* Forster-Hahn, 1995, p. 174–9.
17. G. [Walter Gensel?], 'Menzel's Begräbnis', 1904–5, p. 252.
118. Meyer, 1876, p. 1–10, 41–53. Meyer (following Anton Sprenger) emphasizes that only Menzel's art stands in 'einer nähern Beziehung zu nationalen Interessen' and that 'des spezifisch Preussische . . . sich eines Tages als identisch mit dem recht und echt Deutschen und als dessen Retter und Rächer enthüllt und bewährt hat.' p. 8
19. Donop, 1895, p. 7.
20. For investigations of the role played by the exhibition strategies of the Nationalgalerie in the imaging of a new national identity for the Reich and in representing the history of the modern, *cf.* Forster-Hahn, 1996.
21. *Cf.* Forster-Hahn, p 255–83; and Forster-Hahn, 1991, p 49–54..
22. H.R. 1905, p. 361–4, and especially 363.
23. Gensel, 1904–5, p. 321–5, but especially 321. Gensel is one of the few critics who rejects the view that Menzel 'anticipated' Impressionism.
24. Hugo von Tschudi in a letter to the Ministry dated 27 November 1902. Archiv der Nationalgalerie, *Acta Generalia*, 10, vol. VII, 1302/02, 14/03, 132/03.
25. Rosenhagen, 1905, p. 259.
26. Meier-Graefe, 1906, 2nd rev. ed., Munich, 1914 (written in the summer of 1905). Hugo von Tschudi, 1905 B, p. 215–314. For a discussion of the role of

Meier-Graefe, see also Robert Jensen, 1994, p. 235–63, and Patricia Berman, 'The invention of history: Julius Meier-Graefe, German modernism, and the genealogy of genius', in Forster-Hahn, 1996.

27. Laban, 1906, p. 266, from the opening address on the aims and purposes of the exhibition: 'Es handelte sich um nichts Geringeres, als die deutsche Kunst der letztvergangenen Epoche . . . bis zum Anfang des Impressionismus . . . in der öffentlichen Meinung zu rehabilitieren'. Franz Dülberg, 1906, p. 161, assesses the undertaking as 'eine Bereicherung des geistigen Nationalgutes . . .'.

28. Dülberg, 1906, p. 161: 'Es ist damit ein neuer Zweig des künstlerischen Schaffens, eine Art öberkleidungskunst inauguriert worden . . .'

29. Seidlitz, n.d., p. 44.

30. Hamann, 1906, p. 104: 'Eine Reihe von Sachen um 1850 herum sind ganz im impressionistischen Sinne dieser Zeit gemalt, formal wie inhaltlich . . .'

31. Max Liebermann's widely publicized dipute with Henry Thode in 1905 was typical of the polemical debates surrounding the modern: 'Wenn aber ein Professor an einer der ersten Universitäten Deutschlands in einer rein künstlerischen Angelegenheit mit persönlichen Insinuationen, wie 'Mangel an nationalem Empfinden', 'Nachnahmen der Französen', . . . und andern aus der Rüstkammer der Antisemiten entnommen . . . Waffen den Feind zur Strecke zu bringen versucht. . .' Max Liebermann, 'Der Fall Thode', in *Die Phantasie in der Malerei*, 1983, p. 161, originally published in the *Frankfurter Zeitung*, 1905.

32. Woldemar von Seidlitz, n.d., p. 44–5.

33. *Cf.* Forster-Hahn, 1988, p. 221–32.

34. *Cf.* Forster-Hahn, 1978, p. 275.

Fig. 115. One of the Menzel Rooms at the Nationalgalerie, 1908

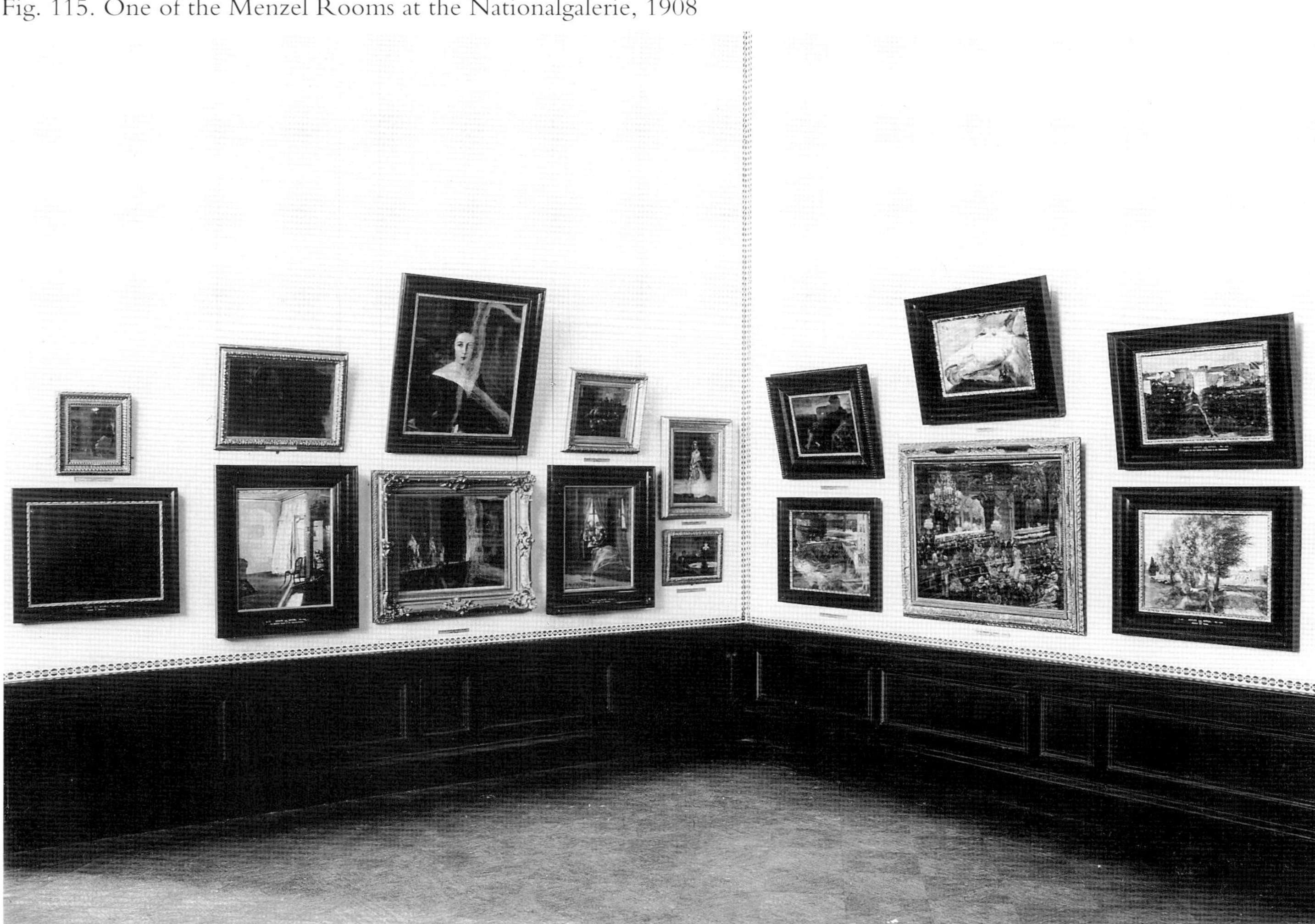

Menzel and French painting of his time: two conceptions of the historical genre

Thomas W. Gaehtgens

The problem of Menzel's relationship with French art has never ceased to occupy the thoughts of art critics, and it has yet to be resolved. Nobody who has worked on Menzel's artistic output has been able to avoid taking a position on this aspect of his work, but their conclusions have little in common. This disagreement is not solely the outcome of a diversity of methodological approaches. Indeed, the artist himself did nothing to make the task of historians and critics any easier; he left behind few written comments, and his work is not sufficiently explicit in itself to clarify the issue.

Even before his first journey to France in 1855, Menzel was fascinated by French art. Although art collections in Berlin and Potsdam provided him with only a few contemporary French works to study, there was no shortage of significant eighteenth-century paintings; these included the major works of Watteau, such as *L'Enseigne de Gersaint* (Gersaint Shopsign; fig. 117) and *L'Embarquement pour Cythère* (Pilgrimage to Cythera; fig. 116). He admired these and was able to reproduce the figures and the costumes. Menzel played an important role in the rediscovery of French *Rococo*[1]. It was probably Watteau who provided Menzel with his first major encounter with French culture, which in turn introduced him to Frederick the Great, the historical figure who was to play a central role in Menzel's artistic activity for several decades to come. There again, it may have worked in the opposite direction: it could have been his admiration for the King of Prussia that led him to study Watteau.

Before devoting an uncommissioned series of paintings to the life of the king, Menzel had produced, between 1839 and 1942, a series of drawings for Franz Kugler's *History of Frederick the Great*. This put him in competition with a great French artist, Horace Vernet, whose illustrations for Laurent de l'Ardèche's *History of Napoleon*, published in 1839 and subsequently translated into German, had been a great source of inspiration for him[2].

He was not, however, to come into contact with French painting, that is to say with French artists and, more generally, with the artistic activity of the French capital, until he travelled three times to Paris, in 1855, 1867 and 1868. Although there are a few letters and other documents, including those of his friend, companion and interpreter, Paul Meyerheim, only limited information relating to these journeys has survived. Little is known of what Menzel saw, of what made any impression on him, or of what took place during the meetings he had in Paris; only his friendship with Ernest Meissonier (1815–91) has been established with some degree of certainty. However, there is evidence to suggest that Menzel's work was successfully exhibited in France on several occasions. Indeed, art critics were fulsome in their praise for it, and he received a number of official prizes[3].

The most important evidence relating to Menzel's relationship with French art is to be found in the paintings referring to journeys to France. In Paris, as was his habit, he produced sketches of all the subjects he could find and, when he returned home, most frequently to Berlin, these helped him to complete a number of oil paintings on French subjects. These included *The Théâtre du Gymnase* (1856; cat. 80), *Policeman and Lady in the Tuileries Gardens* (1856; cat. 79), *Afternoon in the Tuileries Gardens* (1867; cat. 123), *Meissonier in his Studio at Poissy* (1868; cat. 126) and *Weekday in Paris* (1869; cat. 127).

In their analyses of Menzel's life and work, art historians have sought to identify the painter's artistic influences. They agree on the key role Paris played in the nineteenth century as the most important centre of artistic creation that left a mark on Menzel's development. This is not disputed. Moreover, the writers have scoured his works for a specific sign of a shift from Realism to Impressionism taking place. But during the time of his visits to Paris, their scholarly zeal has not been confined to formal aspects of artistic expression. Only recently, in fact, a number of writers have stated with some vigour that, first and foremost, Menzel's stays in Paris gave him a chance to live life to the full in a big city, though even this experience has been interpreted in a number of different ways. Some authors have thought that Paris, then the most lively city in Europe, awakened in Menzel an interest in social analysis, if not social criticism[4]; it is quite clear that these ideas were strongly influenced by the debates over political and social interpretations of Realism in France and elsewhere. Other writers, by contrast, believe that Menzel did not see this Babel, at the

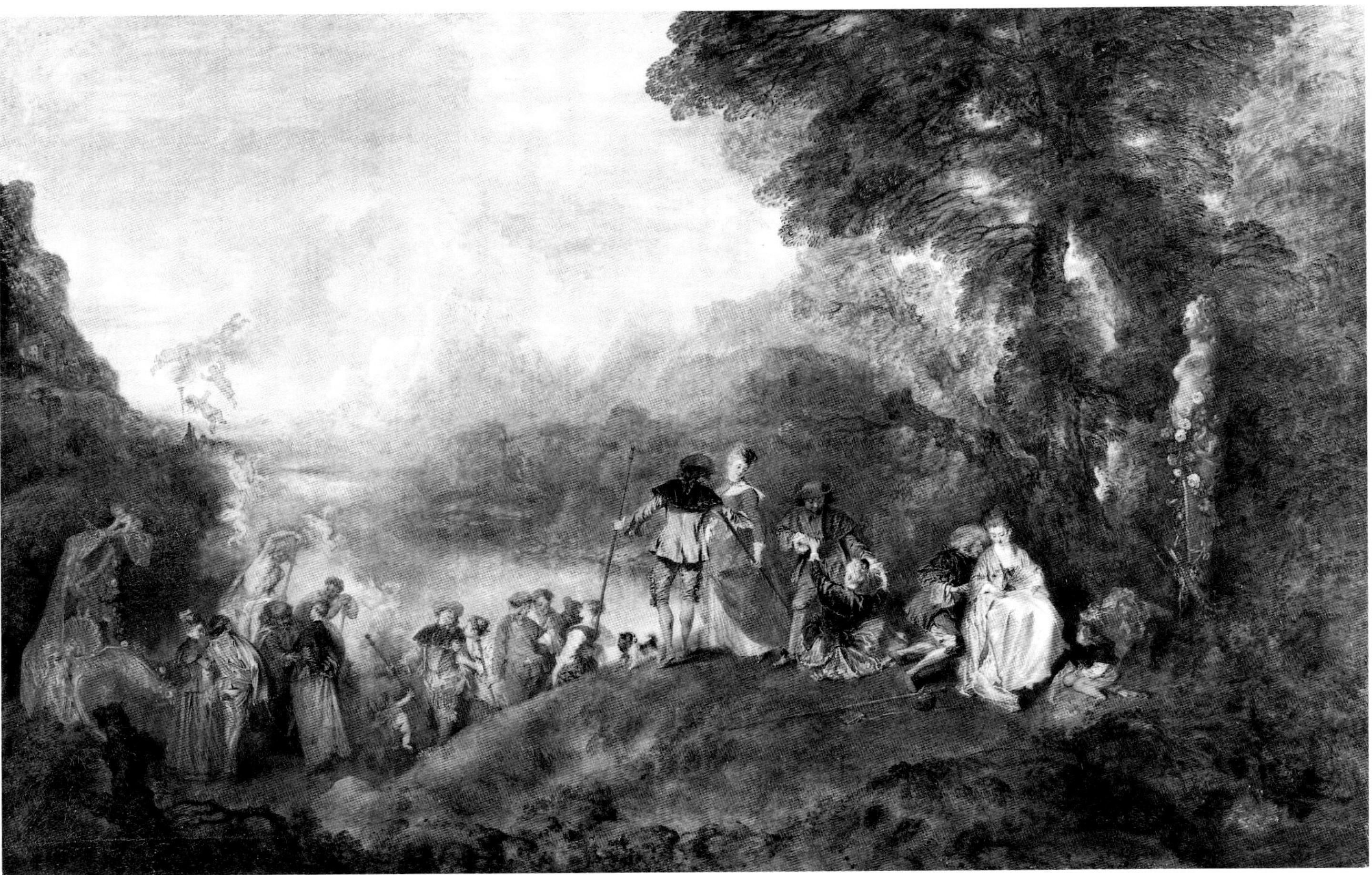

Fig. 116. Antoine Watteau, *Pilgrimage to Cythera*, 1717, oil, Paris, Louvre

time the most modern metropolis in Europe, in political terms at all[5].

Contrary to popular opinion, itself based on many quite different ways of seeing things, it is my belief that, in the course of his artistic development, Menzel showed, if not an element of independence, at the very least a high degree of autonomy, and even stubbornness. He was not indifferent to French art, nor did he resist the charms of the capital city. However, the time he spent there did not bring about a radical change in his conception of art or in the overall orientation he gave his painting. On the contrary, and this is very important, Paris was where he came into contact with artists who shared his sensitivity, and where he found painter colleagues with whom he could establish close working relationships. The most fruitful of these was with Meissonier.

Unlike Max Liebermann, who spent the 1870s in Paris studying Realism, Menzel visited the French capital only when there were exhibitions of his work. He never sought to prolong his stays, and there is no evidence that he was greatly influenced by contemporary French painters; neither the work of Courbet nor that of Manet left any mark on his painting.

From childhood, Menzel had followed a very different path from Liebermann. Self-taught, he had had to provide for his own needs and those of his family from a young age. He could not afford to pay for academic training in Berlin, let alone spend years in Paris completing his education with celebrated French masters. Nevertheless, Menzel had fully developed his pictorial technique and determined his artistic convictions long before his first trip to Paris in 1855.

Françoise Forster-Hahn has convincingly demonstrated how the illustrations in the *History of Frederick the Great* had turned the French models into a style that strongly typified Menzel (*cf.* figs 101–11). He steered

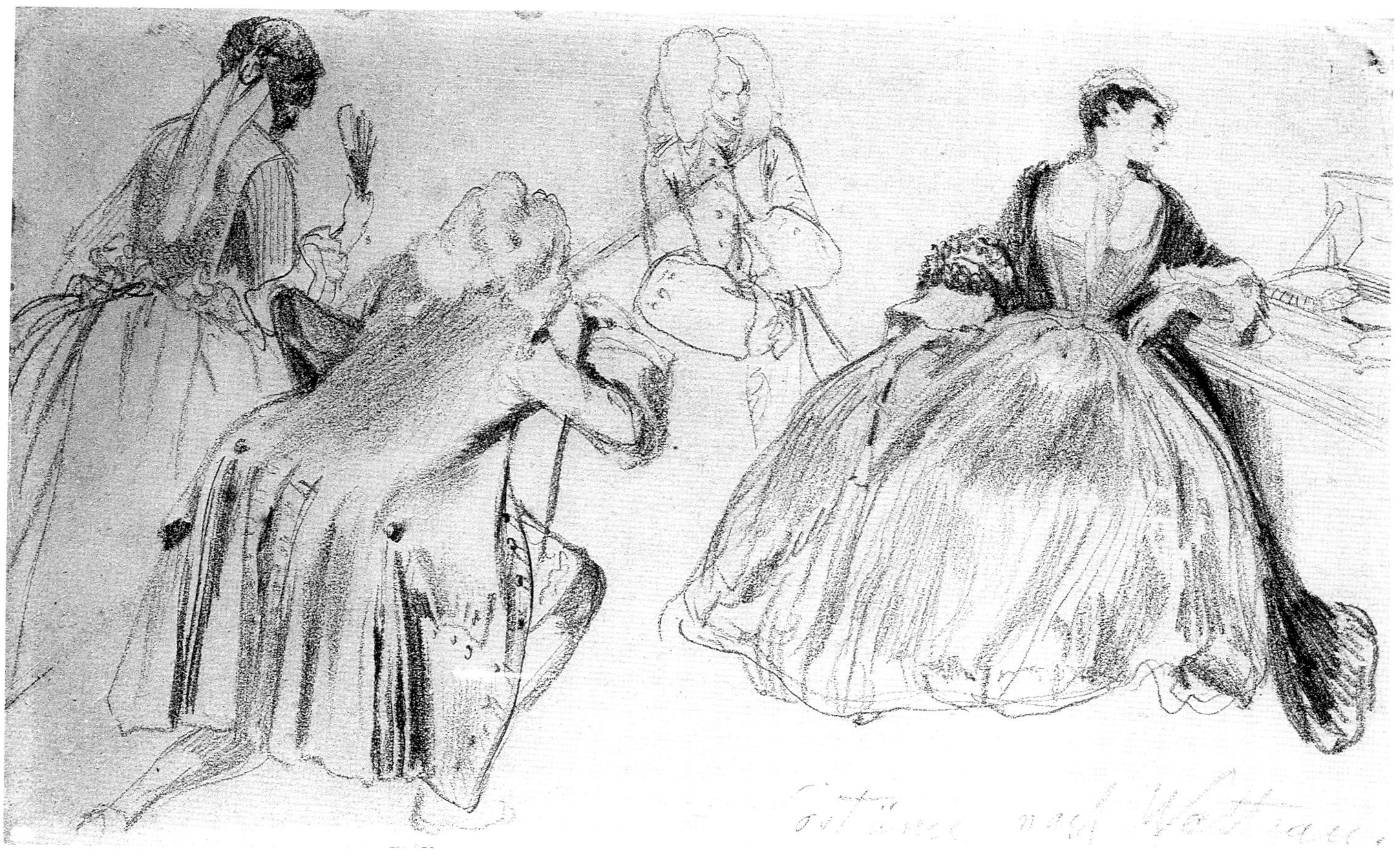

Fig. 117. Characters after Watteau's *Gersaint Shopsign*, 1839–40, pencil, Berlin, Kupferstichkabinett (Kat. 1469 a)

clear of hero cult idealization, and used the wood engravings to make Frederick's life into something tangible. He did not observe the rules of academic composition, which insisted that the hero should occupy centre stage and adopt a striking pose or perform a memorable deed[6]. On the contrary, he complied scrupulously with written and pictorial documentation from the time of Frederick the Great, and thereby gave his illustrations a strong, authentic flavour. Menzel is known to have spent long hours in libraries studying the period in great detail.

Menzel's strictly anti-academic views clearly ran counter to the entire artistic conception of the milieu in which he lived and, significantly, it was also completely incompatible with the French tradition of history painting. The most grandiose event in the spirit of this tradition was Louis-Philippe's attempt to recount history through a cycle of monumental paintings executed for Versailles. In commissioning this work, the king's intention had been to foster a national, patriotic image of history with which all political currents could identify. The Gallery was opened with great pomp in 1837, and was dedicated 'To all the glories of France'. News of the king's initiative spread throughout Europe, and reproductions of the paintings were disseminated in the form of engravings published as a series and in illustrated catalogues. Menzel was undoubtedly aware of their existence[7].

Kugler and Menzel presented Frederick the Great as a monarch feared and hated by princes, but loved and venerated by his people[8]. Hitherto, their history in the form of images corresponded to de l'Ardèche's book on Napoleon or to the illustrations of Horace Vernet. The French people's worship of Napoleon, that combined Republicanism and loyalty to the emperor, served in Prussia as a model for inspiring veneration for Frederick the Great, trying to present him as a Man of the Enlightenment. As for the bourgeoisie, he had become the depository of their long-nurtured hopes for a liberal Constitution[9].

As political events in France and Prussia gathered pace, the artistic media introduced by Vernet and Menzel diverged radically. As Françoise Forster-Hahn has shown, Menzel's illustrations attempted to involve the spectator directly in the event. The artist often made use of contemporary engravings, and here placed the king centre stage, thereby reshaping the entire scene by giving it a specific psychological focus. Menzel drew from the standpoint of an eye-witness in the street, and did not create distance[10]. He also avoided symmetrical compositions, preferring the more powerful impact of immediacy and real life. While Vernet created heroes and kept spectators at a distance, Menzel sought to involve them in the action. This conception of art was not only opposed to Vernet's, it did not comply with the French academic tradition and thus was not to be seen in paintings commissioned by Louis-Philippe for Versailles.

Menzel went to Paris for the first time in 1855. We know little of this first visit. He stayed for only two weeks, having come for the Universal Exhibition to show his *The Round Table at Sanssouci* (fig. 100); the painting clearly enjoyed little success as critics made next to no mention of it[11].

Nor do we have much idea of Menzel's own impressions of the Exhibition. Ingres had a whole section to himself, and Delacroix exhibited a large number of paintings, but if Menzel formed any views about these, we do not know what they were. As for the Courbet Pavilion, which the artist had built outside the Exhibition Hall in order to show his work, we can only assume that Menzel visited it. However, if he had been favourably impressed by the great French Realist on that occasion, or later, in 1867, it is most likely that he would have said so.

Menzel completed his painting of *The Théâtre du Gymnase* (cat. 80) in Berlin in 1856; in Paris, the previous year, he had done preparatory drawings of it in his sketchbook. The painting records a visit that Menzel paid to this theatre, and one sketch, which was made at the time of the visit, depicts the view as the artist saw it. All the evidence suggests that he was particularly struck by the effects of the colours and the light. The foreground, which includes the front rows of the auditorium and the orchestra, in dark brown, contrasts with the brightness of the stage; more powerful colour accents are contained in the light-coloured wall of the boxes, the red of the wings and the blue of the actress' dress. The angle that Menzel chose is unusual, and the fine centring enables the spectator to imbibe the whole atmosphere of

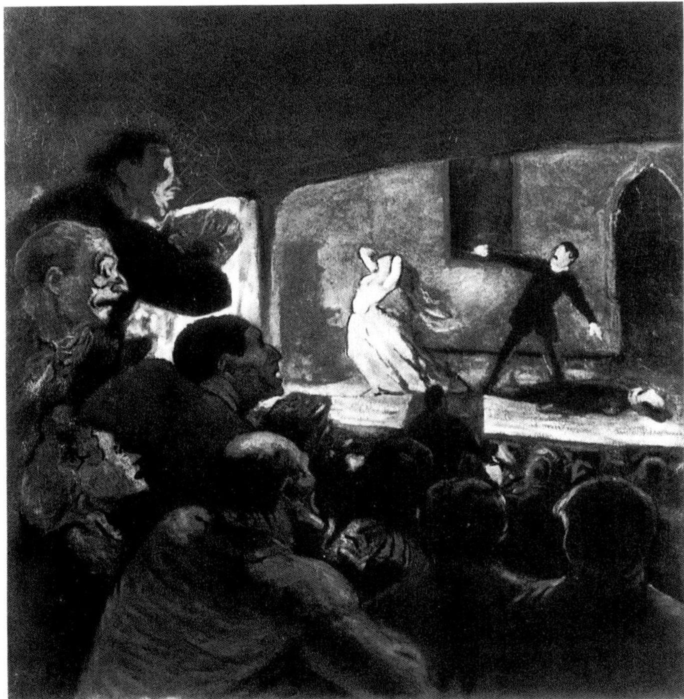

Fig. 118. Honoré Daumier, *The Drama,* c. 1860, oil, Bayerische Staatsgemäldesammlungen, Neue Pinakotek

the theatre. The impression of spontaneity is further enhanced by the fact that Menzel deliberately gave the painting the appearance of being a sketch; it was a technique that he used consciously and contrary to his habit as a stylistic device.

This painting provides no break in style with earlier works, but it nonetheless represents a new orientation. In all probability, Menzel saw it as no more than an experimental piece, and he never showed it publicly. At all events, it is a good example of the importance he accorded images of daily life, which was a trend that had already been glimpsed in drawings and smaller studies. The series of illustrations on Frederick the Great had been imaginary historical drawings, but now Menzel resolutely turned his attention towards subjects of a more contemporary nature. He does not seem, however, to have been directly influenced to do so by French painters; the theatre pictures of Daumier and Degas, for example, did not appear until some time later. It was Paris itself that drew Menzel's attention to a new kind of theme which might be described as the 'contemporary genre'.

Menzel's *The Théâtre du Gymnase* is not a simple genre scene, and it is also more than a simple representation of everyday life. In fact, it depicts a particular moment in a play, in which the viewer of the painting participates, assuming the identity of a member of the audience. Yet, we cannot be certain, however, whether Menzel depicted a real play. The sketch (fig. 4) was obviously drawn in the theatre itself, but the issue of whether it shows an actual performance is unclear because its left margin is cut across and it does not include the woman in the splendid blue dress (fig. 1). Even if the accuracy of the scenic representation remains difficult to prove, there is an overall impression of authenticity. In other words, Menzel has not moved away from the style of his Frederick the Great illustrations: the spectator is ushered into the Théâtre du Gymnase-Dramatique on the Boulevard Bonne-Nouvelle, and the artist shows him to a balcony seat and presents a successful melodrama for him. This painting is nevertheless highly innovative, in that much of the reality is personally experienced, rather than simply presented. innovative.

Curiously, research carried out so far on Menzel has taken little interest in this visit to the theatre. To say the least, it is most surprising that Menzel, who spoke little French, did not opt instead for a musical evening out. The opera or, even better, the Bouffes Parisiennes, successfully directed by Jacques Offenbach, would surely have provided the German visitor with more appealing entertainment. But Menzel does not seem to have gone to the Théâtre du Gymnase-Dramatique without a reason. The melodramas that were presented there enjoyed huge popular success; operas and operettas were social affairs that were the preserve of the *grande bourgeoisie*, a class that Menzel refused to join, at least at that time. By contrast, melodrama to musical accompaniment was more likely to satisfy his curiosity about French theatrical life. Plays by the likes of Balzac, Scribe, Dumas fils, Sand and Sardou were regularly put on during the 1840s and 1850s and, unlike works staged at the Comédie Française, those presented at the Gymnase did not address Classical themes with a lofty moral content. On the contrary, they had a freshness deriving from the inclusion of scenes from real life; other ingredients such as suspense, humour, sensational effects and drama made for a theatrical genre that might be compared to the historical genre in painting.

Menzel is therefore unlikely to have presented a key dramatic moment in this work: he depicted neither an act of despair nor a happy ending. Such a climax , which constituted the very essence of history painting according to Classical academic teaching, had no value in his eyes. The matter under discussion between the three characters on stage is of no importance. In this respect, Menzel was markedly different from Daumier; the latter's theatrical scenes feature a decisive point in the action at which the audience holds its breath in suspense. In fact, it is precisely because this key dramatic moment is absent that Menzel succeeds in creating the illusion of reality, and enables viewers to feel they have come to the Théâtre du Gymnase for an evening's entertainment.

It would be a mistake to conclude that Menzel's painting came out of a confrontation with French art, and more specifically with the art of Courbet. Courbet's style is far too distinct for Menzel to be influenced by it in any way[12]. His artistic development had been determined long before, and he had no need of external impetus; in artistic terms, Paris did not modify his conception of art but it was his presence in the city that, like some grandiose, weighty event, made the real impression on him.

On returning to Berlin, Menzel did not abandon his Frederick the Great engravings in favour of the 'contemporary genre'; *The Théâtre du Gymnase* simply remained a kind of stylistic exercise that he did not let the public see. For the time being, he threw his energies into completing *Night Attack at Hochkirch* (fig. 120), a work he had started in 1850 and which he now planned as his next historical genre painting. Although this work deals with an established historical event, it is not presented as a classical history painting; in fact, the night attack and the ensuing battle scarcely figure. The moment is decisive but the action is not emphasized. The focus, which is directed exclusively at the close relationship between Frederick and his soldiers, is firmly established through the king's presence on the front line. The Prussian defeat following the Austrians' surprise night attack is accorded no narrative description; instead, the almost magical cohesion between the king and his people, between the general and his troops, is treated as if it were an invocation[13].

Menzel did not return to Paris until 1867; this was on the occasion of the Universal Exhibition, where his Hochkirch painting was shown to an international public. During the four weeks he was in Paris, he met Ernest Meissonier on several occasions, and also visited him in his studio at Poissy. On his return, a number of drawings enabled him to complete a small painting in oils showing Meissonier from the back in the process of painting at his easel. His dog is lying at his side, and behind him stand a young woman and Menzel's friend Meyerheim looking closely at a small sketch in oils (cat. 126).

Menzel had previously met Meissonier in October 1862, when the latter was on a visit to Berlin. Meyerheim, Menzel's friend, reports that Meissonier had been very impressed by Menzel's unfinished painting showing Frederick the Great and his generals before the Battle of Leuthen (cat. 90): 'Meissonier was effusively

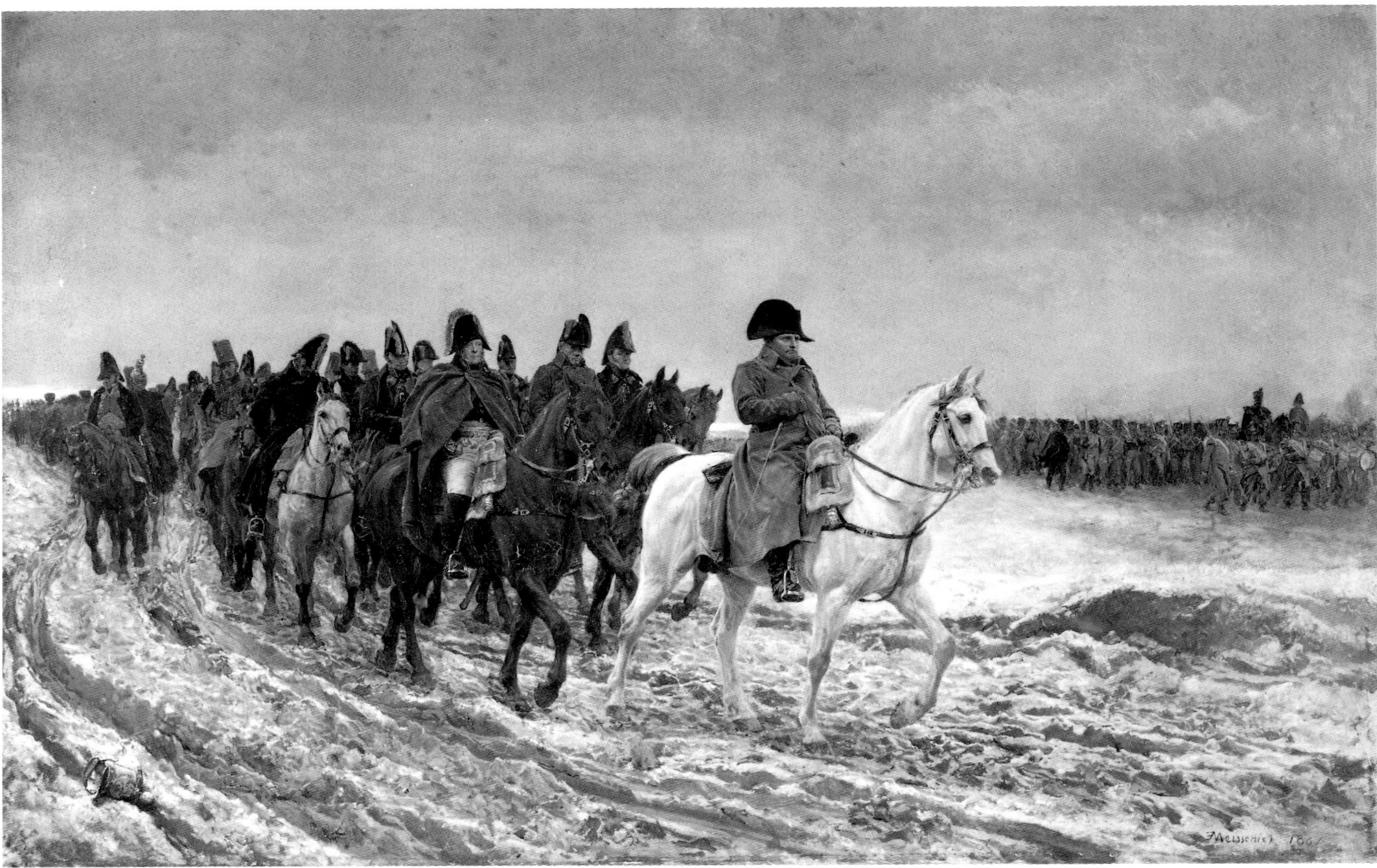

Fig. 119. Ernest Meissonier, *1814, The French Campaign*, 1860–4, oil, Paris, Musée d'Orsay

Fig. 120. *Night Attack at Hochkirch*, 1856, oil, formerly in Berlin, Nationalgalerie, lost during World War II

enthusiastic about this painting; such an intelligent feel for colour, atmosphere and technique was totally unknown in Paris. On his return to Paris, he immediately started work on his *Napoleon's Retreat from Russia* : this contained the same frost-bitten generals, the same silhouette of an army against a grey background, and the same snow-covered, rutted ground that had appeared in Menzel's work'[14]. Whether Meyerheim's account should be believed without question is open to doubt. He was certainly mistaken when he said that Meissonier had painted Napoleon during the retreat from Russia, since the latter made it very clear that his work depicted Napoleon's defeat in France in 1814[15] (fig. 119).

It is hardly surprising, at all events, that Menzel and Meissonier saw eye to eye. Menzel had great admiration for Meissonier, and the French painter returned this regard in equal measure. Both were eager to treat their subjects in as much detail as possible, and to adopt the historical genre in their work.

If, however, we are to make a serious comparison between these two paintings, we need to study more deeply both the points they have in common and their differences. Constance Hungerford has convincingly demonstrated how Meissonier's work may be approached in terms of the account given by Thiers[16]. Meissonier drew not only the theme and the emotional horror from Thiers' description of the Russian campaign, but also the emotional horror which he would depict with his powers of dramatic expression. He sought to convey Napoleon's loneliness, and the affection shown by his officers and troops, who obeyed him to the bitter end, even in defeat, and who, through their solidarity, made victory possible yet again[17].

Thiers had earlier recounted the story in precise detail,

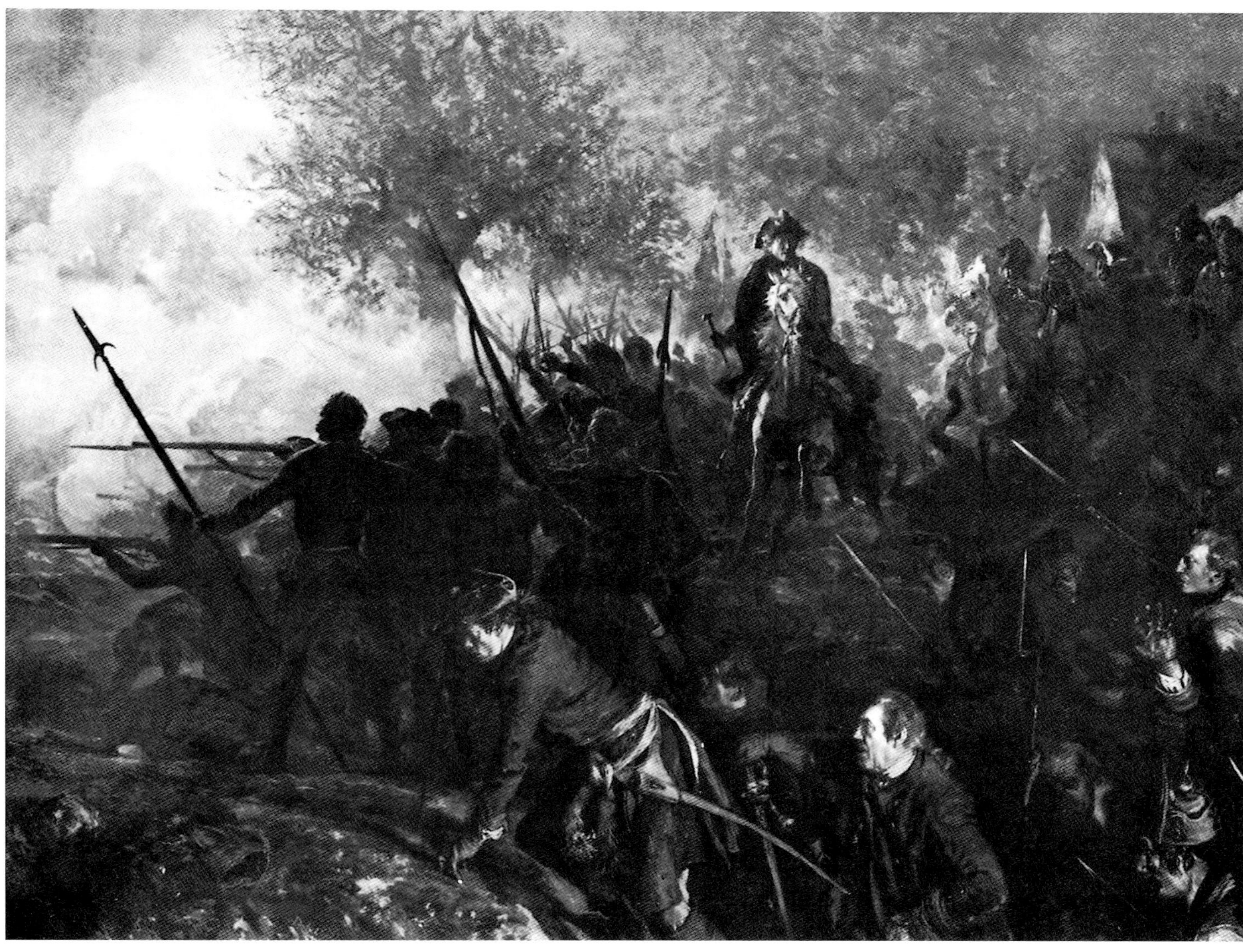

relying on a wide range of historical facts. Now, by reassembling these facts with precision and making use of the studies of models, Meissonier, too, endowed his reconstructions with historical accuracy. However, he did not present a particularly decisive or 'historical' moment, but instead sought to describe the physical and psychological realities of history. Just as Menzel gave a new gloss to Kugler's text, so Meissonier sought in his painting to make Thiers' history intelligible through the senses: 'The role of painting', he said, 'is to come to the aid of history. Thiers speaks of the flash of sabres, and it is this that the painter engraves in the heart of the viewer'[18].

The favourable impression that Menzel's *Address at Leuthen* (cat. 90) made on Meissonier during his stay in Berlin in 1862 could not, as Meyerheim believed, have been solely attributable to the artist's pictorial technique. He must also have been struck by the way in which the subject was presented – the physical presence of people gathered round their commander-in-chief who, as the 'first among equals', had come to them on the eve of a decisive battle. Nothing in the painting evokes the sense of a moment of paramount importance, yet it is quite clearly a historic event. The spectator enters the painting, not to participate in the discussion, but to experience a historic moment. Claude Keisch gives a superb account of the harsh, painful story behind the execution of *Address at Leuthen*, and even goes so far as to see the viewer's involvement as a positively democratic feature[19].

Meissonier's *1814, the French Campaign* shares a number of features with Menzel's painting. The wintry atmosphere and the detailed treatment of the portraits and costumes provide points in common between the two painters in terms of subject-matter and pictorial technique. Another common feature is their wish to make history tangible, and thereby awake the spectator's interest.

And yet the two works are fundamentally different. While the absence of any decisive moment of action in Menzel's painting increases the space and accommodates the spectator, Meissonier's places Napoleon in the very centre of the canvas as a vanquished hero. The pathos exhibited by the defeated emperor inspires veneration and admiration, and keeps the spectator at a distance, whereas Menzel's slightly higher viewpoint involves the spectator directly in the action. By contrast, Meissonier's low viewpoint highlights the principal character; in this way, he turns his back on the historical genre and produces a history painting. Meissonier, the genre painter, had turned into a painter of history, and imposed upon himself a requirement appropriate to this genre: '. . . art having to have an aim, having to provide moral teaching . . ., art having to express great thoughts, dedications and noble examples'. Among the paintings that reflected this ideal, Meissonier also included *1814, Dismal Reversal*[20]. French academic tradition obliged Meissonier to rid himself of his social interests if he wanted to become a history painter; Menzel had no interest in such ambitions.

The works that best illustrate the 'Menzel and France' theme are *Afternoon in the Tuileries Gardens* and *Weekday in Paris*; they were both painted immediately after his visits to France in 1867 and 1868, and they were probably matching pieces. Both paintings were soon hailed as masterpieces by critics, according to criteria that only later became established in art history. For example, on visiting the Menzel Exhibition in 1885, the critic Adolf Rosenberg regarded them as a decisive breakaway in the painter's artistic development which, according to him, had probably taken place in Paris. Rosenberg also remarked that free Naturalism showed through in the concentration of human forms that typified big cities. 'They are, so to speak, instantaneous, ephemeral images in which nature, which constitutes the background, is the sole durable element'[21]. Naturalism and Impressionism had in the meantime become recognized styles. Menzel's art was seen as a precocious contribution to these currents and closely linked to them. These two paintings, which were conceived *en plein air* in the centre of the city, seemed typically French in terms of both subject-matter and out-of-doors working methods; they could not possibly have been done without the influence of Paris. With the benefit of hindsight, however, this view needs to be placed in context .

Manet's *Music in the Tuileries* (cat. 81) has often been thought of as an inspirational source for Menzel's *Afternoon in the Tuileries Gardens*[22]. In fact, the two painters had very little in common, and it is by no means certain that Menzel ever saw Manet's painting. Menzel claimed to have painted his two views of the French capital 'from memory'. They were certainly not executed in the open air but, using a tried and tested method, in his studio and on the basis of drawings. As a result, he deliberately established a distance between the the experience to be captured and the completion of the painting, a reconstruction of a moment in contemporary history. In its organization, the painting is very similar to the Hochkirch work. The picture of the Tuileries is characterized by large numbers of people standing in the shade of trees; these soften the colours, and create powerful contrasts of light and shade in those parts of the garden that are illuminated by the sun. The scene is viewed slightly from above as if the painter was observing it from a terrace: the precise layout is difficult to reconstruct, although the main pathway of the Tuileries, with the Palace in the background, are to be seen on the right-hand side of the painting.

Unlike Manet's painting, Menzel's appears to be more an assemblage. While the French work consists of a balanced composition in which individuals and groups refer to each other in the foreground, Menzel's painting eschews this approach completely. Manet created a genre painting based on respect for academic conventions, whereas Menzel appears to have confined himself to painting a general outline and concentrating on the detailed representation of the various groups. The free surfaces, for example in the foreground to the right, remain empty, and the man in the bottom right-hand corner seems to have been added at the last moment to fill up the space. As Werner Hofmann so eloquently wrote of Menzel's creative methods, 'Nothing relies on an established order, nothing is ruled by composition, nothing leads to a definitive synthesis. The story is told spontaneously by decisions, accidents and errors'[23].

The same method appears to have been used in *Weekday in Paris*. Yet again, Menzel refrained from giving the picture a prominent central focus, preferring a diagonal construction to a frontal composition; he chose the framing, but decided against excessively clear margins at the borders. The overall effect is totally different from that achieved by Manet. Menzel's intention had been to bring the reality to life for the spectator, who becomes a person strolling through the park, entering the Tuileries, and able to choose between the shaded avenue to the left and the sun-drenched pathway to the right. The individuals and groups in the painting are not remotely interested in the viewer: they are not turned towards him and have no connection with him. The day carries on as usual: there is nothing especially picturesque to look at, and the foreground is even swathed in darkness. The person looking at Menzel's pictures is cast in the role of someone strolling through the Tuileries, or of a pedestrian on the streets of Paris. The work of art and the model of nature are but one. In Menzel's paintings, aesthetic pleasure is entirely condensed into the illusion of reality.

By contrast, Manet gave his composition more the form of a painting or an academic work of art. The characters, some of whom are portraits, turn towards the spectator and pose. The whole work is imbued with a sense of internal order. The picture uses a subject as a pretext to turn it into an aesthetic creation. Manet imposes sensory perception on the spectator, cut off from the reality of the object portrayed; forms and colours have their own aesthetic quality, irrespective of the recognizable objects that they describe.

Françoise Forster-Hahn has shown that the most instructive approach to Menzel's painting is to be found in the work of the eminent French critic, Edmond Duranty. Through his concept of Realism, which was extensively discussed in many books and articles, Duranty revealed himself to be critical of the academic approach. He demanded that art should focus on contemporary issues and take account of the social reality of the time. Duranty had studied Menzel's work very closely at a number of exhibitions, and his theoretical ideas found concrete form in the German's painting. In 1880, in the *Gazette des Beaux-Arts*, he published a very detailed article on Menzel's work, and referred to it frequently in his subsequent writings[24].

Duranty was insistent that a revival in painting was only possible if 'Truth' was scrupulously respected. Menzel had succeeded in painting both historical and contemporary themes convincingly because he himself had a profound sense of the present. It was Duranty's view that Degas, who had an equally high opinion of the German painter and had copied *Supper at the Ball* (cat. 168), and Menzel were rare among modern painters in that they had observed and depicted their contemporaries in their respective social environments[25].

It is dangerous, however, to interpret Menzel's art within the context of the theoretical debate on Realism in art then taking place in France. It is true that this interpretation reflected the intensity of Franco-German relations in artistic matters during the nineteenth century – and one that went way beyond national prejudices – but a number of misunderstandings relating to artistic conception also emerged. In fact, Duranty simply analysed Menzel's art in such a way as to suit his own purposes.

What is unclear is whether Menzel's painting can be interpreted using Duranty's concept of Realism. There is nothing in a painting to suggest that the reality that the artist experienced was approached analytically. Menzel does not dissect the object itself, but rather the forms of representation. Far from relying on a Romantic conception of art, one that uses an object in order to give concrete shape to an abstraction, Menzel tried to represent reality just as he perceived and experienced it. For him, drawing and painting were ways of appropriating his environment. Aesthetic charm lies in illusion. It is a new form of the ancient theme of imitation, or trickery of the senses, that is to be found in Menzel. Therefore, his realism could not be likened to any form of social awareness. He only mastered the model supplied by nature by imitating it, and did so by an action that the artist had to practise constantly as if it were a trade.

If a concept, such as Duranty's theory of Realism, could find expression in art, it was more likely to do so in Manet or Degas. The reason is that their works are the fruit of an analytical process whereby the work of art finds its form in true pictorial reality following a transformation of perception. Menzel's works are the fruit of a process of inverse creation. For him, at least in theory, Zola's notion that art reproduces nature through the artist's personality acting as a prism is not pertinent. Quite obviously, Menzel's art is also anti-academic. He goes way beyond the literary concepts of Romanticism; what is more, instead of merely presenting his personal feelings in his paintings, he also sought to give the spectator an opportunity to live the same visual experience.

It is difficult to imagine a greater artistic divide than that separating David's *Coronation of Napoleon I* (fig. 122) and Menzel's *Coronation of King William I at Königsberg* (fig. 121). There can be no doubt that Menzel knew the work of his illustrious predecessor, if only in the form of a reproduction or an engraving made after the painting. The two works are related through their theme, and it may be that, before choosing how he was going to represent King William's coronation, Menzel studied David's monumental work in considerable detail. There is no reason to suppose that Menzel felt anything but admiration for David's painting, yet the two works are very different.

Of course, we now know that Menzel had to consent to compromises while completing his great opus. He did not have total freedom in his choice of mode of representation, because he had to abide by a propaganda policy laid down not only by his sponsor but also by the latter's advisers. The mystical lighting and the raised sword were essential motifs designed to illustrate in the

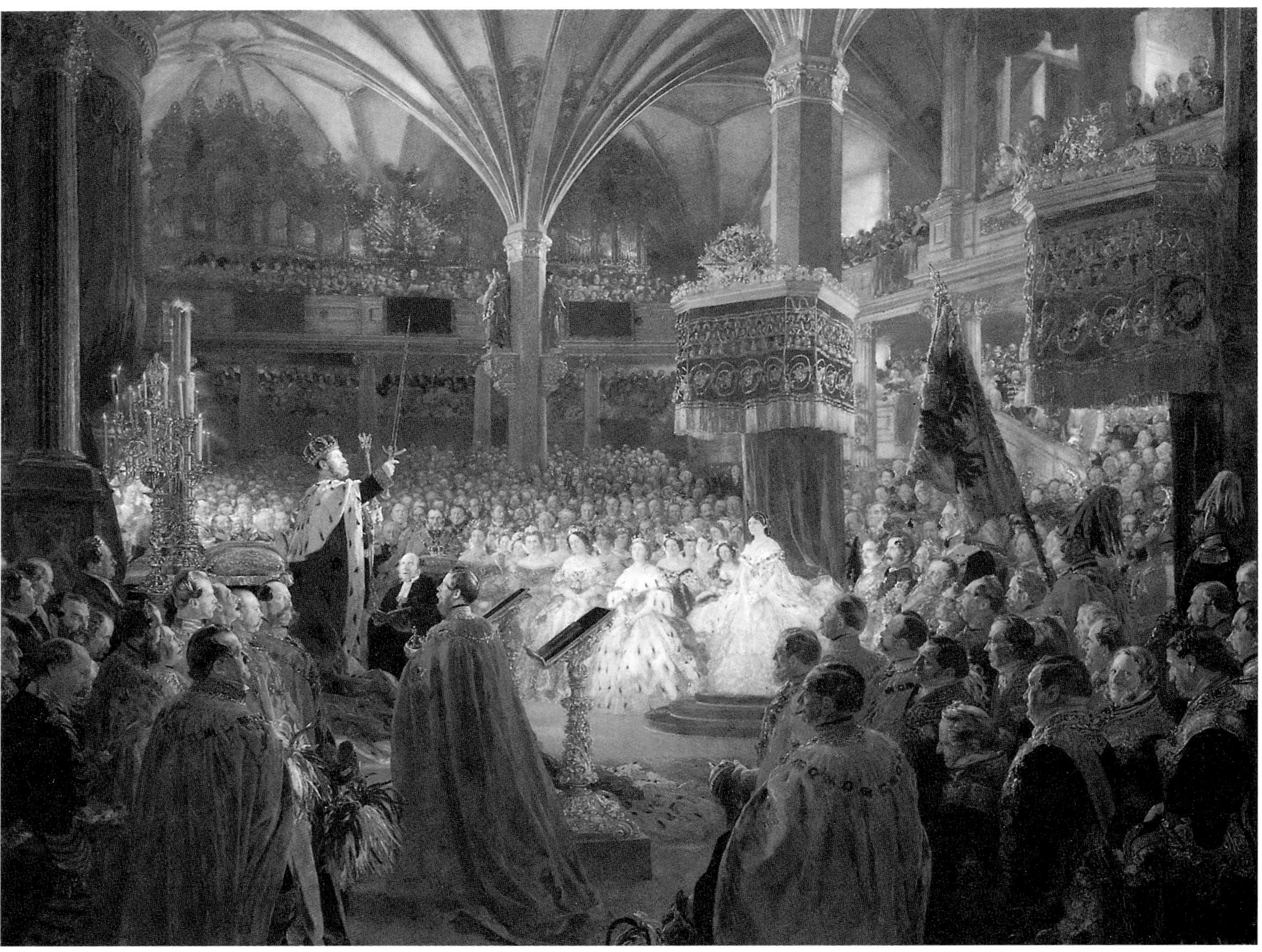

Fig. 121. *The Coronation of William I at Königsberg*, 1865, oil, Potsdam, Stiftung Preussische Schlösser und Gärten

most striking manner possible the King of Prussia's divine right to rule[26].

Just the same, this painting, on which Menzel worked for so many years, does not contradict his basic conception of art. In fact, the major difference between his work and David's sums up precisely what distinguished Menzel's work and painting in the French academic tradition.

David's work is a historical painting *par excellence*: it depicts a contemporary event, the central feature of which is a historic act performed by a hero of exceptional qualities, and all the remaining narrative motifs are subordinated to a central event on which all the lines of the composition converge. Clearly, the event itself did not take place precisely as it is depicted here; it was simplified and made easier to understand by the artist, and interpreted in accordance with the academic theory of historical painting.

By contrast, Menzel transposes his experience into the picture: leaving political compromises to one side, everything happened as he describes it. However, there was one area where he had to make changes, and that was the gap he had to create in the first row of dignitaries so as to allow the principal event to be seen. For the rest, he conceived the picture as if it were a still from a film, and once again demonstrated his commitment to minute detail and authenticity. As Duranty said, 'He was neurotic about the truth'[27]. The idea that a work of art could comply with the rules that the artist obeyed in his artistic representation of reality, as French academic tradition demanded, was entirely foreign to him. Compared with French works of art, Menzel's oeuvre reflects his personal originality. His development as an artist took him to Paris but, once he was there there, nothing induced him to change direction.

1. Schmidt, 1957, p. 317-324; Eckhardt, 1987, p. 251–8.
2. *Cf* also a detailed and still up-to-date interpretation by Forster-Hahn, 1977, p. 242-61; *cf.* also Paret, 1988, p. 26–60.
3. Forster-Hahn, Exhibition Catalogue Berlin A, p. 27–48.
4. Jensen, 1982, p. 40–1.
5. Jensen, 1982, p. 40.
6. *Cf.* on this subject Gaehtgens and Fleckner, 1993.
7. Franz Kugler organised a conference in Berlin in 1846 on his impressions of his visit to Versailles: 'Lectures on the historical museum at Versailles and a presentation of the historic events in painting'. The conference took place on 7 March 1846 at the Berlin Society of Sciences, Berlin; *cf.* also Gaehtgens, 1985, p. 338 et seq.
8. Wolff, 1914, p 21; Forster-Hahn, *op cit*, p. 245.
9. *Cf.* Becker With, 1975, and also Forster-Hahn and Paret, *op cit*.
10. Forster-Hahn, *op cit*, p. 247 and 255. 'When constructing scenes, Menzel found most of his inspiration in popular imagery. He transformed the anecdotal aspect of this into historical moments, and in this way demonstrated remarkable powers of observation and skill at endowing characters and situations with a psychological characterisation.'
11. There is, however, an observation in *Deutsches Kunstblatt* that reflects the confusion surrounding the *genre* in which Menzel's paintings should be classified: 'Menzel has a fluent style, skill and wide-ranging talent. He has tried his hand at a variety of objects and forms including painting, drawing, lithography, studies of contemporary manners, arabesques and vignettes. In Berlin, he is much in demand for his *genre* paintings, although this has not stood in the way of his becoming a member of the Royal Academy of Arts. The concept of the hierarchy of talents and *genres* would appear to be less rigid in Prussia than it is France; in Prussia, Descamps and Meissonier would be Academicians.' The review's correspondent confirms the above remark, and suggests that the rules governing the hierarchy of *genres* had a different impact in Berlin and in Paris; *cf.* 'Aus dem Pariser Ausstellungspalast', *Deutsches Kunstblatt*, 6th year, No 32, 9 August 1855, p. 288–90; *cf* also J du Pays, *L'illustration*, 3 November 1855, p. 297.
12. Here, it is important to agree to the following persuasive, if inevitably somewhat contradictory, comment made by Forster-Hahn: 'Neither Courbet's painting nor the aesthetic programme had a direct influence on Menzel, but they may well have confirmed him in his independent path and given him the freedom to produce a painting as unconventional and unmodern as *Théâtre du Gymnase*. . .' Forster-Hahn, *op cit* p. 35.
13. Menzel described the painting in the following terms: 'A characterisation of the relationship between the hero-king and his troops – an army whose boundless devotion in a wholly desperate situation can only inspire admiration for their sovereign's magnificent and awe-inspiring strength of character.' Menzel in a letter to Frederick-William IV, 1 October 1856, quoted by Keisch, 1987, p. 264.

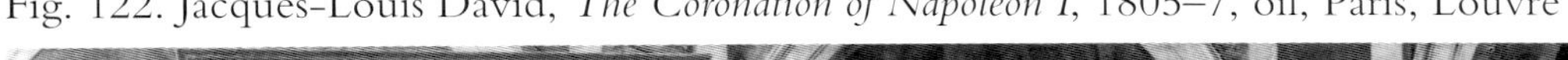
Fig. 122. Jacques-Louis David, *The Coronation of Napoleon I*, 1805–7, oil, Paris, Louvre

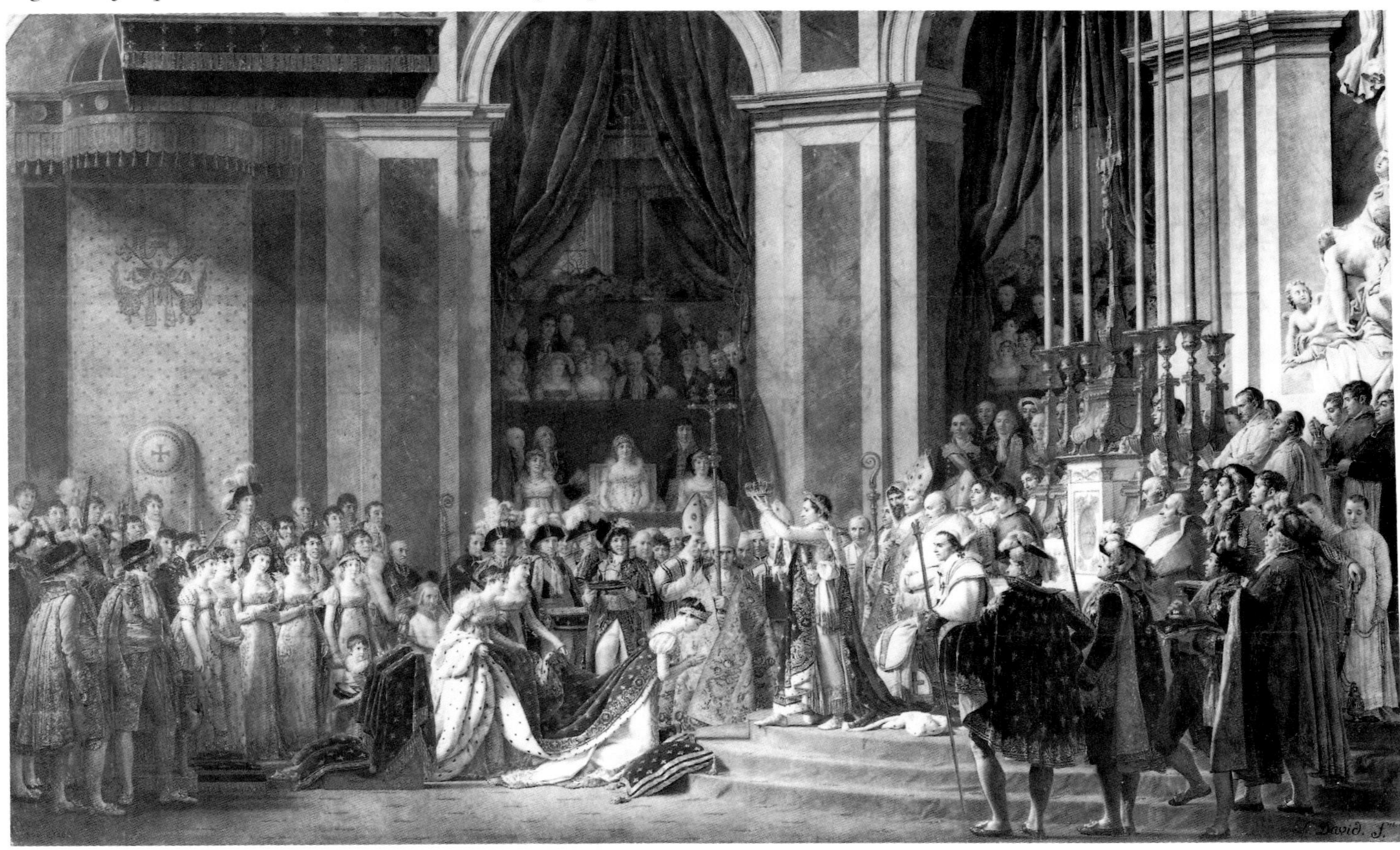

14. Meyerheim, 1906, p. 76–9.
15. Meissonier described the moment captured in the painting as follows: 'While completing the sketch in 1814, I thought of Napoleon returning from Soissons without his general staff after the Battle of Laon', and further on, '1814 was the time of Napoleon's campaign in France, and not 'the retreat from Russia' as is sometimes suggested. No one believes in him any longer. Doubt has taken hold. He alone believes that all may not be lost.'; Gréard, 1897, p. 241; Hungerford, 1980, p. 98–107; Exhibition Catalogue Lyon, 1993.
16. As Meissonier has confided, 'I surrounded myself with papers and immersed myself in Thiers.' Quoted by Hungerford, 1980, p. 102.
17. 'Thiers was Meissonier's main conceptual source, supplying him with the overall theme and the specific detail of the close relations between Napoleon and his officers. Thiers gets the credit for suggesting a new view of Napoleon's personal and historic situation in 1814, and he also provided Meissonier with enough details to enable him to marshall his resources with maximum effectiveness, and thereby present this interpretation of the Emperor.' *Ibid* p. 102.
18. Gréard, 1897, p. 172.
19. In addition to the painting's directly tangible content, 'this abnegation of historical distance – fictitious spontaneity simulated by artistic devices, the slanted angle, this way of perceiving things concealed in everyday events – is a positively democratic feature!', Keisch, 1987, p. 267.
20. Gréard, 1897, p. 250.
21. Rosenberg, 1985–6, p. 230.
22. Forster-Hahn also sees a number of graphical representations as models that may have inspired the theme of Menzel's painting, *op cit*, p. 39.
23. Hofmann, Exhibition Catalogue, Paris, 1984–85, p. 34.
24. Duranty, 1880, p. 210–17, vol 22, p. 105–25.
25. '. . .what we need is the defining characteristic of the modern individual, the way of dressing, the social habits, at home or in the street. . .' Quoted in Forster-Hahn, *op cit*, p. 29.
26. 'Zur Entstehung des Krönungsbildes', Exhibition Catalogue, Berlin, 1980A, p 48–60; Lammel, 1988, p. 121–59; Zangs, 1992, p. 179–89.
27. Duranty, 1880, p. 110.

The draughtsman – and master of the glance

Marie Ursula Riemann-Reyher

'It is fundamentally absurd to ask whether something comes from oneself, or from others, or whether one acts by oneself, or through others. One needs to have great strength of purpose, and the skill and perseverance to see it through. Nothing else is of any importance'[1]. These words, ascribed by Eckermann to Goethe, apply perfectly to Menzel and to his artistry, and can be documented to a fundamental and unparalleled degree in his drawings. For Menzel drawing was synonymous with life; every gaze cast and captured in a drawing was itself a breath from which this slightly built man drew the triumphant power necessary for his own preservation. One must look elsewhere, however, beyond his *Fleiss*, his diligence or application – a quality often attributed to Menzel and laden with moral overtones in the original German – for the reasons for his prolific artistic productivity. In his prodigious drawn *oeuvre* in which he constantly sought to capture the fleeting moment, he never once cried out 'Stay now!'[2]

The demon that animated and sustained Menzel was his art, in which he sought to grasp, to capture, the real. 'He was wholly what he was exclusively and always in the present moment. The only thing that mattered for him was the word most recently uttered'[3]. This judgment voiced by Max Jordan at the time of the artist's death merits further consideration.

On leaving Silesia, a distant province recently incorporated into Prussia, Menzel's father brought his family to Berlin in 1830 with a view to ensuring the best training for his eldest son. He hoped that Berlin would further the development of his own lithography business, but above all that his fifteen-year-old son would be able to benefit from an academic education. Years later, Menzel referred to the death of his father two years after arriving in Berlin as a 'decree of destiny'[4]. Drawing was a starting point for his lithographic work, and allowed him to support his family financially; in addition to being a duty, however, it was also the elixir that enabled his individuality to take shape. Given his difficult financial situation, he might easily have carried on working as a lithographer but his charismatic nature, at once enterprising and creatively restless, prevented this. Indeed from an early age Menzel was guided by a spirit that led him to perform every task with commitment and application, characteristics that were not to diminish during his long life.

In the early stages, it seemed unlikely that Menzel's career would follow a straightforward path. He himself stated that 'Although my artistic creativity began as soon as I was able to hold a piece of chalk, it did not immediately set me on the path of becoming an artist . . . What I have been able to achieve, essentially on my own, resulted from an early drive to embark on self-taught work which later enabled me to study without a teacher. . . Periodic attempts to alter this state of affairs proved unsuccessful. Instead, I soon found myself pushed further along my own path – in the history class at school, for example, where I enthusiastically drew my first composition inspired by . . . Roman history, all very serious and executed painstakingly in pencil'[5]. The boy's remarkable talent for drawing persuaded his father to modify his original plan to launch him on an academic career. Having received his father's 'authorization for his intended goal'[6] of following his artistic ambitions, training in Berlin was now to follow. However, as Menzel wrote at the age of thirty-eight, he was gripped by a 'very specific anxiety . . . to enter the stately portals of the Academy'. This 'exhausting process of refining', as he described his autodidactic efforts, then continued in Berlin, but the unexpected death of his father changed everything. Now confronted by the demands of making a living, 'hitherto enthusiastic occupations' and intentions of receiving an academic artistic education, fell by the wayside. In the spring of 1833 when he finally decided to 'appease his conscience' by 'matriculating at the Academy', he was promptly accepted into the drawing class that drew from plaster cast models. It seemed to be 'already too late for unquestioning acceptance of available education . . . On the other hand it was clearly far too early for independence from the time-tested validity of ancient models'. Menzel's 'irregular attendance' at the drawing class lasted for six months, and 'after some discouraging results and disappointments' he left the Academy. Apart from his work as a lithographer, study on one's own meant only one thing: drawing. Independently he discovered the foundations of his art as a draughtsman in the models with whom he had an affinity, through teachers whom he had to choose himself, and above all in nature and in the world around him. Menzel refused to give consideration to the difficulties inherent in self-education. 'What is so remarkable about someone who achieves something only to save himself from drowning? Someone who has 'no need of it', who nonetheless makes a great effort . . . deserves admiration'[7]. The copying of pictures of popular engravings, such as those published in the *Pfennig-Magazin*[8], was an important early drawing exercise. Examples can be found in a sketchbook of 1835–6, along with studies of concert or theater performances executed from memory, an exercise many artists engaged in for training their visual memory[9].

His earliest drawings dating from 1828 include several portrait studies and studies of his father's hands. In 1829, in gratitude for a contour portrait executed with a well-sharpened pencil, his father's sister, Johanna Martini, gave him two drawing primers by J.D. Preissler, published in 1721–5 and 1734 respectively and copiously illustrated with engravings[10]. These books were perhaps among the first to enter his personal library which was considered worthy of mention by Friedrich Eggers in an 1854 description of the artist's studio. Menzel also owned a volume of 115 engravings after portraits by Van Dyck, as well as a volume of 88 engravings by Riepenhausen after Hogarth[11]. Of course Schadow's 1834 publication *Polyclitus*, a standard work of reference for art students, was probably also known to him[12], although he replaced Schadow's stylizations with studies directly from nature. Late in life, like Schadow before him, he noted the measurements of his models alongside his drawings and studies.

As a young man committed to his spiritual and artistic development, Menzel received support from a number of important figures in Berlin with whom he remained on good terms for many years afterwards. Louis Sachse, forward-thinking art dealer and lithographer for whom Menzel's father had already done some work, commissioned the eighteen-year-old artist to execute twelve pen lithographs to illustrate Goethe's poem *Künstlers Erdenwallen* (The Artist's Earthly Pilgrimage; *cf.* fig. 88). Menzel's enthusiastic execution of the commission drew a favorable review from Schadow in the *Allgemeine Preussische Zeitung*, and subsequently he was unanimously elected into the *Verein der jüngeren Künstler* (Association of Young Artists). The linear style of these lithographs is firmly in the graphic tradition of Peter von Cornelius and there are specific analogies that can be drawn with Cornelius' pen drawings for Goethe's *Faust*, engraved by Ruscheweyh and published in 1816. Dürer had been Cornelius' inspiration, whose example he followed in inventing novel forms to accompany verbal images, but Cornelius was not Menzel's only guiding spirit when it came to lithographic *arabesques*. The young Menzel found another veritable source of educational and cultural guidance in the house of Carl Heinrich Arnold, a rich businessman and amateur painter who had briefly studied in David's atelier in Paris. Menzel met him during the winter of 1833–4 at the evening drawing sessions held at the Academy. In the convivial circle that gathered around Arnold in his residence at the Montbijouplatz, Menzel made the acquaintance of many of Berlin's eminent artists and scholars. Not only did this give him the opportunity to study Arnold's collection of drawings and engravings, but Arnold himself also encouraged the young man to take up painting.

It was Franz Kugler, however, who was to play the key role in Menzel's development as a draughtsman. Writer, intellectual, and keen follower of events in the art world of Berlin, Kugler was the first to recognize 'Menzel's richness of imagination, his confidence in representing the human form, his thorough academic (mainly historical) training, and his animated sense of poetry [. . .] all combined to a degree rarely encountered'[13]. On Kugler's recommendation Menzel was commissioned to execute four hundred illustrations for his *Geschichte Friedrichs des Grossen* (History of Frederick the Great) (*cf.* figs 101–5). This sign of confidence brought Menzel to a peak in his draughtsmanship in hundreds of drawings that demonstrate the wide range of his intense studies. He studied historical and archival sources, drew relevant sites in Berlin, Potsdam and Dresden, and sketched examples of Baroque architecture long before the style was considered worthy of study in academic circles. Wherever possible, Menzel sketched remaining vestiges of the precious century; he also studied French illustrators, not only his immediate rival Horace Vernet and his illustrations for *Histoire de l'Empereur Napoléon* by L'Ardèche but also Jean Gigoux's illustrations for Lesage's *Gil Blas*, and Auguste Raffet's wood engravings for de Norvin's *Histoire de Napoléon* of 1839[14].

It was, however, however, the rich pictorial and graphic art of the Rococo period that informed his renderings of the eighteenth century. His graphite drawings executed with fine lines reflect his familiarity with Watteau, Fragonard, Hubert Robert and Pesne. He also studied Anton Graff and Daniel Chodowiecki, and discovered artists like Johann Georg Ziesenis and Johann Christoph Frisch.

Shortly after Kugler's book appeared, its success brought him a further commission for wood engravings for the *Werke Friedrichs des Grossen* (The Works of Frederick the Great; *cf.* figs 106–11), a task which occu-

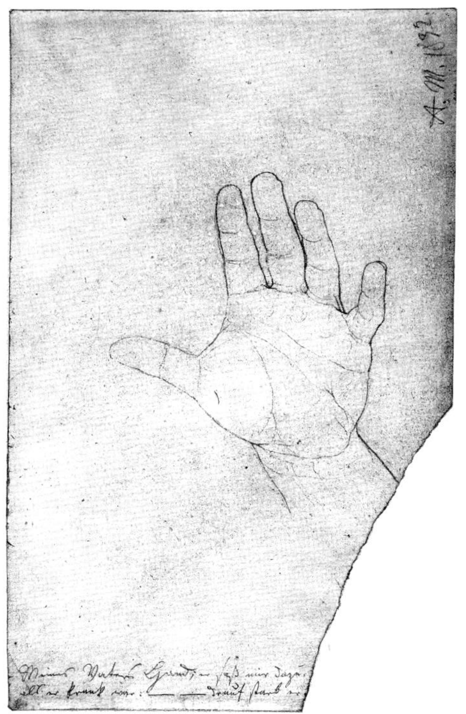

Fig. 123. *Father's Hand*, pencil, Berlin, Kupferstichkabinett (N 993)

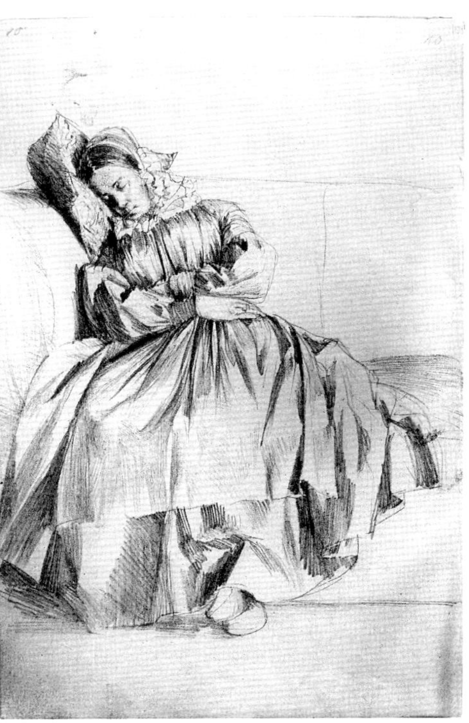

Fig. 124. *Menzel's Mother Sleeping*, 1836–46, pencil, Berlin, Kupferstichkabinett (sketchbook 7, p. 10)

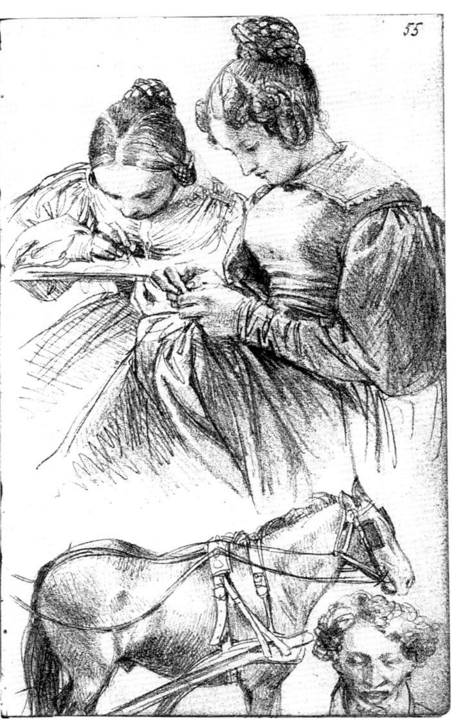

Fig. 125. *Two Women Embroidering*, 1836, pencil, Berlin, Kupferstichkabinett (sketchbook 4, p. 55)

pied him until 1849. If Menzel herein achieved the peak of his graphic inventiveness and skill at narrative illustration, the style of these drawings remained closely related to that which had marked the drawings for *Geschichte Friedrichs des Grossen.*

A sketchbook dating from the period 1839 to 1846 reflects the diversity of tasks with which he was engaged in this period, as well as stylistic changes. In the drawings that he did for Kugler, Menzel abandoned his stiff, sometimes almost wiry, linear style that recalled the work of Georg Friedrich Kersting or Friedrich Wasmann, replacing it with a style marked by slacker, more relaxed, strokes. Now areas of shade are drawn either in subtle contrast or in bold juxtaposition, capturing the varied textures of Biedermeier fabrics. The subjects of these drawings are most often taken from the world immediately around him, and there are occasional glimpses of the influence of Schadow's elegant draughtsmanship. Although it was Schadow who later criticized Menzel for his 'elegant style', Menzel adopted Rococo stylizations in order to characterize the period of Frederick the Great. In doing so he wished to convey to as wide a public as possible a sense of authenticity. Having himself battled against this 'styleless' Rococo epoch, Schadow naturally felt the need to comment. Schadow who had once praised the young and to him unknown illustrator of *Künstlers Erdenwallen*, now mistakenly maintained that the illustrations to Kugler's text were a step backward for the young Menzel, describing them as mere 'scribbles' and 'scrawls'[15].

Like his other drawings of the period, the contents of the sketchbook reflected Menzel's unshakable commitment to work; it is as if the sketchbook expressed his desire for survival. At the same time, Menzel's small family circle consisting of his mother, brother and sister continued to serve as a subject for him. He saw the inevitable craft aspect of art as part of its greatness[16], an opinion that brought him close to that of the Romantic painters. Moreover, the long hours he spent drawing from nature were for Menzel an exercise in discovering reality. Behind every slight, almost coincidental event captured by his pencil there lay a striving for greater meaning. It did not matter to him whether or not the drawings later served as studies for other works, they were the essential components of a body of work that, in its entirely, attained a coherent significance. They were, on the one hand, the signs of a single individual destiny; on the other they were also testimony to a century

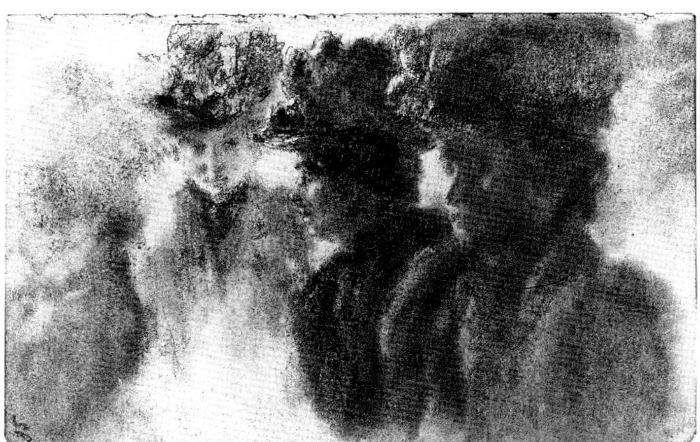

Fig. 126. *Three Women*, 1899–1902, pencil, Berlin, Kupferstichkabinett (sketchbook 74, p. 35)

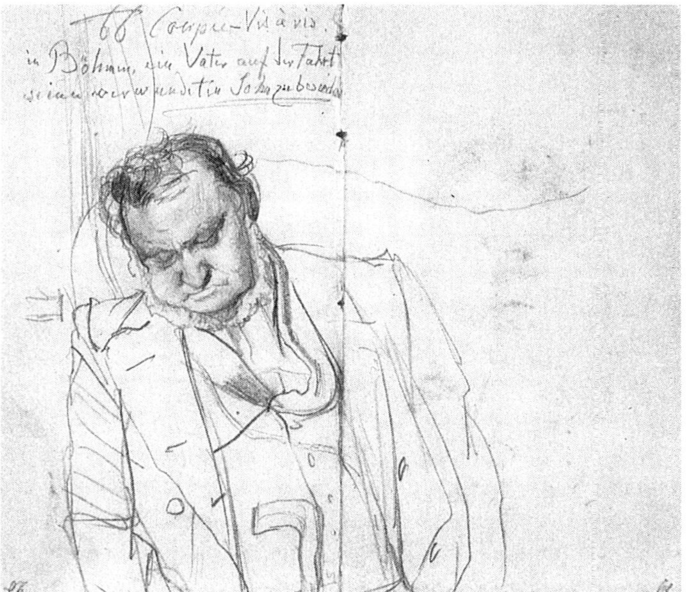

Fig. 127. *Man Asleep in a Railway Compartment*, 1866, pencil, Berlin, Kupferstichkabinett (sketchbook 29, p. 19–20)

whose fracturing of reality Menzel was perhaps one of the last artists to measure and preserve by elevating it to an historic dimension.

Even his earliest drawings were notable for the occasional, and apparently paradoxical, juxtaposition of sundry objects, which seem to have no relation to one another, but which seem to convey, simply because of their placement, a particular sentiment such as solitude, sadness or serene tranquility. This phenomenon may also be observed in his late works, although by this time his drawing style had changed quite substantially.

In 1844, probably after he had returned from a visit to his native Silesia, Menzel wrote: 'I now spend all my time painting (after nature, something I never did previously), engraving and drawing[17]'. This trip opened his eyes towards the painterly, though one must also note the influence of a Blechen or a Constable, both of whose work he was familiar with, the latter if only in two works. Since the mid-1840s Menzel had been producing paintings of a small format, mostly landscapes or interiors, which have often been characterized as 'pre-Impressionist'. This new, immediate sense of the differentiated play of colour and light was also reflected in drawings of the period. They become more self-assured and, one might say, more painterly. The stump is used alongside the pencil to create a range of tones; delicate modulations of grey begin to acquire more importance than the line. Areas of light and shade are created as the black of the lead pencil is smeared with the stump so that all lines softly fade.

Among the many graphite drawings of the 1840s are many that reveal only at second glance that they are less studies than complete, autonomous compositions, like the drawing of the artist's bed (cat. 17). It becomes evident that there is very little that is casual, or coincidental, about the artist's glance; here looking and thinking become one. The solid wood bed frame, the sheets and down blanket allow the pencil to be used diversely and to great effect, though it is the viewer's perception of casualness that overrides the materialism of the objects depicted. The same qualities that appear in the intimate paintings of the period, in which the small-scale format and the selected interior view emphasize the private, where also the momentary appearance of things is perceived as evocative of mood, are also features of the drawings of the period. Each moment that is fixed in a composition – in which the breath of life, so to speak, is discernible – invites not only viewing but reflection; a dialogue occurs on two levels.

In examining Menzel's work it appears that he frequently chose to depict new subjects or to experiment with new techniques but only when he felt he had complete command of the current set of challenges in painting or drawing. Aside from this external motivation that led him in the direction of change, there was the additional motivation of trying to overcome spiritual uncertainties. Uncertainties diminish in the act of creating by taking on a tangible existence of their own. In this way the path is cleared, allowing for new subjects and experimentations.

In the late 1840s, Menzel turned his attention to planning a series of paintings depicting the reign of Frederick the Great (*cf.* cat. 48, 49, 52, 56). During the 1850s he replaced preparatory sketches in pencil with pastel

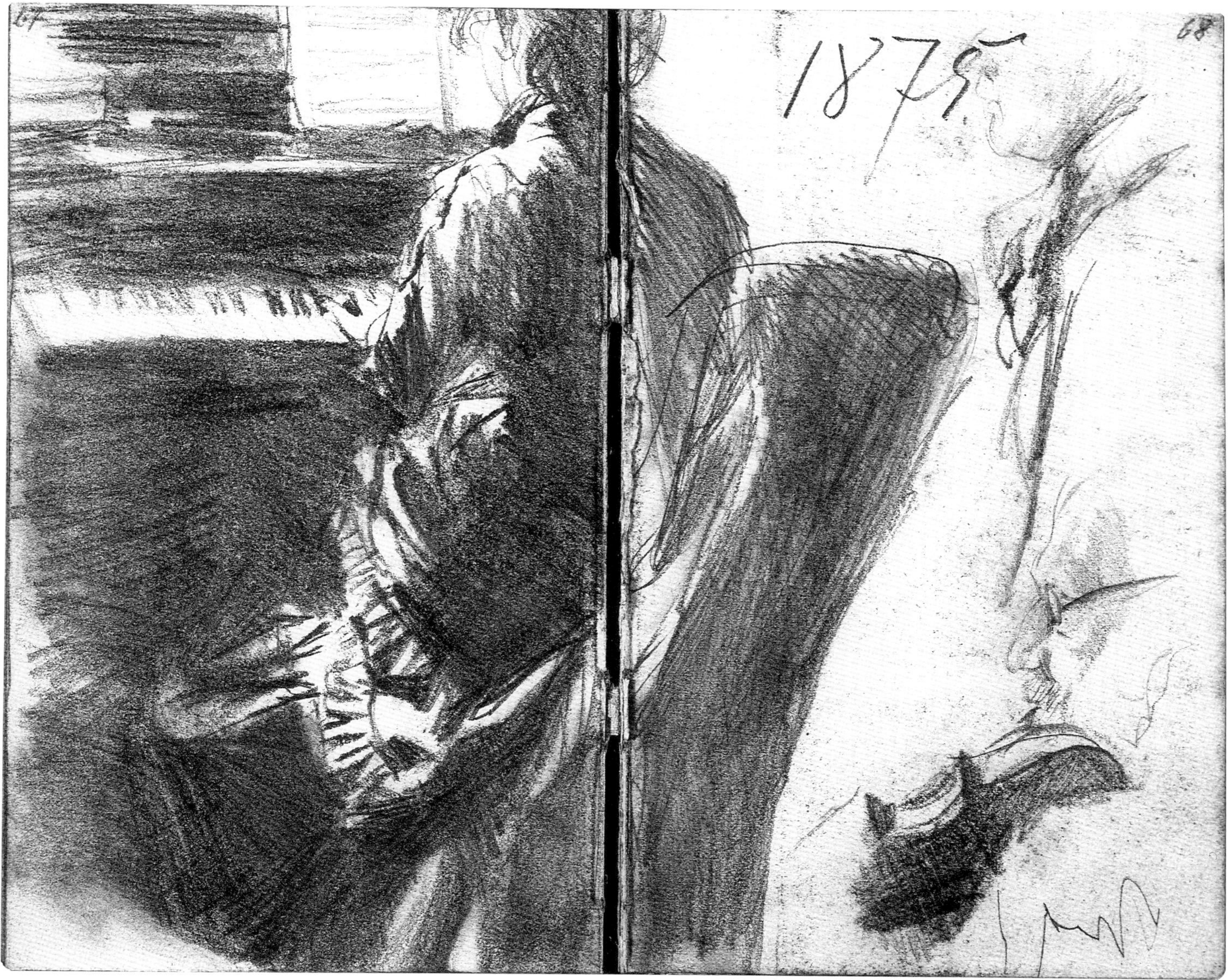

Fig. 128. *Woman at a Piano, Seen from the Back, and Detail of a Violinist* , 1875, pencil, Berlin, Kupferstichkabinett (sketchbook 48, p. 67–8)

studies, whose sumptuous surface he perhaps felt better suited the Rococo period he was depicting[18]. The majority of the drawings executed as studies for these paintings – frequently his brother or sister sat as models – are done in pastel. He often elected to use dark-toned paper as a background, allowing lighter pastel shades to stand out to greater effect. Dating from this period are also many pastel drawings depicting scenes from everyday life – people on the street, attending a concert, or in a railway compartment (*cf.* fig. 127) – and with his first long journey in 1852, many portraits were added to his repertoire. Because of inadequate techniques available for fixing pastels, the fragility of working in pastels led him to give up working in this medium[19]. He also took up watercolours in these years, producing many accomplished landscapes and portraits in this medium[20].

His favored medium for drawing, however, remained the graphite pencil. Unlike many artists of his time, Menzel did not view the pencil as a mere tool for sketching. Rather, throughout his career the variations and nuances he was able to call forth in this medium created effects that had never previously been seen in graphite drawings. Predictably, Menzel was also tempted to achieve similar results in etching. He was not satisfied merely to experiment in this medium, he also wanted to 'achieve results'[21]. It is difficult to say whether the melancholy landscapes of the 1840s, often devoid of figures, are more successfully executed in pencil or as etchings. A great admirer of the etchings of Rembrandt, the 'only one' for whom he had real admiration[22], Menzel ultimately returned to his pencil drawings, perhaps in the knowledge that it was in this medium that he would leave his most important legacy.

The influence of artists whose work was well-known to Menzel, such as Daniel Chodowiecki or Franz Krüger, was of tangential significance as he remained committed to an independence of spirit, drawn again and again to the natural world around him. His intensive dedication to a manner of drawing that became more and more painterly over time, which set him apart and even isolated him from his contemporaries, perhaps links him more closely to young Realists such as Wilhelm Leibl.

Let us turn to a few self-portraits which form only a very small group within his vast *oeuvre*, numbering only about ten. One of the most daring is a drastically foreshortened likeness, a reflection in a hand-held mirror held horizontally[23]. The wild, faun-like deformation of the face is accentuated by aggressive lines seemingly thrust rather than drawn onto what appears to be a cardboard support for drawings or paintings. When Friedrich Eggers saw the drawing, he associated it with ideas inherent in the age by drawing a parallel to the 'glove of Esau', which Menzel sheds: 'Outmoded traditions mask what is in nature, and deceive the untrained eye', writes Eggers, maintaining that only he is who knows the real is 'truly ideal'[24]. Menzel's own concerns were slightly different. Already as a twenty-one-year-old he wished to see objects depicted 'characteristically and ingeniously' rather than with awkward exactitude: as he commented laconically, 'not everything is truthful to nature, that is scrupulously copied'[25]. Nor did he intend that his means of studying reality should lead to the 'truly ideal'. With each new artistic experiment, he made a step towards a new artistic conception of reality.

Another self-portrait depicts Menzel standing behind his siblings and a cousin at the piano (cat. 61). Julius Meier-Graefe, a younger contemporary of Menzel, was perhaps the person to be most profoundly moved by the artist's work after his death, yet also disturbed by Menzel's assembled *oeuvre*. At times voicing brilliant assessments, at times overstated condemnations of select works, Meier-Graefe remarked that this drawing exhibited a strong basis in the real, in which appearances take on a permanence. He singled it out as a 'rare drawing' because it seemed not to have been executed in haste, in contrast to other drawings by Menzel: 'it departs from the usual, and reveals the master's true ability to achieve completion'[26]. Menzel's keen observational skills seem linked in Meier-Graefe's interpretation to a desire for a finished 'style'.

Moving on to a third self-portrait Menzel depicts himself in a half-length view holding a palette in his left hand and turning his head over his right shoulder to confront the spectator with intense eyes. The edge of the lens cuts through the pupil of his right eye. Aside from a few hatched strokes in the area of the overcoat and collar to create volume, the face, hair and beard consist only of contour lines which appear to suggest a conscious sense of determination[27]. The drawing is undated, though one is tempted to place it in the same period as the only known self-portrait in oil, representing Menzel in profile at his easel in close proximity to his brother and sister seated on a sofa. Although the painting has been dated to 1848 in the Menzel literature[28], the sturdy pencil strokes evident in the drawing, particularly in the treatment of the hand, as well as the authority of the artist's expression, may well place it in the late 1850s. There is an uncanny resemblance between the Baroque pose of the artist in this drawing, and that of Anton Graff in a self-portrait with his family in front of Sulzer's portrait then hanging in Friedrichsfelde Castle[29].

All subsequent self-portraits are drawings. The most unusual of these, found in a sketchbook from 1876, quite deliberately divides the face in two, an unabashedly frontal view showing just one eye. Fragmented forms are common in Menzel's work, occupying his attention well into the late drawings[30]. It can be assumed that he saw in the fragment the most logical way to make visible the momentary. Menzel captured transience most convincingly by recognizing its fragmentary essence. Dating from the period immediately after completion of the all-encompassing, monumental painting *Das Eisenwalzwerk* (The Iron Rolling Mill), the self-portrait appears to reject the possibility of representing the world as a closed totality. Indeed had not photography already called such art into question?

A new stage in his development as a draughtsman is revealed in the over 130 portrait studies for the large painting *The Coronation of William I* (fig. 121). For these he used a mixed technique in which he applied gouache or a thin wash of colour over the preliminary graphite drawing (cat. 94). Remarkable is the degree to which Menzel captures the unique physiognomies of his sitters in an unidealized, perhaps even disillusioned manner. With the consummate completion of this commission Menzel, then in his fiftieth year, carved out for himself a degree of freedom and a position of respectability as an artist in society that enabled him thereafter to select his own pictorial themes and subjects.

He devoted himself completely to the present and, in *The Iron Rolling Mill* reached a pinnacle of his art, not only in painting, but in the preparatory drawings for the composition as well (cat. 160). The over one hundred drawings reveal the extent to which Menzel was fascinated by technology, the industrial world, and by the people who worked in the enormous, new factories of the day (cats 150, 151, 153–9). The fact that he chose a larger format to represent theses figures, and that he exchanged his artist's pencil for a cruder carpenter's pencil, is clear evidence of the sympathy he brought to the task. His deep, personal involvement is strikingly present in all the drawings, and is undoubtedly one of the decisive factors in sustaining interest in, and admiration for, this work. Lichtwark reported that two whole walls of the artist's studio were devoted to reproductions of the works of Michelangelo, including photographs of David, Moses, and two prophets from ceiling of the Sistine Chapel[31]. It is conceivable that Menzel drew the inspiration for his imposing figures of workers from Michelangelo's monumental human figures. And it is certainly no coincidence that while working on this painting Menzel returned to his study of antique sculpture (*cf.* cat. 146), particularly to the classical figures on the pediment of the Parthenon. With the width of the carpenter's pencil he outlined with broad lines the larger forms, using the pencil point for sharper lines that appear almost scratched into the paper. The stump is not utilized; there is no need for its resultant softness in a composition which depicts the vehement power of human movement. Even in the drawings he executed in the studio, one senses the rumble of the massive machinery that he witnessed and the nervous excitement of his visits to the Silesian mill in 1872. It is likely that the models were not individuals chosen at random, but workers at the Royal Foundry in Berlin. The director of the foundry was the father of his brother-in-law Krigar, and it is known that before its closing in 1874 Menzel executed some sketches on site. An echo of Menzel's preparatory sketches is possibly to be seen in the young Käthe Kollwitz's cycle of etchings, The *Weaver's Revolt* from the 1890s.

By the mid-1880s Menzel had completed all of his oil paintings on the theme of urban life. Following the last of this these, the *Marketplace in Verona* (cat. 179) with its artfully constructed composition depicting the noisy tumultuousness of the masses, he painted only small-scale pictures. After 1892 he used only gouache, more easily managed than oil paint. In 1901 he worked for the last time in colour, in the small gouache, the *End of Yom Kippur.* Preparatory pencil drawings dating from this period served to give his late gouaches and oils an immediate impression of reality, a vital sense of the moment and an aura of authenticity. Only in the precision of details is there a spiritual rapport with the late work in colour. The capturing of detail by an observant eye and the committing to paper of everything seen – this often included noting down minute details such as measurements and colours – reflected a kind of ever-restless curiosity. Transferred to painting, only the bare essentials remained of this profusion. By comparison with the few late works in colour, the pencil drawings occupy an increasingly important place in his artistic creativity. The graphite pencil becomes the single-most important tool. Together with the small sketchbooks that he could slip into his pocket – he always carried at least one – Menzel always carried pencils with him on the long trips he took until his last summer in 1904. It was in these sketchbooks that he collected his observations. His focus was on light and shade, and on perspective: two aspects that could best be studied with the possibilities offered by work in pencil. On the tiny pages of these sketchbooks, things that drew the artist's glance are captured with calm but intense observation.

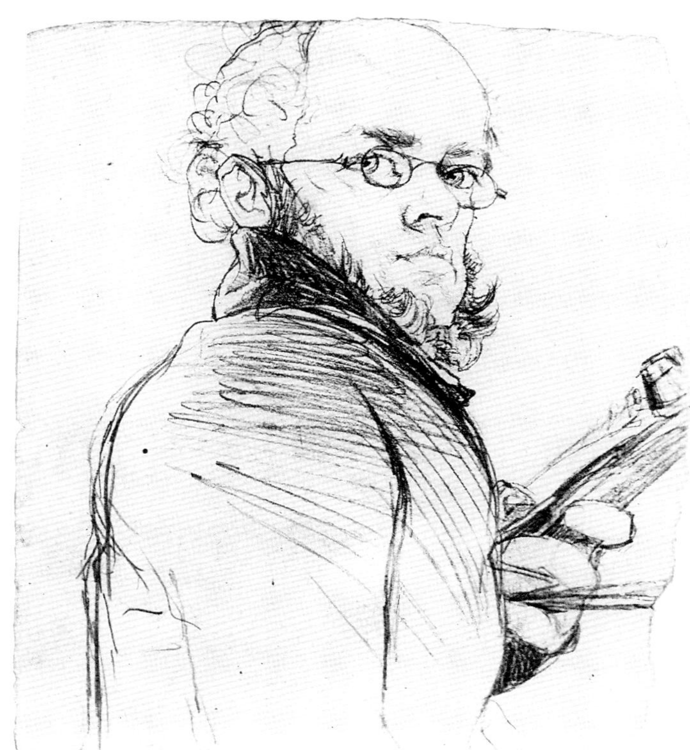

Fig. 129. *Self-portrait Holding a Palette*, *c.* 1850–5, pencil, private collection

The sketchbooks dating from Menzel's later years

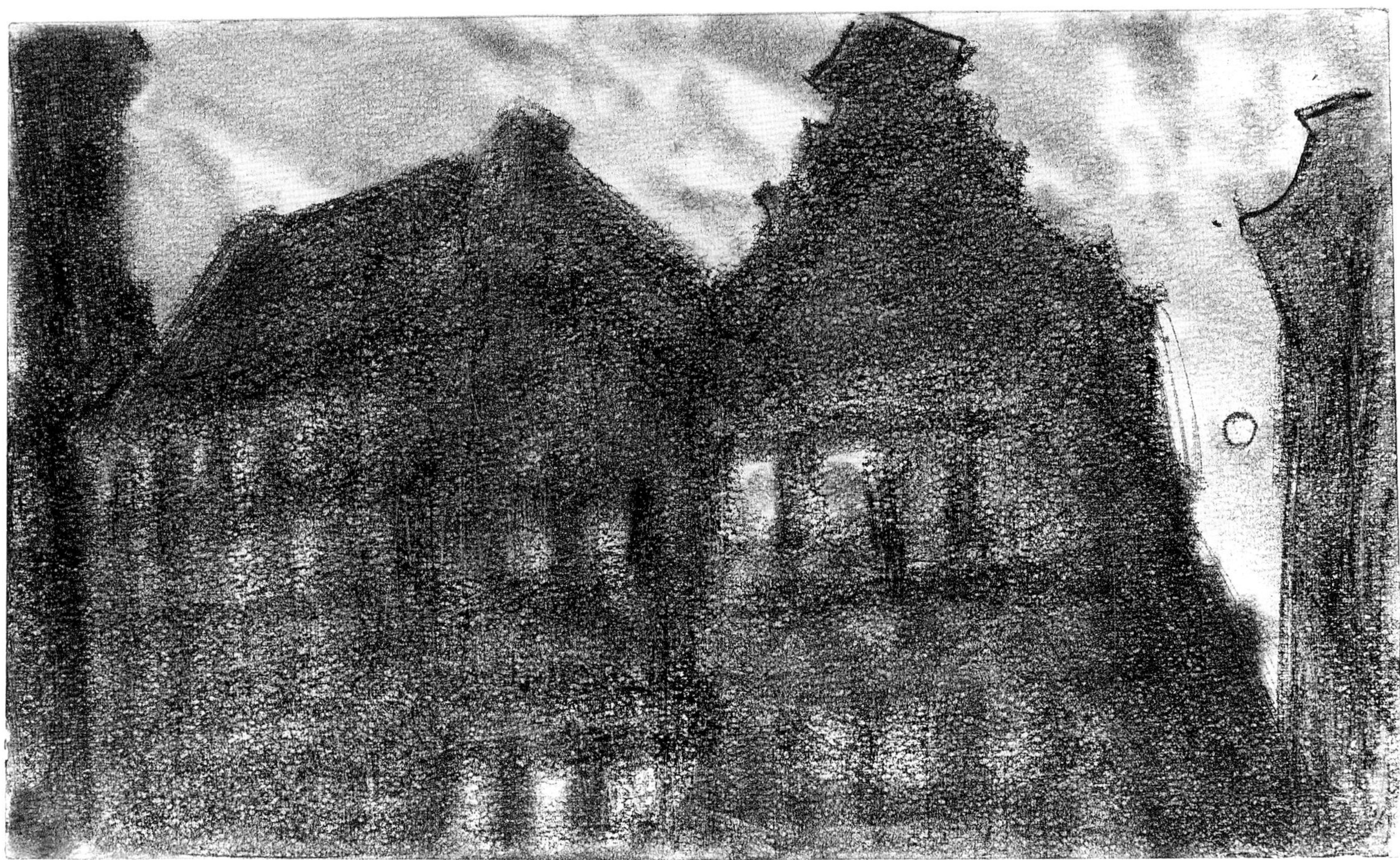

Fig. 130. *Houses in the Moonlight*, *c.* 1890, pencil, Berlin Kupferstichkabinett, Berlin (N 2606)

were notebooks the size of pocket diaries, bound in leather or cardboard, bought by the artist when and as he needed them. These small, fragile objects contain the invaluable source material for a lifetime. He was left-handed, or at least he preferred to do sketches with his left hand, though he displayed equal skill with either hand from an early age. Most often he started on the last page, thereby seeking to avoid smudging drawings as they took shape[32]. Even then, the pencil images, as fragile as the paper on which they were executed, bear distressing scars from the passing of time, caused additionally by the frequently careless treatment to which they have been exposed since the artist's death; the astonishing painterly composition and delicacy of the studies preserved in the sketchbooks have lost much of their original vitality. Menzel rarely used pen and ink for drawings, and the nature of graphite drawings, particularly in the way that Menzel carried them out, has disadvantages in terms of preservation. Menzel himself wrote of his small sketchbooks,'They contain many things that are extremely personal to me'[33].

The frequently mentioned loneliness that afflicted Menzel as an old man was most likely the result of being passed over by a younger generation of artists. Theodor Fontane wrote, 'Menzel, the leading celebrity of our circle, is in excellent health despite his seventy years and remains full of drive and energy for his work. But it also has to be said that fashions change, and the younger generation – none of whom can hold a candle to him – treat him as if he were a famous mummy or ancient relic to whom one raises one's hat but without offering any additional gestures of veneration'[34].

Menzel's skill with pencil and stump reached new heights in the late drawings. Working with extraordinary vehemence until the end, he nonetheless used the graphite pencil with gentleness and a light tough, skilfully manipulating grey and black tones. His genius can be discerned in the way in which he transformed reality into signs, making of seemingly unimportant or fragmented forms something of profound significance. Here the influence of Japanese prints with their miniature precision and irregular perspectives, that Menzel would have been able to see and study at in the 1880s at his dealer's, Hermann Pächter[35], can be seen in the late drawings.

Although Menzel continued to draw dramatic views of Baroque architecture during his journeys, in the late drawings he was often attracted by the strange, the peculiar. Darkly lit, picturesque street corners and alleys, dilapidated houses and sheds are subjects of the late drawings: everywhere he saw ruin, destruction, ugliness. These drawings exhibit an uncanny charm, his virtuosity producing an abundance of novel variations. In his landscapes he was captivated by trees whose bizarre contortions become humanized with branches stretching like arms to the sky. The drawings Menzel made in St Peter's cemetery in Salzburg are jolting. What could have caused him to depict the desolation of the graves in the way he did? Menzel certainly no longer saw the 'intact world' as Ferdinand Olivier and Julius Schnorr von Carolsfeld had done in their 'romantic' views of this cemetery.

It was only in the last decade of Menzel's life that a distinct calm sets in. He no longer perceived things around him with the same detachment he had shown in earlier years. Now his eyes fixed on human beings with apparent benevolence and compassion. The loneliness that old age imposed on him in no way prevented him from remaining an unusually alert observer. In addition to his relentless desire to work, an interest in social and psychological matters encouraged him to receive models at his studio every day. Mostly these were old men and women who came to Menzel's third floor studio, waited on the steps and earned a little money for sitting for him. It was a remarkable, final theme. For the most part he drew half-length portrait studies of groups of individuals or heads of elderly men and women with great painterly sensitivity (*cf.* cat. 215–18). The graphite pencil is used to create gentle, finely differentiated shadings for the last time. A strange, simulated perspective hardly distinguishes between near and far; fundamentally important is only the spiritual expression of unrelated faces placed side by side. In an almost dream-like way, as if seen through a fog, the faces glance at or past one another. Their enigmatic facial expressions ranging from joy to sadness are perhaps those that moved Menzel as he drew.

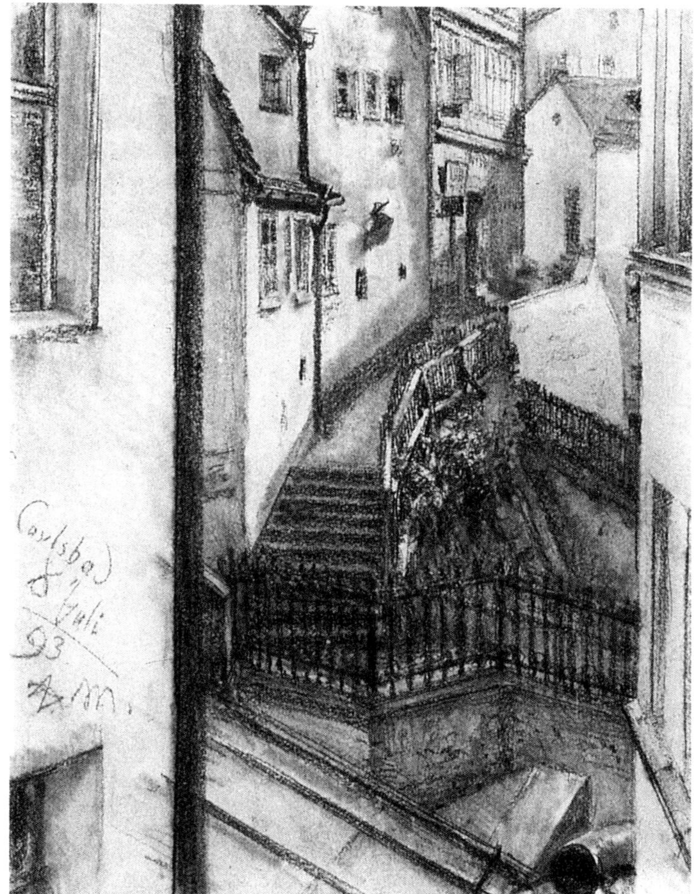

Fig. 131. *Narrow Street with Steps in Carlbad*, 1895, pencil, Berlin, Kupferstichkabinett (SZ Menzel, N 170)

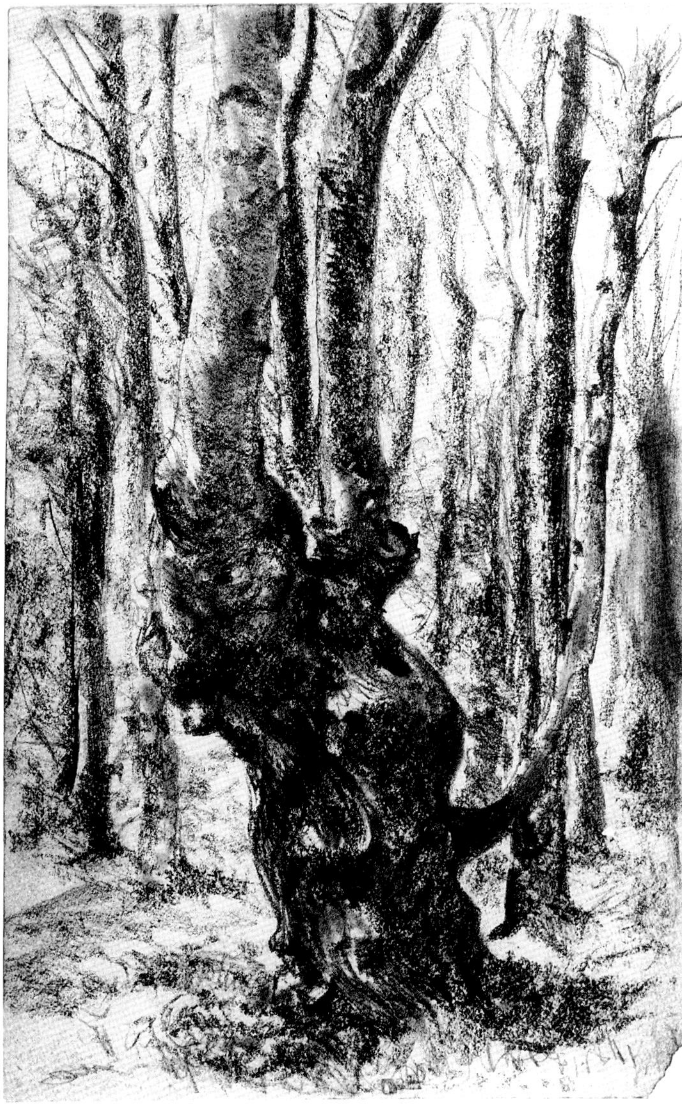

Fig. 132. *Tree trunks*, *c.* 1880–90, pencil, Warsaw, Muzeum Narodowe

1. Johann Peter Eckermann, *Gespräche mit Goethe*, Berlin and Wiemar, 1982, p. 663.
2. An allusion to the final prayer that Faust addresses to the passing moment as he is on the point of dying: 'Stay now! You are so beautiful!' (Goethe, *Faust* Part II, line 11 582) [N.d.T.]
3. Jordan, 1904–5, p 265.
4. Letter to Karl Bormann, 6 May 1882, Wolff, 1914, p. 226. '. . . a pressing destiny bore down on me: without doubt you are not yet mature enough to marry, but you are mature enough to be head of the family. It was thus that destiny spoke and carried my father off. And today I must proclaim, "Blessed are the tempests of life! (although I do not wish them on anyone)."'
5. *Cf.* Pecht, 1887, p. 331. One of these early pencil drawings by Menzel is entitled *Publius Cornelius Scipio und Lucius Caecilius Metellus. Nach einer Aufgabe des Hrn. Prof. Dr. Büsching.* (Publius Cornelius Scipio and Lucius Cecilius Metellus. Homework given by Professor Büsching) and bears the signature 'Adolph Menzel alt 13 Jahr inv.:& del: 46:50cm' (Adolph Menzel aged 13, inv.:& del: 46 x 50 cm).
6. This and subsequent quotations are taken from a *curriculum vitae* written by Menzel himself on 8 November 1853. He was elected to the Academy on 30 April 1853. Quoted by Lammel 195, p. 54 *et seq.*
7. Letter to Ludwig Pietsch, 24 December 1879, Wolff, 1914, p. 221. These words of Menzel refer to his late friend, the painter Eduard Magnus.
8. This magazine was both popular and, as its title (*Penny Magazine*) suggests, cheap. The Swiss publisher and bookseller, Johann Jakob Weber, brought out the *Pfennig-Magazin* in 1833 through the Bossange père subsidiary in Leipzig. Weber, who had settled in Leipzig in 1830, later published Franz Kugler's *Geschichte Friedrichs des Grosen.*
9. *Cf.* Sketchbook 1, p. 11. References to 'Erinnerung' (from memory) are most frequent in the early drawings; numerous theater sets were also done from memory.
10. *Cf.* Stargardt Sale catalogue, Berlin, 1938, cat. 399, No 249. *Cf.* Jordan 1905, p. 2.
11. *Cf.* Menzel's notes on a drawing for Kugler's *Geschichte Friedrichs des Grossen* and *Werke Friedrichs des Grossen*. Berlin, Kupferstichkabinett (SZ Menzel cat. 129).
12. *Cf.* Stargardt Sale catalogue, Berlin, 1938, cat. 399, No 246 and 247.
13. Kugler, 1911, Vol, 2.II, p. 1725.
14. *Cf.* Entrup, 1995.
15. *Cf.* letters of 3 April 1840 to Weber and of 6 September 1840 to C H Arnold, Wolff, 1914, p. 43 and 48. *Cf.* also Eckardt, 1989, p. 36–46.
16. Letter to Fritz Werner, 10 March 1856, Wolff, 1914, p. 171: 'It is so true that the more a person is suited for art, the more he is disheartened by the craft aspect of his work. But all art is craft, something that has to be learned with difficulty, and that is where the greatness of art lies.'
17. Letter to C. H. Arnold, 25 April 1844, Wolff, 1914, p. 79.
18. Menzel used this technique more as a draughtsman than as a painter. The pastel technique was used most extensively in France during the Rococo period.
19. *Cf.* Meyerheim, (1906) 1992, p. 161.
20. Letter to C. H. Arnold, 21 January 1842, Wolff, 1914, p. 64. On the subject of his initial, unsuccessful attempts at painting in water colours, Menzel wrote: 'It I was a bit of a know-all, I would say that I gave up watercolours because the colours fade. In fact, I am in the same position as someone who has been twice thrown by his new horse, and has to climb back on again. I am damned put out.'
21. *Cf.* letter to C. H. Arnold, 22 July 1843, Wolff, 1914, p. 78.
22. *Ibid*, p. 79: '. . . most of all Rembrandt who is, and continues to be, the only one. The more one studies him, the more respect one has for him, and not for his lighting effects, but for his composition, his understanding of nature and his sense of form! We hear from those dunces – I mean those pedantic gentlemen with their heads stuck in dictionaries – that he did not known how to draw! In the sense that these gentlemen in Munich and Düsseldorf mean, no, he certainly did not!'
23. Berlin, Kupferstichkabinett (SZ Menzel cat 3).
24. Eggers, (1854) 1924, p. 7–8. Esau's younger brother Jacob received the blessing of his blind father when his mother dressed him in fur – Eggers refers to this as the 'glove of Esau' – to simulate Esau's rougher skin. *cf.* I. Moses, Chapter 27.
25. Letter to Wilhelm Puhlmann, 5 November 1836, Wolff, 1914, p. 15.
26. Meier-Graefe 1906, p. 54.
27. At one time, this self-portrait was thought to have disappeared. It was then exhibited at the Academy of Art, Berlin, in 1955; at that time, it belonged to Ingrid Brebeck, the granddaughter of Menzel's sister, who lived in Berlin. The drawing is now part of a private collection in Hamburg.
28. The self-portrait in oil with his brother and sister is thought to have disappeared. It appears in Kirstein, 1919, in the frontispiece on p. 116, together with

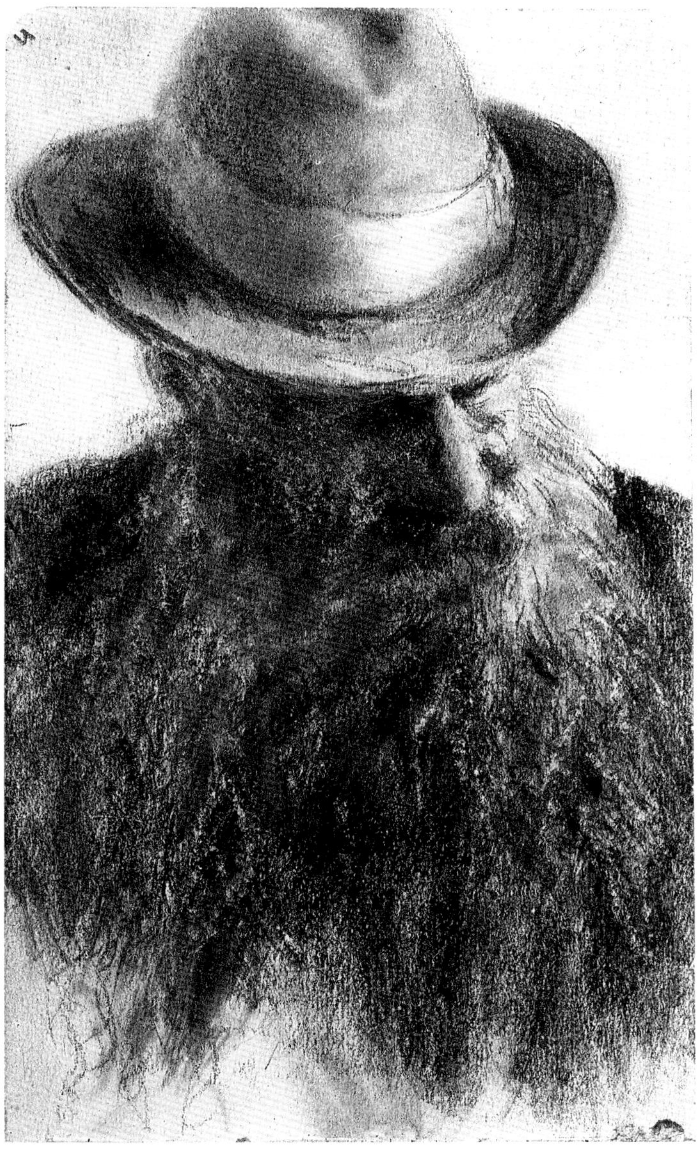

Fig. 133. *Bearded Old Man Wearing a Hat*, 1903, pencil, Berlin, Kupferstichkabinett (sketchbook 77, p, 4)

the name of the owner at the time, Marcus Kappel of Berlin.

29. Anton Graff, *Self-portrait with family in front of the portrait of Johann Georg Sulzer*, oil, 1785. Since 1949 this has been in the possession of the Museum Stiftung Oskar Reinhart in Winterthur. *Cf.* Franz Zelger, Stiftung Oskar Reinhart, Winterthur, Vol I, No 85, reprod. p. 185.

30. Berlin, Kupferstichkabinett, Sketchbook 51, p. 69–70. *Cf.* Schmidt, 1858, p. 97-119.

31. *Cf.* Lichtwark's description of Menzel's studio, 11 March 1896, (1924) 1992, p. 297.

32. Max Jordan is the first to mention that the artist was left-handed. *Cf.* Jordan, 1905, p. 14.

33. Recalling a visit to Menzel on 24 December 1904, Paul Lindenberg remembers the artist saying, 'I am always accompanied by a sketchbook like this, whenever I go for a walk or make a journey. I have filled up over 50 of them. They are my memories. They contain things that are extremely personal to me.'

34. Letter to Hermann Wichmann, 7 July 1894, Fontane, 1980, vol. II, p. 343.

35. *Cf.* Lichtwark, 1972, p. 140.

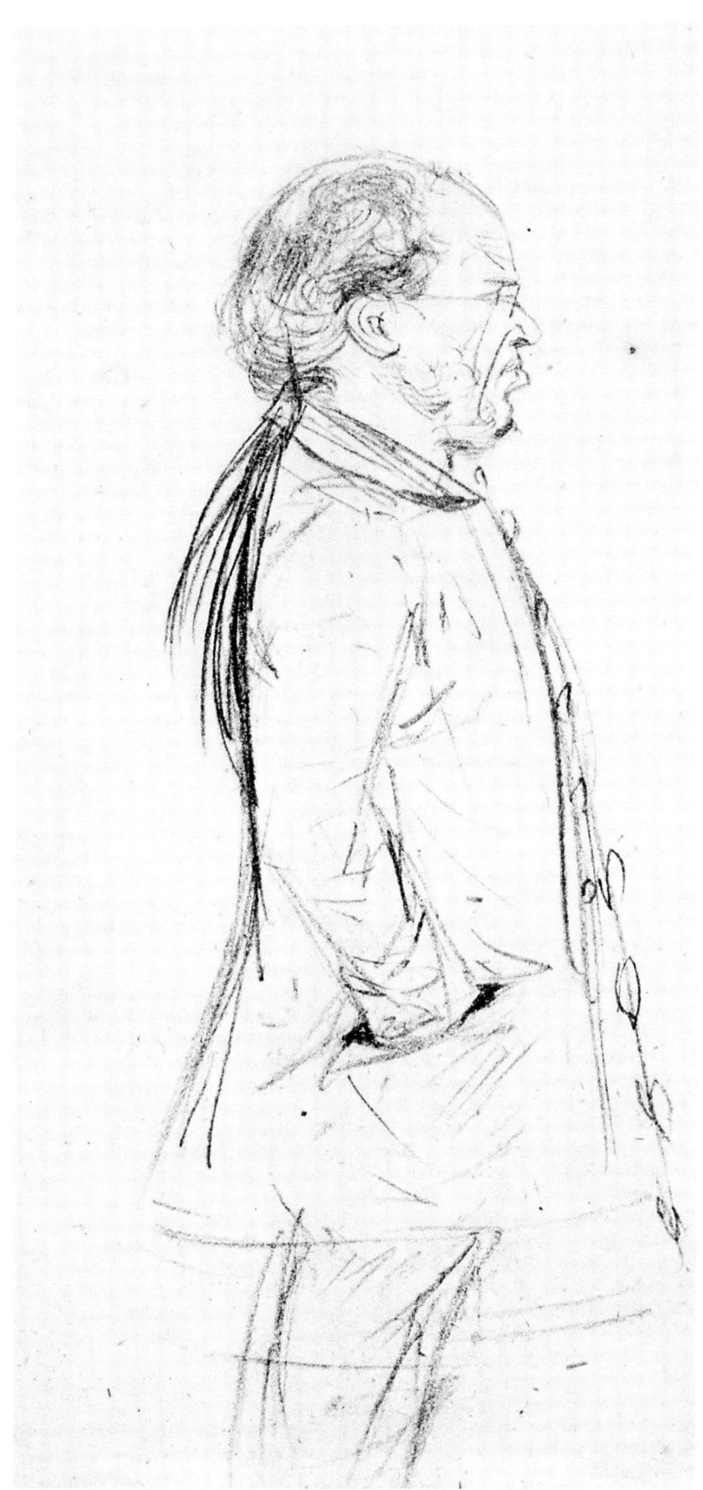

Fig. 134. *Self-portrait with a Morose Expression*, *c.* 1860, pencil, Berlin, Kupferstichkabinett (SZ Menzel, Kat. 2)

Menzel's modernity

Peter-Klaus Schuster

1. The labyrinthine city

In 1995, a strange contest was held at the Grand Palais in Paris: between Caillebotte and Poussin. This extraordinary event, intended to attract the attention of the general public, contrasted the contingent and the absolute in art. And, in the eyes of perceptive critics, it was Poussin – great champion of the absolute, of Classicism purified of every incidental element, whose work is reckoned to represent a return to antiquity *à la française* – who emerged the loser in the contest for public favour[1].

'Victory' went to Caillebotte – by a long chalk considering the number of visitors – an amateur painter who, in a few remarkable canvases, captured the appearance of late nineteenth-century Paris with icy precision. Caillebotte's perspective is that of an outsider, who discovers a sublime monumentality in the humdrum everyday sights of the modern urban landscape. Workmen planing a floor display the violent energy of human carnivores. Men in top hats walking along beside the geometric metal girders of newly built bridges have the air of curious tourists in the exotic land of modern technology. And a rainy day on the Boulevard Haussmann suggests a melancholy outing into the great empty spaces of bourgeois triviality. Every element of Caillebotte's paintings can be identified and dated with accuracy. It would be no surprise to read the inscription 'Schneider-Creusot' on his iron girders. With extreme precision, he pinpoints a randomly chosen time and place, which – beyond the established conventions of classical culture, beyond even the colour harmonies of the Impressionist world – exercises an obsessive fascination, in both its details and in overall impact[2]. The spectator feels like a witness at the scene of the crime, a setting precisely determined by the artist. At the same time, he has the sense of being in the heart of a mysterious city, which looking alone cannot assimilate.

Another elusive city, bigger even than Paris, is Berlin. Not constructed on an exact and easily remembered grid pattern, having no natural landmarks (such as a hill or promiment, flowing river), Berlin grew up into a labyrinth of streets, waterways and rails, meandering through the flat, sandy landscape. When he visited Berlin in 1806, Stendhal expressed astonishment at the idea of a city built on sand[3]. Sinuous and vaguely defined, beginning with the historical core of palace, cathedral, opera house, university and a few museums, in the nineteenth century Berlin spread out in all directions, with the building of new streets, squares, houses, churches, stations, schools, barracks, schools and stereotyped factories. In the industrial era, Berlin became an immense patchwork, endlessly repeating its original pattern. The patchwork was constantly being undone and restitched at various points. Hence the difficulty that still exists in getting one's bearings.

Menzel is the observer of this amorphous city. His friend, the writer Theodor Fontane, pointed out at the time that Menzel was possible only in Berlin, to which he owed everything. It is impossible to imagine Menzel in the country, in a village or in a small town[4]. Menzel, the tireless recording eye of the city, wearer of gold-rimmed spectacles, would take opera glasses with him when he went out drawing. His pencil was described as an 'optic nerve in action'. He could draw as skilfully with his left hand as with his right[5]. It was this Menzel whom Jules Laforgue – French tutor to the empress at the court of Berlin in 1884 – admired as 'an eye of formidable pen-

Fig. 135. Gustave Caillebotte, *Paris Street, Rainy Day*, 1877, The Art Institute of Chicago, Worcester Fund

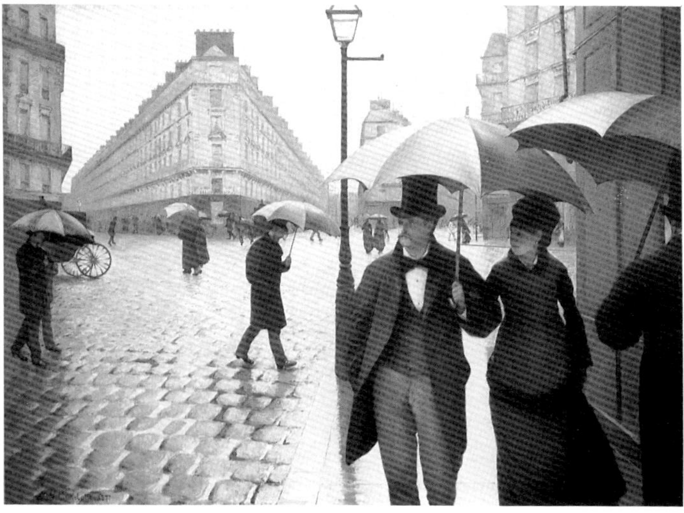

etration' and 'Germany's greatest painter'[6]. This Menzel, so attached to the labyrinthine development of Berlin as a growing European metropolis, should have taken his place, as one of the masters of modernity, among the foremost artists of the nineteenth century.

2. Menzel's diversity

But it was not to be. After his death, Menzel was more and more neglected abroad, and even in Germany his modernity was only partially recognized. The paintings of Menzel's youth, shown for the first time in 1905 at the commemorative exhibition at the Nationalgalerie, have always been considered extremely modern. Their impressionism is apparent, several decades *avant la lettre*, especially in the miraculous atmospheric colour of the *Balcony Room* (cat.18). 'What would the French reaction have been', – writes Meier-Graefe, 'if Menzel had conceived the idea in 1856, the year in which *The Théâtre du Gymnase* was painted, of sending this painting, and others such as the 1845 *Balcony Room*, to the Salon?'[7] The young Menzel was undoubtedly modern in outlook, and this included politics. As a liberal member of the middle class, he was openly in sympathy with the 1848 Revolution, and created for the victims of this revolution in his *Lying in State of the March Dead*, a painting heralding politically committed art. Until a ripe old age, Menzel always refused to subordinate himself to the State authorities. Thus, he opposed Bismarck, who had forbidden German artists to take part in the Universal Exhibition of 1889 in France. Together with his younger colleagues Uhde and Liebermann, Menzel exhibited his work in Paris in defiance of all patriotic opposition[8]. Menzel's industrial paintings were to become the quintessence of his modernity. *The Iron Rolling Mill* (cat. 160), finished in 1875 and acquired by the Nationalgalerie in the same year with the alternative title *Modern Cyclopes*, was certainly the most exciting painting in the barely inaugurated temple of contemporary art. But alienation, the darker side of industrial progress, could also be detected in the setting of his *Studio Wall* (cat. 65), and this came to be seen as the leitmotif, highly relevant to the times, of Menzel's art[9].

So, although in his modernity Menzel lived up to the aesthetic credo 'one must belong to one's time', from which Baudelaire, Daumier and Manet also drew inspiration, in other respects we find a disappointing contrast. His pitiless judgement of the paintings of Manet and other Impressionists he had got to know at the Berlin salon of Felicie Bernstein, cousin of Charles Ephrussi, has often been quoted. 'Dear Madam', wrote Menzel in apologizing to his hostess, 'I am very sorry to have used such violent language about paintings you admire so much. But I am fully convinced of what I said'[10]. It was Meissonier, not Manet, that Menzel chose to visit on his trips to Paris (*cf.* cat. 126). Not Degas, but his friends Alfred Stevens and Giovanni Boldini were the painters closest to his own artistic idiom. Again, we find Menzel in Berlin expressing fellow-feeling with official Salon painting. He briefly showed benevolence towards the young Liebermann, whereas in his old age he expressed 'special admiration' for the history painter Anton von Werner, director of the Academy, whose works had the precision of postcards[11] (*cf.* fig p.17). Nevertheless, Menzel certainly took a sufficiently objective view of Manet's exhibition in 1867 and the paintings the future Impressionists sent to the Salon in 1867 and 1868. His long visit to Courbet's 'Pavilion of Realism' is well attested. Moreover, his works were regularly shown in the exhibitions organized by the Berlin Secession, under the auspices of its president Max Liebermann, though these came from private collections and he contributed nothing himself.

One cannot avoid sensing that there were several Menzels, an impression that is confirmed in the political field. After 1839, Menzel, the bourgeois liberal, plunged into the aristocratic, rococo world of Frederick the Great. Taking advantage of the king's growing popularity and creating the image of a sovereign solicitous of his subjects' well-being, Menzel promoted the idea of a Prussia imbued with French Enlightenment ideals. Once this artistic vision of a close link between power and spirit was formed, we find Menzel, loaded with honorary titles, carrying out commissions for the Hohenzollerns and working as a portraitist at the court in Berlin, now set on its course towards the German imperial crown. 'To the herald of the glory of Frederick the Great' were the words on the wreath laid by Wilhelm II on Menzel's coffin[12]. A great admirer of the painter, the young emperor had bestowed on him the highest honours, including a title. Moreover, above the writing desk in the emperor's study hung Menzel's painting of the *Night Attack at Hochkirch* (fig. 120), serving as a constant reminder. It portrays Frederick the Great at the moment of one of his worst military defeats, like a ghostly rider in the midst of his exhausted, traumatized troops. The painting's disjointed structure conveys the historical disaster with vivid reality. The history painter obsessed with detail is shown to be a visionary realist.

The disturbing diversity of Menzel's work and the influence he exercised during his lifetime here seems concentrated as by a magnifying glass. He was both the favourite painter of a conservative political élite, almost

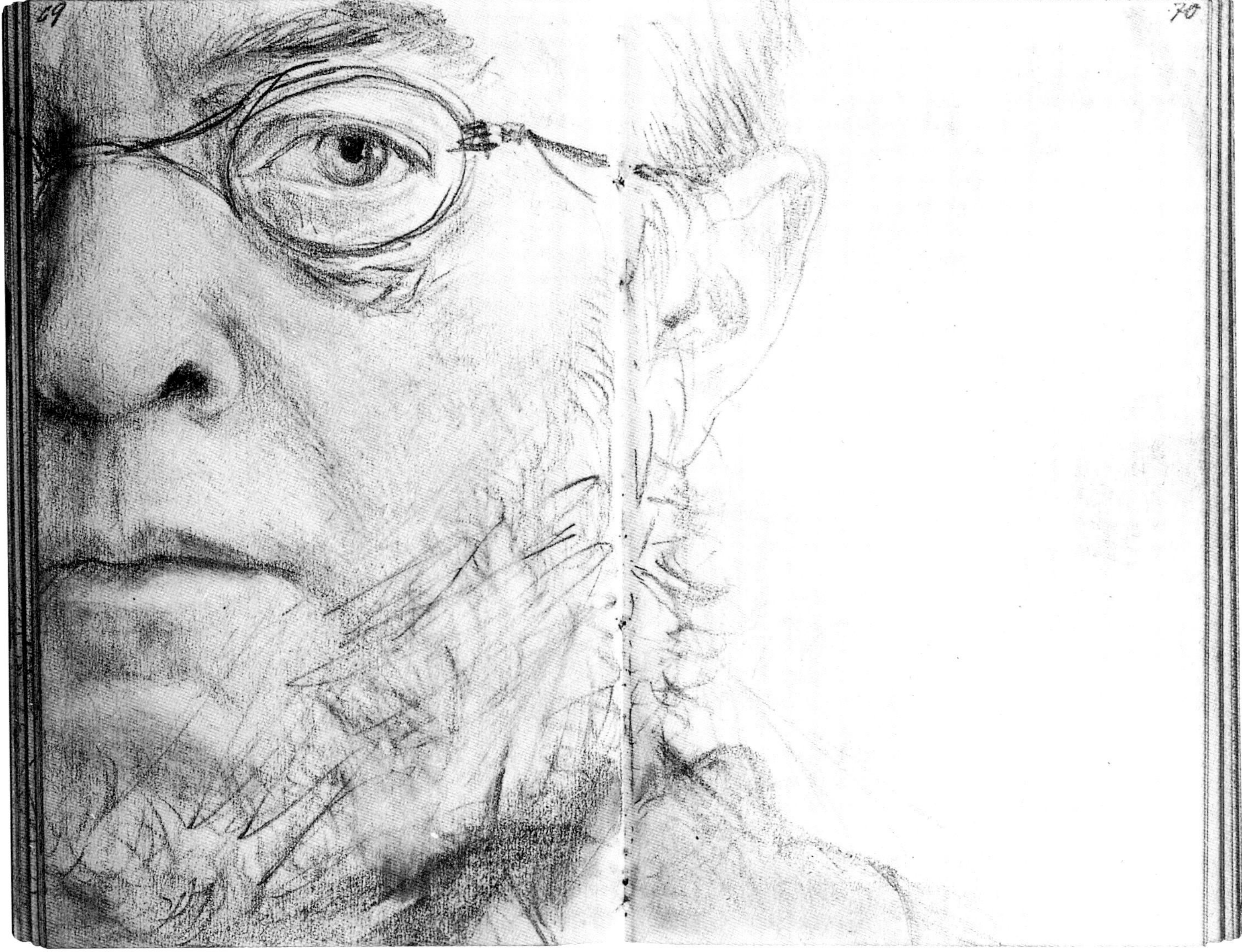

Fig. 136. *Partial Self-Portrait*, 1876, pencil, Berlin, Kupferstichkabinett (sketchbook 51, p. 69–70)

the emperor's official painter, and the preacher who warned of the imminent decline of Prussia, just as it stood on the brink of becoming a world power. This awareness of crisis is evident in *Night Attack at Hochkirch*, where, flaunting convention, the painter sacrifices continuity in the elements of the picture to add in scenic snapshots, optical sections of the chaos of war. This disjointed, multifaceted history painting is reminiscent of a panorama, or even of the cinema, which, to convey the unfolding of such dramatic action, must needs have been invented during Menzel's lifetime.

3. Modern trends

Positivism

Our perplexity in the face of Menzel's diversity is echoed in a poem written by Fontane to mark the painter's seventieth birthday in 1885. Questioned about Menzel by Frederick the Great, Fontane answers:

Indeed, who is Menzel? Menzel is many things,
If not everything; he is in any case
A great Noah's ark, animal and human being:
Turkeys, geese, parrots and ducks,

Schwerin and Seydlitz, Leopold von Dessau,
The old Zieten, wet nurses, apprentice locksmiths,
Catholic churches, Italian squares,
Shoe buckles, bronzes, rolling mills,
Town councils with or without chain of office,
Morose ministers in cashmere trousers,
Ostrich feathers, court balls, lobster mayonnaise,
The Emperor, Moltke, Countess Hacke, Bismarck . . .[13]

Laforgue and others also resorted to such catalogues to describe Menzel's artistic universe[14]. They thus confirm Fontane's essential argument: Menzel is everything. The painter himself reinforced this definition in an oft-quoted saying: 'Every drawing is useful, and drawing everything is useful, too'[15]. In one of Menzel's plates for the youthful work *Book of Life*, published in 1835, 'everything' is shown being poured out from two horns of plenty by the goddess Fortune, taking the form of a multiplicity of random objects. In fact, they are structured in terms of rich and poor: the prosaic instruments associated with manual labour fall heavily from the horn of plenty in the goddess's left hand, while the horn on the right showers forth the sweet attributes of glory, honour and wealth. Thirty years later, the fullness of life, or more exactly of history, appears unchanged in Menzel's *Studio Wall* (cat. 137): a multiplicity of objects forming a cosmos of fragments of plaster, apparently arranged haphazardly and without hierarchy by the painter. Everything is included: from a dog's head, via the mask of a poet, to the body of Venus. Referring indiscriminately to past and present, Menzel's plaster casts bear witness to an eagerness to grasp hold of everything available in the visible world.

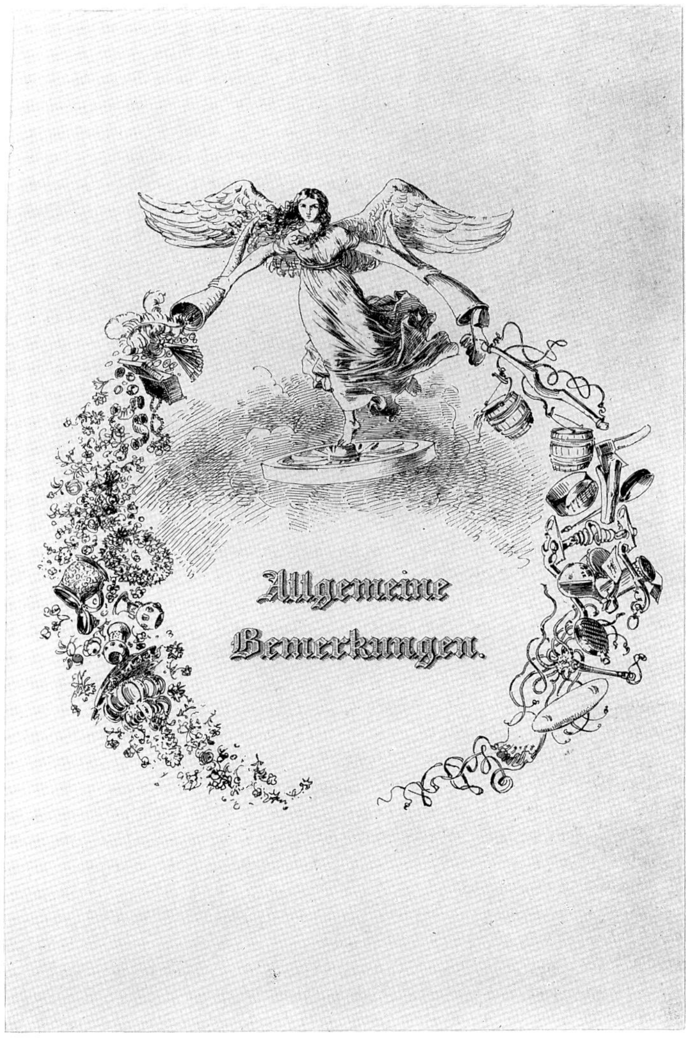

Fig. 137. Title page for chapter 6 of the *Book of Life*, 1836, lithograph (B 138)

Menzel's drawings, heaped together in cardboard boxes in his studio, were his major source of artistic detail. This studio (fig. 140), bizarrely overflowing with an encyclopaedic collection of objects, archive of a universal vision of both past and present, never failed to fascinate visitors. Depending on the visitor's bent, the last studio in the Sigismundstrasse, which he had occupied for years, gave the impression of total chaos, picturesque bric-à-brac, a pile of dirty rubbish left to its own devices, or a reserve of artistic motifs. In 'possibly the ugliest artist's studio to be found in Berlin', some saw 'a disturbing setting' where a painter, scientist and vivisectionist possessed by his objects surrounded his visual prey with the 'skeletons' of his unfinished works. Visitors commonly stressed the sobriety, simplicity and humility of Menzel's studio, located on the fourth floor of a house giving on to a courtyard, 'isolated above the apartments with human occupants'[16].

It is impossible to avoid a comparison with Virchow's laboratory at the Charité hospital (fig. 139). The world-famous doctor, anthropologist and hygienist, who had undertaken archaeological digs with Schliemann and represented a progressive party in the Reichstag, is seen surrounded by a multitude of anatomical specimens, plaster casts and folios. Here we have the laboratory of a positivist man of science, comparable with that of Menzel, who was of roughly the same age and has always been seen as a dismantler of the visible world and a researcher 'with the eye of an anatomist'[17]. Typifying the spirit of the age, the photograph of Virchow in his laboratory was featured on the cover of the *Berliner Illustrierte Zeitung*, a popular illustrated Sunday newspaper, under the title 'Portraits of modern Berliners'[18]. What was modern in this case was the systematic and painstaking method of enquiry, pursued in an objective spirit – reality examined and dissected right down to the last fibre.

Photography

Although a positivist in art by analogy with modern science, Menzel tended to become increasingly anachronistic in his manner of appropriating the world. For, in the context of the breathtaking progress of photography, nothing was more outmoded than the scrupulous realism painstakingly achieved with pencil and paintbrush, when the same could be arrived at, instantaneously and far more accurately, simply by taking a photograph. Despite his positivist, modern outlook in matters scientific, Menzel appears archaic in his artistic means and intentions. In 1921, Max Liebermann summed up in a striking sentence (which anticipates Walter Benjamin's reflections on the modern media) the problem posed by the artistic realism of the painter and the realistic pretentions of photography. If Menzel 'had received from nature most supreme qualities as an artist', as Liebermann put it, 'would he have been able to attain the freedom of a Rembrandt in the age of the the invention of photography?'[19]

This question acquires its full force when we realize that, in 1864, Menzel's brother, Richard, took over one of Berlin's most flourishing photographic reproduction studios, the Gustav Schauer Verlag. Following the premature death of his brother, Menzel advised his sister-in-law on the running of the business, which also published reproductions of works by Menzel, receiving a gold medal for this activity at the Paris Universal Exhibition of 1878. As it ensured the livelihood of one part of the family, photography was an ever-present reality in the Menzel household. All the more remarkable, then, that Menzel resorted to photography only in preparing his historical paintings. As a positivist historian – 'A Prussian positivist', as he was called[20] – he sometimes familiarized himself with artefacts from the past with the help of photographs. For instance, he owned a collection of photographs of the weapons and armour kept in the Historisches Museum in Dresden[21] (fig. 141) But it is a strange fact that his drawings, compared with the photographic plates, rendered the detail of the objects with far greater precision than could be achieved by the camera. Moreover, by varying the angle, Menzel freed his subjects from the singleness of viewpoint characteristic of photography. He improved on photography and made his subjects live!

It is in exactly this respect that the new medium presented him with a problem. To a man who drew tirelessly from life, photography seemed fundamentally unsuited to taking hold on life itself. For his painting of *The Coronation* (fig. 121), he had been obliged to paint two persons from photographs: one already dead, the other not available to sit for him. He did not meet the second person in the flesh until long after he had completed the painting. Extremely ashamed, according to his later account, at the lack of resemblance between the person and the photograph on the one hand and his portrait on the other, he organized a belated sitting and repainted the offending head[22].

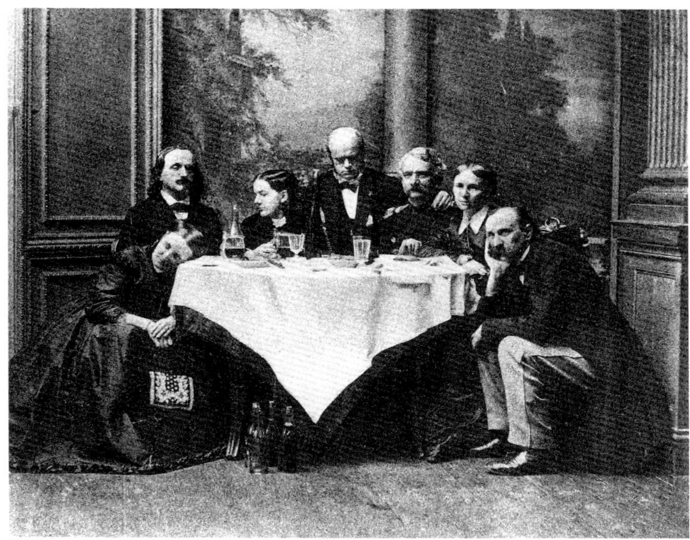

Fig. 138. Menzel with friends, around 1865, anonymous photograph

According to Liebermann, who had an excellent understanding of Menzel, photography is fundamentally unsuited to appropriating reality because of its mechanical objectivity. In contrast, what characterizes the artist is 'the greatest possible subjectivity in the rendering of nature'[23]. However, photography and art are not entirely separate, and this is what lends pertinence to Liebermann's question about Menzel's art in the age of photography. For the advent of photography, with its minute attention to detail, has completely changed our visual habits, and this in turn reinforced Menzel's penchant for minutiae: 'His visual sense, naturally inclined towards the observation and reproduction of the tiniest details, received fresh stimulus from photography'. Given the tendency to disintegration of photographic perception and the very existence of this modern medium, given its public effectiveness, 'we are touched', says Liebermann, 'by this tragic aspect of Menzel's development: he set himself to bridle the free flight of his imagination. One might say that his artistic scruples were

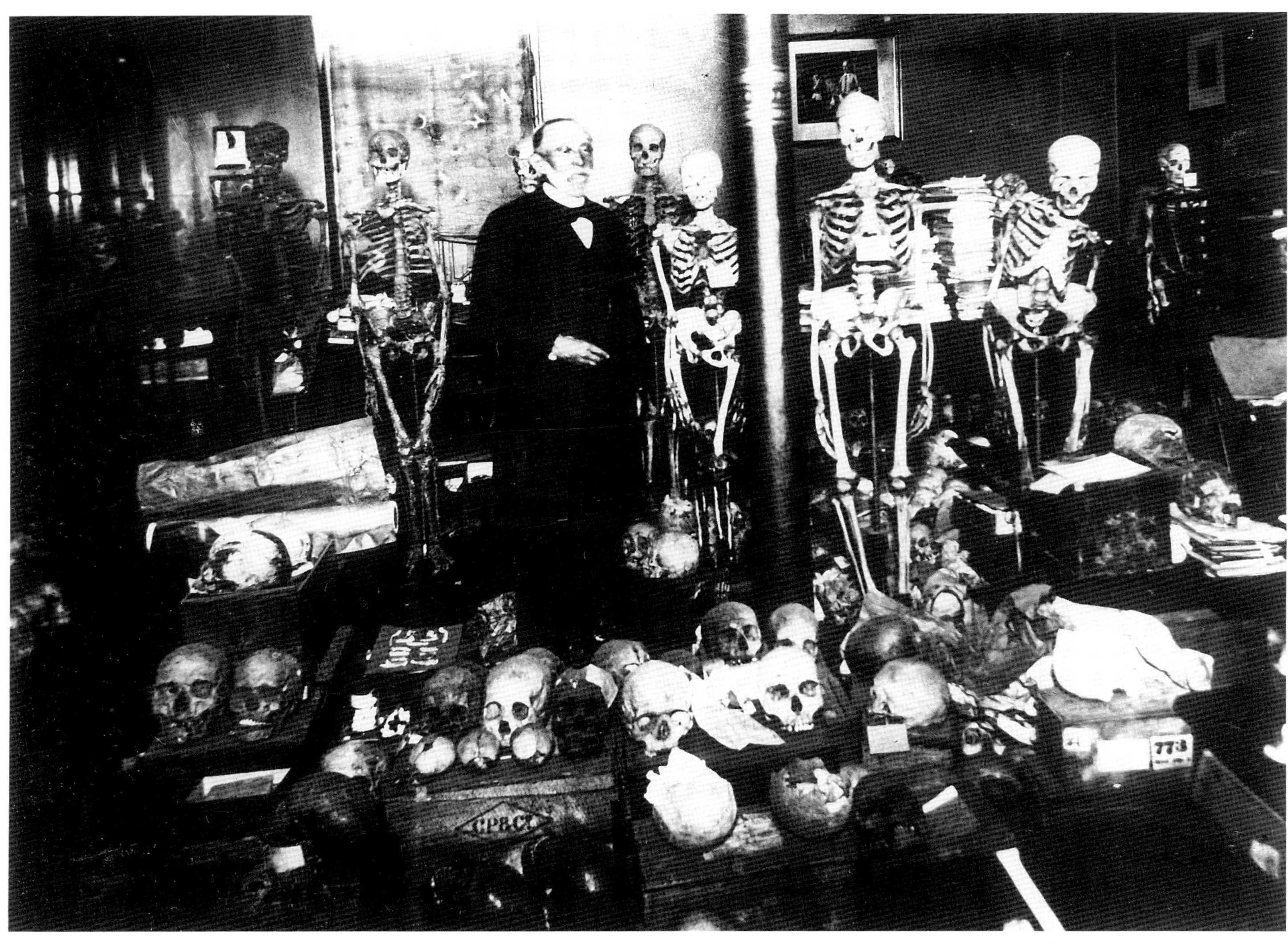

Fig. 139. Virchow in his laboratory at Berlin's Charité Hospital, around 1900, anonymous photograph

Fig. 140. Menzel in his studio, around 1895, anonymous photograph

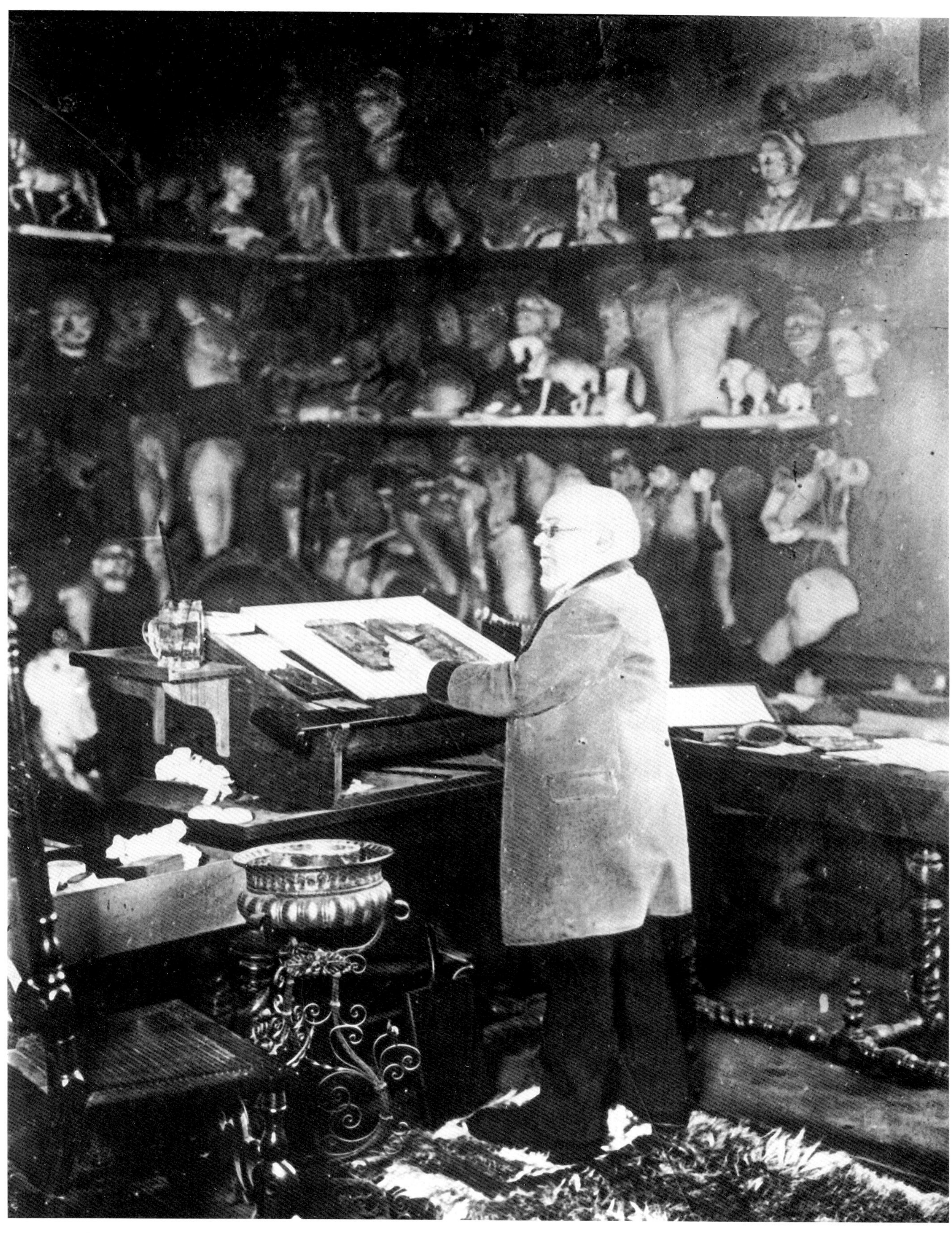

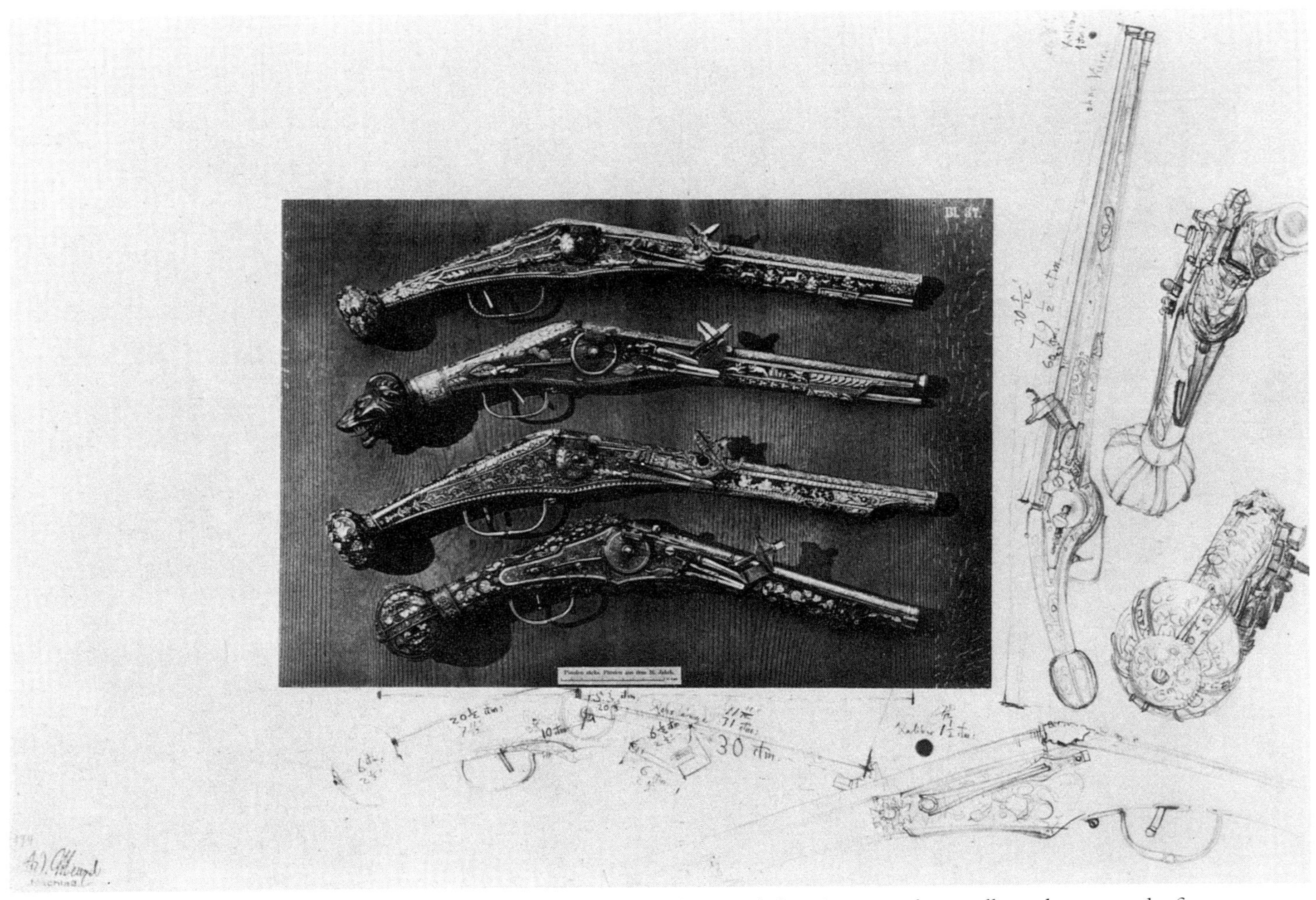

Fig. 141. *Pistols belonging to Princes of Saxony (16th Century)*, black pencil drawings on the cardboard surround of a photograph, Hamburg, Kupferstichkabinett, Hamburger Kunsthalle

employed in dissecting the creations of his genius, threatening to rob his art of life itself'[24].

Industrialization

For Liebermann, what was living in modern art was represented by the merits of French Impressionism. But he knew that modern art had not just one but many manifestations. Therefore, in the essay he wrote on Menzel in 1921, he exhorted 'our distinguished aesthetes' to show themselves 'a little more cautious in their judgement of Menzel'. He was of course getting at Meier-Graefe, who in his partiality saw Impressionism as the high point of the 'history of artistic development'. The same irritation is evident when Liebermann writes, 'Degas spoke to me of Menzel in the most laudatory terms. He considers him to be the greatest living painter and has attempted to copy his *Supper at the Ball* from memory'[25]. Liebermann could conceive of no greater homage to Menzel than that rendered by one of the greatest representatives of the Impressionist movement (*cf.* cat. 168).

Menzel's modernity surpassed even that of the Impressionists, if we are to believe the judgement expressed by Joris-Karl Huysmans. In 1880, Huysmans noted that, even more than the Impressionists, Menzel had made modern life the subject of his art: 'Which artist will now render the imposing grandeur, and follow the way opened up by the German Menzel, by venturing into immense ironworks, into the railway stations that M. Claude Monet has, it is true, already attempted to paint, but without managing to bring out in his vague abbreviations the colossal magnitude of the locomotives and their setting [. . .]?'[26] 'All this modern fever which presents industrial activity' was for Huysmans, an admirer of Caillebotte, the future subject-matter of art, boldly tackled not by the Impressionists but by Menzel alone. It is true that in 1879 Manet had planned to paint large-scale frescoes of daily life in the modern city for the Paris Mairie. He had intended to depict Les Halles and the city's stations and river port[27]. The project fell through, however, as did Menzel's plans to decorate the walls of the new Berlin city hall, opened in 1861. In contrast with the historical cycle that Wilhelm von Kaulbach had painted with antiquarian erudition for the nearby Neues Museum, Menzel had dreamed of a panorama representing contemporary life as an aspect of the history of civilization. But this monumental encyclopaedia of images of contemporary life was also doomed to remain unrealized. 'Missing this opportunity', said Menzel, 'is the thing I most regret'[28].

And yet Huysmans was right: Menzel alone had made the daily life of industry a subject for art. This is true not only as regards his choice of subject-matter, but of the whole of his oeuvre, from the very beginning. Industrial production was, together with positivism and photography, the major cause of fragmentation in nineteenth-century life. Traces of this enforced division of labour are to be found in the 'utilitarian merchandise' produced by Menzel as a young man. For instance, the samples for labels, business cards and other purposes (fig. 142) which Menzel, then sixteen, composed in his father's lithographic workshop in 1831, are a stock of ornamental motifs for advertising projects. They could be used in different combinations for the mass ornamentation needs of a prosaic age.

Another example of spare parts for decorative purposes are the arabesques that Menzel was often asked to design for the title pages of books. The arabesque, venerated by the Romantics as a mysterious hieroglyph of the growth process inherent in nature and in life, was transformed by Menzel for the purposes of the industrial age into an interlacing motif which, though a unity, could also be broken down into its component parts like a piece of engineering. A good example is Menzel's title page for Count Raczynski's *Modern Art in Germany* (fig. 143). With mischievous irony, Menzel here hints at the state of total immobilization into which recent German art had fallen. Led into error by false erudition and fake sensibility, represented by a trio of bards piously playing the harp before a critic with an ass's head, official German art in the early years of the nineteenth century, as industrialization gathered pace, was, as Menzel saw it, declining into empty virtuoso embellishments contrary to nature. In Menzel's estimation, neither academic artists nor the academic Romantics represented by the Nazarenes were attaining the heights of arabesque art achieved by Dürer, who had been capable of apprehending reality in all its breadth[29]. With the progress of industrialization, German art was succumbing to the charms of an isolation which had only the appearance of calm contemplation. It lacked growth and unity in harmony with the dynamic emergence of the modern age that was to engulf it, consisting rather of the abandoned arabesques of an art that had become rigid.

This entire dismantling process, whether conducted by scientific investigation or by painstaking observation, was to culminate in a new synthesis of fragments into a whole: such was the resolutely modern aesthetic that Menzel deduced from the division of labour in industrial society. He himself practised this principle for his illustrations to Kugler's *History of Frederick the Great*. The tasks were shared out among a number of collaborators, and the opulent illustrated volume that resulted was a work of art totally in keeping with the spirit of the industrial era[30] (*cf.* figs 101–5).

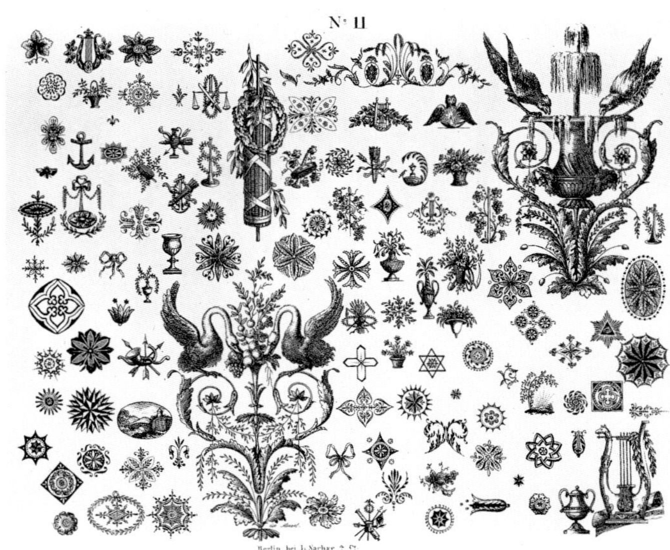

Fig. 142. *Samples for labels, business cards and other purposes*, 1831, lithograph (B 87)

This dismantling of the whole and the re-establishment of links between the component parts is the very hallmark of the modern age. Menzel showed his awareness of it at an early stage in depicting the landscape divided by the new railway line between Berlin and Potsdam (*cf.* cat. 35). Menzel was also the first German artist to depict travel by train as a mass phenomenon. Of the many railway carriage interiors he painted, *Travelling*

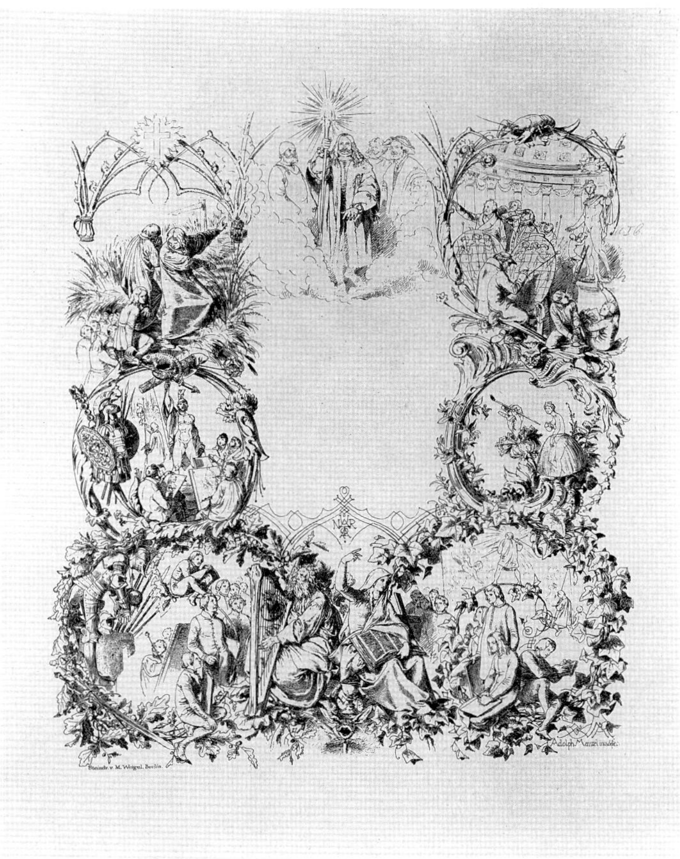

Fig. 143. Title page to Count Athanasius Raczynski's *Modern Art in Germany*, 1836, lithograph (B 125)

through the Countryside (fig. 143), from around 1892, is particularly rich in detail. People are portrayed sleeping or observing the scenery, torn from their familiar world, ensconced in the opulent arabesque forms of the upholstered first-class seats. In works of this kind, Menzel shows the alienation of a society that has become divorced from nature and from itself. Only the sleeping child and the ticket inspector outside the window are truly at ease. In contrast, the busy activity of the people travelling together amounts to a portrayal of *curiositas*, the hunger for novelty, that takes hold of a society borne along by industrial progress towards a future of constant change. On the one hand, an allegory of learned artifice stagnating in an arabesque, on the other that of a purely touristic, voyeuristic attitude to nature, concerned only with externals. In these two examples of the way in which he dismantled the field of vision – arabesque and realistic depiction – Menzel makes visible the corresponding failings of present-day consumer society.

This precise rendering of fragmented simultaneity, the palpable paradox of a totality in decomposition, *concordia discors* as the emblem of modern times, is all equally apparent in Menzel's work when, instead of criticizing the alienation of modern society, he glorifies the division of labour as the quintessence of contemporary life – as he does in *The Iron Rolling Mill* (cat. 160). Menzel's composition clearly shows how industrial production is divided up into several stages, with the various groups of people playing their different roles within an overall organizational framework. Some are engaged in productive work at the roll train, while others stand ready to begin a later stage of the process. Others again are taking a break or washing. All are exerting themselves with zeal, discipline, skill, and not without dignity. The whole is broken down into its component parts. The painter therefore plays the role of a conscientious positivist observer. By making preparatory studies of each type of worker, he achieved a synthesis in the final painting. He appears as the sovereign anatomist and director of an ill-defined entity; he finds his strength of conviction precisely in its organized disorder and applies it to representing the modern production process. For Menzel, the division of labour characteristic of industry therefore corresponded to an artistic process whose aim was to reproduce the whole from its constituent parts. But this division, like his syntheses, was also reflected in the subjects he tackled, whether he was criticizing or praising the society of his time, its many forms of human alienation, its incredible vitality and the new opportunities and experiences it afforded, the infinite diversity of which could, again, be apprehended only in part.

4. Subjective viewpoint

Positivism, photography and industry – these forms of specialization in research, perception and production that sum up all that was modern in the nineteenth century – had their equivalent in the insatiable eye of Menzel as draughtsman. Menzel drew everything and, in his role of scientific draughtsmen, sought mastery over all the identifiable and verifiable components of both past and present. Hence the impression he gives of scrupulous realism, authenticity and objectivity. He was often reproached for this, not only by Liebermann but also by Tschudi. In this passion for realistic detail – over-scrupulous as far as his critics were concerned – they saw a distancing from real life. Such was the opinion of Hugo von Tschudi, the rediscoverer of the work of Menzel's youth: 'The most interesting thing about Menzel's images are his studies; the truth of the detail is greater

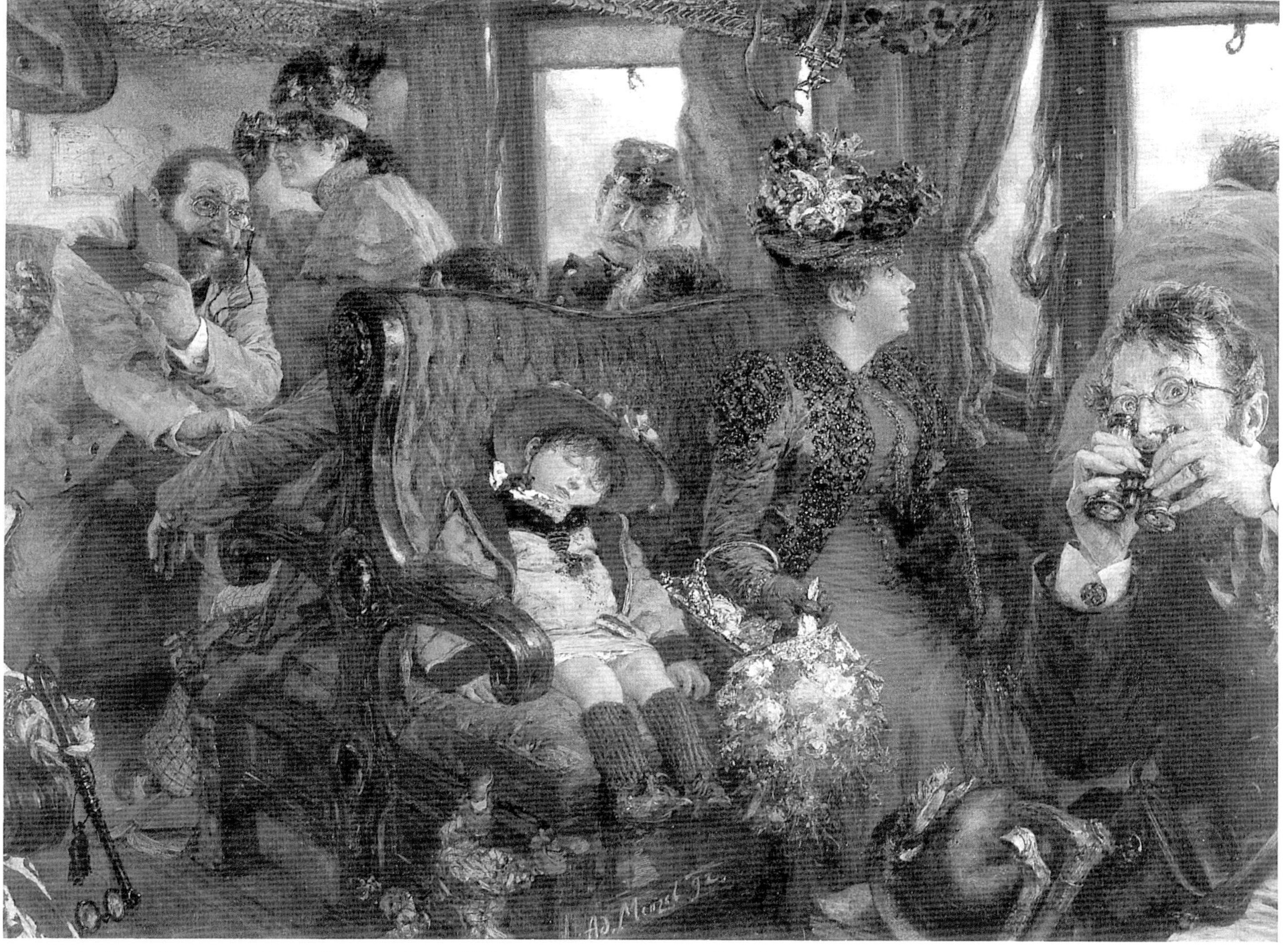

Fig. 144. *Travelling through the Countryside* , 1892, gouache, private collection

than that of the whole'[31].

Menzel would not have agreed with this analysis. For him, truth was only to be found in detail. Menzel gathered together – or, to use a more exact term, synthesized – this host of singular observations by adopting a perspective of extreme subjectivity. Speaking of this brings us to a concrete fact: Menzel's height. A mere four feet seven inches tall, he was very small indeed. In *An Evening Together* (cat. 28), he is depicted in the foreground with his back to the spectator, his head slightly raised, straining to see across the surface of the table. Menzel observed the world from below, like a child. Able to make fun of himself, he several times disguised himself as a child for fancy dress parties[32]. In a similar facetious spirit is the photograph (fig. 138) showing Menzel standing as if he were the tallest among a group of people who are in fact slumped down in their chairs at the table.

Menzel's position was obviously that of an outsider. It could be said that his small stature excluded him from the adult world. He observed with the penetrating gaze of a stranger. At the same time, a certain intimacy derives from the unexpected level of his viewpoint. It was as if he were spying on the person before him. His sister sleeping on the settee (cat. 47) appears nearer than she would have done to a taller onlooker. The imprecision in distance from the subject caused by the adoption of unusual perspectives, the sudden switch from above to below, can transform simple observation into aggression. This intensity of approach to a subject from an extremely subjective viewpoint is something that Menzel shared with Degas[33]. When a scene is viewed slightly from below, the perspective gives the impression that we are observing through the eyes of the person represented. And this optical empathy has a surprising effect: the spectator perceives Menzel's characters as immediately present. He sees the lines that life has imprinted on their faces and all the elegant or prosaic details of their clothing, as if they had been captured from close up in passing and projected into the picture.

As well as the unusual viewpoint and its surprising lack of consistency, this way of capturing individual fragments of reality is highly characteristic of Menzel's work. Like a child looking down and seeing things on the ground close to and from a narrow angle, so in Menzel's *Children's Album* we see the rat, narrowly framed, as it runs away from the observer along the gutter (cat. 111). In other gouaches, we have the impression that we are looking up, like a child, when a door is opened by an adult. Or we are in the enchanted world of a fairy story, where big and small are only relative. It was in this spirit, somewhere between childish amazement, mockery and parody, that Menzel painted *Travelling through the Countryside*. Foreshortening, obsession with detail and total lack of realism are the attributes of this indulgent view, from a point roughly on a level with the sleeping child, of the world of adult tourists thrown into agitation by the beauties of nature. Duranty's 'neurotic preoccupation with the truth' is here ironically transformed, as in *Alice in Wonderland*, into wondering astonishment, that of the child who dreams of the madness of the 'objective' way in which reasonable adults experience the world.

Menzel's drawing of *Kurhausstrasse at Kissingen after a Storm* (cat. 192) carries his eccentricity of perspective and method of foreshortening to an extreme. This view from above, quintessence of the subjective viewpoint that distances things to the point of vertigo, may well have given Menzel a special visual satisfaction, a kind of compensation. His studios were always located on an upper storey. The final one, in the Sigismundstrasse, was at the top of the building, on the fourth floor. From an elevated viewpoint, perception changes, becomes more selective. The alternation of sharply defined and blurred outlines gives rise to calculated effects of voids and solids in the finished picture. As well as framing his subject in a surprising way, Menzel was a master of the drama of voids and solids, and all stages in between. Thus, *Kurhausstrasse at Kissingen after a Storm* depicts the melting snow as a maelstrom sweeping diagonally across the picture, whose graphic structure anticipates twentieth-century movements in abstract art. In its consistency, a kind of amorphous porridge, it hovers between saturation and an almost monochrome void. Only by contrast with the angle of the house in the top left can be made out, on the surface riffled with graphite, the appearance of a road in winter.

Balcony Room is most definitely an allegory of painting and this subjective viewpoint (cat. 18). All the elements previously mentioned – foreshortening, voids and solids, enigmatic point of view – are combined as if in a stylistic manifesto and made to overlap one another. For instance, the delicately painted void of the wall is disconcerting because the objects reflected in the mirror, which should appear on or in front of the wall with the same sharpness, are either hazy or totally absent. From his subjective stance, Menzel painted what the spectator would have seen on entering the room. Things near to him, such as the mirror and the image it reflects, appear sharper, while more distant objects, like the ground, become more blurred the nearer they are to the wall. An allegory of painting or, to be more exact, an 'allegory of the real', *Balcony Room*, by making reality enigmatic, unmasks the illusory nature of painting and the subjectivity of the eye we bring to it[34].

From one of Menzel's apartments, there was a view of the palace of Prince Albert (*cf.* cat. 164). The most extraordinary thing about this view from above is the oblique foreshortening of the garden, with the workmen caught napping, and the transition from solid to void (fig. 145). It takes time for the spectator to realize that his eye, having wandered to the right of the palace, has not met the sky but is resting on a firebreak wall lit by the sun. Making use of tiny windows, the painter accentuates the surprising emptiness of this very ordinary feature, which fills the horizon beside the palace. Again, Menzel anticipates twentieth-century art: the surreal emptiness of firebreak walls that were used to convey the unreal and inhospitable character of Berlin in works of the Neue Sachlichbeit (New Objectivity) movement, the post-1945 townscapes of Werner Heldt and, in our own day, the art of K.H. Hödicke.

Menzel also anticipates future developments in his high-angled views of Berlin's burgeoning building sites, which must have come close to his own house. His view of a *Rear Courtyard and House* (cat. 13) is a typical example, though it is not possible to identify the precise location. Again, Menzel's subjective viewpoint lends mystery to the image of reality. We do not really know if the dark shape in the background is merely a reflection in a large puddle or a real building standing on the dry ground beyond the pool of water, or if both hypotheses are true (*cf.* detail fig. 146). The destabilizing influence of the reflection – an upside-down effect before its time – is reinforced by the disturbing pictorial quality of the motif. In contemporary terms, this is what we might expect to find in the work of Anselm Kiefer or Georg

Baselitz. On the other hand, the building site in the foreground with its long pipes and plaster debris between fragments of wall is reminiscent of the piles of materials so dear to Beuys, for instance his *Last Space with Introspector* (fig. 147), a souvenir of his native Cleves, in the form of inanimate objects[35]. Menzel's striking transitions from one set of objects to another bear comparison with the technique used by Beuys. In Menzel's work, as in a real-life collage, the heap of rubbish on the building site coexists with the washing fluttering in the breeze in the back garden next door.

The abrupt switch from one sphere to another, for example the close juxtaposition of objects commonplace and pleasurable, is a new feature of Menzel's outlook. In his 1867 *View of a Small Courtyard* (fig. 148), for instance, the rust-coloured building on the left with its four blank windows and the dappled shade thrown by the leaves on the sunlit wall suggest an oasis of summer happiness in the desert of city bustle. Then our sudden awareness of the scratching hens and the pump re-establishes the ordinariness of the courtyard, the narrow world of the tenants, and their fondness for their bit of lower middle-class countryside in the heart of the town.

The scrutinizing gaze Menzel brings to the sunny atmosphere of this rear courtyard is also apparent in his romantic views of Berlin by night. *Moonlight on the Friedrichsgracht in Old Berlin* (cat. 76) is no less enigmatic than his *View of Anhalt Station by Moonlight* (cat. 24), seen from between two houses. The moonlit façade of the house on the left is characterized by flapping curtains and other strange objects mysteriously emerging from the windows. Here again, in a view from above which seems

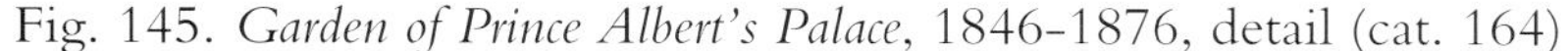

Fig. 145. *Garden of Prince Albert's Palace*, 1846-1876, detail (cat. 164)

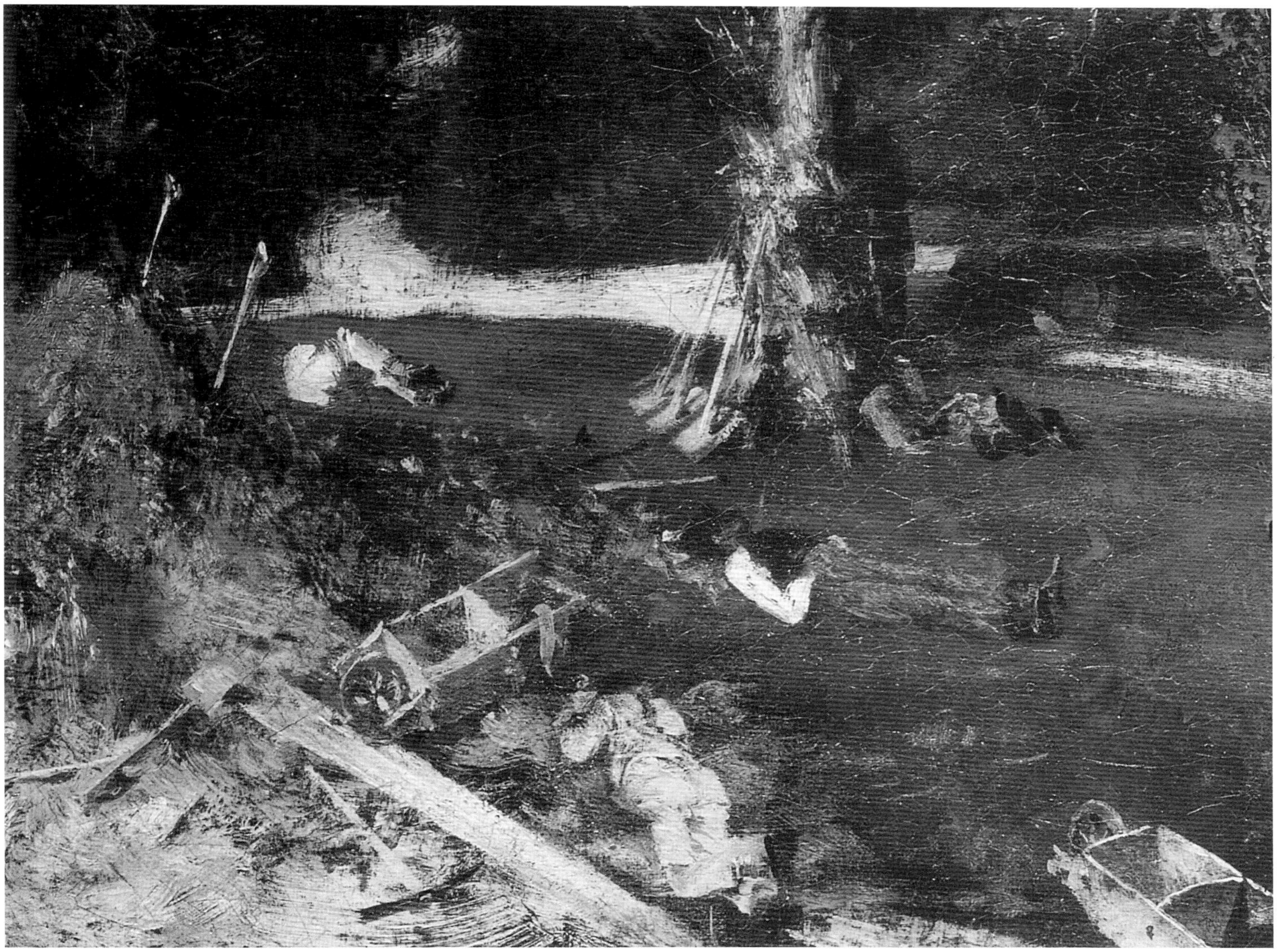

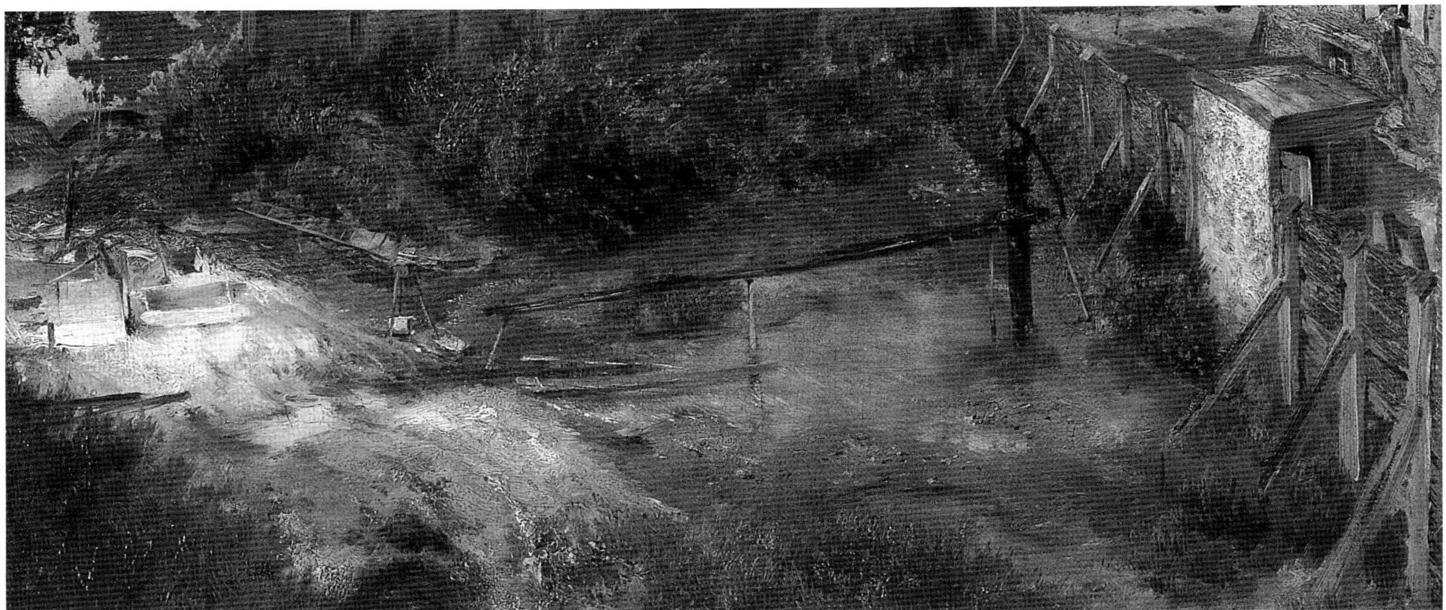

Fig. 146. *Rear Courtyard and House*, 1844, detail (cat. 13)

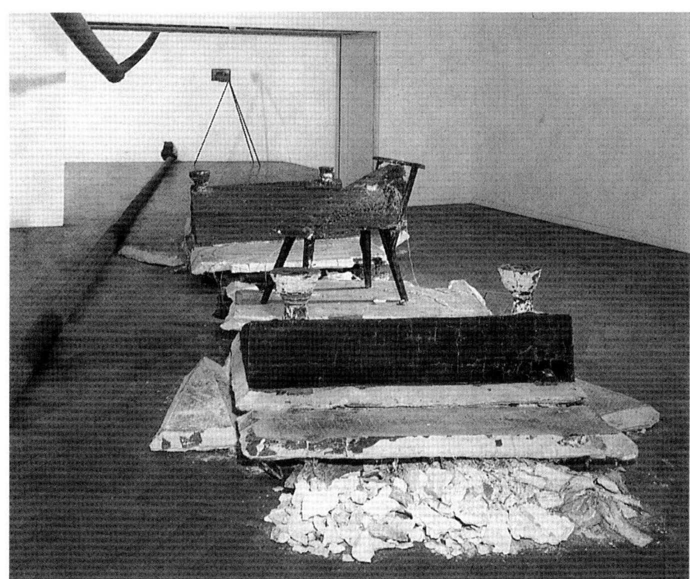

Fig. 147. Joseph Beuys, *Last Space with Introspector*, Stuttgart, Staatsgalerie

to have been selected at random, we encounter the disorderly and unfinished city: Berlin endless and disorientated in its disturbing nocturnal silence, void of inhabitants but packed with strange objects given up to their own devices, which Menzel has recorded at this particular spot. But in his view of buildings brightly lit by moonlight (*cf.* cat. 109), the scrutinizing but subjective eye with which Menzel looks upon the world is to some extent that of a voyeur. On each floor, the life of the great city, broken down into its component parts, is being acted out in a different way: sociability, solitude and banality. Here Menzel anticipates George Grosz, whose drawings of Berlin at the time of the Great War (fig. 149), in revealing what is going on behind each window, give the lie to the illusion of bourgeois respectability.

Menzel's social criticism, unlike that of his future admirer George Grosz, is never direct, aggressive or hurtful. In Menzel's case, as in the naturalistic novels of his friend Theodor Fontane, a lucid – and therefore critical – view of reality is often mixed with humour and a sense of parody. And sometimes even a touch of transfiguration, if this term – also characteristic of Fontane's novelistic modernity – is taken to mean the opposite of a lack of objectivity the deliberately subjective dimension of the perception specific to the observer[36]. For instance, Menzel's *Departure of King William I for the Army, 31 July 1870* (cat. 134), far from being a profession of patriotic fervour, is rather an ironical representation of such sentiments. Menzel transforms his main subject, the passing of the royal couple, into a matter of secondary interest. And it is certainly not by chance that the face of

Fig. 148. *View of a Small Courtyard*, 1867, gouache, Berlin, Nationalgalerie (held in trust for a private collection)

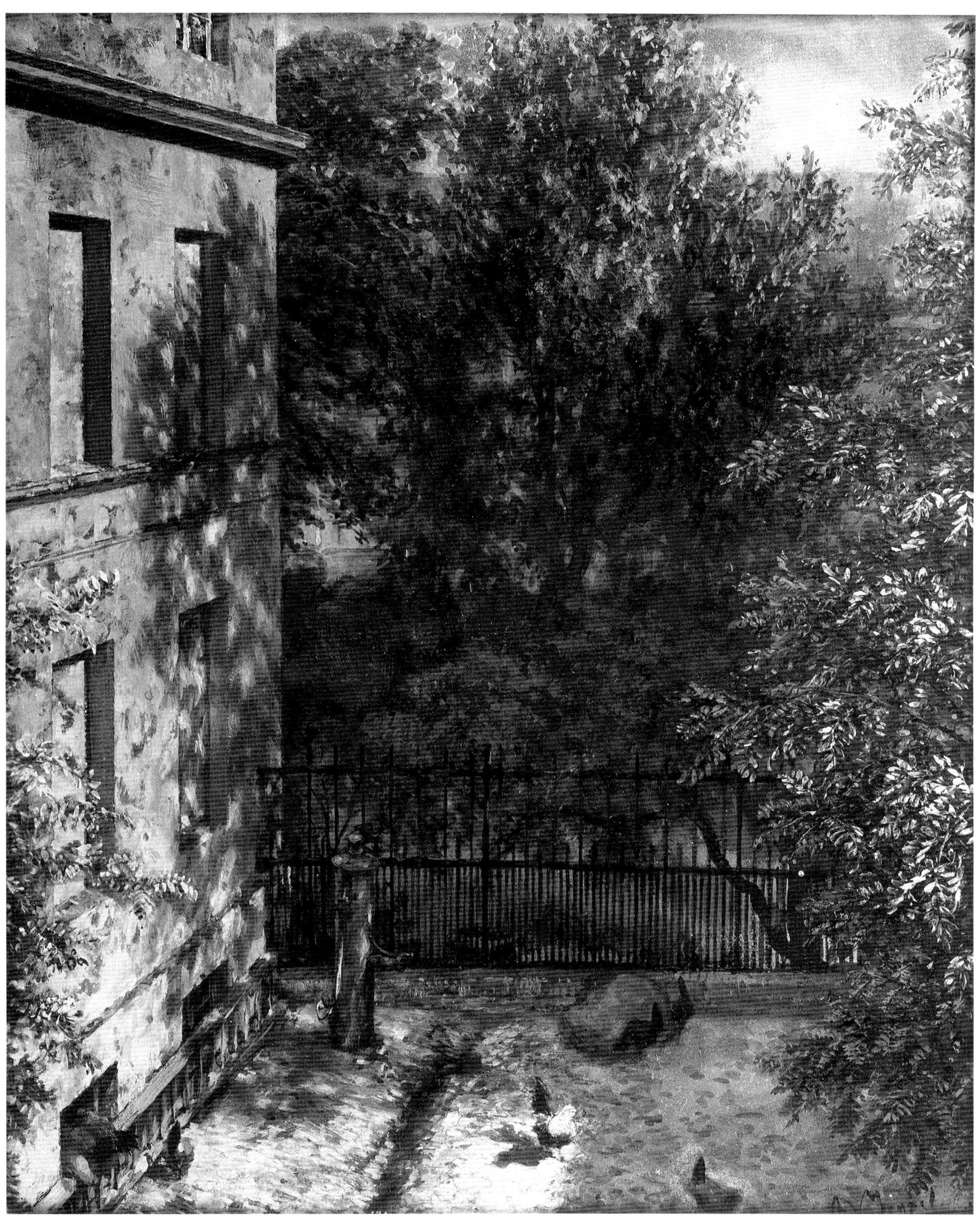

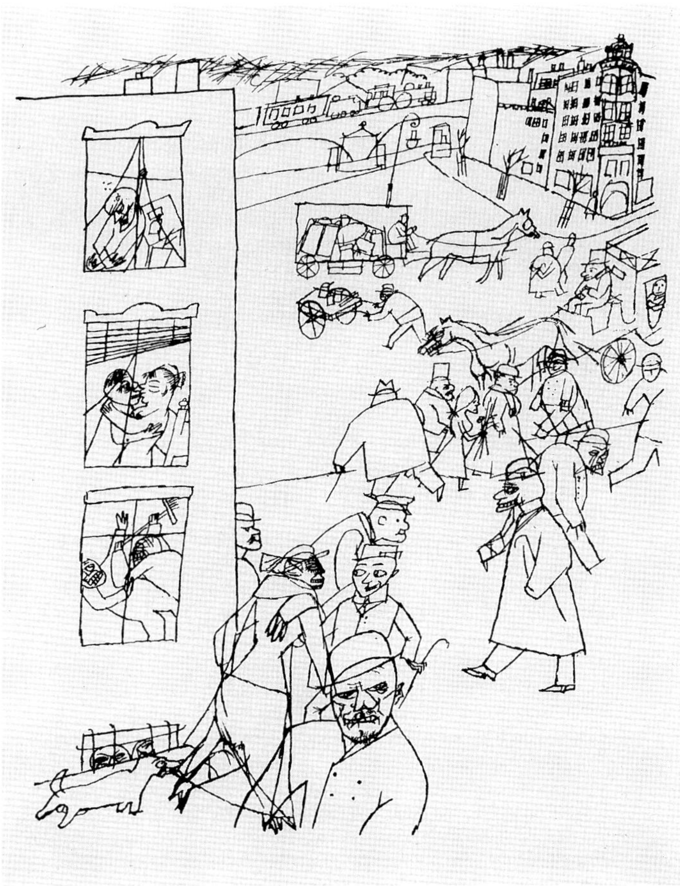

Fig. 149. George Grosz, *The Ways of Men*, 1915, lithograph from *Weise Blätter*

the queen in the carriage is obscured by a handkerchief. Anonymous handkerchiefs also flutter strangely at the window at the top right (*cf.* detail in catalogue section). And the woman gripped with fervent enthusiasm at the shop doorway in the bottom of the picture seems to be receiving a blow from the iron fist of the angel supporting the street light. The same 'snapshot quality'[37], with its double message, a way of fixing the fleeting moment while hinting at a deeper meaning, is also evident in Menzel's obvious allusion to death and injury, conveyed by the Red Cross flags among the festive banners of the celebration.

A year earlier, Menzel had put together a kaleidoscope of visual axes and divergent viewpoints to depict the city crowds in his *Weekday in Paris* (cat. 127). Based on many studies, to which he remained faithful to the smallest detail, this work was painted in his Berlin studio and represents a purely imaginary crossroads in Paris. It is this universal quality that distinguishes Menzel from Caillebotte, whose depiction of the solitude of the great city can be precisely localized to the crossing of the Rue de Turin and the Rue de Moscou. In contrast to Menzel's, Caillebotte's figures have an anonymous, stereotyped look, and their fashionable elegance corresponds to the ideal of beauty based on the 'heroism of modern life'[38] propagated by Baudelaire and Manet. The pictorial versions of urban alienation propounded by Caillebotte rest on the emptiness of the urban environment and the stoical nonchalance of a distant and élitist middle class. In contrast, Menzel shows the excessively vulgar chaos of the social whole, with all its stratifications, professions, generations and races. Here is modern life in its commonplace beauty, diversity and isolation. The crowd amid the traffic of a great city, surrounded by advertisements and merchandise, building sites and cafés, relentlessly driven by needs of various kinds.

In visualizing this urban dynamic, Menzel did not follow the example of salon Impressionism typified by Boldini's 1874 scene of Parisian street life (fig. 150). He did not resort to spirited brushwork, nor to optical artifices such as doubling the horses' legs, as Boldoni did to simulate movement. Nor did he line up a series of subjects as in a comic strip. Instead, Menzel wove together his motifs to create a kind of tapestry, so that the eye has to home in on each motif individually in order to identify it with precision. Here we have the disconcerting interweaving of a *horror vacui*, ranging from the strikingly modern representation of tatters of peeling poster in the left-hand foreground to the charming balcony scenes in the top of the picture. Menzel's *Weekday in Paris* is particularly expressive of the city as a catalyser of energies, a picturesque jostling – as Fontane described it – of everything and anything. In its anarchic profusion, the painting is also a visual metaphor of the feverish vitality of modern life. Described as 'an aggregation of pieces into a fragment', this kaleidoscope of simultaneous impressions undoubtedly lacks the dimension of explicit social criticism[39]. Nevertheless, the obsessive detail with which Menzel represents the particular is not without general value. For here he offers us the visual metaphor of a modern society in which, in terms of Darwinian social evolution, it is the fittest who come out on top. Like Schopenhauer, to whom he pays homage[40] in the pantheon of his *Studio Wall* (cat. 137), in his image of the city Menzel illustrates his philosophical conviction that life has meaning only in terms of self-preservation and the capacity for domination by the human will. In this respect, and unlike Impressionism, Menzel represents the fleeting moment in a way that looks beyond the moment itself. In other words, the incomparable abundance of motifs he managed to synthesize, by virtue of his subjective viewpoint, into a complex whole, a *concordia discors*, enabled Menzel to demonstrate the contingency of the absolute, and to commend self-preservation in its most concrete aspects as the only meaning of life.

What applies to his paintings of modern life is no less true of his representation of the past. Menzel's illustrations as a young man for Kugler's *History of Frederick the Great* already show his ability to synthesize a host of drawings, graphical renderings of the historical places associated with the king, from a great variety of written and iconographical sources. By virtue of his subjective viewpoint, Menzel was able to turn this diverse raw material, which he had mastered with great accuracy, into images with a force of suggestion so powerful that the spectator seems to be seeing the king directly, as in a snapshot of daily life. Kugler particularly appreciated the 'daguerrotypical reality' of Menzel's historical settings, believing this to be the hallmark of their modernity[41]. For Menzel, who judged photographs to be deficient in life, the snapshot effect he produced was always the fruit of a complex creative process. The artist viewed the personality of the king he revered with a well-documented eye. Again, it is the contingency of the absolute, in this case the apparently accidental daily banality of the form in which historical greatness is manifested, which confers on the image of Frederick created by Menzel a character infinitely more living and durable than any historical work on the subject, including Kugler's biography[42].

The extent to which the amazing originality of Menzel's subjective viewpoint also marked his ventures into the world of the rococo is demonstrated by the extreme virtuosity of his gouache *Crown Prince Frederick Pays a Visit to the Painter Pesne on his Scaffolding at Rheinsberg* (cat. 93). It is amazing how Menzel, whose eye was compared during his lifetime to a Kodak camera[43], here anticipates the subjective possibilities of photographic art, which nobody had yet exploited, and, looking even further ahead, those of the movie camera.

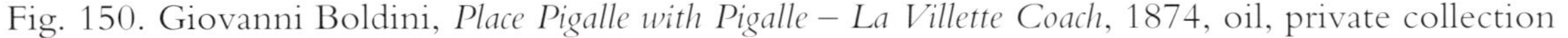

Fig. 150. Giovanni Boldini, *Place Pigalle with Pigalle – La Villette Coach*, 1874, oil, private collection

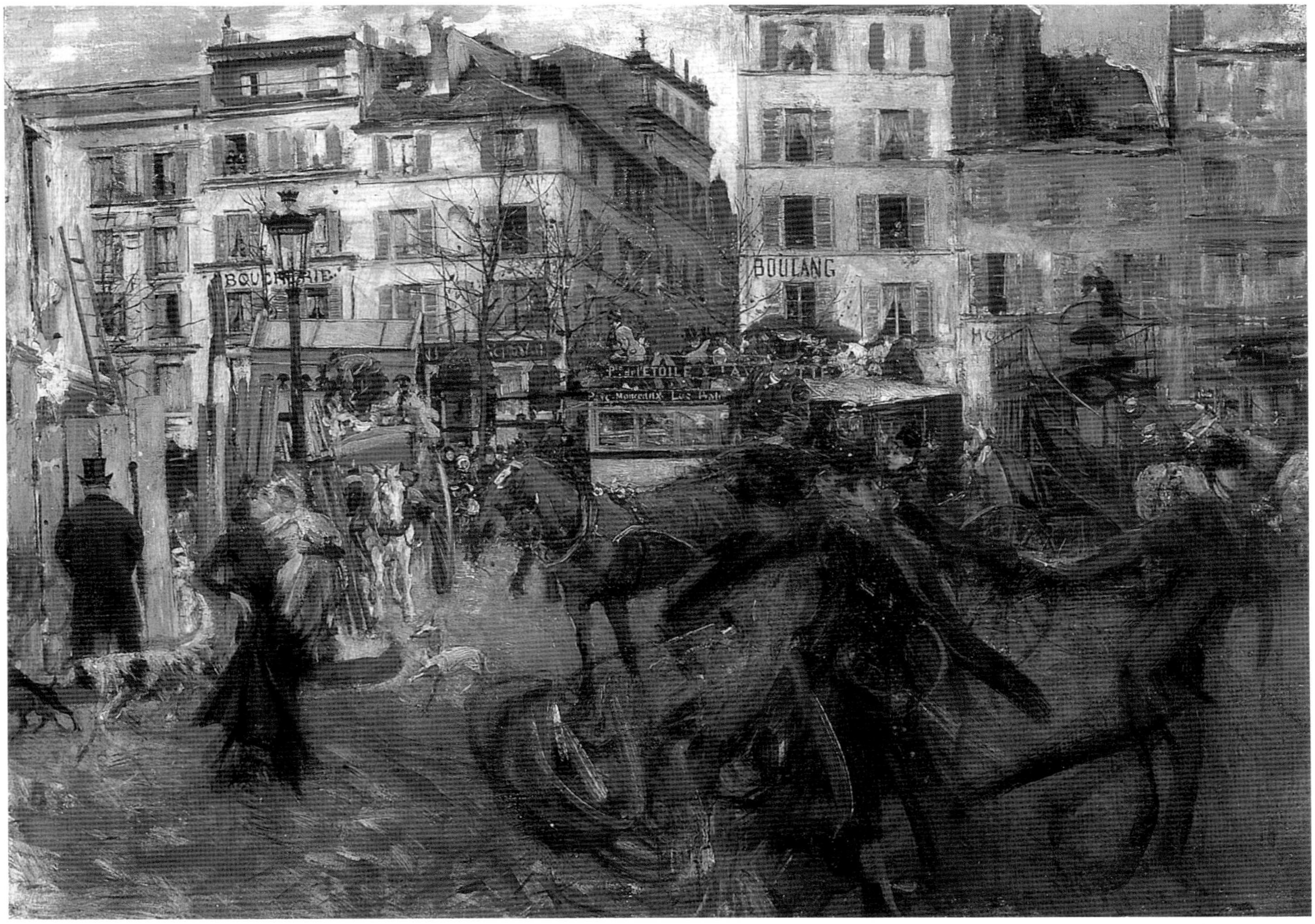

In this exceptional picture, as the vanishing point is located just above the dummy's head, the spectator has the impression that he is climbing the scaffolding with the prince. Given its criss-cross structure, the scaffolding forms an unexpected, quite unconventional backdrop, making us immediately aware of the spontaneous character of this surprising visit.

Once again, Menzel used this way of lending animation to the scene to make it into an exalted pictorial allegory of the living and life-giving character of naturalistic art. The paradox in this case is that the characters are in period dress. Pesne, with whom Menzel identified himself in one of his preliminary studies, leaves the academic dummy lying, not paying it the slightest attention. The dummy becomes an impotent symbol of a classical, cultivated, formalist art. Pesne, meanwhile, is perched high on the scaffolding, painting from a real flesh-and-blood model. To inspire and encourage him in his task, he has music: a traditional remedy for the artist's melancholy, to which Menzel, too, often had recourse. Among the elements likely to inspire the artist, there is also wine, another helper which Menzel did not disdain. It is no coincidence that the wine glass, set down on the chair, is framed four-square by the window, against a background of sunlit natural beauty. The final sharp expression of the vigour and cheerfulness of an art practised with all the senses is the grotesque motif of the paintpot full of brushes being knocked over. It could be said that the paint is spreading over the picture. This theme, famous in art history, of an object falling within the picture space, which was used from Rembrandt to Hogarth in pointed contravention of the rules of classical painting, is here taken up by Menzel as an exaltation of his subjective outlook, whereby his art draws inspiration from the ideal of the snapshot, from spontaneity and life, which is also the ideal of the modern artistic sensibility.

This resurrection of the 'world of Fritz', as Fontane referred to Menzel's work on Frederick the Great in his birthday poem, was not without influence on the official style of Menzel's own day, the age of Emperors Wilhelm I and Wilhelm II. Menzel did much to make the neo-rococo the ideal of taste in Berlin in the 'Gründerjahre' period. It has rightly been pointed out in the case of Manet how much his recourse to the Renaissance was in fact a witty cover for historicism of his own time[44]. The same is true of Menzel. All the caryatids and Atlases at the Palace of Sanssouci, which he had popularized by his illustrations of the life of Frederick II, could be found in the young capital of the Reich in the form of inflationist sculpture adorning the neo-baroque architecture of the new buildings of the Kurfürstendamm. Menzel was adept at turning the impotent actuality of the past against his own age as it sought to live in the midst of former glories. It has rightly been remarked[45] that would have been unusual for court society to have accepted being represented as they are in *Supper at the Ball*, 1878 (cat. 167), a mischievous transformation of the rococo of Frederick's time into the vain mass entertainment of Emperor Wilhelm's Berlin.

As a positivist historian making caustic criticism of historicism, Menzel was never so to the point as in his gouache *Beati Possidentes* (Happy Owners) of 1888 (fig. p. 155). A *nouveau riche* couple, displaying all the self-satisfaction born of their prosperity, are having work done on their house and garden. As in the arabesques embellishing the title page of Count Raczynski's *Modern Art in Germany* (fig. 143), artists, historians, gardeners and other assistants are shown dispersed all over the picture and shaping nature with art, giving the house an artistic appearance, and lining their own pockets to boot. What appears at first sight to be a Dutch bourgeois genre painting of around 1600, is in fact a shaft aimed at newly rich Berlin. A comparison with the Renaissance villa built in 1885 at Charlottenburg (fig. 152) for Wilhelm Bode, a specialist in Renaissance art and the painting of Frans Hals and the future director-general of the Berlin State Museums, shows just how right Menzel was. In his view, these 'Gründerzeit' villas were simply freshly painted forgeries. Escaping from the world into an ideal past – it is no coincidence that the villa depicted by Menzel is completely isolated by high walls – meant that the prosperous classes of the young empire were deliberately turning their backs on the ideals of truth and nature, together with humanity, that Menzel sought to promote as the only valid ideals of the period. On the contrary, the industrial prosperity of Germany, and particularly of Prussia, was leading to imitative provincialism and complacent megalomania. Rarely has humorous bonhomie been depicted as less good-natured than in Menzel's *Beati Possidentes*. 'The Berliner', writes Fontane, expressing the same sort of concern in a letter to a friend of Menzel's in 1894, 'remains a selfish, narrow-minded provincial. The town grows and grows, millionaires are two a penny, but . . . Berlin is ruled by imitation, the lowest common denominator, respectable mediocrity'[46].

Fig. 151. *Beati Possidentes* (Happy Owners), 1888, gouache, Georg Schäfer Collection, Euerbach

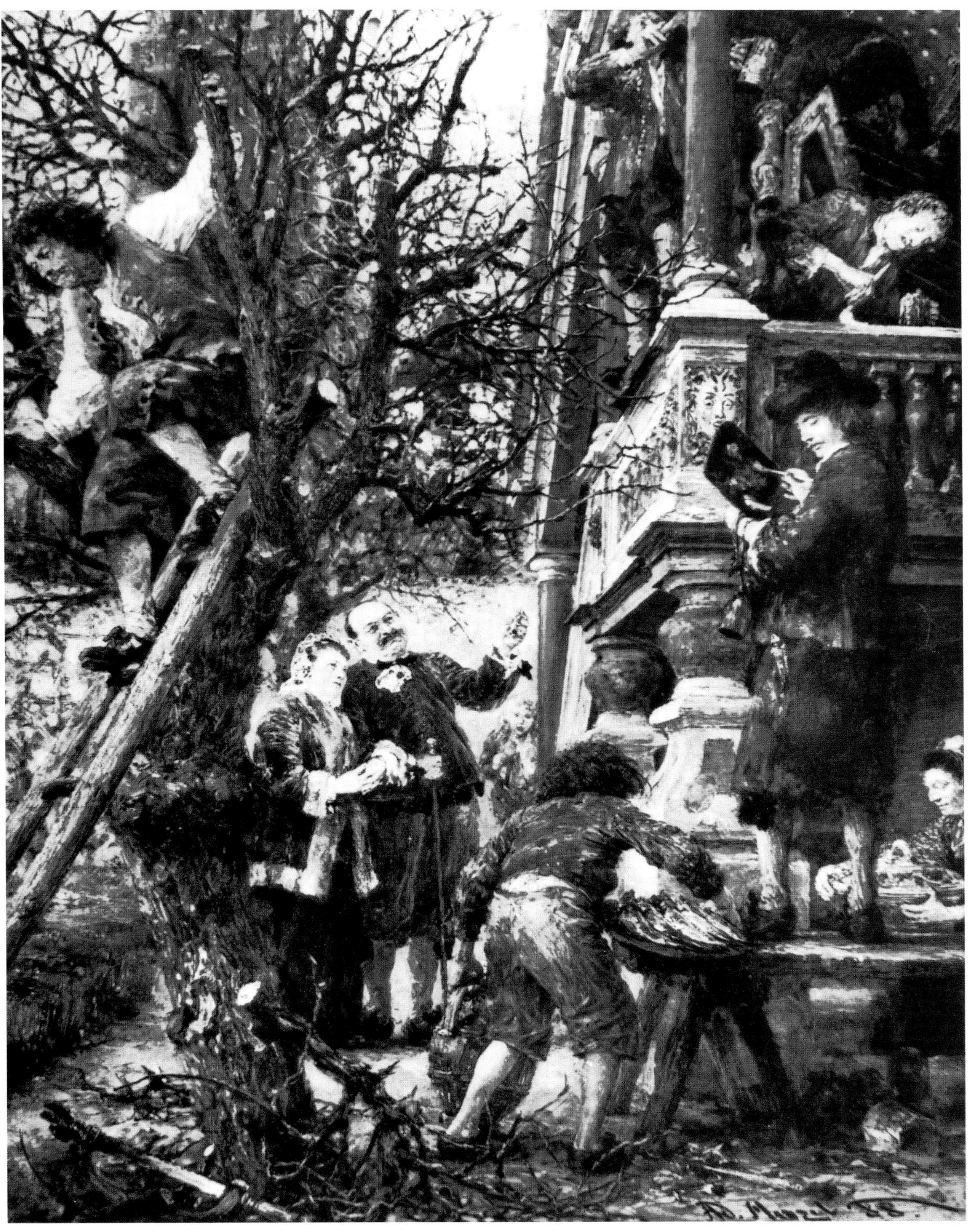

5. Menzel's universe

Our survey of Menzel's work in terms of his subjective viewpoint has revealed its fundamentally bipolar structure. Isolation and multiplicity, precise rendering of detail and calculated synthesis giving rise to a diverse and living unity, are the opposing poles of Menzel's practice as an artist. It is this double position that makes Menzel's reaction to the realities of his time so topical. The nods he makes in the direction of modern trends – positivism, photography and industry – bear witness to his modernity, as does his depiction of the labyrinths of city life and of history. They show that the principle of decomposition was already fundamental to life in the nineteenth century. In a world where daily life had become extremely complex and confusing, in a world of parataxis, verifiable connections and a living vision of things must necessarily be arrived at via intimate knowledge of all the details. Details then became both the fragments and the building blocks of a lost unity needing to be reconstructed. When we get to the bottom of all the great idealist, philosophical or scientific systems that come under the heading of positivist empiricism, to the basis of all the conventions handed down by religion, the State and society under the heading of industrialization, there is a sense of the totality and diversity of life, and of its loss, that can only be recovered in an absorption with detail and the innumerable possibilities of reconstruction and dismantling of its forms. Life, as Menzel showed early on in his depiction of Fortune, consists of infinite details poured over our heads from her cornucopiae in an endless stream. An exact realist like Menzel therefore sought to go into detail and, with his accurate knowledge of it, represent the whole as a unity made up of its constituent components.

Fig. 152. Villa Bode, Uhlandstrasse, Berlin-Charlottenbourg, built by Hans Grisebach in 1885, anonymous photograph

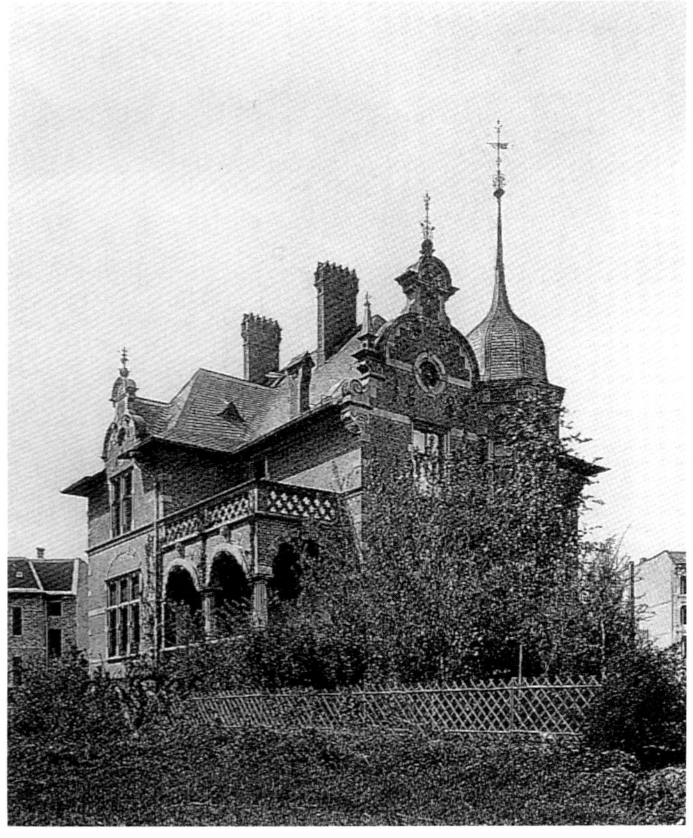

But Menzel's modernity in this respect did not mean just an uninterrupted and feverish extension of his attention to an endless profusion of contemporary and historical realities. The essential point is perhaps that Menzel's universe also included a great diversity of modes of representation and therefore many different ways of achieving a balance between the parts and the whole. But his composition, which gives so strong a sense of fragmentation, could suggest profusion as well as a distancing from life, dynamism as well as the disintegration of the condition of things and of vital constellations, and all in a deliberate and perfectly ambivalent manner. On the other hand, the studies of Menzel's early career, painted with such mastery, are just as enigmatic in their amazingly heterogeneous details. The alleged contradiction between the works of a happy youth, fruit of a simple virtuosity of expression, confined exclusively to the private sphere, and Menzel's later works of an official character, problematic owing to their compositional sophistication – this apparent contradiction then finds its resolution in a world of multiple artistic possibilities. Menzel had them all at his fingertips, switching abruptly from one to the other and so contriving subversive surprise effects. As we have seen, he used Romanticism to criticize Romanticism. He transformed the naturalistic *veduta* into an atmospheric townscape of essentially romantic character. History painting became on-the-spot reportage with the qualities of a documentary film. An apparently impressionistic interior turned out to be a pictorial allegory of the enigma of reality. In his historical painting, Menzel also celebrated realism as truly living art. And if his pictures of the industrial world, incomparable in their realism, tend on the contrary to magnify factory work and confer on it the status of a myth of modern life, his *Children's Album* is a no less realistic representation of the world as an enchanted, fairy-tale realm.

In Menzel's universe, the different parts cannot be set

in opposition to one another. His painting of the industrial world cannot be seen as superseding an outmoded form of history painting. Nor is Menzel's technique of fragmentary composition more modern, because of its implied criticism of social alienation, than his depiction of fairy stories: in the latter role he is just as keen an observer of the social and individual world. With Menzel, it is always a question of a highly subjective perception of the world in all its dimensions – present and past, diversity and particularity – and the representation of that world by extremely diverse means. The real miracle of Menzel and his universe is his ability to master and make use of all subjects and all modes of representation. It is this capacity that Fontane was referring to – and not only the infinite range of his subject-matter – in the famous dictum: Menzel is everything.

Faced with such richness and heterogeneity, one cannot but be astonished at Menzel's prodigious productivity in reacting without fail to the profusion of diverse impressions offered by the outside world. An inexhaustible appetite for work was undoubtedly one of the principal Protestant virtues on which Menzel's world was founded. It is significant that the criticism he levelled at his own first oil paintings, executed with such mastery, was the same as his criticism of Impressionist works: that they were lazily executed and slapdash. The second pillar of his art was the insatiable curiosity with which he viewed the world, a universal attention akin to that of a reporter. Menzel was in fact an admirer of *Punch* and collected great piles of the magazine[47]. But the nature of his curiosity precluded his undertaking long journeys, for the simple reasons that he 'had still not finished with Germany'[48]. And this fear of not being able to get to the end of it aroused in Menzel a sense of anguish at the prospect of death. He was not very happy with Fontane's poem marking his seventieth birthday, because it accorded him only another ten years[49]. He eventually reached the age of eighty-nine, leading a life devoted entirely to observation, yet curiously withdrawn. For Menzel needed an extreme form of discipline. He needed to shut himself away almost all day long in his studio, to be able, as Fontane had rightly seen, to transform the innumerable stimuli of the city into an oeuvre of unlimited scope[50].

The task undertaken by Menzel (undoubtedly Berlin's most famous eccentric) in his studio was not a description of reality but a production of reality using a whole range of techniques of representation. This stylistic pluralism was itself ideally suited to the period. The extent to which Menzel exactly matched the flood of images beginning to overwhelm major cities is shown by Jules Laforgue's astonished description of Berlin's pillar-shaped billboards. In 1887, he noted that they were covered with 'every possible kind of advertisement, in wild promiscuity'[51]. Menzel's work is the first response, in the field of art, to the disparity of visual forms of communication in the modern city, and to the way in which the observer is conditioned by them. It is true that, behind this world of artistic representations, for Menzel there lies the idea that the strength of the artist is that of a demiurge capable of unlimited creation. Above and beyond modern sobriety, Menzel's artistic positivism and his permanent attachment to detail are marked by a solemn pathos, which led even his contemporaries to compare his art to a religion. For Menzel, then, the whole is not just the sum of the parts, but each part itself reveals the whole which it bears in itself[52]. Behind this idea lies one of the fundamentals on which Menzel's artistic universe rests: the conviction that art is less to do with reality than with truth. 'Beauty is to be found where truth is. Truth is everything'[53]. When he could find no way of producing a credible representation of truth, Menzel, though capable of carrying off anything on a purely visual level, could not but leave his pictures uncompleted, as he himself said. This is as true of the *Lying in State of the March Dead* as of *Frederick the Great Addressing his Generals before the Battle of Leuthen* (cat. 90).

It is this ideal of truth, the attempt to convey the truth of the real world, which gives the palette of Menzel's subjective viewpoint its scope, and is the basis for the diversity of his subjective participation in what he represents, whether through coded messages, irony, poking fun, humour or transfiguration. Ottomar Beta was well aware that Menzel the realist was 'at the same time dreamer, satirist, symbolist and contemplative'[54]. In all these fields, Menzel appears as a true realist, thanks to his accurate perception of detail and the artistic synthesis he achieves using the procedures already described as deriving from his subjective viewpoint. As early as 1819, Schopenhauer, in his principal work, *The World as Will and Idea*, had stated that history painting discharged its 'endless task' by 'bringing to our attention scenes of life just as they are, both those that are of great importance and those that are not. No individual or action can be without significance or importance: in them and through them, the idea of humanity gradually develops. Painting should therefore exclude nothing of what makes up human life'[55].

This corresponds to Fontane's plea for the incidental in art. Fontane was an admirer of Schopenhauer as of Menzel and explicitly took the painter's art of detail as a model for his realistic novels. Of the aesthetics of detail he gave this laconic formulation: 'The incidental is obviously nothing if it is only incidental, if it conceals nothing. But if it conceals something, it will be no less than the essential, for it will always give you what is truly human'[56]. From declarations of this kind, it has been deduced that Fontane was the source of Warburg's celebrated formula, whereby God is to be found in detail[57]. Whether this is true or not, in these words Fontane gave a precise formulation of that contingency of the absolute which, together with his subjective viewpoint and synthesis of component parts into a whole, constitutes Menzel's modernity. Truth, reality and life are revealed only in the particular instance. And it is only in the particular, only through the *concordia discors* of all these details, arrived at via his subjective viewpoint, that Menzel's universe acquires its force of persuasion and suggestion, its vitality.

The dialectic of the contingence of the absolute enables us to explain why Menzel's art is dependent on his store of observations. Menzel, insatiable eye scrutinizing Berlin, cannot apparently be dissociated from the place of his observations. This is why he has been compared to the giant Antheus, whose strength deserted him if he was lifted off the ground[58]. But if Menzel's modernity lies in the aesthetic of the incidental, in the contingency of the absolute, made credible by art, how legitimate is his art beyond the confines of his experience? Would it not be true to say that Berlin, visual treasure-house of such vital details, is in fact Menzel's prison? This would indeed be the case if reality were at the heart of the painter's art. But the purpose of his art, which is to reveal not reality but truth in each of its particular manifestations, makes Menzel's artistic universe a modern *orbis pictus*, a visual encyclopaedia expressive of ever-renewed knowledge of human life.

There is no question, in Menzel's *orbis pictus*, of putting into practice reasonable rules for living of the kind we find in the Enlightenment narratives painted by Hogarth and Chodowiecki[59]. Nor did Menzel believe in the advent in history of reason as such, a faith conveyed in the veritable historical treatises painted by Kaulbach. In the case of Menzel, such Hegelian totalities are superseded, after the disappointments of 1848, by the idea, encouraged by Schopenhauer, that the will to live asserts itself with the greatest brutality and is manifest in all individuals. Life has no other meaning than its own renewal and its tireless vitality, which can be experienced and observed by individuals only from their subjective points of view. In Schopenhauer's view, man, who appears to be a protagonist but who, in the final analysis, is no more than a powerless component of the violent vitality of life, has no recourse but to an art submerged in detail, if he is to give a human face to the anarchic flow of the world[60]. Or, to return to Fontane's words pointing to the incidental as the fundamental element of modernity: 'But if it conceals something, it will be no less than the essential, for it will always give you what is truly human.' Menzel's work, seen in this light, is an encyclopaedic attempt to save the incidental, be it ever so insignificant, by means of art. His subjective viewpoint, and its power to perform a synthesis which transforms the component parts into a whole, to represent the contingence of the absolute with an obsessive concern for detail – it is this, as we have seen, that constitutes the modernity and truth of Menzel's art. In the contest between Poussin and Caillebotte, Menzel would have been firmly on the side of the contingent. But a contingent that Menzel turned into an absolute, revealing life and humanity in all its diversity and with all its contradictions. It is this reciprocal interplay of contingent and absolute that elevates Menzel's modernity to the status of what we have called 'Menzel's universe'.

1. *Cf.* Werner Spies, 'Poussin in exile', *Frankfurter Allgemeine Zeitung*, 17 January 1995.
2. Varnedoe, 1989.
3. Quoted from Bluhm/Nitsche, 1993, p. 16.
4. Theodor Fontane, letter to Georg Friedlaeneder, 21 December 1884: 'Indeed, Berlin for him was a necessity. Menzel fifty years in Filehne would no longer be Menzel. . .'. Quoted in Reuter, 1968, I, p. 499 ff.
5. *Cf.* Lammel, 1992, p. 104.
6. Laforgue, 1884, p. 82.
7. Meier-Graefe, 1906, p. 141.
8. Liebermann, 1978, p. 147.
9. Hofmann, 1982, p. 31 ff.
10 Quoted from Lichtwark, 1924, II, p. 184. Regarding Menzel and the Impressionists in the Bernstein Collection *cf.* also Teeuwisse, 1986, p. 98 ff.
11. *Cf.* Lammel, 1992, p. 23.
12. Feist, 1980, p. 21.
13. Quoted from Reuter, 1968, II, p. 778.
14. Laforgue, 1984, p. 77 ff. Regarding Menzel's attitude to animals, *cf.* Lammel, 1992, p. 92 ff. In this tradition of listing: Grisebach, 1984, p. 18 ff.
15. Reply to an enquiry by the review *Die Gegenwart*, 1897, p. 200.
16. Regarding Menzel's studio, see the comments made by his visitors, *cf.* Lammel, 1992, p. 73 ff., p. 267, p. 275, p. 302 ff., p. 311, p. 353 ff.
17. According to Julius Norden, 1900. *Cf.* Lammel, 1992, p. 312.
18. Reproduced in Glatzer, 1933, p. 136.
19. Liebermann, 1978, p. 134.
20. According to Jan Veth, 1904, quoted from Lammel, 1992, p. 312.
21. *Cf.* on this subject Schaar, 1982, p. 200 ff.
22. Numerous comments on Menzel and photography in the work of Paul Meyerheim, *cf.* Lammel, 1992.
23. Liebermann, 1978, p. 134.
24. *Ibid.*, p. 135.
25 *Ibid.*, p. 136.
26 Joris-Karl Huysmans, *L'art moderne/Certains*, 10/18. 1975, p. 134.
27. *Cf.* Reff, 1982, p. 87.
28. Menzel made these remarks in the presence of Ottomar Beta, quoted from Lammel, 1992, p. 27 ff.
29. *Cf.* Busch, 1985, p. 87.
30. *Cf.* Paret, 1988, p. 34 ff.
31. Tschudi, 1912.
32. Heyse, (1912) 1992, p. 148–9.
33. *Cf.* Hofmann in the introduction to the catalogue of the exhibition held in Hamburg, 1982, p. 7.
34. *Cf.* Busch, 1985, p. 278 *et seq.* I owe the interpretation of *Balcony Room* as an 'allegory of painting' to Sabina Slanina.
35. *Cf.* Zweite, 1991, p. 30.

36. Regarding 'transfigurative' realism, *cf.* Brinkmann, 1967, p. 39 ff. As regards Menzel, *cf.* Radziewsky, 1982, p. 17 ff.
37. According to Jensen, 1982, p. 108.
38. *Cf.* Steinhauser, 1994, p. 9 ff., p. 55 ff.
39. Jensen, 1992, p. 106.
40. Jensen, 1992, p. 110. On p. 80 of this book, it states that: 'Menzel, the Prussian protestant, regarding whom there is no evidence of any kind of religious sentiment, whose letters and sayings indicate rather a stoical scepticism in the Schopenaurian sense. . .' A detailed study of Menzel and Schopenhauer is yet to be written.
41. *Cf.* Forster-Hahn, 1977, p. 242–55.
42. *Cf.* Paret, 1988, p. 62 ff.
43. The comparison was made by the Berlin painter Albert Hertel (1911–12) 1992, p. 104.
44. Steinhauser, 1994, p. 14.
45. *Cf.* Schmidt in the catalogue to the Berlin exhibition of 1955, p. 189.
46. Letter of 21 December 1884 to Georg Friedlaender, quoted from Reuter, 1968, I, p. 499–500.
47. Quoted from Lammel, 1992, p. 360.
48. Reported by Paul Meyerheim, (1906) 1992, p. 224.
50. Fontane, letter of 21 December 1884 to Georg Friedlaender: '. . . but see too how he [Menzel] lived in Berlin. He shut him self away in his studio from 9 to 9, and only when other people were going to bed did he go to the court with his sash or to Huth's place in his opera hat. All his life he was a master of the art of concentration, and that is why he pursued the career of an artist without ever being career-minded.' Quoted from Fontane, 1981, p. 295.
51. Jules Laforgue, *Berlin, La cour et la ville*, 1922, p. 92.
52. Quoted from Beta, (1898) 1992, p. 72. *Cf.* on this point Elke von Radziewsky, 1992, p. 28.
53. Quoted in this form by Evers-Milner, (1940) 1992, p. 151.
54. Ottomar Beta's formulation, (1898) 1992, p. 15.
55. Translation of a passage quoted by Paret, 1988, p. 15.
56. Quoted from Brinkmann, 1967, p. 59. Regarding Fontane and Menzel, *cf.* Ihlenfeld, 1969, p. 108 ff.
57. *Cf.* on this point Dieter Wuttke, in Aby Warburg, *Ausgewählte Schriften und Würdigung*, Baden-Baden, 1979, p. 614–24.
58. Veth, (1904) 1992, p. 312.
59. *Cf.* Arndt, 1994, p. 113 ff.
60. *Cf.* Schulz, 1981, p. 403 ff.

Catalogue

Note to the reader

The works are discussed in chronological order as far as possible, and themes are grouped together when this allows. Studies precede the final work. We have opted to group themes in only three cases, *The Coronation of William I at Königsberg*, *Children's Album*, and *The Iron Rolling Mill*; in these cases, the purpose was to highlight the origins of the works in question.
Most of the drawings and gouaches are kept in the Kupferstichkabinett of the Berlin Museums, although they have been housed there for only a few years. When it opened in 1876, the Nationalgalerie began its collection of drawings, apart from paintings and sculptures, but this was transferred to the Kupferstichkabinett in 1992. This new system coincided with a move to bring together collections that had previously been distributed between Museum Island in East Berlin and the Dahlem Museum in West Berlin.

The complicated numbering of Menzel's drawings (it consists of figures preceded by the letters Kat., N and Nr.) requires an explanation. The system is based on the dates of acquisition: the 1712 drawings acquired between the years 1880 and 1902 appear in a catalogue drawn up by Lionel von Donop and published in the latter year, and these are the numbers that are referred to here using Kat. In 1906, the Nationalgalerie acquired a large number of works from the artist's studio, and these drawings, of which there were approximately 4500 in addition to the sketchbooks, were given numbers preceded by the letter N. All subsequent acquisitions received numbers preceded by Nr.; this system begins with the number 1713.

Catalogue authors:
Andreas Heese (A.H.)
Claude Keisch (C.K.)
Marie Ursula Riemann-Reyher (M.R.-R.)
Elisabeth Vogl (E.V.) (cat. 1 only)

1

The Game of Chess

1836

Oil on canvas
42 × 42cm
Signed and dated bottom left: *Menzel p. / 1836*
Germany, private collection
Exhibited in Berlin only

Provenance: Mr Eltschig, merchant, Berlin; Mr Eltschig's widow, née Neumann, Berlin; *c.* 1880 inherited by her sister, Auguste Neuber, née Neumann, Berlin ; then by the latter's daughter, Margarete Scharlock; between 1908–9 and 1948 Dr Erich Moewes, state councillor; private collections; 1960 on sale in Frankfurt am Main; 1960 E. Weber, Frankfurt; 1962 acquired by the current owner.
Exhibitions: Berlin, 1836, no. 600; Berlin, 1837; Bamberg, 1968; Augsburg, 1981–2 (not in cat.).
Bibliography: Kugler, 1837, p. 282; Tschudi, 1905 A, p. IX (unnumb., no reprod.); Wolff, 1914 p. 10 *et seq.*; *Frankfurter Rundschau*, 23 January 1960, p. 6, reprod.; *Die Weltkunst*, XXXII, 1962, no. 4, p. 16, reprod. p. 28; Jensen, 1982, p. 20, fig. 11; Zangs, 1992, p. 43 *et seq.*

The Game of Chess was Menzel's first painting in oil, and was sold shortly after completion. It was then forgotten, and subsequently thought to have been lost. Hugo von Tschudi was able to see it on only one occasion, in 1909.

Two letters written by Menzel himself tell us something about events leading up to this work. Although he was still complaining to his friend, Carl Heinrich Arnold, in February 1836 about 'a large number of intervening [graphic] works' which were preventing him from painting, he was able to say, on 8 October 1836: 'So there! I have finished my painting – there is nothing more to be done! No doubt Biermann has told you that I have continued to work with paint as thick as my finger, although I started off with such delicacy and tried so hard to keep myself in check. It still turned out to be something half kneaded and half mixed together, but Biermann thinks that I came out of it well enough. My only consolation is that it will not look too out of place among the rubbish on show at the exhibition [Academy of Arts 1836][1]. At least I have had some experience of painting, and that was my main aim. My second attempt will, I hope, be better'[2].

After the exhibition at the Academy of Arts, *The Game of Chess* was shown only once in Menzel's lifetime, and that was at the premises of his dealer, Sachse, in 1837. Franz Kugler wrote at the time – and this was two years before their collaboration which was to have such a momentous influence on Menzel's artistic career – that the painting still bore 'the unmistakable mark of an experiment'[3]. At the age of 20, Menzel was under the spell of 'historical genre painting', which, representing scenes from daily life in previous eras, proved hugely popular in the 1830s. Moreover, his work in this field as a young man influenced his subsequent ideas for historical painting. For instance, his refusal to idealize events of historical importance by dissociating them from daily reality gave rise to reservations about his illustrations for the *Geschichte Friedrichs des Grossen* (History of Frederick the Great). As soon as the cycle on the life of Frederick the Great was interrupted, the artist focused more attention on the representation of contemporary life. With that, he began to introduce historical genre subject-matter into his work, and that triggered a number of lively, small-format paintings on seventeenth-century themes (*cf.* cat. 166, 188). The gouache entitled *Contribution* (fig. 153), dated 1885[4], gives us the clearest idea of the changes that had taken place in the 50 years since *The Game of Chess*, and of what had survived intact.

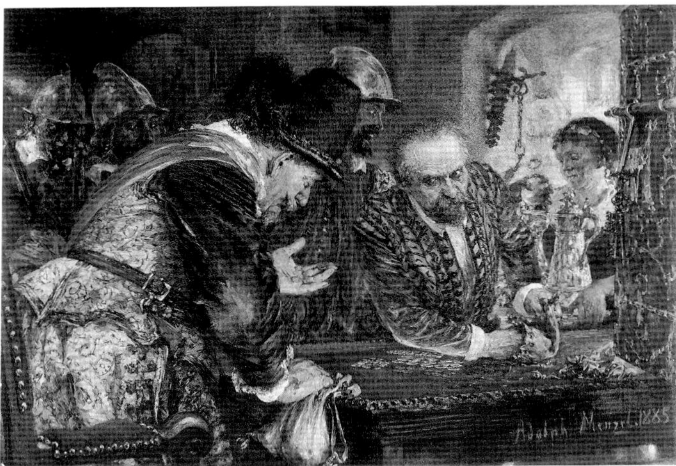

Fig. 153.
Contribution, 1885,
gouache, Berlin,
Kupferstichkabinett
(N 1802)

The Game of Chess takes the viewer back to the days of the Thirty Years War. Two gentlemen are seated in a passageway playing a game of chess, and light is coming in through a bull's-eye glass window. One of the players has hung his hat, shoulder-belt and sword on the wall, and put down his bag; the other player has remained fully dressed, and is holding on to his sword. The player on the right is waiting resignedly for the final, decisive stage of the game, and his opponent, with a triumphant look in his eye, is about to move the black queen. The tension that has been built up is about to break. In the background, two women are talking animatedly with another gentleman wearing arms, and a crooked ladder leads up to the loft. The scene is illuminated by a warm, but subdued, light, though an additional source of light appears to be coming from outside the picture, and from the direction of the viewer. Menzel never ceased to be intrigued by the interactions between various sources of light; remarkably, on this occasion, the colours, which have been applied in thick layers, have retained their freshness and luminous intensity.

Most depictions of games of chess represent the board with its characteristic black and white squares, but in this case Menzel selected a viewpoint which is at an

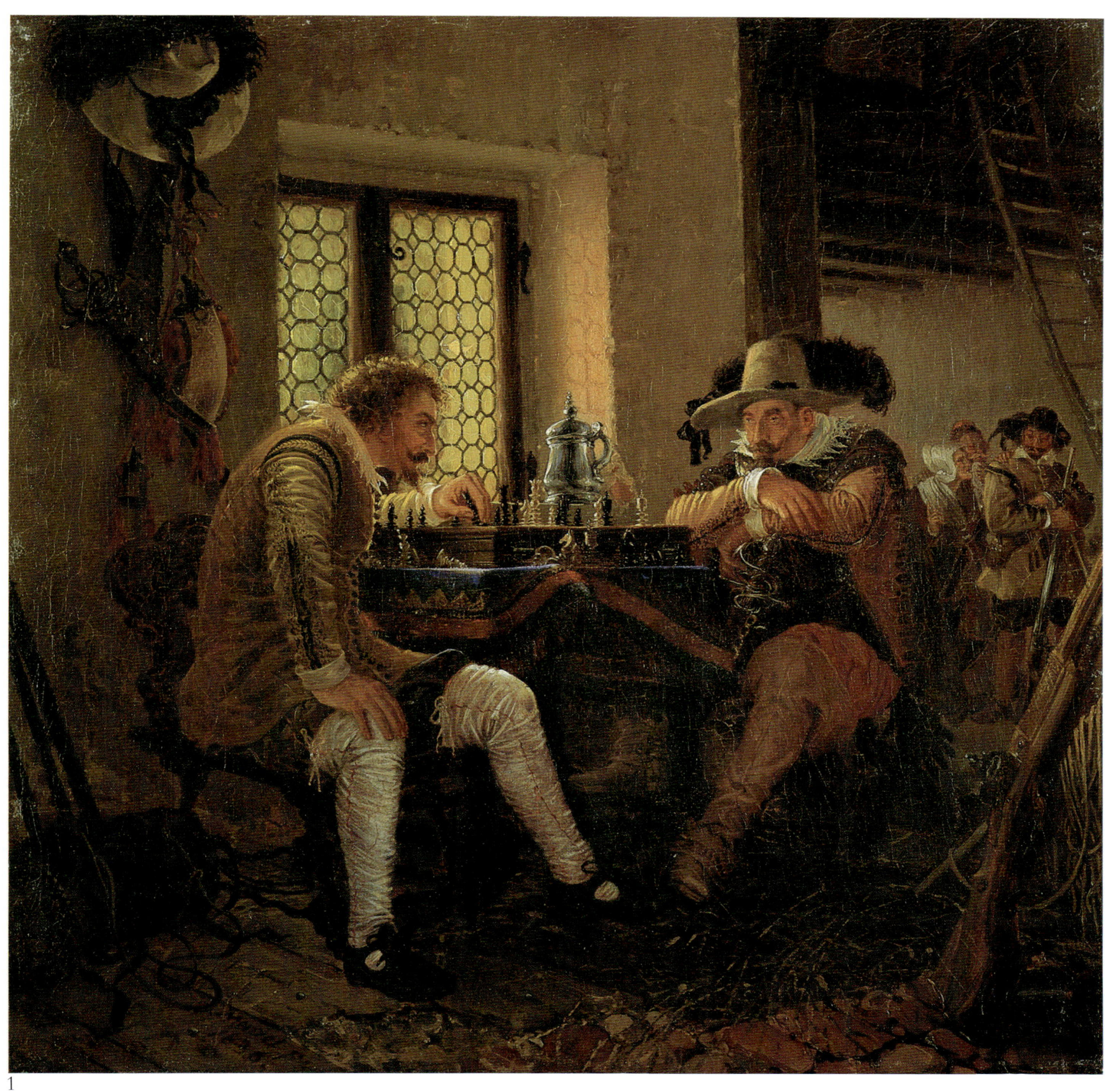

1

angle to the table, and thereby conceals the board. However, it is still easy to see the nine black and five white pieces still in play, and the superior position enjoyed by the player on the left.

Chess had been played extensively for many centuries, and it was certainly very popular in Berlin. There had been an association of chess players in the city since 1806, and documentary evidence refers to the existence of a Chess Society since 1828. The motif presented in this painting recalls Dutch interior scenes of the seventeenth century, and Menzel was undoubtedly aware of a group portrait by Johann Erdmann Hummel which bears a passing resemblance to this work. E.V.

1. Letter to Carl Heinrich Arnold, 23 February 1836, Wolff, 1914, p. 4.
2. Letter to Carl Heinrich Arnold, 8 October 1836, Wolff, 1914, p. 10–11.
3. Kugler, 1837, p. 282.
4. 1885, Tschudi, 1905 A, no. 651; Kupferstichkabinett, Berlin (SZ Menzel Nr 1802).

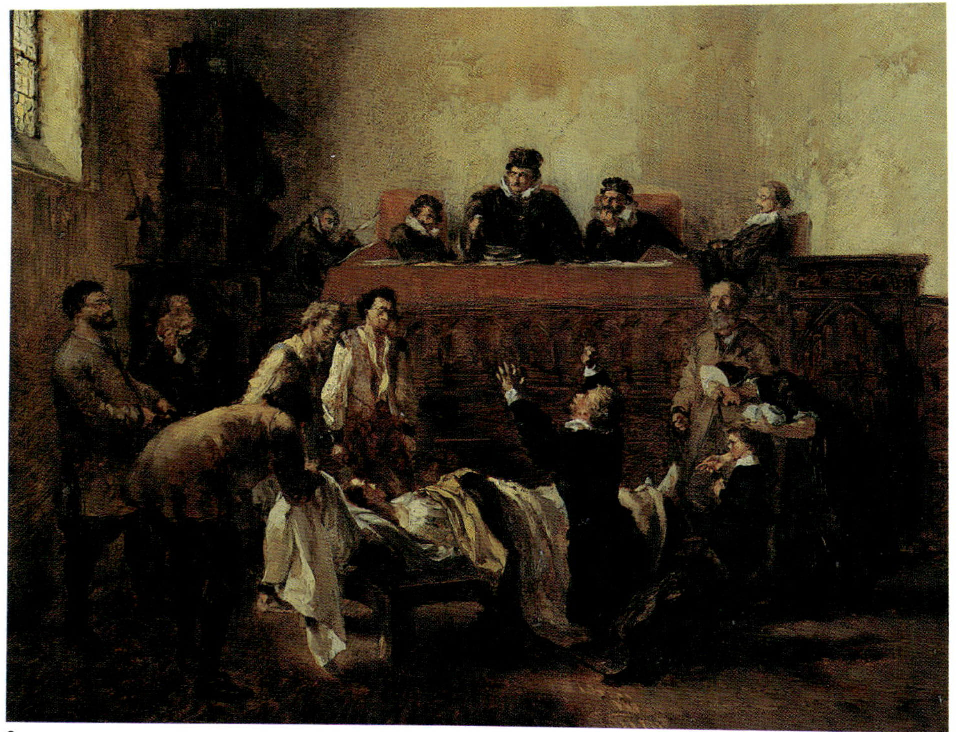
2

2
Day of the Hearing. Sketch
1838

Oil on canvas
29.1 × 36.1cm
Signed at the bottom left: *Menzel*
Berlin, Nationalgalerie (A I 896)
Exhibited in Berlin only

Provenance: 1905 Count of Pourtalès, Munich; R. Wagner Gallery, Berlin; acquired by the museum in 1906.
Exhibitions: Berlin 1895 A, Nr. 120; Berlin, 1905, no. 88; Berlin, 1935, no. 1; Berlin, 1980 A, no. 1, reprod. p. 210.
Bibliography: Tschudi, 1905 A, no. 5; cat. NG, 1907, no. 990; Scheffler, 1922, p. 143; Justi, 1932, p. 133; Scheffler, 1938, p. 55 *et seq.*; cat. NG, 1986, no pag., fig. 66.

Menzel chose this 'curious subject'[1] for the second of his large-format paintings 'only because it provided an opportunity to carry out studies of a variety of physiognomies'. The first, which had also been set in the time of the Thirty Years War[2] and was of almost identical dimensions, had been painted in 1837. The scene represented in this sketch deals with the then fashionable theme of robbers and imprisonment. Kneeling before the corpse of his murdered wife, and accompanied by his child who does not yet understand the meaning of mourning, a widowed husband brings an action against the murderer; he vents his despair with such vehemence that the court is obliged to call for silence. However, might there not be a case here for shelving the traditional story, and interpreting the drama afresh? Could this man be a father instead of a husband? In the final painting, one of the accused looks more like a lover than a highwayman and that might suggest a slightly different interpretation of the subject.

A study dated 1838 shows the woman lying on the stretcher with the porter leaning over her[3], just as he does in the oil sketch. When the large-format painting was produced immediately afterwards, this group – and no other section – was substantially changed, and the highly dramatic servant and shroud were removed. What the composition thereby lost in short-lived anguish, it made up for in balance and clarity.

The final painting was shown in 1839 and in Gottfried Schadow, the sculptor who was also director of the Academy of Arts in Berlin, it found its first admirer. He was not to be the last. Over twenty years later, by which time the artist had completed many masterpieces, an influential critic described this picture as 'of all Menzel's paintings – and we know nearly all of them – . . . the most important and, in all respects, the most beautiful'[4]. Comparisons were made with Delaroche and Gallait. In fact, the influence is very clear, and the historical context and the artistic trends are also comparable, although Menzel's enthusiasm for historical scenes made famous by Gallait and de Keyser did not become apparent for many years to come. By contrast, Julius Meier-Graefe described *Day of the Hearing* as one of Menzel's 'indifferent works' and one of the 'poor, banal paintings' of his early period[5]. It had been commissioned by a merchant named Herrmann; then, after passing through the hands of a number of owners, the painting was not seen again until early this century.

In the middle of the nineteenth century, and in the Berlin and Düsseldorf Schools in particular, historical genre subjects were enormously popular; one of the reasons may have been that this mixed genre challenged the traditional standards of history painting. Working from reconstructions of daily life in previous eras, it was possible to think afresh about the dramatic representation of political or military events. This strongly affected Menzel's paintings that illustrated the life of Frederick II; it also explains why he was accused (and with particular force by Max Schasler) of aligning himself with genre painting and its variations without ever breaking free from history painting as such. C.K.

1. Letter to C. H. Arnold, 30 April 1839, Wolff, 1914, p. 28.
2. *The Enemy Arrives*, Tschudi, 1905 A, no. 1; whereabouts unknown. Both paintings are approximately one metre wide.
3. Munich, Staatliche Graphische Sammlung (36015); cat. Hamburg, 1982, no. 2, reprod. It is unlikely that the sketch in oils could date from any earlier than this.
4. Schasler, 1863, p. 369.
5. Meier-Graefe, 1906, p. 85.

3

Eduard Meyerheim
Portrait of Adolph Menzel as a Young Man
c. 1839

Oil on canvas
42.7 × 36.6cm
Berlin, Nationalgalerie (NG 995)
Exhibited in Paris and Berlin only

Provenance: 1880, Paul Meyerheim, son of the painter; acquired by the museum in 1884.
Exhibitions: Berlin, 1880, no. 36; Celle, 1949–50, no. 92; Kassel, 1964, no. 73.
Bibliography: Cat. NG, 1907, no. 995; Bildnissammlung, 1915, no. 53; Bildnissamlung, 1929, no. 45; cat. NG, 1976, p. 285, reprod.; Scheffler, 1912, reprod. p. 139; Lammel, 1993 A, p. 31, fig. 23 (detail).

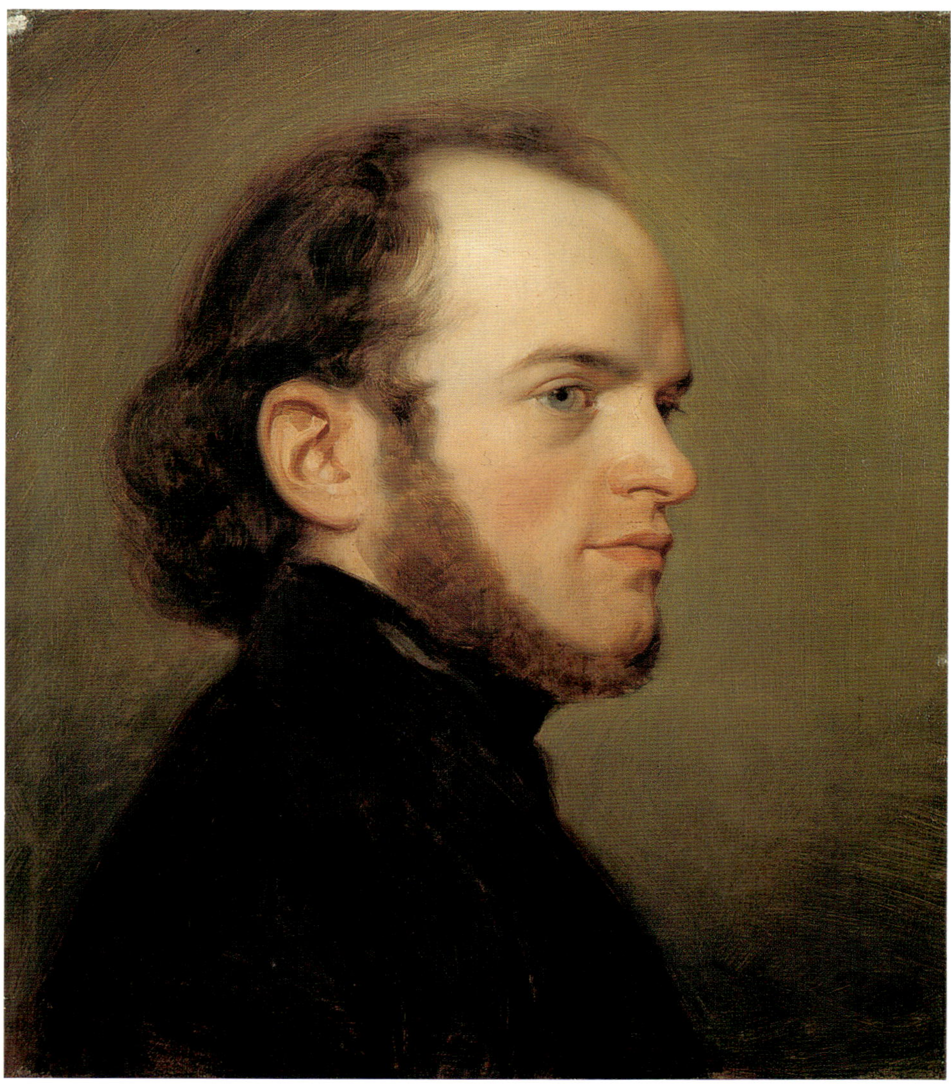
3

During the winter of 1834, artists including Schinkel, Rauch, Drake and Eduard Magnus began meeting as an informal group on Sunday evenings in the home of wallpaper manufacturer Carl Heinrich Arnold[1]. It was here that the genre painter Eduard Meyerheim (1808–79) and Menzel came into contact. Menzel was seven years younger, and had recently been making a name for himself with his series of lithographs on Goethe's *Künstlers Erdewallen* (The Artists's Earthly Pilgrimage). He also had a high opinion of the charming works produced by Meyerheim, despite the fact that the latter's skill was very different from his own: 'He was the first to regard with a poetic eye, and to represent with artistry, the lives of the little people of northern Germany, the people from the Harz Mountains and Thuringia in particular. . . . He is the father of the idyll of German art.' It was in these terms that Menzel described Meyerheim when putting him up for the Order of Merit (in the *Friedensklasse*, for art, science, literature etc.). Their friendship endured, and extended to include a broad circle of family members; a beautiful portrait in watercolours of Mrs Meyerheim (1847) is an eloquent testimony to this[2]. Later on, the circle also included Paul, Eduard's son, who was to be Menzel's companion for over a half a century, accumulating a splendid collection of mementoes of the artist.

This head-and-shoulders portrait shows Menzel still as a young man, and wearing a noble and serious expression; it also underlines the artist's burgeoning spirit and sound judgement. However, there is no indication of Menzel's short stature: in his youth his contemporaries rarely alluded to this; in his old age they often did! The only record we have of the youthful Menzel standing is a watercolour by Eduard Magnus[3]; it depicts the artist as a young man of twenty-one and dressed carefully with a touch of the dandy. For the work reproduced here, Meyerheim selected a flattering angle from a slightly lower viewpoint. This perspective, together with the square of the shoulders, make for distance and objectivity, while the sideways look is mindful, intelligent and shrewd. The young artist's impressive forehead is striking and prematurely balding.

The date of this portrait can only be determined by relating tangential events. Menzel had been wearing a beard along the line of his jaw since the mid-1830s but, if an anecdote is to be believed, he splashed blue paint on himself one day, and he had had to shave off his beard and not show himself in public for two weeks[4]. The year 1843[5] has been suggested for this portrait, but it is not convincing: a portrait of Menzel painted that year by Eduard Magnus[6] was already lacking the youthfulness that Meyerheim captured. The portrait in the Nationalgalerie conveys two aspects of the same man: on the one hand, the author of the large pen lithograph, *Lord's Prayer*[7], the man who was able to combine realism and religious allegory in a single, extravagant arabesque and simultaneously interpolate a masterly theological interpretation[8]; on the other hand, the young artist in 1839, confident of his talents and eager to reform German illustrative art and wood engraving. C.K.

1. Arnold, (1905) 1992, p. 129.
2. Berlin, Kupferstichkabinett (SZ Menzel Nr 1778); exhib. cat. New York, 1990, no. 5, col. reprod.
3. Berlin, Kupferstichkabinett (Magnus Nr 14); Lammel, 1993 B, fig. 20.
4. Lammel, 1993 B; in the 1880 exhibition catalogue, this painting is placed between works dated 1844 and 1845.
5. Arnold, (1905) 1992, p. 129–30.
6. Private collection; Lammel, 1993 B, fig. 22.
7. 1837, Bock, 1923, no. 193.
8. Kurth, 1905.

4

Frederick the Great's Study in the Palace of Potsdam

1840

Pencil
20.8 × 12.9cm
Signed and dated at the bottom right: *A.M.40.*
Berlin, Kupferstichkabinett (SZ Menzel Kat. 74)
Exhibited in Paris and Washington only

Provenance: Hermann Pächter (R. Wagner Gallery, Berlin); acquired by the museum in 1889.
Exhibitions: Berlin, 1905, no. 424; Berlin, 1955 A, no. 182; Berlin, 1980, no. 175; New York, 1990, no. 16.
Bibliography: Donop, 1902, no. 74; Liebermann/Kern, 1921, p. 11, col. pl. 2; exhib. cat. Hamburg, 1982, p. 10, fig. p. 11.

In 1834, the pen lithographs inspired by Goethe's poem *Künstlers Erdenwallen*[1] (Artist's Earthly Pilgrimage) had provided Menzel with his first major success. Then, five years later, following Franz Kugler's intervention, a wonderful new project came his way. This was a commission for about four hundred wood engravings illustrating the *Geschichte Friedrichs des Grossen* (History of Frederick the Great)[2], a 'popular book' to be published in Leipzig by Weber. Menzel took his inspiration from the wood engravings by Horace Vernet for the *History of Napoleon* by Laurent de l'Ardèche[3] (Paris, 1839).

Kugler showed great wisdom in choosing Menzel, an almost unknown young artist who shared his passion for history conceived as an authentic reconstruction based on a painstaking study of primary sources. Menzel's engravings were lively and invigorated by the new aesthetics; what is more, they not only provided an excellent accompaniment for the splendid text, but also interpreted it freely, sometimes departing substantially from the original. It was this that gave the work its enduring qualities; moreover, almost three hundred years after Dürer, it also provided German wood engraving with a new impulse that was long overdue.

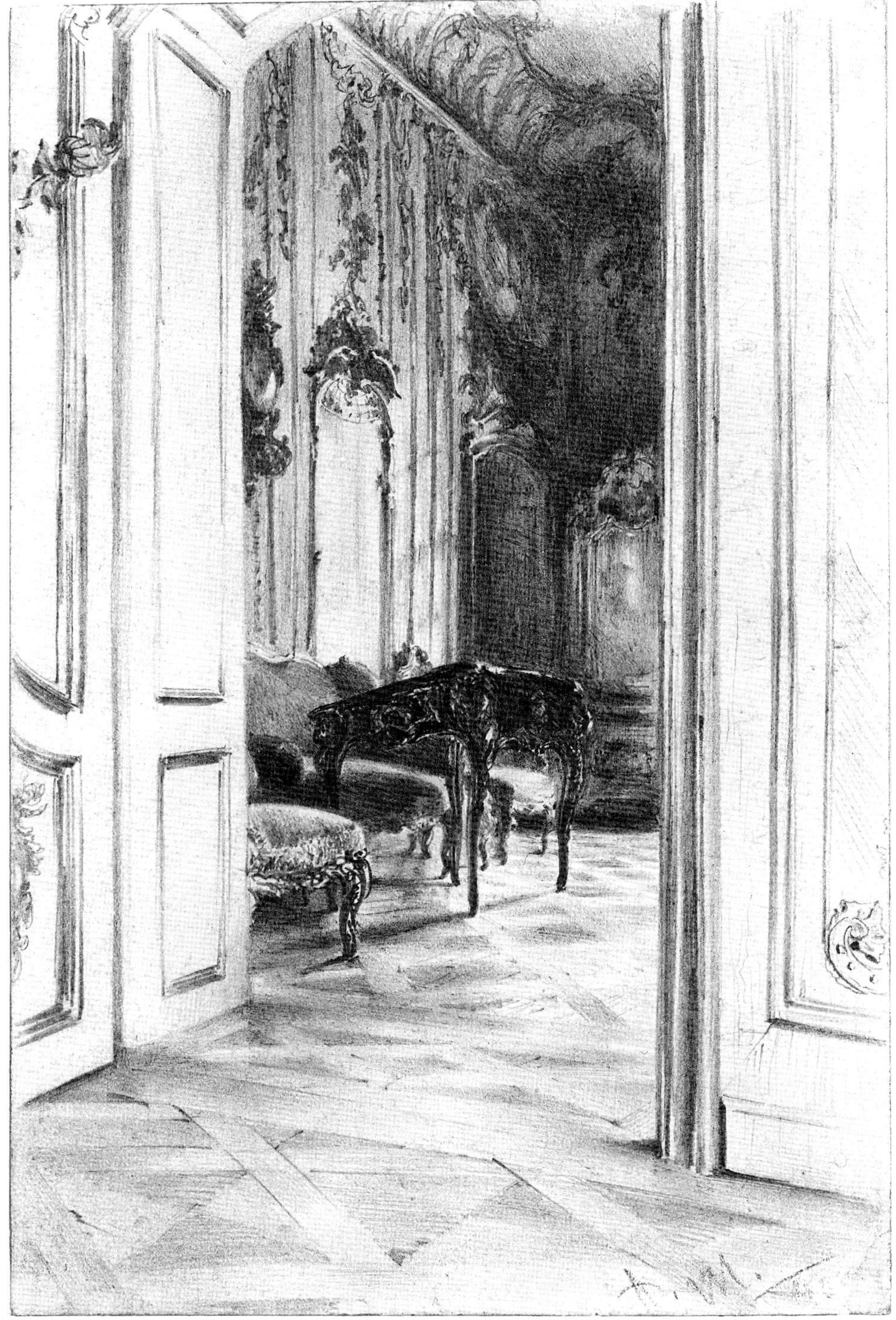

4

Menzel's copious correspondence with Weber, his publisher, testifies to the considerable efforts that he made to find wood engravers who measured up to his artistic demands[4]. Mindful of his experience with Parisian wood engravers, whose skills had been blunted by the routine nature of their work, and who did not reproduce his drawings with sufficient precision, Menzel actually trained these new engravers in Berlin himself for as long as they were engaged on this commission. The final work appeared in twenty instalments between 1840 and 1842. It received a controversial reception from Johann Gottfried Schadow, the director of the Berlin Academy, who publicly described Menzel's work as 'scrawl'[5], but it later became well known and firmly established Menzel's reputation.

Menzel relied on numerous studies for which he used a large number of varied sources[6]; these enabled him to achieve 'as much authenticity as possible'[7]. For this purpose, he devised a new style which comprised elegant form and a kind of adaptation of Rococo, and it is hardly surprising that the Classically minded Schadow was shocked. Menzel often journeyed to Potsdam to do drawings in two of Frederick the Great's palaces, the New Palace and Sanssouci[8].

Fig. 154. *History of Frederick the Great: the King at his desk*, 1839–42, wood engraving

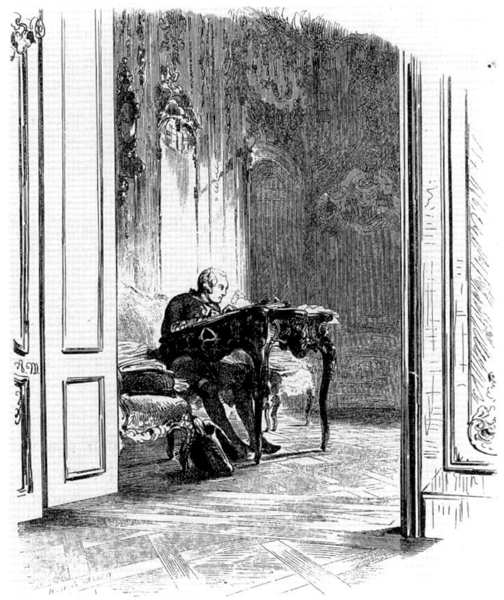

The king's study shown here is in a third palace, the city palace at Potsdam. Menzel had already drawn the divan and desk designed by J.M. Kambly[9], but the surface of the desk is more at an angle both on the later drawing shown here and on the wood engraving[10] (fig. 154). Menzel was too much of a Realist to alter his subjects just to suit artistic requirements. Otherwise, the engraving is almost identical, except that the dimensions of the room were compressed: the composition thereby loses some of its tension, but there is compensation in the accentuated angle of the desk and, behind it, the seated figure of the king looking for all the world like a humble servant of the State.

Menzel took a keen interest in the transfer of his drawings. In a letter to his publisher, he wrote: 'For the drawing of Frederick writing in his study, I would like the engraving of Frederick himself, the floor inside the study and the shadowy background, including the wall clock, to be done by Georgy. This small work must be done with the greatest of delicacy. When doing the background, Georgy should use the shadowy atmosphere of the Battle of Mollwitz (which he engraved himself) as his model, and be mindful of the details in this work'[11]. M.R.-R.

1. Title page and eleven lithographs, published by Sachse, 1834, Bock, 1923, p. 109–15.
2. 398 wood engravings for *History of Frederick the Great* by Franz Kugler, Leipzig, Verlag der J.J. Weberschen Buchhandlung, 1840. For the historical background, *cf.* Bock, 1923, p. 285 et seq., p. 427-824.
3. A German edition was published by Weber in Leipzig in 1841.
4. Much of this correspondence is reproduced in Wolff, 1914. A few unpublished letters are kept in the central archives of the Staatliche Museen zu Berlin.
5. *Cf.* Eckhardt, 1989.
6. Most are kept in the Kupferstichkabinett, Berlin.
7. Letter to Weber, 23 April 1839, Wolff, 1914, p. 27. On the subject of 'authenticity', *cf.* also a letter to C.H. Arnold, 30 April 1839, Wolff, 1914, p. 29.
8. *Cf.* on this subject, a letter to Wilhelm Puhlmann, 22 October 1840, Wolff, 1914, p. 52 and to Weber, 31 October 1840 (unpublished), central archives of the Staatliche Museen Preussischer Kulturbesitz, Berlin.
9. Berlin, Kupferstichkabinett (SZ Menzel Kat. 1690). Another drawing of the study (pencil, 16.4 × 11.3 cm) is drawn on the back of a handwritten letter (Reemtsma Collection, Hamburg), reproduced in Bremen, 1963, no. 44.
10. Bock, 1923, no. 599.
11. Letter to Weber, 20 November 1840, (unpublished), central archives, Staatliche Museen Preussischer Kulturbesitz.

5

The 'Green Stairway' at the Royal Palace of Potsdam

1842

Pencil
20.9 × 12.7cm
Berlin, Kupferstichkabinett (SZ Menzel Kat. 98)
Exhibited in Paris and Washington only

Provenance: Hermann Pächter (R. Wagner Gallery, Berlin); acquired by the museum in 1889.
Exhibitions: Berlin, 1905, no. 448; Berlin, 1980 A, no. 184, reprod.
Bibliography: Donop, 1902, no. 98.

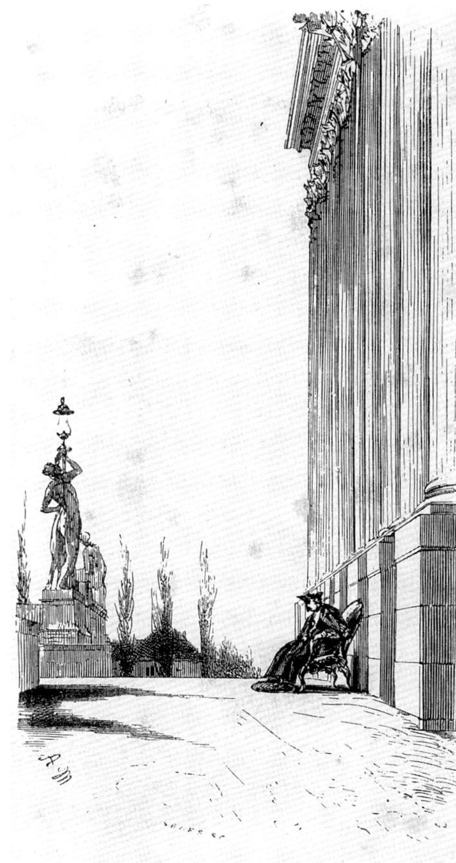

Fig. 155. *History of Frederick the Great: the Sick King*, 1839–42, wood engraving

In his comments on the illustrations for the *History of Frederick the Great*[1], Menzel wrote that he had drawn the inclined pathway at the royal castle at Potsdam, known as the 'Green Stairway', from real life; he did a number of exteriors in this way. This drawing was used for the penultimate chapter entitled 'Frederick's final days', and the author describes how the king, now a sick man and in the last year

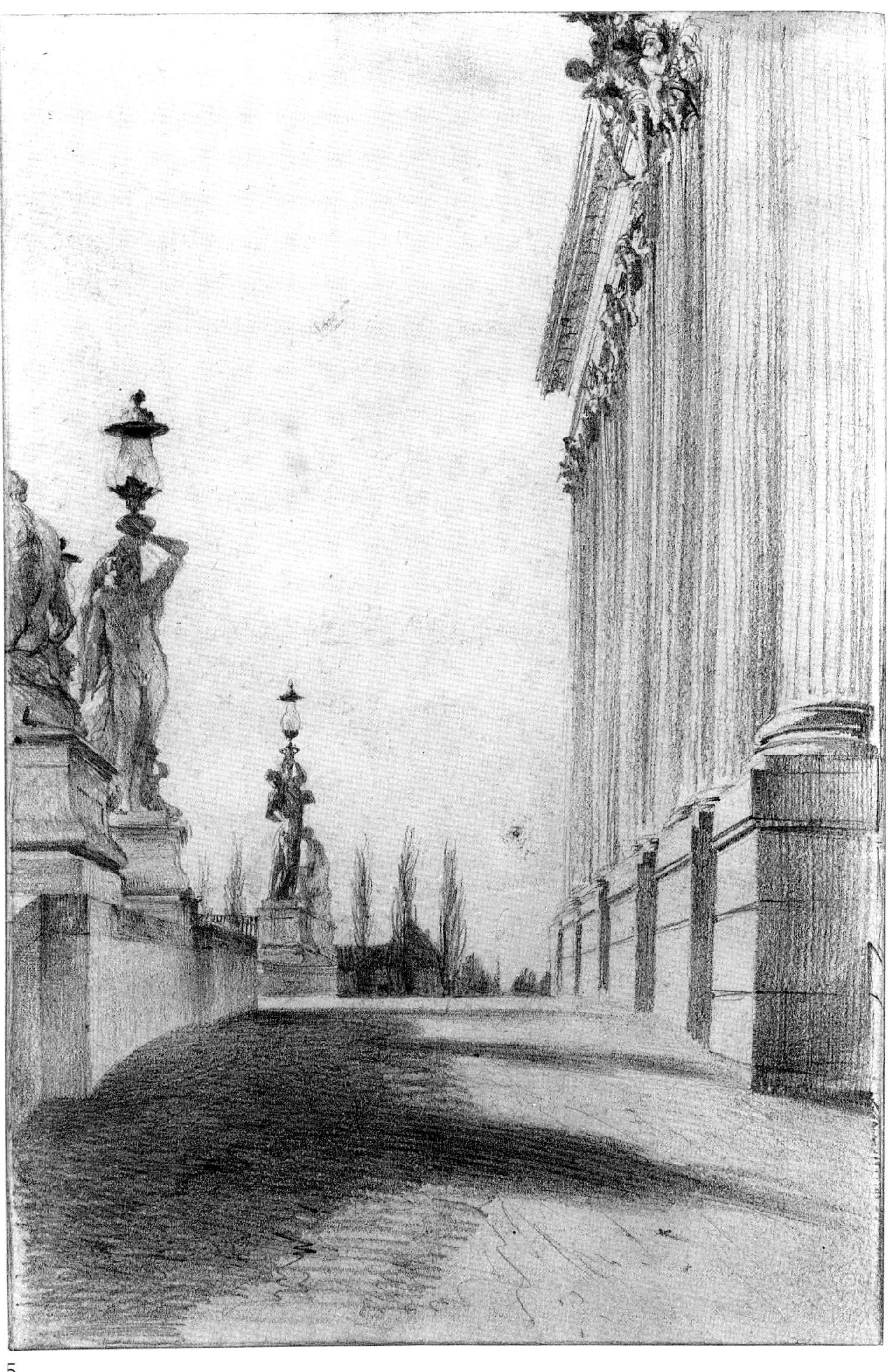

5

of his life, had himself carried out on to this pathway in an armchair to enjoy the last rays of the setting sun. The twentieth instalment of this series, which contains this engraving[2] (fig. 155), was published in 1842, and we can therefore date this drawing accurately[3]. The preparatory drawings for this book were mostly done with a sharp pencil, and are marked by careful hatching. M. R.-R.

1. In an appendix to the book.
2. Bock, 1923, no. 808.
3. Completion of the work is referred to in a letter from Menzel to C. H. Arnold, dated 19 July 1842, Wolff, 1914, p. 71 et seq.

6–9
Four Landscape Drawings
1842–3

Commissions began to multiply in the early 1840s, and the young Menzel was somehow able to fulfil them all, and even find time to draw a large number of fine landscapes.

A sketchbook that had been started in 1839, when the artist was 24, was used for the ensuing seven years. It illustrates the diversity of his work at this time, and also records the few moments of calm he allowed himself; these are admirably captured in the studies of landscapes[1]. He had begun work on the illustrations for the *History of Frederick the Great* in 1839, and a thirty-volume edition of the *Werke Friedrichs des Grossen* (Works of Frederick the Great) three years later. To turn down this royal commission would have been unthinkable, even though he had agreed with Louis Sachse, his publisher and dealer, to work on documenting the uniforms of Frederick's armies, a huge task that was to occupy him until 1857. And that was not all. After a number of unsuccessful attempts, Menzel also returned to his painting of *The Interruption* (cat. 19), which he had started in 1843 and did not finish until 1846. He had put it to one side in order to 'familiarise [himself] in the meantime with etching. I am extremely keen to achieve something in this field'[2]. Before even starting work on *Experiments in Etching*, a series of etchings depicting mostly landscapes and published by Sachse in 1844, Menzel had already completed a good many.

It is true that the isolated little house (cat. 7) was used in the etching entitled *Landscape with Three Huts*[3], but the opportunity to reproduce these drawings was certainly not their only function. Despite the immense amount of work that the artist had undertaken, these works surely grew from a deep, inner need, and observation of nature surely compensated for his ambitious efforts in the new field of wood engraving. It might be said that, in a great act of liber-

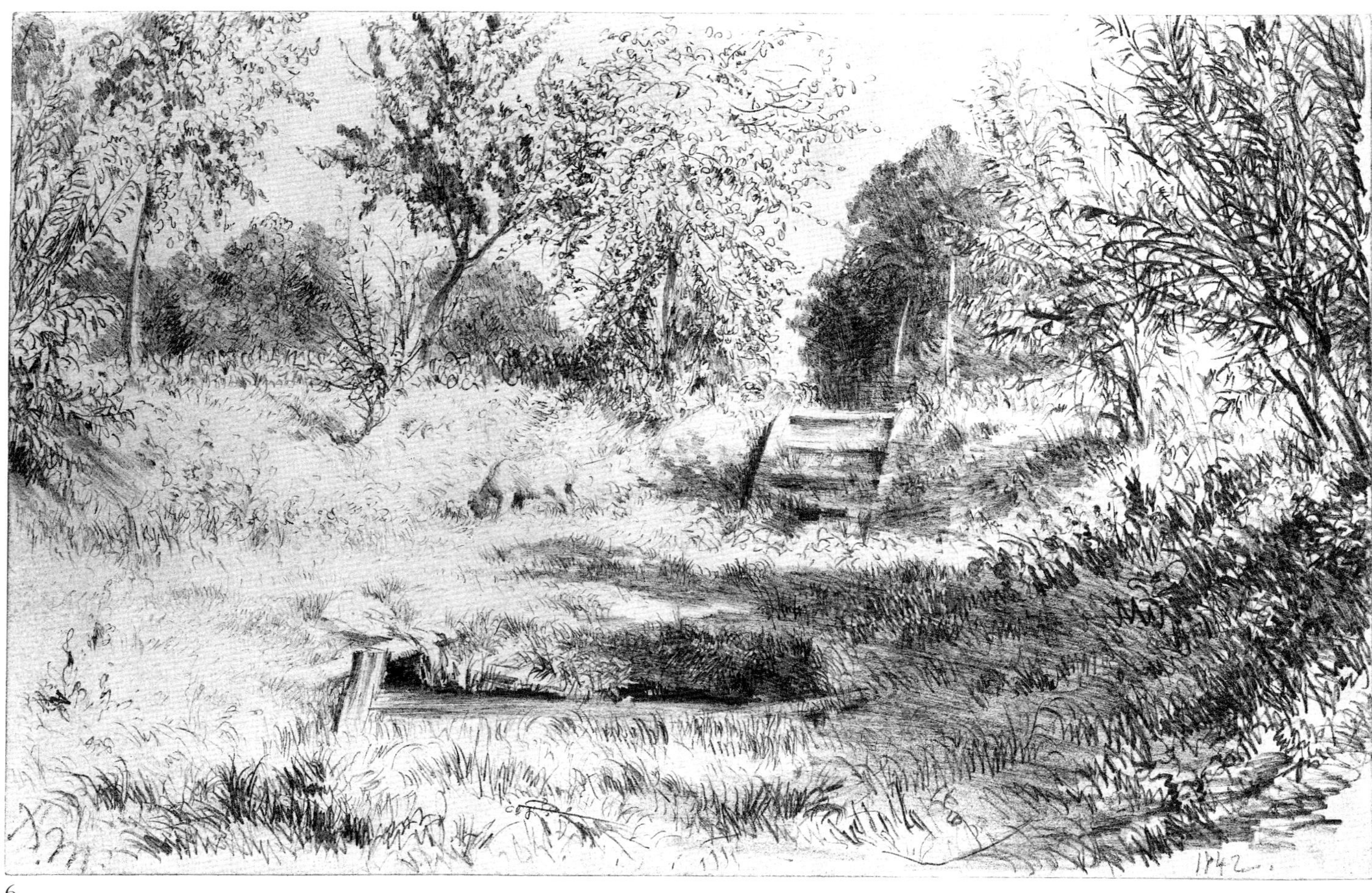

6

ation, the nature that the artist contemplated turned into a mirror of his soul. In *Fields, Trees and Sheep Grazing* (cat. 6) his pencil painstakingly traced the intricate foliage of the trees, and warm shades were supplied by delicate hatching. The whole drawing exudes calm and serenity, very much in the manner of other drawings in the sketchbook of the same period. The three drawings that follow this one (cat. 7–9) are marked by a restrained melancholy; this is suggested by the delicate insistence of the pencil strokes and the emptiness of the composition, but also by the more passionate lines which taper away to nothing – dark blacks contrasting with gentle greys. Lastly, the broken trunk of a willow and a tangle of snapped branches suggest an early spring atmosphere far removed from Romantic commonplaces. Menzel's landscapes were never again to express his feelings with the intensity of those of his young adulthood. In those days, the idea of the emptiness of a flooded field taking over the entire surface of a drawing, or a few little houses on the opposite bank acting as symbols of hope, aroused in him no inhibitions.

M.R.-R.

1. Berlin, Kupferstichkabinett, Sketch book 7, (1839-46); *cf.* Riemann-Reyher, 1996.
2. Letter to Carl Heinrich Arnold, 22 July, 1843, Wolff, 1914, p. 78.
3. Sheet 5 in *Essays in etching*, Bock, 1923, no. 1142.

6
Fields, Trees and Sheep Grazing
1842

Pencil
12.7 × 20.4cm
Signed at the bottom left: *A.M.* Dated at the bottom right: *1842.*
Berlin, Kupferstichkabinett (SZ Menzel N 382)
Exhibited in Berlin only

Provenance: Painter's studio; 1905 Emilie Krigar-Menzel; acquired by the museum in 1906.
Exhibition: Berlin, 1905, no. 3213.

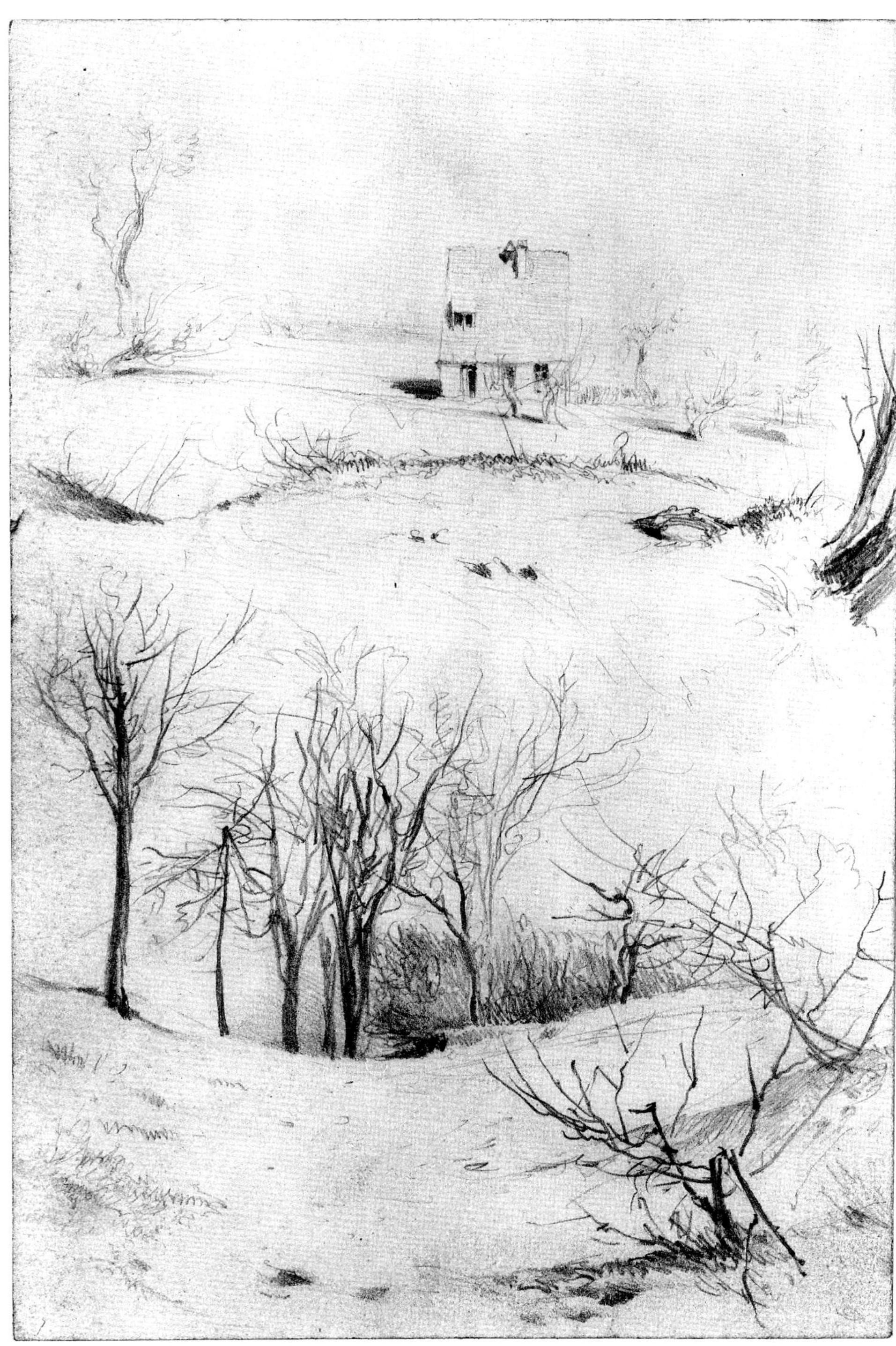
7

7
House and Bare Bushes
c. 1842–3
Pencil
20.9 × 13cm
Berlin, Kupferstichkabinett (SZ Menzel N 415)
Exhibited in Paris only

Provenance: Painter's studio; 1905 Emilie Krigar-Menzel; acquired by the museum in 1906.
Exhibition: Berlin, 1905, no. 3224c.

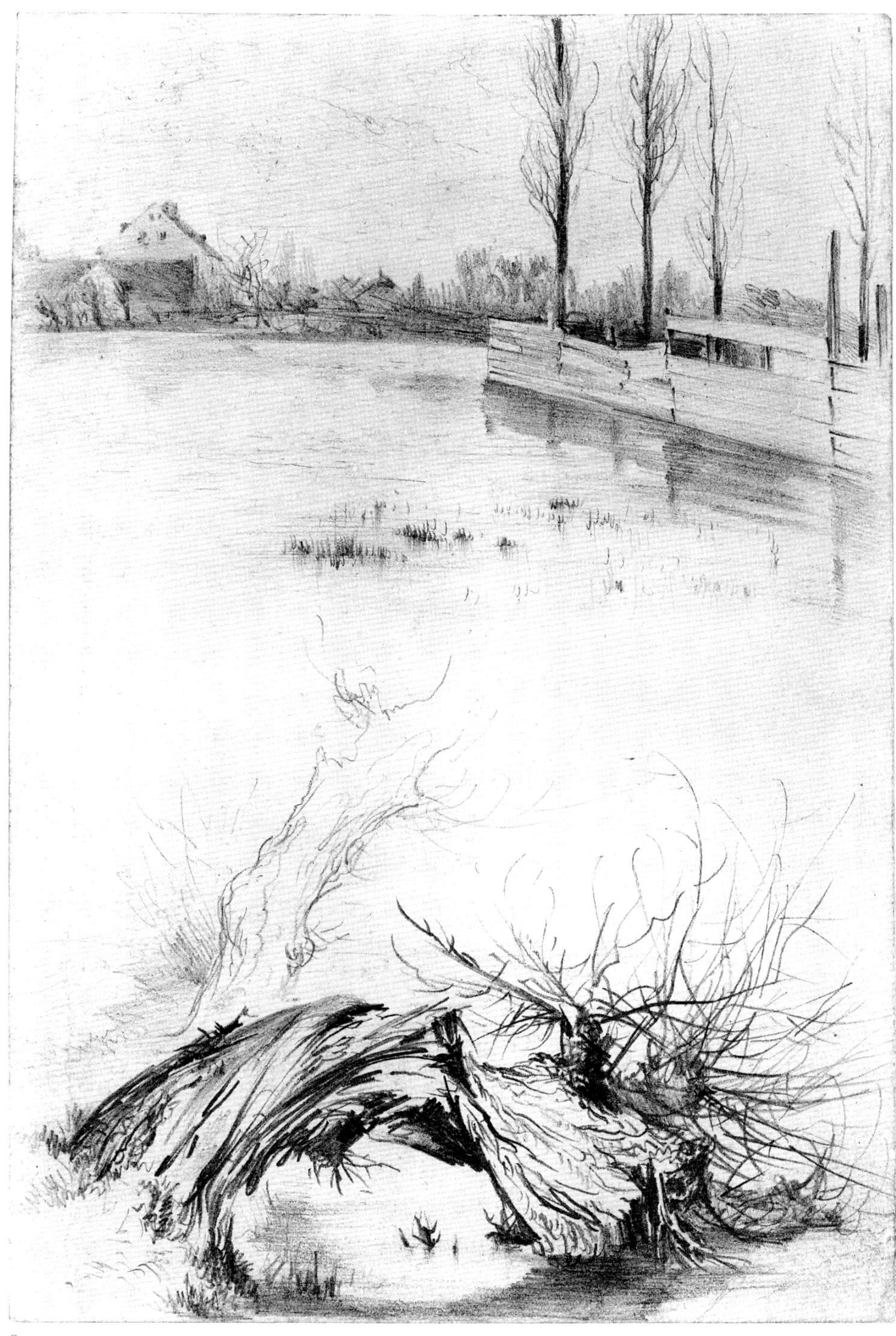
8

8

The Schafgraben Flooded

c. 1842–3
Pencil
21 × 15cm
Berlin, Kupferstichkabinett (SZ Menzel N 310)
Exhbited in Paris and Washington only

Provenance: Painter's studio; 1905 Emilie Krigar-Menzel; acquired by the museum in 1906.
Exhibitions: Berlin, 1905, no. 3202a; Copenhagen, 1985, no. 15, reprod. p. 19; New York, 1990, no. 2, col. reprod. p. 57.

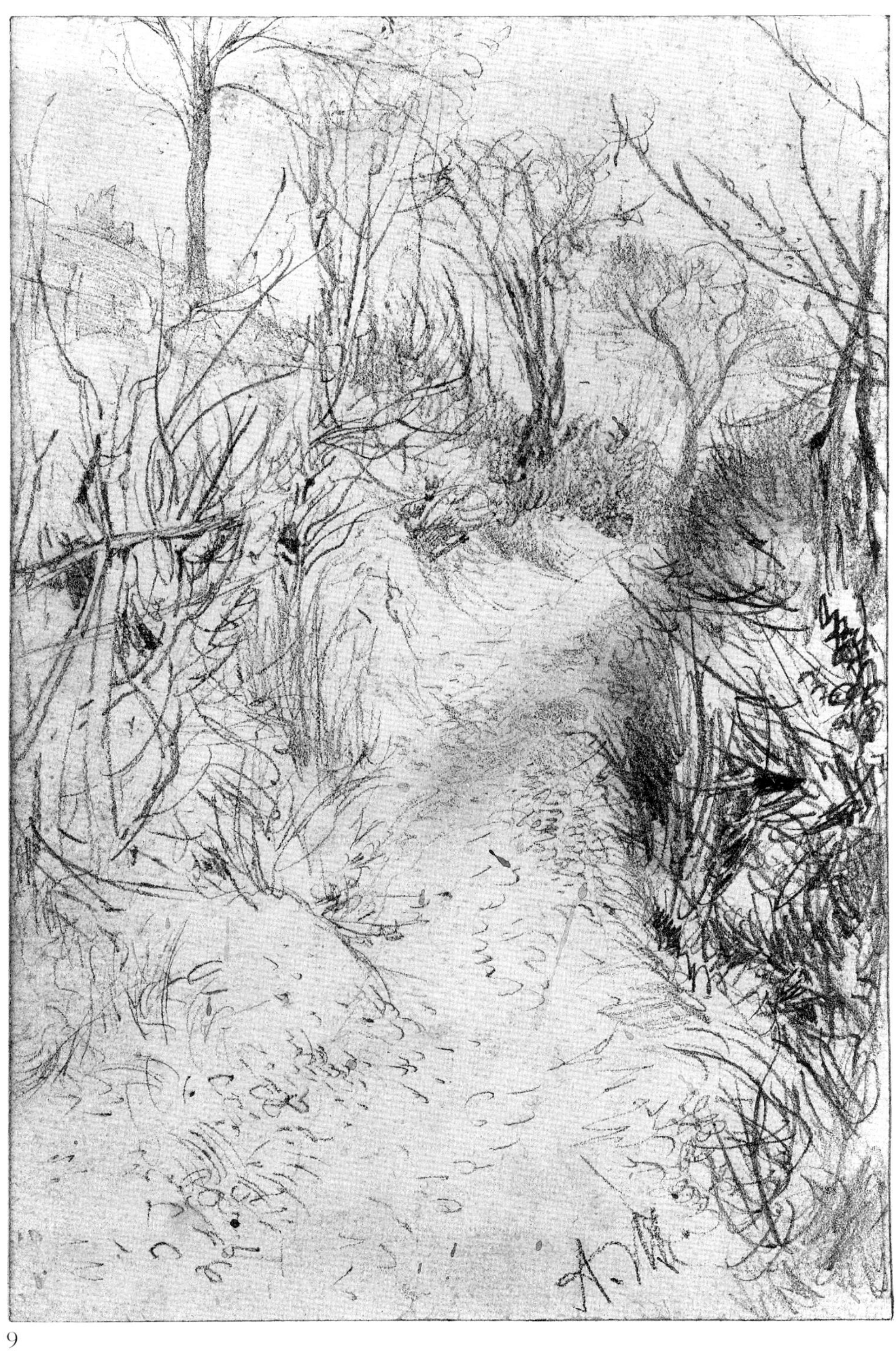

9

9

Path Lined with Bare Hedges

c. 1842–3
Pencil drawing
20.5 × 12.9cm
Signed at the bottom right: *A.M.*
Berlin, Kupferstichkabinett (SZ Menzel N 2668)
Exhibited in Berlin only

Provenance: Painter's studio; 1905 Emilie Krigar-Menzel; acquired by the museum in 1906.
Exhibition: Berlin, 1905, no. 2840.

10

Woman Sleeping

c. 1843–4
Oil on canvas
17 × 21cm
Berlin, Nationalgalerie (A III 776)
Exhibited in Berlin only

Provenance: Painter's studio; Emilie Krigar-Menzel; acquired by the museum in 1906.
Exhibitions: Berlin, 1905, no. 104; Berlin, 1955 B, no. 6.
Bibliography: Tschudi, 1905 A, no. 9; cat. NG, 1968, p. 140; cat. NG, 1976, p. 253, reprod.

It is quite possible that the *Woman Sleeping* is a rare representation of Menzel's mother. Emilie Menzel née Okrusch was widowed early and died of a fever in 1846. However, although the subject is seen here to be relaxed and in a deep sleep, she would still appear to be much younger than in the drawing dated 30 January 1842[1], which depicts her as she approaches her fiftieth year. Clearly, then, this study in oils does not attempt to attain the accuracy of a portrait. Its date is also difficult to establish as the chronology of all Menzels paintings in oils done in the early 1840s is uncertain. Although there are some reliable dates from 1844 onwards, we do not know when Menzel started to represent his day-to-day impressions in colour. Perhaps he found he had the time to do so after he had completed the illustrations for Kugler; and at the same time he may have found the courage to represent such fragmentary experiences in oils. Here, traditional imperatives were of less importance, but they were not entirely absent as there was between the oil sketch and other genres of painting a rigid and undisputed hierarchy of techniques; it was a totally different artistic area. However, one of the key innovations that Menzel brought to this work consisted precisely of blurring the edges of these demarcations. Landscape painters were already permitted momentary observation and a contraction of the visual field within the restricted format of the 'sketch' or 'study' in oils, but it did not follow that the same went for the depiction of people. The impression that *Woman Sleeping* makes is

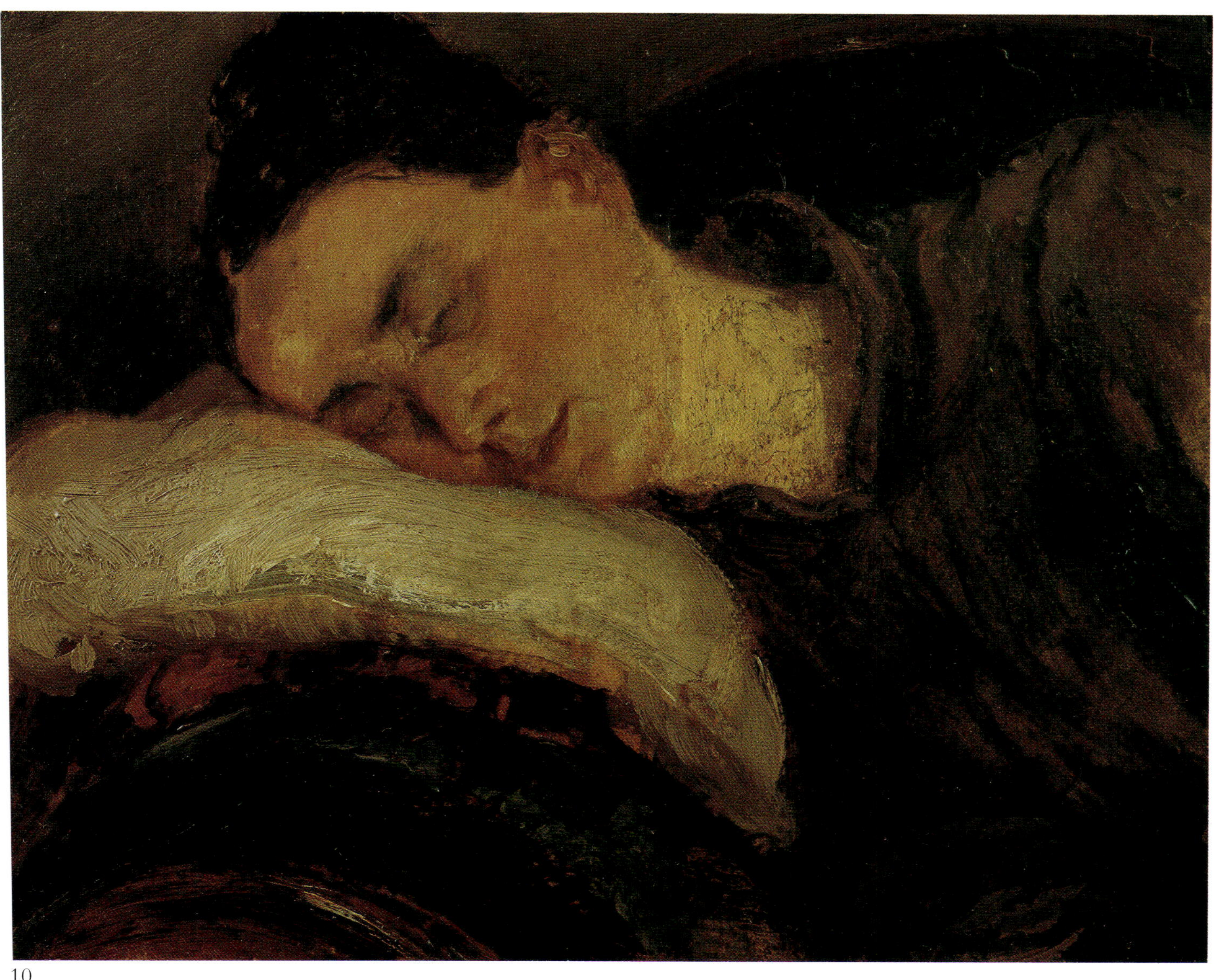

10

that of a note in a private journal transcribed into painting, and was one of many memories of members of close family and immediate circle that Menzel recorded. It has been remarked that his models are often shown sleeping; the reason is that the daytime was when he did his commissions and everyone else went about their business, and only the evening was left for more intimiate settings.

This painting sets out to be a 'part representing the whole'. It is deliberately fragmentary and unbalanced, and makes its impact through a contrast between the superimposition of voluminous forms and the dynamism of other elements. The head is curiously separated from the slender torso, and nestles so gently on the cushion that it leaves scarcely an indentation; it seems to have been perceived as autonomous. The painting recalls Brancusi's *La Muse Endormie*.

Just the same, the artist's brushwork does not seem to have acquired the assurance and expressive suppleness that marked his work in the mid-1840s: his touch is too heavy-handed, and the paint too thick. Nor is there any hint yet of the transposition of real colours into the range of brown tones that later characterized *Young Boy Sitting at a Table* (cat. 27). He does not transgress the limits of monochrome painting. C.K.

1. Whereabouts unknown. Lammel, 1993 B, fig. 7.

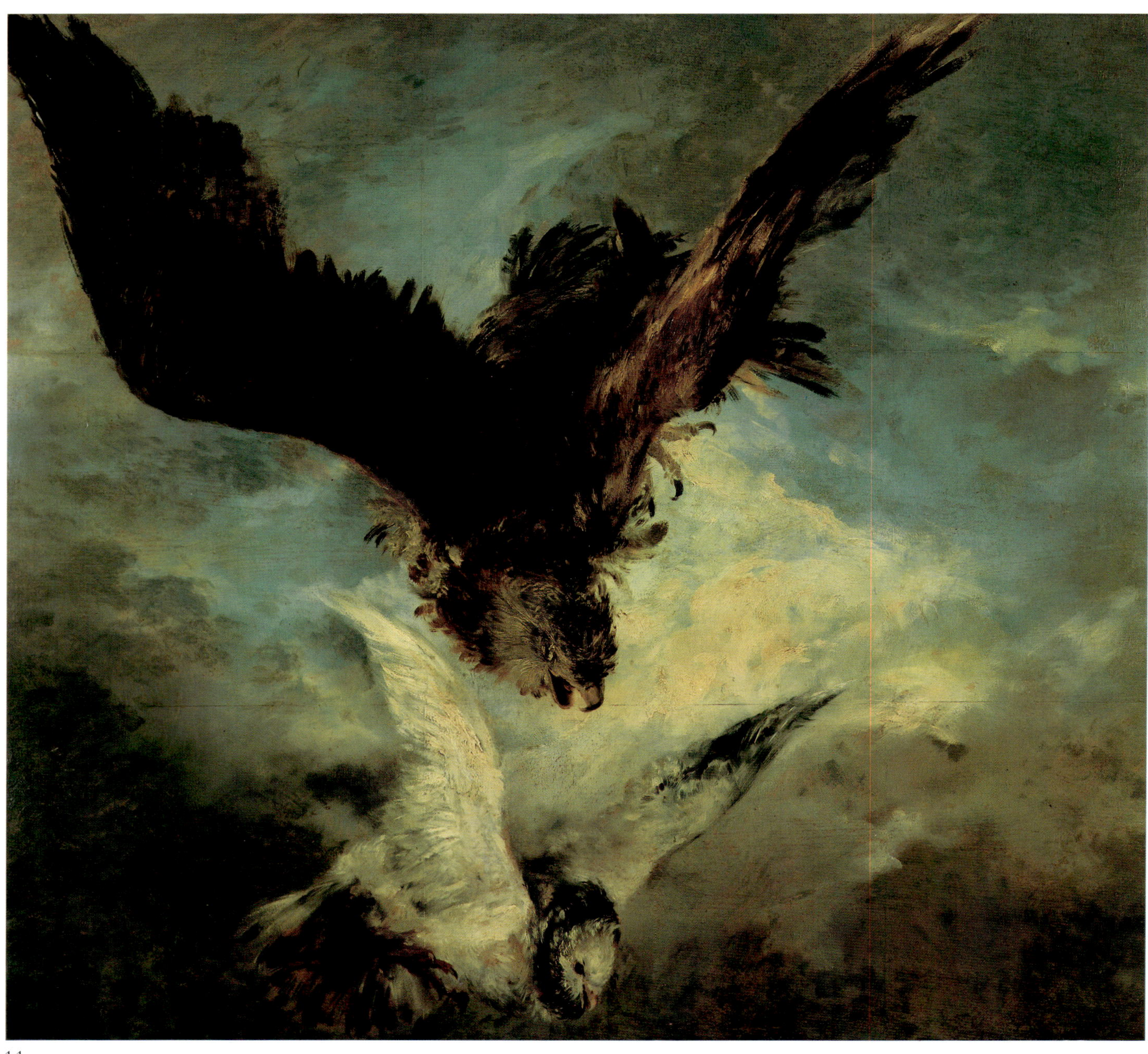

11

11

Falcon Swooping on a Dove

1844

Oil on paper (several sheets juxtaposed), wood backing
102.7 × 119cm
Berlin, Nationalgalerie (A I 960)
Exhibited in Berlin only

Provenance: 1887 H. Paasche, judge at the court of summary jurisdiction, Liegnitz (Silesia), whose widow, later living in Berlin-Friedenau, still owned the work in 1905; Ernst Zaeslein Gallery, Berlin; acquired by the museum in 1906.
Exhibitions: Berlin, 1905, no. 5708; Berlin, 1980 A, no. IV, reprod. p. 138.
Bibliography: Tschudi, 1905 A, no. 58; M.R., 1906, pl.; cat. NG 1907, no. 981; Scheffler, 1912, p. 121 *et seq.*; Kern, 1915–16, reprod. p. 81; Scheffler, 1922, p. 144; Waldmann, 1941, p. 45, fig. 26; cat. NG 1986, no pag., fig. 65.

Hitherto, this painting has always been dated 1846, but it clearly goes back to 1844, an important year with which three paintings in this catalogue are associated. At this time, when Menzel was twenty-eight years old, he went to live with his father's relatives who had settled in Jauer and Striegau, Silesia; given the number of portrait and landscape drawings he completed there, he must have spent some considerable time in the area. This prolific output did not curtail his activities in the locality, and on the occasion of a shooting competition he took on a casual commission to paint this work as a target; the painting was to be presented to the winner after the competition was over. Many years later, the owner of the painting sent Menzel a photograph of it, and subsquently received the following ambivalent reply from the elderly artist: 'In the early 1840s, I did indeed paint the target you describe; it was for a shooting match organized by a club whose honoured guest I was on several occasions. I have no wish to see it ever again. On the contrary, I would have felt happier if it had been peppered with bullets by the club's many excellent marksmen – they have all completely passed from my memory'[1].

This recalls a number of other critical, and sometimes summary, opinions that Menzel, now a famous but embittered old man, made of his youthful works. Happily, on this occasion, it did not prevent someone from looking after a work whose author, despite the absence of a signature, had never been forgotten in the remote province of Silesia; the impact marks were later retouched at an unknown date, but certainly before 1905.

In order to accept this commission, Menzel was obliged to study how birds fly. He depicts the falcon as it executes a sharp turn, its tail acting as a rudder[2]. For the rest, the painting's ultimate destination encouraged him to finish it as quickly as possible, and the result recalls both Rubens[3], whose name Menzel adopted in the 'Tunnel Over the Spree' literary circle, and Rembrandt. Menzel's virtuoso technique does full justice to both the violence of the mortal combat against a backdrop of the sky peeping through the clouds, and the birds with their fantastical dragons' heads and plumage standing on end. Colour is used without restraint – sometimes with delicacy, and sometimes thickly with the very end of the brush – and the paint is applied to produce a sense of chaotic energy; delicate attention is paid to details, such as the sleek feathering of the bird's head. In fact, the deployment of colour is never limited by an outline, and is consistently the source that the painter uses most extensively to achieve expression.

A few years later, Menzel produced a woodcut of a single eagle fighting a pair of double-headed eagles. This symbolic image appeared on the frontispiece of the third volume of the *History of Frederick the Great*[4] (fig. 156), and was an allusion to

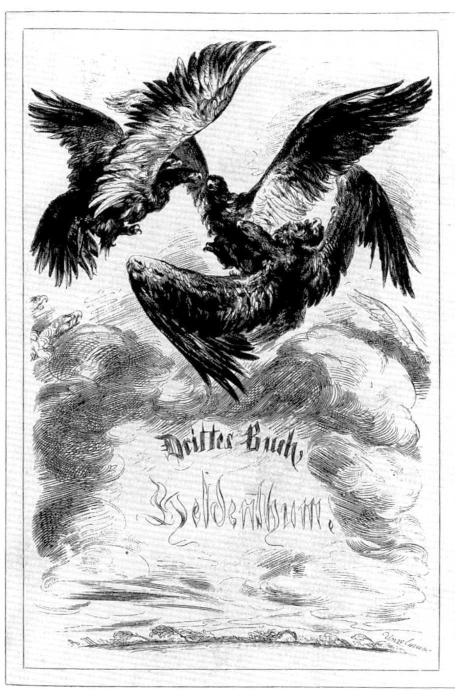

Fig. 156. *History of Frederick the Great*, illustration on the title page of the third book (*Heroism*), 1839–42, woodcut

the hostilities which divided Prussia from Austria and Russia. The theme of birds fighting reappeared in the satirical allegory, the *Sheet Commemorating the Berlin Tunnel Society Carnival*[5] (1852); this shows an owl attacking a parrot. C.K.

1. Letter to H. Paasche, 13 May 1887, Central Archives, Menzel Archives, XI, no. 13, Staatliche Museen zu Berlin. Although Menzel does not mention a date, he must have meant 1844.
2. M. R., 1906. Apparently on Menzel's instructions.
3. In 1845, in collaboration with his friend Theodor Hosemann, Menzel made a large-format copy of the *Adoration of the Magi* by Rubens.
4. Bock, 1923, no. 617.
5. Bock, 1923, no. 391.

12

Head of a Bearded Workman in Profile

1844

Oil on paper, board backing
40.1 × 29.6cm
Nationalgalerie, Berlin (A III 765)

Provenance: Hermann Pächter (R. Wagner Gallery, Berlin); acquired by the museum in April 1889.
Exhibitions: Berlin, 1895 A, no. 121; Vienna, 1896, no. 269; Hamburg, 1896, no. 2; Berlin, 1905, no. 22; Celle, 1949–50, no. 62; Berlin, 1950–1, no. 49; Berlin, 1955 B, no. 7; Erlangen, 1971, no. 92.
Bibliography: Donop, 1902, no. 1411; Tschudi, 1905 A, no. 58; cat. NG, 1907, no. 970; Hütt, 1965, fig. 61 (col.); cat. NG, 1976, reprod. p. 254.

May we accept the terminology used by Menzel's contemporaries, and describe this kind of painting as a 'study'? The half-turned face is the only feature that one might not expect to find in a portrait, and the artist was patently striving to convey the subject's individuality. Indeed, the man's clearly proletarian origins are so marked – he was obviously not a professional model – that the initial temptation is to associate this surprising choice with the revolutionary climate that prevailed in 1848.

The absence of a signature or a date is extraordinary in a work that the painter sold himself instead of holding in reserve, and it is all the more astonishing to find the entry 'A. Menzel 1844' in the catalogues accompanying the 1895 and 1896 exhibitions. The explanation is probably not that this is a mistake (and certainly not that the signature was later cropped)

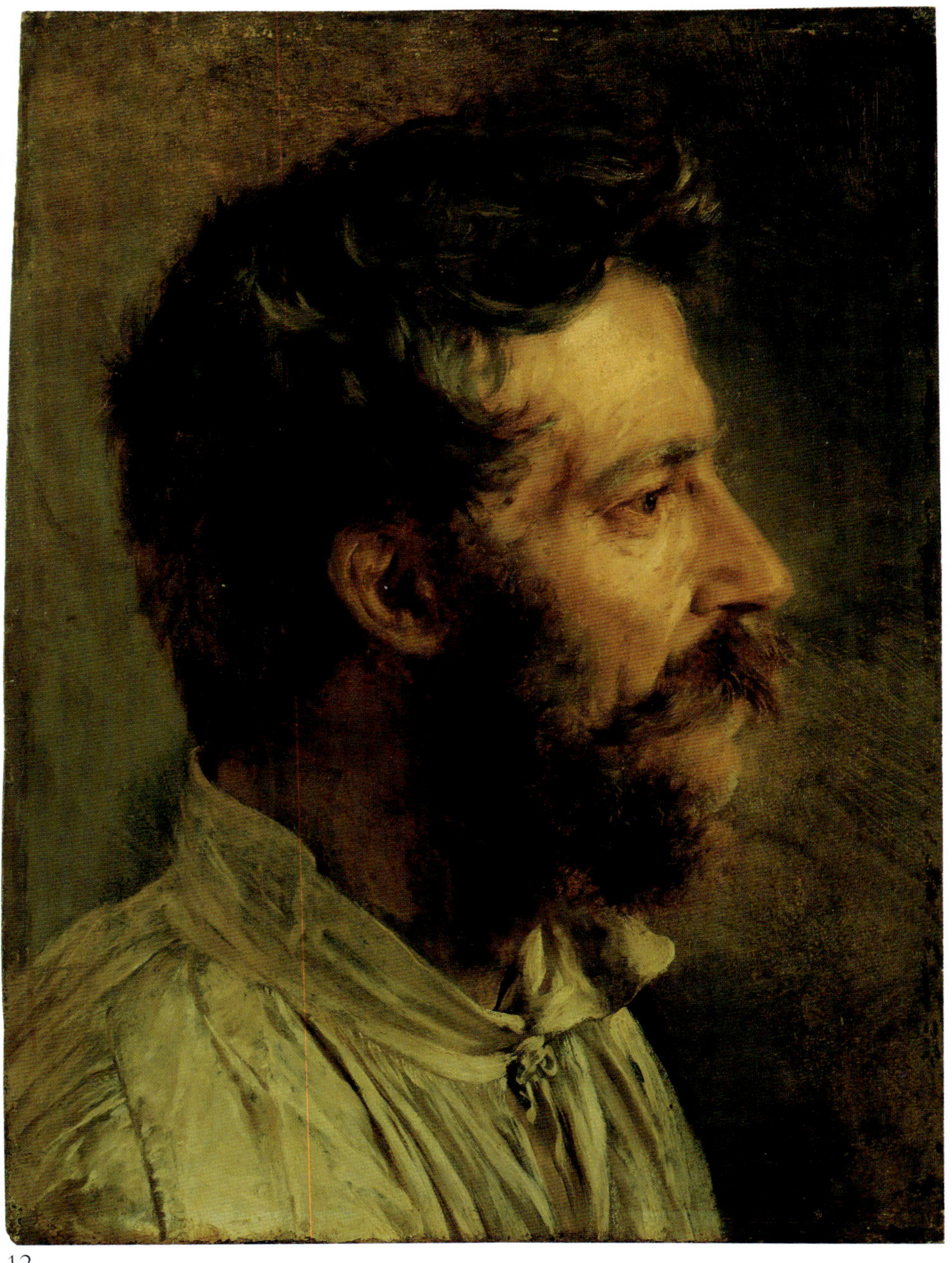

12

but is linked to the fact that the paper on which Menzel painted this work, and many others in his early years, was pasted on to board, the back of which the artist signed; this was subsequently replaced by another piece of board which is exceptionally solid and heavy, and is certainly not the original[1]. The technique is quite compatible with the year 1844, as *Falcon Swooping on a Dove* (cat. 11) demonstrates.

This portrait of a worker, the first in Germany and possibly anywhere in Europe, therefore acquires an even more striking significance than any possible link with the Revolution of March 1848 might suggest. The reason for this is an uprising in early May 1844 of home-working weavers in rural parts of Silesia, who had been ruined by decades of competition from industrially manufactured cloth. The whole of Germany was shocked by their abject state and expressed great sympathy for them; their revolt was subsequently seen as a forerunner of the 1848 Revolution. It was at about this time that Heinrich Heine, for whom Menzel had immense admiration, published his celebrated poem *The Silesian Weavers*; it contained the lines: 'With our dark eyes, devoid of tears, Seated at the loom we bare our teeth. Germany, we weave your shroud, We cast on you a triple curse . . .' Before the Revolution was fully under way, the Düsseldorf painter Carl Wilhelm Hübner, had exhibited his dramatic genre painting *The Weavers of Silesia*[2] (fig. 157); when this was shown in Berlin, it made such an impact that, 'out of pity, substantial orders for cloth were passed to the needy Silesian weavers'[3].

During this period, Menzel's interest in his native Silesia was inevitably revived as it coincided with his stay in Jauer and Striegau. The nerve centre of the uprising, the mountainous regions of Peterswaldau and Langenbielau to the south of Breslau, the main town of the province, was not far away; from here, reports came of certain 'excessive behaviour' on the part of apprentices, journeymen and pupils. The precise date of Menzel's stay is not known, but there is evidence to suggest that it was in the springtime[4]. It follows that the young artist had direct experience, not perhaps of the high point of the weavers' uprising, but certainly of the general concern, compassion and anxiety that surrounded it; Menzel could not have avoided becoming aware of the Fourth Estate.

The question arises whether this portrait depicts a member of the proletariat from the Silesian countryside or a labourer in the city. It is difficult to say, despite the fact that these two social groups were very different and their economic interests quite separate. Furthermore, a number of migrations were beginning to take place at this time, and factories in Berlin were already recruiting large numbers of Silesian workers. At all

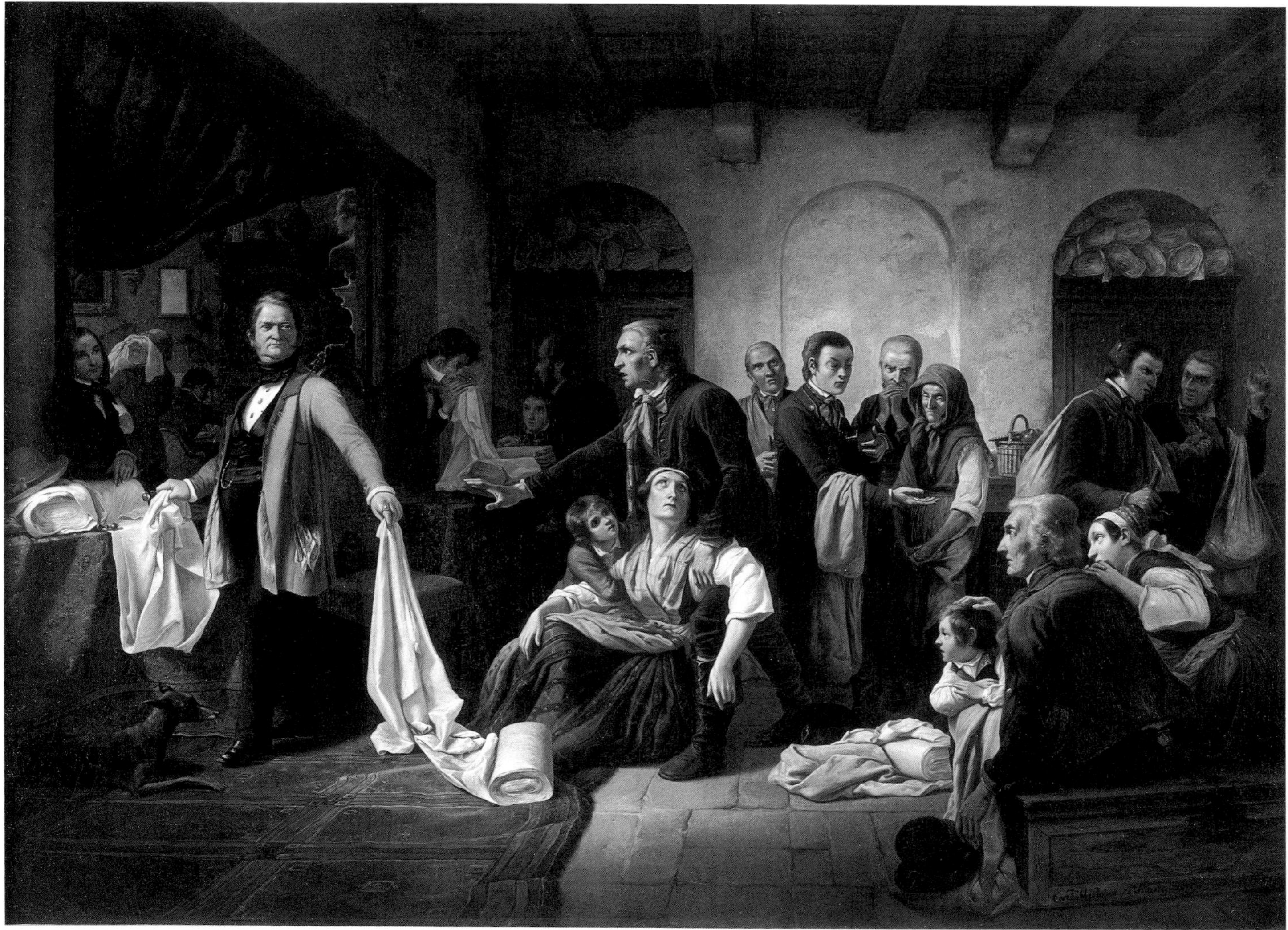

Fig. 157. Carl Wilhelm Hübner, *The Silesian Weavers* 1844, oil, Düsseldorf, Kunstmuseum

events, in 1844, Menzel's paintings captured the unexpected symmetry of the Industrial Revolution's impact: on the landscape (*cf.* cat. 13) and in this man's face. C.K.

1. This view is further supported by the fact that the catalogue for the Berlin exhibition of 1905 and Tschudi, 1905 A both state that the technique used was 'oils on wood'. The cardboard that is currently attached is very heavy and thick, and could easily be taken for wood. Quite possibly, and before 1905, it replaced the lighter cardboard that had been used during the 1890s.
2. This painting has disappeared. There is a copy in the Kunstmuseum, Dusseldorf. *Cf.* exhib. cat. Dusseldorf, 1979, no. 110, reprod. p. 75.
3. Hagen, 1857; quoted by Hanna Gagel, exhib. cat. Dusseldorf, p. 75.
4. Riemann-Reyher, 1992, p. 22.

13

Rear Courtyard and House

1844
Oil on canvas
44.5 × 61.5cm
Nationalgalerie, Berlin (A I 957)

Provenance: Probably sold to an unknown buyer during the painter's lifetime; Fritz Gurlitt Gallery, Berlin; acquired by the museum in 1906.
Exhibitions: Berlin, 1935, no. 6; Celle, 1949–50, no. 57, p. 7; Berlin, 1950–1, no. 44; Berlin, 1955 B, no. 12, fig. 18; Kiel, 1956, no. 55;

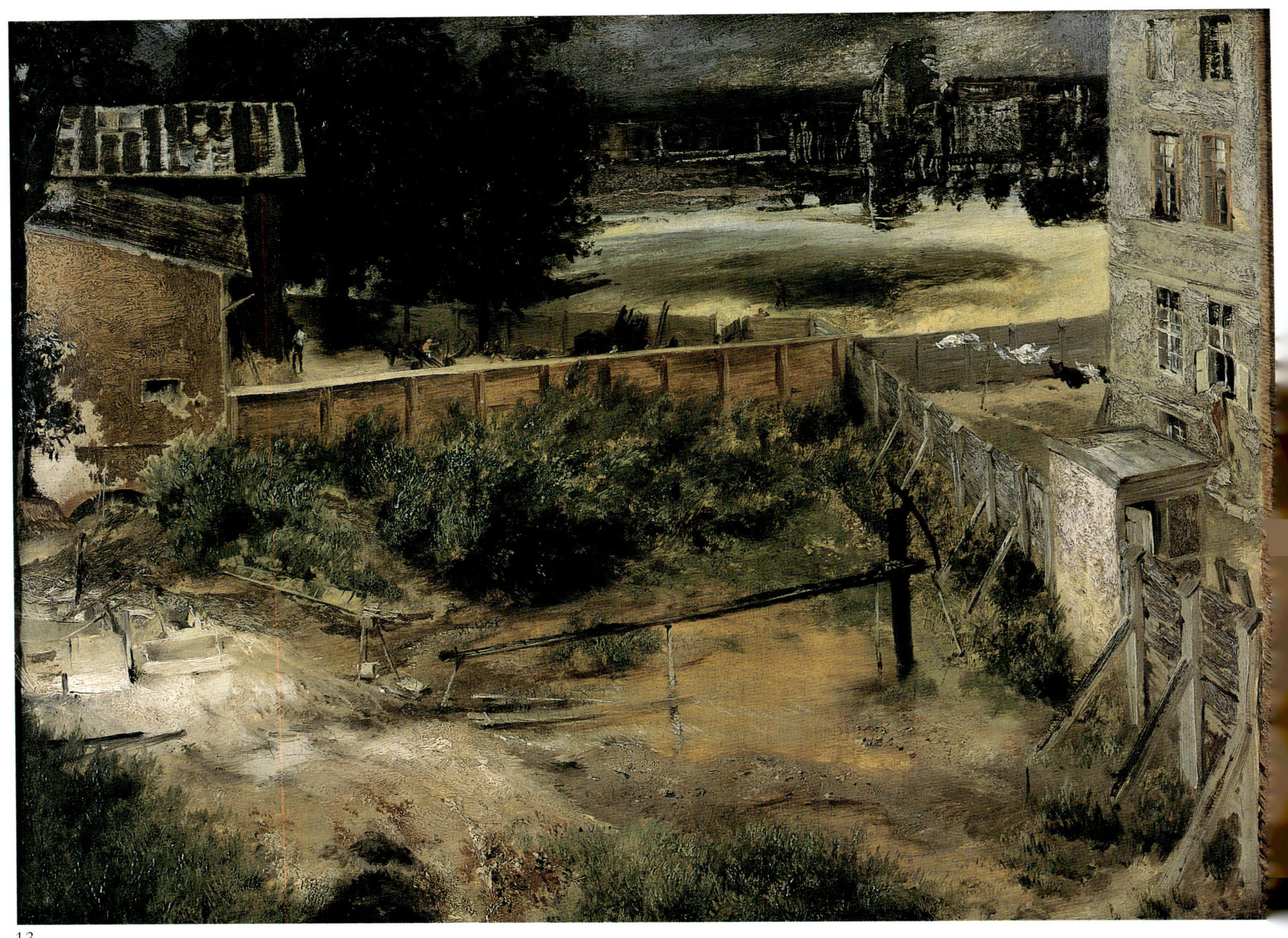

13

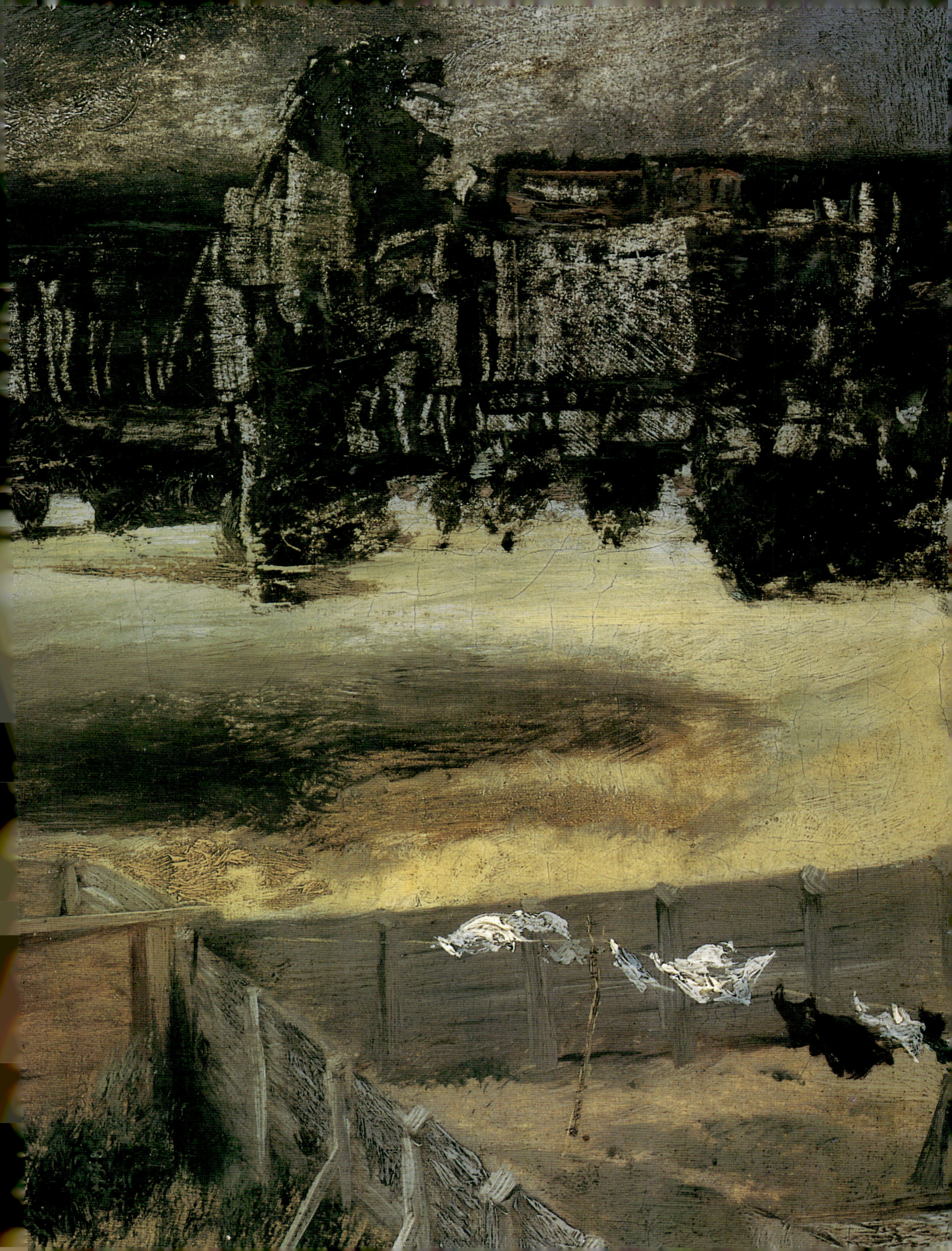

Frankfurt, 1975, no. 29, reprod.; Paris, 1985, no. 95, reprod.; Berlin, 1987 B, no. 93, reprod.
Bibliography: Not mentioned by Tschudi, 1905 A; cat. NG, 1907, no. 988; Kern, 1915–16, p. 86, reprod. p. 101; cat. NG, 1976, p. 260, reprod. p. 261.

Rolf Bothe[1] consulted contemporary building plans to compare the scene represented in this painting with what Menzel would have seen from the window of his apartment. It is clear that the view from this house at 18 Schöneberger Strasse, where he lived from April 1845 to March 1847, would have been quite different. However, there were 'old buildings, outhouses and dilapidated courtyards' around the house at 4 Zimmerstrasse, which Menzel left at the end of March 1845, and Bothe has accordingly dated this painting, which was previously linked with works completed around 1846, one year earlier. In fact, if due account is taken of the season, we need to move the date back to 1844 at least. During this decisive phase in Menzel's development, chronological revisions of this type are important because few of the tiny urban landscapes and the intimate paintings that he produced until as late as 1848 are dated, and none of them prior to 1845. *Rear Courtyard and House* therefore provides a landmark which in turn enables us to date works that preceded, or were contemporary with, *Balcony Room* (cat. 18) with a little more accuracy.

Clearly defined volumes, in the true sense of the word, only appear near the painting's margin: to the right, in a device using a receding perspective, a grey wall dotted with joyless windows gives on to a tiny courtyard and a small building containing latrines; to the left, and similarly off-centre, there is a kind of shed standing in a hazily delineated field. Lastly, there is a fence at right angles, although it is unclear what links it to the painting as a whole. Most of the composition depicts a depressed area; ochre land that has been turned over, a small workshop strangled by undergrowth, the supports holding the fence upright, and a watering device whose wooden conduits traverse the courtyard as far as the plot of land. Objects at the far end of the courtyard are indistinguishable, and the eye falls on the children playing.

The background appears to be divided, as if containing a picture within a picture. The brown tones of the asphalt, which Menzel normally deployed in a fine scumble on a light background before working the colour in[2], has remained visible, mixed with black. There are also signs of considerable scratching; Menzel must have subsequently retained this technique on the grounds that it extracts all material properties from an already thin layer of paint. Nonetheless, it has here managed to create a kind of visionary image which floats almost in the manner of a mirage; it also boasts an element of suspense that contrasts sharply with the pure, realistic presentation of the façade and windows to the right. C.K.

1. Exhib. cat. Berlin, 1987 A, no. 93.
2. Gronau, 1987, p. 286–8

14
Moving out of a Cellar
1844

Pencil
13.1 × 20.8cm
Note on top right: *von oben aus 2 Tr. hoch* – Signed and dated above note: *A.M. /44.* – At the bottom right: *Umzug aus einem Keller.*
Berlin, Kupferstichkabinett (SZ Menzel N 673)
Exhibited in Berlin only

Provenance: Painter's studio; 1905 Emilie Krigar-Menzel; acquired by the museum in 1906.
Exhibitions: Berlin, 1905, no. 4094; Vienna, 1985, no. 93, fig.
Bibliography: Wirth, 1965, fig. p. 58.

Everything is quiet again, the dust has settled, and a great mound of furniture and objects piled up at random has been formed in front of the house after the cellar has been cleared. A cupboard, a table, a chair, a bed, a basin, even rabbit hutches and all kinds of small items: everything required to furnish a flat. The move must have taken place in a rushed, disorganized way, with scant regard for the furniture. On the left a little girl is crouching on the piled-up planks: apparently her doll has been thrown down on a table and forgotten. There is something sad about the pile of furniture, and the separation of the child from her doll which could well have been her favourite toy.

While this composition has a symbolic aspect, it is still also an exercise in perspective. The opportunities afforded by the bird's-eye view and the resulting foreshortening are what prompted Menzel to make this drawing. Paul Meyerheim[1] tells how Menzel, to escape the tedious classes in perspective held at the Academy, arranged for the laws of space formulated by his friend, the architect Johann Heinrich Strack, to be explained to him. Within a few days his technique was so perfect that he kept inventing increasingly difficult exercises for himself.

Even without the signature which was added later *Moving out of a Cellar* is very much at home in 1844. In his 1839–46 notebook[2] there is a sketch of two horses in harness with the note 'From two flights of stairs up': the style and title are very close to those of *Moving*. Then the motif of a pile of planks crops up again in an engraving dating from the same period, *The Pile of Wood*[3] (fig. 159). In its first state in particular (with no background) it is like an ordinary genre scene. Yet the people grouped round the pile of wood are also a symbolic incarnation of the different ages of man.

In the early 1840s Menzel's works often conveyed a symbolic content of this kind: we need only recall *Still Life with Books and Skull*[4]. This expresses not only 'the disintegration of the world of objects'[5], but more particularly here represents a disintegration in human relationships. A.H.

1. Meyerheim, (1906) 1992, p. 220.
2. Berlin, Kupferstichkabinett, sketchbook 7, p. 72.
3. Bock, 1923, no. 1141, fourth item in *Radir-Versuche* (Experiments in Etching).
4. Stuttgart, Staatsgalerie; exhib. cat. Hamburg, 1982, no. 4.
5. Keisch, exhib. cat. Vienna, 1985, p. 158.

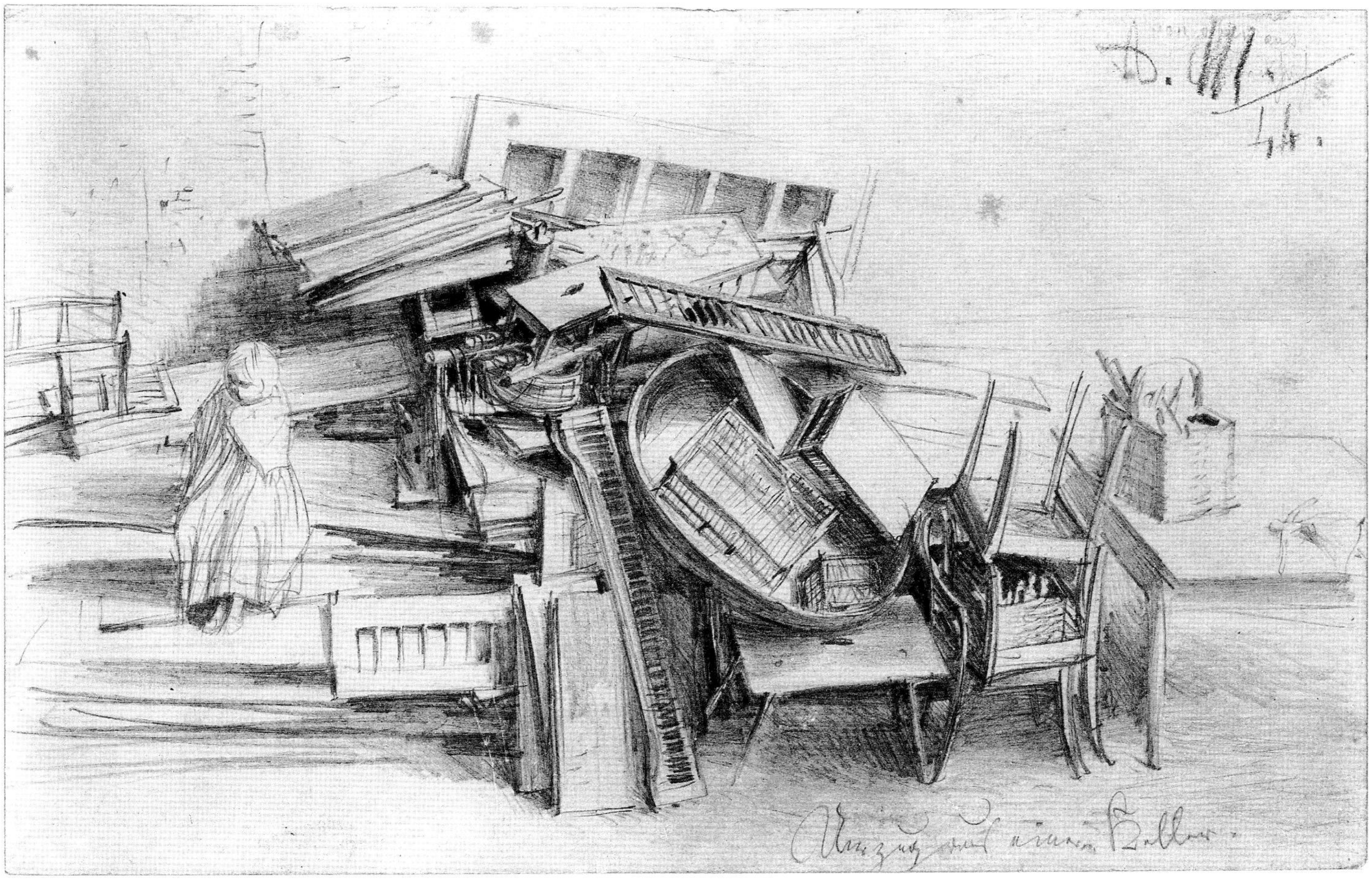

14

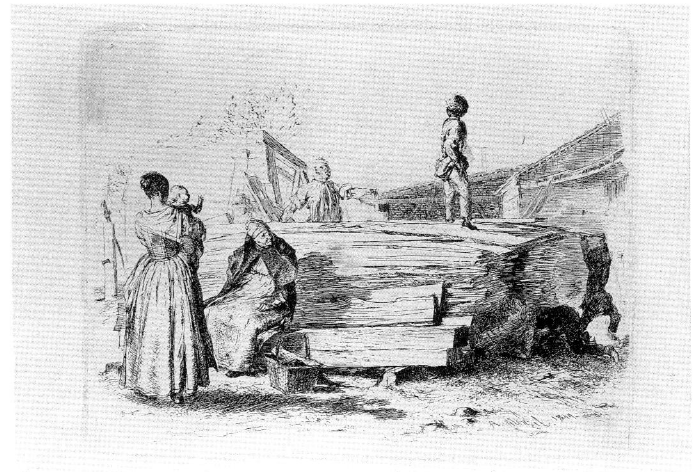

Fig. 159. *Experiments in Etching: The Pile of Wood*, 1844, etching

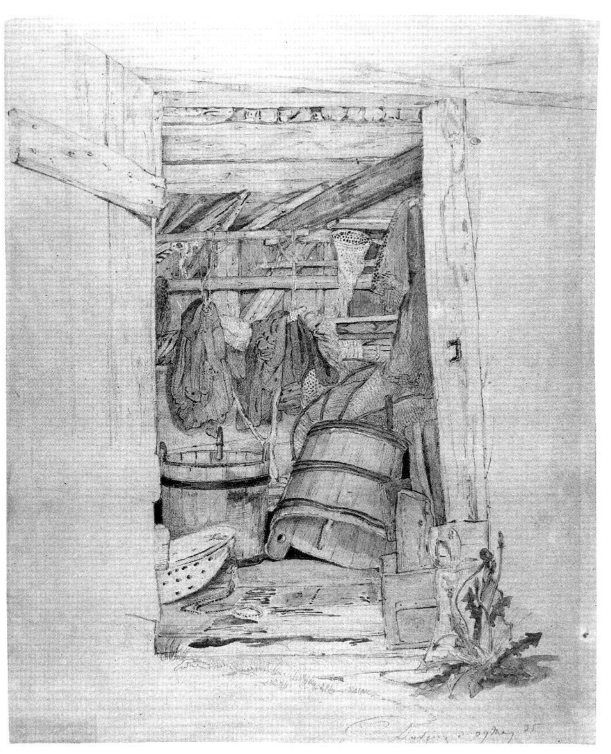

Fig. 158. Anonymous (South Germany), *Interior of a Fisherman's Shed*, 1835; pencil, Stanford, Stanford University Museum of Art

15

Dr Puhlmann's Bookcase

1844

Pencil

26.9 × 21cm

Signed and dated at the bottom left: *Ad. Menzel 44. Potsdam.*

Berlin, Kupferstichkabinett (SZ Menzel N 1027)

Exhibited in Paris and Washington only

Provenance: Painter's studio; 1905 Emilie Krigar-Menzel; acquired by the museum in 1906.
Exhibitions: Berlin, 1905, no. 4107; Berlin, 1955 A, no. 142; Berlin, 1980 A, no. 151, reprod.; Vienna, 1985, no. 93, reprod.; New York, 1988, no. 118; Vienna, 1990, no. 136.
Bibliography: Exhib. cat. Hamburg, 1982, no. 4.

For Menzel, inanimate objects, the products of human work, were also part of nature whose vagaries he followed 'patiently, . . . knowing for certain that the more he obeys it, the better he will master it and be sure of constraining it in full freedom', as Friedrich Eggers wrote in 1854 after visiting his studio[1]. He was trying to penetrate the oddities and peculiarities of forms, and knew how to capture their coded messages and transpose them into drawings using an ambivalent, pictorial language peculiar to him, sometimes verging on the surreal. Here he is still trying to convey an overall view of a bookcase; in later years he would yield more and more to the passion for collecting which prompted him to immortalize the flotsam and jetsam thrown down higgledy-piggledy by civilization by means of his drawings (cf. cat. 190). How untidy this bookcase is! It belonged to his friend, Dr Puhlmann, who lived in Potsdam; they met in the mid-1830s and remained good friends until Puhlmann's death. Already in 1838 he had drawn the compartments of a set of bookshelves where skulls lying beneath handwritten papers also conjure up the paraphernalia of a doctor[2]. With his reflective nature Menzel could have been no stranger to the ideas underlying *vanitas* paintings which often found their way into the illustrations of the *Works of Frederick the Great* (drawn between 1843 and 1849). But Menzel himself was certainly a 'bibliomaniac' too, with the autodidact's thirst for learning. There are many references indicating that he was very well read, and it would be interesting, not to say revealing, to catalogue his books. Here are Eggers' comments on Menzel's library: 'A tall bookcase with a helmet on top of it contains eighteenth-century authors, ranging from folio volumes bound in pigskin to small visitors' books and genealogical almanacs. Most of them are history books, and their owner knows them from cover to cover; he treats them as his working tools and their presence is at odds with Rückert's dictum according to which people acquire books to get out of reading them.' What literature meant to Menzel is also revealed in a letter to his brother and sister who had obviously complained and said they were missing him when he had yet again put off his return from Kassel, where he was detained by his great historical composition. 'My dears,' he wrote, 'in idle hours when you are at home alone do you too make use of your well-stocked little library? It contains an abundance of soothing balms and remedies for all sorts of ills . . . .'[3]

M. R.-R.

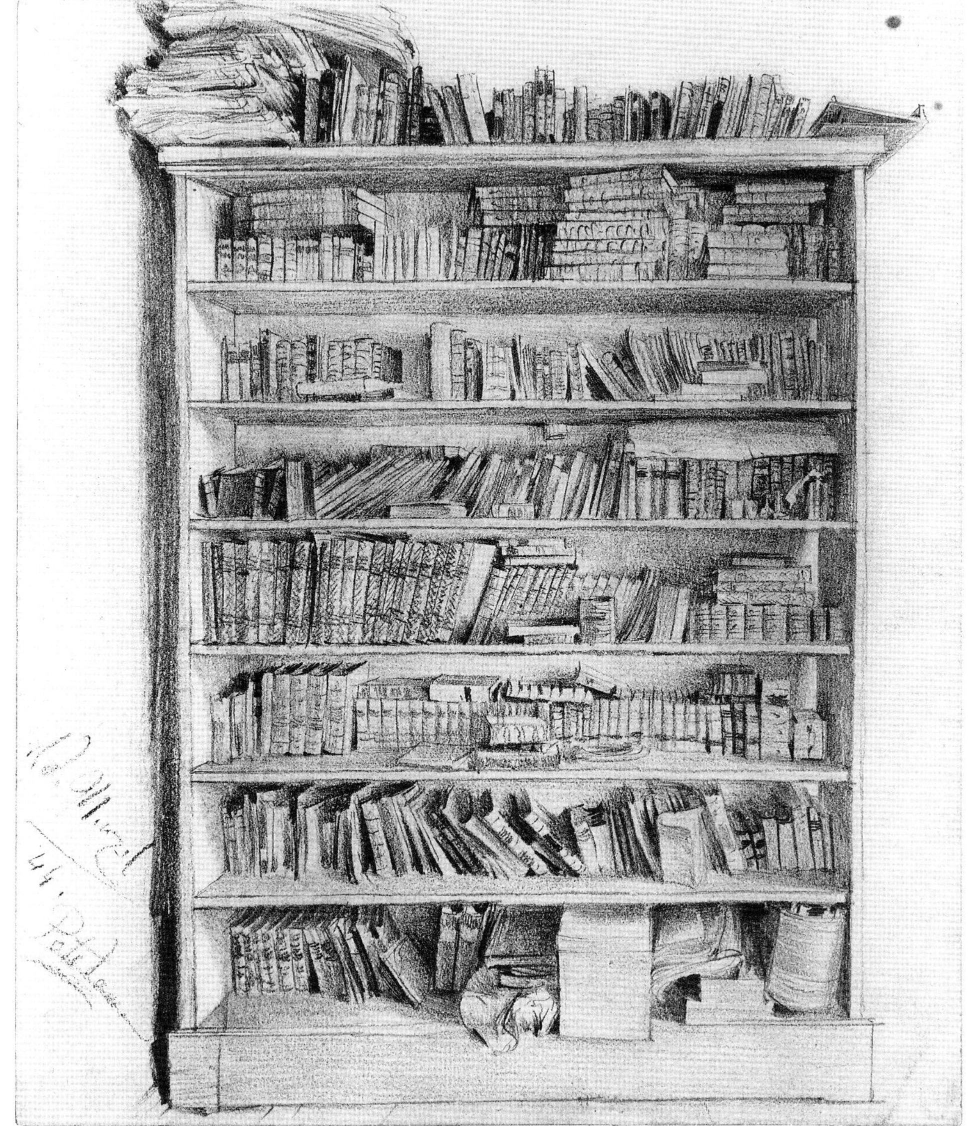

15

1. Eggers, 1854, quoted after 1925 reprint, p. 6.
2. Stuttgart, Staatsgalerie, Graphische Sammlung.
3. Letter to his brother and sister, n.d. [*c.* 11 February 1848], Wolff, 1914, p. 124.

16

Road along a Park Wall

c. 1845
Pencil
12.9 × 20.5cm
Berlin, Kupferstichkabinett (SZ Menzel N 383)
Exhibited in Berlin only

Provenance: Painter's studio; 1905 Emilie Krigar-Menzel; acquired by the museum in 1906.
Exhibitions: Berlin, 1905, no. 3202f; Berlin, 1955 A, no. 135; Copenhagen, 1985, no. 16; New York, 1988, no. 119, fig.; Vienna, 1990, no. 138, fig.

The period Menzel spent in Silesia with his family at the start of 1844 was obviously a decisive experience; it encouraged the new pictorial perception which was beginning to take shape in the young painter's mind. Three years later Menzel was still comparing immediate impressions of nature, 'shadows of clouds, stretches of sunshine and colours', with 'something similar' he had seen in Silesia[1]. Once back in Berlin he started painting again, producing the first of the little pictures which attracted so much comment after his death; the landscapes among them must also be considered as direct impressions of nature (cat. 13, 21, 22, 23). Among the drawings of this period are the

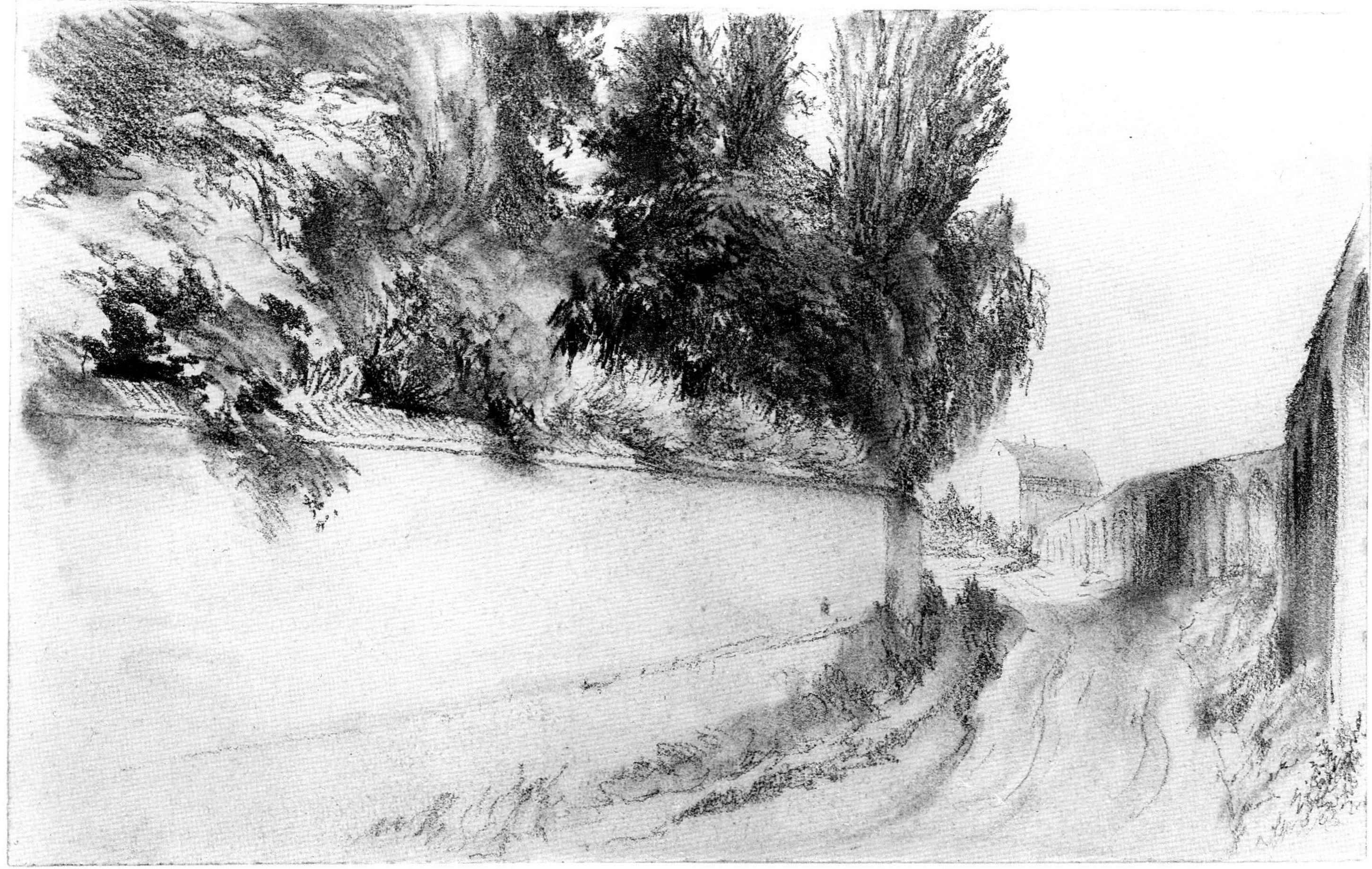

16

Road along a Park Wall and *Cemetery among the Trees* (cat. 26), or the 1845 drawing of a young woman on a ferry near a wooded river bank[2]. All have a lightness about them, a special atmosphere, conveyed by means more painterly than graphic. The spirit emanating from them is relaxed and free, almost light-hearted. Before using his pencil, and Menzel was already choosing a rather softer one, a stump has been used to prepare the areas of light and shade. Only then do the lines come in to complete and consolidate the composition. The foliage of the trees blends into generous surfaces rather than being broken up into a thousand carefully suggested leaves (cf. cat. 6). The hesitancy and groping which sometimes characterized his drawings of landscapes done shortly before seem to have been overcome around the mid-1840s. As his work progressed, pure landscape would soon be superseded by new motifs, and among the many studies carried out during his summer travels landscapes would increasingly often become topographical in character.

M. R.-R.

1. Letter to his brother and sister, 11 August 1847, Wolff, 1914, p. 109.
2. Berlin, Kupferstichkabinett (SZ Menzel N 1366).

17
Unmade Bed
c. 1845

Black stone and stump on greenish-grey paper
22.1 × 35.3cm
Signed at the bottom left: *A.M.*
Berlin, Kupferstichkabinett (SZ Menzel N 319)

Provenance: Painter's studio; 1905 Emilie Krigar-Menzel; acquired by the museum in 1906.
Exhibitions: Berlin, 1905, no. 5055; Berlin, 1980 A, no. 286, fig.; Vienna, 1985, no. 95, col. fig. p. 67; New York, 1988, no. 120; Vienna, 1990, no. 140.
Bibliography: Donop, 1908, p. 1; Kurth, 1941, p. 38 *et seq.*, p. 95.

From his youth Menzel showed a fascination for the concrete. It was in his work as a draughtsman in particular that throughout his life he unremittingly cultivated his predilection for endowing the representation of inanimate objects with a surreal dimension. These 'found objects' live only outwardly from their materiality. Very often they suggest coded messages, allegories of a completely personal nature, exposing the deceptive outward aspects of reality. The illustrations for the *Works of Frederick the Great* as well as many other drawings on a variety of subjects are characterized by a hidden meaning assigned to the object. He seemed to find envelopes of all kinds particularly well suited to being assigned a new, secret life; emptied, deprived of life, they are an extreme expression of 'still life', without in any way aspiring to the aesthetic effect of a still life. The magic inherent in these reproductions of empty casings, for example clothes thrown down at random, shoes that have been taken off, empty oyster shells, skulls, or even unoccupied beds, comes from their ambiguity. Menzel found an opportunity to express his thoughts – sometimes critical – in the first drawing work he did, although he was restrained by the convention of a commission. In an 1836 sketchbook[1] the different variations of crumpled cushions, or a divan covered by a sheet, show Menzel as a young artist

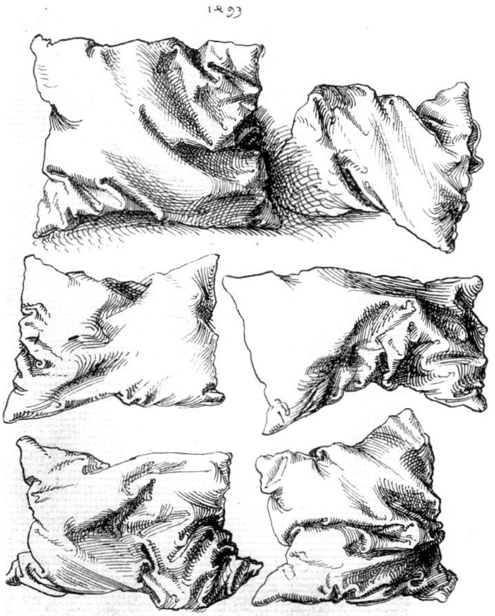

Fig. 161. Albrecht Dürer, *Cushions*, 1493, pen and Indian ink

Fig. 160. Carl Johann Arnold, *Menzel's Bed*, 1846, pencil, location unknown

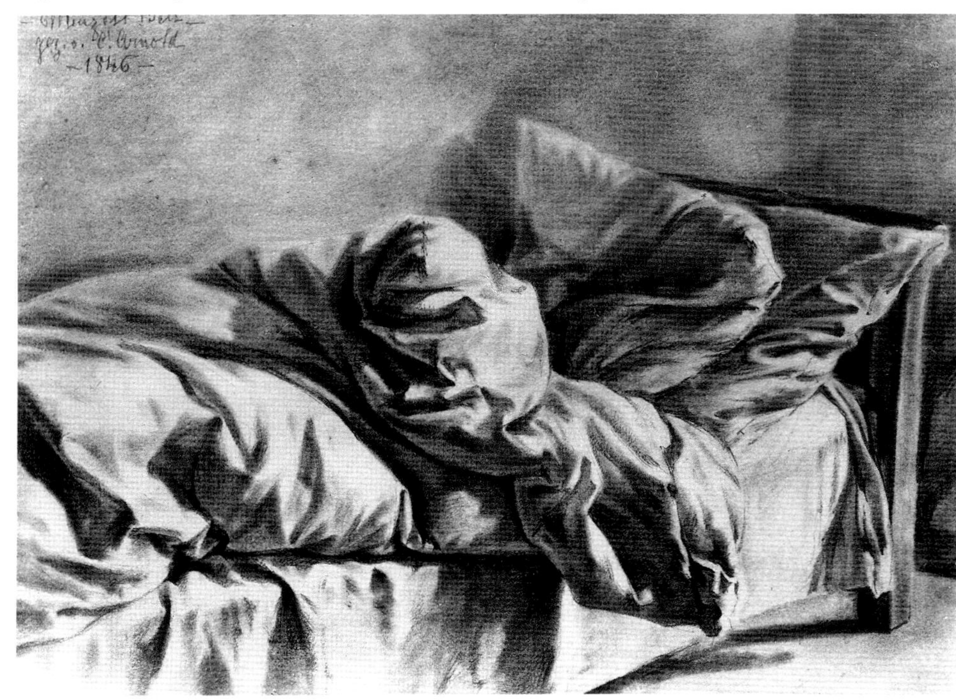

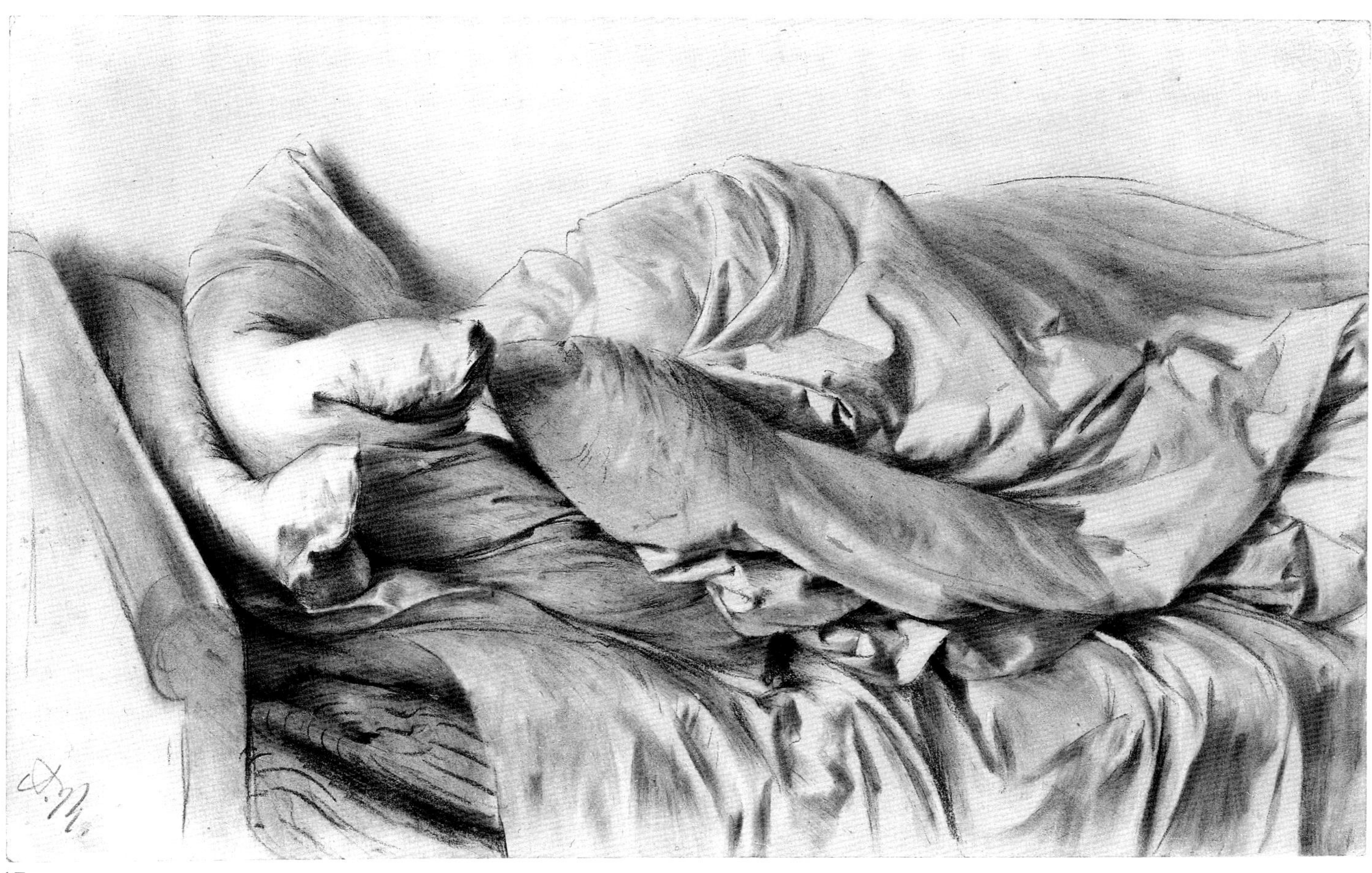

17

struggling to convey the specificity of objects, even if he could not yet achieve the standard of execution of the drawing exhibited here. At the start of his career, when he was earning his living by means of lithography, he studied Dürer's engravings. We do not know whether he was familiar with the self-portrait with the cushions, and the six cushions depicted on the reverse side, which Dürer had drawn in 1493[2] (fig. 161).

At the beginning of the 1840s he made a few drawings of his brother in a disarranged bed, studies after a model Cato, sliding in agony from his couch, which were to feature on the vignette engraved on wood for the *Works of Frederick the Great*[3]. In 1847 he painted a striking view of his bedroom at 43 Ritterstrasse (*cf.* cat. 34). The bed with a thin blanket carelessly pulled over it very much dominates the foreground. A preoccupation which Menzel would never subsequently lose is very soon evident in the suggestiveness of a seemingly fortuitous arrangement such as is presented in the *Unmade Bed*, distinguishing his interiors from the welcoming simplicity of Biedermeier interiors. The charm of this drawing of the bed is also due to the tacit eloquence of its reality, commonplace yet displayed in a provocative manner.

M. R.-R.

1. Berlin, Kupferstichkabinett, sketchbook 3.
2. Winkler, 1936, nos 27 and 32.
3. Berlin, Kupferstichkabinett (SZ Menzel N 1574 and N 1575), for the engraving Bock, 1923, no. 947; *cf.* also the vignette for the *Epistle to the Bed of the Marquis d'Argens*, Bock, 1923, no. 954.

18

Balcony Room

1845

Oil on board
58 × 47cm
Signed and dated at the bottom right: *A.M./45.*
Berlin, Nationalgalerie (A I 744)

Provenance: R. Wagner Gallery, Berlin; acquired by the museum in January 1903.
Exhibitions: Düsseldorf, 1904, no. 5; Berlin, 1905, no. 4, pl. facing p. 64; Berlin, 1906, no. 1142, fig. p. 133; Berlin, 1935, no. 2; Wiesbaden, 1947, no. 54, p. 9; Celle, 1949–50, p. 11; Wiesbaden, 1952, no. 151; Berlin, 1955 B, no. 8, fig. 6; London, 1956, no. 162, col. fig.; Berlin, 1960, fig. facing p. 29; Cologne, 1971, no. 67, pl. IV; Frankfurt, 1975, no. 26, col. fig.; Paris, 1976–7, no. 136, fig.
Bibliography: Cat. NG, 1903, no. 845; Tschudi, 1905 A, no. 23; *Gazette des Beaux-Arts*, 1904, vol. III/32, p. 424, fig. p. 425; Jordan, 1905, p. 102; Tschudi, 1905 B, p. 226, col. pl. opp. p. 221 (p. 16, col. pl. opp. p. 10); Marguillier, 1906, p. 83 *et seq.*; Meier-Graefe, 1906, p. 96 *et seq.*, p. 98–100, p. 116, p. 183; Scheffler, 1912, p. 118–21, fig. p. 119; Kern, 1915–16, p. 84, fig. facing p. 81; Justi, 1920,p. 135–8; Scheffler, 1922, p. 151 *et seq.*, fig. p. 55; Waldmann, 1941, p. 14–15, p. 43, fig. 7; Beenken, 1944, p. 179 *et seq.*, fig. 40; Chapeaurouge, 1960, p. 146 *et seq.*, fig. 83; cat. NG, 1976, p. 255, col. fig. p. 15; Busch, 1985, p. 278–82.

Since it was first able to be viewed publicly this has been regarded as the embodiment and acme of the art of Menzel as a young man. Pictorial art is here gently beginning to break away from narration and symbol. An almost empty room in which just a few everyday items of furniture distributed according to a very equivocal law of chance arrest our gaze, the only event a slight puff of wind, and light the only protagonist: rays of light coming through the curtain – exactly at the median axis – and shining on to the ground. Rather than referring to the contours of the objects or their colours this painting is conceived as a chromatic organism. This led Hugo von Tschudi to despair of the ability of the 'clumsy word' to do justice to the extremely subtle 'miracles' of such art[1]. Although he said that with his 'modern eye' he regretted only the absence of the 'air being subdued by tone', he immediately revised this opinion, quoting 'one of our most illustrious painters' – who other than Liebermann? : 'But just think! There is no air in a bedroom'[2].

In the same spirit, among the wood-engravings intended for Kugler's book, landscapes in which action is barely perceptible break up the course of the narrative. Also among them is the picture of Frederick's study at Sanssouci[3] (*cf.* cat. 4), an 'empty' interior, even if it admirably implies the presence of a person; it is inhabited by a generous light diffused through the French windows which seem like the source of life. Depicting empty rooms had represented a genre of its own since the beginning of the nineteenth century, especially in watercolour. However, it was mainly a matter of using a perspective based on a central axis faithfully to reproduce rooms complete with their furniture and pictures, usually the rooms of the aristocracy. It is those very elements which Menzel removes from the visual field, revealing only fragments.

For a long time after Tschudi and Meier-Graefe, any interpretation of *Balcony Room* concentrated exclusively on the way light is conveyed by colour; it is only in the last few years, looking instead at the depiction of space, that we have begun to ask questions about the lack of a homogeneous construction of perspective. Two incompatible heights are in fact suggested for the viewing point, and the ground seems to slide from underneath the viewer's feet[4]. No lateral delimitation helps to define the foreground and the comment Heinrich von Kleist was prompted to make in 1809 with regard to Caspar David Friedrich's *Monk by the Sea* comes to mind: 'With only the frame acting as foreground, when looking at it you have the feeling that your eyelids have been cut off.' Moreover the objects are depicted with very varying degrees of precision. Oscillating between clear, palpable expression and the summary suggestion of a phantom-like half-presence, we approximate to everyday experience, involving a graduated, selective perception: while concentrating on one object it takes in others in an ever more blurred way the further they are removed from the main element. It may be added that this visual experience, 'simultaneously extremely subjective and extremely objective'[5], was not unknown to the theorists of the day: thus Rudolf Wiegmann, a professor at the Düsseldorf Academy, recommended those pursuing an illusionist effect to imitate 'the varying adaptation of the retina dependent on the remoteness of the object to be perceived', to allow for the fact that the eye cannot take in two objects at a distance from one another simultaneously and with equal precision, and therefore to paint the periphery less sharply in focus than the main object[6].

This has remarkable implications for the formal structure of the picture. Immediately the perception of the object seems to be broken up into several stages, the suspension of time – a fiction which had been one of the crucial rules of painting since the Renaissance – is called into question. This of course ties in with the event introduced by the movement of the curtain – at odds with the traditional immobility of bedrooms, which were depicted like still lifes. Thus the dimension of time is evident at two levels: in the event and in perception.

On top of this there is the deliberately non-symmetrical arrangement of the objects in the pictorial space. Everything, little as that is, is on the right-hand side, partly in a state of palpable reality, partly merely reflected in the large mirror. Alluding to things outside the pictorial field by means of a mirror was an old device: from Jan van Eyck's *Arnolfini Marriage* to the subtly enigmatic compositions of the Berlin artist Johann Erdmann Hummel (and on to the American Richard Estes . . .). However, the reflected image had always been used to complement an already ample supply of information; in *Balcony Room* on the other hand the image in the mirror gives a considerably clearer and more coherent idea of the nature and function of this room than much of the rest of the composition' and, immediately we start to

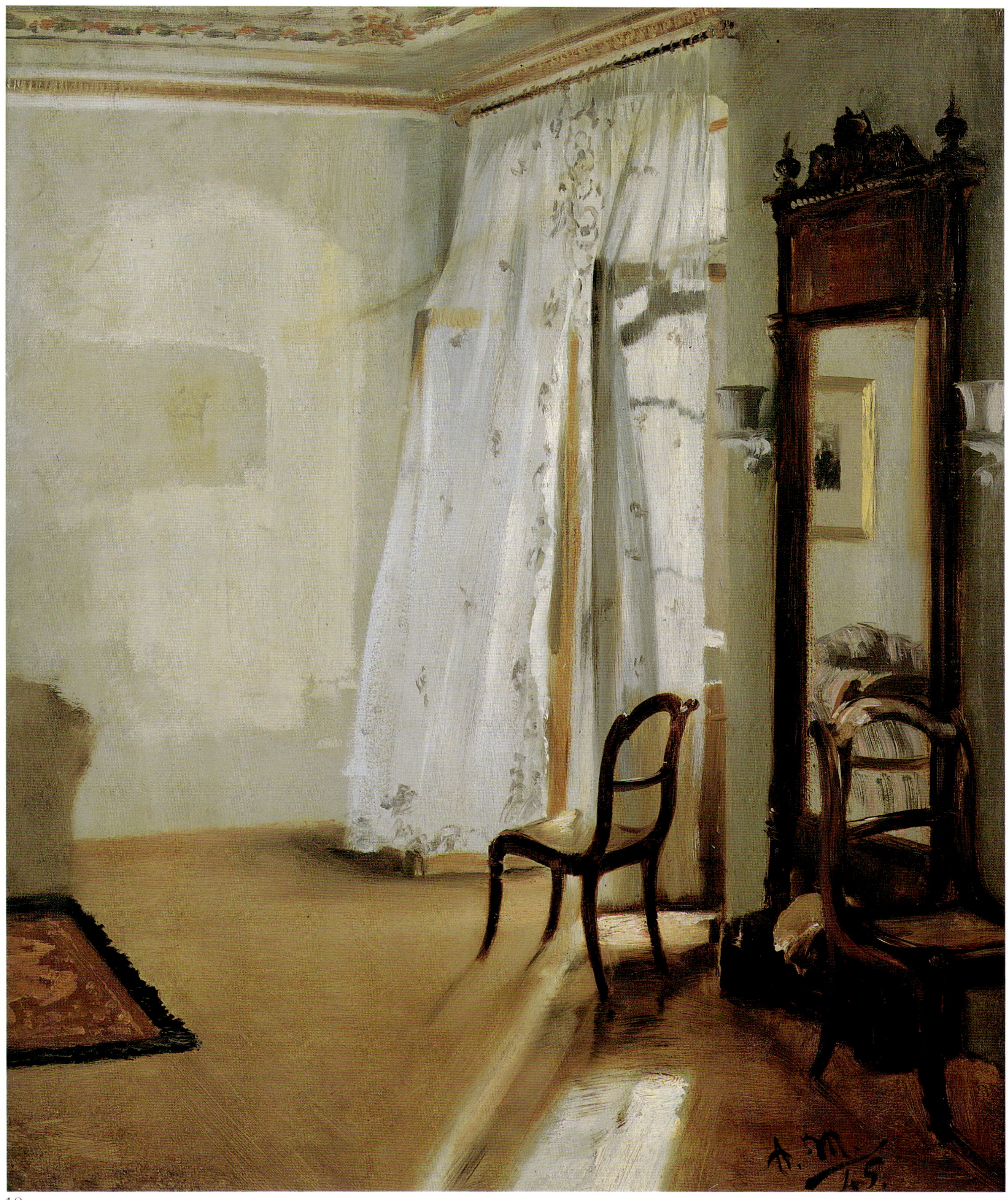
18

consider only what is actually in our field of vision, disregarding objects brought into view by means of artifice, this turns out to be desperately sparse.

The two chairs turned back to back seem to have been placed at random, as when moving into a house or giving the room a thorough clean. And the meaning of the light patch on the bare wall in particular remains an enigma: a reflection of sunlight? Did the house-painter break off work there, or did Menzel himself leave his picture 'unfinished'? Thus half of the picture exists without material substance: a signifier without a signified. Likewise the dividing wall would suggest its thickness better if the sofa on the left edge was a little more than a faint shadow; but that is in fact what has been avoided. Everything combines to suggest that the sofa did not remain 'unfinished' because the painter had lost interest, but because the pictorial logic rejected all plasticity at this point. C.K.

1. Tschudi, 1905 B, p. 226 *et seq.*, quotation p. 227 (pp. 16–17, quotation p. 17).
2. Tschudi, 1905 B, note p. 17.
3. Bock, 1923, no. 783.
4. Busch, 1985.
5. *Ibid.*
6. Wiegmann, 1855, pp. 197–200.

19

The Interruption (The Visit)

1845–6

Oil on canvas
111.5 × 90cm
Signed and dated on the left, on the side of the instrument: *Adolph Menzel/1846.*
Karlsruhe, Staatliche Kunsthalle (2611)
Exhibited in Berlin only

Provenance: Painter's studio; 1905 Emilie Krigar-Menzel; *c.*1910–20 (until before 1926) Theodor Schall, Berlin; Mayer-Krude, Berlin; Rudolf Lob, Boston; Parke & Bernet sale, New York, 4.11.1971, no. 33, fig.; Fritz and Peter Nathan, Zurich; acquired by the museum in 1973.
Exhibitions: Berlin, 1846, no. 592; Zurich, 1917, no. 79, fig.; Sofia, 1918; New York, 1981, no. 60, col. fig.
Bibliography: Tschudi, 1905 A, no. 29; Tschudi, 1905 B, p. 228 *et seq.* (p. 18 *et seq.*); Meier-Graefe, 1906, p. 94; Wolff, 1914, p. 78, p. 88, p. 96; Scheffler, 1922, p. 166; Scheffler, 1938, p. 63f; Waldmann, 1941, p. 15–16, p. 44, fig. 10; Karlsruhe, 1973, p. 163 *et seq.*; Karlsruhe, 1984, p. 62, fig. 58 (col.); Karlsruhe, 1988, p. 220, col. fig. p. 221; Börsch-Supan, 1988, p. 393 *et seq.*, col. pl. 95.

'1846: an oil painting, the first since the break in 1839, depicting two woman friends spending a musical evening together, disturbed by a social call from visitors who are coming in'[1]. We can see that in his first official curriculum vitae, written when he was accepted into the Academy of Arts, Menzel only took account of works intended for exhibition or sale. This 'break' after the *Day of the Hearing* (cat. 2) included *Rear Courtyard and House* (cat. 13) or *Balcony Room* (cat. 18)!

The canvas was started in 1843 and was already 'fairly well on' in the summer[2] and could temporarily be 'left on one side'; he did not take it up again until the end of 1845[3]. A few lines Menzel wrote when he was working on a transparency in the style of Rubens attest to the immense joy the young artist – who had meanwhile gone back to working on small illustrations, this time for the *Works of Frederick the Great* – derived from working in as large a format as possible: 'a delight . . . never have I experienced such pleasure'[4].

Using an imposing format, *The Interruption* portrays a fairly insignificant event in a dramatic mode, with a certain amount of exaggeration, as if reproducing a scene in a theatre. (But compare it with *The Théâtre du Gymnase* [cat. 80] painted ten years later!) Like the facial expressions and gestures, the decor of the room (part of a chateau?) seems overdone, down to the almost grotesque ornamentation of the harmonium, inspired by baroque mannerism. The drawing-room, with its complicated plan, as permeable as a set constructed from flats, opens out both to the outside and on to an antechamber, and to add to these complications there is a 'problem' of lighting. The young painter's ambition could not be satisfied with the flames from the candles and the bright shafts of light they project on to the young ladies, nor the moonlight coming through the window, and the contrast between the warm tints and the icy blue; on top of that he needed the reflection of the lamp in the next-door room and the glow from behind the door. On the other hand, in an ironic twist, the chandelier is not lit. We are reminded of Johann Erdmann Hummel's provocative constructions of space and light. And it was in fact in 1846 that Hummel, Menzel's elder by forty-six years, exhibited a second version of his *Game of Chess*[5] with this very revealing note: 'Conceived following the laws of perspective, optics and catoptrics.' Although very far removed from this extreme cerebralism, Menzel was happy to resort to other expedients: 'In order to make an exact study of candlelight, he had built a miniature room with a tiny piano in it on which he had placed two tiny candles and a miniature doll . . . In the first sketch a young woman was pacing up and down the room; later on he changed his mind in favour of unexpected visitors appearing in the background'[6]. (It has been thought that the lady making her entry accompanied by a gentleman might be Caroline Meyerheim, whose painter husband was a friend of Menzel's[7].)

The Interruption was shown at the exhibition of the Berlin Academy in 1846: more than half a century later the art critic Ludwig Pietsch still recollected it as an 'unforgettable painting in the modern genre'. Pietsch remembered the lukewarm response of the public, but also the 'pure delight' of a painter friend who from that time on was 'completely besotted' with Menzel[8]. Tschudi on the other hand found this work 'with its anecdotal slant and the construction of its interior rather behind its time[9]'. Meier-Graefe was even harsher, judging it a 'complete failure' for the very reason that there are 'so many different lighting effects'. It was not until Emil Waldmann came along that it was again spoken of warmly; he pointed out the unity of the plastic values and of the colours 'bathed in light and themselves giving off light'. 'That light

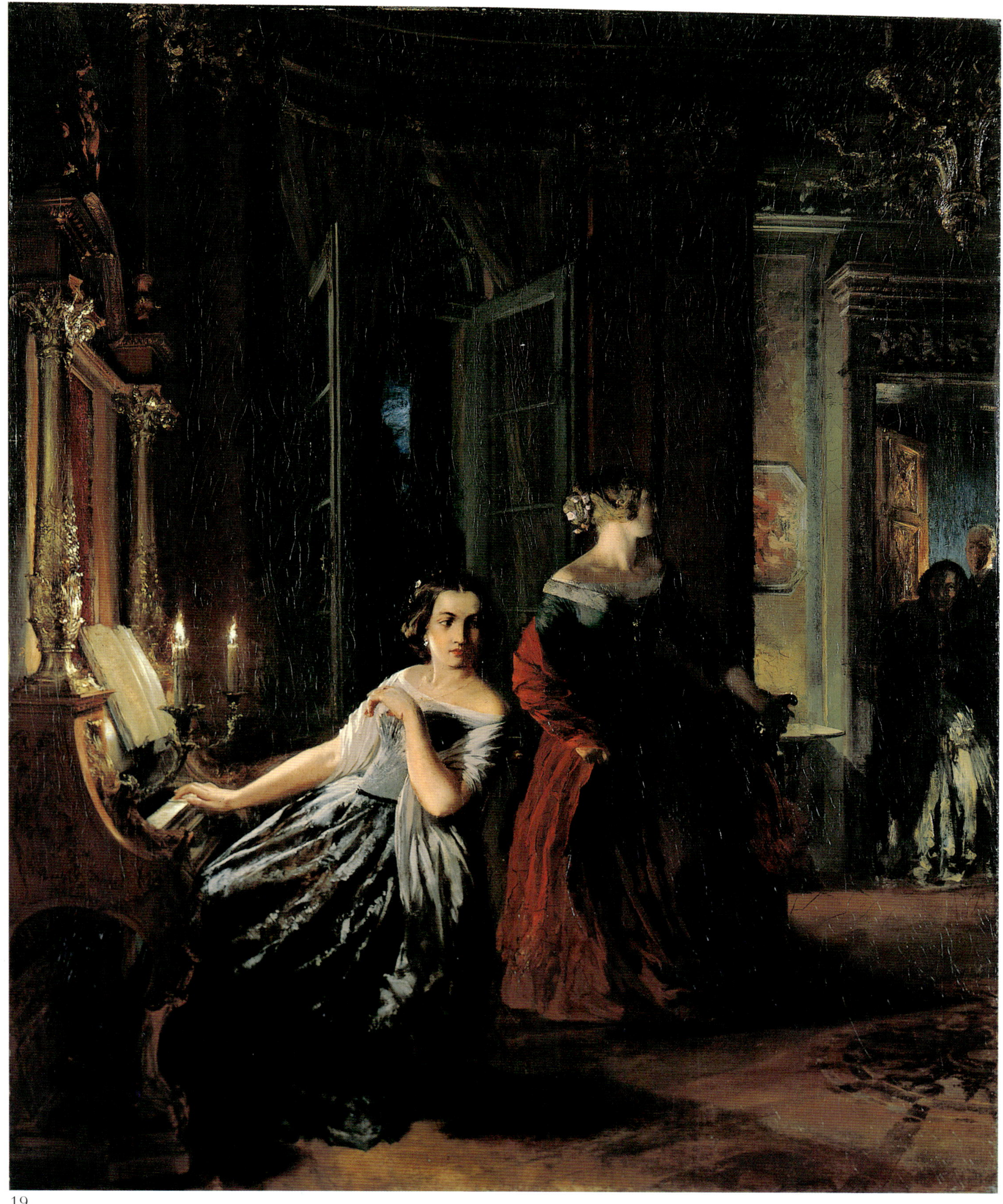
19

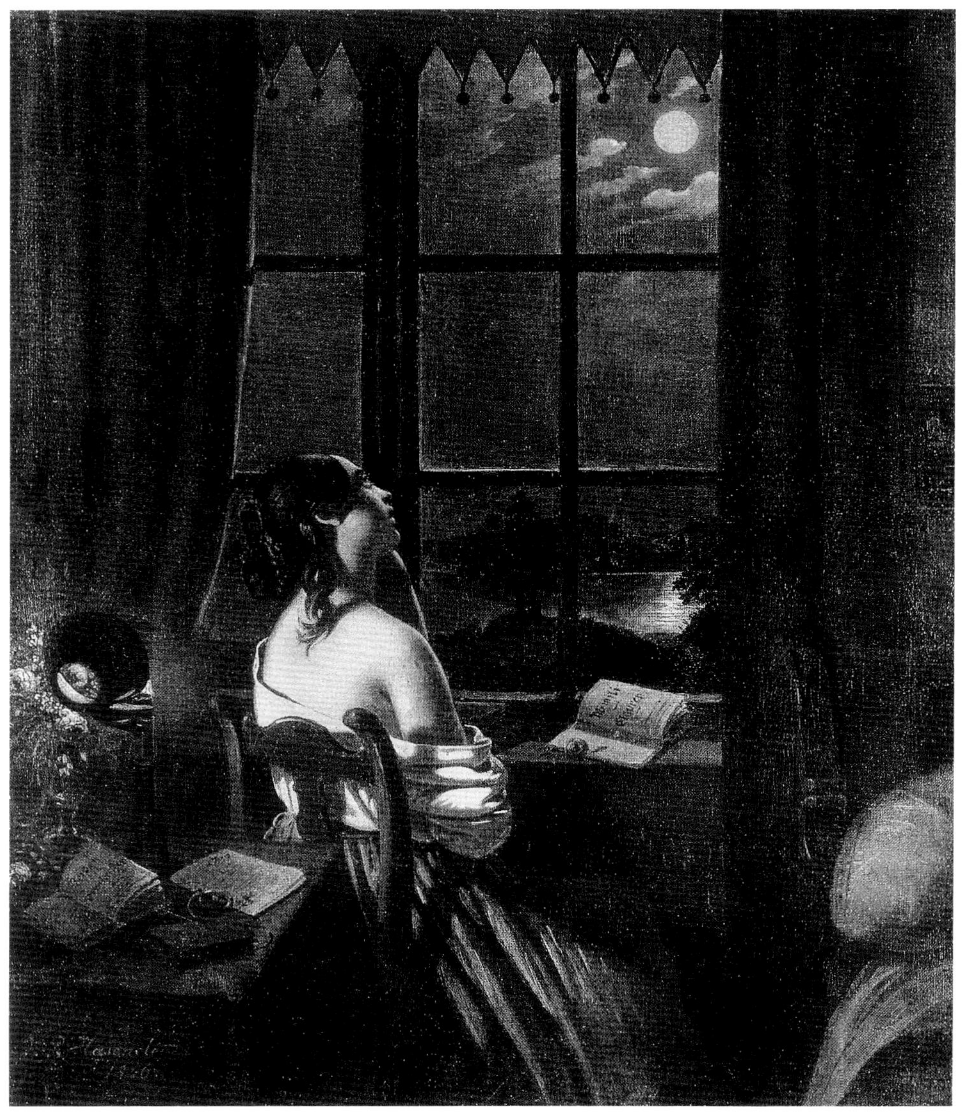

Fig. 162. Johann Peter Hasenclever, *Sentimental Woman*, 1846, Düsseldorf, Kunstmuseum

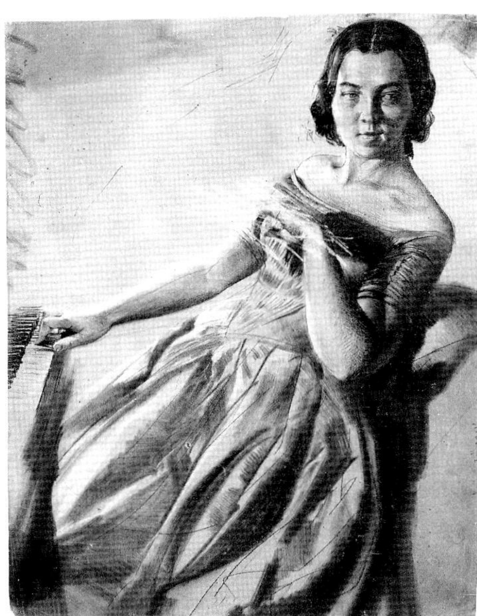

Fig. 163. *Frau Maercker at the Piano*, 1846, pastel, Berlin, Kupferstichkabinett (N 1123)

and that colour are as solid as walls.' And it is in this manner that the picture reveals its importance: the light that catches fire here radiates through Menzel's work in several forms until the period of *The Iron Rolling Mill* (cat 160).

Even so, the 'residue' of theatricality, conventional in that it is not justified by the subject and deplored by Waldmann, is indicative of the precarious balance which Menzel would always seek between preserving the narrative substance, and making it subordinate: it may be that something really crucially important in the sense of a melodrama is coming into the lives of these two women through this unexpected visit – the couple in the background may have a role in the 'intrigue'; but no detail makes the viewer party to what is going on and they remain outside the action. A similar phenomenon again occurs in Menzel's final paintings which feature a large number of characters and a multiplicity of tiny incidents arising from everyday life; this creates a vague sense of confusion which does not encourage us to share in the emotions or identify with the characters depicted. C.K.

1. Curriculum vitae written for the Academy of Arts on 8 November 1853. Repr. in exhib. cat. Berlin, 1955 B, pp. 8–11, p. 10.
2. Letter to Carl Heinrich Arnold, 22 July 1843, Wolff, 1914, p. 78.
3. Letter to Carl Heinrich Arnold, 29 December 1845, Wolff, 1914, p. 88.
4. *Ibid.*
5. First version, *c.*1818–19, Berlin, Nationalgalerie; second version, 1846, Hannover, Niedersächsische Landesgalerie.
6. Carl Johann Arnold, (1905) 1992, p. 133. As a young man Arnold had been given the sketch as a present.
7. Exhib. cat. Karlsruhe, 1984. Preliminary drawings: Berlin, Kupferstichkabinett (SZ Menzel N 1123, for the seated woman; SZ Menzel N 1122, for the woman turning round). Mrs Maercker served as a model for both women.
8. Pietsch, (1905) 1992, p. 323–4.
9. Tschudi, 1905 B, p. 198.

20

The Grand Masters Siegfried von Feuchtwangen and Ludger von Braunschweig. Sketch for the Marienburg Paintings
1846

Oil on canvas
93.5 × 78.5cm
Signed and dated (vertically) at the bottom left: *Adolph Menzel 1846* – Annotated beneath each of the figures: *Siegfried / Luderus*
Berlin, Nationalgalerie (A III 502)
Exhibited in Berlin only

Provenance: Ignaz von Olfers, director-general of the Berlin Museums, entrusted the sketch to the Kupferstichkabinett, probably after the frescoes had been executed; 1888 Department of Paintings; 1890 Nationalgalerie.
Exhibitions: Berlin, 1895 A, no. 122; Berlin, 1905 A, no. 20; Berlin, 1980 A, no. II, fig. p. 211.
Bibliography: *Die Dioskuren*, 1, 1856, p. 164; Donop, 1902, no. 120; Tschudi, 1905 A, no. 25, fig.; NG cat., 1907, no. 1063; Forstreuter, 1967, p. 12–14, pl. facing p. 26; Boockmann, 1982 A, p. 32 *et seq.*, p. 118, fig. 43; Boockmann, 1982 B, p. 127 *et seq.*; Riemann-Reyher, 1992, p. 68–73.

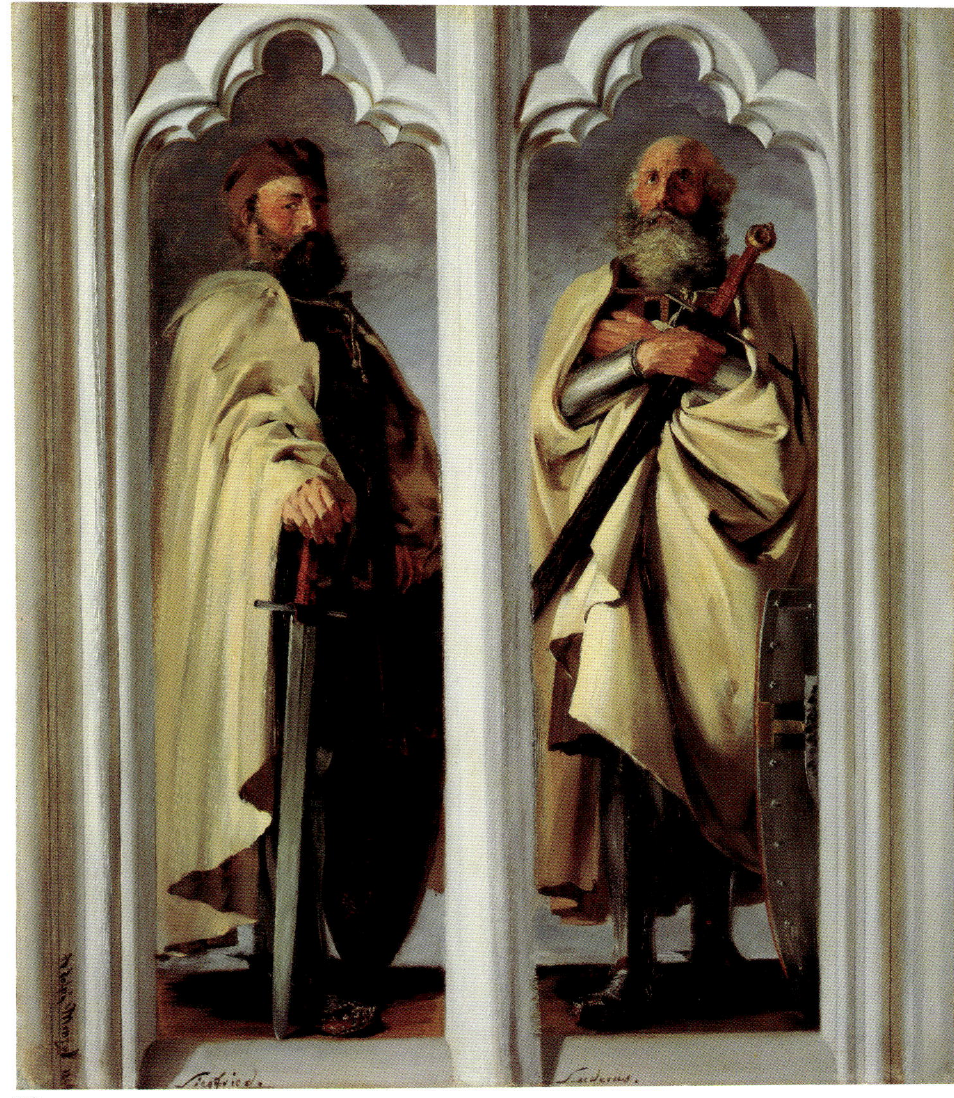
20

There were nine years between the initial concept and the execution of the wall painting which was Menzel's contribution to the decor of the Marienburg fortress (fig. 164). By this means he was associated at the age of thirty with one of the ambitious national monuments projects developed in Prussia after 1815 – the most important being the completion of Cologne cathedral, which had remained unfinished since the Gothic period. Since 1309 (at the initiative of that same Siegfried von Feuchtwangen whose image Menzel painted) the Marienburg (Malbork) on the Nogat near Danzig had been the main headquarters of the Teutonic Order founded in 1190; in the thirteenth century the order conquered huge areas of what used to be Prussian territory – now belonging to Poland and Russia – and became a major regional power thanks to numerous wars and far-flung and elaborate trading links. But the decline of the order of knights started in the fifteenth century and in 1466 it had to concede much of its territory, including the Marienburg, to Poland. The order lost more and more of its political and military influence and was abolished in Germany by Napoleon, so that it continued to exist only in Austria and Belgium. The castle of its Grand Masters had fallen into ruin and narrowly escaped the demolition which had been under consideration from before 1800, thanks to the Berlin architect Friedrich Gilly, who had drawn attention to the building. From 1815 the first president of western Prussia, Theodor von Schön, perseveringly set about having it restored and transformed into a 'national monument', a 'Prussian Westminster'. Moreover, for him this was not a reference to the Teutonic Order's policy of annexation, but more to an ideal concept of the State, linked with the attempts to introduce liberal reforms into Prussia after 1806. Crown Prince Frederick-William for his part was quickly and permanently won over to von Schön's plans and envisaged turning the castle into the representative symbol of a Romantic corporate State; he even considered founding a new chivalric order.

The summer refectory is one of three refectories located within the main building, the palace of the Grand Masters. After it had been enhanced by sumptuous storied stained-glass windows in 1828 there had been a plan for five wall paintings (in the recesses of the blind win-

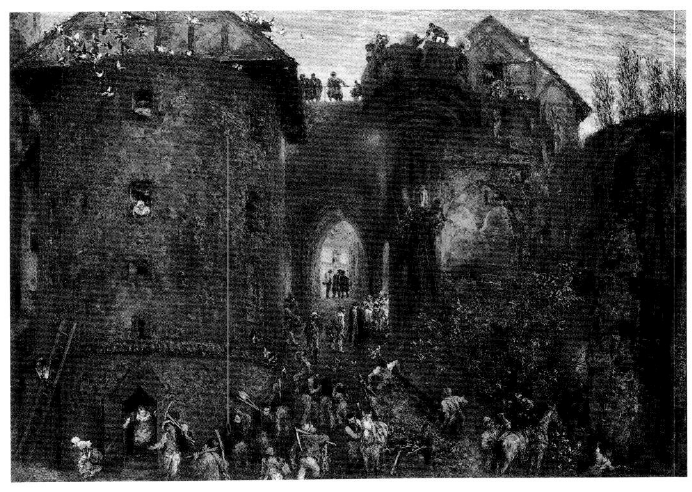

Fig. 164. *The Marienburg*, 1897, gouache, Berlin, Kupferstichkabinett (N 4596)

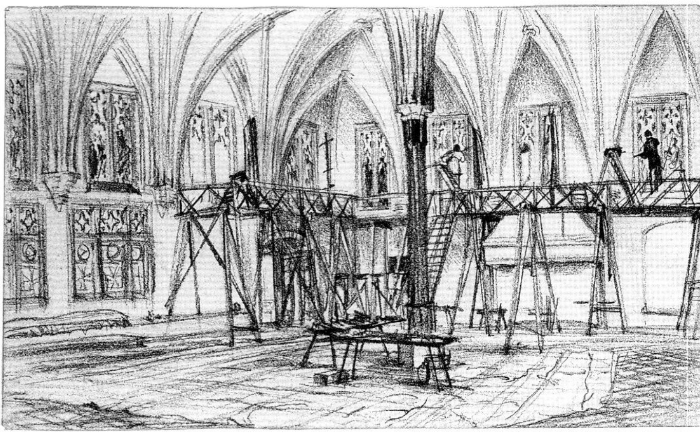

Fig. 165. *Painters on Scaffolding in the Summer Refectory at Marienburg*, 1855, pencil, Berlin, Kupferstichkabinett (N 151)

dows) with ten full-length portraits of the Grand Masters; according to von Schön's original project, which was to be rejected by the king, they were to be given the features of the first advocates of Prussian reform. Five artists shared the commission, and Menzel was entrusted with the figures of Siegfried von Feuchtwangen (who held office 1303–11) and Ludger von Braunschweig (1331–5). In a letter to Menzel, von Schön, who wanted an idea to be associated with each portrait, wrote: 'The portrait of Siegfried von Feuchtwangen – the first Grand Master to be based at Marienburg – should be a dignified expression of fulfilment and happiness. That of Grand Master Ludger von Braunschweig should depict the sublimity of a life dedicated to the Idea in poetry and song.' Indicating some historical reference books to the painter and noting the lack of any authentic portraits, he added: 'The artist can give his genius free rein. The two characters are entrusted to you and you have complete freedom in bringing them back to life'[1].

As the king was financing the commission the colour sketch had to be sent to the director-general of Berlin Museums, Ignaz von Olfers, before July 1846. But the years of crisis leading up to 1848, the Revolution and finally the Restoration meant the project was forgotten, and for a time von Schön seemed to prefer the elderly Peter von Cornelius to the artists he had previously approached. It was not until 1854 that Menzel was asked to draw the cartoons and rethink the figure of Ludger von Braunschweig, which had been turned down by his client[2]. He seems to have carried out this task with rather bad grace. This is evident in the figure accompanied by a bear which replaced the fine old man clutching a sword to his breast, and the model of the fortress held by his companion is a rather problematical addition. Nor does Menzel seem to have used the sketch as his inspiration for the faces; probably it had not been returned to him.

The mural painting was not executed until 1855 (fig. 165), when it was done in nine days employing a technique very much in vogue at the time, stereochromy, also used by Wilhelm von Kaulbach at the Neues Museum in Berlin. On this occasion the painter visited the superb fortress and met von Schön, then eighty-three years old, 'captivating my interest like a very fine old fossil, still giving off sparks'[3]. Before going directly to Paris, where he was due to visit the Universal Exhibition, anxious as always to have personal documentation, he did not forget to have a 'good photograph'[4] taken of his work. Fortunately the mural painting survived World War II and has recently been restored.

A year later, just as Menzel was celebrating his triumph in Berlin with the art review picture of *Night Attack at Hochkirch*, the art review *Die Dioskuren* wrote that the portraits of the Grand Masters were 'in no way satisfactory'. The sketch, on the other hand, with the freedom and sumptuousness no doubt learnt from Rubens, with the bursts of light on the clothes and steel, the highlights on the edges, the splendour of the yellows and the shading of the greys, give an extremely sensuous image of the past. This can be confirmed by comparing this with the sketch of two other Grand Masters executed by Eduard Daege (until very recently attributed to Carl Wilhelm Kolbe), also at the Nationalgalerie. C.K.

1. Quoted by Forstreuter, 1967.
2. The cartoons belonged to the Nationalgalerie and disappeared in 1945 (SZ Menzel Kat. 719, 720). Preparatory drawings: N 1121, 1426, 4186, 4187; Kat. 721 (dated 1855).
3. Letter to Paul Heyse, 19 October 1855, reprod. in Riemann-Reyher, 1992, p. 70.
4. Letter to Paul Heyse, n.d. [early 1856]. Munich, Bayerische Staatsbibliothek.

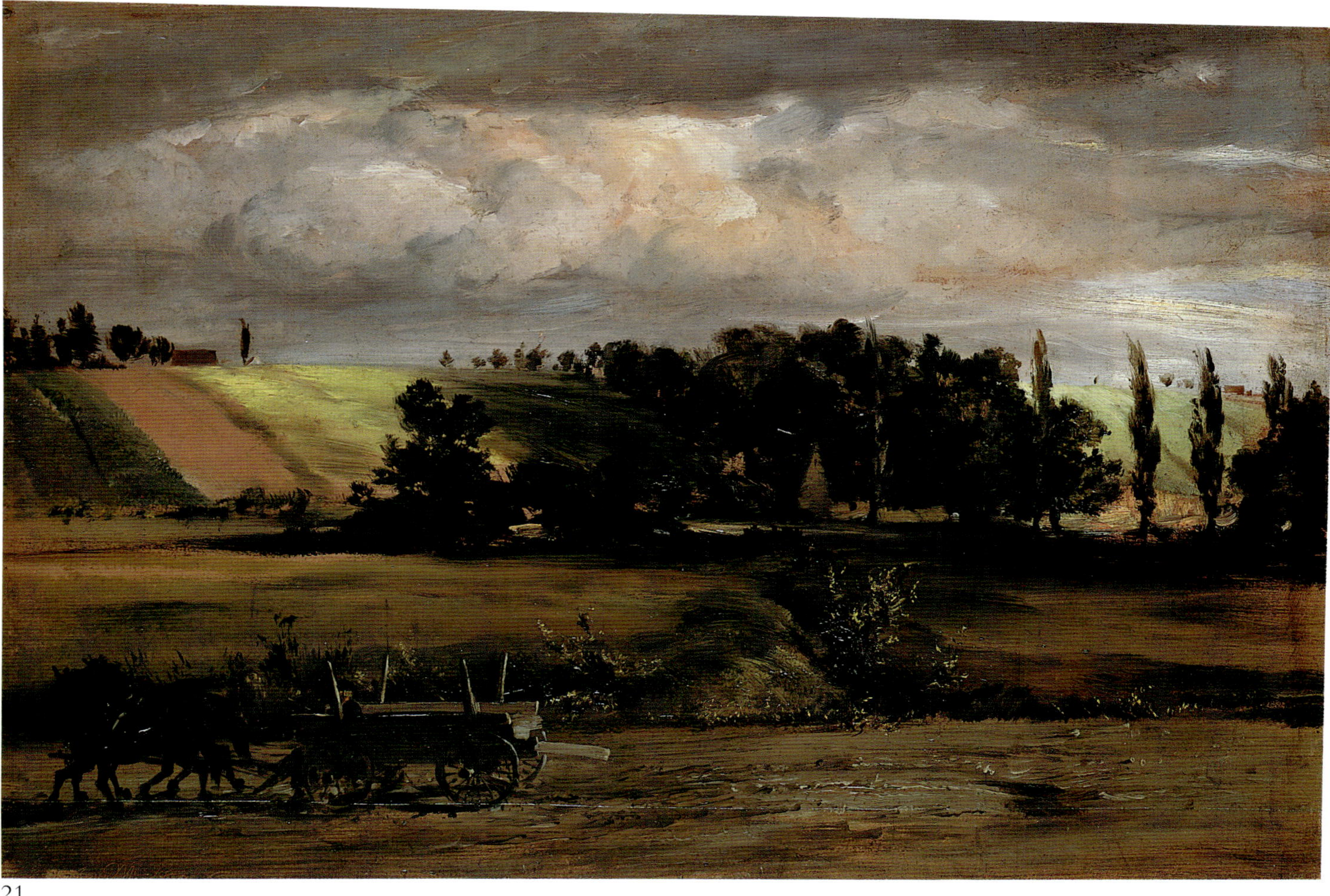
21

21
Storm over Tempelhofer Berg
1846

Oil on paper
31 × 47cm
Signed and dated at the bottom left: *AM 1846*
Cologne, Wallraf-Richartz-Museum (WRM 1126)
Exhibited in Paris only

Provenance: Painter's studio; 1905 Emilie Krigar-Menzel; Otto and Grete Krigar-Menzel; Theodor Schall, Baden-Baden; Museumsverein Köln; acquired by the museum in 1914 (gift of the Museumsverein Köln).
Exhibitions: Cologne, 1922, no. 114; Berne, 1936, no. 96, reprod.; Marburg, 1946, no. 32; Cologne, 1953–4, no. 22; Berlin, 1955 B, no. 18, fig. 21; Paris, 1976–7, no. 138, reprod.
Bibliography: Not mentioned by Tschudi, 1905 A; Tschudi, 1905 B, p. 232 (p. 22); Scheffler, 1922, p. 148, reprod. p. 49; Scheffler, 1938, p. 58, reprod. 159; Waldmann, 1941, p. 12, p. 44, fig. 12; Andree, 1964, p. 89, reprod. p. 243; Hütt, 1981, fig. 37 (col.); Jensen, 1982, p. 54, col. pl. 4; Cologne, 1986, vol I, fig. 732; vol II, p. 222, col. reprod. p. 223.

Like the motif used in *On the Kreuzberg, near Berlin* (cat. 31), the subject for this painting lay quite close to the city gates, and a short distance from Menzel's apartment in Schöneberger Strasse; in those days, Tempelhofer Berg (the old name for Kreuzberg) was turning into a suburb, if not a town in its own right. This work underlines the still dominant rustic features, and the untamed forces of nature are highlighted by storm clouds that have not quite blotted out the sunlight. Thick, but light-coloured, clouds are gathering over the brow of the hill, which itself imparts light of rare clarity, and the fields would suffer from stifling monotony were it not for the dying rays of the sun. The house shaded by the trees in the middle ground is already enveloped in shadow.

The spectacle could have been captured from a carriage speeding past. Colour skims from the surfaces of the pathways and fields as they fly by and, *a priori,* it is surprising to find that the only object that can be seen to be moving, the cart, is reproduced with the greatest precision, despite the fact that it is off-centre. Nonetheless, the spectator is being handed a clear invitation to identify with the cart and the direction it is taking. The uneven, even ill-matched, treatment of the different sections of the painting reflects the disjointed approach to pictorial work and non-linear technique that Menzel favoured as a young man; as Werner Busch (1985) has cleverly demonstrated, Menzel followed imprecisions of perceptions as closely as possible. Even the occasional repetition (in itself an unusual technique for the German artist) of horizontal parallel motifs within an oblong format – the regular alignment of trees in the middle ground – seems to reinforce the impression of a vehicle moving quickly down a straight road.

C.K.

22

Building Site with Willows

1846

Oil on canvas
41 × 55cm
Signed and dated at the bottom right *A.M. 1846*
Berlin, Nationalgalerie (A I 900)

Provenance: Richard Menzel; 1865 Elise Milner, Menzel's widow, Gross-Lichterfelde; acquired by the museum in 1906.
Exhibitions: Berlin, 1905, no. 80; Berlin, 1906, no. 1175b, reprod.; Berlin, 1926, no. 96; Boston, 1909, unnumb. (p. 56), unnumb. pl.; Berlin, 1935, no. 6, reprod.; Wiesbaden, 1947, no. 56; Wiesbaden, 1952, no. 153; Berlin, 1955 B, no. 10, fig. 19; Kiel, 1956, no. 56; Zurich, 1959, unnumb., no pag.; Paris, 1961, no. 44; Dusseldorf, 1967, no. 228; Hamburg, 1976, no. 307, reprod.
Bibliography: Tschudi, 1905 A, no. 30; Tschudi, 1905 B, p. 229–31; pl. facing p. 228 (p. 19–21, pl. facing p. 18); cat. NG, 1907, no. 986; Scheffler, 1912, p. 121, reprod. p. 118; Kern, 1915–16, p. 84, p. 86, reprod. p. 82; Justi, 1920, p. 140 *et seq.*; Scheffler, 1922, p. 12, p. 148, reprod. p. 47; Justi, 1932, p. 130 *et seq.*; Scheffler, 1938, p. 57 *et seq.*, reprod. p. 162; Waldmann, 1941, p. 13, p. 44, fig. 14; Hütt, 1981, fig. 30 (col.).

When the French man of letters Bernardin de Saint-Pierre (1737–1814), visited Berlin, he expressed great affection for the willows lining the banks of the Spree. Many years later, Menzel most frequently drew them along the Schafgraben, not far from where he lived[1] (figs 166,167). This waterway, a diversion canal of the River Spree, had been laid out in 1705. It described an arc around the town from south-east to west, and small beaches, some industrial buildings and a gasworks had been built on its banks. The move from rural life to industrialization was marked by a degree of uncertainty, a phenomenon remarked on by a guidebook to Berlin dated 1834 which described its main bridge as 'a bridge made of wood, but with an iron parapet'[2].

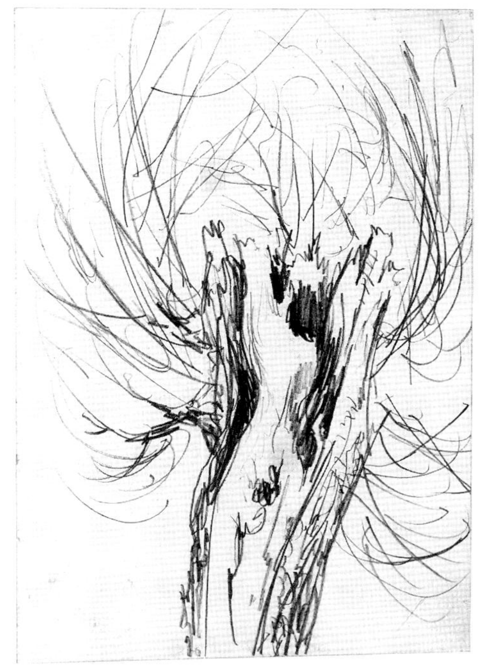

Fig. 166. *Willow*, c. 1844, pencil, Berlin, Kupferstichkabinett (N 2332)

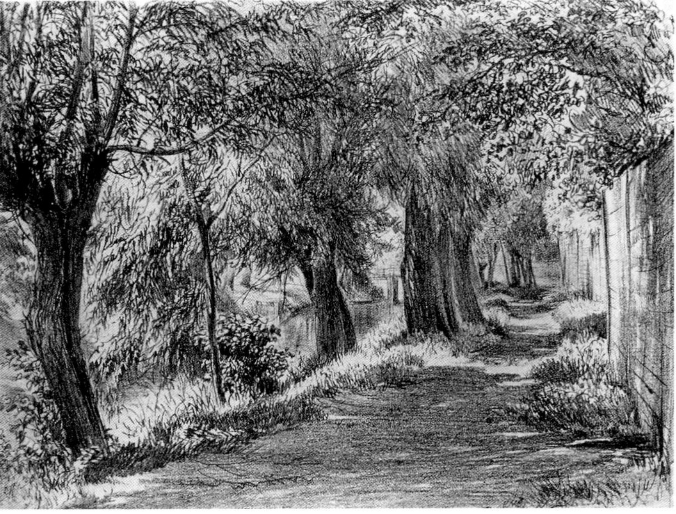

Fig. 167. *The Schafgraben*, 1843–6, pencil, Berlin, Kupferstichkabinett (sketchbook 8, p. 28)

Apart from *Building Site with Willows*, this landscape also inspired an etching notable for its overwhelming and mysterious silence (fig. 86). There are also numerous drawings of isolated willow trees with their trunks laid waste, their branches sketched in or indicated with simple, bold lines. These studies are united in a wood engraving in Kugler's book[3]. The painting is a faithful copy of a pencil drawing, although the latter takes up more space[4].

Depicting scaffolding and the untreated surfaces of newly constructed brick walls imparted a fragmentary, transitory impression, and was quite new to painting in Berlin. It is true that Realist painters of the Biedermeier period such as Eduard Gaertner, Friedrich Wilhelm Klose and Ludwig Deppe had emphasised the minutiae of new, sparsely decorated edifices, and buildings with back yards and unprepossessing façades[5]; however, they did not embrace the incompleteness, or the building sites or the way the town was encroaching into the countryside.

If we recall the abundance of people and events represented in Menzel's second period, the frequent absence of people and movement in his earlier work is all the more surprising. This painting, by contrast, is marked by a sense of intense human activity: horses being taken to water, and workers putting up a

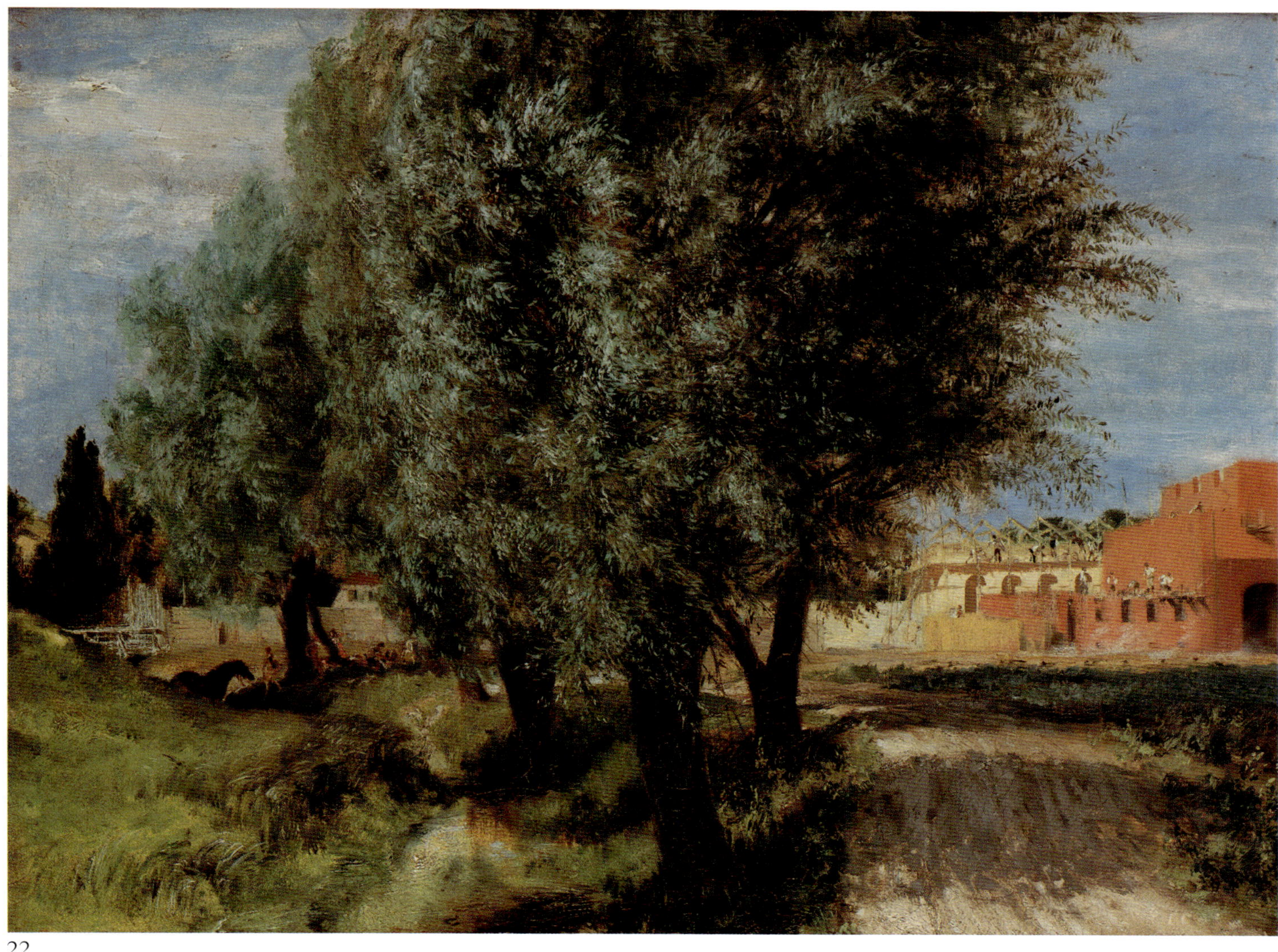

22

brightly coloured building; closer at hand, a bumpy, sandy path – one can almost breathe the dust and the warmth of summer – rushes helter-skelter down to the water's edge. By contrast, the willows seem to be toppling over towards us, and sparkling silver reflections on the nearest tree – splashes of greeny-blues and bluey-greens of many shades – dominate much of the foreground.

Paintings such as this with their wealth of sunlight signally fuelled the debate on Menzel the 'Impressionist'. However, trying to answer an incorrectly articulated question only adds to the confusion. Hugo von Tschudi's refusal to make Menzel into 'a kind of miraculous guide' on the basis of these works was unsuccessful. Instead, he pointed to Blechen, who had (on one occasion) found a factory that was worth painting. In his view, Menzel had in no way anticipated Impressionist *plein-air* painting. His interest focused on matters relating to light, and not on the way colours changed – and certainly not on the modification of local colour by the atmosphere and light conditions obtaining at a given moment. The fact of the matter was that Menzel did not really take any interest in *plein-air* painting at all; he simply made passing references to it from time to time. What is more, it played little or no part in his development[6].

So far as we are aware, this painting was never shown in Menzel's lifetime, but he parted with it at quite an early stage in his career; by the early 1806s at the latest, it was in the possession of his brother, Richard. C.K.

1. Also known as the Landwehrgraben, and what is now the Landwehrkanal.
2. Ziedlitz, 1834, p. 695.
3. Chapter 34 (Bock, 1923, no. 713).
4. Kupferstichkabinett, Berlin (SZ Menzel N 337). Tschudi, 1905 B places this on a site close to the future Hafenplatz.
5. Exhib. cat. Berlin, 1987 B.
6. Tschudi, 1905 B, p. 231 (p. 21).

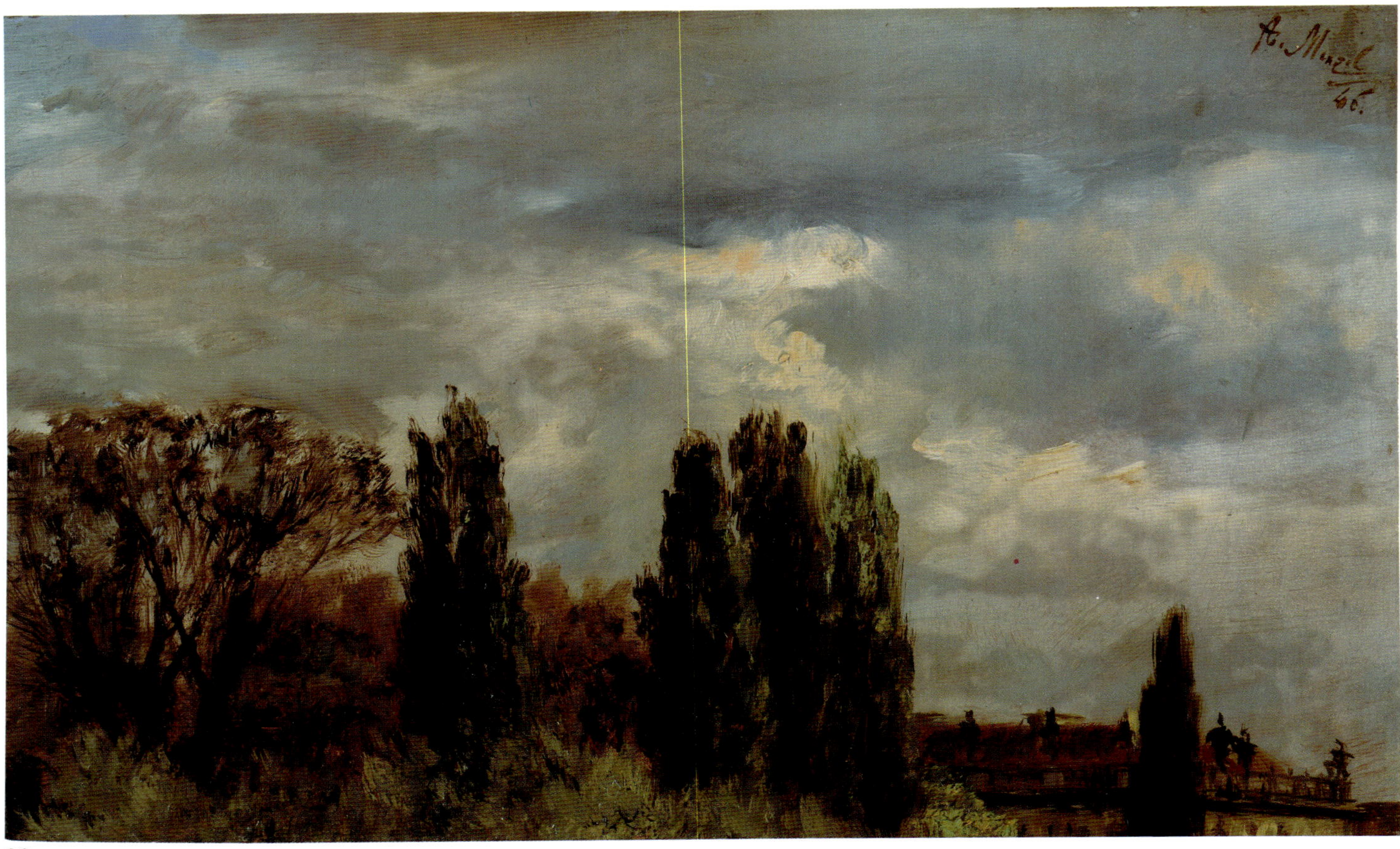

23

23

View over Prince Albert's Palace Park

1846

Oil on paper, canvas backing
24.7 × 40cm
Signed and dated at the bottom right: *A. Menzel – 46.*
Berlin, Nationalgalerie (A I 988)

Provenance: 1896 private collection; 1905 Martin Kappel, Berlin; acquired by the museum in 1907.
Exhibitions: Vienna, 1896, no. 274; Berlin, 1905, no. 51; Berlin, 1906, no. 1143; Paris, 1976–7, no. 137, reprod.; Berlin A, no. III, col. reprod. p. 132; Berlin, 1987 A, no. F 40, reprod.
Bibliography: Tschudi, 1905 A, no. 27; cat. NG, 1908, no. 1106; Scheffler, 1912, p. 122 *et seq.*, reprod. p. 120; Kern, 1915–16, p. 95 *et seq.*, reprod. p. 99; Scheffler, 1922, p. 146, reprod. p. 36; Justi, 1932, p. 130 *et seq.*; Scheffler, 1938, p. 57, reprod. p. 155; Busch, 1985, p. 286, fig. 95; cat. NG, 1986, no pag., col. pl. XII.

From the house on Schöneberger Strasse Menzel would have been unable to see the garden of Prince Albert's palace. It was too far away. At best, he might have been able to catch a glimpse of it from an apartment on Anhalter Strasse where, if an unreliable source is to be believed, he may have stayed briefly – Menzel frequently moved house as a young man. What is quite certain, however, is that he could not have seen it in 1846. Referring to the large-format version of the same

Fig. 167. *The Schafgraben*, 1843–6, pencil, Berlin, Kupferstichkabinett (sketchbook 8, p. 28)

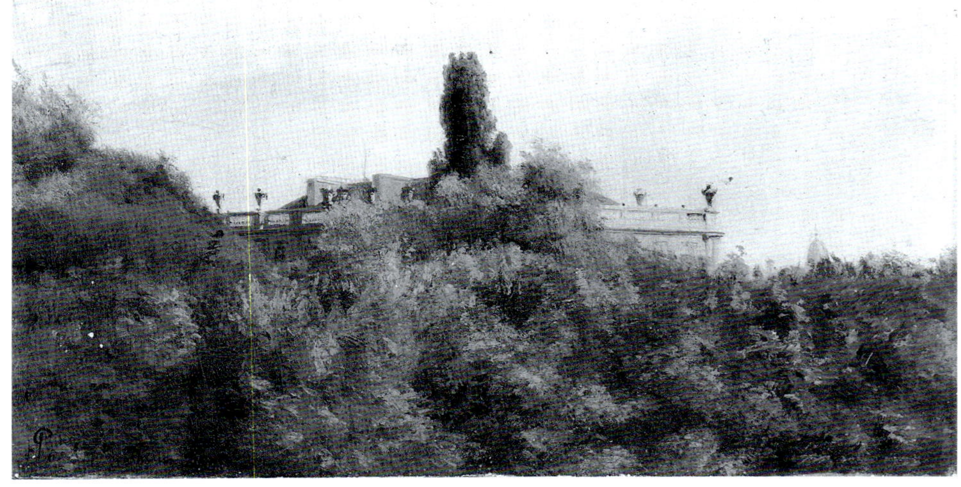

view (*cf.* cat. 164) which he started at the same time, he claimed to have painted it 'from the balcony of [his] apartment'; this is a very curious remark.

The ultimate fate of the palace on Wilhelmstrasse reflected both Germany's glories and its misfortunes. It was originally built for a French businessman, François Mathieu Vernezobre, who was ennobled by Frederick-William I and died in 1748. Alterations were later carried out by Schinkel for Prince Albert of Prussia; the principal additions included a large indoor riding arena, and stables in the Gothic style for to 90 horses belonging to the Prince, a keen horseman. The palace also became famous for its grand staircase in cast iron. In 1937, the German SS selected it for their headquarters, and it was from there they they spread their reign of terror throughout Europe. The palace was badly damaged by bombing in 1944, and it was eventually pulled down after the war.

Of the building as it appeared in the 1840s, the painting shows only a narrow strip representing the roof encircled by a balustrade of large decorative stone vases; this technique formed part of the tradition of studies of clouds (*cf.* cat. 59). They required a concrete motif (what might be seen as an element of measurable reality) in order to establish a landmark, and make it easier to approach the cluster of colours that the sky consisted of in these pictures – and which would otherwise be difficult to identify. In contrast with the clump of trees which suggest a hill, the building appears to be sinking beneath the surface of the earth. The trees include some poplars, a species often planted in towns because they grew quickly and were not associated with Classical symbolism of any sort. No less ordinary is the light-grey sky which is a mass of clouds save for a gentle, dissolving beam of light that illuminates the heavens as if by magic.

At about the same time, Menzel started work on a much larger, more ambitious version of this subject which he retouched some 30 years later (*cf.* cat. 164). C.K.

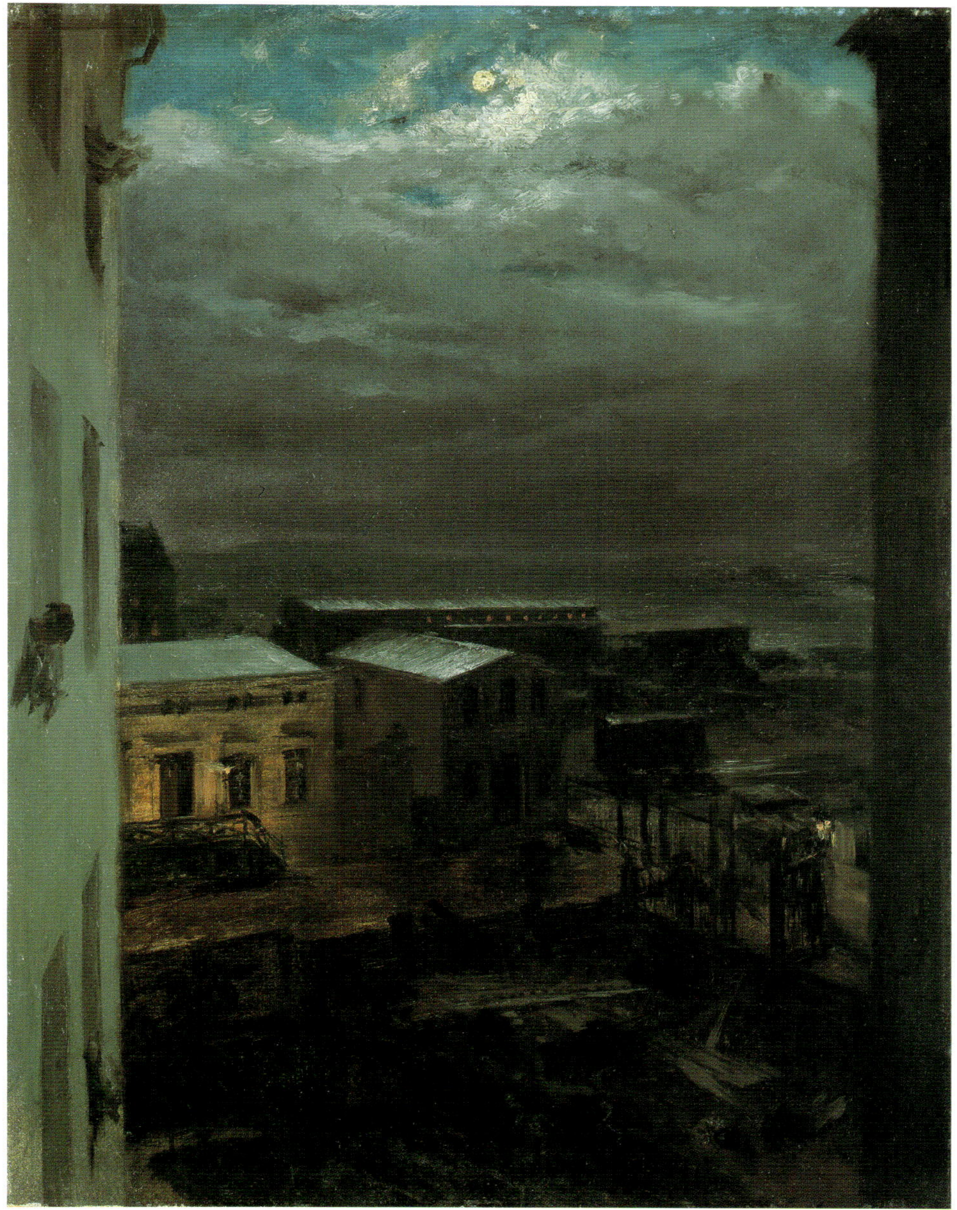

24

24

View over Anhalt Station by Moonlight

c. 1845-6

Oil on paper, wood backing
46 × 35cm
Winterthur, Museum Stiftung Oskar Reinhart
Exhibited in Berlin only

Provenance: Ludwigs-Galerie, Munich; acquired in 1932 by Oskar Reinhart, Winterthur (his collection was turned into a foundation which was opened in 1951).
Exhibition: Berlin, 1993, no. 93, col. reprod.
Bibliography: Not mentioned by Tschudi, 1905 A; Wirth, 1965, p. 26, fig. 9; Schmoll, 1970, p. 124, reprod. p. 125; Hütt, 1981, fig. 29 (col.).

From March 1846 to March 1847, Menzel lived at 18 Schöneberger Strasse, 'on the second floor'[1], from where he could have had this view of the railway station. Schöneberger Strasse itself had been laid out in 1843, shortly after Anhalt Station was built over land previously known as Töplitzwiese, a broad meadow where cows once grazed. The railway line out of Anhalt Station ran south-east (the terminus was at Köthen); it had been constructed in 1836. The station, which was opened in 1841, was a relatively modest affair, and it was pulled down in

1875 to make way for a monumental construction by Franz Schwechten. However, a number of important facilities had been introduced at the time: these included a large passage through the city's customs wall, a new city gate and thoroughfare linking it with the centre, and two roads and the station esplanade which were paved and provided with electric lighting. All in all, the mid-1840s were a period of rapid development for the district.

From his window, Menzel could see the wings of a three-storey building that was used for incoming passengers. However, he did not paint it, and opted instead for some small outbuildings and, in the foreground, a piece of land that is blurred and covered with rubble and other detritus. Rarely has the temporary been conveyed in a painting with such subtlety. The extraordinary views overlooking the backs of buildings painted by Ludwig Deppe in 1820 and by Johann Erdmann Hummel in 1835 were still subject to the discipline of parallelism, an approach that Menzel had long abandoned. For the rest, although the subject matter is disparate, art brings 'order' to the composition in the form of a central, imperceptibly inclined axis which falls from the moon on to the illuminated gable of one of the buildings. It is a cold, dry moon, one that floats inside a narrow strip of midnight-blue and over the top of lacklustre clouds, and casts a feeble light on to the roughcast of the wall on the left of the yard. In response, street lamps evoke warmth, calm and mystery. The sky has been stripped of all Romanticism in this painting, and all signs of human activity have been transfigured and enveloped within a truly inspired atmosphere.

The view is framed by two walls which form a kind of corridor. One's mind instinctively goes to those ubiquitous nineteenth-century compositions that incorporate a window together with the view, and one remembers the famous back yards behind Berlin's apartment buildings. In this painting, the space is left open on one side, but one wonders what subject-matter could realistically have been represented here. The eye only picks up the far-off extremities of the two walls[2], and a much broader scene should really be visible; of everything that the view properly encompasses, only a small fragment is represented here. The composition has no foreground. It also lacks the starting-point for the perspective, that fundamentally reliable definition of space which Menzel did not discover for another 20 years, and in another painting of a view from a window. This painting is also part of the Reinhart Collection[3].
C.K.

1. Letter to C. H. Arnold, 1 March 1845, Wolff, 1914, p. 83.
2. Menzel painted many views of the courtyard without a wall on either side; *cf.* the gouache entitled *View over a Small Courtyard* (undated, Tschudi, 1905 A, no. 562, on loan to the Nationalgalerie) and the following footnote.
3. *View from the Window in Marienstrasse*, 1867, Tschudi, 1905 A, no. 563; Museum Stiftung Oskar Reinhart, Winterthur.

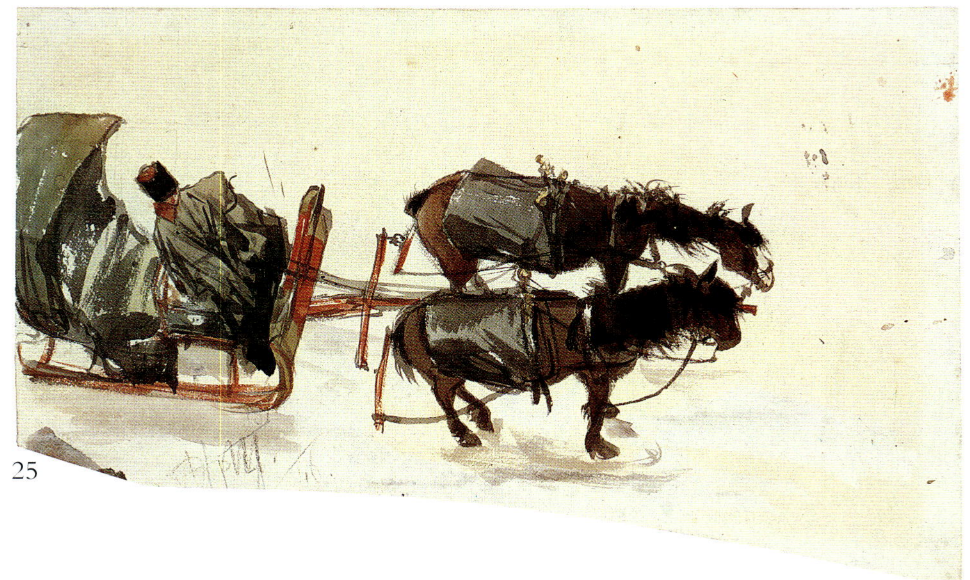

25

25
Sleigh with Horses
1846
Watercolour
16.8 × 26.3cm
Signed and dated at the bottom left: *Ad.M.46.*
Berlin, Kupferstichkabinett (SZ Menzel Kat 121)

Provenance: Dr Wilhelm Puhlmann, Potsdam; acquired by the museum after his death, in 1882.
Exhibitions: Berlin, 1905, no. 471; Berlin, 1980 A, no. 3, col. reprod. p. 157; New York, 1988, no. 122; Vienna, 1990, no. 139.
Bibliography: Donop, 1902, no. 121; Tschudi, 1905 A, no. 191; Liebermann/Kern, 1921, p. 3, no. 8.

This charming watercolour must be one of the many occasional works which Menzel produced at great speed and loved to give to his friends. The spontaneous glance out of a window is an astonishingly frequent feature of his drawings, and not surprisingly his eyes occasionally alighted on horses and carriages. In the sketchbook that he used between 1839 and 1846, and which accompanied him throughout those seven years, there are no fewer than 40 sketches of horse-drawn carriages[1]. On two occasions, he notes: 'Seen from two flights of stairs up' or 'High viewpoint from the second floor'. Sometimes, it has to be said, the aerial perspective came close to becoming the factor that determined the shape of the whole composition (*cf.* cat. 184). Menzel drew and painted horses during the 1840s more than at any other time, and initially did so while working on the illustrations for the *History of Frederick the Great*. When the author, Franz Kugler, passed on criticisms that his publisher, Weber, had voiced about the horses, Menzel was quick to acknowledge his shortcomings[2]; a letter addressed to his friend Wilhelm Puhlmann testifies to the considerable efforts he made to achieve mastery in a field with which he was still not familiar. When he sent Puhlmann the fourth instalment of the *History of Frederick the Great*, he commented that it included 'some fine horses': 'My horsetrading skills leave something to be desired, but they will improve. For the time being, I examine any old nag I can find from top to bottom'. He is known to have made inquiries about the autumn manoeuvres at Potsdam; he undoubtedly did so with a view to studying horses in closer detail[3].

M.R.-R.

1. Berlin, Kupferstichkabinett, Sketch book 7.
2. Kugler, 1911, Vol 2, p. 1723–6.
3. Letter to Wilhelm Puhlmann, 28 August 1840, Wolff, 1914, p. 47–8.

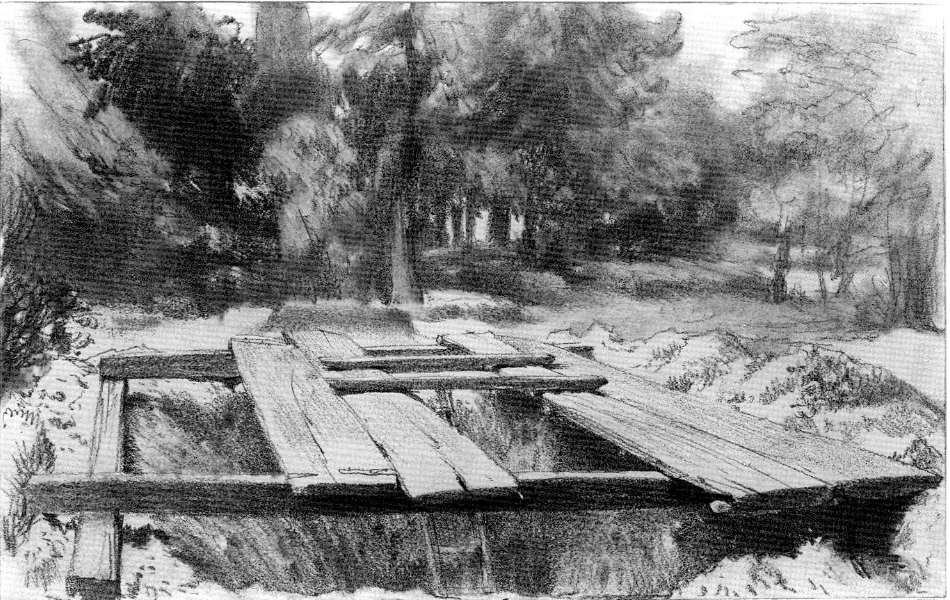
26

26
Cemetery among the Trees, with an Open Grave
1847

Pencil
12.9 × 20.4cm
Berlin, Kupferstichkabinett (SZ Menzel N 395)
Exhibited in Washington only

Provenance: Painter's studio; 1905 Emilie Krigar-Menzel; acquired by the museum in 1906.
Exhibition: Berlin, 1905, no. 3215.

Contour and traditional hatching disappeared from Menzel's drawings in the second half of the 1840s, and were replaced by light and shade. Like *Road along a Park Wall* (cat. 16), this drawing avoids all picturesque effects. The eye is first drawn towards the gently swaying branches of trees standing in a park-like setting, but the attention is then held by the open grave situated between the trees and the viewer. Completed a year after the death of Menzel's mother, this drawing is likely to be an expression of the artist's personal grief.

M.R.-R.

27
Young Boy Sitting at a Table
1846–7

Oil on canvas
20 × 49cm
Berlin, Nationalgalerie (A III 775)

Provenance: Painter's studio; 1905 Emilie Krigar-Menzel, acquired by the museum in 1906.
Exhibitions: Berlin, 1905, no. 5821; prior to 1945, in store at Breslau Museum; Wiesbaden, 1952, no. 150; Berlin, 1955 B, no. 16, fig. 11.
Bibliography: Tschudi, 1905 A, no. 21; Meier-Graefe, 1906, p. 93; Waldmann, 1941, p. 11, p. 43, fig. 4; cat. NG, 1976, p. 260, reprod.

Without doubt, the young boy leaning over the table and drawing with such concentration is Carl Johann Arnold (1829–1916); he was the son of Menzel's friend and first mentor, Carl Heinrich Arnold, an amateur a painter and wallpaper manufacturer from Kassel. It fell to Menzel to teach his friend's son drawing and perspective; the lessons lasted for three months during 1846 and were resumed in 1853, and Menzel often had his young man's work sent over to him. The advice he offered in his letters gives us an idea of the principles that had guided his own artistic training. Surprisingly, Menzel speaks very little of drawing and much more of painting, strongly recommending pastel work and lauding the merits of stump-drawing, an art form condemned by the Academy of Arts under Schadow. At the time, Carl Johann Arnold was both Menzel's student and his model, particularly for *Kassel Sketch* (1847–8). Although Menzel had real teaching skills, as his efforts with the Berlin wood engravers demonstrated, 'Little Carl' was to be his only pupil; moreover, Menzel never gave classes at the Academy, and generally counselled young people against taking up art as a career. Carl Johann Arnold turned out to be a painter of modest pretensions, but many years later he wrote up his impressions of his mentor; these were published only recently[1]. A large portrait (1847) of Carl aged 18 has his thick curls cut in a similar style (*cf.* cat. 39).

Many examples of this subject were to be seen in Menzel's home, versions of this theme appear on many occasions, notably on a sheet of his sketchbook of 1837[2] which was used six years later for an etching entitled *Family around the Lamp*[3]. In November 1846, Carl Johann Arnold returned the compliment and drew his teacher in the same posture,

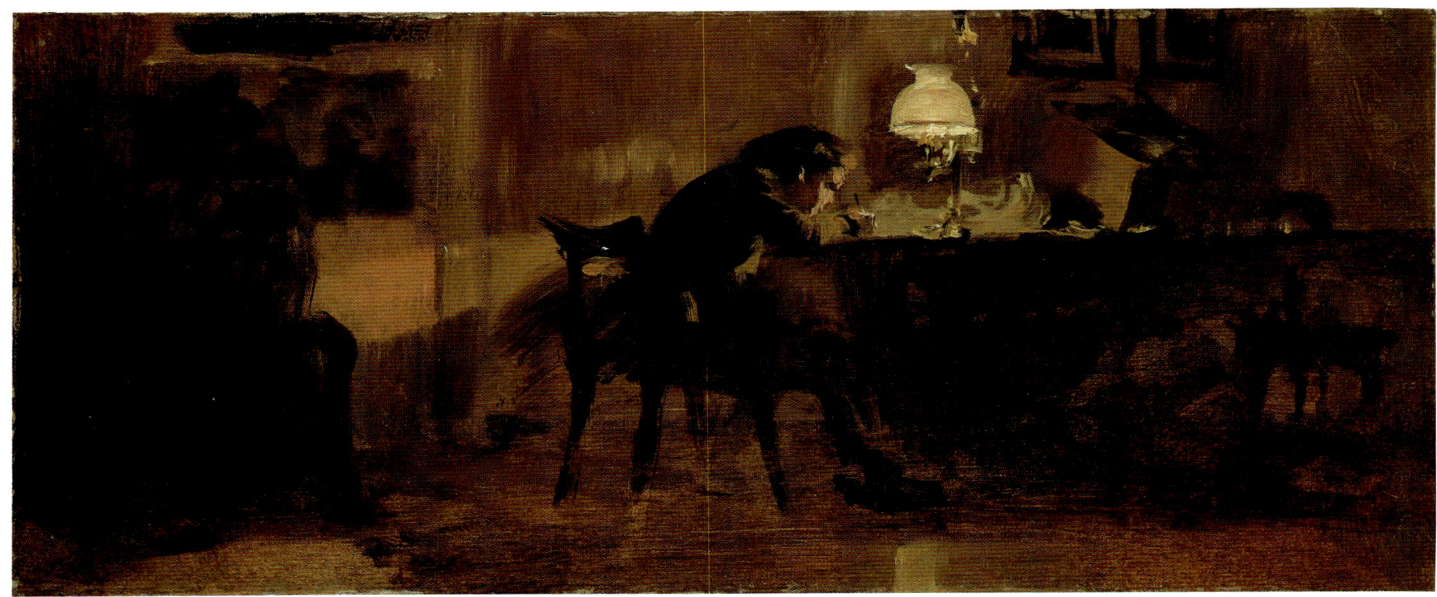

27

under a lamp, leaning over the table and drawing diligently[4] (fig. 170). In fact, the similarity highlights the painting's underlying originality. No form is given any undue emphasis to the detriment of the work as a whole, and the young boy hunched over the table is like a shadow among shadows. In fact, he is the only shadow, which is then swept away by a whirlwind of energetic brushstrokes and hasty sketching. The furniture, too, is unsteady, papers are falling from the table for no apparent reason, and nothing seems to be calmly in its place. And yet, all this upset and violation of established rules is simply an expression of the colour which ranges from informal *macchia* to figuration, and fades away to the left in a confusion of rounded strokes. The curious panoramic format, which is ideal for the representation of a small interior, suggests a rapid movement of the eye, and a film-like sweep of perceptions of varying character. The viewer has the impression of being presented with several changes of rhythm, attentiveness and mood.

Nearly the entire work is painted in a reddish-brown. On the lamp there is a lemon-yellow tinge which produces a pink reflection on the boy's face, and this is enough to establish a chromatic system of reference that eschews all local colour. This technique is quite foreign to the tradition of monochrome painting that had held sway since the early days of oil painting. In *Ballet Rehearsal on Stage* by Degas[5] (1874), the colours are erased in order to achieve a more plastic effect. By contrast, Menzel dissolves them in chiaroscuro, leaving just enough evidence to show that they were once there.

A similar nocturnal atmosphere is to be fund in *Drawing-Room with Mr von Maercker*[6]; in this painting, which is also undated, the subject seems to be no more than a fugitive figure who has been added at the edge of the composition. C.K.

Fig. 169. *Weigel the Lithographer at Work*, *c.* 1836, pencil, Berlin, Kupferstichkabinett (N 971)

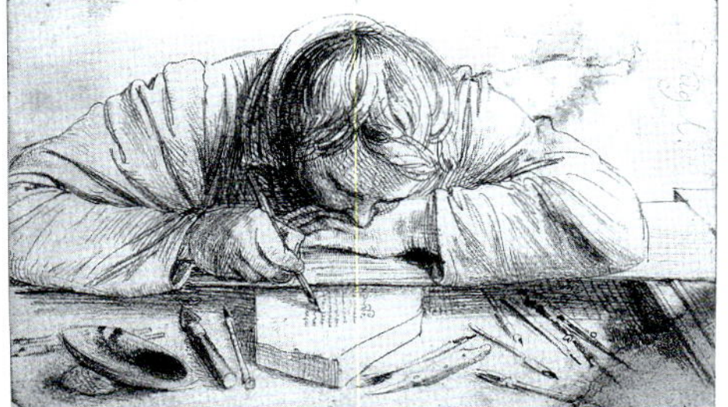

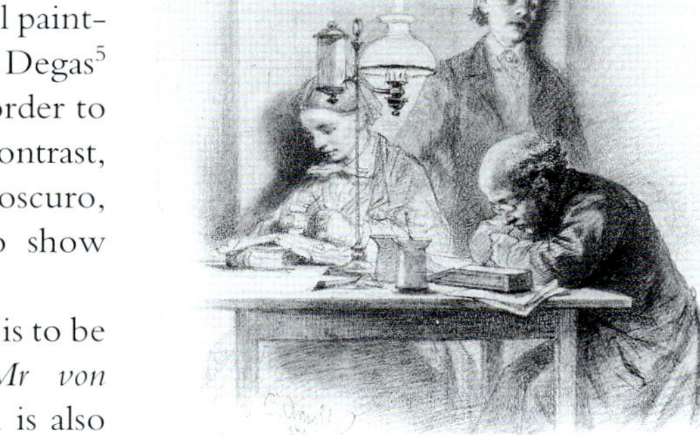

Fig. 170. Carl Johann Arnold, *Menzel Drawing, with his Brother and Sister*, 1846, pencil, Berlin, Stadtmuseum

1. By Gisold Lammel; *cf.* Arnold, 1992.
2. Forster-Hahn, 1978, pl. 5.
3. 1843, Bock, 1923, no. 1132. *Cf.* exhib. cat. Berlin, 1984, no. 225, reprod.
4. One of the two known versions is in the Stadtmuseum, Berlin: Lammel, 1993 B, fig. 25; the other is in Kirstein, 1919, reprod. p. 15.
5. Musée d'Orsay, Paris.
6. Georg Schäfer Collection, Euerbach.

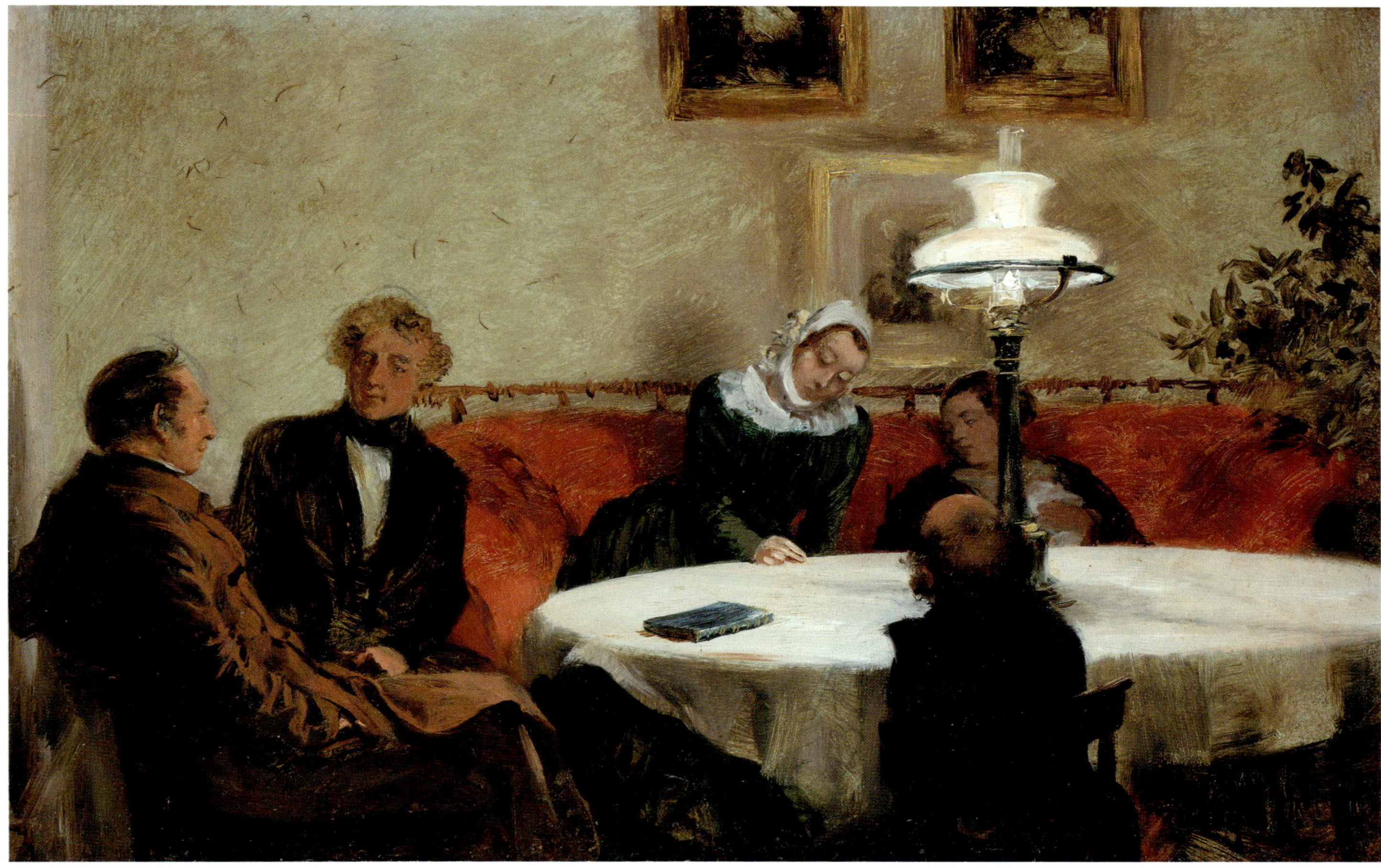

28

28

An Evening Together

c. 1846–7

Oil on paper, board backing
25 × 40cm
Signed at the bottom right: *A.M.*
Berlin, Nationalgalerie (A I 861)

Provenance: Julius Aufseesser, Berlin; acquired by the museum in 1905.
Exhibitions: Berlin 1905, no. 2; Berlin, 1906, no. 1169, reprod.; Berlin, 1935, no. 16, reprod.; Wiesbaden, 1947, no. 58, pl. XIII; Wiesbaden, 1952, no. 156; Berlin, 1955 B, no. 15, reprod.; Munich, 1962, no. 62; Bremen, 1976, no. 83, reprod.
Bibliography: Cat. NG, 1907, no. 976; Tschudi, 1905 A, no. 59; Scheffler, 1912, p. 124 *et seq.*, reprod. p. 122; Kern, 1915–16, reprod. p. 100; Justi, 1921, p. 11, fig. 6; Waldmann, 1922, fig. 5; Scheffler, 1922, p. 155–6, reprod. p. 73; Justi, 1932, p. 130 *et seq.*; Scheffler, 1938, p. 60 *et seq.*, reprod. p. 163; Waldmann, 1941, p. 15, p. 45, reprod. 27; Hütt, 1981, p. 61, fig. 44 (col.); Wirth, 1990, p. 272, fig. 347; Jensen, 1982, p. 66, col. pl. 10.

When the Menzels lived at 18 Schöneberger Strasse, between the spring of 1845 and March 1847, they struck up a friendship with their neighbours, the Maercker family. What little we know of the lawyer Carl Anton (von) Maercker (1803–71) goes back to the time when this small painting was done. During 1847–8, Maercker was the director of Berlin's Criminal Court and, following the popular uprising of March 1848, stood 'in front of the Anhalt Gate as Commandant of the Guard'[1] (people's militia); then, in the summer of that year, he was appointed minister of justice in the short-lived cabinet of Rudolf von Auerswald. The 'June Ministry', as it soon came to be known, was set up in response to popular unrest which was seen as a threat to the monarchy; its purpose, after the fall of the liberal ministry that took office in March, was to keep the democratic forces in check. Relations with Menzel do not appear to have deteriorated at the time, and the portraits of the Maercker children are traditionally dated 1848[2]; two years later, Maercker left Berlin for Halberstadt. If information provided by Tschudi is correct[3], the person sitting next to Maercker, an unimpressive-looking gentleman wearing a brown overcoat, is a lawyer friend of his.

The composition is dominated by red and white, and is embraced by a dull greenish-grey that is strengthened by the dark green of Mrs Maercker's dress. Here and there, traces of a drawing show through the surface: the heads of the two men have also been sketched in with a few quick pencil strokes, but these ultimately provide no more than an approximate representation.

Menzel's compositions of this type were a far cry from ordinary genre painting, a style consistently marked by narrative clarity; here, we have an impression of a scene captured instantaneously, and almost by chance. It has no definite centre or order, or apparent focus, and no feeling seems to dominate; moreover, the focal points of the composition alternate in a disconcerting manner and threaten the unity of the entire group. Two thoughtful-looking men, whose relationship appears to be marked by mutual reserve, seem to have just interrupted their conversation; meanwhile, absent-mindedly and only just keeping her balance, a woman with a bandaged cheek (Mrs Maercker is known to have suffered frequently from toothache) drums her fingers mechanically on the table while her friend, Emilie Menzel (who regularly fell asleep) is slumped on the couch wearily looking on. The only character in any way animated is the small man in the foreground. The slightly irreverent downward viewpoint enables us to identify the prematurely bald head of the painter himself[4]; his arm explores the space behind the back of the chair as if he is looking for some support. Nobody seems to notice him, and even less attention is paid to the dog which appears to be pulling the white cloth off the table. The animal has not been painted in, and only the folds in the material tell us that it is there at all. The characters are marked off from one another, and even the moderator lamp, a modern kind of gas lamp of which the Menzels had a large number, does not bring them together. The room appears to be partly illuminated by an additional lamp. Two axes intersect at the foot of the lamp: on the one hand, the surfaces that are parallel to the painting itself – the wall, the couch and the paintings – and the alignment formed by the the faces; on the other, the vertical axis formed by the person seen from behind, the foot of the lamp and Emilie leaning to one side. The artist's head and elbow loom out of the painting's imaginary space, creating a subversive dynamic.

Compared with family scenes from the Biedermeier period, which were characterized by harmony and peace and described a well-ordered world, this painting harbours something of an enigma. Moreover, the choice of subject-matter, drawn from the painter's own private family life, makes no difference. This tiny work actually found a buyer during Menzel's lifetime. If only we knew who! C.K.

1. Letter to C. H. Arnold, 23 March 1848, Wolff, 1914, p. 131.
2. Tschudi, 1905 A, no. 205–7; whereabouts unknown. Neither of these pastels is dated.
3. Kirstein, 1919, an equally well informed contemporary source, also identifies these people but reverses them. However, the man in the brown coat cannot be Maercker because we know him from his slim appearance in a small painting entitled *Room with minister of justice von Maercker)* (Georg Schäfer Collection, Euerbach).
4. One of those 'daring self-reflections'! *Cf.* on this subject Korte, 1973–4.

29

Portrait of Mrs Maercker

c. 1846–88

Oil on canvas
37.5 × 28cm
Signed at the bottom right: *A.M.*
Winterthur, Museum Stiftung Oskar Reinhart
Exhibited in Berlin only

Provenance: Painter's studio; 1905 Emilie Krigar-Menzel; Mrs Flesch, Frankfurt am Main; Fritz Nathan, St-Gall; acquired in 1948 by Oskar Reinhart, Winterthur (his collection was turned into a foundation which was opened in 1951).
Exhibitions: Berlin, 1905, no. 64; Leipzig, 1905, no. 16; Basle, 1932, no. 40; Winterthur, 1933, no. 47; Berne, 1940, no. 167; Berlin, 1993, no. 65, col. reprod.
Bibliography: Meier-Graefe, 1906. p. 96; Tschudi, 1905 A, no. 54; Tschudi, 1905 B, p. 216, reprod. p. 251 (p. 6, reprod. p. 41); Scheffler, 1922, p. 156 *et seq.*, p. 174, reprod. p. 77; Scheffler, 1938, p. 61 reprod. p. 161; Waldmann, 1941, p. 32, p. 45, fig. 23; Hütt, 1981, fig. 43 (col.); Vignau-Wilberg, 1981, no. 79, reprod.

A chalk study on tinted paper[1], dated 1846, shows only the model's head, and its size is surprising given the work's small format. The artist complied with a note he wrote in the margin ('the hand a little closer to the mouth'), and he also made other changes including the head leaning forward, the neckline concealed under a thick, red shawl, and the addition of a handkerchief. Otherwise, Mrs Maercker has the same clothes as she wore for a study in a similar style, *The Visit.* From this, we may infer that the latter study also served as a basis for the portrait; unfortunately, we do not know when. The Maercker family did not leave Berlin until 1850, and Menzel's links with them appear to have continued after he left his apartment in Schöneberger Strasse in March 1847; it is possible that the portrait, which was not a commission and remained in the artist's possession, was completed somewhat later.

This work may also be seen as a counterpoint to the portrait of Clara Ilgner (cat. 46), a work that was only slightly larger. Both paintings place the women in affluent settings, although this one chooses the intimacy of the drawing-room. The luxuriant motifs of the carpet, the couch and the tapestries enveloping Mrs Maercker leap out of the warm half-light, and create an atmosphere of almost oriental sumptuousness, although this is softened by the whiteness of her gown and the handkerchief. The book and the padded stool would normally be no more than ornamental accessories, were it not for the fact that the painting suggests the fleeting moment. Unlike Clara Ilgner, the grandly dressed subject of this work is turned away from the viewer, and appears to be addressing, in thoughts rather than words, a person who is standing outside the painting's field. The rules of portrait composition are therefore broken, and the purpose here is to achieve a mixed genre better suited to conveying a state of mind. C.K.

1. Kunsthalle, Hamburg; exhib. cat. Hamburg, 1982, no. 16, reprod.

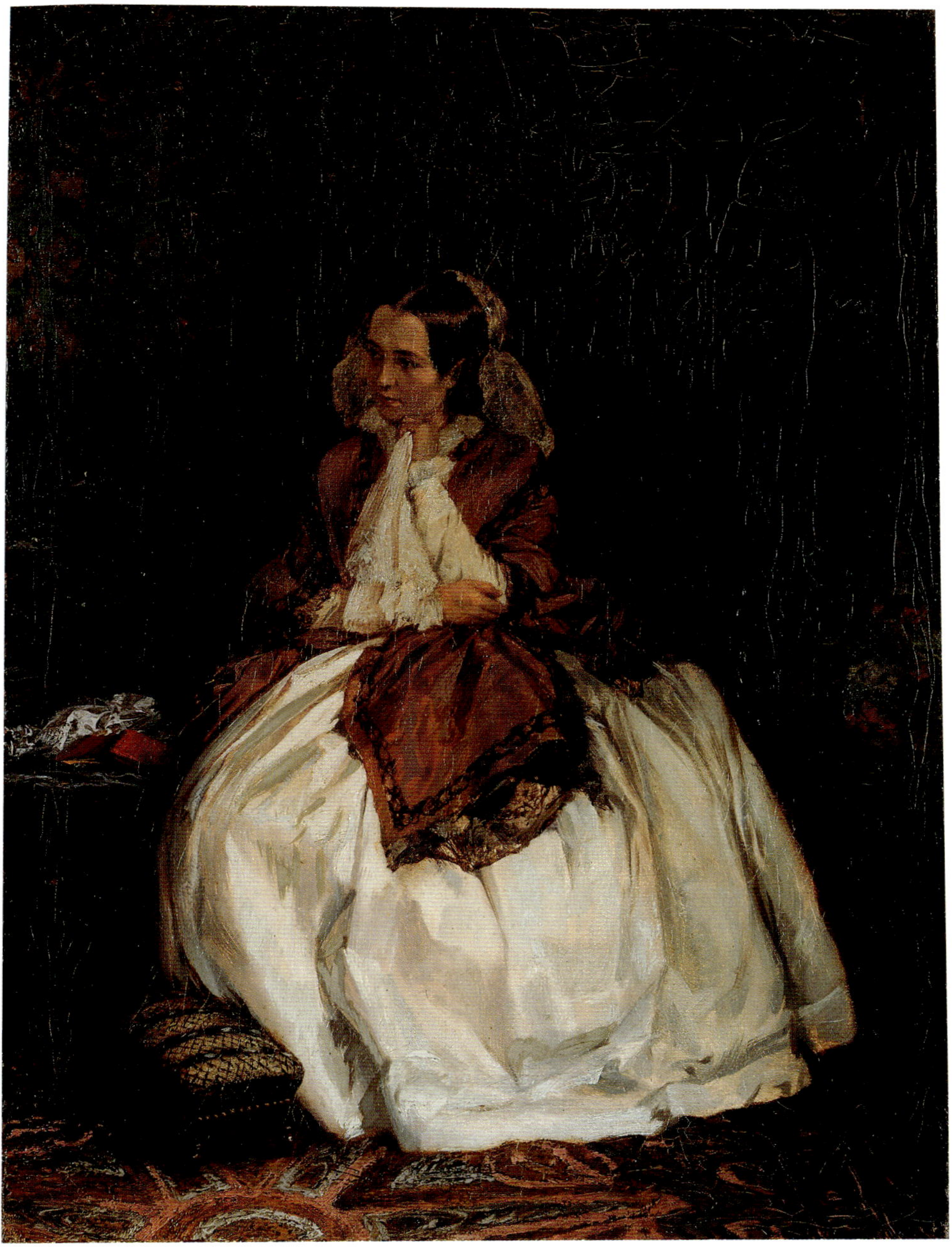

29

30

House on the Kreuzberg, near Berlin

c. 1845–6

Pencil
20.5 × 26.4cm
Berlin, Kupferstichkabinett (SZ Menzel N 1365)
Exhibited in Paris only

Provenance: Painter's studio; 1905 Emilie Krigar-Menzel; acquired by the museum in 1906.
Exhibitions: Berlin, 1905, no. 3197; Berlin, 1980 A, no. 165, reprod. p. 242; Copenhagen, 1985, no. 17.

Menzel produced this drawing, which is typical of the style of the late 1840s, from a slightly elevated viewpoint. The half-timbered house in the medium ground is an inn; it is situated near a neo-gothic monument commemorating the wars of liberation against Napoleon I, and built by Karl Friedrich Schinkel on a hill, the Kreuzberg, to the south of the town. The monument is to the right, and emerges out of a shaded clump of trees; the town is to be seen in the distance. A slightly modified version of this drawing was used for the background of a painting (cat. 31). M.R.-R.

31

On the Kreuzberg, near Berlin

1847

Oil on canvas
89.5 × 114.5cm
Signed and dated at the bottom left: *Menzel 47*
Berlin, Stadtmuseum (VII 59/869 x)
Exhibited in Paris only

Provenance: Acquired in 1905 (from the painter's studio) for the Municipality of Berlin; handed on to the Märkisches Provinzialmuseum, Berlin, in 1906.
Exhibitions: Berlin, 1903 A; Berlin, 1905, no. 26; Berlin, 1906, no. 1172, reprod.; Zurich, 1917, no. 80, reprod.; Berlin, 1935, no. 12; Berlin, 1980 A, no. V, reprod. p. 133.
Bibliography: Beta (1899) 1992, p. 57 *et seq.*, Anon, 1902–3; Heilbut, 1902–3; Jordan, 1905, p. 102; Tschudi, 1905 A, no. 32; Delmar, (1905) 1992, p. 113–6; Tschudi, 1905 B, p. 232, reprod. p. 299 (p. 22, reprod. p. 89); Meier-Graefe, 1906; p. 89; Kern, 1915–16, p. 86; Beta, (1899) 1992, p. 57 *et seq.*; Lichtwark, (1924) 1992, p. 306; Wirth, 1965, p. 28; Timm, 1974; Hütt; 1981, Fig. 33 (col.); Uebel, 1986, p. 4, p. 10 *et seq.*, p. 14; Berger, n.d., p. 25–7, reprod. p. 24.

In August 1847, Menzel left for Kassel to work on a mediaeval subject, *Kassel Sketch*. This was going to occupy him for several months, and he had to leave the work shown here unfinished in Berlin. Of all his landscapes, this is the biggest; even *Garden of Prince Albert's Palace* (cat. 164), the other painting with which he hoped to win exhibition honours for *plein-air* painting, was smaller.

Today, the Kreuzberg dominates a lively and very popular district of Berlin, but it used to be open countryside. Menzel took up position on one side of the hill, and turned away from Schinkel's famous war memorial. He also ignored the Tivoli, a pleasure garden designed on the Parisian model, and made only the most fleeting of references to the many

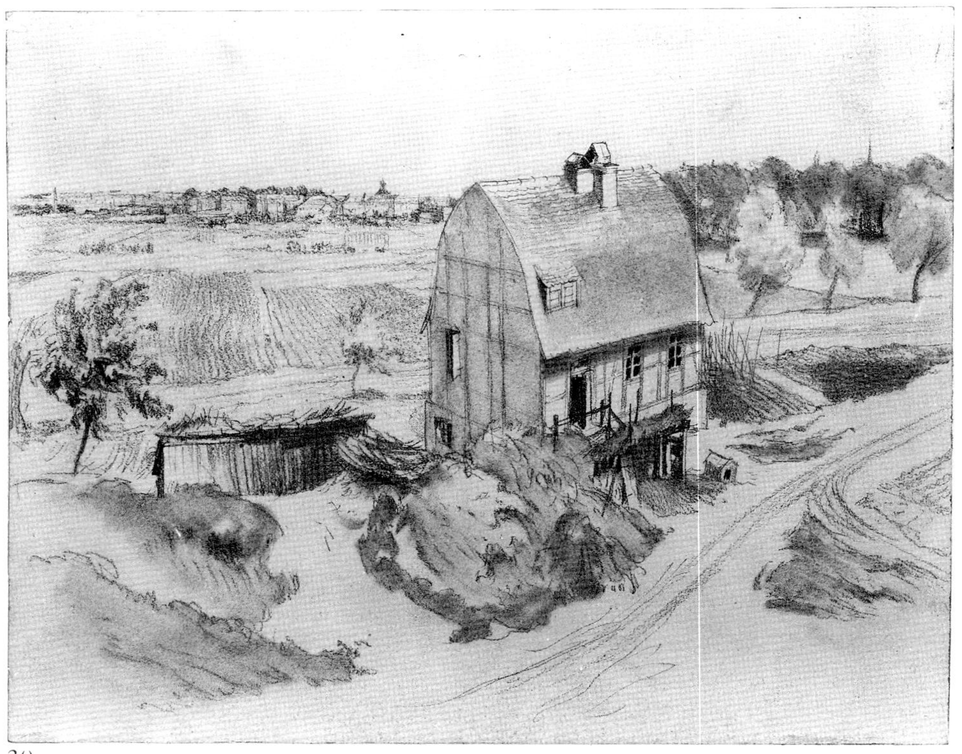

30

gardens and summer pavilions that had been springing up since 1828. The viewer's eye is taken from half-way up the hill across the 'remarkably picturesque desert' with its 'slopes and crevices', and enlivened only by 'children sliding down the fine sand from the monument'[1]. A few years later, while making his preparations for his painting of the battle of Hochkirch, Menzel drew models in uniform climbing sand quarries similar to those in this drawing. To the left, there is an area known as the 'Düsterer Keller' ('Dark Cellar') and a ravine a short distance beyond an old vine; this was later surrounded by trees[2], and it then became popular with apple-pickers. It was here in 1810 that Prussian patriots gathered secretly under the leadership of Karl Friedrich Friesen and Friedrich Ludwig Jahn and, through their people's gymnastic clubs, laid the ground for resistance to the Napoleonic occupation. Also at the beginning of the nineteenth century, a entrepreneur mason by the name of Johann Caspar Bergemann had turned his farm into an inn and smoking-den which enjoyed much popularity until about 1860. This is the imposing half-timbered house in the middle ground. Menzel actually remembered that it had once been called 'Zum Bogen' ('The Bend'): 'It was an inn run, I think, by Fingeradi, and was popular in those days with better-off members of the bourgeoisie.' For the rest, 'the stream in the foreground on the right and the willow trees are complete invention'. The buildings in the background are also likely to be fruits of the artist's imagination, but testify to the onward march of a less impassioned civilization than that represented by the splendid old half-timbered house.

By rejecting the opportunities presented by the subject of an ever-expanding city, Menzel spurned the conventional view of Berlin which had been established since the end of the eighteenth century, frequently found on locally manufactured porcelain[3]. The house 'at the bend' is depicted from the same viewpoint on such vases but the eye takes in the outline of the town clearly and completely. The town is also to be seen in one of Menzel's drawings (*cf.* cat. 30); which depicts the inn close-up, but does not hint that it might be an affluent inn. The omission was therefore deliberate; what, then, was the work's 'real' aim? To the right, a full third of the painting's surface is given over to the foreground, whereas the background may only be seen to the far left; meanwhile, the chaotic middle ground establishes no sort of link between these two sections. The roughness of the terrain is not enough to justify the abrupt change of perspective of the type that occurs between the half-timbered house and the buildings in the distance. This was all quite revolutionary for 1847, Menzel's intentions only slightly less so.

Friends visiting Menzel at the turn of the century learned that the artist had originally planned that the foreground should be taken up by a group of nannies and some children playing. In fact, if we examine the painting from an angle, it is now possible to distinguish among layers of repainting a woman lying down and a child[4]. Even as late as 1902, Menzel had not given up the idea of placing them back in the picture; as he pointed out, 'I have kept all my studies from that period'[5]. Indeed, he always carefully looked after the preliminary studies that preceded his works, and kept them all together.

'It is true, my dear sir, I have frequently been offered considerable sums for this landscape – very frequently indeed. If it had been painted by a French master, it would not have hung in his studio for a single week – at least, that is what I am told'[6]. Ottomar Beta was the first to draw the public's attention to this unknown masterpiece, in 1899. However, it was not until 1903 that Menzel allowed himself to be persuaded to part with it without making any further changes. Moreover, he seems to have felt obliged to explain that he had finally acknowledged his inability to re-capture the 'style of his youth' and rework a canvas as large as this with his failing eyesight[7]. This did not prevent him, when in the process of actually selling the paint-

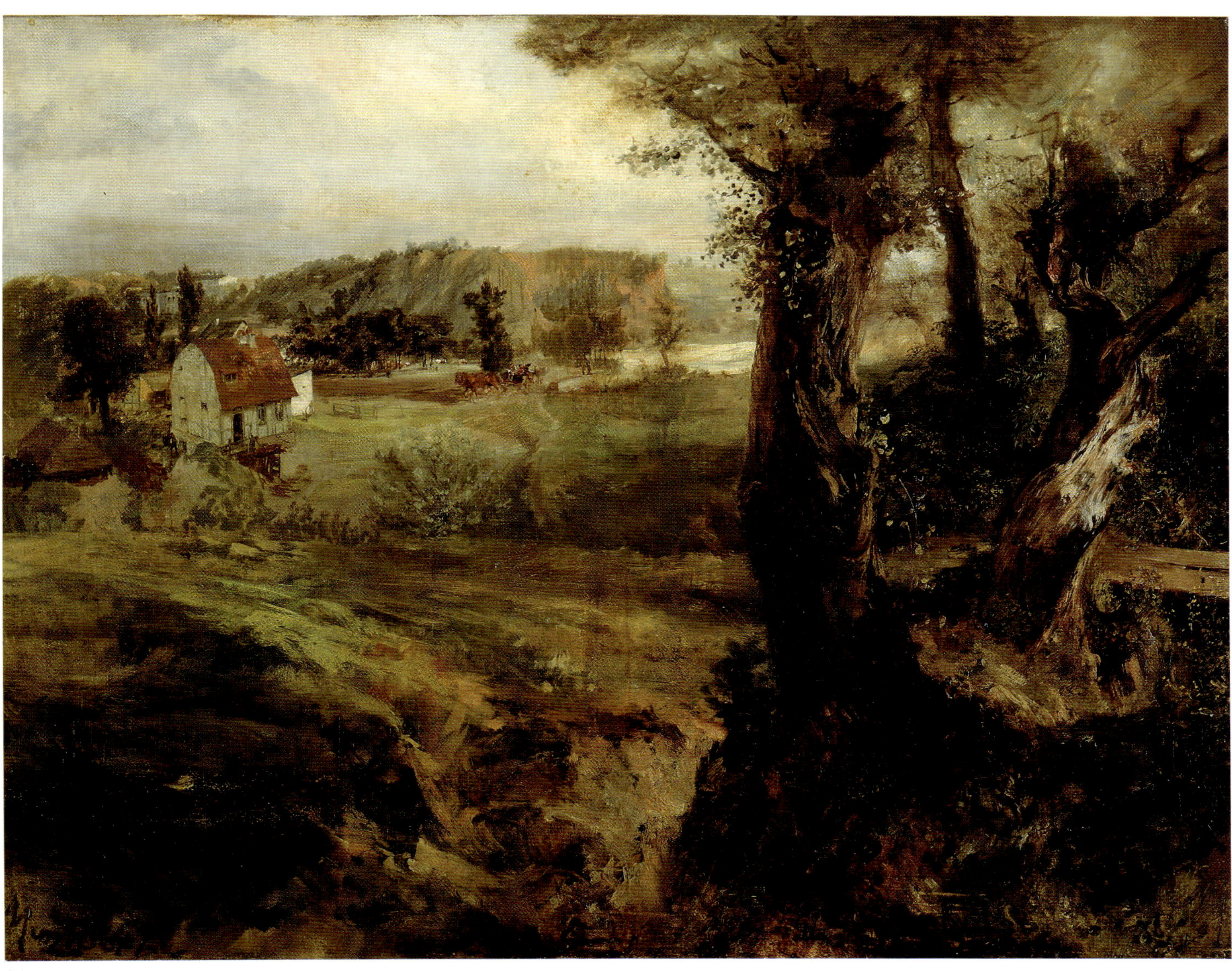

31

ing, from stipulating that he reserved the right to make changes.

When it was exhibited for the first time in 1903 (together with cat. 73), it made such an impression with its 'pictorial freshness that one is tempted to prefer it to its celebrated successors'. The magazine *Kunstkritik* quoted a 'recent observation by a noted pioneer of Impressionism: "If chance had led Menzel to Paris when he was still a young man, and if he had stayed there for twenty years, he would have become the German Manet"'. On the other hand, Julius Meier-Graefe, a great admirer of the French pictorial tradition, and therefore all the more critical of the rawness that contributed to Menzel's power, felt that this painting had the same shortcomings as *The Berlin – Potsdam Railway*. He considered the latter work, with its 'dirty colours', to be 'untidy', 'unrestrained' and 'more cavalier than inspired'. The trees recall Rubens, but there are also reminders of Constable's thickly applied paint, his splashes of light, and energetically and dramatically shaped tree trunks. The formal aspects of Menzel's work still defy categorizaton as does his application of colour – sometimes thickly, sometimes ostentatiously, and sometimes (like the space between the middle-ground trees) blurred to the point of transparency. The fact that the painting is 'unfinished', even though this was the result of force of circumstances, was entirely characteristic of the artist. C.K.

1. Meyerheim, (1906) 1992, p. 168.
2. This was probably close to the present site of Arndtstrasse and Nostitzstrasse. *cf.* Berger, n.d., p. 25.
3. Three crater-shaped vases painted by Johann Hubert Anton Forst. A copy is owned by the Order of St John, Berlin.
4. Timm, 1974.
5. Lichtwark, (1902) 1992, p. 306.
6. Beta, (1899) 1992, p. 57.
7. Delmar, (1905) 1992, p. 115 et seq.

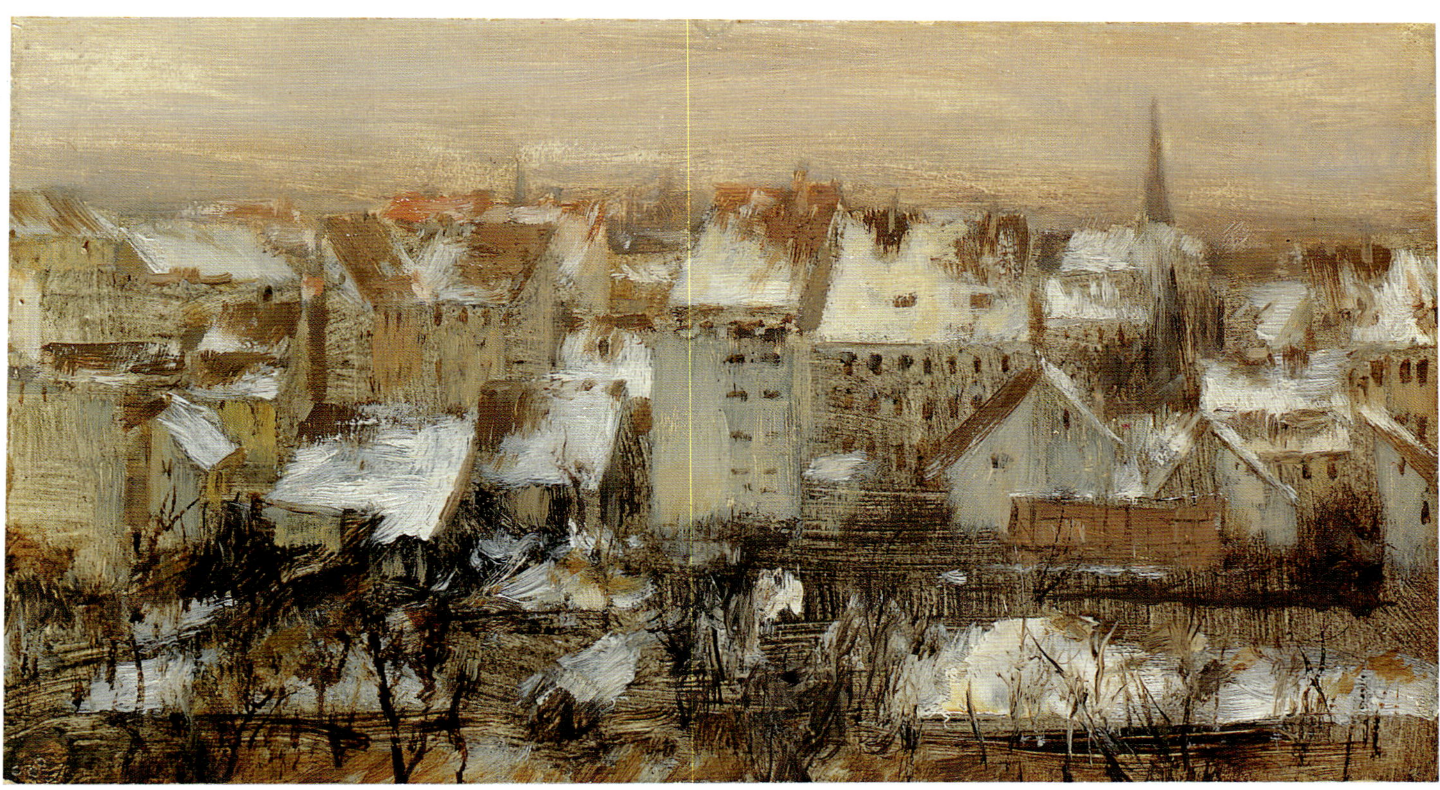

32

32

Back Yards in the Snow, Berlin

1847

Oil on paper, board backing
13 × 24cm
Winterthur, Museum Stiftung Oskar Reinhart
Exhibited in Berlin only

Provenance: Painter's studio; 1905 Emilie Krigar-Menzel; 1906 Neumann Collection, Berlin; Fritz Nathan, St-Gall; acquired in 1938 by Oskar Reinhart, Winterthur (his collection was turned into a foundation which was opened in 1951).
Exhibitions: Leipzig, 1905, no. 25; Berlin, 1905, no. 75; Berlin, 1928, no. 9, reprod. p. 11; Berne, 1940, no. 166; Berlin, 1993, no. 66, col. reprod.
Bibliography: Tschudi, 1905 A, no. 31; Scheffler, 1922, p. 150, reprod. p. 40; Wirth, 1965, p. 68, fig. p. 61 (col.); Vignau-Wilberg, 1979, no. 77, reprod.; Hütt, 1981, fig. 51 (col.).

Several other paintings, including *The Artists's Bedroom in Ritterstrasse* (cat. 34) show very much the same view from the window in his apartment at 43 Ritterstrasse; this was in a district of Berlin called Luisenstadt, and was where Menzel lived from Easter 1847 to the beginning of 1862[1]. At the time, Luisenstadt was undergoing major changes, and rural areas including gardens and fields alternated with newly built or half-finished roads[2]. Friedrich Eggers, who knew the apartment well, described the surroundings as follows: 'The main window, which is slightly raised . . ., gives on to a vast expanse of land. This is divided into gardens overflowing with abundant foliage, and marked off by the back yards of buildings in adjacent districts, and a rabbit warren of houses in the town proper, interspersed with numerous towers and cupolas'[3]. This description applies also to another painting (*cf.* cat. 33); the painting reproduced here shows only houses under construction on the south side of Oranienstrasse.

The two small unsigned and undated pictures probably come from the same period as *The Artist's Bedroom.* At all events, there is nothing to suggest that Menzel's interest in views observed from windows lasted for long. This view over the snow-covered roofs was probably the first, and was completed in March, shortly after the artist and his family moved in. Dating it to the following winter is out of the question as Menzel did not spend it in Berlin; as time passed, other subjects commanded his whole attention. It is a little surprising, however, to see a steeple in the distance; this presumably belonged to St Peter's Church in Old Kölln. In fact, the church was in the process of being rebuilt following a number of serious fires, and the work, which was directed by Heinrich Strack, a member of Menzel's circle of friends from his younger days, lasted from 1847 to 1855. It is just possible that Menzel conjured up his friend's future plans in his imagination, and incorporated the tower, as yet unbuilt, into this view of the district. This explanation makes more sense than a later date.

Hitherto, wintry atmospheres and the coloured reflection of snow had rarely been represented in painting. It is true that compositions of German Romantic painters such as Friedrich, Carus, Blechen and Lessing had depicted forests and cemeteries covered with thick blankets of snow as if weaving shrouds that stopped time. However, this symbolism meant nothing to Menzel, who instead painted the snow as it thawed, a transitory process as when the white cloak rips. He also observed the light – the pinkish tinges of damp air – as it dispersed and landed on surfaces that were still white themselves. Soon afterwards, he was to recapture these observations in a historical painting (*cf.* cat. 37), and his last major composition of this type incorporated yet another superb depiction of winter (*cf.* cat. 90).

C.K.

1. Not, as is normally claimed, until 1860. A letter to William I dated 7 January 1862 once again gives 43 Ritterstrasse as his address (Geheimes Staatsarchiv Preussischer Kulturbesitz, 2.2.1 N° 20337).
2. Günther, 1981.
3. Eggers, 1854.

33

View of Back Yards

1847

Oil on paper, board backing
27 × 53cm
Signed at the bottom right: *A. Menzel.*
Berlin, Nationalgalerie (A I 1057)

Provenance: Probably in the collection of one of Menzel's friends, the painter Eduard Magnus (died 1872); Dr Ernst Magnus, councillor of state, Berlin; in storage at the Nationalgalerie in 1907; acquired by the museum in 1909.
Exhibitions: Berlin, 1906, no. 1176, reprod.; Berlin, 1935, no. 9; Celle, 1949–50, no. 59, p. 8; Berlin, 1950–1, no. 46; Berlin, 1955 B, no. 21, fig. 26; Zurich, 1959, no pag.; Paris, 1961, no. 47, reprod.; Berlin, 1966, no. 37; Hamburg, 1976, no. 258, reprod.; Paris, 1984–5, no. 96, reprod.; Berlin, 1987 B, no. 94.
Bibliography: Not mentioned by Tschudi, 1905 A; cat. NG, 1907, no. 994; Scheffler, 1912, p. 121, reprod. p. 124; Kern, 1915–16; p. 90, reprod. p. 98; Justi, 1921, pp. 10–11, fig. 4; Scheffler, 1922, p. 150, reprod. p. 39; Justi, 1932, p. 130 *et seq.*; Scheffler, 1938, p. 58 *et seq.*, reprod. p. 158; Hütt, 1981, fig. 31 (col.); Busch, 1985, p. 288, fig. 96.

The same group of disparate and down-at-heel buildings that appeared in the small painting hanging in the museum at Winterthur (cat. 32) is reproduced here; the tones are appropriately seasonal, but the colouring is different – as if in anticipation of Monet's series. Painters of the Romantic period such as Caspar David Friedrich, Emil Ludwig Grimm and August Kopisch had also shown Menzel how to represent a given place at different times of the year. There are considerable variations in detail between the two paintings. These mainly relate to the larger houses and the distribution of towers in the distance, and there is therefore a considerable incentive to find out whether the views that Menzel had from his windows – or, to be more precise, the views that he presents to us – were painted from real life. Liberties taken when painting from memory on the contrary lead to a physical distancing from the subject.

This work incorporates a number of features of the town that the winter painting ignored; these include the new cupola of the castle, the steeples of the churches of St Mary and St Nicholas, and the Luisenstadt Tower. This painting is also sharper than its more blurred predecessor, and highlights the confusion that reigned the length of Oranienstrasse at the time: this is mostly captured by fire-break walls close to the village buildings, and areas cleared for the construction of new houses standing next to a smaller half-timbered house that has been spared. In the foreground, there are tiny gardens which seem to have been added in blurred, brown strokes. This wash-painted brown is to be found over almost two-thirds of the picture, and is in sharp contrast with the geometrical precision of the work's upper section. A similar distribution of different pictorial approaches in clearly demarcated areas is also to be found in many other works of Menzel (*cf.* cat. 130).

In this respect, Menzel went much further than Carl Blechen if we compare this work with *View over Roofs and Gardens*[1] (fig. 171), which Blechen had painted a little over 10 years earlier. Blechen's framing is much tighter. Views over gardens and buildings with back yards – usually from a high viewpoint – had become well established in painting in many countries since the beginning of the nineteenth century[2]. Two painters from Berlin who contributed to this movement were Ludwig Deppe and Wilhelm Brücke. Johann Erdmann Hummel's *Berlin Seen from Marienstrasse*[3] (1835) is among the paintings that are closest to Menzel's work in terms of objects represented and the framing selected. The 'sketch' or 'study' alibi is not enough to justify the choice of so unspectacular a subject, even though it is treated within a fine, delicate structure in a Biedermeier style, and uses a well-ordered perspective.

However, even by comparison with such pioneering work on theories which Naturalist painting (referred to as 'art of the gutter' by William II) appropriated fifty years later, the link that Menzel established between these two kinds of subject – a view over tumbledown buildings and back yards, one might say provocatively interrupted by a panoramic view of prestigious dwellings – is extraordinary. That very year, the same juxtaposition was used again in *The Berlin–Potsdam Railway* (cat. 35).

C.K.

1. Nationalgalerie, Berlin.
2. Exhib. cat. Berlin, 1990, p. 277–80.
3. Formerly in the Märkisches Museum. Lost during the war.

Fig. 171. Carl Blechen, *View over Roofs and Gardens*, *c.* 1833, Berlin, Nationalgalerie

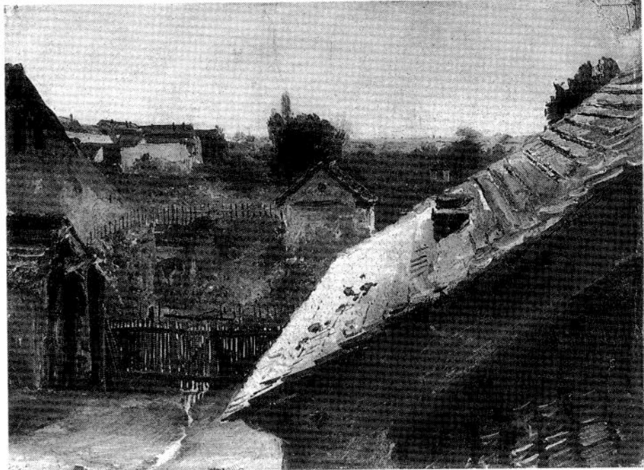

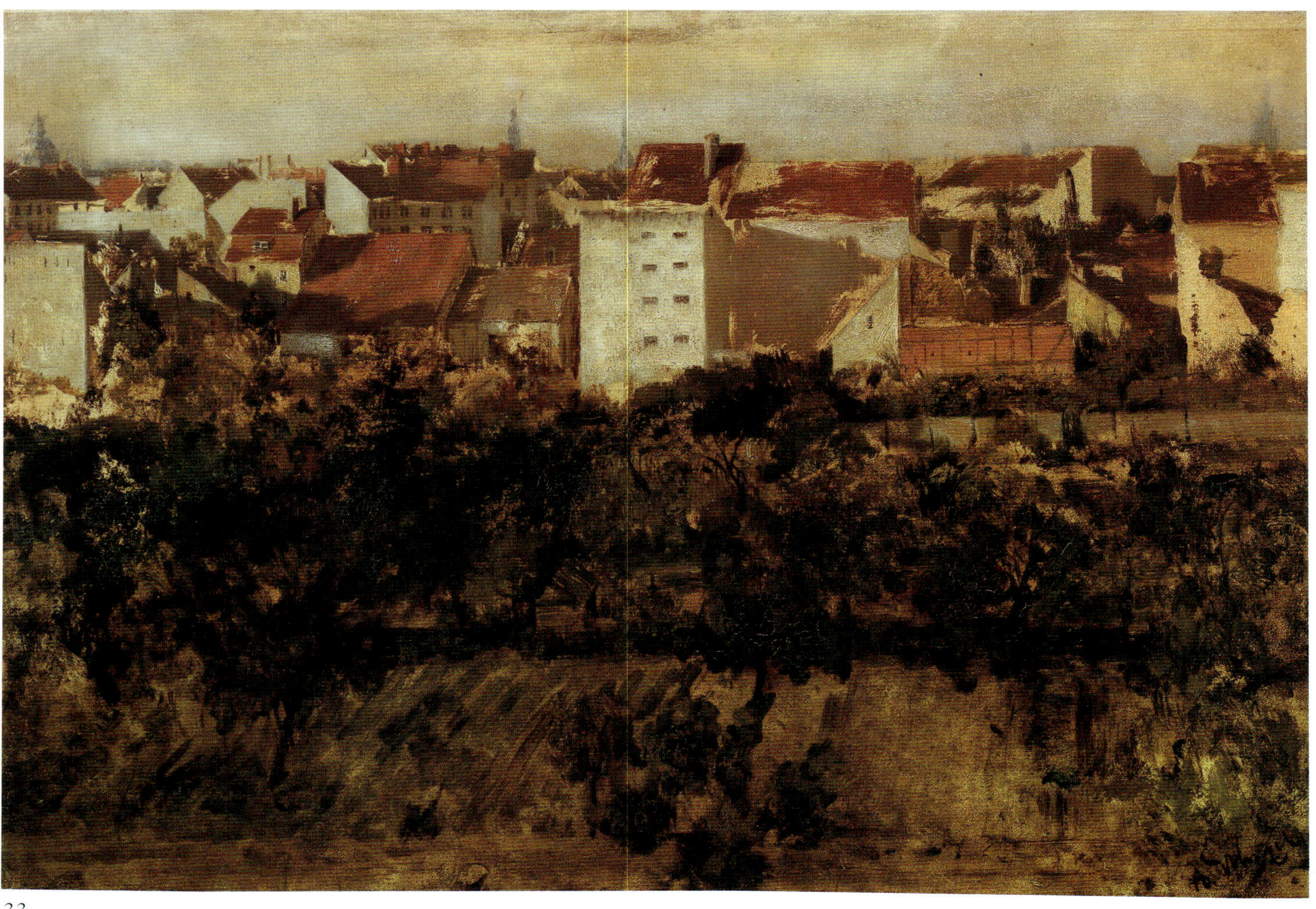
33

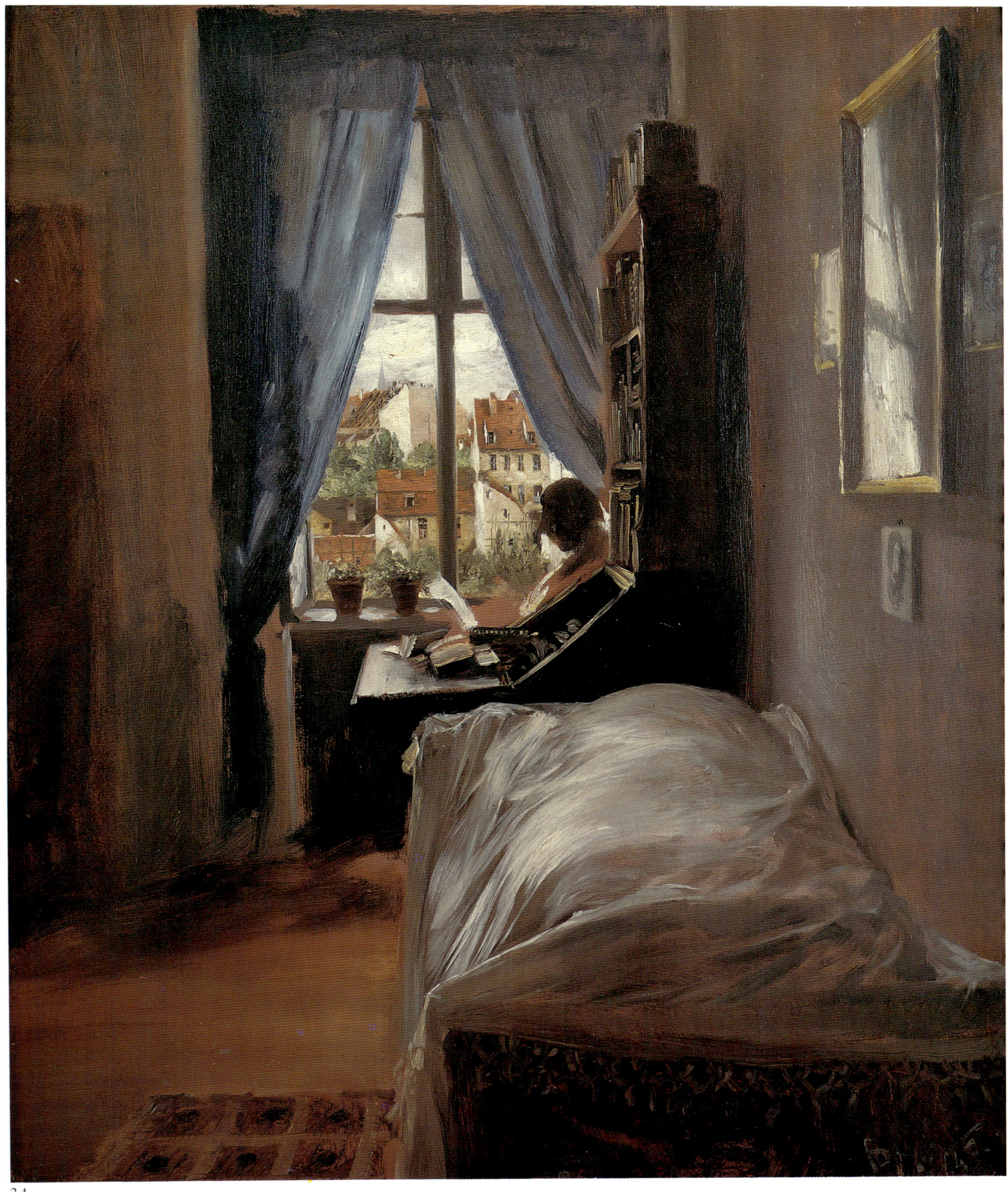

34

34

The Artist's Bedroom in Ritterstrasse

1847

Oil on canvas
56 × 46cm
Signed and dated at the bottom right: *A M 47*
Berlin, Nationalgalerie (A I 860)

Provenance: The painting was sold in the artist's lifetime: the owner's identity does not appear in the 1905 exhibition catalogue, and in Tschudi only with the initials 'M.C.O, Berlin'; acquired by the museum in 1905 with the R. Wagner Gallery, Berlin acting as intermediary.
Exhibitions: Berlin, 1878; Berlin, 1906, no. 1145, reprod. p. 133; Berlin, 1935, no. 7; Celle, 1949–50, no. 58, p. 8, p. 11, fig. 2; Berlin, 1950–1, no. 45, reprod,; Hamburg, 1982, no. 18, col. reprod.; Berlin, 1955 B, no. 14, fig. 7; Paris, 1961, no. 45; Hamburg, 1982, no. 18, col. reprod.
Bibliography: Tschudi, 1905 A, no. 35; Tschudi, 1905 B, p. 227, reprod. p. 267 (p.17, reprod. p. 57); Meier-Graefe, 1906, p. 96 *et seq.*; cat. NG, 1907, no. 977; Scheffler, 1912, p. 123 *et seq.*; Kern, 1915–16, p. 84; Justi, 1921, p. 11, fig. 5; Scheffler, 1922, p. 152, reprod. p. 57; Justi, 1932, p. 130 *et seq.*; Scheffler, 1938, p. 60 *et seq.*; Chapeaurouge, 1960, p. 148, fig. 84; Jensen, 1982, p. 60, col. pl. 7; Busch, 1985, p. 286, fig. 93.

Xavier de Maistre's *Journey around my Room* was far from the only work of its type to grace literature, and artists' domestic arrangements have filled painting no less abundantly. However, instead of focusing narrowly on individual objects and recalling tales associated with them, Menzel condensed, abridged and gathered them all together.

The same bedroom, albeit differently furnished, featured in a pen-and-ink ink drawing in 1858[1]. It is a room in the Ritterstrasse apartment, and through the window we can see some of the houses that appear in the *Back Yards* pictures (cat. 32, 33), although they are slightly altered and seem closer.

The format is similar to that used in *Balcony Room* (cat. 18), which had been painted two years earlier, and one is tempted to ask if it was coincidence, or whether Menzel might have been planning a pair[2]. At all events, the two paintings met quite different fates. Although we have no documentary evidence of *Balcony Room* being exhibited until 1905, there can be little doubt about which work is being referred to in the following description of a painting shown in 1878: 'A work whose beautifully lit yard recalls Vermeer's *A Street in Delft*'[3]. *The Artist's Bedroom* was probably sold shortly afterwards.

Both in this painting and in *Stairway Landing in Nocturnal Lighting* (cat. 42), Menzel plays – consciously perhaps – with the Romantic variant of the window motif; in this case, it is not at the geometric centre of the picture, where one might expect to find it. Moreover, all the vertical lines hang down, suggesting a rapid journey through a tunnel; they also thrust towards the window, foreshortening the perspective, the perspective devices of the bed and the carpet, despite the fact that they do not meet at the horizon, which may be seen at a high point outside. Here, the eye is taken along a horizontal line, there it drops, and this involves a change of viewpoint or, at the very least, a movement of the head. The pictorial interpretation lacks all unity. For example, the window seems to be embedded in the wall because of its disjointed appearance, itself the result of the use of small brushes, and of bright colours, each one isolated by a strong white; there is nothing in the foreground that prepares us for this. Inside the room, the colouring is muted and, in places, the artist appears to have done little to alter the brown background. An early twentieth-century art historian commented on the surprise the artist must have felt when he observed that the white bed covering was the same colour as the polished open flap of the desk. The time in the afternoon when the painting was conceived expunged the difference between these objects' real colours . . .'[4]. This can seen only by contrasting it with the exterior, and the picture's chromatic unity is only called into question after the colours have been subjected to a detailed examination.

This modified pictorial approach reflects a new position from which the painting should be viewed; in other words, by passing through the framework provided by the window, the eye becomes more penetrating. Over a short distance, it slides superficially over objects, stopping here and there. It also ignores the resistant hardness of the wall to the left, and symbolically gathers together the desk and the person reading by the window (in all probability, Menzel's brother, Richard) in a brilliant shower of dashes of colour. Then, as soon as it espies the image outside the window, the eye becomes more focused and begins to inspect the details of the houses and roofs stretching away into the background[5].

There is no evidence of a woman's orderly hand Biedermeier-style in this room. As in *Unmade Bed* (cat. 17), the disorderliness of the bed suggests physical proximity and the residual warmth of a body, as well as an object recently abandoned after use. The eiderdown has been left behind on the bed in a shapeless pile, and the fine fabric has not been smoothed down; this fabric covers the protuberant mass in an irregular manner, sometimes in small, neat folds and sometimes in broader folds. It is only transparent where it is stretched, and it then acquires the muted bluey-grey that was so typical of Menzel's painting in the days prior to his works on Frederick the Great. It is a colour that contains both rococo delicacy and the pallid supernatural – the idea of horror concealed beneath banality. This was a Romantic notion that was frequently depicted, and particularly in the works of E.T.A. Hoffmann.

In no other work by Menzel do idyllic and threatening concepts sit in such close proximity to one another. The bedroom is the venue for 'disturbing strangeness', for dreams and for anxiety. Even the man reading by the window, on whom all lines may be said to be converging, remains in the shadow as a vague silhouette; meanwhile, a point immediately behind him marks the beginning of 'openness', light, and a clear and rational world.

Menzel was seventy-three years old when Van Gogh painted his room at Arles[6]. Van Gogh's bed and window are in the same place, but the conception of colours and volumes is completely different, and one suspects a totally different conception of life. The sight lines reflect a violent and accelerated perspective which envelops the entire room, but they are opposed by an obstacle of substance (the headboard) and they ultimately fade towards a blind window, a motif with which Menzel was very familiar. C.K.

1. His drawing adorns a letter dated 26 July 1858 to Hermann Krigar, Müller, 1935, p. 382.
2. Busch, 1985.
3. A[dolf] R[osenberg], 1878, p. 103.
4. Kern, 1915–16.
5. Werner Busch, 1985, initiated an interpretation of Menzel based on the psychology of perception.
6. The best known version (1888) hangs in the Art Institute of Chicago.

35

The Berlin–Potsdam Railway

1847

Oils on canvas
42 × 52cm
Signed and dated at the bottom right: *A.M. 1847.*
Berlin, Nationalgalerie (A I 643)

Provenance: Dr Wilhelm Puhlmann, Potsdam; when he died in 1882, his heirs kept this painting back from the collection of works sold to the Nationalgalerie; the architect H.H. Meier of Bremen, a noted collector; R. Wagner Gallery, Berlin; acquired by the museum in 1889.
Exhibitions: Düsseldorf, 1904, no. 4; Berlin, 1905, no. 5; Berlin, 1906, no. 1144, reprod.; Berlin, 1935, no. 8; Wiesbaden, 1952, no. 154; Berlin, 1955 B, no. 20, fig. 25; Zurich, 1959, unnumb. no pag., col. pl.; Paris, 1961, no. 46, col. reprod.; Bremen, 1976, no. 84, reprod. 71; New York, 1981, no. 62, col. reprod.
Bibliography: Cat. NG, 1900, no. 780; Tschudi, 1905 A, no. 33; Jordan, 1905, p. 102 *et seq.*; Delmar, (1905) 1992, p. 117; Marguillier, 1906, p. 84; Meier-Graefe, 1906, p. 71, p. 88 *et seq.*; Tschudi, 1905 B, p. 232 *et seq.*, pl. facing p. 254 (p. 22 *et seq.*, pl. facing p. 44); Scheffler, 1912, p. 123, reprod.; Kern, 1915–16, p. 98, reprod. p. 94; Justi, 1921, p. 11; Scheffler, 1922, p. 148, reprod. p. 43; Scheffler, 1938, p. 58, reprod. p. 167; Waldmann, 1941, p. 12, p. 44, fig. 15; Hütt, 1981, fig. 35 (col.); Jensen, 1982, p. 62, col. pl. 8; Busch, 1985, p. 288, fig. 97; Lammel, 1993 B, p. 103–8, fig. 54.

The first railway line connecting Berlin and the surrounding area was opened in September 1838, eight years after the construction of the Liverpool–Manchester line and three years after the first railway line anywhere in Germany between Nuremberg and Fürth. The excavation works had lasted for fourteen months, but formal applications and plans had begun back in 1833. However, by the time Menzel painted this stretch of track, which had originally been intended to be very short, it had already been extended to Magdeburg and, in the meantime, the Anhalt (1841) and Frankfurt and Stettin (both 1842) lines had also come into service. They were all financed out of private funds, and only nationalized at a later date. The locomotives on the Potsdam train were manufactured in Newcastle and, when Menzel saw them, he may have been reminded of one of his earliest commissions – a lithograph depicting four railway trains of English design[1]. The station had been built not far from the Schafgraben, which Menzel included in many of his drawings, paintings and etchings (*cf.* cat. 8, fig. 86).

The vast area spread out at the gates to the town, and its appropriation by private property companies, did more to disfigure it than to improve it. No one had ever experienced the like. However, Menzel was the first to see that it had the makings of a pictorial subject and, in this, his work had few rivals: the best was Max Klinger's *The Walker* (1878)[2]. Clearly, what was being turned into an enormous building site had mostly been worked land rather than wild countryside, and the impact of industrial expansion must have caused less concern than we might like to think. Curiously, though, it was the curve in the line – it plays a dominant role in Menzel's painting – that most offended people's aesthetic sense. In fact, it was unavoidable because of the nature of the terrain between Zehlendorf and the Schafbrücke, and people found consolation in the thought that the line would lose 'neither in beauty nor in prestige due to the fact that it was not visible in its entirety because of the countryside it ran through'[3]. According to Irmgard Wirth, Menzel did a drawing[4] in 1845 of what was later the site of Groschgörschenstrasse Station, and it was turned into a painting two years later. It has the same framing and identical content, including the Berlin skyline in the background; however, additions came in the form of the train and the engine pouring out smoke. Other small modifications, including a different distribution of volumes and a marginally higher viewpoint, turned a well-balanced, linear drawing into a painting with a troubled, uneven air. Meier-Graefe, who never ceased to make comparisons with French art, called this expressiveness 'crude and precipitate' and 'more cavalier than inspired'. As he used to say, 'It is all too trite!' Which just goes to show how misunderstood Menzel was, even by those who had discovered his talent. At exactly the same time, Auguste Marguillier in Paris was writing that it was 'maybe Menzel's greatest work'.

It was *The Berlin–Potsdam Railway* that encouraged Hugo von Tschudi to ask Menzel if he knew the work of John Constable. 'At that time,' replied Menzel, '(the date escapes me), there was an exhibition of several of his works at the Hôtel de Russie and I was able to examine them very closely'[5], This new subject recalls J.M.W. Turner's *Rain, Steam and Speed. The Great Western Railway, 1844*[6], which was painted only three years before Menzel's work and, unlike *The Berlin–Potsdam Railway*, was shown immediately; news of Turner's latest painting, and of the respect and admiration that it inspired, also reached Berlin[7]. Whereas the energetic swirls, dreamlike pathos and powerful Romantic connotations of the Turner elevate the natural to the status of supernatural, Menzel's blunt, prosaic aesthetic underlines the intrinsic value of the new phenomenon of railways.

This turned out to be Menzel's only painting to deal with the railway and the countryside, although the first representations of passengers in railway carriages came close on its heels (*cf.* cat. 87). At the very end of his life, however, Menzel did

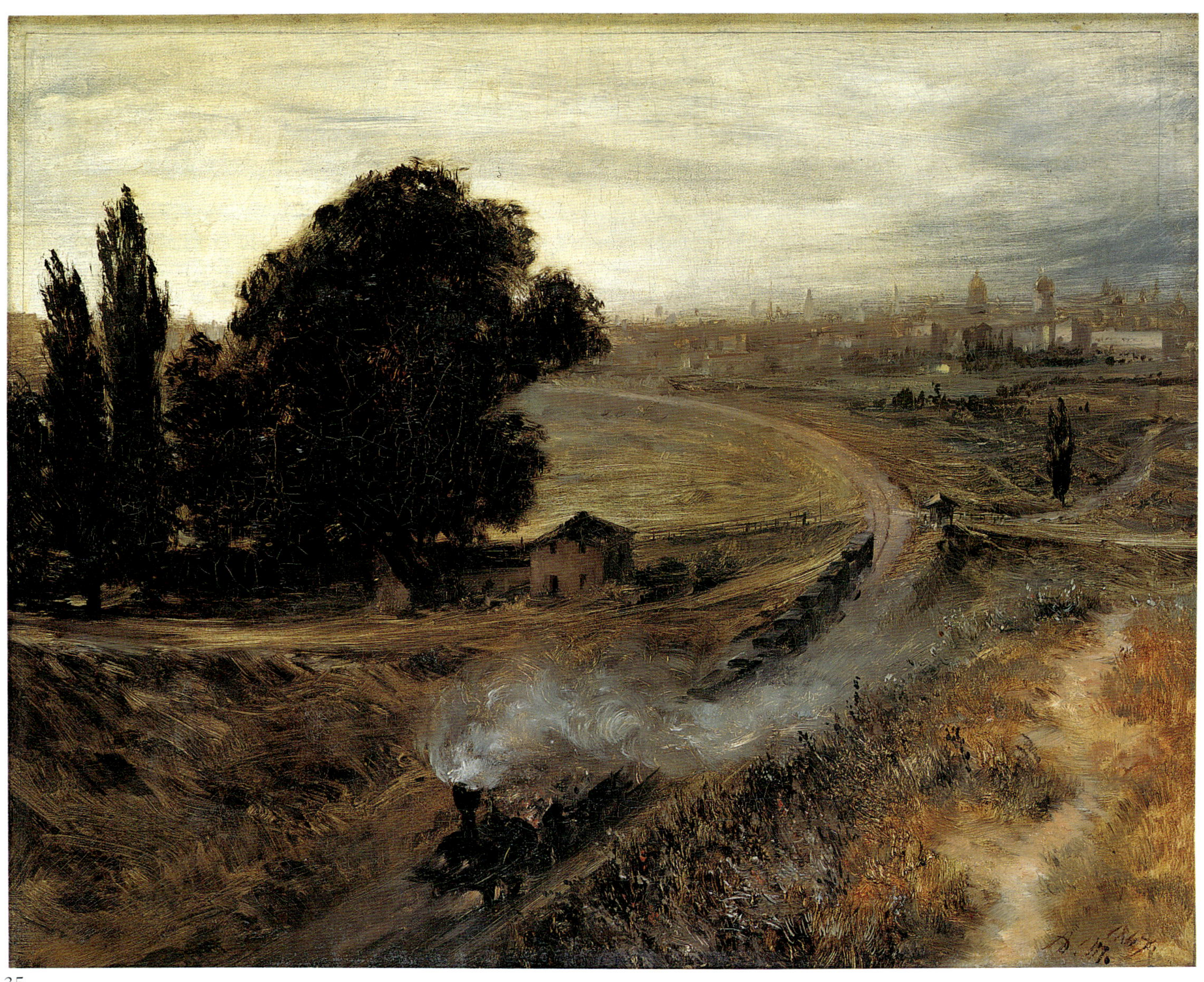

35

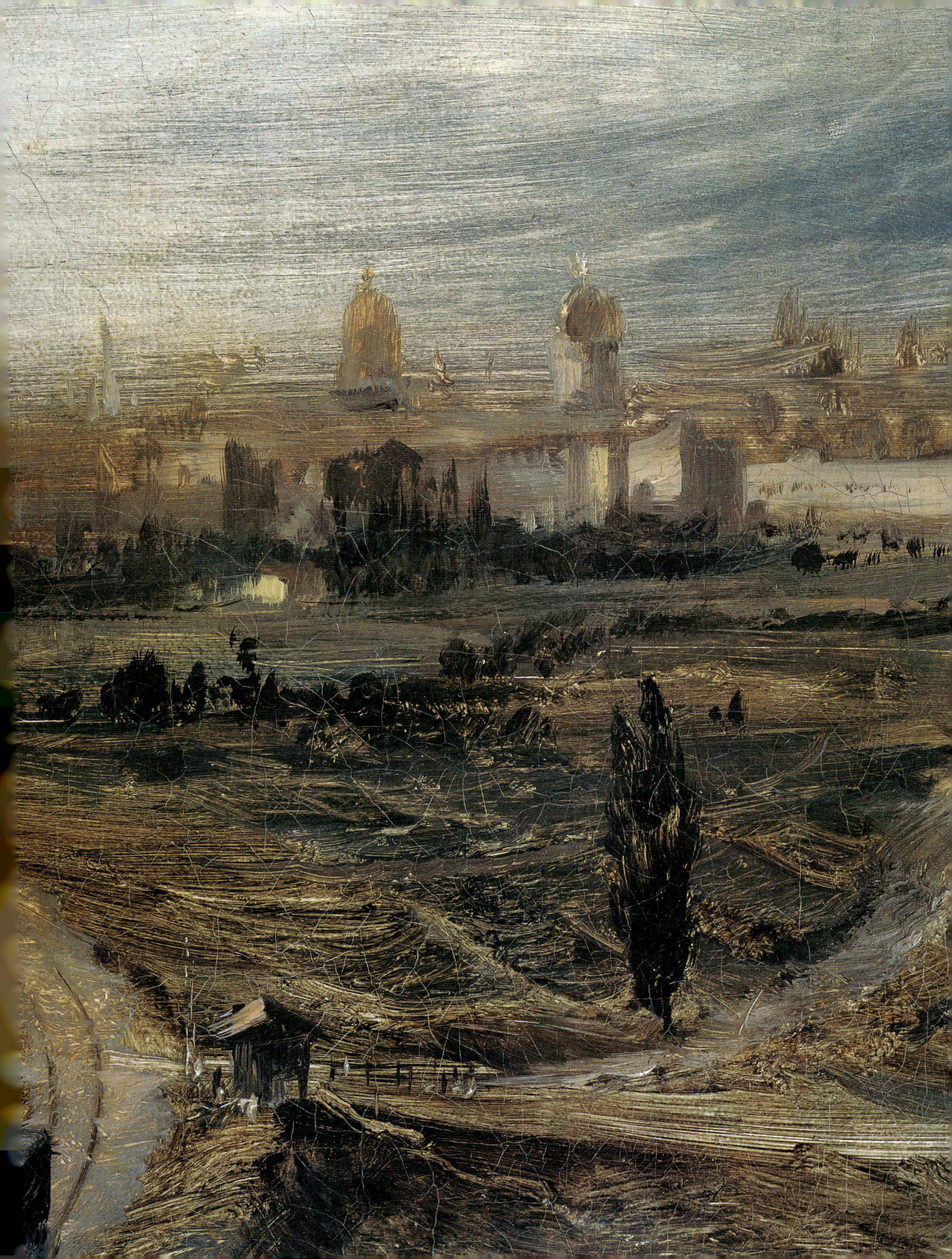

take one final look at the exteriors of carriages, and produced a drawing of a view as he leaned out of the window of a compartment[8].

The Berlin–Potsdam Railway was the first, and for a long the time only, painting by Menzel that Hugo von Tschudi bought as director of the Nationalgalerie, Berlin. Shortly before taking up the post, he had written an essay in which he set out an ambivalent critique of Menzel on the occasion of his eightieth birthday; in it, he stripped Menzel's work down to its 'rational' elements, contrasting this with Böcklin's poetic' approach[9]. C.K.

1. For the *Berliner Kinderwochenblatt*, Bock, 1923, no. 23.
2. Nationalgalerie, Berlin, (A II 818).
3. Taken from a 1835 application relating to the construction of the Berlin-Potsdam railway line, *Cf. Berlin et ses chemins de fer*, 1896, p. 136.
4. Kupferstichkabinett, Berlin (SZ Menzel Nr 1750); *cf.* exhib. cat. Berlin, 1980 A, no. 154, reprod. p. 243.
5. Tschudi, 1905 B, note at the foot of p. 23. *cf.* also cat. 164 in this book.
6. National Gallery, London.
7. E[rnst] F[örster]: 'The art exhibition at the Royal Academy in London', *Kunstblatt*, no. 22, 1844, p. 324.
8. Kupferstichkabinett, Berlin.
9. Tschudi, 1896.

36

Living Room with the Artist's Sister

1847

Oil on paper, board backing
46.1 × 51.7cm
Signed and dated at the bottom left: *A.M. /47.*
Munich, Bayerische Staatsgemäldesammlungen, Neue Pinakotek, (8499)
Exhibited in Paris and Berlin only

Provenance: 1905 painter's studio; 1905 Emilie Krigar-Menzel; 1907, Margarete Krigar-Menzel; presented by the latter to the Bavarian State in 1908; following a dispute as to the legitimacy of the gift, the painting was acquired by the museum in 1937.
Exhibitions: Berlin, 1905, no. 67; Munich 1908, no. 545 a; Berlin, 1935, no. 10; Winterthur, 1947, no. 69; Berlin, 1955 B, no. 17, fig. 17; London, 1956, no. 163.
Bibliography: Tschudi, 1905 A, no. 37; Tschudi, 1905 B, p. 227, reprod. p. 221 (p. 17, reprod. p. 11); Meier-Graefe, 1906, p. 93; Scheffler, 1922, p. 152, p. 154, reprod. p. 51; Waldmann, 1941, p. 11, p. 44, fig. 11; Wirth, 1965, fig. 21; Hütt, 1981, fig. 46 (col.); Jensen, 1982, p. 64, col. pl. 9; Eschenburg, 1984, p. 291, reprod. p. 290; Munich, 1989, p. 229, col. pl. XIV; Wirth, 1990, p. 272, col. pl. 38.

Menzel completed numerous paintings that suggested the end of the day, and which included lights penetrating the gloom and the blurred inconsistency that marks people at this hour. Recalling the many months that he had spent with the Menzels, Carl Johann Arnold (*cf.* cat. 27) wrote that they worked 'well into the evening': 'on one occasion, his sister, who had called us to table more than once, founded herself in a spot where the lighting was unusually interesting. This provided the opportunity for a study, which took some time'. A very similar setting had appeared in a sketchbook in 1838[1].

In this charming painting, the wall and the door meet in the foreground like corridors and carry the eye into the room beyond, thereby reinforcing the sense of illusion; meanwhile, the girl's pretty head, leaning gently against the upright, slips timidly into the same undefined area. The inquisitive look in her eyes, which are directed to the right of the canvas, suggests a space and activity just where the viewer is standing; in this way, the viewer is involved in the picture. However, the foreshortening of the left-hand flap of the door takes the eye beyond the young girl and towards the table, and to the woman sitting with the light behind her. These strongly contrasted sections are linked by an oblique line which takes in the two sources of light – one bright and radiant, the other subdued. Perhaps we did not have to wait after all for Picasso's *Minotauromachia* to bring us the symbolism of a young girl holding a candle! Lastly, the woman sitting by the lamp could well represent the artist's mother, who had died the previous year; indeed, the whole composition, with its atmosphere of mysterious silence, might be a work in commemoration of her. In this painting, Menzel's art made significant advances. He now applied colour with great freedom, and short, vigorous brushstrokes alternated with longer, more flexible ones; the result was a truly poetic sense of space, light and colour that completely eschewed local colour. Not even the source of light from below gives the impression of being a sign of virtuosity. It is a technique that recalls Degas, but the Frenchman was 20 years his junior; that being so, it is not unreasonable to wonder whether anyone at all could have used this approach before Menzel. At all events, he went on to use the device on a number of occasions subsequently.

When Meier-Graefe saw this painting, he was reminded of Corot. This is understandable, and Menzel also respected Corot's work although he could not have known it until 1855. Later on, we know that his studio in Sigismundstrasse had a photograph of a work by Corot[2] on the wall, next to reproductions of Velázquez, Holbein and Schlüter. C.K.

1. Kupferstichkabinett, Berlin, Sketch book 6, p. 33.
2. Lichtwark, (1896) 1992, p. 298.

37

Gustav Adolph Greets his Wife outside Hanau Castle

1847

Oil on canvas
55 × 68cm
Signed and dated at the bottom left: *Menzel 1847*
Leipzig, Museum der bildenden Künste (I. 849)
Exhibited in Berlin only

Provenance: Richard Menzel; 1865 Elise Milner, Richard Menzel's widow, Gross-Lichterfelde (died 1906); Mathilde Rabl Gallery, Berlin; acquired by the museum in 1906.
Exhibitions: Berlin, 1885, no. 4; Berlin, 1895 A, no. 36; Berlin, 1905, no. 78; Berlin, 1928, no. 8, reprod.; Berlin, 1980 A, no. VII, reprod. p. 134.
Bibliography: Duranty, 1880, II p. 109 *et seq.*; Jordan, 1890, p. 39; Jordan, 1895, p. 26, p. 67; Pietsch, (1905) 1992, p. 338; Tschudi, 1905 A, no. 34; Jordan, 1905, p. 42; Wolff, 1914, p. 100. p. 105; Meier-Graefe, 1906, p. 85, p. 89;

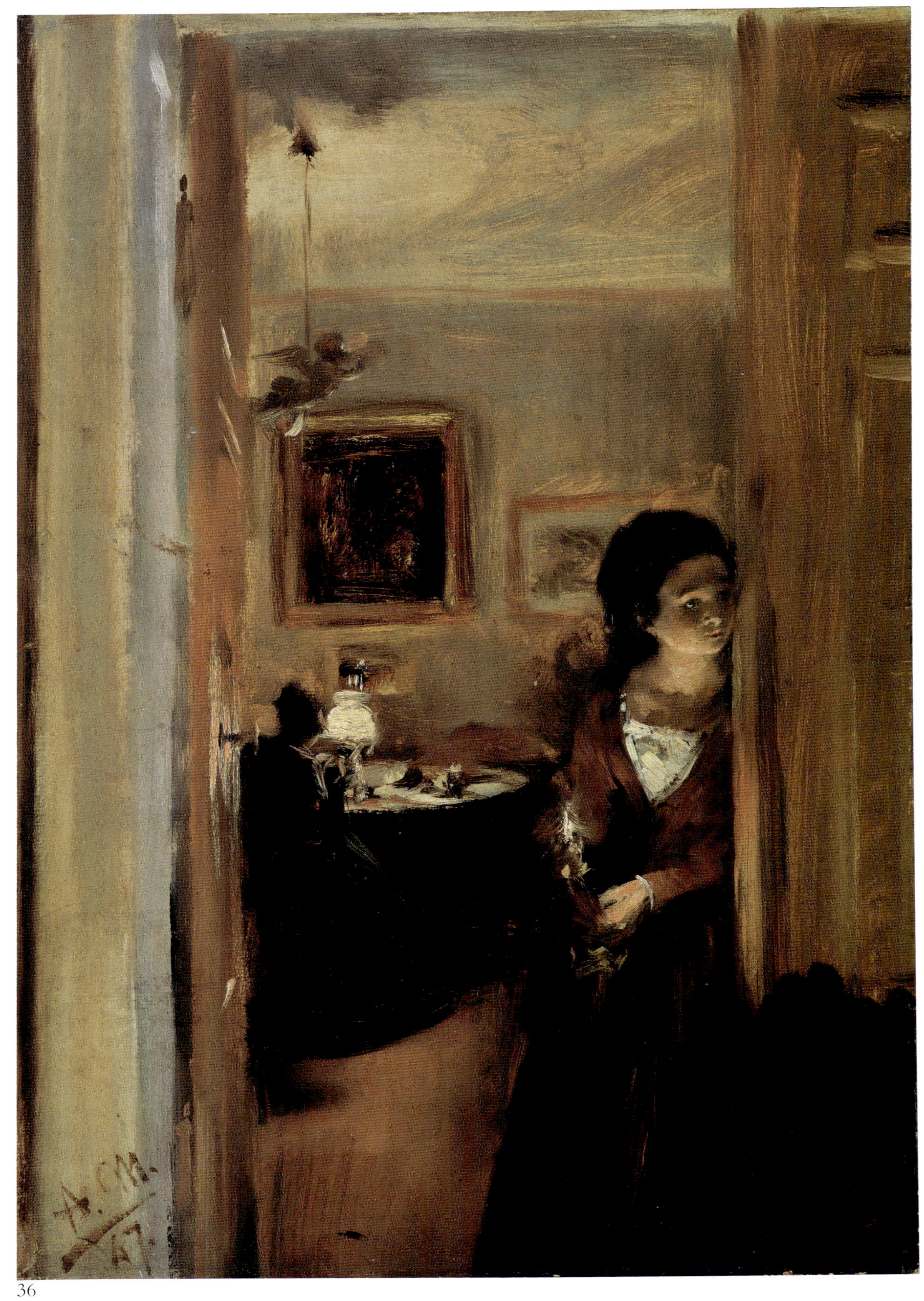

36

Scheffler, 1922, p. 166, p. 176; Scheffler, 1938, p. 64; Dörr, 1988; Keisch, 1988, p. 76 *et seq.*; Lammel, 1993 A, p. 132, fig. 83; Lammel, 1933 B, p. 13–15, col. pl. 1.

In Carl Heinrich Arnold, the young Menzel had a friend and protector on the committee of the Kassel-based Society of Arts. Arnold had been trying to persuade the Society to award Menzel one of its projects since 1845, and was eventually able to pass on a commission for a historical composition. After several delays, the sketch in oils was conceived and completed in under four weeks (April–May 1847). Although it was a very elaborate painting, Menzel had not carried out any preparatory studies for the portraits and architectural details, despite the fact that he considered this to be essential for a large-format work. 'To avoid any misunderstandings,' he wrote to the Society of Arts, 'I wish to state that I have left many elements relating to perspective and other matters in the sketch, and I reserve the right to return to it at a later stage'[1].

Menzel had once again had a free hand in selecting his subject and, in line with the theme he chose for the stained-glass window in Magdeburg Cathedral[2], he opted for an episode from the Thirty Years War; this was a scene from the life of King Gustav II Adolph of Sweden, the Protestant leader throughout the hostilities. As he wrote to the Society of Arts, 'Art has hitherto sought to show simply the heroic dimension of this king, who achieved lasting glory in the service of Germany. On this occasion, I thought it proper to highlight his human side, which is no less impressive'[3]. For this purpose, he chose the moment at which the king is reunited with his wife, the Brandenberg princess, Marie Eleonora, in January 1632. Gustav Adolph's death later that year at the Battle of Lützen cast a sad shadow over this scene of conjugal affection. However, Cornelia Dörr has drawn attention to a political feature that Menzel's contemporaries might well have identified – the fact that the meeting did not take place at Hanau. The king and his wife were in fact reunited nearby, and the couple made their way to the castle later on. This was followed by another meeting at Erfurt, and it proved to be their last. So why did Menzel choose Hanau? It was the town to which William II, the Elector of Hesse, had lived in retirement with a mistress well below his station. The 'family quarrel in the Electorate of Hesse' that this situation aroused had serious repercussions for domestic and foreign policy, and Menzel may have learned of this from a well-informed soldier, General Joseph von Radowitz. The picture, which opposed the model of an 'exemplary' king to the elector's reputation for depravity, was not completed, and the Society of Arts amended their commission. Menzel's response came shortly afterwards in the form of the *Kassel Sketch*, a work on a mediaeval theme.

The subject-matter and the presentation establish quite clearly that, like many artists, Menzel was greatly impressed by the historical paintings of the Belgian artists Louis Gallait and Edouard de Biëfve; they had created a major stir when they exhibited in Berlin in 1842, but it was also at about that time that Menzel began to overtake them. It may be true that 'on this occasion, red is a typically theatrical colour'[4], but the significance of his work lies elsewhere.

'In those far-off days,' wrote Duranty, 'Menzel did not insist on the conventional elegance and fine attire of today's people of quality. He had seen in Holbein's paintings many lords and ladies of the time of Henry VIII dressed like butchers and butcher's wives, and Holbein was an artist in whom he had a lot of trust.' Menzel's concept of history had been marked by the very considerable amount of time he had spent illustrating Kugler's *History of Frederick the Great*; in these wood engravings, he had sought to provide a clear, coherent storyline, and had added certain unexpected or accessory elements to make it more credible and accessible to the reader. The central event is not presented directly to the viewer; the eye must first bypass obstacles, perhaps a half-open door, or peer into distant countryside. In this way, the continuum of life is unbroken, and this picture of Gustav Adolph transposes this conception of graphic art into the domain of painting. A range of grotesque details provide an ironic counterpoint to the royal couple's joyful meeting, and secret, mundane factors underpinning the display of 'public' intimacy are exposed in the most indiscreet manner. The 'grandeur' of the event is accordingly muted. In the ensuing fifteen years, many of which were given over to historical painting, Menzel did not develop this principle with any great enthusiasm: it was greatly diluted, for instance, in the earlier paintings of Frederick the Great, which had been conceived as genre works, although it was much sharper and more polemical in *Address at Leuthen* (cat. 90). Here, however, Menzel did not aim at irony or investigation; he simply located an important historical event in a clear context, in a space where 'essential' and 'secondary' details are interwoven, while providing a crossroads for several lives which did not have to come together at this point[5]. The *Departure of King William I for the Army* (cat. 134), completed a quarter of a century later in a contemporary setting, contains a wide range of similar themes.

The event at Hanau takes place in the open air. It was the first time Menzel had chosen the winter – characterized by snow on the ground and a tangle of bare branches half-visible through the mist – for a history painting. However, some twelve years later, he borrowed these pictorial elements for *Address at Leuthen*, although on this occasion he used them in a much more accomplished manner. The painting also reminds us of Caspar David Friedrich, Courbet and Monet.

C.K.

1. Letter to the Society of Arts in Cassel, 24 May 1847, J. A. Stargardt, Berlin, sales cat. 659, 16-17 March 1995, no. 558.
2. *The Meeting Of Tilly with the Preacher Bake*. The project was subsequently turned down. *Cf.* Lammel, 1993 B, p. 148 et seq., fig. 94.
3. *Cf.* footnote 1.
4. Meier-Graefe, 106, p. 89.
5. *Cf.* Keisch, 1988.

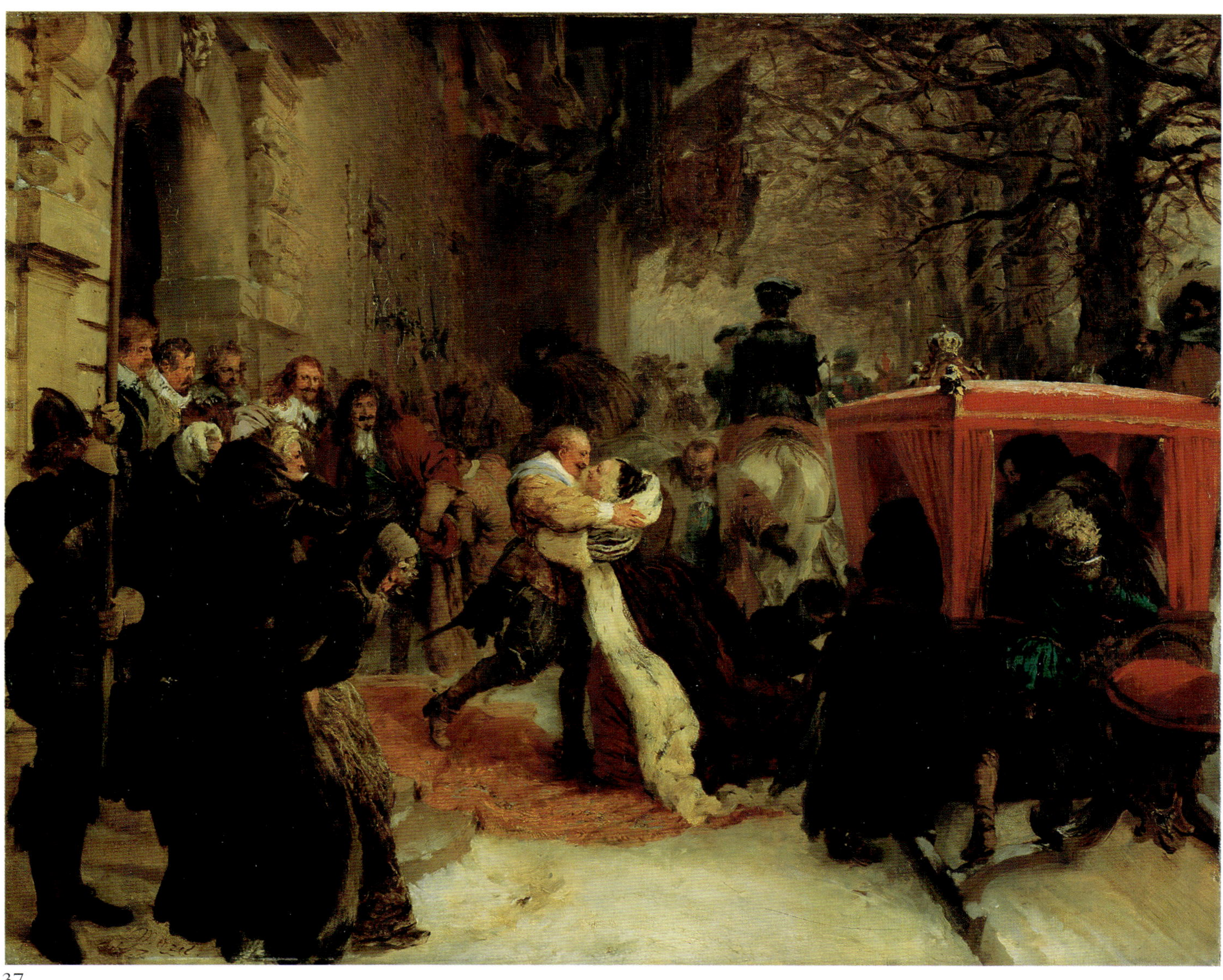

37

38

Portrait of a Young Girl

c. 1847–8

Black chalk
38.3 × 29.7cm
Berlin, Kupferstichkabinett (SZ Menzel N 242)
Exhibited in Paris and Washington only

Provenance: Painter's studio; 1905 Emilie Krigar-Menzel; acquired by the museum in 1906.
Exhibition: Berlin, 1905, no. 4727.

This portrait is of a young girl aged about ten sitting at a table with her arms crossed, and looking attentively and seriously at the artist. She is wearing a striped dress, and her hair, which has two partings, is tied at the back of her head. Menzel looks down on his model from a higher viewpoint, and lighting is coming in from the left.

In 1845, the Menzel and Maercker families (*cf.* cat. 28, 29) were neighbours at 18 Schöneberger Strasse and, after the Menzels moved to 43 Ritterstrasse in 1847, they stayed in touch. We know this from three watercolours of the Maercker children[1]; they were probably painted in 1848. In one of these[2], the little girl is wearing exactly the same dress as in this drawing, and we may infer that also studied Horace Vernet's illustrations for *Life of Napoleon*. Following on from these early experiences, Menzel always maintained a close affinity with all innovatory French artists. A.H.

1. Tschudi, 1905 A, no. 205, 206, 207.
2. Tschudi, 1905 A, no. 205.
3. Tschudi, 1905 A, no. 206.
4. Kupferstichkabinett, Berlin (SZ Menzel Kat 1261).
5. Letter to Carl Heinrich Arnold, undated, [1836], Wolff, 1914, p. 10; letter of 29 December 1836, *ibid.*, p. 13-14.

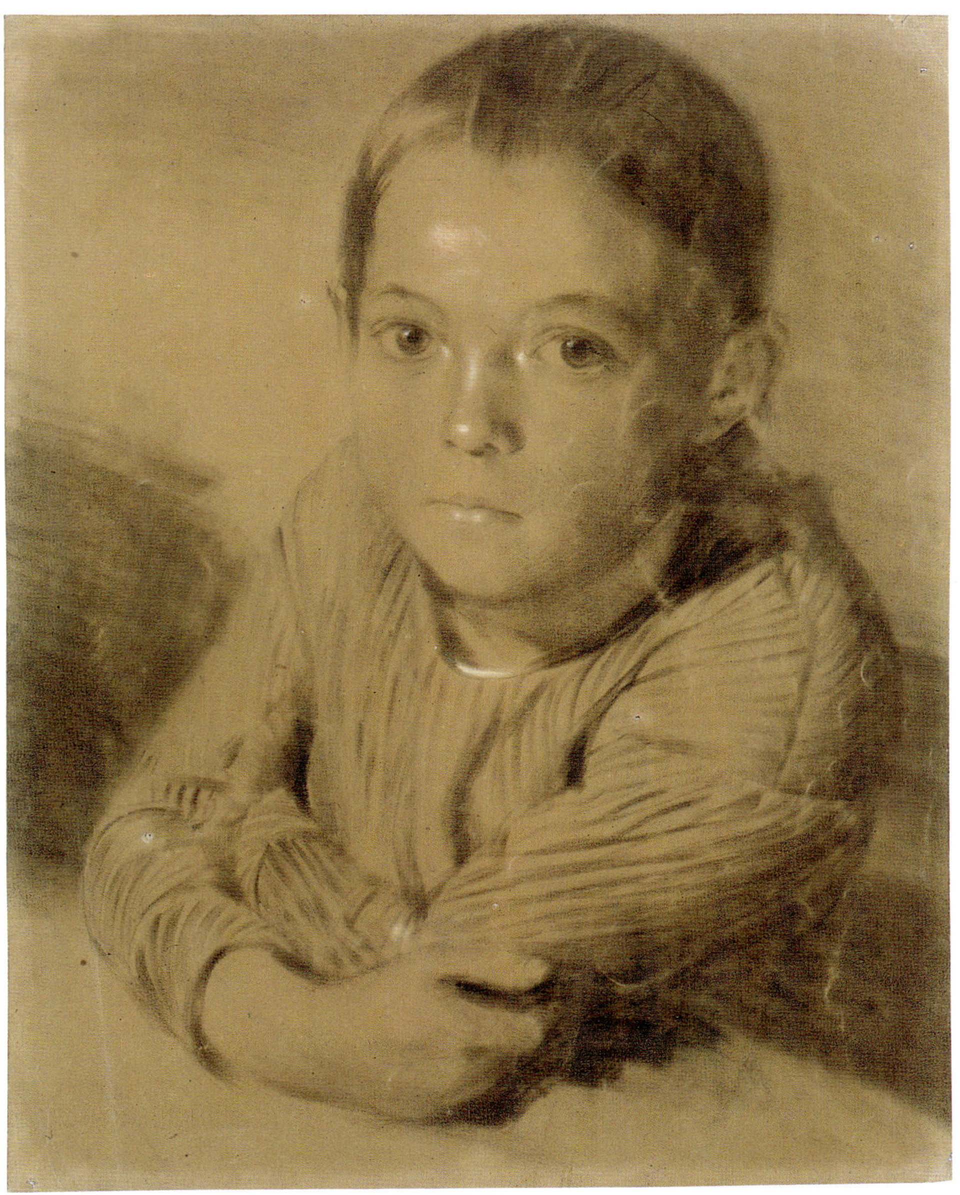

38

this is a drawing of the lawyer's daughter. Her face, with its eyes set far apart, is also to be seen in a third watercolour[3].

As far back as 1841, Menzel had done a portrait of a little girl of his immediate circle who adopted a similar pose and look. This work, which he completed using a hard, sharpened pencil of the type he had favoured in his early years, was of Sophie, daughter of Dr Puhlmann, the doctor at staff headquarters[4]. Some six years later, when the drawing reproduced here was finished, the brushstrokes are softer and broader. By this time, Menzel had learned to use pastels, and this black chalk portrait of young Miss Maercker puts one in mind of a number of French portraits painted at about this time; these might include Jean-François Millet's very natural and intimate representation of Catherine Lemaire (1849). Menzel had also known the work of the Barbizon School of painters since 1836 and, in a letter to his friend Carl Heinrich Arnold referred to new modes of expression that these artists had discovered[5]. And shortly afterwards, while preparing for his illustrations of *History of Frederick the Great*, he

39

Carl Johann Arnold

1847

Pastel
45.2 × 32.7cm
Signed and dated on the left: *A.M.1847*
Berlin, Kupferstichkabinett (SZ Menzel Nr. 1723)

Provenance: Carl Johann Arnold, Weimar; acquired by the museum in 1906.
Exhibitions: Berlin, 1905, no. 5714; Berlin, 1980 A, no. 5, reprod. p. 159.
Bibliography: Tschudi, 1905 A, no. 196; Kirstein, 1919, p. 30 *et seq.*, reprod. p. 32; Scheffler, 1922, p. 160, reprod. p. 79; Hütt, 1981, fig. 22; Lammel, 1992, p. 127–47, reprod. p. 143; Lammel, 1993 A, p. 31 *et seq.*, fig. 27.

In early 1847, Menzel wrote to his friend, the wallpaper manufacturer Carl Heinrich Arnold, 'I have just put the frame on young Carl's head; I worked on this for the last few evenings of his stay, and afterwards made a few corrections.' He then added a few words for Arnold's son, Carl Johann, then aged 17 (*cf.* cat. 27): 'My dear young Carl, I advise you to spend the evenings doing pastel drawings in the style of portraits on ancient medallions – and life size, of course, because that is the only way you can truly benefit from the exercise. It is extremely instructive, both with a view to doing oil paintings and for capturing flesh tones'[1]. Two months later, he added detailed instructions, encouraging the young man to use 'fantastic lighting' and describing the use of pastels in great detail[2].

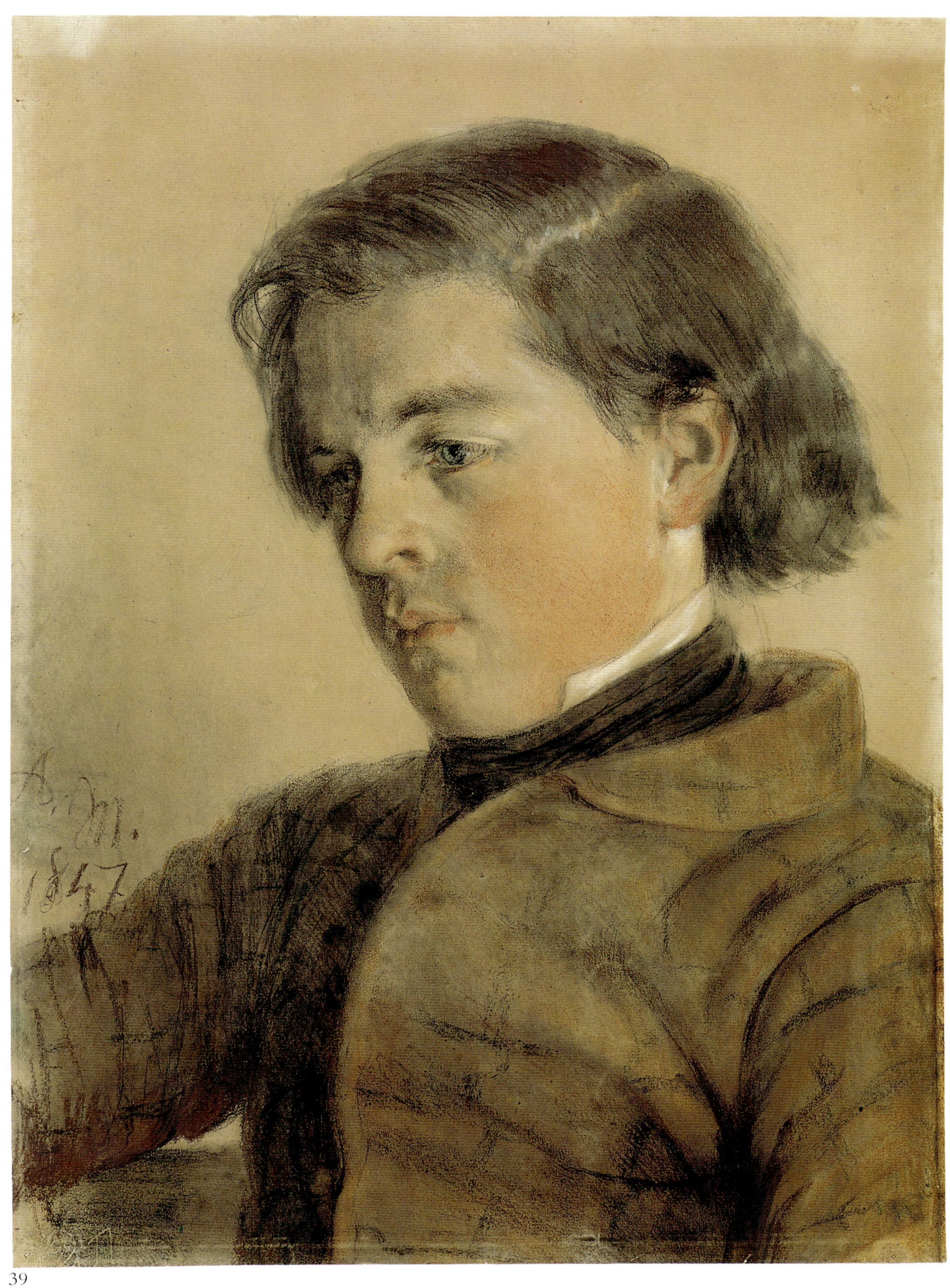

39

Carl Johann Arnold spent the last months of 1846 with the Menzels for the purpose of taking private lessons in drawing and painting. His stay was overshadowed by the death of Menzel's mother, and we may be able to detect the impact of this in the gentle, but sad, look in the young man's face.

There is a problem in identifying this and related works. The first of the two letters quoted above is illustrated with a sketch after the portrait that Menzel had framed. However, this sketch is not what is normally referred to as a pastel, and is in fact another portrait of Carl Johann that was drawn in black chalk while he was in Berlin[3]. It would appear that Menzel used the word 'pastel' to describe both techniques. The two drawings were probably still in his studio at the beginning of 1847, and he then must have taken the pastel to Kassel in the autumn when he started work on *Kassel Sketch*[4].

Menzel painted most of the portraits of people in his immediate circle during the 1840s and 1850s. In fact, he only did portraits of those close to him, and never accepted any commissions of this type. This explains their sense of authenticity and the sympathy that they evoke. A.H.

1. Letter to C. H. Arnold, 13 February 1847, Wolff, 1914, p. 101.
2. Letter to C. H. Arnold, 23 April 1847, Wolff, 1914, p. 104.
3. Kupferstichkabinett, Berlin (SZ Menzel Kat 1312).
4. This depicts Sophia of Brabant and her son, the future landgrave Henry (the founder of the princely house of Hesse), entering Marburg. The painting once hung in Magdeburg Museum, but it was destroyed at the end of World War II.

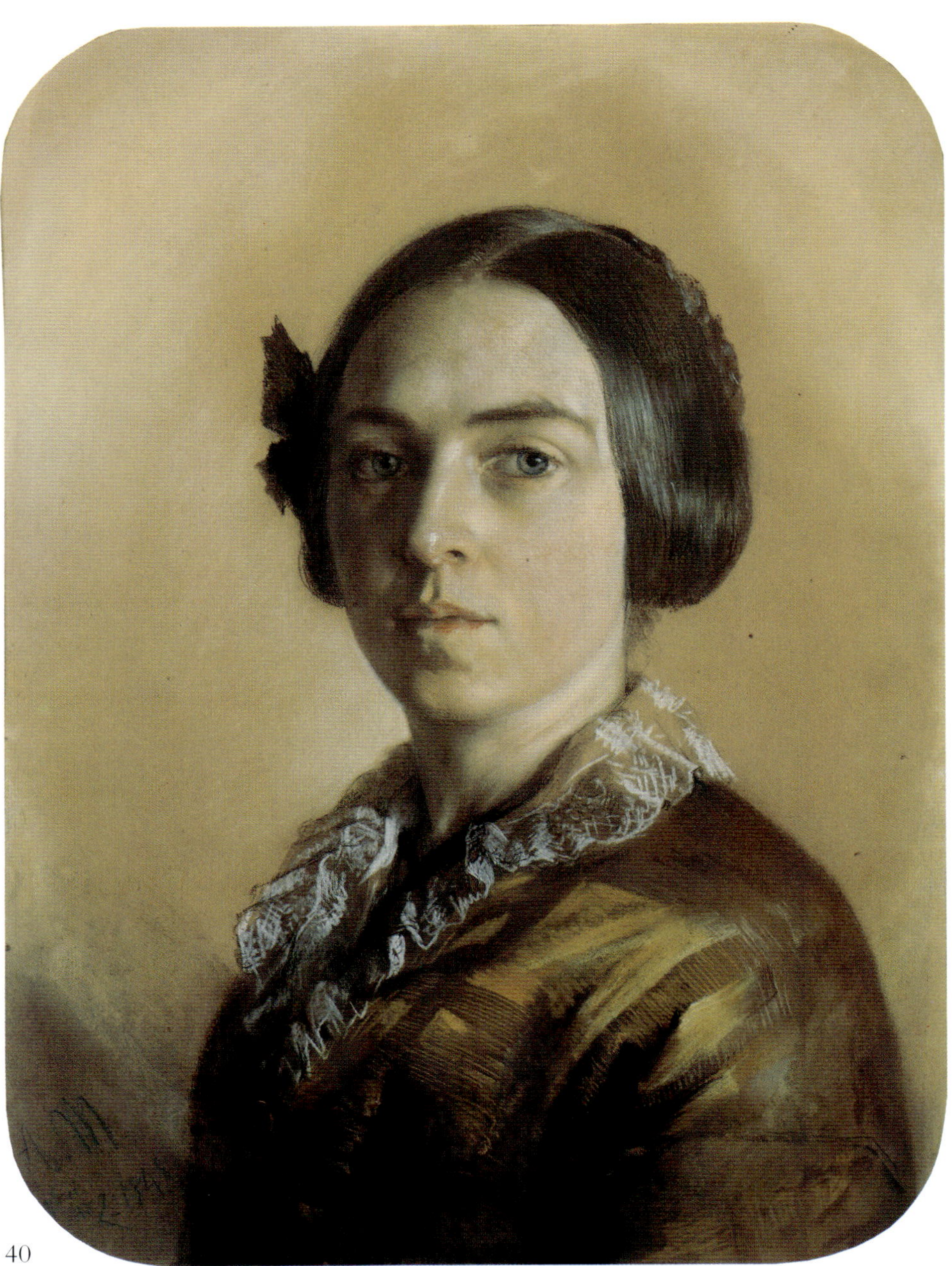

40

40

Caroline Arnold

1848

Pastel

45 × 23.8cm

Signed and dated at the bottom left: *AM März 1848*

Zurich, Arturo Cuéllar collection

Provenance: Caroline Arnold, later Baroness Treusch von Buttlar'Brandenfels; Baroness Stephanie Treusch von Buttlar-Brandenfels, Plathe sur-la-Rega, Pomerania

Bibliography: Tschudi, 1905 A, no. 197; Tschudi, 1905 B, fig. p. 241.

When Menzel was thirty-five, he justified his refusal to accept commissions for portraits in the following terms: 'It is not my job to do portraits of all and sundry to suit the public taste or to ape fashion[1].' As the years passed, he was good as his word and his best portraits exclusively represent members of his family or of his friends' families. He also completed this portrait of Caroline Arnold in pastel[2], a medium of which he had been very fond since he started the series featuring

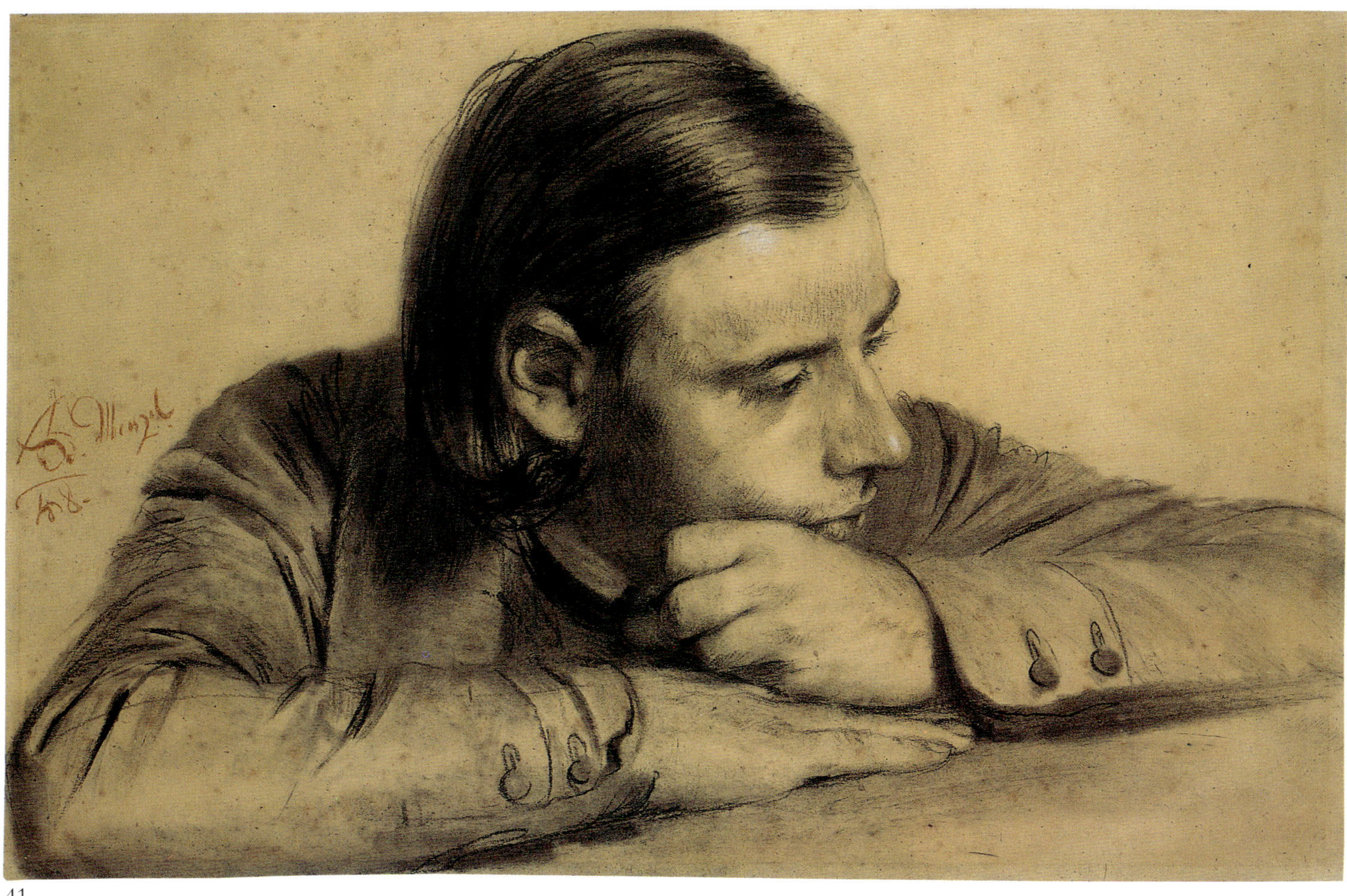

41

Frederick the Great and the rococo period. Caroline Arnold was the elder daughter of Carl Heinrich Arnold, himself an amateur painter and friend of Menzel. Arnold's youngest child, his son Carl Johann, was sent to Menzel for art lessons for some considerable time. The two friends had met at the evening drawing sessions at the Academy in 1833 and, through Arnold, Menzel met the leading artists and intellectuals in Berlin. Their friendship survived the Arnolds' move to Kassel, and Menzel produced pastel drawings of his friend's three children[3] (*cf.* cat. 39).

There was already in existence a pencil drawing of the younger sister, Friederike, which had been done in 1841 on the occasion of her birthday, and an oil portrait[4] dated 1846; in both of these delightful works, she is looking at the viewer with a lively, direct expression. Of Caroline, by contrast, we have only the drawing reproduced here and another pastel[5]. She had posed similarly for both of these head-and-shoulders portraits, and it may well be that, like the two portraits of their brother (cat. 39), the undated pastel was the precursor. The beautiful, wide-open eyes seem to look straight through the viewer, and do not cancel out the severe, almost impenetrable, expression of her face. Caroline was born on 5 January 1821 in Cassel, and died in 1883; in 1853, she appears to have married Lieutenant-General Baron Ludwig Treusch von Buttlar-Brandenfels. Menzel must have done the portrait on 21 March while he was still in Kassel, and a few days before he returned home.

M.R.-R.

1. Letter to C. B. Lorck (J. J. Weber), 9 February 1850, Wolff, 1914, p. 145.
2. According to Meyerheim, Menzel abandoned this technique later on, mainly because he found it difficult to ensure that the pastel adhered. Meyerheim, (1906) 1992, p. 161.
3. *Friederike Arnold*, 1847, pastel (incorrectly called Caroline in critical works), 45.5 × 34.5 cm; Tschudi, 1905 A, no. 194; Georg Schäfer Collection, Euerbach.
4. *Friederike Arnold*, 23 September 1841, pencil, 20 × 13.8 cm; Germanisches Nationalmuseum, Nuremberg (5812). Same title, oils on canvas, 47 × 61 cm; Nationalgalerie, Berlin.
5. *Caroline Arnold*, undated, pastel, 43.5 × 30.3 cm; Kupferstichkabinett, Berlin (SZ Menzel Kat 1326).

41

Richard Menzel, the Artist's Brother

1848

Black chalk
25 × 37cm
Signed and dated in the middle at the bottom: *Ad. Menzel.48.*
Zurich, Dr Peter Nathan and Barbara Nathan collection

Provenance: Probably the Krigar-Menzel family; Fritz Nathan, Zurich; 1955 Willi Dünner, Winterthur.
Exhibitions: Berlin 1955 B, no. 28, fig. 8; Winterthur, 1955, no. 396, pl. XLV; Bremen, 1963, no. 36, reprod. p. 32.
Bibliography: Scheffler, 1955, fig. p. 34; Hütt, 1981, fig. p. 32; Hochhuth, 1991, p. 48, reprod.

The intimate posture adopted by the artist's brother suggests thoughtfulness, sensitivity, and even despondency, and gives this portrait a melancholic, almost Romantic, feel. He was eleven years younger than Adolph and, next to such an energetic and ambitious elder brother, he must have found it very difficult to find a role for himself in life. After their parents died, Adolph assumed his full responsibilities and looked after his sickly brother – and slightly older sister – with much love and attention. The many letters that Menzel wrote in 1847 during his eight-month stay in Kassel show the deep-rooted sense of solidarity that bound the two brothers and their sister[1]. In an effort to improve his health, Richard went to live on a farm in Oderbruch during 1860–1, and it was there that he probably met his wife-to-be, Elise Preuss; she was the daughter of one of the king's farmer's, and they married on 23 July 1864. After studying photography, he settled in Berlin and managed the art publishing and photography firm of Gustav Schauer, which he and Adolph had bought together[2].

Richard died one year after getting married, on 14 July 1865. Adolph drew him on his deathbed[3]. After the burial, Ludwig Pietsch wrote about the artist to a common friend in the following terms: 'It was terrible to see this strong, serious man racked by the most awful pain over "his child"; it was what he called the brother he had brought up and looked after from an early age. This bereavement will be a turning-point in his life'[4].

The most intense and striking of Menzel's portraits are those of his brother and sister. He frequently drew them and painted them – his brother particularly – when they were young. And in 1844, when he did portraits of his Silesian parents in the Biedermeier style, he included his brother, who was then only 18 years of age[5], wearing a serious expression. Then, in 1846, the year in which their mother died, he did a painting of Richard in profile and leaning slightly and looking behind him, as if turned in upon himself[6].

During 1848, he painted Richard at least four more times[7]. In one of these, Richard looks very slim in his large cloak and, with his small oval glasses, gives the impression of being a youthful intellectual. Of the remainder, the last one of all, which dates from 1860 (10 July, according to a note made by Menzel), is a head-and-shoulders portrait. It shows him almost from behind and adopting a determined posture, sitting bolt upright and looking into the far distance; he was now sporting a beard and looking healthy and confident. This was a happy time in his life, although he had only a few more years to live[8]. M.R.-R.

1. Wolff, 1914, p. 109 et seq.
2. Riemann-Reyher, 1992, p. 134 et seq.
3. The drawing is annotated on the back as follows: '16 July 1865', legal stamp relating to the family estate; lead drawing. 8.3 × 13.3 cm; private collection, Munich. *Cf.* Berlin, 1955, B, no. 178.
4. Ludwig Pietsch to the writer Theodor Storm, 19 July 1865, Storm, 1939, p. 151. *Cf.* also Menzel to Wilhelm Rieffstahl, Kösen, 2 August 1865, Wolff, 1914, p. 201.
5. Wolff, 1914, reprod. facing p. 112. Annotated: *Nov. anno 1844*; whereabouts unknown.
6. Tschudi, 1905 A, no. 26; Georg Schäfer Collection, Euerbach.
7. The three others were: *Richard Seated at Table*: Tschudi, 105 A, no. 55; Georg Schäfer Collection, Euerbach (Nationalgalerie until 1945); *The Artist Standing near the Easel, and Richard and Emilie opposite him Sitting on the Couch*: not mentioned by Tschudi, *cf.* Kirstein, 1919, frontispiece; *RIchard Standing near a Table (?), Leaning back in his Long Cloak, his Arms Crossed, an Object (?) in his right hand*: lead drawing, Kupferstichkabinett, Berlin (SZ Menzel N 1684).
8. Kunsthalle, Hamburg, *cf.* exhib. cat. Hamburg, 1982, no. 80, reprod.

42

Stairway Landing in Nocturnal Lighting

1848

Oil on paper, board backing
36 × 21.5cm
Signed and dated: *A. Menzel 1848*
Essen, Museum Folkwang (G 116)
On show only in Paris and Berlin

Provenance: 1905 F.S. Archenhold, Berlin-Treptow, astronomer, director of the Observatory; Theodor Schall, Berlin; sold by Schall to Paul Cassirer, Berlin, 26 October 1926, no. 28; Dr Georg Hirschland, Berlin; acquired by the museum in 1939.
Exhibitions: Berlin, 1905, no. 39; Berlin, 1921; Marburg, 1946, no. 31; Berlin, 1955 B, no. 26, fig. 16; Berlin, 1970, no. 68; Moscow-Leningrad, 1974, no. 24; Frankfurt, 1975, no. 30, reprod.; Paris, 1976–7, no. 143, reprod.; Berlin, 1987 A, no. F.40.1, col. reprod. p. 240.
Bibliography: Tschudi, 1905 A, no. 51; Mackowsky, 1917, p. 97; Essen, 1971, no. 116, pl. 26; Hütt, 1981, fig. 40 (col.); Wirth, 1990, p. 271, fig. 348.

Balcony Room (cat. 18) ushered in two major characteristics of Menzel's work in an astonishing way: they were the additional factors of objects in space, and the void (in the true sense of the word), which is developed here in a most radical manner. If we were looking at a photograph, we might be forgiven for thinking that this was a case of the shutter release having been pressed by mistake. The whole composition is full of negations: a staircase whose descending steps cannot be seen, and the top of which stops at the level of the floor mat and is shrouded in shadow; a light that illuminates smooth parts of the wall but makes it difficult to make out contours or outline. In brief, the main subject is totally deceptive.

The window is situated in the very middle of the painting. Only the double overlapping of the staircase stringers masks and subverts (in the truly Romantic sense of the word) the composition's geometry. Moreover, the central subject's centre of gravity is quite unexpectedly situated in the lower part of the picture, and this gives the viewer the feeling of descending and makes it easier to see the curve in the landing as it skirts the window. In other words, the apparent destination will only be brushed against by chance – *en passant*. The window also boasts a number of interesting features including a semicircular arch and the upper panes of glass arranged in the form of an aureole. However, the situation is quite absurd: the window, which has been located with such care, is locked, and beyond the glass it is total darkness, and we do not know if that is because it is night time or whether the shutters are closed. In this way, the altar-like composition is deceptive, and the feeble light that dimly illuminates parts of the staircase comes, not from the window, but from the small wall lamp to one side. Practical matters relating to everyday life are embodied by the staircase which comes up as far as the foreground, and they prevail over an ideal entrenched in silence and the metaphysical elements. It is a locked-up world, living space is narrow and has no outlet, and the way points downwards. This small painting borrows from a formula used by Caspar David Friedrich, whose work was well known in Berlin[1], and contrasts the Romantic's faith with modern scepticism and almost the experience of nothingness.

This painting also reminds us of Friedrich for another reason: that is that his *Woman on the Staircase*, a late work that preceded Menzel's[2] by a little over ten years, similarly causes its subject to be erased. Light shines from behind a turning in the stairway and, in the shadow, we can see the outline of the person who is climbing the stairs in the direction of the light. It was precisely this hope that that the after-life will resolve problems that Menzel was so opposed to.

The date of this painting is a matter of some debate. In the course of this year of revolution, Menzel's initial enthusiasm rapidly fell away, and this could well be the source of the work's emotive and symbolic content. C.K.

1. The bookseller, Georg Reimer, owned a substantial number of Friedrich's work. Some of his collection was sold by auction in 1844; the remainder is still with his family.
2. Private collection; on permanent loan to the Kunsthalle, Hamburg; Börsch-Supan; 1973, no. 334, reprod.

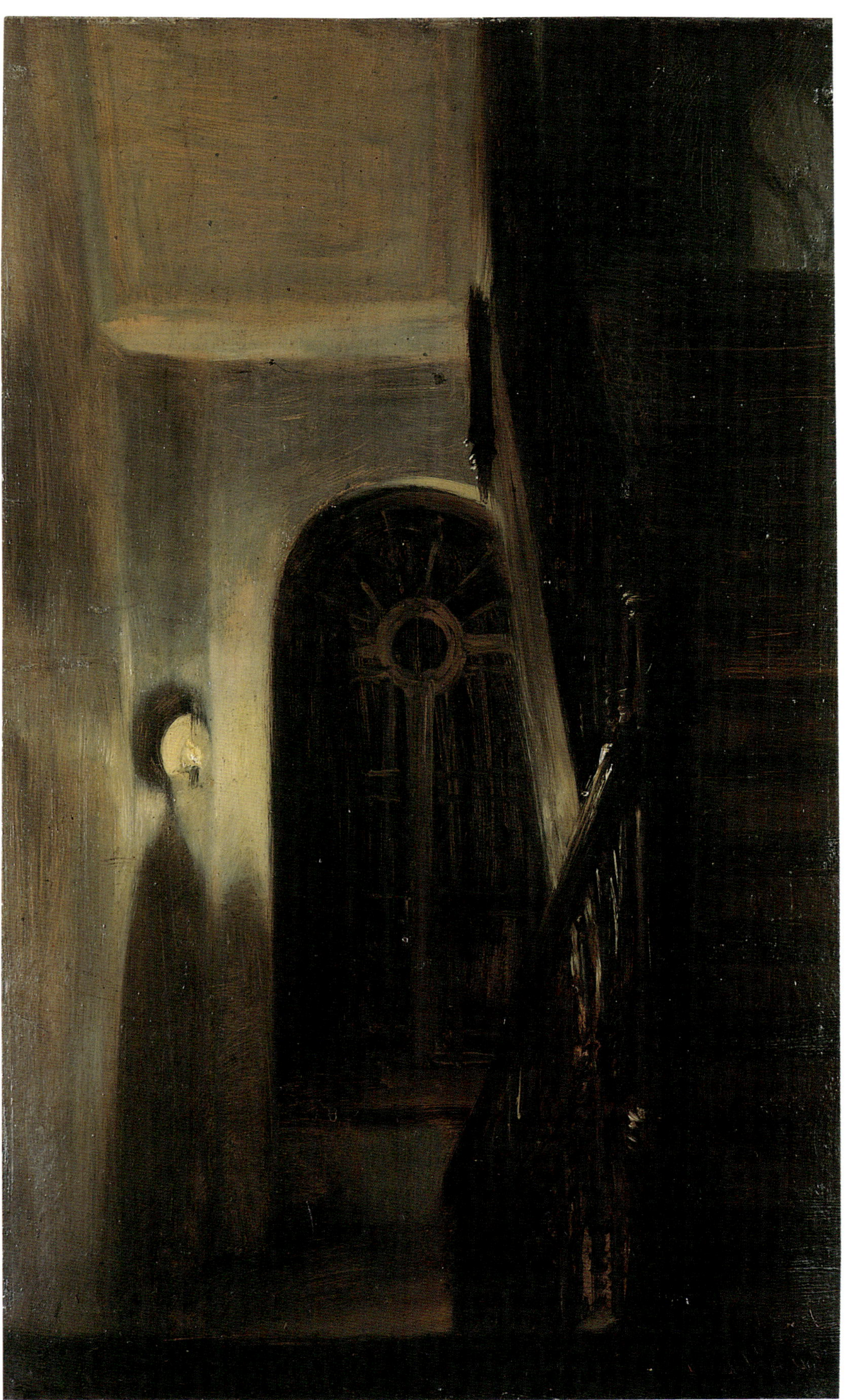

42

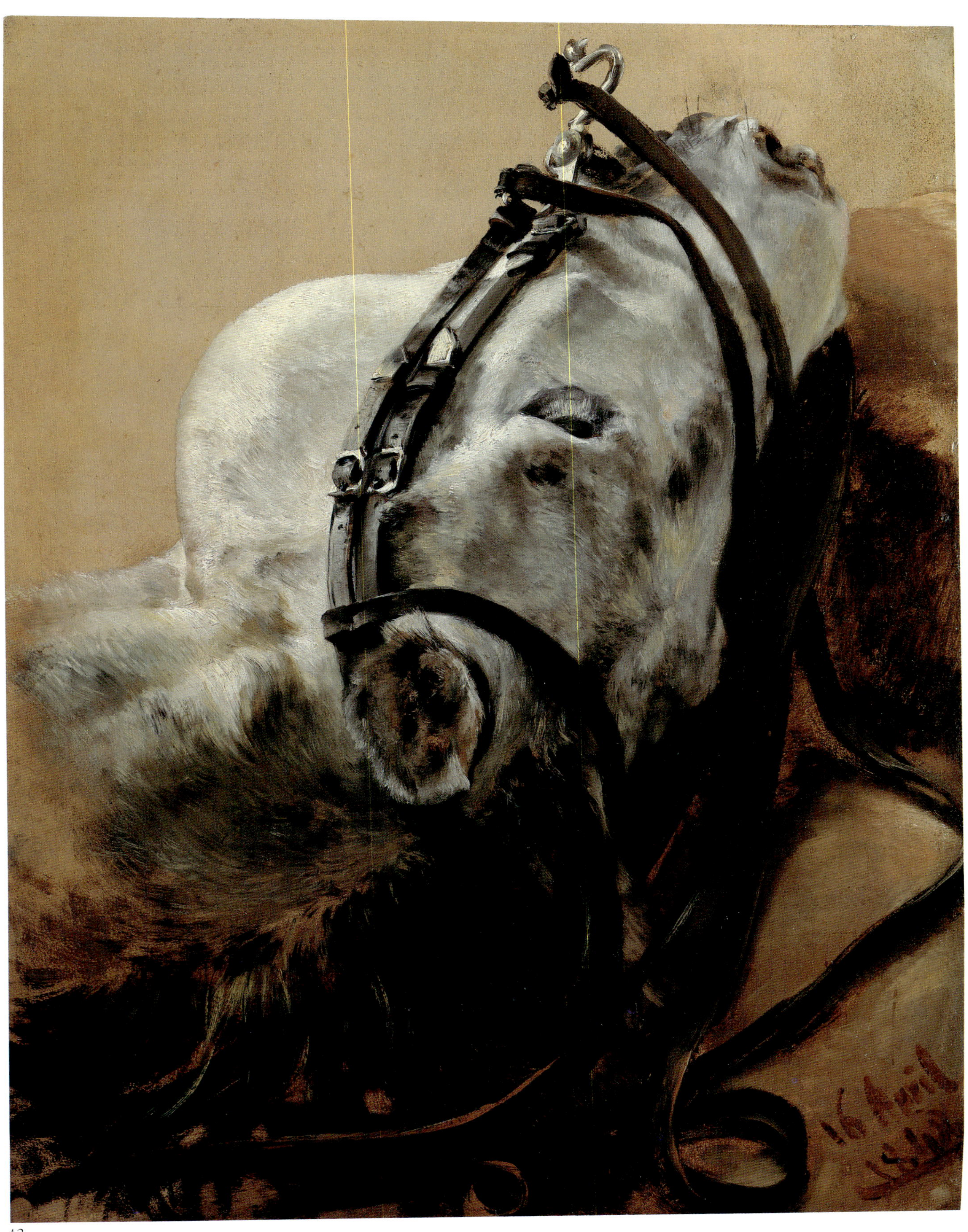

43

43
Head of Horse Wearing Bridle, Lying Down
1848

Oil on paper, board backing
64.2 × 50cm
Date on bottom left: *16 April 1848*
Berlin, Nationalgalerie (A III 510)

Provenance: Painter's studio; 1905 Emilie Krigar-Menzel; acquired by the museum in 1906.
Exhibitions: Berlin, 1861 (uncertain identification); Berlin, 1905, no. 107 c; Berlin, 1980 A, no. IX, reprod. p. 137.
Bibliography: Schasler, 1861 (uncertain identification); Tschudi, 1905 A, no. 47, reprod.; cat. NG 1907, no. 993; Scheffler, 1912; cat. NG, 1986, no pag., fig. 68.

There are at least seven studies of horses dating from 1848[1], with five others probably made shortly after this period[2]. Three of them depict the heads of dead horses. One of Menzels letters says, 'Last week, with a great song and dance and a terrible stink, I painted some horses' heads life-size, which I had sent for from the abattoir. It was very instructive'[3].

The scenes of battles and encampments so frequent in the *History of Frederick the Great* had already drawn the young illustrators attention to horses. As early as 1840, his curiosity was such that he would 'stand and watch any old nag' in order to study it (*cf.* cat. 25). An oil study[4] of one of these modest, inelegantly proportioned horses, of the kind that carried merchandise through the streets of Berlin, in harness, could not reasonably be dated after 1845. In fact the depiction of the heroic spirit of the battle horse exists side by side in his visual universe with studies of the domestic animal.

During his long stay at Kassel from late 1847 to early 1848, Menzel spent a lot of time drawing horses on the princes stud farm. In the artists opinion, it was 'just about the most interesting and edifying thing' on offer in the town (where there was also a magnificent picture gallery[5]). The vast historical composition on which he was then working included two life-sized horses, with the rump of one of them placed disrespectfully in the middle foreground. In contrast, the paintings of the Frederick the Great cycle contain few horsemen, and none of their mounts have the passionate expression or the overflowing frenzy of the contemporary Delacroixs Romanticism. Poignancy is only evident once, and Menzels state of mind in the spring of 1848 no doubt had something to do with this.

Immediately on his return to Berlin, Menzel carried on with the studies started at Kassel, without a specific aim this time. But his recent experiences of the revolt, and of death and the idea of sacrifice and victimization so prevalent at this time may well have inspired his choice of dead animals[6], as well as the dramatic form of expression of the most beautiful of these paintings. No closer link can be established. The fact remains that an engraving at the start of a chapter of the *History of Frederick the Great* quotes the ancient image, so familiar to French Romantics, of the horse as the symbol of freedom[7]. The animal is galloping with its reins wrenched off. The horse Menzel painted on 16 April 1848 still wore them. It is not the animal's anatomy the painter is portraying in his depiction of its tilted-back head, scant mane and closed eye. Its white coat, painted with all the subtlety and softness the painter could muster (even the very fine hairs around the nostrils), and the sinuous curves of the precisely formed leather, together with the hard reflections from the metal are surely an elementary symbol of the contrast between nature and servitude[8].

Fig. 172. Théodore Géricault, *Two Severed Heads*, Ssudy for *The Raft of the Medusa*, 1818–19, oil, Stockholm, Nationalmuseum

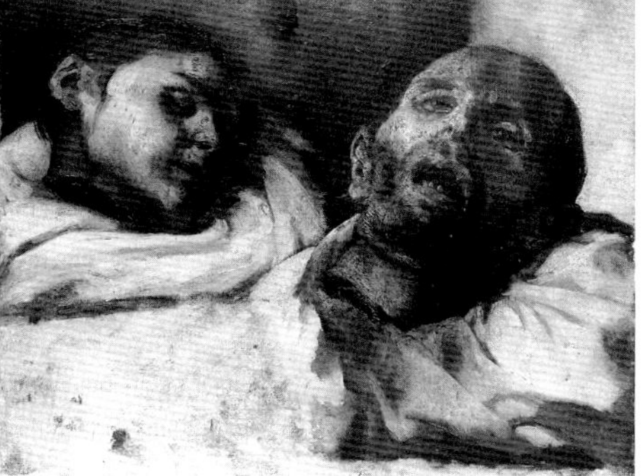

This painting, which can be viewed in the painter's studio (*cf.* fig. 31), is reminiscent of the heads and limbs of convicts which Géricault had brought to his workshop when preparing *The Raft of The Medusa*, and of the full-sized studies in oil that he made of them, in a pale light, often emphasizing the carelessness with which these human remains were thrown higgeldy-piggeldy on a table (Fig. 172). Pathos stems from the horror – the image of a suffering which transcends death. C.K.

1. Tschudi, 1905 A, no. 39, 42, 43, 47, 48, 50 plus one at the Kunstalle in Hamburg.
2. Tschudi, 1905 A, no. 14, 20, 40, 41, 57.
3. Letter to Carl Heinrich Arnold, 3 May 1848, Wolff, 1914, p. 134.
4. Tschudi, 1905 A, no. 14, reprod.; Berlin, Nationalgalerie.
5. Letter to his brother and sister, 15 September 1847, Wolff, 1914, p. 111.
6. This idea was put forward by Marie Riemann-Reyher, *cf.* exhib. cat. New York, 1900, No. 6.
7. Chapter 6; Bock, 1923, no. 482.
8. The study reproduced in Tschudi, 1905 A, no. 43 (Winterthur, Stiftung Oskar Reinhart Museum) is very similar, depicting the same animal, without its reins.

44
Head of a Horse in Right Profile
1848

Oil on paper, canvas and board backing
35.2 × 59.6cm
Signed and dated at the centre right: *A. M. 48*
Nationalgalerie, Berlin (A III 509)
Exhibited in Berlin only

Provenance: Painters studio; 1905 Emilie Krigar-Menzel; acquired by the museum in 1906.
Exhibitions: Berlin, 1861 (identification uncertain); Berlin, 1905, no. 107b; Berlin, 1980 A, no. VIII, reprod. p. 136.
Bibliography: Schasler, 1861 (identification uncertain); Tschudi, 1905 A, no. 42, reprod.; cat. NG, 1907, no. 994; Scheffler, 1922, p. 144, reprod. p. 62; Justi. 1932, p. 131; cat. NG, 1986, s.p., fig. 67; Forster-Hahn, 1988, fig. 8.

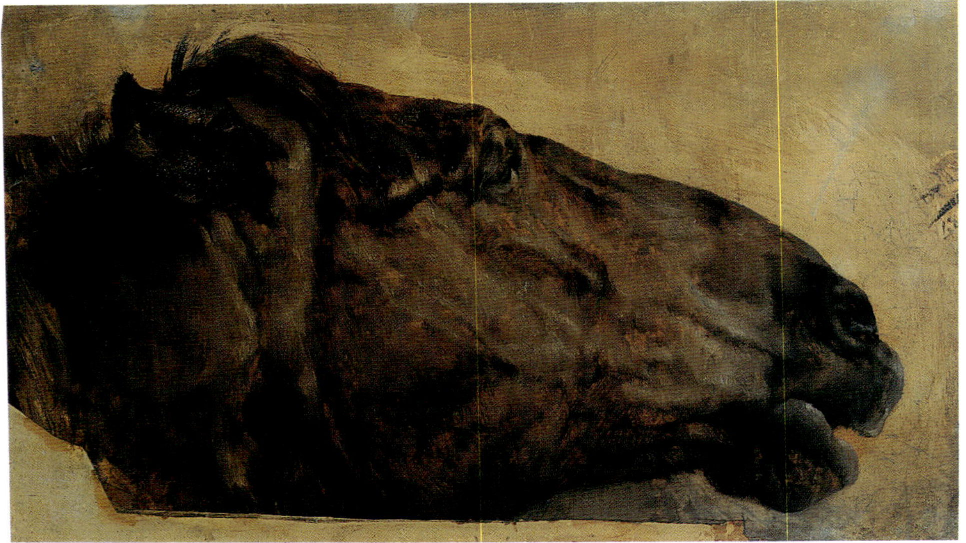

44

Along with several other studies of horses, this painting was hung on a different wall from the *Head of Horse Wearing Bridle, Lying Down* (cat. 43), above another of Menzels bureaux in his last studio. Nearby is hung *Lying in State of the March Dead* (fig. 65). C.K.

45

Plaster Model Storeroom in the Altes Museum

1848

Coloured chalks
46.2 × 58.8cm
Signed and dated at the bottom left: *Ad.Menzel. 26.August 1848* – Annotated with: *Aufbewahrungssaal während des Museumsneubaues 1848*
Berlin, Kupferstichkabinett (SZ Menzel Nr 1761)

Provenance: Max Liebermann, Berlin; purchased by the museum in 1907.
Exhibitions: Berlin, 1899, no. 225 (withdrawn from exhibition); Berlin, 1905, no. 278; Berlin, 1979, no. 142; Berlin, 1980 A, no. 9, col. reprod. p. 173; Vienna, 1985, no. 107, col. reprod. p. 68; Copenhagen, 1985, no. 100, reprod. p. 63; Berlin, 1987 A, no. G.10.
Bibliography: Jordan, 1895, p. 67; Tschudi, 1905 A, no. 215; Kaiser, 1956, p. 61, fig. 35.

With his hopes dashed of seeing the claims of Liberalism converted into something with more substance, Menzel fell into a reflective phase. In March he wrote a long letter to his friend in Kassel, deeply emotional in tone, relating his long walk through the town transformed by the uprising, and marked by signs of street fighting. His account, which culminates in the description of the exhibition of the bodies of the victims and the funeral procession to the burial place, shows no sign of resignation nor bitterness in face of such vain sacrifice[1]. Shortly after, he insisted on his democratic convictions in a letter to his friend in Potsdam, an army doctor: 'Although you are on the side of the military and I am a partisan of the people . . .', and he admitted to his friend in Kassel: 'For the first time I am suffering from what I was indifferent to before – my failure to grow into a fine strapping lad.' It came naturally to him to channel all his energies into his activities. In his letter to Arnold he describes the horses' heads from the abattoir which he painted from life (cat. 43, 44) and talks of a sketch in colour, which he had not yet decided on how to use[2]. This was *Lying in State of the March Dead*, as yet unfinished. By September, his words sound more resigned: 'Once more, I have expected too much of humanity; to my (justifiable) indignation against the upper class has been added indignation against the lower. The rifle has only been put on the other shoulder'[3]. The reasons for leaving the work aside are not straightforward. Lichtwarks report of a conversation with Menzel in 1902 seems to simplify the true complexity of his motives[4].

Three weeks after writing the letter dated 15 September, Menzel signed the large chalk drawing depicting the room in which the plaster models belonging to the Altes Museum were stored. It was situated on the first floor of the museum, designed by Schinkel and finished in 1828 (before its inauguration in 1830). The three aisles intended for the storage of sculptures, their subdued colours and reddish columns are recognizable. During the building of a passage at first-floor level allowing access to the neighbouring museum then being built (Stüler's Neues Museum), the collection of plasters belonging to the museums had been stored there temporarily before they were placed in their final positions in the Neues Museum. One is immediately struck by the replica of Pasquinos famous group. The grandiose pathos of this unsophisticated Hellenistic-style sculpture seems a material manifestation of Menzel's intuitive thoughts. It shows Menelaus, the leader of the Greek army, laying siege to Troy, and carrying the body of Patrocles, Achilles companion, away from the battlefield.

Two drawings relating precisely to this group are the only preliminary works known[5]. One, in chalk, is very detailed in its execution, with white highlights, and shows the group from the front, so that the base serving as a support is invisible. Rather than being a mere reproduction of a statue, it is the material, carnal quality that prevails, soft and melancholy, in the young man, contrasting with the angry, accusing expression of Menelaus. The other study, drawn with energy, gives more or less the same view of the sculpture as the final composition, emphasizing its dramatic violence. On the same piece of paper, Menzel uses the figure of Patrocles again and addes a bust of Hermes to it, which does not appear in the pastel version. In the foreground of the latter lies the plaster of the marble throne of the Parthenon, under the group[6]. The other statues cannot all be identified with certainty. Behind the lions head adorning Pope Clement XIII's tomb, by Canova[7], the discus-thrower from the Vatican Museum appears, with half of his body visible. Behind this is the gentleman of the robe making an offering, from the same collection. Further back may be the Lemnia Athene with the head of the Giustiniani Athene preserved at Kassel. Menzels interest in plaster models went back to his early days in the plaster casting class at the Academy, where he was a keen pupil, as he wrote later: 'The great novelty for me here lies in all these beautiful plaster casts'[8].

In the chalk drawing, all these sculptures seem to be arranged around the main group. This must surely be the real motif? Perhaps Menzel was not only impressed by the Baroque pathos of Pasquinos group, but also wanted to express his own thoughts regarding the remembrance of victims. He could not have known August Wredows statue at this stage, which represented a young warrior taken to Olympus by an angel of victory, inspired by Pasquinos group. It was not placed on the Schlossbrücke (the bridge designed by Schinkel, linking Unter den Linden to the royal palace) until several years later. M.R.-R.

1. Letter to Carl Heinrich Arnold, 23 March 1848, Wolff, 1914, p. 126 and ff.
2. Letter to Doctor Puhlmann, 7 April 1848, and letter to C.H. Arnold, 3 May 1848, Wolff, 1914, p. 132–133.
3. Letter to C.H. Arnold, 15 September 1848, Wolff, 1914, p. 136.
4. Lichtwark, (1924), 1992, p. 303–5.
5. Kupferstichkabinett, Berlin.
6. Museum of the Acropolis, Athens.
7. In Saint Peters Basilica, Rome.
8. Letter to Ludwig Pietsch, 'Monday evening' [30 December 1879]. Reprod. in Wirth, 1986, p.88.

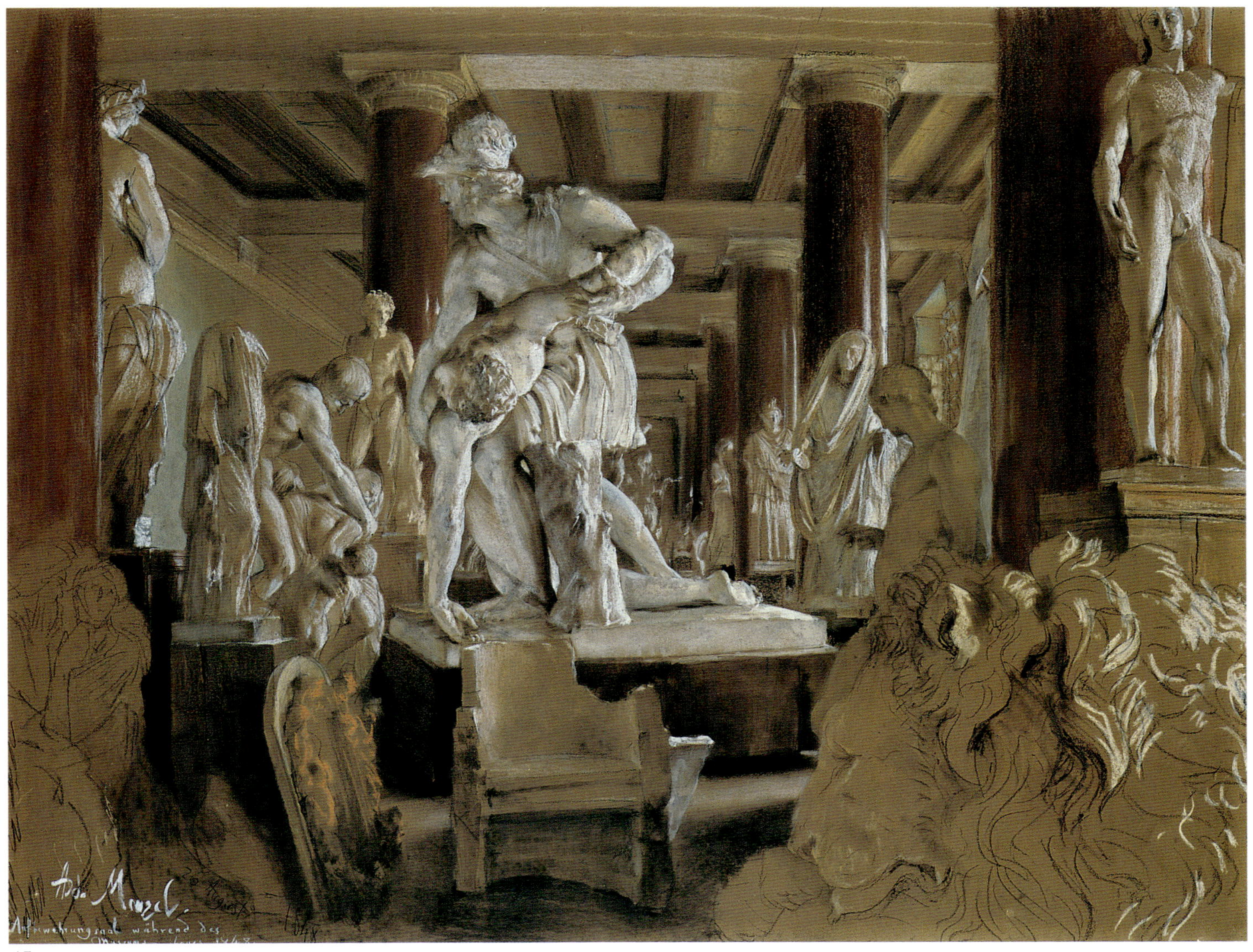

45

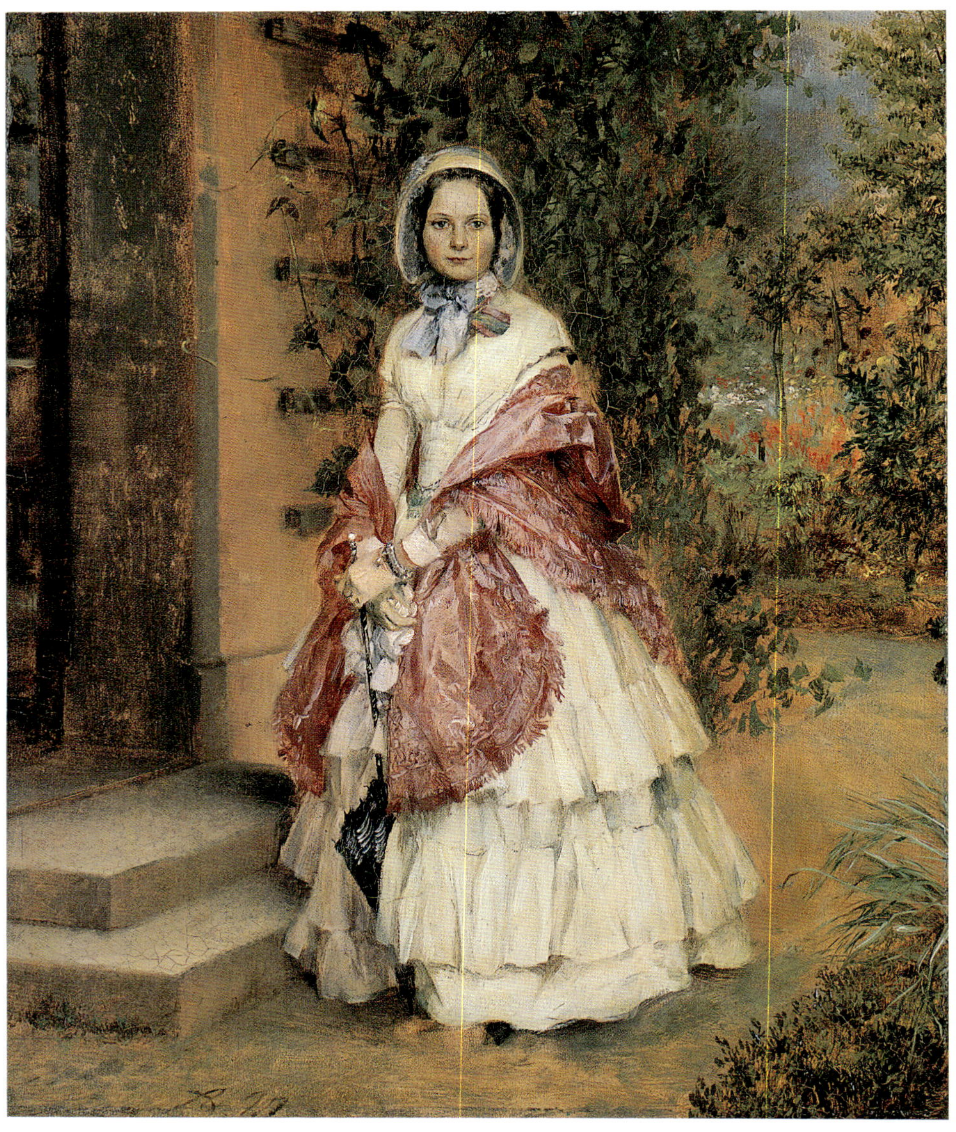

46
Portrait of Clara Ilgner, later Frau Schmidt von Knobelsdorf
1848

Oil on canvas
44 × 36cm
Signed at the bottom left: *A.M.*
Berlin, Nationalgalerie (A I 897)

Provenance: Elisabeth and Meta Ilgner, Berlin, models sisters; acquired by the museum in 1906. *Exhibitions:* Berlin, 1895, no. 234; Berlin, 1906, no. 1171, reprod.; Berlin, 1935, no. 15; Wiesbaden, 1952, no. 157; Berlin, 1955 B, no. 32, fig. 12; Kiel, 1956, no. 58; Munich, 1962, no. 63, reprod.
Bibliography: Tschudi, 1905 A, no. 53; Tschudi, 1905 B, reprod. p. 81, reprod. p. 291; Meier-Graefe, 1906, p. 95 *et seq.*; cat NG, 1907, no. 989; Kern, 1915–16, reprod. p. 83; Justi, 1921, p, 12, fig. 8; Justi, 1932, p. 131; Scheffler, 1938, p. 61; Waldmann, 1941, p. 45, fig. 22; Beenken, 1944, p. 395 *et seq.*; Hütt, 1981, fig. 39 (col.); Jensen, 1982, p. 68, col. pl. 11.

Menzel painted few portraits, even in the 1850s and when commissioned as here. This facet of Menzels artistic activity reached its culmination, and essentially its conclusion, in the 132 people depicted in the painting of the *Coronation* (fig. 121). What he did do however is enough to refute the opinion of Hugo von Tschudi that Menzel lacked the key to the human soul[1].

Unlike the portrait of Madame Maercker (cat. 29), the setting of the young woman on the threshold of her house and the stylish outfit she wears in readiness to go out do not conflict with the conventions of the genre. English portraits of the end of the eighteenth century, although of a larger format, used a similar technique. The person portrayed is ascribed an area in which their life is revealed, and of which they are the main ornament. In this case, the splendour of the flowers in the garden are opposed to the beautiful silk fabric, as the freedom of nature is opposed to the golden cage of the easy life of the city dweller[2]. Enclosed within the restricted confines of her cabriole hat, the young womans face fixes the onlooker with a gentle, attentive expression, in keeping with the rules of etiquette she has learnt. Even her hands are imprisoned in her gloves.

The woman in this picture is not, as was supposed, the wife of the cabinet minister in June 1848. At the time when Menzel painted this portrait, she was seventeen and was still Clara Ilgner. Several years later, she married an officer, Schmidt von Knobelsdorf (who was no relation to the architect of the château of Sanssouci). It is said that the painter, then aged thirty-three, was so severely affected by the announcement of this marriage that he never painted the portrait of a standing woman again. Whether we should rely on family hearsay is another matter[3]. C.K.

1. Tschudi, 1896, p. 43.
2. *Cf.* the gouaches *Sweet liberty* and *Sweet servitude* in the *Children's album* (Kupferstichkabinett, Berlin).
3. Information generously given by Joachim von Wartenburg.

47
Emilie Menzel Asleep
c. 1848

Oil on paper, canvas backing
46.8 × 60cm
Hamburg, Hamburger Kunsthalle (1267)
Exhibited in Paris and Washington only

Provenance: Mlle E. Maercker, Halberstadt; acquired by the museum in 1912.
Exhibitions: Berlin, 1905, no. 54; Berlin, 1955 B, no. 29, fig. 10; London, 1956, no. 165; Paris,

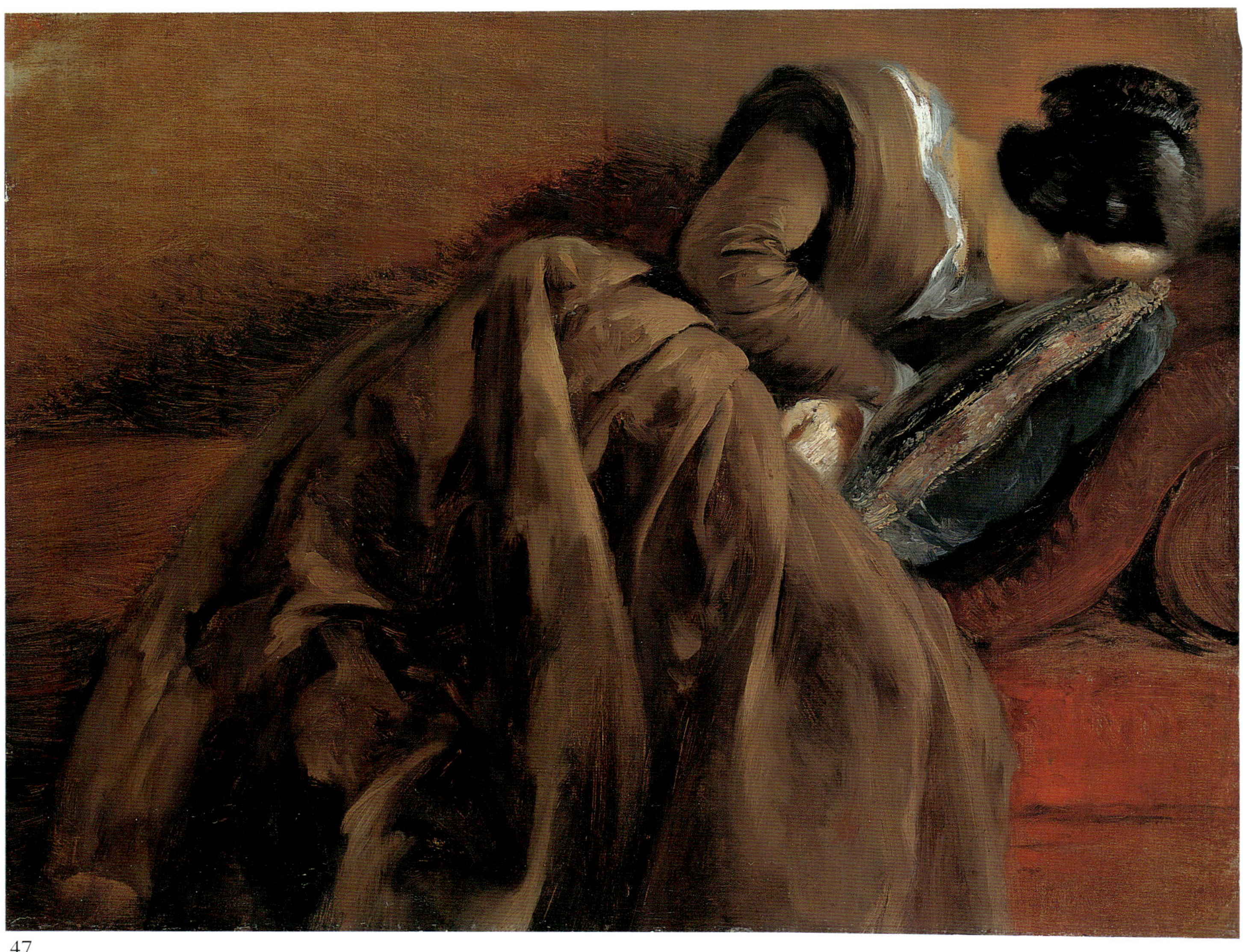

47

1976–7, no. 145; Berlin, 1981, no. 5.170; Hamburg, 1982, no. 45 with col. reprod.; Paris, 1984–5, no. 97, reprod.
Bibliography: Tschudi, 1905 A, no. 49; Meier-Graefe, 1906, p. 94 *et seq.*; Waldmann, 1941, p. 45, fig. 18; Krafft/Schümann, 1969, p. 215 with reprod.; Hentzen, 1969, no. 233 (text by Wolf Stubbe); Forster-Hahn, 1978, p. 259–61, fig. 2; Jensen, 1982, p. 70, col. pl. 12; Howoldt, 1993, p. 12, col. fig. p. 13.

Menzel decided to remain a bachelor early on, and shared a flat with his sister, eight years younger than he, who lived two years longer, and his sickly brother (*cf.* cat. 41) whose fragile health was a frequent source of concern. Family visits, evenings at the theatre, excursions and journeys were undertaken together, and the family members gathered together in the evening around the gas lamp often served as models for him. So for a long time, Menzel drew continual inspiration from his intimate entourage. In this respect he was very like Picasso. At the end of the eighteenth century, in Germany, this practice was adopted in a modest way by the young Wilhelm von Kobell in Munich, and also in Berlin by Daniel Chodowiecki, the only artist Menzel would acknowledge as his inspiration[1]. Chodowiecki already appreciated the natural grace of people caught unawares in poses so different from the standard studies used by professional models.

In the sketchbooks of the 1840s, Menzel was even at this stage drawing his brother or sister asleep on the sofa with a sense of curiosity and wonderment, often using unexpected perspectives. The painter never forgot that motif, interpreted poetically (*cf.* cat. 75) or, later, satirically (as in the gouache *Travelling through the Beauty of Nature*; fig. 144[2]). Completely inactive, unaware of social context or even of their own existence, the individual is transformed into still life. The face, limbs and clothes, no longer in their habitual forms and poses and reduced, like any material, to their earthly substance, reveal their malleability. Transitoriness disappears in immobility, and sleep always suggests the proximity of death. There are also the erotic connotations that Werner Hofmann found in Courbet, though on a far more discreet level.

The woman sleeping in the Hamburg picture is lying in an uncomfortable and clearly temporary position. She has buried her face in a cushion whose braiding must hamper her, and she is lying with all her weight on her bent left arm and on her shoulder. Her head, which is in the corner of the picture, gives way to the striking still life formed by the abundant folds of her dress, appearing like a colossal pyramid in the foreground. The juxtaposition of the blue cushion, the red arm of the sofa and the silky brown hair form a second still life, whose solid structure can be compared with the soft imprecision of the same motif in the *Woman Asleep* (cat. 10). The design is calculated and conspicuous. Its arbitrary order is imposed, in a way as significant as it is surprising, on a subject favouring this apparent casualness, this aesthetic of the irregular so dear to the young Menzel. *Emilie Asleep* is his response to Classical art, which he defies as he cites it. All this from no more than the fruit of furtive observation.

Emilie, with her chin resting on her hand, is depicted in a similar, but more dreamy pose in a chalk drawing dating from roughly the same time[3]. On the other hand, it seems unlikely that the etching entitled *Dressmaker Asleep*[4] (1843) is of his sister, who was then only twenty.

C.K.

1. I am the pupil of no living being, other than him." Menzel to Friedrich Pecht, 1 July 1879. Letter reproduced in Kirstein, 1919, p. 115.
2. Tschudi, 1905 A, no. 675; private collection.
3. Tschudi, 1905 A, no. 183; Kupferstichkabinett, Berlin (SZ Menzel N 4091).
4. Bock, 1923, no. 1134.

48 49 52 55 56 62 63 64 90

The Frederick the Great Cycle

A very long time before he had started the first of the eleven compositions which were to make him famous as a painter – not just as an illustrator and engraver – the young Menzel, at the age of twenty-five, dreamed of creating an entire series, possibly in the spirit of those eighteenth-century English works, such as the Boydell Shakespeare gallery, a series of paintings of different formats, planned from the start to be reproduced graphically. As early as 1840, while he was working on the illustrations for Kugler's book, *History of Frederick the Great*, with tremendous enthusiasm for his hero and for what he described as the 'pictorial' possibilities of the subject, he admitted that he hoped 'one day to have the great good fortune to be able to paint a cycle of large historical paintings on this period'[1].

At what time did this project, submerged in the intense activity of the 1840s, really begin to take shape? Probably a little earlier than the date usually given, but a slight shift in the timescale is not without importance.

In January 1849, Menzel spoke in a letter of a 'long series' of pictures he

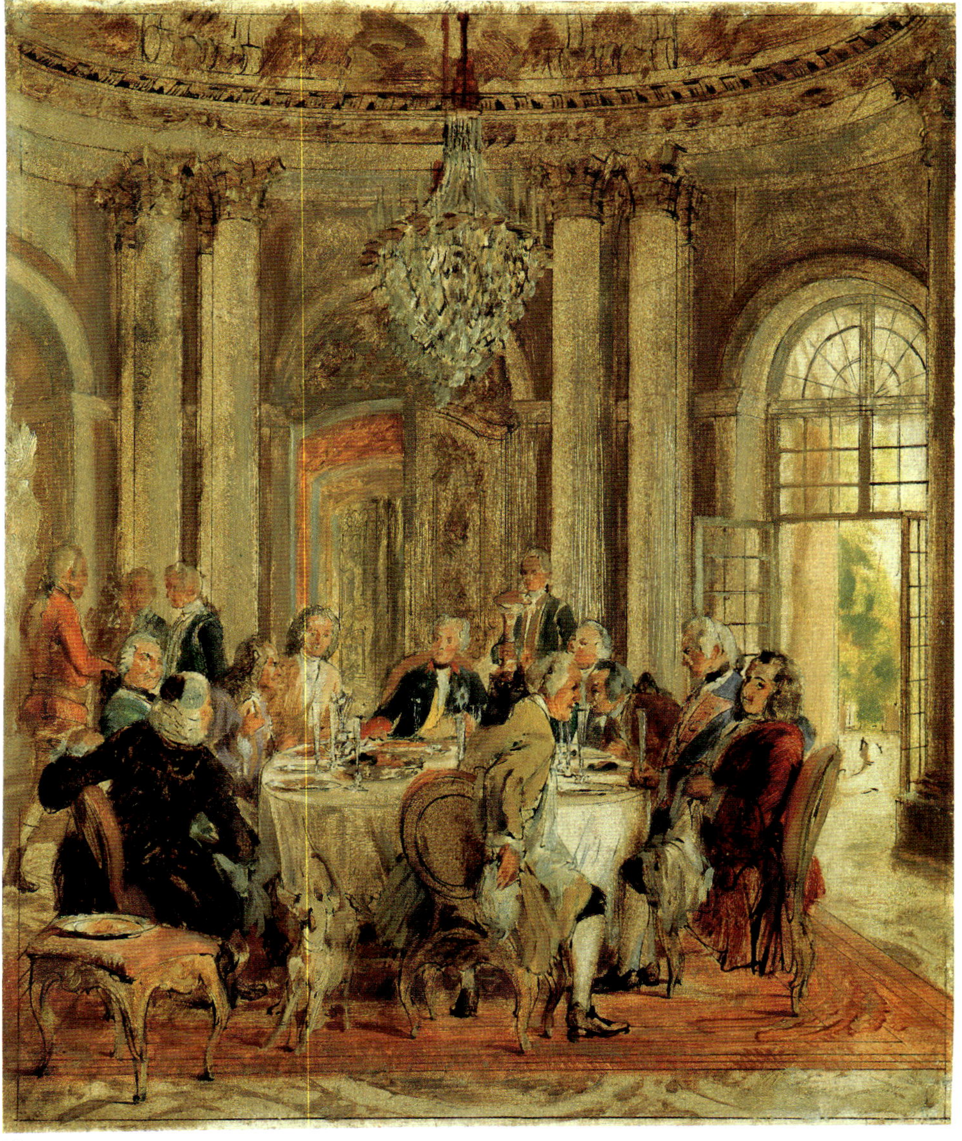

48

wanted to paint[2]. He had just started work on *The Petition* (cat. 52), 'that's to say, standing in front of the easel', as he expressly described it. That presupposes that the sketch (and no doubt the preliminary studies of the people) had been made previously, during 1848. This applies not only to this composition, which is certainly the first in the series according to its date of completion, but not according to its date of conception! Because 'initially it was an idea which came to me when I was making the preliminary studies for another painting', he stated a little later[3]. We can conclude that in addition to the *Petition* project, at least one other was already well advanced.

Which was it? In the years to follow, Menzel had three projects close to his heart, on which he spent variable amounts of time. He would stop work on one for several months in order to get ahead with another. (This could have been due to the constraints of his studio, in which he was unable to set out several large canvasses at the same time in a suitable light.) The picture whose conception precedes *The Petition* 'had just been started' in May 1849[4]. As far as one can tell this was *The Flute Concert* (cat. 56), as he stated on this subject that work on it would have to be 'interrupted because of the picture of *The Round Table at Sanssouci*'[5]. So this painting must have been started in the summer or autumn of 1849, as it was not exhibited until the end of March 1850 at the Academy. The painter then no doubt went back to *The Flute Concert* for several months, before turning, in August 1850, to *Night Attack at Hochkirch*[6] (fig. 120). Another change, six months later, due to a firm order, when Menzel returned to *The Flute Concert*[7], in order to finish it on 1 September 1852, leaving the field clear again for *Night Attack at Hochkirch*.

The piecing together of these rather involved facts reveal that the three ideas (except that for *The Petition*) developed in parallel in the painters mind, and not one after another. Two points arise from this. Firstly, the date of completion of the large battle scene (1856) is not sufficient to classify it among the later works of the Frederick the Great cycle. It was probably from the start, not from 1850 only, that the painter thought of depicting the 'Sanssouci philosophy' just as effectively in the form of an enlightened monarch who was patron of the arts, as in the form of the commander-in-chief of the army. The cycle depicting the 'great king' suggests a polarity, which may not be surprising in the light of the long years already devoted to this subject. Secondly, the start of work should be dated not in 1849, but in 1848. Before the conception of *The Petition*, at least one other painting had taken sufficient shape in his mind for the 'preliminary work', in other words the architectural studies, even the models, to be well on the way by the end of 1848. This composition is undoubtedly *The Flute Concert*, the first picture the painter worked on immediately after *The Petition*. Even if *The Round Table* (cat. 48) were inserted later in the series, it was probably thought of at the same time, in so far as the two works complement each other in their opposition (with similar dimensions).

So the Frederick the Great cycle, or rather, a dream from the past taking material form, was not conceived of during the period of general depression following the notorious failure of the Revolution, but during the period of revolutionary fervour, when only a little of its intensity had been lost. Even during the period when the artist painted *The Petition*, in 1849, after the dissolution of the Prussian National Assembly, and the 'granting' of a constitution by the king in December of the previous year, ideas of freedom had not been surrendered in the slightest degree. Certainly the stronghold moved from Berlin to other parts of Germany, but this was just the time to forge a vision of a united nation. Press and private correspondence echo this highly charged atmosphere, which was to last until late 1849, and which was due to the feeling that things were still undecided – even in Berlin[8]. Menzel's bouts of more or less radical democracy did not last long, but they affected his activities at the Association of Berlin Artists[9]. Perhaps in his search for it he had taken his 'indignation against the lower classes' too literally, that disappointment with the masses ('Once more, I have expected too much of humanity') expressed in the frequently quoted letter of 15 September[10]. During these months of confusion the basic feeling, whether on the right or left, was one of bitter distress and bewilderment, of a loss of confidence in all political factions.

It was in this context that the Frederick the Great cycle was conceived of, some months, or perhaps some weeks, after Menzel had started to give shape in his *Lying in State of the March Dead* (fig. 65) to his vision of a 'painting of present history, in which it is vital to assert peoples rights'[11]. If this picture was never finished, this was not initially, whatever may be said later, the result of a conscious decision, taken once and for all. Doubtless the present and the past coexisted for a time in his mind as possible subjects for the painting of history, before practice imposed a choice in favour of the past.

The contradictory personality of Frederick II has given rise to very diverse interpretations. Previously, the German Empire, in the spirit of the 'Prussian legend', had made him the champion of a state avid for victory, had glorified his military exploits and cleverly exploited Menzel's works (this reinterpretation of the painters work was a cause, latterly, for dubious praise) and the representatives of progressive and liberal ideas had honoured him as an enlightened monarch. He was viewed as the friend of philosophy and the arts, the author of *Against Machiavelli*, the ardent defender of religious tolerance, the person who established modern economic and administrative structures – so many qualities confirmed by historical facts that one risks not taking account of other equally significant facts. In relation to the political torpor of the years before the March revolts, Frederick was simply the exemplary good monarch. His biography by Franz Kugler is based on this image, and illustrated by Menzel with the avowed aim of making a 'book for the people'. During the course of this work, the young artist developed deep down an image of the king to which he would always remain attached, an image formed of energy and will, spirit and stoicism in face of suffering. The human, individual, even private dimension is a vital aspect of this image, inspired by the bourgeoisie. It was nourished, as Françoise Forster-Hahn explains (1977), by the writings of liberal personalities such as the historians J.D.A. Preuss (1834), Friedrich Förster (1840) or Carl Friedrich Koeppen (1842), who pro-

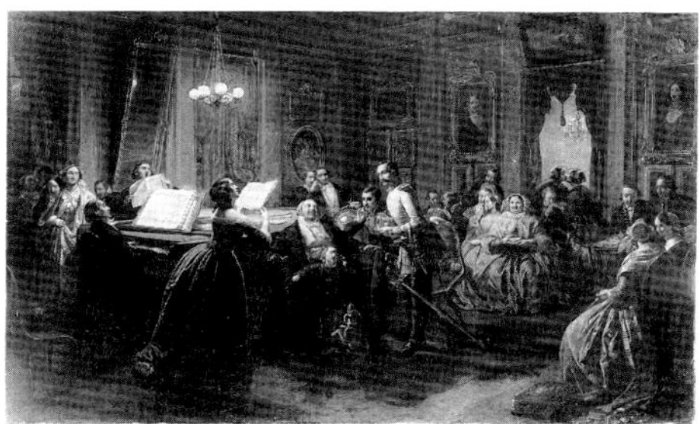

Fig. 173. Johann Peter Hasenclever, *Teatime*, 1850, oil, Potsdam, Stiftung Preussische Schlösser und Gärten

jected the political hopes of their times into the past.

In his much-quoted words, Menzel states his aim of depicting 'the prince hated by princes and revered by the people . . ., old Fritz, who lives in the people'[12], 'the man of the people', 'whose memory is sacred beyond all others to the bourgeoisie'[13]. While Menzel was working on this book, Frederick-William III was replaced after forty-three years on the throne by his son, upon whom rested hopes of renewal and of gaining a constitution. They were soon disappointed. This monarch, with his romantic inclinations, dreamed of returning to the social order of the past, and Frederick became an opposition figure once more. When the attempts of the bourgeoisie to escape through their own efforts in the form of a short-term revolutionary alliance with the urban proletariat failed, due in part to that proletariats fear of extremism, the appeal to the enlightened monarch took a new turn and the accent was then on change without the risk of radical upheaval.

Menzel probably did not escape this state of mind. The fact that 'he sometimes had to squander a theme worthy of an oil painting – !!' by making his small woodcuts of it for the *History of Frederick the Great*[14] does not explain in itself why his ideas for pictures had their origins in these woodcuts. Similarly, the aesthetics of these pictures, which aroused reservations, if not opposition, for a very long time, were based on the progressive ideas of the period before the March revolts. The same arguments put forward in the dispute over the paintings of Belgian history, around 1842–3, and strongly politically biased (the young Hegelians playing a considerable role in this debate), may also serve to defend the method by which Menzel managed to actualize historical reality, in an effort to achieve authenticity in the depiction of the world of objects, as well as souls. C.K.

1. Letter to Carl Heinrich Arnold, 6 September 1840, Wolff, 1914, p. 49.
2. Letter to Carl Heinrich Arnold, 16 January 1849, Wolff, 1914, p. 158.
3. Letter to Carl Heinrich Arnold, no date, Wolff, 1914, p. 141. Dating possible through the exhibition for charity" described in this letter. The pictures of famous painters of Belgian history were exhibited in it, plus a number of artists from Berlin, as well as *The Petition*. This exhibition took place in May at the Academy of Art (Berlinische Nachrichten von staats- und gelehrten Sachen, no. 110 and 114, 12 and 17 May 1849).
4. *Cf.* the previous note.
5. Letter to Carl Heinrich Arnold, 26 December 1851, Wolff, 1914, p. 154.
6. Letter to Carl Heinrich Arnold, 8 January 1851, Wolff, 1914, p.152; Friedrich Eggers, Deutsches Kunstblatt, 1851, p. 150.
7. Letter to Carl Heinrich Arnold, 26 December 1851, Wolff, 1914, p. 154.
8. *Cf.* for example Weber, 1973, an interesting selection of letters written by representatives of each of the political groupings.
9. For detailed information, *cf.* With, 1979, p. 205–7.
10. Wolff, 1914, p. 136.
11. Letter to Carl Heinrich Arnold, 4 January 1847, Wolff, 1914, p. 100.
12. Letter to J.J. Weber, 17 July 1839, Wolff, 1914, p. 32.
13. Letter to J.J. Weber, 24 February 1839, Wolff, 1915, p. 21.
14. 'Series of marginal notes' drawn up on the 28 October 1887 by Max Jordan (Staatliche Museen zu Berlin, central archives, Menzel archives, file VII, no. 2).

48

The Round Table of Frederick II at Sanssouci. Sketch

1848

Oil on pen and ink, on paper, canvas backing
34 × 27.8cm
Berlin, Nationalgalerie (A III 503)

Provenance: Hermann Pächter (R. Wagner Gallery, Berlin); acquired by the museum in 1889.
Exhibitions: Berlin, 1863?; Berlin, 1895, no. 129; Hamburg, 1896, no. 88; Vienna, 1896, no. 268; Berlin, 1935, no. 20; Berlin, 1980 A, no. X, reprod. p. 139; Paris, 1994, no. 171, col. reprod.
Bibliography: Donop, 1902, no. 156; Tschudi, 1905 A, no. 66; Waldmann, 1941, p. 22–24, p. 45, fig. 28; cat. NG, 1986, s.p., fig. 71; Lammel, 1988, p. 36-43, fig. 18 (col); Zangs, 1992, p. 87 *et seq.*

In the second of the four volumes of the *History of Frederick the Great* by Kugler, who dealt with the ten years of peace after the two Silesian wars under the title *Glory*, there appears the famous chapter 22, 'The philosopher of Sanssouci', from which were taken the subjects of the two most famous paintings of Frederick II. In both cases the large pictures show the keen interest of the draughtsman. Menzel does not depict specific events but describes the life of culture, devoted to philosophy, science and the arts, which unfolded on a daily basis at the 'pleasure chateau of the royal vine' built by Frederick near Potsdam. 'At Sanssouci, all the elements necessary for the most exquisite delectation of intellectual things

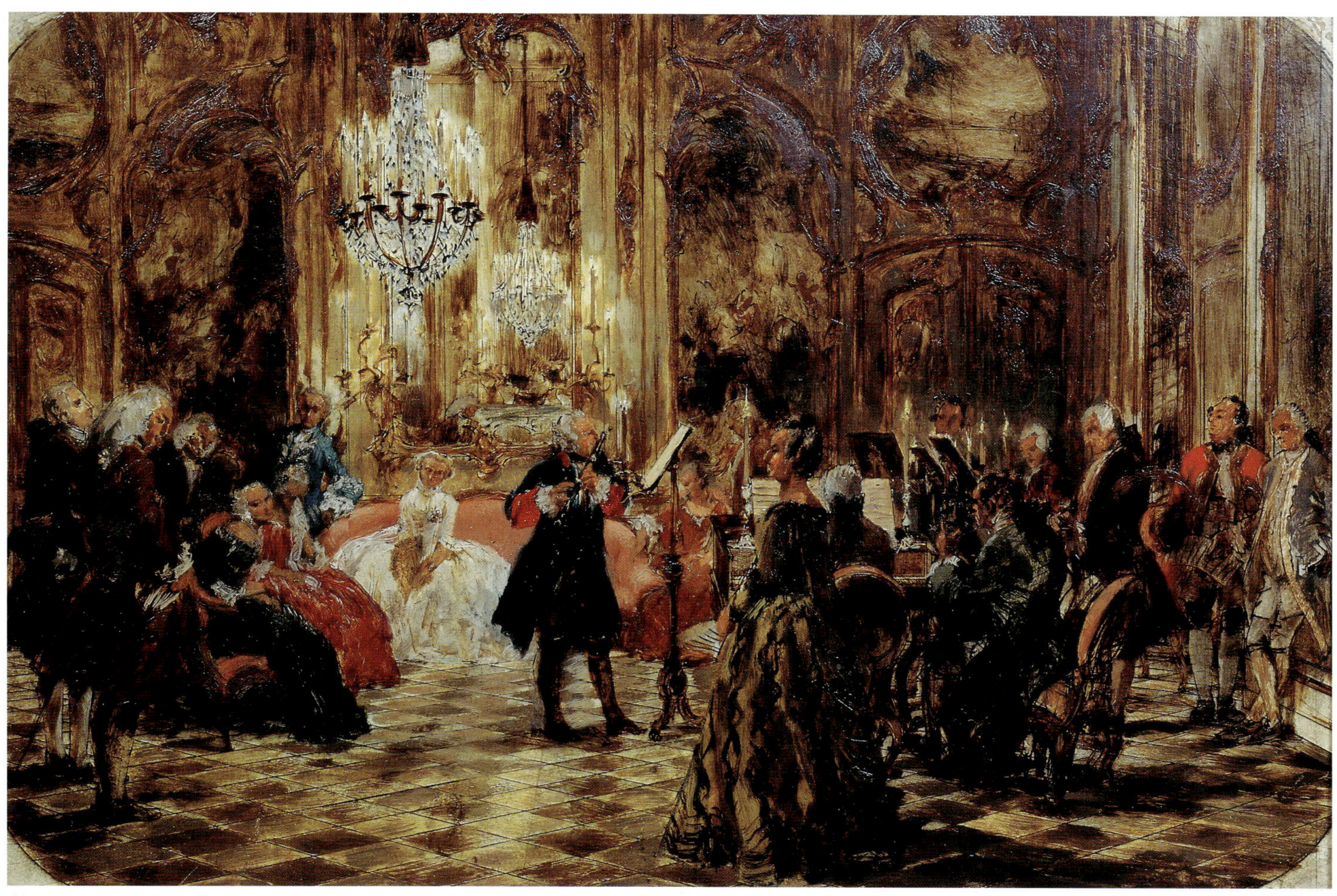

49

were brought together', it reads, before the explanations of the all too human quarrel with the person who at times was the centre of the circle: Voltaire. The writer lived at Potsdam for three years, from 1750 to 1753, as chamberlains servant and regular sounding board and advisor to the king on the subject of his poetry and prose works.

The text provides only general information for the woodcut (almost full-page format) depicting the royal supper[1]: 'It was only at the evening meal that the circle of intimate friends was accustomed to gather together for pleasure and amusement. At these gatherings, it was all wit and intellect.' Voltaire and Frederick faced each other as sovereigns of the mind. The woodcut shows a supper lit by chandeliers though, in the picture, it is still light. The great French windows of the round marble salon at Sanssouci open into the obscure space outside; the lower edge of the picture cuts off the guests. The king is addressing Voltaire directly. At the round table (where no person present has special privileges) are seated the soldiers (George and Jakob Keith [*cf.* cat. 139–40], General von Stille, General von Rothenburg) and men of intellect: in addition to Voltaire, the Marquis Jean-Baptiste d'Argens, the Venetian Count Francesco Algarotti (philosopher and art connoisseur), the doctor Julian de La Mettrie. Nearly all are foreign, more or less political refugees. Their welcome in Prussia is evidence of Frederick IIs spirit of tolerance and liberal-mindedness.

The subtle arrangement seats the king in the middle, but gives him the role of observer. The action involves two speakers leaning towards each other across the table, Voltaire and Algarotti. While the animated head movements of the other guests do not seem to indicate that they are following this dispute, the attention given to it by Frederick lends it special significance. Around 1800 the graphical industry had already produced a similar image (*cf.* fig. 99). The painter who chronicled the life of Voltaire, Jean Huber, had also painted a round table with famous contemporary figures dining and avidly discussing matters in the presence of the philosopher at Ferney, where he spent his old age[2].

Before it was reproduced on a grand scale, this oil sketch was traced and marked into squares[3], a careful procedure contrasting with the improvisation that Menzel latterly allowed himself. During the execution of the picture, however, the three figures in the foreground and the king were modified again.

The painting (fig. 100) was exhibited for the first time in 1850 with the significant title 'Frederick the Great with his friends and companions'. The unaccustomed allusion to rococo style, and the liberal spirit are noticeable. The diary of August Varnhagen von Ense, a civil servant dismissed in his youth for his democratic sympathies, says: 'Intellect and vigour inspired Prussia then. Now we have a rotten synod, false piety and hypocrisy . . . I curse this decline daily'[4]. The painting was bought by the Association of Friends of the Arts of Prussia, where it hung in the gallery until it entered the Nationalgalerie in 1873[5].

C.K.

1. Bock, 1923, no. 605.
2. Oxford, The Voltaire Foundation.
3. Berlin, Kupferstichkabinett (SZ Menzel Kat 157); Lammel, 1988, fig. 19. Other preliminary drawings, notably Kat 158–68, N 1954.
4. 2 October 1853. Quoted from Ellwart, 1985, p. 19. Ellwart, 1988, p. 124.
5. This painting was one of those lost by the Nationalgalerie at the end of the second World War.

49

The Flute Concert at Sanssouci. Sketch

1848

Oil on pen and ink, on paper, canvas backing
31.5 × 43.8cm
Berlin, Nationalgalerie (A III 504)

Provenance: Herman Pächter (R. Wagner Gallery, Berlin); acquired by the museum in 1889.
Exhibitions: Berlin, 1863?; Berlin, 1895 A, no. 132; Hamburg, 1896, no. 91; Vienna, 1896, no. 266; Berlin, 1935, no. 24; Berlin, 1980, no. XI, reprod. p. 140; Berlin, 1987 A, no. G 3, reprod.
Bibliography: Donop, 1902, no. 666; Tschudi, 1905 A, no. 77; cat. NG, 1907, no. 969; Wolff, 1914, p. 154; Justi, 1920, p. 167; Waldmann, 1941, p. 25, p. 46, fig. 34; Beenken, 1944, p. 307; Rave, 1943; Forster-Hahn, 1977, p. 253 *et seq.*; cat NG, 1986, s.p., fig. 72; Hermand, 1985, p. 23, fig. 11; Lammel, 1988, p. 44, fig. 21 (col.); Zangs, 1992, p. 101.

'I can justly say that I have never made things easy for myself, but I've never taken on anything quite like this with (more than anything else) the lighting constraint – candlelight on all sides and from the top'[1].

The chosen place is the concert room at the château of Sanssouci, with its paintings of scenes from Ovid by Antoine Pesne alternating with the stucco ornaments of Johann August Nahl. In the woodcut for Kuglers book on the same theme[2], which brings together in a smaller space a lesser number of figures (all cut off) beneath the bright light of a chandelier and candlelight, composed in a similar way to that of the painting, the king looks youthful and kind and is wearing a sumptuous brocade outfit. In the painting he looks more mature, thinner and is wearing a simple uniform jacket. While the women are anonymous in the woodcut, the painting depicts 'one of the evening concerts that he used to give for his sister, the Margrave Wilhelmine von Bayreuth, on the occasion of her last visit (1750)'[3]. These details allow us to imagine that the memoirs of the knight Chasot (*cf.* cat. 63) served as a textual source. The latter did in fact attend concerts given by the king from 1734 on, and he is depicted in the background of the painting. He recounts the visit of the two margraves to Berlin in August 1750, when the king had gathered together a number of German princes, with great pomp[4].

After the *Round Table,* this picture gives a new perception of the flourishing culture of Fredericks time. Moreover, since it was a question of complementing the first painting, all the figures around the king have been changed. Among the musicians, who watch the flautist fixedly, waiting their turn at the end of his solo, can be recognized Carl Philippe Emmanuel Bach, seated at the harpsichord; standing on the right is the concert master Franz Benda; leaning behind him, a little apart, is Frederick IIs flute teacher, Johann Joachim Quantz. The conductor of the orchestra, Carl Heinrich Graun[5], has slipped off into the audience and is on the left, near the mirror. The presence beside the musicians of the old Countess Camas, a confidante of the king, shows the care taken to depict an ideal group of intellects, beyond differences of rank[6]. Her bird-like face, as spiritual as it is ugly, lies on the median axis of the painting. Her counterpart on the left, under the chandelier, is the Margrave Wilhelmine, wearing a dazzling white dress, and seated, head bent, like an elegant and dream-like apparition, on the salmon pink sofa. This sister, whom Frederick loved greatly, was intelligent and gifted in artistic matters. Frederick corresponded with her until her premature death, which drove him to despair. On her left is the other sister, Amalia. The mathematician and physician Pierre de Maupertuis, president of the Academy of Sciences, absent-mindedly raises his eyes to the ceiling. On the left edge of the picture is Baron Jakob Friedrich von Bielfelt, and in front of him the heavy silhouette of the operatic director Gustav Adolf von Gotter.

Older representations of this subject can be found. But the comparison with the engraving by Peter Haas, which Menzel must have known as a reprint (1840) shows the richness and nuance of his composition, and above all its innovation – the psychology, not only shown by attitudes and expressions but linked with subtlety to the surrounding atmosphere, to the changing 'tonality' of the light. Thus the rhythmic series of candle flames matches the group of musicians, while reflections from the chandelier fall on the audience. Only the king on the right has both a candle and chandelier reflection in the mirror. Where have similar effects been created? Possibly in a composition by Gabriel de Saint-Aubin, *The Concert*[7]. In the more directly accessible Berlin tradition, we should bear in mind the compositions depicting card players by Johann Erdmann Hummel[8], whose

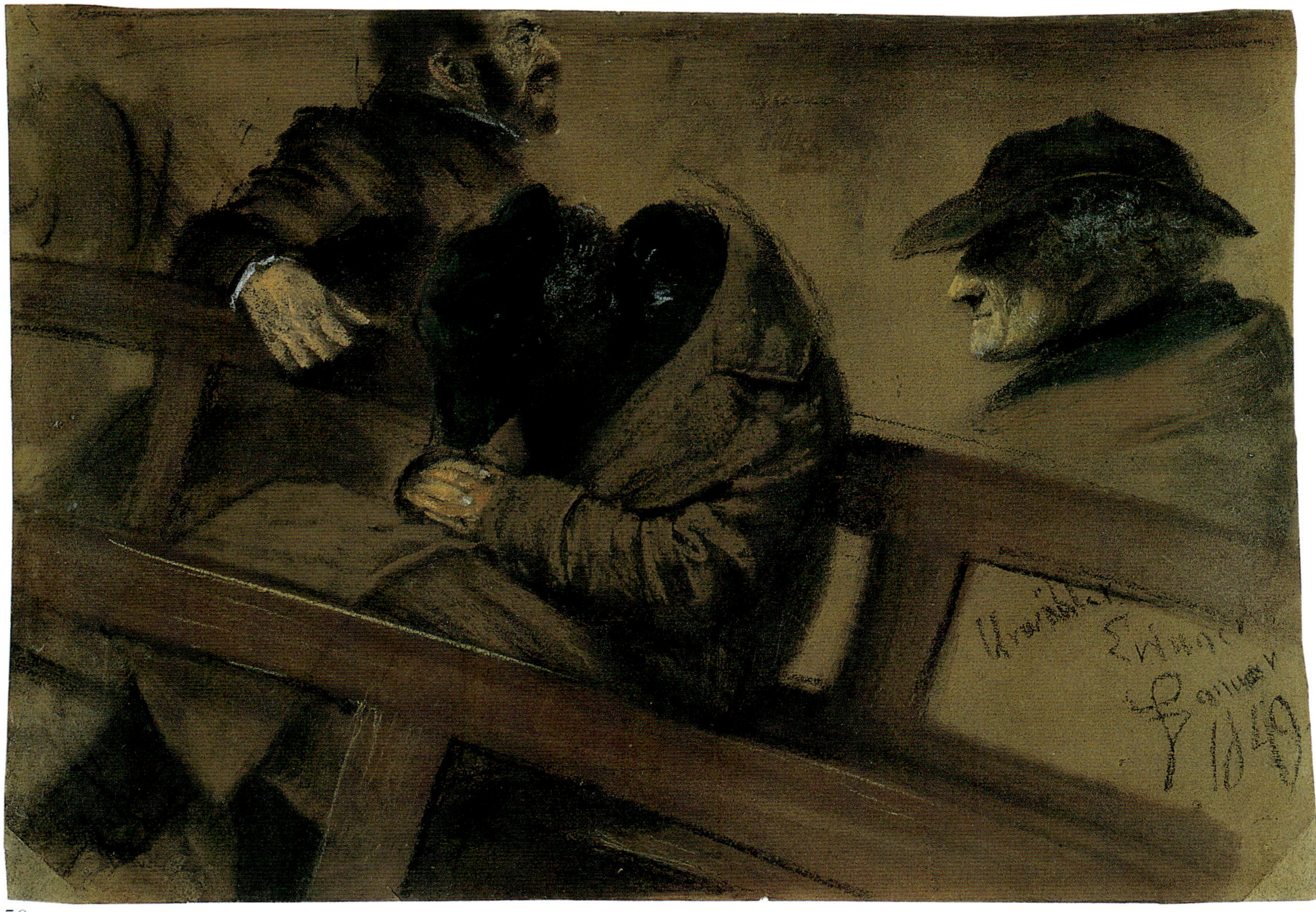

50

minute, excessive rationality is transformed into a mysterious rigidity which cannot compare with the poetic density of Menzels atmospheres. We should also remember the incomparable evidence of the old masters – Rembrandt. Finally, an artist from Düsseldorf, Johann Peter Hasenclever, had a predilection for the play of lamplight, in the Dutch tradition of imitation of Caravaggio. In 1850 he finished the large format *Tea Time*[9] (fig. 173), whose composition, peppered with contemporary satire of political resonance, has sufficient parallels with *The Flute Concert* to allow the distance between prose and poetry to be measured. The fact that where Menzel has a shimmering chandelier, Hasenclever has a gas-lamp shedding a milky light, gives an initial indication of the difference. C.K.

1. Letter to Carl Heinrich Arnold, 26 December 1851, Wolff, 1914, p. 154.
2. Bock, 1923, no. 606. The scene is located this time at the royal castle of Potsdam. At the end of the book is a second illustration of the flute concert, showing an older king and Franz Benda, caricatured (Bock, 1923, no. 796).
3. F[riedrich] E[ggers], [chronicle], *Deutsches Kunstblatt*, 2, no. 19, 10 May 1851, p. 150.
4. *Cf.* Schlözer, 1856, p. 112 and ff. and appendix p. 212–13. Menzel knew of Chasots memoires.
5. And not his brother, Johann Gottlieb, who was not leader of the orchestra, but violin soloist, asked latterly to lead the orchestra (konzertmeister). Information kindly supplied by Michael OLoghlin, Paddington, Australia.
6. Hermand, 1985, p. 38 and ff.
7. *Etching by Antoine-Jean Duclos.*
8. *Cf.* also cat. 19.
9. 97 × 152cm, Potsdam, Stiftung Preussische Schlösser und Gärten. Soiné, 1990, no. 217 and p. 192–4.

50

Two Voters and Study of One of the Heads

1849

Pastel

17 × 24cm

Annotated and dated at the bottom right: *Urwähler Erinner: Januar 1849*

Private collection

Provenance: 1905 Julius Aufseesser, Berlin; private collections; 1963 Stein collection, Cologne.

Exhibition: Bremen, 1963, no. 38.

Bibliography: Tschudi, 1905 A, no. 219.

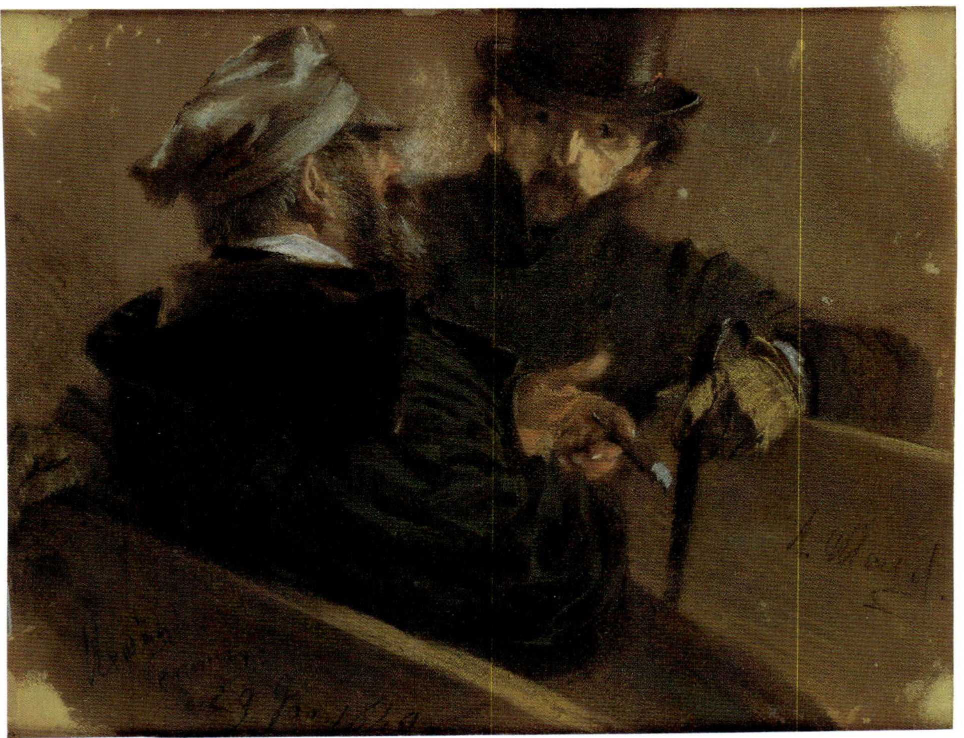

51

51

Conversation between Two Voters
1849

Pastel
18 × 23cm
Signed in the middle on the right: *A.Menzel.* – Annotated and dated at the bottom left: *Urwähler Erinner: 29 Jan. 1849*
Berlin, Berlin (NG 2/52)
Exhibited in Berlin only

Provenance: Private collections; Asta von Friedrich, Berlin; acquired by the museum in 1952.
Exhibitions: Berlin, 1905, no. 5741; Berlin, 1955 B, no. 35; Bremen, 1963, no. 39; Berlin, 1965, no. 21; London, 1965, no. 11; Würzburg, 1966, no. 7; Berlin, 1981, no. 5132; Hamburg, 1982, no. 44, col. reprod. p. 90; Berlin, 1984, no. 45; Cambridge, 1984, no. 37;
Bibliography: Tschudi, 1905 A, no. 217; Zimmerman, 1953, p. 2, fig. 8; Kaiser, 1956, p. 64; fig. 34; Hütt, 1965, fig. 11; cat NG, 1976, p. 268, reprod.; Honisch, 1979, p.150.

Just as he had expressed his views at great length in a letter to Carl Heinrich Arnold on what he had seen in Berlin immediately after the March 1948 uprising (*cf.* cat. 45), Menzel reflected a little later on the political consequences of these events, in particular the introduction of the parliamentary vote. Between the fighting and disarmament of the population on 12 November 1848 (which marked the true end of the revolution, followed on 5 December by the dissolution of the National Assembly), elections were held on 1 and 8 May, with poll tax-based suffrage according to the 'three class system'. Immediately after, fighting broke out in the interior of the country, leading to the victory of the reactionary forces. Prussia gained its constitution, but it was granted by the king.

Menzel recalled the elections in a letter: 'Yesterday it was election day throughout the State. In my ward voting went on from eight in the morning till nine at night (with a half-hour break at midday), which was fairly acceptable, since in some wards voting went on till midnight or two in the morning. In some areas, voting had finished by the afternoon. These were the primary elections – this week those elected have got to choose their MPs for Prussia and Frankfurt. Leaving aside the importance of this event, there was so much that was interesting and fine to see in the preliminary assemblies alone!'[1].

Each citizen over the age of twenty-four had the right to take part in the primary elections and to choose a certain number of delegates, who met every morning at the committee meeting held in the Schauspielhaus concert hall at Schinkel, for the final election of members of parliament on 8 May.

After these events, Menzel drew numerous small sketches in pencil showing armed citizens and voters as well as the discussions preceding the election of members of parliament[2]. After these hastily drawn sketches of January 1849, Menzel drew some pastels depicting voters from memory, as he was accustomed to do at this time. Forty years after the elections, Fontane recalls his polling station in a wool storehouse in Neue Königstrasse, where everyone turned up, with only a few exceptions, in their everyday clothes (mostly craftsmen, innkeepers and cellarmen). Later he described these amusing events with a hint of nostalgic irony[3]. It was a slow, difficult process, as the voters, who were still new to the whole procedure, had difficulty in making up their minds. So it is not surprising to see exhausted men depicted in Menzel's chalk drawings, involved in long discussions, as in one pastel[4] prepared by a small sketch containing numerous figures, or in another which shows an elderly man asleep sitting down, with his chin on his chest (and beside it a study of the head of the same man awake, in profile), and a man with a beard who seems to be involved in an animated discussion. There is also a pencil drawing for the second composition shown, depicting two men conversing, one with a cigar in his mouth and wearing a cap, showing his allegiance to the political left, and the other wearing a top hat and yellow gloves, suggesting the political right.

This chalk drawing of early 1849, and therefore after the defeat, shows none of the excitement aroused by this atmosphere of hoped-for political change which was evident in the letter, but rather suggests a climate of scepticism and resignation which took a progressive hold. M.R.-R.

1. Letter to Carl Heinrich Arnold, 3 May 1848, Wolff, 1914, p. 133.
2. Berlin, Kupferstichkabinett.
3. *Cf.* Fontane, 1982 A, p. 70.
4. Essen, Museum Folkwang.

52
The Petition
1849

Oil on canvas
60 × 75cm
Hechingen, Burg Hohenzollern
Exhibited in Washington and Berlin only

Provenance: 1863 Baroness von Wilken, Dresden; 1885 Countess von Nostitz-Wallwitz, Dresden; 1904 private collection, Dresden; 1912 collection of the Emperor William II (at the Berlin palace); Hohenzollern family.
Exhibitions: Berlin, 1849; Berlin., 1863; Berlin, 1885, no. 24; Dresden, 1887; Dresden, 1903 B; Dresden, 1904, no. 2349; Berlin, 1912, no. 219, pl. 86 (no. 70 of small catalogue); Berlin, 1929, no. 970; Berlin, 1935, no. 17; Berlin, 1955 B, no. 38, fig. 27; Berlin, 1986, no. VIII, 21 b.
Bibliography: Jordan, 1980, p. 42; Jordan, 1895, p. 28, reprod. p. 27; Beta (1898) 1992, p. 40; Beta (1899) 1992, p. 63; Jordan, 1905, p. 46, reprod. p. 47; Tschudi, 1905 A, no. 60; Scheffler, 1922, p.170; Scheffler, 1938, p. 66 *et seq.*; Waldmann, 1941, p. 21; Beenken, 1944, p. 305, fig. 104; With, 1975, p. 152–5; Ellwart, 1985, p. 10–14; Lammel, 1988, p. 34–6; Zangs, 1992, p. 95–7.

The first painting in the 'long series' (*cf.* the introductory comments to the Frederick the Great cycle) shows the king of Prussia as exemplary administrator of his territories and a conscientious and just father to his country. 'Tradition has it that one of the trees in front of the palace at Potsdam was where supplicants stood to attract the kings attention. It became known as the tree of grace.' This was how Menzel spoke of an illustration for the forty-second chapter of the *History of Frederick the Great*[1]. *The Petition*, however, does not show that tree. The scene with two supplicants is transposed into open countryside. In the distance can be seen the New Palace which the king had built later. As for the atmosphere of the painting, Menzel seems to have had in mind another engraving illustrating Kuglers book, the landscape with reapers which introduces chapter twelve (Bock 525). While the king approaches on horseback, followed by two officers, a young village couple in their best clothes wait under a willow. The young man is hesitant and his companion tries vehemently to persuade him. (Kugler, who devoted several chapters to the kings good deeds towards his subjects as he grew older, reproduces the long account of a young theologian from Thuringia who was given the task of taking complaints to the king. Seized with fear, he was literally dragged before the sovereign by two officers, to be treated with all the more benevolence.) At the time this painting was executed, around 1848, when political complaints took the form of daily petitions addressed to the king and to the National Assembly, and when, in the country in particular, the bonds of feudal dependence and taxes of all kinds were questioned, those contemporary with the picture could only interpret it within the context of current realities. Also, the idea of a vital alliance with the peasants permeated Prussian liberalism, with the obvious intention of erecting defences against the radical movements that had sprung up from the poverty-stricken rural populations[2]. The peasants depicted by Menzel visibly belong to the better-heeled section of the population.

In the picture, the approaching king occupies the centre space exactly. There is a similar figure, frontal and on horseback, in *Night Attack at Hochkirch*, but the expression is quite different. (Could *Hochkirch* be the composition which was being prepared when the idea for *The Petition* took shape?[3] Probably.)

However, the onlookers gaze must pass over the vast wide-open space to alight on the king, in the middle foreground, before the bend in the track. The couple in the extreme foreground of the picture, under the willow, may have been drawn there simply to act as a 'repoussoir'. But the painter has concentrated all his attention on them. They are in full light, an oblique morning light which shines between the figures, illuminating a hem here, a forehead there, or a fold in the sheet of white paper, and it adds a salmon hue to the pale pink tones of the large areas of shadow on the young girls dress. The left side of the picture is much more conventional. Inspiration is clearly lacking, and the painter was visibly pressed by a deadline. The exhibition organized at the Academy by the young painters of Berlin was an important event, for which the banker Wagener had brought out his collection of large history paintings commissioned from two hotly debated Belgian painters. On this occasion, Julius Schrader was also showing his painting *Frederick the Great after the Battle of Kolin*, representing the hero in defeat, a little like the *Napoleon at Fontainebleu* by Delaroche. Later, Menzel would hang a reproduction of Schraders painting in his studio.

Menzel recounts that the proposal for the king to buy *The Petition* was never followed through. According to him, the painting was forgotten about for almost a year, in the hands of the general museums director Ignaz von Olfers. This 'courtier, who harked back to the good old days, wanted me to flatten and tidy up the track on which the king was approaching. He did not feel it was worthy of the court. But, dear sir, I could not agree to that – I preferred to suffer a years privations'[4]. This was the first of a number of conflicts over the illustrations of Frederick the Great (*cf.* also cat. 82, 90), which Menzel viewed as a profession of faith, and over which he would not allow the slightest limitation of his artistic autonomy. C.K.

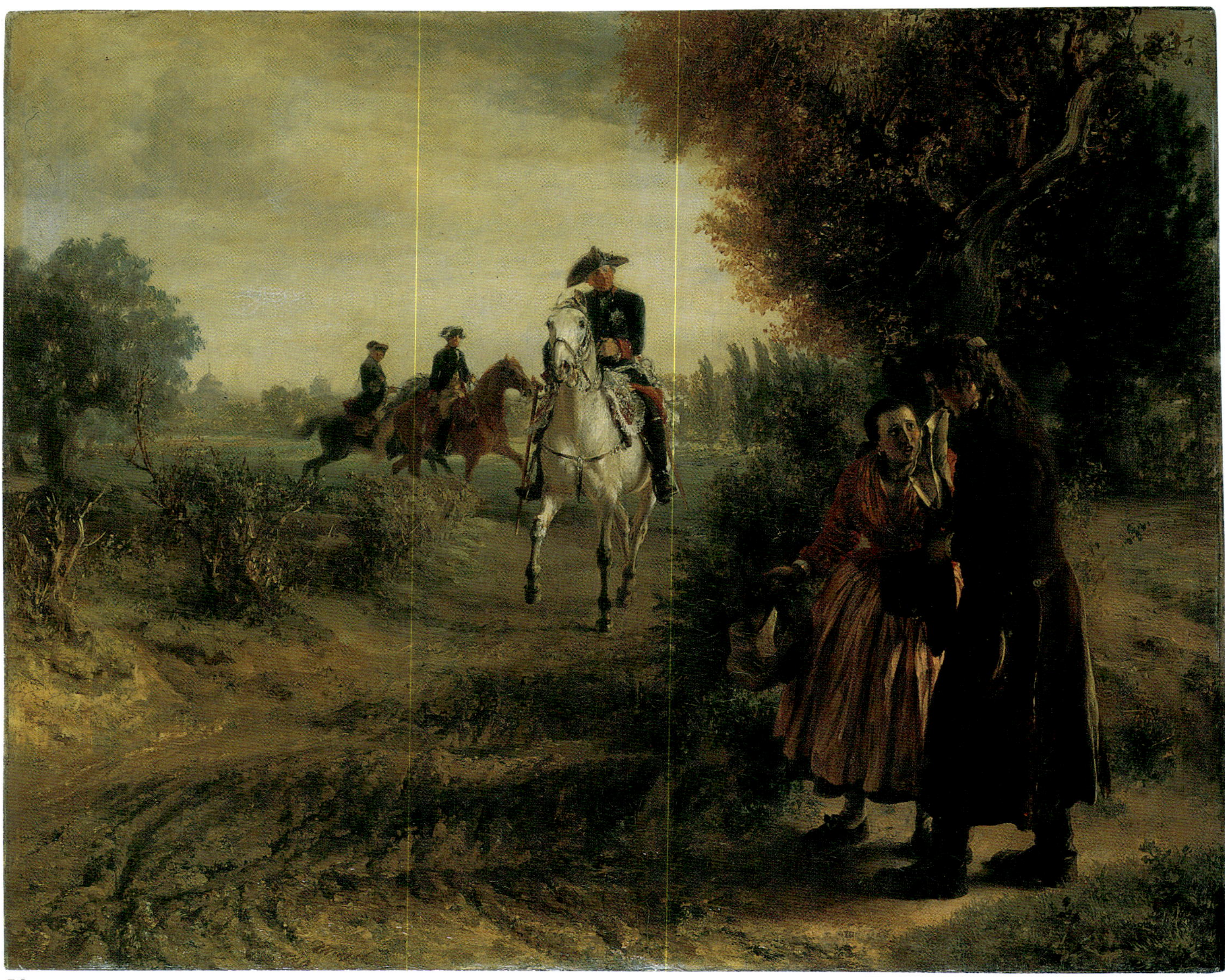

52

1. Bock, 1923, no. 788.
2. Ellwart, 1985, p. 13.
3. Letter to Carl Heinrich Arnold, no date, [May, 1849], Wolff, 1914, p. 141 (*cf.* preliminary remark in this catalogue, p. 231.
4. Beta, 1899, p. 63.

53
Congratulatory Address by Berlin City Council to Prince Frederick William
1850

Watercolour and gouache
80 × 60cm
Signed and dated at the bottom right: *Adolph Menzel. 1850.*
Potsdam, Stiftung Preussische Schlösser und Gärten, Aquarellsammlung (2177 A)
Exhibited in Berlin only

Provenance: Prince Frederick-William of Prussia, later the Emperor Frederick III; Berlin, Hohenzollernmuseum; after 1945, with its current owner.
Exhibitions: Berlin, 1861; Berlin, 1885, no. 26; Berlin, 1895 A, no. 64; Hamburg, 1896, no. 27, p. 32; Vienna, 1896, no. 245; Düsseldorf, 1904, no. 26; Berlin, 1905, no. 115.
Bibliography: Eggers, 1850; Pietsch, 1861; Wessely, 1873, p. 9; Jordan, 1895, p. 33–4, p.50; Tschudi, 1905 A, no. 218; Seidel, 1914, p. 11; Wolff, 1914, p. 147; Lammel, 1993 A, p. 138.

Menzel had barely finished the two hundred woodcuts for the *Works of Frederick the Great* when he was commissioned by Berlin city council to paint a congratulatory address to the kings nephew, Prince Frederick-William, for his coming of age.

From his early days as a lithographer, Menzel was familiar with this kind of diplomacy in pictorial form, so common in the nineteenth century, and used on a wide variety of occasions. Greatly appreciated, and increasingly fashionable in the second half of the century, pictures of this type expressed the bourgeoisie's growing awareness of its value. Derived from ornamental engraving, they were usually created with the help of printing techniques, and also watercolour, or even oil, if necessary. The composition, in its simplest form, followed a standard layout: a picture or some text was set in an illuminated frame, often very refined and rich in allusions, and forming the main ornamentation. At the height of his career as a painter, Menzel received a number of commissions of this kind, and his principle of 'transforming everything into an artistic task'[1] inspired him, even in this relatively minor genre, to create some extraordinary compositions. While adhering to the traditional format of a central text and surrounding ornamentation more closely than in certain later addresses (*cf.* cat. 129, 187), his fertile imagination wove a whole fabric of allusive metaphors, not always easy to interpret. Much later, yet in the same vein, he created lithographs such as *Our Father* in 1837, and the *Companion of Freemasonry Certificate* one year later, to which is attached an album leaf for Emil Loffhagen, in the form of a marvellous wash drawing (fig. 174)[2]. He used watercolour for the first time for the town council commission. Its delicate tones immediately suggest youth. A very fine network of climbing plants stretches over the top of the drawing, divided into three sections containing the three main scenes. Two festoons consisting of coral, shells and snails frame the text to left and right. The extreme popularity and widespread diffusion of such decorative trailing plants was due in part to the rediscovery of the drawings of Albrecht Dürer in 1808, illustrating the prayer book of the Emperor Maximilian (1459–1519), which the lithographer Johann Nepomuk Strixner had reproduced with such great understanding[3].

In addition to the climbing plants, the three scenes of the young prince are separated by four statues representing his most famous ancestors: from left to right, Frederick-William, the Great Elector, Frederick-William I, known as the 'soldier king', Frederick the Great and Frederick-William III.

Frederick-William was the only son of Prince William of Prussia and his wife Augusta, born Princess of Saxe-Weimar-Eisenach. He was born on 18 October 1831 at the New Palace at Potsdam, where he died on 15 June 1888 of cancer of the larynx. Isolated from politics because of his liberal ideas, he was unable to put them into practice during his brief reign (as Frederick III), which only lasted for ninety-nine days.

He can be seen on the left, seated beside a private tutor, accompanied by a fencing master (all wearing vaguely 'mediaeval costumes of the early sixteenth century). From 1844 on, the archaelogist Ernst Curtius gave him private lessons, awakening his interest in history and initiating him, during a trip to northern Germany, into the Hanseatic society of Lübeck, his country of origin. Over the course of many summers, the prince shared his life with friends of his own age, some of bourgeois origins, when he studied law, political sciences and history at Bonn between 1849 and 1852.

The central scene is an allusion to the mediaeval rite of dressing, and at the same time the symbol of goodbyes and of friendship. The prince states his loyalty as he shakes his friends hands. A powerfully built woman, dressed in white, with a crenellated crown on her head, offers him a sword lying on a cushion. She has her back to us. The bear lying at her feet indicates that this is Berolina, the deity of the city of Berlin.

The third and last scene probably alludes to the 1848 Revolution, followed by the young prince with such interest. The March insurgents were the first dead people he had seen. The scene is reminiscent of the traditional representations of St Michael. The Brandenburg, heart of the Prussian monarchy, is saved by saved by a winged Victoria who strikes the devil with her lance. The spirit of evil sniggers under the skirt of a woman with long blonde hair wearing a red and white dress, the Brandenburg colours, while its tail twines round the climbing plants at the top and its paw strikes the fallen crown.

Forming the basis of these scenes are the four naked river gods, which are the incarnation of the great Prussian rivers. They are rocking in fishermens nets. Departing from tradition, Menzel does not represent the provinces by women. Instead the rivers, which make the land fertile, are personified by naked, bearded men, evoking the 'wild men' of the coat of arms of the State of Prussia. On the left is the Vistula, an old man looking at his broken sword, while a crowned eagle digs its claws into his shoulder. The god of the Elbe is being crowned by a virgin. This is an allusion to the sculptures in the cathedral at Magdeburg (situated on the Elbe), representing the wise and foolish virgins. The god of the Oder leans on a small boat. Behind him appears the crowned eagle of the Brandenburgs with an oar. Beneath its open wings, a dwarf dressed in black symbolizes working in the mines of Upper Silesia. Finally, the Rhine god is holding a windlass and brandishing a goblet. With good humour he watches a dwarf wearing a skullcap and a leather apron. Does he represent the important iron industry of the Rhineland or is he a cellarman? As if this were not enough, one discovers small figures everywhere – cupids, animals. There are some preparatory studies in pastel for some of the figures and for the river gods. In spite of the deadline, Menzel did not want to botch the work[4]. When Ludwig Pietsch saw it exhibited in Berlin at the Künstlerhaus in 1861 he commented on the 'surprising subtlety of the execution in the form of a miniature, ... the dazzling beauty'. He also remarked that the 'ideal form and true Romanticism of the river gods' was not

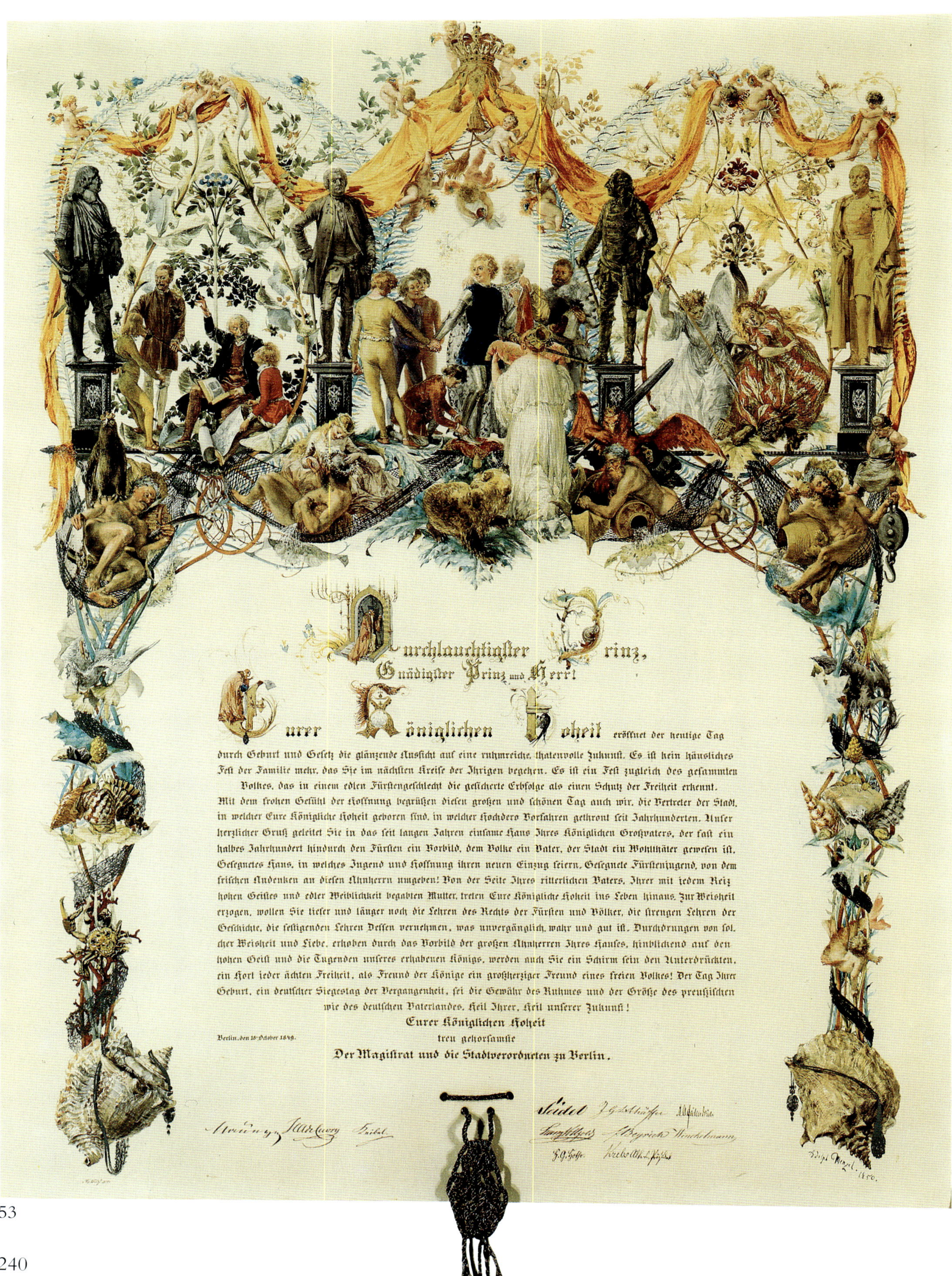

Durchlauchtigster Prinz,
Gnädigster Prinz und Herr!

Eurer Königlichen Hoheit eröffnet der heutige Tag durch Geburt und Gesetz die glänzende Aussicht auf eine ruhmreiche, thatenvolle Zukunft. Es ist kein häusliches Fest der Familie mehr, das Sie im nächsten Kreise der Ihrigen begehen. Es ist ein Fest zugleich des gesammten Volkes, das in einem edlen Fürstengeschlecht die gesicherte Erbfolge als einen Schutz der Freiheit erkennt.

Mit dem frohen Gefühl der Hoffnung begrüßen diesen großen und schönen Tag auch wir, die Vertreter der Stadt, in welcher Eure Königliche Hoheit geboren sind, in welcher Hochdero Vorfahren gethront seit Jahrhunderten. Unser herzlicher Gruß geleitet Sie in das seit langen Jahren einsame Haus Ihres Königlichen Großvaters, der fast ein halbes Jahrhundert hindurch den Fürsten ein Vorbild, dem Volke ein Vater, der Stadt ein Wohlthäter gewesen ist. Gesegnetes Haus, in welches Jugend und Hoffnung ihren neuen Einzug feiern. Gesegnete Fürstenjugend, von dem frischen Andenken an diesen Ahnherrn umgeben! Von der Seite Ihres ritterlichen Vaters, Ihrer mit jedem Reiz hohen Geistes und edler Weiblichkeit begabten Mutter, treten Eure Königliche Hoheit ins Leben hinaus. Zur Weisheit erzogen, wollen Sie tiefer und länger noch die Lehren des Rechts der Fürsten und Völker, die strengen Lehren der Geschichte, die festigenden Lehren Dessen vernehmen, was unvergänglich, wahr und gut ist. Durchdrungen von solcher Weisheit und Liebe, erhoben durch das Vorbild der großen Ahnherren Ihres Hauses, hinblickend auf den hohen Geist und die Tugenden unseres erhabenen Königs, werden auch Sie ein Schirm sein den Unterdrückten, ein Hort jeder ächten Freiheit, als Freund der Könige ein großherziger Freund eines freien Volkes! Der Tag Ihrer Geburt, ein deutscher Siegestag der Vergangenheit, sei die Gewähr des Ruhmes und der Größe des preußischen wie des deutschen Vaterlandes. Heil Ihrer, Heil unserer Zukunft!

Eurer Königlichen Hoheit
treu gehorsamste
Der Magistrat und die Stadtverordneten zu Berlin.

Berlin, den 18. October 1849.

53

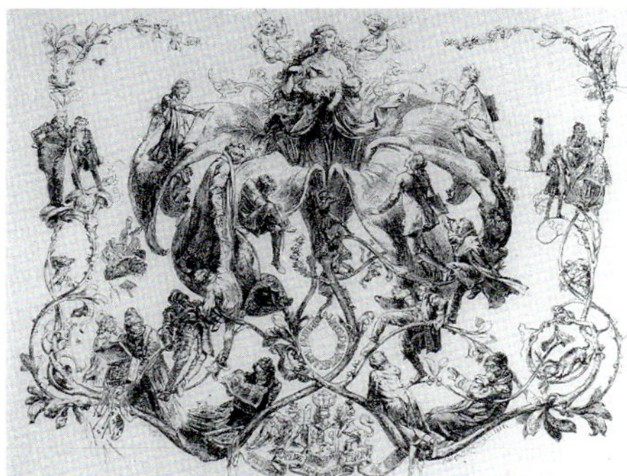

Fig. 174. *Album for Alfred Emil Loffhagen*, 1838, pen and Indian ink, location unknown

in this painters domain. Pietsch thought Menzel's style was 'spiritual and modern, situating it in the second Rococo period[5]. M.R.-R.

1. Letter to Otto Greiner, 6 February 1890, Wolff, 1914, p. 227.
2. Bock, 1923, no. 193 and 195. The drawing for Emil Loffhagen seems to have been lost. *Cf. Zeitschrift für bildende Kunst,* n.s. 7, 1896, reprod. p. 55.
3. In the spiritual vignettes which Menzel had just finished for the *Works of Frederick the Great*, he was inspired by the way in which Dürer had freely, and often humorously, interpreted the text in his drawings.
4. Berlin, Kupferstichkabinett (SZ Menzel, Kat 1139, N 1463, 3590, 3591, 3788, 4255) and Hamburg, Kunsthalle (1978/22). In a letter to Puhlmann written on 30 May 1850, he says: If I come and visit you for a day or two I will not be able to finish the work for the town council to meet the deadline to which I am committed in writing. Wolff, 1914, p. 147.
5. Pietsch, 1861 B.

54

Rococo Fireplace

c. 1850–1

Pastel on brown paper
44.4 × 27.6cm
Berlin, Kupferstichkabinett (SZ Menzel Kat 1595)
Exhibited in Paris and Washington only

Provenance: Hermann Pächter (R. Wagner Gallery, Berlin); acquired by the museum in 1889.
Exhibitions: Berlin, 1905, no. 1865; Berlin, 1955 A, no. 278; Berlin, 1980 A, no. 26, reprod. p. 226.
Bibliography: Donop, 1902, no. 1595; Drescher/Kroll, 1981, no. 473.

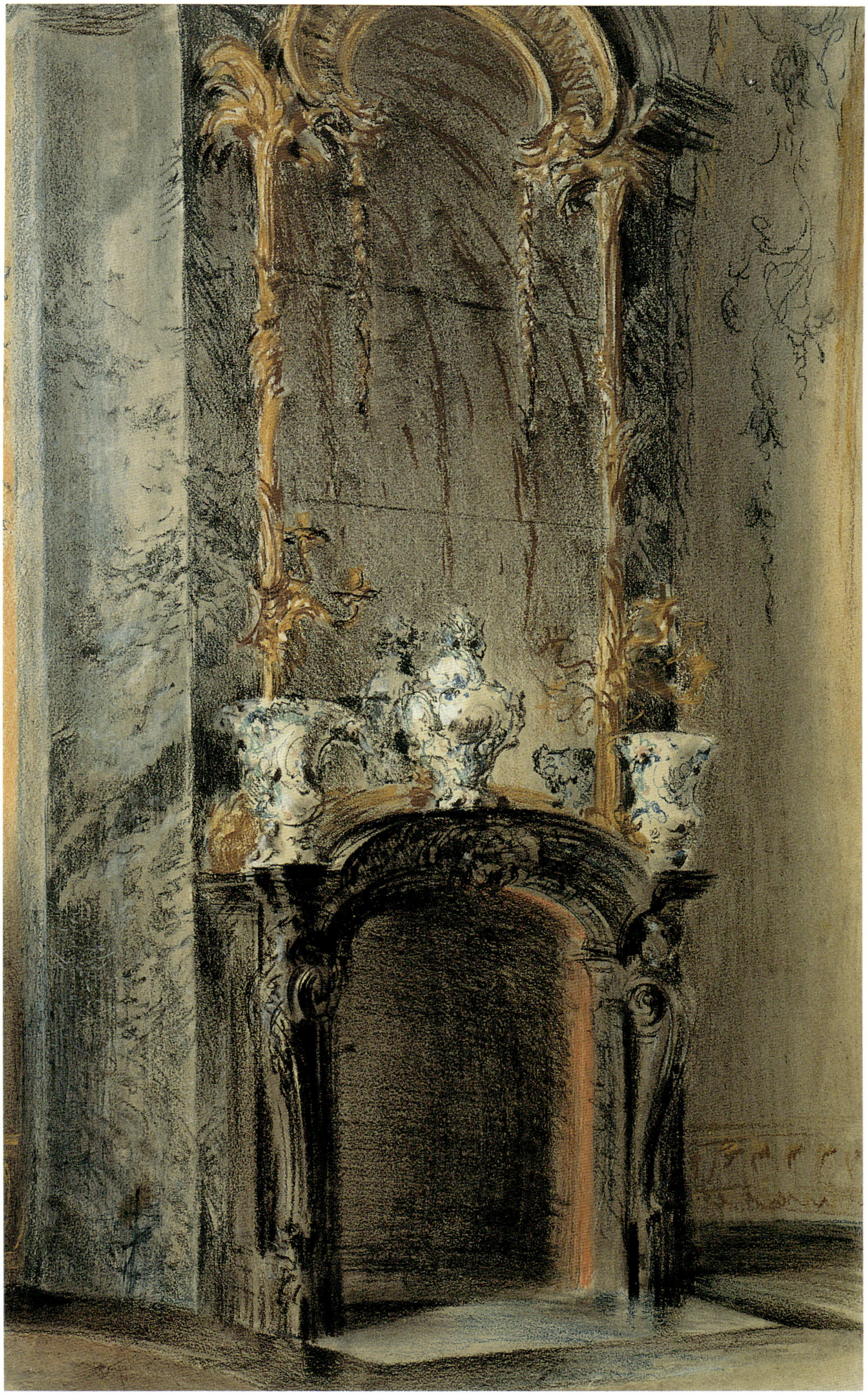

54

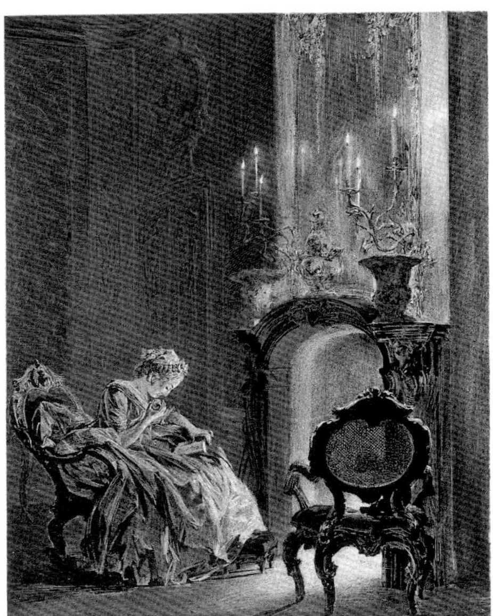

Fig. 175. *Woman Reading by the Fire*, 1851, lithograph (mezzotint)

The Oval Room at the New Palace at Potsdam was designed in 1766 by Carl von Gontard, and formed part of the king's guest accommodation, situated on the ground floor. The surround of the black marble fireplace with its curved mantel resting on scrolls has two krater-type vases on it plus a lidded vase in the middle. Their strong colours distinguish them from their surroundings. It is not known if Menzel found the same group of Saxony porcelain vases on the mantelpiece mentioned in a description of 1786[1]. The undulating shapes of the gilded rococo mirror frame are echoed on the left in a marble panel, while the wallpaper on the right is only roughed in, as is the multicoloured floor. This drawing, with the same date as the studies for *The Flute Concert* and *The Round Table,* was used for the lithograph *Lady Reading by the Fire* (fig. 175[2], the fourth illustration in the collection *Experiments on Stone with Brush and Scraper*, published in 1851. Lit up by the fire as well as by the two chandeliers which emerge from the rocaille of the mirror frame, the reader is wearing a rococo-style dress and is seated in an armchair. She seems to be nibbling a sweetmeat of some kind. A second unoccupied armchair obstructs the view of the hearth.

In the lithograph Menzel turned the fireplace the other way round. There exist two preliminary studies for the armchairs[3], which were also used in *The Flute Concert*. The motif of a woman reading was common at this time, either reading a letter[4] or reading while knitting[5]. The gouache *In the Light of the Reading Lamp*[6] is very close to the lithograph in terms of its lighting. A.H.

1. Nicolai, 1786, t. 3, p. 1239; adapted from Drescher/Kroll, 1981.
2. Bock, 1923, no. 402.
3. *The empty armchair*: Berlin, Kupferstichkabinett (SZ Menzel Kat 691). – *The ladys' chair*: Berlin, Kupferstichkabinett (SZ Menzel Kat 671).
4. Berlin, Kupferstichkabinett (SZ Menzel Nr. 1801).
5. Berlin, Kupferstichkabinett, notebook 7 (1839-1846), p. 8.
6. Again Berlin, Nationalgalerie (SZ Menzel kat 651), missing since 1945.

55

Model Study for Wilhelmine von Bayreuth

c. 1851–2

Coloured chalk
38.6 × 44.1cm
Berlin, Kupferstichkabinett (SZ Menzel Kat 673)
Exhibited in Paris and Berlin only

Provenance: Hermann Pächter (R. Wagner Gallery, Berlin); acquired by the museum in 1889.
Exhibitions: Berlin, 1905, no. 999; Berlin, 1980, no. 218; Vienna, 1985, no. 6; Copenhagen, 1985, no. 4; New York, 1990, no. 21.
Bibliography: Donop, 1902, no. 673; Hermand, 1985, p. 47, fig. 31; Lammel, 1988, p. 42 *et seq.*, fig. 28.

The study was made for *The Flute Concert* (cat. 49) after Menzel had drawn in the main outlines of the painting. There was no doubt that Frederick II's favourite sister, Wilhelmine, Margrave of Bayreuth, in whose honour the concert was given, captivated everyones attention and she rightly occupies the well-lit space in the background. Emily, the artist's beloved sister, posed once more for this study[1]. However, it is not the person herself who is the subject of this study, but her clothing. The great volume of the dress, which seems to have a life of its own, takes up half of the drawing. The red sofa with its shallow back, plus the background, only slightly modified by the colour of the paper, form the part of the drawing that is static. Above the moving landscape of the fabric rise the torso and slightly inclined head, with a serious expression on the face. The melancholy look is underlined and given credence by the figure itself, which seems to be hiding in the abundant material. Menzel clearly emphasizes the plasticity of the dress – the raised folds and creases in the fabric are highlighted in white chalk, and the inner folds in black chalk, while the colour of the paper acts as the background. In this way the fabric seems to have a lightness and movement which contrasts with the heaviness of the human body.

There may be an echo here of Menzel's study of the works of Antoine Watteau, several years before, certainly in the nature of the subject itself. Clearly Menzel was aware that he belonged to the nineteenth century. Even if he borrowed the treatment of Watteaus figures, he neither could nor wanted to bring back 'the magic of the eighteenth century', which no longer had a place in a 'completely different era', the nineteenth century[2]. This magic is obliterated in Menzels strongly rationalist outlook, which leaned towards the reality of the bourgeois world. A.H.

1. *Cf.* the drawings *Emilie crouching down* (Vaduz, Ratjen collection) and *Emilie asleep* (Hamburg, Kunsthalle [1267]).
2. Schmidt, 1957, p. 320 and 324.

56

The Flute Concert of Frederick the Great at Sanssouci

1850–2

Oil on canvas
142 × 205cm
Signed and dated at the bottom right: *Adolph Menzel Berlin 1852*
Berlin, Nationalgalerie (A I 206)

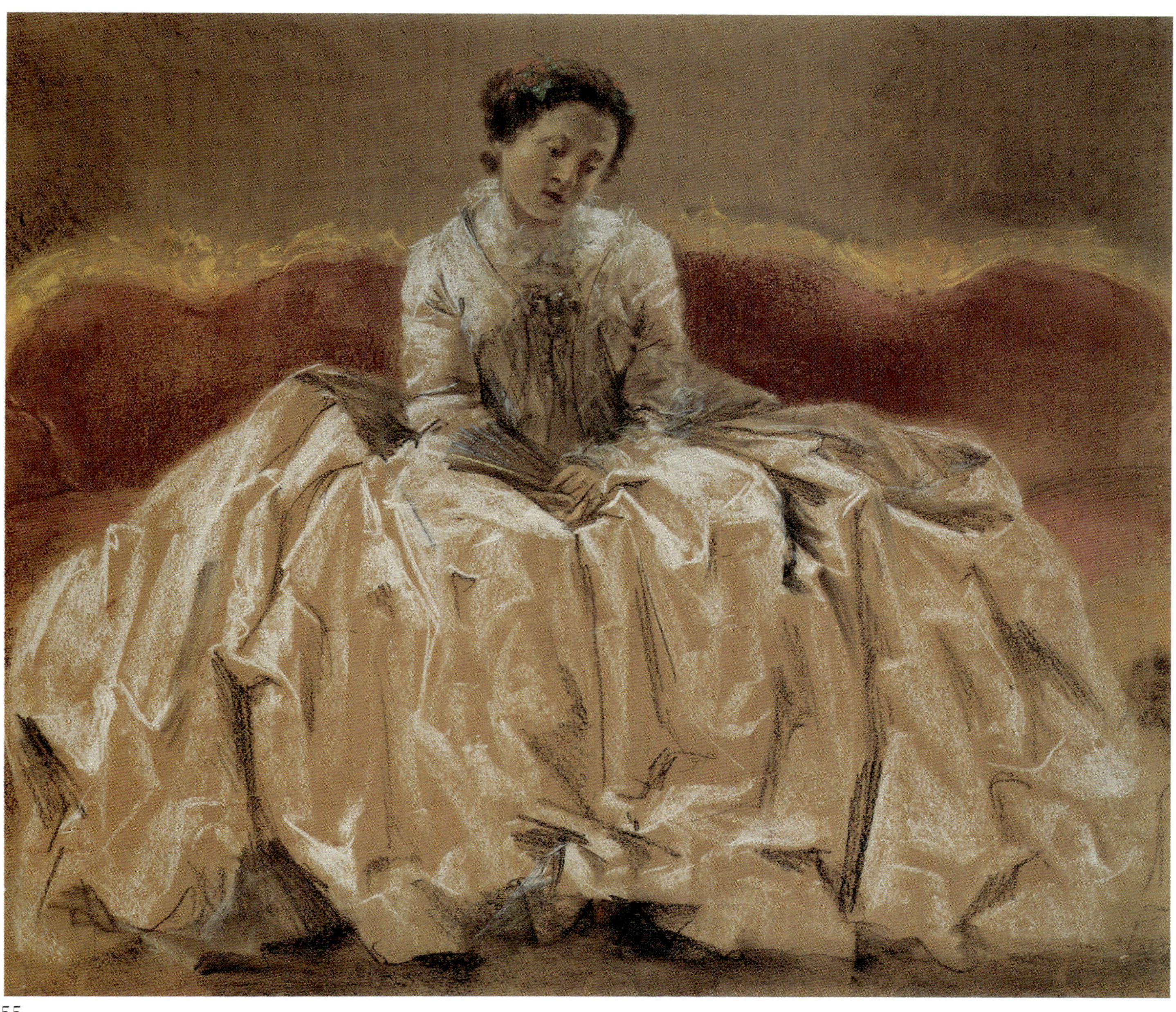

55

Provenance: The work had already been started when it was commissioned (before April 1851) by the sugar manufacturer Jacobs, at Potsdam. It was sold *c.* 1870 to the banker Magnus Herrmann, Berlin, who sold it to the Nationalgalerie in 1875.
Exhibitions: Berlin, 1852, no. 362; Berlin, 1857; Berlin, 1863; Paris, 1878; Berlin, 1895, no. 42; Düsseldorf, 1904, no. 3; Berlin, 1906, no. 1154, reprod. p. 135; Berlin, 1912, no. 221, pl. 88 (no. 92 of small cat.); Berlin, 1935, no. 23; Wiesbaden, 1962, no. 159; Berlin, 1955 B, no. 44, fig. 28; Berlin, 1986, no. VIII.8 d, col. reprod.
Bibliography: Eggers, 1851; Sternberg, (1852) 1935, p. 4 *et seq.*; Schasler, 1857, p. 93; cat. NG, 1879, no. 219; Jordan, 1890, p. 43 *et seq.*; Jordan, 1895, p. 29–30, p. 67; Jordan, 1905, p. 48–50; Jordan, 1905 (1992), p. 265; Herrmann, (1905) 1992, p. 39 *et seq.*; Tschudi, 1905 A, no. 79; Meier-Graefe, 1906, p. 28 *et seq.*, p. 97; Scheffler, 1912, p. 126 et seq.; Wolff, 1914, p. 154; Justi, 1920, p. 167–9; Scheffler, 1938, p. 67 *et seq.*, reprod. p. 178; Waldmann, 1941, p. 25–6, p. 46, figs 35–37, col. pl. V; Rave, 1943; Bergsträsser, 1969; With, 1975, p. 156–72; Forster-Hahn, 1977, p. 253–5, fig. 29; Jensen, 1982, p. 82 *et seq.* col. pl. 18; Hermand, 1985; Ellwart, 1985, p. 27–38; Lammel, 1988, p. 43–6; Zangs, 1992, p. 99–103.

This painting was undoubtedly in progress by the Spring of 1849, after *The Petition* was completed, but it was soon left to one side for work to continue on *The Round Table*. Work was again interrupted briefly in the spring or summer of 1850, in order to give priority to the *Hochkirch* painting[1]. In the following year, the manufacturer Jacobs from Potsdam commissioned the painting, which had already been given one coat of paint, and the artist worked on it until the

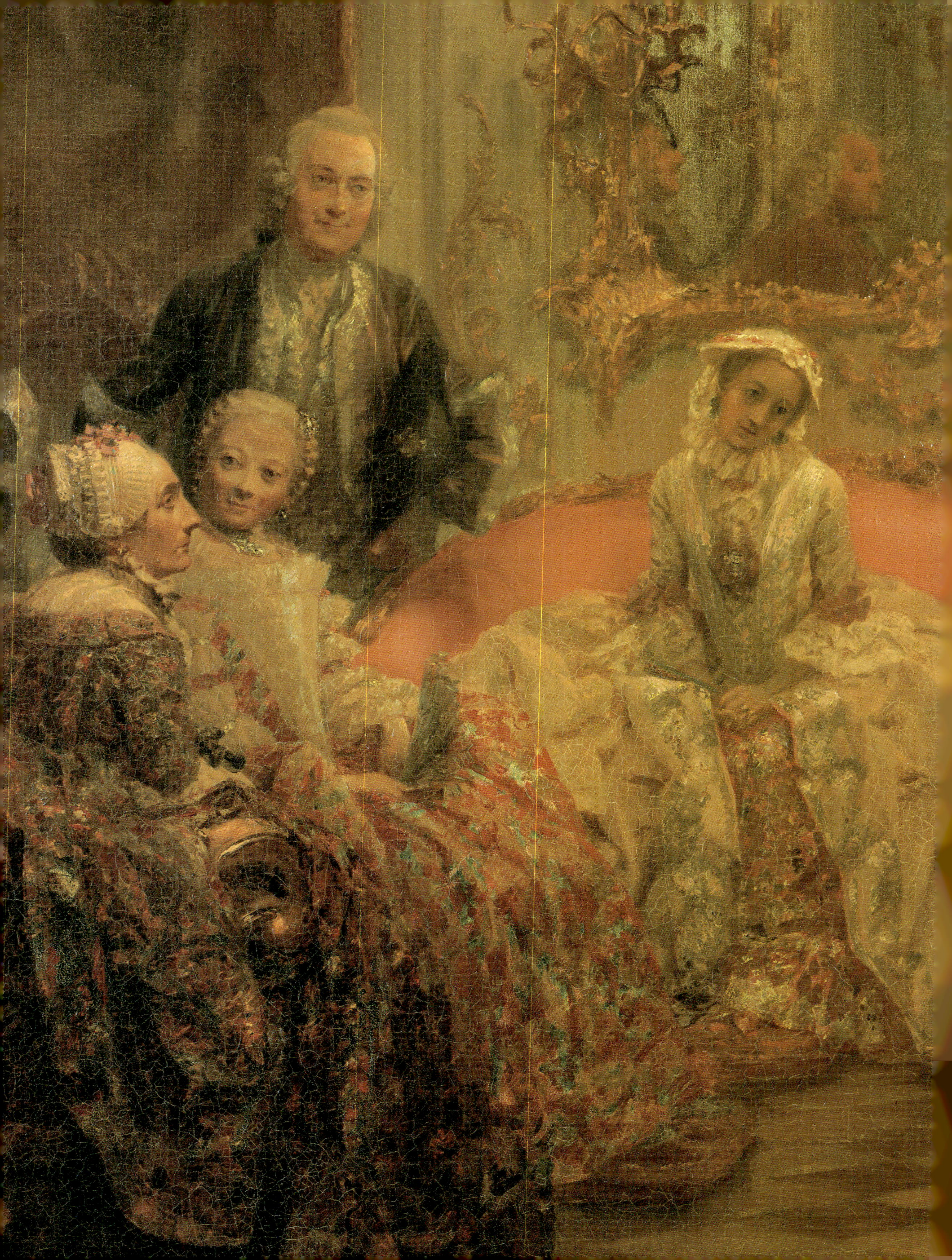

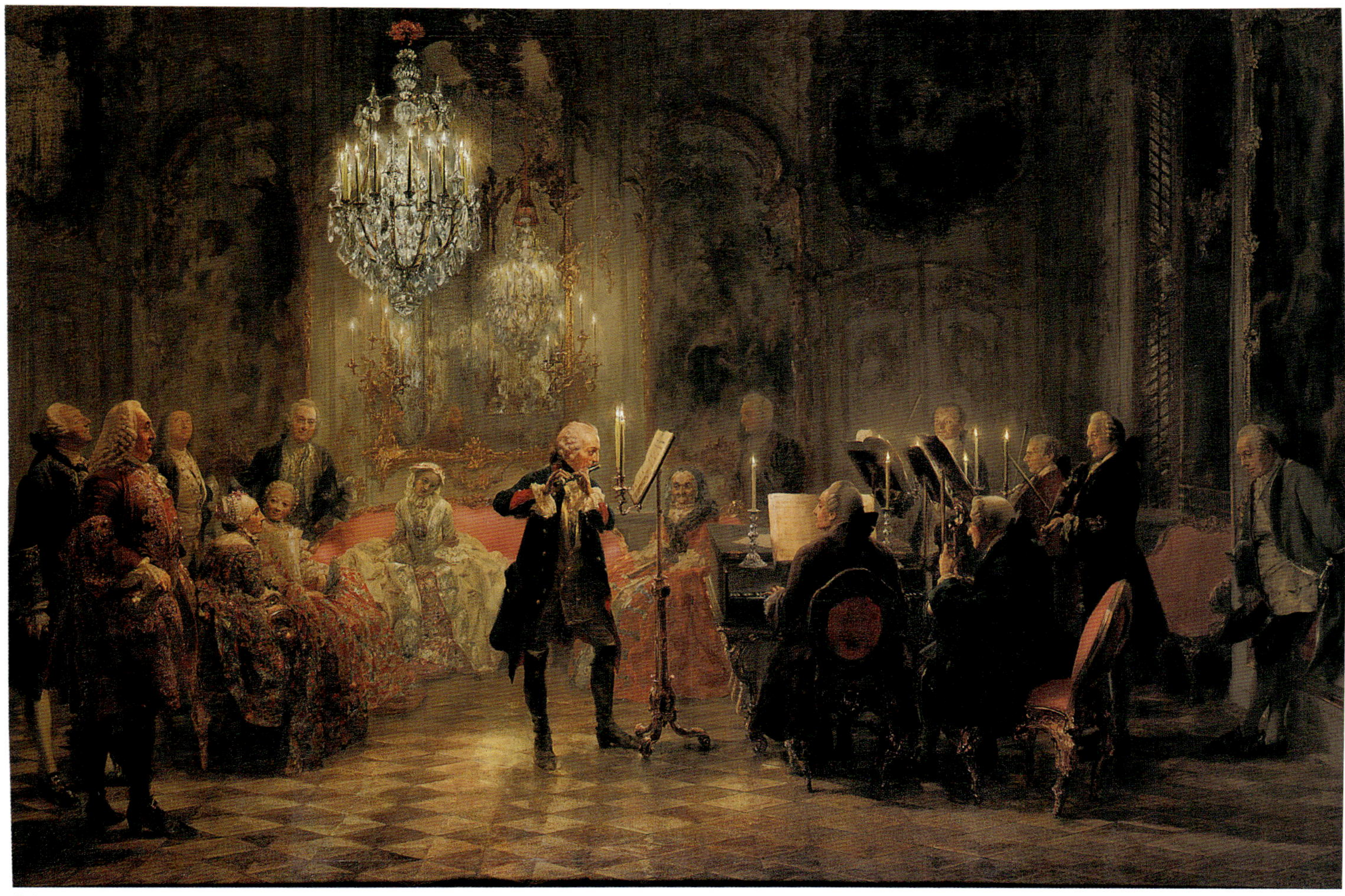

56

beginning of August 1852, in a concentrated effort which left him exhausted[2]. He used a plan to work out the position of each figure in the room[3]. In comparison with the oil sketch, the spaces are far more precisely defined. This point is reinforced by a significant modification: the strange motif of a woman crossing the foreground of the painting is abandoned, so that an ordered semicircle is created around the king. This is evidently a concession to conventional ideas on composition. There is none of the conflict of form that characterizes *Gustav Adolph at Hanau* and *Harangue at Leuthen* (cat. 37, 90) – *The Flute Concert* seeks harmonious balance.

The studies of the models have also been preserved, most of them made in coloured chalk on coloured paper, as were the studies for all the paintings in the Frederick the Great cycle[4]. Finally, Menzel drew a sketch for the frame itself, which has been missing since 1945. Three large and very detailed drawings[5] show rococo-style shapes.

This composition forms a contrast with *The Round Table,* of similar dimensions, but whose format has been turned round widthways. Instead of the daylight so suited to witty discussion, a cleverly tiered artificial light envelops the musical entertainment. Above the audience is candlelight, which the mirror reflects and spreads softly. This light is diffracted and multiplied by the glass pendants of the chandelier. Close to the musicians, a severe row of single candlesticks form an eloquent contrast.

The painting was very well received, and even Max Schasler, the severest of Menzel's critics, thought it 'the artists most beautiful and brilliant painting'[6], praising 'its naturalness, the living reality and real presence of the subject depicted', though not without mentioning a 'lack of style and 'epic moderation' which prevent this form of art from achieving the greatness of a history painting[7]. Those who confined themselves to the demands of the genre believed they could see in it the development of the 'characteristic', the individual trait, the danger of the 'grotesque', and even those who looked kindly upon it could not help lamenting the absence of beauty, of the ideal[8].

Yet *The Flute Concert* remained Menzels most popular painting. *Tableaux vivants* were composed using it as a model. During the costumed celebration held by the Academy students in honour of Menzel's seventieth birthday, the protagonists played a piece by Philipp Emmanuel Bach[9]. Another example was the celebration in honour of Frederick the Great organized by William II at Sanssouci in 1895. But the ageing Menzel was his own severest critic over his most popular work: 'the king looks like shop assistant playing a flute on Sunday to amuse his family . . .. Besides, I only painted it because of the chandelier. In *The Round Table* it is not lit – in this painting it is'. He meant by this that the work was only created for its picturesque effect and not because it had profound content. 'Sometimes I regret having painted it. But anyway, half my life is made up of regret. One more won't make any difference[10]. Later generations were able to appreciate the painting better. Menzel began to be seen as a 'truly creative painter'. For Max Osborn, *The Flute Concert* is one of the 'high spots in painting, achieving the perfect fusion between historical representation and pictorial essence'[11]. In the year Menzel died, Lovis Corinth painted *Under the Chandelier*, apparently in homage to *The Flute Concert*[12]. C.K.

1. F[riedrich] E[ggers], [chronicle], *Deutsches Kunstblatt*, 2, no. 19, 10 May 1851, p. 150.
2. Letter to Adolf Schöll, 18 January 1853, Deetjen, 1934, p. 31.
3. Berlin, Kupferstichtkabinett (SZ Menzel Kat 665).
4. Berlin, Kupferstichkabinett (SZ Menzel Kat 428, 667-693, 1417, 1631). The studies of musicians N 616-622, 660-664 are also related.
5. One is at Hessische Landesmuseum in Darmstadt, and until 1945 two were at the Kupferstichkabinett in Dresden. *Cf.* Bergsträsser, 1969.
6. Schasler, 1857, p. 85.
7. *Ibid.* p. 93.
8. For example, Sternberg, (1852) 1935, p. 5.
9. Voss, 1885-6, p. 102.
10. Delmar, (1905) 1992, p. 107–108.
11. Osborn, 1903-4, p. 437–40.
12. Vienna exhib. cat., 1992, no. 18, col. reprod.

57

Breaking the Journey at an Inn

1851

Oil on paper
38.2 × 52cm
Signed and dated on the back (cut into the wood of the frame): *M 1851.*
Berlin, Nationalgalerie (A I 958)
Exhibited in Berlin only

Provenance: Fritz Gurlitt Gallery, Berlin; acquired by the museum in 1906.
Exhibition: Berlin, 1955 A, no. 60.
Bibliography: Tschudi, 1905 A, no. 89; cat. NG, 1907, no. 979; cat. NG, 1976, reprod. p. 271.

Nuances of tone have been lost as the bitumen has darkened, and it is difficult to distinguish the action. A clergyman (?) has just got out of the carriage followed by two servants with a lantern. With his head bent over his muff, he is hastening towards the door of the inn. He is accompanied by a proud, adventurous-looking figure, whose hat, worn at an angle, and his enormous fur collar are more appropriate to the sixteenth century, while those helping, including the middle-class citizens in the background, are undoubtedly based on Menzel's contemporaries. Suitcases and other travel items lie here and there – but in the bottom left corner there is an unusual and austere composition consisting of a hat which has been tied around with string and a freestone lying across it, at the bottom of the steps. These are strangely out of place in a picture of this kind. Will we ever know the opera or melodrama from which this scene was taken? The houses look as if they are part of theatre decor. The scene, however, is transfigured by differing degrees of low light. A lantern casts its white, rather dramatic light on the feet of the men, yet at the same time spreads a reddish reflection over their faces; there is light from a lamp discreetly placed high in the top left corner of the picture, and a dreamy, warm light shines through the windows. It is akin to *The Théâtre du Gymnase* (cat. 80) and brings to mind another scene of similar darkness, though more markedly anecdotal in nature, *Drinkers around a Large Table* (on which a singer is seated, with a guitar)[1]. E.T.A. Hoffman was thought to be the source for Menzels painting, in the absence of any further information. C.K.

1. Painted in oil on paper, Tschudi, 1905 A, no. 89; Berlin, Kupferstichkabinett (SZ Menzel N4474).

58

Night in the Forest

1851

Oil on canvas
50.9 × 65cm
Signed and dated at the bottom left: *Menzel /51.*
Zurich, Kunsthaus (1975/14)

Provenance: 1895 Ernst Seeger, Berlin (friend and patron of Wilhelm Leibl in particular); 1905 Robert von Mendelssohn, banker in Berlin; 1955 Dr Christoph Bernoulli, Basle; acquired in 1975.
Exhibitions: Berlin, 1895 A, no. 39; Berlin, 1905, no. 59; Berlin, 1906, no. 1151, reprod.; Berlin, 1928, no. 25, reprod.; Berlin, 1955 B, no. 58.
Bibliography: Tschudi, 1905 A, no. 71; Meier-Graefe, 1906, p. 90, p. 121; Hochhuth, 1991, col. pl. p. 88.

The viewer's gaze follows the edge of the wood and goes along the coppice, until it reaches a clearing. The shadows of three tree-trunks separate the foreground from the background and are created solely by light brown scumbling, used over most of the canvas, while the background scene is painted with a thicker layer. It is above all in the foreground that disparate *taches* dominate, where the brown, violently scraped with a spatula, undergoes innumerable new transformations – small islands of a heavier colour appear in it, in which there are cracks. The painter's touch, very bold, but always delicate and prone to reworking, avoids any detail. Specific elements can only really be identified in the branches of the trees. The result suggests a dream rather than tangible reality.

Of all the landscapes painted by Menzel, *Night in the Forest* is the one that

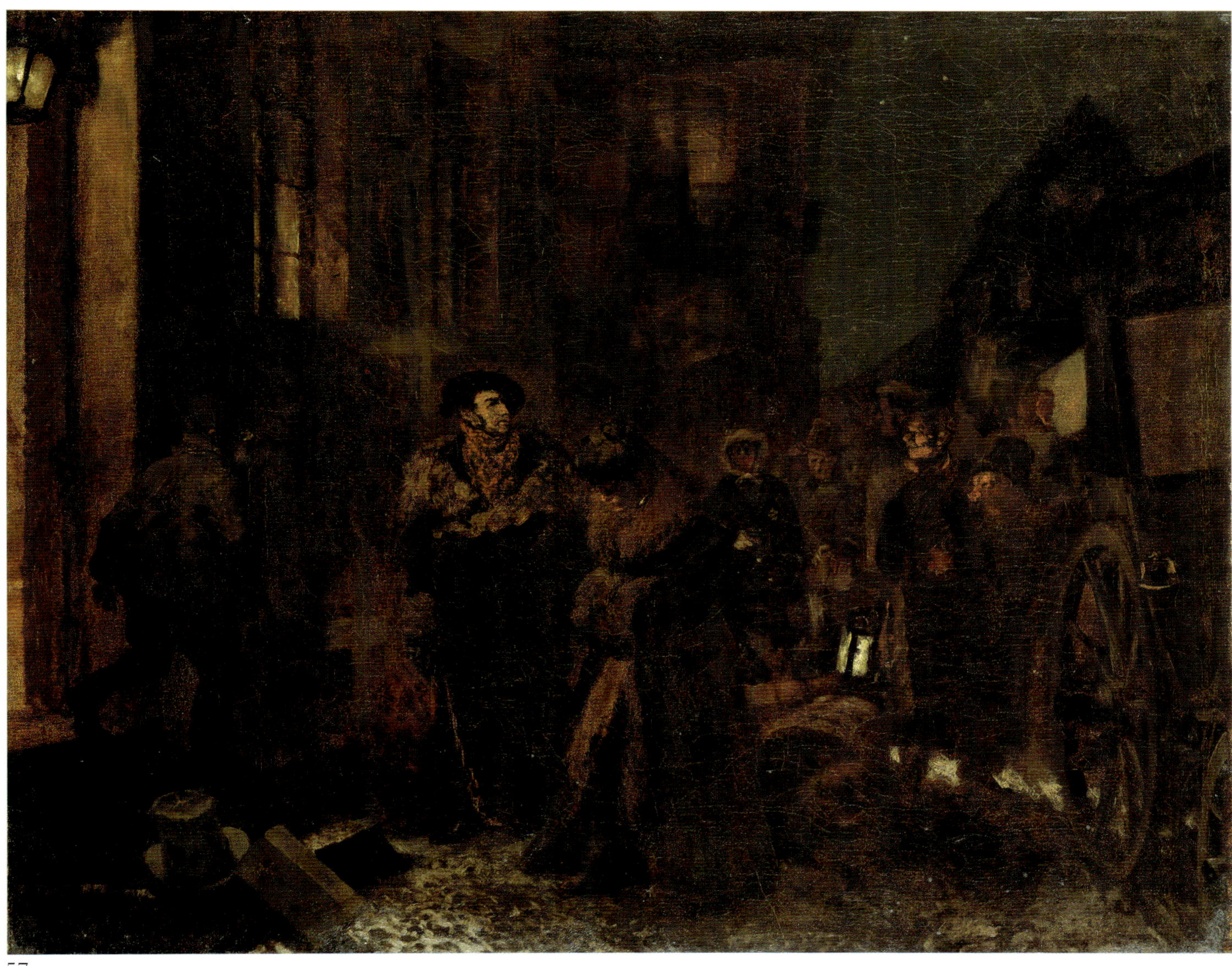

57

the demanding critic Meier-Graefe considered to be 'the most remarkable'. He wrote that 'when the painting is viewed close up, the canvas is like a palette on which the dark tones have been mixed arbitrarily. But as soon as the viewer moves further away, the magic of the colours appears, as they blend together', giving us 'a vision of the silent atmosphere of a soft summer night'. Meier-Graefe also added that the spectator is confronted with 'a psychological enigma . . . : Menzel is usually so objective, and only reluctantly considered a great artist – how was he able to see like this and have this kind of enthusiasm?'

Yet it is not unusual in Menzel's work to see the concrete shapes of objects spring from ambiguous patches of paint. A draughtsman by training, he often used pencil for the stump drawing, and covered the paper with grey clouds that were only defined more precisely later. Similarly a few brushstrokes at random often served as a starting point for a water colour or gouache. Even in the oil paintings of his later years, created piece by piece like a mosaic, the contours of surfaces that were temporarily left white appear to have inspired him. But nowhere else is there such a bold challenge in floating colour, disassociated from any specific form or shape, nor has the 'prefigurative' nature of his work been so solidly and intentionally preserved as it is in *Night in the Forest*, which is no more than an outline, although it bears the traces of several different stages of work. In places the colour was scraped on, then worked over again when it was dry. This delight in scraping and scoring the paint surely suggests hidden aggression (*cf.* also cat. 90), but the painter is able to integrate this into his creation, as is clear from the start (*cf.* cat. 13) and also in certain drawings done in his old age, such as the *Allegory of the Berlin Academy's Jubilee*[1] (1896).

It is a significant coincidence that the year in which *Night in the Forest* was painted was the same in which Menzel

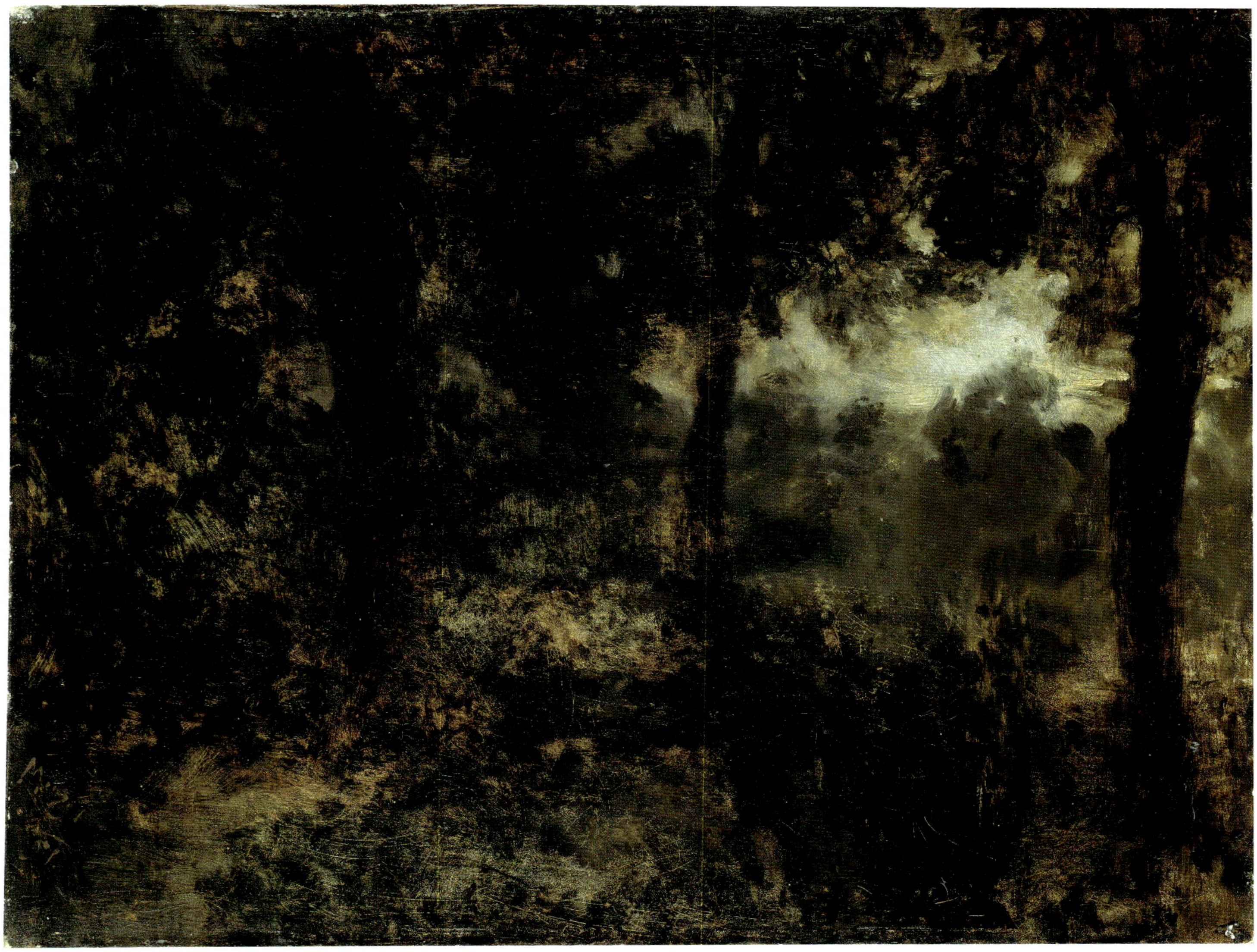

58

produced *Experiments on Stone with Brush and Scraper*, a series of seven lithographs in which the highlights are created by scraping the already applied black ink.

On the other hand, there is no similarity with the *Drawings of a Scribbler* by Justinus Kerner[2], nor with the *Pictures Created from Coffee Stains* produced during the same period, but in another district of Berlin, by Wilhelm von Kaulbach (creator of the historical frescoes in the Neues Museum) and his collaborators[3]. These focus on form, however random, and seek the shortest route between the indeterminate and the determined, according to the technique inherited from antiquity by Leonardo da Vinci, drawing inspiration from the shape of a cloud or from crumbling roughcast to create fantastic images. For the same reason, there is no similarity with Victor Hugos equally contemporaneous phantasmagorical drawings.

It is more relevant to consider a series of six brush drawings by Carl Blechen, four of which are in Berlin[4], in which the blending of grey and black arouses the same uncertainty as to the object represented (fig. 176). One of them has a few significant details added with a finer brush, but this does not lessen the importance of these 'unfinished' drawings. If several were left in that way it is logical to suppose it was intentional, and that the

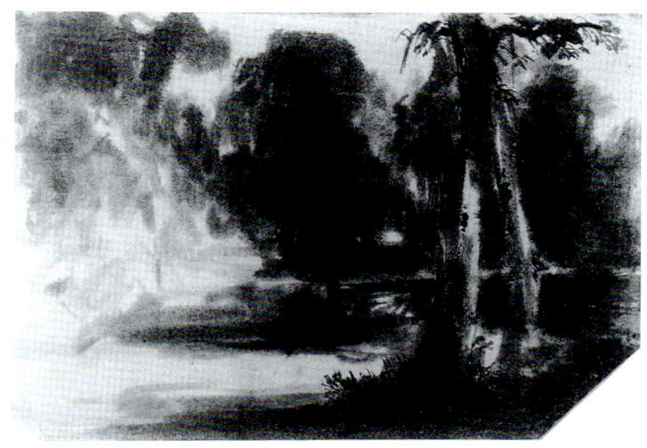

Fig. 176. Carl Blechen. *Trees by the Water*, *c.* 1830–6, Chinese ink and wash, Berlin, Kupferstichkabinett (Nr. 910)

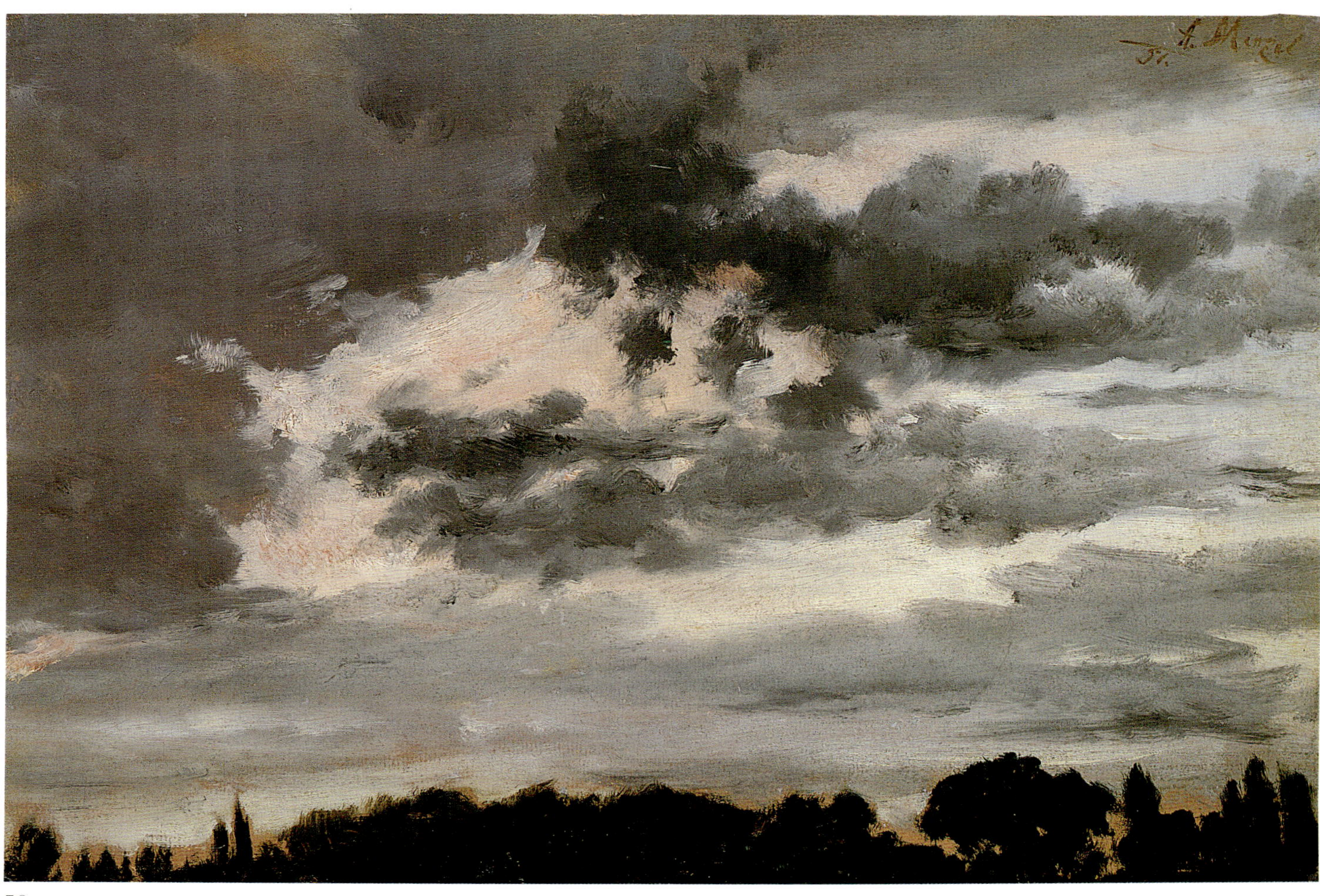

59

artist was attracted by less formal expression.

If Menzel had not signed this painting, one might hesitate to think that the artist considered the painting to be finished, in view of his perfectionism, particularly in his later years, when he was often tempted to add extra detail to works at a later date. It is of special interest, as it reveals how varied and even contradictory Menzel's criteria and intentions could be. If he sold the picture before 1895 and allowed it to be exhibited, then he must have been satisfied with it. But when did he sign it? He hardly ever allowed a canvas to leave his studio without signing his name and the date. Unsigned works were generally those discovered after his death. But he must have signed the painting late, as we learn in the story of the picture *At the Kreuzberg*[5] (cat. 31). It should not be overlooked, on the other hand, that his method of working assumed complete freedom to rework and modify, and that his canvasses, whether finished or not, could be worked on again at a later date (*cf.* cat. 164). So he could have decided later not to go any further with it, and the date attributed would apply to a stage in its creation originally thought of as provisional. This happened on various occasions, the best example being in the case of the *Lying in State of the March Dead*.

C.K.

1. Berlin, Kupferstichkabinett (SZ Menzel Nr 1803); Vienna exhibition catalogue, 1985, no. 118, reprod.
2. Kerner, 1857.
3. Frisch (ed.), no date [1880].
4. Berlin, Kupferstichkabinett (Blechen Nr 907–910) as well as two drawings (location unknown). *Cf.* Rave, 1940, no. 1993–98 and Vienna exhibition catalogue, 1990, no. 109 and 110, reprod.
5. Delmar, (1905) 1992, p. 113.

59

Cloud Study

1851

Oil on canvas
28 × 40cm
Signed and dated at the top right: *A. Menzel 51*
Berlin, Nationalgalerie (A I 903)

Provenance: before 1898, Weidenbusch collection, Frankfurt am Main (sold in 1898; Gustav Horn, industrialist, Braunschweig; acquired by the museum in June 1906 by the R. Wagner Gallery, Berlin, as intermediary
Exhibitions: Dresden, 1904, no. 2355; Berlin, 1905, no. 5727; Berlin, 1906, no. 1152, reprod. p. 136; Berlin, 1935, no. 22; Celle, 1949–50, no. 63, p. 7; Berlin, 1950–1, no. 50; Berlin, 1955 B, no. 57; Hamburg, 1982, no. 55, col. reprod.; Vienna, 1989, p. 743, reprod. p. 334.
Bibliography : Tschudi, 1905 A, no. 72; Tschudi, 1905 B, p. 229, reprod. p. 215 (p. 19, reprod. p. 5); Meier-Graefe, 1906, p. 88, p. 181; cat. NG 1907, no. 982; Kern, 1915–16, p. 92 and 95, reprod. p. 93; Justi, 1921, p. 12; cat. NG, 1976, reprod. p. 271; Jensen, 1982, p. 78, col. pl. 16.

The cloud study[1], a real genre in its own right within Romantic landscape painting, was born of the desire to capture the most changeable natural phenomenon, which evaded academic strictures in a palpable and clearly defined way. The ever-present idea of the cosmos, the acute awareness of the passing of the present moment and the interest in natural sciences all contributed to this intense but ephemeral flowering. Studies of cloudy skies are less frequent in Menzels painted body of work than one might expect[2], but they are numerous in his sketchbooks, used at various times throughout his career. It is surprising to see the insistence with which he sought to define contour, defining the floating shadow created in the stump drawing, using light but accurate strokes. The oil study of the same subject was thought early on to be an echo of the influence of Johan Christian Clausen Dahl on the young Menzel, who possibly visited the famous Norwegian, then living in Dresden[3]. Added to this influence was the presence in Berlin of the works of Carl Blechen, to which the art dealer Louis Sachse was able to give him easy access. On Menzels horizon appeared both Dahl and Blechen, two painters in whose work Romanticism was indissolubly linked to Realism and Luminism.

Where was this stormy sky painted? Perhaps in Prince Albert's garden[4] (*cf.* cat. 23), but by 1851 Menzel was no longer staying nearby. In addition, instead of being a green urban area, the treetops form a dense, narrow strip at the bottom of the picture, evoking a large country park. It might have been Potsdam, where Menzel went often, as much for his studies for the Frederick the Great cycle as to visit Wilhelm Puhlmann, army doctor and founder of an art society in this town with its royal residence. He was without doubt the closest of Menzels friends, with whom he exchanged warm, humorous letters.

It was probably this study that was exhibited in 1904 with the title *Evening Sky over Potsdam*. The title is interesting for more than biographical reasons. In sky studies, sometimes the day and time of observation were noted down, emphasizing an interest in the weather. On the other hand, for Menzel the redness of the setting sun, the cloud formations, the last ray of light and the heavy areas of shadow are not a subject for analysis. His wide brush translates them into a single colourful sweep. Curiously, the title tells us the location – a piece of information difficult to square with the appearance of the sky, since only topography and architecture can define a place objectively. The title chosen later makes the painting a unique spectacle, showing the fortuitous nature of a perception. When memory becomes a field of reference, it is the emotional biography of the artist that comes to the forefront. C.K.

1. Badt, 1960.
2. *Cf.* in particular a small undated painting (not mentioned by Tschudi, 1905 A), Dresden, Gemäldegalerie Neue Meister.
3. Meier-Graefe, 1906; Kern, 1915-16.
4. Tschudi, 1905 B.

60

The Artists Room in Ritterstrasse

1851

Oil on board
32 × 27cm
Signed and dated at the bottom right: *A.M. /51*
Switzerland, private collection

Provenance: Private collections; 1955 Emil Bührle collection, Zurich.
Exhibition: Berlin, 1955 B, no. 50.
Bibliography: Not mentioned by Tschudi, 1905 A; Kern, 1920; Wirth, 1965, fig. 20.

Paintings depicting empty rooms reappear at regular intervals over a period of six years: *Room with a Balcony* in 1845 (cat. 18), *The Bedroom* in 1847 (cat. 34), the small painting entitled *The Room of a Secondhand Bookseller*[1] in 1848. Also associated with this group is the *Interior with Herr Maercker, c.* 1848[2], a night-time scene which has to be looked at twice before the viewer notices the person in the room, who is bending over in a corner and turning his head. Three years later came this painting, the last in the series. Whether the room depicted was really the painters, if not certain, is at least likely. Guido Josef Kern had already commented on the poor lines and ugly proportions of the rooms in the Ritterstrasse apartment, and he realized that this room, which is far too small and has only one window, was obtained by dividing a larger room in two. This seems surprising when the Ritterstrasse was flanked by modern buildings of good appearance, and Menzel occupied a 'very spacious' apartment there 'on the third floor of an 'expensive-looking building'[3]. As the *Room of a Secondhand Bookseller* shows, Menzel did not paint his own apartment exclusively. The caption on the back of this small picture tells us of the circumstances in which this kind of work was created: '. . . painted by me from memory in the summer of 1848, after waiting on my own for the return of the bookseller, because of an old book'.

On this sunny summer day, both curtains are drawn. A yellowish shutter is down on the outside, only allowing bright light into the dark room through

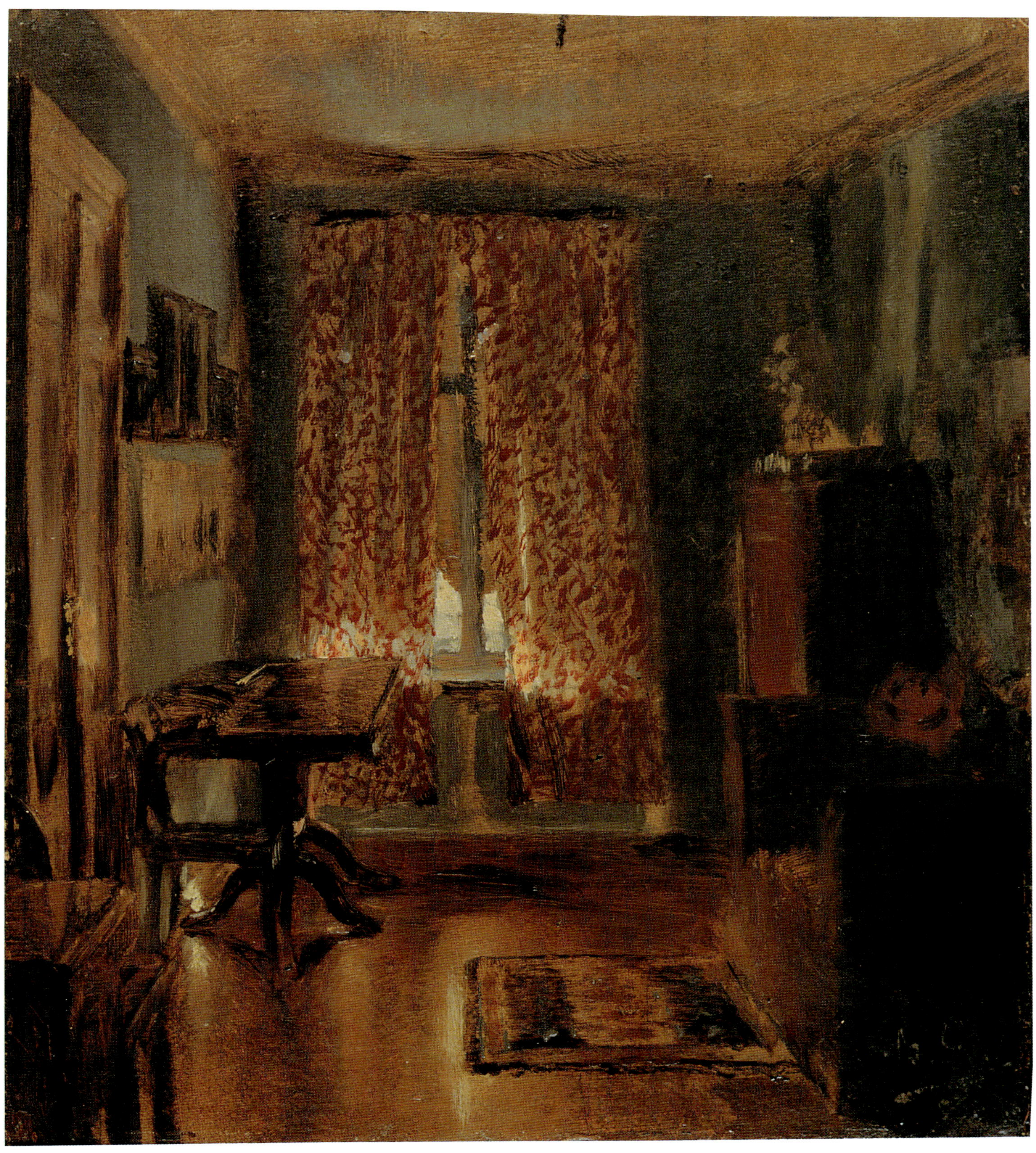

60

the bottom, and through the curtains with their lively red pattern. The light spreads over the floor, touches the door on the left, the bottom of the table leg and the flat front of the cupboard. The painter is interested only in the intangible charm of the atmosphere – objects are merely suggested, and some can be identified only from the context, like the striking bust, defined by a few light *taches* casually outlined. Once again, Menzel uses a brown wash in several areas, emphasizing motifs in the same tone, but more compactly. The pale, veiled grey so common in the paintings of these years appears in places, on the ceiling, for example. Where the colour is applied more thickly, the brown becomes a brick red or a deep, shadowy chestnut colour (like the armchair on the right, and the cupboard with the bust on it). A green reflection on the right and another on the left, changing from mustard to sulphur yellow, blend with the sombre, matt grey of the walls shaded from the sunlight.

C.K.

1. Tschudi, 1905 A, no. 45; Munich, Neue Pinakothek.
2. Tschudi, 1905 A, no. 44; Euerbach, Georg Schäfer collection.
3. Eggers, 1854, p. 2.

61
Menzel with his Brother, Sister and a Relative next to the Upright Piano
1851

Pencil
22.5 × 28.5cm
Signed and dated on the bottom right: *A.M. 22 Dezember 1851.*
Berlin, Kupferstichkabinett (SZ Menzel Nr 1744)
Exhibited in Paris and Washington only

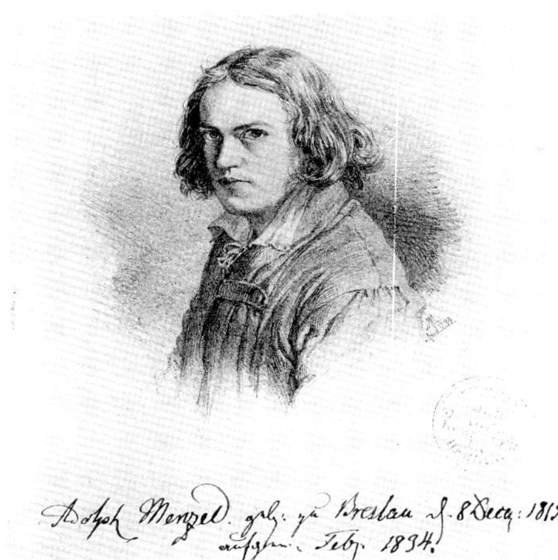

Fig. 177. *Self-portrait*, 1834, pencil, location unknown

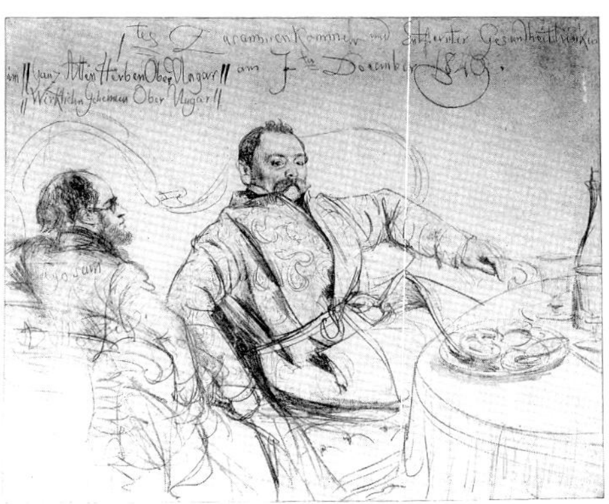

Fig. 178. *Menzel and Count Flemming at Breakfast*, 1849, pencil, Berlin, Kupferstichkabinett (Kat. 1)

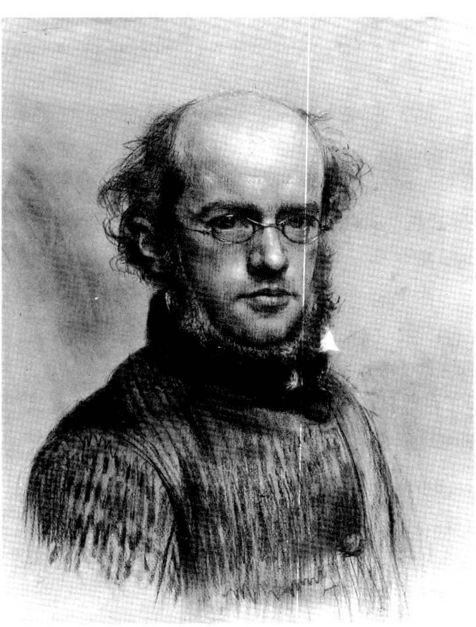

Fig. 179. Probably Adolph Menzel (attributed to Fritz Werner), *Self-portrait*, 1853, chalk with white highlighting, Berlin, Stadtmuseum

Provenance: Fritz Martini, Berlin; acquired by the museum in 1906.
Exhibitions: Berlin, 1905, no. 5369; Berlin, 1980, no. 406, reprod. p. 234; Vienna, 1985, no. 31, reprod.; New York, 1990, no. 11, reprod.
Bibliography: Kirstein, 1919, fig. p. 17; Scheffler, 1922, p. 181–2, fig. p. 161; Hütt, 1981, fig. 1; Lammel, 1993 B, fig. 6.

Some years before this drawing was made, around 1848, during his period of small landscapes and interiors, Menzel had painted his self-portrait with his brother and sister. The small painting, missing for a long time[1], showed him standing beside the easel, holding his palette and handrest in the right hand, and a paintbrush in the left. His head, in profile, is turned towards his brother and sister sitting facing him on the couch. The work reflects the painter's self-assurance, in its expert composition and nimble execution. The drawing shown here is also significant. Then aged thirty-six, Menzel is behind the upright piano at which his brother and sister are seated. A relative, Constance Martini, is knitting. Adolph had been practising portraiture since he was thirty, and excelled at it, as can be seen in the numerous portraits of the Arnold family[2]. The portraits are only of one person, either relatives or members of the Martini family, whom he visited in 1844 in Jauer in Silesia. They show the sensitivity with which Menzel depicted their features, in spite of a certain Biedermeier rigidity[3]. The self-portrait with his brother and sister at the upright piano must have been offered to his relatives in Silesia, and Menzel made a replica of it, as he sometimes did[4]. The purpose of the drawing explains the official nature of its composition, showing Menzel face on. He drew himself twice more in this pose, but not until 1882, for an official occasion (*cf.* cat. 177). Although he is somewhat in the background, there is no doubt of his importance as head of the family and originator of the drawing.

M.R.-R.

1. Missing. Reprod. in Kirstein, 1919, frontispiece. According to a note p. 116, it then belonged to Marcus Kappel, Berlin.

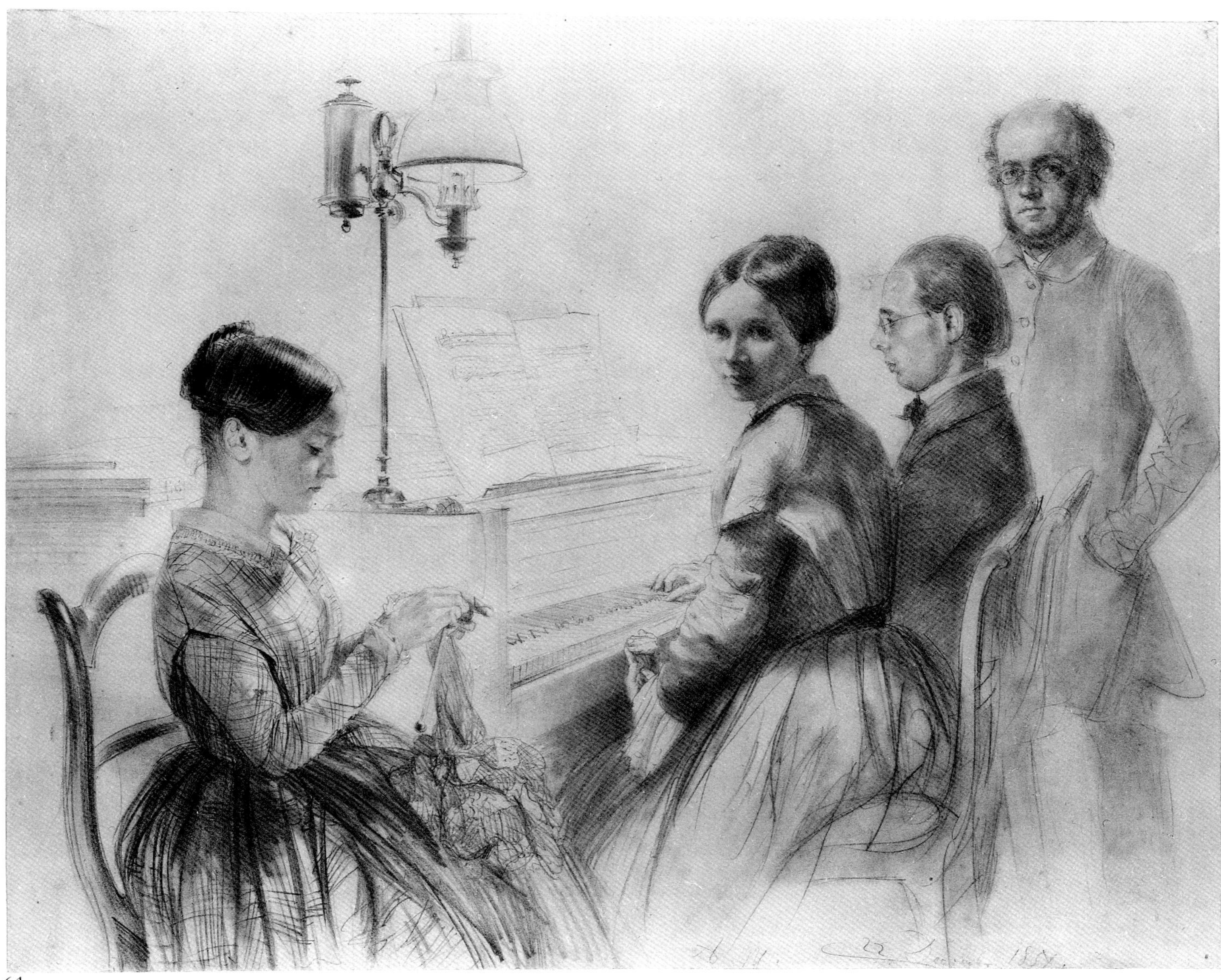

61

2. Portraits from 1828, Berlin, Kupferstichkabinett (SZ Menzel N 1672, 1673); *Friederike Arnold*, signed and dated: *Cassel d: 23 Sept. 1841,* Nuremberg, Germanisches Nationalmuseum (5812); *Mrs. Antonie Arnold*, 1841, Bremen/Berlin, private collection.
3. Portraits of Karl, Pauline and Constance Martini, Berlin, Kupferstichkabinett (SZ Menzel Nr 1746, 1747, 1748, 1749). In 1906 the Nationalgalerie bought these drawings of Constance's nephew, Fritz Martini. A drawing of the younger brother, Paul Martini, is in a private collection in Hamburg.
4. Berlin, Kupferstichkabinett, (SZ Menzel N4519); *cf.* also Berlin exhibition catalogue, 1955 A, no. 46.

62
Study of Model for Frederick II in an Armchair
1852

Chalk with white highlights
32.4 × 28.4cm
Berlin, Kupferstichkabinett (SZ Menzel Kat 155)
Exhibited in Berlin only

Provenance: Hermann Pächter (R. Wagner Gallery, Berlin); acquired by the museum in 1889.
Exhibitions: Berlin, 1905, no. 505; Berlin, 1955 A, no. 264; Berlin, 1980, no. 220; Vienna, 1985, no. 8; Copenhagen, 1985, no. 6; Berlin, 1987, no. G.4; New York, 1990, no. 22.
Bibliography: Donop, 1902, no. 155; Lammel, 1988, p. 47, fig. 36.

This drawing is one of the studies that preceded the small-format painting *Frederick the Great and the Dancer Barbarina* (1852; cat. 63). The model for Frederick II is an imposing man in eighteenth-century uniform, sitting in a rococo arm-chair. He is looking and turning to the left. He is holding a stick casually in his left hand, the pommel of which is sketched in rapidly. Menzel used this drawing almost exactly in the painting. Only the leg position became more flexible and elegant, and he used pairs of buttons on the outfit. In the chalk drawing, great importance is attached to the expression, which in the painting indicates Frederick II looking at the dancer Barbarina. The centre of attention in the drawing is the model's pair of eyes looking to the side. The entire composition is logically directed towards the whites of the eyes. These areas of brightness on a face darkened by a three-cornered hat were used in the painting to reflect the spectators looks as they admired the beautiful dancer. A.H.

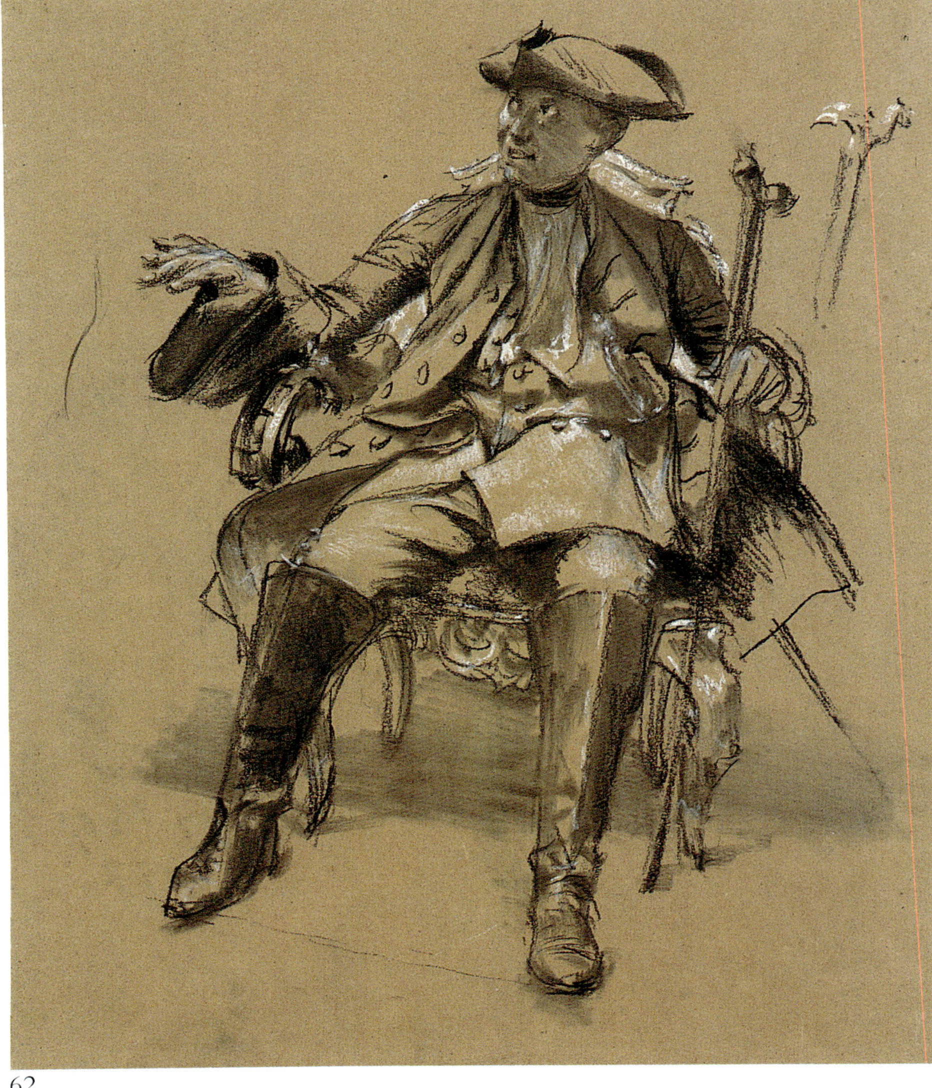

62

63

Frederick the Great and the Dancer Barbarina

1852

Oil on canvas
34 × 26cm
Signed and dated: *Adolph Menzel. Berlin 1852*
Frankfurt am Main, Kunsthandel Peter Fichter
Exhibited in Berlin only

Provenance: Commissioned in December 1851 by Goupil in Paris; in all likelihood refused; 1855, Sachse gallery, Berlin; acquired by the pharmacist Carl Ludwig Kuhtz (1809–89), well-known art lover, secretary of the Association of Friends of the Arts of Prussia (*Verein der Kunstfreunde in Preussen*); Kuhtz sale through Rudolph Lepke, Berlin, 15 February 1898; 1905 and 1912 Robert Warschauer, Berlin-Charlottenburg; private collections.
Exhibitions: Danzig, 1855; Berlin, 1855; Berlin, 1863; Berlin, 1885, no. 5; Berlin, 1895 A, no. 123; Düsseldorf, 1904, no. 21; Berlin, 1905, no. 94; Berlin, 1912, no. 223 (no. 69 of small catalogue); Berlin, 1928, no. 28, reprod.; Wolfsburg, 1956, no. 124, fig. 22; Erlangen, 1971, no. 39, reprod.
Bibliography: *Deutsches Kunstblatt*, 6, 1855, p. 392; Jordan, 1895, p. 30, p. 67; Jordan, 1905, p. 50 *et seq.*; Tschudi, 1905 A, no. 81; Waldmann, 1941, p. 24, p. 46, fig. 39; Lammel, 1988, p. 47 *et seq.*, reprod. p. 52; Zangs, 1992, p. 105 *et seq.*

In the spring of 1852, the following appeared in the journal *Deutsches Kunstblatt*: 'Adolph Menzel has received a commission from the well-known French art dealer Goupil for two genre paintings, with subjects from the rococo period, so familiar to the artist. Such commissions for our artists from France were a great rarity until now, while the reverse happened frequently'[1]. This related to *Frederick the Great and the Dancer Barbarina* and to *Frederick the Great and Fouqué*, which were in progress in June[2]. It was probably the Berlin art dealer Louis Sachse who acted as intermediary, as he had been acquainted with Menzel since 1833. A lively mind and always seeking something new, he had moved previously from working as secretary to the erudite Wilhelm von Humboldt to being a political prisoner because he belonged to a secret society. He claimed to have Huguenot ancestors who had fled to Prussia, and he visited Paris regularly in order to sell French art in Berlin (he brought back the new daguerrotype technique from Paris around 1839). It was his permanent desire to establish a reciprocal arrangement between French and German art that was honoured in the last sentence of the article in the *Kunstblatt*. But his optimism was misplaced, as Goupils order went wrong. Undoubtedly the two paintings remained in Paris for a considerable time without being sold and were finally returned, since in 1855 they went on sale at Sachses – at the exact moment when Menzel gained his revenge over Paris with the success of his *Round Table*.

The pair of matching paintings, separated today, contrast the young king, full of life, with the aged king burdened with care. The dancer Barbarina (her real name was Barbara) Campanini (1721–99), from Parma, had first been successful in Paris, London and Venice, from where Frederick II had literally snatched her away under the most incredible circumstances so as to obtain her for Berlin. From 1744 to 1748 she was greatly admired on the opera stage recently built by Knobelsdorff. The fascination she held for Frederick for some time had, according to Voltaire, already started, and was due to the fact that she had 'a mans legs'. She undoubtedly lost favour with the king when she married the son of a senior Prussian civil servant in 1749. Ignoring the royal anger, she remained in Prussia and died a countess. Among the portraits that Antoine Pesne, court painter to Frederick II, painted of her, the most remarkable is the great full-length painting that the king had hung in his writing room at the castle in Berlin[3]. Menzel was freely inspired by the bearing, dress and jewellery of the dancer, although he showed her in profile.

While he was working on this painting[4], the *History of Opera and of the Royal Opera House in Berlin* by Louis Schneider appeared. The latter was an actor, a knowledgeable historian and very versatile author, well known to the painter, with whom he occasionally cooperated[5] Curd von Schlözer, who was writing the biography of the knight Chasot[6] (*cf.* cat. 49) was able to help his friend the painter too. He knew from Chasots memoirs that he regularly left his garrison in Mecklenburg to go to Berlin for the carnival, and that he was one of the dancers greatest admirers. In his book he quotes a contemporary, the priest Denina, who claimed 'to be certain that, with the exception of General Rothenburg and Count Algarotti, Chasot had always been one of the chosen few that the king was accustomed to invite to those small supper parties after the opera . . . The king seemed to take pleasure in presenting these three friends, and Chasot in particular, as the famous lovers of the dancer'. It was precisely these three figures that Menzel placed around the seated king: Count Algarotti (kneeling), Rothenburg (on the right) and Chasot (in the background). All three are also depicted in *The Round Table* (cat. 48).

Is the similarity of the group to the Judgement of Paris coincidental? The seated king, with an expression of subtle malice verging on the demoniacal on his face, may be seen as the focus of a six-pointed star. As in the equally piquant *The Heir to the Throne pays a Visit to the Painter Pesne on his Scaffolding* (cat. 93), Frederick is enjoying the superiority of the onlooker, without taking part directly. C.K.

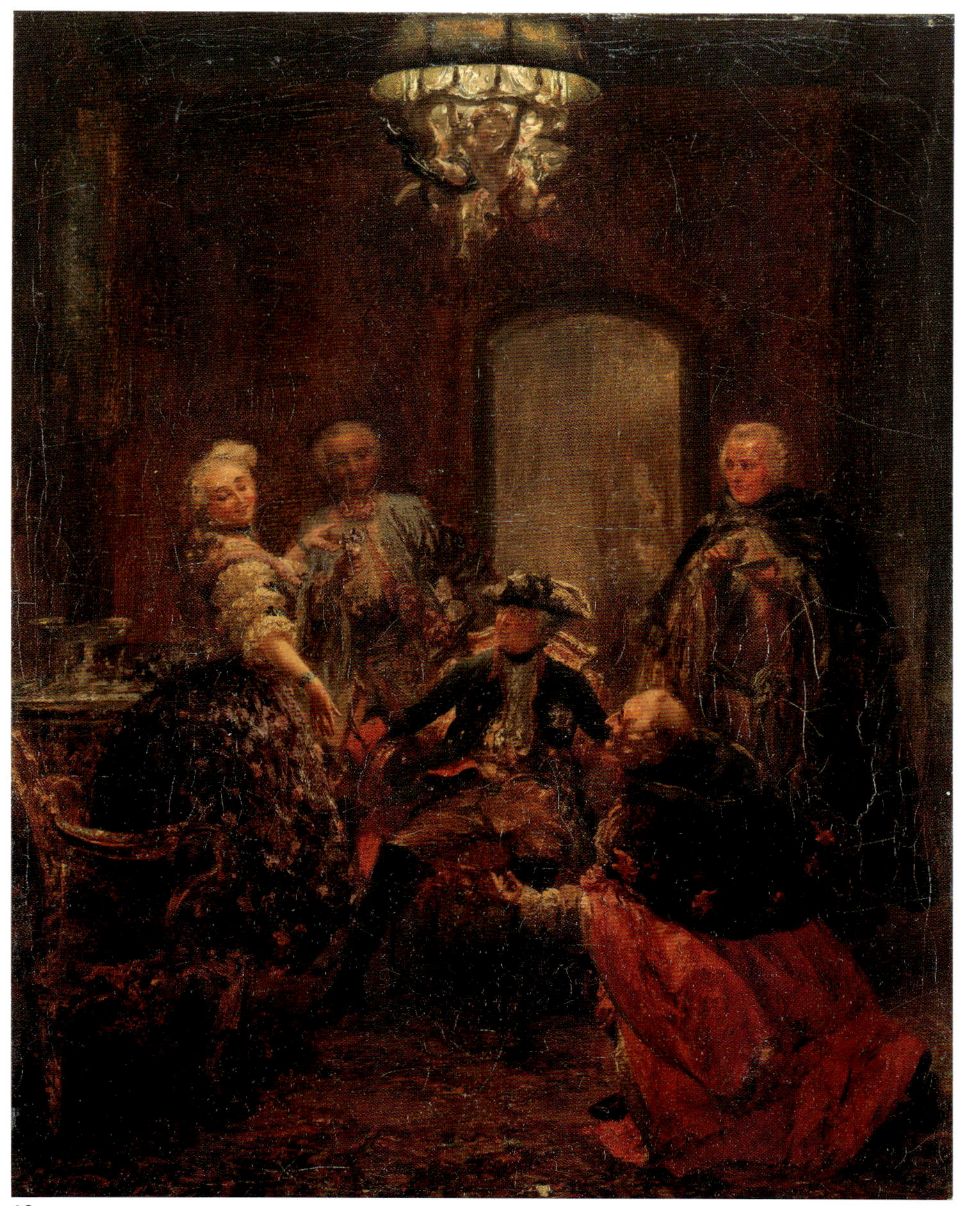

63

1. Eggers, 1852, no. 10 of 6 March, p. 85.
2. Letter to Carl Heinrich Arnold, 4 June 1852, Wolff, 1914, p. 156.
3. Painted around 1745. Berlin, Schloss Charlottenburg; Berckenhagen, 1958, no. 46b, fig. 173. Three drawings by Menzel after Pesne, at the Kupferstichkabinett in Berlin (SZ Menzel Kat 1121–1123).
4. Several preparatory drawings at the Kupferstichkabinett in Berlin (SZ Menzel Kat 553, 772, 1359), as well as the drawing described here (*cf.* cat. 62); perhaps also Kat 439.
5. On the subject of Barbarina, p. 100 and ff.
6. Schlözer, 1856, p. 101–10.

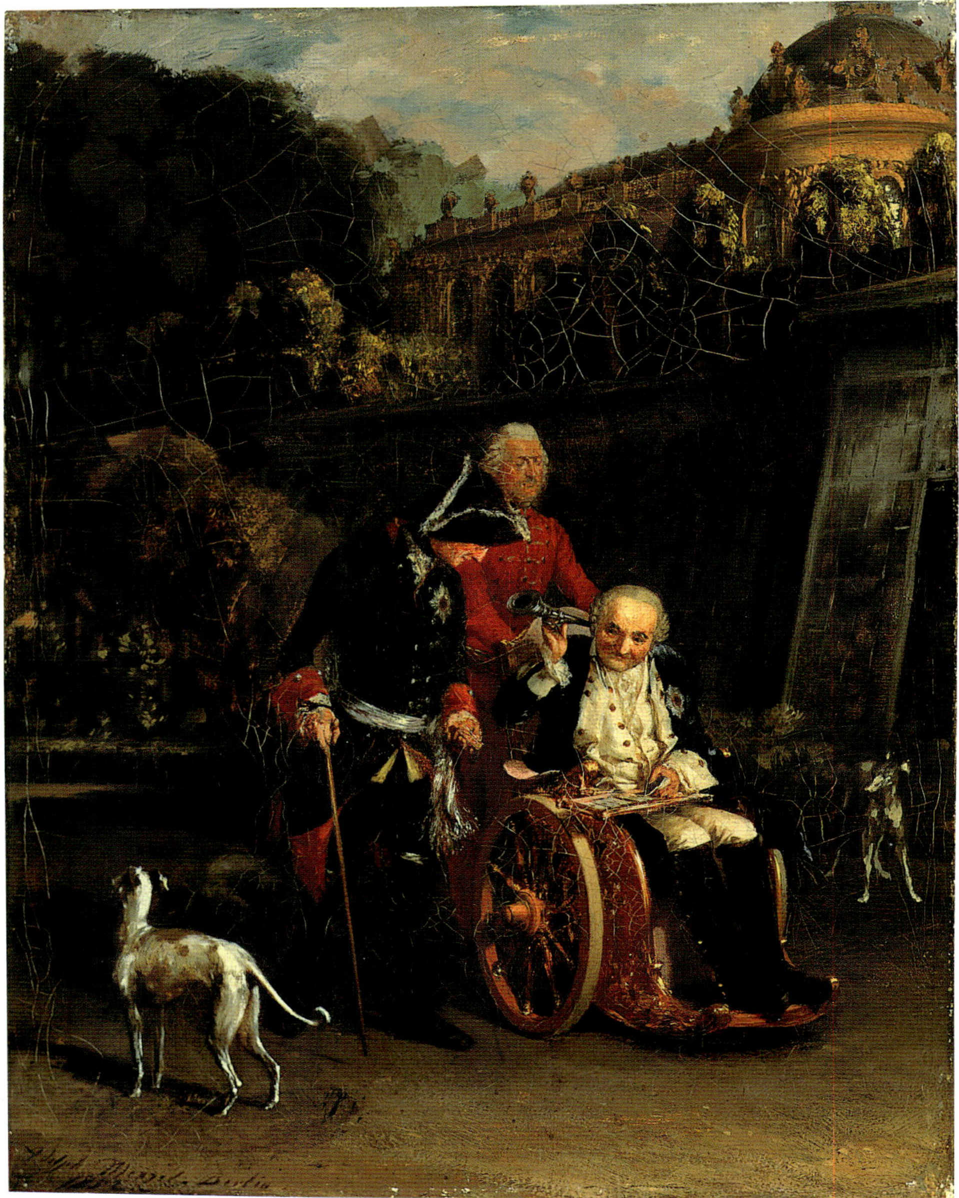
64

64

Frederick the Great and General Fouqué

1852

Oil on canvas
34 × 26.5cm
Signed and dated at the bottom left: *Adolph Menzel. Berlin 1852*
Poznan, Museum Narodowe (Mo 430)
Exhibited in Berlin only

Provenance: Galerie Louis Sachse, Berlin; acquired in 1855 by Count Athanasius Raczynski. This Polish aristocrat, long in in the Prussian diplomatic service, collector and author of *Modern Art in Germany*, opened his gallery to the public in 1847; between 1883 and 1902 the collection was presented to the Nationalgalerie; in 1903 it was given to the museum of Poznan.
Exhibitions: Danzig, 1855; Berlin, 1855; Berlin, 1905, no. 34; Berlin, 1980 A, no. XII, reprod. p. 215; Munich, 1992, no. 36, no. 6 col. reprod.
Bibliography: Deutsches Kunstblatt, 1855, p. 328; Jordan, 1905, p. 50 *et seq.*; Tschudi, 1905 A, no. 80; Lammel, 1988, p. 47–9; Zangs, 1992, p. 105 *et seq.*

The penultimate chapter of the biography of Frederick the Great written by Kugler, introduced by a vignette depicting the Temple of Friendship which the ageing king has had built in honour of his sister Wilhelmine, describes at length how he had monuments constructed to the memory of his deceased companions, while remaining faithful to those still living, such as Lord Marshall Keith (*cf.* cat. 139, 140) and Generals Zieten and Fouqué. Following the example of Kuglers text Menzels painting and its matching work aimed to emphasize the human, touching side of the King of Prussia, as in *The Round Table* and *The Flute Concert*.

General Heinrich August de la Motte-Fouqué (1689–1774), grandfather of the Romantic poet who created the famous *Ondine*, had already served under the orders of the 'Elder of Dessau' before he became the close friend and mentor of the young Frederick. At the court of Rheinsberg, he had been the grand master (known as 'The Chaste') of Bayard, the secret order of knighthood founded by the heir to the throne, whom he subsequently assisted, always at a crucial point in his campaigns. Later, weak with age, he retired to the town of Brandenburg, where he was given a priory, but a significant correspondence and mutual visits maintained their relationship. 'In order to enjoy walks with his friend, Frederick made him sit in a specially designed chair, in which he was pushed through the gardens of Sanssouci while the king walked at his side. When Fouqué's hearing failed, he arranged for all kinds of sound amplifying ear trumpets for him. When he had difficulty in speaking, a machine was invented with which he could finish the words he could no longer pronounce, by assembling the letters.' All this led Theodor Fontane to define Fouqué's 'historical and poetic importance', even the 'distinctive feature of his greatness' as the fact that he 'allowed the great kings human and compassionate side to find its full expression[1]'.

Menzel portrayed the general several times – a bust in 1833[2], then a woodcut (in the series *In the Time of Frederick the Great. Hero of War and Peace*[3]), in which he appeared, full of energy, in his wheelchair.

A woodcut illustrating Kugler's book (fig. 180) preceded the painting, but it depicts a great sunlit vista seen through a marble colonnade built by Knobelsdorff in Sanssouci park (and demolished several years after the kings death). Using a technique increasingly frequent as the book goes on, the figures are in the distance and seem to appear from behind a couple of columns. The painting locates the action on one of the vine terraces overhanging the chateau of Sanssouci. The group is put together in the same way, although they are closer to the viewer. One of the greyhounds of which Frederick was so fond is acting as a guard (the dogs were also 'friends', whose portraits were painted, and who were buried with full honours). The wheelchair, the ear trumpet and the writing tool are depicted with as much clarity as the inanimate legs (which in the woodcut are hidden under a blanket). The enthusiasm and complexity of the conversation contrasts with the indifference of the lackey.

It is surprising that, contrary to the woodcut, the group forms a classic triangle. If Frederick is leaning his head over, it is more to favour the triangle than because he wants to be heard clearly. However, it is a person of lower rank, and moreover, secondary to the action, who unexpectedly forms the point of the triangle. This kind of formal irony can be observed on many occasions in Menzel's work (*cf.* cat. 179). C.K.

1. Fontane, 1969, p. 565 and ff.
2. Lithograph, Bock, 1923, no. 57.
3. 1855–6, Bock, 1923, no. 1076.

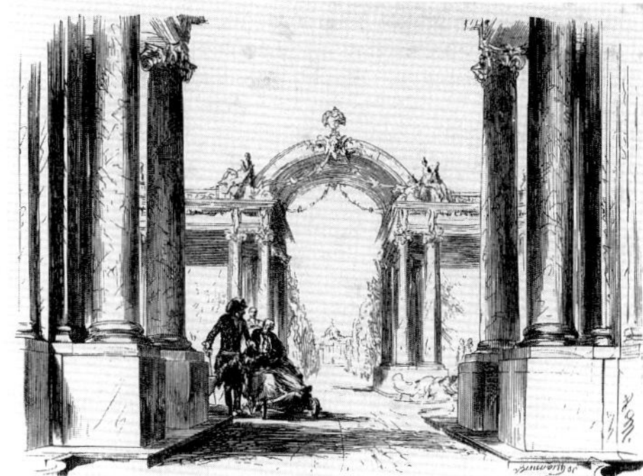

Fig. 180. *History of Frederick the Great: Frederick and Fouqué*, 1839–42, wood engraving

65

Studio Wall

1852

Oil on paper, wood backing
61 × 44cm
Signed and dated at the top right: *A.M.20.März 1852*
Berlin, Nationalgalerie (A I 904)

Provenance: 1904 R. Wagner Gallery, Berlin; acquired by the museum in 1906.
Exhibitions: Vienna, 1896, no. 285; Düsseldorf, 1904, no. 23 a; Berlin, 1905, no. 93; Berlin, 1906, no. 1153, reprod.; Berlin, 1935, no. 25; Wiesbaden, 1947, no. 59; Wiesbaden, 1952, no. 158; Berlin, 1955 B, no. 61, fig. 43; Kiel, 1956, no. 60; Frankfurt, 1990, no. 56, reprod.
Bibliography: Cat. NG, 1907, no. 987; Tschudi, 1905 A, no. 83; Tschudi, 1905 B, p. 236, pl. facing p. 300 (p.26, pl. facing p. 90); Meier-Graefe, 1906, p. 125–7; Scheffler, 1912, p. 128, reprod. p. 125; Justi, 1921, p. 12, fig. 9; Scheffler, 1922, p. 178–9, reprod. p. 151; Justi, 1932, p. 130 *et seq.*; Scheffler, 1938, p. 72; cat. NG, 1976, p. 272, reprod.; Hofmann, 1977 B, p. 141 (1982, p. 31, reprod. p. 32).

'All these life-size studies of limbs and plaster masks lit from beneath – all by lamplight! – that you can see on the walls of my studio', Menzel later claimed he had painted in preparation for the ambitious battle painting *Night Attack at Hochkirch*, started in 18501, so as to 'give myself practice, using my large, wide brush, in the large-scale application of thick paint in the very special light created by the surrounding flames'[2]. Only *Studio Wall* is known from this period, not 'all these studies' to which Menzel refers, and, while the connection with *Hochkirch* is undeniable, the great canvas itself is only one of the stages of the long 'picturesque journey' through the night, lit by candles, lamps, street lights or torches, engaged upon by the young Menzel. It was a journey that never really ended.

There is a detailed description of the painting studio in the Ritterstrasse – barely distinguishable from Menzels other studios – by his friend Friedrich Eggers, dated 1854. We learn that 'on the shelving there was nothing but a few attempted casts of antique sculptures, forms cast from life, and in particular all kinds of death masks, which took up more and more space'. This description indicates the clear difference between two kinds of visual aid that the disciple of working from life used – the model (in all senses of the word, but especially in relation to the Classical ideal) and a life substitute[3], which Menzel favoured. This observation was confirmed by a view of a corner of the studio, dated around 1900, this time in Sigmundstrasse[4], in which a number of casts of human limbs can be seen, together with various statuettes, some of which seem to be less than life-size. We know from photographs that other plaster casts were hung on various parts of the studio walls. A photograph by Zander and Labish (fig. 31) shows the hand of a muscular man, on the right in the shadow, hanging beside the skull which appears in the painting. The painter kept the hand all his life.

Other similar elements can be seen in the frame around a drawing loaded with symbolism, *His Studio*[5] (1890). References to the artist's existence, plaster

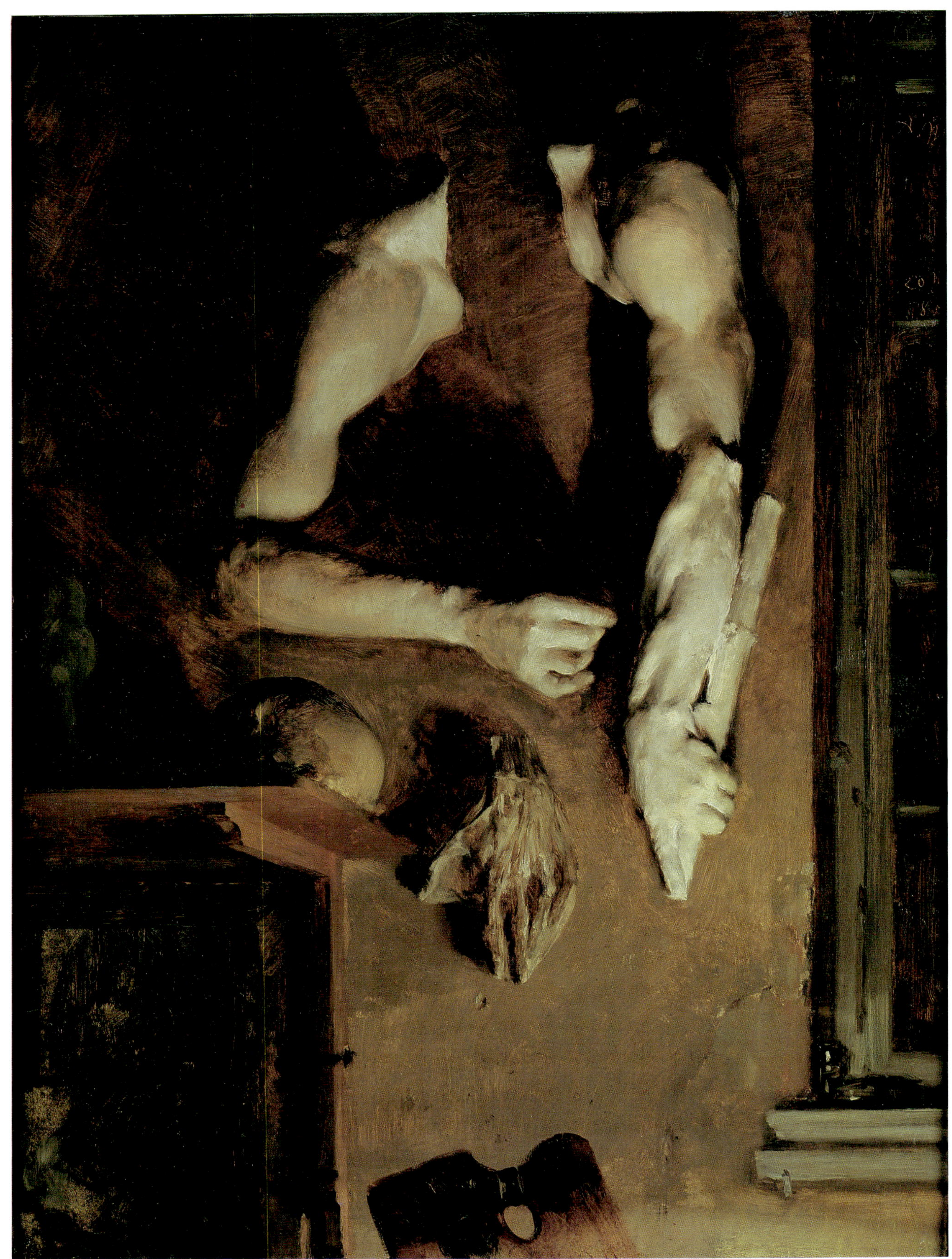

65

casts, weapons and other objects appear with the bust of one of the Fates. There are also rams skulls – real ones, no doubt, like the human skull on the left in the painting. To the end, Menzel did not withdraw from his critical attitude towards the academic method, which had each student draw first of all from stationary models, before reproducing the living form. When asked by a journal what were the advantages and disadvantages of this method of teaching, he answered with a play on words: 'All drawing is beneficial, and so is drawing all things'[6].

In a now classic text, Werner Hofmann interpreted the Hamburg *Studio Wall* (cat. 137), painted twenty years later, as a 'coded manifesto', as 'a realist's response to the canonical system of form given such stature by the Academy, and he showed that Menzel's critical view of the Academy is already evident in the prints from Menzel's youth, beginning with a series of lithographs entitled *The Artist's Earthly Pilgrimage*, which appeared in 1833–4. In the *Studio Wall*, the 'aesthetics of the fragment so dear to Menzel are triumphant, according the nobility of art to the disjointed and divided, and more generally challenging the traditional hierarchy of elements in a work of art. In this work Menzel demonstrated the superiority of painting, where lighting and colour bring inanimate plaster casts to life. (Normally these pieces were only used as models for painting through the intermediary of a drawing.)

This is also valid for the first *Studio Wall*, of less imposing size, barer and with more sober subject-matter and lighting effects. However, in the Hamburg masterpiece, the very studied composition appears to follow a precise iconographic scheme, while the Berlin version owes more to the moment, to spontaneous inspiration. The macabre tone cannot be overlooked in this picture either – in the stumps of torn-off arms, arranged so that they seem to be seeking the parts lost in order to reconstitute the whole; in the cut-off hand hanging between them like a sexual organ, near the skull and pointing towards the palette, which in itself escapes the pull of this area of glacial rigidity because it disappears off the edge of the painting. Paradoxically, only the fragmentary objects are fully visible, while the others, the palette, the window on the right and the shelf on the left (whose perspective does not match the height of the window sill), are cut off by the edges of the composition. If the light brings this ghostly substitute to life, it must be noted that it is an 'artificial' light. Are we in the room of Faust the alchemist, or of a Doctor Caligari? The large, truncated window jars slightly. It is bolted and dark like *Landing in a Nocturnal Light* (cat. 42), suggesting the existence of other worlds which will remain inaccessible. C.K.

1. Only completed in 1856. Tschudi, 1905 A, no. 106. Bought immediately by the king, it passed to the Nationalgalerie after the deposition of William II; lost since 1945.
2. Hertel, (1911-12) 1992, p. 91.
3. On the use of these, see exhibition catalogue, Paris, 1990, p. 67-71.
4. Hamburg, Kunsthalle; Howaldt, 1993, fig. p.43.
5. Private collection; exhib. cat. Hamburg, 1982, no. 174, reprod.
6. 'Alles Zeichnen ist nützlich, und Alles zeichnen auch!' Answer to an enquiry by the review Die Gegenwart, 51, Nr. 13 (27 March 1897, p. 200.

66

Art Lover in front of The Flute Concert by Menzel

c. 1852

Pastel
25.9 × 16.5cm
Berlin, Kupferstichkabinett (SZ Menzel N 935)
Exhibited in Washington and Berlin only

Provenance: Painter's studio; 1905 Emilie Krigar-Menzel; acquired by the museum in 1906.
Exhibitions: Berlin, 1905, no. 4621; Berlin, 1955 A, no. 253; Berlin, 1980 A, no. 25; Vienna, 1985, no. 32, col. reprod. p. 59; Copenhagen, 1985, no. 30; Vienna, 1990, no. 145.
Bibliography: Tschudi, 1905 A, no. 241; Hütt, 1981, fig. 57.

The traditional subject of a person viewing a painting appears throughout Menzels body of work. Early on, the last lithograph of the series entitled *The Artist's Earthly Pilgrimage* (1833–4), inspired by Goethe, shows a fashionable public holding forth before the work of the artist, who has died in poverty. Aspiring to the ideal, his understanding of the public really has failed him at the critical time. When Menzel used this subject again in *At the Louvre* (cat. 122) or in *Meissonier in his Studio* (cat. 126), he lines up with the viewers, who are presented as connoisseurs this time. The satirical side of the motif, the contrast between ideal and reality expressed many times by Daumier, does not interest him. The lack of success of the historical composition entitled *Kassal Sketch* (1847) revealed to him the weaknesses of his work, and he suffered greatly over this for a long time. Next, he drew two people viewing works of art, similar perhaps to those who had examined his sketch. Although the work in question in the painting is not clearly visible, one can guess that it is a picture by Menzel which is being scrutinized by these two gentlemen, with their hands on their hips and the air of real experts[1]. Eighteen years later, when he came across the *Kassel Sketch* again, Menzel admitted that he 'blushed red with embarrassment when he saw it'[2].

Yet, undeterred, he soon drew up his plan for the paintings of Frederick the Great. It may be that Menzel wished to portray himself in the rear view depicted in the pastel, a short man carefully examining a detail on the canvas close up. Werner Schmidt identified the picture in the background as *The Flute Concert*. The figure, shown from an unflattering angle, recalls the rear view of the figure in the foreground of the painting of 1846–7 entitled *Intimate Soirée* (cat. 28). Here it is possible to make out the vague outline of Count Gotters red doublet, an anonymous lady-in-waiting and Princess Amelia. *The Flute Concert* is already framed, and the painter is perhaps examining it for the last time before the critics see it. The picture is resting on an easel, and the scene could

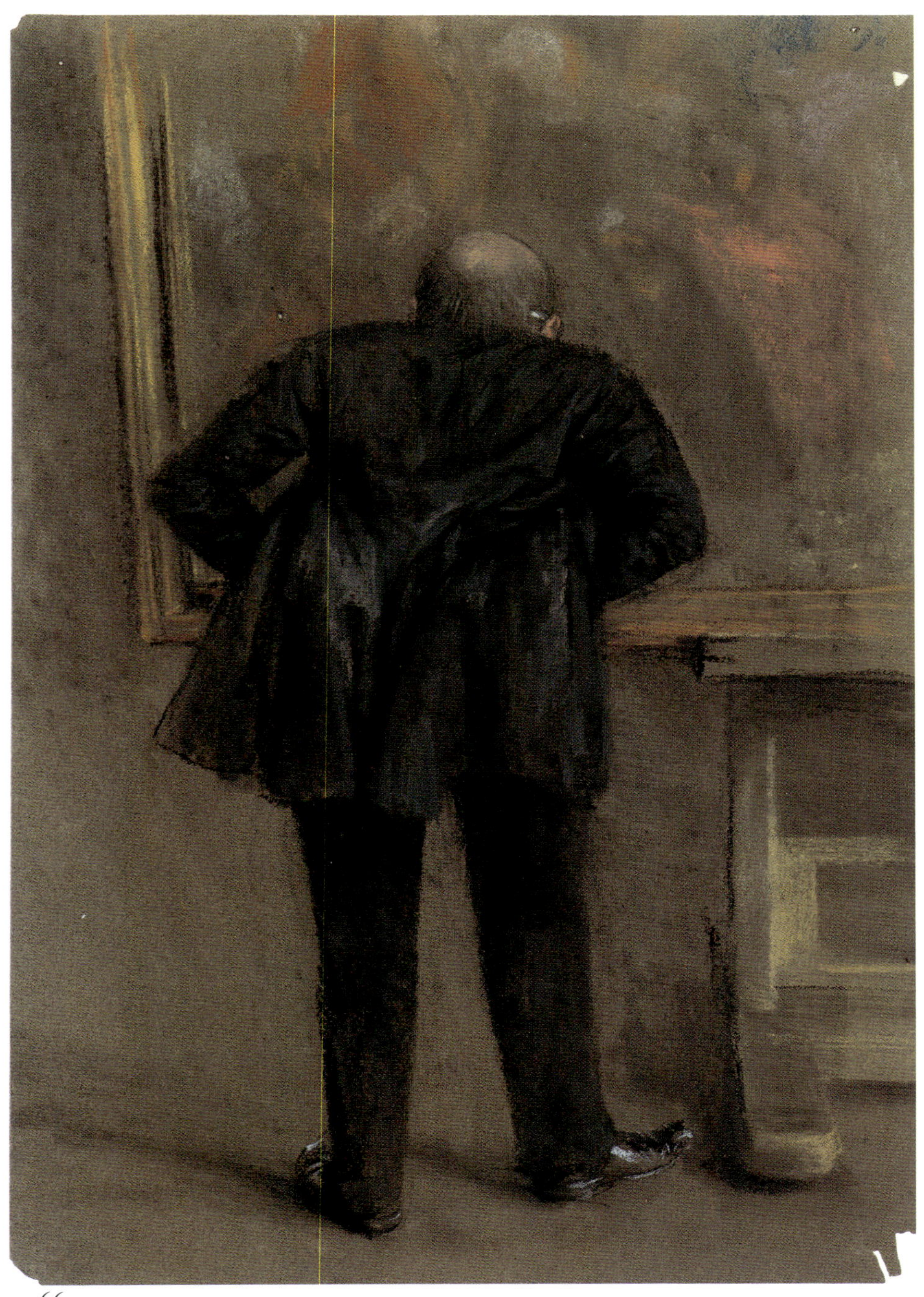

66

well be in a studio. Not without self-criticism, the artist is putting himself in the limelight at the time when he had begun to paint the series of historical paintings of which he had such high hopes. M.R.-R.

1. 1847, coloured chalks; Euerbach, George Schäfer collection.
2. Letter to Hermann Krigar, 23 August 1866, Wolff, 1914, p. 206.

1. Tshudi, 1905 A, no. 316; location unknown. A third variation is in Munich (private collection).

67
Lady with Opera Glasses
c. 1850

Coloured chalks
28.2 × 19.4cm
Annotated: *Erinn:*
Berlin, Kupferstichkabinett (SZ Menzel Kat 650)
Exhibited in Paris and Washington only

Provenance: Dr Wilhelm Puhlmann, Potsdam; acquired by the museum after his death, in 1882.
Exhibitions: Berlin, 1885, no. 149; Berlin, 1905, no. 130; Berlin, 1955 A, no. 251; Berlin, 1980 A, no. 12, col. reprod. p. 170; Vienna, 1985, no. 25, col. reprod. p. 58; Vienna, 1990, no. 142.
Bibliography: Donop, 1902, no. 650; Tschudi, 1905 A, no. 254; Scheffler, 1938, p. 54.

Lightness of touch, enhanced with a degree of anecdotal elegance, is characteristic of the pastels of the 1840s to 1850s. After that, economy of method and form tended to disappear. Menzel was a fervent lover of the theatre and of concerts, especially in his youth, often finding his subjects in the public themselves. The word 'Erinnerung' frequently appears on work done subsequently, sometimes meaning 'from memory' sometimes referring to rapid pencil sketches done on site, which he used to mark with a cross when he had used them.

Here, the lady is seen from above and at an angle (probably from an opera box), with a sideways profile which is almost a rear view. Her right arm, towards the viewer, is wrapped in a shawl. She is holding a pair of opera glasses in her left hand, which is invisible due to the extreme foreshortening, and the glasses seem to start out of her head as if they were telescopic. A second pastel, dated 1853, shows a lady with opera glasses and a shawl, from almost the same perspective[1]. She is wearing a small, ruched headdress decorated with ribbons, and is lifting the opera glasses to her eyes with her right hand. The colour seems to have been applied in a more compact way than it is here, where the delicate, airy touch corresponds to an earlier period. Colour and composition both tend to become more compact over the years.

M.R.-R.

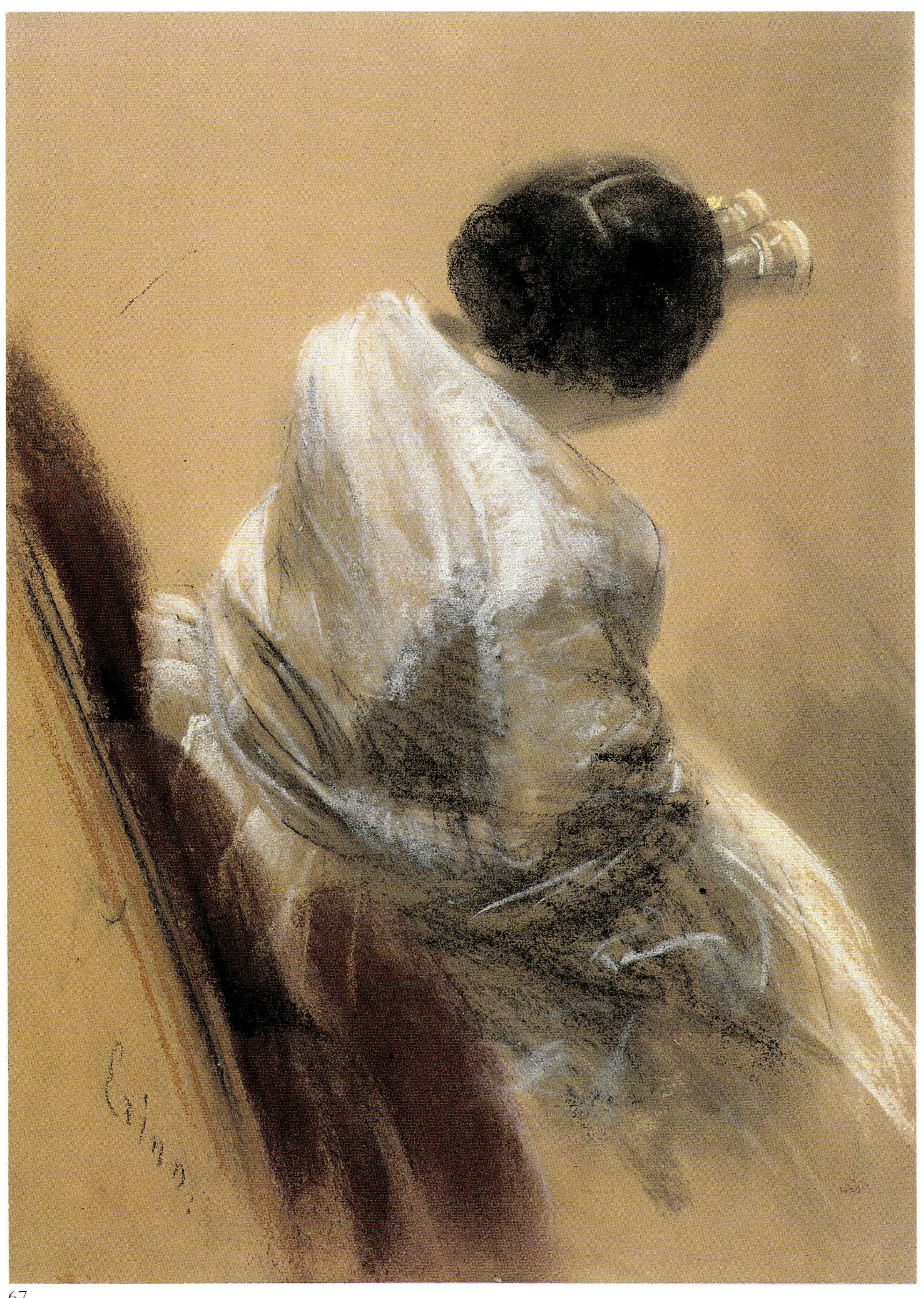

67

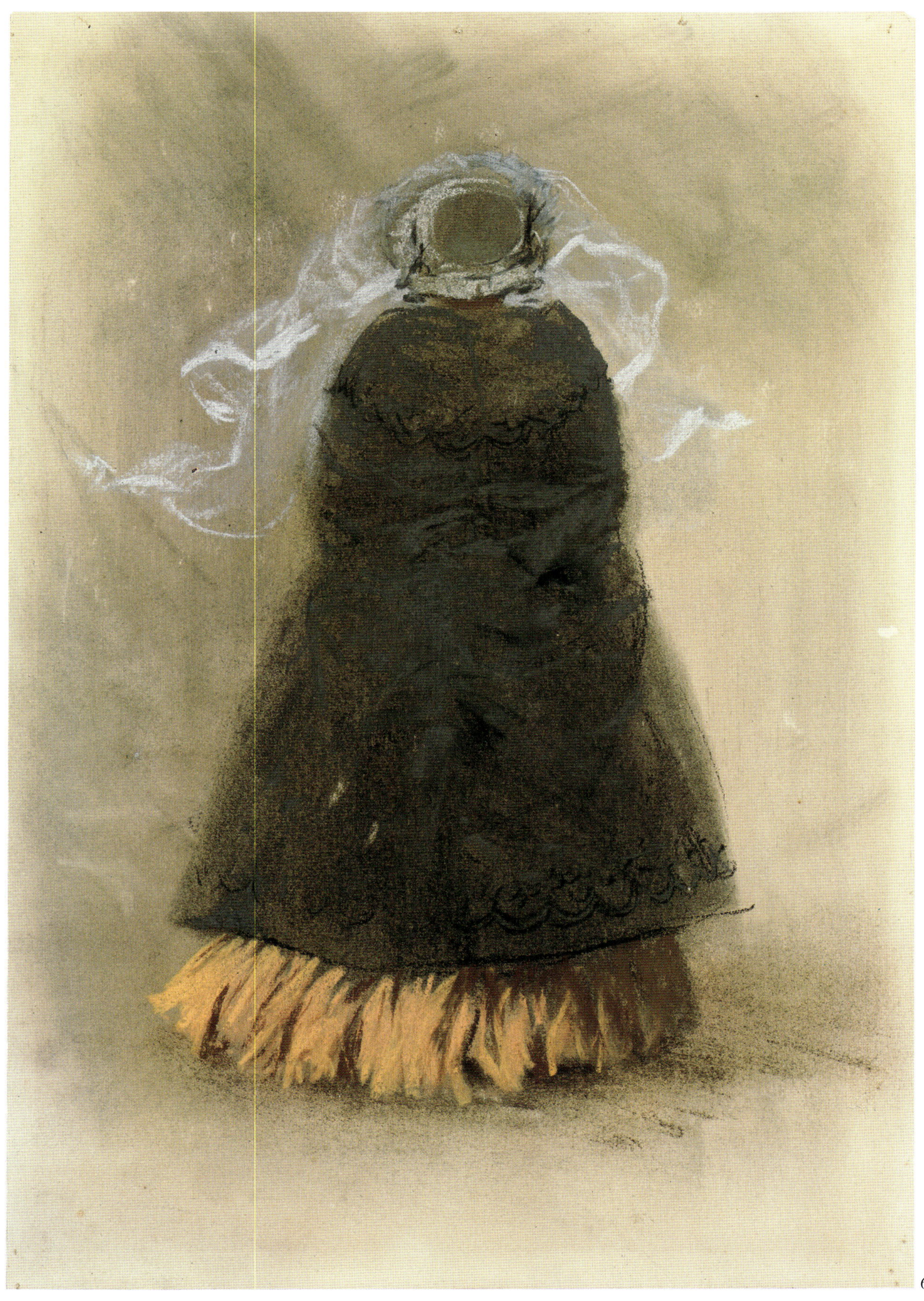
68

68

Lady with Hat and Veil, Viewed from Behind

c. 1850–5

Pastel
26.8 × 18.4cm
Berlin, Kupferstichkabinett (SZ Menzel Kat 652)
Exhibited in Paris only

Provenance: Dr Wilhelm Puhlmann, Potsdam; acquired by the museum after his death, in 1882.
Exhibitions: Berlin, 1905, no. 152; Berlin, 1980 A, no. 22, reprod. p. 314.
Bibliography: Donop, 1902, no. 652; Tschudi, 1905 A, no. 258.

As this woman strolls along we see a rear view of her veil which billows out and envelops her body. The opposition between lightness and heaviness could not have been better expressed in this relationship between the veil and the pyramid formed by the body. Drawings like these were made in the artists studio – from quick pencil sketches or 'from memory' as Menzel stated in an often-quoted inscription (*cf.* cat. 67). How could he have done otherwise? It is unlikely that he would have carried pastels on his person to create such an elaborate drawing. The use of pastels, at a concert for example, would have been extremely awkward, and the light would not have been adequate. Here, the dark, diffuse background suggests the verge of twilight, and the dark tones of the coat and cape reinforce this impression.

There are no preparatory drawings for this pastel study, but in the sketchbook used on the Baltic trip in 1851[1] there are pencil studies which served as a starting point for studies in colour comparable to this drawing, in particular *Two Walkers Facing the Sea*[2]. Rear views of figures are frequent in Menzels work around 1850, either admiring a work of art (*cf.* cat. 66), listening to a concert or quite simply sleeping. A.H.

1. Berlin, Kupferstichkabinett, notebook 11 (1851-3), p. 82 and 84.
2. Tschudi, 1905 A, no. 300; Berlin, Kupferstichkabinett (SZ Menzel Kat 642).

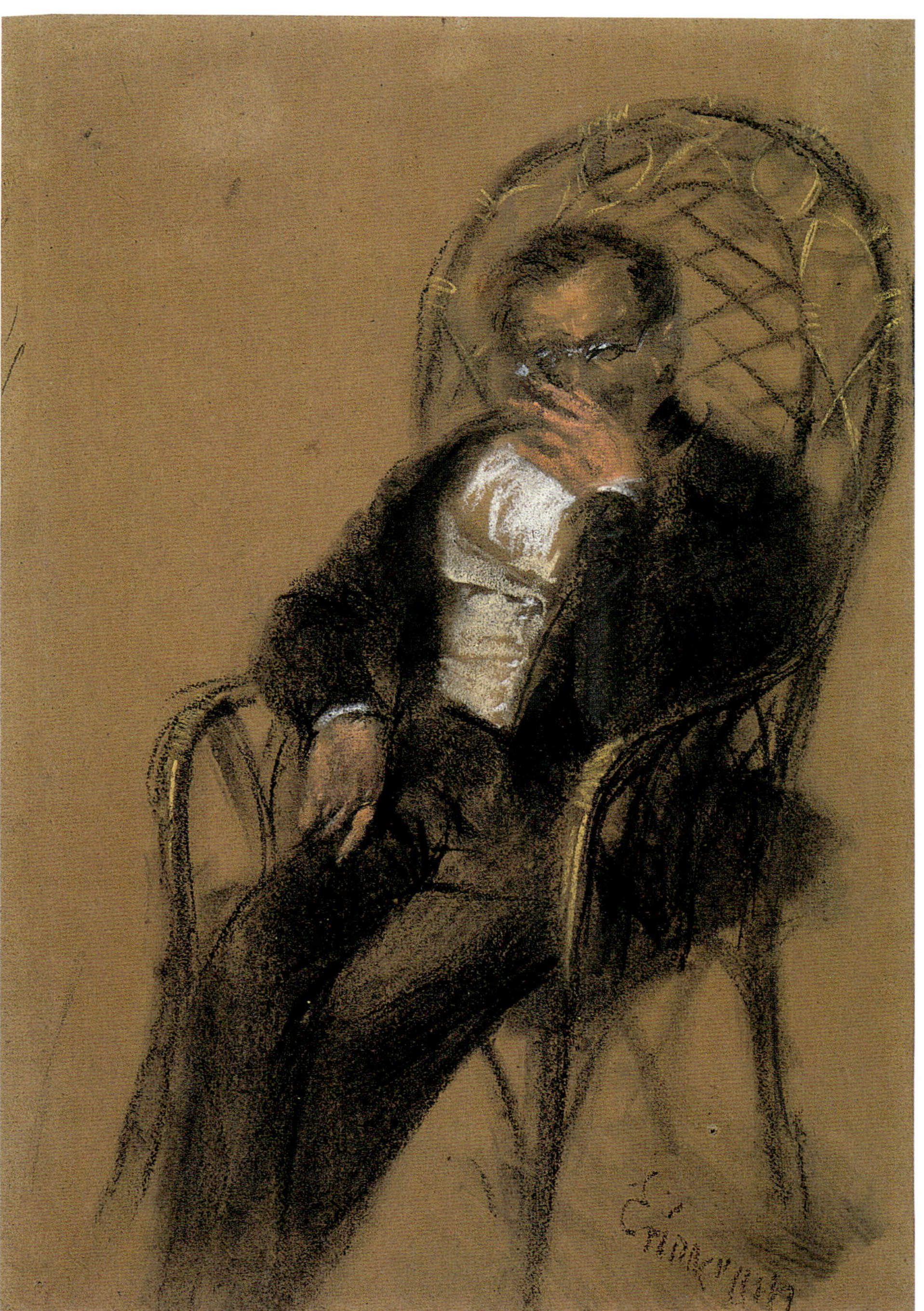

69

69

Man with Cigar

c. 1850–5

Coloured chalks
22.9 × 15.4cm
Annotated at the bottom right: *Erinnerung:*
Berlin, Kupferstichkabinett (SZ Menzel Kat 655)
Exhibited in Washington and Berlin only

Provenance: Dr Wilhelm Puhlmann, Potsdam; acquired by the museum after his death, in 1882.
Exhibitions: Berlin, 1905, no. 135; Berlin, 1955 A, no. 64; Berlin, 1980, no. 13.
Bibliography: Donop, 1902, no. 655; Tschudi, 1905 A, no. 235; Kirstein, 1919, reprod. p. 110; Hütt, 1981, p. 66, fig. 49.

The drawing in coloured chalks was worked 'from memory', as Menzel did frequently from 1847 to 1855 to capture a passing moment. A man lost in thought is smoking a cigar in a rattan armchair. The title, *Sketch from a Party* that Gustav Kirstein gave to this drawing rather accentuates the impression of dreamy solitude and the figure is literally isolated in his context.

Menzel observed a situation which he had perhaps seen at a gathering at the house of Doctor Wilhelm Puhlmann. Clearly this drawing was preceded by a situation of this kind, as Menzel often sent his works to his friend the army doctor. Upon the death of Puhlmann, the drawing, which formed part of a lot in his estate, was bought by the Nationalgalerie. It is impossible to identify the person depicted, deep in thought, and protecting his face from the intrusion of a viewer with his hand. He looks up unwillingly, like a person watching from a safe vantage-point. People smoking at a salon usually moved ponderously, which made the scene easier to capture. The theme of the smoke is frequent in Menzel's work of this time. Later, he associated it much more closely with the theme of the satisfied bourgeois[1]. But in these fragments of memory, in addition to the outer signs of the imperturbable complacency of the bourgeoisie in 1848, there is also a hint of criticism levelled at the inadequacy of the individual and the tensions within society. The fundamental connection with Daumier is articulated here. Even if they worked with completely different media, both artists have 'an illustrative element, which reaches the level of a representation of humankind as strongly social[2]. A.H.

1. *Cf. The member of Parliament*, Berlin, Kupferstichkabinett (SZ Menzel N 4265).
2. Scheffler, 1915, p. 164.

70

The Jewish cemetery in Prague

c. 1852–3

Oil on canvas
69.5 × 57.3cm
Berlin, Nationalgalerie (A III 511)
Exhibited in Berlin only

Provenance: Painters studio; 1905 Emilie Krigar-Menzel; acquired by the museum in 1906.
Exhibitions: Berlin, 1905, no. 9; Berlin, 1980 A, no. XIV, reprod. p. 217.
Bibliography: Tschudi, 1905 A, no. 84; cat NG, 1986, s.p.

The Flute Concert was finished by 1852. The painter, then thirty-seven, was exhausted, and 'although he wasnt ill, he badly needed a jaunt abroad'[1]. With Emilie, he undertook his first long trip, lasting six weeks, travelling as far as Salzburg and passing through Nuremburg and Munich on the way. From there, he followed the Danube by boat to Vienna, with a stop-off at Ratisbon. Later, he would often revisit these towns.

Still avid for artistic experience, he admitted that the ancient art in the museums 'moved him to the marrow', but 'without whimpering' he added resolutely. On the way back, the Jewish quarter in Prague, where they stopped off, left him with very vivid memories. As well as the cemetery, he also painted the interior of the Old-New Synagogue in 1853[2], taking up this theme again later[3]. There is nothing surprising about this attraction, as several months before the visit to Prague, one of his compositions, *Jesus among the Doctors*, painted at the end of 1851 for the annual exhibition of transparent panels at the Berlin Academy, and soon distributed in the form of a lithograph[4], aroused deep emotion in Berlin. For reasons of ethnographic realism he exaggerated the Oriental appearance of the Pharisees to the point of caricaturing them. The heads of old Jews painted around 1855 could be interpreted as a new look at the problem, and an attempt to avoid exaggeration this time using a more direct approach.

The Jewish cemetery of the old town of Prague presents a spectacle as moving as it is picturesque even today, with its profusion of gravestones. Originally they came from a larger area and were brought there, turned over and left half-buried on the sides of the hill. Few places have such a powerful sense of the ephemeral, which gave rise to the 'cemetery poetry' of the German Baroque poets and the Pre-Romantics, and which inspired the Romantic painters. However, *The Jewish Cemetery* bears no relation to this. In the work of Caspar David Friedrich (whose *Monastery Cemetery in the Snow* was in the castle in Berlin) and that of Karl Friedrich Lessing, in Düsseldorf, historical allusions (monks, Gothic architecture in ruins) are a constituent part of the symbolic message. Menzel, on the other hand, chose to use the basic symbolism suggested by the disorder and dilapidation of the tombstones, and the melancholy air of the twisted tree-trunks.

The pictorial language is close to *Night in the Forest* and, although the work is not signed, it was not out of displeasure that it was left in this state. It is incontestably incomplete in academic terms. The thin layer of paint has been scraped in some places and the background shows through. Fairly extensive areas are painted with a large brush, with no relief, and brush hairs seem to have fallen into the paint at times. From a distance, all the shapes lose their contours and the trees with their unusual foliage twist and snap against the white autumn sky. Menzel painted a picture of desolation. On the other hand, the cubic presence of stones leaning one on top of the other, the simplification of forms and the very pronounced contrast between light and shadowed surfaces have an equivalent in the left foreground of *Breaking the Journey at an Inn* (cat. 57). *The Jewish Cemetery* could not have been painted much later.

C.K.

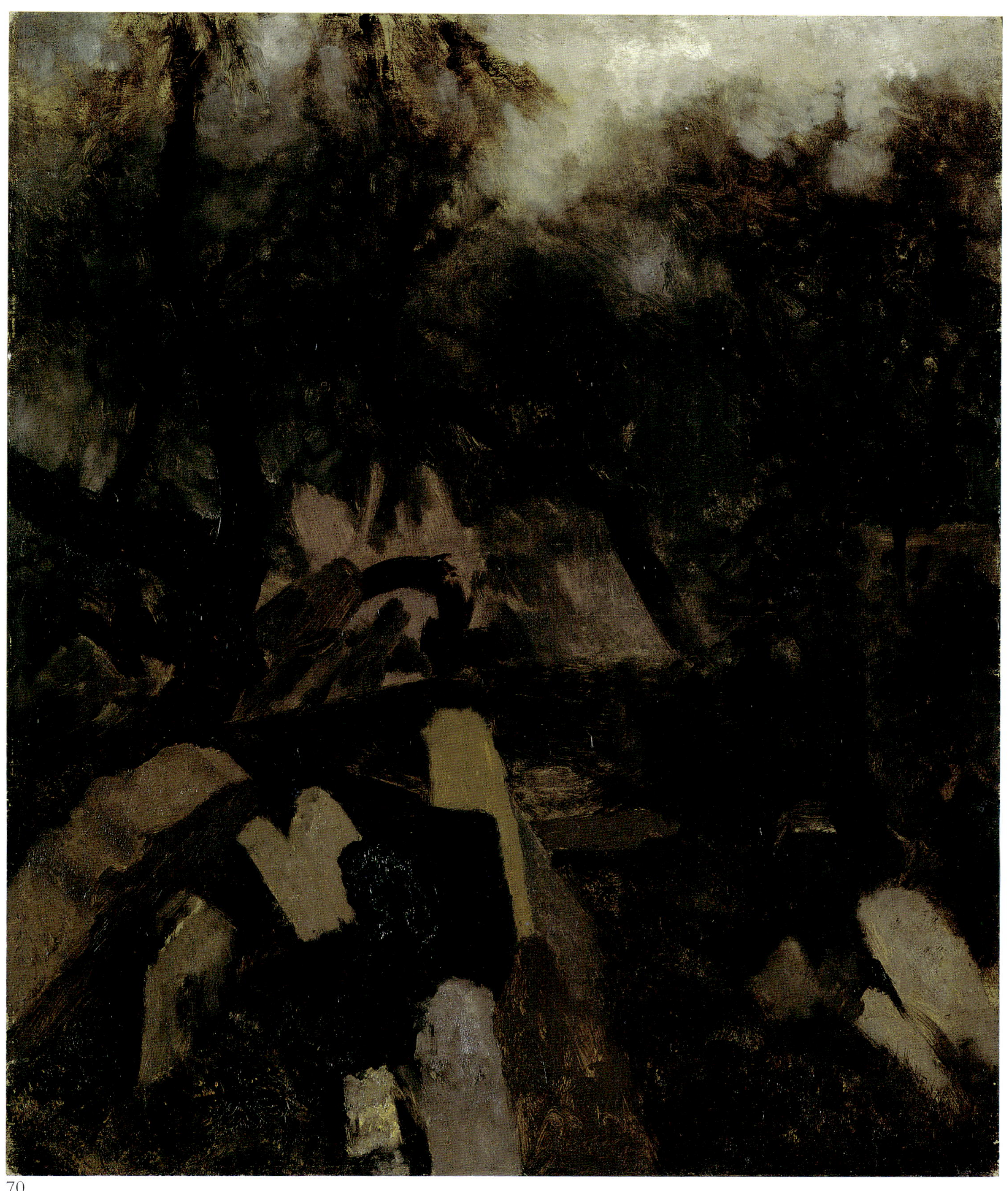

70

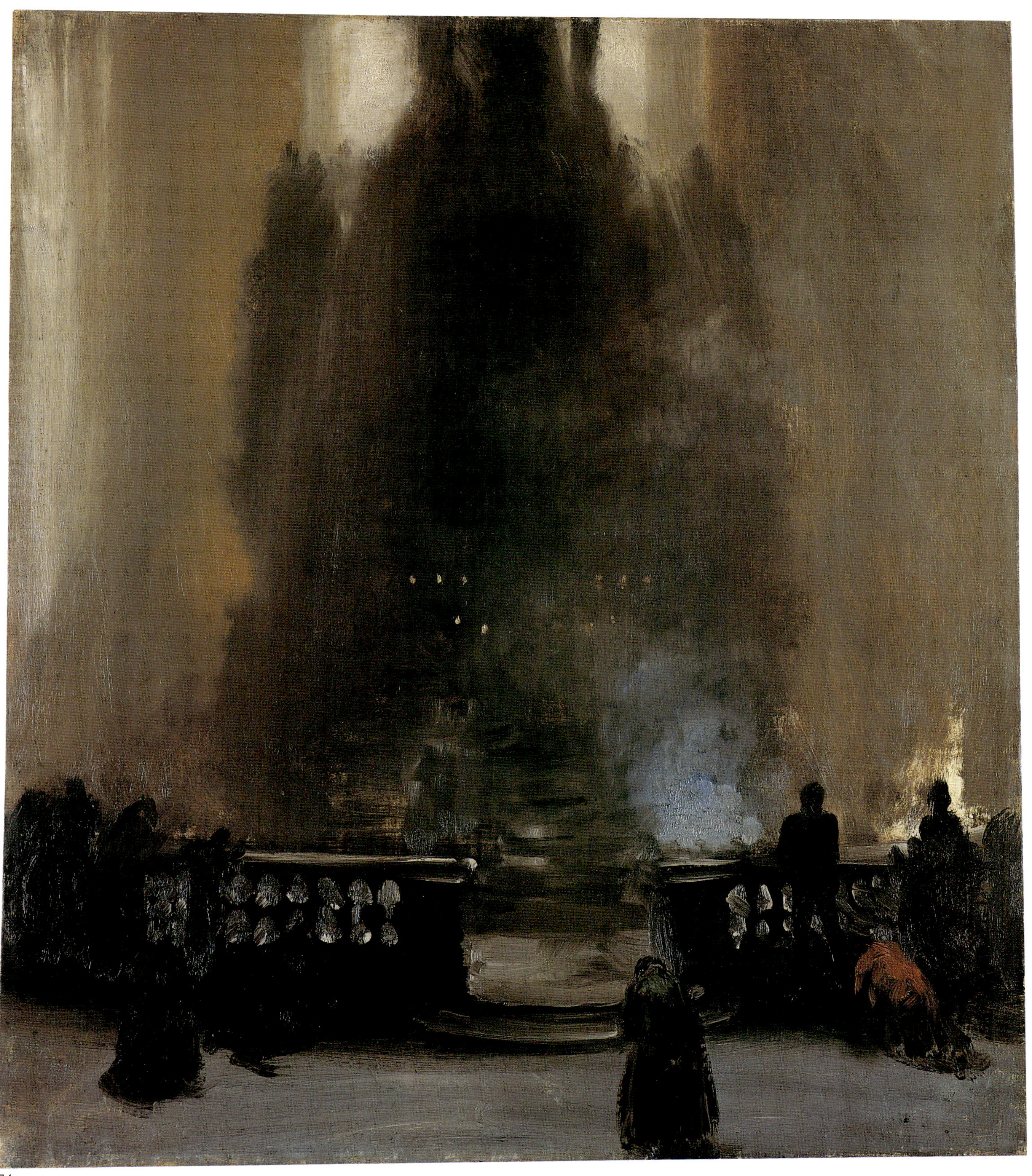

71

1. Letter to Adolf Schöll, archaeologist at Weimar, 18 January 1853, Deetjen, 1934, p. 31. This letter is also the main source for what follows.
2. Tschudi, 1905 A, no. 88; Cologne, Wallraf-Richartz-Museum.
3. Gouache painted after a second visit in 1866: Tschudi, 1905 A, no. 666; Euerbach, Georg Schäfer collection. Later, in 1901, a gouache entitled *End of the Yom Kippur festival*, Tschudi, 1905 A, no. 685, in the same collection.
4. Large rough sketch in gouache and pastel (1851) in the Kunsthalle in Hamburg (exhib. cat. Hambrug, 1982, no. 56, col. reprod.); lithograph, 1852, Bock, 1923, no. 406.

71

Church Interior

c. 1852–5

Oil on canvas
70.5 × 60cm
Berlin, Nationalgalerie (A III 507)

Provenance: Painters studio; 1905 Emilie Krigar-Menzel; acquired by the museum in 1906.
Exhibitions: Berlin, 1905, no. 102; Berlin, 1980 A, no. XIII, reprod. p. 213.
Bibliography: Tschudi, 1905 A, no. 11; cat NG, 1986, s.p.

The same effect that one sees in Menzel's drawings is used here, where the stump drawing spreads areas of grey shadow over the paper before the details are put in in pencil. Here on the background prepared with an ochre-toned scumble, the grey ghost of the baroque altar appears first. Only tiny points of light – altar candles – allow the situation to be identified. The colour of the whitish window and the blue rising smoke is more compact. But the most imposing presences are those of the altar railing, whose polished surface reflects the light brightly, and of the faithful before it. They are all anonymous, although of varying density. Probably without intending it originally, Menzel once more embroiders the theme of dualism by opposing two different states of pictorial existence. The half-fading apparition of the inaccessible contrasts with the foreground, palpable and present. It is reminiscent of Caspar David Friedrich (*cf.* cat. 42), who opposes the foreground and the background of his landscapes in a comparable way. This kind of 'pure' painting creates a deeply Romantic situation.

The front view, unusual for Menzel, underlines the irregular distribution of the figures. Twenty years later, a similar motif would be used quite differently in a gouache depicting *The Main Altar* in the Damenstiftskirche in Munich[1], which is an oblique view with a profusion of details and anecdotal features.

C.K.

1. 1873, Tschudi, 1905 A, no. 604; exhib. cat. Kiel, 1981, no. 143, reprod.

72

Church Interior with Woman at Prayer, before a Rococo Iron Grille

c. 1852–5

Oil on board
25.8 × 33.5cm
Munich, Bayerische Staatsgemäldesammlungen, Neue Pinakothek (8502)
Exhibited in Paris only

Provenance: In the painter's last years, Gustav Kirstein saw 'a small painting from Menzel's youth – the interior of a baroque church with a woman kneeling' at his studio; before 1932, Ludwigs-Galerie, Munich; acquired by the museum in 1932.
Exhibitions: Berlin, 1861; Leipzig, 1905; Erlangen, 1971, no. 27.
Bibliography: Pietsch, 1861 A; Tschudi, 1905 A, no. 17; Kirstein, 1919, p. 86; Hütt, 1981, col. pl. 42; Eschenburg, 1984, p. 294, reprod.

Menzel had nostalgic memories of the baroque churches of his childhood in Breslau. He had his first artistic experiences and impressions within them: 'And in the venerable shadows of the churches, in the dust and candle smoke, how many martyrs intended for devotion were transformed by magic, in the imagination of the small boy, into masterpieces of art'[1]. There was no equivalent in Protestant Prussia. The young Menzel drew and painted the interior of the Cloister Church in Berlin several times[2]. Repeated journeys to southern Germany and Austria, from 1852 onwards, once again led him to sumptuous baroque churches which never ceased to inspire him. It was almost always the interior which captivated his attention, and like his other subjects, he neglected the celebrated views of the whole in favour of out-of-the-way corners.

'. . . delightful small church interior at Innsbruck: a richly ornate iron grille in front of an altar, and a clear ray of sunshine passing through the railing falls on its red cloth with a truly blinding luminosity'[3]. This description is by Ludwig Pietsch (the first critic to show enthusiasm for Menzel's paintings without a narrative subject), and it provides us with additional information on the location of this travel souvenir. It is not certain to which church in Innsbruck it relates, and probably Menzel did not wish to reproduce concrete architecture exactly. As it happened, elaborate rococo wrought-ironwork was only just starting to be appreciated by his contemporaries. In contrast with *Early Mass in a Salzburg Church* (cat. 73), where the praying figures attract the attention, the woman depicted here with her back to us, anonymous and in the corner of the picture, serves only as a kind of marker to assist in orientation. The work is a pictorial aphorism. Its narrow central image has been chosen so that the trajectory of the thin beam of light crosses the space obliquely. The phenomenon is visibly ephemeral – is a door about to open? As if to make a matching pair with *Room with a Balcony* (cat. 18), the light is the main event here. In the calm, warm colours of the half-darkness in this silent church, where the rococo style communicates its profane splendour, only the present reigns.

C.K.

1. Menzel's reply to a questionnaire on the occasion of his acceptance into the Academy of Arts. *Cf.* Oettingen, 1908, p. 184.
2. Notably a painting of 1837, acquired in 1892 by the Dresden gallery, Tschudi, 1905 A, no. 36.
3. Pietsch, 1861.

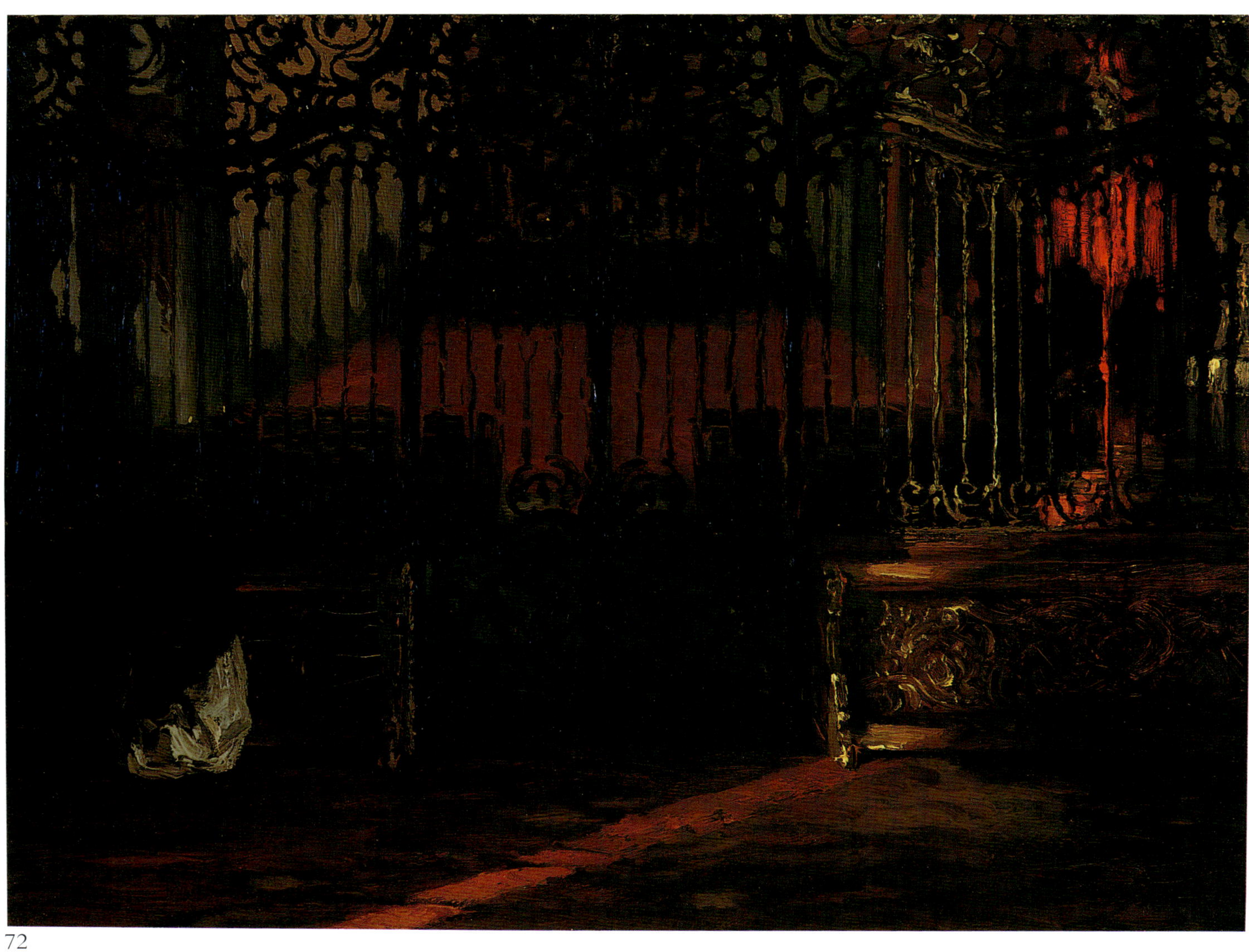

72

73

Early Mass in a Salzburg Church

1855

Oil on canvas
58.4 × 68.3cm
Signed at the bottom right: *A. Menzel*
Vienna, Österreichische Galerie im Belvedere (3699)
Exhibited in Berlin only

Provenance: Sold by the painter in 1903; acquired by Frau M. Müller-Hahn, Stuttgart; Th. Fischer Gallery, Lucerne; acquired by the museum in 1939.
Exhibitions: Berlin, 1857; Berlin, 1861; Berlin, 1903 A; Berlin, 1905, no. 81; Berlin, 1928, no. 22, reprod.; Vienna, 1940, no. 16; Vienna, 1951; Berlin, 1955 B, no. 47, fig. 39.
Bibliography: Schasler, 1857, p. 64; Pietsch, 1861; *Kunstchronik*, series no. 14, 1902–3, col. 355; Heilbut, 1902–3; Tschudi, 1905 A, no. 82; Tschudi, 1905 B, p. 236 (p. 26); Waldmann, 1941, p. 11, p. 46, fig. 40; Wirth, 1974, p. 67, fig. 70; Jensen, 1982, p. 80, p. 136, pl. 17; Koja, 1992, p. 52, p. 54.

The monument depicted here has not been identified. The traditional title was given to the work by the painter himself[1], and his information is rarely wrong. It may be that 'Salzburg' does not refer to the town itself, but to the region of Salzkammergut, which Menzel discovered in 1852 during his first visit to southern Germany and Austria: 'Ah! this spot is paradise!'[2] he exclaimed. Whatever the case may be, this subject has not been found in Salzburg, nor in Munich, which was also a possibility[3], and the chapel gates in the church at Breslau can be ruled out too[4]. It is quite likely that memories and sketches of different churches have been brought together synthetically[5]. The painter is seeking a type, a characteristic situation. The sub-

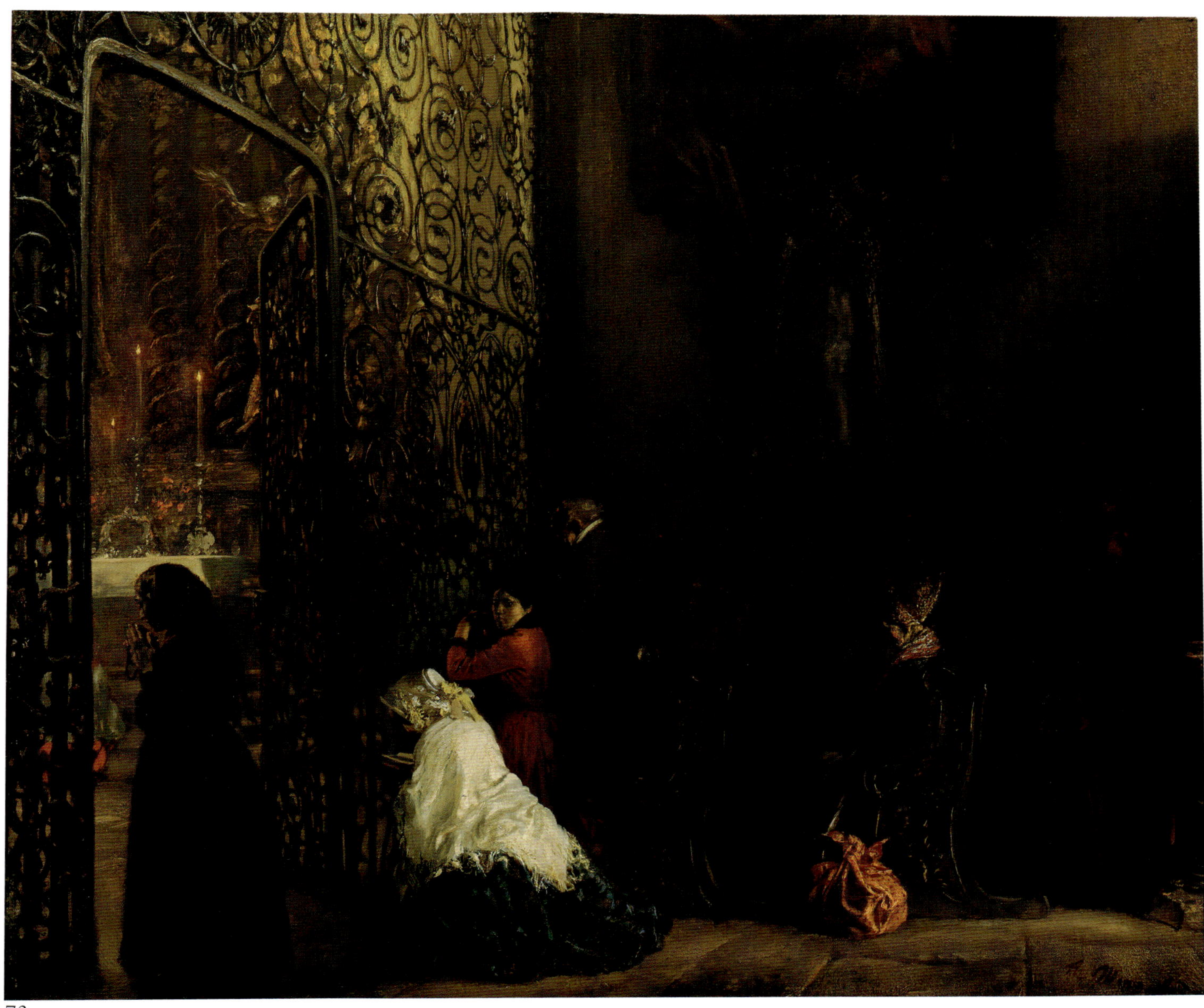

73

ject of the faithful at prayer in front of the wrought-iron baroque grille is used again in a gouache of 1876[6].

In comparison with the previous work (cat. 72), *Early Mass* is rich in narrative elements. Ludwig Pietsch admired their variety, as well as the striking authenticity of social types and situations. The dates of the two paintings are fairly close, yet the first is an echo of the young Menzel, while the second already paves the way for the descriptive density of his gouache paintings and canvasses of the later years, devoted to contemporary life.

To date the work, we must refer to the only information given from that time[7]. In the history of Menzel's critical reception, *Early Mass* has a special place because of its chance presentation in the legendary Künstlerhaus exhibition of 1903. Two canvasses – the second was the Kreuzberg landscape (*cf.* cat. 31) – plus a series of drawings were enough to cause astonishment at 'Menzel's early works. The anonymous critic of the *Kunstchronik* reported that *Early Mass* was 'thick with dust' in the painter's studio prior to this. In fact, it had been framed and hung above a writing desk in Menzel's studio from about 1895 onwards[8], but the critic comments that the painting 'had been visibly reworked or cleaned before the exhibition, which was damaging'. It seems no-one could dissuade the painter from retouching his canvas, which was also the case with the Kreuzberg landscape. But the *Early Mass* was as little known as *The Théâtre du Gymnase*. Like this painting, it had already been exhibited in 1861, and in his account of the period Ludwig Pietsch affirms that 'he already knew the painting from an exhibition organized in the early 1850s'[9]. If one considers that the choice of drawings differs very little from those already presented on other occasions, it seems that the two Künstlerhaus exhibitions were looked on as a turning point, solely because the time was right for a reassessment of Menzel's work.

Max Schasler's opinion, given in 1857, should not be ignored. After rejecting the subject, which he felt lacked interest, he insisted that Menzel's great strength lay in his exact portrayal of physical features, while colour had always been 'his weak suit, and it seems unfortunately that this weakness is getting worse rather than improving. The . . . painting has a dominant grey-black tonality, as if it were sooted up, lacking strength and warmth, with no local distribution of tones. In short, it has no real palette'. C.K.

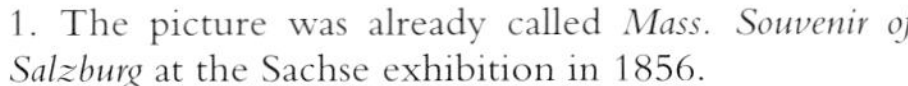

1. The picture was already called *Mass. Souvenir of Salzburg* at the Sachse exhibition in 1856.
2. Letter to Adolf Schöll, 18 January 1853, Deetjen, 1934, p. 31.
3. Wirth, 1974.
4. Jensen, 1982.
5. Wirth, 1974. A page from a sketchbook (already published by Wirth, 1974, p. 17 shows the method clearly – there is a young woman in a white shawl kneeling, from *Early Mass*, but also the rear view of a man, standing with his legs apart, from cat. 71, Sketchbook 12 (1852), p. 30.
6. Tschudi, 1905, no. 126; since 1955: Düsseldorf, private collection.
7. In *Kunst und Künstler*, 1902-3, no doubt from the Künstlerhaus exhibition inscription.
8. Photograph by Zander and Labisch, Berlin; Berlin, Kupferstichkabinett; exhib. cat. Berlin, 1984, reprod. p. 514.
9. No doubt he is referring to the one in 1857.

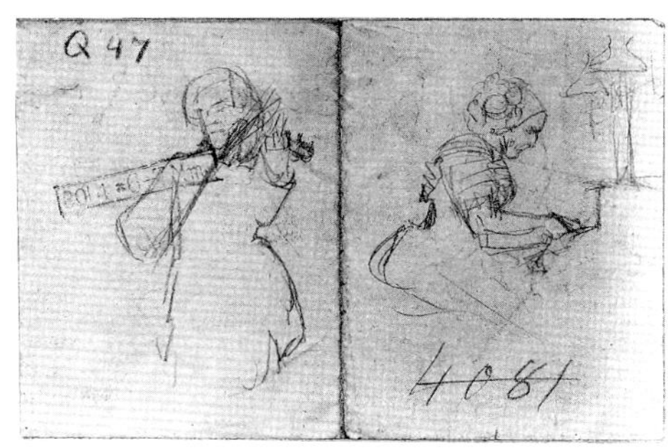

Fig. 181. *Clara Schumann and Joseph Joachim*, 1854, pencil, Berlin, Kupferstichkabinett (N 621)

74

Clara Schumann and Joseph Joachim in concert

1854

Coloured chalks
27 × 33cm
Signed and dated at the bottom left: *A.M. Erinnerung 20 Dez 54.*
Zurich, collection of Doctor Peter Nathan and Barbara Nathan
Exhibited in Paris only

Provenance: Emilie Krigar-Menzel, Berlin; 1907 Doctor Otto Krigar-Menzel, Berlin; 1958 M. Henry E. Hirschland, Rochester, NY; Georg Hirschland, Essen; Evelyne Dolk-Hirschland, Rochester, NY; Doctor Fritz Nathan, Munich.
Bibliography: Kirstein, 1919, p. 26–7, p. 116, fig. p. 24; Scheffler, 1922, p. 164, fig. p. 127; Scheffler, 1938, fig. p. 175; Scheffler, 1955, fig. p. 135; Wirth, 1965, p. 85, fig. 27; exhib. cat. Hamburg, 1982, fig. p. 119; Hochhuth, 1991, col. reprod. p. 91; Lammel, 1993 B, p. 83 *et seq.*, fig. 68.

Menzel drew this picture from memory, as he noted in the margin. A quick pencil sketch[1] was perhaps made during a concert given by the two musicians and attended by Menzel. Curiously, Clara Schumann, who was thirty-five, looks like an old woman in this sketch, and Joachim has no trace of the youthful vitality so often talked of at the time. A pastel study, in which Joachim is depicted alone and in the same posture as in this drawing, appears to be an imitation rather than a work by Menzel himself[2].

These details jotted down from memory are particularly evident in the chalk drawings of the 1850s. The majority are scenes portraying picturesque figures and reflecting events in the artist's everyday life or of his early travels. In his youth particularly, Menzel was an enthusiastic theatre-goer and rarely missed an important musical event. Like reading, music was the elixir of life to him. Although he did not play an instrument himself, he had some musical ability, and made sure his brother and sister kept up their piano lessons. The domestic practice of music in the Menzel family was further reinforced when his sister married the royal director of music, Hermann Krigar, in 1859. Through him, Menzel was able not only to discover the works of Schubert, Schumann, Wagner and Dvorák, but also to meet Johannes Brahms and Joseph Joachim personally. Krigar's training began in Berlin with Spontini, and then continued at Leipzig with Mendelssohn and Schumann. He established a quartet with Joachim, and occasionally rehearsals took place in the Krigar-Menzel house. For some time soirées at the Academy of Singing had become a habit for the Menzels. It was Joseph Joachim who, after Menzel's death, delivered a eulogy and paid musical homage to the deceased on the occasion of an Academy of Vocal Music concert. He also 'played an adagio by Haydn for Menzel in the afterlife . . . at a memorial service celebrated in the cupola of the Altes Museum'[3].

In this chalk drawing Menzel concentrates on recalling two exceptional artists, absorbed and unselfconscious as they play. The portraits depict the characteristic features of their faces very accurately. The golden light of the candle flame, which is echoed in the luminous yellow of Clara Schumann's dress, suggests the exquisite rarity of this kind of evening.

1854 was a tragic year for Clara. In February Robert Schumann threw himself into the Rhine and, although his life was saved, the growing shadow of his insanity kept him confined to the psychiatric institution at Endenich, near Bonn,

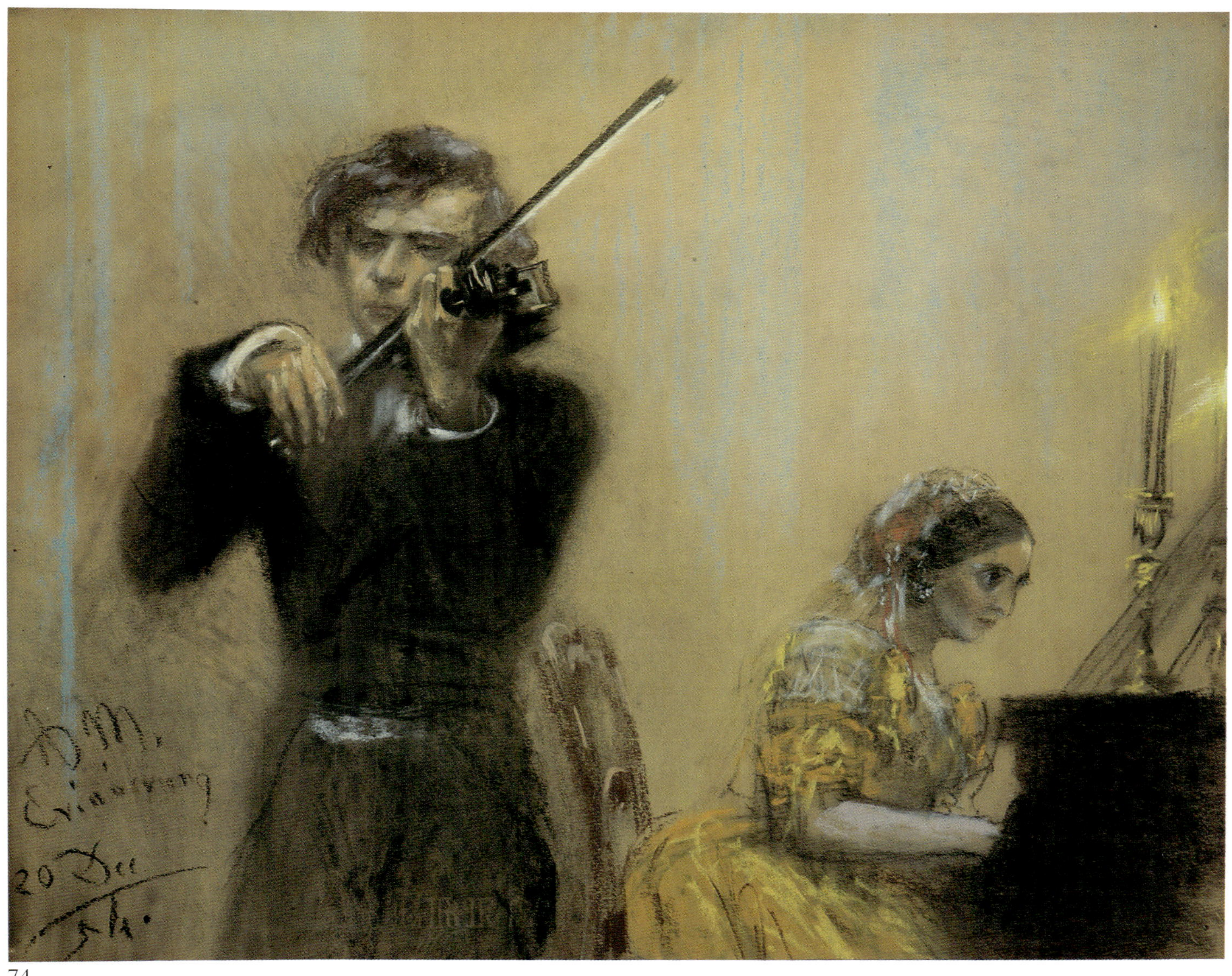

74

where he died two years later. Clara had just given birth to her seventh child, and was obliged to give concerts in order to support her family. The young Brahms, and Joachim above all, gave her their support. At the end of the year, Clara undertook a series of concerts with Joachim which took them to several towns in northern Germany. On 10 and 16 December, they gave two concerts at the Academy of Vocal Music in Berlin. The *Neue Zeitschrift für Musik* reported that 'the Berlin daily newspapers described these two evenings as the most significant event in the performing arts for as long as they could remember'. And also: 'They played Bach's Sonata in A minor and the Kreutzer Sonata for violin and piano by Beethoven; symphonic studies by Schumann and Brahms' Sonata in F minor (Frau Schumann); Bach's Chaconne and Beethoven's Romance in G major (Joachim). The second concert was even more magnificent – they played Schumann's Sonata in D minor and Beethoven's Sonata in G major (opus 30) for violin and piano; Mendelssohn's B-flat variations (opus 83), a fantasy (opus 8) by W. Bargiel, Chopin's Nocturne in C minor, a rondo from the Sonata in C minor by C.M. von Weber (Frau Schumann); a prelude and fugue for solo violin by Bach and Bach's Prelude in E major, variations from Paganini's Capriccio (Joachim). We hope that the distinguished pair – the two great musical powers, as the *National-Zeitung* calls them – will organize a third evening'[4]. It is not known whether Menzel attended the first or second of these concerts, or both. There was not a third concert in Berlin, but one was organized in Potsdam on 14 December, between the two in Berlin[5]. On 20 December, when Menzel did this drawing from memory, the two artists were already in Leipzig. They gave a concert on 21 December at the Gewandhaus. Before the Berlin concerts,

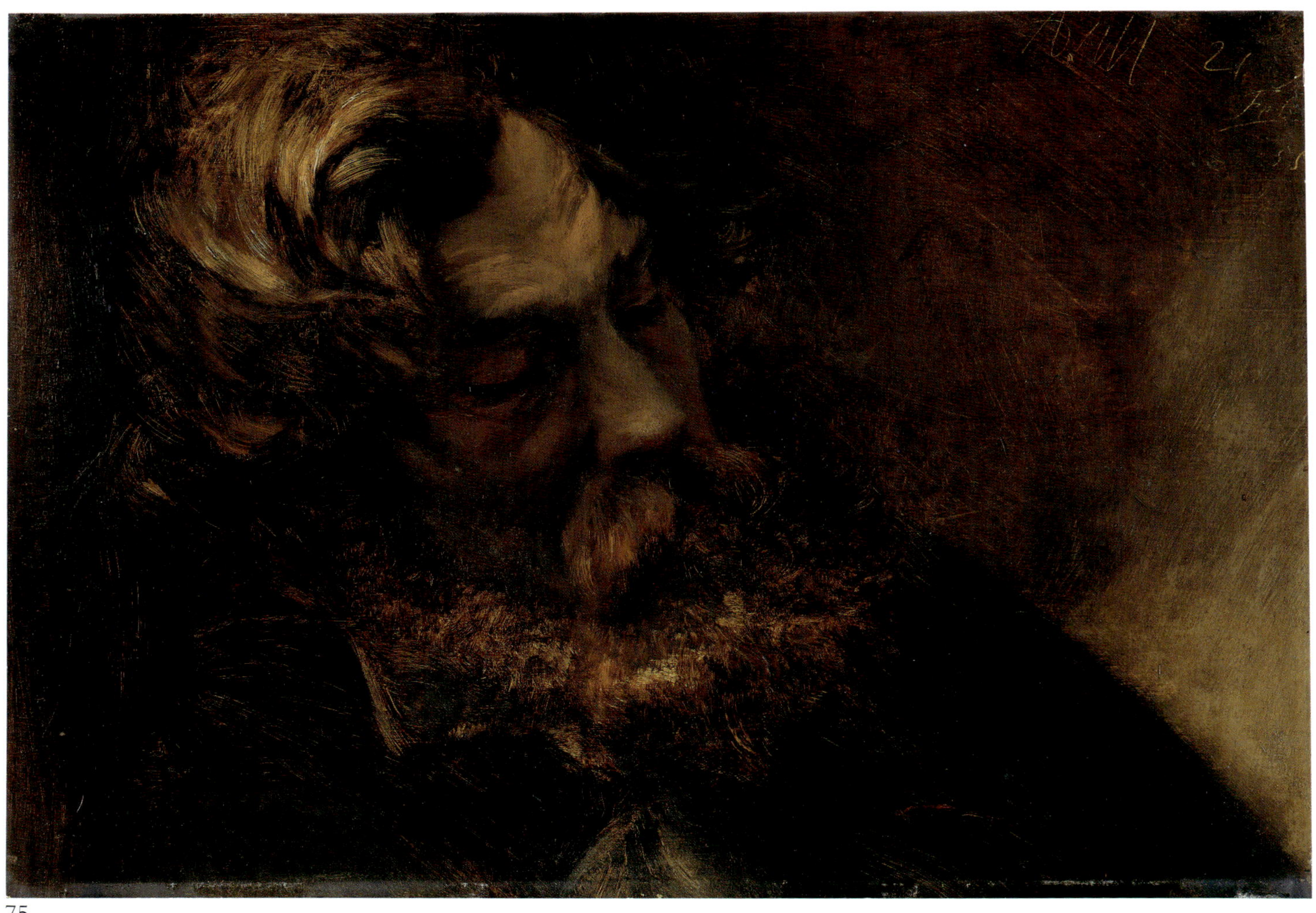
75

Joachim, who was twenty-seven, had written: 'I pray to heaven that the concerts bring in some money. I am certain that Frau Schumann's talent will inspire admiration. I revere her sincerely, and her unfortunate husband too, and am glad to support her in the concerts, although I am repulsed more than ever at having to earn a living by making a public exhibition of myself . . .'[6].

Later, Menzel drew a portrait of Robert Schumann at his own initiative, which was made into a lithograph by Gustav Feckert. In 1861, he wrote a few ironic words on this subject: 'I have been pushed in the direction of ideal values by all the new local press, which has taken up the cause of aesthetics [Menzel is alluding to the repeated criticism of his 'realism' by Max Schasler, published in the review *Die Dioskuren*], and in this small work I have moved away from the tendency towards an art which has no content, instead embracing universal reality by painting a life-sized portrait of Robert Schumann, without ever having met him'[7]. M.R.-R.

1. Berlin, Kupferstichkabinett (SZ Menzel N 621), reprod. in Wolff, 1916, p.43.
2. Hamburg, private collection; reproduced several times since 1965.
3. Moser, 1910, vol. 2, p. 321.
4. *Neue Zeitschrift für Musik* (Robert Schumann was the founder), no. 26, 22 December 1854, p. 283-4. *Cf.* Kirstein, 1919, p. 116, reference to Litzmann, 1902, vol. 2, p. 359 (describes a concert on 20 December).
5. Letter to the musician Bernhard Cossmann, Berlin, 12 December 1854, *Letters to and from Joseph Joachim*, gathered and edited by Joseph Joachim and Andreas Moser, Berlin, 1911, vol. 1, p. 237.
6. Letter to Herman Grimm, Hanover, about 5 December 1854, *op. cit.* p. 235.
7. Letter to Wilhelm Puhlmann, 1 April 1861, Wolff, 1914, p. 181: Menzel told his friend that he would send him the lithographed portrait of Schumann for his birthday.

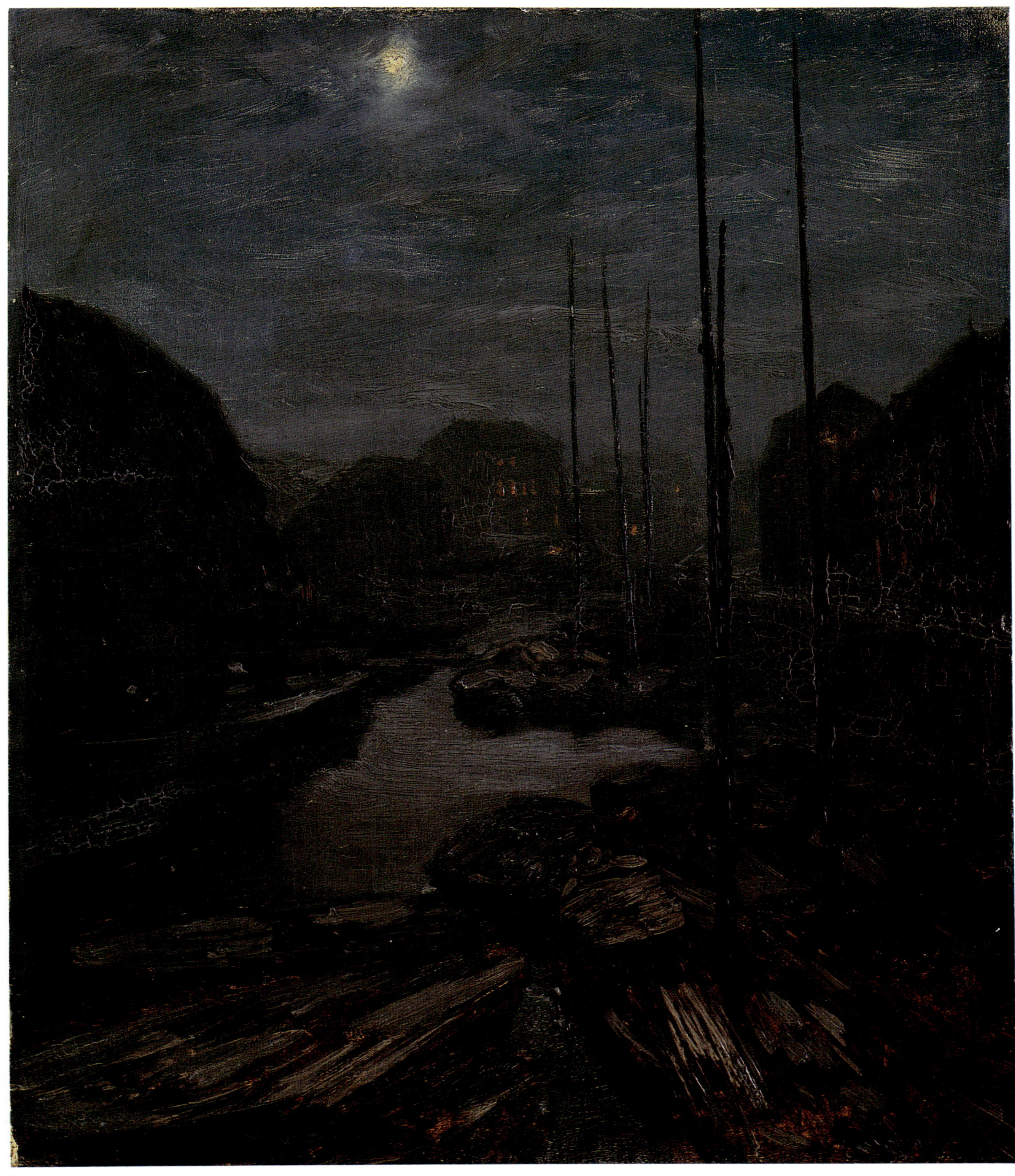

76

75

Man Asleep

1855

Oil on paper, board backing
37 × 52.3cm
Signed and dated at the top right (engraved on the painting): *A.M. 21 Feb 55*
Berlin, Nationalgalerie (A I 959)

Provenance: Hermann Pächter (R. Wagner Gallery, Berlin); acquired by the museum in 1889.
Exhibitions: Hamburg, 1896, no. 7; Vienna, 1896, no. 280; Berlin, 1905, no. 9; Berlin, 1980 A, no. XVII, reprod. p. 144.
Bibliography: Donop, 1902, no. 1410; Tschudi, 1905 A, no. 98; Meier-Graefe, 1906, p. 90; cat NG, 1986, no pag., fig. 70.

Around 1855 Menzel painted a series of 'studies' of heads of old bearded men, including Jews, as he had already observed them in 1851 in preparation for his painting *Jesus among the Doctors*. The standard classification of works by genre is deceptive. Certain paintings using anonymous models have no less significance than the masterpieces related to *Room with a Balcony*, which were also formerly catalogued as studies. Similarly, a number of portraits of old men were painted in Rembrandt's studio, some of which were large format, due to the painter's love of the landscape of their faces and their impenetrable psychology. *Man Asleep* also recalls these paintings in the softly blended light which shines on curls of hair and touches the forehead, while most of the face is in shadow. In the near foreground, leaning towards the viewer with the falling shoulders forming a single oblique plane, the life-sized head could be oppressive if sleepiness and the dim light did not counteract this tendency. Amid this uncustomary imprecision, in which it seems as if everything to which portraiture aspires is called into question, discretion and suggestiveness triumph. In 1906, Meier-Graefe compared this painting to *Night in the Forest* (cat. 58) because of its lyrical touches, and saw in it a hint of a Rubens study. C.K.

76

Moonlight on the Friedrichsgracht in Old Berlin

c. 1855

Oil on canvas
39.5 × 33cm
Berlin, Nationalgalerie (A II 150)
Exhibited in Paris and Berlin only

Provenance: Paul Cassirer Gallery, Berlin; acquired by the museum in 1916.
Exhibitions: Berlin, 1980 A, no. XV, reprod. p. 145; Berlin, 1987 A, no. F41, col. reprod. p. 240.
Bibliography: Not mentioned by Tschudi, 1905 A; cat. NG, 1918, no. 1284; Mackowsky, 1917–18, p. 100–3, reprod. p. 101; cat. NG, 1986, no pag., fig. 69.

This painting seems to be one of those which were sold while the painter was alive (and perhaps at a fairly early stage, when he did not bother to sign every work before he parted with it), and it remained unknown even to the art historians who catalogued the works in 1905. The Friedrichsgracht, an arm of the river Spree whose course was altered in 1681, bounds the colony of fishermen to the West in Kölln, one of the two core towns, dating back to the middle ages, that formed the city of Berlin. The district is near the Ritterstrasse where Menzel lived in the 1850s. Hans Mackowsky, who expressed the poetry of the painting so well in terms of an autumn night, dated it towards the end of the 1850s, and recalled the life-sized portrait by the painter Daniel Chodowiecki, whom Menzel revered, and whom he imagined in 1895, drawing in front of the parapet of the Jannowitzbrücke, not far distant[1].

The landscape in the Nationalgalerie directs the eye from a bridge – probably the extension of the Rossstrasse – towards the south, passing over boats whose masts disappear into the distance, into space, and leading it along the river edged with houses deep in mist, until a bend in the river (near the Spittelmarkt) obscures the background with buildings. The veiled moon is hanging in the dark blue, in which dark blocks of brownish colour, denser and more matt, distinguish the houses from the smooth surface of the water. The few lights shining from their windows are transformed into extremely thin orange rays. In the middle ground, some high-masted boats form a further part of this sphere of dark reflections, which they link to the foreground, indicated by impulsive streaks of colour. Yet no observation of detail stands out from the whole in this lyrical nocturne, more evocative than mimetic, which could not have been created before the subject was conceived. C.K.

1. Tschudi, 1905 A, no. 118; Euerbach, Georg Schäfer collection.

77

Head of a Worker Wearing a Cap

1855

Oil on canvas, wood backing
35 × 27cm
Signed and dated at the bottom right: *A.M. 1855*
Rome, Doctor Benno Griebert
Exhibited in Berlin only

Provenance: G. Zaeslein Gallery, Berlin; Carl Nicolai Gallery, Berlin; 1928 sale to Hugo Helbing, Munich, no. 135, pl. 7; 1955 Arthur Henneke, industrialist, Düsseldorf.
Exhibitions: Berlin, 1955 B, no. 70; Berlin, 1991, unnumb., reprod. p. 237.
Bibliography: Tschudi, 1905 A, no. 97 a; Kaiser, 1953, p. 97, fig. 78; Kaiser, 1956, p. 67 *et seq.*, fig. 40; Hütt, 1965, fig. 62; Hütt, 1981, p. 142, fig. 107.

Throughout his life, Menzel explored the physical appearance of the worker, and his world (*cf.* cat. 12, 147–60, fig. 5). This continuity is not the least of the surprising characteristics which made him an artist exceptional in his generation, and more generally, in his century. It relates to the universality of his observation, which not only takes in the most diverse subjects, but scrutinizes the historical layers of society. A head like this one encapsulated the most recent transformations which pointed towards the future. It should be noted that, when this second

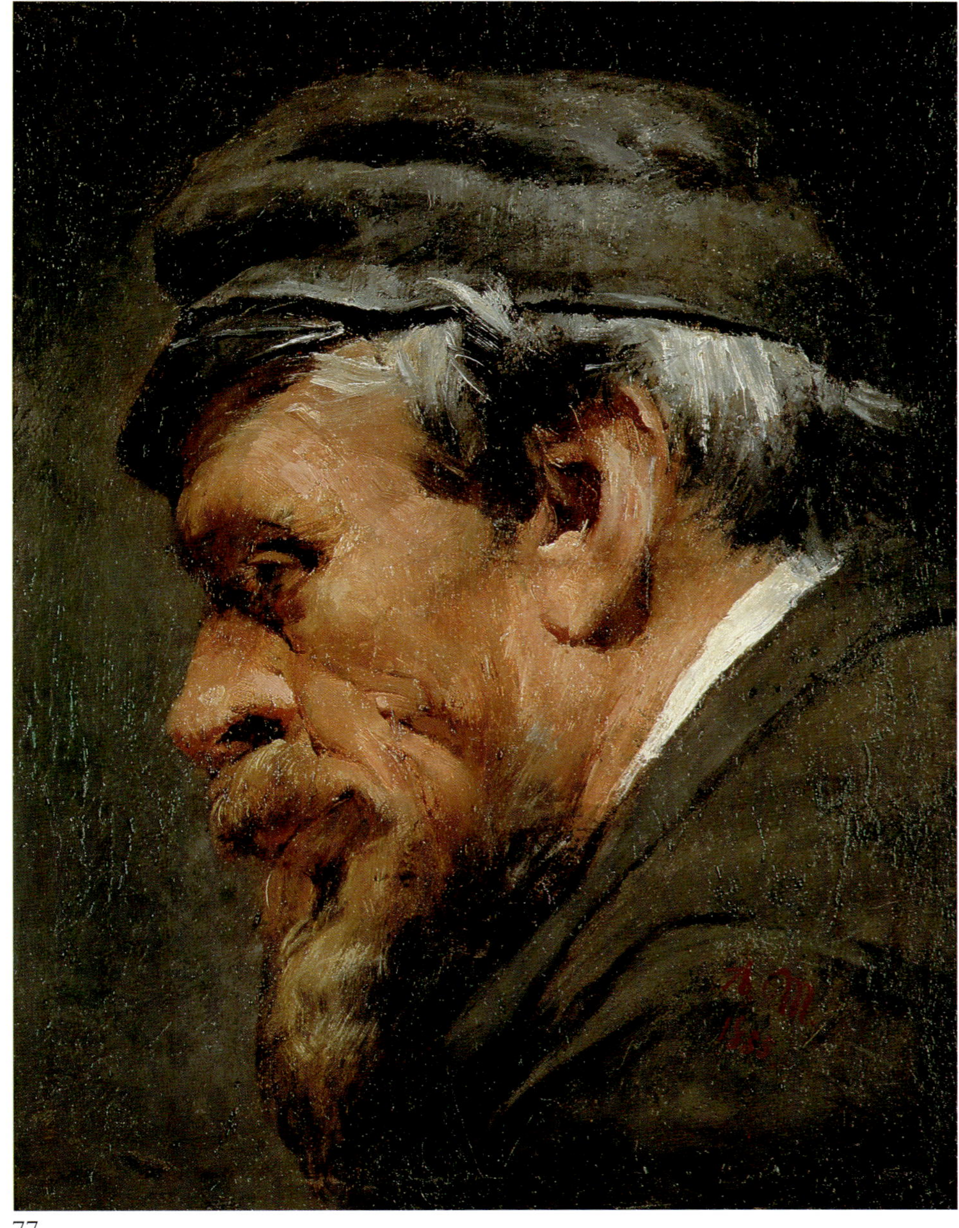

77

portrait of a worker had been finished, an ambitious historical painting project was in progress, *Night Attack at Hochkirch*. On the other hand, the artist painted this canvas some years after the enthusiastic description by Friedrich Eggers, a close friend of Menzel, of pictorial subjects observed in a metalworking factory[1]. It is true that Eggers only speaks of 'powerful figures', of 'the natural and primary movement of athletic limbs', and of varied groupings – he is happy to look from a distance. Using an imposing format, Menzel turns his attention to the palpable characteristics of an individual face, which is so close as to be almost oppressive. The cap is emphasized, to show that the man belongs to the working class. His head, leaning slightly to the side, appears to have been isolated and enlarged. This effect is not the exclusive attribute of a 'study' – the Viennese portrait artist Friedrich von Amerling more than once gave preference to the incidental, familiar appearance of the *profile perdu*[2]. In 1846, Menzel had painted his brother Richard at the same angle[3], and the turning away of the head does not lessen the psychological appeal in this portrait, nor in that of the worker. The painter usually circumvented the outer appearance of things, both literally and figuratively, and he does the same in his portraits. In 1854, he painted the bust of the *Old Messenger Woman*[4] in the form of a portrait, although an anonymous one. Here again, the lower strata of the urban population break into traditional painting. A very marked individuality is depicted in the source of mysterious light, reminiscent of Rembrandt. There is also an astonishing affinity of these portraits with those of the Munich painter Joseph George Edlinger (1741–1819), whose works he could surely not have seen in Berlin. Moreover, the unknown people who appear in these sombre portraits with their muddy colours as the poor are in reality members of the petty bourgeoisie. C.K.

1. Riemann-Reyher, 1976, p. 4. *Cf.* cat. 147–60.
2. Notably the portrait of Carl Vogel von Vogelstein, 1837 (Berlin, Nationalgalerie).
3. Euerbach, Georg Schäfer collection.
4. Euerbach, Georg Schäfer collection.

78
Recollection of Paris
1855

Pastel
29.3 × 39.1cm
Signed and dated at the bottom right: *Erinnerung. Menzel 1855*
Hamburg, Hamburger Kunsthalle (5475)
Exhibited in Paris only

Provenance: Dr Helmut Janus, lawyer and notary, Essen; acquired by the museum in 1991.
Exhibition: Berlin, 1955 B, no. 74.
Bibliography: Siner, 1904, p. 157; Howoldt, 1993, p. 28, col. reprod. p. 29.

On 1 August 1855, Menzel and his sister arrived at the Marienburg (in West Prussia), which was in the process of restoration, in order to paint, over a

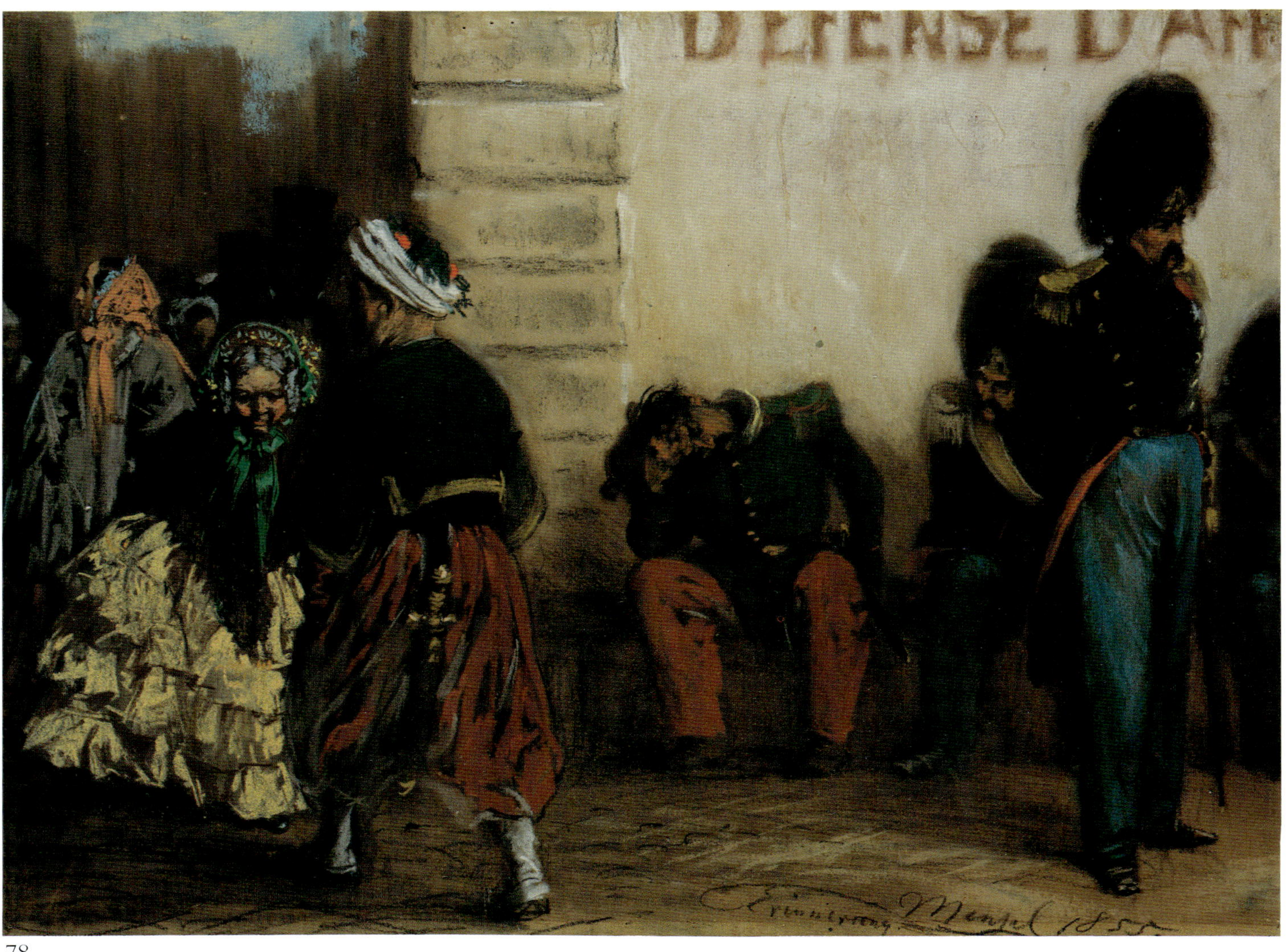

78

period of nine days, the life-sized figures of two Grand Masters of the Teutonic Order (*cf.* cat. 20). As he wrote to a friend: 'After the pleasure of work, . . . the travail of pleasure'[1]. In fact the journey had only just begun, since Menzel retraced his steps, reaching Cologne, and then, after a detour in the Black Forest, he visited Strasbourg and Paris. In the second half of September, he saw Paris at the time of the Universal Exhibition and visited the first international painting exhibition and Courbet's Pavilion of Realism. After his return from 'Babel', he wrote to Puhlmann that he was quite incapable of expressing his impressions, and in his usual comic manner, invited him to visit him if he wished to broaden his knowledge on the subject of 'lackeys, ruins of the homes of gentlemen, the illuminations, castles, vines, chamber pots, innkeepers bills, machines, foul railways that fly through the air, works of art, fountains, etc. . .'[2].

It is doubtful that the chaos of the capital city daunted him. One thing is for certain: his realist aesthetic found great encouragement in his first stay in Paris. *The Théâtre du Gymnase* and *Policeman and Lady in the Tuileries Gardens* (cat. 80, 79) provide rare artistic evidence of his journey. This coloured chalk drawing was suggested to him by several quick sketches[3] of the soldier wearing a busby and standing, the soldier sitting with his head in his hand, and the lady in the crinoline dress. The word 'Erinnerung' added to so many of Menzel's works indicates that the subject was drawn from memory. In the resulting snapshot, only the corner of a large public building is retained, upon which is written 'POSTERS PROHIBITED'. But only part of the writing is visible, and the overall composition has the same fragmentary, momentary effect. Two soldiers are sitting on the stone plinth at the bottom of the wall, and a third is cut off by the edge of the drawing. A standing figure is turning to the right. A Zouave on the other side is heading for the road where two ladies are walking, and further away, a man is wearing a top hat. The impression is of a busy street. In the back-

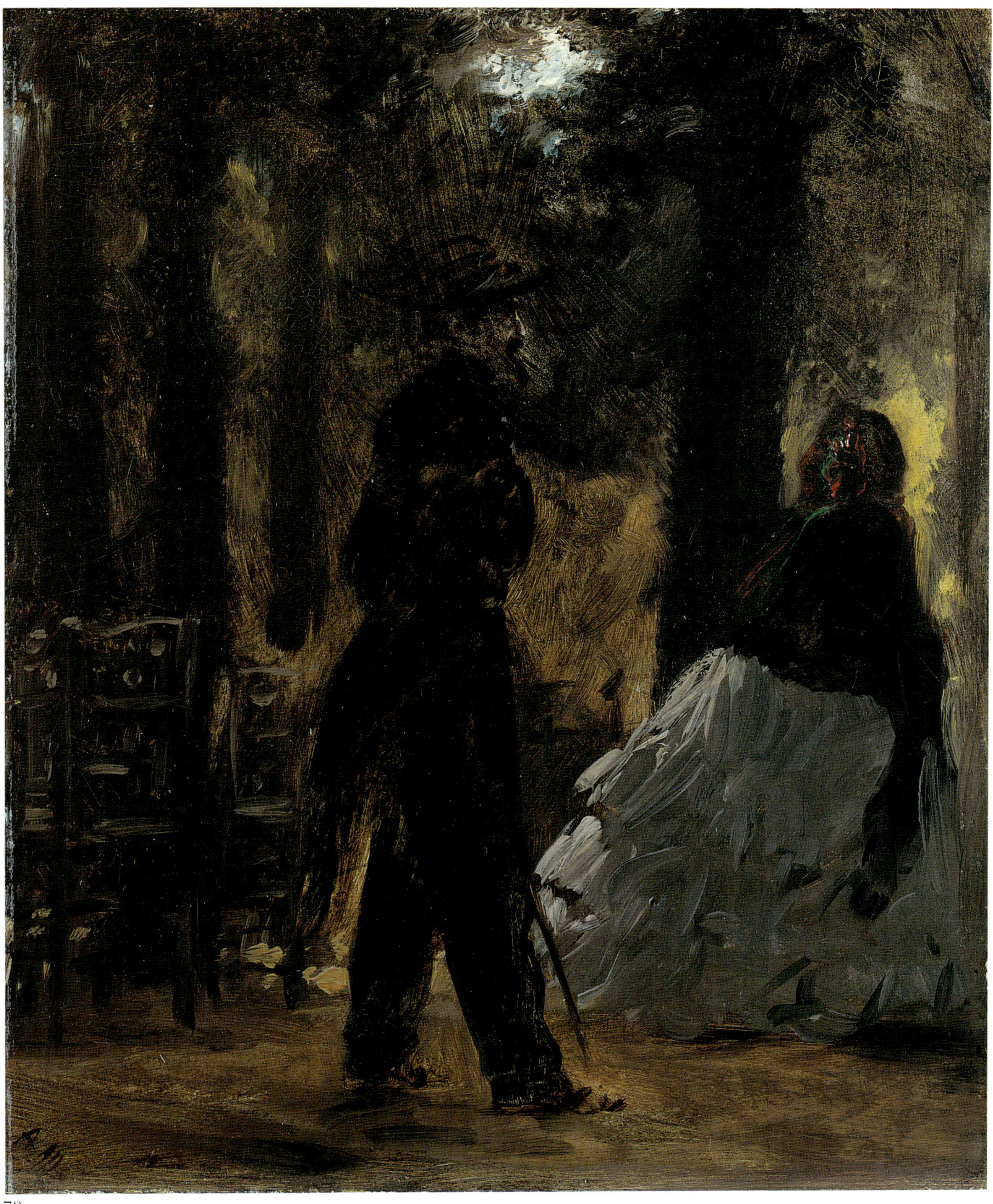

79

ground a tiny area of blue sky with white clouds can be seen. This extreme reduction of the sky would become a characteristic of later urban landscapes. The background is covered vertically with layers of brown, suggesting a row of high buildings bordering a street.

The strong colours of the blue and red trousers, the yellow and intense blue-green, are also used in the pastel *At Church*, which portrays men and women sitting in pews[4]. The deep tones in some places and the overall tendency show that Menzel was soon to turn away from pastel painting in favour of a mixed technique, using gouache in particular. This drawing portrays figures turned towards each other, one set against the other, with no real link between them. This prefigures the urban landscapes painted ten years later, after two more trips to Paris, in which individuals would merge into an anonymous crowd (cat. 123, 127).

M.R.-R.

1. Letter to the writer Paul Heyse, 19 October 1855, Munich, Bayerische Staatsbibliothek, Heyse VI archives (Menzel).
2. Letter to Dr Puhlmann, 29 September 1855, Wolff, 1914, p. 168.
3. Berlin, Kupferstichkabinett, sketchbook 14, p. 126, p. 131, p. 141. According to Singer, 1904, the drawing was exhibited in 1904, with another one hundred and fifty or so works.
4. Berlin, Kupferstichkabinett (SZ Menzel N 317).

79

Policeman and Lady in the Tuileries Gardens

†1856

Oil on board
23 × 19cm
Signed at the bottom left: *A.M.*
Berlin, Nationalgalerie (F 243)

Provenance: Dr Wilhelm Puhlmann, Potsdam; acquired by the museum after his death, in 1882.
Exhibitions: Berlin, 1895 A, no. 134; Hamburg, 1896, no. 93; Vienna, 1896, no. 273; Berlin, 1905, no. 21; Berlin, 1935, no. 32; Celle, 1949–50, no. 67, p. 8; Berlin, 1950–1, no. 52; Berlin, 1955 B, no. 76, fig. 33; Paris, 1984–5, no. 99, reprod.
Bibliography: Donop, 1902, no. 661; Tschudi, 1905 A, no. 109; cat NG, 1907, no. 971; Scheffler, 1912, p. 130, reprod. p. 128; Waldmann, 1922, fig. 10; Scheffler, 1922, p. 179–80, reprod. p. 155; Scheffler, 1938, p. 72 *et seq.*; Waldmann, 1941, p. 47, fig. 47; cat NG, 1976, p. 276, reprod.

This small picture is unique in German painting and in international painting of its time. It is at once a spontaneous transcription of the moment (in my opinion), a painting of changing light and an image of modern life. Undoubtedly the reduced format permits the kind of daring which would have been forbidden in Salon painting. The artist deliberately ignores anecdote. Gavarni would have drawn material for a description of social customs from this subject, and Daumier would have dwelt longer upon the figures. Menzel is content to skim over the scene. He seems to have wanted to capture a fleeting, accidental impression in his painting. Often, this situation became the rule in his last 'pictures' done in pencil, which consist of a reflection on the theme of memory and the effort of memorization. The scene communicates little. The beautiful woman in the crinoline dress, almost shapeless, is viewed only from behind. Another insubstantial, ghostly figure crosses the front of the picture to reach the median axis. The profile establishes no link with the volumes of the composition, and here one recalls the lady in the foreground of the sketch for *The Flute Concert*. In the almost white patch at the top, in the luminous yellow behind the woman, in the clarity of outline of her dress, the strong light of a summer day, piercing the foliage, produces an array of changing colours.

C.K.

80

The Théâtre du Gymnase

1856

Oil on canvas
46 × 62cm
Signed at the bottom left: *Menzel. 1856*
Berlin, Nationalgalerie (A I 901)

Provenance: 1902 Adolf Rothermund, Dresden-Blasewitz; acquired by the museum in 1906.
Exhibitions: Berlin, 1861; Berlin, 1903 B, no. 1; Dresden, 1903 A; Dresden, 1904, no. 2372; Berlin, 1905, no. 5701; Berlin, 1906, no. 1157, reprod. p. 132; Boston, 1909, unnumb. (p. 56), pl. (unnumb.); Berlin, 1935, no. 30; Wiesbaden, 1947, no. 60, p. 9; Wiesbaden, 1952, no. 160, reprod.; Berlin, 1955 B, no. 77, fig. 35; London, 1956, no. 166; Cologne, 1971, no. 69, col. pl. V; New York, 1981, no. 63, col. pl.; Paris, 1985, no. 100, reprod.
Bibliography: Pietsch, 1861; Norden, 1900 (1992), p. 82; Jordan, 1905, p. 102; Tschudi, 1905 A, no. 107; Tschudi, 1905 B, p. 236, col. pl. facing p. 299 (p. 26, col. pl. facing p. 89); Meier-Graefe, 1906, p. 186 *et seq.*; cat. NG, 1907, no. 984; Meier-Graefe, 1906, p. 129–38, p. 142 *et seq.*, p. 167, p. 182–4, p. 211; Scheffler, 1912, p. 130 *et seq.*, reprod. p. 127; Kern, 1915–16, col. reprod. facing p. 96; Kirstein, 1919, p. 28, p. 116; Justi, 1920, p. 144–6, pl. 7; Scheffler, 1938, p. 73, p. 111, p.134, reprod. p. 176; Waldmann, 1941, p. 17–19, p. 39, p. 47, figs 48–9, col. pl. II; cat. BG, 1976, p. 274, p. 276, reprod.; Forset-Hahn, 1980, p. 32–5; Hütt, 1981, fig. 70 (col.); Jensen, 1982, p. 86 *et seq.*, col. pl. 20.

One wonders why contemporaries only learned of about Menzel's first stay in Paris, allegedly a secret, when the *Théâtre du Gymnase* was shown in 1903[1]. Not only had the picture already been shown in 1861, but a short piece in the *Kunstblatt* had announced the trip to the public, and upon the artist's return a full account of it was written[2]. Menzel's participation in the 1855 Salon took on a special importance due to the Universal Exhibition which formed the framework for all events that summer. He visited it, the second of its kind, for two weeks in September, and from then on he chose the name 'Babel' to describe the 'capital of the nineteenth century' – Paris – and he still used this name twelve years later. One can only speculate on which works and painters attracted his attention (*cf.* Thomas W. Gaehtgens in this catalogue, p. 113 *et seq.*).

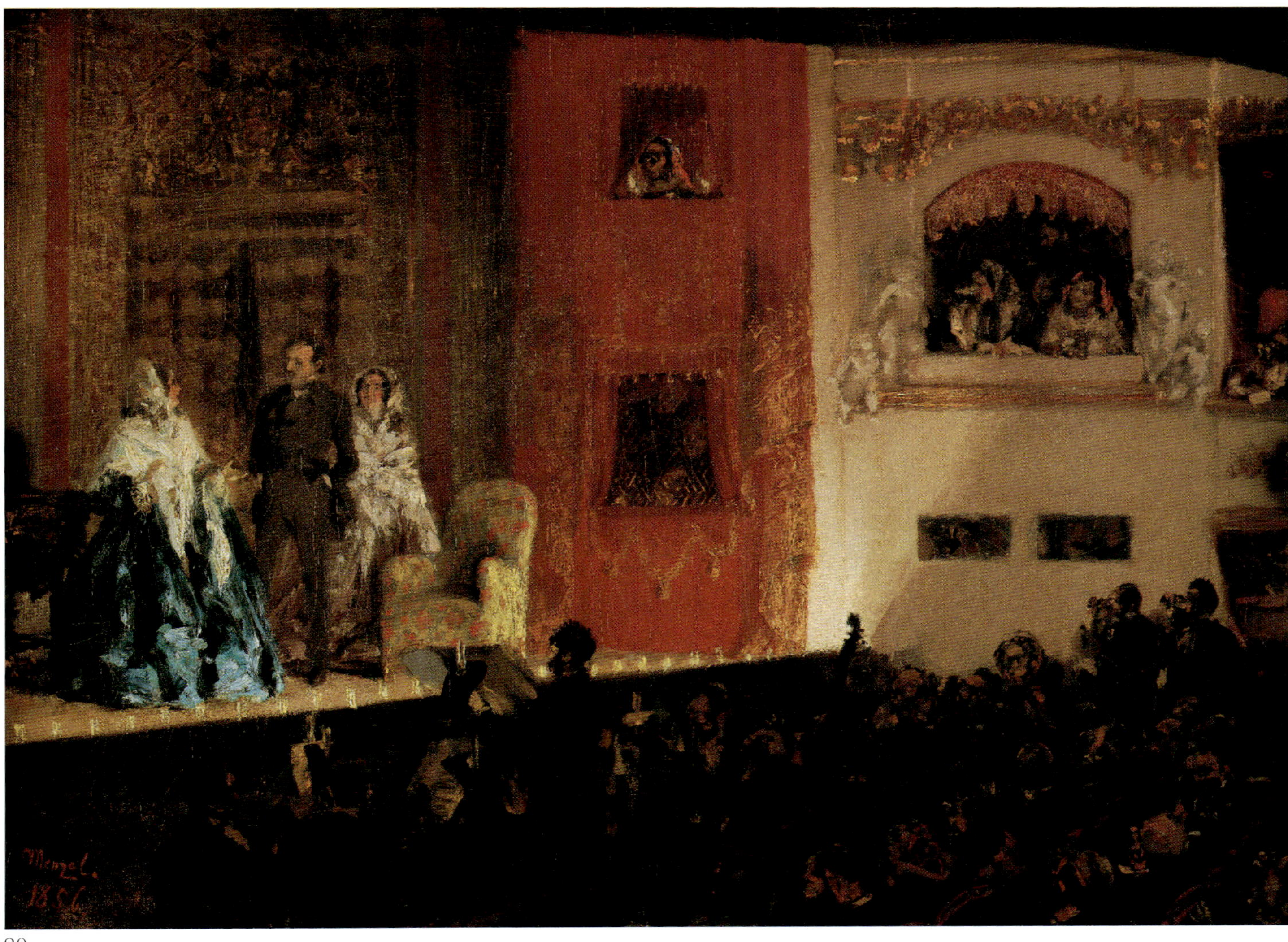

80

A year later, when *Night Attack at Hochkirch* was finished, the starting point for the picture was a double page in the sketchbook[3] he had used in Paris. It shows the inside of the Théâtre Madame built by Auguste Rougevin, inaugurated in 1820 and soon to change its name[4] (fig. 4). The light comedies of Eugène Scribe were put on here, and even if the presence of a small orchestra suggests another genre, either melodrama or musical comedy, the play is definitely a fashionable' contemporary one.

Although the basic details of the sketch are used, the enlarged composition gains in breadth and rigour. The stage dominated by the flaming red of the box takes up almost two-thirds of its width. The actors, who have increased in number by one, have additional importance; people are watching from their boxes and the leader of the orchestra extends above the framework of the stage, as does the scroll of the double bass, linking the two parts of the theatre – a procedure later familiar to Degas.

Menzel's picture is often linked with Daumier's *The Drama*[5] (and they could have been compared today at the Nationalgalerie if William II had not stood in the way of the purchase; fig. 118). No connection is possible if, as stated most frequently, the Frenchman's work was painted about 1860. But the subject was in the air, and provided an opportunity to portray urban life, as did the depiction of cafés (or open-air cafés in Menzel's case), with all their fleeting gatherings and false atmosphere under artificial daylight, with strange, unreal scenes detached from daily life. Menzel echoes Daumier in the critical representation of society, the contrast between the unselfconscious liveliness of the audience and the stiff attitude of the group on the stage, which projects a refined, polished image of the people themselves.

All the figures that appear in the work of Degas and of Toulouse-Lautrec until the end of the century had already appeared in Menzel's paintings, together with the oblique viewpoint and layout on the canvas, which gives each of the three parts of the picture – stage, orchestra, boxes – a peripheral place. Four years after *The Flute Concert*, *The Théâtre du Gymnase* suggests a modern antithesis to this history painting. With comparable initial elements – performers and public, artificial light, a world of appearances and leisure apart from daily life – it is not only the focus on a central figure that is abandoned, but also the psychological differentiation. The public is a crowd, the actors an artistic composition in which individuality is obliterated. Menzel did not seek the tension of the emotions behind actions, neither on the stage nor among the audience (while it is a main theme in Daumier's works; *cf.* Gaehtgens, p. 117), and renounces individualization in favour of a mass effect. In the detail, there is a great deal of disorder and divergent movement, which are not linked together. Even the action on the stage is somehow incidental. Watching the play is interpreted as a kind of avid consumption, with the opera glasses as weapons in a futile chase. And as if the viewer himself were armed with a similar weapon, he sees the three figures on the stage in more vivid colours and with greater clarity than the musicians in the orchestra pit and the spectators in the auditorium, although they are closer.

The ordered distribution of surfaces is dramatized by the sensational use of the three primary colours, red, yellow and blue, and by the effect of distance given by lighting from below. The colour is reminiscent of Delacroix. But what was the canvas like in its early stages? The question arises because it was reported that Menzel 'until his last years, before the picture left his studio, added faces to the figures [of the audience] to make them more "interesting"'[6].

When the painting was shown for the first time, Ludwig Pietsch marvelled at the feeling of real life portrayed by the scene, and commented on 'the battle between the light on the building from above and that on the stage from below'. 'What character', he added, 'in all the heads of the players in the orchestra seen from above!'. When this was written, the painting was five years old, and Menzel was already preparing to give a quite different 'character' to a crowd of spectators. Several weeks before, he had received the commission for the painting of the *Coronation* (*cf.* cat. 94–9). In the eyes of the generation who discovered the 'young Menzel', *The Théâtre du Gymnase* is one of the key works. Meier-Graefe devoted an entire enthusiastic chapter to it in his monograph (otherwise highly critical), and Ludwig Justi felt it to be 'perhaps the most valuable work in our collection – inasmuch as one wishes to compare it'. C.K.

1. According to Jordan, 1905, p. 102 and Kirstein, 1919, p. 28; it was only in 1902 that the ageing Menzel, who understood nothing of the journalistic chatter about the picture resolved the enigma.
2. Letter to Wilhelm Puhlmann, 29 September 1855, Wolff, 1914, p. 168.
3. Berlin, Kupferstichkabinett, (sketchbook 14, p. 132).
4. The theatre auditorium was changed in 1972.
5. *Munich, Neue Pinakothek.*
6. Kirstein, 1919, p. 116.

81
Upturned Kettle
1856

Oil on canvas
32 × 42cm
Signed and dated at the top right: *A.M. 1856*
Private collection
Exhibited in Berlin only

Provenance: 1955 Wilhelm Döring, Aix-la-Chapelle.
Exhibition: Berlin, 1955 b, no. 79.
Bibliography: Not mentioned by Tschudi, 1905 A; Kern, 1951.

Menzel never painted traditional still-life pictures of the kind found in baroque painting in multiple variations, an aspect of which endures in Biedermeier's floral compositions. To Menzel the grouping of objects on a table did not symbolize universal order, and he sought a purely decorative effect even less. What intrigues him is the disintegration of an order, the provisional situation, observed in passing and unpremeditated, but not without deep astonishment. It is true that in his illustrations for the *History of Frederick the Great* and *Works of Frederick the Great* there are numerous vignettes representing still life with an aphoristic concision, tending towards the allegorical, which could scarcely be considered as preparatory stages to those painted shortly after[1]. A literal symbolism is not sought, but rather a hidden and enigmatic suggestiveness in this copper kettle, strangely placed in unstable equilibrium on a surface which cannot be clearly defined. It seems to want to stand up on its spout, and defy static law, which the lid is obeying all the more strictly and ostentatiously. The pictorial space is not bounded on any side, being rather like a lunar landscape full of mysterious reflections of light. 'Throughout his long life,' says Paul Meyerheim, 'the artist worked a lot at night, by the light of his oil lamp, which he undertook to clean himself'[2]. This is also a painting at night, and the darkness seems to be its secret theme. It was conceived when the picture of *Night Attack at Hochkirch* was on the point of being finished after six years' work[3], and the experience with generous colour, applied over large areas, had its effect. The highlights have a pasty texture (though they are matt pink in tone), while the taut, smooth roundness of the container has a very bright reflection from a powerful beam of light, which gives the impression of thick colour (as in the *Students' Torchlight Retreat* (cat. 86). It is a dialogue with Rembrandt, whose fame had increased in the middle of the century; Menzel was able to find his works on several occasions, in Berlin, Dresden, Munich, Vienna or Paris.

If the foreshortening of the opening in the kettle and the handle are unconvincing, it is precisely through this apparent incorrectness that the object acquires an autonomous existence in space. Exceptions to the stereometric rule, frequent and intentional in Menzel, notably in

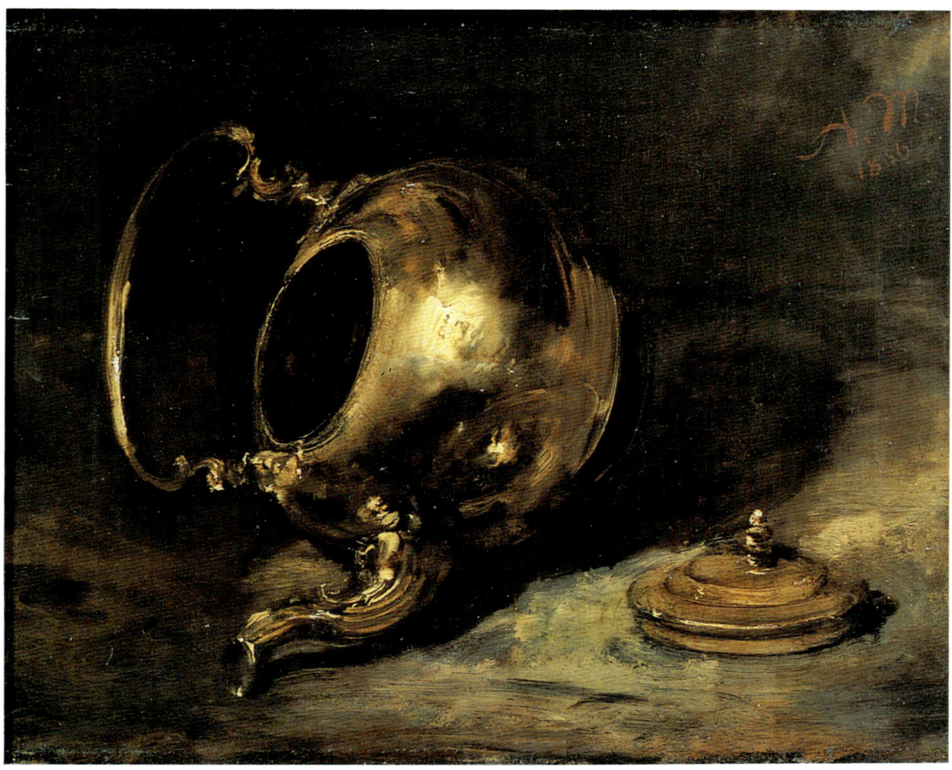

81

paintings of interiors, are none other than a manifestation of the 'movement which shifts lines', and these are constantly challenged and their position changed by the movement. The construction in harmonious perspective assumes immobility, which is an exception to the rule. Showing it as complex, Menzel suggests that movement is always possible, and that the relationship between objects is always provisional.

The everyday object too has pathos, even a theatrical effect. This small picture is closest to *Studio Wall* (cat. 65) in its form and spirit, but it also points the way to *Fantasies from the Arms Room* (cat. 117–9). C.K.

1. *Cf.* cat 65 and Tschudi, 1905 A, no. 87.
2. Meyerheim, (1906) 1992, p. 174.
3. Delivered late for the Berlin Academy exhibition, 14 October 1856.

82

Good Evening, Gentlemen! (Frederick the Great at Lissa). Sketch

1856

Oil on paper, canvas backing
32.6 × 25.6cm
Berlin, Nationalgalerie (A III 506)

Provenance: Hermann Pächter (R. Wagner Gallery; acquired by the museum in April 1889.
Exhibitions: Berlin, 1863?; Hamburg, 1896, no. 85; Berlin, 1905, no. 18; Berlin, 1906, no. 1167; Berlin, 1935, no. 38; Berlin, 1908 A, no. XIX, reprod. p. 142; Berlin, 1987A, no. G 5, col. reprod. p. 82.
Bibliography: Jordan, 1895, p. 68; Donop, 1902, no. 802; Tschudi, 1905 A, no. 116; cat. NG, 1907, no. 968; Waldmann, 1941, p. 26–30, p. 40, p. 47, fig. 52; Forster-Hahn, 1977, p. 249, fig. 13; Ellwart, 1985, p. 84; Lammel, 1988, p. 75, fig. 63 (col.).

With the skill of a good dramatist, Kugler inserts an episode that is both lively and captivating in chapter 28 of his biography of Frederick the Great, entirely devoted to the battle of Leuthen (*cf.* cat. 90). Between the account of the fighting and the terrifying solemnity of the chorus of offerings of thanks intoned by exhausted, wounded and dying Prussians, the victorious king leaves in haste in a scouting party with a small troupe of hussars, and reaches the town of Lissa, still in Austrian hands. He enters the château without being intercepted by Austrian officers who come to meet him in large numbers, and he says coolly: 'Good evening, gentlemen! You weren't expecting to find me here. Is there any room for us to stay the night?' He continues the discussion while he awaits the arrival of his soldiers.

In reality the adventure was far less daring. The Austrians had already been put to flight, and the château's owner, the Baron von Mudrach, was known to the king and very pleased to see him again[1]. Although the daring lay more with the historians, the anecdote soon became known, and provided one of the themes requested by the young King Frederick-William III for his 'Gallery of Historical and Patriotic paintings' (Academy exhibition of 1800, in Berlin) – and of all of them it is the only one to which Menzel returned a year later. A sketch of this composition is recognizable in the work of Johann David Schubert, a painter from Dresden[2], with its dramatic lighting in front of the backlit figure. But where there was a certain uniformity, Menzel introduced disorder, and the figures who rush down the staircase create a feeling of volume at the bottom as well as the top. He did not go back to his illustration in Kugler's book[3], which had a much simpler structure.

The picture was begun in spring 1856 at the same time as the *Meeting of Frederick the Great with Joseph II at Neisse*[4]. It is the exception in the series of portraits of Frederick. The subject 'Frederick at Lissa' had been 'desired' by the person commissioning the painting[5] for local reasons – Victor de Hohenlohe-Schillingsfürst had been Duke of Ratibor since 1840 and no doubt held on to the idea that the

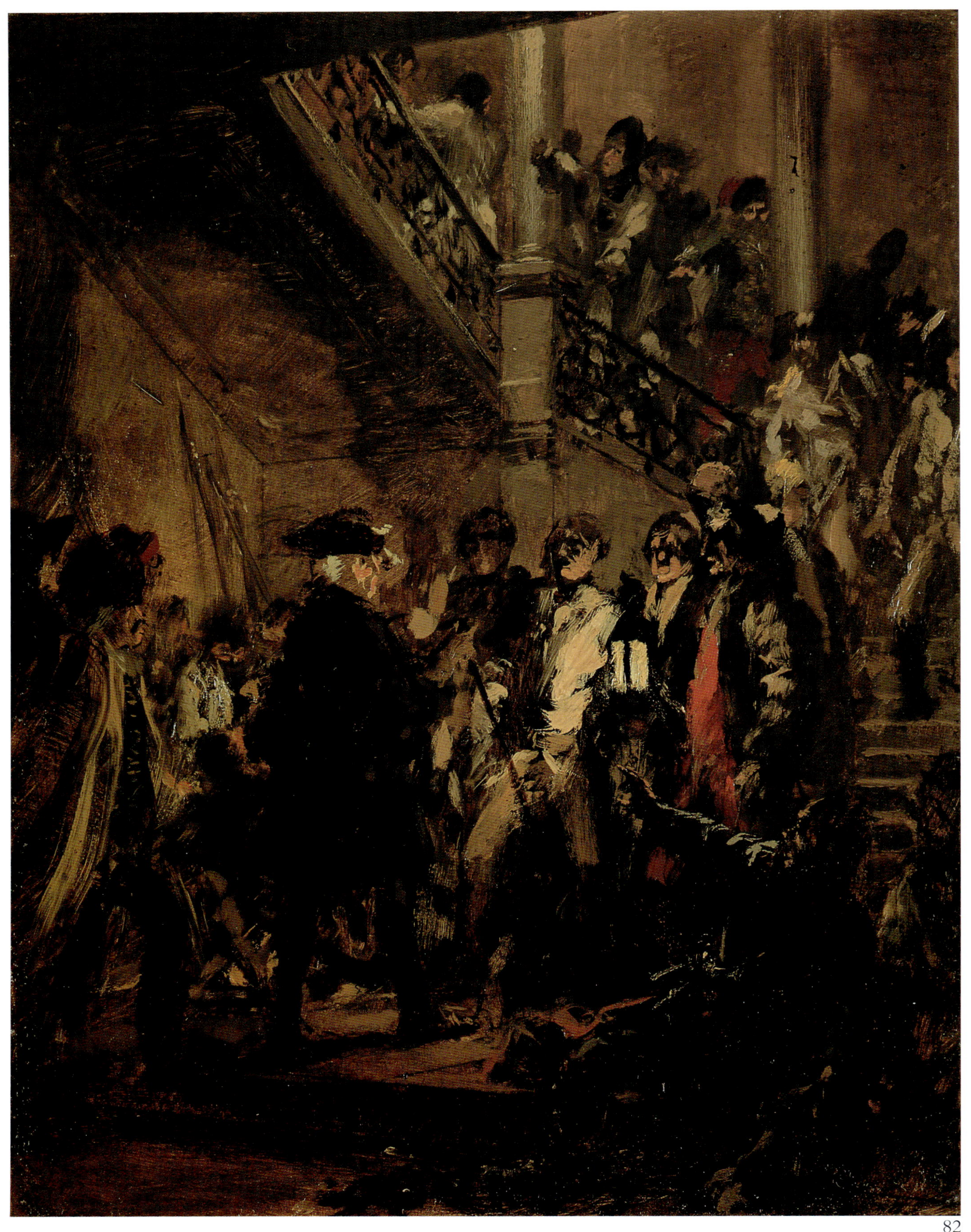
82

subject related to the relations between Frederick II and Silesia. But nothing was agreed about details and when the duke and duchess saw the unfinished painting, the duchess found the scene too 'muddled'. Her wish to use a later episode, the presentation of the officers to the king, was not fulfilled, but Menzel did not in the end apply the final glaze. We know that he realized from that time on, as he stressed when he was older, in an interview with Alfred Lichtwark, that the dynamics and spontaneity of touch, the pace and feeling, had to be perceptible. 'It should give the effect of a fleeting vision', he said.

The transition to large format should have endowed the picture with a reality which was only a suggestion in the sketch. There were a number of changes, the most striking being the one affecting the two main figures. They both lose their hesitant, indecisive attitudes, they move faster, the gesture of doffing the hat and of holding up the lantern are intense and dramatic. The officers behind the lantern holder are leaning avidly to one side. The whole composition gains in its profusion, use of space, and dynamism. The function of the colour sketch becomes clear – to suggest the use of space in the picture and try out groupings and lighting in relation to figures without anticipating how the picture would develop. This relationship between the sketches and the pictures can be seen in all the paintings of the Frederick the Great cycle, and the earliest ones owe their freshness to this suggestiveness. As the years went by, Menzel feared losing himself in his sketches more and more, and the painting of the *Coronation* is the last to have been prepared in the usual sense of the word. Later, he declared 'that it spoilt his appetite to paint an oil sketch; it was as if one were eating the bread and butter before dinner'[6]. Instead he opted to carry out significant reworkings on the large canvas. The 'unfinished' painting was unknown to the general public, even when the Zurich collector Henneberg put it in his gallery of history paintings. It was only in 1902 that it was purchased by the Hamburg Kunsthalle. It had the same effect on contemporaries as *Night Attack at Hochkirch* on a writer on later Romantic art – confusion reigned 'in the picture itself (and not just in what is being portrayed)'[7]. Menzel viewed the emphatic and highly polished images of Frederick critically. 'As far as I'm concerned, the king is a hero, and a hero without a halo. I see him as he was, with his worn clothing and the sheath of his sword, which he had patched up himself with some sealing wax, like a great mind in a mortal shell'[8]. C.K.

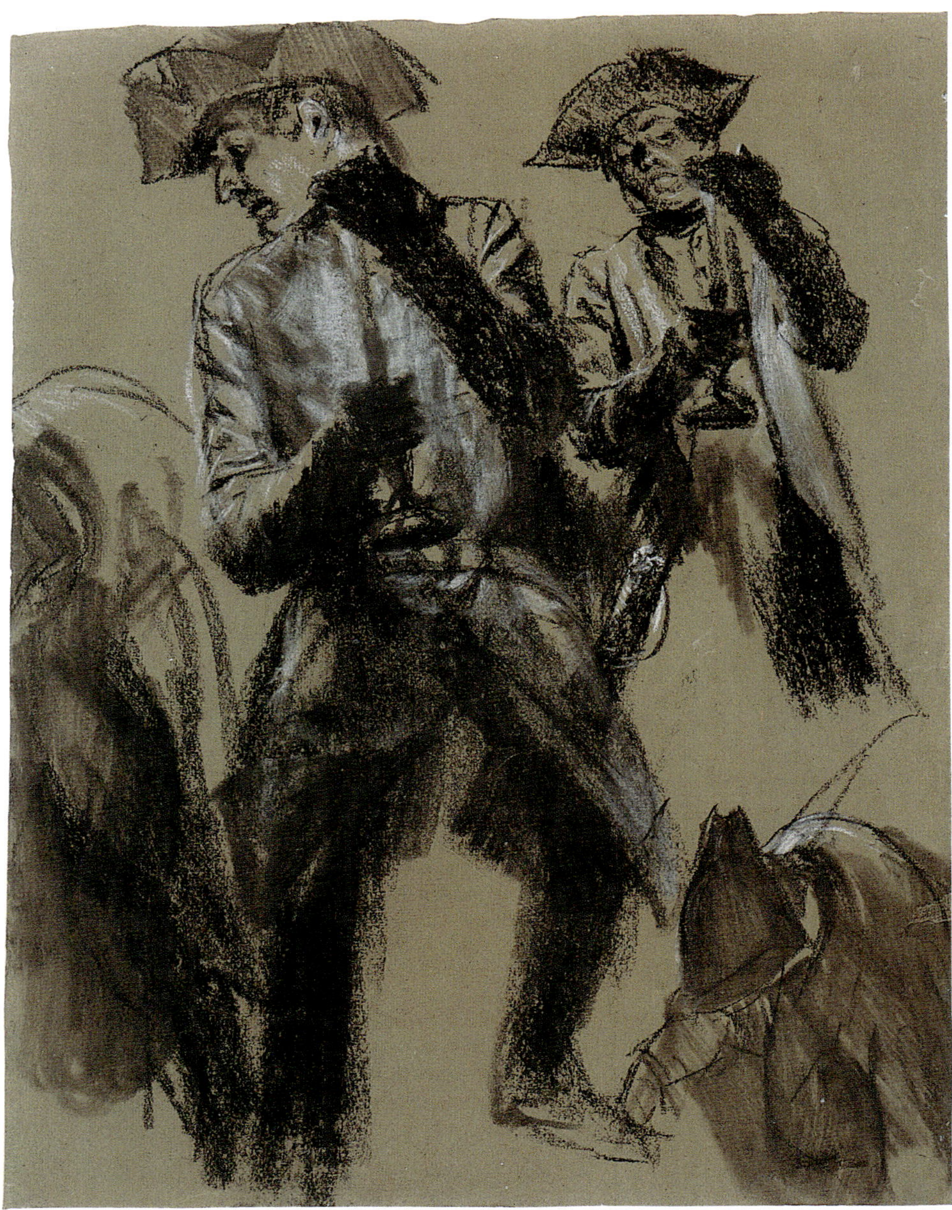
83

1. Helmut Börsch-Supan, exhib. cat. Berlin, 1986, no. VIII.13 and VIII.13g.
2. Exhibition catalogue Berlin, 1986.
3. Bock, 1923, no. 659.
4. Finshed in 1857; Tschudi, 1905 A, no. 112; Berlin, Nationalgalerie.
5. Letter to Fritz Werner, 27 March 1856, not reproduced in Wolff, 1914, Staatliche Museen zu Berlin, central archives.
6. Meyerheim, (1906) 1992, p. 164.
7. Förster, 1860, p. 300.
8. Beta, (1899) 1992, p. 70.

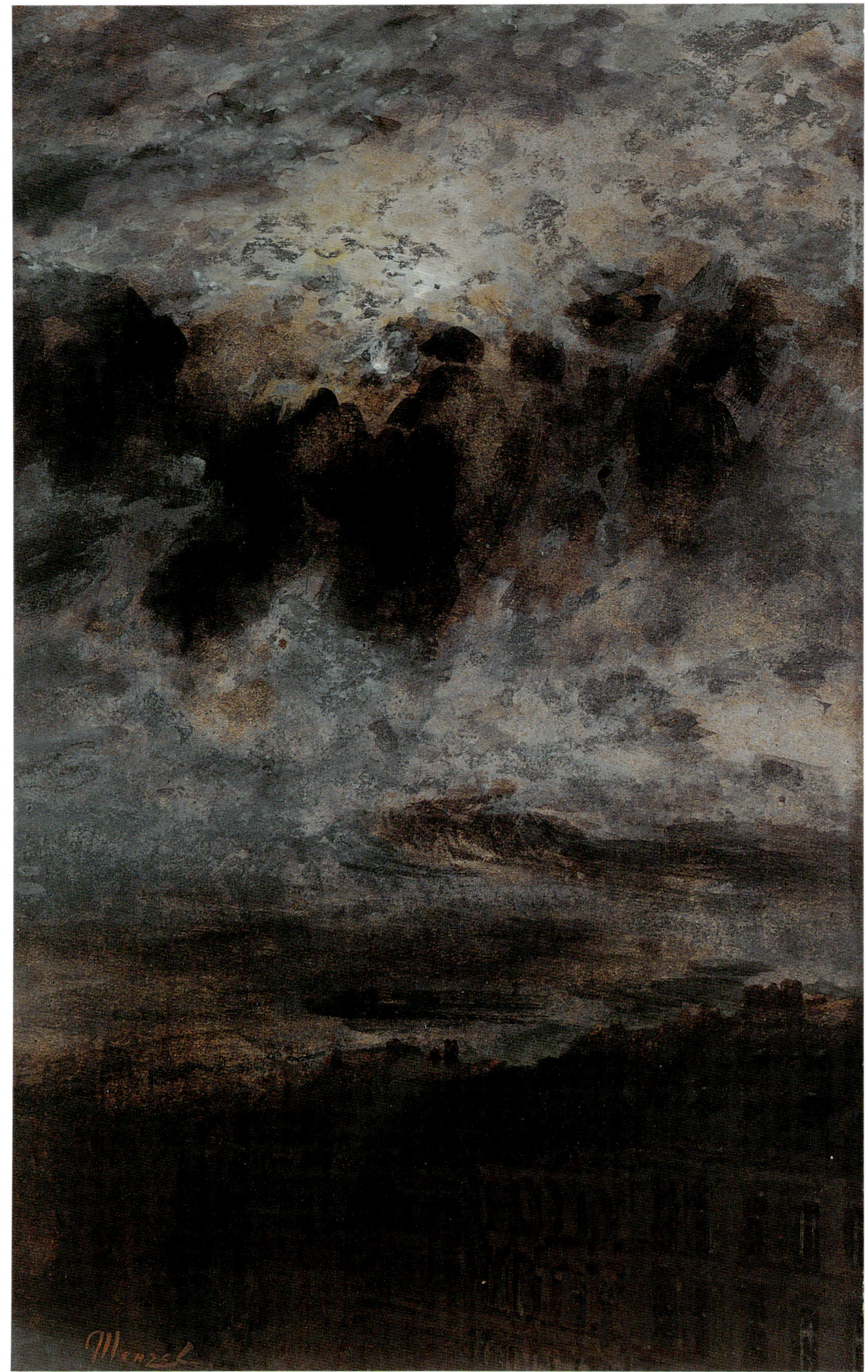

84

83

Officer Carrying a Candle

1857–8

Black chalk with white highlighting
28.7 × 21.9cm
Berlin, Kupferstichkabinett (SZ Menzel N 4431)
Exhibited in Berlin only

Provenance: Painter's studio; 1905 Emilie Krigar-Menzel; acquired by the museum in 1906.
Exhibitions: Berlin, 1905, no. 3513; Copenhagen, 1985, no. 9, reprod. p. 15; Berlin, 1987 A, no. G.6; New York, 1990, no. 24, col. reprod.

This is one of the chalk studies for the unfinished composition *Good Evening, Gentlemen!* (cat. 82). A model in eighteenth-century costume posed as the Austrian officer coming down the stairs with a candle in his hand, facing the viewer. The figure is 'thought out in depth', as Menzel used to say, with two different head movements. He did not even appear in the oil sketch, although he plays a vital role in the final composition, as his sideways glance directs the attention to the action on the upper levels of the staircase. A.H.

84

Looking at the Moon (Moonlight on the Rooftops of Berlin)

c. 1855–60

Gouache
31.9 × 19.5cm
Signed at the bottom left: *Menzel.*
Private collection

Provenance: Private collections; 1980 Gerda Bassenge Gallery, Berlin; acquired in 1980.
Exhibitions: Berlin, 1980 B, no. 3, reprod.; Kampen, 1995, no. 1, col. reprod.
Bibliography: Simson, 1986, frontispiece (col.).

The elongated format of this painting enables a recollected impression of a street veiled by night to be retained at the very bottom. The street is only hinted at by the outlines of the upper levels of some fairly ordinary buildings, suggesting at the same time that someone is looking determinedly above it all. Visionary transport, abandonment to whatever it is that moves the soul in the atmosphere of a landscape, objective observation of a meteorological phenomenon – so many complementary and contradictory approaches. In places the colour is thinned to the fluidity of watercolour, while it is applied drily in other areas, and flecks the sky. Mousse-like fluffiness spreads, dissolves, covers the only element demanding rational attention, the circle of the bright moon. A comparable affection for a natural phenomenon can be found in the narratives of the Austrian Adalbert Stifter.

What is the date of this small masterpiece? Once more, one must beware of the traps inherent in Menzel's chronology. In terms of format, subject and concept, parallels can be seen at once with certain pages of the *Children's Album: Thatched Roof with Storks' Nest* (cat. 110), or *Corner of a House in Moonlight* (cat. 109), for example. The first must have been painted after 1866–7, while we have no information to date the second. If the *Children's Album* was begun in 1861 or shortly after, it is possible that older works (or those started beforehand) were inserted. There is only a vague basis for comparison. The same vagueness applies to *Moonlight on the Friedrichsgracht* (cat. 76), which it would be useful to compare. *Looking at the Moon* lies between the lyricism of this painting and the more analytical approach to *Corner of a House in Moonlight*, which has several epicentres. So how can an exact date be worked out? In the 1850s, Menzels art was characterized by the simultaneity of contrasts. If one thinks of *View of Anhalt Station by Moonlight* (1846; cat. 24), *Looking at the Moon* seems more distant, more artificial, with its jagged clouds and multitude of small, isolated shapes. *Night in the Forest* (1851; cat. 58), however, shows the degree of importance of the 'informal' world of shadows in Menzel's work from the start of the 1850s. The choice of varied modes of expression, different signatures within one and the same overall work, the black patches applied roughly over the disc of the moon, are all reminiscent of the Zurich painting. There is also *Cloud Study* (cat. 59), of the same year, although the texture is quite different.

Fontane wanted to show how Menzel vacillated between 'genius and caricature', and how he could sometimes lose his way, and in 1857 he recalled 'the sheet of black paper with the following comment written on it: *Berlin by Night*. With enough imagination, one could distinguish clearly the cupola of the castle and the towers of the Gendarmenmarkt, but for most mortals, it was merely a large blot of ink, thats all!'[1]. If the poets memory of the towers and cupola is correct, he must be thinking of another, similar composition. But this description indicates the degree of difficulty encountered even by contemporaries when faced with such paintings. C.K.

1. Letter from Fontane to Wilhelm von Merckel, 21 December 1857, Erler, 1987, p. 226.

85

After the Torchlight Procession. Extinguishing of Torches on the Dönhoffplatz[1], Berlin

1858

Oil on canvas
55.5 × 73.5cm
Signed and dated at the top right: *Menzel. 1858.*
Berlin, Nationalgalerie (A I 1096)

Provenance: Richard Menzel; 1865 Elise Milner, widow of Menzel, Gross-Lichterfelde; 1906 Käte Cajettan, her daughter, Berlin-Charlottenburg; acquired by the museum in 1910.
Exhibitions: Berlin, 1861; Berlin, 1905, no. 79; Meier-Graefe, 1906, p. 181; Berlin, 1935, no. 37; Berlin, 1980A, no. XXI, reprod. p. 150.
Bibliography: Pietsch, 1861 A; Pietsch, (1905) 1992, p. 338; Tschudi, 1905 A, no. 115; Tschudi, 1905 B, p. 236, reprod. p. 233 (p. 26, reprod. p. 23); cat. NG, 1912, no. 1153; cat. NG, 1986, no pag., fig. 78; Lammel, 1993 B, p. 80, col. pl. 17.

In Menzel's preparation for the monumental painting *Night Attack at Hochkirch*, the way had been paved for this study of light spreading across the night, in which the flames spring up or are extinguished by a smoke which they illuminate and colour, and figures move against dramatic backlighting. However, once this canvas was finished, the exploration of fire and light continued to preoccupy Menzel. It is hard to disbelieve stories of the policeman who was told to awaken the painter if there was a fire during the night. Such studies do exist to bear this out[2]. But the two paintings inspired by the torchlight retreat and housed at the Nationalgalerie had another impulse, over and above a 'purely pictorial interest'. The event depicted was important, even if, as usual, the painter fixed upon a relatively minor aspect.

Prince Frederick-William, the nephew of Frederick-William IV (latterly crown prince himself for a long time, and 'emperor for ninety days' in 1888), married Queen Victoria's daughter in January 1858 in London, and had returned to Berlin with her on 8 February (Menzel also painted a gouache of onlookers perched in the trees[3]). Public celebrations lasted a week. One such celebration, and an unforeseen one at that, was the homage paid by the students of Berlin. The three higher education establishments (the University, the School of Architecture and the School of Arts and Crafts) had come together to organize nine hundred people carrying torches, who walked from the Brandenburg Gate to the royal palace. 'While the Germans sang celebratory songs', they waited for the royal couple to appear on the balcony. 'The sight of this sea of torches lifted the spirits, and Her Royal Highness was overwhelmed; then her illustrious husband spoke to those present about the Highlands of her native country'[4]. After the extinguishing of the torches, painted by Menzel, the people sat round to have a drink, which a journalist described as 'the true culmination of the event'. 'All the toasts and speeches given bore the hallmark of Germany and

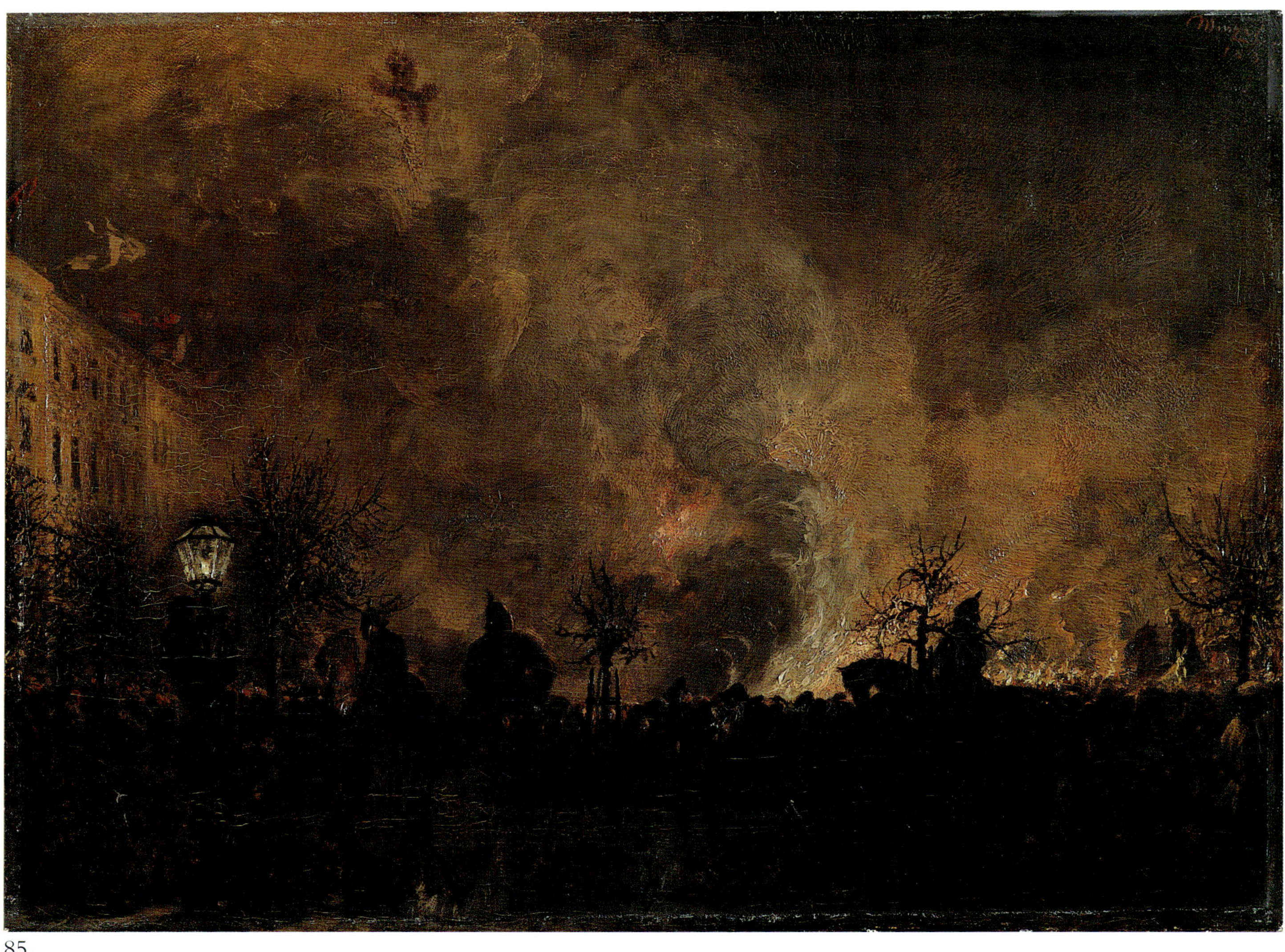

85

of brotherhood. After this first communal public appearance by the students, separated for a long time by an awareness of caste, the ideas spread by the student groups created during the war against Napoleon were reaffirmed, 'German action' was called for, and solidarity was established with 'our German brothers in Schleswig-Holstein'. For years, the end of Dutch sovereignty over these two duchies had been claimed to be a step towards the national unification of the Germans, but it was also, in 1848, one of the military objectives of the Prussian hegemony[5] (objectives which were achieved in several stages up to 1866).

The event painted by Menzel had ambivalent meanings. Everyone knew that the king was ill and, shortly after, the 'new Era' was to begin, a phase of political hope linked to the regency of Prince William, the father of Frederick-William. The poignant clair-obscur of this painting therefore also suggests political agitation[6].

A woodcut relating to chapter 37 of Kugler's biography of Frederick the Great shows a torchlight retreat organized by the Berliners in honour of the king upon his return from the Seven Years' War. Here the individuals are clearly different, and are depicted in great detail in the brightness of a single, gigantic cloud of flame, while the canvas shows a dark mass, with the figures of mounted police and a young man up a street lamp standing out above the rest. As if the painting of clouds (cat. 23, 59) were enriched with a new variant, the smoke rises, lit by a reddish light, and covers two-thirds of the canvas. Only the narrowing of the perspective on a house gives any depth to the space. The light from the gas lamp, weak, but a deep lemon yellow, is set against the fire hidden from view by the assembled people, thus providing a yardstick against which to measure the chromatic values of the light. C.K.

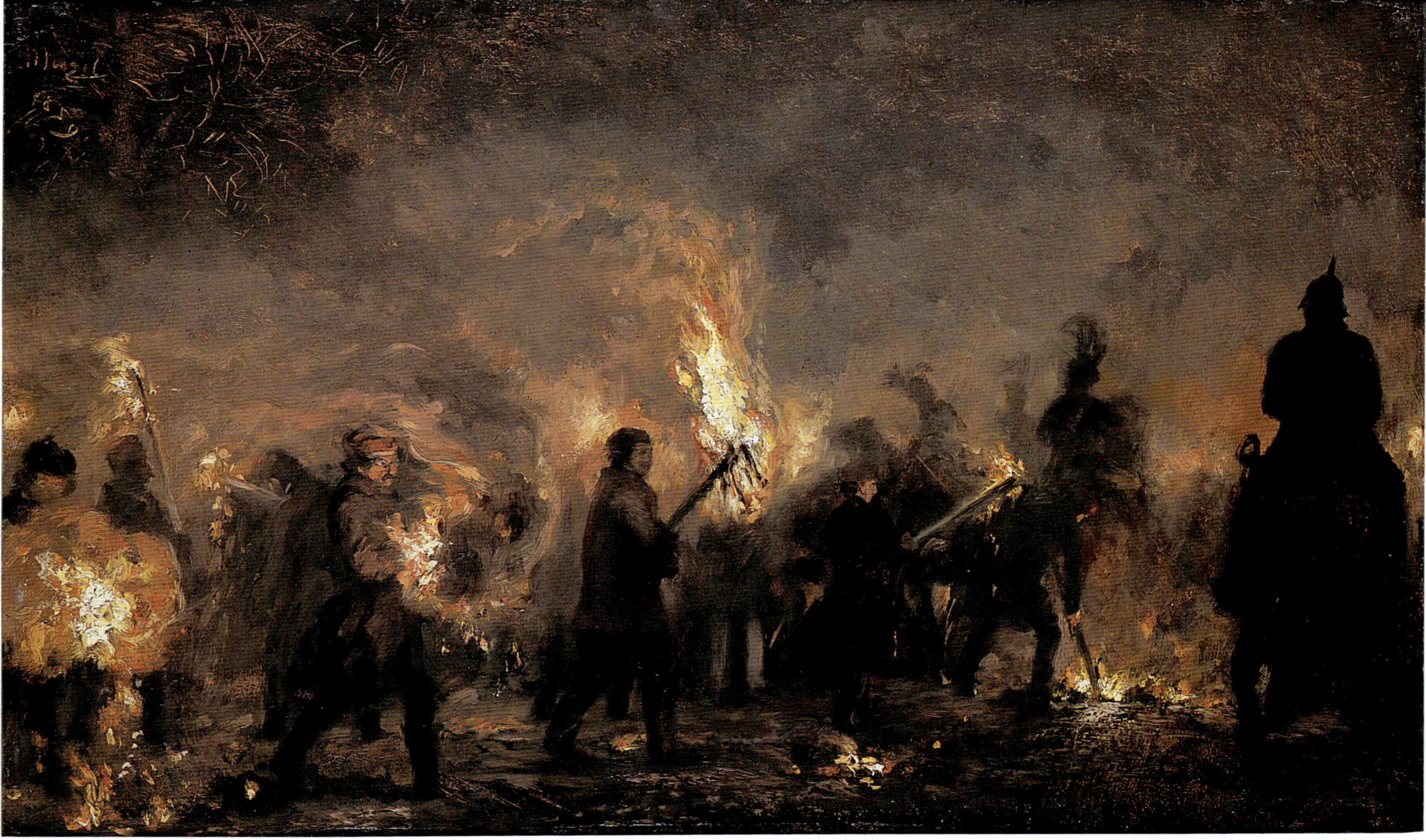

86

1. Since the painting reappeared in 1905, it has always borne the words on the Akanischer Platz. Ludwig Pietschs commentary of 1861 was forgotten, although it contained the exact topographical location and also indicated the occasion when this torchlight retreat took place.
2. This was how he painted a fire at a large house in 1863 (gouache, Berlin, Kupferstichkabinett [SZ Menzel N 232], dated 4 June.
3. Berlin, Kunstamnt Wilmersdorf.
4. [Untitled], *Vossische Zeitung*, 16 February 1858, p.
5. The subsequent quotations are also taken from this article.
5. The conservative journal *Neue Preussische (Kreuz) Zeitung* of 16 February, recounting the same event, printed the long and pious discourse addressed to the royal couple, and omitted to mention the political speeches.
6. A small gouache, *Souvenir of the return of the royal couple to Berlin* (Berlin, Kunstamt Charlottenburg) shows onlookers perching in the branches of a tree to get a better view of the ceremony, obstructing the painter's view from the window of the palace.

86

Students' Torchlight Procession

1859

Oil on board
31 × 54cm
Signed and dated at the top left: *A. Menzel 1859*
Berlin, Nationalgalerie (A I 961)

Provenance: 1896 private collection ('Cl.L.'); 1905, A.Israel, Hamburg; acquired by the museum in 1906.
Exhibitions: Hamburg, 1896; Celle, 1949–50, no. 68, p. 8; Berlin, 1950–1, no. 53; Berlin, 1955 B, no. 85, fig. 41.
Bibliography: Tschudi, 1905 A, no. 119; Tschudi, 1905 B, p. 236 (p. 26); Meier-Graefe, 1906, p.181; cat. NG, 1907, no. 991; Justi, 1920, p.147; Scheffler, 1922, p. 180, reprod. p. 157; cat. NG, 1976, reprod. p. 278; Jensen, 1982, p. 92, col. pl., Lammel, 1995B, p. 80, col. pl. 16.

This picture was probably started at the same time as its pair (cat. 85), and finished later. It depicts the same action, but from a closer vantage point. As if wanting to pinpoint the source of the fire which rises up behind the small crowd in the other version, here the same mounted police survey the still-roaring flames as they are being extinguished. No contemporary would have been unaware of the classical analogy with the spirit of death (with the lowered torch), which could be found in every cemetery. Menzel was too familiar with allegories and symbols to paint such a subject without forethought. This connotation may also justify the disturbing single flame in the exact centre of the picture, solemn and absolute (although the picture is supposed to represent a jubilant crowd). The agitation of the figures, who scarcely stand out against the darkness, seems to suggest an impending evil. This is why, without knowing its true aims, a political 'revolt' has been read into the painting[1]. In its dramatic rhythm and reddish enveloping light, but also in the exuberance of the paintbrush, this small-format painting echoes the very large compositions *Night Attack at Hochkirch* and *Good Evening, Gentlemen!* (cat. 82).

However, even Menzel's friend and admirer, the writer and occasional art critic Theodor Fontane, only considered it as a study. He wrote: 'I could never acknowledge that *Students' Torchlight Retreat* could be a proper painting – it is a number of hats, caps, helmets, and a lot of smoke and darkness, with the light of glowing embers in the midst. And it is no use quoting Rembrandt. In art, we do not accept this identification of man with chimney sweep. But since such lighting effects achieved with such virtuosity are not an aim in themselves, but a means to achieving an end, our judgement has been modified . . .'

One might also mention the famous battle painting, finished three years before this 'study'![2] C.K.

1. Jensen, 1982; Lammel, 1993 B.
2. Die diesjährige Kunstausstellung, [1863], Fontane, 1970, p. 212–13.

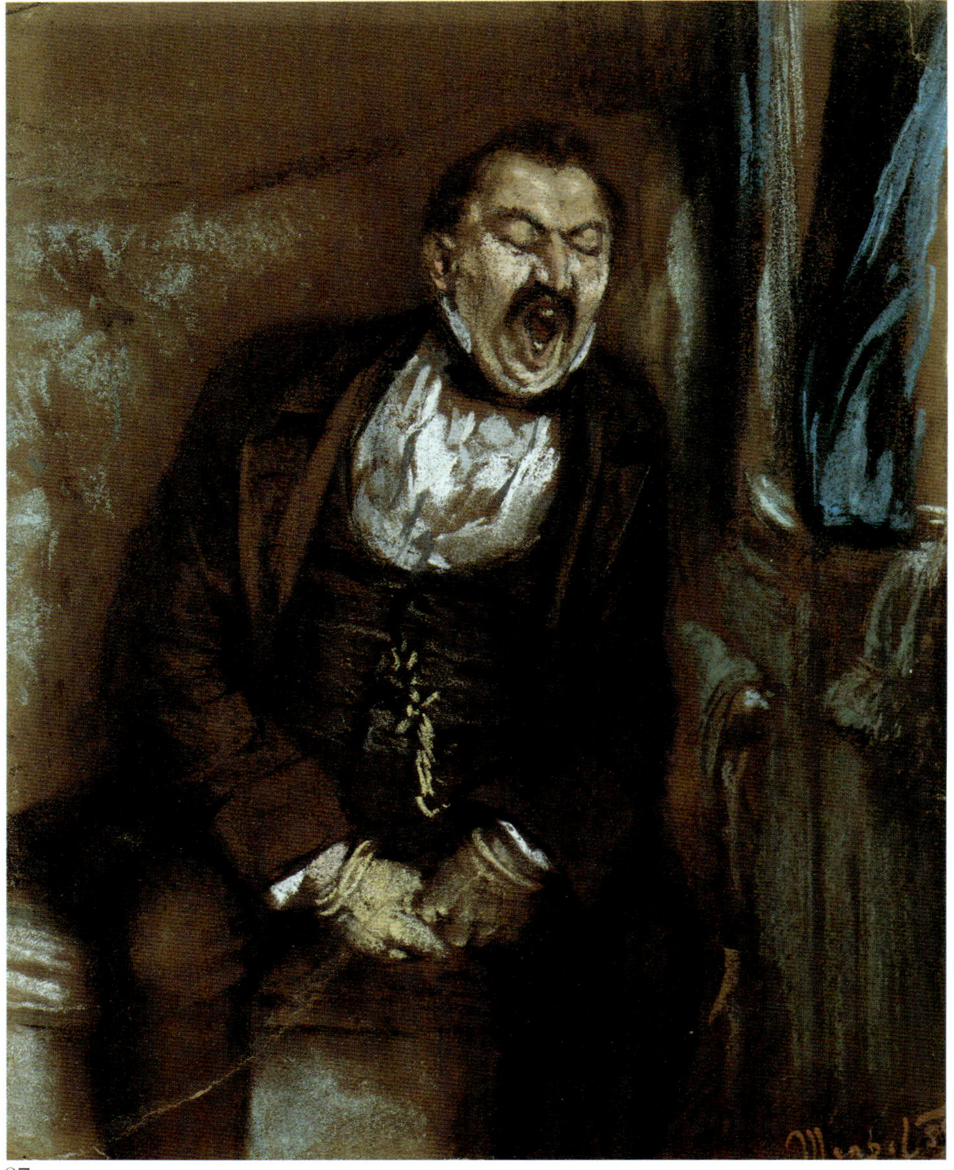

87

87

Man Yawning in a Train Compartment

1859

Pastel
23 × 18cm
Signed and dated at the bottom right: *Menzel 59.*
Berlin, Kupferstichkabinett (SZ Menzel Nr 1742).

Provenance: Edgar Hanfstaengl the younger, who took over the direction of the Munich photograph and art book publishing house created by his grandfather Franz Hanfstaengl; acquired in 1907 with its pair and a third work, a gouache.
Exhibition: Berlin, 1980 A, no. 43, reprod. p. 319; Vienna, 1985, no. 35, reprod. p. 105; Vienna, 1990, no. 146.
Bibliography: Jordan, 1895, p. 68; Tschudi, 1905 A, no. 350; Bredt, 1920, reprod. p. 36; Weinhold, 1956, p. 193; Vogl, 1984, no. 13, reprod.; Lammel, 1993 A, p. 161, fig. 10 (col.).

This pastel is full of lively colours, and was the last picture created by Menzel using the pastel medium on its own. It shows a man in a train, yawning with a disconcerting lack of consideration. There was also a matching picture depicting a woman looking out of the compartment window[1]. Underlining the grotesque aspect of the scene in the same way, a gouache dated 1851[2] depicted a couple in a train compartment, the man asleep with his mouth open and his hat pulled down over his ears, and his wife looking through the window with a tired and melancholy expression, after a 'night of travelling', as the title indicates. Hermann Beenken wrote about this man stretched out without restraint: 'In this traveller, whose body is so grossly and rudely affected by the loss of a night's sleep, humanity is shown as the ugliest thing in Creation'[3]. Often in his later portrayals of travellers, Menzel had to move the anecdotal to the foreground, as in the gouache *A Five-Minute Stop* or *Early Morning on the Night Express*[4] (1877). Once again the artist, as ever attentive to human weakness, shows the uninhibited stretching and yawning of a traveller, and the fear of his wife, lying down under the blankets, while a serving man

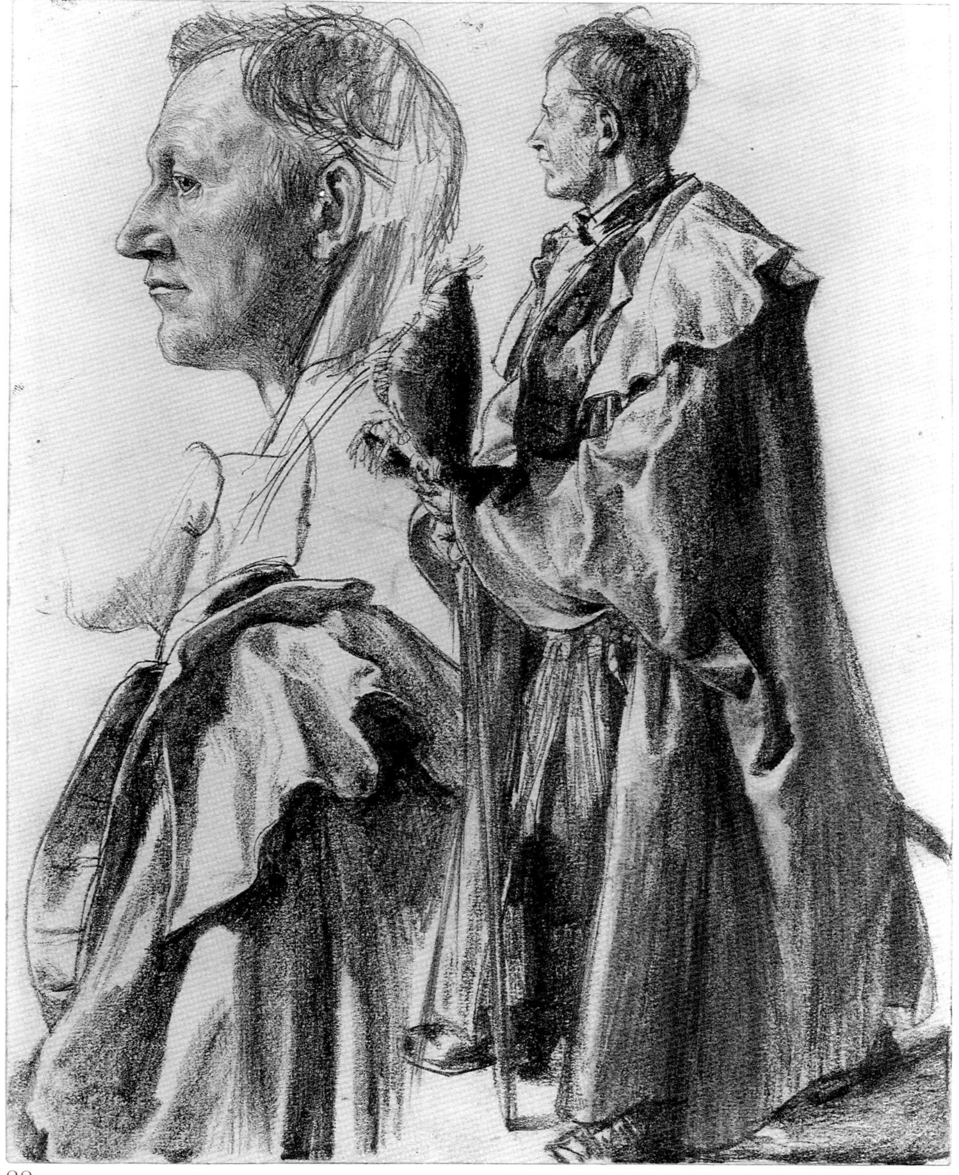
88

opens the door as they stop at a station, and offers them coffee.

In company with Honoré Daumier and some English painters, Menzel was among the first to include early rail travel among his contemporary subjects. While in Daumier's drawings and canvasses of the 1850s in particular, the social connotations and a certain dramatic solemnity counterbalance the comical aspect, Menzel preferred to emphasize the grotesque aspects of this new passion for travel. With irony and a profound sense of contrast, he took the most varied and unexpected reactions to these escapades in the last of his compositions containing numerous figures, *A Journey through the Beauty of Nature*[5] (fig. 144). A benevolent sympathy colours his apparently pitiless observation of people, who only have in common their submission to the contingencies of this modern means of transport, which Menzel himself used each summer. A number of his drawings and sketches are valuable as documents showing bourgeois tourism in Germany at this time. M.R.-R.

1. Tschudi, 1905 A, no. 351; Berlin, Nationalgalerie (missing since 1945).
2. Tschudi, 1905 A, no. 302; location unknown.
3. Beenken, 1944, p. 330.
4. *Not mentioned by Tschudi, 1905 A; location unknown; cf.* Meyerheim, (1906) 1992, p. 188 and ff., reprod.
5. *Tschudi, 1905 A, no. 675; private collection.*

88

Study of Model for an Officer

c. 1859–60

Pencil
32.2 × 24.4cm
Berlin, Kupferstichkabinett (SZ Menzel Kat 822)
On view only in Paris

Provenance: Hermann Pächter (R. Wagner Gallery, Berlin); acquired by the museum in 1889.
Exhibition: Berlin, 1905, no. 1145.
Bibliography: Donop, 1902, no. 822; Keisch, 1987, p. 270, fig. 5, p. 265.

Two more detailed studies showing the head and shoulders and the folds of the large turned-down collar were added to this view of a man standing, in profile, with a three-cornered hat in his hand. The oil sketch for *Address at Leuthen* (cat. 90) shows that this figure was intended to be on the right edge of the composition, but was never painted. Two other drawings of the same person are even closer to the oil sketch, and were used to prepare for this study[1]. Up to this point, Menzel had prepared for the paintings in the Frederick the Great cycle by making chalk drawings on coloured paper. He only began to use pencil for *Leuthen*. This technique undoubtedly allowed him to make far more advanced studies of facial expressions before painting them. A.H.

1. Berlin, Kupferstichkabinett (SZ Menzel, Kat 823, 824).

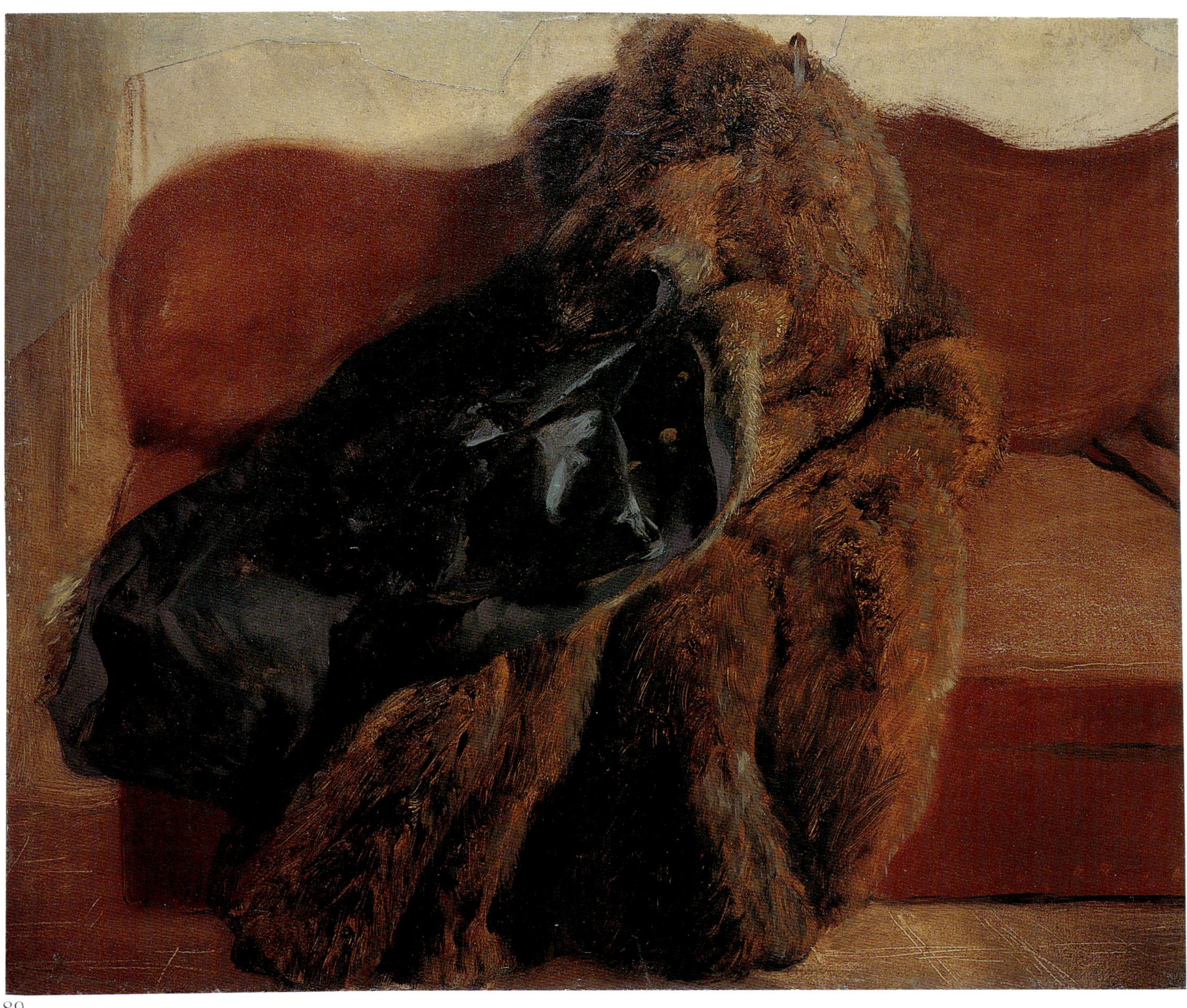

89

89

Fur Coat on a Sofa (The Artist's Pelisse)

c. 1859

Oil on paper, board backing
38.6 × 44.5cm
Munich, Bayerische Staatsgemäldesammlungen, Neue Pinakothek (8507)
Exhibited in Paris and Berlin only

Provenance: 1905 painter's studio; 1905 Emilie Krigar-Menzel; 1907 Margarete Krigar-Menzel; gift of the latter to the Bavarian State in 1908; acquired by the museum in 1937, following a difference of opinion regarding the legitimacy of the gift.

Exhibitions: Munich, 1908, no. 545i; Berlin, 1955 B, no. 41; Erlangen, 1971, no. 28; Frankfurt, 1975, no. 27, reprod.
Bibliography: Tschudi, 1905 A, no. 19; Waldmann, 1941, p. 11; Hütt, 1981, fig. 47 (col.); Eschenburg, 1984, p. 291 *et seq.*, reprod.

This heavy, fur-lined coat has been flung on the red sofa. It looks as if it is part of a uniform yet, in a photograph taken at the end of the 1850s, the painter is wearing a coat resembling this one, which would confirm the traditional title of the painting. The soft outlines of the light-coloured settee seem to lean into the background in relation to the fur, whose real size is hard to guess, as an optical illusion makes it seem to be about to slide out of the picture. Here the painter is showing the effects created by the different materials, fabric and fur, in the convulsive downward movement of the fabric and the bunched-up bulk of the fur, on the ends of which the light creates a soft reflection here and there. Once more, a shapeless object, bereft of structure or framework, is chosen as the subject of the picture.

Contrary to the usual dating of the

work in the late 1840s, I prefer to locate this study at the same time as *Address at Leuthen*, in which a fur coat, slipping from the shoulders of one of the generals, is a powerful influence in the composition. Menzel did preparatory work for this subject with several drawings, and it is quite possible that he also practised it in the form of a painting.

C.K.

90

Frederick the Great's Address to his Generals before the Battle of Leuthen

1859–61

Oil on canvas, outlines (semi-erased) in white chalk
318 × 424cm
Berlin, Nationalgalerie (A II 839)
Exhibited in Berlin only

Provenance: Painter's studio; gift of the heirs of Emperor William II; after the 1905 exhibition, kept at the Nationalgalerie; gift formalized in 1907; remained the property of William II until 1934.
Exhibitions: Berlin, 1905, no. 98; Berlin, 1906, no. 1170, reprod.; Berlin, 1935, no. 35; Berlin, 1980, no. XXII, reprod. p. 214.
Bibliography: Jordan, 1890, p. 47; Jordan, 1895, p. 32 *et seq.*, p. 68; Beta (1898) 1992, p. 30; Beta (1899) 1992, p. 61 *et seq.*; Delmar, (1905) 1992, p. 120; Jordan, 1905 (1992), p. 267; Tschudi, 1905 A, no. 121; Tschudi, 1905 B, p. 236 *et seq.*, pl. facing p. 236 (p. 26 *et seq.*, pl. facing p. 26); Meyerheim, (1906) 1992, p. 13, p. 15, p. 30, p. 62–4, p. 73; Meier-Graefe, 1906, p. 188–91; cat. NG, 1907, no. 975; Scheffler, 1912, p. 132 *et seq.*, reprod. p. 129; Wolff, 1914, p. 175, p. 176 *et seq.*; Hamann, 1914, p. 158; Scheffler, 1922, p. 176, reprod. p. 149; Justi, 1932, p. 138; Deetjen, 1934, p. 34; Scheffler, 1938, p. 69, reprod. p. 180; Waldmann, 1941, p. 26–30, p. 36; Ellwart, 1985, p. 84–87; cat. NG, 1986, s.p., fig. 76; Keisch, 1987; Gronau, 1987; Lammel, 1988, p. 77–85; Zangs, 1992, p. 141–4; Lammel, 1993 B, p. 33–9, fig. 16.

The large areas of blank canvas and scratched faces on the last of the compositions devoted to the life of Frederick II, and the most ambitious in both dimensions and aesthetic, indicate a tragedy. In spite of its unfinished state, the attention given this work by contemporaries arose from Max Jordan's decision in 1890 to include it, if not among the plates, at least in the text of his monumental work on Menzel: '. . . like a gigantic torso with the head missing', he wrote. 'it provides enough stimulus to allow the imagination to fill in the rest. Even the severe Meier-Graefe also acknowledged 'the dignity of form'.

The battle of Leuthen had, in just a few years, been the subject of a number of monographs[1], with which Menzel must have been familiar. In addition, one of his friends in the 'Tunnel' circle, Christian Friedrich Scherenberg, had written an epic poem in alexandrines on the subject. By the end of 1757, the Seven Years' War, which had set Prussia against a coalition led by Austria and France, had already brought a devastating series of alternating victories and defeats. Near the village of Leuthen, in Silesia, the battle for which Frederick was preparing would be decisive. 'Either the Austrians had to be attacked immediately, at any cost, to drive them out of Silesia, or Prussia had to resign itself to losing the province for ever'[2]. With only a third of the number of troops held by the Austrians, Frederick was victorious on 5 December, using a famous tactic which became known as the 'oblique order'. The loss of life was terrible. Two days before, at daybreak, he had gathered together his generals to explain the risks to them, and also the importance of the undertaking. Mixing persuasion with threats, Frederick went so far as to allow those who dared not follow him to leave him immediately.

'This is a case of painting a moral effect', stated Menzel straightaway[3], and his choice of words is significant. It is a matter of 'painting' not 'producing' (as one might expect), nor of 'depicting'. He wanted to create a pictorial fact parallel to the subject, an internal drama. It is a question of life and death, although we are not shown men fighting, poignant poses, weapons, smoke.

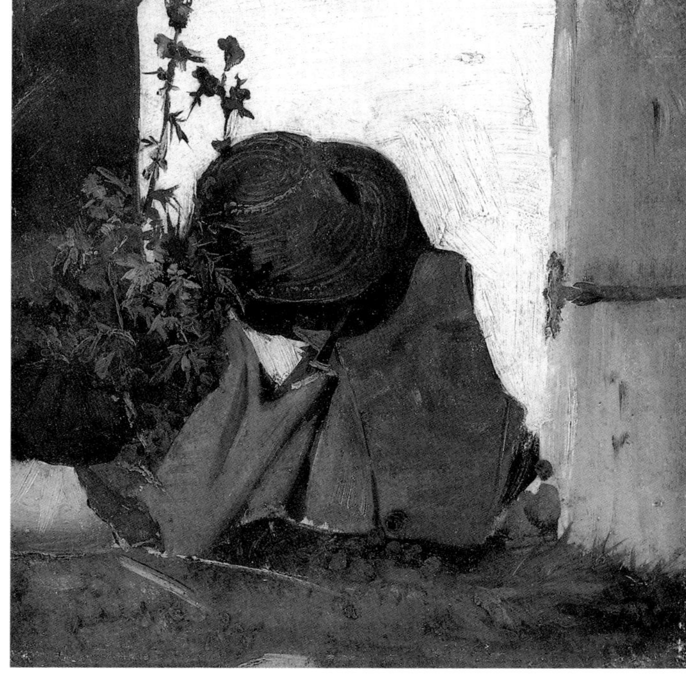

Fig. 182. Franz Lenbach, *Clothes and Hat*, 1854, oil, Hannover, Niedersächsische Landesgalerie

At the heart of this work lies the aesthetic conflict between psychological research and large format, to which were linked quite other expectations[4]. From the oil sketch onwards, Menzel sought the appearance of the everyday, stifling the temptation to theatricality, in a step

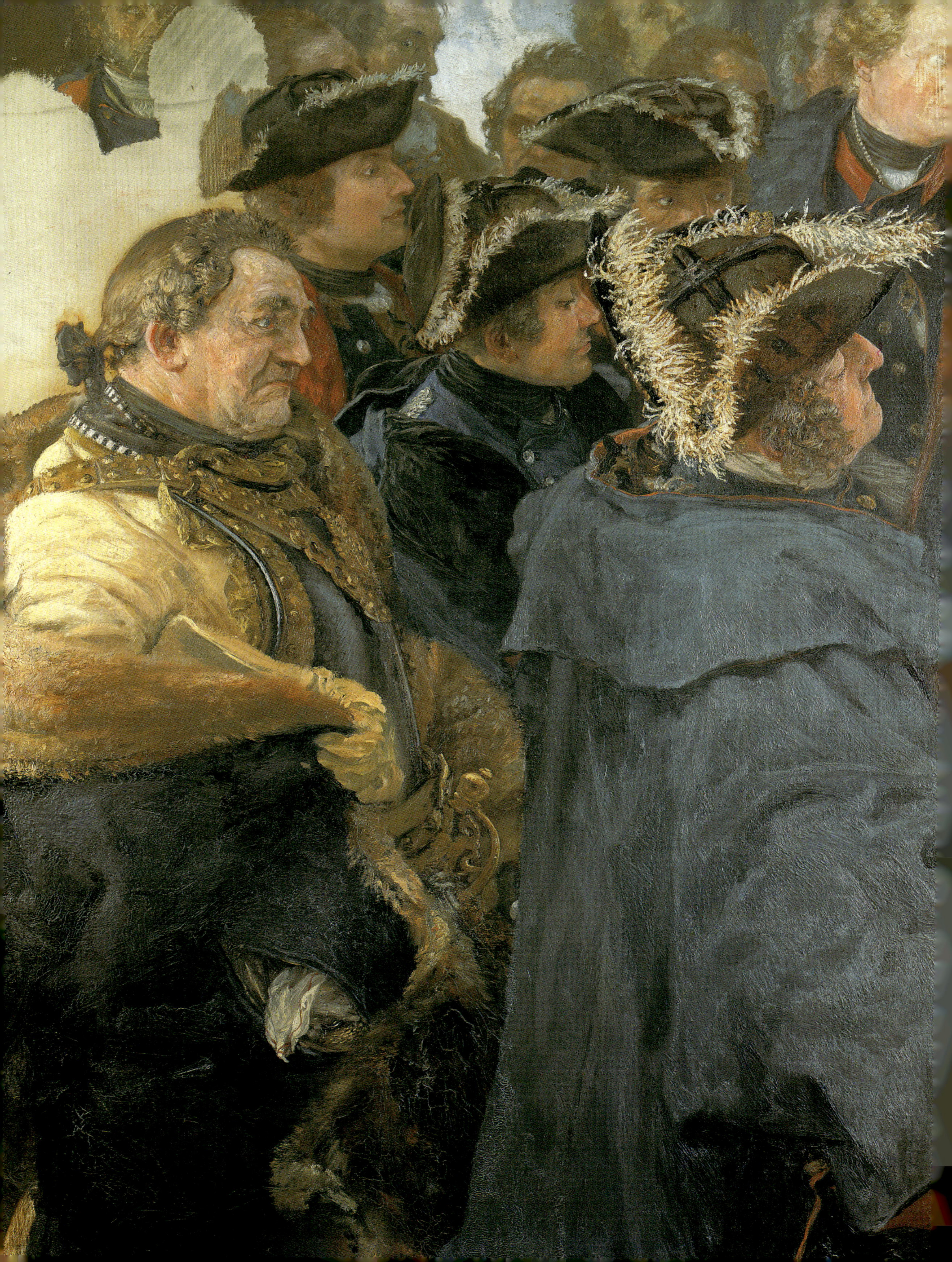

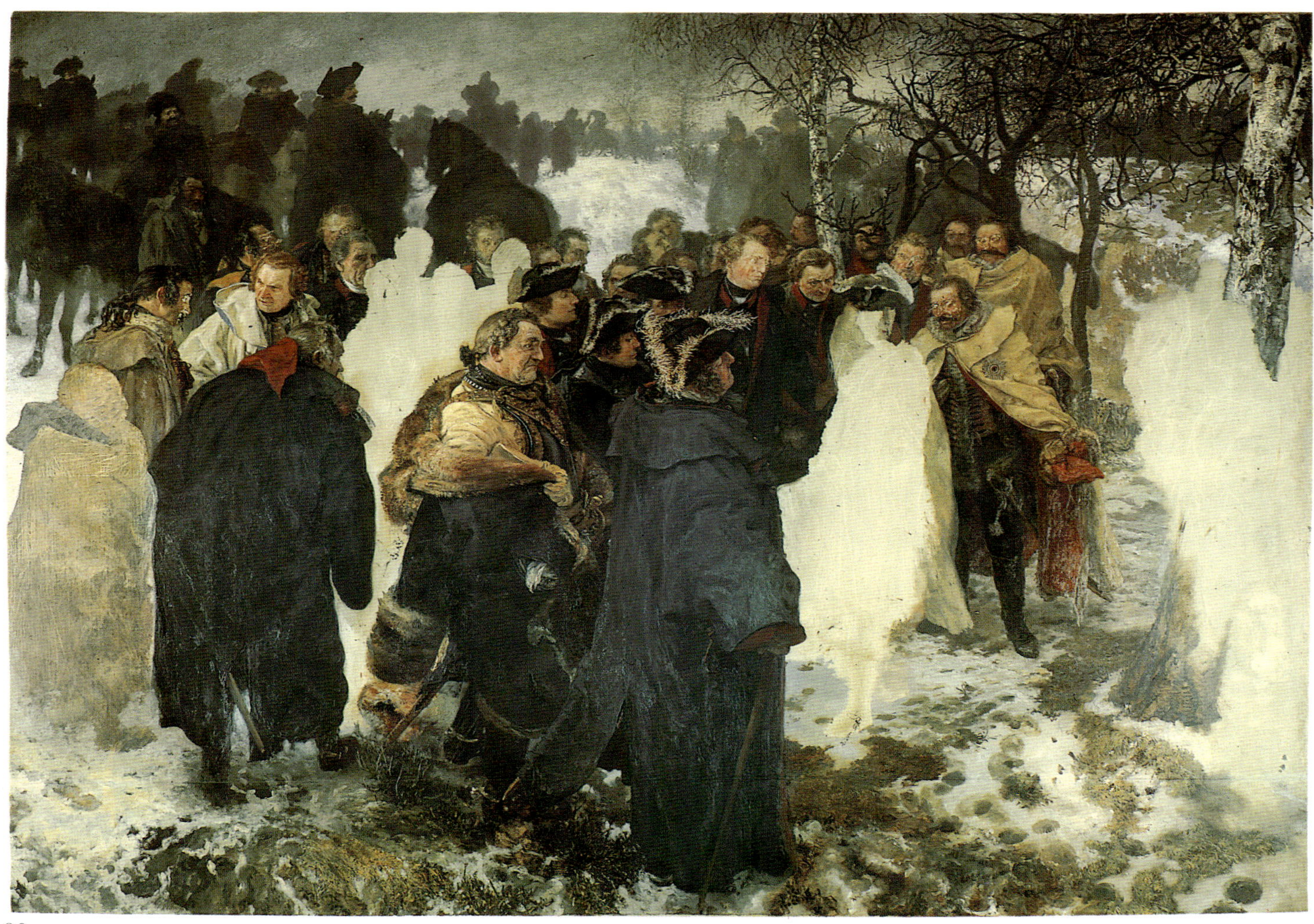

90

which might be likened to Manet when he painted *The Execution of the Emperor Maximilian* several years later. Menzel had already dealt with the subject of Leuthen twice before. In a lithograph dated 1835[5], he placed the king on an elevated piece of ground, so that he seemed to dominate the generals who surrounded him at a respectful distance. For the illustration in Kugler's book[6] (fig. 184), they formed a tight circle around the king, and his speech looked more pressing and impulsive. Yet the group was isolated from the landscape, and appeared in impeccable order. In the thumbnail sketch painted in 1859, the figure on the left with his head turned, viewed from behind, prefigures the disparity of anxious movements which is reinforced in the final canvas. Here, instead of the normal trajectory of the viewer's gaze *di sotto in sù*, the onlooker takes in the entire scene at once, which puts all the protagonists on an equal level. The landscape was painted first, with its trampled snow, clods of earth and flattened grass which pushes up in places, the labyrinthine branches extending over the grey sky, the bluish, violet and pinkish-grey tones of the riders enveloped in fog and disappearing, shapeless, on the horizon (this area seems to foreshadow Monet). The landscape takes part in the action. The agitation of the riders preparing to leave suggests the start of trouble, the cold can be seen and sensed and the large overcoats of the generals (so different from their elegant appearance in the engravings) indicates their condition. One of them, the general of the mounted soldiers, Lentulus, tries hard to pull a heavy pelisse over his shoulder, inattentive to what his leader is saying, while behind him other figures are grouped together in isolated conversation. What vigour there is in his gesture, and how foreign to the action! What overwhelming weight, what formal autonomy are attributed to the figure in the blue overcoat and three-cornered hat (probably Prince Maurice of Dessau), who stands on the central axis and is in the forefront of the scene, literally breaking through the fictional frontier between the image and the viewer[7]. The king (whose place, like those of other figures, was left blank) is reduced to a secondary role, not in the action, but in the spectacle itself. So the action seems unbalanced, off-centre, and the so-called historical event is revealed to be no more than a retrospective abstraction, while reality is presented as a fabric of contingencies.

In this composition Menzel developed the suggestions inherent in the burlesque elements of *Gustav Adolph at Hanau* (cat. 37), but with great passion and seriousness. The pictures of the Frederick the Great cycle had toned down this conception of history, which little by little reappeared. *Address at Leuthen* was definitely a challenge, and Menzel went even further in choosing a gigantic format, adding a large section to his canvas to increase the height.

It seems that Meissonier admired this picture during a stay in Berlin in 1862, and gained some useful ideas for his *French Campaign* (fig. 119). In seeking reasons why Menzel did not complete the picture, it has even been suggested that he was discouraged because Meissonier had copied 'all the effects'[8]. But artistic jealousy is not enough to explain what happened. Menzel set to work[9] full of energy in the spring of 1859, speaking later of 'more and more fervent dedication to the great canvas'[10], and feeling rather too optimistic in the spring of 1861, as was often the case, that he would finish it for the next Academy exhibition in 1862[11]. Then the sudden commissioning of the painting of the *Coronation* (*cf.* cat. 94–9) interrupted the project. Yet it is astounding to see *Address at Leuthen* hung in the room in the castle next to the temporary studio allocated to Menzel for the immense canvas of the *Coronation*. Had the king decided to keep it as well? He would have been virtually the only intended recipient of such a large work. If things went slowly at first, new impetus was provided in 1867, when the painting was requested for the newly founded Nationalgalerie. Menzel had it photographed and retouched one of the proofs to demonstrate his intention[12]. But this project came to nothing, like the one to integrate *Address at Leuthen* into the interior decor of the city hall in Berlin, and the various requests from art lovers. The work was left unfinished for decades, hanging on the wall in Menzels studio. Finally, in exasperation, he scraped over the faces and eyes of some of the figures. The worst affected was the portrait of Zieten, the famous general of the hussars (on the right of the king), a figure of which the painter was very fond.

A photograph taken in 1905 provides an explanation. The summary sketch in white chalk of the missing figures can be seen on the light-coloured canvas where it has been scraped, and is preserved to this day. But there is also, on the picture itself, a sketch of the figures already finished, but in different places. There was a fundamental revision, in which the two main generals were placed in the background, restraining their pervasive insolence, and forming a more homogenous semi-circle around the king, better to underline his authority. The person who requested this rethinking of the entire conception of the work can be deduced from a picture portraying the same subject in a theatrical and authoritative manner, painted by Fritz Roeber for the Halls of Fame of the Berlin Arsenal (fig. 183), in whose composition William I intervened[13]. It is likely that the monarch did the same with Menzel's canvas, around 1867, the artist giving in for a short time and trying a different layout for the figures. It was unpardonable weakness in his view, especially since it was a work undertaken at his own initiative! The painting started so magnificently remained at a standstill, and underwent the punishment described. In conversations recorded around 1900, there are implicit accusations and a wan bitterness[14]. 'After all', said the old man to a journalist, 'half of my life consists of remorse'[15]. C.K.

Fig. 183. Fritz Roeber, *Frederick the Great on the Eve of the Battle of Leuthen*, 1889, oil, previously exhibited at the Ruhmeshalle of the Berlin Zeughaus

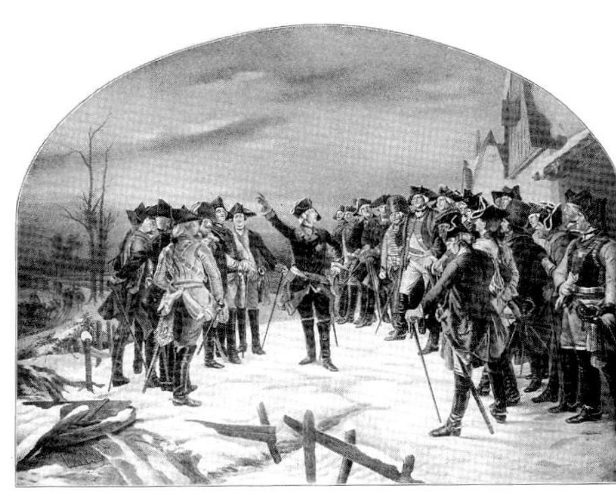

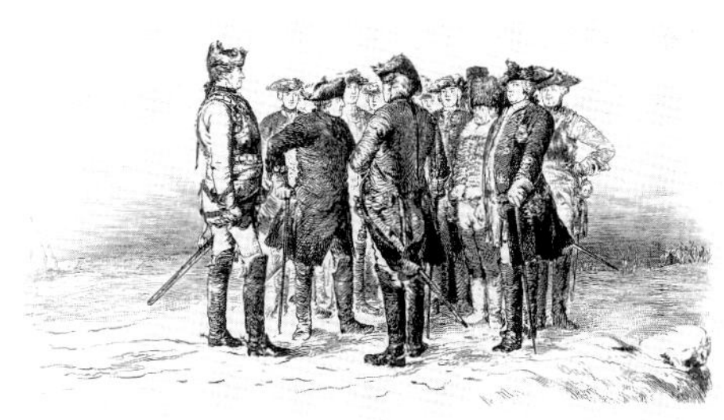

Fig. 184. *History of Frederick the Great: Frederick Instructs his Generals before the Battle of Leuthen*, 1839–42, woodcut

1. By J. Heilmann (1849), Joseph Kutzen (1851 and 1857), Adolf Müller (1857).
2. Frederick II: History of the Seven Years War I, *Works of Frederick the Great*, vol. IV, Berlin, 1847, p. 183.
3. To Adolf Schöll, 1 July, Deetjen, 1934, p. 34.
4. As Hamann saw it in 1914.
5. Bock, 1923, no. 80. Part of the series *Memorable events in the history of Brandenburg and Prussia.*
6. Bock, 1923, no. 654. *Cf.* a similar subject in the same work, Bock, 1923, no. 540.
7. Without knowing *Harangue at Leuthen,* Duranty thought that the generals painted by Menzel were stocky, short-legged or enormous, hewn in large outlines, bearing a resemblance to part of our revolutionary generation of 1789, common, but full of fire.
8. Meyerheim, (1906) 1992, p. 195 and ff.
9. In addition to the oil sketch (Berlin, Nationalgalerie) and the drawings kept in Berlin (Kat 418, 419, 423, 449–51, 485, 516, 518–21, 524, 525, 794–811, 813–19, 821–24), a drawing of eight profiles of generals should be noted (Edinburgh, National Galleries of Scotland; reprod. in exhib. cat. Hamburg, 1982, no. 73) and another at Albertina in Vienna (reprod. in Ebertshäuser, 1976, p. 1018).
10. Letter to Fritz Werner, 3 February 1860, Wolff, 1914, p. 175.
11. Letter to Fritz Werner, 27 May 1861, not published (Staatliche Museen zu Berlin, central archives).
12. These photographs have not been found, although the accompanying letter is kept in the Staatsbibliothek in Berlin (unpublished).
13. The passages containing his critique are quoted in Keisch, 1987, p. 278. The painting was lost in World War II.
14. In particular in Beta, (1898 and 1899) 1992 and in Delmar, (1905) 1992. *Cf.* Keisch, 1987, p. 276.
15. Delmar, (1905) 1992, p. 108.

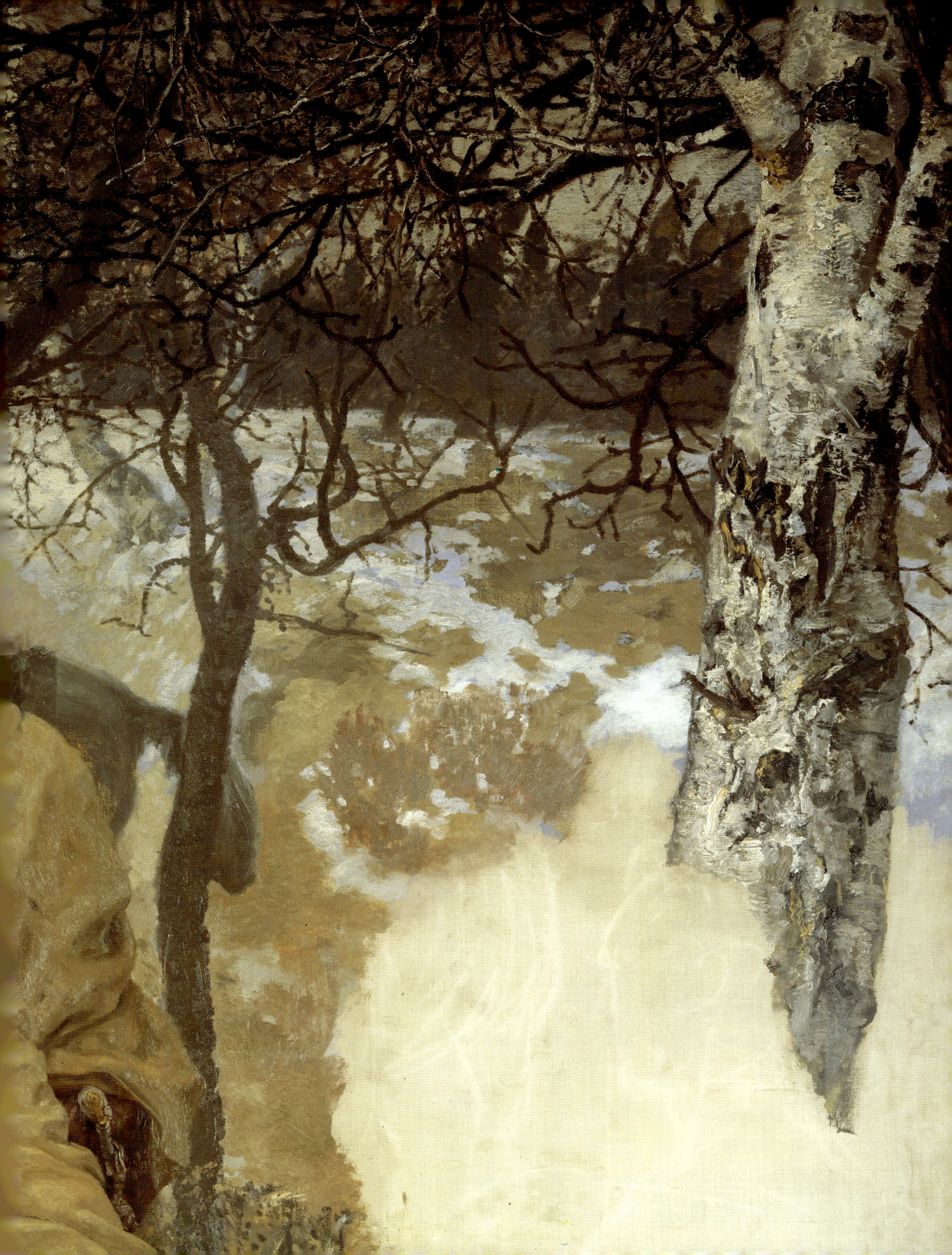

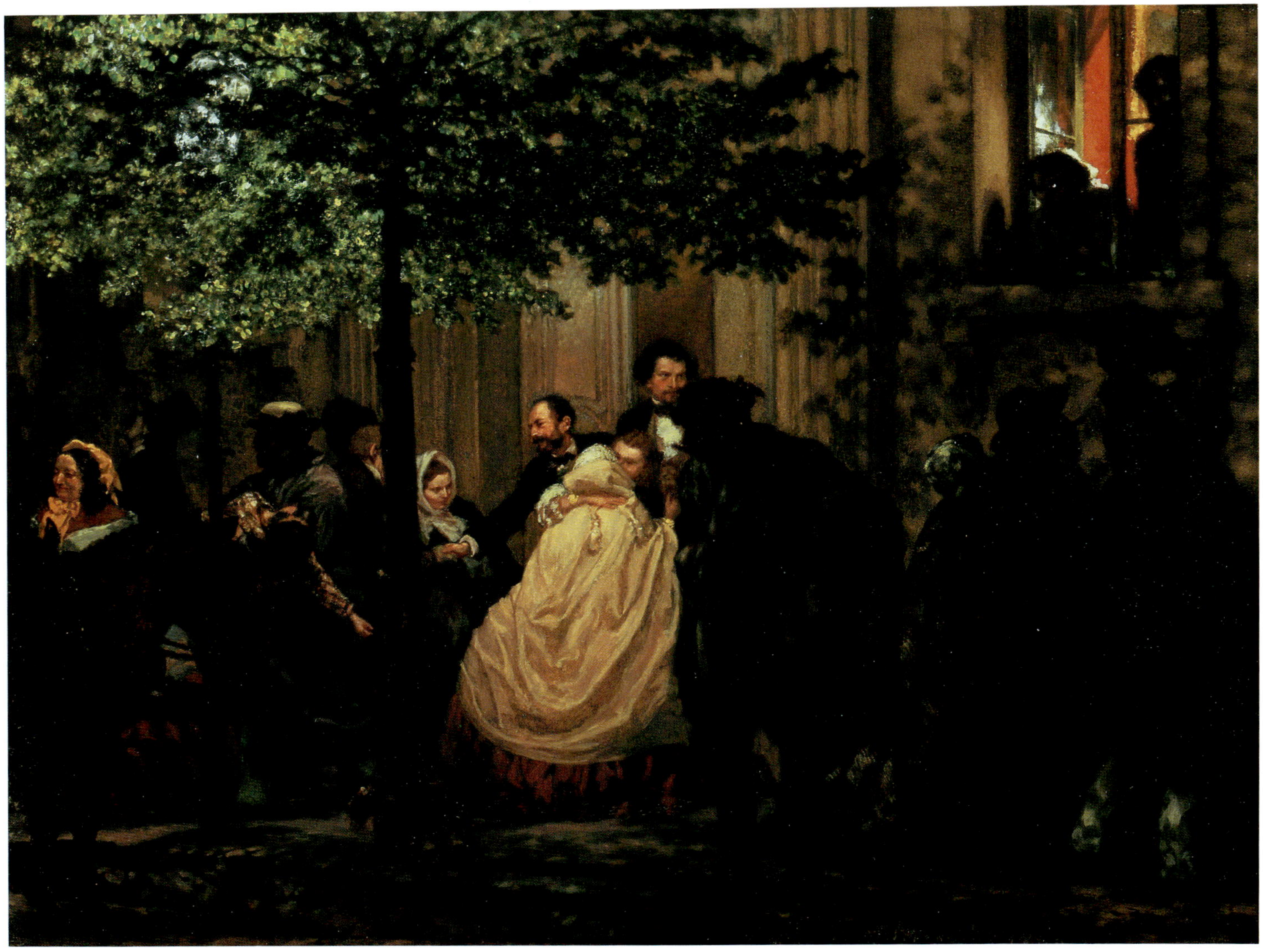

91

91

The End of the Evening

1860

Gouache
20 × 32cm
Signed and dated at the bottom right: Menzel. 1860
Pittsburgh, The Carnegie Museum of Art, Heinz Family Acquisition Fund (92.8)
Exhibited in Washington only

Provenance: Commercial advisor E. Kahlbaum, Berlin; 1905 Frau E. Kahlbaum, Berlin; private collections; acquired by the museum in 1992.
Exhibitions: Berlin, 1861; Berlin, 1905, no. 264.
Bibliography: Pietsch, 1861 B; Tschudi, 1905 A, no. 359; Bredt, 1920, p. 87 *et seq.*, reprod. p. 87; Lippincott, 1992.

After ten years, at the start of the 1860s, Menzel finally abandoned the painting of history and the era of Frederick II. Several factors had brought this about. Firstly, it was undoubtedly the problem that he had with the painting of the *Address at Leuthen* (cat. 90), which remained unfinished. Also, he had been very hurt by the pitiless criticisms expressed by the defenders of idealistic history painting over some of his other canvasses. The modernity of the psychological approach in the Frederick the Great paintings was not recognized until much later. The existential crisis into which Menzel had been plunged ended after some time, when the commission for the painting of the *Coronation* was received. When it was finished, he devoted himself unrestrainedly to contemporary subjects, free once and for all from the constraints imposed by commissions. From 1859 to 1862 he painted nine small gouache pictures for the Berlin commercial advisor Kahlbaum, among which were four genre scenes taken from the life of the heir to the throne Frederick, as a final gesture (*cf.* cat. 93) and five contemporary subjects, including *The End of the Evening* (*cf.* also cat. 92).

In this scene he portrays guests leaving their host's house, the image of city conviviality, in a lively scene of men and women departing, some lit by a bright lantern in the branches of a small lime tree, others engulfed in the darkness of the street. Everything that makes it a genre painting blends in an admirable lightness of colour, sometimes matt, sometimes warm and luminous, in which the recognizable and the indistinct alternate in a manner characteristic of Menzel's painting (*cf.* cat. 58).

Policeman and Lady in the Tuileries Gardens (cat. 79) is definitely the painting most similar to this work, in that its rough application of colour in the dark areas makes the light areas stand out even more. Not only are the figures surrounded by the light and the dusk, but the soft breath of a summer night seems to suffuse the whole. The warm tones of the earth colours are also reminiscent of *The Théâtre du Gymnase* (cat. 80). Menzel's visit to Paris in 1855 left its traces in a new choice of subjects, as well as in colour and application of paint. The artistic debate on new content based on reality was begun in Paris by Maxime Du Camp at the start of the 1850s. In Berlin, it was led by Friedrich Eggers in the *Deutsches Kunstblatt* in 1852, and changes in taste around 1855 were observed in the literature of Theodor Fontane[1].

Paul Meyerheim, the son of the family of painters with which Menzel spent a lot of time, describes this scene of departure, which, according to Meyerheim, Menzel sketched immediately[2]. One sketchbook shows more than five drawings[3] of three subjects relating to the picture[4]. There are also two studies of Fräulein Schaumann, standing to the right of the lime tree, with a pale scarf around her neck. She was the daughter of a private advisor and lived at Ritterstrasse 43, where the Menzel family also lived until the end of 1860. With a few exceptions, most of the figures are anonymous. Menzel's brother, so often painted and drawn by him, especially in that year[5], is turning to the left and shaking a man's hand. The man behind him might be Friedrich Eggers, standing in front of the door. The two women hugging each other could be Frau Meyerheim, with her hair down, and Menzel's sister Emilie. They are the other way round in the drawing[6]. Emilie, who is wearing a *coiffe* on her dark head, is hugging the person seen from behind, and her wedding ring is clearly visible on her right hand. M.R.-R.

1. Fontane, 1982 A, III/1, p. 145.
2. Meyerheim, (1906) 1992, p. 171.
3. Berlin, Kupferstichkabinett (SZ Menzel N 543, 1782, 2425, 3366, 3437).
4. Berlin, Kupferstichkabinett, sketchbook 22 (1860-62).
5. Hamburg, Kunsthalle. *Cf.* exhib. cat. Hamburg, 1982, no. 80.
6. Berlin, Kupferstichkabinett (SZ Menzel N 3366).

92
Two Builders at Work
1860

Gouache
36 × 22cm
Signed and dated at the bottom left: *Menzel 1860*
Regensburg, Ostdeutsche Galerie (18498)
Exhibited in Berlin only

Provenance: Commercial advisor E. Kahlbaum, Berlin; 1905 Frau E. Kahlbaum, Berlin; private collections; acquired by the museum in 1992.
Bibliography: Tschudi, 1905 A, no. 355; Lammel, 1993 B, p. 99, col. fig. 26.

Between 1859 and 1862 Menzel painted nine gouaches for the Berlin collector Kahlbaum. Four of them portray fictional scenes from the time of Frederick the Great, when he was the crown prince at Rheinsberg. Two of these, *A Boat Trip*[1] and *Crown Prince Frederick Pays a Visit to the Painter Pesne on his Scaffold in Rheinsberg* (cat. 93) herald the abandonment of the 'Frederick' theme favoured for so long. With this commission, Menzel's interest in contemporary subjects is evident. Five pictures present scenes from everyday life, three of which were painted on the basis of memories of his journey to Thuringia, Innsbruck and the Zillertal in the Tyrol. *The End of the Evening* (cat. 91) derives from a familiar Berlin scene and, to judge from the sketches in the same sketchbook[2], he observed the construction site that inspired this gouache in Berlin too. The way in which he used such drawings is illustrated in a letter dated 1860 to his friend Fritz Werner on the subject of his trip to the Tyrol a year earlier, and on the series painted for Kahlbaum: 'Afterwards I spent at least two months painting pictures in oils, chalk, watercolour, using the notes I took when I was there'[3].

Menzel always drew workers. Here for the first time he uses colour for the subject. As is often the case, the composition, which looks simple at first sight, is the result of subtle reflection on colour and layout. The very marked rectilinear structure of the walls is softened by the contrast with the old, worm-eaten planks and the dust, or smoke, round about them. Burning red stands out from dark brown. Man and work seem to be in perfect harmony, which is not the case in *The Iron Rolling Mill*, a later portrayal of the industrial world. Here, bricklayers and ironworkers recall once more the time of harmonious cooperation between craftsmen. In 1861, Menzel made twelve woodcuts for *Der Blitzschlosser zu Wittenberg* (The Lightning Conductor Maker at Wittenberg) by Berthold Auerbach, which appeared in a popular calendar[4]. The figure of the artisan had already appeared in this gouache, and does so again in a series of studies drawn in an ironmaker's workshop at the start of the 1860s[5]. M.R.-R.

1. 1855, Hamburg, private collection.
2. Used in 1860–2. Berlin, Kupferstichkabinett, sketchbook 22.
3. Letter to Fritz Werner, 3 February 1860, Wolff, 1914, p. 175.
4. Bock, 1923, no. 1085.
5. Berlin, Kupferstichkabinett, (SZ Menzel N 678, 680, 801–7).

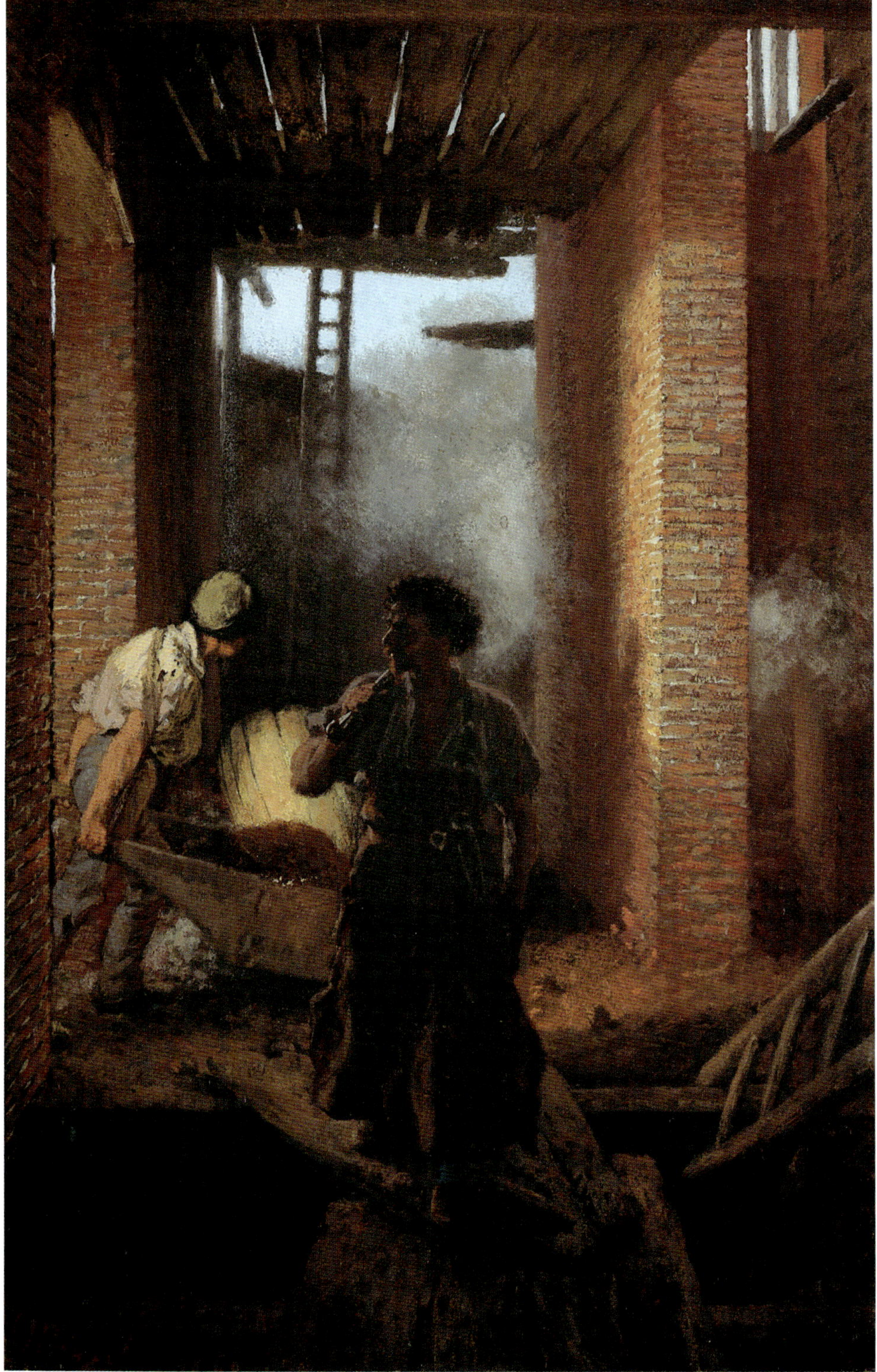

92

93

Crown Prince Frederick Pays a Visit to the Painter Pesne on his Scaffold at Rheinsberg

1861

Gouache on paper, board backing
24 × 32cm
Signed and dated at the bottom left: *Menzel 1861*
Berlin, Nationalgalerie (on permanent loan from the German Federal Republic)

Provenance: Commercial adviser E. Kahlbaum, Berlin; 1905 Frau E. Kahlbaum, Berlin; private collections; deposited by the German Federal Republic at the Nationalgalerie in 1967.
Exhibitions: Berlin, 1861; Berlin, 1863; Berlin, 1895 A, no. 248; Berlin, 1912, no. 230 (no. 69 of small cat.), pl. 93; Berlin, 1955 B, no. 96, fig. 32; Wolfsburg, 1956, no. 126; Berlin, 1965, no. 37, reprod.; Wurtzburg, 1966, no. 10; Berlin, 1986, no. VIII.3, col. reprod.
Bibliography: Pietsch, 1861; Jordan, 1895, p. 42–4, p. 69, reprod. p. 39; Jordan, 1905, reprod. p. 67; Tschudi, 1905 A, no. 409; Meier-Graefe, 1906, p. 193; Lammel, 1993 B, p. 44, p. 46, col. pl. 4.

For a virtual Menzel gallery in miniature, commissioned by the commercial advisor Kahlbaum, the painter, approaching fifty, seemed to be following a kind of programme. He used gouache, a technique he had begun to favour for increasingly complex and ambiguous compositions. But above all he brought together an almost equal number of historical and contemporary subjects, corresponding to the transition between the two great phases of his work taking place at that time. Two years later, when nearly all his paintings and wood engravings of the time of Frederick II were exhibited, he left aside this source of inspiration. The systematic choice of scenes for the historical paintings of the Kahlbaum cycle (as well as the composition described here, *A Trip on the Water at Rheinsberg*, *Court Ball at Rheinsberg*, *Court Lackeys and Hussars in the Antechamber*) seems to indicate a depoliticization of the royal personnage.

When he was taking a cure at Rheinsberg, Menzel had the opportunity to observe the architecture of the castle altered and rebuilt by the crown prince to entertain an artistic court. It was an inten-

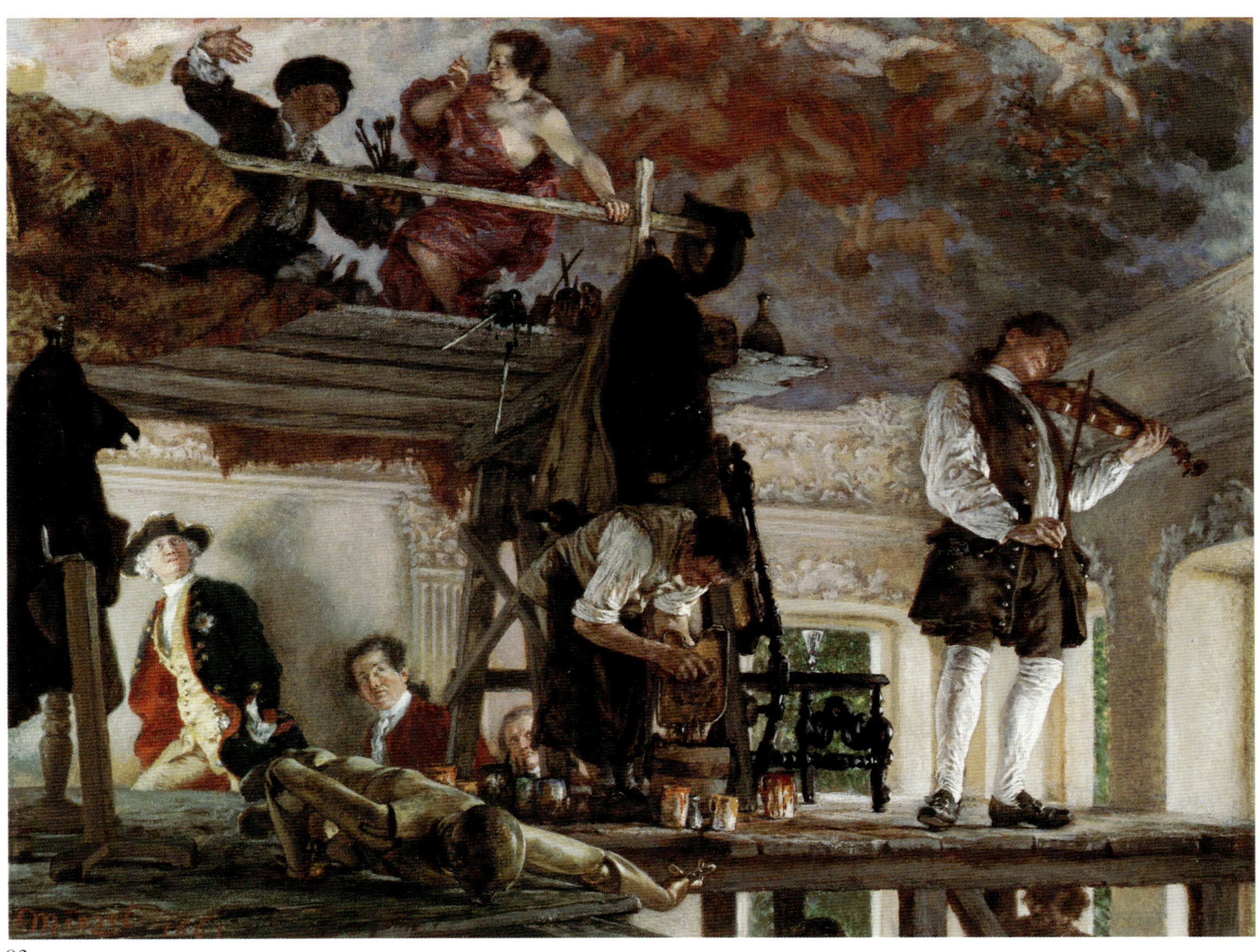

93

tional departure from Frederick's unpopular father's austere, inelegant style. He did not enjoy it for long, since almost as soon as the work was finished, he came to the throne and immediately went to war.

Menzel portrays Antoine Pesne, summoned from Paris in 1710 by Frederick's grandfather as court painter, in which position he remained until his death. Here he is painting the ceiling of the ballroom with an allegory of Apollo chasing the Night, which the prince's friends did not fail to interpret as an allusion to the forthcoming change of monarch[1]. On the scaffold large pots of the paint used for such works wobble on the uneven planks. While Franz Benda lifts the spirits and senses with his viola-playing, Pesne, perched at a vertiginous height above him, demonstrates a dance step to a model. No one, not even the assistant cleaning a palette, notices the arrival of the fascinated prince, illuminated in the sunlight. The first of his companions is the architect of the castle, Georg Wenzeslaus von Knobelsdorff (whose portrait was copied from one of Pesne's pictures).

The picture's system of foreshortening its elements, subdividing an improbable, suspended space, without concrete boundaries, is a stunning virtuoso exercise. The view from below does not allow the distance from the floor to be measured, and the *trompe l'oeil* ceiling seems to be at a distance when in fact it is very close. The architecture opens on to the outdoors in an unexpected place. The vanishing lines, as well as those of the scaffold, justify the caricaturesque foreshortening of the fallen dummy in the forground. The three visitors appear from nowhere, as the steps of the staircase are invisible. Does the viola player realize he is on the edge of the precipice, like a sleep-walker? Totally isolated, with the light on the brown and white of his modest clothes, as it is on the yellow, red and blue of the crown prince's outfit, the viola player uses the empty space to the right of the painting like a resonating space. His solitary reverie is reminiscent of Watteau's *Gilles*. The silent music is not in rhythm with the lively movement dominating the left half of the picture,

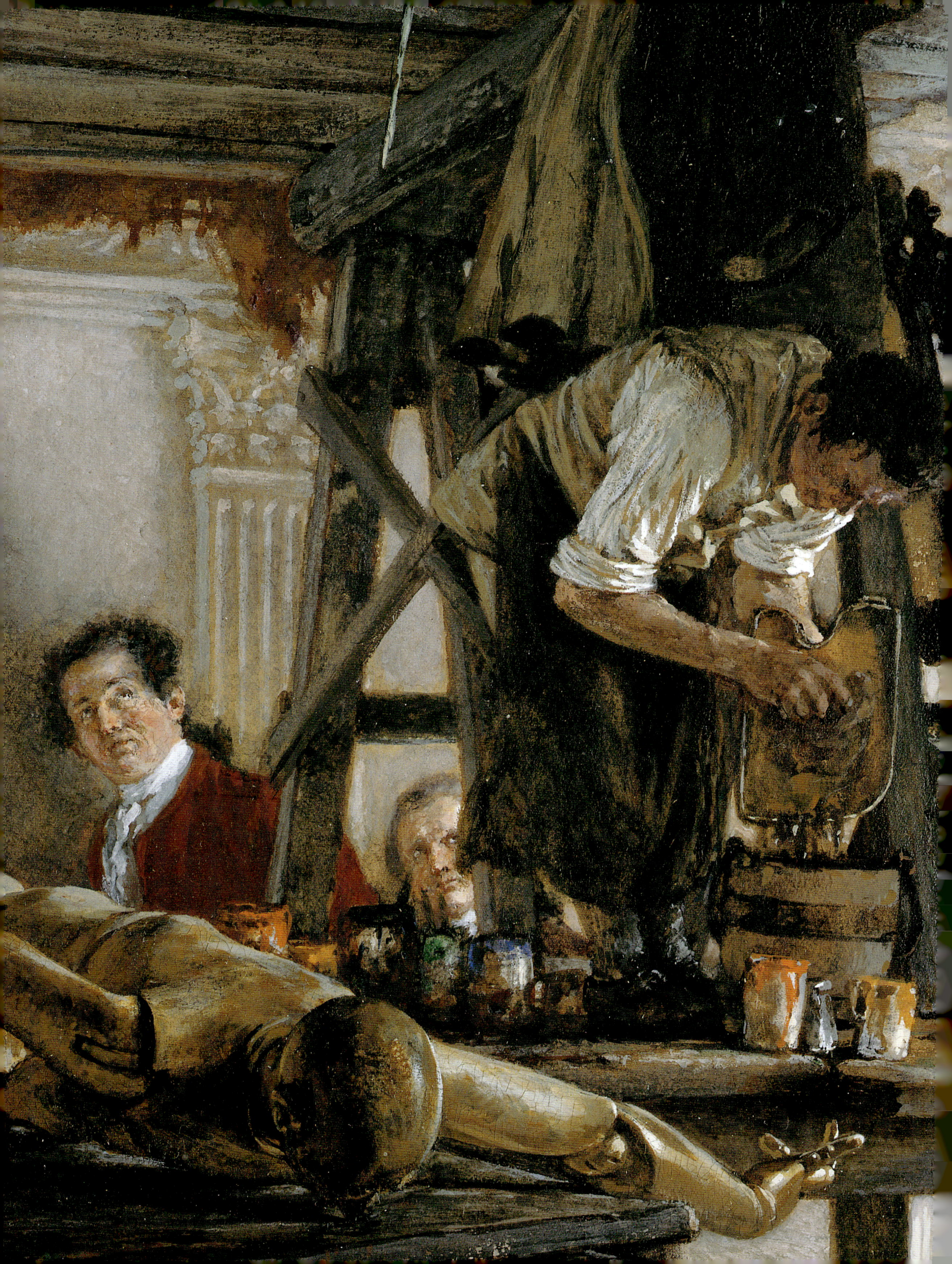

which can be seen in three different areas, or four if one takes into account the movement around the wooden dummy. The different figures are unaware of each other's presence, and only Frederick and his companions take notice of the merry scene above them without, however, being able to see it. It is just the central axis, defined by the pole, the coat and the assistant, that brings together the different parts of the picture, in a rather abstract way.

The depiction of a work site in Schinkel's great painting *View of the Apogee of Greece*[2] has a similar construction that projecting skywards without any visible point of support. Menzel may have been making an ironic allusion to this evocation of antiquity, by distorting one of its essential elements in favour of his rococo comedy, studied from close up, and in truth more humorous than graceful. The picture contains another allusion, this one imperceptible to the general public. Behind the painter's assistant, half hidden by clothes, is an elaborately carved chair, quite unexpected in a place where it is threatened by splashes of paint. It is not a period piece, and this break with style is intentional, for the chair is Menzel's, a manufactured piece of furniture later adapted to suit his height, which can be seen in the photographs of his last studio. Menzel is literally presenting himself here as the 'painter of Frederick the Great', and it is no surprise to find that he also drew himself in the happy dance pose of Pesne, with a paintbrush between his teeth[3]. In this context, the dummy lying forgotten on the ground is significant too, since for centuries dummies had been used in the Acedemies for studies of clothing. The painter shows a clear preference for the living model and life drawing[4]. C.K.

1. In his biography of Frederick (Chapter 11), Franz Kugler quotes a letter from Baron Bielfeldt, who was unequivocal on the subject. One of Menzel's illustrations relates to this passage, and represents a scaffold similar to the one in the 1861 gouache.
2. 1825, location unknown. Copy by Wilhelm Ahlborn (1836) in the Nationalgalerie, Berlin.
3. Berlin, Kupferstichkabinett (SZ Menzel Kat 830). The drawing was considered as a study for the gouache painting described here. Traces of colour left by a paintbrush suggest that it was laid on a table used for watercolours. Nevertheless, its use remains obscure. It is probably a free allusion to the gouache, Menzel identifying himself once more, and with a certain irony, with the famous court painter. Lammel, 1993 B, fig. 5 (col.). Another drawing shows Menzel with the same perspective of looking up from below (Nuremberg, Stadtgeschichtlicht Museen), and also has traces of watercolour on it . It would be satisfying to link it with the Berlin drawing, if the pencil were not noticeably thicker and the style later. Eckhard Schaar noted that it relates to the gouache *Beati possidentes (*Blessed landowners) of 1888 (exhib. cat. Hamburg, 1982, no. 168, reprod.).
4. Preparatory drawings at the Kupferstichkabinett in Berlin (SZ Menzel Kat 831-834, 1033, 1335, 1386, N 1731).

94–99

Studies for The Coronation of King William I at Königsberg

1861–4

The commission in October 1861 for the great painting of *The Coronation of William I* (fig. 121) is generally considered to be the turning point in Menzel's work, the start of an official career (to which he only applied himself passively, without accepting State commissions), and the second phase in his overall work, in which modern subjects dominate. The main problem with this painting is the conflict between the demands of the history painting and an objective viewpoint, stimulated by contemporary reality.

Before coming to the throne on 2 January 1861, William I had been regent for over two years. When he became king, he soon disappointed any hopes of economic and political liberalization he may have for a while awakened. The idea of reviving the support of East Prussia with the coronation ceremony in Königsberg, abandoned for a century and a half, was accepted unwillingly by those who detected an authoritarian concept of royalty 'by the grace of God', directed against 'the yoke of parliamentary government'.

Whether commemorating the event with a painting had been thought of at the last minute, or whether it had taken a long time to decide on the choice of painter, Menzel, who had only just recovered from a long illness, was approached only one week before the ceremony. He must have decided to accept immediately, and rushed to the borders of Prussia where, with the help of his friend Fritz Werner, he was able to gather information about the church at the castle where the coronation was to take place. Standing on a pew, he shared the observation with Werner, using a carefully worked out method. Originally he appears to have chosen the moment when the king places the crown on his head but, like Jacques-Louis David half a century before, he decided against that idea as being too secular, and opted for the moment when the king repeats the formula in the sermon given to him by the court preacher Adolf Thielen.

Of all the drawings brought back to Berlin, the gouache (cat. 94), with its sparkling red and gold, is the most picturesque. The oil sketch (cat. 95), done after Menzel had returned to Berlin, is the second of four drafts for the project, submitted in succession for the king's judgement. Each time, from December 1861 to July 1862, modifications were requested[1], and the watercolours of the English painter George Thomas and even of the princess royal were recommended as models (*cf.* fig 186).

The most significant of the objections made related to the foreground: the rows of people viewed from behind who obstructed it were to be removed, and redistributed in triangular groups on each side, leaving a space into which Menzel inserted the imposing figure of the crown prince in the red coat of the Order of the Black Eagle (he was previously on the right, facing the king). This figure, who encapsulated certain liberal values, was thus placed in the limelight. The idea may have been Menzel's, in an effort to accommodate the new design, but it contradicted his search for authenticity: 'He rejoiced at being able to move away from historical truth, which until then he had made it his duty to respect. . . .'[2]

This rejoicing may have been a little ironic. It was a question of moving from one genre to another, from the faithful depiction of a contemporary event to a history painting touched with idealism. Once this hurdle was passed, more licence was permitted, and later Menzel managed to persuade the king to adopt a different posture, brandishing the broadsword on high and holding the sceptre in his left hand – an authoritative gesture, but one which fits admirably into the rhythm of the composition. The royal banner on the right balances the gesture with its slanting position (previously it was vertical).

Most of this reworking, even the insertion of the crown prince, took place after the extremely detailed preparatory drawing had been traced on to the canvas. A photograph of it exists, which seems to indicate the intention from the beginning to consider the painting of *The Coronation* from a historical point of view by documenting the stages of its preparation. Finally, everything was brought together in an enormous album[3], containing over one hundred and fifty studies (mostly portraits), studio photographs and photographs of the canvas accompanied by the inscription 'The finished work', plus a long autographed account of the process of creation, of a type that Menzel wrote for several of his major pictures.

The work was finished at the end of 1865 and, after some exhibitions in Germany, was at first hung in the art gallery of Berlin palace[4], then exhibited abroad several times. Its political significance was always commented upon. When there was a question of sending it to the Universal Exhibition in St Louis in 1904, its painter was sceptical: 'Will the Americans really appreciate this subject? And supposing one day some man goes to the exhibition with a stone in his pocket???'[5] On the other hand, a whole series of contemporary portraits arose out of this solemn composition, gripping in their pitiless veracity, which makes no concessions to the historical genre. C.K.

1. More details will be given in an article to appear in 1997.
2. Report made by the church minister August von Bethmann Hollweg to the king, 11 February 1862, Geheimes Preussisches Staatsarchiv, 2.2.1., no. 20337, fol. 21.
3. This was acquired by the Nationalgalerie in 1880. Only four portraits are not present, which today belong to the Georg Schäfer collection, Euerbach.
4. It is preserved today at the New Palace at Potsdam.
5. Letter to an unknown recipient, 2 January 1919, Kirstein, 1919, p. 89.

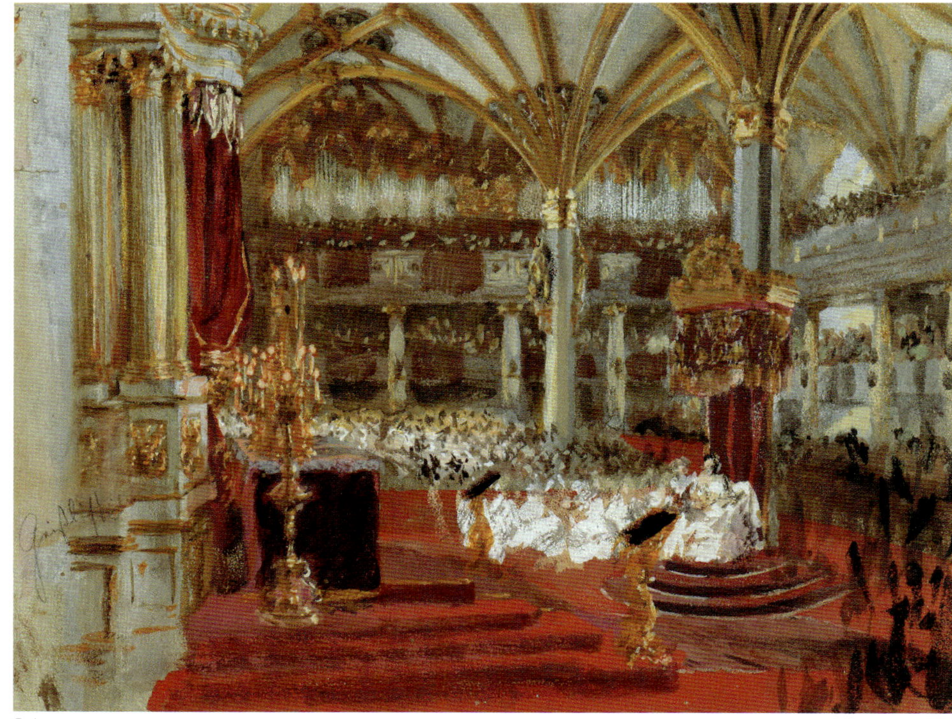
94

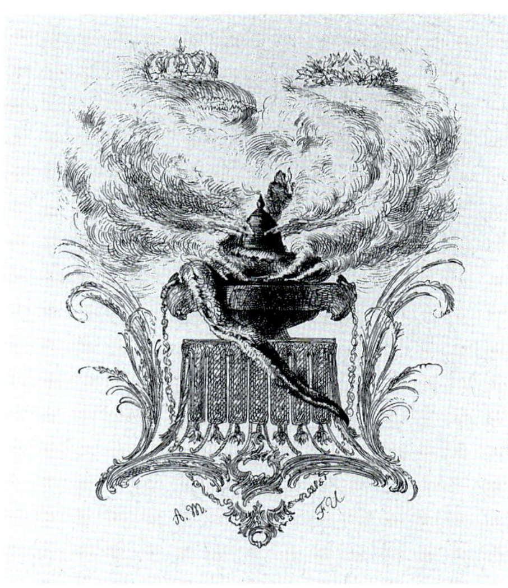
Fig. 185. Illustration to the *Works of Frederick the Great*, 1843–9, woodcut

94

Sketch for The Coronation of King William I at Königsberg

October 1861

Gouache
22.5 × 29cm
Annotated at the bottom left: *Geistlichkeit*
Berlin, Kupferstichkabinett (SZ Menzel Kat 841)
Exhibited in Paris only

Provenance: Hermann Pächter (R. Wagner Gallery, Berlin); acquired by the museum in 1880.
Exhibitions: Berlin, 1905, no. 112; Berlin, 1980 A, no. 249, p. 49 *et seq.*, reprod. p. 254; New York, 1990, no. 27, col. reprod. p. 113.
Bibliography: Donop, 1902, no. 841; Tschudi, 1905 A, no. 420; Grohn, 1976; Lammel, 1988, reprod. p. 121.

This sketch, which is obviously the first of a series of four, shows the interior of the church at Königsberg castle, built around 1600, with its slender pillars and late Gothic vaulting. Its originally baroque decoration is further enriched by the splendour of the coronation scene.

The figures in the foreground, and that of the king, have not yet been put in. The interior space of the church seems higher and vaster than it actually was. (The church was destroyed towards the end of World War II.) M.R.-R.

95

Sketch for The Coronation of King William 1 at Königsberg

November 1861

Oil on canvas
74.5 × 100cm
Signed at the bottom left: *Menzel 1861*
Berlin, Nationalgalerie (A I 310)
Exhibited in Berlin only

Provenance: Hermann Pächter (R. Wagner Gallery, Berlin); acquired by the museum in 1880.
Exhibitions: Vienna, 1873; Berlin, 1885, no. 8; Berlin, 1895 A, no. 125; Hamburg, 1896, no. 84; Vienna, 1896, no. 270; Berlin, 1935, no. 40, reprod.; Berlin, 1980 A, no. XXIV, reprod. p. 147.
Bibliography: Cat. NG, 1880, no. 481; Jordan/Dohme, 1890, p. 57; Jordan, 1895, p. 39, p. 69; Jordan, 1905, p. 63; Meyerheim, (1906) 1992, p. 164 *et seq.*; Tschudi, 1905 A, no. 127; Waldmann, 1941, p. 48, fig. 60; Hütt, 1981, fig. 99; Lammel, 1993 B, p. 67, col. pl. 10.

In this version, the king thought he looked 'too old (with a white beard) and lacking in nobility and majesty'. He wanted to look larger, and appear to be moving less abruptly, with the sceptre held higher. He felt the church was too narrow, and the congregation took up too much space[1]. The new draft, finished by 7 January and housed today in Hannover[2], took these objections into account. The foreground, however, was not divided in two until the last sketch, a watercolour painted in February, belonging formerly to William II[3], in which the artist introduced an intense lighting effect. C.K.

1. Report by the church minister, 6 December 1861, Geheimes Preussisches Staatsarchiv, William 1 fund, Rep 51J, Bethmann Hollweg letters, fol. 7 and ff.
2. Gouache, Tschudi, 1905 A, no. 422; Hanover, Niedersächsische Landesgalerie.
3. Tschudi, 1905 A, no. 420; location unknown.

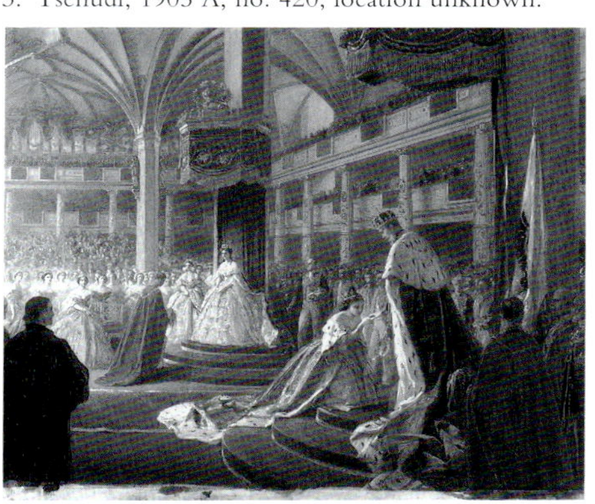

Fig. 186. George H. Thomas, *Homage of the Prince and Princess Royal to King William I and the Queen at the Coronation, 18 October 1861*, 1861, oil, collection of H.M. The Queen

95

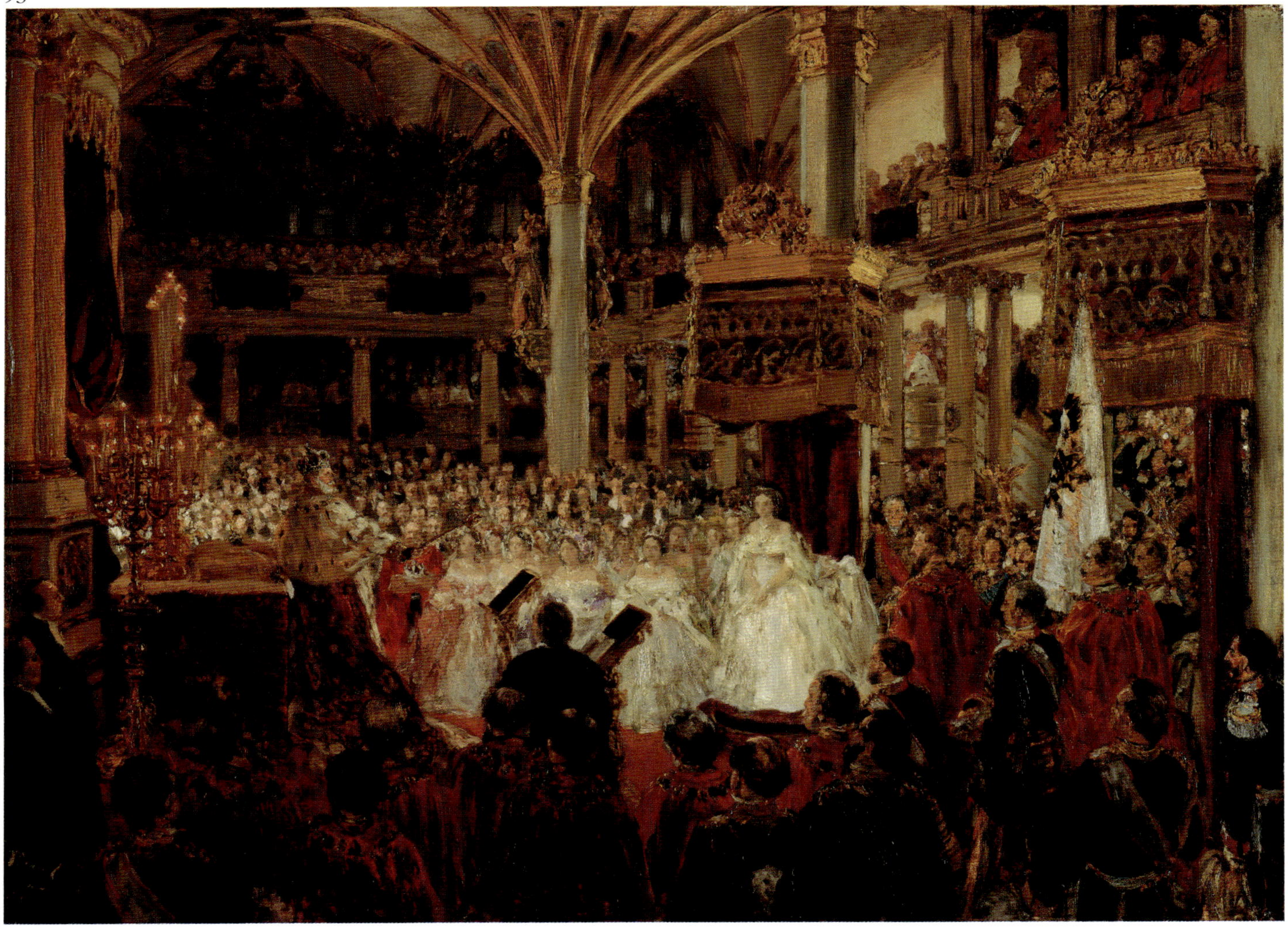

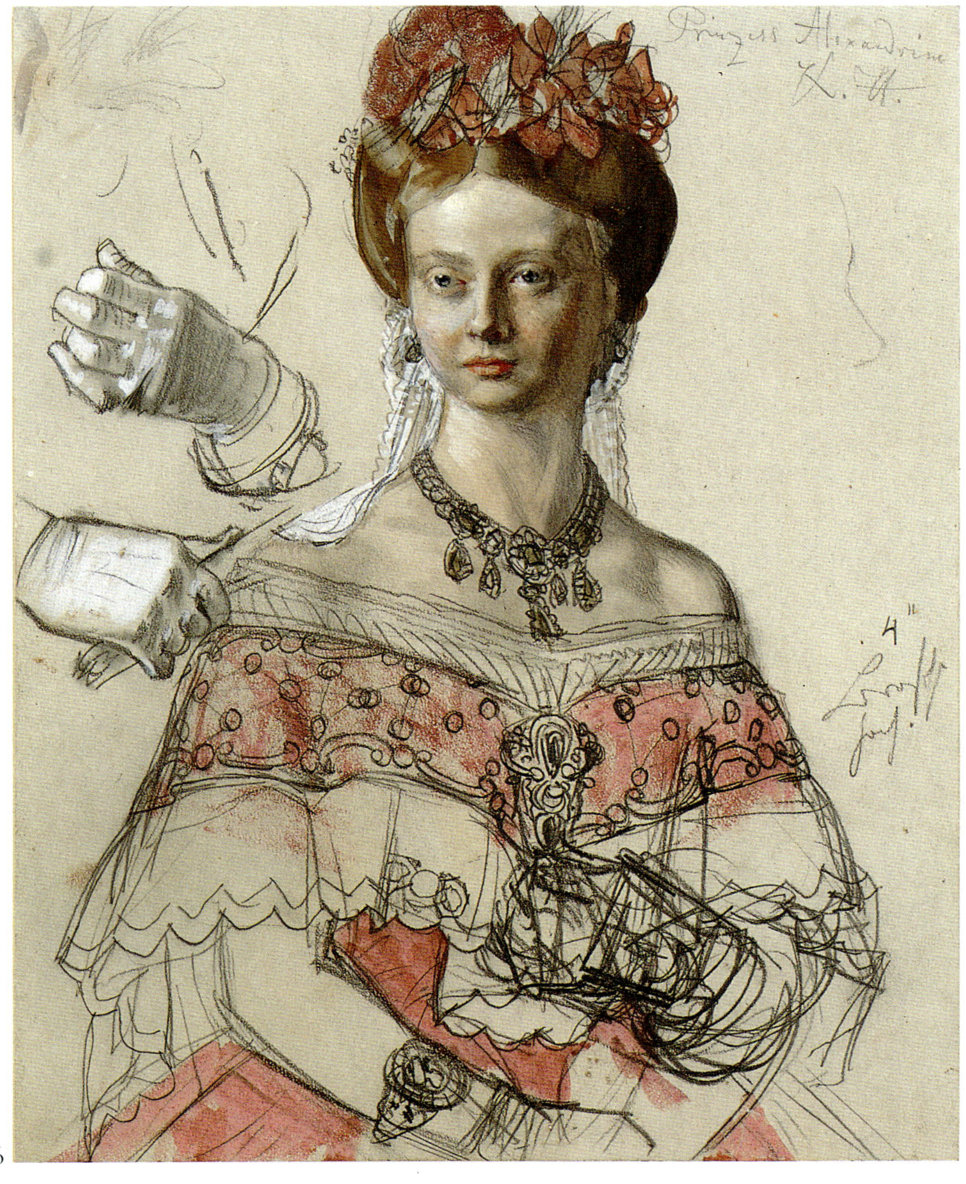

96

96

Princess Alexandrine of Prussia

c. 1863–4

Gouache
29.5 × 23.1cm
Annotated at the top right: *Prinzess Alexandrine K.H. – 4" Brosche hoch.*
Berlin, Kupferstichkabinett (SZ Menzel Kat 968)
Exhibited in Paris only

Provenance: Hermann Pächter (R. Wagner Gallery, Berlin); acquired by the museum in 1880.
Exhibitions: Berlin, 1905, no. 1289; Berlin, 1980 A, no. 257, reprod. p. 372; Copenhagen, 1985, no. 36, reprod. p. 27.
Bibliography: Donop, 1902, no. 968; Tschudi, 1905 A, no. 432.

Portrait sessions for the 132 people represented in the *Coronation* painting began on 19 March 1863 in the guard room at Berlin palace, which had been made available to Menzel as a studio since 6 April 1862. The great glory of the painting derives mainly from these preparatory portraits in gouache which were transferred *alla prima* on to the canvas. The portrait of this princess displays a very rare phenomenon: intense reproduction of each detail of her face in all its individuality, not idealized but, rather, without illusion – simultaneously inexpressive yet with an imposing presence. Alexandrine (born in 1842) was the daughter of Prince Albert, the king's younger brother, for whom Schinkel had refurbished the palace in the Wilhelmstrasse in Berlin (*cf.* cat. 23, 164). She appears in the middle ground of the *Coronation* painting, at the end of a row of ladies, to the right of General and Count Karl von Groeben, who is carrying the queens crown on a cushion (and was the first to have his portrait painted, according to Menzel). The painter clarified the position of the princess' hands in a separate study, and transferred it directly to the painting.

M.R.-R.

97

Baron von Patow, Minister of State

1864

Watercolour and gouache on pencil
29.4 × 22.3cm
Annotated and dated at the bottom right: *Staatsminister von Patow 2 Febr. 64.*
Berlin, Kupferstichkabinett (SZ Menzel Kat 938)
Exhibited in Berlin only

Provenance: Hermann Pächter (R. Wagner Gallery, Berlin); acquired by the museum in 1880.
Exhibitions: Berlin, 1885, no. 51; Berlin, 1895 B, no. 612; Vienna, 1896, no. 198; Düsseldorf, 1904, no. 31; Berlin, 1905, no. 1259; Berlin, 1955 A, no. 291; Berlin, 1980 A, no. 263, reprod. p. 261; Vienna, 1985, no. 44; reprod. p. 115; Copenhagen, 1985, no. 39; New York, 1990, no. 29, col. reprod. p. 117.
Bibliography: Donop, 1902, no. 938; Tschudi, 1905 A, no. 501; Lammel, 1988, p. 137, fig. 107.

Baron von Patow (1804–90) started work in the Prussian Ministry of Finance in the 1830s. The owner of a stately home, he was already a delegate of the *Landtag* (State Assembly) of Niederlausitz in 1839. In April 1848 he became Minister of Commerce, Industry and Public Works in the Camphausen cabinet, and after the dissolution he was appointed the first president of the province of Brandenburg. He ran for the conservatives, supported

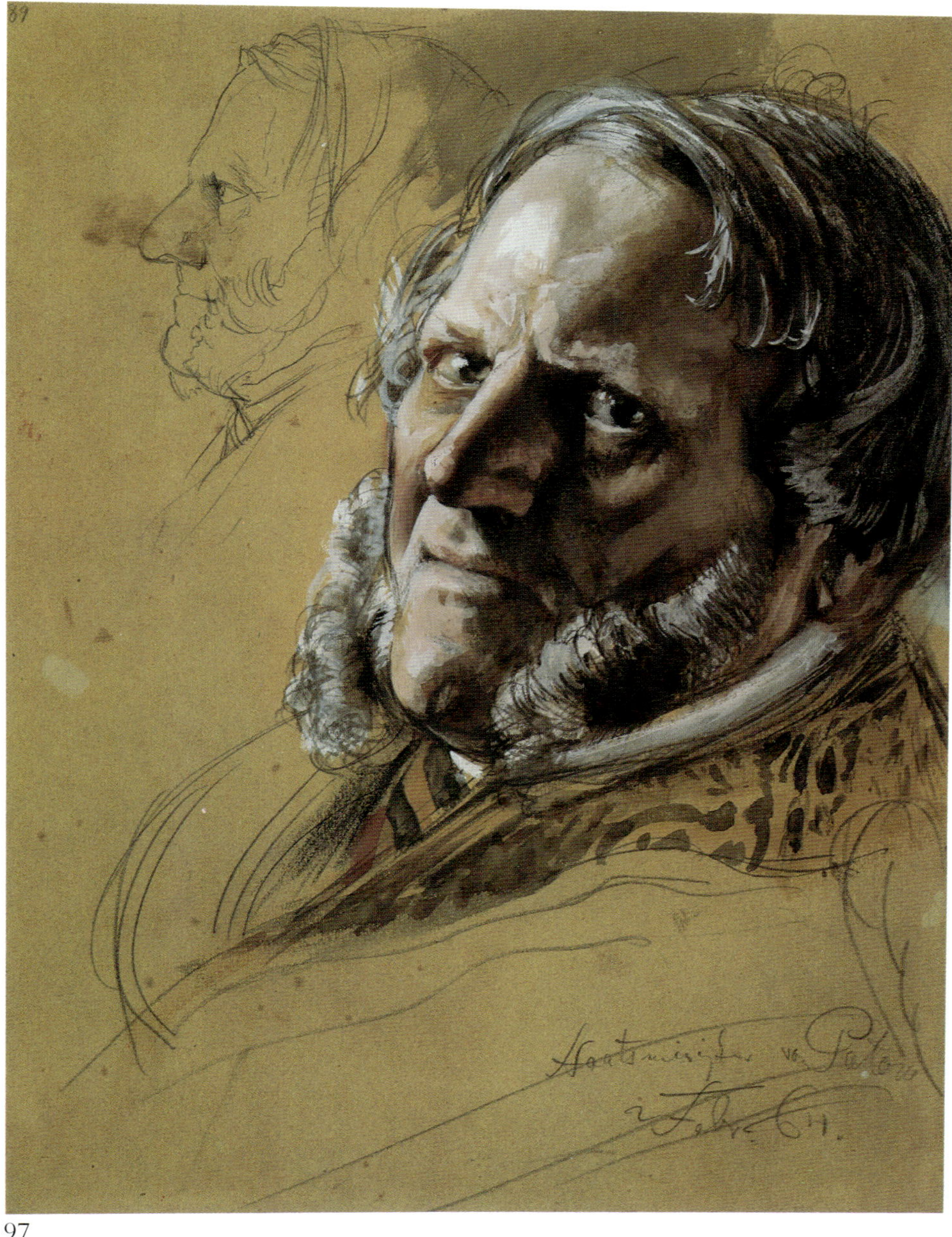

97

the opponents of the democratic Left and departed from public service at the end of 1849. In November 1858, King Frederick-William IV was ill and had to delegate his duties to the Prince Regent William. A 'new era' began, a liberal phase which scarcely lasted until William ascended the throne. During this period, in which long-awaited reforms were promised, von Patow was Minister of Finance in the Hohenzollern cabinet, for which he served as main representative in Parliament, and brought in a general property tax in order to reform the army. When the reversal that put an end to the 'new era' came, he took refuge in parliamentary activity. Later he became the first president of the province of Saxony. In *The Coronation* he appears in the foreground, on the right, among the government ministers. The extra profile study underlines Menzel's interest in physiognomy, although he also drew the full-length figure[1]. M.R.-R.

1. Berlin, Kupferstichkabinett (SZ Menzel Kat 937).

98

Baron von der Heydt, Minister of State

1864

Watercolour, gouache and pencil on yellowish-brown paper
29.6 × 22.4cm
Annotated and dated at the top right: *Staats = Min:von der Heydt Kopf circa 8⅝″ Grösse gute 5′7¼″ 12. Febr. 64.*
Berlin, Kupferstichkabinett (SZ Menzel Kat 912)
Exhibited in Paris only

Provenance: Hermann Pächter (R. Wagner Gallery, Berlin); acquired by the museum in 1880.
Exhibitions: Berlin, 1885, no. 52; Berlin, 1895 B, no. 614; Dresden, 1904, no. 2335; Berlin, 1905, no. 1233.
Bibliography: Donop, 1902, no. 912; Tschudi, 1905 A, no. 482.

Baron August von der Heydt (1801–74), a banker from Elberfeld, was a member of the United Parliament (Vereinigter Landtag) in 1847 and previously of the parliament of the Rhineland province. After 1848, he became Prussian Minister of Trade, Works and Public Affairs until the reshuffle in 1862. Having moved on to be Minister of Finance, he resigned a few months later when faced with the authoritarian policy of Bismarck. However, the talent he showed in financing the war against Austria earned him another term as Minister of Finance from 1866 to 1869.

In the painting of *The Coronation*, von der Heydt, the then Minister of Trade, is placed next to the Minister of Finance, von Patow, whom he replaced temporarily in 1862. In the light of what followed, Menzel offers a remarkable interpretation of the political rapport between these two men, which only became established a year after the coronation. Von der Heydt, on the periphery of the group of ministers, is situated on the edge of the picture in relation to the onlooker. There is a pencil sketch showing him standing, which was used as a model for the painting. The note '5'7¼' at the top of the watercolour refers to this drawing, which shows the minister in profile, as in the painting. A.H.

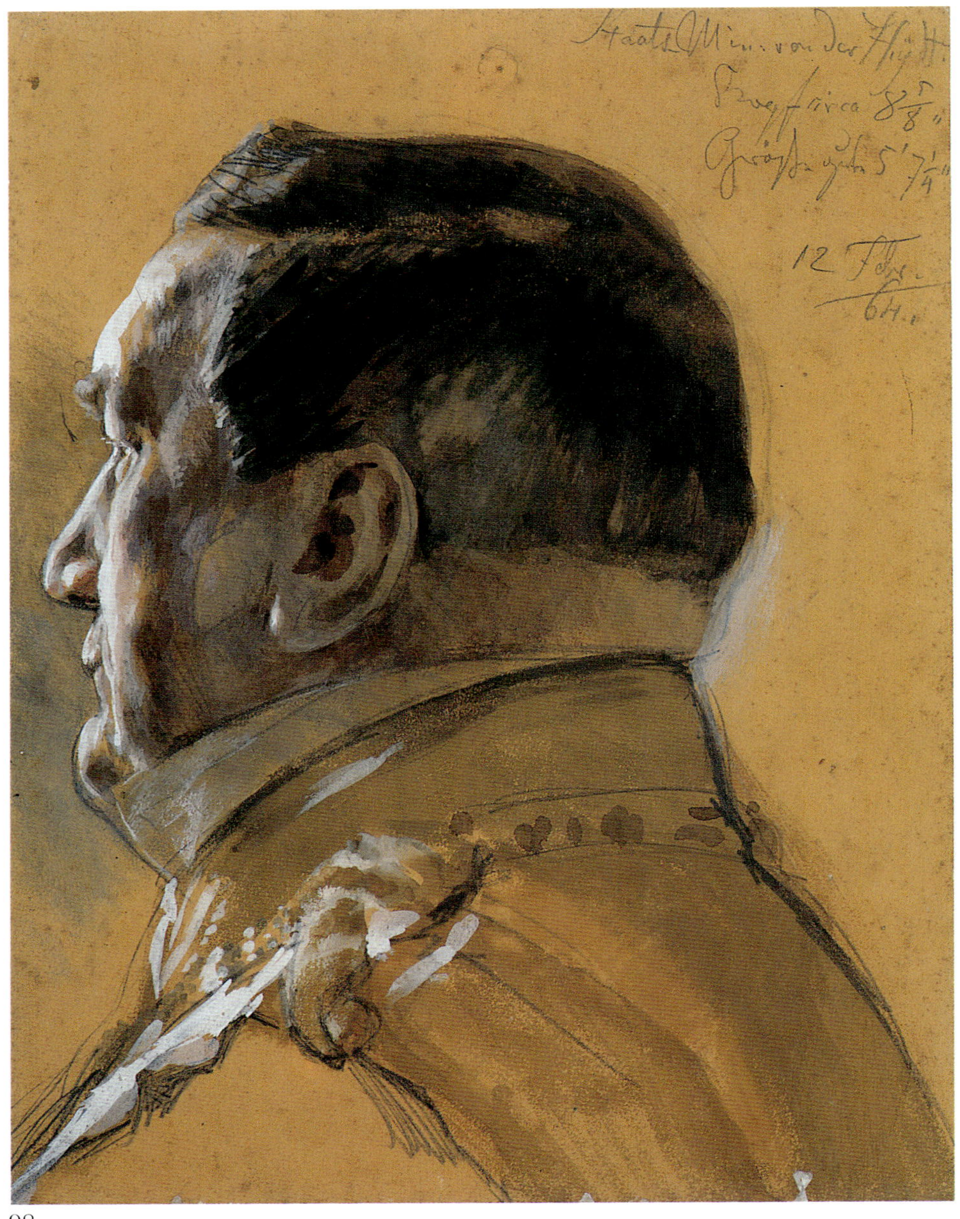

98

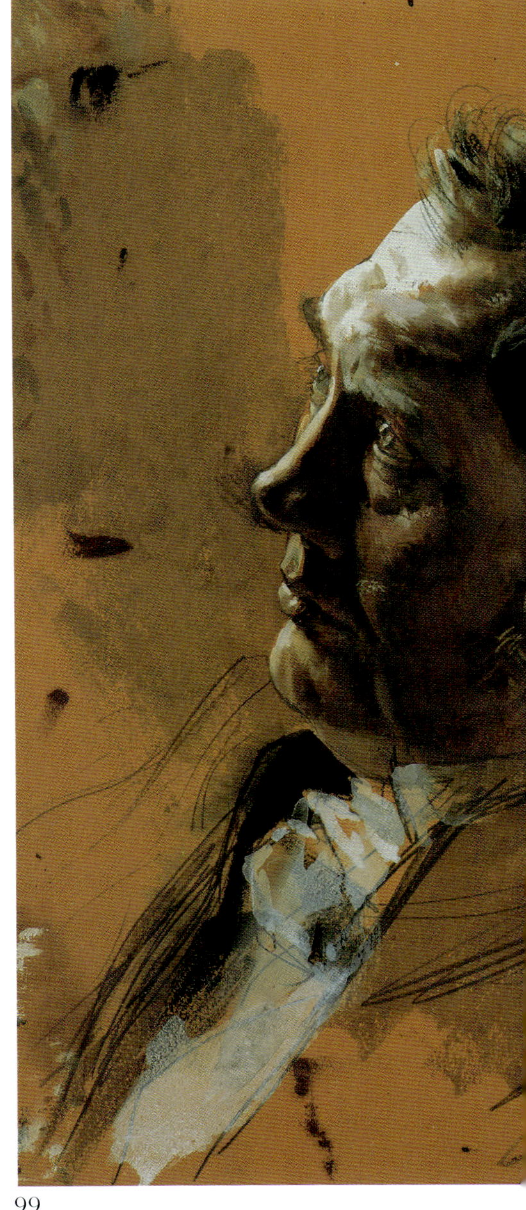

99

99

Count von Schwerin, Minister of State

1864

Watercolour and gouache on pencil
30.1 × 22.5cm
Annotated and dated at the top right: *Staats:Min.Gr Schwerin 13 Febr.64*
Berlin, Kupferstichkabinett (SZ Menzel Kat 992)
Exhibited in Berlin only

Provenance: Hermann Pächter (R. Wagner Gallery, Berlin); acquired by the museum in 1880.
Exhibitions: Berlin, 1885, no. 208; Berlin, 1895 B, no. 615; Vienna, 1896, no. 208; Dresden, 1904, no. 2336; Berlin, 1905, no. 1313; Vienna, 1985, no. 45, reprod. p. 115.
Bibliography: Donop, 1902, no. 992; Tschudi, 1905 A, no. 519; Lammel, 1988, p. 121 *et seq.*, fig. 105.

Count von Schwerin (1804–72) entered the government as a legal expert, and was subprefect (*Landrat*) at Anklam from 1833 onwards. In March 1848, he became Minister of Cultural Affairs in the liberal Camphausen administration, from which he resigned in June with the other ministers. A member of the Prussian Chamber of Deputies (parliament) from 1849, he belonged, with Patow (cat. 97), to the liberal faction. Appointed as Minister of the Interior in July 1859, he was relieved of his responsibilities in March 1862 and returned to the Chamber of Deputies, where he fought for constitutional rights at the head of the 'former liberals'. In his last years, he was a municipal councillor in Berlin. Schwerin married the daughter of Friedrich Schleiermacher, the theologian and philosopher. His portrait appears in the same pose in the *Coronation* painting, in the midst of the group of ministers. M.R.-R.

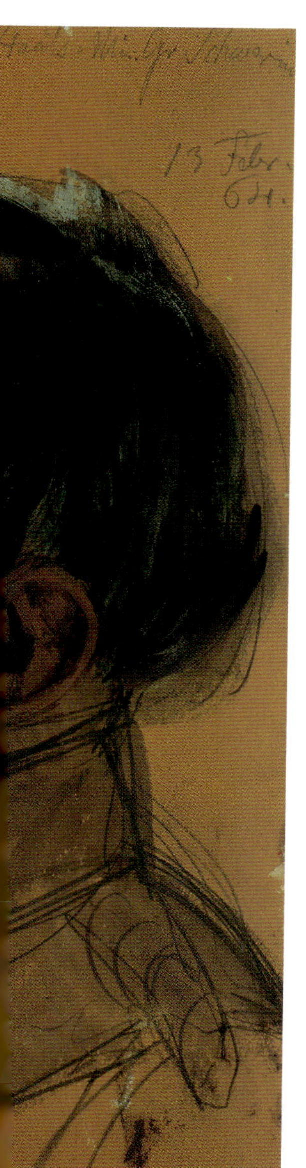

100
At the Opera
1862

Oil on paper, board backing
51.5 × 43.2cm
Signed and dated at the bottom left: *Menzel 1862.*
Hamburg, Hamburger Kunsthalle (1268)
Exhibited in Berlin only

Provenance: R. Wagner Gallery (H. Paechter), Berlin; acquired in 1898 (gift of *Verein von Kunstfreunden von 1870*).
Exhibitions: Düsseldorf, 1904, no. 10; Berlin, 1905, no. 30; Berlin, 1955 B, no. 98; Erlangen, 1971, no. 62, reprod.; Moscow/Leningrad, 1974, no. 29; Frankfurt, 1975, no. 35.
Bibliography: Tschudi, 1905 A, no. 123; Meier-Graefe, 1906, p. 200; Scheffler, 1922, p. 198; Waldmann, 1941, p. 36, p. 48, fig. 59; Wirth, 1965, p. 94; Krafft/Schümann, 1969, reprod. p. 218; Hütt, 1981, fig. 103; Jensen, 1982, p. 96, col. pl. 25; Howoldt, 1993, p. 36, col. reprod. p. 37.

The theatre or, more precisely, its public, inspired Menzel to paint his first pictures of urban crowds. Around 1850, a few pastels depicted isolated members of the audience in adjacent rows of the theatre, but with *The Théâtre du Gymnase* (cat. 80) and the slightly later *Country Theatre in the Tyrol*[1], Menzel focused on the noisy but homogenous audience. And some years later he depicts figures that are near to the foreground and seem to have been chosen arbitrarily, in a chance encounter. In Paris, Menzel had admired the 'constant movement . . . of humanity, where all races mingle, as well as all the very subtle nuances of class and social dignity, good and bad taste in clothes, people of imposing stature and those who are weak and puny, etc. etc.!'[2] These words are characteristic of the ageing Menzel's distanced viewpoint, his quick but accurate observation and insatiable eye for the new and unfamiliar. This is evident in *At the Opera*, which heralds his paintings of court balls. None of the figures show any

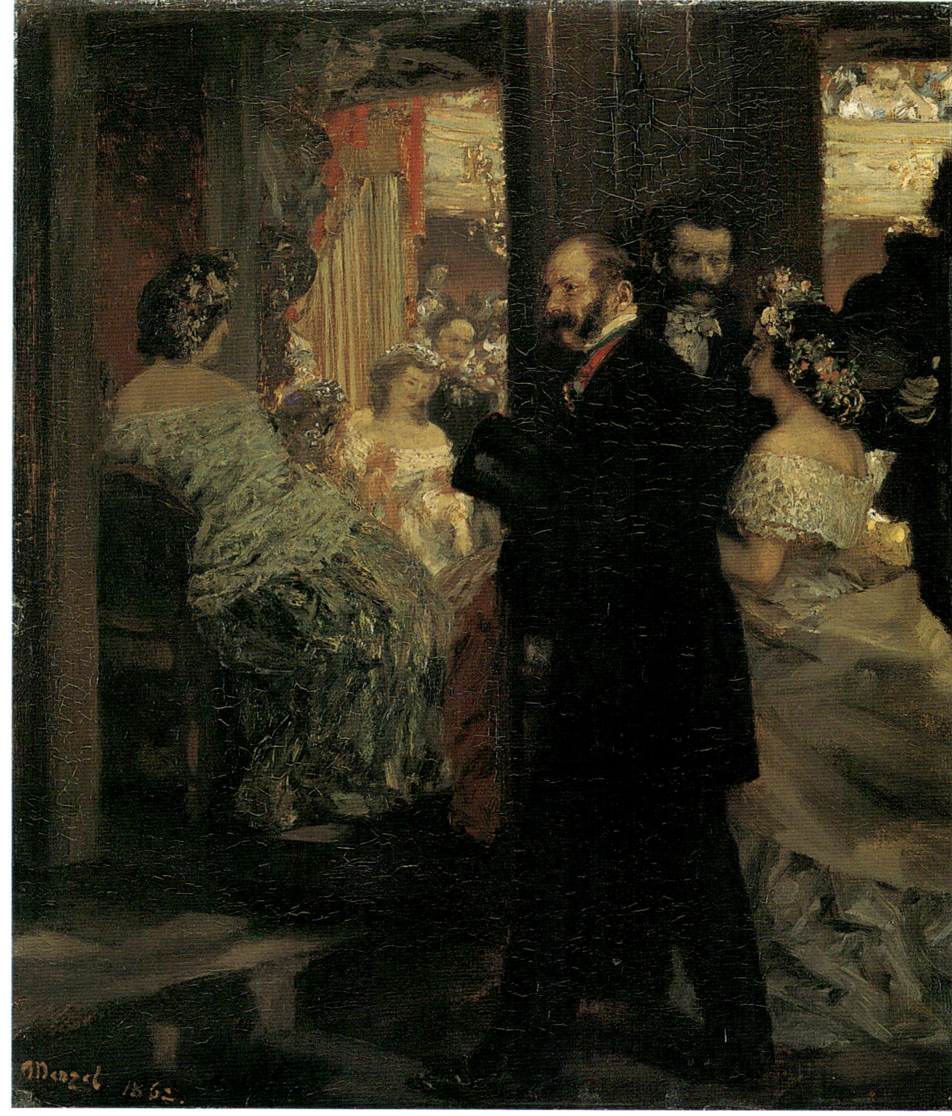

100

of the musical feeling which the painter expressed so often himself. The opera is a pretext for a society occasion, yet the interplay is confusing. Although each of the figures has his or her own story, we will never know the exact details, as in real life. For example, we will not find out why the lady on her husband's arm passes the shadowy person against the wall so hastily, without even glancing at him – few painters of Menzel's generation would have left it to the imagination. The picture is like a book that cannot be opened.

The spatial situation is confused too. The couple walk along the first balcony, passing in front of the open door of a box, which itself leads the eye towards the inner curve of the balcony. In the royal box a pretty woman in white tilts her diadem-crowned head to one side. Immediately to the right, a second open door reveals bright light. In the absence of a theatre plan, fragments of spaces seem to have no link yet are placed next to each other. In a technique reminiscent of Degas, much later, several areas are portrayed in which the action is ostensibly divergent. C.K.

1. 1859, Tschudi, 1905 A, no. 122; Hamburg, Kunsthalle.
2. Letter to Hermann Krigar (after a solemn concert in Paris) 3 June 1867, Wolff, 1914, p. 207.

101
Market in Winter
1862

Gouache and coloured chalks
32.4 × 26.8cm
Signed and dated at the bottom right: *Menzel. 1862*
Berlin, Stadtmuseum (GHZ 83/37)
Exhibited in Berlin only

Provenance: 1905 Heinrich Breithaupt, Berlin; Breithaupt family, Augsburg and Berlin; private collection; Magdalena Haberstock; acquired by the museum in 1983.
Exhibitions: Berlin, 1905, no. 222a; Berlin, 1990, no. 575, col. reprod. p. 264.
Bibliography: Jordan/Dohme, 1890, pl. 43; Tschudi, 1905 A, no. 412; Bredt, 1920, p. 38 *et seq.*, reprod; Bothe, 1984, p. 32; Lammel, 1993 A, p. 172, fig. 14.

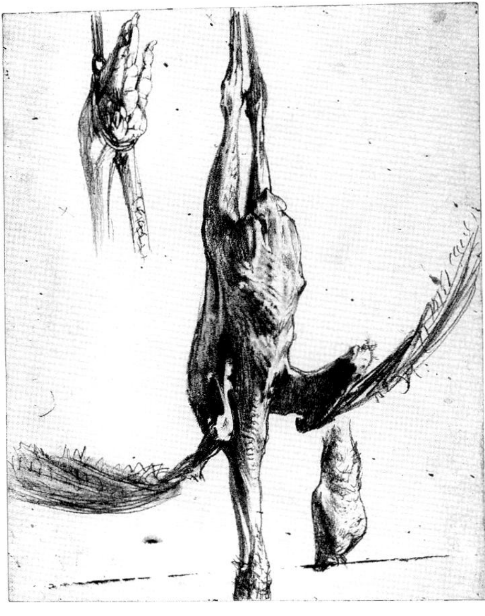
Fig. 187. Plucked Turkey, 1862, pencil, Berlin, Kupferstichkabinett (N 1472)

For the first time Menzel chose to depict the busy street of a large town, and did so in a way that was to become characteristic of his work. In a narrow space, the figures are crowded against each other in front of the stalls of different shops. There is no real communication, however, and the people passing seem isolated from each other. Only the winter cold and an intense light surrounds them uniformly. In the centre a woman wrapped in a shawl is carrying a child in one arm and a basket of food in the other. An old man wearing a pelisse, but still looking frozen, walks in her direction. Behind them is the reddish face of a bearded man wearing a tall hat, and to the right of him can be seen the head of a woman coming out of a fabric shop, recognizable from the crinoline underwiring hanging on display, with various fabrics of different colours. A little boy is totally absorbed in the contemplation of the shop windows of poultry, game and fish merchants, on the right of the picture. There are two known studies for the plucked turkey hanging up, one of which is marked with the exact measurements by the painter[1] (fig. 187). In the background, other passers-by can be vaguely distinguished beneath the bare trees in the street and the pallid red winter sky. Without any special emphasis, the social differences between the people rubbing shoulders randomly in the street are faithfully observed – even in his last drawings of heads, Menzel continued to base his compositions on this effect of the unexpected. He painted an even more elaborate picture of the busy life of large towns in 1869 (*cf.* cat. 127) and another in 1884 (*cf.* cat. 179). An evening view of *Christmas Market in Berlin*, painted in gouache in 1866, once again shows figures wrapped up against the cold, which appear to form part of a single, large crowd in front of the brightly lit shops and the darkness of the street, flanked by tall houses[2]. M.R.-R.

1. Berlin, Kupferstichkabinett, (SZ Menzel N 1471, 1472). Menzel drew plucked poultry several times, particularly in his sketchbook 36 (1871-5), p. 32 and 42.
2. Tschudi, 1905 A, no. 556; private collection; Hochhuth, 1991, fig. 112.

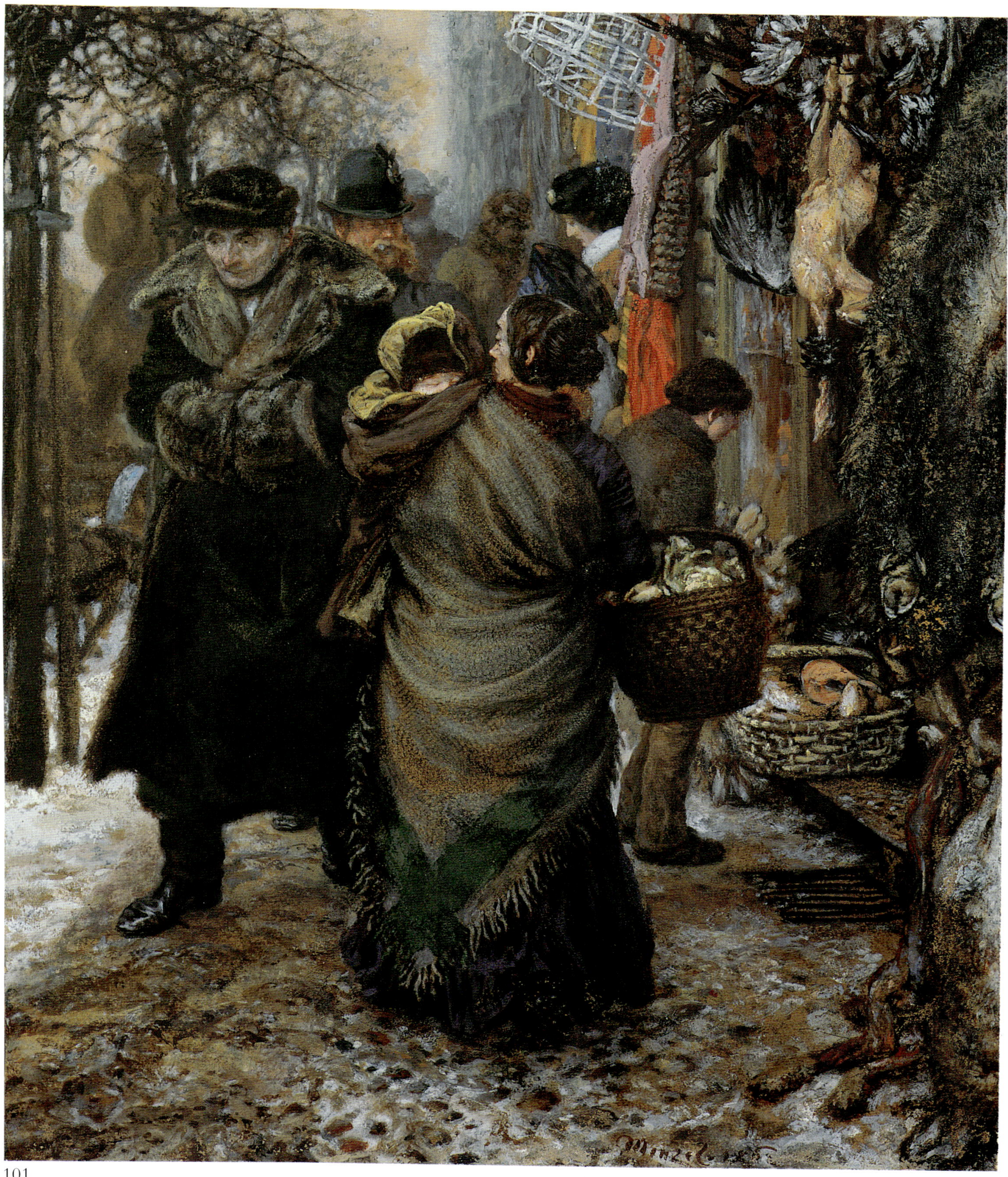

101

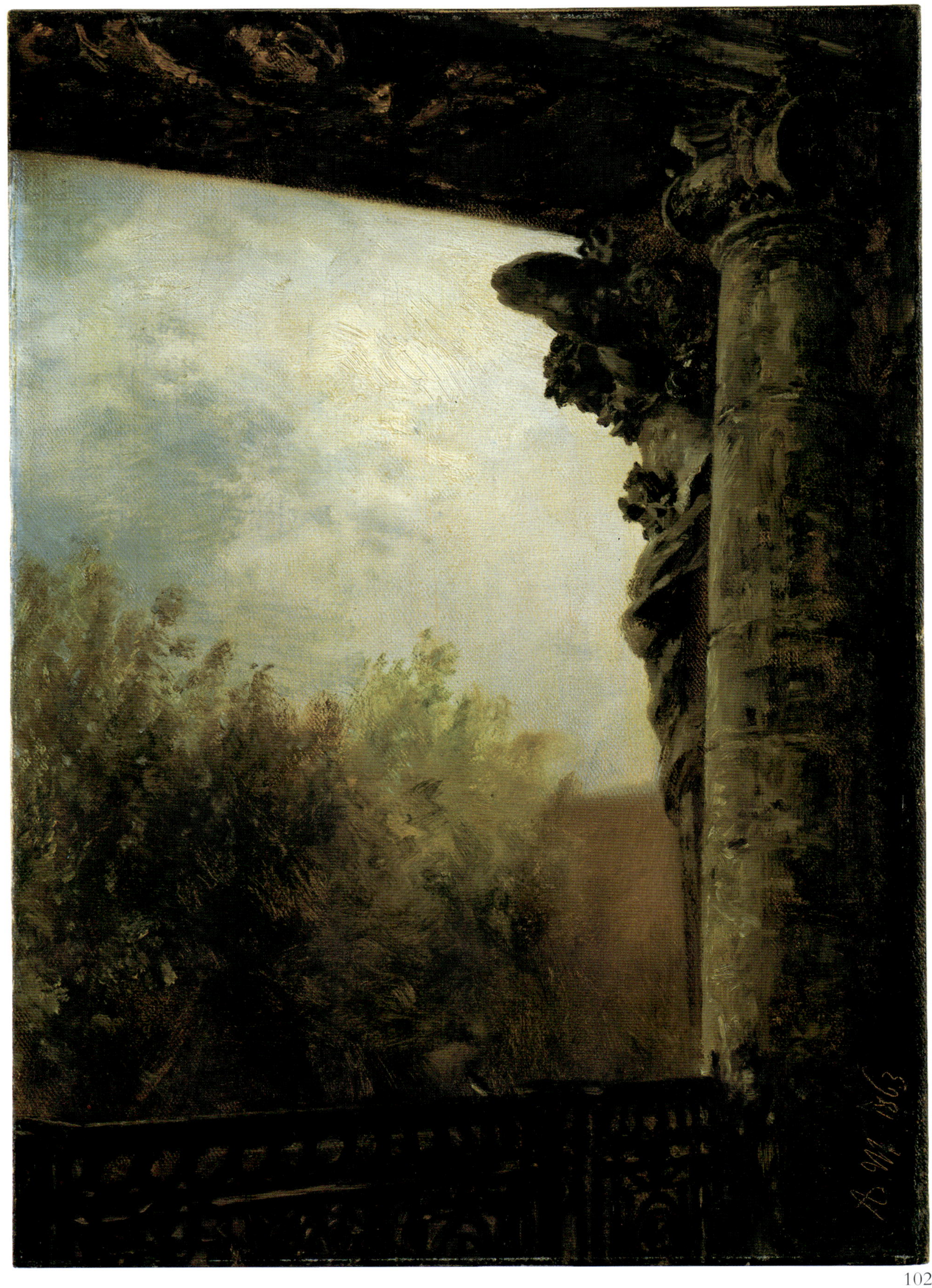

102

102

View from a Window of the Royal Palace in Berlin

1863

Oil on canvas
52.6 × 37cm
Signed and dated at the bottom right (scratched into the paint): *A.M. 1863*
Munich, Bayerische Staatsgemäldesammlungen, Neue Pinakothek (8502)
Exhibited in Paris and Berlin only

Provenance: Painter's studio; 1905 Emilie Krigar-Menzel; 1907 Margarete Krigar-Menzel; acquired by the museum in 1937.
Exhibitions: Berlin, 1905, no. 65; Leipzig, 1905, no. 17; Berlin, 1955 B, no. 99, fig. 46; Berlin, 1987 A, no. G 18; Berlin, 1987 B, no. 95, col. reprod.
Bibliography: Rosenberg, 1879, p. 269; Tschudi, 1905 A, no. 124; Tschudi, 1905 B, reprod. p. 222, p. 12; Scheffler, 1922, p. 190, reprod. p. 175; Eschenburg, 1984, reprod. p. 297.

After some difficulty, and various unsuccessful attempts to find somewhere for the artist to work, the large studio in which Menzel was to paint the picture of *The Coronation* was only found two months after the event had taken place. In January he had already complained impatiently, 'The weeks go by one after another, the *impression of reality* is receding and already a quarter of the year has passed (!). I have hardly even made a start yet!'[1] From April 1862 onwards Menzel worked in the former guard room, then recently vacated, which acted as a temporary store for items from the arms room. Here he received high-ranking personnel to sit for their portraits. This phase of the work did not begin until March 1863 in spite of the 'frantic life' he had led up to then ('I am always in my studio in the palace from morning until night'[2]), which indicated the difficulty he had in finalizing the composition, with all the reworking required both from the artist's point of view and from others too. Then things progressed more quickly and, during the course of the year the left half of the painting was completed[3]. All the works Menzel dedicated to Frederick the Great were also exhibited during this productive year, as if the artist were drawing up a statement of accounts.

His mood may have become more retrospective as he approached the age of fifty. He turned once more to a kind of painting he had left aside for a long time, yet which had played an important role at the start of his career. He began to paint views framed by windows again. Several years after he finished the picture described here, Menzel painted views of the courtyard of the house where he then lived, in Marienstrasse[4]. He took advantage of his daily presence at the palace to draw interiors. In 1866 the historical armour that surrounded him in his temporary studio inspired a series of magnificent watercolours (*cf.* cat. 117–19). At the culminating point of the *Coronation* picture he painted the view from a window whose location is quite important.

The guard room was in the north wing, facing the large garden (the Lustgarten), in the part of the royal palace designed by Andreas Schlüter around 1700; it was on the first floor, just beneath the sumptuous knights' room where the throne was installed. On the outside, the bay of this room was enhanced by a monumental overhang (portal V). The balcony, which was accessible from the knights' room through an arched doorway, was supported by two powerful male caryatids which framed a large French-style barred window, without a balcony, on their level. The opening shown in the picture was in the middle bay of Menzel's studio and was therefore part of his immediate environment, where he painted. One of the columns framing the window with a part of the caryatid in front can be recognized.

The specifically political importance of this room was that it contained the throne. Prestigious and official Unter den Linden avenue approached it directly. In the light of this it is possible to assess the intentional casualness in the depiction of an angled view of part of the baroque statue – again lacking in profile – in front of which the architecture is reduced to a sloping corridor whose asymmetry removes any sense of direction. When, in contrast, Menzel's compatriot Johann Heinrich Hintze painted a view from Berlin's Royal palace[5], he not only included interior decor – carpet, curtains, paintings on the walls – but also chose a view facing south, depicting part of old Kölln in detail, and in the centre the equestrian statue of the Great Elector by Andreas Schlüter. That was political iconography asserting itself.

Menzel gives a much more diffuse and incidental view of the landscape. It appears closer than it could have been in reality, and the foliage of the trees in the gardens blocks the view beneath a grey, everyday sky. The reddish shadow of the venerable 'pharmacy wing' (the Renaissance wing of the castle) can be glimpsed. It is surprising to see a bird perched on the wrought-iron balustrade. It not only provides a sense of scale, but introduces the natural world in among the stones, and suggests the ephemeral. At the same time, it indicates a capricious choice of preferences. It defines the spatial axis (that otherwise is void) in an asymmetrical picture which balances heavy stone with air. When far more imposing elements are hidden from view, the smallest feature is afforded the greatest attention.

C.K.

1. Letter to a civil servant in the Ministry of Culture, 7 January 1862, Santa Monica, The Getty Center for the History of Art and Civilisation Archives.
2. Letter to Adolf Schöll, 16 January 1863, Deetjen, 1934, p. 36.
3. Pecht, 1887, p. 354 and ff.
4. Two gouaches, 1867; Tschudi, 1905 A, no. 562; private collection, housed at the Nationalgalerie. – Tschudi, 1905 A, no. 563; Winterthur, Museum Stiftung Oskar Reinhart.
5. Watercolour, Euerbach, Georg Schäfer collection; Schmoll, 1970, p. 126 and ff., fig. 187.

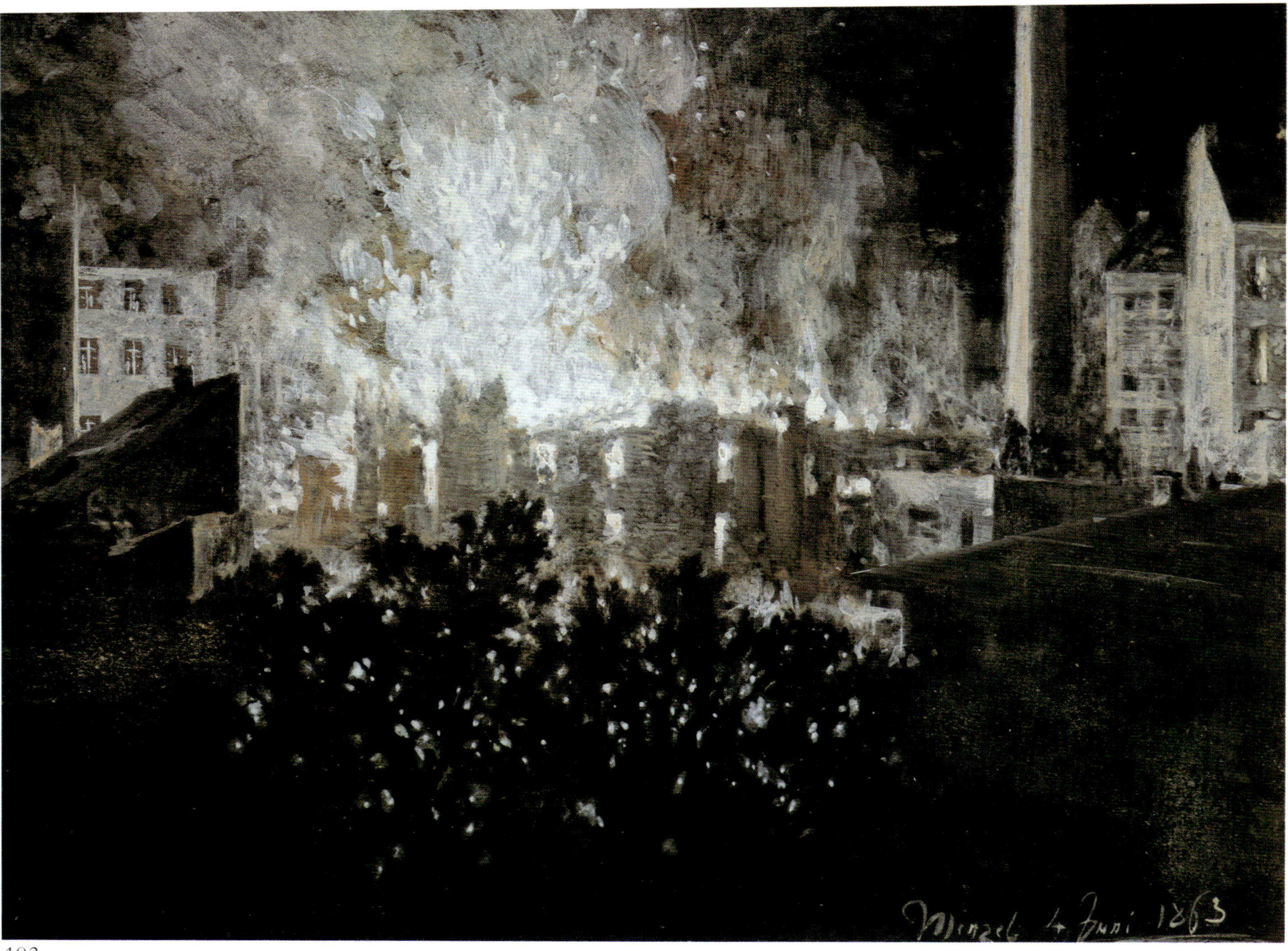

103

103
Factory on Fire
1863

Gouache
29.9 × 39.5cm
Signed and dated at the bottom right: *Menzel: 4 Juni 1863.*
Berlin, Kupferstichkabinett (SZ Menzel N 232)
Exhibited in Paris and Washington only

Provenance: Painter's studio; 1905 Emilie Krigar-Menzel; acquired by the museum in 1906.
Exhibitions: Berlin, 1905, no. 4640; Berlin, 1980, no. 47; Vienna, 1985, no. 37; Copenhagen, 1985, no. 32; New York, 1990, no. 14.
Bibliography: Tschudi, 1905 A, no. 415; Kirstein, 1919, p. 59–60, fig. p. 61; Liebermann/Kern, 1921, p. 9, col. pl. 34.

Menzel's 'Notes for my heirs'[1] mentions the existence of a picture entitled *Blaze*, in the penultimate portfolio 'with a mixed content – gouache studies', in addition to the two *Hands* (cat. 115, 116) and the study *Evening Light* (probably cat. 84). The note 'grisaille' written here is a clear reference to this painting. It was possibly the last in which Menzel tested his skill in portraying the phenomenon of fire (*cf.* cat. 85, 86). In it he has captured the link between beauty and destructive violence in a particularly impressive manner. The view of the tiny group of firemen at the foot of the tall chimney, which is still standing, suggests that, when the flames have been put out by the fine jet of water, the already ravaged walls of the building will be completely destroyed. The dark setting, twinkling with points of light in the foreground, superbly points up the dramatic nature of the event. In comparison, the fire at the Renz circus, of which Menzel made an oil sketch in November 1853, rises up over a low wall running parallel with the lower edge of the picture, appearing as an even cloud of flame against the night sky in the background[2]. M.R.-R.

1. Menzel's will, reproduced in Wolff, 1916, p. 35 and ff., and in Kirstein, 1919, p. 92 and ff.
2. Oil on canvas, 21 × 33cm; Tschudi, 1905 A, no. 85; location unknown.

104

Zulus

c. 1863

Watercolour and gouache
27.5 × 30.3cm
Signed at the top left: *Ad Menzel.* – Annotated on the tiger on the curtain: *Niemand wandelt (u)ngestraft unter Palmen*
Hamburg, Hamburger Kunsthalle (1277)
Exhibited in Paris only

Provenance: Property of Menzel's photographer Rudolphy, who obtained it from the painter; acquired by the museum in 1910 through Behrens will.
Exhibitions: Berlin, 1955 B, no. 131; Erlangen, 1971, no. 105; Hamburg, 1982, no. 67.
Bibliography: Tschudi, 1905 A, no. 398; coll. cat. Hamburg, 1969, p. 218; Lammel, 1993 B, p. 175–7.

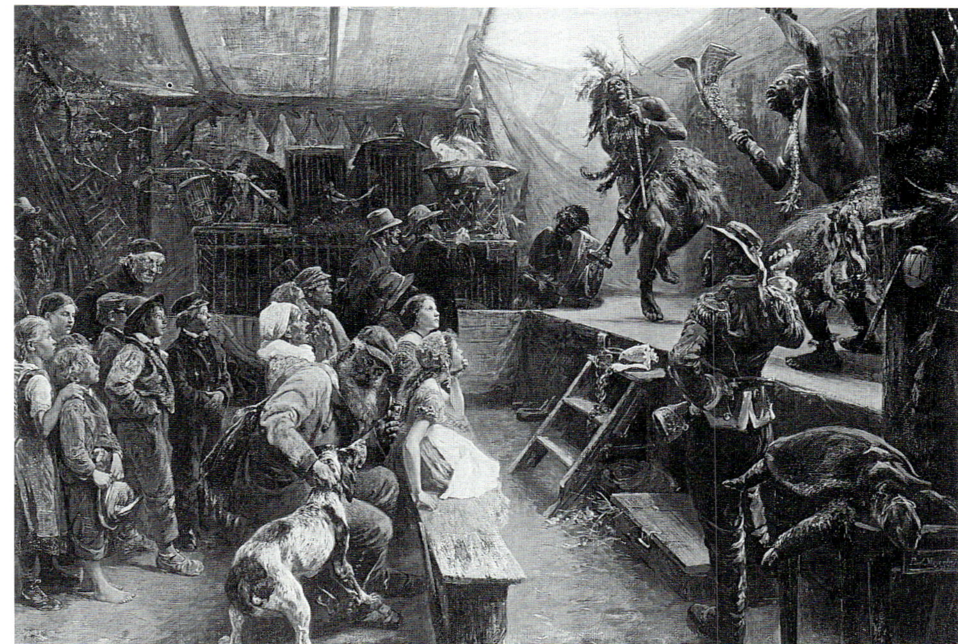

Fig 188. Paul Meyerheim, *Zulu Dancers at a Fair Booth*, 1873, oil, location unknown

Menzel caught the gesture and facial expression of the crouching figure and dancers in a series of quick sketches that appear in a sketchbook from 1855[1]. Menzel used this sketchbook in the spring, when he was still in Berlin, and also in the summer during a journey first to Marienburg and then to Paris via the Rhineland. It is therefore difficult to deduce where he saw this subject. Three pastels, two of which depict big cats eating, and the third showing a lion tamer, are also related to the studies in this sketchbook[2]. One of the pastels is dated 14 March 1855, so it may be assumed that all the animal studies appearing after this in the sketchbook and indicating a visit to a zoological garden or even a circus, were drawn when the artist was still in Berlin, as well as the sketches of Zulus also in this series. But Menzel's sketches generally follow only an approximate chronology, so it should not be ruled out that he saw these people during the Universal Exhibition in Paris.

The widespread interest in ethnology, which took the form of a modern science in the 1820s, was often expressed in exhibitions given by various ethnic groups highly valued by the most diverse strata of the population. Paul Meyerheim, who had made exotic animals, zoos, fairs and that eminently bourgeois invention, the circus, the favoured theme of his art, painted a spectacle of Zulu dancers under a big top in 1873 (fig. 188). Two black people dance frenetically on an improvised stage to the rhythm of a drum beaten by a man on his haunches, analogous to the scene in Menzel's drawing. But while Meyerheim presents a highly detailed view of the fair booth invaded by

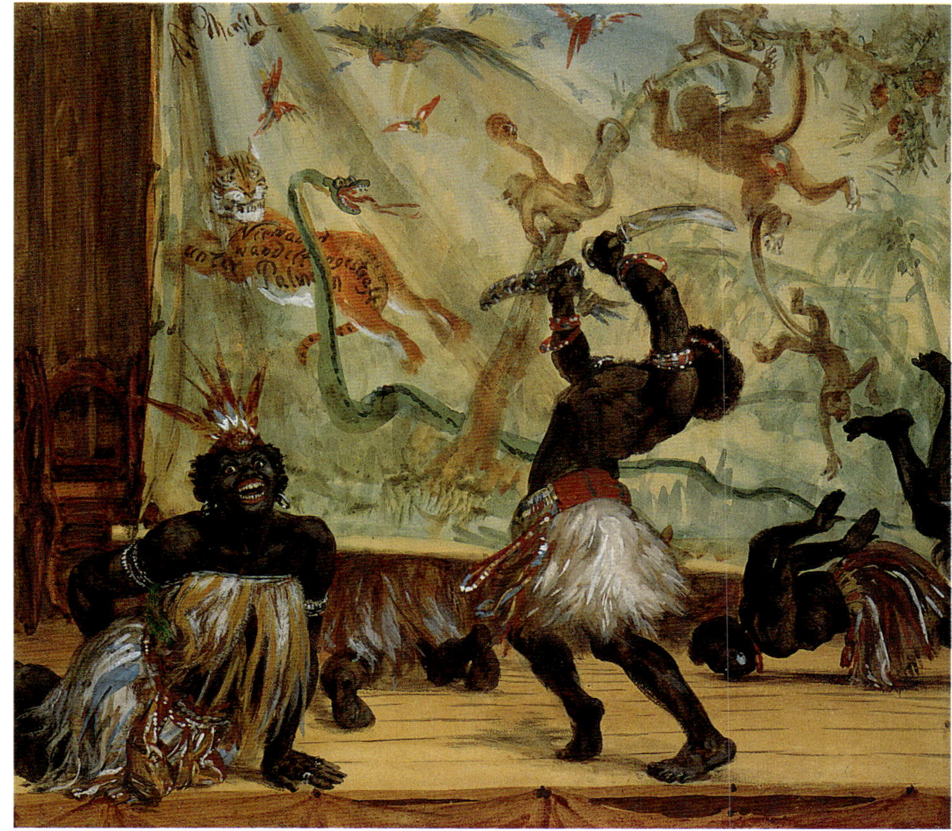

104

an eager public, according to the conventions of the genre, Menzel portrays only a slight fragment, forcefully abridged in places. On the right edge the figure kneeling is cut off, and two legs without a body irrupt into the picture. On the left, near the painted ceiling, the likening of the scene to a fair booth is only suggested by the head of a lion in a cage, barely recognizable behind the two chairs piled on top of each other. In spite of these realistic elements, the scene has a naturalistic feel.

It is difficult to know what the words 'No-one walks among the palm trees with impunity, which are written on the tigers back, mean. Menzel did not intend Goethes fashionable phrase to be taken literally[3]. If we allow that the works of the two friends, whose themes so often overlapped, relate to an event reported by Max Ring[4], Menzels ironic device could allude to this Berliner who left home and was found by his wife hiding behind a black mask at a popular entertainment. The hypothesis of a later date for this picture, which would put back the genesis of Menzels drawing by ten years, would have to account for the use of earlier sketches. This would be strange, at the least, if the drawing did relate to a later event. So it seems wise, until further information becomes available, to agree with Tschudi[5] in situating the drawing in the context of the *Childrens Album*.

M.R.-R.

1. Berlin, Kupferstichkabinett, sketchbook 14 (1855), p. 13 and 15.
2. Berlin, Kupferstichkabinett, (SZ Menzel N 4448 [dated 14 March 1855] and 4478) and Munich, Graphische Sammlung (1932/67).
3. *Cf.* exhib. cat. Hamburg, 1982, no. 67, in relation to *The Zulus,* where there is a commentary on Goethes words (Es wandelt niemand ungestraft unter Palmen.) taken from Ottilies diary in *Specific Affinities*, 2nd part, Chapter 7.
4. *Cf.* Lammel on this subject, 1993 B, p. 155 and ff., the full presentation of the episode described by Ring, 1883, p. 273-280.
5. Tshudi, 1905 A, no. 398.

105–14
Children's Album
1863–83

The forty-four gouaches which form the *Children's Album*, together with the frontispiece, were all painted between 1863 and 1883. Menzel started to create this series of small pictures for his sister's children, Margarete, born in 1860, whom he called Gretel, and Otto, born in 1861. Letters and drawings show the keen interest he had in their development. Menzel had planned from the beginning not to give them the pictures he painted on each birthday directly, but to keep them in order to 'share' their true value when the children came of age.

Menzel had been very fond of his sister Emilie since they were young (as he was of his brother Richard, who died prematurely), and he had already guaranteed her a secure future after the death of their father in 1832. Later he vowed the same loyalty and attention to his sister's family, when fairly late on she married a very cultivated musician, Hermann Krigar, court composer and conductor of the orchestra. Menzel followed the Krigar family several times when they moved house, and went on trips with his sister, continuing to share the house with Emilie when his brother-in-law died. When his niece and nephew were small, he joined in summer trips to Friedrichsaue, on the outskirts of Berlin. The Krigars owned some cultivated land at Albrechtshof, in the Tiergarten district, then still in the country. From there, they went to the 'Moritzhof', an inn nearby. One of the drawings in the *Children's Album* depicts a scene in this typically Berlin open-air café with its dance floor (cat. 108). The discordant, disjointed aspect of his composition only vaguely echoes the subjects of the early French Impressionists. Menzel could not have seen them until a later date. The serenity created by the colour, applied lightly and diaphanously in the background of this painting, is balanced by bright local colour and the opposing movements of some of the figures on the canvas, and in particular the chairs leaning awkwardly against the table. If the gouache entitled *Drying the Washing* (cat. 106) seems more balanced in terms of normal pictorial construction, certain elements, like the boys fighting and the dog rolling on the ground, also create dissonance here.

With a few exceptions, the paintings in this series are of animal subjects. Menzel, whom Paul Meyerheim reports as being a great animal lover, drew them everywhere[1]. On individual sheets of paper, or in sketchbooks, there are numerous animal studies used in the *Children's Album*. He drew them on his regular visits to zoological gardens in Berlin, Cologne, Paris or Munich. The scene *Deer at the Zoo* is one of his first three works dated 1863 (cat. 107). Here, the viewer has the impression that they are also in the cage with the animals, while the zoo visitors appear in the background, behind the bars. On the right of the picture all that can be seen are the points of their umbrellas, with which they are trying to stroke the deer.

Menzel liked to compensate for the fact that he lived in a large town by choosing domestic country animals as his subjects. He took an interest in the smallest and most insignificant animals of the forest and fields, including even a *Rat in the Gutter* in his pictorial world (cat. 111). When he was very young, in 1836, he drew thirty lithographs for the illustrated magazine for children *Little Boys and Girls Companion*, nearly all of which portrayed animals[2].

The town and its inhabitants is only used once in the series of gouaches, in *Corner of a House in the Moonlight* (cat. 109). In the 1860s the liveliness of the big city can be found in several of Menzel's canvasses, finding its most powerful expression in *Weekday in Paris* (cat. 127). *Christmas Market in Berlin*[3] also shows, in comparison with *Corner of a House*, that Menzel never ceased to find new ideas in aspects of urban life. Although in *Looking at the Moon* (cat. 84)

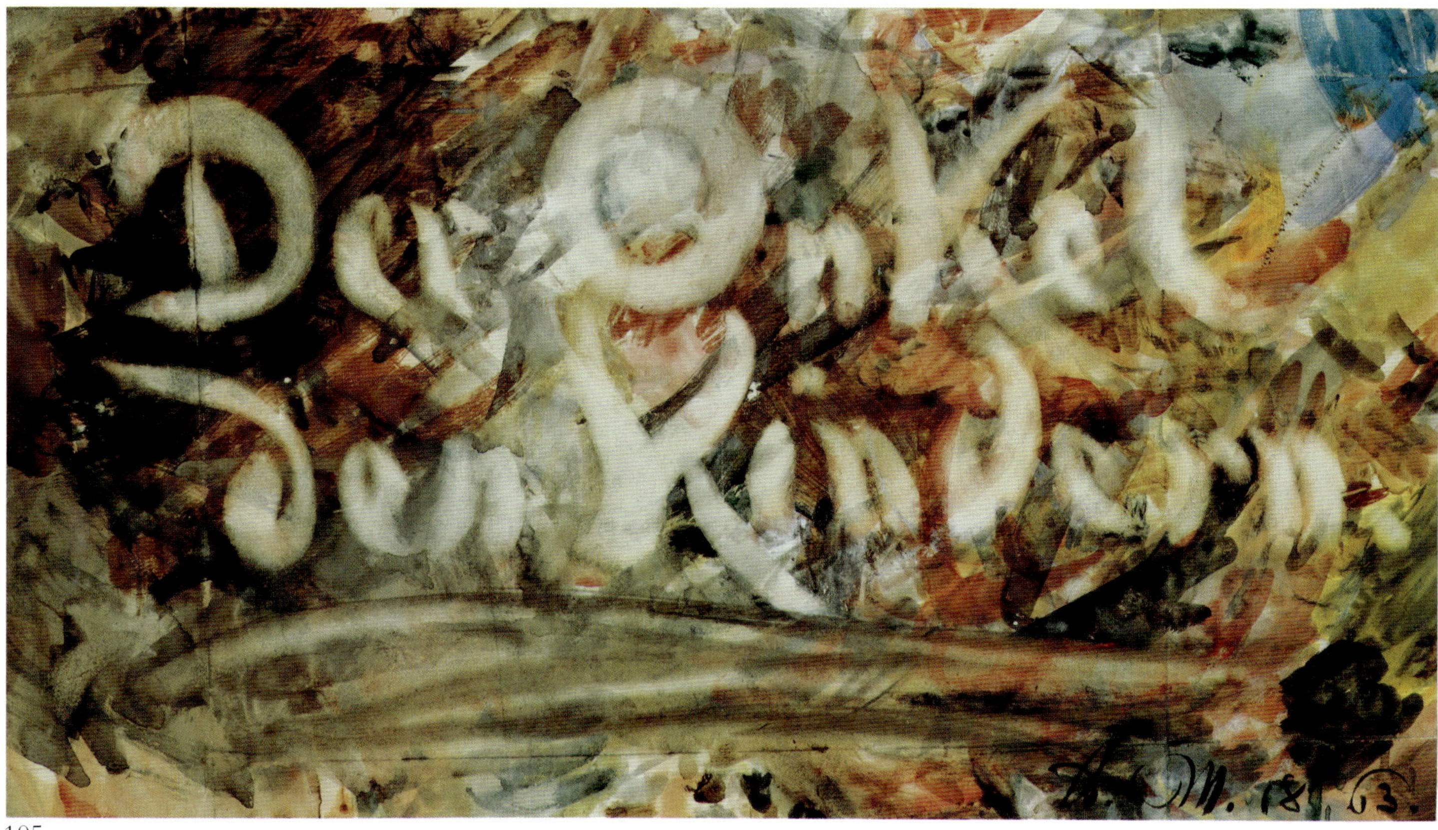

105

the town is almost unrecognizable in the lower part of the picture, which is dominated by the sky, in *Corner of a House* the moonlit sky is only a thin slit between two straight houses, and windows lit by artificial light compete with its brightness. It is interesting to contrast the country twilight shown in the drawing *Thatched Roof with Storks Nest*, in which nature, the trees and the large roof supporting the nest blend in a feeling of calm and security (cat. 110).

Each of Menzel's drawings contains something exciting, which in combination with the simultaneous and virtuoso handling of gouache and watercolour, is the source of their special charm. In addition, the varying format of the compositions creates suspense, emphasizing the unexpected in the whole.

After visiting an exhibition in Paris, Menzel wrote to Krigar in 1867: 'If I had known what I know today, I wouldn't be apprehensive about seeing certain things [exhibited] here. Even some pages from the 'Albogen'![4] This was what he called the *Children's Album* within his family. It was a combination of the words *Al*bum and Bilder*bogen* (picture book). In fact, in 1868 Menzel produced two pages of pictures for Gustav Weise's publishing house in Stuttgart[5]. One of them was called *After the Holiday*. Full of animals and children, it is entirely devoted to impressions of nature in the country, and of country life. His sister, niece and nephew are depicted riding donkeys. The link with the *Children's Album* is obvious – in both cases Menzel hopes to enable town children to appreciate the natural world.

After the death of his brother-in-law in 1880, it may have been his sister's sixtieth birthday that in 1883 spurred Menzel to sell the album to his dealer, Hermann Pächter, for the benefit of her children, who were by then adults.

The artist added four compositions, or more precisely two pairs, just before he sold the work, probably in view of an exhibition which was to be organized at the Nationalgalerie to celebrate fifty years of his artistic activity. In the exhibition drawings were to be displayed to the public for the first time. One picture shows an *Owl in a Thicket* (cat. 114) and a *Robin and Hoopoe in a Thicket*[6], while the two others are clearly a matching pair representing the 'destinies of parrots', *Sweet servitude*[7] and *Sweet liberty*[8]. Out of the forty-four gouaches, three are dated 1863, one 1864, another 1868 and the works just mentioned bear the date 1883. According to Tschudi, most of the pictures were retouched in 1883. A lot of preliminary studies can be found in the sketchbooks of the 1860s, but others were done a little before 1883. In 1889 Hermann Pächter sold the *Children's Album* to the Nationalgalerie[9], after exhibiting it for the last time in 1885, at the Pavillon de la Ville de Paris. Five important pictures in the series have been missing since World War II10.

M.R.-R.

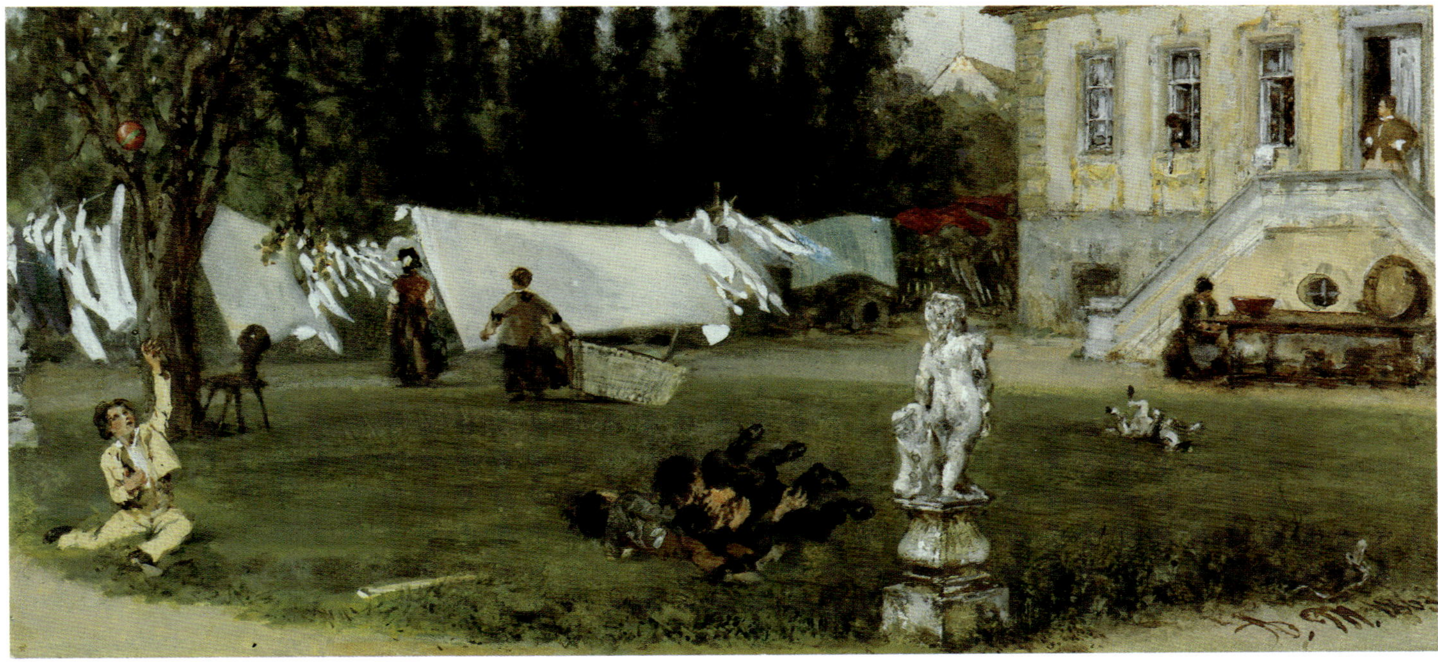

106

1. Meyerheim, (1906) 1992, p. 186.
2. Bock, 1923, no. 148 to no. 177.
3. 1866, Tschudi, 1905 A, no. 556; location unknown.
4. Letter to Hermann Krigar, paris, 3 June 1867, Wolff, 1914, p. 208.
5. Bock, 1923, no. 1094.
6. Tschudi, 1905 A, no. 401.
7. Tschudi, 1905 A, no. 403.
8. Tschudi, 1905 A, no. 382.
9. On the circumstance of this purchase, *cf.* Jordan, (1905) 1992, p. 269.
10. The *Zebra* (Tschudi, 1905 A, no. 483), the *Pheasants in the trees* (Tschudi, 1905 A, no. 373), the *Cow lying in the shed* (Tschudi, 1905 A, no. 365) and *Forest floor with squirrels* (Tschudi, 1905 A, no. 396).

Fig. 189. *Balloonist*, 1846, pencil, Berlin, Kupferstichkabinett (N 671)

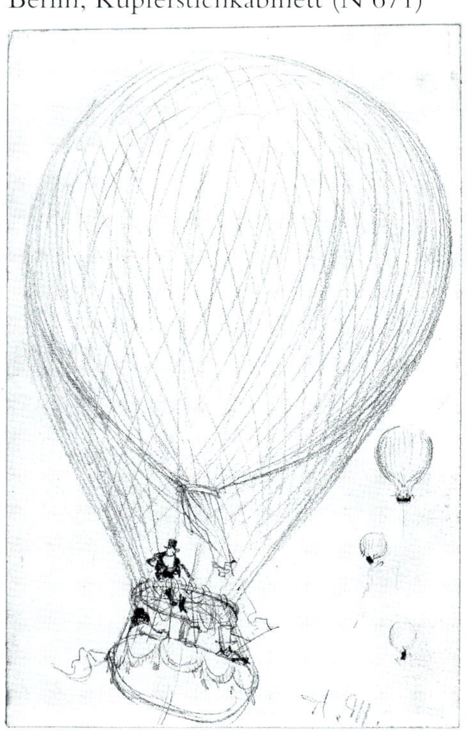

105
Title Page
1863

Watercolour
18.1 × 30.7cm
Signed and dated at the bottom right: *A.M.1863.*
Berlin, Kupferstichkabinett (SZ Menzel Kat 1012a)

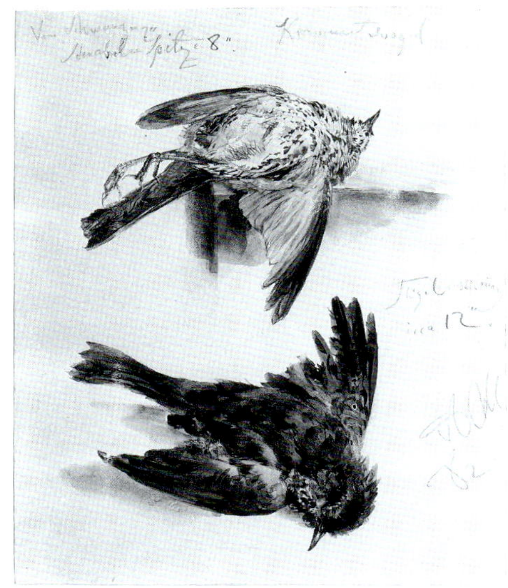

Fig. 190. *Dead Fieldfares*, 1882, watercolour and gouache, Berlin, Kupferstichkabinett (N 210)

Provenance: Dr von Burchard, State advisor; acquired in 1912 (only painting from the *Album* to have been purchased separately).
Exhibitions: Berlin, 1980 A, no. 60, reprod. p. 323; Vienna, 1985, no. 78, reprod. p. 150.
Bibliography: Kirstein, 1919, reprod. p. 45.

106

Drying Yard

1863

Gouache
13.4 × 28.1cm
Signed and dated at the bottom right: *A.M.1863.*
Berlin, Kupferstichkabinett (SZ Menzel Kat 1055)

Provenance: 1883 Hermann Pächter (R. Wagner Gallery, Berlin); acquired by the museum in 1889.
Exhibitions: Paris, 1885, no. 293; Berlin, 1885, no. 93; Berlin, 1895 B, no. 557; Vienna, 1896, no. 215; Düsseldorf, 1904, no. 47; Berlin, 1905, no. 188; Berlin, 1980 A, no. 94, col. reprod. p. 191; Vienna, 1985, no. 79, reprod. p. 150; New York, 1990, no. 38, col. reprod. p. 136.
Bibliography: Jordan, 1895, p. 69; Donop, 1902, no. 1055; Tschudi, 1905 A, no. 360; Kaiser, 1956, p. 112 *et seq.*, fig. 81.

107

Deer at the Zoo

1863

Gouache
21.1 × 26cm
Signed and dated at the bottom right: *A.M.1863.*
Berlin, Kupferstichkabinett (SZ Menzel Kat 1028)
Exhibited in Paris and Washington only

Provenance: 1883 Hermann Pächter (R. Wagner Gallery, Berlin); acquired by the museum in 1889.
Exhibitions: Paris, 1885, no. 295; Berlin, 1885, no. 101; Berlin, 1895 B, no. 556; Vienna, 1896, no. 214; Dresden, 1904, no. 2361a; Berlin, 1905, no. 161; Berlin, 1980 A, no. 71, col. reprod p. 195; Copenhagen, 1985, no. 69, reprod. p. 47; Vienna, 1990, no. 147.
Bibliography: Dumas, 1885, pl. (unnumb.); Jordan, 1895, p. 69; Donop, 1902, no. 1028; Tschudi, 1905 A, no. 361; Wirth, 1965, p. 134; Hütt, 1981, p. 98, fig. 77.

107

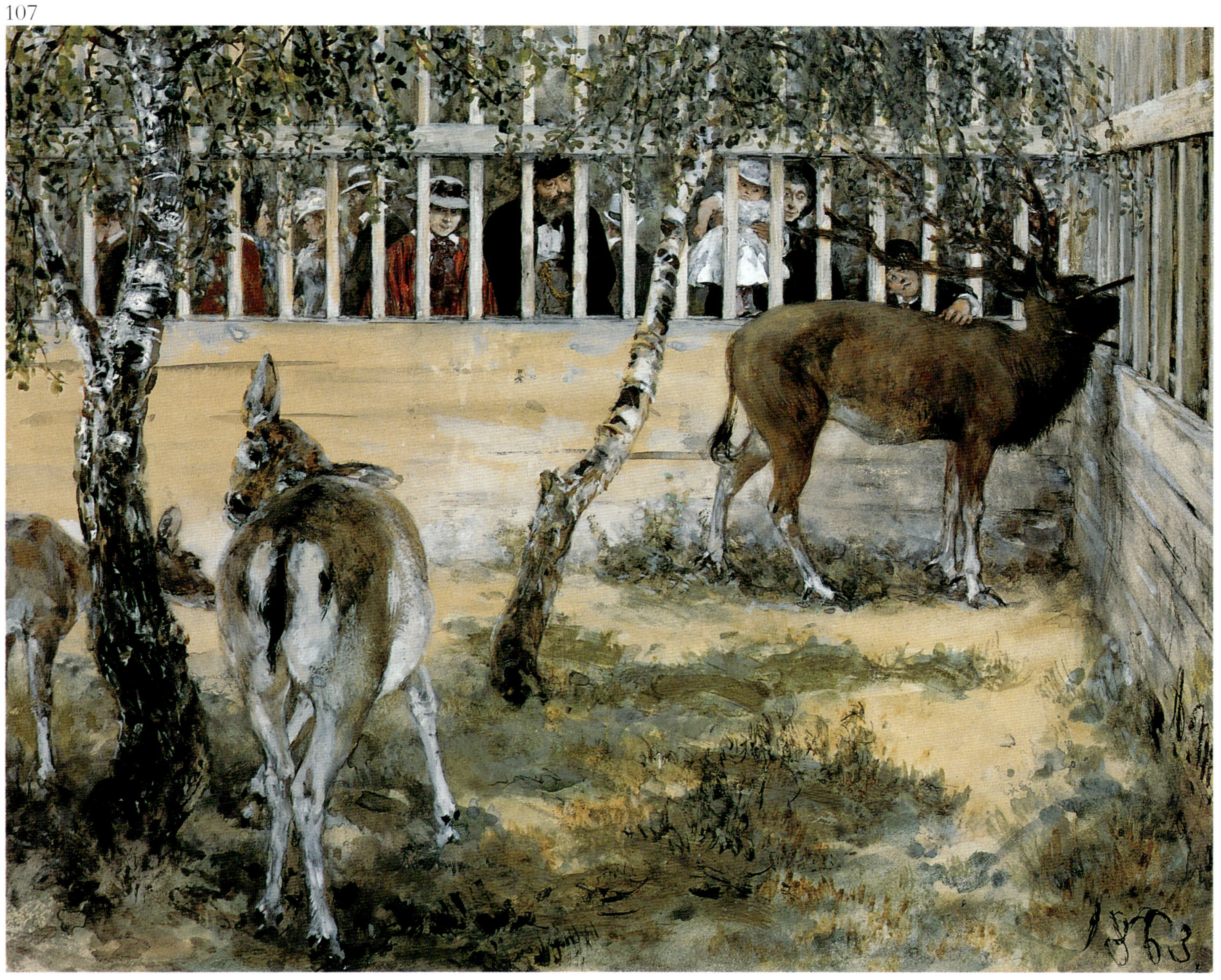

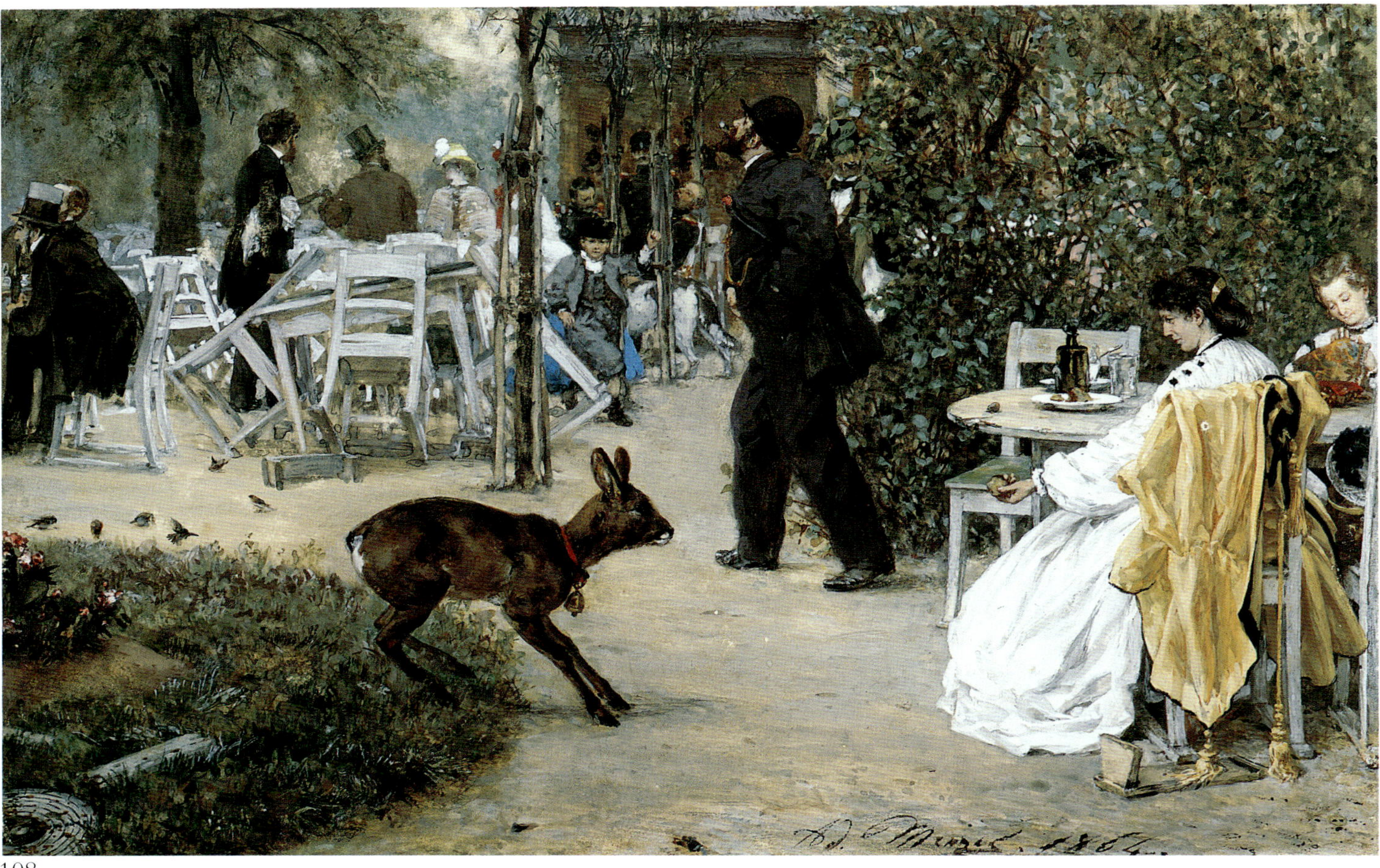

108

108
The 'Moritzhof' Inn
1864

Gouache
23.4 × 36.1cm
Signed and dated at the bottom right: *Ad.Menzel 1864.*
Berlin, Kupferstichkabinett (SZ Menzel Kat 1014)

Provenance: 1883 Hermann Pächter (R. Wagner Gallery, Berlin); acquired by the museum in 1889.
Exhibitions: Paris, 1885, no. 289; Berlin, 1885, no. 92; Berlin, 1895 B, no. 558; Vienna, 1896, no. 223; Düsseldorf, 1904, no. 51; Berlin, 1905, no. 147; Berlin, 1980 A, no. 62, reprod. p. 209; Vienna, 1985, no. 80, reprod. p. 151; Copenhagen, 1985, no. 70, reprod. p. 48.
Bibliography: Jordan, 1895, p. 69; Donop, 1902, no. 1014; Tschudi, 1905 A, no. 362; Kirstein, 1919, p. 45, reprod. p. 44; Kaiser, 1956, p. 112 *et seq.*; fig. 82; Wirth, 1965, p. 125, fig. 47; Hütt, 1981, p. 98, fig. 76.

Moritzhof was the most extensive and charming of the green areas near the Landwehrkanal, not far from Tiergarten and the newly created zoological garden. 'For a long time, until the 1870s, it remained a garden restaurant with a café, very popular with families from Berlin', states a contemporary account written by one of Menzel's friends. He added: 'A circle of writers and national-liberal civil servants often met there for coffee, and discussed current politics for several hours, playing with ivory tops or having games of chess'[1]. In the evening, people drank milk curds with breadcrumbs and caster sugar, served in glass bowls, as they watched gondolas passing by on the canal[2]. M.R.-R.

1. Pietsch, 1893, p. 178. *Cf.* Pietsch, 1898, p. 184 and ff.
2. Nalli-Rutenburg, no date, p. 65.

109
Corner of a House in the Moonlight
c. 1863–83

Gouache
27.8 × 21cm
Signed at the bottom left: *Ad.Menzel*
Berlin, Kupferstichkabinett (SZ Menzel Kat 1016)

Provenance: 1883 Hermann Pächter (R. Wagner Gallery, Berlin); acquired by the museum in 1889.
Exhibitions: Paris, 1885, no. 283; Berlin, 1885, no. 118; Berlin, 1895 B, no. 596; Vienna, 1896, no. 216; Berlin, 1905, no. 149; Berlin, 1980 A, no. 64, col. reprod. p. 205; Vienna, 1985, no. 87; col. reprod. p. 65; Copenhagen, 1985, no. 77; New York, 1990, no. 46, col. reprod. p. 153.
Bibliography: Jordan, 1895, p. 71; Donop, 1902, no. 1016; Tschudi, 1905 A, no. 393; Scheffler, 1915–22, p. 90 *et seq.*, reprod. p. 181; Wirth, 1965, p. 30 *et seq.*

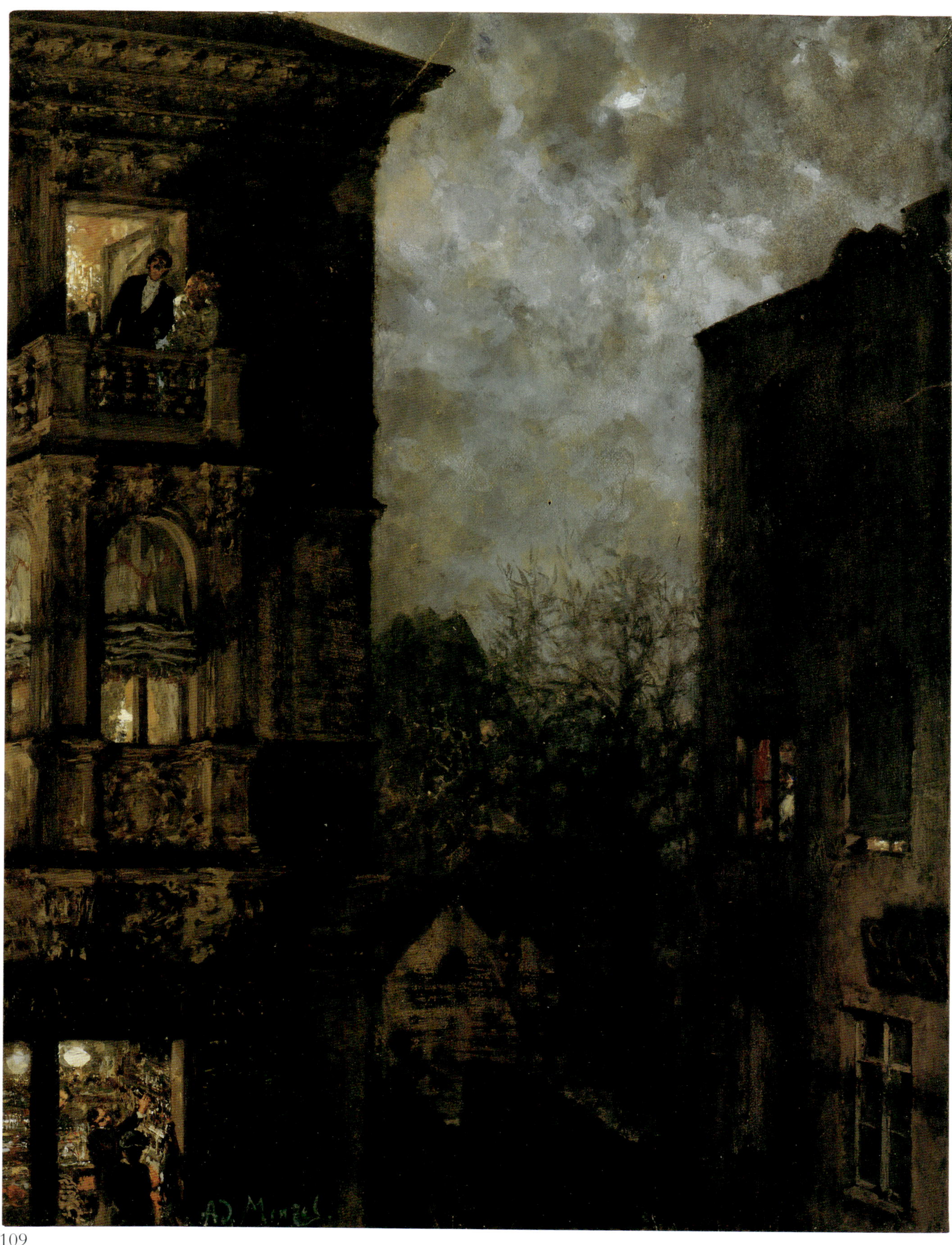

109

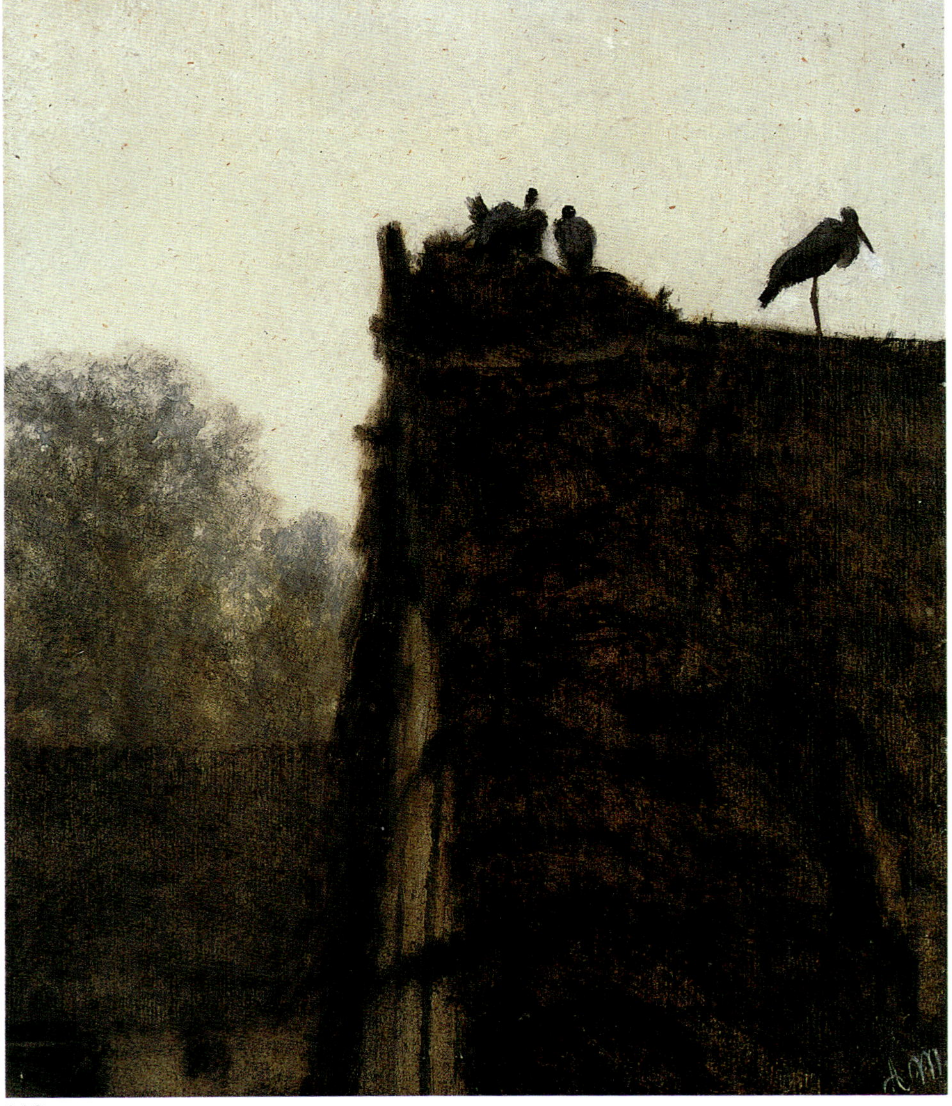

110

110

Thatched Roof with Storks' Nest

After 1866

Gouache
23.3 × 19.1cm
Signed at the bottom right: *A.M.*
Berlin, Kupferstichkabinett (SZ Menzel Kat 1015)
Exhibited in Paris and Washington only

Provenance: 1883 Hermann Pächter (R. Wagner Gallery, Berlin); acquired by the museum in 1889.
Exhibitions: Paris, 1885, no. 312; Berlin, 1895 B, no. 567; Berlin, 1905, no. 148; Berlin, 1980 A, no. 63, reprod. p. 323; Vienna, 1985, no. 88, reprod. p. 155; New York, 1990, no. 40, col. reprod. p. 140.
Bibliography: Jordan, 1895, p. 71; Donop, 1902, no. 1015; Tschudi, 1905 A, no. 394.

Menzel used a sketch from his 1866–7 sketchbook (Berlin, Kupferstichkabinett, sketchbook 28).

111

Rat in the Gutter

c. 1863–83

Gouache
8.3 × 14.2cm
Signed at the bottom right: *A.M.*
Berlin, Kupferstichkabinett (SZ Menzel Kat 1022)

Provenance: 1883 Hermann Pächter (R. Wagner Gallery, Berlin); acquired by the museum in 1889.
Exhibitions: Berlin, 1895 B, no. 595; Berlin, 1905, no. 155; Berlin, 1955 A, no. 367; Berlin, 1980 A, no. 68, reprod. p. 324; Vienna, 1985, no. 90, reprod. p. 156.
Bibliography: Jordan, 1895, p. 71; Donop, 1902, no. 1022; Tschudi, 1905 A, no. 391.

There are two studies for the metal grating in the 1863–4 sketchbook (Berlin, Kupferstichkabinett, sketchbook 25).

Fig. 191. *Storks Nest on a Thatched Roof*, 1866–7, pencil, Berlin, Kupferstichkabinett (sketchbook 28, p. 73)

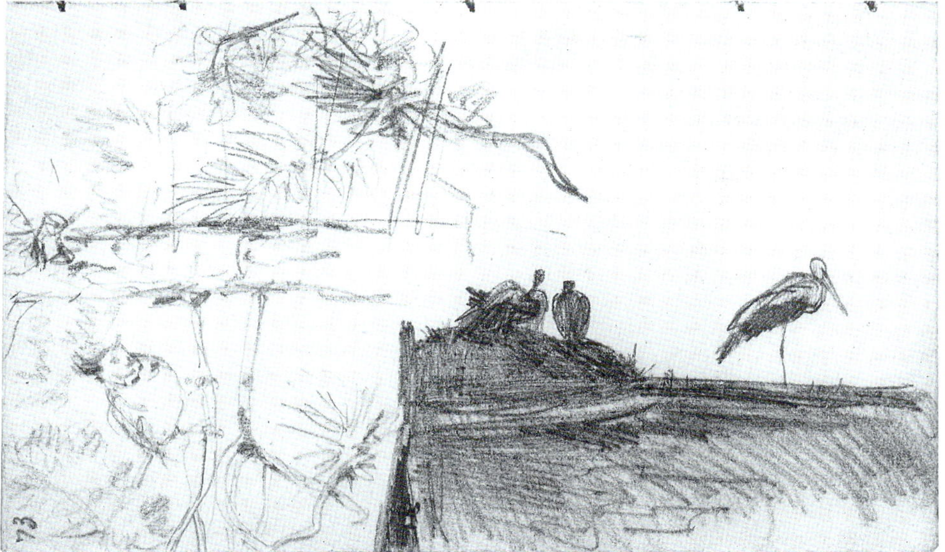

112

Cassowary

c. 1863–83

Gouache
25 × 11.1cm
Signed at the bottom right: *A.M.*
Berlin, Kupferstichkabinett (SZ Menzel Kat 1035)
Exhibited in Paris and Berlin only

Provenance: 1883 Hermann Pächter (R. Wagner Gallery, Berlin); acquired by the museum in 1889.
Exhibitions: Paris, 1885, no. 284; Berlin, 1895 B, no. 580; Düsseldorf, 1904, no. 48; Berlin, 1905, no. 168; Berlin, 1980 A, no. 78, col. reprod. p. 192; Vienna, 1985, no. 86, reprod. p. 154.
Bibliography: Jordan, 1895, p. 71; Donop, 1902, no. 1035; Tschudi, 1905 A, no. 367.

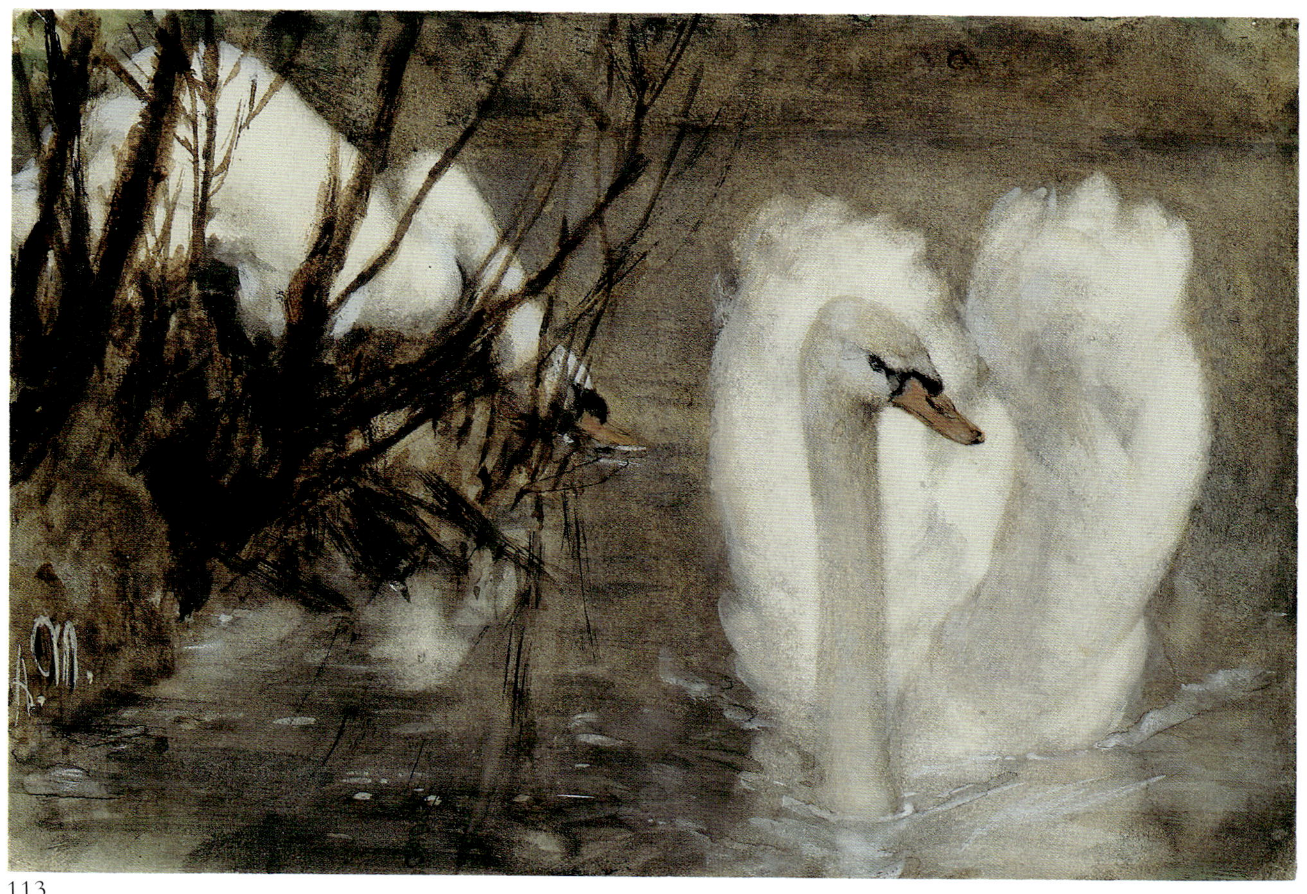

113

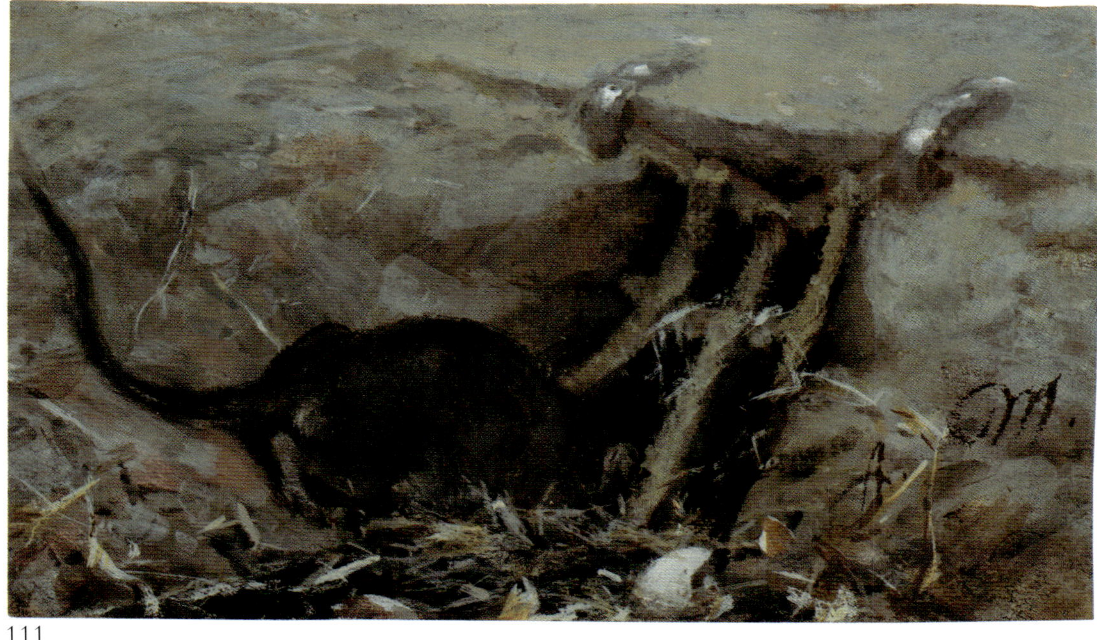

111

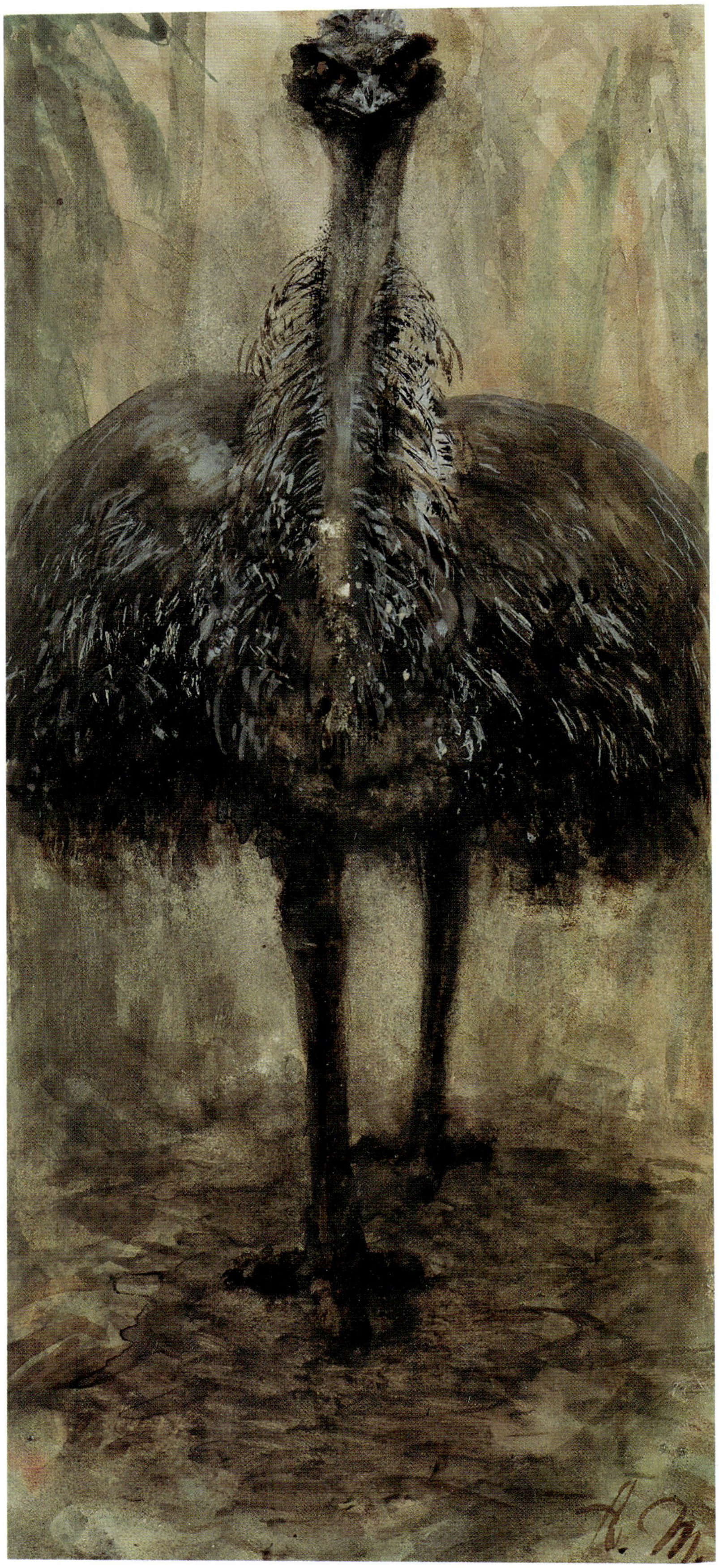

112

113

Two swans

After 1868

Gouache
12 × 7.1cm
Signed at the bottom left: *A.M.*
Berlin, Kupferstichkabinett (SZ Menzel Kat 1038)
Exhibited in Paris and Berlin only

Provenance: 1883 Hermann Pächter (R. Wagner Gallery, Berlin); acquired by the museum in 1889.
Exhibitions: Paris, 1885, no. 281; Berlin, 1885, no. 112; Berlin, 1895 B, no. 563; Vienna, 1896, no. 227; Düsseldorf, 1904, no. 50; Berlin, 1905, no. 171; Berlin, 1980 A, no. 80, col. reprod. p. 201; Vienna, 1985, no. 84, col. reprod. p.64; Copenhagen, 1985, no. 74; New York, 1990, no. 42, col. reprod. p. 145.
Bibliography: Jordan, 1895, p. 71; Donop, 1902, no. 1038; Tschudi, 1905 A, no. 404; Bredt, 1920, p. 81, reprod. p. 80; Hütt, 1981, p. 98, fig. 81.

There is a drawing in the 1868 sketchbook for the swan on the right (Berlin, Kupferstichkabinett, sketchbook 31).

114

Owl in a Thicket

1883

Gouache
29 × 17.1cm
Signed and dated at the bottom centre: *Ad.Menzel.83*
Berlin, Kupferstichkabinett (SZ Menzel Kat 1053)

Provenance: 1883 Hermann Pächter (R. Wagner Gallery, Berlin); acquired by the museum in 1889.
Exhibitions: Paris, 1885, no. 303; Berlin, 1885, no. 94; Berlin, 1895 B, no. 592; Vienna, 1896, no. 218; Dresden, 1904, no. 2370; Berlin, 1905, no. 186; Berlin, 1980 A, no. 93, col. reprod. p. 206; Vienna, 1985, no. 91, col. reprod. p. 66.
Bibliography: Jordan, 1895, p. 71; Donop, 1902, no. 1053; Tschudi, 1905 A, no. 402

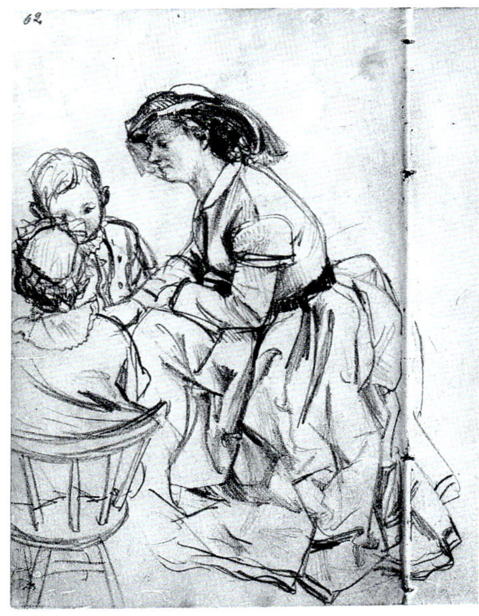

◁ Fig. 192. *Emilie with Otto and Grete,* 1864–5, pencil, Berlin, Kupferstichkabinett (sketchbook 27, p. 62)

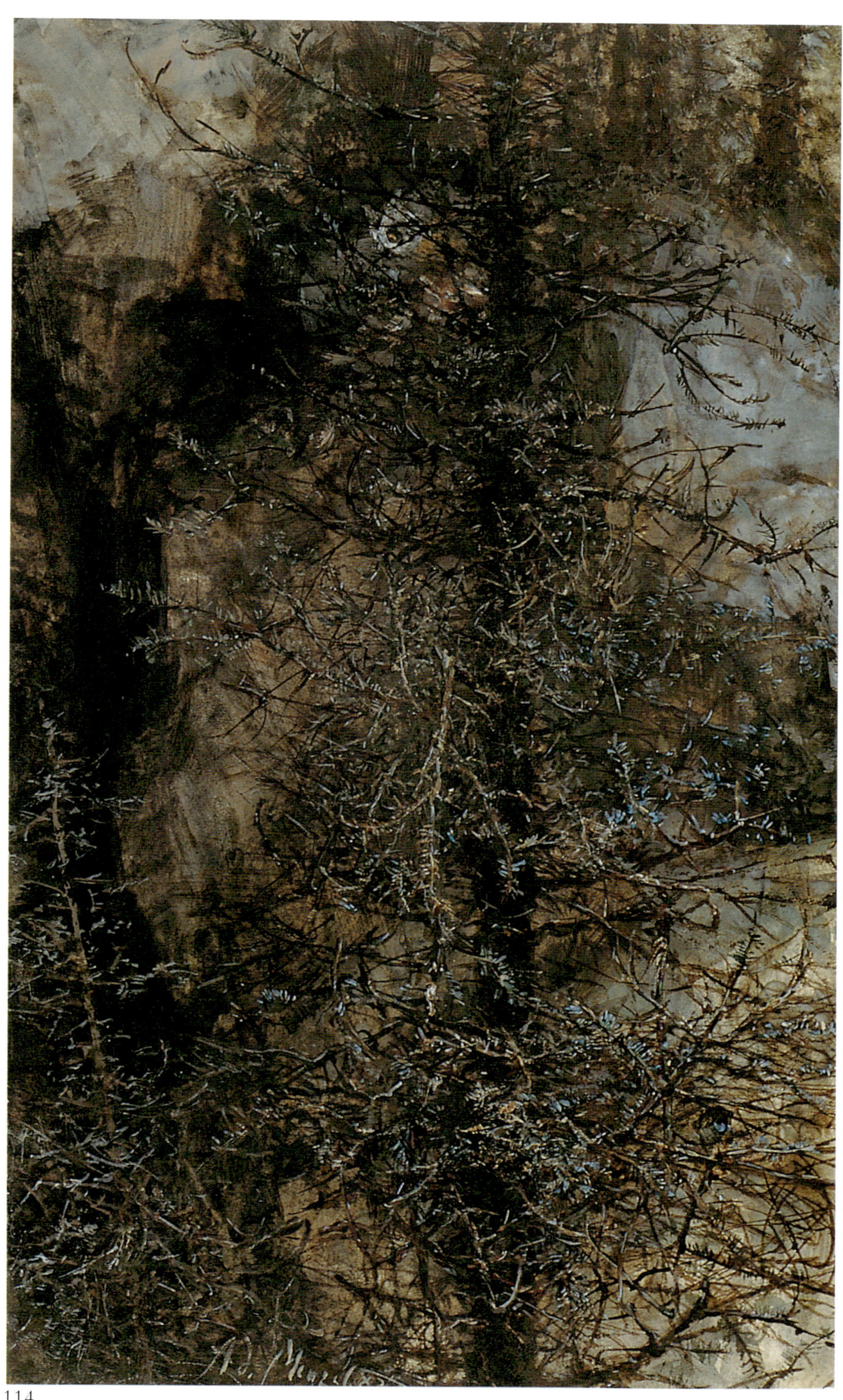

114

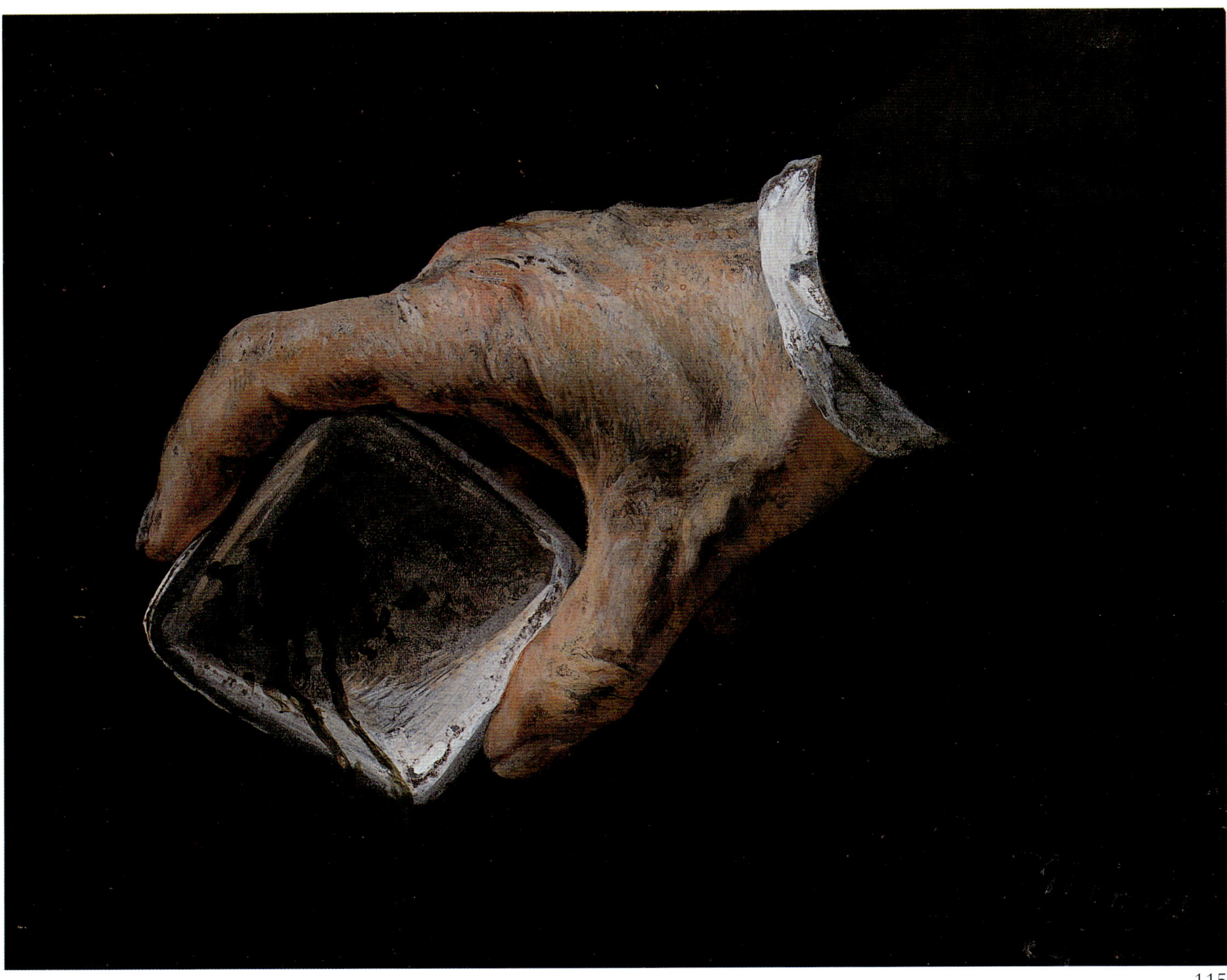

115

115
Hand Holding a Paint Dish
1864

Gouache
20 × 25cm
Signed and dated at the bottom right: *Menzel 64*
Berlin, Kupferstichkabinett (SZ Menzel Nr 1733)
Exhibited in Paris and Washington only

Provenance: Hermann Pächter, Berlin; Ernst Seeger, Berlin, important collector and patron of Wilhelm Leibl; acquired by the museum in 1906.
Exhibitions: Hamburg, 1894; Berlin, 1905, no. 2776; Berlin, 1955 B, no. 101; Berlin, 1984, no. 55; Cambridge, 1984, no. 44.
Bibliography: Jordan/Dohme, 1890, reprod. p. 56; Tschudi, 1905 A, no. 417; Meyerheim, (1906) 1992, p. 170; Scheffler, 1922, p. 189, fig. p. 177; Berlin, 1934, no. 1683, p. 90; cat. NG, 1976, p. 279, reprod.; Honisch, 1979, p. 150.

116
Hand Holding a Book
1864

Gouache
25 × 18cm
Signed and dated at the top right: *Menzel 64.*
Berlin, Kupferstichkabinett (SZ Menzel Nr 1734)
Exhibited in Washington only

Provenance: Hermann Pächter, Berlin; Ernst Seeger, Berlin, important collector and patron of Wilhelm Liebl; acquired by the museum in 1906.
Exhibitions: Hamburg, 1894; Berlin, 1905, no. 2777; Berlin, 1955 B, no. 100; Berlin, 1984, no. 56.
Bibliography: Joprdan/Dohme, 1890, reprod. p. 57; Tschudi, 1905 A, no. 416; cat. NG, 1934, no. 1648, p. 90; cat NG, 1976, p. 280; Honisch, 1979, p. 150.

When he was thirteen, Menzel the apprentice lithographer drew his father's hand holding a knife, and his father's open hand when he was confined to bed shortly before his death[1]. This motif re-appears several times later in his work. Menzel used his own hands as models for these two gouaches painted with his left hand, depicting the right. In the 1862-3 sketchbook, several minutely detailed pencil studies acted as studies for these gouaches[2]. The studies are of both his small, delicate hands in different positions. In 1848 he had previously drawn his own hand in pastel, later adding the following comment: 'My right hand drawn with my left hand'[3]. A number of contemporary reports state that he had always been fascinated with drawing his two hands, from his youth[4]. It was said in general that he drew with his left hand and painted with his right, but he himself contradicts this, emphasizing when talking about light in his work, as he did in 1876, that he painted with his left hand, for 'nearly all of my pictures on Frederick'[5]. He made the same declaration years later about a gouache done for the town of Hamburg (cat. 187). Perhaps Menzel was reacting to the numerous stories on this topic, which would not have escaped his attention, and wanted to show that he was originally left-handed[6], or perhaps he simply wanted to emphasize the expert lighting effects.

In his memoirs, Meyerheim commented on the gouache of the hand and pot: 'The white he used was called "Snow flower", which he ground with rainwater in a very old square dish which used to contain toothpaste. Using his left hand he painted his right holding the dish in watercolour and life size'[7]. In his treatise on the apprenticeship of painting, Lovis Corinth found the gouache depicting Menzel's hand a particularly characteristic example of this technique: 'The way of painting and applying colour is exactly the same as for oil painting, but the artist doesn't work on a layer of wet paint. The dry colour can be painted over as often as is necessary. One is not obliged to paint all in one go, because it dries. Menzel was extremely skilled in using gouache in miniature paintings the size of a hand as well as in life-sized studies of hands and other parts of the body. One of his own hands, holding a dish, is engraved on my memory as one the greatest masterpieces of our time'[8]. M.R.-R.

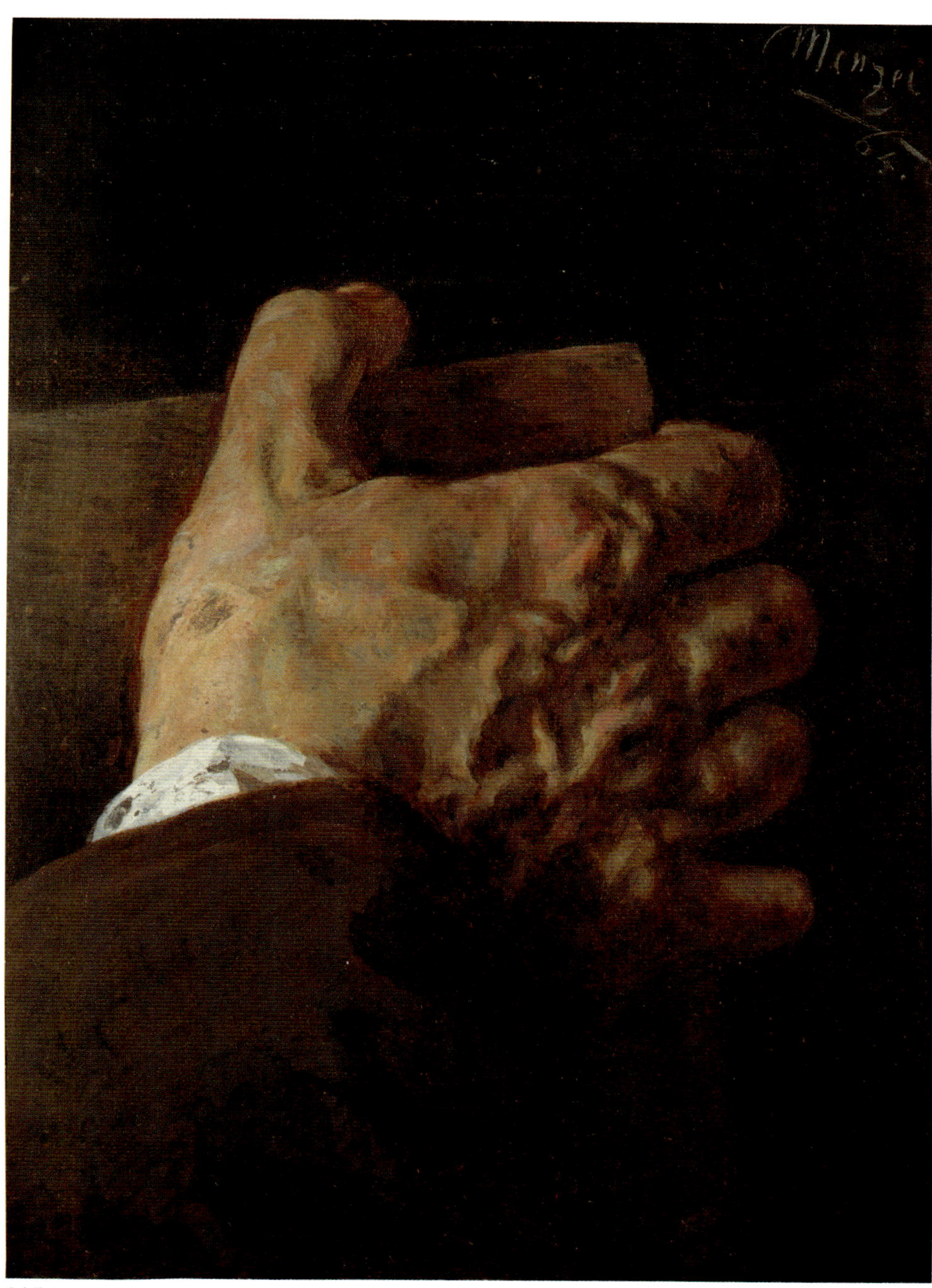

116

1. Berlin, Kupferstichkabinett (SZ Menzel N 993).
2. Berlin, Kupferstichkabinett, sketchbook 24, p. 9, p. 11.
3. Hamburg, Reemtsma collection.
4. *Cf.* for example Meyerheim, (1906) 1992, p. 174.
5. Letter to an unknown recipient (perhaps his dealer, Hermann Pächter), September 1876: 'I painted the picture with my left hand, like, for example, my sermon in the forest, and nearly all my paintings of Frederick.' *Cf.* cat. 125.
6. *Cf.* the thesis (in preparation) of Ulf Küster on Menzels early work (University of Freiburg, Breisgau).
7. Meyerheim, (1906) 1992, p. 170.
8. Lovis Corinth, *Das Erlernen der Malerei,* 2nd ed., Berlin, no date [1909], p. 121.

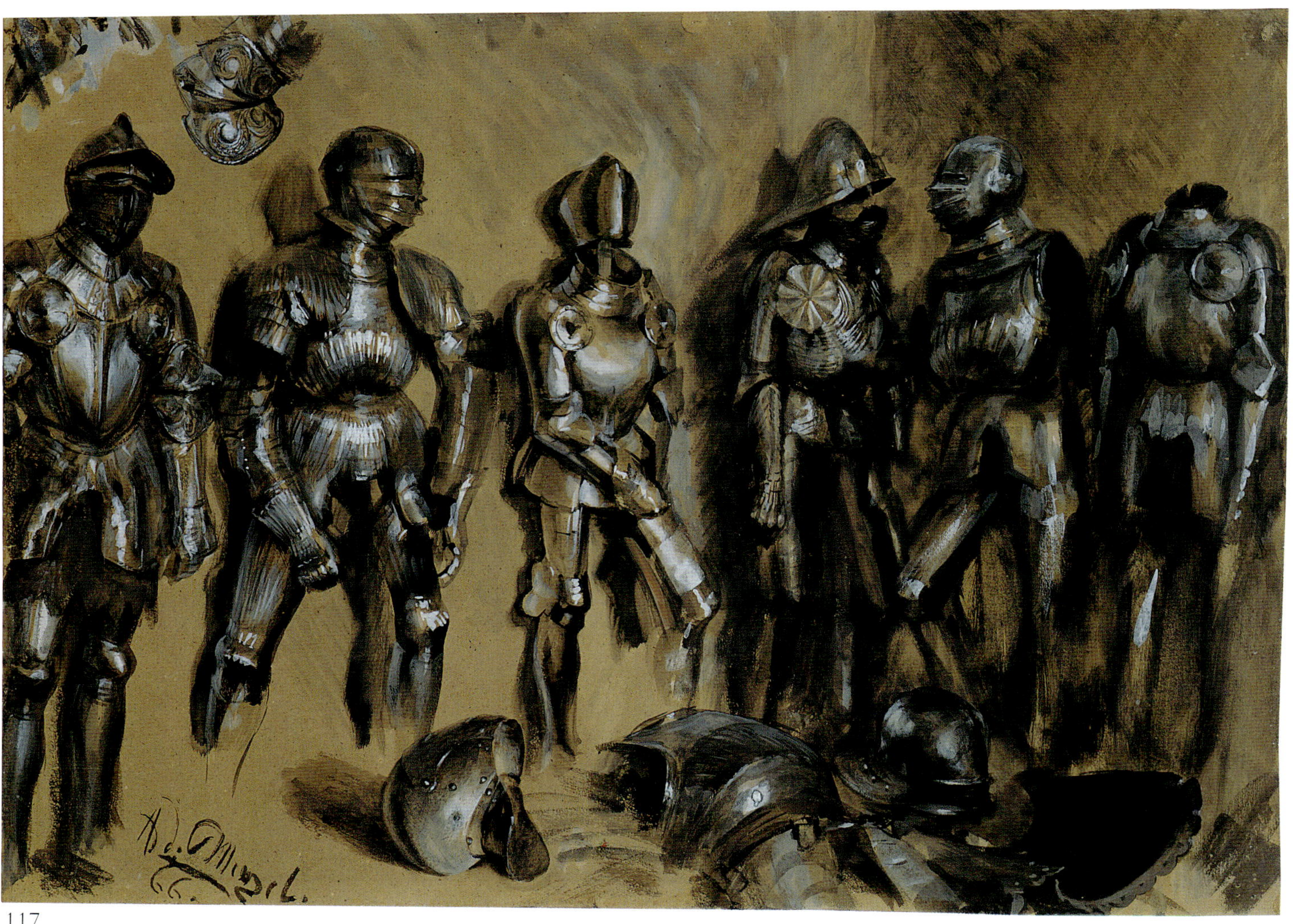

117

117–19
Fantasies from the Arms Room
1866

From the spring of 1862 onwards, Menzel occupied a large room in the royal palace in Berlin where the scaffolding for the execution of the great painting of *The Coronation of William I* could be erected. The guard room, which had been allocated to him (*cf.* cat. 102), had first of all to be emptied of its contents. A letter to his friend Dr Puhlmann is decorated with a sketch (in the same red ink he used to mark out the working drawing for his composition) showing men putting up the gigantic canvas and scaffolding, and emptying the room of a collection of arms and armour which had been stored there. 'There is a din going on all around me . . . . I must keep an eye on these chaps'[1], he wrote next to the sketch, in which a soldier was drawn dragging the imposing, yet puppet-like, armour with difficulty. What remained of these objects, mainly from the Renaissance, formed part of the painter's working environment in the four years he devoted to the *Coronation* painting. He left the studio at the start of 1866.

The great canvas was complete by mid-December. In just a few weeks, spilling over into 1866, he produced about twenty watercolours and gouaches

117
Six Suits of Armour Standing against a Wall
1866

Gouache
38.3 × 52.3cm
Signed and dated at the bottom left: Ad.Menzel.66.
Berlin, Kupferstichkabinett (SZ Menzel N 4472)

Provenance: Painter's studio; 1905 Emilie Krigar-Menzel; acquired by the museum in 1906.
Exhibitions: Berlin, 1885, no. 59; Berlin, 1905, no. 4593; Berlin, 1980 A, no. 51, reprod. p. 321; Vienna, 1985, no. 111, reprod. p. 177; Copenhagen, 1985, no. 103, reprod. p. 64.
Bibliography: Tschudi, 1905 A, no. 546

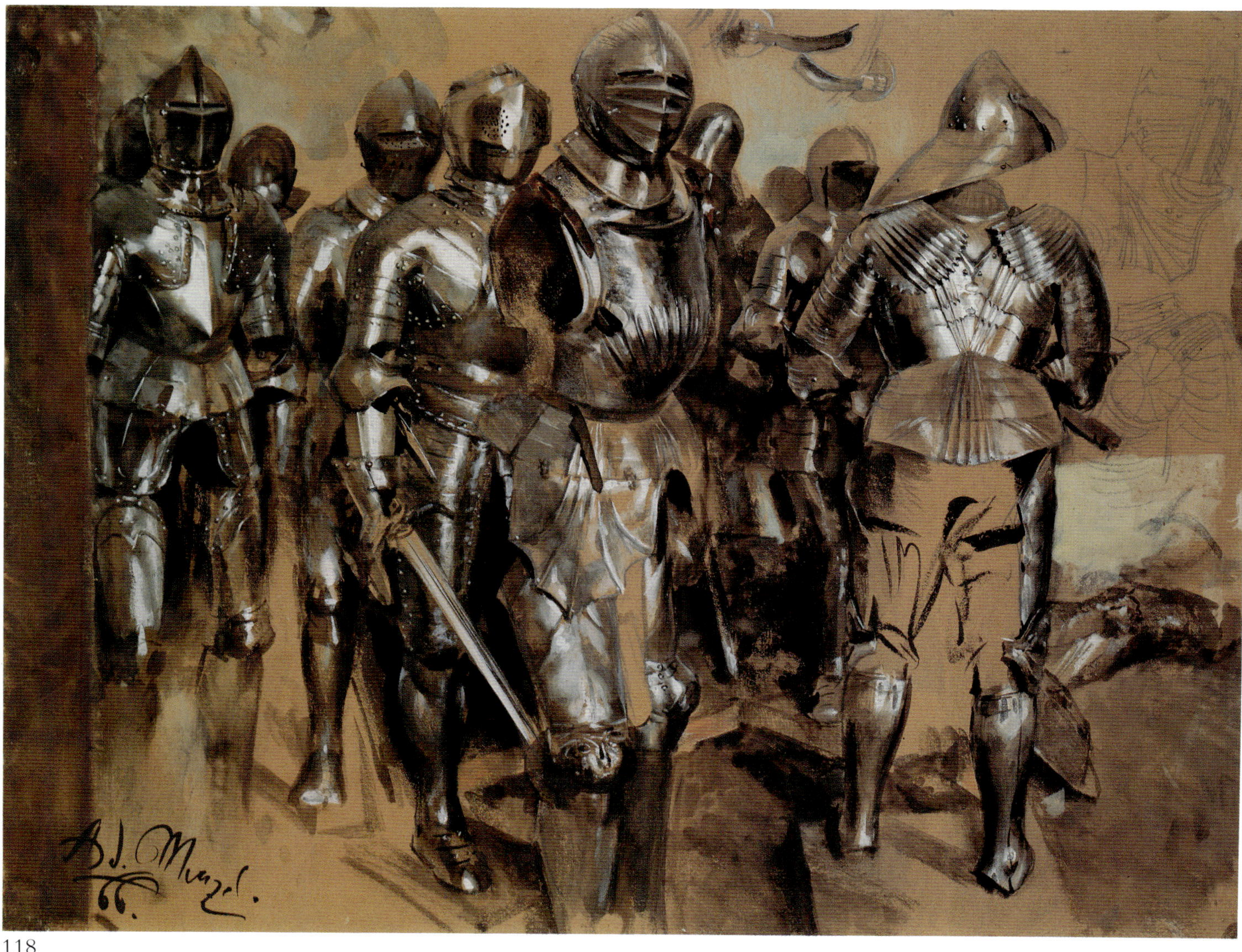

118

118

Suits of Armour Standing

1866

Gouache and pencil
43.9 × 56.7cm
Signed and dated at the bottom left: *Ad.Menzel.66.*
Vienna, Graphische Sammlung Albertina (34.803)
Exhibited in Berlin only

Provenance: Painter's studio; 1932 Caspari gallery, Munich; acquired by the museum in 1934.
Exhibitions: Berlin, 1885, no. 59 or 59a?; Munich, 1932, no. 2, reprod.
Bibliography: Not mentioned by Tschudi, 1905 A; exhib. cat. Hamburg, 1982, reference work at no. 92.

inspired by the armour, helmets and pointed weapons[2]. Images like these had been familiar to him for a long time, since his studies of weapons and costume for the lithographic illustrations of the history of Prussia and Brandenburg, and in particular for the woodcuts illustrating the *History* and the *Deeds of Frederick the Great*. Still surrounded by armour, 132 people had posed for Menzel in two years. These portraits, defying any ideal, have always been considered as an exceptional phenomenon. Immediately after, the painter seemed to invoke ancestral spirits and breathe new life into the assembled armour. In the second half of the century, William I, at the height of the great mission he felt called upon to undertake, encouraged the cult of the hero and of war, and pan-Germanic ideas. There was a general interest in the past, which held the key to German identity. Mediaeval arms and armour were used as ornaments inside homes, and notably in the studios of artists, who incorporated them in their paintings.

An extraordinary capacity to make inanimate objects live is apparent in these virtuoso pictures. Under the painter's eye, and in a magical light, a fantastic dance begins. In three superb large drawings in particular, which contain an abundance of figures, the armour is grouped into varied formations like armies on the

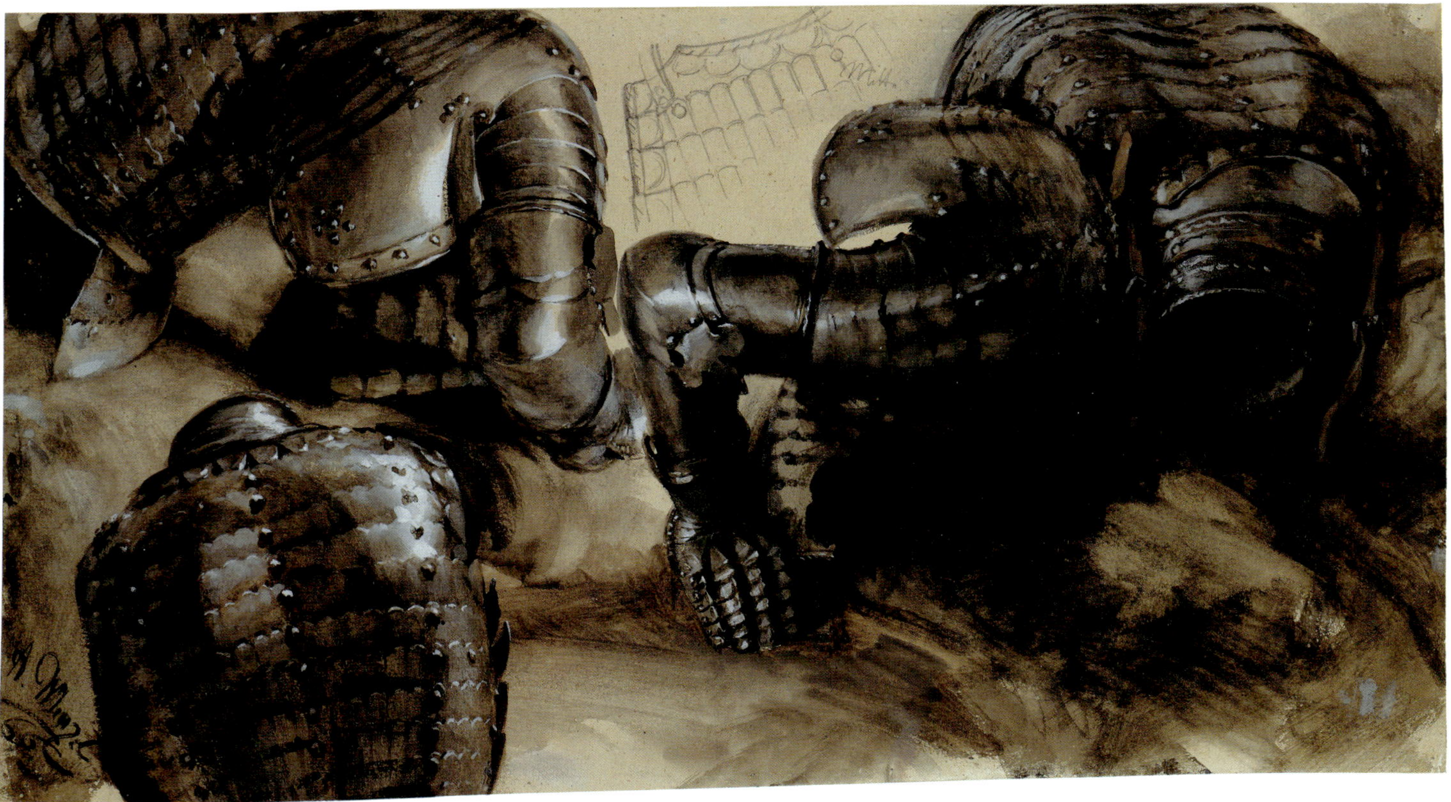

119

119

Cuirasses Lying Down

1866

Gouache

29.3 × 51.2cm

Signed and dated at the bottom left: *A.Menzel 66*

Berlin, Kupferstichkabinett (SZ Menzel N 4473)

Provenance: Painter's studio; 1905 Emilie Krigar-Menzel; acquired by the museum in 1906.

Exhibitions: Berlin, 1905, no. 4597; Berlin, 1955 A, no. 298; Vienna, 1985, no. 113, reprod. p. 178; Copenhagen, 1985, no. 104, reprod. p. 65; New York, 1990, no. 32, reprod. p. 123.

Bibliography: Tschudi, 1905 A, no. 550.

Fig. 193. *Two Helmets with Visors and a Cuirasse*, 1866, pencil and watercolour, Berlin, Kupferstichkabinett (N 4446)

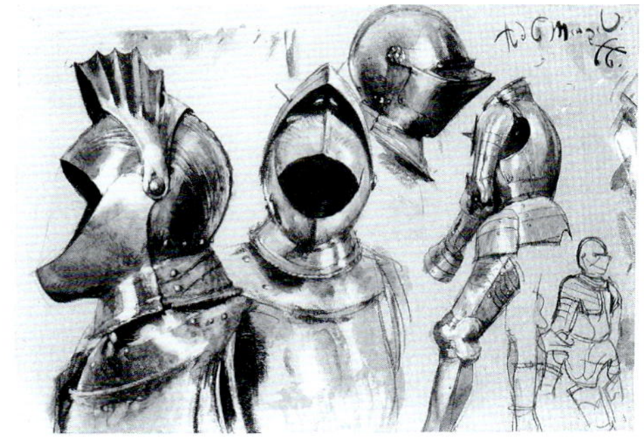

move. In 1892, Menzel sold one to Albert Lichtwark for the Kunsthalle in Hamburg. The second went to the Albertina in Vienna, and the third, perhaps a little less prestigious, was acquired by the Nationalgalerie with studio funds (cat. 117, 118). Max Liebermann bought a smaller picture[3].

In spite of their metallic sheen, the cuirasses seem almost unreal, like empty envelopes, or cocoons abandoned by mysterious, recently metamorphosed moths (cat. 119). These drawings were exhibited in 1866 under the title *Fantasies from the Arms Room* at the same Academy exhibition in which *The Coronation* was on display. Max Schasler, a critic always hostile to Menzel, wrote: 'Without wishing to deny their technical virtuosity and originality of conception. I am unable . . . to find anything to my taste in them. Firstly, they are not "paintings", but simple studies hanging there (I was going to use another term) with great nonchalance, although wrought by an astoundingly expert hand. Secondly, the dominant impression they leave is so subjective and capricious that one might admire the "genius" of the artist, but can, objectively, find no interest. The same effect is produced by the lithograph *Fantasies from the Arms Room* intended for the 1867 *Album of German Artists*'[4]. It was hard for Menzel's contemporaries to acknowledge such innovative work, so very different from his official pictures and born of his own initiative as a way of finding his true expression. He also made concessions to the tastes of his time, as in the lithograph quoted by Schasler and entitled *Guess Who*[5], in which a beautiful woman in Renaissance costume tries to lift a knight's visor. The pleasure Menzel took in painting these gretaly admired genre scenes, in historical costume, is confirmed by numerous small pictures of the life of the knight, with ironic or amusing touches[6]. M.R.-R.118

1. Letter to Wilhelm Puhlmann, 2 April 1862, text printed in exhib. cat. Berlin, 1955 A, no. 294. Drawing reproduced in exhib. cat. Berlin, 1980 A, p. 50.
2. Most of these are in the Kupferstichkabinett in Berlin.
3. Tschudi, 1905 A, no. 554; Berlin, Kupferstichkabinett (SZ Menzel Nr 1753).
4. *Die Dioskuren*, 11, 1866, p. 378.
5. Bock, 1923, no. 86.
6. As regards these compositions in general, Meier-Graefe makes some appropriate remarks, 1906, p. 200 and ff. when he compares them among others to what he calls Japanese Impressionists

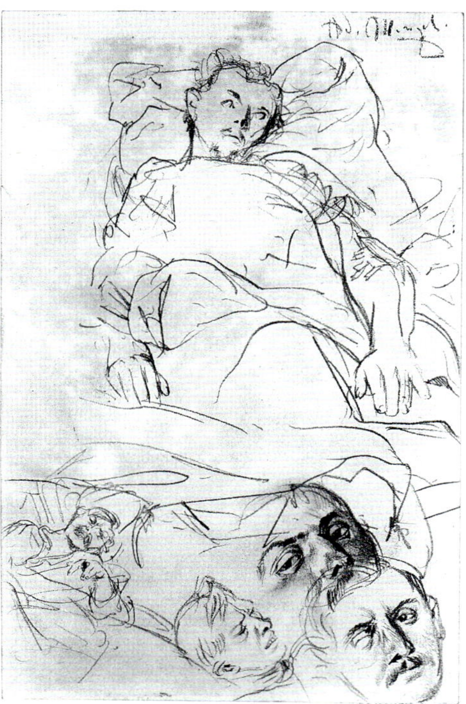

120

Two Dead Soldiers Laid out on Straw

1866

Pencil and watercolour
18 × 27.2cm
Signed at the centre bottom: Ad. Menzel – Annotated: *Leichenkammer zu Königinhof 21 Juli 1866.*
Berlin, Kupferstichkabinett (SZ Menzel N 1740)

Provenance: Painter's studio; 1905 Emilie Krigar-Menzel; acquired by the museum in 1906.
Exhibitions: Berlin, 1905 A, no. 5233a; Berlin, 1980 A, no. 54; Vienna, 1985, no. 49; Copenhagen, 1985, no. 40; Vienna, 1990, no. 148.
Bibliography: Tschudi, 1905 A, no. 540; Lammel, 1988, p. 160 *et seq.*, fig. 117.

Fig. 194. *Wounded Soldier. Study of the Military Hospital at Königinhof*, 1866, pencil, Berlin, Kupferstichkabinett (N 3930)

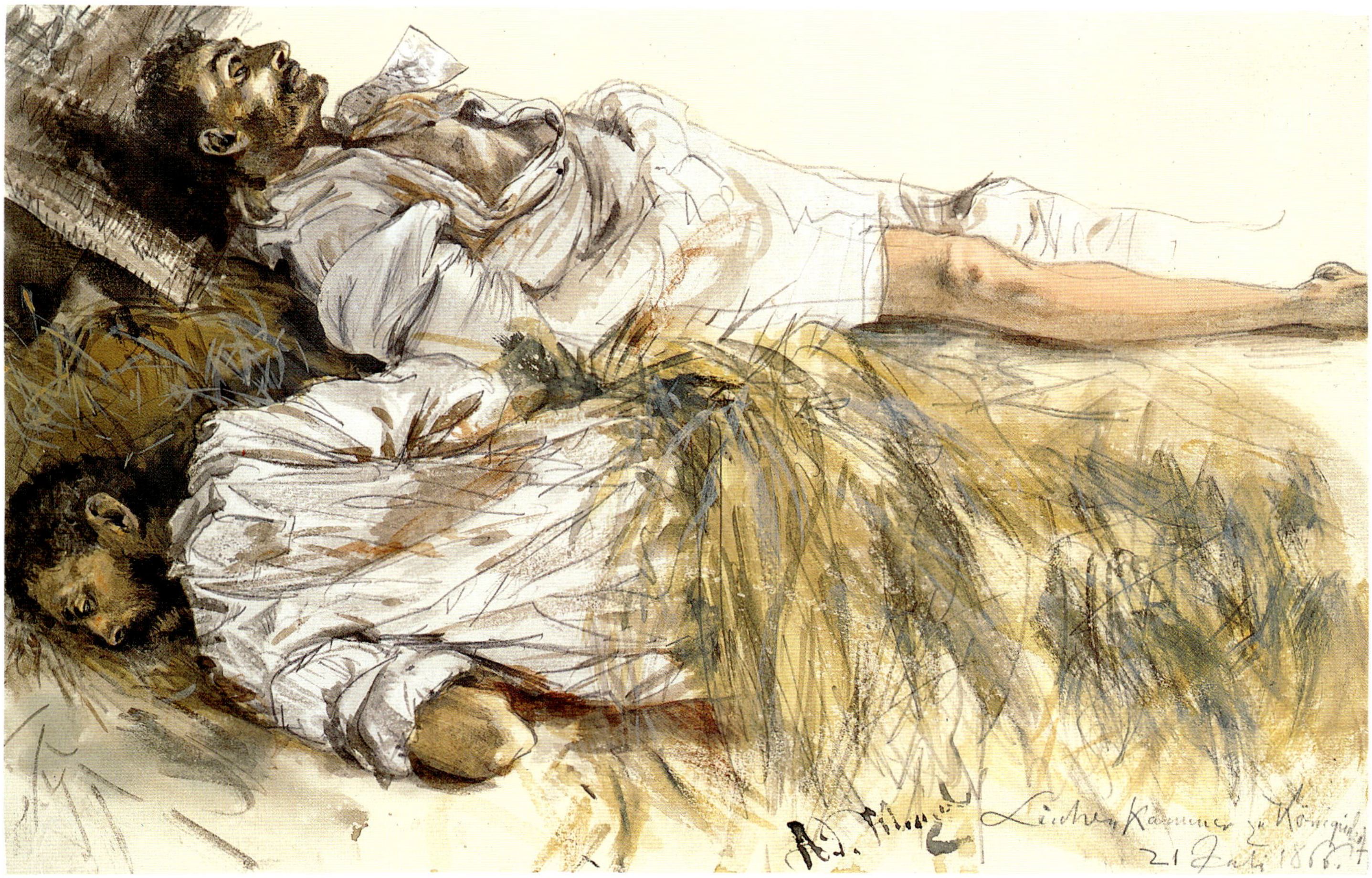

120

121
Two Dead Soldiers in a Barn
1866

Pencil and watercolour
18.6 × 27.3cm
Signed at the top right: *Ad. Menzel* – Annotated: *Leichenkammer Königinhof 21 Juli 1866.*
Berlin, Kupferstichkabinett (SZ Menzel N 1741)

Provenance: Painter's studio; 1905 Emilie Krigar-Menzel; acquired by the museum in 1906.
Exhibitions: Berlin, 1905, no. 5233b; Berlin, 1980 A, no. 53; Vienna, 1985, no. 50; Copenhagen, 1985, no. 41; Vienna, 1990, no. 149.
Bibliography: Tschudi, 1905 A, no. 538; Lammel, 1988, p. 160 *et seq.*, fig. 116.

These two paintings are the first of Menzel's works to be marked by the presence of war and death. The dread they arouse pervades the graphic work on the deeds of Frederick the Great. Menzel drew soldiers in combat and on the point of death, although he had never seen any. It was one of the rare exceptions to his principle of authenticity. However, he knew Frederick's *Reflections and Rulings on War* very thoroughly and had interpreted the prince's words in a brilliant, ironic and subtle manner in his illustrations to the *Works of Frederick the Great* (1843–9). He painted a provocative image of death for *Instructions to my Artillery: How to Adjust their Fire to the Occasion*, in depicting a cannonball emerging from the end of a cannon directed towards the onlooker, and projecting deadly flashes of light with its fixed and unseeing eye. But Menzel must have obtained the 'instructions' by consulting treatises and frequenting arms rooms. His interest in the fire of battle in the violent clash between the Prussians and Austrians in Bohemia during the summer of 1866 is not surprising. For Prussian partisans, the desire for a national sovereign state was necessarily linked to the prospect of war. Menzel had not been unaffected by the general feeling of exaltation – all Prussia was expected to do its duty. Because of his very short stature, he had been released from his military obligations yet, until 1866, when he was determined to see the atrocities of war with his own eyes, he had not been free of the 'feeling of duty', of the 'thirst to find out about things, even if it was not on the smoking battlefield itself', as he wrote to a friend. He continued: 'That was how I came to cross the battlefield of Königsgrätz – past the small wood with its sinister reputation, I went through Sadowa-Chlum – the place where there were great cavalry confrontations, etc.'[1]. Menzel had seen the horrible remains of the carnage in which the Prussians had

121

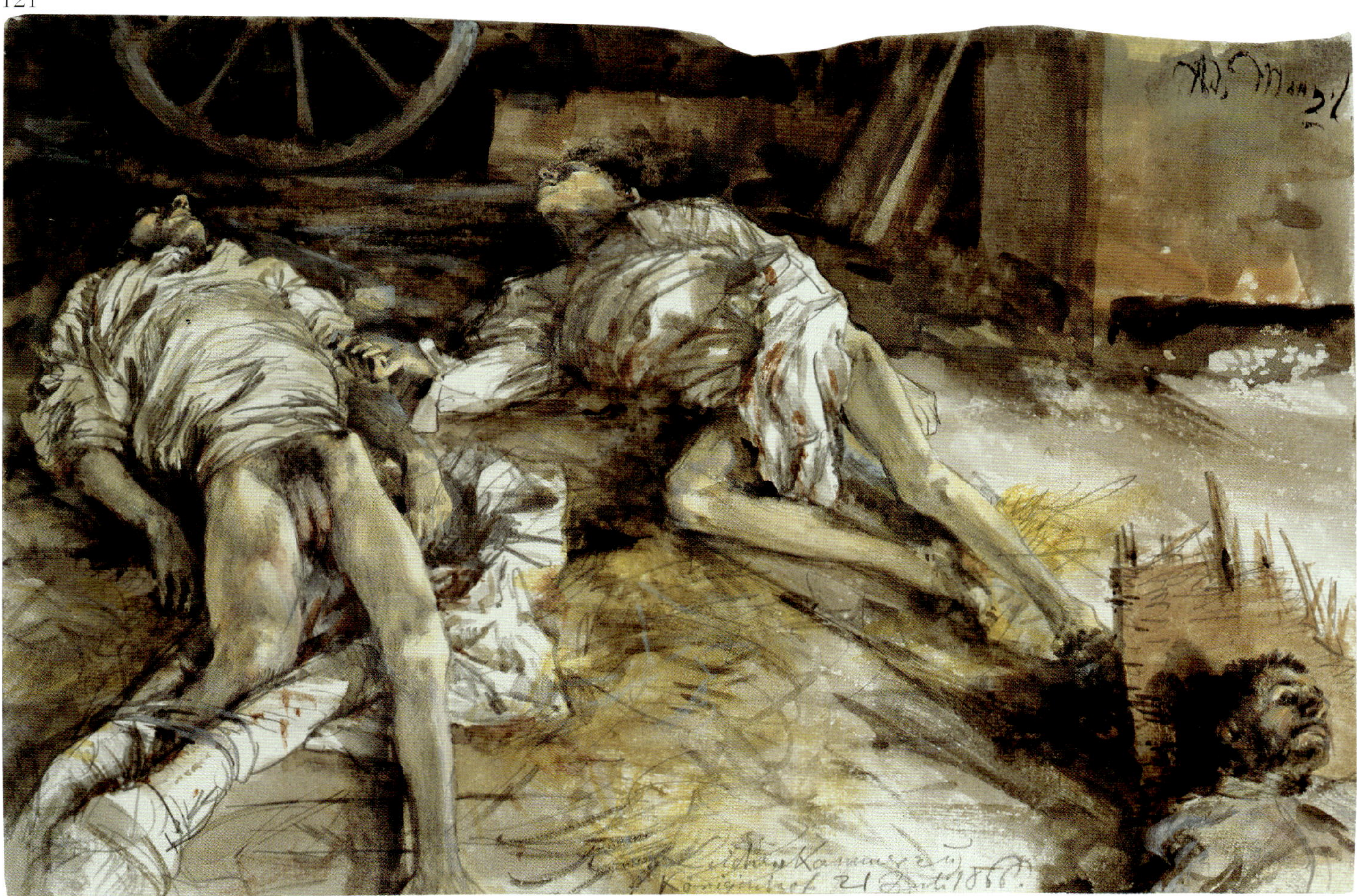

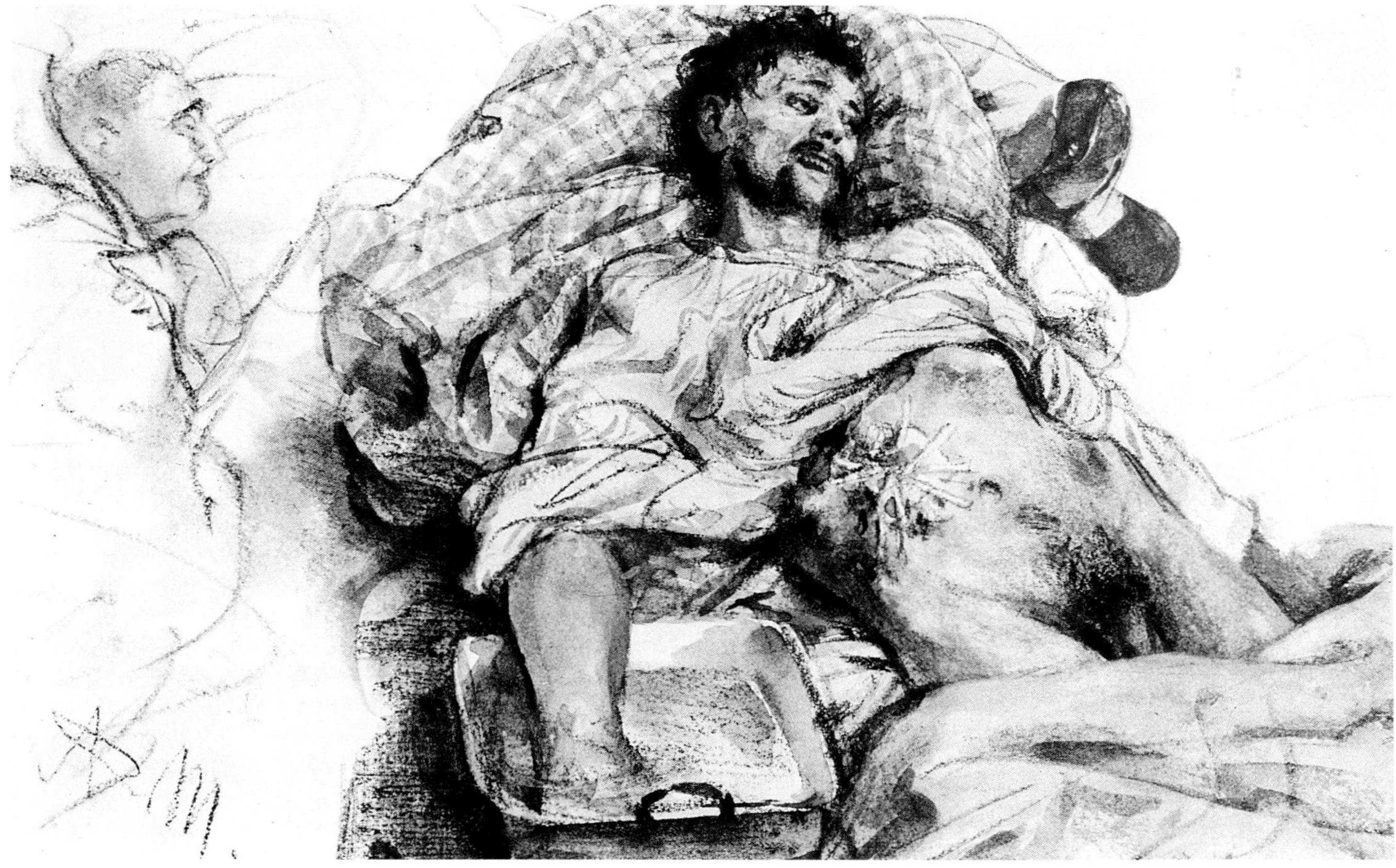

Fig. 195. *Dying Soldier*, 1866, pencil and watercolour, Euerbach, Georg Schäfer collection

emerged victorious from the decisive battle of 3 July, close to Königsgrätz, between the small villages of Sadowa and Chlum. The 8th regiment of Austrian cuirassiers had attempted to cover the retreat of their defeated army. Menzel left on 16 July, several days before the cessation of the hostilities between Prussia and Austria, and had reached Königinhof, near Königsgrätz, on 19 July. Three days later, transport disruption forced him to return to Prague, via the battlefields.

The letters of forced enthusiasm Menzel wrote on his return to Berlin at the end of July contrast with the artistic echoes of his impressions in the drawings and watercolours of the military hospital at Königinhof where he stayed for three days, 'sparing himself nothing' in terms of 'horror, distress and stench'[2]. These drawings of the wounded, dead or dying were both objective and compassionate, strongly revealing the shock and emotion Menzel felt (fig. 194). There is a third drawing of a dying soldier[3] (fig. 195) in addition to the two of dead soldiers, as well as watercolours and studies of the wounded in a sketchbook[4]. In these works Menzel created a powerful indictment of war, and his personal testimonial is unique in German art of the time. The unceremonious realism of these works already speaks in the language of the twentieth century. These pages remained unknown during Menzel's lifetime and, although they could be seen at the commemorative exhibition at the Nationalgalerie in Berlin, interest in them has only recently been renewed. It is useful to compare them with the watercolour drawing dated December 1848 by a contemporary, the French Pierre Andrieu (1821–92), a pupil of Delacroix, in which he depicts the victim of barricade fighting in the Paris riots in February. The body, which is demonstratively nude, is carried by partisans with imprecatory gestures. In contrast, it is clear that Menzel has renounced all anecdote[5].

In 1878, when Friedrich Pecht asked him why he had not painted any work on the wars of 1866 and 1870, Menzel summed up his feelings in a way which sheds light on the artistic motivation behind his visits to the battlefield. He recalls with embarrassment the 'naïve audacity' with which he painted *Night Attack at Hochkirch*[6], without 'any kind of realistic study or observation', which is 'the vital condition upon which any undertaking in art rests'. He ended: 'The requirements of patriotism have been covered by others and, after all, is it necessary to paint the horror?! *Anno 66 (post festum)* I went to Bohemia![7] . . .' The heavy silence of these suspension marks reveals, rather than regret, the acquired conviction that no painting could ever portray the devastating horror of war. In the second half of his life, Menzel never again used war as a subject for his art.

M.R.-R.

1. Letter to Hermann Krigar, Prague, 24 July 1866, Wolff,1914, p. 204.
2. *Cf.* the letters to his cousin Heinrich Paul, 31 July 1866, and to Wilhelm Puhlmann, 2 August 1866, Wolff, 1914, p. 204 and ff. Both men had taken part in the war.
3. Tschudi, 1905 A, no. 539; Euerbach, Georg Schäfer collection.
4. Berlin, Kupferstichkabinett.
5. Paris, Carnavalet museum; reprod. in exhib. cat. Berlin, 1990 B, no. 3a/1.
6. 1856, Tschudi, 1905 A, no. 106; missing since the Second World War.
7. Letter to Friedrich Pecht, 9 December 1878, Berlin.

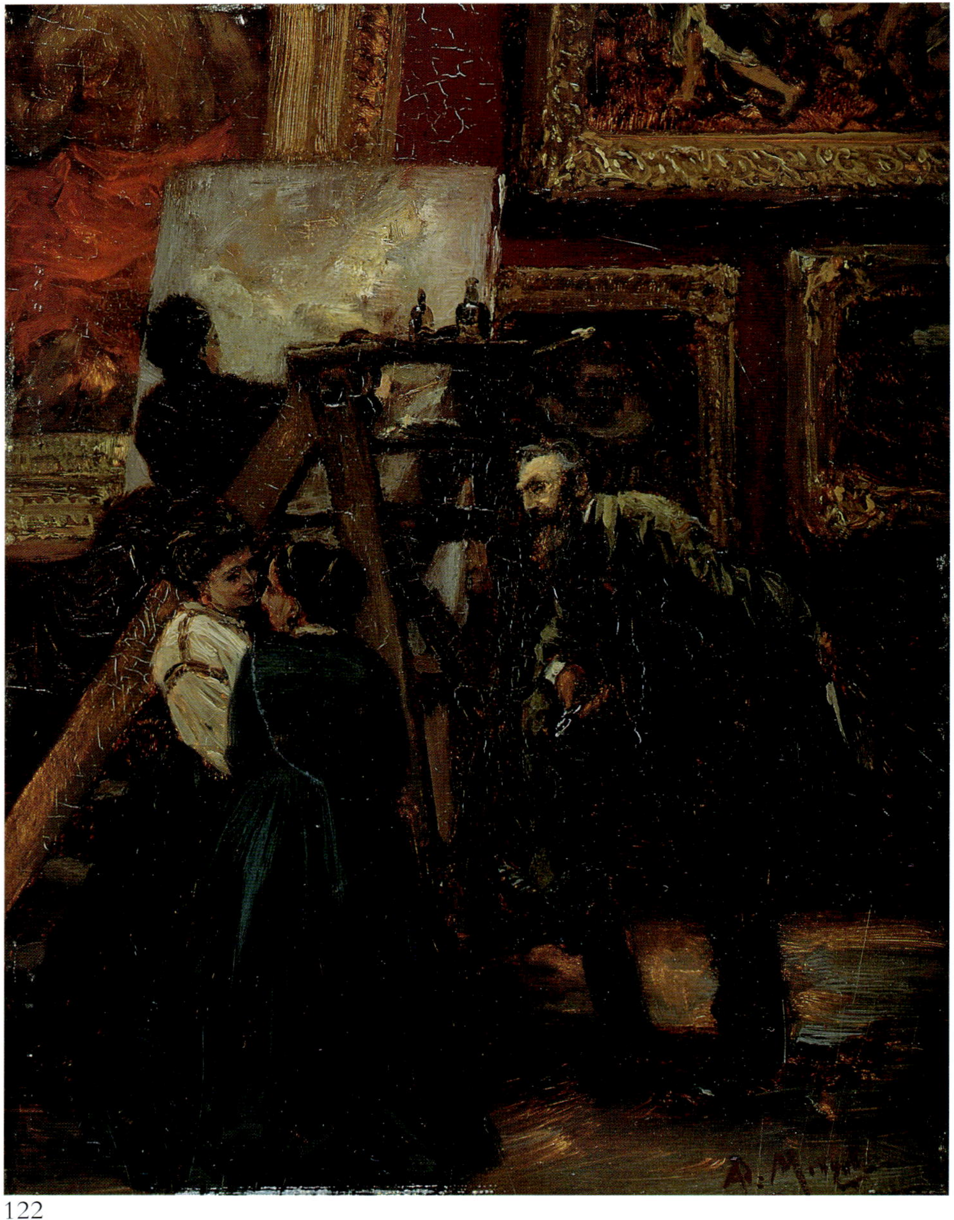

122

122

At the Louvre

1867

Oil on wood
23.6 × 18cm
Signed at the bottom right: *A.Menzel.*
Hamburg, Hamburg Kunsthalle (2457)
Exhibited in Washington only

Provenance: Very probably owned from the start by the Viscomtesse de Calonne, whom Menzel met in Paris in 1867. She was the friend of the painter Louis Ricard (*cf.* cat. 126), who painted two portraits of her (housed at the Musée d'Orsay). In May 1868, Menzel had sent each a picture as a present. The Viscomtesse immediately exchanged the picture intended for her, depicting 'cultivated artists', easily recognizable as *At the Louvre*, for the *Red Proletarian* – apparently missing – that Ricard had received. He was the next owner[1]. In 1895 the painting already belonged to Erdwin Amsinck, Hamburg; acquired by the museum in 1921 (legacy of Erdwin Amsinck and his wife Antonie, neé Lattmann).
Exhibitions: Berlin, 1895 A, no. 239; Hamburg, 1896, no. 24; Berlin, 1905, no. 35; Berlin, 1955 B, no. 108; Erlangen, 1971, no. 75; Hamburg, 1982, no. 98, col. reprod.
Bibliography: Tschudi, 1905 A, no. 130; Hamburg, 1969, p. 219, reprod.; Howoldt, 1993, p. 38, col. reprod. p. 39.

The activity of the copyist lies between the study and the sale of art. Both aspects, orientated towards the old masters, flourished in Paris, 'capital of the nineteenth century'. At the Louvre, as at so many great museums of the nineteenth century, copyists, who were often women, were part of the everyday scenery, and cluttered up rooms with their materials to the extent that visitors could not see some of the works on display. The theme gave Menzel another opportunity to dodge possible allusions to elevated ideas – art and history are reduced to a simple corridor of gilt frames on a Pompeian-red wall. No one is taking in the works of art in the picture. Standing around a cumbersome, everyday pair of steps, the figures are engaged in a rather absent-minded discussion. The activities of the art world are relegated to the middle ground.

It would be interesting to know which paintings Menzel chose for the background. In the middle there appears to be a portrait of a woman wearing a ruff and, at the top left corner, the red habit of a penitent St Jerome. No one has been able to identify these paintings. Once more, the authenticity for which Menzel is so acclaimed is deceptive. C.K.

1. Letter from Viscountess de Calonne to Menzel, 21 May 1868, Nuremberg, Germanisches Nationalmuseum.

123

Afternoon in the Tuileries Gardens

1867

Oil on canvas
49 × 70cm
Signed and dated at the bottom right: *Adolph Menzel Berl. 1867*
Dresden, Staatliche Kunstsammlungen (2442 A)

Provenance: 1868 Fritz Meyer; 1885 Frau Meyer (widow); 1905 Elika Meyer, Berlin; 1914 Professor Richard M. Meyer, Berlin; acquired by the museum in 1935.
Exhibitions: Berlin, 1868, no. 487; Paris, 1885, no. 229; Berlin, 1885, no. 9; Berlin, 1928, no. 38, reprod.; Berlin, 1980 A, no. XXVI, reprod. p. 151.
Bibliography: Die Dioskuren, 1868, p. 331; Gonse, 1885, p. 520 and 522; Jordan, 1890, p. 63, pl. 56; Jordan, 1895, no. 16, p. 46, p. 69; Jordan, 1905, p. 69; Tschudi, 1905 A, no. 129; Justi, 1932, p. 130 *et seq.*; Waldmann, 1941, p. 35, p. 48, fig. 66; Beenken, 1944, p. 333; Forster-Hahn, 1977, p. 265 et seq.; Forster-Hahn, 1980, p. 32–5; Hütt, 1981, fig. 89–91 (col.); Jensen, 1982, p. 100, p. 138, col. pl. 27; Zangs, 1992, p. 197–202; Niessing, 1993.

Menzel's second stay in Paris during the 1867 Universal Exhibition is well documented, both by his own letters and in detailed descriptions given by Paul Meyerheim. Twelve years earlier Menzel had spent two weeks in Paris, but this time he stayed for nine. We know he visited the Salon several times ('today it will be this alone; it would be madness to miss it')[2], and also the Louvre, and that he was impressed by the landscape painters of the school of Fontainebleau, Daubigny and Théodore Rousseau in particular. He also had a friendly relationship with Meissonier (*cf.* cat. 126), and visited Courbet's great retrospective with attention and some enthusiasm, since he admired his work with the palette knife and Courbet needed no persuasion to explain his technique to him[3]. He also assiduously frequented the 'Liederkranz', a circle of German artists who met in the Rue Lamartine, and possibly it was there that the reputation of the painter d'Ornans as being 'rather gross' was confirmed at a farewell evening for Knaus and Meyerheim[4].

When he returned, Menzel set to work immediately on this painting. It was finished before the end of the year, and inaugurated the mature painter's series of urban landscapes. In fact, it was not the first of its kind. *Lying in State of the March Dead* (fig. 65) had been painted twenty years before, and he rekindled the old concept. The fact that he began to paint as soon as he returned from Paris indicates the jolt he must have had. His youthful efforts, with no lineage, took on new meaning.

Tschudi[5] suggested a rapport with Manet's *Concert at the Tuileries*[6] (fig. 81), which Menzel could well have seen at the retrospective which Manet had organized in full awareness of its value, in parallel with that of Courbet. Since then constant parallels have been made between the two works, and they do belong to the same genre of representation of urban society. In France this theme can be traced back to the time of the Directory, to Debucourt and Boilly, made commonplace by nineteenth-century reproductive illustrations. Menzel might also have known watercolours by Constantin Guys, favoured by Baudelaire because of his theory of 'the heroism of modern life'. But these are surely further from his art than Manet's canvas, which is almost twice the size of Menzel's painting.

Manets composition consists of two opposing parts. The right foreground is crossed by all kinds of objects and the figure of a child, while the area on the left of the twisted tree trunk, with easily identifiable portraits of people looking at the onlooker, gives a contrasting feeling of clarity. It exposes the scene ostentatiously and almost like a quotation. The space is filled evenly, from the foreground to the calm horizon in the distance, dark and light nuances alternating with a regular rhythm, with red accents scattered over the surface of the canvas, showing different levels of depth.

In Menzel's painting, details appear like quotations from his Parisian colleague: the child crouching down in the same place in the foreground (a second child coming to find him is further away), the man leaning forward slightly and wearing a top hat, offering the same left profile to the onlooker, partially covered by a tree. But there is an abyss between the two works as regards the rest. Effortlessly, Manet carries the aesthetic of the old masters across the river on to the far bank of modern life, while Menzel is weighed down by tradition. Everything seems related to the model, but is denser, with more substance and colour. But the dark and light depend directly on the lighting instead of deriving from the immediate properties of the colour. His foreground seems to be full of sudden intrusions, people hurrying – none of whom bear any relation to the onlooker – who seem to embody confusion, 'lack of concentration' in all senses of the word. Narrow paths tear into the space, leading to imprecise shadows on the right, and to an undefined sunny brightness on the left. The central group under the tree moves towards the foreground like a sharp corner penetrating space, a motif that Menzel liked to use. To right and left, figures seek to depart from the foreground – which slips away from the viewer's gaze. The young man on the right recalls a figure from *Lying in State of the March Dead*, but it is not just the spatial organization of the painting, characterized by deep gashes, which is not repeated in this picture.

Max Jordan intended to be complimentary when he spoke of the instant vivacity of the rendering as creating an impression 'normally only captured by the camera obscura'[7]. When the work was presented to the public for the first time – with the title *Sunday in the Tuileries Gardens, from Memory* – a critic gave it a curious rubric: 'Genre painting – ethnographic and rococo genre'. Together with *Country Theatre in the Tyrol*[8], an earlier work shown in the same exhibition, *Afternoon in the Tuileries Gardens* led Max Schasler to offer one of his ambiguous opinions: 'The two paintings, notably in a format which is only appropriate to small genres, are treated as a kind of sketch, but with a lot of verve. The very varied motifs are full of characteristic authenticity, even if they only appear allusively. This kind of painting shows Menzel's predilection for darker tones, which are not lacking in strength and naturalness for all that'[9]. It did not stop a collector from buying it immediately.

It seems, however, that the painting was not popular at the 1885 Paris exhibition. According to Louis Gonse, 'the artist seems lacking in concentration, disorientated, outside his normal setting and environment'[10]. It is significant, however, that Menzel's setting and environment never offered more material, after his first effort in 1848, for the representation of large towns. The feeling of alienation which he felt in 'Babel', as he often called Paris, and in Verona, where his incomprehension of the language left him bereft of any sense of belonging, marks a visible stage on the journey towards modern themes.

C.K.

1. Letters to Hermann and Emilie Krigar, 3 and 29 June 1867, Wolff, 1914, p. 206–9; Meyerheim, (1906) 1992, p. 196-209.
2. Letter to Hermann and Emilie Krigar, 29 June 1867, Wolff, 1914, p. 209.
3. Meyerheim, (1906) 1992, p. 196–8.
4. Werner, 1993, p. 175.
5. Tschudi, 1905 B, p. 236 (p. 26), note 1.
6. 1862, London, National Gallery.
7. Jordan, 1905.
8. Painted in 1859, Tschudi, 1905 A, no. 122; Hamburg, Kunsthalle.
9. *Die Dioskuren*, 1868, col. 331.
10. Gonse, 1885, p. 522.

Fig. 196. *In the Tuileries*, 1867, pencil, Berlin, Kupferstichkabinett (sketchbook 28, p. 95)

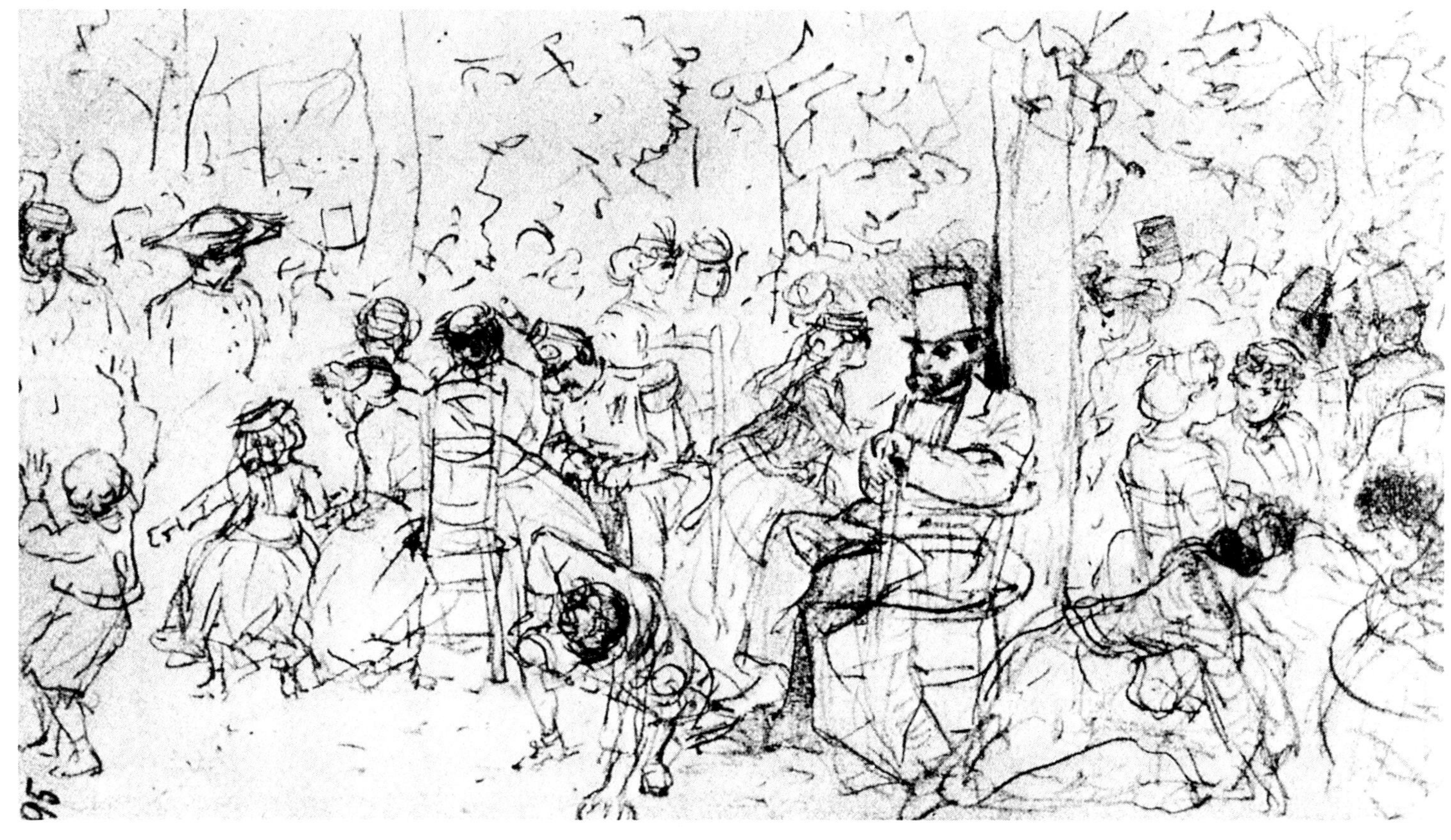

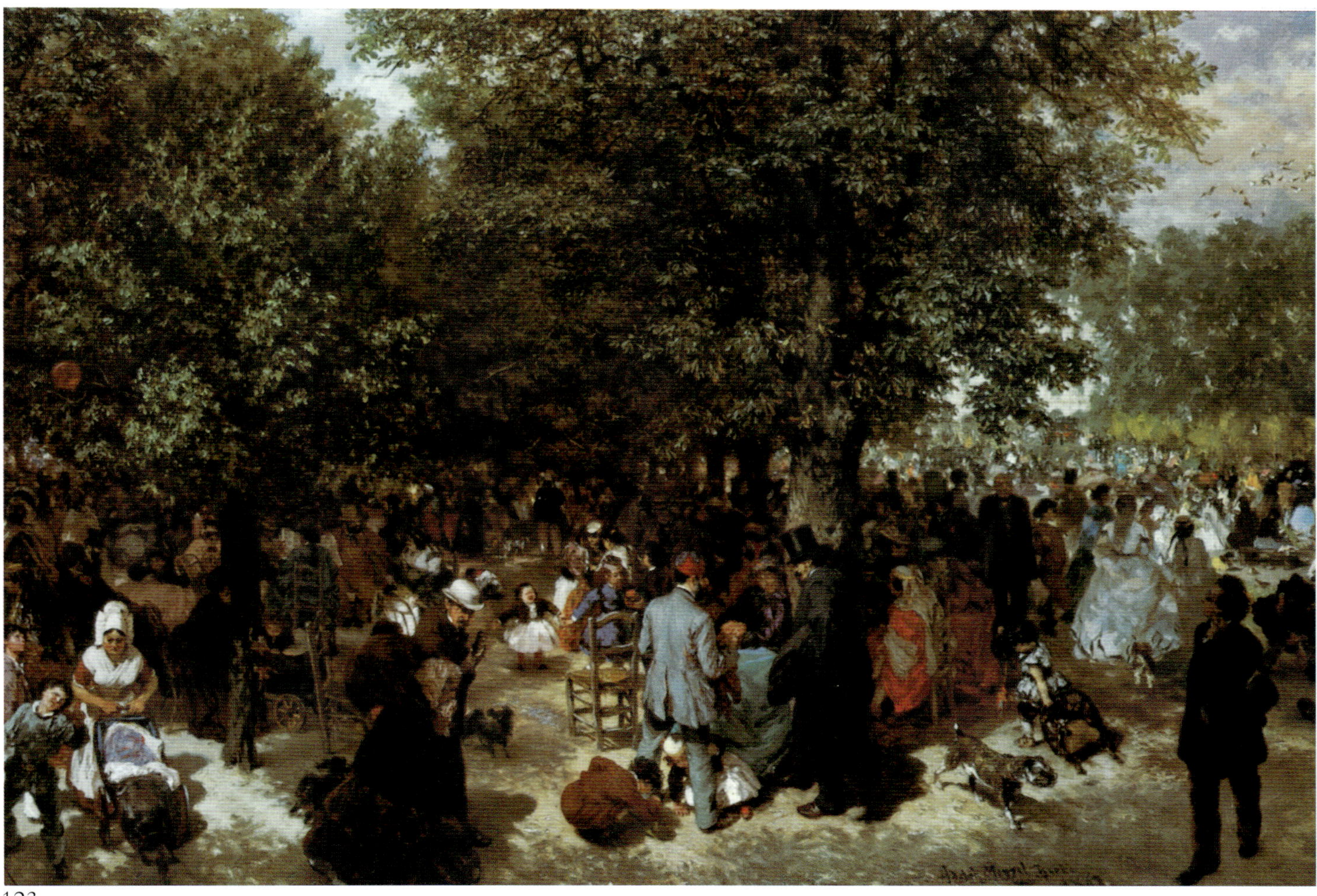

123

124
Borussia
1868 (January–February)

Oil on canvas
112.5 × 61.5cm
Signed and dated at the bottom right: *Menzel 1868* – Annotated on the back: *Prof. Menzel / Luisenstr. 27*
Berlin, Berlin Museum (on permanent loan from the German Federal Republic, GEM 66/43)
Exhibited in Berlin only

Provenance: Franz Mendelssohn, banker and commercial advisor in Berlin, who had bought the five paintings from the bazaar stall to help the poor in eastern Prussia (at Berlin Royal palace in 1868); 1905 still in his ownership.
Exhibitions: Berlin, 1885, no. 11; Berlin, 1905, no. 58.
Bibliography: Anon., 1867–8; Duranty, 1880, II, p. 108; Jordan, 1895, p. 33 *et seq.*, p. 69; Tschudi, 1905 A, no. 134; Lammel, 1993 A, p. 188, col. pl. 16; Beneke/Gramlich, 1994, no. 468, reprod.

Sometimes a foreigner can stand back from a work and be more objective about it. This was the case with Duranty[1], who saw in *Borussia* 'some of the rounded forms and drapery of Michaelangelo and Rubens', of the ancient Venetians and of Dürers *Melancholy*, which was so frequent in German nineteenth-century art. On the other hand, he also saw an 'unexpected and original note in the veiled, sad softness of the head, some royal portrait no doubt'. With the exception of the last remark, Duranty was right. There is another reference to venerable traditions in the unfurled cloak, made popular on pious virgins of the end of the middle ages. Yet the manifest refusal to idealize in any way flies in the face of tradition, as does the lack of unity of the image, which fails to determine a distance in relation to the onlooker. In spite of the raised viewpoint, the viewer here is surrounded by the extras in a *tableau vivant* where the plump, blonde principal actress seeks vainly to hide the awkwardness of her uncomfortable disguise. A year after the death of Peter Cornelius, the last great defender of Nazarene monumental art, Menzel locates the scene not as a historical ideal, but on the stage, which seems only too real, producing an ephemeral spectacle in which a touch of superior irony does not affect its basic seriousness.

A link between this *Borussia* and superficially comparable personages has been sought in vain, stimulating a patriotic identification with such figures as Germania, which abounded in German painting and sculpture after 1871. While the Romantic painters of the Nazarene circle of the first half of the century inte-

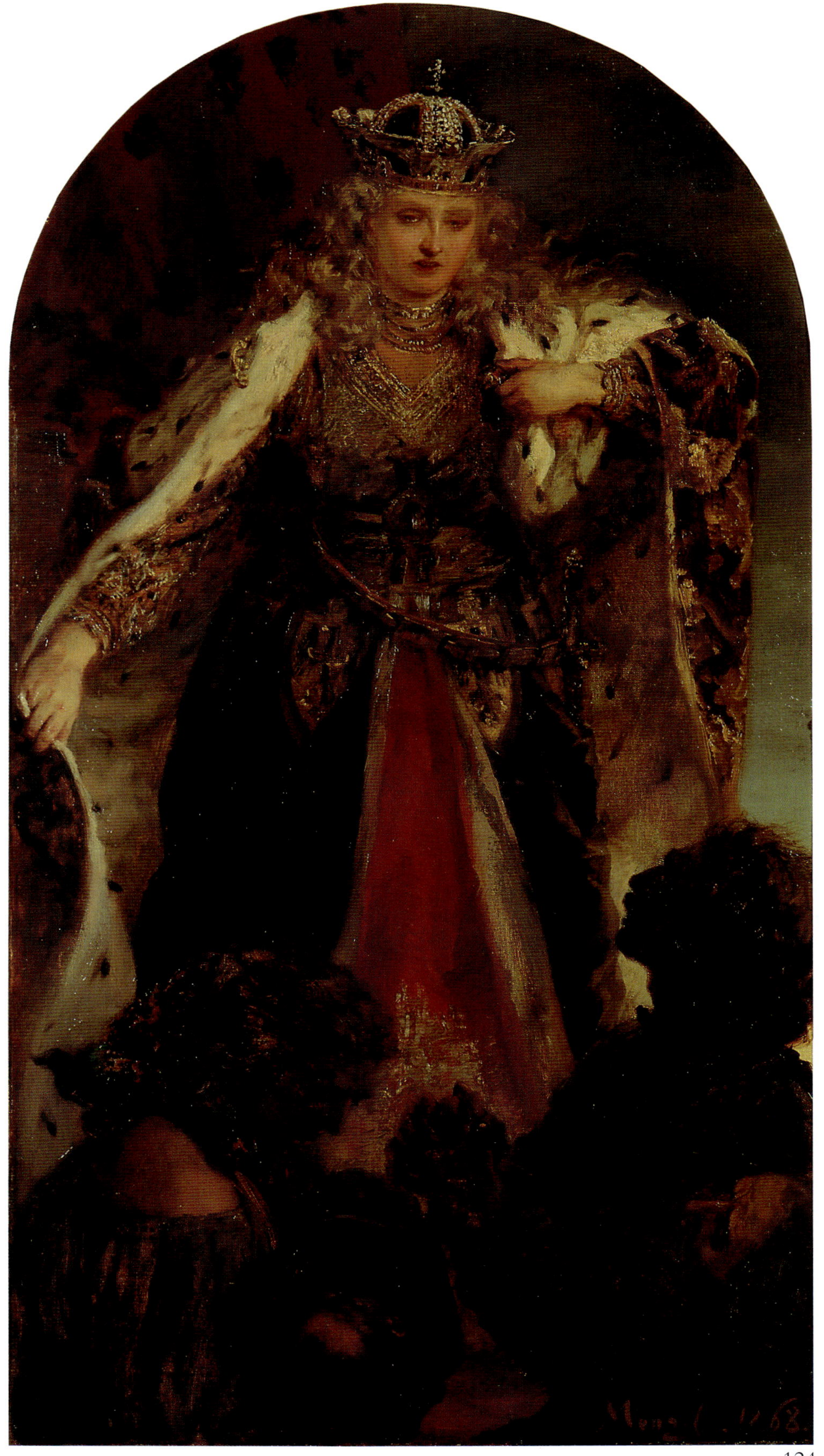

124

grated the personification of Germany in a pair of sisters or friends with elegiac touches (Italia and Germania), the Germania of the young empire was always isolated, wearing a breastplate, aggressive, as she was in the once famous paintings of Lorenz Clasen, *Germania on Guard on the Banks of the Rhine* and Hermann Wislicenus' *The sentinel beside the Rhine*[3]. The drawn sword is her main attribute, while in Menzel's painting, she is still wearing her fur cloak, and the tall figure is turning not towards a hostile horizon, but to the people, represented by a family. She has a caring, sympathetic expression as she starts to throw off her ermine cloak, seizing her precious necklace in readiness to sacrifice it.

It was not the victories in the wars of 1864 and 1866 (against Denmark and Austria), ensuring Prussia's final supremacy among the German states, which were aimed at here. The picture was painted for a charity sale for 'the welfare of the natives of East Prussia'[4], organized in February 1868 in the art gallery of Berlin palace. A wooden stall had been erected in the form of a pentagonal niche with elaborate mouldings and topped with a cupola. On the walls had been hung five pictures representing the provinces of the realm of Prussia (to which one of them, on the geographical periphery, had lent its name. 'The initial idea was to surround a Borussia plagued by poverty with all the other Prussian provinces ready to give assistance, representing for the first time the newly annexed territories next to the original and ancient provinces.' So Menzel's allegory does not evoke the Prussian monarchy but personifies one of its provinces, the former Prussia (separated from Germany in 1945)[5].

This explains the intensity of feeling conveyed by the soft, warm light enveloping the woman and from which she seems to rise up like a supernatural apparition, while, logically, the other figures remain against the light.

By way of comparison, a wood engraving illustrating the *Works of Frederick the Great*[6] shows Germania on a rock above dark clouds in which the numbers of the fatal year 1806 appear like a wake of fire. Her only attribute is her mural crown. This unarmed woman with her breast laid bare, is a mother, not a warrior. The German principalities which adorn the certificate of honorary citizen for Bismarck in 1871[7] appear to conform more to the usual type, in the form of a group of women wearing crowns. The Germania on the diploma painted for Moltke on the same occasion[8] stands under an elaborate canopy, wearing her crown. These figures are attired with pomp, yet any warlike characteristics are absent, in spite of the circumstance. One might also compare the figure of Hammonia in cat. 187. C.K.

1. Duranty, 1880, p. 108.
2. 1860, Krefeld, Kaiser Wilhelm Museum.
3. 1873, Berlin, Deutsches Historisches Museum.
4. Cf. Lammel, 1993 B, p. 188, for the different supportive action in which Menzel took part.
5. Pomerania and Posnania were added, painted by Fritz Kraus, Saxony and Silesia by Wilhelm Amberg, Rhineland, Nassau, Hesse, Westphalia and Schleswig-Holstein by Gustave Richter and Hanover by Carl Becker.
6. Bock, 1923, no. 900.
7. Tschudi, 1905 A, no. 595.
8. Tschudi, 1905 A, no. 596.

125

Sermon in the Beechwood at Kösen

1868

Oil on canvas
70 × 58cm
Signed and dated at the bottom left: *Adolph Menzel. Berlin 1868.*
Budapest, Szépmüvészeti Müzeum (386 B)
Exhibited in Paris and Berlin only

Provenance: 1870 Albert Arons, banker (who in 1834 had given his support to the financing of the Berlin–Leipzig railway line, a project which was postponed in favour of the development of the Berlin–Potsdam line); 1924 Frau Leo Arons; Bruno Cassirer, Berlin; acquired by the museum in 1926.
Exhibitions: Berlin, 1870, no.538; Vienna, 1873; Berlin, 1885, no. 13; Berlin, 1891, no. 727; Berlin, 1895 A, no. 49; Dresden, 1904, no. 2339; Berlin, 1980 A, no. XXVII, reprod. p. 216; Hamburg, 1983-4, no. 421, reprod.
Bibliography: Duranty, 1880, II, p. 122; Jordan/Dohme, 1890, p. 63, pl. 61, Kirstein, 1919, p. 113; Jordan, 1895, no. 17, p. 46, p. 52, p. 69; Beta, (1898) 1992, p. 51; Beta, (1899) 1992, p. 72; Tschudi, 1905 A, no. 132; Meier-Graefe, 1906, p. 208 *et seq.*, p. 212; Jensen, 1982, p. 102, p. 138, col. pl. 28.

Kösen was situated not far from Naumburg, through which flows the River Saale, rich in Romantic connotations and immortalized by a popular song written by none other than Franz Kugler. From 1815 onwards, the town was frequently visited as a spa, and after 1860 offered salt water baths to the public. Menzel had often used such a remedy, as indicated in the long letters he wrote when he was taking the waters at Freienwalde in 1861, and stayed at Kösen several times with his family after 1865. The parish was created after 1860, on account of the growing number of people taking the waters there, and for a long time there was only a temporary place of worship. Services were held in a beech clearing, whose foliage formed a kind of vault, on the road to the picturesque mediaeval ruins of Rudelsburg. These services were sometimes organized by the Gustav-Adolph foundation, created in 1832, which collected funds to finance missions in non-European countries[1].

A sketch[2] formed the basis for this

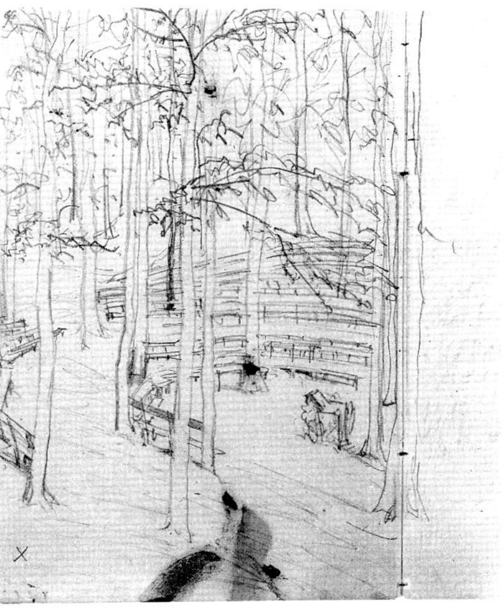

Fig. 197. *Beech Clearing at Kösen*, 1864–5, pencil, Berlin, Kupferstichkabinett (sketchbook 27, p. 66)

composition (fig. 197). It shows a beech clearing from the same angle, but without any people in it. Menzel did several other drawings at Kösen. In 1865, he painted a gouache, *Young Bathers in the Saale near Kösen*[3], and three years later, as if in synthesis of his observations, he produced the painting of Budapest whose original title had the additional note 'Adapted from memory', a term often used by Menzel which underlined the authenticity of the elements of the picture. Clearly what attracts his attention is the coming together of two phenomena, the crowd of people and the countryside, which is occupied, used, transformed and above all ignored with a totally modern casualness, challenging the ideal of 'nature' inherited from Romanticism. Here Menzel is paving the way for his urban landscapes full of crowds. The modernity of his vision is evident if we recall a canvas by Max Liebermann, his great admirer. In his *Commemoration Ceremony at Kösen*[4], painted twenty years later, a large empty space in the foreground and the balance of several vertical parallel lines created an air of calm and concentration. In the congregation of the faithful, no one stands out in particular. A man with his hand resting a little too

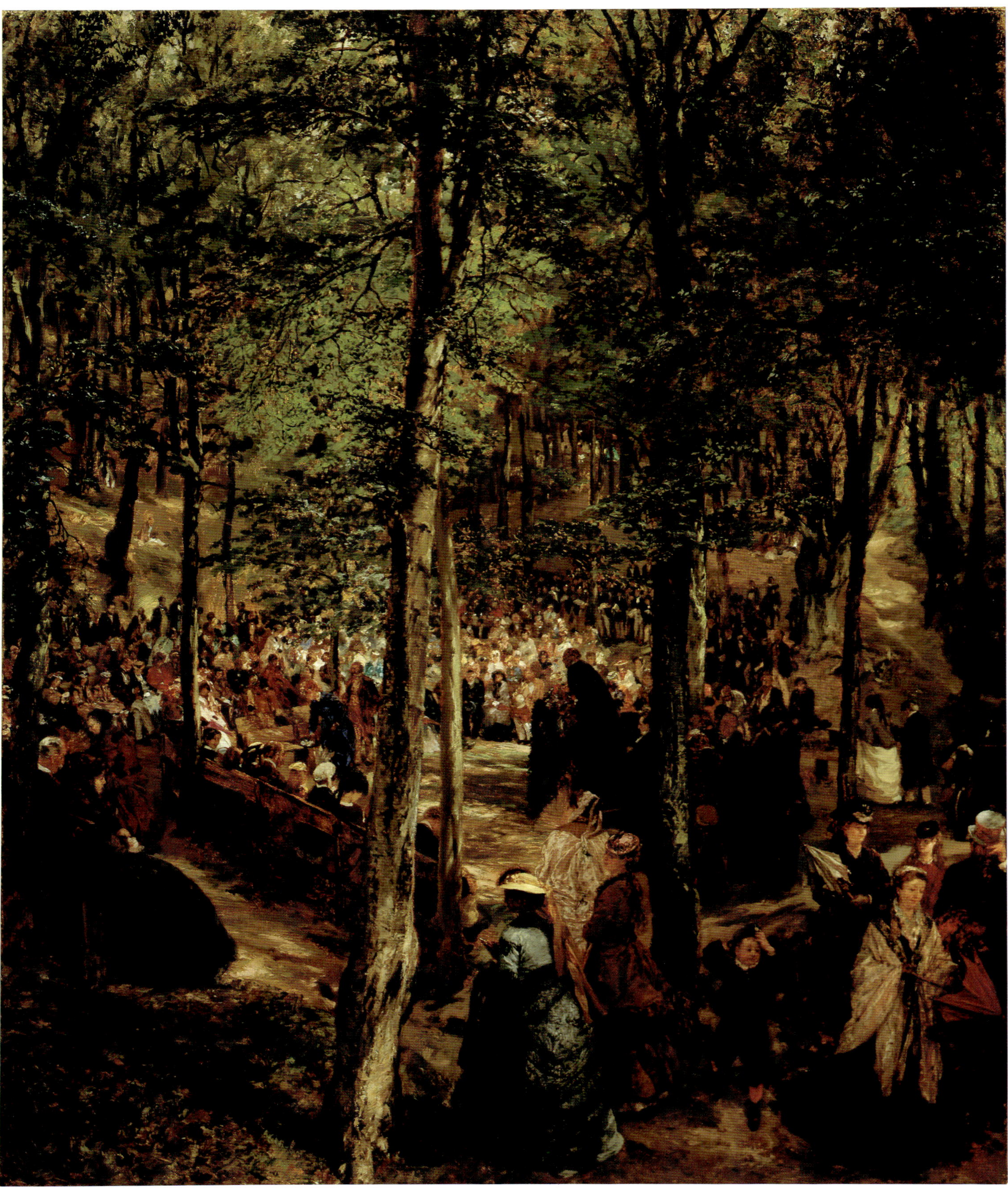

125

comfortably on his hip, towards the back part of the middle ground, is only just noticeable. In contrast, in Menzel's painting, the whole composition, from foreground to background, is movement, inattentiveness, centrifugal force, social chit-chat and bourgeois vanity. While a lady of some social standing hastily looks for her place in the front row, others leave, breaking up the angle of the painting. An empty space occupies the centre of the composition, but it is also dominated all the more freely by an extremely fragmented light, which seems to have to force its way through the large space between the treetrunks and thickets. C.K.

1. Information provided by Lutz Toepfer, Bad Kösen.
2. In sketchbook 27 (1864-5), p. 66. Another preparatory drawing: Berlin, Kupferstichkabinett (SZ Menzel Kat 1058).
3. Tschudi, 1905 A, no. 419; today in a private Spanish collection.
4. In memory of the emperor Frederick III, who died in 1888. One of the two versions is in the Tate Gallery in London, and the other used to be on view in the Budapest museum not far from Menzels work, but it was destroyed in 1945. The happy confrontation was replicated temporarily during the Hamburg exhibition of 1983-4, with the help of the London version.

126

Meissonier in his Studio at Poissy

1869

Oil on canvas
22.3 × 29.9cm
Signed and dated at the bottom, to the right of centre: *Adolph Menzel Berl. 1869*
San Francisco, The Fine Arts Museum (Jacob Stern Permanent Loan Collection)
Exhibited in Washington only

Provenance: According to the painter[1], the picture was purchased by an American as soon as it was finished. According to Meyerheim, it went missing until it was rediscovered by Hermann Pächter; 1905 Jacob Stern, San Francisco.
Bibliography: Vollmar, 1904–5 B, p. 183; Tschudi, 1905 A, no. 136; Meyerheim, (1906) 1992, p. 208 *et seq.*; Forster-Hahn, 1980, p. 36, reprod. p. 37; Jensen, 1982, p. 104, p. 139, col. pl. 29; Lammel, 1993 B, p. 169, fig. 111.

Paul Meyerheim, who accompanied Menzel at the Universal Exhibition until he 'was so tired he could drop', described the painter's second stay in Paris in 1867 in great detail[2]. Thanks to him we know that Menzel had a very high opinion of Courbet, whom he had met personally. He said that all Courbet's paintbrushes should be confiscated, as only the work he did using his palette knife was excellent. Meyerheim also tells us that Menzel knew the painter Louis Gustave Ricard (1823–73) very well. His portraits were greatly valued, and Meyerheim describes him as 'an epigone, an alchemist, an assayer', and as 'one of the nicest people, and a real virtuoso in the art of conversation'. Ricard did a portrait of Menzel[3], and Menzel did the same in return, which he described as 'the figure of a bogey-man'[4]. In *Meissonier in his Studio at Poissy*, Ricard is standing in the background next to Mme Meissonier. Menzel's visit to Ernest Meissonier is also described in detail by Meyerheim. Meissonier was exactly the same age as Menzel, and had been extremely successful for a long time due to his historical genre paintings which brought him in large amounts of money. He had then spent several years painting history proper. In the year of the visit, 1867, Charles Blanc wrote that there was no equivalent to his style. Since 1846 he had owned a beautiful country house in Poissy, with a stable to house his horses and to assist his animal studies. Théophile Gautier wrote that 'some of the rooms themselves are worthy of framing. They are as valuable as the masters paintings, of which they are the copies'[5]. The painter, who, like Menzel, was short of stature, can also be seen in a photograph from *c.* 1860–3 (fig. 199) leaning against the door of his summer studio, the one in the Menzel painting. The photo shows the same easel and one of the greyhounds given to him by Alexandre Dumas fils.

Meissonier had a great affinity with his German visitor whom he had already met in Berlin, and it is recorded that he admired the *Address at Leuthen* (cat. 90)[6]. They had a common passion for history

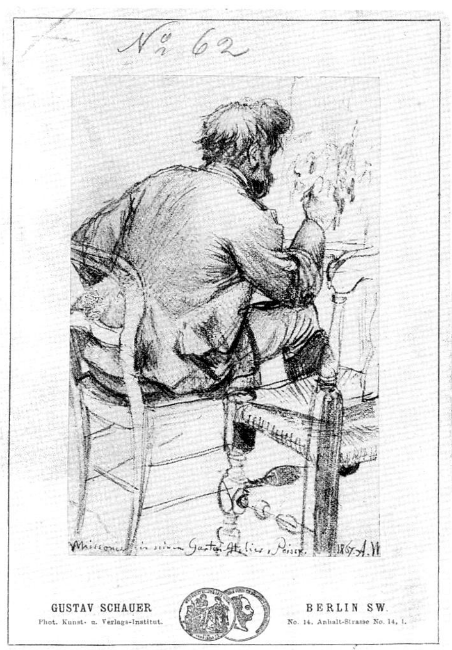

Fig. 198. Meissonier Working on *Solferino*, 1867, pencil (photograph)

Fig. 199. *Meissonier in his Studio at Poissy*, *c.* 1860–3 photograph

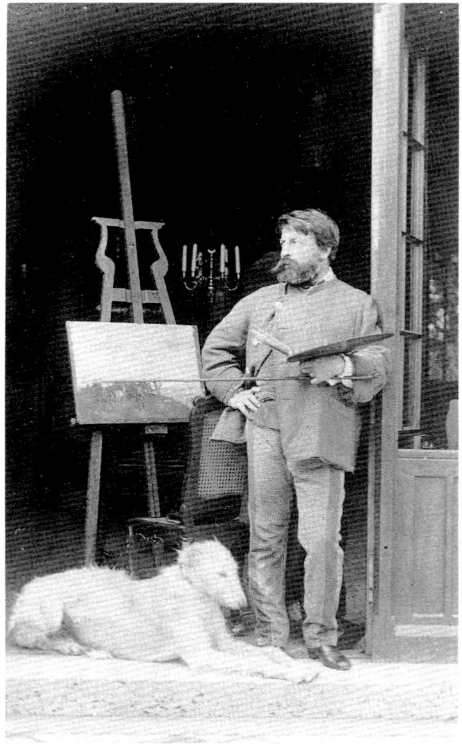

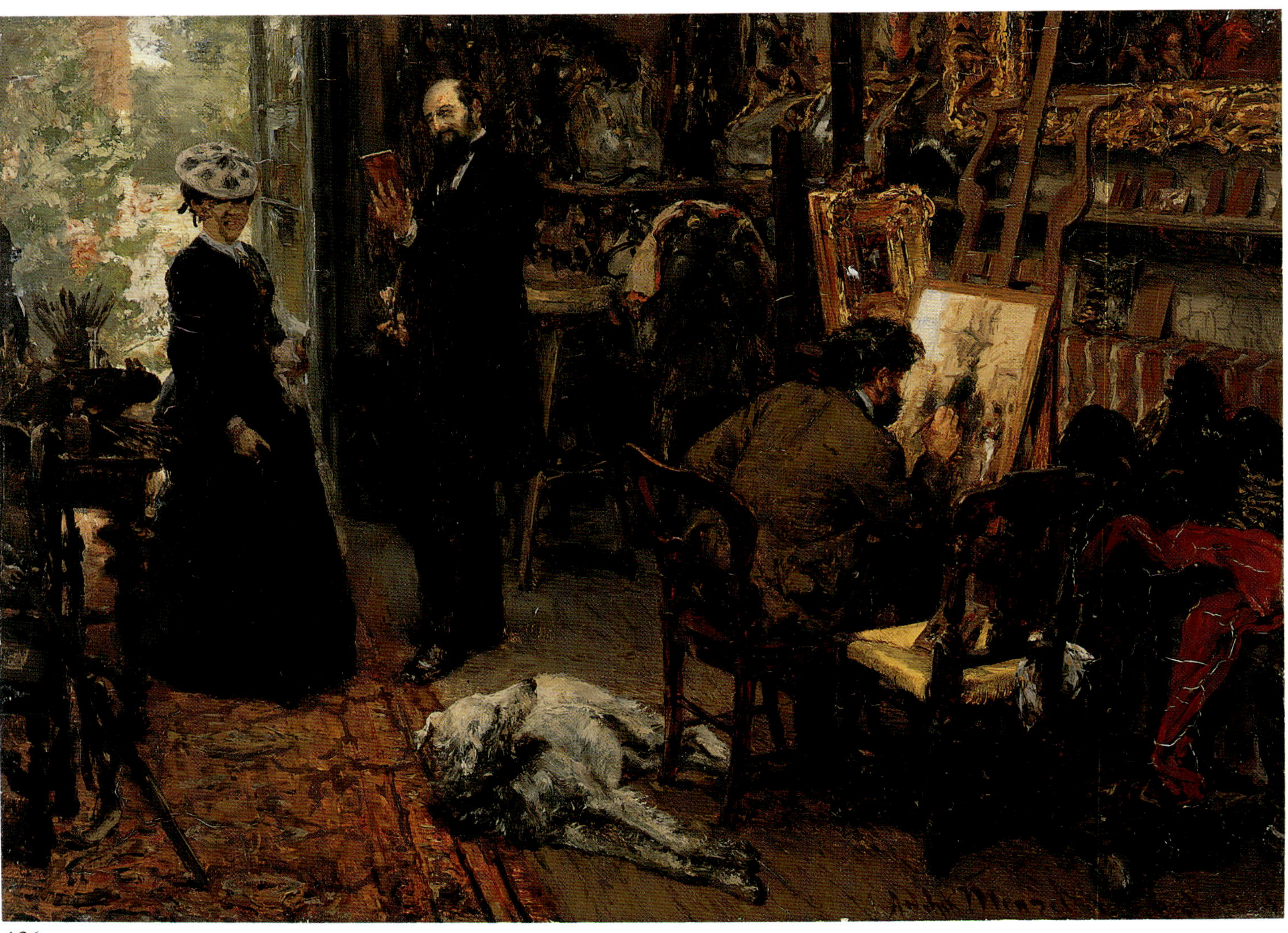

126

and a liking for small-format works. If Meissonier, a virtuoso of reproduction, had a greater liking for detail, their experience of the 1848 Revolution was remarkably parallel. While Menzel was working on *Lying in State of the March Dead*, Meissonier was painting the corpses of the barricade fighters lying in the street. Their work was a kind of confession for them both[7].

However, a standing self-portrait of Meissonier, exhibited in 1867, depicts him as a dignified Venetian gentleman wearing a red velvet overcoat[8], and nothing illustrates more clearly what separates the two artists. Menzel must have seen this portrait, yet his painting contrasts with this majestic composition in its restlessness, in the scene where the presence of the elegant guests emphasizes the painter's total absorption in his activity, his hair tousled and his jacket crumpled. The luxurious interior decor, particularly on the right of the picture, creates a disconcerting cluttered effect, and contrasts with the narrow view outside. The woman coming into the room seems to bring the outdoor brightness with her. In the background is visible one of the sculpted studies of a horse which Meissonier modelled in the 1860s for his paintings on the Napoleonic era. (Later, he would share Menzel's keen interest in the snapshots of horses trotting and galloping taken by Eadweard Muybridge).

Menzel kept until the day he died the small bronze elephant by Barye which Meissonier had given him. The little sculpture appears as a symbol in a drawing done in his old age, entitled *End of the Game* (fig. 114), depicting the empty studio in the Sigismundstrasse[9]. As if it suddenly takes on a life of its own, the animal tries to escape from the picture and overturns a stool, possibly foreshadowing the painter's death. When Menzel created this allegory in 1895, Meissonier had already been dead for four years. The 1870–1 war had violently destroyed their friendship. Like many of his compatriots, Meissonier had severed all relations with Germany. Not content with refusing the Prussian Order of Merit[10], he renounced any further contact with Germans and proudly declared: 'No German has set foot in my house since the war, nor shall do[11]. 'Menzel and all my other contacts had the honour of coming to my house. I have not seen them since 1871 and I will never see them again'[12].

A drawing done in 1867 shows Meissonier sitting down[13] (fig. 198) , and two others of Meissonier and his dog appear in a sketchbook[14]. C.K.

1. Vollmar, 1904-5 B, p. 93.
2. Meyerheim, (1906) 1992, p. 194-210, plate facing p. 102.
3. Letter to Ludwig Pietsch, Paris, no date [1867], Nuremberg, Germanisches Nationalmuseum.
4. Giraud, 1932, p. 302. Jensen, 1982 was right in recognizing Ricard in the portrait of a bearded man (Euerbach, George Schäfer collection) which he had already published without identifying it (exhib. cat. Kiel, 1981, no. 90, reprod.). It was confirmed by the reproduction in Girauds book.
5. Quoted by Agnès Dupasquier-Guignard, exhib. cat. Lyon, 1993, p. 68.
6. Meyerheim, (1906) 1992, p. 195.
7. *Recollection of the civil war.* He offered the sketch for the watercolour to Delacroix (now in a private collection). The small format version in oil is in the Louvre. *Cf.* exhib. cat Lyon, 1993, p. 162-165, and exhib. cat. Hamburg, 1978-9, p. 88-90.
8. *Reading,* location unknown. Reprod. in Gréard, 1897, p. 217.
9. Location unknown (reprod. p. 111).
10. Gréard, 1897, p. 127.
11. *Ibid.*, p. 307.
12. *Ibid.*, p. 308.
13. Munich, Staatliche Graphische Sammlung.
14. Berlin, Kupferstichkabinett, sketchbook 28, p. 12, p. 101.

127

Weekday in Paris

1869

Oil on canvas
48.4 × 69.5cm
Düsseldorf, Kunstmuseum (4433)
Exhibited in Paris and Washington only

Provenance: 1869 Lepke Gallery, Berlin; 1869–74 collection of the great industrialist and 'king of the railroad', Bethel Henry Strousberg, in Berlin; after the latter's spectacular bankruptcy, the work passed to the banker Adolph von Liebermann, who was in turn obliged to give it up in 1875; James Duncan collection, London; 1886 Eduard I. Behrens, Hamburg; in the 1920s stored at the Kunsthalle in Hamburg; Paffrath gallery, Düsseldorf; acquired by the museum in 1935.
Exhibitions: Berlin, 1869; Berlin, 1870, no. 537; Munich, 1883; Hamburg, 1887; Berlin, 1895 A, no. 51; Hamburg, 1896, no. 5; London, 1903; Düsseldorf, 1904, no. 13; Berlin, 1955 B, no. 109, fig. 53; Berlin, 1980 A, no. XXVIII, reprod. p. 218; Paris, 1984–5, no. 104, reprod.
Bibliography: Jordan, 1890, pl. 65; Heilbut, 1891, p. 99–101, pl. facing p. 110; Jordan, 1895, no. 18, p. 46, p. 69; Tschudi, 1905 A, no. 135; Heilbut, 1905, p. 226; Meier-Graefe, 1906, p. 214–16; Scheffler, 1922, p. 198; Waldmann, 1941, p. 35, p. 48. fig. 67; Andree, 1968, p. 72–5; Forster-Hahn, 1978, p. 267 *et seq.*; Hütt, 1981, fig. 95–6 (col.); Jensen, 1982, p. 106 *et*

127

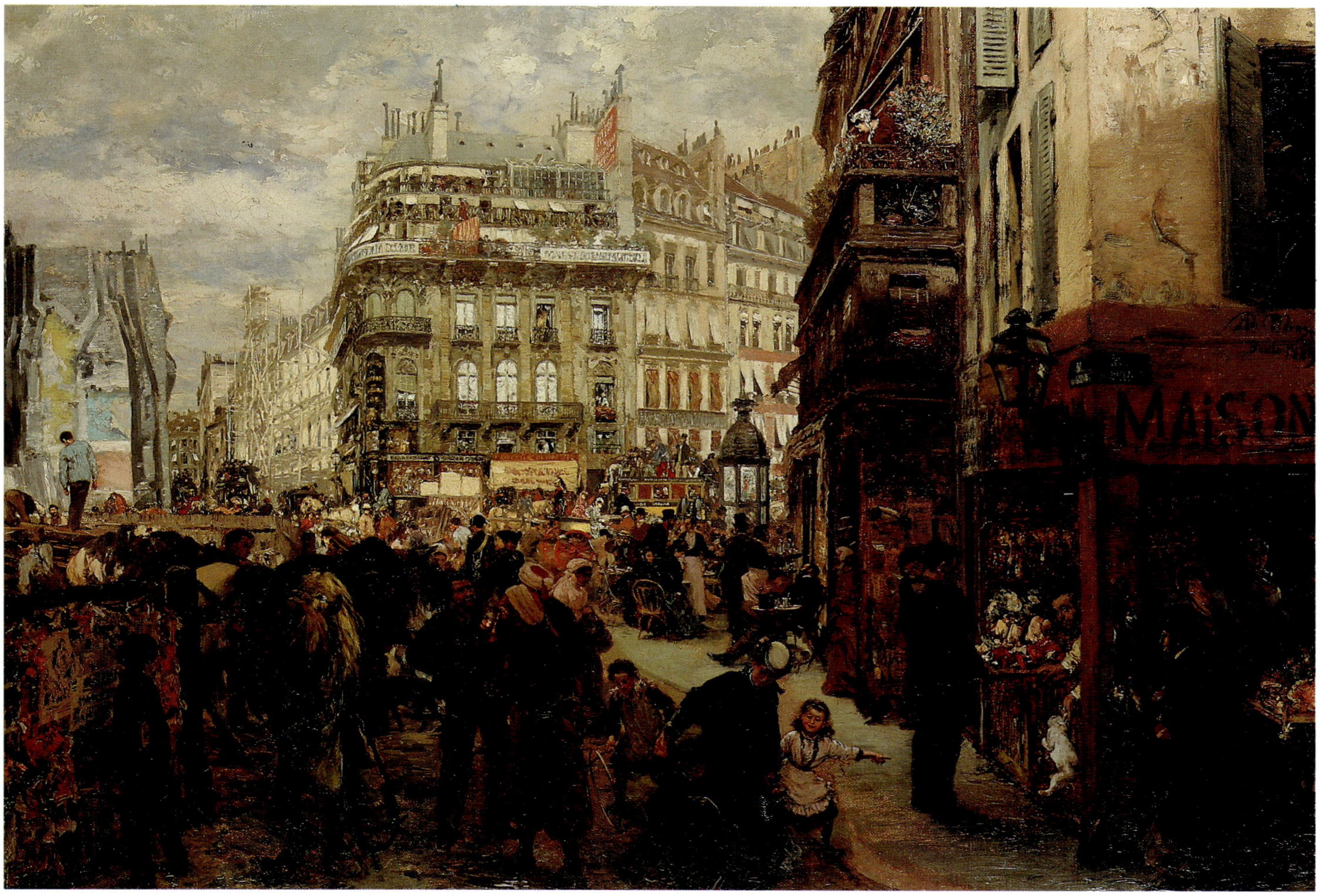

seq., col. p. 30; Wirth, 1990, p. 290, p. 292, fig. 364; Zangs, 1992, p. 199–202.

In terms of its size and theme, *Weekday in Paris* might have been conceived as a complement to *Afternoon in the Tuileries Gardens*[1] (cat. 123), but it was painted when the latter had already been sold. Like all the paintings of Menzel's mature years, it immediately found a buyer. It is characteristic of the reception Menzel's work received that the first two resales of the picture were due to the bankruptcy of the great Berlin businessmen who owned it.

'It is a fragment made up of fragments', wrote Emil Heilbut in 1891, who then undertook an unusual task, but one appropriate to this work. He described it down to the very last detail, without leaving out the figures farthest away in the background, nor the people at the windows nor the bus passengers, taking eight printed pages to do so. Later, he was to emphasize the links between subject-matter and form in Menzel's painting. In his view, the focus on the Zouaves in their brightly coloured clothes (*cf.* also cat. 78) was a sign of Menzel's philistine 'penchant for the bizarre'. However, when a Zouave lights a pipe and the light from the match illuminates his dark, weather-beaten skin in *Weekday in Paris*, the 'penchant for the bizarre' becomes a 'penchant for the picturesque'[2].

The lack of unity of the whole is even more striking in this picture than it is in *Afternoon in the Tuileries Gardens*. It is not exceptional for the composition to be a compilation of fragmentary observations of diverse origin, nor for the drawings used to be taken from different occasions[3]. Yet the fact that this is immediately obvious, and is even accentuated intentionally, gives a feeling of strangeness to both the detail and the picture overall. 'Menzel', wrote Meier-Graefe, does not move back from the surface of his canvas 'to relate all the rest to the immoveable limits of the painting, but takes a new point of view for each detail, in order to arrive at the model, not at the painting. He . . . moves close to each figure, studies it, chats and then abandons it to continue with same vain conversation with the next'[4]. This remark is a kind of reproach ('The source of his zeal is a burning passion for man, the source of new discoveries, which are sterile for the artist'), but it accurately describes the concrete progress of the painter in creating a multiplicity of perspectives, as well as the effect of his painting, perceived in its most modern and disquieting guise. It is as if an entire range of incompatible things have been brought together in the composition. The space which is the road is invaded by busy people – the jam-packed platforms of three buses are carrying those who could find no room inside, and the animal world erupts into urban civilization in the form of a draught horse. Each person attends to his business. In the foreground the painter has seized on a group preparing to leave in a hurry. The notices attached to the railing, to the wall and the ornamental advertising pillar, the coloured and disparate interior of a house cut in half before it is completely demolished, all emphasize the impression of a collage, of things which are broken up, which characterizes the whole. The plunging lines of the houses on the right with a woman on the balcony will reappear two years later in the *Departure of King William I for the Army* (cat. 134).

When this picture was exhibited for the first time in the Lepke Gallery in Berlin, it was in the company of works by French painters such as Meissonier, Bouguereau, Rosa Bonheur, Decamps and Vibert[5]. As a sign of friendship towards Meissonier, (*cf.* cat. 126), Menzel included his friend in the middle ground, sitting at a café terrace, from a drawing made of the Henri IV café. C.K.

1. Forster-Hahn, 1978.
2. Heilbut, 1903.
3. Rolf Andree, 1968, identified them. Berlin, Kupferstichkabinett: figure studies, SZ Menzel N948, 949, 2976, 2975; some sketches from sketchbooks 28 (1866-7) and 30 (1867-8); a series of sketches from sketchbook 31 (1868).
4. Meier-Graefe, 1906, p. 228.
5. *Die Dioskuren*, 14, 1869, p. 221.

128

Choirstalls in Mainz Cathedral

186

Gouache
31 × 24.5cm
Signed and dated at the bottom right: *Ad. Menzel Mainz 1869*
Mainz, Landesmuseum (GS 1959/18)
Exhibited in Paris and Berlin only

Provenance: Painter's studio; 1905 Emilie Krigar-Menzel, Berlin; Ingrid Brebeck, granddaughter of Emilie Krigar-Menzel, Eutin; acquired by the museum in 1959.
Exhibitions: Berlin, 1905, no. 295; Berlin, 1955 B, no. 112.
Bibliography: Tschudi, 1905 A, no. 573.

The extraordinary magnificence of the baroque choirstalls of Mainz Cathedral, completed in 1767 by Franz Anton Hermann, inspired Menzel to paint three works in colour. He probably sketched a plan of the stalls on site, in his 1869 sketchbook[1], a technique he sometimes used to get a feel for the space. During the year that he visited Mainz in the summer, he painted an oil sketch showing the imposing choirstalls with a priest and choirboys[2], using bold, passionate lines. A gouache also dates from this period, depicting the whole length of the choirstalls flooded with sunlight, with a verger in the foreground[3], together with the tall picture shown here which only gives a detail, the statue of a bishop above the door. The undulating forms of the statue and the two angels at its side dance against the light on the entablature as if they are on a wild sea. The male caryatids supporting the entablature, which are on each side of the door must have attracted Menzel's attention, as he used a similar motif in his *Diploma for the Fiftieth Anniversary of the Heckmann Factory* (cat. 129). M.R.-R.

1. Berlin, Kupferstichkabinett, sketchbook 33, p. 45–6.
2. Not mentioned by Tschudi; Berlin, Nationalgalerie.
3. Tschudi, 1905 A, no. 573; location unknown.

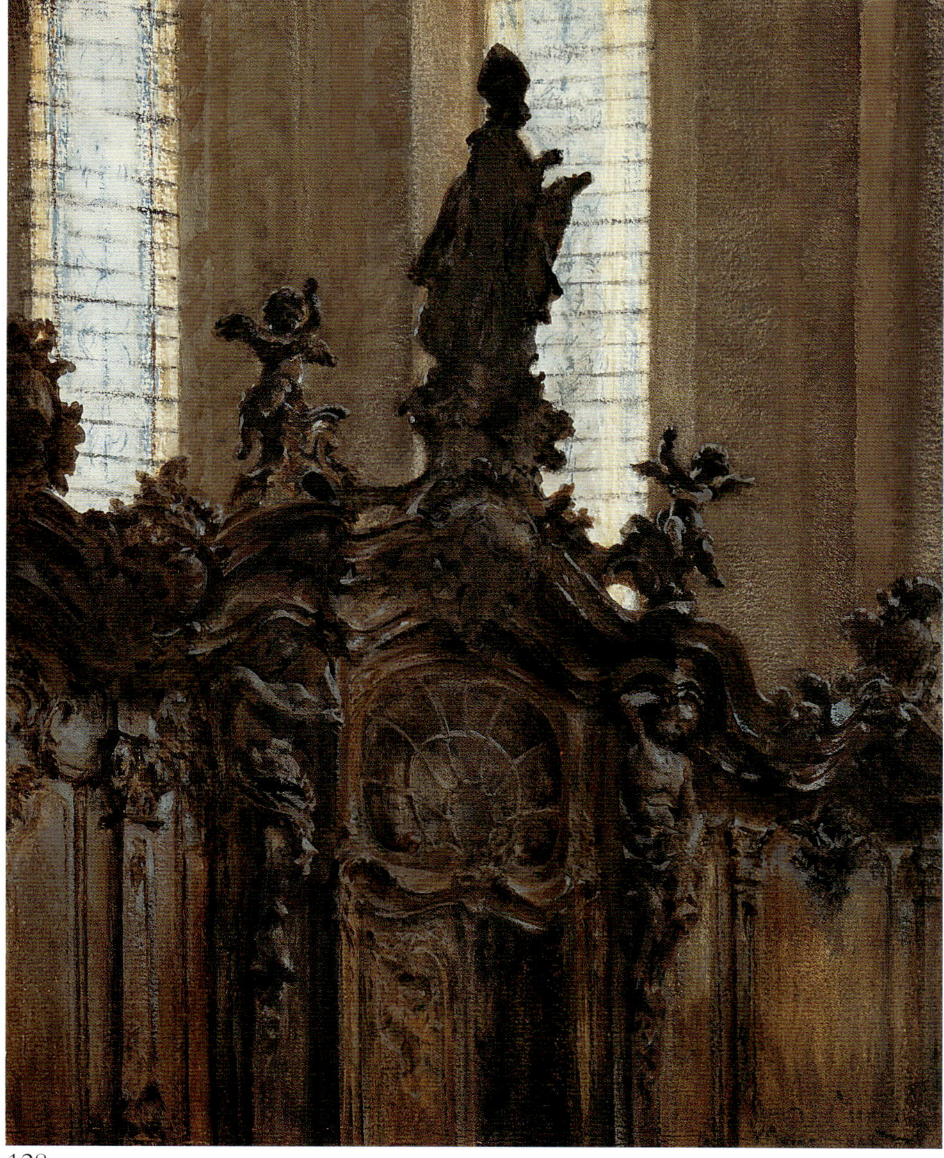
128

129

Diploma for the Fiftieth Anniversary of the Heckmann Factory
1869

Gouache
50 × 61cm
Signed and dated at the bottom right: *Adolph Menzel Berlin 1869*. Text below the two scenes: *Tausend Jahre sind ein Tag – 50 aber ein halb Jahrhundert* – Beneath, in letters forming a chain: *Aller Anfang ist schwer*
Berlin, Kupferstichkabinett (SZ Menzel Nr 1777)

Provenance: Carl Justus Heckmann, industrialist, Berlin; Georg Heckmann; acquired by the museum in 1911.

Exhibitions: Berlin, 1885, no. 67; Paris, 1885, no. 237; Berlin, 1895 A, no. 85; Düsseldorf, 1904, no. 76; Berlin, 1905, no. 248; Berlin, 1955 A, no. 381; Berlin, 1980 A, no. 58, col. reprod. p. 186; Vienna, 1985, no. 114, col. reprod. p. 70; Copenhagen, 1985, no. 105, col. reprod. p. 66; New York, 1990, no. 50, reprod. p. 165.
Bibliography: Jordan/Dohme, 1890, vol. I, p. 70; Jordan, 1895, p. 51 *et seq.*, p. 69; Tschudi, 1905 A, no. 570; Scheffler, 1922, p. 165, reprod. p. 119; Kaiser, 1953, p. 16 *et seq.*, Kaiser, 1956, p. 98, fig. 63; Riemann-Reyher, 1976, p. 3 *et seq.*; Hütt, 1981, p. 150, fig. 120; Jensen, 1982, p. 41, fig. 38; Lammel, 1993 A, p. 34, p. 139 *et seq.*, fig. 8 (col.).

In Menzel's book of receipts, dating from 1858 to 1904, he entered the following in November 1869: '. . . for the commemorative composition in gouache: 1, 983 thalers and 20 silver sous'[1]. In the same year he had received a commission for an illustrated diploma commemorating the fiftieth anniversary of a brass, copper and iron factory, whose founder Carl Justus Heckmann, had just been appointed private commercial advisor (Geheimer Kommerzienrat).

The diploma created for Heckmann far surpasses the majority of Menzel's other work of this kind in its originality and freshness (*cf.* cat. 53, 187). Its uniqueness lies in the deliberate blending together of a frame in the fashion of the time with two scenes of workers taken from the Heckmann factory and portrayed with realism. This internal conflict between convention and personal tendency is apparent throughout Menzel's entire work, and perhaps is the source of its originality. Here it unfolds to a very great extent, within a special piece of work. No sketch is known for the imaginative frame, in contrast with those for the modern working scenes with their light effects created by smoke and fire, which were prepared in the minutest detail. A liking for this kind of ornamentation had developed, under the influence of the rediscovery of Dürer's prayer book at the start of the century. Its impact had increased after the celebrations for the tricentenary of his death in 1828, and Menzel used this predilection while playing with it. Here the frame serves to draw attention to the two views of the foundry, with workers melting the metal in the furnace on the left, and casting it on the right. Menzel's first sketches made on an industrial production site appear in the 1869–71 sketchbook[2]. Detailed studies of location come from the Hermann factory itself, situated at Schlesische Strasse in Berlin (fig. 200), and are reproduced faithfully in the diploma. Menzel's fascination with such a contemporary theme does not diminish until *The Iron Rolling Mill*.

The apparent discrepancy between the realistic scenes and the decoration later gave rise to many incomprehending

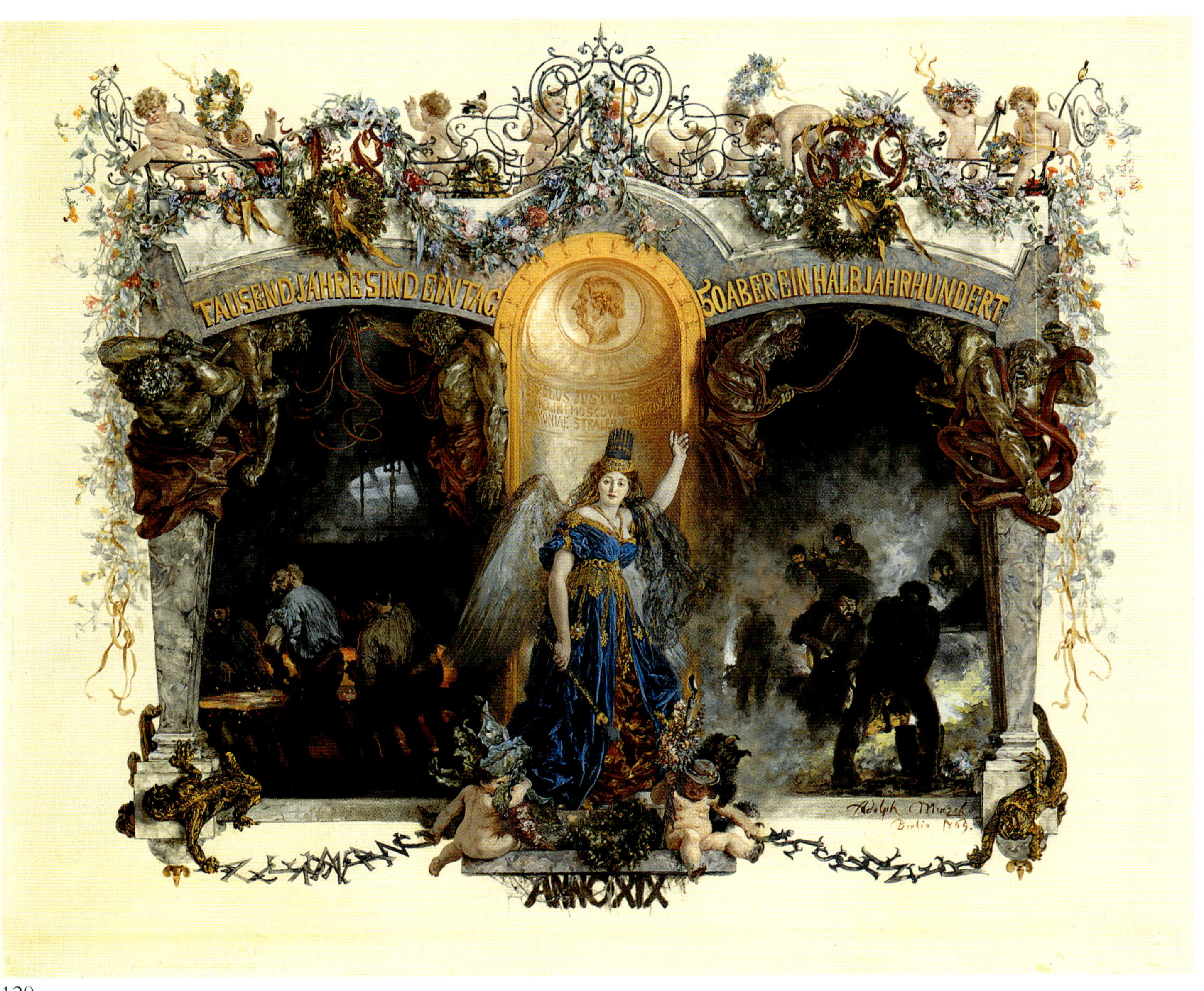

129

judgements of the work. If the decorative frame is examined carefully it can be seen to be a subtle enigma, drawn with a lightness of touch. Its unravelling forms its special charm. The composition is based on marble architecture. Behind the vaguely baroque ornamentation, the façade of the factory can be seen, and a kind of terrace is supported by six male caryatids, who look rather like cyclops. Entwined in metal ropes, they evoke the antique statue of Laocoön and his two sons crushed by serpents. The large door-like openings allow the viewer to look into the factory halls. A gilded niche separating them forms the median axis of the composition, inside which a winged woman is standing. Her left arm reaches upwards to the semicircular surface of the apse, where the founder of the company appears in a medallion, with the names of towns relating to the companys international business listed below. The womans attributes – her iron crown, chains and cog-wheels on her dress – suggest Fortune, or perhaps she represents some female owner of the firm. The inscription 'A thousand years are but a single day – but fifty are half a century' (Menzel's adaptation of Psalm 90, verse 4) appears on the architraves, and in response a chain of forged letters forming a garland on either side of the year of the firms foundation, 'Year XIX', state: 'All beginnings are hard'. Heckmann began his career as a coppersmith, and set up in business in Berlin in 1819. There are other allusions to the art of the forge, and also to the peasant origins of the family, which later was among the richest in Berlin. A letter from Fontane to his wife, dated 19 October 1869, indicates the familiarity felt by Menzels contemporaries with a picture abounding to this degree with allusions: '. . . At six o'clock I went to the Rütli circle at Menzel's house, where we weighed up the pros and cons of Glucks *Armide*. Eventually Menzel showed us a new watercolour (similar to the Monbijou one) which he had painted for old Heckmann's fiftieth anniversary. Brilliant! Its one of his most beautiful works of this kind, quite ingenious, with splendid colours, and easy to understand. A success at all levels. What pleasure it gave me to be able to shake his hand sincerely and straightforwardly[3].

M.R.-R.

1. Unpublished, private collection.
2. Berlin, Kupferstichkabinett, sketchbook 34. A very first sketch of a worker near a power hammer, accompanied by several blacksmiths appears in a sketchbook (no. 18, p. 40–1) of 1855, and was possibly drawn in Paris.
3. Fontane, 1968-71, vol. I, p. 1968 and ff.; the Monbijou watercolour – this relates to cat. 53, then exhibited at the Hohenzollern museum in the Monbijou castle at Berlin.

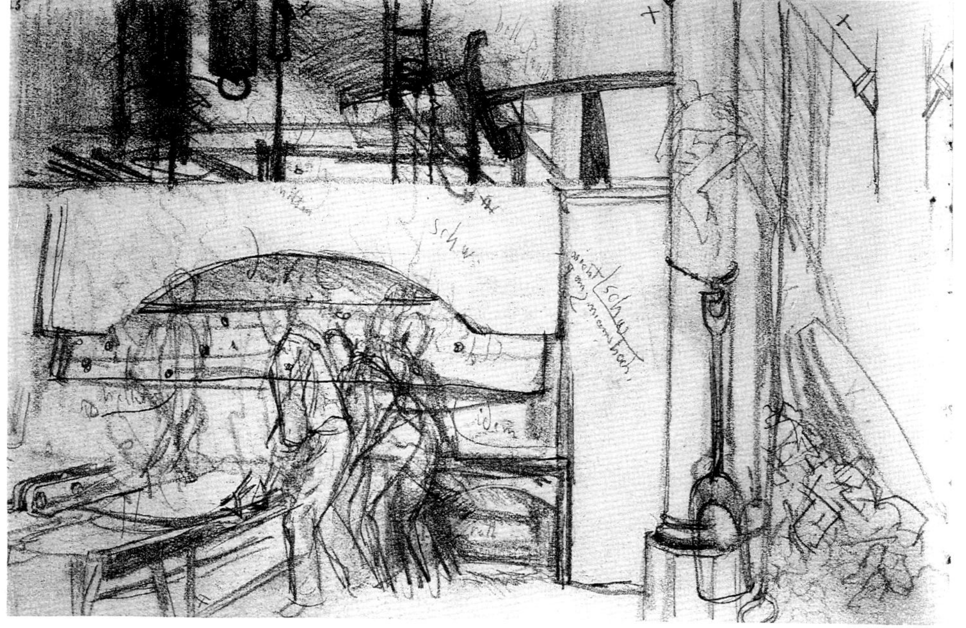

Fig. 200. *Workers at the Heckmann metal factory*, 1869–71, pencil, Berlin, Kupferstichkabinett (sketchbook 34, p. 35)

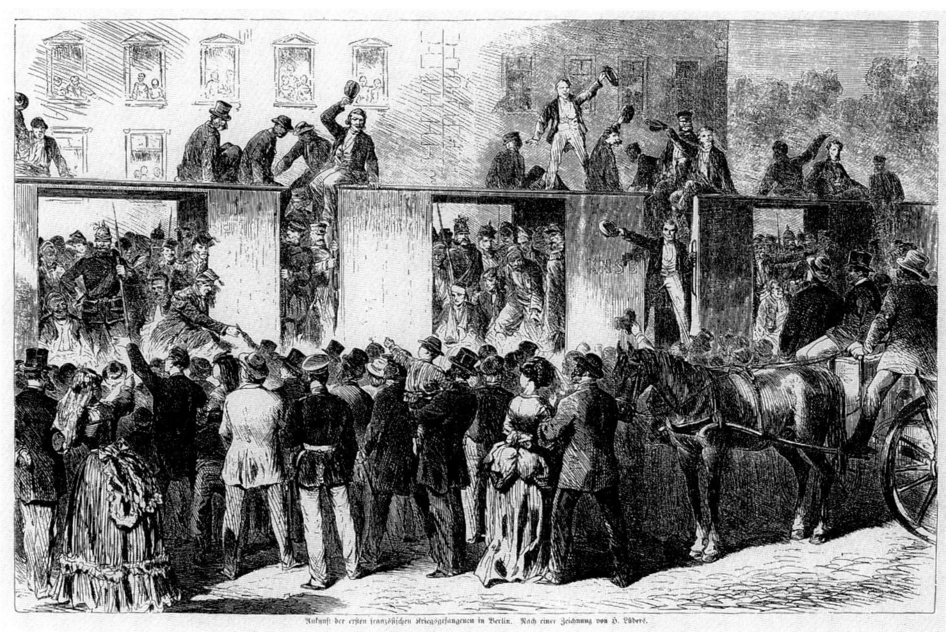

Fig. 201. Hermann Lüderes, *Arrival of the First French Prisoners in Berlin*, woodcut, illustration appearing in the *Leipziger Illustrierte Zeitung*, 20 August 1870

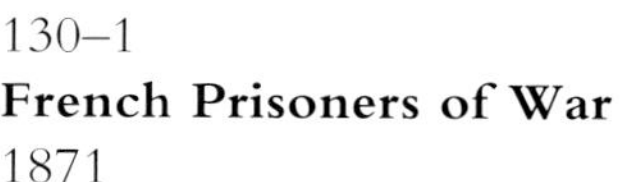

130–1

French Prisoners of War

1871

When Menzel saw the battlefields of the Austro-Prussian war, he knew 'from where Schlüter had got his masks of the Arsenal'[1] (*cf.* cat. 120, 121). When he spoke of this recent war to his friend, the army doctor Puhlmann, he hid his feelings behind sarcasm, talking of 'consumption of men', and setting against it 'the ridiculous affairs and illnesses of little men' who had not been involved in it, like him. 'Yet Germania needs a lot of good painters, etc., not so much for all those mediocre battle pictures. Something as unique as our army should not be its only asset'[2]. 'The job of a soldier and its frightful consequences were present in Menzel's work from the time of his interest in Frederick the Great. But after the painting of *Night Attack at Hochkirch* (1856), he had never gone back to the theme of war. Years later, when Friedrich Pecht asked him why he had not painted a picture of the wars of 1866 and 1870, he replied, 'Should one really paint such horror?[3] His participation in the events of 1870–1 was limited to a small painting, *Departure of King*

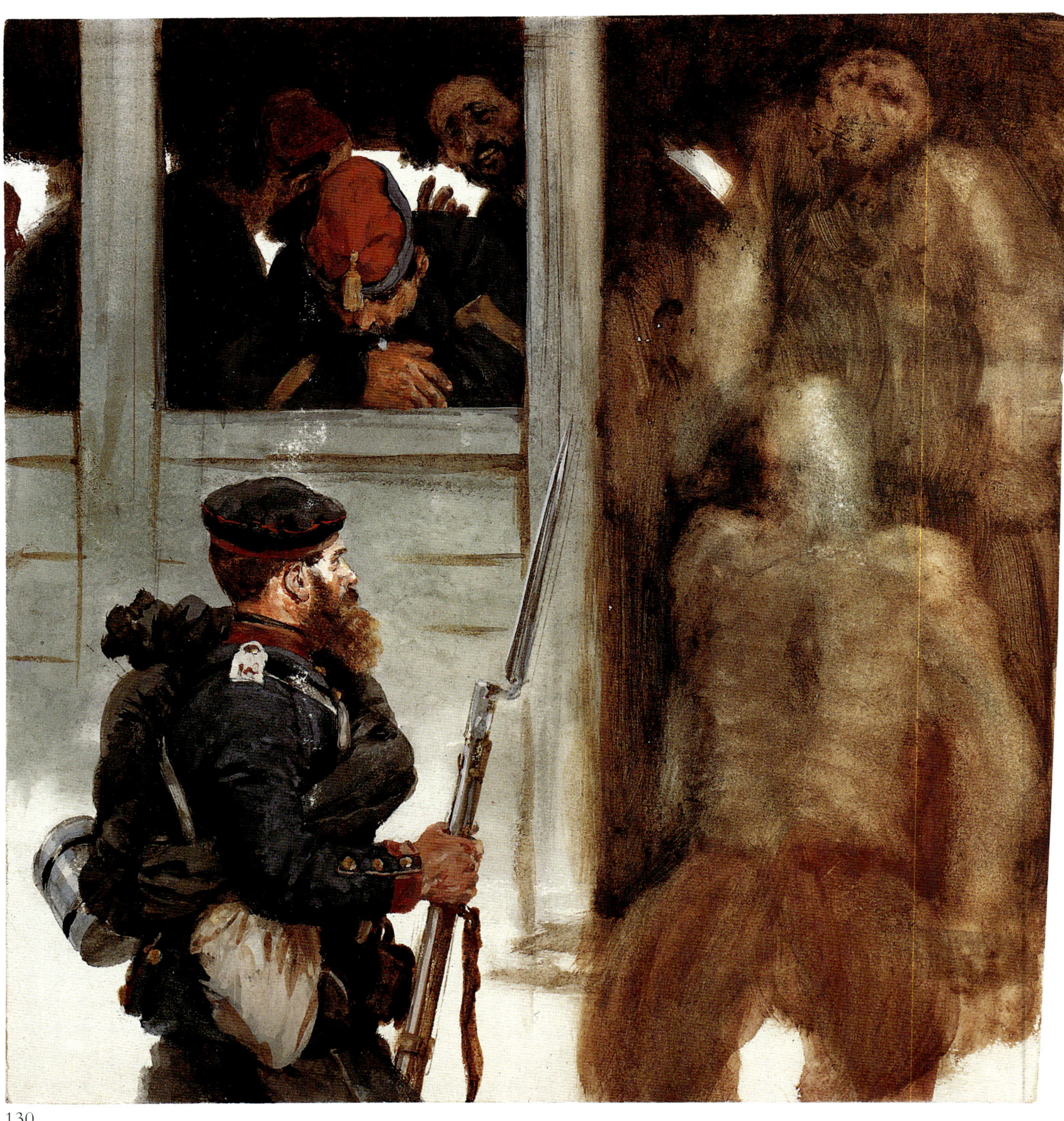

130

William I for the Army, 31 July 1870, in which he gave a subtle psychological portrait of the crowd in Unter den Linden avenue (cat. 134). On 16 June 1871 he had taken part in the decoration of the Academy situated on the triumphal route, along with other Berlin painters, and had painted two congratulatory addresses commissioned by the town magistrate for Bismarck and Moltke, who were named as honorary citizens (*cf.* cat. 132, 133). But his independence of spirit became clear several years later, when in spite of State resistance, he shipped his works to Paris, to

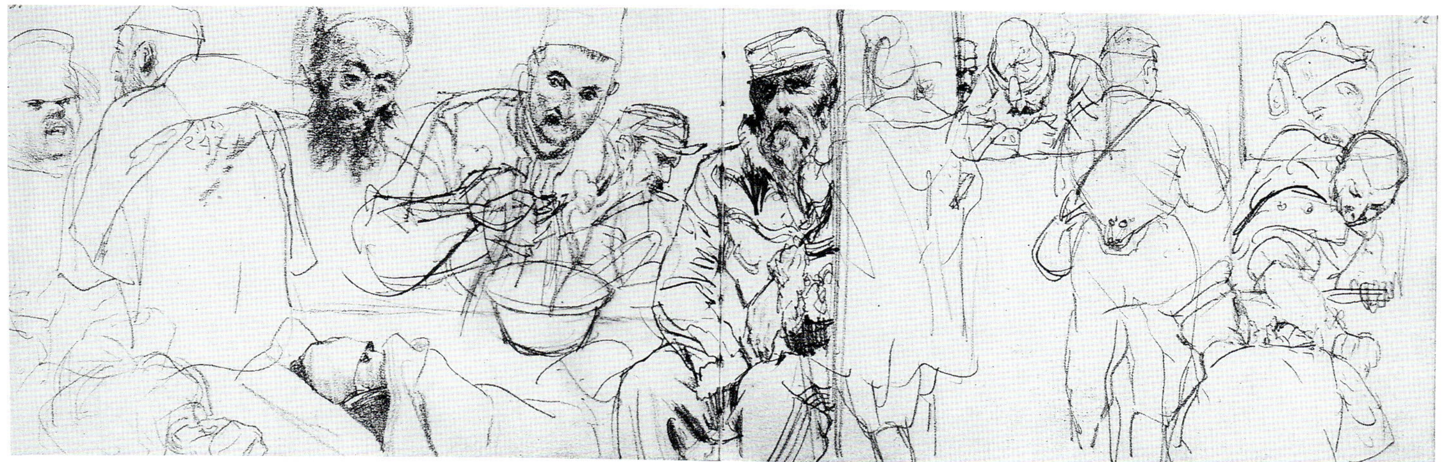

Fig. 202. *French Prisoners*, 1870–1, pencil, Berlin, Kupferstichkabinett (sketchbook 34, p. 11–12)

131

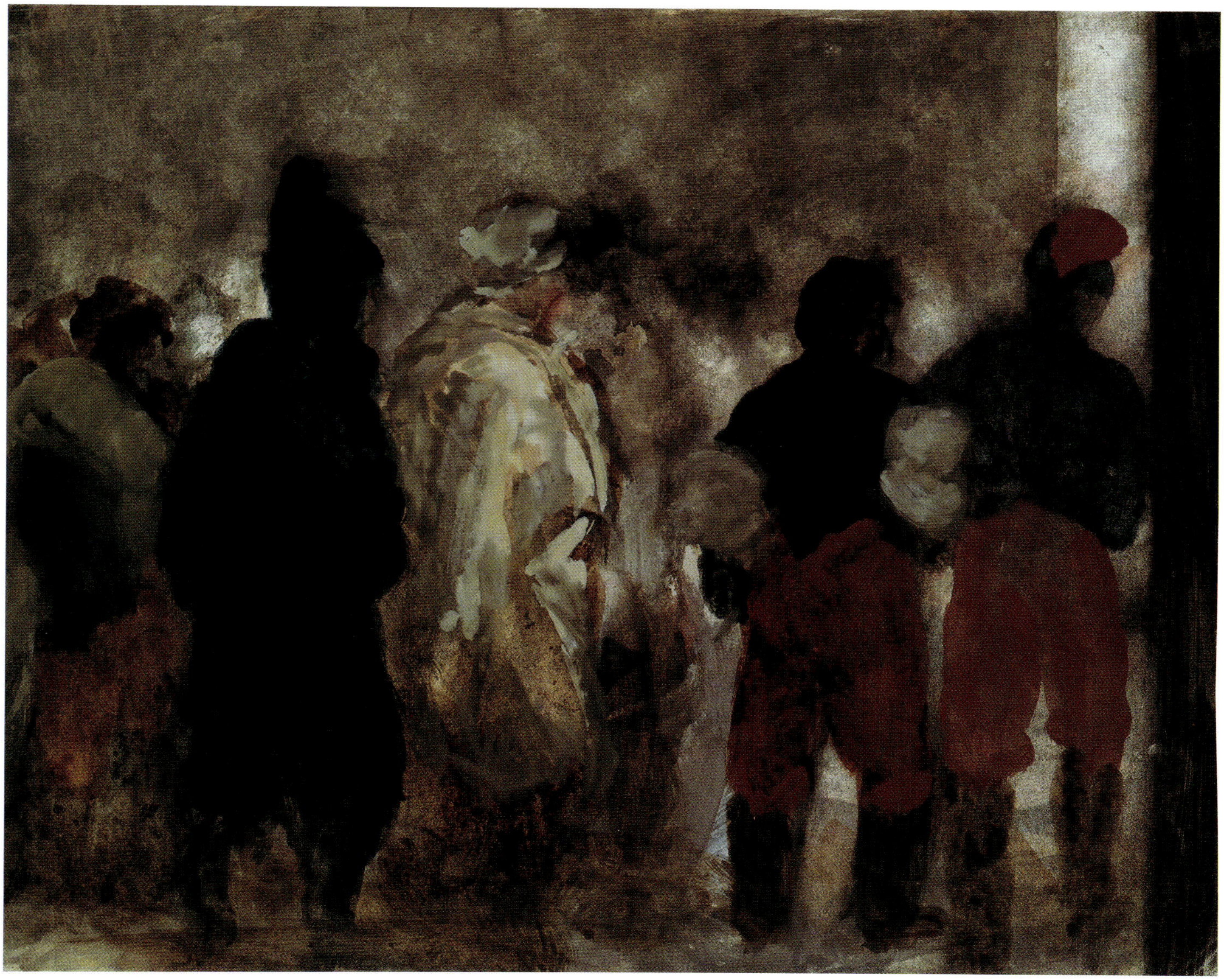

the Universal Exhibition, for the centenary of the French Revolution.

It may not have been entirely the taste for the sensational which took him like a journalist to the station in east Berlin in January 1871 to wait for the French prisoners of war in the hope of finding new subjects. Compassion for suffering is expressed in the sketches he did of those wretched men. In January William I proclaimed himself emperor at Versailles. Shortly after, prisoners arrived (fig. 201) and were taken to the fortress at Spandau. A letter from Menzel to his young friend and colleague Paul Meyerheim states that he waited for them for hours.

He was finally able to watch their arrival after obtaining the special privileges required[4]. He sketched many of these sad figures (fig. 202), a lot of whom were Moroccan, getting off the train and in the room where women whom Menzel and Meyerheim knew were distributing food to the prisoners. He noticed the red and blue of their striking Zouave hats, as they are depicted in the two later compositions. These two paintings illustrate his technique of stretching the watercolour considerably, which only revealed vague shapes, then covering the paper, layer by layer, with gouache, right down to the smallest detail. The pencil sketch of a man getting out of a train, whose laced up jacket is drawn accurately, served as a model for the blurred figure with a dark mark on his chest, as already shown in the drawing[5]. Two autonomous images have been created from the sketches in this book, the arriving prisoners getting out of the train carriage, and the journey towards a dark future, suggested in the matt, provisional nature of the colour. M.R.-R.

1. Letter to Doctor Puhlmann, 2 August 1866, Wolff, 1914, p. 205. Masks of the Arsenal – this refers to stone masks of dying soldiers, by Andreas Schlüter (after 1696) in the courtyard of the Arsenal in Berlin.
2. Letter to Wilhelm Puhlmann, 15 November 1870, Wolff, 1914, p. 213.
3. Letter to Friedrich Pecht, 9 December 1878, Landesarchiv, Berlin, reproduced in Kirstein, 1919, p. 108.
4. Letter to Paul Meyerheim, 25 January 1871, Wolff, 1914, p. 214.
5. *Cf.* sketchbook 34, 1869–71, p. 3, Berlin, Kupferstichkabinett.

130
Soldier of the Prussian Landwehr and French Prisoners
1871

Gouache
21 × 19.7cm
Berlin, Kupferstichkabinett (SZ Menzel N 598)

Provenance: Painter's studio; 1905 Emilie Krigar-Menzel; acquired by the museum in 1906.
Exhibitions: Berlin, 1905, no. 4032; Berlin, 1955 A, no. 54; Berlin, 1980 A, no. 98, reprod. p. 329; Vienna, 1985, no. 51, col. reprod. p. 61; Copenhagen, 1985, no. 42, col. reprod. p. 30; New York, 1990, no. 35, col. reprod.
Bibliography: Tschudi, 1905 A, no. 591.

131
French Prisoners of War on the March
1871

Gouache
21.1 × 19.2cm
Berlin, Kupferstichkabinett (SZ Menzel N 1023)

Provenance: Painter's studio; 1905 Emilie Krigar-Menzel; acquired by the museum in 1906.
Exhibitions: Berlin, 1905, no. 4032; Berlin, 1955 A, no. 309; Berlin, 1980 A, no. 97, col. reprod. p. 181; Vienna, 1985, no. 52, reprod. p. 120; Copenhagen, 1985, no. 43, col. reprod. p. 30; New York, 1990, no. 34, col. reprod. p. 126.
Bibliography: Tschudi, 1905 A, no. 550.

The reverse side of the sheet is completely covered with different brightly coloured brushstrokes in blue, green, yellow and red, as well as earth tones. Before Menzel started painting, he had obviously used the back of the paper to test his colours while he was working on another watercolour or gouache.

This reflects the words of his friend Paul Meyerheim on the subject of his friend's technique: 'While his oil paintings took shape on the canvas like a mosaic, his watercolours were often developed on an old piece of paper used for cleaning his paintbrush. He would shade off the chaos of colours a little and, carefully sticking this smooth paper, which no one else would have used to paint on, on to a piece of board, he started to work on the watercolour. The cardboard was itself attached to a drawing board, inside a wooden box on which he had fixed a piece of wood to rest his hand. All of this took place on a small table, as the master only ever worked standing up'[1]. As an example, the title page from *Children's Album*, dated 1863 (cat. 105), was created using this method. It has no concrete subject and the toned down letters of the title stand out on the multicoloured surface. Brushmarks are sometimes visible on the edges of some gouaches, with this area later covered by the frame. M.R.-R.

1. Meyerheim, (1906) 1992, p. 170.

132
Painters Preparing a Transparent Panel
c. 1871

Brown ink and gouache
33.4 × 25cm
Berlin, Kupferstichkabinett (SZ Menzel N 1180)
Exhibited in Washington and Berlin only

Provenance: Painter's studio; 1905 Emilie Krigar-Menzel; acquired by the museum in 1906.
Exhibition: Berlin, 1905, no. 4408.
Bibliography: Lammel, 1993 A, fig. 50.

The colour in this monochrome painting is largely faded, and it is definitely not a memoir of the work on large transparent paintings done each year at Christmas time, as it was thought up to now. These paintings, with musical accompaniment by the cathedral choir, were for the benefit of widows and orphans, and Menzel took part in the event four times, the last of which was in 1857[1].

The scene here was probably painted on another occasion. In May 1871, the artists of Berlin prepared to decorate the public route to be used by the Prussian troops for their triumphal entry, between Hallenser Tor and the Lustgarten. In addition to great painted awnings five streets long and hung across the road, the façade of the Academy was decorated with immense portraits of the commanders-in-chief of the army, which covered all the upper windows. With his colleagues Gustav Richter, Carl Becker, Otto Heyden and Georg Bleibtreu, Menzel contributed to the series by painting the figures of Bismarck and Moltke. Areas were made available to the artists to carry out this work, notably in the unfinished building of the Campo Santo by Stüler[2].

The place depicted cannot be identified from the watercolour. A kind of scaffold has been built behind a large opening, possibly a door. A plank has been laid across the gap, on which a painter is standing with a paintbrush in his hand, and underneath this a man wearing a hat is helping a woman to bend underneath the plank to get through. A pencil sketch of this scene shows all the characteristics of Menzel's style of the 1870s[3]. The lines seem to have been drawn quickly and vigorously with the thin, hard side of a carpenter's pencil, a technique used only from this late time on. The vague blurred effect of the scene is also characteristic of his last period, as Menzel no longer wanted to present accurate detail in his paintings. M.R.-R.

1. On the transparent panel for Christmas in Berlin, *cf.* letter to C.H. Arnold, 26 December 1851, Wolff, 1914, p. 153. Menzel took part in this in 1844, 1851, 1853 and 1857, as reported in the paper *Vossische Zeitung*. (This information was given by Birgit Verwiebe. *Cf.* her thesis on transparent paintings, Greifswald, 1989.)
2. Werner, 1913, p. 58 and ff.
3. Berlin, Kupferstichkabinett (SZ Menzel N 3367).

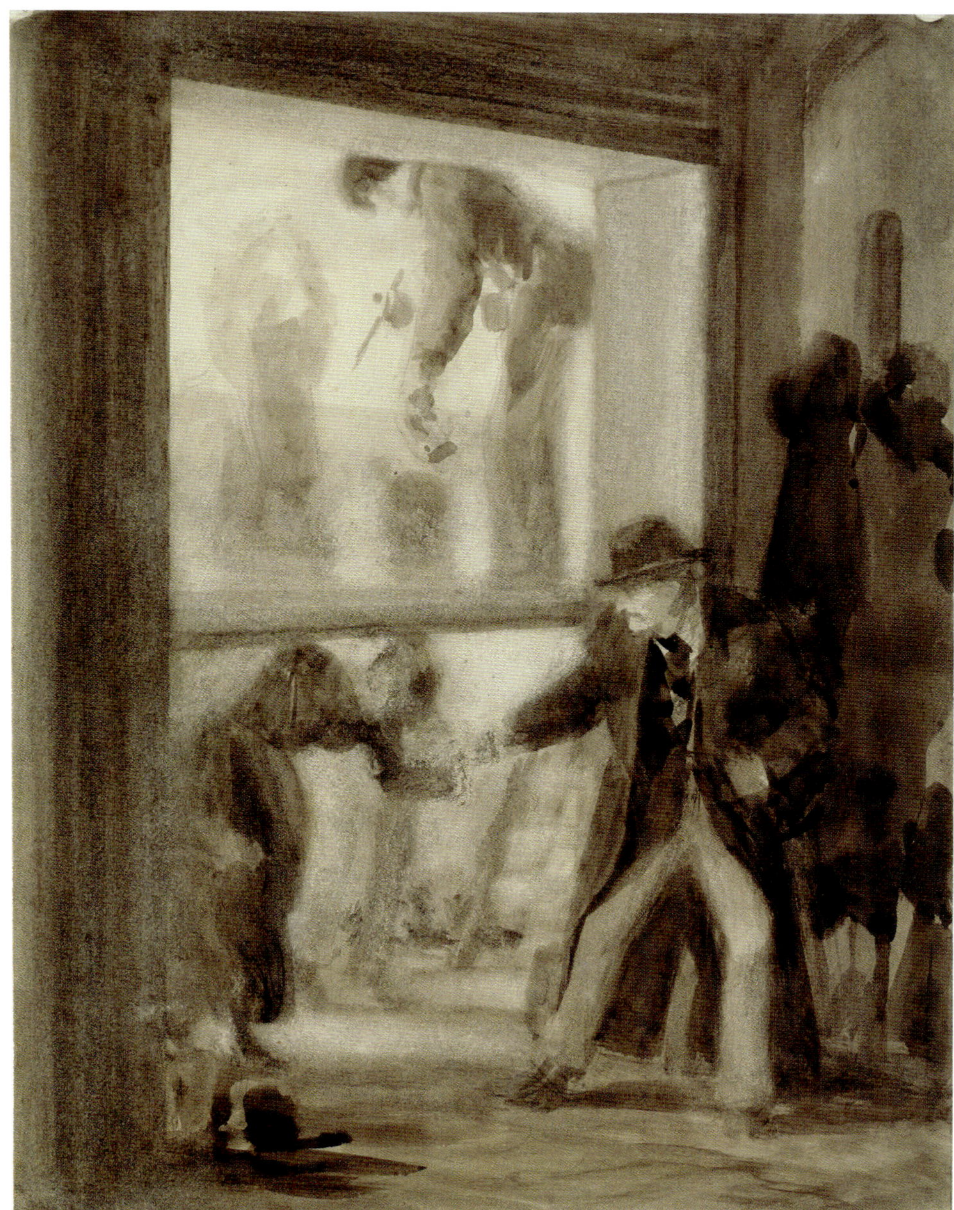
132

133
Moltkes Binoculars
1871

Pencil and gouache
26 × 40cm
Signed at the top right: *Ad. Menzel* – Annotated: *Feldmarschall Gr: v. Moltkes Fernglas (und: Futteral) dessen er sich im Kriege von 1870–1 bediente.*('Field-marshal Gr.: v. Moltke's binoculars [and: case] which he used in the 1870–1 war'. Various measurements.
Berlin, Kupferstichkabinett (SZ Menzel N 1022)

Provenance: Painter's studio; 1905 Emilie Krigar-Menzel; acquired by the museum in 1906.

Exhibitions: Berlin, 1895, no. 149; Hamburg, 1896, no. 155; Berlin, 1905, no. 3999; Berlin, 1955 A, no. 302; Berlin, 1980, no. 279; Vienna, 1985, no. 98; Copenhagen, 1985, no. 84; New York, 1990, no. 33.
Bibliography: Tschudi, 1905 A, no. 592; Berlin, 1984, p. 18 *et seq.*, reprod. p. 19.

The study for Moltke's binoculars and case was made on the edge of a larger than life-sized portrait of Helmut von Moltke standing, which Menzel painted at the same time as a portrait of Bismarck with a similar date. These two works

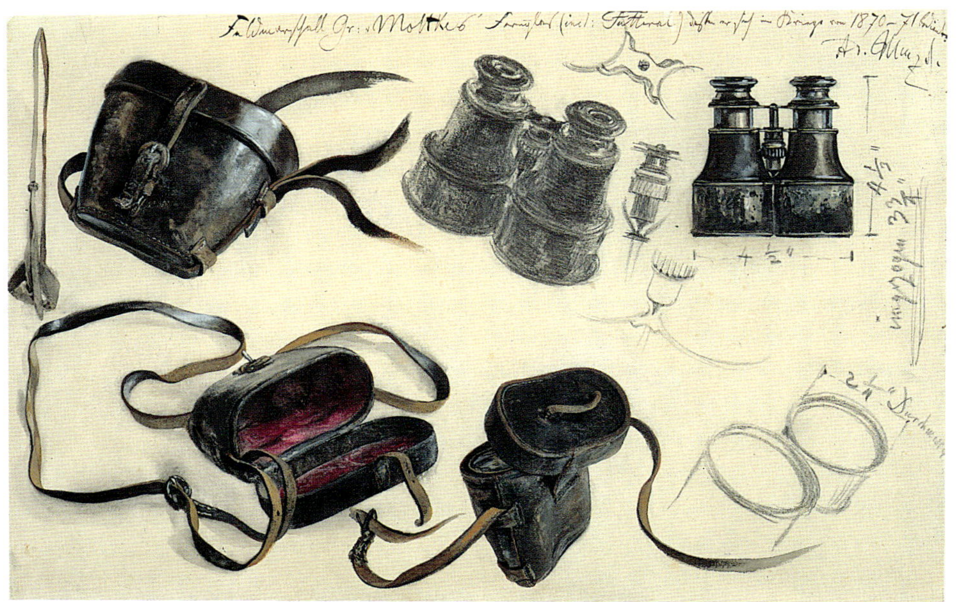

133

were to adorn the Academy building on the day of the entry of the victorious Prussian armies into Berlin on 16 June 1871, after defeating France[1]. Menzel's two pictures covered the windows of the building beside three other portraits of conquering generals painted by other artists. They were just a detail of the artistic ornamentation of the *via triumphalis* which led from Belle-Alliance-Platz through the Brandenburg Gate and along Unter den Linden to the palace, passing by the Academy building. Numerous other Berlin painters apart from Menzel were involved in the decoration of this route and painted monumental canvasses which were arranged like transparent panels. Paul Meyerheim later remembered the speed at which everyone worked, while Menzel, for his part, calmly began his portrait of Moltke: 'Beneath a leaden sky, wrapped up in his overcoat, he stood on the battlefield with his opera glasses [sic] in his raised right hand, for which the master had made no end of detailed watercolour studies done with microscopic precision. . . . While we were all on tenterhooks, Menzel squandered his time painting the decorative charms around Moltke in chocolate brown and yellow ochre'[2].

Meyerheim adds that, after these great events, Menzel spent more time on Bismarck's portrait, to finish it off. It is possible that he painted the study for Moltke's binoculars at that time. The study does not have the look of a preliminary drawing, like certain sketches for Molktes greatcoat[3]. It has more in common with the series of works inspired by numerous inanimate objects which never ceased to fascinate the painter, and which Menzel excelled at imbuing with a secret life of their own. In the portrait of Moltke standing with his spiked helmet and overcoat, the binoculars he is holding in his hand would be almost a secondary attribute if Menzel had not intended to suggest through them the generals clairvoyance. The binoculars which Meyerheim described much later in 1910 as 'opera glasses', in a very unmilitary manner, represent Moltke's own personality in this drawing – they are the witnesses of the war in which he used them.

It seems as if Menzel turned an object over and over in his hands (*cf.* cat. 189). The visibly worn case, with its magenta lining, lies open. Beside it are the metal binoculars, black and scuffed, viewed from the front and from the side. Even if the annotations in the foreground, giving the dimensions, seem to confer a legitimacy on this work, the simple documentation has the silent eloquence of still life. The expression of the concrete nature of things, found equally in other drawings (of military equipment, a fur, shoes, a bed or a library), does not just capture the simple material aspect of objects, it reflects something of the person to whom the object belongs, or of the artists way of thinking.

At the request of the Berlin judicial authorities, Menzel began to paint a richly ornamented address in homage to Moltke in 1871, as he had for Bismarck, which he did not finish until 1872[4].

M.R.-R.

1. Not mentioned by Tschudi; Potsdam, Stiftung Preussische Schlösser und Gärten.
2. Paul Meyerheim, Two monumental paintings by Adolph Menzel rediscovered, *Vossische Zeitung*, no. 46, 28 January 1910. Quoted in Lammel, 1993 A, p. 148.
3. Berlin, Kupferstichkabinett.
4. Friedrichsruh, Bismarck-Museum; *Moltke-Adresse*: the work probably was lost in the Second World War. It was formerly in Kreisau, in Silesia.

134

Departure of King William I for the Army, 31 July 1870

1871

Oil on canvas
63 × 78cm
Signed and dated at the bottom right: *Ad. Menzel Berlin, 1871*
Berlin, Nationalgalerie (A I 323)

Provenance: Commissioned by the banker Magnus Herrmann; an initial attempt to purchase it by the Nationalgalerie before 1877 failed due to the extremely elevated price demanded by the owner. Acquired by the museum in December 1881 via Hermann Pächter (R. Wagner Gallery), to whom Herrmann had sold it that year.
Exhibitions: Berlin, 1871; Berlin, 1876 A, no. 492; Vienna, 1876–7; Vienna, 1882; Munich, 1883, no. 1321 b, reprod.; Berlin, 1885, no. 15; Berlin, 1895 A, no. 53; Hamburg, 1896, no. 15; Munich, 1896; Vienna, 1896, no. 279; Berlin, 1935, no. 42; Wiesbaden, 1952, no. 161; Berlin, 1955 B, no. 116, fig. 54; Berlin, 1960, no. 1, reprod.; Cologne, 1971, no. 70; Berlin, 1979,

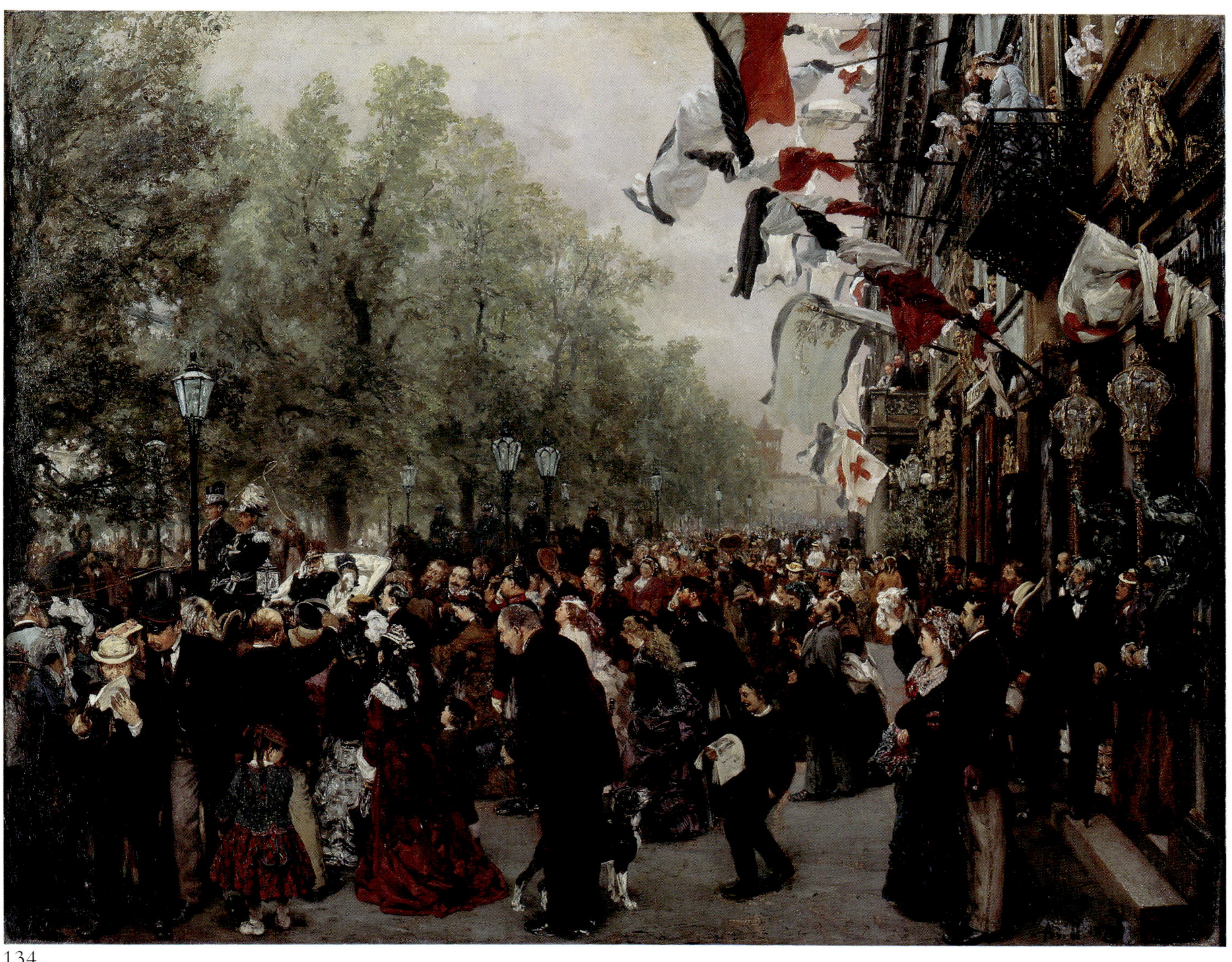

134

no. 176, col. reprod.; New York, 1981, no. 64, col. reprod.
Bibliography: Schasler, 1871, p. 230; Rosenberg, 1877; Rosenberg, 1879 A, p. 271; Pecht, 1881–2, p. 109, reprod.; cat. NG, 1883, no. 490; Jordan/Dohme, 1890, p. 64 *et seq.*; Jordan, 1895, no. 19; p. 47–9, p. 70; Tschudi, 1905 A, no. 140; Jordan, 1905, p. 70; Delmar, (1905) 1992, p. 112; Herrmann, (1905) 1992, p. 250; Meier-Graefe, 1906, p. 213 *et seq.*; Justi, 1921, p. 31–32; Waldmann, 1922, p. 10; Scheffler 1922, p. 91; Justi, 1932, p. 138; Scheffler, 1938, p. 115 *et seq.*; Waldmann, 1941, p. 34 and 48, fig. 68–9; Beenken, 1944, p. 332 *et seq.*; Jensen, 1982, p. 108, col. pl. 31; Lammel, 1988, p. 159 *et seq.*, reprod. p. 161; Zangs, 1992, p. 207–13; Lammel, 1993 B, p. 70–2, col. pl. 13.

'Unter den Linden (Under the Lime Trees), an avenue that starts at the emperor's palace, is the pride and joy of the people of Berlin. It is their favourite place to walk, it is where fashionable people meet, where the crowds gather, the *via sacra* of the people, the triumphal route of the courageous army, the government forum, the pantheon of the gods and of illustrious men. There, the most beautiful palaces can be admired, the most wonderful artistic monuments, the best hotels, the most luxurious shops and alluring shop windows. . . .'[1] Contemporary opinion agrees on this subject, although the enthusiasm coloured with patriotism of an 1883 writer is different from the astonished curiosity of Heinrich Heine in 1828. It is different in the extent of the transformations undergone in this prestigious avenue from the Biedermeier era to that of the empire. The title *The Berlin Linden, Afternoon of 31 July 1870* with which the picture was exhibited for the first time, conceals the historical event beneath the promise of a portrait of the town (and matches the structure of the image perfectly). In his series of compositions depicting urban roads filled with crowds, Menzel only painted one of the Prussian capital, and it is the only one which uses the pretext of an historic event, yet has so little in common with history painting. It is interesting that, in 1847, when Menzel was preparing an immense picture with a mediaeval subject, he felt the need for a 'painting of contemporary history, whose legitimacy should be claimed unwaveringly'[2]. His first attempt in that area was the *Lying in State of the March Dead* (fig. 65), and the second was the painting of the *The Coronation* (fig. 121). *The Departure* distances itself from the upper echelons of society depicted in it.

As soon as heard that war was declared once more, the painter immediately put an end to his summer visit to the mountains of Saxony. On the very day that he returned to Berlin, he witnessed the emotion caused by the departing king travelling towards Potsdam station[3] amid the enthusiastic clamours of the Berliners, which Menzel observed from the first-floor window of a restaurant in Unter den Linden. William I rejoined the army, after declaring an amnesty for people accused of 'political crimes and infringements'. He did not announce that he had become supreme commander of the troops of all the states in the Germanic confederation until he was well on his way, beyond Mainz.

A year later, the work was complete. Menzel had 'painted it with my left hand, as for example, in my *Sermon in the Beechwood at Kösen* (held by Mr Arons) [cat. 125] as well as nearly all my works on Frederick'[4]. The comment is important, because Menzel had learnt to paint with both hands, although he was naturally left-handed. In general he drew with his left hand and painted with his right, but there were significant exceptions. A work started with the left hand (and consequently on the left of the window) had to be continued in the same way to retain the incidence of light from the right. The place where the picture was hung had to imitate this situation, to allow the onlooker to perceive the relief of the thickly applied paint under the same conditions.

According to Max Jordan, the painter had been 'on the south side of the Linden, near the Russian ambassadors palace'. This was late Neoclassical in style and was near the Brandenburg gate. Yet the buildings depicted are elegant and brand new Neo-baroque, the detail of which had already appeared in the illuminated diplomas, and in particular the one painted two years before for August Heckmann (*cf.* cat. 129). There may be a hotel in the foreground yet, whatever it is, Menzel does not faithfully reproduce actual architecture but alludes to the type of building which was becoming prevalent at that time on both the east and west of the Friedrichstrasse, and the town he portrays, although fictitious in detail, is representative overall.

One point is troubling, however. If we look for orientation, and consider that the buildings in the background are quite near, we should not be surrounded by modern, affluent-looking buildings, but should be further east, more or less at the royal palace or the opera, because the brick tower of the recently built City Hall seems so close. Yet the imposing castle in front is only a veiled shadow. It is a strange illusion! Behind the King of Prussia who would become Emperor, his ancestral home, the seat of his throne, is obliterated by that of the municipality. The field of vision does not contain any of the prestigious buildings connected to the court, which border the road leading from the royal palace to the Brandenburg Gate. It is the city bourgeoisie that fills the space. In their overzealous reverence and cheering of the flags of Prussia and the German confederation, the people are celebrating themselves rather than the sovereign. The couple in the barouche, with the queen in tears, reflect a private, moving moment, even if the helmet which the king actually wore[5] has been substituted for one with a more warlike appearance.

Franz Krüger, senior to Menzel, had already painted several pictures of military parades, the first of which was completed in 1829 or 1830[6], where the attention was turned away from the military ceremony and directed towards the crowd of spectators made up of portraits of unknown Berliners. Their apparently casual placing in the picture belies a carefully orchestrated scene which conveys a harmonious image of social order. The same does not apply to a work which could easily be the French equivalent or match for Menzel's painting, *The Departure of the Militia* by Alfred Dehodencq (1870–1; fig. 203)[7]. The painter had seen the regiments depart after the first French defeats and had expected to see 'resolute, serious men. 'He found a mêlée, panic, drunken revelry, and returned exhausted, distraught and hopeless. . .', then he painted the picture during the siege of Paris. 'It is not enthusiasm, it is drunkenness, and patriotism seems like a joke'[8]. This composition has a centrifugal dynamic, chaos and spontaneity, which are a vital part of depictions of urban crowds, from the critical point of view.

No other painting by Menzel has such a dualistic perspective. The view along the façade is vertiginously foreshortened and broken up by the flags. It is a grotesque view from below the next balcony, craftily disguised by the dense crowd which spreads over the whole width of the foreground. The top cornice appears to be vertical. In this upper level, what separates the two houses, still visible lower down, can no longer be painted accurately, confirming the impossibility of taking in the scattered elements of the composition in a single glance in this right third of the picture. The problem is also concealed by the poignant spectacle of the flags which swell, flap and unfurl. Some black, white and red German flags wrapped round their poles by a gust of wind fall back gently and seem incapable of flying again. Could it be intentional that the blue and white flags bearing the Brandenburg eagle seem more shapeless? What a difference between these and the tricoloured flags flapping freely which Monet, Pissarro and their friends used so often in their pictures! To question patriotic spirit even further, a Red Cross flag has surreptitiously been slipped in among the others[9], evoking the victims of the war, who were ever-present in Menzel's mind (*cf.* cat. 120, 121).

Menzel's friend, the banker Magnus Herrmann who commissioned the work,

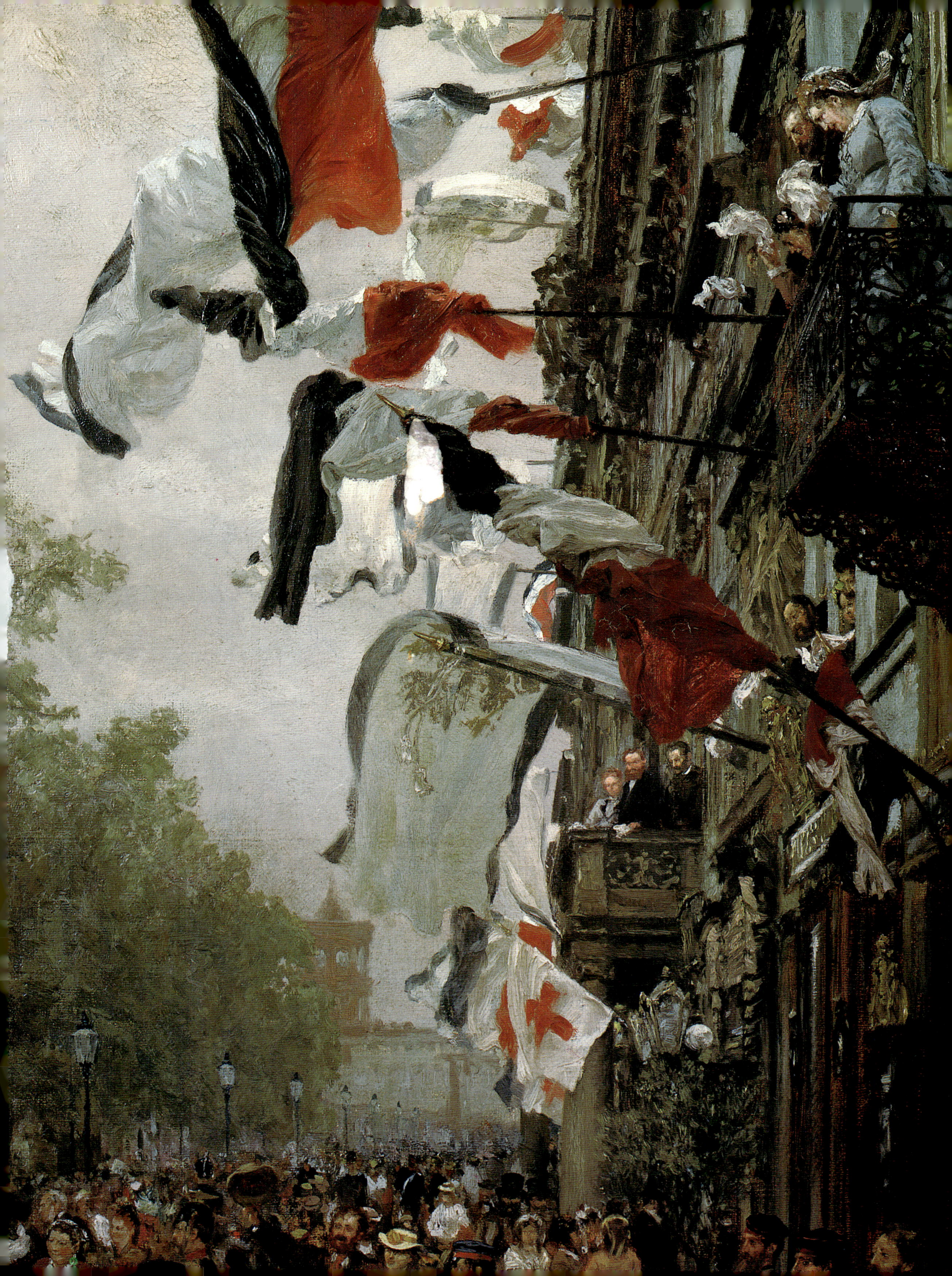

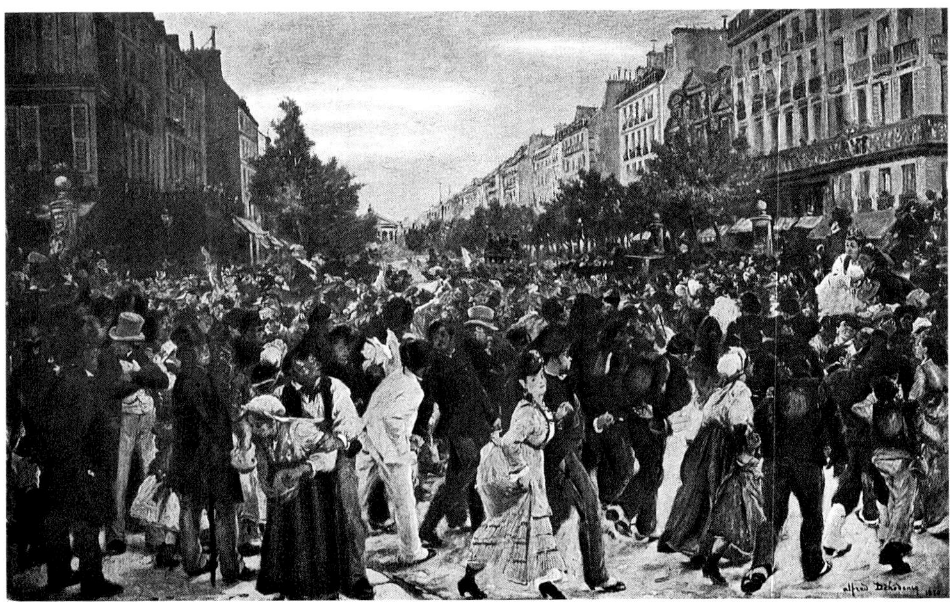

Fig. 203. Alfred Dehodencq, *Departure of the Militia*, 1870–1, oil, location unknown

is alleged to be depicted with his wife on the balcony in the background (*cf.* cat. 2, 174, 175). A drawing of the couple was transferred to the painting without any changes[10]. Herrmann's daughter and son-in-law, the painter Albert Hertel, then twenty-eight, are in the right foreground[11] (thirty-four years later Hertel would give one of the funeral speeches in Menzels honour).

At the time the painting was being exhibited Berlin was celebrating Prussia's victory and, several months later, William I was proclaimed emperor. Menzel had long ago established his authority, but that did not silence the critics. The influential director of the review *Die Dioskuren*, Max Schasler, an embittered 1848 supporter, for whom any trace of realism and 'materialism' in art implied the threatening spectre of social democracy[12], and who had always been ambivalent towards Menzel's work, praised his stunning pictorial 'virtuosity on the one hand, and on the other criticized the 'triteness of the faces'. 'If the artist', he persisted, 'judged it useful to allow the queen to cover her face with her handkerchief, this is explained better, in my opinion, by the fear that his natural uncouthness would prevent him from capturing the expression exactly, rather than by tactfulness'. The 'discord between drawing and colour' was due to the incoherent touch, which forces the onlooker to move further back to appreciate the 'total effect than the size of the painting allows'[13].

Much later, when Meier-Graefe was preparing to condemn the work, the official Anton von Werner stated in his funeral speech for the painter that Menzel had 'touched the hearts of his people in this painting'[14]. But this refers to monarchist feelings. Friedrich Pecht, an admirer of the painter, thought it more accurate to mention (and deplore) the absence of patriotic resolution in the picture: 'There is too much sentimental philistinism'[15]. Theodor Fontane warmly congratulated the painter for having 'brought grandeur into everyday life (when so many "historians with the paintbrush" injected the high life with their own ordinariness)'[16]. Leaving aside any hierarchy of genres, this formula in which 'grandeur penetrated everyday life', in which lies the essential interest of the painting, corresponds quite well to Menzel's conception of history and how he depicted it. C.K.

1. Ring, 1883, p. 102.
2. Letter to Carl Heinrich Arnold, 4 January 1847, Wolff, 1914, p. 100.
3. Kirstein, 1919, p. 78.
4. Menzel speaking to an art dealer, October (?) 1876, Berlin, Staatsbibliothek.
5. Zangs, 1992, p. 208, quotes a passage from the diary of Baroness Spitzemberg on this subject.
6. Berlin, Nationalgalerie.
7. Séailles, 1910, p. 156 and ff., reprod. p. 167.
8. *Ibid.*, p. 156.
9. Zangs, 1992, p. 211, stressed that the Red Cross flag is almost at the vanishing point of the perspective and noted this too in direct relation to the disabled people on the diploma presented to William I by the town council after the 1866 victory (Tschudi, 1905 A, no. 555).
10. Berlin, Kupferstichkabinett, (SZ Menzel N 1650). Other preliminary drawings: kat 1059, 1060, 1387, N 1580, 2164, 2281, 3035, 3611. Albert Hertel also once had a study (exhib. cat. Berlin, 1905, no. 5332). There is another at the Städelsches Kunstinstitut, Frankfurt-en-Main (Ebertshäuser, 1976, II, p. 1099).
11. Jensen, 1982, p. 139, thinks that the man in the hat is the commissioner of the painting.
12. '. . . and when one thinks that the consequences of these theories lead to such atrocities as the murder of princes, etc. . . .': here the author is speaking of philosophical materialism, Schasler, 1879, p. 39.
13. *Die Dioskuren*, 1871, p. 230.
14. Werner, 1905, p. 13.
15. *Deutsches Kunstblatt*, 1881-2, p. 109.
16. Letter from Fontane to Menzel, 2 July 1871, Fontane, 1979, p. 382.

135

Bilse Concert

1871

Gouache
17.8 × 12cm
Signed and dated at the top right: *Ad: Menzel 71.*
Berlin, Kupferstichkabinett (SZ Menzel Nr 1781)

Provenance: Frau Rehse, Oldenburg; 1935 bequest to the museum.
Exhibitions: Berlin, 1905, no. 317; Berlin, 1980 A, no. 96, col, reprod. p. 183.
Bibliography: Tschudi, 1905 A, no. 593; Lammel, 1993 A, p. 88, fig. 4 (col.).

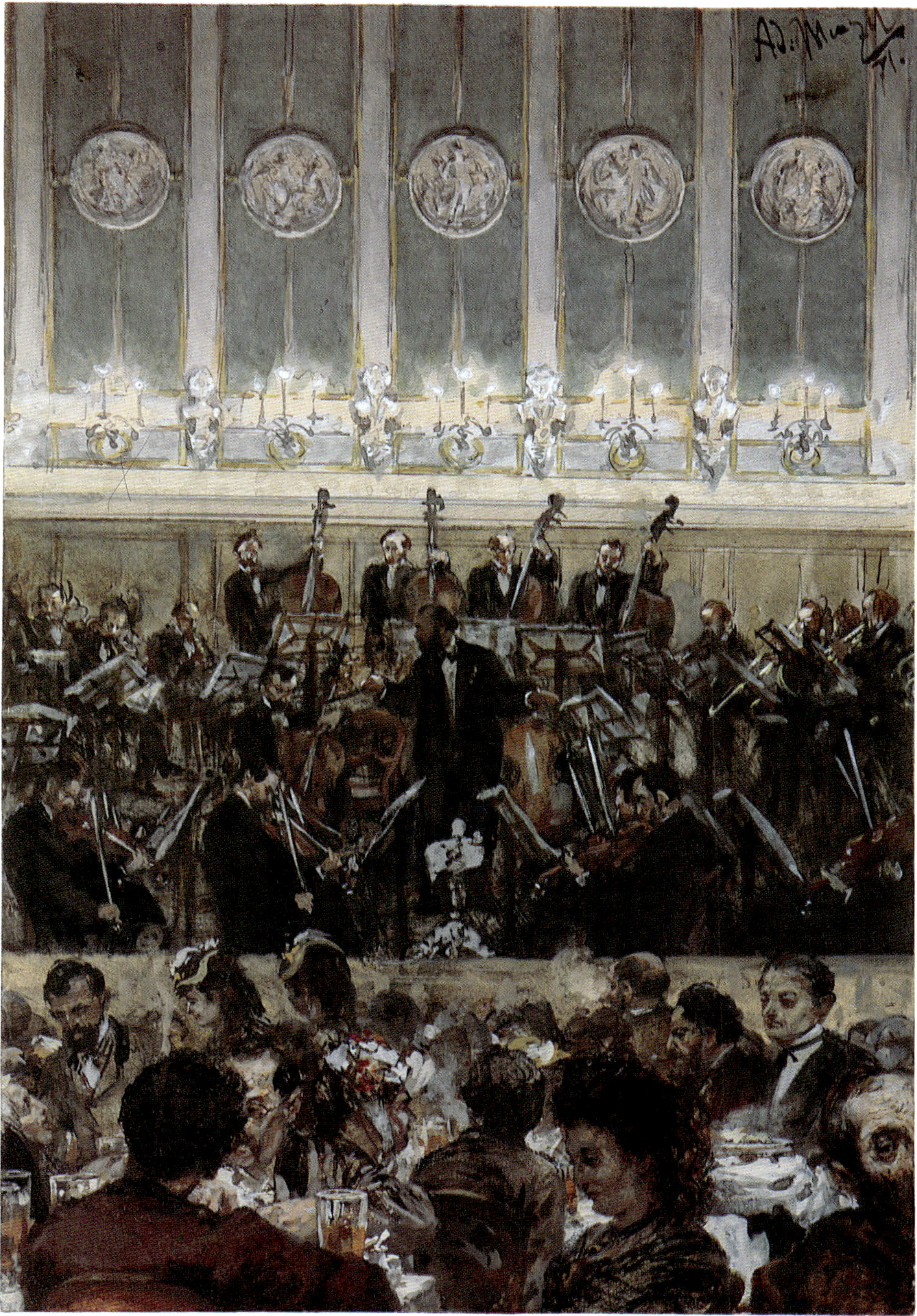

135

This gouache dates from the glorious years when this orchestra played in Berlin. Its division into three well-defined sections may correspond to three levels of meaning. The wall of the room is subdivided into several ornate panels containing a bas-relief in the form of a medallion, and is demarcated by alternating busts and candelabra. This upper level corresponds to what is sublime in art. The scenes inside the medallions may be mythological. Below, the composers immortalized by the busts appear to be watching over the quality of execution of their works. Between them are placed the only light sources in the room, as if spreading the spirit of lyrical art among the common mortals. In the second section, at a lower level, the orchestra surrounds its conductor Benjamin Bilse. He is standing, with his musicians below him. Their concentration is reflected in their sweating faces. The podium forms a frontier with the room, where movement and bustle is clearly visible. The public is busy eating, drinking, smoking, even listening to the music, while a waiter carries in steaming hot soup. Gerhart Hauptmann related that people were accustomed to communicate by gestures during the concert so as not to spoil the enjoyment of others. This lowest level belongs to people intent on absorption, in all senses of the word, abandoning themselves to everyday pleasures far from Olympus and its gods. Menzel's comments on the theatre are confirmed in this picture. The observation of actors, of their costumes and events on stage, and the effects of artificial light absorbed him to such a degree that he never managed to follow the plot.

Benjamin Bilse (1816–1902) had conducted an orchestra of forty musicians at Liegnitz in Silesia since 1842. His subsequent fame, established during his long annual tours, rested on the rigour of his work. He conducted for the first time in Berlin in 1847, then in 1851 and 1864. After causing a sensation in Paris during the Universal Exhibition of 1867, Bilse decided in the autumn to move to Berlin with his orchestra, using the new Konzerthaus at 48 Leipzigerstrasse, near the Dönhoffplatz. At that time, Bilse con-

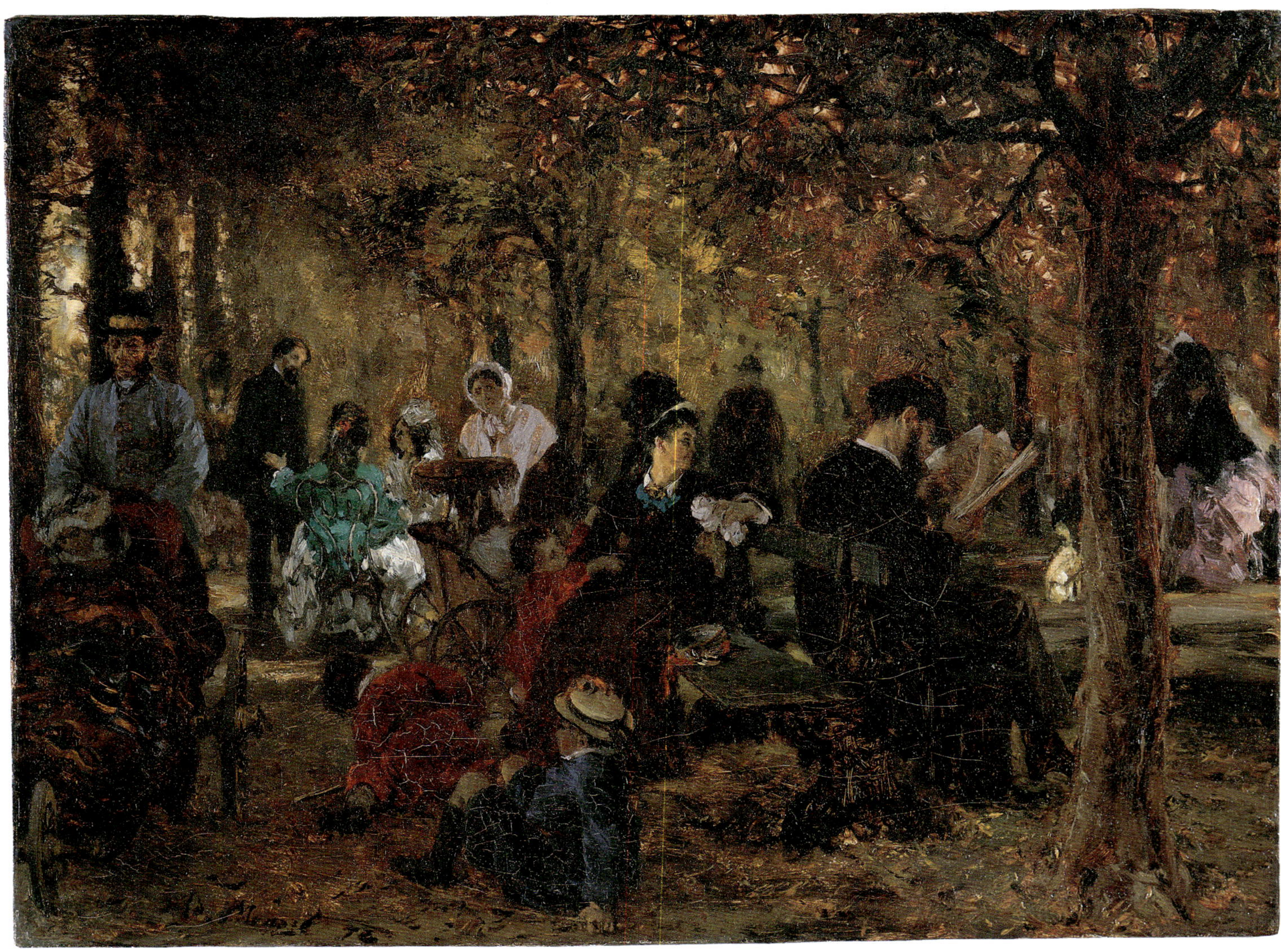

136

ducted up to one hundred musicians in what were described as 'monster concerts'[1]. His large repertoire called for a demanding and knowledgeable public, but he also enjoyed an extraordinary popularity because of the concerts given in public gardens, which he had learned about when he listened to Johann Strauss the elder in 1842. He promoted modern composers vigorously. In 1873 and 1875 Richard Wagner himself conducted Bilse's orchestra, and he was appointed conductor to the Prussian court in 1876.

Without intending to do so, Benjamin Bilse became the founder of the Berlin Philharmonic by in 1882 sacking some of his musicians who had expressed doubts about the financing of a planned visit to Warsaw. These musicians came together using the name 'Philharmonie', but it was not until 1887, after joining with the 'Meininger' that they found a conductor of genius in Hans von Bülow.

It is not surprising that the theme of music recurs so often in Menzel's work (*cf.* cat. 49, 56, 61, 74). The marriage of his sister Emilie to the conductor of the royal orchestra Hermann Krigar in 1859 encouraged his liking for music, as the family continued to live under the same roof. A.H.

1. Unverricht, 1952, p. 400.

136

Recollection of the Luxembourg Gardens

1872

Oil on canvas

21.5 × 28.5cm

Signed and dated at the bottom left: *A. Menzel 72*

Moscow, Pushkin Fine Art State Museum (3539)

Exhibited in Paris only

Provenance: Paris, Drouot sale[1]; before 1883, banker Wilhelm Itzinger, Berlin; Frau Itzinger; sold at auction in 1889; Serguei Tretiakov, Moscow; 1892 Moscow, Tretiakov gallery; 1925 State Fine Art Museum, Moscow.

Exhibitions: Berlin, 1883, no. 411; Berlin, 1885, no. 16; Berlin, 1891, no. 727b; Moscow, 1930, no. 119; Moscow, 1963, p. 50, unnumbered; Cologne/Bonn, 1978, p. 22 *et seq.*, unnumb., reprod.; Berlin, 1980, no. XXIX, reprod. p. 219; Moscow, 1994, (no cat.).

Bibliography: Jordan, 1890, p. 67, pl. 72; Tschudi, 1905 A, no. 142, reprod; Waldmann, 1941, pl. 72.

Only Menzel's later work found any international acclaim, and represents the artist today in a few foreign collections. After *Meissonier in his Studio at Poissy* (cat. 126), which went to the United States, this last picture inspired by Parisian life seems to have belonged to a Paris art lover before going to Moscow. It is much smaller than *Afternoon in the Tuileries Gardens* (cat. 123), and the composition seems initially to be an abbreviated version of it. The distribution of groups and certain motifs are similar, most strikingly in the case of the governess with a pushchair at the far left of the 1867 work, replaced in the 1872 painting by a valet pushing a wheelchair towards the onlooker in the same way. Yet the picture has less anxiety and disparity. The perspective is not from a high angle and the space and number of figures are noticeably reduced, with the main characters close together in the foreground with no threat of disappearing into the crowd. A young woman sitting on a bench ignores the children jostling her and turns to look at something that a stranger is reading. There is no better illustration of the fleeting encounter, of anonymity scarcely challenged by a moment of curiosity.

This miniature is undoubtedly the gentlest of Menzel's later works, and has the best blend of colours and subtle and discreet plays of light. The central group is not unlike those of Renoir, but the surroundings are a different world. The presence of technological elements is marked – the wheels, the iron chair of a style recently introduced in Paris gardens[2], the bench which projects its bare surface into the foreground, and whose back seems almost aggressive. C.K.

1. Jordan, 1890, p. 67.
2. Menzel drew some similar chairs in Monceau park in 1867 (Berlin, Kupferstichkabinett, SZ Menzel N 4323).

137

Studio Wall

1872

Oil on canvas
111 × 79.3cm
Signed and dated at the bottom right (scraping): *Menzel Octob/72*
Hamburg, Hamburger Kunsthalle (1266)
Exhibited in Paris only

Provenance: Eduard L. Behrens, Hamburg, who made a gift of the painting to the museum in 1898.
Exhibitions: Paris, 1885, no. 232; Berlin, 1885, no. 17; Hamburg, 1896, no. 17; Berlin, 1905, no. 31; Berlin, 1906, no. 143, reprod. p. 123; Berlin, 1955 B, no. 120, fig. 44; London, 1956, no. 167, reprod.; Cologne, 1971, no. 71, fig. 31; Hamburg, 1982, no. 102, col. pl. p. 175.
Bibliography: Rosenberg, 1889, pp. 210–11; Hamburg, 1896, p. 31–2; Lichtwark, (1896) 1992, p. 299; Meier-Graefe, 1906, p. 126; Meyerheim, (1906) 1992, p. 37; Scheffler, 1915, p. 203, reprod. p. 197; Pauli, 1924, p. 10–11, reprod. p. 8; Waldmann, 1941, p. 29; Novotny, 1960, p. 161–2; Krafft/Schümann, 1969, p. 219; Hentzen, 1969, pl. 238; Riemann-Reyher, 1976, fig. 3; Hofmann, 1982, p. 31–9, reprod. p. 33.

The *Studio Wall* is among the most remarkable works of Menzel's later period. It arouses the desire to 'open the magic box', to lift the veil of its mystery. It may be wiser to avoid an in-depth analysis of the work and let art win the day.

Although the young Menzel soon tired of the Academy's 'plaster cast class', he delighted in 'all those beautiful casts . . . quite new to him'[1]. He began to collect them and kept his 'finds' each time he moved house. They attracted the attention of visitors, displayed on a Pompeian-red wall in his studio[2]. His first *Studio Wall* of 1852 shows only unusual casts (*cf.* cat. 65). In 1848 he wrote to Dr Puhlmann in an old-fashioned manner, as a joke: '. . . I will not therefore hide from you my visit to the statuary at Drake's yesterday. I inspected his Venus and, finding it to my liking, I immediately ordered Drake, on the authority which you accorded me, to take the aforementioned Venus and have it sent to me here in the room I occupy in the Ritterstrasse, a room which enjoys a most desirable situation and which is registered in the mortgage records of this town *cost:* I don't know how much'[3]. This may refer to the plaster cast of a female bust in the centre of the picture, and Friedrich Drake, a long-time friend of the painter, must have helped him to obtain it[4]. The bust was not by Drake, but was a reproduction of a Venus de Milo belonging to the Berlin collection of plaster casts, as later writers supposed. The Venus in Menzel's picture is unrecognizable, under a kind of footlight, as if awakened to new, more authentic life.

The 1872 *Studio Wall* is closely linked to *The Iron Rolling Mill*, which Menzel started work on in that year. It would be too dismissive merely to see this unusual composition as a light study for the larger painting, as Meyerheim's memoirs suggest[5]. Before new considerations emerged in relation to the *Studio Wall*, Karl Scheffler had already suggested back in 1938 that the picture had a deeper, hidden meaning. When he spoke of an 'enduring monument' created by Menzel, he seemed to have a memorial in mind[6].

The friendship between the art historian Friedrich Eggers and Menzel was an important element in the creation of *The Iron Rolling Mill* (160). With his description of August Borsig's steelworks in 1852, Eggers encouraged his friend to turn to more up-to-date subjects[7]. But it was not until twenty years later, the year when Eggers, died on 11 August 1872 aged fifty-two, that *The Iron Rolling Mill* was begun. *Studio Wall* is dated as October. According to the ambivalent opinion of Fontane on the friendship between the two men and on Eggers personality, light and shadow intermingled. They were both friends of the 'Tunnel over the Spree' group and of the more intimate 'Rütli' group. Eggers was Menzel's first critic, and wrote warmly about the artist's personality and work at a time when Menzel was struggling for recognition[8].

He was the first to describe Menzel's studio in the Ritterstrasse at great length in the journal *Deutsches Kunstblatt* in

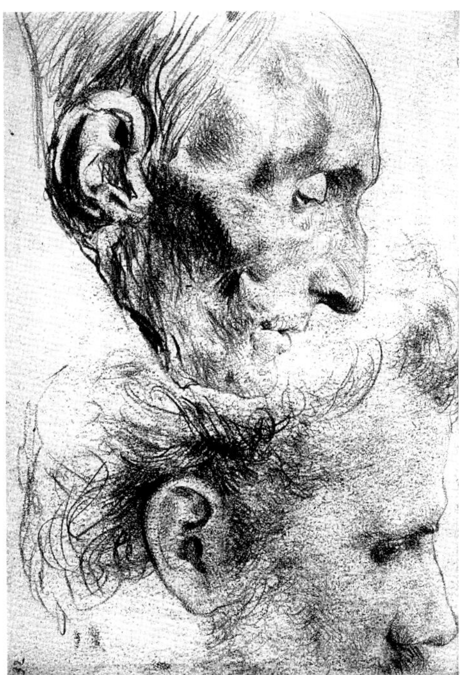

Fig. 204. Death Mask of Friedrich Eggers and Head of Man, 1872, pencil, Berlin, Kupferstichkabinett (sketchbook 38, p. 32)

1854. His description of one of the studio walls seems like a first sketch for the future composition: 'As well as Menzel's studies in oil, watercolour and pastel, there is a collection of plaster casts of human limbs and heads. Next to the sketches, the yellowish engravings in the style of Raphael are rare, and on the shelves there is nothing except a few casts of antique sculptures admired by everyone. Most of the place is filled with casts taken from nature, especially the most varied death masks, because of the two mistresses of art, Antiquity and Nature, Menzel undoubtedly favours the latter. . . .'[9] This reflection, revealing divergences in artistic conception which may well have been the source of more than one difference of opinion between the two men, might have been the inspiration for the composition of this unusual votive image. Behind these rows of masks are hidden Menzel's 'maxims and reflections' regarding the friendship and concepts of art of the two men[10]. Werner Hofmann rightly detected this when he spoke of a demonstration of the superiority of painting over sculpture. In fostering this ambiguity Menzel had discovered a way of expressing his personal and at times critical ideas, right from his first graphic works, over and above the conventions imposed by a commission. These 'finds' only have life by all appearances from the fascination with the real. They emit secret signals, become personal metaphors, showing the deceptive images of reality.

The still-life *Studio Wall*, an emblematic image of thoughts on death, is at the same time the apotheosis of pure painting (executed not only in daylight but, as is the case here, under artificial light). Everything in it, the death masks, the fragmentary nature of the plaster casts, the juxtaposition of objects apparently grouped randomly, can be interpreted as signs conveying the ephemeral nature of things and progressively blurring certainty of form. Upon the death of his friend Eggers, Menzel honoured his memory and painted his death mask, hanging in the centre of the picture, next to the female torso. Their mutual friend Drake probably made the death mask[11]. Menzel had already drawn Eggers on his deathbed on 11 August 1872[12]. His sketchbook of the same year[13], which only contains studies of workers at a rolling mill, also has the profile of a death mask turned to the right, with mouth and eyelids open, as in the drawing of the dead man (fig. 204). The high forehead and sharp nose of this once handsome face do not deceive. The mask must have been placed in the centre of the composition intentionally. M.R.-R.

1. *Cf.* cat. 45, note 5.
2. *Cf.* Kirstein, 1919, p. 84.
3. Letter to Wilhelm Puhlmann, 7 April 1848, Wolff, 1914, p. 132.
4. His friendship with Drake dated from the time of his visits to Carl Heinrich Arnold, when the latter still lived in Berlin, in the mid-1850s. Drake, the pupil of Christian Daniel Rauch, was a member of the Tunnel over the Spree, and married the sister of the painter Eduard Meyerheim. In 1844, Menzel drew Drake's plaster models in chalk. The models represented the female allegories of the eight Prussian provinces for the White Room of Berlin Castle (Euerbach, Georg Schäfer collection).
5. Meyerheim, (1906) 1992, p. 174. All the authors who support this view drew on Meyerheim, namely Hertel, (1911-12) 1992, p. 91; Scheffler, 1938, p. 72; Lichtwark, (19 June 1892) 1924, I, p. 92. They all consider the first *Studio wall* as a lighting study for the *Hochkirch* painting of 1856, which is highly unlikely. Lichtwark is even further from the mark when he sees the 1872 *Studio wall* as a lighting study relating to *Hochkirch*!
6. Scheffler, 1938, p. 120.
7. *Cf.* cat. 147-160, note 4.
8. On the subject of Fontane's opinion of Eggers, *cf.* in particular the description (which also relates some memories of Heinrich Seidel, a friend of Eggers) in the chapter devoted to him in his autobiography *Between twenty and thirty*; and also his opinions (given to his wife) which suggest that the relationship between Eggers and Menzel was sometimes strained, *cf.* letter of 5 April 1880 (Fontane, 1968-71, I, p. 120 and ff.). On Eggerss critique, Bruno Meyer wrote: After the creation of *Deutsches Kunstblatt* in 1850, Menzel, who was Achilles, found his Homer in Eggers. (Meyer, 1876, p. 1-10). He appreciates that Eggers's comments on Menzel and his preconceived ideas on aesthetics may not always have allowed him to make an appropriate judgement.
9. Eggers, 1854, p. 2.
10. A study on Eggers and Menzel is in preparation.
11. Like Friedrich Drake, Menzel attended the funeral preceding the transfer of the mortal remains to Eggers's home town of Rostock. *Cf.* Fontane, 1872. However, it is not proven that Drake made the death mask.
12. Prague, Narodní Gallery.
13. Berlin, Kupferstichkabinett, sketchbook 38, p. 32.

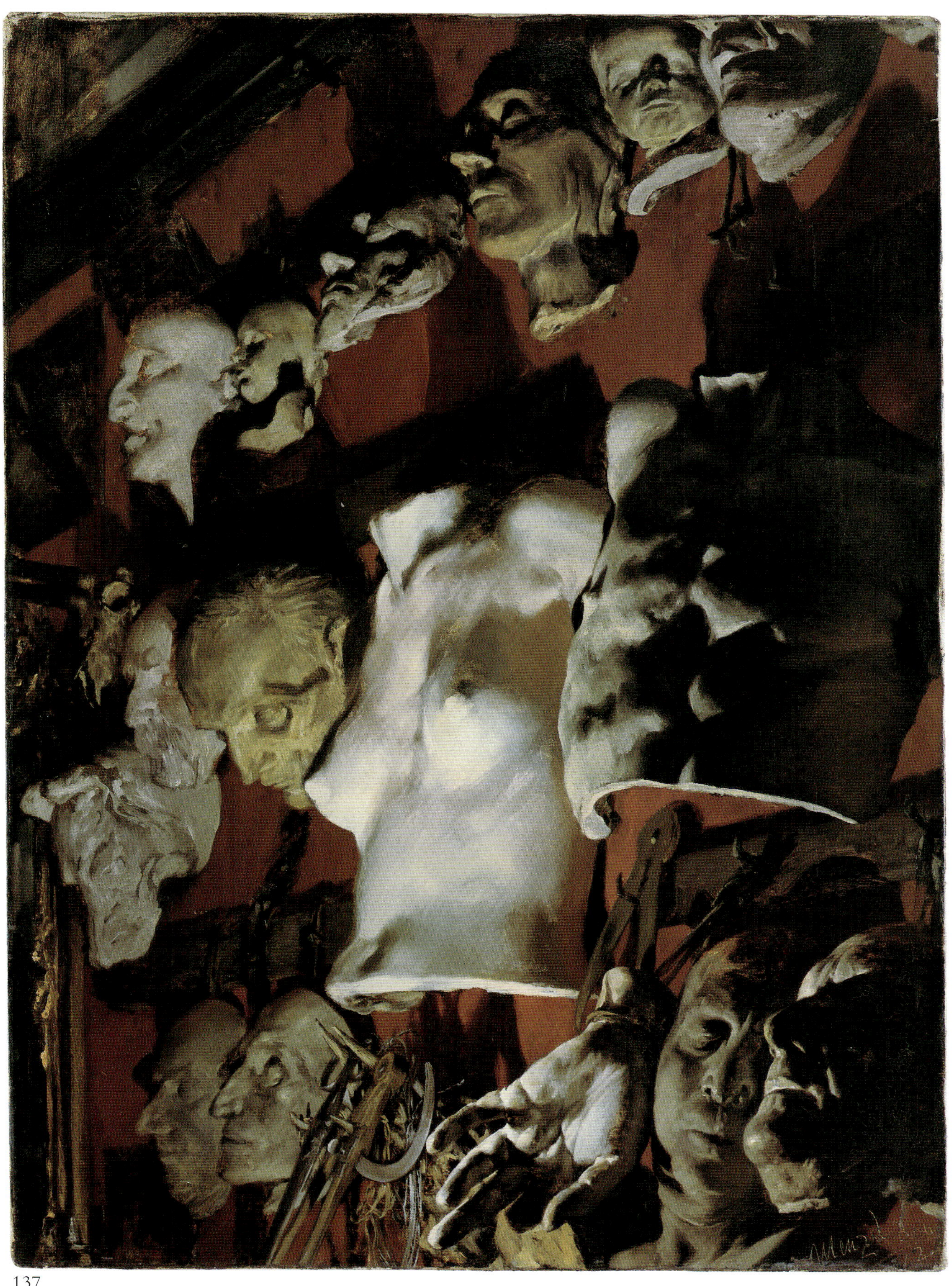

137

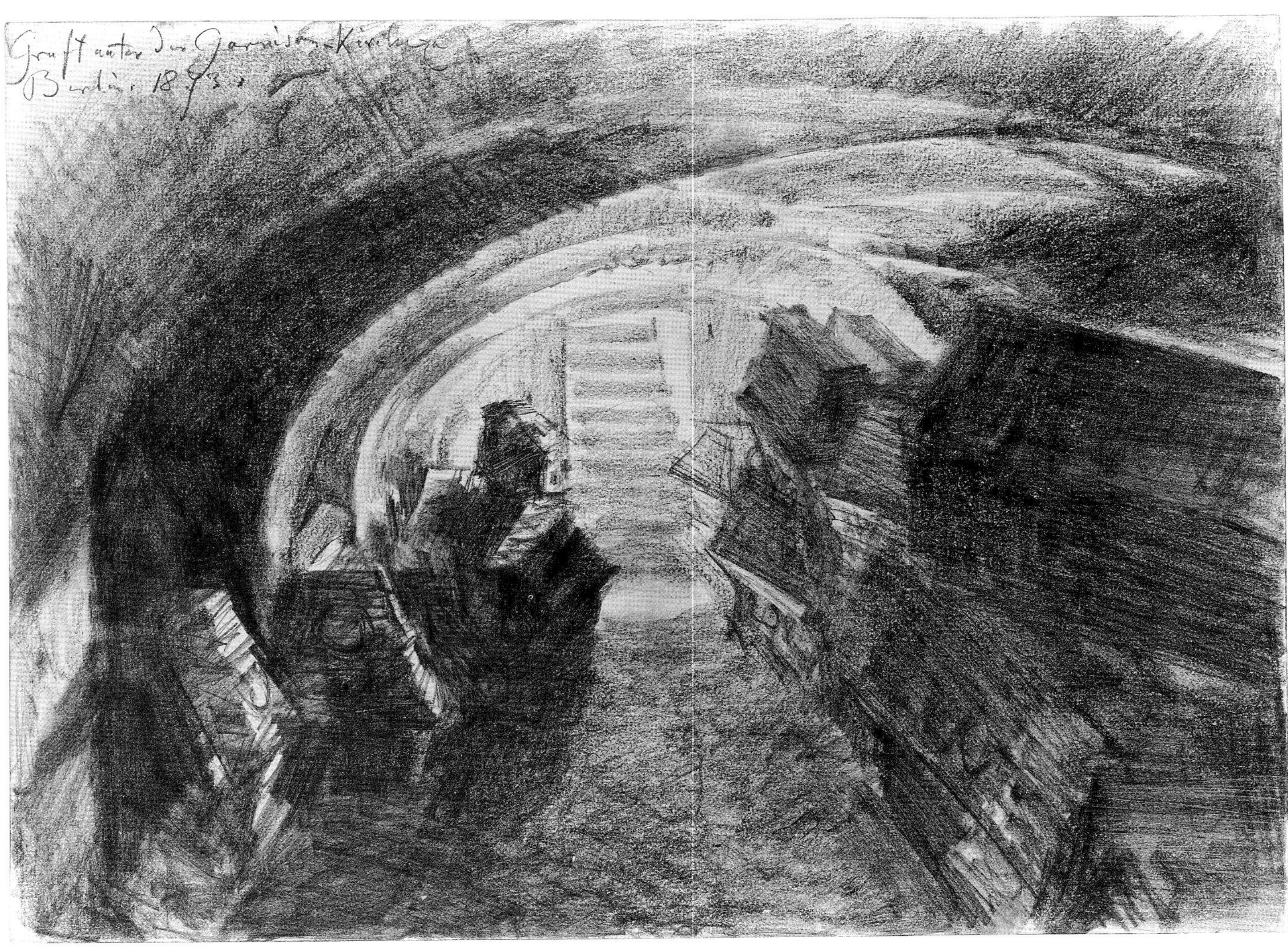

138

138

Vault beneath Garrison Church in Berlin

1873

Pencil
23.8 × 33.2cm
Annotated at the top left: *Gruft unter der Garnison-Kirche zu Berlin. 1873.*
Berlin, Kupferstichkabinett (SZ Menzel N 4441)
Exhibited in Paris and Berlin only

Provenance: Painter's studio; 1905 Emilie Krigar-Menzel; acquired by the museum in 1906.
Exhibitions: Berlin, 1905, no. 5234; Berlin, 1955 A, no. 388; Vienna, 1985, no. 99, reprod. p. 166; New York, 1990, no. 36, col. reprod. p. 131.

The church attached to the Berlin garrison was in the former Neue Friedrichstrasse on the area of the first fortifications. Founded in 1701 under the direction of Martin Grünberg, it was transformed by Philipp Gerlach between 1720 and 1722. A year later a large vault was constructed under this sober building built in the shape of a Greek cross, for the interment of soldiers and their relatives, with another built in 1786. Although they had been used for only a hundred years, by 1830 the vaults were full and, for reasons of hygiene, it was decided to close them. So in 1873 the most famous Prussian servicemen were transferred to the Hohenzollern vaults under Berlin cathedral, at the initiative of the newly constituted imperial house. The garrison vault had to be opened up and an attempt to identify the sarcophagi had to be made before they were transferred.

It was not the first time that Menzel had been present at the opening of tombs. The drawing of an open coffin in the Notre-Dame church in Halberstadt, which he used as a model for a gouache, dates from 1852[1]. In 1857 he saw the corpse of General von Winterfeld, entombed in 1758, of whom he did a portrait in the early 1850s[2]. The oil grisaille painted in 1878 also comes to mind, which shows Frederick II before the open coffin of the Prince-Elector[3], as do various drawings of the 1880s entirely devoted to vaults, crypts and tombs. Once again these reveal how

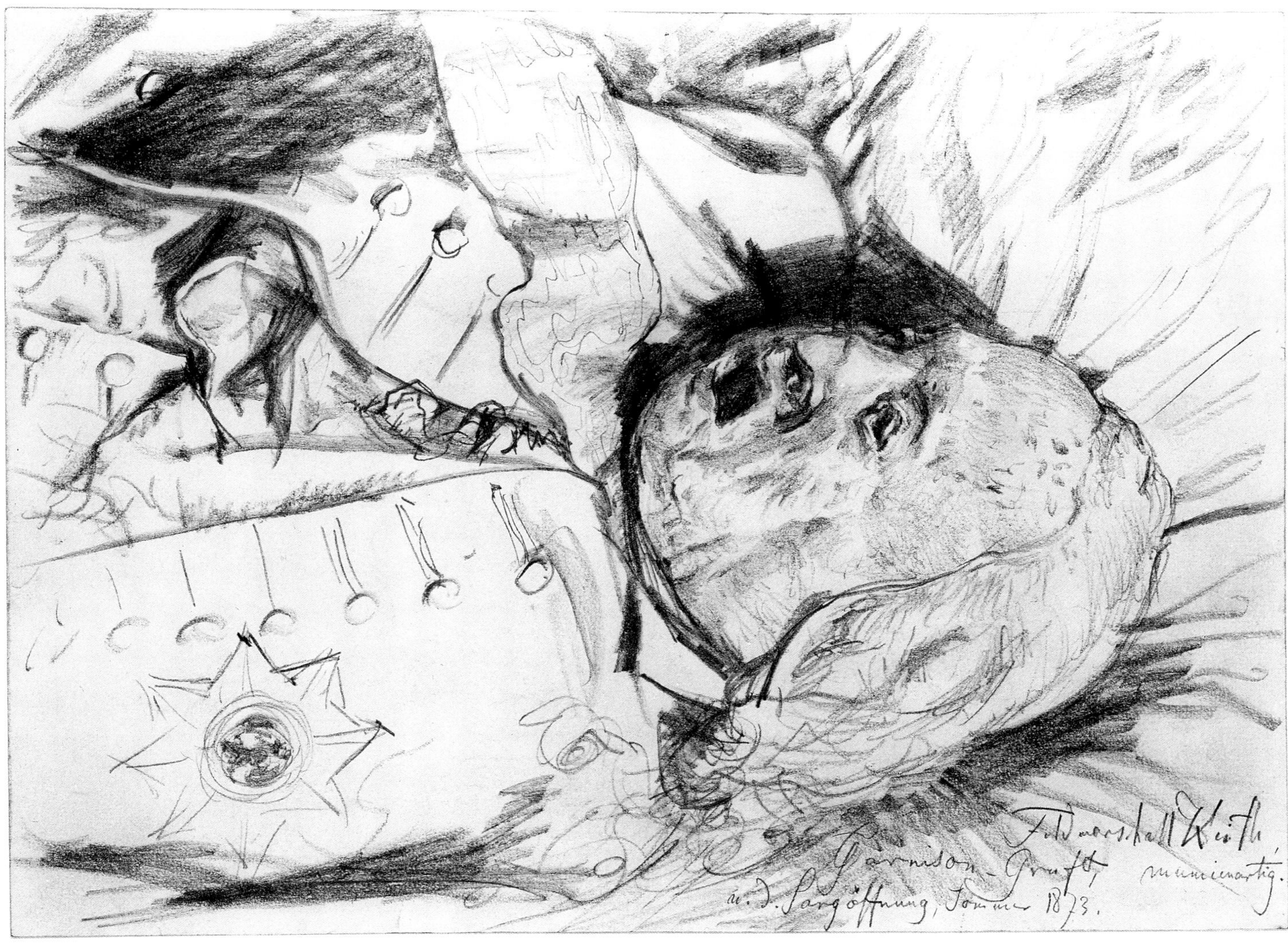

139

attractive the complex light in these situations was to Menzel (*cf.* cat. 181). The random piling up of the sarcophagi, fixed in pencil, is like a documentary tour. This drawing is a kind of introduction to a whole series of portraits of corpses. One cannot help grasping the lugubrious nature of the confrontation when the first coffin was opened. No one and nothing disturbs the silence of the place, where the dead are stacked one on top of the other with no respect for rank. This layout is reproduced in another drawing from a different angle[4]. The disorder is paralleled in Menzel's hasty, agitated lines which fix his impressions of the place on paper. A ray of light comes from the bottom of the steps and lights the scene inadequately. The light can only be reached by passing beyond the dead bodies. A.H.

1. Berlin, Kupferstichkabinett (SZ Menzel N 1181).
2. For the series of woodcuts *In the time of King Frederick* (Bock, 1923, no. 1069).
3. Tschudi, 1905 A, no. 149.
4. Berlin, Kupferstichkabinett (SZ Menzel N 4440).

139

Body of Field-Marshal Keith

1873

Pencil
23.8 × 33.2cm
Annotated and dated at the bottom right: *Feldmarschall Keith, mumienartig. Garnison-Gruft, n.d. Sargöffnung, Sommer 1873.*
Berlin, Kupferstichkabinett (SZ Menzel N 252)

Provenance: Painter's studio; 1905 Emilie Krigar-Menzel; acquired by the museum in 1906.
Exhibitions: Berlin, 1905, no. 5234f; Berlin, n.d., no. 56; Berlin, 1980 A, no. 281, reprod. p. 262; Vienna, 1985, no. 101, reprod. p. 168; Copenhagen, 1985, no. 86, reprod. p. 54.

'In 1873, in the presence of the parish council and Professor Adolph Menzel, I opened many coffins among the nine hundred in the church of the Berlin garrison, in order to identify the bodies. In one of the coffins we found a completely preserved field-marshal, with his hair and Black Eagle decoration on his chest. Menzel said at once: "It's Keith, I recognize him from his likeness!" It was indeed him – a bullet had pierced his mouth', wrote Colonel von Prittwitz in 1883, contesting the widespread opinion that Keith had been mortally wounded in his 'heroic chest'[1].

James Keith, who fell during the Seven Years War in 1758 at the battle of Hochkirch, had served Prussia since 1747. He was born in 1696, the son of an ancient family of the Scottish nobility and was forced into exile in 1715. He served different European powers before moving to Potsdam at the age of fifty-one. Frederick II greatly esteemed this cultivated and cautious man, who was part of his 'round table' and listened to his advice. Not only his military successes were glorified by Bernhard Rode when he linked him with four other generals in the series of allegories painted for the choir of the garrison church.

Menzel drew him at an angle to hide the frightful wound, yet without concealing the cruelty of death. The marshal's individual features seem to have interested him, probably all the more because he had already painted his portrait[2] on the basis of idealized portraits of his face, while the body was done from studies of a model. The unique opportunity presented itself of comparing his 1851 portrait of Keith with the disfigured, lifeless yet real corpse twenty-two years later[3]. Menzel sought the reality of the past not in the accounts of historians, but in the mortal remains of Fredericks time. A.H.

1. Siefart, 1908.
2. In the series of engravings *In the time of King Frederick* (1856, Bock, 1923, no. 1065-1076).
3. Bock, 1923, no. 1068.

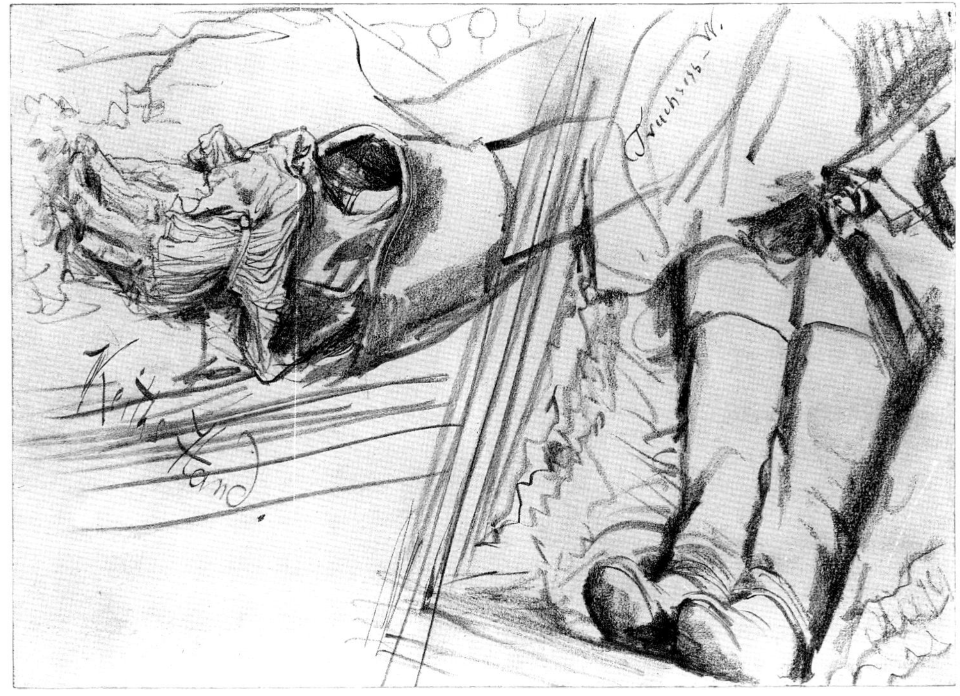
140

140
The Hand of Keith and the Legs of Count Truchsess von Waldburg
1873

Pencil
23.8 × 33.2cm
Annotated on the left: *Keiths Hand* – At the top right: *Truchsess-W.*
Berlin, Kupferstichkabinett (SZ Menzel N 250)
Exhibited in Paris only

Provenance: Painter's studio; 1905 Emilie Krigar-Menzel; acquired by the museum in 1906.
Exhibitions: Berlin, 1905, no. 5234d; Vienna, 1985, no. 102, reprod. p. 168.
Bibliography: Lammel, 1988, p. 166, fig. 120.

The disorder in which the bodies in the garrison vault were found is reflected in the characteristic layout of this drawing. Two disparate details are put together on the same sheet of paper. An oblique gaze which ignores the rest of the body is directed upon the mummified hand of Field-Marshal Keith, while the legs of the mummy of a Count Truchsess von Waldburg are viewed from high above. This approach is quite typical of Menzel's sketchbooks. The drawings of the garrison vaults were noted down in one of those sketchbooks which contain the customary hasty bringing together of subjects and their enigmatic association on the page. The rapid use of the pencil is obvious in all of this series, in which at times a fiercely drawn line has scored the paper. The identity of Count von Waldburg is explained in another drawing[1], showing the upper part of the counts corpse lying in the sarcophagus with his hands folded across his stomach, apparently holding a rosary. The head is once again sketched at the side. The iron cross with which he is decorated indicates the context of the Napoleonic wars. Menzel suggests a link between James Keith, who fell in the Seven Years War, and a dead man from the Napoleonic era. A.H.

1. Berlin, Kupferstichkabinett (SZ Menzel N 250); exhib. cat. Vienna, 1985, no. 103.

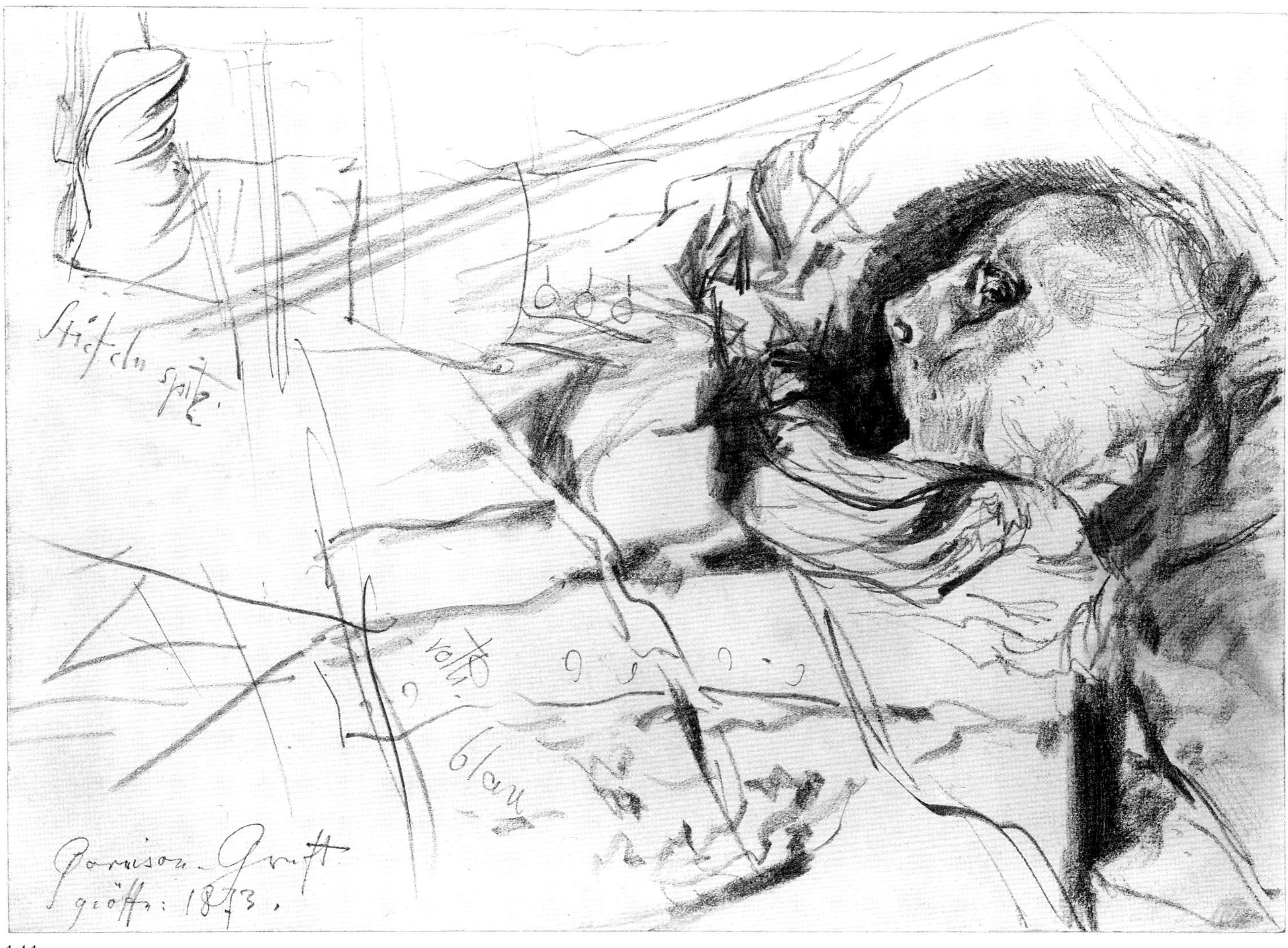

141

141
Head of a Dead Man, and Boots
1873

Pencil
23.8 × 33.2cm
Annotated on the left: *Garnison-Gruft geöffn: 1873. Stiefeln spitz. roth. blau*
Berlin, Kupferstichkabinett (SZ Menzel N 251)
Exhibited in Washington and Berlin only

Provenance: Painter's studio; 1905 Emilie Krigar-Menzel; acquired by the museum in 1906.
Exhibitions: Berlin, 1905, no. 5234e; Berlin, 1955 A, no. 390; Vienna, 1985, no. 100, reprod. p. 167; Copenhagen, 1985, no. 85, reprod. p. 53.

This time the attention of the artist was drawn by the sloping skull of the mummy, the wide-open mouth on the coffin pillow and the surrounding shadow. We can make out a scarf, though the uniform has been sketched in a few quick lines. In the empty upper space Menzel added a pair of boots, plus the significant detail: 'Pointed boots'. Their contours cross over those of the coffin, quickly sketched beforehand. Menzel was a meticulous collector of documents and historical facts and the shape of the boots or colour of the uniform were very important to him. It was due to such details that the artist was able to identify a person or reconstruct a context. A.H.

142
Body of an Officer
1873

Pencil
23.8 × 33.3cm
Annotated at the top left: *Auf dem Sargdeckel nur die Buchstaben Gd v G. 1794. Uniform wei· Rab: roth* – At the bottom left: *Garn: Gruft, geöffn: 1873.*
Berlin, Kupferstichkabinett (SZ Menzel N 253)
Exhibited in Paris only

Provenance: Painter's studio; 1905 Emilie Krigar-Menzel; acquired by the museum in 1906.
Exhibition: Berlin, 1905, no. 5234g.

We may never know who lies behind the initials 'Gd v G. 1794'. It must have been a high-ranking officer who was buried in

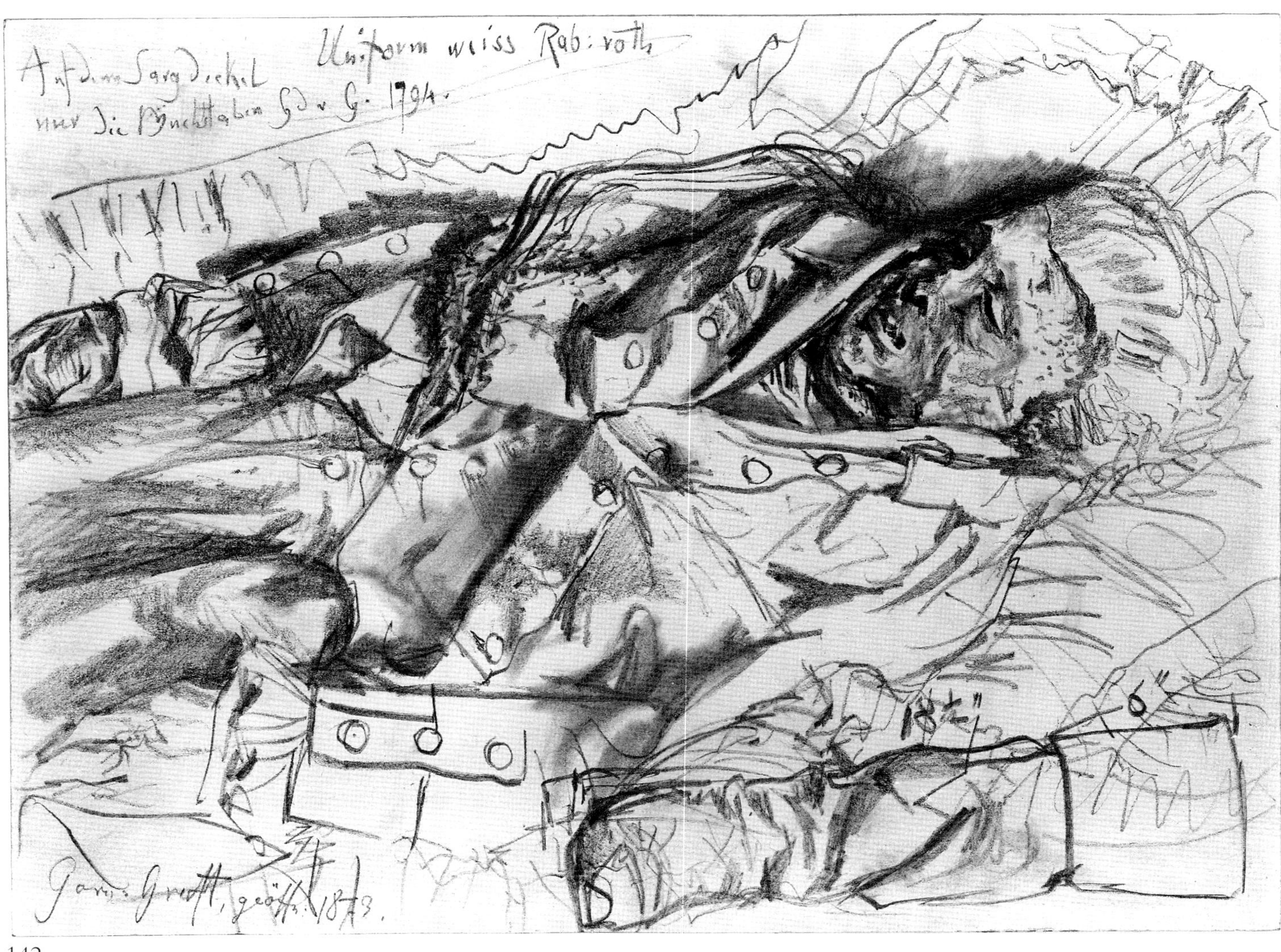

142

his white gala uniform. Menzel drew him up to the thigh, as he was found, laid out in the coffin lined with fabric. Everything is included, detailed notes at the bottom of the drawing, stains on the other side of the lace, as well as the boots with even the measurements taken down.

Faced with the cadaver, the artist chose a penetrating perspective. The macabre aspect of these drawings has been underlined[1], which not only characterize the subject represented but also the situation itself, the act of opening up the vault and inspecting the sarcophagi before their transfer. Menzel was not in the least disconcerted. His objective approach released him from the scruples which may have been appropriate in such a situation. The exceptional nature of the event absorbed his attention to such a degree that he made all these drawings at one sitting, which bear the imprint of an intense, expressive dialogue between the artist and the interred body, beyond the time which separated them. Some years before, in 1866, when Menzel painted a watercolour of the bodies of soldiers who had just died in the military hospital at Königinhof and were thrown on the ground instead of being laid on a bier, deep feeling comes over: '. . . after 15 days' immersion in terror, suffering and stench. Now I know where Schlüter obtained his masks for the Arsenal[2]. On the other hand he had learned long before to speak of the dead without the least respect, as in the case of Wallenstein, when he planned on a journey to 'go and see the laughing face of the old man from Friedland in his coffin at Gitschin'[3]. A.H.

1. Keisch, exhib. cat. Vienna, 1985, p. 165.
2. Letter to Doctor Puhlmann, 2 August 1866, Wolff, 1914, p. 205.
3. Letter to Heinrich Paul, 31 July 1866, Wolff, 1914, p. 204.

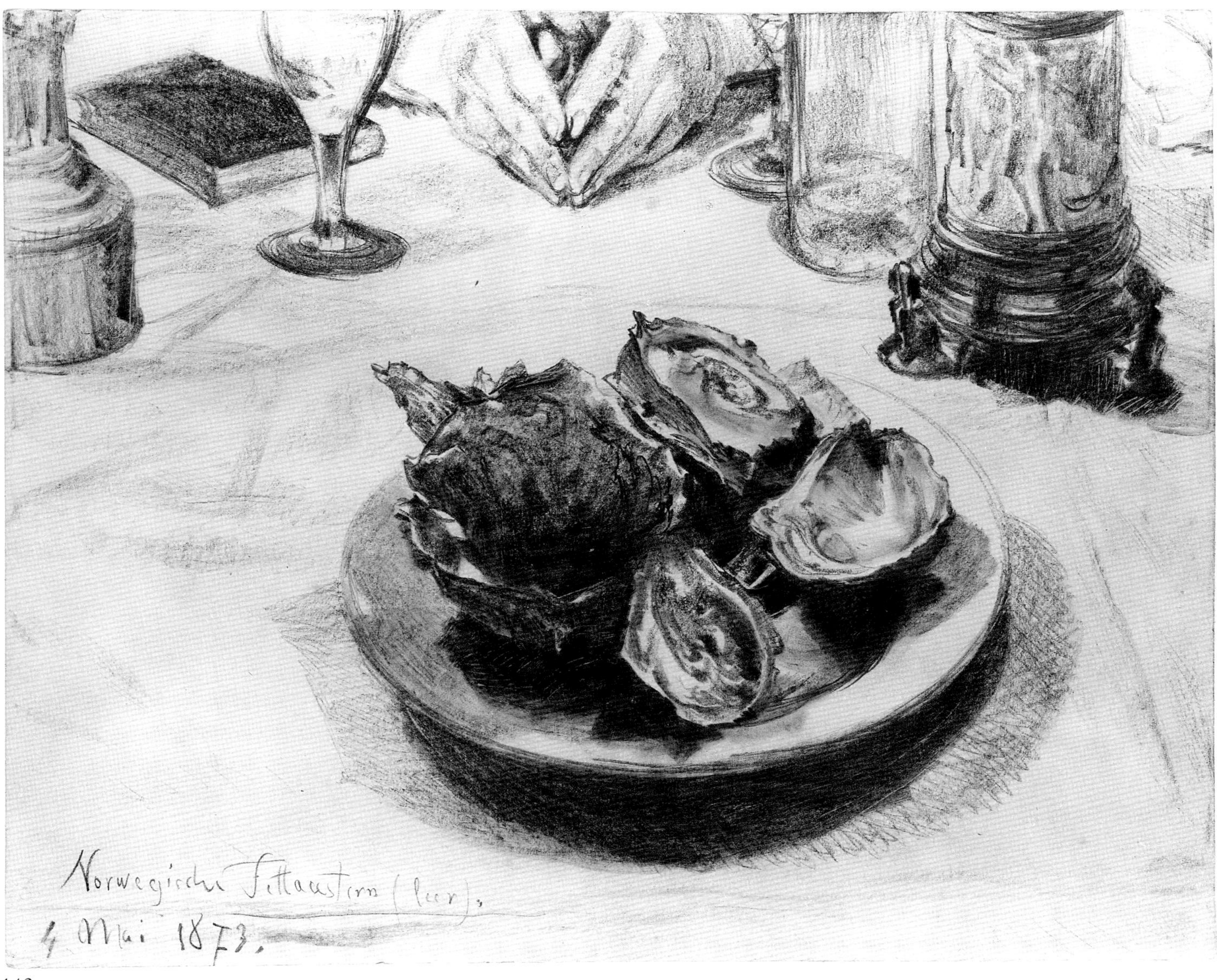

143

143
Norwegian Oysters
1873

Pencil
26.8 × 34cm
Annotated and dated: *Norwegische Fettaustern (leer). 4. Mai 1873.*
Berlin, Kupferstichkabinett (SZ Menzel N 262)

Provenance: Painter's studio; 1905 Emilie Krigar-Menzel; acquired by the museum in 1906.
Exhibitions: Berlin, 1903 A, Berlin, 1905, no. 6412; Berlin, 1955 A, no. 386; Vienna, 1985, no. 104, reprod.
Bibliography: Beta, 1898, II, p. 50; *Kunst und Künstler*, vol. 1, 1902–3, p. 320.

Menzel's eye creates a poignant representation worthy of his most famous works, as he did with the decomposed bodies of the heroes discovered in the garrison vault in the same year (*cf.* cat. 139–42). As he got older he increasingly used a carpenter's pencil, which he had already used for studies for *The Iron Rolling Mill*. Once more, it is the 'found' object, the inanimate and slightly misplaced article, which fascinates him. Whether these objects are liturgical shoes, a viola d'amore or the case of a pair of binoculars, his eye manipulates them and makes it hard to avoid the interpretation given in the drawing. Under the plate of oysters the word 'empty' appears, and this sensation of the void is strengthened by the empty space around the plate. The view from above and the sharp, seemingly random breaking off of the subject at the top edge of the picture reinforce the strange isolation of the objects represented – clasped hands, glasses, containers and a small book. (Another drawing[1] shows empty shells on a plate surrounded by other shells, two open and three closed.) In the drawing shown here, a space suggested by a shadow on the edge of the plate dissolves immediately in the absence of perspective around the shells.

According to the date given on the two pages, they must have been drawn at

Vienna, during a visit to the Universal Exhibition, which began at the beginning of May. Meyerheim recalls the strange culinary habits of the painter. He often had dinner very late, and sometimes fell asleep in the middle of it. 'When he woke up, Menzel tried to eat what was left of his dessert but, realizing it was cold and inedible, he laid his knife and fork on top, pushed it away from him a little and took out his sketchbook from his pocket to draw this strange still life meticulously'[2].

Menzel used the subject of oysters again, in 1879. In a historical genre scene entitled *The Oyster Eater* (or *Just One More!*), they occupy the entire corner of the table at which a gentleman from the baroque era is sitting and asking the innkeeper to refill his glass[3]. M.R.-R.

1. Berlin, Kupferstichkabinett, (SZ Menzel N 263).
2. Meyerheim, (1906) 1992, p. 183.
3. Tschudi, 1905 A, no. 623; location unknown. *Cf.* Werner, 1913, p. 251; with *The oyster eater* Menzel contributed to an album given by the Royal Academy to its president Friedrich Hitzig, for fifty years of service.

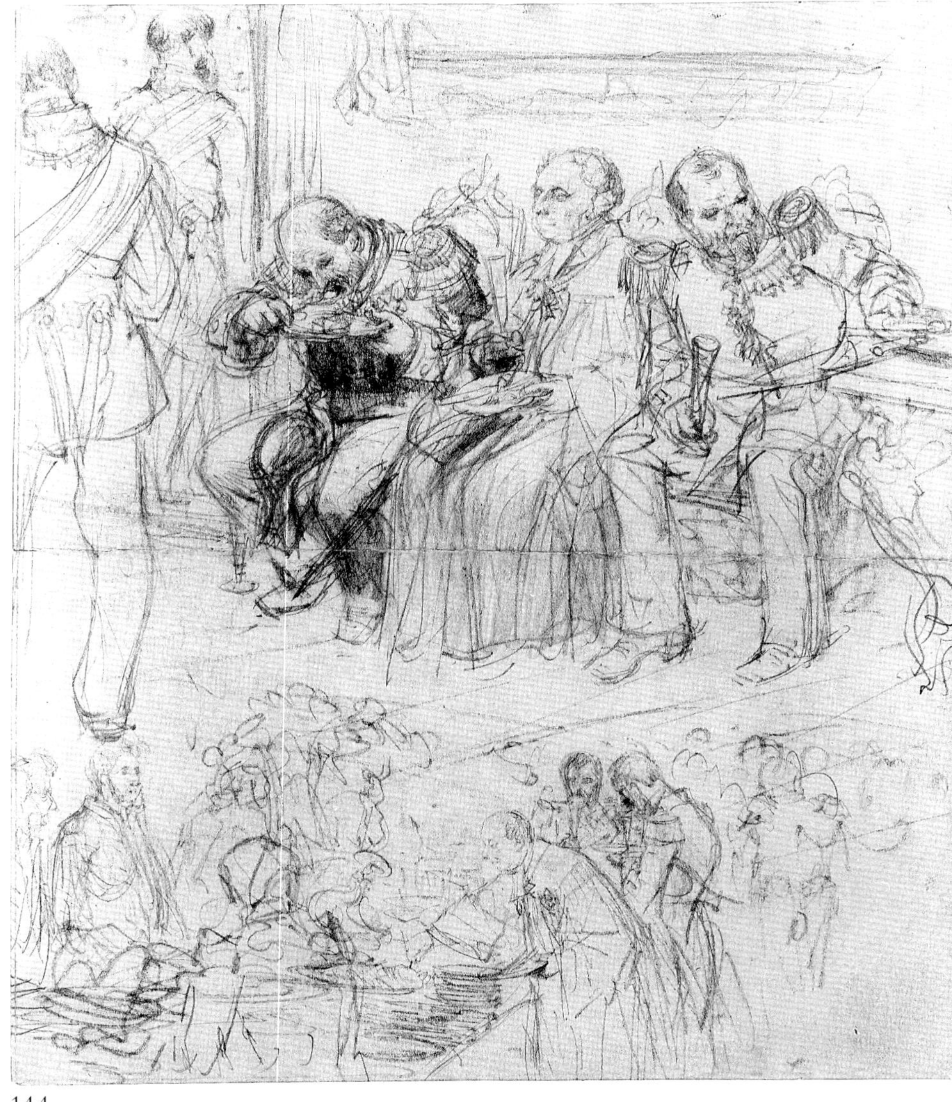

144

144
A Ball at Court (Scene at the Buffet)
1873

Pencil
28.3 × 22.7cm
Berlin, Kupferstichkabinett (SZ Menzel N 1476)

Provenance: Painter's studio; 1905 Emilie Krigar-Menzel; acquired by the museum in 1906.
Exhibitions: Berlin, 1905, no. 6671; Vienna, 1985, no. 55.

After he had painted the picture of *The Coronation* (*cf.* cat. 94–9), Menzel was regularly invited to court festivities. He often used the back of announcements and party invitations, which were usually quite generous, to do his sketches. He used to fold them so that he could fit several sketches in side by side on the same sheet.

The two officers sitting on the right and left are shown differently in *Supper at the Ball* (cat. 167), in contrast with the clergyman sitting in the middle. Menzel 'pursues' the clergyman in his drawing, first sitting vacantly between his two neighbours enjoying the feast, and then helping himself to food from the buffet. The features of the army chaplain and consistorial high councillor Peter Thielen are recognizable, a figure who had already appeared looking fresher and younger in the picture of *The Coronation*. A painter and a clergyman meet here, two people from bourgeois society for whom a court ball could only have had a minimal interest, for different reasons. Menzel the observer found a whole range of subjects there which enriched his portrayals of city life. It is not without discreet irony that he drew the preacher helping himself at the buffet, or depicted the difficulties of eating food in the most uncomfortable positions. A.H.

145 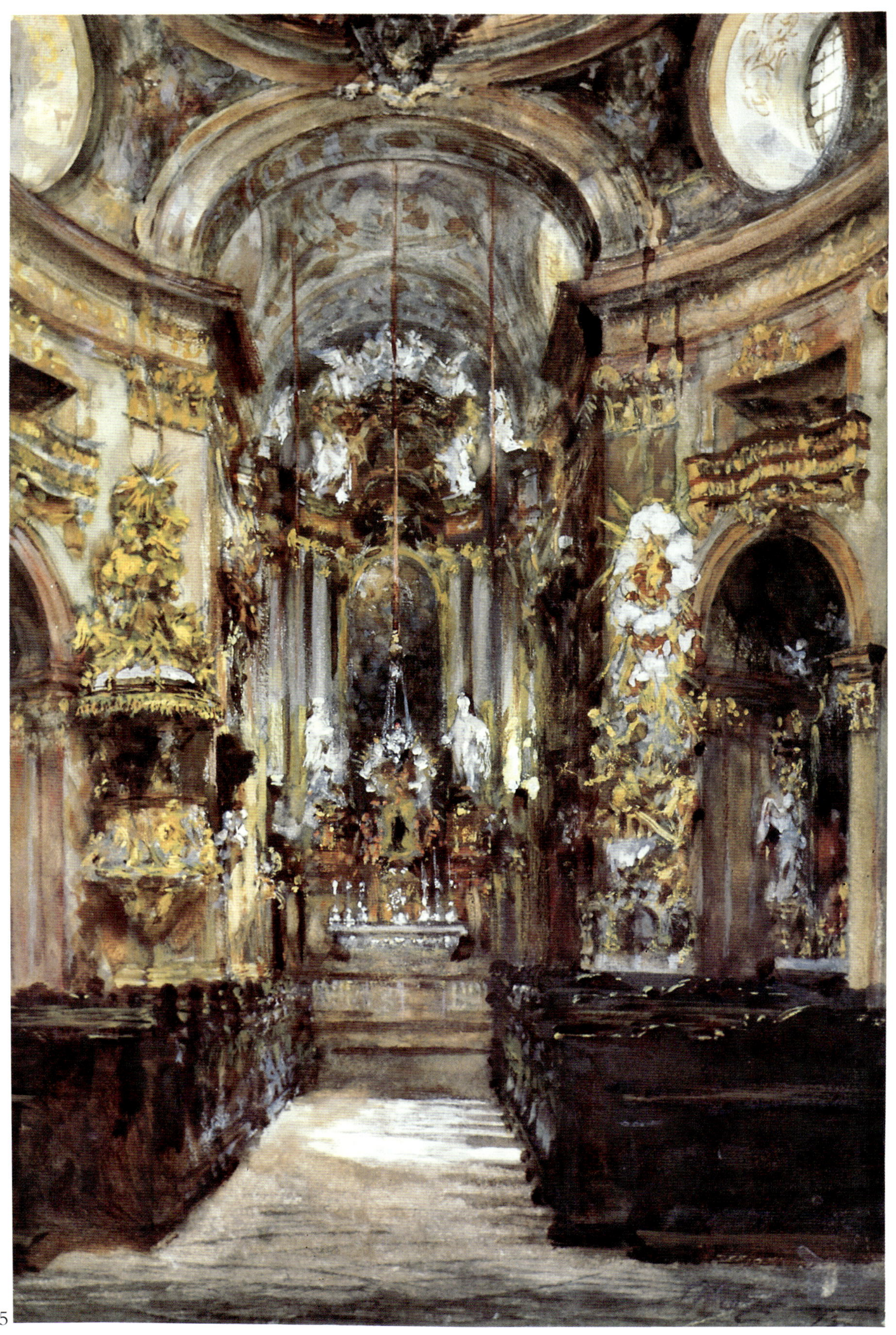

145

Interior of Saint Peter's Church in Vienna

1873

Gouache
40 × 26cm
Signed and dated at the bottom right: *Menzel 73*
Liberec, Oblastní Galerie (C 208)

Provenance: Victor Rheinse, Berlin; acquired by the museum in 1913.
Exhibitions: Prague, 1955, no. 130; Berlin, 1956, no. 140.
Bibliography: Schwedeler-Meyer, 1929, p. 146, reprod.; Vintner, 1964, p. 116, fig. 5; Hütt, 1965, fig. 50; Wirth, 1974, p. 135 *et seq.*

In the summer of 1873, during a long journey through Upper Austria, Menzel went through Vienna, a place he already knew, and which he would revisit several times in the future. It was the year of the Universal Exhibition. Soon after his return to Berlin, he painted not only two subjects from Hofgastein[1] and a view of the Ladies Collegiate church in Munich[2], but also *The Indian Café at the Universal Exhibition*[3] and this *Interior of Saint Peter's Church*, the oldest parish church in Vienna, near the Graben (*cf.* cat 206), rebuilt to a central plan by Lukas von Hildebrandt. The eye starts in the middle of the scene and moves over the pews to alight on the main altar, which is slightly to the left of the median axis of the composition and disturbs its symmetry a little. The rostrum built by Matthias Steinl at the beginning of the nineteenth century is to the left of the *trompe l'oeil* architecture adorning the main altar by Antonio Galli-Bibiena, although the Trinity grouped on the sounding-board is indistinct. Facing, on the altar of St John of Nepomuk, also designed by Steinl, the dramatic scene of the saint thrown into the Moldau is not clear either. Only a general impression of shapes is given. The special radiance, the exceptional nature of the object, is rendered like a mental state, in a brief moment of 'natural authenticity'[4]. In this way Menzel often goes against the subjective vision to arrive at an objective formula.

This baroque interior is without doubt the only one Menzel painted without figures in it. The effect is created only by the silence and play of light which spreads across the floor from the glass roof to the cupola over the altar, calming the agitation of form and colour. M.R.-R.

1. Interiors of a country inn Zur wei·en Taube, Tschudi, 1905 A, no. 601 and 602; Berlin, Kupferstichkabinett (SZ Menzel N 256) and Euerbach, Georg Schäfer collection. 2. Tschudi, 1905 A, no. 604; Euerbach, Georg Schäfer collection.
3. Tschudi, 1905 A, no. 599; location unknown.
4. Letter to Wilhelm Puhlmann, 5 November 1836, Wolff, 1914, p. 15.

146

The Barberini Faun

1874

Pencil
40.1 × 26.2cm
Signed and dated at the bottom right: *Menzel 74.*
Berlin, Kupferstichkabinett (SZ Menzel N 203)
Exhibited in Paris only

Provenance: Painter's studio; 1905 Emilie Krigar-Menzel; acquired by the museum in 1906.
Exhibitions: Paris, 1885, no. 106 (*Satyr from the Barbonico Museum*); Berlin, 1905, no. 4551; Berlin, 1980 A, no. 285; New York, 1990, no. 61.

Although he briefly attended plaster cast classes at the Academy, Menzel soon turned away from studies bearing the stamp of Classicism to find models in nature and in historical documents. However, he never stopped drawing the masterpieces of antiquity. The Berlin collection of plaster models, which were quite unique at the time, consisted of several thousands of pieces made up largely from the Academy's teaching materials, and Menzel drew them several times (*cf.* cat. 45). In 1873 and 1874, when Menzel was drawing The Barberini Faun at the Munich Glyptotek, a series of drawings came to light at the Neues Museum, which had been in possession of the collection of Berlin plaster sculptures since the early 1850s. They had been finally deposited there after temporary location at the Altes Museum. The drawings show the river god Cephissus, one of the Classical figures on the west front of the Parthenon, with other sculptures from the same monument[1]. The comparison with an older study of the same subject which Menzel had drawn in 1846 as a vignette for *Epistle to La Motte Fouqué*[2], clearly shows the evolution of his style. The two figures are in opposition: fine lines, drawn with sharp pencil in the first drawing, and vigorous lines and the supple plasticity of the carpenter's pencil in the second. When Menzel began to work on *The Iron Rolling Mill* he sought large forms exclusively. The studies of workers and male nudes drawn from models coincide with the years prior to the completion of this picture. In this context, we can appreciate that the grandiose physique of the sleeping faun was of exceptional interest to Menzel. During his stay in Munich in the summer of 1874, he drew two representations of confusing density[3]. He did not treat the young, vigorous faun's abandonment to sleep in a Classical way, but in total conformity to his time, more as a psychic phenomenon, by modifying the sleeper's features only. Menzel transformed the expression of animal exhaustion, the half-open mouth and knitted brows, into serene relaxation, with almost a smile playing round the lips. The fascination he must have felt for this sculpture of a faun from the late Hellenistic period (220 BC) can be explained also by his liking for the lively nature of the Baroque, whose origin lay less in contemporary enthusiasm for Neo-baroque than in his own nature, as often conveyed by his writing. Menzel definitely did not see the faun for the first time in 1874, but in 1852, on his first extensive study trip. In a letter to Paul Heyse dated 1854, he mentions the faun in a humorous tone as a 'horrid child'[4] in relation to 'an ill-considered idea'.

It is interesting that Menzel's drawings depict the figure of a faun which no longer exists today. The torso of the satyr was discovered between 1623 and 1628 in the ditch of the San Angelo castle in Rome. Its left leg was missing, as well as

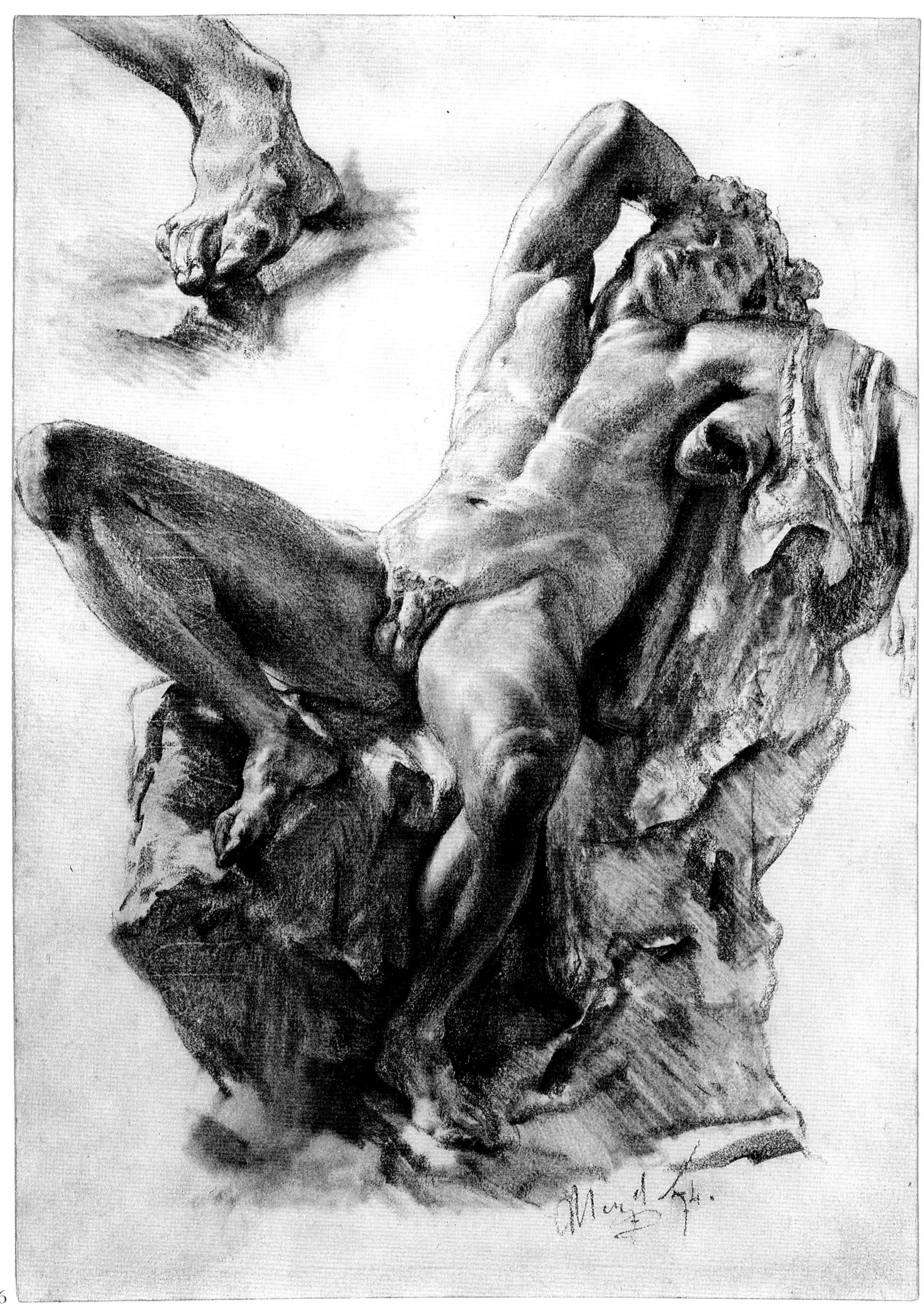
146

part of the right leg, the left forearm, the tips of the fingers and nose, part of the fur and the back half of the rock. Part of what was missing was found in fragmentary form. The satyr was named after the royal family of Barberini, from whom its first owner, Pope Urban VIII, was descended. It was sold at the end of the eighteenth century to the sculptor and dealer Vincenzo Pacetti, who completed it in his own way, only preserving the base of additions made by Bernini. After some incredible commercial transactions, it went to Munich in 1820 to the collection of Crown Prince Ludwig, who had been fascinated by this exceptional sculpture since he saw it in Rome in the winter of 1803–4, and had been trying to buy it for years[5]. The drawing of the faun shown here cuts off the left arm completed by Pacetti and almost suggests the reconstruction of the sculpture (without the arm) which has been on show in the Glyptotek, with some intermediate modifications, since 1983. M.R.-R.

1. Berlin, Kupferstichkabinett (SZ Menzel N 215-217, 899).
2. Bock, 1923, no. 925; *Works of Frederick the Great*. vol. XI, p. 22.
3. The second unsigned version is in the Staatliche Graphische Sammlung in Munich; it once belonged to the writer Ludwig Pietsch. Menzel may have seen the marble replica by Edme Bouchardon at the Louvre.
4. Letter to Paul Heyse, 18 August 1854, Munich, Bayerische Staatsbibliothek, Heyse archives.
5. *Cf.* Walter, 1993.

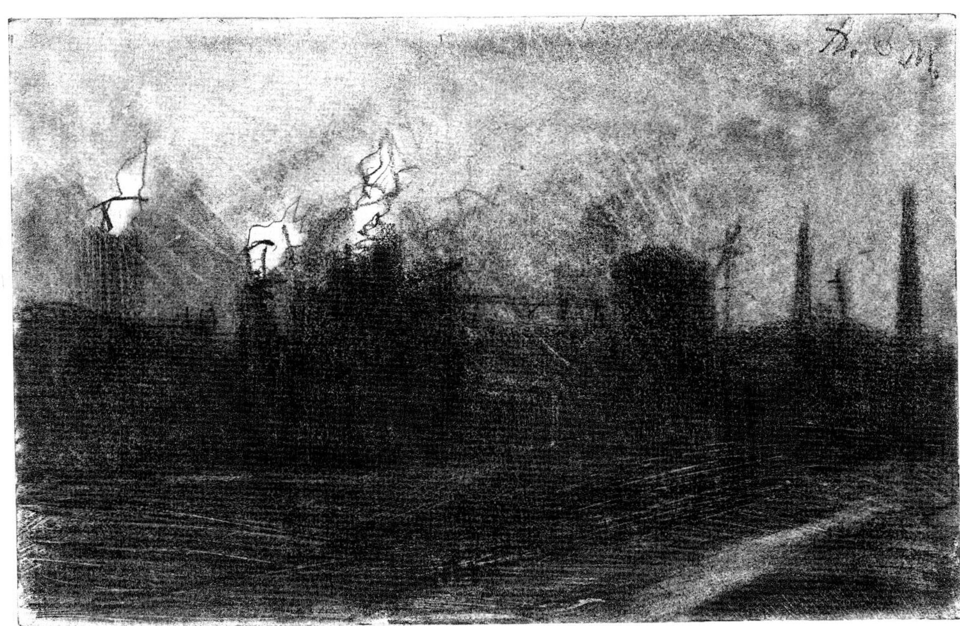

147

147

The Chimneys at Königshütte, Spitting Flames (Industrial Landscape at Königshütte)

1872

Pencil
12.2 × 19.1cm
Signed at the top right: *A.M.*
Berlin, Kupferstichkabinett (SZ Menzel N 3195)
Exhibited in Paris and Washington only

Provenance: Painter's studio; 1905 Emilie Krigar-Menzel; acquired by the museum in 1906.
Exhibitions: Berlin, 1905, no. 3354; Paris, 1976–7, no. 140; Vienna, 1985, no. 69, reprod. p. 138; Copenhagen, 1985, no. 61, reprod. p. 41; Vienna, 1990, no. 140.
Bibliography: Kurth, 1941, p. 38 *et seq.*, p. 95; Berlin, 1994, no. VII.36.

Like another similar drawing[1], this drawing prefigures the generous use of chiaroscuro in the 1880s. The factory with tall chimneys, in daylight, is viewed from a realistic angle.

1. Berlin, Kupferstichkabinett (SZ Menzel N 3260).

148

Great Hall of the Rolling Mill. Königshütte

1872

Pencil
23.8 × 32.9cm
Signed at the bottom left: *Ad. Menzel* – Annotated: *Bei der Walzarbeit alles Balken u. Stangenwerk roth angeschienen. Alles dahinter erscheint dunkel. Alles Gitterwerk oben auf dieser Seite heller als der grau Hintergrund.* ('When the rolling mill is working all the girders and system of rods are lit up red. Everything behind is dark. The entire iron trellis system above is lighter from this side than the grey background'.)
Berlin, Kupferstichkabinett (SZ Menzel N 155)

Provenance: Painter's studio; 1905 Emilie Krigar-Menzel; acquired by the museum in 1906.
Exhibitions: Berlin, 1905, no. 3261; Berlin, 1980 A, no. 313, reprod. p. 385; Vienna, 1985, no. 72, reprod. p. 142; Copenhagen, 1985, no. 63, reprod. p. 43; New York, 1990, no. 52, col. reprod. p. 168.
Bibliography: Exhib. cat. Berlin, 1976, p. 8 *et seq.*

The space indicated with impetuous lines corresponds almost exactly to the painting (cat. 160), but it was considerably enlarged on both sides as well as in the foreground.

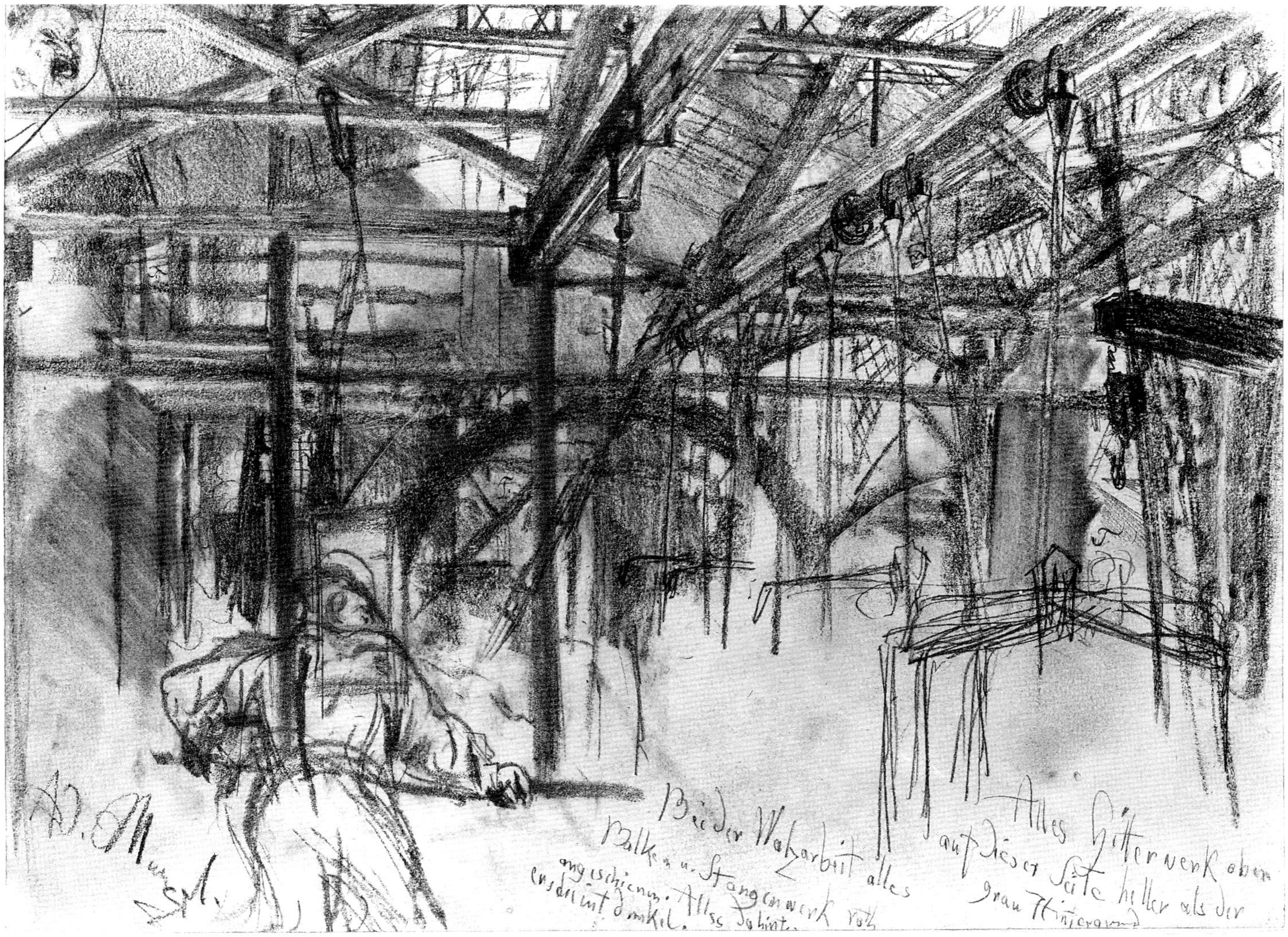

148

149

Engine Room in the Rolling Mill

1872

Pencil
22.3 × 30.5cm
Signed at the centre bottom: *AM*
Berlin, Kupferstichkabinett (SZ Menzel N 1381)
Exhibited in Paris and Berlin only

Provenance: Painter's studio; 1905 Emilie Krigar-Menzel; acquired by the museum in 1906.
Exhibitions: Berlin, 1905, no. 3311; Vienna, 1985, no. 70, reprod. p. 139.

This lively and clearly spontaneous sketch was undoubtedly drawn in the engine room itself.

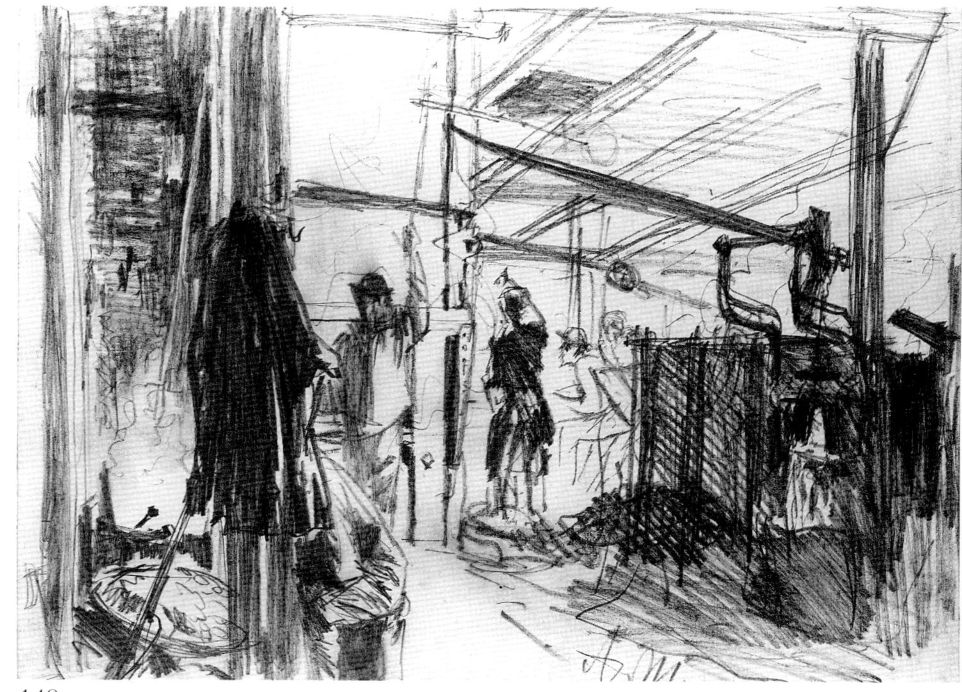

149

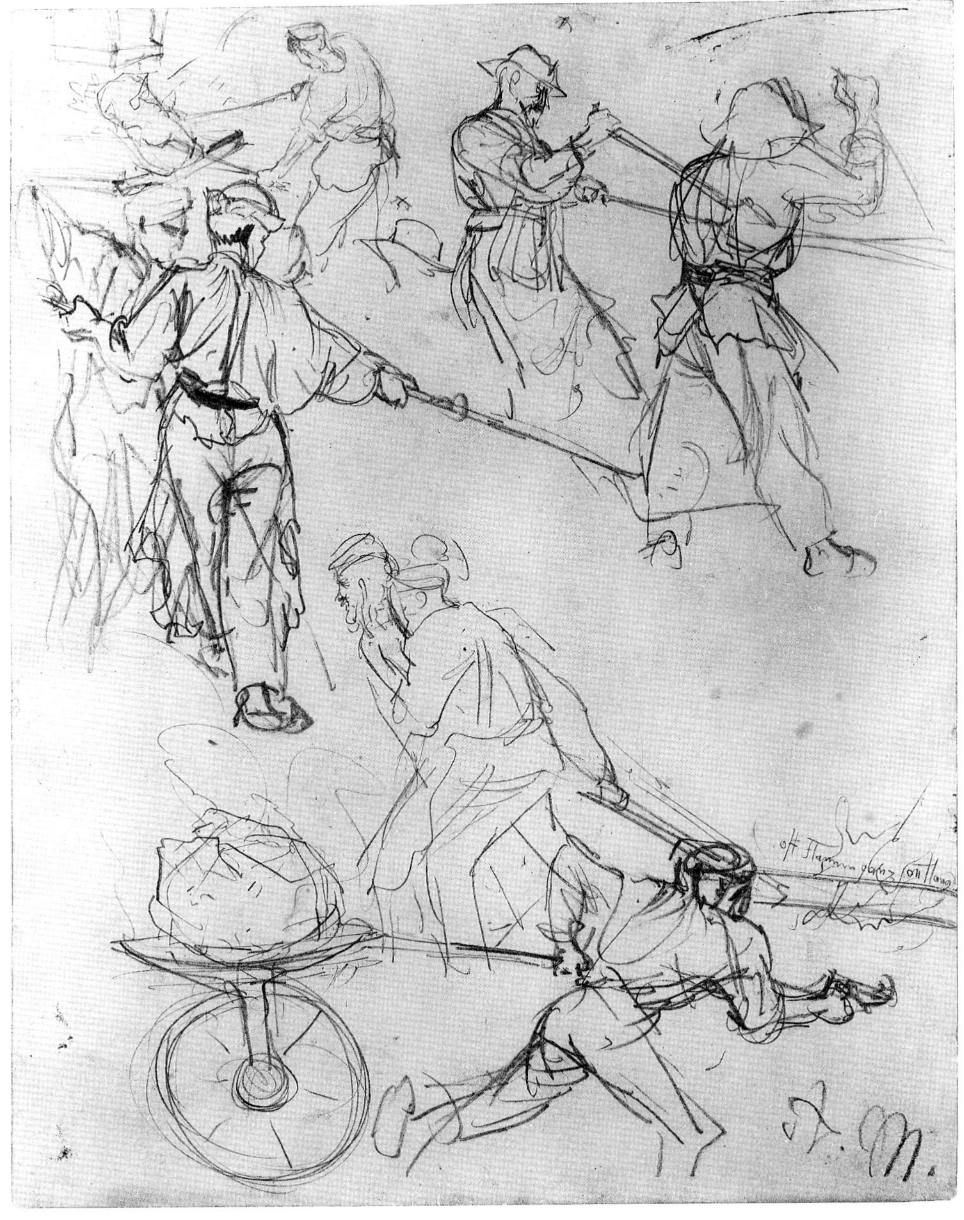

150

Sketch of Workers at the Rolling Mill
1872

Pencil
30.5 × 22.5cm
Signed at the bottom right: *A.M.* – Annotated: *oft Flamm ganz . . . .*
Berlin, Kupferstichkabinett (SZ Menzel N 1375)
Exhibited in Paris only

Provenance: Painters studio; 1905 Emilie Krigar-Menzel; acquired by the museum in 1906.
Exhibition: Berlin, 1905, no. 3291.
Bibliography: Kaiser, 1953, p. 60, fig. 44.

Numerous sketches of small figures like these show workers busy in various ways, as they appear in the painting.

151

Transport Truck
1872

Pencil
22.3 × 30.5cm
Signed at the top left: *Ad. Menzel* – Annotated: *Zangenwagen für "packtirtes" Eisen* (plus measurements in feet and inches).
Berlin, Kupferstichkabinett (SZ Menzel N 1371)
Exhibited in Paris and Berlin only

Provenance: Painter's studio; 1905 Emilie Krigar-Menzel; acquired by the museum in 1906.
Exhibitions: Berlin, 1905, no. 3272; Vienna, 1985, no. 71, reprod. p. 141; Copenhagen, 1985, no. 62, reprod. p. 42; New York, 1990, no. 51, col. reprod. p. 167.
Bibliography: Exhib. cat. Berlin, 1976, p. 8 *et seq.*.

This page was probably brought back from Königshütte. In the inventory of the contents of his studio in Menzel's will, there is: 'A box containing studies for my oil painting *The Rolling Mills at Königshütte*, with the sketches done on site and the studies from a model'[1]. In this study and the following one (cat. 153),

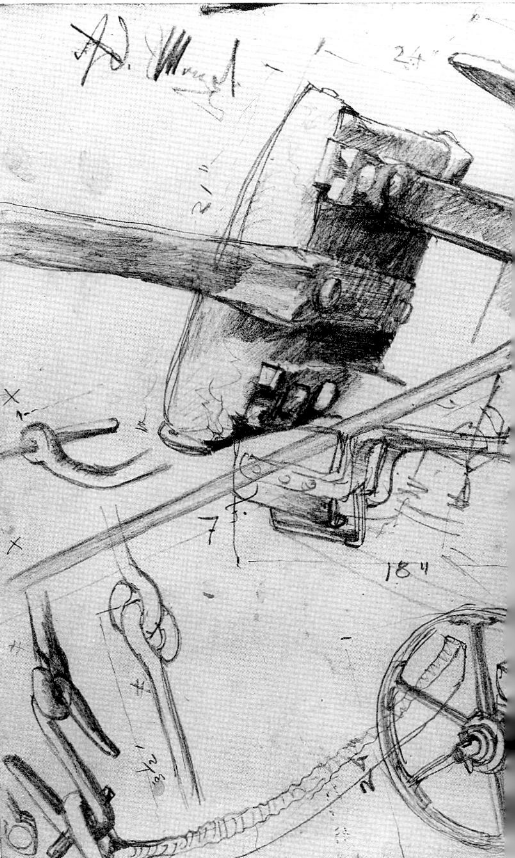

151

Menzel borrowed an idea from Courbet, who wanted to trivialize art by transposing the everyday subject observed with accuracy.

1. Text reproduced in Kirstein 1919, p. 92-8; quotation p. 94.

152

Self-portrait with Worker near the Steam-hammer

1872

Gouache
16 × 12.5cm
Signed and dated at the top left: *Ad. Menzel 72*
Leipzig, Museum der bildenden Künste (1972-6)
On view only in Paris and Berlin

Provenance: Helene and Lucius Spengler, Davos; Annemarie Maurer-Dinckler, Leipzig; Heinz Senger, Neubrandenburg; gift of the last to the museum, 1972.
Exhibition: Berlin, 1976, no. 5.
Bibliography: Tschudi, 1905 A, no. 597; Hütt, 1981, fig. 110; Mehnert, 1990, no. 111, reprod.

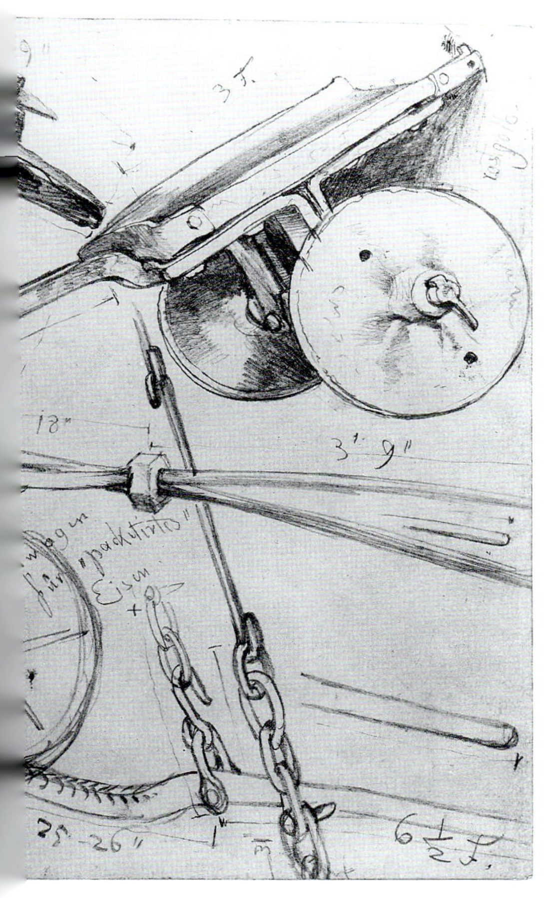

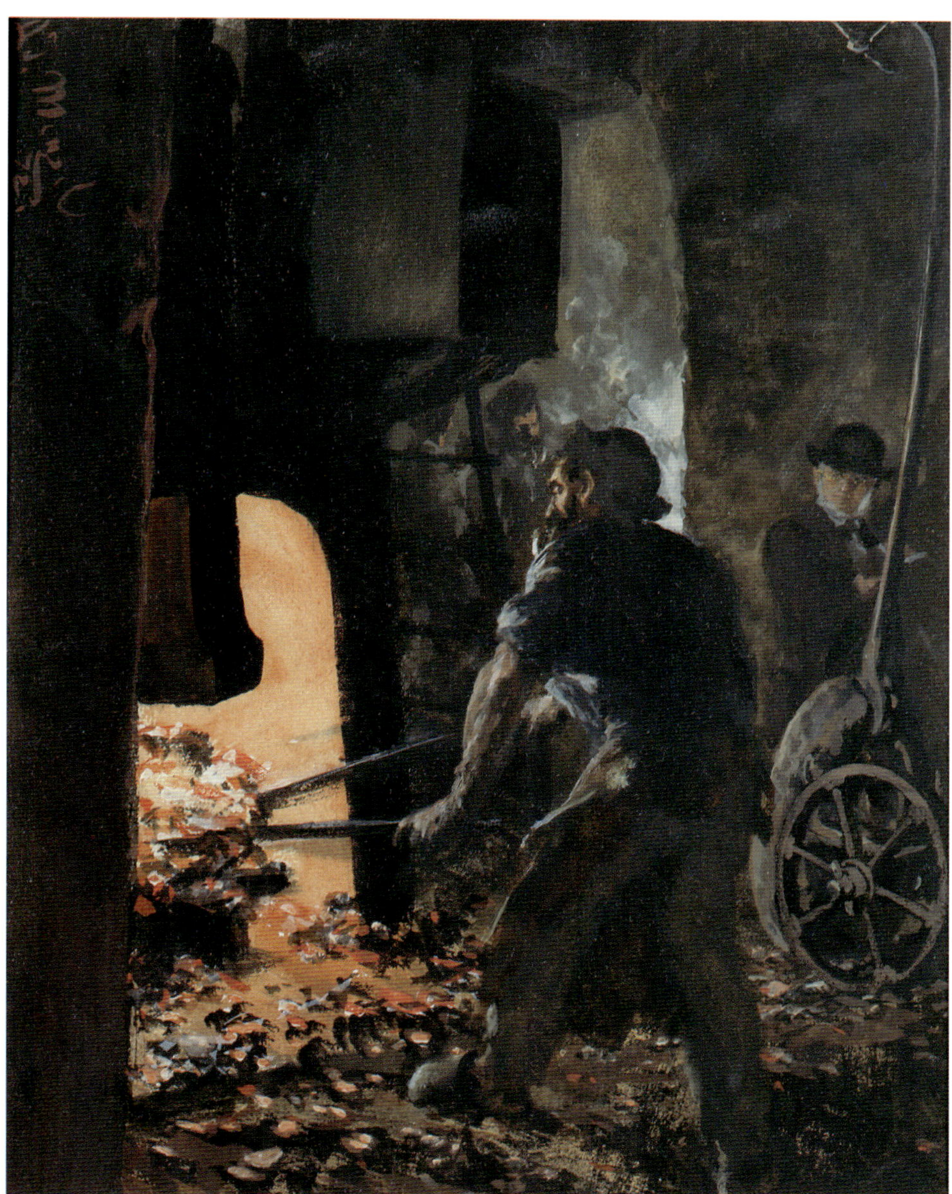

152

It is likely that this painting was done after Menzel's time at Königshütte. He bore in mind his quest for authenticity before starting the large painting in his studio. The main figure in this composition is the worker in the foreground, standing in front of the red, incandescent opening to the steam-hammer and, in a three-quarter view, stokes the embers with a long rod. On the right of the picture the painter, half-hidden by a truck, stands in front of a dark wall, wearing a hat and holding a sketchbook in his hand. There is a sketch showing an exact overall view of the steam-hammer with this annotation: 'Steam-hammer in mechanical workshops from an elevation drawing'[1]. He probably obtained this drawing through a cousin in Silesia[2]. However, technical knowledge always gives way to painting. Later, underlining the limits of authenticity, Menzel stated, on the subject of *The Iron Rolling Mill*, that he considered 'the accuracy with which all the accessories were drawn . . . simply as a necessary consequence' of his attempt to 'enjoy the spectacle of that place in a purely pictorial way'[3]. He continued: 'Even while I was working on this picture, this type of layout within the firm was already out of date'[4]. Two other men appear vaguely in the background of this small composition, in the light cast by the fire which illuminates the worker's silhouette. Amid the suggestive promiscuity of figures in a small space and emphasized by contrasts of light, the small motionless figure of Menzel adds an accent of objectivity. A pencil sketch almost twice as big and comparable in terms of style to the studies made at the workshops in Königshütte should be considered a preliminary study for the Leipzig picture[5]. The worker's position in front of the steam-hammer is already defined, but in its pictorial transposition the composition centres on the worker and the self-portrait adds an additional message. An apparently unfinished colour study of a rolling mill[6] could also be related to the gouache. Alongside Menzel's first work on the theme of the rolling mill should be mentioned his last, a gouache which he painted in 1900 entitled *Visit to the Rolling Mill*[7] (fig. 206), in which the direct clash of social classes takes on an almost satirical keenness not present in the *Diploma for Heckmann* (cat. 129). There, the sophisticated allegories in the decoration, rubbing shoulders unexpectedly with scenes taken from the world of the worker, create a feeling of disorientation. M.R.-R.

1. Berlin, Kupferstichkabinett (SZ Menzel N 1397).
2. Letter to Albert Paul, 13 April 1874, Wolff, 1914, p. 217.
3. Letter to the editor of *Biographisches Künstler-Lexikon*, 17 November 1882. Stargardt sale catalogue, Berlin, 436 (1940), no. 902.
4. Letter to the authors of *Das Werk Adolph Menzels* in three volumes, 7 March 1880. Henrici sale cat., Berlin, LXXIX, no. 233.
5. Euerbach, Georg Schäfer collection.
6. Tschudi, 1905 A, no. 575; Berlin, Kupferstichkabinett (SZ Menzel N 3357).
7. Tschudi, 1905 A, no. 680; Berlin, Kupferstichkabinett (SZ Menzel Nr 1839).

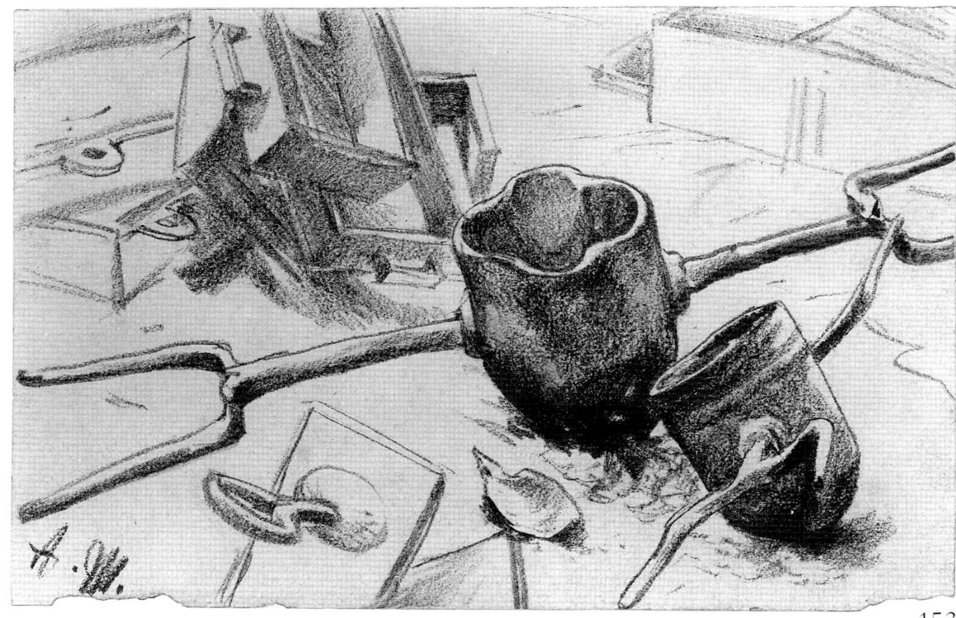

153

153
Casting Ladle
c. 1872–4

Pencil
13 × 20.8cm
Signed at the bottom left: *A.M.*
Berlin, Kupferstichkabinett (SZ Menzel N 811)
Exhibited in Washington only

Provenance: Painter's studio; 1905 Emilie Krigar-Menzel; acquired by the museum in 1906.
Exhibition: Berlin, 1905, no. 4154.
Bibliography: Exhib. cat. Berlin, 1976, p. 8 *et seq.*

The harvest of drawings reaped from Menzel's stay in Königshütte was completed by studies from the former royal foundry in Berlin, which was closed down in 1874. These drawings, often dating from that year and bearing an indication of the place, were executed using a particularly thick, granular lead. The drawing shown here is part of that group. It is similar to another which depicts three casting ladles, one large and two small, in front of a wall, upon which Menzel noted: 'Kön. Eisengie·erei 74'[1]. On the lower edge of the picture towards the centre, a surprising still life composed of different small tools creates a link with the group of workers busy eating.

1. Private collection. Reprod. in Ebertshäuser, 1976, p. 1125.

154
Pulling a Casting Truck
c. 1872–4

Pencil
32.5 × 24.5cm
Signed at the centre right: *Ad. Menzel*
Berlin, Kupferstichkabinett (SZ Menzel N 156)

Fig. 205. Paul Meyerheim, *Opening to the Main Furnace in the Mechanical Construction Building of the Borsig factories*, 1874, oil, Berlin, Stadtmuseum

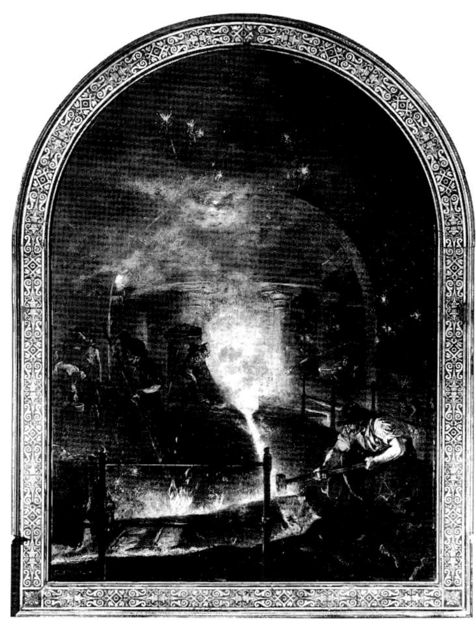

Provenance: Painter's studio; 1905 Emilie Krigar-Menzel; acquired by the museum in 1906.
Exhibitions: Berlin, 1905, no. 3264; Berlin, 1980 A, no. 314, reprod. p. 385; Vienna, 1985, no. 73, reprod. p. 143; New York, 1990, no. 53, reprod. p. 171.
Bibliography: Kaiser, 1953, p. 62, fig. 46.

This could be a study made in Berlin from a model. The posture corresponds to that of the worker who appears in *The Iron Rolling Mill* in front of the casting, pulling the salamander on a casting truck. Only the head has been slightly modified. There are other studies for this figure[1], and for the following worker.

1. Berlin, Kupferstichkabinett (SZ Menzel Kat 1070, N 157, 161, 261, 1376, 3153).

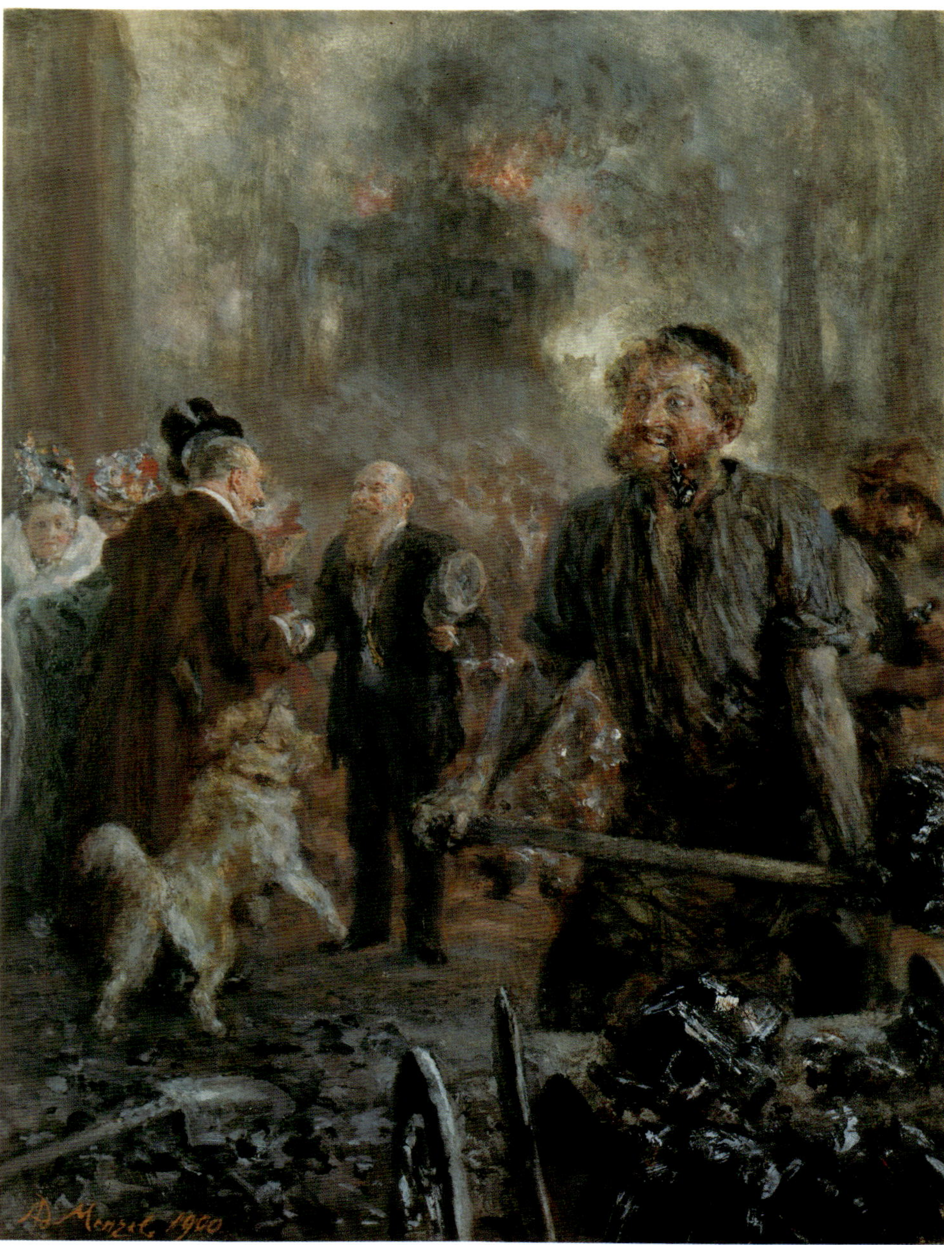

Fig. 206. *Visit to the Forge*, 1900, watercolour and gouache, Berlin, Kupferstichkabinett (Nr. 1839)

155

Worker Holding the Shaft of a Truck in front of the Rolling Line

c. 1872–4

Pencil
40 × 26.2cm
Signed at the centre bottom: *A.M.*
Berlin, Kupferstichkabinett (SZ Menzel N 4456)
Exhibited in Washington and Berlin only

Provenance: Painter's studio; 1905 Emilie Krigar-Menzel; acquired by the museum in 1906.
Exhibitions: Berlin, 1905, no. 3267a; Berlin, 1980 A, no. 333, reprod. p. 273.
Bibliography: Kaiser, 1953, p. 35, fig. 19.

Often it is impossible to tell whether a figure study was made on site or from a model. But it is likely that most of the expressive drawings of men in the central group[1] in the painting were not made at Königshütte. There are also portraits for some of the workers. The one of a worker with a moustache and wearing a small leather hat belonged to Edgar Degas but is now in a private American collection (fig. 5). Degas acquired the drawing in 1881 at the Duranty sale, which he had organized. Menzel had met Degas, who admired his work, in 1867, at the circle of the painter Alfred Stevens (*cf.* cat. 168).

1. Variants on this study: Berlin, Kupferstichkabinett (SZ Menzel Kat 3267, N 158, 1379, 4458, Nr 1792) as well as a drawing in the Kunsthalle in Hamburg (exhib. cat. Hamburg, 1982, no. 105, reprod.).

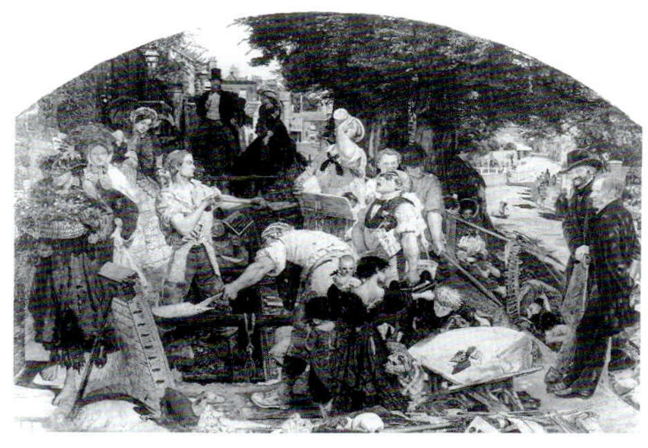

Fig. 207. Ford Madox Brown, *Work*, 1852–63, oil, Manchester, City Art Gallery

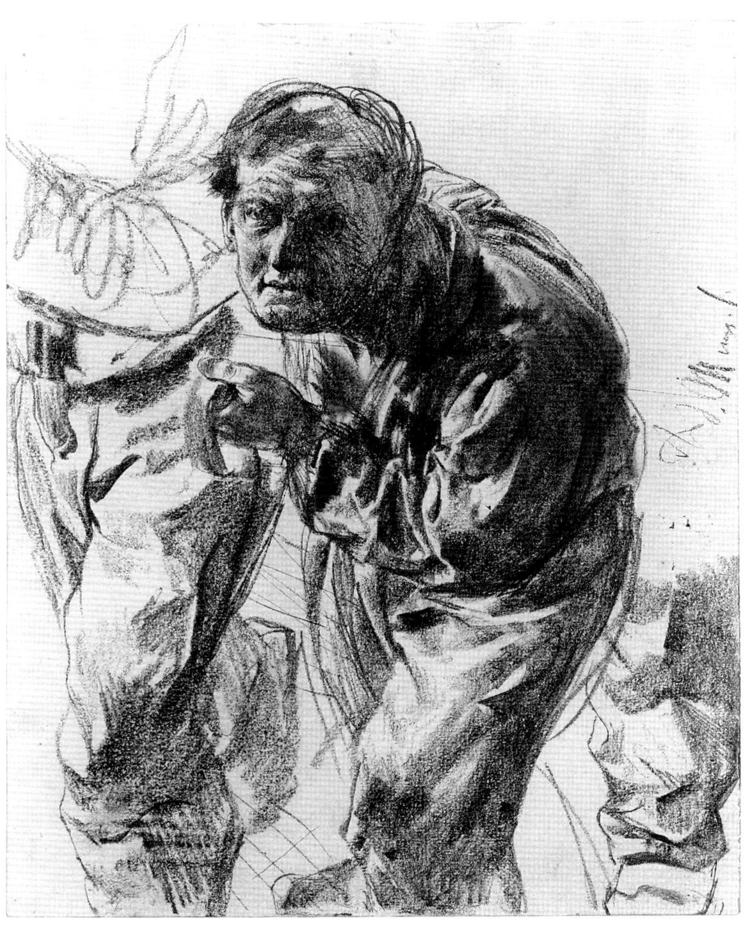

154

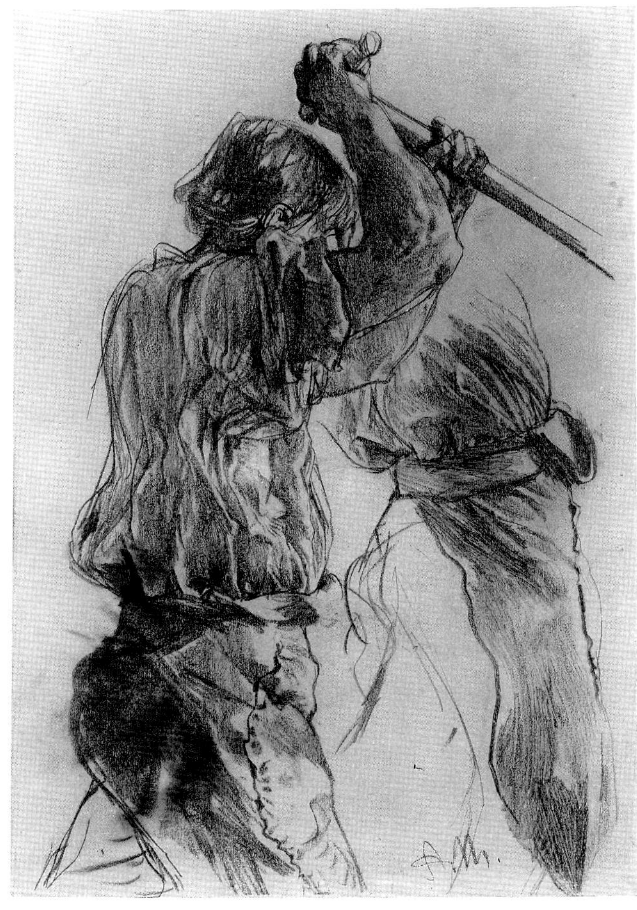

155

Fig. 208. Letter from Menzel to Max Jordan (April 1879), correcting the description of *The Iron Rolling Mill* in the first edition of the Nationalgalerie catalogue of 1876, Berlin, Staatliche Museen zu Berlin, central archives

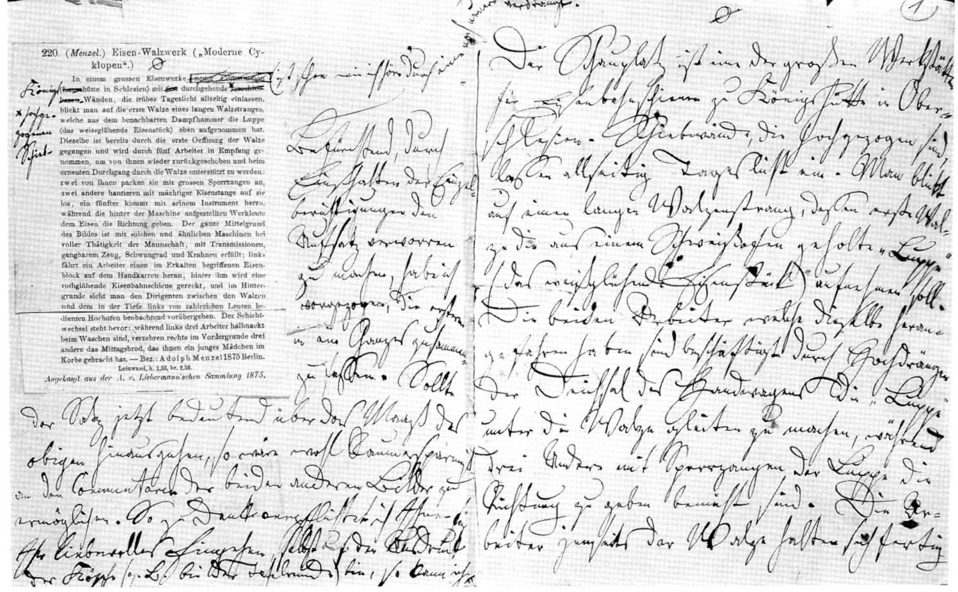

220. (*Menzel.*) Eisen-Walzwerk („Moderne Cyklopen".)

In einem grossen Eisenwerke [illegible] ([illegible]hütte in Schlesien) mit [illegible] durchgehends [illegible] Wänden, die trübes Tageslicht allseitig einlassen, blickt man auf die erste Walze eines langen Walzstranges, welche aus dem benachbarten Dampfhammer die Luppe (das weissglühende Eisenstück) eben aufgenommen hat. Dieselbe ist bereits durch die erste Oeffnung der Walze gegangen und wird durch fünf Arbeiter in Empfang genommen, um von ihnen wieder zurückgeschoben und beim erneuten Durchgang durch die Walze unterstützt zu werden: zwei von ihnen packen sie mit grossen Sperrzangen an, zwei andere hantieren mit mächtiger Eisenstange auf sie los, ein fünfter kommt mit seinem Instrument herzu, während die hinter der Maschine aufgestellten Werkleute dem Eisen die Richtung geben. Der ganze Mittelgrund des Bildes ist mit solchen und ähnlichen Maschinen bei voller Thätigkeit der Mannschaft, mit Transmissionen, gangbarem Zeug, Schwungrad und Krahnen erfüllt; links fährt ein Arbeiter einen im Erkalten begriffenen Eisenblock auf dem Handkarren heran, hinter ihm wird eine rothglühende Eisenbahnschiene gereckt, und im Hintergrunde sieht man den Dirigenten zwischen den Walzen und dem in der Tiefe links von zahlreichen Leuten bedienten Hochofen beobachtend vorübergehen. Der Schichtwechsel steht bevor: während links drei Arbeiter halbnackt beim Waschen sind, verzehren rechts im Vordergrunde drei andere das Mittagsbrod, das ihnen ein junges Mädchen im Korbe gebracht hat. — Bez.: Adolph Menzel 1875 Berlin.

Leinwand, h. 1,53, br. 2,53.

Angekauft aus der A. v. Liebermann'schen Sammlung 1875.

156

Worker Holding the Shaft of the Casting Truck (with Details)

c. 1872–4

Pencil

40.1 × 26.2cm

Signed at the bottom left: *Ad. Menzel*

Berlin, Kupferstichkabinett (SZ Menzel N 1380)

Exhibited in Paris and Washington only

Provenance: Painter's studio; 1905 Emilie Krigar-Menzel; acquired by the museum in 1906.

Exhibition: Berlin, 1905, no. 3309.

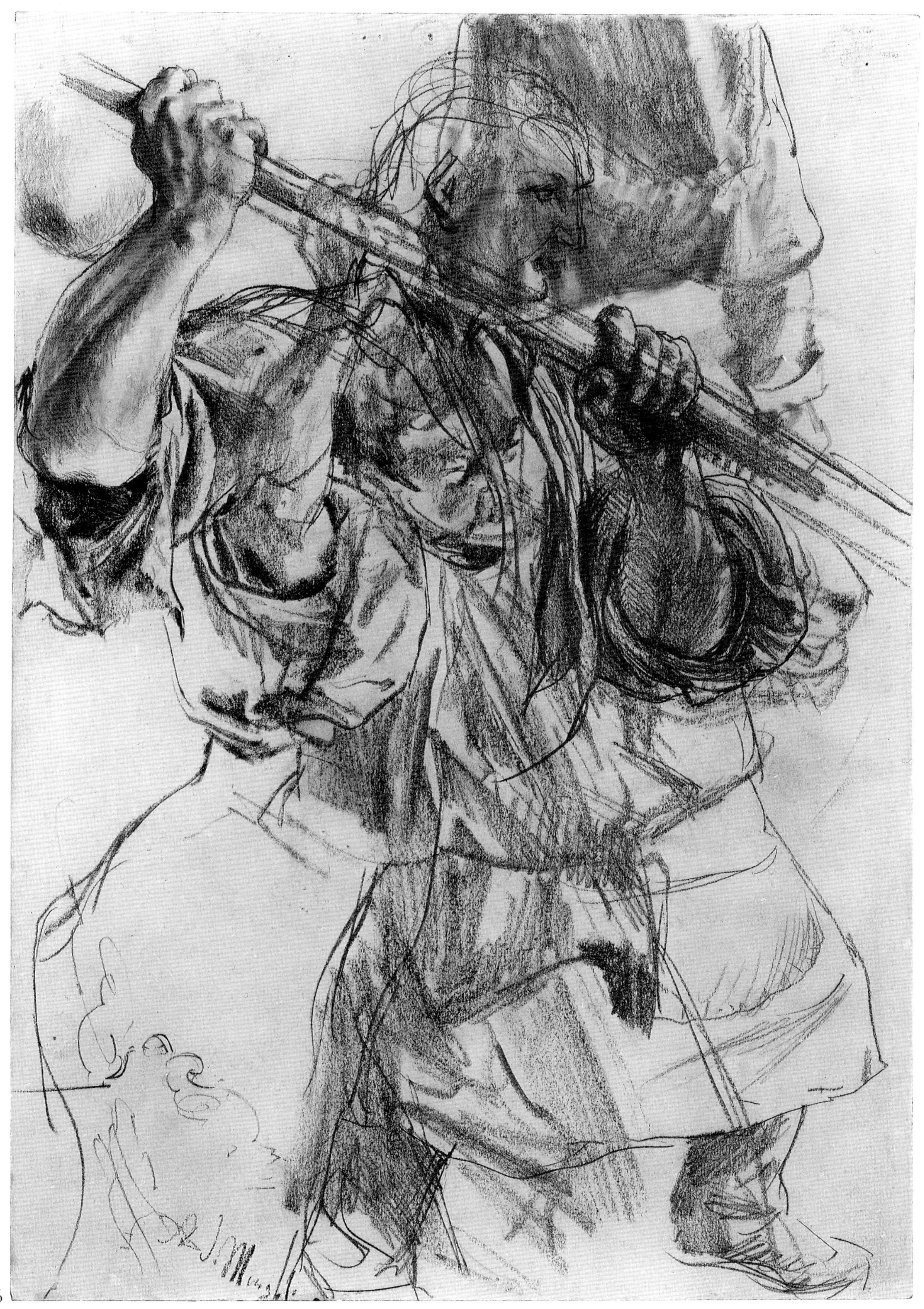

156

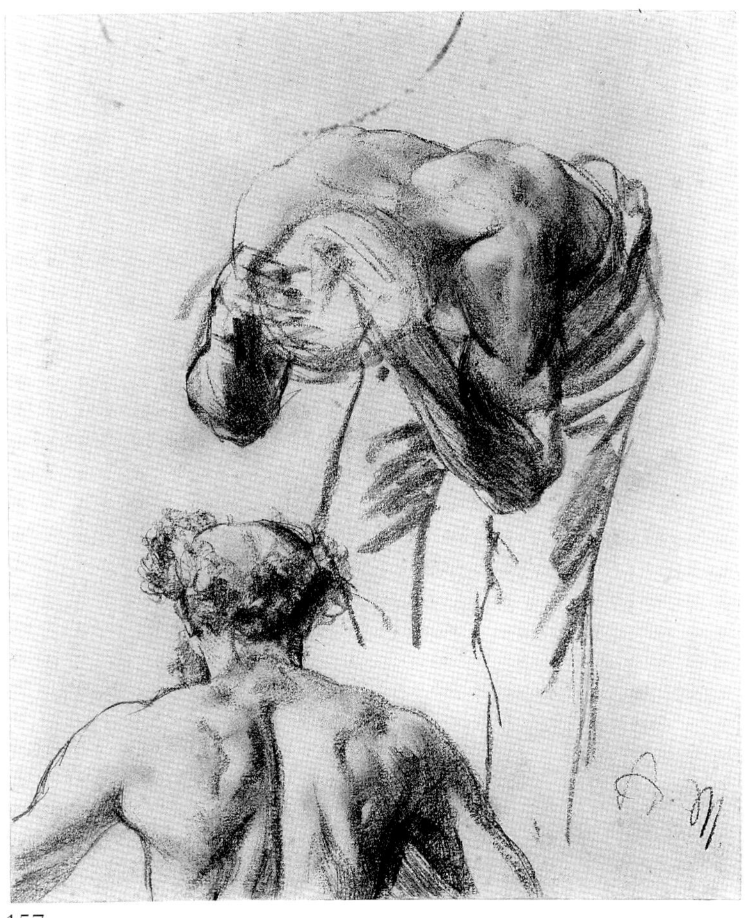

157

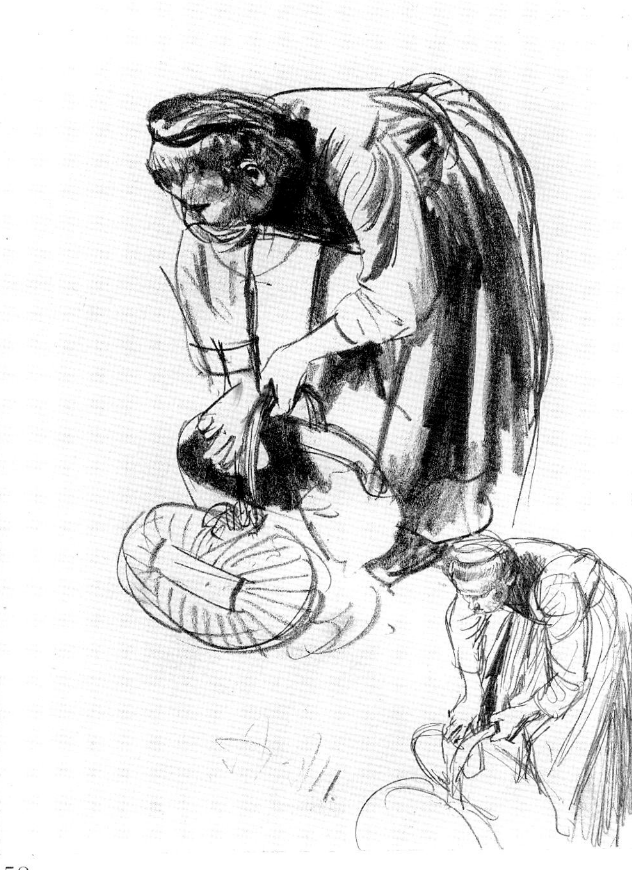

158

157
Worker Washing Himself
c. 1872–4

Pencil
32.3 × 24.5cm
Signed at the bottom right: *A.M.*
Berlin, Kupferstichkabinett (SZ Menzel N 1387)
Exhibited in Paris and Washington only

Provenance: Painter's studio; 1905 Emilie Krigar-Menzel; acquired by the museum in 1906.
Exhibitions: Berlin, 1905, no. 3330 or 3269; Berlin, 1980 A, no. 322, reprod. p. 387; Vienna, 1985, no. 75.
Bibliography: Kaiser, 1953, p. 72, fig. 58.

For the group of workers washing, there also exist a certain number of studies from a model for the group of workers eating, and of the woman bringing them food[1].

1. Berlin, Kupferstichkabinett.

158
Woman with Basket of Food
Around 1872–4

Pencil
37.9 × 25cm
Signed at the centre bottom: *A.M.*
Berlin, Kupferstichkabinett (SZ Menzel N 1395)
Exhibited in Washington only

Provenance: Painter's studio; 1905 Emilie Krigar-Menzel; acquired by the museum in 1906.
Exhibitions: Berlin, 1905, no. 3366; Vienna, 1985, no. 74, reprod. p. 144.

This is another study from a model. The woman is not looking at the viewer as in other studies[1] and in the final composition. A reference outside photography must be sought for this remarkable effect of instantaneity. In the foreground of the painting by François Bonhommé, *Calamine Washing Plant*[2], a woman is depicted looking out of the picture, enhancing the effect of authenticity[3]. Menzel might have seen this subject in Paris in 1859.

1. Berlin, Kupferstichkabinett (SZ Menzel N 1393, 1394, 164).
2. Jarville, museum of the History of Iron.
3. *Cf.* also exhib. cat. Berlin, 1976, p. 7 and ff.

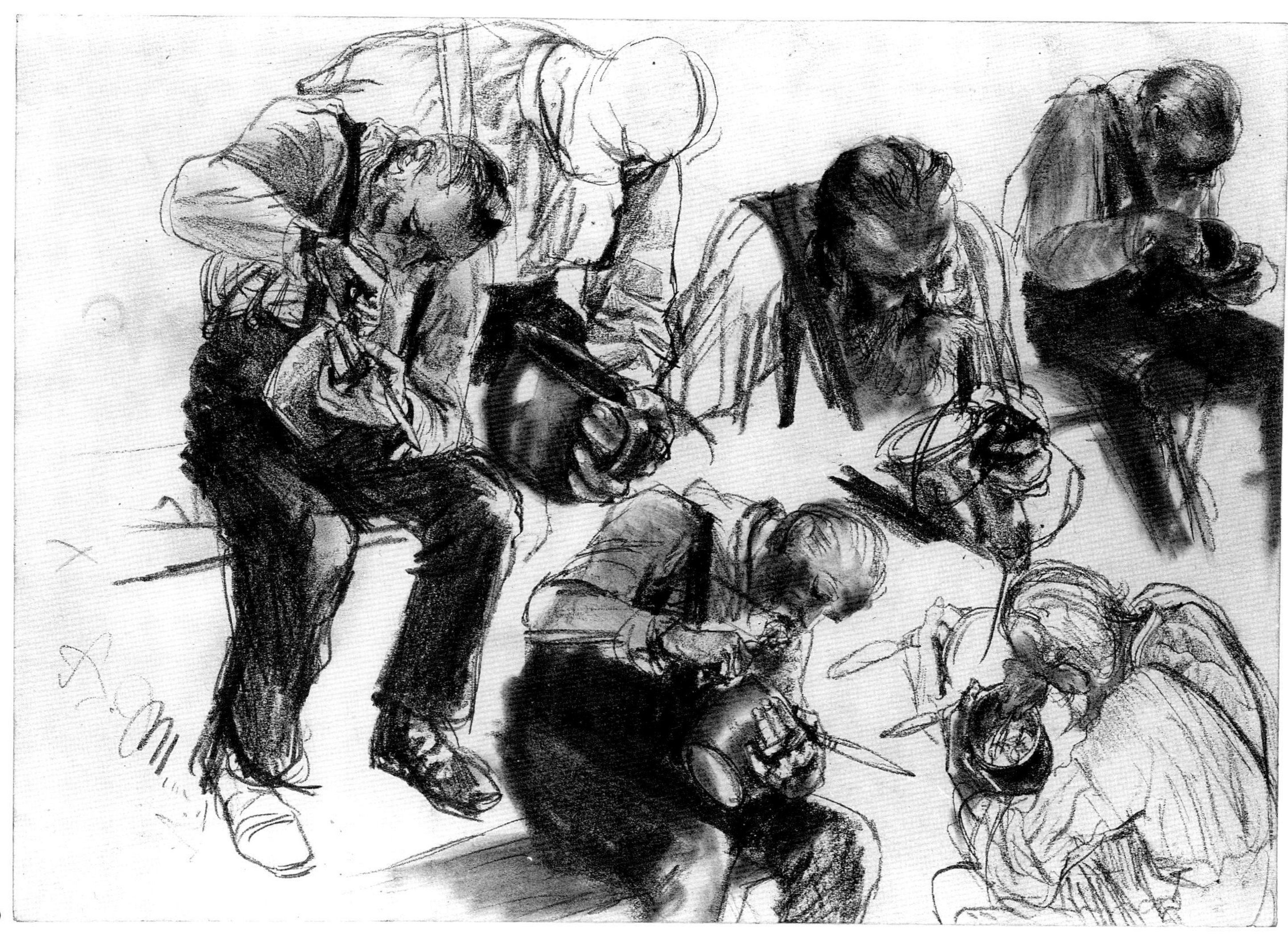

159

159
Worker Eating, Several Views
c. 1872–4

Pencil
26.5 × 37cm
Signed at the bottom left: *A.M.*
Berlin, Kupferstichkabinett (SZ Menzel N 166)

Provenance: Painter's studio; 1905 Emilie Krigar-Menzel; acquired by the museum in 1906.
Painter's studio; 1905 Emilie Krigar-Menzel; acquired by the museum in 1906.
Exhibitions: Berlin, 1905, no. 3806; Berlin, 1980 A, no. 319, reprod. p. 386; New York, 1990, no. 56, reprod. p. 176.

160
The Iron Rolling Mill (Modern Cyclops)
1872–5

Oil on canvas
158 × 254cm
Signed and dated at the bottom left: *Adolph Menzel. Berlin 1875*
Berlin, Nationalgalerie (A I 201)

Provenance: Begun without a commission and paid for about 1872 by the banker Adolph von Liebermann; delivered at the start of 1875 and resold in October to the Nationalgalerie.
Exhibitions: Berlin, 1876, no. 493; Paris, 1878; Munich, 1879; Paris, 1885, no. 18; Berlin, 1886, no. 2461; Berlin, 1895 A, no. 55; Vienna, 1896, no. 283; Berlin, 1906, no. 1163, reprod. facing p. 134; Münster, 1980, p. 26–7, reprod. p. 27; Berlin, 1980 A, no. XXX, reprod. p. 152–3; Berlin, 1987 A, no. H.11, reprod. p. 29.

Bibliography: Rosenberg, 1875, col. 372–3; cat. NG, 1876, no. 220; Rosenberg, 1877, col. 102; Gonse, 1885, p. 519–20; Jordan/Dohme, 1890, vol. 3, p. 65 *et seq.* pl. 89; Jordan, 1895, pp. 48–9, p. 70, pl. 24; Beta, (1898) 1992, p. 40; Meissner, 1902, p. 76–7, reprod. p. 69; Osborn, 1904, p. 437 *et seq.*; Tschudi, 1905 A, no. 144; Jordan, 1905, p. 71–4; Anon., 1905, no. 71; Scheffler, 1912, p. 134; Kirstein, 1919, p. 79; Justi, 1920, p. 171–4; Justi, 1932, pp. 138–9, fig. 54; Scheffler, 1938, p. 115; Waldmann, 1941, p. 37, p. 49, figs 70–1; Winkler, 1941, no. 7, col. pl.; Kaiser, 1953, fig. 1, col. pl. 68; Riemann-Reyher, 1976, fig. 6; Janke/Wagner, 1976, note 50; Weiss, 1983, vol. 1, p. 352 *et seq.*; Forster-Hahn, 1981, p. 122–9, reprod. p. 129; cat. NG, 1986, fig. 79, col. pl. XIX; Riemann-Reyher, 1992, p. 155 *et seq.*; Lammel, 1993 B, p. 93 *et seq.*

Menzel reached the apogee of his art in this canvas. It was painted between 1872 and 1875, on the threshold of the works

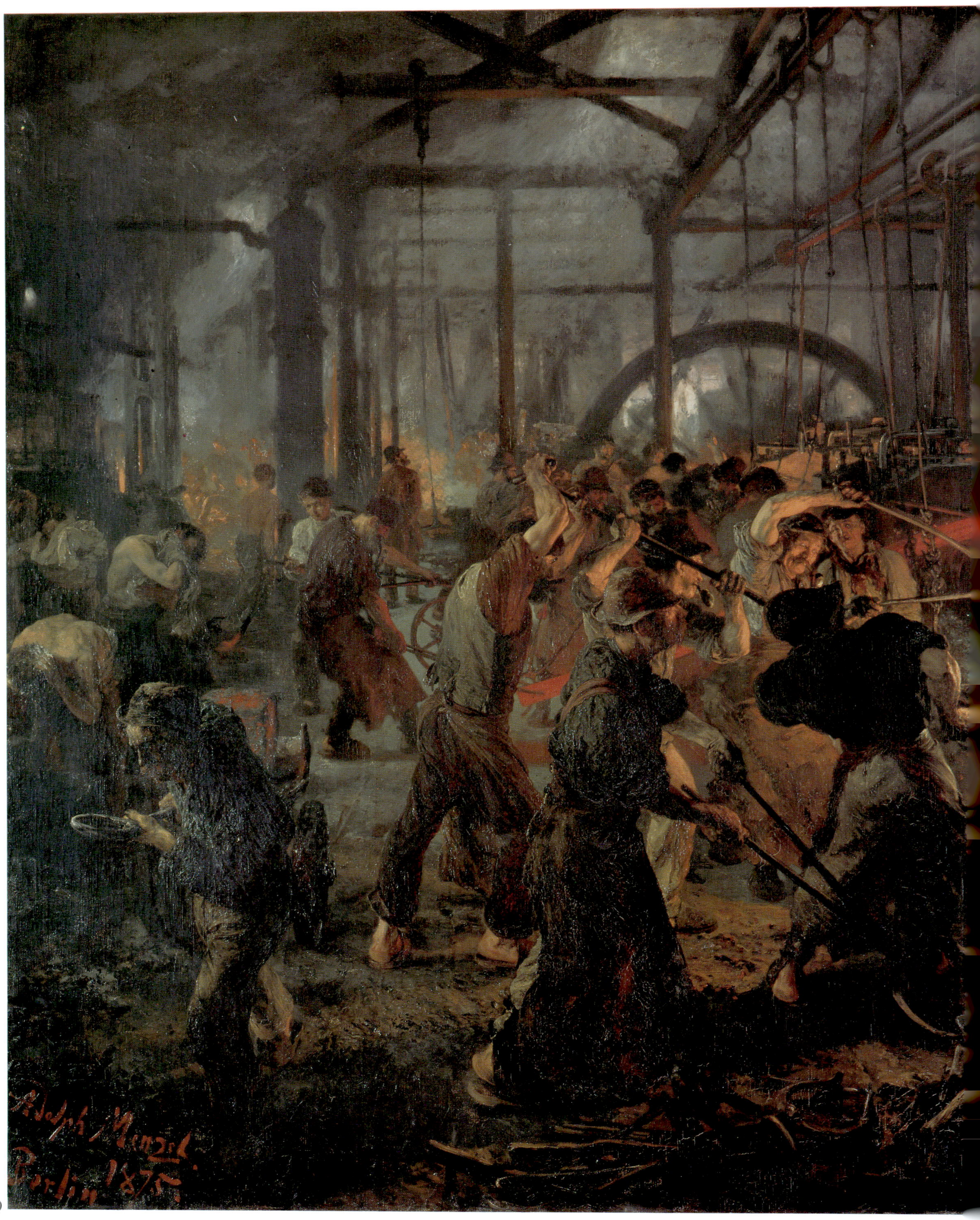
Adolph Menzel.
Berlin 1875.

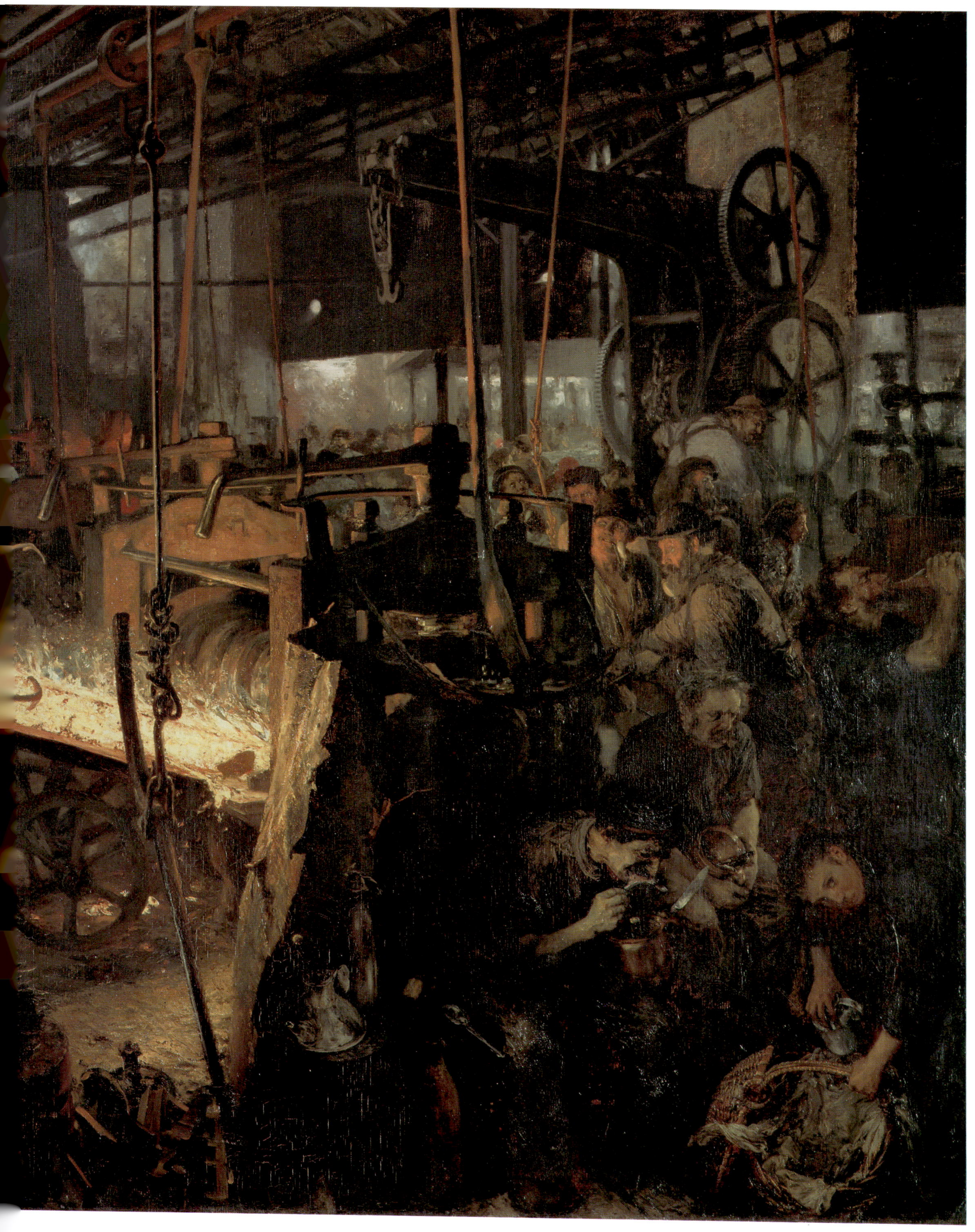

of his old age, and is extraordinary in its richness and complexity. In the second half of his life, Menzel was fundamentally concerned with the themes of his time, and moved in a sometimes conflicting field of action between his creative will and the demands of society, even though he might have escaped the constraints of a commission. 'A disparity which may seem surprising to some', and which he justified by 'a categorical imperative for new starts'[1] grew increasingly in his late works, accentuating contradictory aspects.

This work caused a sensation as soon as it appeared. It was not only due to its exceptional nature, but also to the rare and happy synthesis of these contradictory elements. Menzel had discovered an essential theme, which once more summoned up all his strength. This did not happen by chance, as the numerous studies of the man at work which appear throughout his entire work go to prove.

He had turned to industrial subjects at a time when the benefits of progress seemed unquestionable. Industrialization had accelerated since the German empire had been founded, and had significant social consequences. Within the context of conflicts presaging the second world economic crisis of 1873, Menzel began to prepare a work depicting factory workers, who represented the disturbing 'Fourth Estate', that threat which had made the potent German bourgeoisie renounce its autonomous position of strength and its potential access to power.

At that time Bismarck's government supported the interests of industrial entrepreneurs in order to safeguard international competitiveness, while at the same time refusing to adapt industrial working conditions to human needs. *The Iron Rolling Mill* is the first German painting to use the 'social question' as a theme.

This idea had early roots in the painter's work. Multiple sources of inspiration fed him before finding their culmination in this painting based on the rolling mill for rails at Königshütte, situated in the biggest and most important mining and metallurgical region of Upper Silesia. Menzel was a native of Silesia and was attached to his native area in numerous ways, and therefore had less reason to seek a subject in the great mines of the Ruhr. The Königshütte factory, founded by the State in 1797, had merged with the Laurahütte factory in 1871, which was one of the first large private metalworking plants, founded in 1839 by the Henckel von Donnersmarck family, who were large landowners in Silesia. The former puddling furnace and the Alvenslebenhütte rolling mill were integrated with the zinc mine at Lydognahütte under the name 'Vereinigte Königs- und Laurahütte A.G.' It therefore became the most important of the firms financed by the powerful banker of the Prussian court Gerson Bleichröder.

Menzel was invited to all court celebrations after his work on the picture of the coronation, and found inspiration for his society paintings in the evening gatherings there. In court circles he often had occasion to mix with bankers and industrialists as well as intellectuals and soldiers, particularly at Frau von Schleinitzs salon[2]. Most of the buyers of his paintings in the second half of the century were precisely these bankers or industrialists.

He had seen representations of the world of industry at the Universal Exhibition in Paris in 1855. Side by side with studies for *The Théâtre du Gymnase* in the sketchbooks he used in Paris are two fleeting studies of blacksmiths near an anvil and a worker wielding a pair of tongs in front of a steam-hammer. Courbet springs immediately to mind, whose search for this new kind of art, which he called 'living art', could only have encouraged Menzel. In 1869 he may have seen *The Stone-breakers* again in Munich, a work which was exhibited in Frankfurt for the first time in 1852, with immediate and considerable public success.

Nineteenth-century industrialists had commissioned authentic pictures of their factories for a long time, with the main element in these images always being the installations and machinery, while man played a small and anonymous part. 'Industrial portraits' of this kind had also been devoted to the centre of the iron and coal industry in Upper Silesia. The tradition of the 'industrial landscape', which came from England, was strongly influenced by the great pictures of the painter and lithographer François Bonhommé, known as 'The Blacksmith', in the mid-1840s. These pictures of the different stages of work in the metal industry, using modern furnaces such as Fourchambault, Indret and Le Creusot in particular, showed the upheaval of production methods for the first time. Better still, Bonhommé no longer used figures as accessories. His approach differentiates and individualizes, showing the specific relationship between a man and his activity. These industrial paintings, the first of the genre, and of imposing format, were exhibited at the annual Salons and at the Universal Exhibition of 1855. Menzel probably discovered them then, and probably saw them for a second time during his second stay in Paris for the Universal Exhibition of 1867[3].

He did not neglect any source of information liable to stimulate his curiosity for industrial and technical innovations, and consulted books and popular prints in reviews and newpapers like the *Leipziger Illustrierte Zeitung, Le Monde illustré* or *Le Tour du Monde*. He probably also knew contemporary engravings of Königshütte.

One stage in his progress was the commission given in 1869 by the Berlin Heckmann family for a commemorative diploma for the fiftieth anniversary of their brass, copper and iron factory. Menzel painted scenes from the modern metal industry for the first time on this occasion (*cf.* cat. 129).

However, his first encounter with the metal industry, his first consideration of the subject from a painter's point of view, goes back to 1852. At almost the same time as Maxime Du Camp in Paris, the art critic Friedrich Eggers had started a discussion in the *Deutsches Kunstblatt* on the new artistic content taken from reality. He enthusiastically promoted the search for new subjects inspired by the industrial world and life in the large built-up areas which were then mushrooming. In this context, Eggers described a visit to the Borsig factories at Moabit. August Borsig, who died in 1854 at the age of fifty, soon became the emblematic figure of the entrepreneur. A man of practical experience, he greatly contributed to the economic independence of Germany in relation to England by building the first German locomotive. Eggers's description of the factory, the foundry and machine rooms situated next to the Borsig villa evoke the baroque representations of Vulcan's forge, the god of fire and metal-working, assisted by the cyclops. By elevating the phenomenon of the metal industry to the level of mythology, and having unlimited faith in progress, Eggers left social reality aside. He admired these 'strong, bearded men, their youthful vigour, the natural, authentic movement of the often athletic limbs of robust, well-treated workers!'[4]

But the metalworkers at the Borsig factory were the best paid and best qualified in Berlin at the time. When Eggers spoke of working in shifts, the result of intensified production methods, he only considered it from the aesthetic and documentary point of view: 'It is obvious that there are very different effects at night – one whole day of work here is equivalent to a week . . .' This enthusiastic account may have influenced Menzel's choice of subject for *The Iron Rolling Mill*, whose description is thought to be referred to in 'the immense pictorial subject' in which only one group of cyclops can be distinguished 'who are using powerful tongs to shake the red incandescent mass of iron within the voracious teeth of the machine'. While Eggers ignores any social dimension, Menzel insists on this aspect, with the support of the studies and observations made at Königshütte.

At the end of his account, Eggers speaks of a friend who accompanied him and who was the real person to discover the subject. One imagines that Menzel was that friend, and that during this visit to the Borsig factories, and in the immediate impressions created there, the first spark of the idea for *The Iron Rolling Mill* was kindled. Menzel began the work in 1872, and in the summer of that year Friedrich Eggers died at the age of fifty-two. In October Menzel painted the *Studio Wall*, whose large format is surprising in comparison with the size of his other paintings of a personal nature. It was initially thought of as a lighting study for *The Iron Rolling Mill*[5], but its meaning goes beyond this (*cf.* cat. 137). In the same year Menzel undertook his first and probably only journey to Königshütte, as indicated by several dated drawings. There is also a significant relationship, undetected for a long time, between Menzel's project and a commission given to his friend Paul Meyerheim by Albert Borsig, the son of the man who built the first German locomotive, probably in 1872[6]. A series of seven monumental compositions painted on copper plates and intended for the loggia of the Borsig villa in Moabit, built by Heinrich Stack, was to recount 'the history of a locomotive'[7]. Grouped around a family portrait, six pictures represent respectively: the extraction shaft of a mine, the opening to the main furnace, forging a prelaminated locomotive wheel, then its embarkation at port, and the meeting of the locomotive and the stagecoach. There may have been an initial question of painting allegorical compositions, but this was renounced in favour of realistic scenes. Possibly Menzel had some influence on this change of ideas. He was a close friend of this twenty-seven years younger painter, as he had been with Meyerheim's father (*cf.* cat. 3). The younger painter was already well known and experienced, and had painted numerous frescoes for villas and public buildings in Berlin. He published his memories of Menzel a year after the latter's death. In 1867 he accompanied his friend to Paris, and the artistic exchange between the two painters becomes obvious in *The Iron Rolling Mill*, where Menzel chose for his theme a stage of production which Meyerheim had left aside, the basic laminating process. Menzel's young friend worked remarkably fast and, by 1876, a year after *The Iron Rolling Mill* was completed, the whole cycle of seven paintings was finished.

The two paintings by Paul Meyerheim which are the closest to Menzels work, *Forging a Locomotive Wheel* and *Opening to the Main Furnace* (fig. 205), are dated 1873 and 1874. Meyerheim's immediate interest in the progress of *The Iron Rolling Mill* appears in a letter from Menzel to his friend, which shows the exact date upon which the picture was finished: 'B., 22 Feb. 75. Is it still your wish to be present at the resurrection of the colours in my picture – if so be warned that tomorrow, Tuesday 23 February at 4 oclock, the varnish-laden brush of Herr Schmidt will perform this miracle. But it will be downstairs in my room, remember. Yours, Menzel'[8].

A comparison of the two approaches reveals that Menzel is much more orientated towards reality. His realism emphasizes contradictions implicit in the subject, without idealizing it, which Meyerheim could not prevent himself from doing. The tall, semicircular format restricted Meyerheim to reducing each of his compositions to a small group of vigorous workers. The monumental aspect of the Borsig factory dominates, and the works are magnified by ingenious lighting effects. One worker is drinking, another washing behind the casting opening to the main furnace. This corresponds to the groups of workers eating and washing in Menzel's picture (there is also a man drinking and a woman bringing food in *The Casters* by Eyre Crowe, dated 1869)[9], but the subject has not freed itself from genre painting, nor from the arbitrary nature of everyday things. Similarly, in Meyerheim's other compositions narrative elements tend to water down the interpretation of industrial work. Menzel, on the other hand, portrays the phenomenon of working in shifts by juxtaposing the group of workers washing before they leave the factory with those working, and those eating.

The experience of the gigantic factory at Königshütte gave Menzel a new and meaningful approach to industrial production, and he continued his studies at the famous former royal foundry in Berlin, which was closed in 1874. Some of his drawings are of historic interest, but the social problem was definitely the most visible at Königshütte. Three thousand workers managed seven main furnaces, seventy-one puddling furnaces and thirty-three smelting furnaces as well as four Bessemer converters, and produced 55,000 tonnes of raw iron, 43,000 tonnes of iron in the form of bars and rails, 750 tonnes of raw zinc and 10,000 tonnes of steel per year for the railways. The metal works was extremely important, but the working conditions in Upper Silesia were notorious for being worse than in the Ruhr. The social conflicts among the working population of Upper Silesia during the 1873 crisis were worsened further by the Catholicism of the Polish worker population, and the riots caused by Bismarcks anti-Catholic measures had to be quashed by military force.

Menzel was sensitive to all the upheavals and agitation of his time, and at Königshütte in 1872 he could not have been ignorant of these events, creating a tense environment for his work. He made about a hundred pencil studies, the majority of which are preserved in Berlin, small rapidly drawn sketches representing workers at furnaces, working with steam-hammers, laminating cylinders, but also during their breaks, resting near their workplace, eating or washing at the end of the day. All these scenes basically took place inside one large hall, as Menzel portrayed it in his picture.

There are also drawings of machines and various tools, as well as overall views of the imposing main furnace by day and by night. One of the drawings dated 1872 shows an open mine and the silhouette of the factory on the horizon. In addition to mineral deposits there were also limestone quarries and coal mines at Königshütte. A gouache of 1872 documents the painters stay – he is a small figure in the background drawing a worker wielding a pair of tongs at the steam-hammer opening (cat. 152). The final composition was made in the Berlin studio, where the studies of movement were finished from models.

In 1898, Menzel recalled his time in Königshütte: 'I did these studies in Königshütte in Silesia. I ran the constant of risk of being laminated myself, so to speak. For weeks, from morning to night, I stood among those enormous hand-wheels, conveyor belts and the cast iron and I sketched. Technology, the modern world of cyclops, is very rich in terms of subjects. And Im not just talking about a bit of smoke . . . .'[10]

In the same passage, Menzel reveals that he chose the subject himself: 'The banker Liebermann (the painter's uncle) wanted a picture, and when I suggested painting *The Iron Rolling Mill* in 1872, to which private counsellor Jordan[11] later gave the title *Modern Cyclops*, he was very surprised to start with[12]. This subject was, in fact surprising, as there was nothing like it in German painting. The real object was not to magnify the gigantic enterprise of Königshütte, but to capture the subject of the factory worker from the decisive angle, that of his humanity. For this reason the notion of the 'heroism of modern life' invented by Baudelaire, who was thinking of urban crowds and the rising proletariat, also applies to *The Iron Rolling Mill*. The work foreshadows the monstrosity of an era of machines and masses in which man is reduced to a part within a machine. The sole, apparently secondary, fact that about forty men are depicted in the picture already suggests this idea. At the same time this rolling mill, chaotic at first sight, where the speed of the machines forces the men to hurry, is revealed as a perfectly organized factory with an exact task allotted to each part and to each individual. Menzel shows the extent to which man must submit his most elementary needs to the rhythm of work, as shown by the undignified conditions under which workers' changing of shifts took place. In spite of its authenticity, this work is not an impartial piece of reporting. The experience of reality confers a human dimension upon its reality. The Königshütte workers are the centre of interest and, showing them in their individuality, Menzel has made them the essential part of the work process.

The Iron Rolling Mill belonged to the banker Adolph von Liebermann for only a few months, as the collapse of his business soon forced him to sell his whole collection of German masters, in 1876. In mid-July 1875 he asked the Nationalgalerie to buy some of his paintings, among which was this one. The inauguration of the gallery was planned for 1876, and it owned only one of Menzel's paintings, *The Round Table of Frederick II at Sanssouci*. Max Jordan, the director of the Nationalgalerie, who knew and admired Menzel's work, wanted to buy the painting at any price. But in the request made to the Minister of Culture he had to justify the considerable price of 30,000 thalers (Menzel had received 11,000 from Liebermann). The justification for purchasing the painting written by Jordan is a document of its time, all the more because he had to interpret the picture as a variant of history painting for tactical reasons. It was a question of 'glorification of rough work in modern cultural life', of 'a moving description of the heroism of duty' which 'refrains from intent, 'equalling the most grandiose contemporary history paintings in its moral force. . . .'[13] The intention behind the painting went unseen, and it may have seemed inappropriate to speak of it. It is virtually expressly denied by the words 'refrains from intent'. The letter served its purpose, however, and enabled the gallery to purchase the picture.

Amid the paintings in the Nationalgalerie, which was seen as a true 'temple of Art', *The Iron Rolling Mill* immediately drew public attention. Made heroic by some, condemned by others, it rarely gave rise to an objective opinion, and has a special place in Menzel's work.

In April 1879, he wrote to Jordan to ask him to modify the rather vague description of the painting in the first catalogue in 1876, and to add his clear, concrete text. Jordan kept the description of the painting and it appeared in the 1879 edition, with some small modifications of form: 'The scene is one of the great rail factories at Königshütte in Upper Silesia – daylight comes through the sliding wall compartments, which are raised. The eye alights upon an installation of laminating cylinders, the first of which rolls the cast iron coming out of the smelting furnace. The two workers who have brought it are straightening up the shaft of the casting truck to place the cast iron on the rollers, while three others try to get it in the right position using tongs. On the other side, the workers are ready with tongs and hanging bars, attached by chains from the framework above, to seize the rolled iron, lift it off and put it on more rollers, this time of a different size, repeating the process several times along the line, until it is shaped into a rail. On the left, a mill-hand is taking the moulded iron to cool down, and he shapes it with the steam-hammer. On the same side, in the background, some men are working the puddling furnace. Close by, one can see the site manager. The change of shifts is imminent. In the middle ground half-naked workers wash, and on the right others eat the bread brought by a young girl in her basket'[14].

M.R.-R.

1. Letter to Friedrich Pecht, 9 December 1878, Kirstein, 1919, p. 108.
2. Baron Alexander von Schleinitz: Prussian Minister for Foreign Affairs (1858-61); later Minister to the royal House, he was one of the figures portrayed in the picture of the coronation. Menzel drew a society evening at Mrs Marie von Schleinitz's salon, 29 June 1874.
3. On Bonhommé: Schnerb, 1913, p. 11–12 and p. 132–3; exhib. cat. Bonhommé, 1976; Schrenk, 1975, p. 13 and ff.; Janke/Wagner, 1976, p. 5 and ff.; Weisberg, 1980, p. 51–2 and p. 71 and ff.
4. Eggers, 1852.
5. New approaches: *cf.* Riemann-Reyher, exhib. cat. Berlin, 1976, p. 3-19; Hofmann, 1977, p. 141–8; Hopp, exhib. cat. Hamburg, 1982, p. 174–5.
6. The relationship between Eggers and Menzel on the one hand and *The Forge* on the other have been studied for the first time by Riemann-Reyher. *Cf.* exhib. cat. Berlin, 1976, p. 4–5 and p. 13–14.
7. These paintings are now kept at the Stadtmuseum, Berlin and at the Museum für Verkehr und Technik, Berlin.
8. Letter to Paul Meyerheim, 22 February 1875, Wolff, 1914, p. 218.
9. *Cf.* Lammel, 1993 B, fig. 52.
10. Beta, (1898) 1992, p. 55, p.109.
11. Max Jordan, director of the Nationalgalerie.
12. The idea of modern cyclops used by Jordan and also by Menzel, is given for the first time by Eggers in 1852 (*cf.* note 4), then in shortened form by Karl Marx in the first volume of *Capital* which came out in 1867. Inspired by the name of the firm Cyklops Stahl-und Eisenwerke der Herren Cammel et Co., he wrote ironically: For the cyclops, the prohibition of children and young people working at night seems an impossible thing – it would bring their factories to a halt (*cf.* Karl Marx and Friedrich Engels, *Werke*, vol. 23, Berlin, 1993, 34th ed., vol. 1, p. 227). He also speaks of machines of cyclopic steam (*Ibid.*, p. 395). I would like to thank Uwe Henning, Berlin, for this reference.
13. Draft of a letter from Max Jordan, Staatliche Museen zu Berlin, central archives, *Specialia. A. Menzel* 1, *Journal* Nr. 169/75.
14. Letter to Max Jordan, April 1879, Staatliche Museen zu Berlin, central archives, *Specialia A. Menzel* 1, E 1987/1974.

161

Bricklayers at Work on a Scaffold

1875

Pencil
32.4 × 24.6cm
Signed and dated at the top centre: *Ad. Menzel. 19 März/75*
Berlin, Kupferstichkabinett (SZ Menzel N 1150)

Provenance: Painter's studio; 1905 Emilie Krigar-Menzel; acquired by the museum in 1906.
Exhibitions: Hamburg, 1896, no. 163; Berlin, 1905, no. 3072; Berlin, 1955 A, no. 376; Berlin, 1980 A, no. 295, reprod. p. 267; Vienna, 1985, no. 77, reprod. p. 147.

This composition relates to another drawing also dating from 1875 showing building workers on a very high scaffold[1], and also to a gouache, *Bricklayers on a Building Site* (cat. 162). According to Rolf Bothe, it could be a site at 6 Potsdamer Strasse, beside the building where Menzel lived, although it is not certain that he still lived there then. In 1875 a new wing was built and the façade of the building was changed[2]. Another drawing shows the view of the scaffolding and facing buildings from a window[3]. It has no date, but its style indicates that it is certainly from the same period.

A year later, in 1876, Menzel used the motif of a group of bricklayers resting in *Garden of Prince Albert's Palace* (cat. 164), painted in 1846, based on sketches from this early period. This shows how much Menzel had distanced himself from the pictorial ideas of his youth, and how interested he was in the activity and work in a metropolis in a state of permanent flux.

M.R.-R.

1. Halle, Staatliche Galerie Moritzburg.
2. *Cf.* exhib. cat. Berlin, 1987 B, no. 96.
3. Berlin, Kupferstichkabinett (SZ Menzel N 1368).

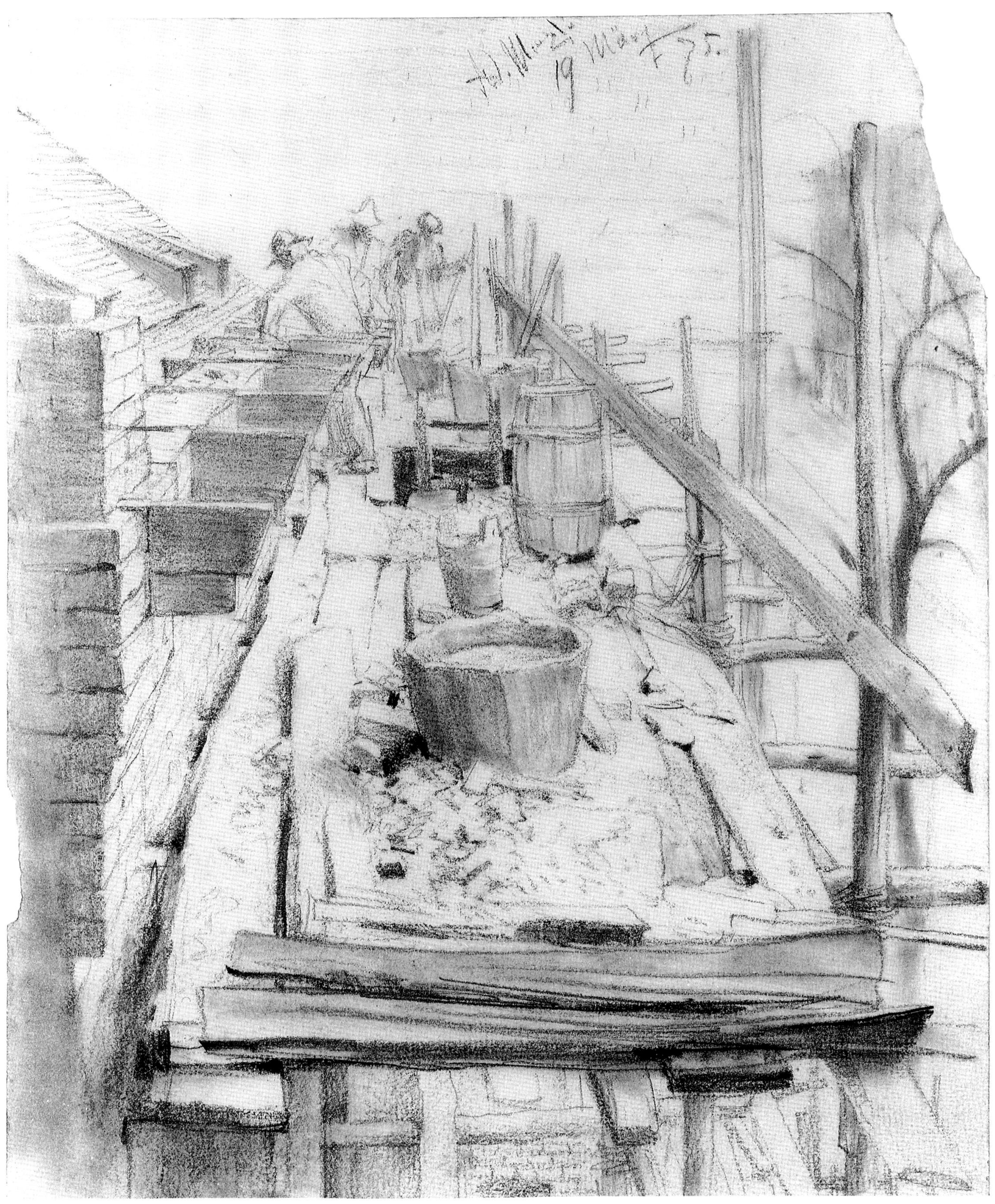

161

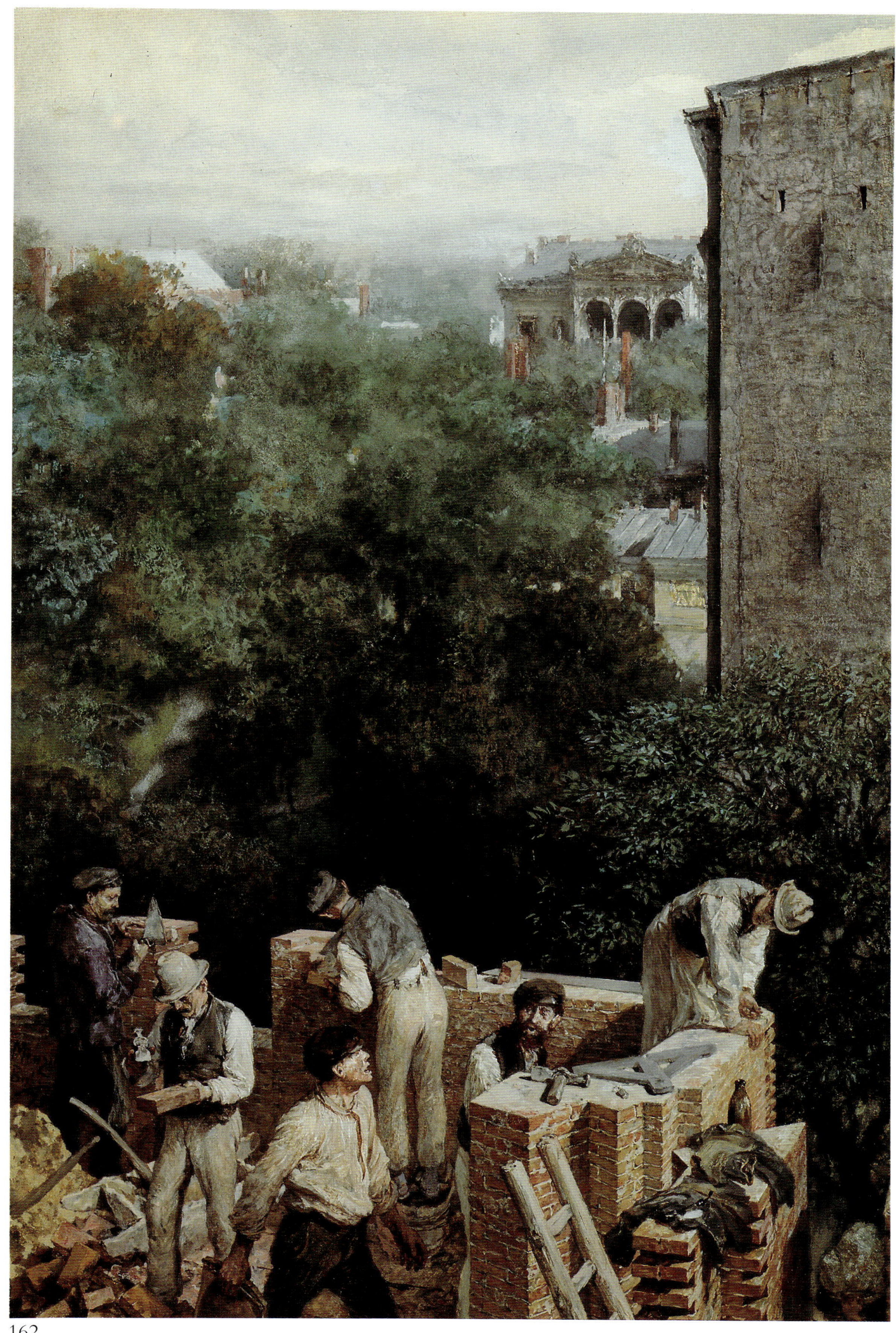
162

162

Bricklayers on a Building Site

1875

Gouache
40 × 26cm
Signed and dated on the left, on the wall: *Menzel Berl. 75*
Essen, Doerte von Bohlen und Halbach

Provenance: Ernst Borsig, Berlin; private collections.
Exhibitions: Berlin, 1877, no. 866; Berlin, 1885, no. 77; Berlin, 1895, no. 99; Hamburg, 1896, no. 62; Vienna, 1896, no. 259; Berlin, 1905, no. 222; Berlin, 1955 B, no. 123; Frankfurt, 1975, no. 36; Berlin, 1987 B, no. 96.
Bibliography: Rosenberg, 1878; Knackfuss, 1895, p. 90, fig. 75; Jordan, 1905, p. 74, fig. p. 82; Tschudi, 1905 A, no. 610; Bredt, 1920, fig. p. 51; Kaiser, 1956, p. 108, fig. 74; Wirth, 1965, p. 31, fig. 15.

Building sites and workers often appear in Menzel's universe, from his youth to his old age (*cf.* cat. 22) and concern him throughout his work (*cf.* cat. 92). He had scarcely finished *The Iron Rolling Mill* when he went back to the theme of the building. On 22 February 1875 he invited Paul Meyerheim to attend the 'resurrection of the colours in my painting [via] the varnish-laden brush of Herr Schmidt'[1]. On 19 March 1875 he signed a drawing of a scaffold with workers (cat. 161). It may be linked to this gouache, and also to another dated 1875 representing workers on the upper platform of a building under construction, which had reached the attic stage[2], even though these are not preliminary studies. On the other hand there are ten studies of workers in the 1874–5 sketchbook[3] which are definitely linked to the gouache. Menzel sketched bricklayers occupied with different tasks, some of whom reappear slightly modified in the colour composition. The measurements of a brick in a bricklayer's hand can be read on one study. The man is wearing a hat and waistcoat in the picture, and is preparing to cut the brick. There are two studies of the bricklayer viewed from behind, whose head and body are leaning to the left. He is standing over a bucket, with a brick in his left hand. The other study is of the foreman[4]. Menzel may have drawn further studies of workers from models; their rather rough and ready style resembles the model drawings for *The Iron Rolling Mill.*

He drew building workers more often than other men at work and, apart from the social interest, it was undoubtedly the building boom at this time in Germany, which was called the 'Gründerjahre' (founders' years), when Berlin was positively transformed, that led Menzel to make so many critical and documentary drawings[5]. But the theme of building did not inspire large paintings. In 1888 he finished his last genre painting, a gouache in the Dutch Baroque style, a composition illustrating the passion for building which went hand in hand with the creation of the German empire. It shows a well-off couple in the garden of a villa about to be completed. Menzel gave this the appropriate title *Beati Possidentes* (Happy Owners)[6].

He sold the painting shown here to Albert Borsig at the end of January 1875 for 2000 thalers. Borsig was the son and successor to the founder of the famous Borsig factories[7]. The industrialist had probably known Menzel since 1872, when he commissioned Paul Meyerheim to paint the cycle of paintings *History of the Locomotive* which was an important source of inspiration for Menzel's *The Iron Rolling Mill.* If we believe the title given to the picture, the house under construction was being built on the site of an old garden. The painter was already aware of the destruction of nature caused by the expansion of the metropolis. Long before this, he had observed the tension between nature, with its fields and trees, and the elegant curve of the railway cutting brutally through the countryside (*cf.* cat. 35). In 1876, when he went back to his picture *Garden of Prince Albert's Palace* from 1846, he destroyed the park idyll by including a group of workers at rest (cat. 164).

It is often difficult to identify the locations for Menzel's pictures exactly. An interesting deduction was recently made, although the chosen perspective, so characteristic of Menzel, confuses attempts to define the site painted. The view looking down on the building suggests the small height of the painter in relation to the roads and park. On the right another building rises above, raising the question of how high the new building will be. The villa in the right background allows the site to be identified as near Menzel's apartment at 7 Potsdamer Strasse (even if he had already moved a little further away in 1875, to 3 Sigismundstrasse). It depicts a villa built in 1868 at 6 Bellevuestrasse, by Friedrich Hitzig, for the factory owner Julius Jacoby[8]. M.R.-R.

1. Letter to Paul Meyerheim, 22 February 1875, Wolff, 1914, p. 218.
2. Halle, Staatliche Galerie Moritzburg.
3. Berlin, Kupferstichkabinett, sketchbook 46.
4. As for the sketchbook: Berlin, Kupferstichkabinett.
5. *Cf.* Brandt, 1928, p. 279.
6. Euerbach, George Schäfer collection.
7. According to an account book Menzel kept between 1858 and 1904 (unpublished, location unknown).
8. *Cf.* Bothe, exhib. cat. Berlin, 1987 B, no. 96.

163

Planning a Journey

1875

Gouache
15 × 31cm
Signed and dated at the bottom right: *Ad. Menzel 1875*
Essen, Folkwang Museum
Exhibited in Berlin only

Provenance: Adolph Thiem 1888; 1905 Paul Cassirer Gallery; 1915 Fritz Gurlitt, Berlin; Probst collection, Berlin; Kunsthaus Mannheim; acquired by the museum in 1938.

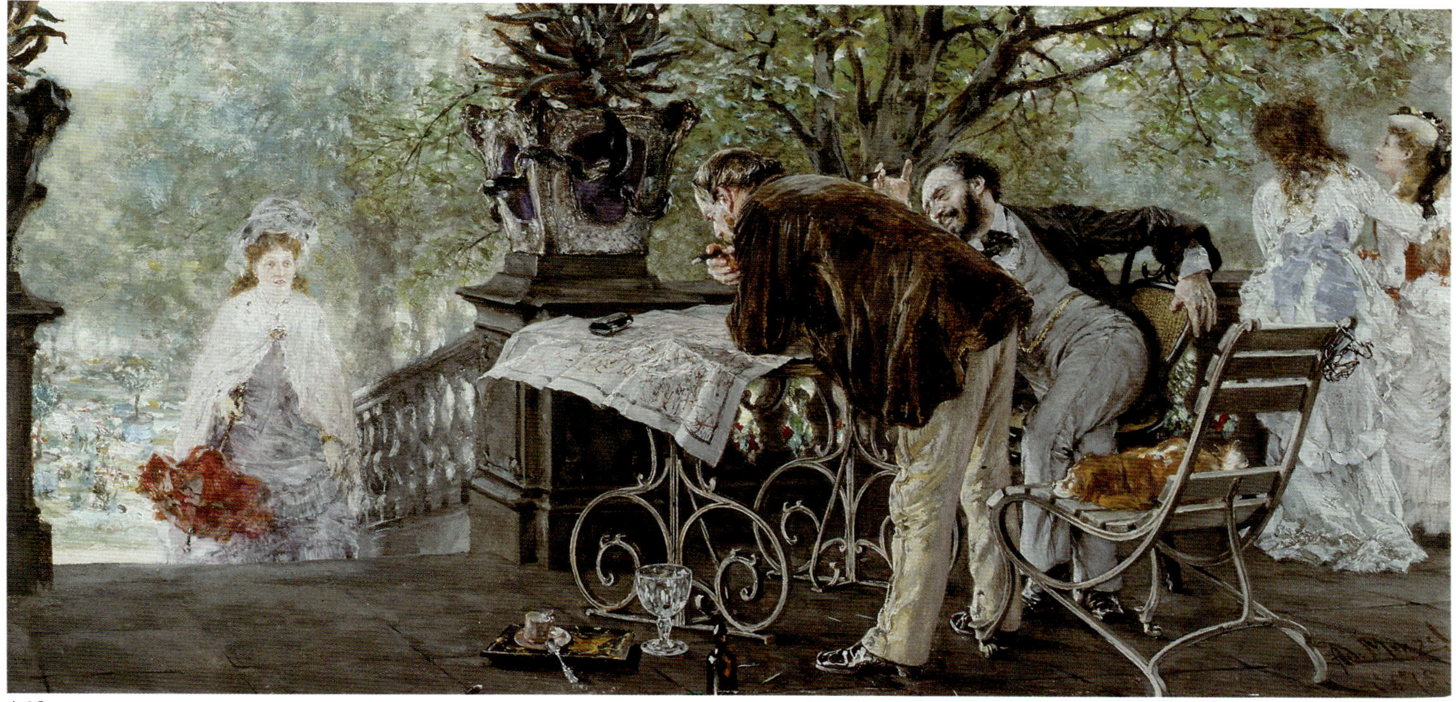
163

Exhibitions: Brussels, 1878, no. 71; Paris, 1885, no. 254; Berlin, 1885, no. 78; Berlin, 1895, no. 100; Düsseldorf, 1904, no. 68; Berlin, 1905, no. 223; Berlin, 1955 B, no. 124.
Bibliography: Dumas, 1885, pl. 254; Jordan, 1895, p. 49; Tschudi, 1905 A, no. 612; Jordan, 1905, p. 74; Vogt, 1965, p. 219, col. pl; Hütt, 1981, fig. 92.

Menzel expressed his impressions of his stay in Paris at the end of the 1860s in two large paintings (cat. 123, 127), and the subject of 'modern life' reappeared in the 1870s in the depictions of Berlin life. Some gouaches of the 1870s are remarkably gay and lighthearted in comparison with older ones such as *End of the Evening* (cat. 91) or even *The 'Moritzhof' Inn* (cat. 108), belonging to the *Children's Album,* so charming in colour and form.

The composition and colours of the gouache described here are delightful and harmonious. Nature and man's attachment to fashion interpenetrate in a profound way in the painter's superb mastery of the medium of watercolour, whose strength resides in the delicacy of the film of paint which renders spatiality secondary. The natural world, suggested by the green-leaved trees, harmonizes perfectly with the delicate pink of the women's clothing and the nuanced tones of the men's outfits. The summer activities of the city bourgeoisie are the pretext for this gouache, as well as for another of the same kind, *In the Park*, of the same year[1]. In the picture sown here, two men on the terrace of their house, or perhaps their hotel at a thermal spa, make travel plans, while the women are in a state of dreamy, hopeful expectation. Duality is conveyed by contrasting colours – all the objects representing the present moment are concentrated mainly around the group of men, in strong colours, while lightness and sensitivity are expressed in the light tones of the figures of the women on the right and left. The gouache *In the Park* has no 'awkward details', and shows two couples near a bench under the undulating foliage of some trees, having a casual conversation. In Menzel's paintings the figures are almost totally anonymous. This picture could convey the vivid impressions of his repeated visits to Hofgastein during the 1870s, at the summer villa of the family of the Berlin banker Magnus Herrmann, and his son-in-law the painter Albert Hertel, whose family was connected with the Krigar-Menzels[2] (*cf.* cat. 174, 175).

In another painting of 1875, entitled *The Stroller*[3], which portrays an old man in the dress of Frederick the Great's time on a country road under some willows, Menzel seems to be glancing back at the time to which he devoted so many creative years. But there is only a superficial melancholy in the pictorial treatment of the landscape with its sparkling, delicate colours. In harmony with the other two paintings, it is evidence that Menzel had turned away from thematic narrowness to abandon himself gladly to the narrative, picturesque plurality of the everyday scene. Although the formats are sometimes small, they have a grandeur reminiscent of Manet. Or perhaps bourgeois society life is observed in its interplay of relationships between men and women as an echo of the Parisian atmosphere, a common link in both artists. There may also be a 'hint of the early Manet'[4] in all his Parisian paintings. M.R.-R.

1. 1875, gouache, 19.5 × 14.7cm; Tschudi, 1905 A, no. 616, reprod; Boston, Fogg Art Museum, Harvard University. *Cf.* Schlagenhauff, 1991, p. 15, col. reprod.
2. *Cf.* Hertel, 1911-12, p. 786–93; Herrmann, (1905) 1992, p. 84–8 and p. 249–54. In sketchbook 36 (1871–5), Berlin, Kupferstichkabinett, there are drawings of the friends playing music. The person standing near a table is the subject of a pencil study, 20.5 × 12.5cm; location unknown.
3. 1875, watercolour and gouache, 20.8 × 29.8cm, 1992 on the market; Tschudi, 1905 A, no. 614; *Cf. The Arts*, May 1905, p. 10, no. 41.
4. Meier-Graefe, (1906) 1914, p. 206. The quotation is as follows: In all Menzel's Parisian paintings there is a slight hint of the early Manet.

Fig. 209. *In the Park*, 1875, gouache, Cambridge, Ma., Fogg Art Museum, Harvard University

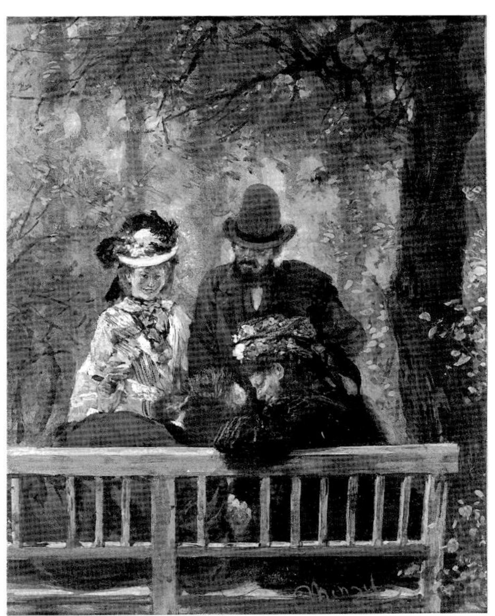

164

Garden of Prince Albert's Palace

1846/1876

Oil on canvas
68 × 86cm
Signed and dated at the bottom left: *Ad.Menzel 46*
Berlin, Nationalgalerie (A I 989)

Provenance: Hermann Frenkel, Berlin banker, owned the work from 1885; acquired by the museum in 1906, although it had already expressed its interest in 1903, but was unable to gain pre-emptive right.
Exhibitions: Paris, 1885, no. 231; Berlin, 1885, no. 2; Berlin, 1886, no. 2460; Berlin, 1895 A, no. 35; Vienna, 1896, no. 275; Düsseldorf, 1904, no. 16, reprod.; Boston, 1909, unnumb. (p. 56), pl. (unnumb.); Berlin, 1935, no. 4; Wiesbaden, 1947, no. 57; Wiesbaden, 1952, no. 155; Berlin, 1955 B, no. 11, fig. 20; Zurich, 1956, unnumb., no pag.; New York, 1981, no. 61, col. reprod.; Paris, 1984, no. 94, reprod.
Bibliography: Jordan, 1895, p. 40; Jordan, 1905, p. 42; Tschudi, 1905 A, no. 28; Tschudi, 1905 B, p. 229, pl. facing p. 260 (p. 19, pl. facing p. 54); Meier-Graefe, 1906, p. 87 *et seq.*; cat. NG, 1908, no. 1107; Scheffler, 1912, p. 122; Kern, 1915–16, p. 96; Justi, 1920, p. 139 *et seq.*; Waldmann, 1922, p. 11; Scheffler, 1922, p. 92, p. 147–8, reprod. p. 37; Justi, 1932, p. 130 et seq.; Scheffler, 1938, p. 57, reprod. p. 154; Beenken, 1944, p. 177 *et seq.*, fig. 43; Wirth, 1965, p. 26; Hütt, 1981, fig. 45 (col.); Jensen, 1982, col. pl. 5; Busch, 1985, p. 286 *et seq.*, fig. 94.

Menzel wrote on the subject of this much larger variant (and probably intended for exhibition) of *View over Prince Albert's Palace Park* (cat. 23): 'In 1846 I painted the oil study "Prince Albert's garden" from the balcony of my apartment at that time, directly from life, with the exception of the foreground which is invented, *as well as* the navvies ['garden' is crossed out] having their afternoon snooze. In fact, two dates apply to this painting as, thirty years later, I changed the sky, which I didn't like, and *re*painted it, in 1876. Then it went into other hands'[1].

These lines are instructive on more than one level. For one thing the painter describes a painting of this size as a 'study', adhering to an out-of-date usage of the word as the reproduction of reality for its own sake, everything which does not communicate a 'content' in the conventional sense of the word. On the other hand, we learn more of Menzel's methods. What seems to be a view from the window is a view from above, without the frame imposed by a window. Thirdly, if the painter was standing on his balcony, the words 'painted directly from life'[2] have their full meaning, refuting the idea, at least in this case, that Menzel drew an open-air subject and then painted it in his studio. It probably varied from painting to painting, which is confirmed by the remark about the 'navvies' asleep. They were not invented but painted from drawings taken from another site (there are bricklayers on scaffolding in the background of *Building Site with Willows* [cat. 22]). Several sketches from 1845 show variations on tired bricklayers asleep in the midday heat (fig. 210), observed on a 'building site from two floors up'[3]. They were incorporated into the picture thirty years later. Menzel continued to work on this theme, which reappeared several years later on the frontispiece of the sketch *Berlin a Hundred Years Ago*[4], this time wrapped in the folds of history and having a symbolic meaning – the workers have finished building Frederick the Great's city.

Last of all, this letter explains the strange, mixed character of the work in indicating its second stage in 1876. It is, however, hard to believe that only the sky was repainted[5]. The overall picture marries, in general, with the painter's later work. A comparison with the smaller version shows this, where the colour is light and soft, applied with panache, and seems diaphanous and almost ethereal in places. The reworked part has a density, clarity, meticulousness and also a certain roughness which is lacking in the pictures of the 1840s. On the other hand, the retouching was done at a time when Menzel was painting only open landscapes of this type. What the painter actually *saw* in 1846[6] and conveyed in paint (a similar view was chosen for *The Garden of the Ministry of Justice* about 1848[7]) found its definitive form in a quite different phase of Menzel's painting. The result hardly conforms to the demands of catalogue numbering. What-

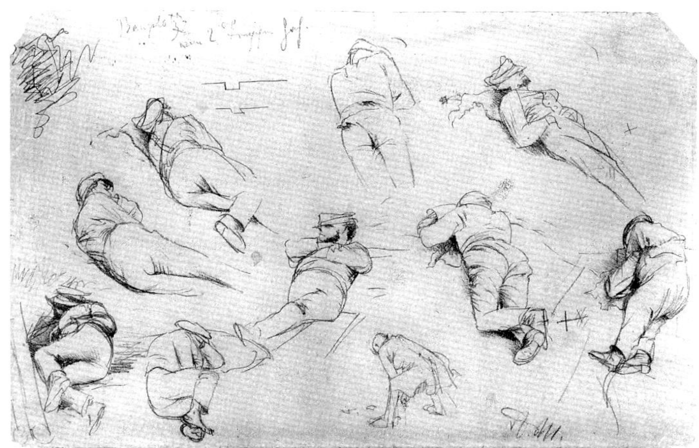

Fig. 210. *Workers Resting*, 1846, pencil, Berlin, Kupferstichkabinett (N 1398)

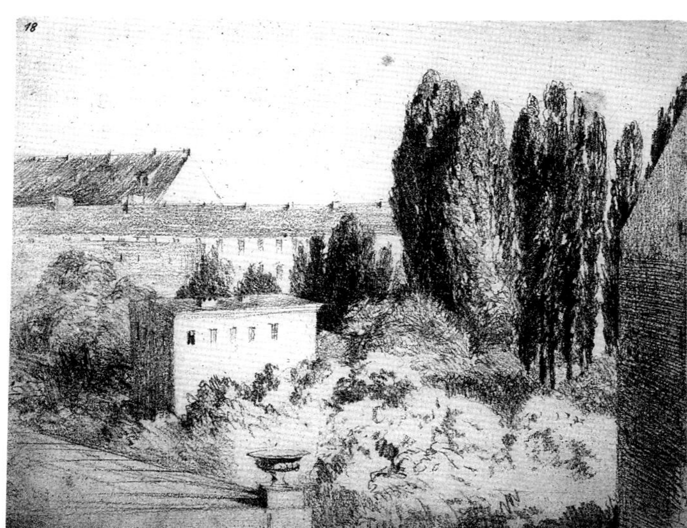

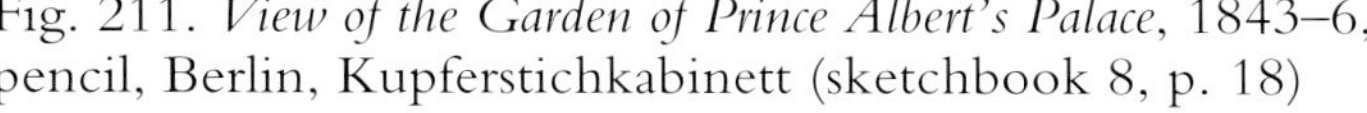

Fig. 211. *View of the Garden of Prince Albert's Palace*, 1843–6, pencil, Berlin, Kupferstichkabinett (sketchbook 8, p. 18)

ever stage of the painter's work one relates it to, it seems to be out of place.

Menzel's penchant for severe self-criticism and reworking older works is reinforced by a profound sense, and experience of, the alternative, and the possibilities it offers. This basic plurality of his approach (to reality as well as to art) which is its strength, needs to be organized. Hence the problem of mixed solutions. The 'bifocality' described by Werner Hofmann in an essay in this catalogue (p. 91 *et seq.*) takes up the challenge. That does not prevent some reworked pictures from showing the effects of the conflict between contradictory perspectives. In its current state, the gouache *Marienburg at Dusk* is the result of retouching just like *The Garden of Prince Albert* – over forty years separated the initial phase from its completion[8] (1855 and 1897). In both cases photographs allow a comparison between the first and final stages. In the gouache *A Place for the Great Raphael*[9] (1855 and 1859) only the main motifs have been altered, while the portrait of Menzel's friend Karl Eitner (1850 and 1901), modified down to the last detail, was finally called *A Visitor Waiting*. The reason for these changes was, in each case, the desire to enrich the painting with innumerable narrative details involving new pictorial elements. The addition of a window casts a reflection from it upon the cheek of one of the figures, which means that the whole face has to be repainted, and so on[10].

Like Tschudi, who spoke of 'Menzel's most important landscape', Guido Josef Kern resisted the temptation to belittle the large canvas, whose structure is far more complex in comparison with the smaller version, which is so fresh. He wrote: 'The artist attaches more importance to the park than to each of the trees, and more to the image of the town than to the park. More important than the image of the town is the countryside which stretches out beneath the warm summer sun'. After Tschudi and Meier-Graefe had detected the influence of John Constable on Menzel in this painting as in others, Kern found confirmation of this in a very detailed, enthusiastic report published in 1839 on the posthumous exhibition of the English painters two pictures in Berlin[11]. C.K.

1. *Series of marginal notes*, drawn up on 28 October 1887 for Max Jordan (Staatliche Museen zu Berlin, archives).
2. For contradictory indications of where the painter was standing, *cf.* cat. 23.
3. Berlin, Kupferstichkabinett (SZ Menzel N 480 and 1401, both dated; N 1333 [plus the copy N 854] and N 1398).
4. 1879, not mentioned by Bock, 1923; exhib. cat. Berlin, 1984, no. 341; the drawing is now at the Berliner Stadtmuseum: Berlin, 1990, no. 577, reprod.
5. Jordan, 1895, adds that the palace was also retouched.
6. A drawing in sketchbook 8 (1843-6) in the Kupferstichkabinett in Berlin, p. 18, shows a quite different view of the park.
7. Tschudi, 1905 A, no. 46, reprod.; in the Kunsthalle in Bremen till 1945.
8. Riemann-Reyher, 1992, p. 77 and ff., reprod. p. 78.
9. Tschudi, 1905 A, no. 335; Nuremberg, Germanisches Nationalmuseum; exhib. cat. Hamburg, 1982, no. 68, reproduces the two versions.
10. Tschudi, 1905 A, no. 227 (1855 version, reprod.), no. 681 (1901 version, reprod.); Norden., (1900) 1992, p. 79 and ff.; Lammel, 1993 B, p. 180 and fig. 94; location unknown.
11. Kern, 1915–16, p. 96 and ff.

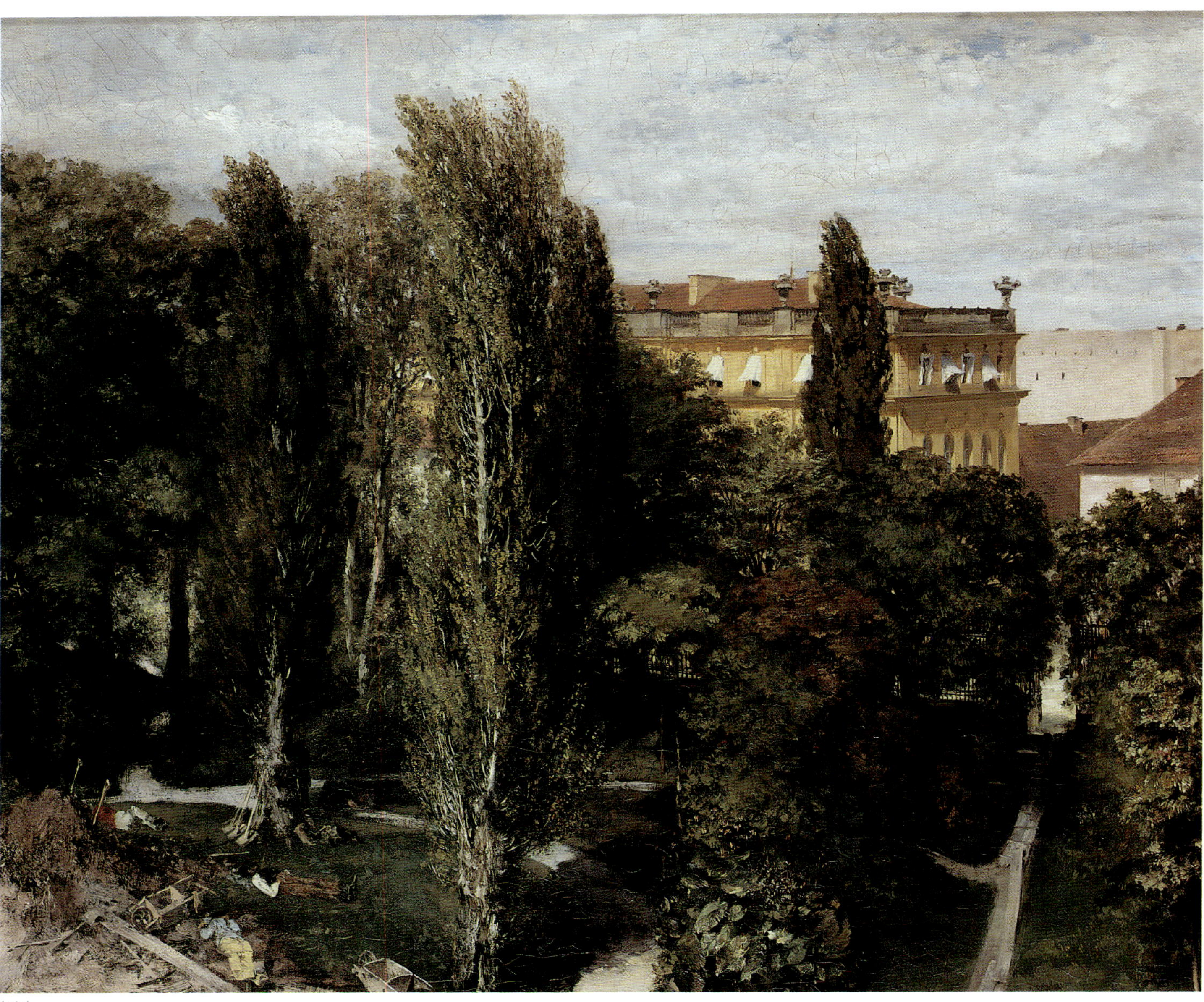

164

165

The Artist's Foot

1876

Oil on wood
38.5 × 33.5cm
Signed and dated at the bottom right: *A.Menzel 76*
Bochum, Bochum Kunstvermittlung
(H.L. Alexander v. Bersword-Wallrabe)

Provenance: 1904 R. Wagner Gallery, Berlin; 1905 Prof. Oeder, Düsseldorf; private collections; became part of the current collection *c.* 1983.
Exhibitions: Düsseldorf, 1904, no. 23 b; Berlin, 1905, no. 85.
Bibliography: Tschudi, 1905 A, no. 145.

The luminous gaze of the painter focuses on unexpected sights. Hugo von Tschudi probably based his statement that Menzel painted his own foot when he was unwell on the artist's own words. From the start of the 1850s, Menzel's pupil Carl Johann Arnold had seen him 'when he was going to have a foot bath, painting a study of his foot, life size, so that he completely forget his initial intention'[1]. The lively curiosity for this subject never lessened and, eighteen years after the painting described here, Menzel drew a large format picture of his half-bare right leg, adding the image of his left foot in a mirror[2]. Its perfect working and apparently autonomous movement, like a puppet, and at the same time the strange animal quality and cartilaginous aspect of this despised part of the body – and for this reason the object of fetishism – exerted a fascination over him comparable to that of old dog-eared books or a wobbly scaffold.

Even works with an aesthetic of the fragmentary do not escape the iconographic field of attraction. When a woodcut by Menzel for chapter 17 of Kugler's book, possibly inspired by Gran-

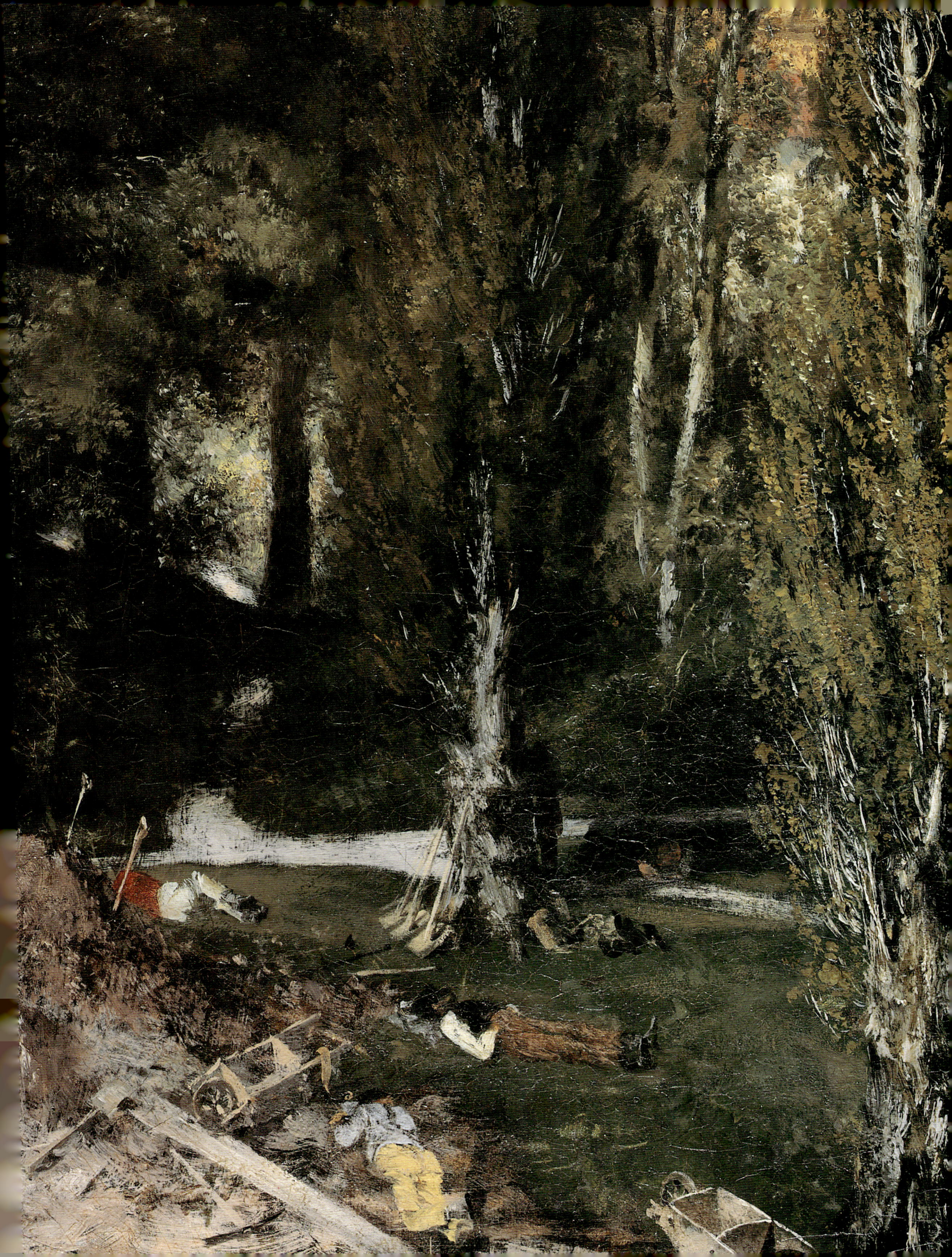

ville, shows the legs of dancers behind a falling curtain, a 'mosaic' of photographic visiting cards by Disdéri picks this up twenty years later[3]. Isolated representations of feet, which appear here and there, even in sculpture, in the second half of the nineteenth century[4] are no more 'studies' in the traditional meaning of the term than Menzels painting, which affords the same attention, the same respect, as for a landscape or a human face. A commitment to sincerity and perseverance inspire this view, like the commitment brought to the body of Christ by, for example, Mantegna. In this respect, the work lines up with those which lend nobility to common objects by isolating them (Courbet's pipe with the inscription 'Courbet without ideal or religion', or the shoes and stool of Van Gogh, etc.). They are expressions of a realism which does not hesitate to seek a plebeian look. In 1865 Thomas Couture painted a young artist who was drawing a pigs head, sacrilegiously using an antique marble head as a stool. One might recall Menzel's decapitated horses heads (*cf.* cat. 43, 44), but the choice of a pig's head is significant. The picture is called *The Realist*[5].
C.K.

1. Arnold, (1905)1992, p. 139.
2. Bock, 1923, no. 564.
3. Exhib. cat. Frankfurt, 1990, fig. 419.
4. Berlin, Kupferstichkabinett (SZ Menzel N 245); exhib. cat. Vienna, 1985, no. 106, reprod.
5. Boime, 1980, p. 331–5, fig. IX.47.

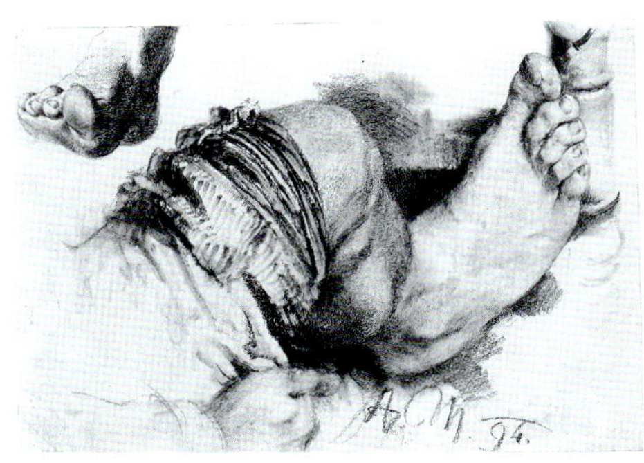

Fig. 212. *Right Leg with the Trouser Rolled up*, 1894, pencil, Berlin, Kupferstichkabinett (N 245)

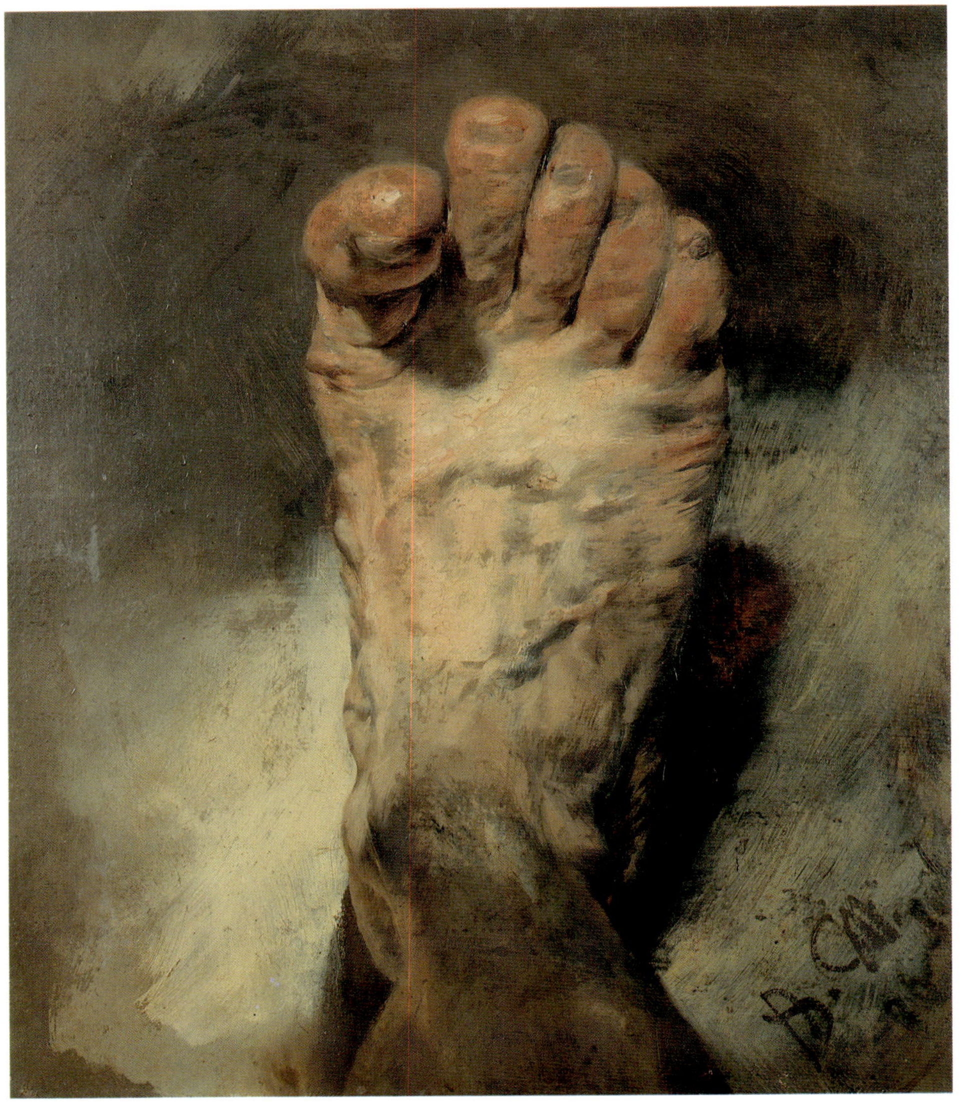

165

166

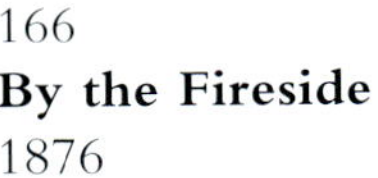

By the Fireside

1876

Oil on canvas
29 × 23cm
Signed and dated vertically along the left side: *A. Menzel 76*
London, private collection
Exhibited in Berlin only

Provenance: 1877 and 1880 H. Goldschmidt, Berlin; 1905 Ottilie Goldschmidt-Przibram, Brussels; private collections.
Exhibitions: Berlin (Rudolph Lepke Gallery), 1876 B; Berlin, 1877, no. 492; Düsseldorf, 1904, no. 17; Berlin, 1905, no. 50; Wolfsburg, 1956, no. 128; Erlangen, 1971, no. 91.
Bibliography: Pietsch, 1877; Duranty, 1880, II, p. 112, p. 114 *et seq.*, pl.(etching by Paul Le Rat) facing p. 260; Tschudi, 1905 A, no. 146; Wirth, 1990, p. 294, fig. 368.

Is this a sacrifice to fashion, a challenge taken up, or a frivolous distraction for the great painter who had just completed *The Iron Rolling Mill*? Or is there a deeper meaning in these historical reconstructions, painted mostly in gouache, where the action takes place in the seventeenth century?[1] The exuberant vitality and pretention of the bourgeois rich who people them, whose ordinariness easily becomes grotesque, is reminiscent of the successful entrepreneurs of the 'Gründerzeit'. Menzel seems to have had to experience this period of bold speculation and spectacular bankruptcies before he could once more take an interest in a century and an anecdotic type of painting he left behind forty years ago (*cf.* cat. 2) in favour of the eighteenth century. The fact remains that he did not take it up again until the second half of the 1870s, no doubt encouraged by the new style of interior decor, the Renaissance and baroque furniture and by the mysterious chiaroscuro created by the thick curtains. In the Sigismundstrasse, he himself was surrounded, not by luxury, but by solid, bulky shapes and frequently by half-light, in spite of the large windows.

The figures in *By the Fireside* move in this sort of context. Although the bottle glass in the windows colours the external light with red and yellow tones, the two real sources of light are hidden: the light from the fireplace, which gives off reddish reflections, and the pronounced contrast of the daylight falling to the right through a nearby, yet invisible, window. It can be seen on the white ruffs of the women and on the skirt of the older woman, while the light on the white collar of the man sitting in front of the fire changes from one source to another. Duranty described how 'reflections slide, climb, rise, explode and die down on clothes, faces, furniture . . .' From a purely pictorial point of view – alternating the chromatic atmosphere from cold, through red to warm – the small painting might be considered to be a sequel to *The Iron Rolling Mill*. But then it would be a highly ironic historical distortion!

This costume scene is not like any painting from the time it depicts. The thought of any painting of the Dutch seventeenth-century genre is enough to reveal a clearly more analytical description of the characters, more individual and momentary, as well as striking differences in staging and layout. The fireplace and the back of the chair form heavy, dark theatrical 'wings' (with the figure of the man sitting down across the foreground acting paradoxically as a foil). Between these props a narrow section of the room opens out and dissolves into a mysterious chiaroscuro. The near miracle of the servant standing in the bicoloured backlighting is created by just a few light touches which modify only the reddish-brown wash of the background.

Ludwig Pietsch, a well-informed critic who was close to the painter, interprets the scene as follows: 'The timid young girl behind the back of the armchair has been sought in marriage by a man she does not love. While her mother tries to convince her reluctant father, the suitor stokes the fire with the poker because he realizes that everything has fallen through'. But his indifference could be interpreted quite differently. He could be a commoner counting on his luck in entering the nobility through marriage. In any case, the rank of the betrothed's father is clearly indicated by his sword. C.K.

1. *The Letter*, 1886, Tschudi, 1905 A, no. 658; New York, The Metropolitan Museum. – *Beati Possidentes*, 1888, Tschudi, 1905 A, no. 667; Euerbach, Georg Schäfer collection.

167
Supper at the Ball
1878

Oil on canvas
71 × 90cm
Signed and dated at the bottom left: *Adolph Menzel Berlin, 1878*
Berlin, Nationalgalerie (A I 1902)

Provenance: The first owner, Adolf Thiem, Berlin, had bought the work before it was finished, and kept it until at least 1888; later, Emil Meiner, Leipzig (who also owned *Marketplace in Verona*) offered the picture unsuccessfully to the Städelsches Museum society for a large amount of money; acquired by the Nationalgalerie in 1906.

Exhibitions: Berlin, 1878, (no. 493 of cat., not exhib.); Paris, 1879; Berlin, 1879, no. 379a; Munich, 1879; Paris, 1885, no. 230; Berlin, 1885, no. 19; Hamburg, 1888; Berlin, 1891, no. 727a; Boston, 1909, unnumb. (p. 56), unnumb. pl.; Berlin, 1935, no. 43; Wiesbaden, 1947, no. 61; Wiesbaden, 1952, no. 162; Berlin, 1955 B, no. 127, fig. 55; London, 1956, no. 168; Berlin, 1960, no. 2; Berlin, 1961, no. 51, reprod.

Bibliography: Rosenberg, 1879 A; Rosenberg, 1879 B, p. 275–9; Duranty, 1880, II, p. 117 *et seq.*; Gonse, 1885, p. 522; Jordan, 1890, p. 72 *et seq.*, pl. 98; Tschudi, 1905 A, no. 148; Jordan, 1904–5, p. 269, pl. facing p. 269; cat. NG, 1907, no. 985; Jordan, 1905, p.79 *et seq.*; Meier-Graefe, 1906, p. 97, p. 216 *et seq.*; Scheffler, 1912, p. 134 *et seq.*, reprod. p. 130; Justi, 1920, p. 174–9; Scheffler, 1922, p. 198–9, reprod. p. 205, p. 207; Waldmann, 1922, p. 11–12, fig. 20/16; Fechner, (1927) 1992, p. 246; Justi, 1932, p. 139 *et seq.*, fig. 55; Scheffler, 1938, p. 83, p. 116 *et seq.*, reprod. pp. 196–7; Waldmann, 1941, p. 36, pp. 38–9, p. 49. figs 75–7; Beenken, 1944, p. 329 *et seq.*, fig. 122; Hütt, 1981, fig. 100; Zangs, 1992, p. 225–33; Forster-Hahn, 1993, p. 89.

The representation of balls and parties is scattered throughout Menzel's work like a leitmotiv. It would perhaps be justifiable to include among these the two last gouaches in the series 'White Rose Festival', even if the people at court are portrayed beneath the chandeliers in historical costume[1]. The large gouache *Salon Recital* was painted earlier[2]. In another gouache, *Ball Scene*[3] (1867), just a few figures fill the picture. Then came *Lull at the Ball*[4] (1870). The space defined is already becoming larger, in preparation for *Supper at the Ball*, where the whole immense depth is used. *Supper at the Ball* was immediately followed by *William I's circle*[5], which like the later ball paintings, seems to be a small-format extract from *Supper at the Ball*. The gouache *Ball at the Rheinsberg court*[6] might anticipate *Supper at the Ball* in historical costume. It has one difference – the anecdotic grotesque (probably inspired by Hogarth) is not compensated for by the charm of the lighting and the mystery of the space.

After his work on *The Coronation*, Menzel often went to court balls at Berlin, which immediately provided him with a new area of study. Jules Laforgue watched his careful observation in the 1880s. He had no hesitation in sketching

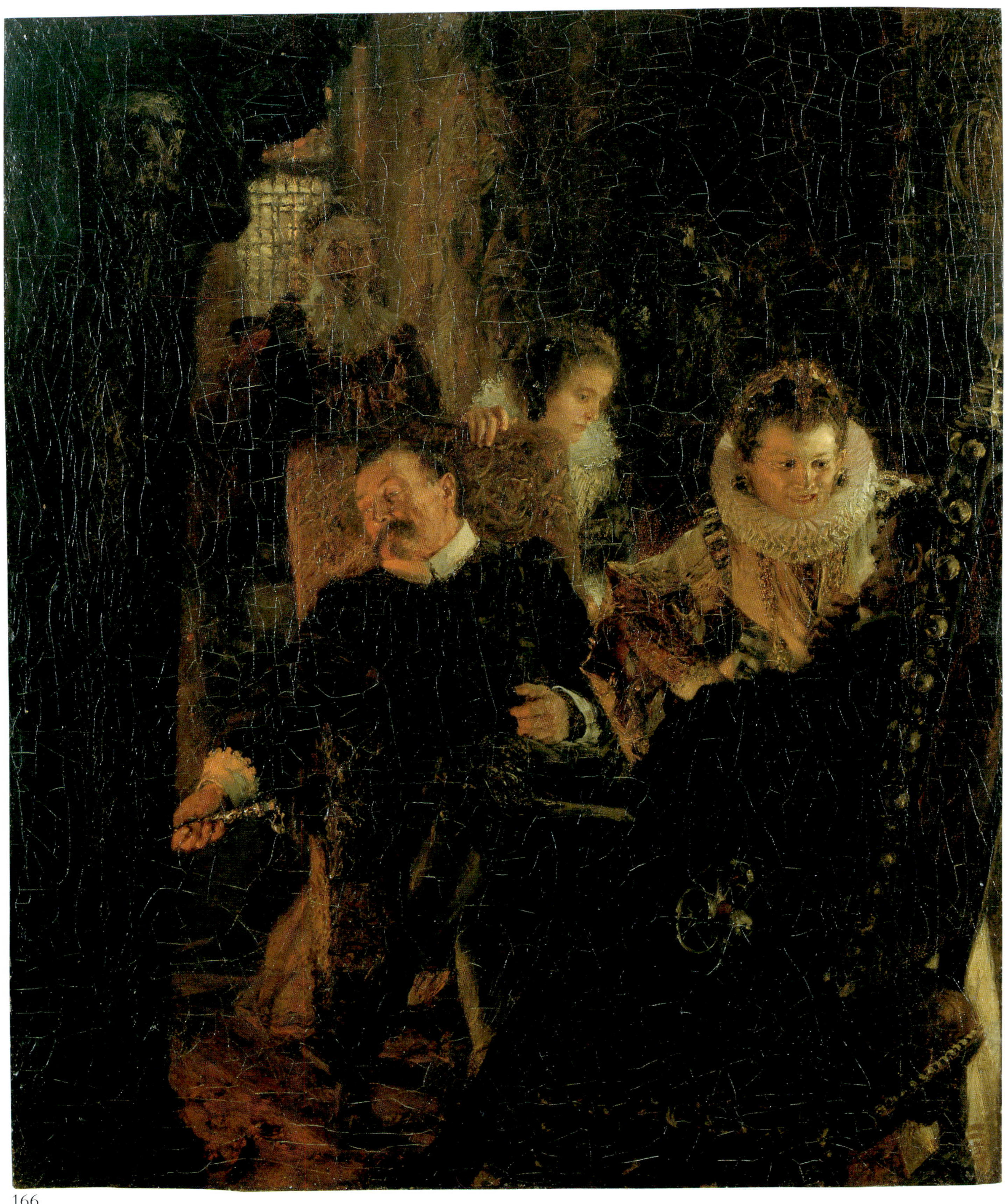

166

where he was, sometimes using the backs of invitations, whose text enables the drawings to be dated. Thus a whole group of works of a specific style was formed, of which *Supper at the Ball* is a synthesis. Few of the drawings made previously were actually used in the picture directly. But some studies from models relating to the very small figures in the painting indicate a constant need for accuracy.

If a sketch of the whole had existed, it would undoubtedly have been preserved with care. After *The Coronation*, Menzel no longer liked to make a rough draft of his compositions. A witness recounts how the picture was created, using the method Menzel followed until the end of his life: he 'did not really compose as such, at least not by sketching on to the canvas, but the objects in the painting appear little by little, as if of their own accord, as work progresses'. 'He had an exact idea in his head of the whole as well as of the detail, which he could work on in sections. At the end an area at the front right of the picture remained empty: 'That doesn't bother me – I will fill it with white – the whipped cream – the ladies!' Meier-Graefe[7] considers this mosaic-like aspect to be a weakness of the work, yet it is the source of its originality. The crowd moving inside the room is captured in the same way as a crowd in the street, as a contemporary critic noted when he wrote that the 'mad rush to the buffet' during the lull between dances was the 'moment when the individual reasserted his rights within the general pulling and shoving of the masses'.

One might imagine that the room depicted, which opens on to a picture gallery lost in vagueness, must be part of the royal palace of Berlin, yet even those who knew this vast and prestigious building before it was destroyed were disconcerted. There are motifs in the picture similar to those decorating the Andreas Schlüter staircase, or those in the 'parade rooms'. Overall, however, the painter has imagined a ballroom in the same Neo-baroque spirit which gave rise to the composite motifs of the diplomas (*cf.* cat. 129, 187). The architecture and decoration of the building form a whole in which the light of the lamps and chandeliers is an integral part, rendered with virtuosity in its numerous gradations, with the rustle of dresses, and busy twirling round of the guests engaged in animated or affected conversation, or just busy with their plates of food. The world of women reigns on the right side, that of men on the left. Discomfort, banality and prestige clash brutally.

The composition is clearly not consistent with the dimensions of the canvas. It is a cleverly articulated painting of society, of a contemporary event. The onlooker expects to recognize some of the figures, but this expectation is not fulfilled. Although each face has clearly defined features, these are not portraits, as well-informed contemporaries indicate. The officer in the light-coloured uniform (almost in the centre of the painting) has been thought to be the Crown Prince Frederick-William[8], patron of the arts, who held Menzel in high esteem and visited his studio several times. But important personalities have no place in this picture: 'The court has retired to the reserved rooms'[9], only the ordinary guests are helping themselves to the buffet.

'From the point of view of colour, this picture is undoubtedly the artists greatest act of bravery', wrote Max Jordan. Adolf Rosenberg is probably referring to the presentation of the work to its first owner when he writes: 'If the room is darkened, and a lamp lit so that its light is concentrated on the canvas through a reflector, the effect of the lighted candles is greatly reinforced'. This is what lead Rosenberg to think that 'Menzel saw his picture in artificial light, conceived of it in that light and probably also painted it for artificial light'. This would explain its yellow tone.

'As for its historical and cultural meaning', the same critic compares the work to *The Round Table of Frederick II at Sanssouci*. Gonse praises the picture as 'one of Herr Menzel's most extraordinary works', full of 'ironic sincerity and, perhaps unintentionally, with cruel satire', which is reminiscent of Hogarth and Daumier – definitely unintentionally! The satire lies in the structure of this crowded image itself rather than in the figures and the ridiculous aspects of their behaviour, and is like a beehive behind glass, creating in the onlooker a feeling of astonishment born of admiration and anxiety, and perhaps, distaste. C.K.

1. Tschudi, 1905 A, no. 327–8. The ten gouaches (Tschudi, 1905 A, no. 319–28) depict episodes from the White Rose Festival which was organized in 1829 in honour of the Tsarina Alexandra, one of the daughters of the King of Prussia, at Potsdam. They were painted between 1853-4, and were offered to Saint Petersburg by Frederick-William IV, where they are still kept today (Hermitage museum).
2. Not mentioned by Tschudi; Munich, Staatsgemäldesammlungen, Neue Pinakothek.
3. Tschudi, 1905 A, no. 561.
4. Tschudi, 1905 A, no. 137; Munich, Staatsgemäldesammlungen, Neue Pinakothek.
5. Tschudi, 1905 A, no. 147; Euerbach, Georg Schäfer collection
6. Tschudi, 1905 A, no. 414; Euerbach, Georg Schäfer collection.
7. Meier-Graefe, 1906, p. 214.
8. Zangs, 1992, p. 338; Forster-Hahn, 1993, p. 89.
9. Jordan, 1905, p. 79.

168
Edgar Degas
Supper at the Ball (after Menzel)
1878

Oil on wood
44.5 × 66.5cm
Strasbourg, Musée d'Art Moderne et Contemporain (MNR 226)

Provenance: Painter's studio; third Degas sale, Georges Petit, Paris, April 1919, no. 30, reprod.; Ochsé collection, Paris; Coutot collection, Paris; Hector Brame collection, Paris; for sale, 1941 Paris; acquired by the Karlsruhe Kunsthalle in 1941, in view of an exchange with the Nationalgalerie in Berlin, which took place in 1943 (the Degas panel for a work by Hackert and one by Slevogt); evacuated; after 1945, kept at Wiesbaden; allocated to the Louvre by the Private Goods Office in 1950; deposited at the Musée d'Art Moderne et Contemporain in Strasbourg in 1951.
Bibliography: Lemoisne, vol. 1, no. 190, reprod.; Keller, 1979.

'What a twinkle in the eye of the painter when he captured, embraced all these creatures, these small grimacing beings who are really important personages, these fat ladies who hold the destiny of the people in their hands, . . . the savage, the deformed hidden under lace and embroidery, this mêlée, the contrasts, the mad rush of instincts and appetites'. Menzel's *Supper at the Ball* inspired Duranty to write this long, magnificent passage in a style similar to Emile Zola, and Degas was filled with equal enthusiasm when the work appeared in Paris.

Duranty's article on Menzel did not yet exist, and no one had planned an exhibition like the one of 1885, when the Parisian dealer Goupil exhibited *Supper at the Ball* in March 1879 (a quarter of a century before, Goupil had not even managed to sell two of Menzel's small paintings in the Frederick the Great cycle; *cf.* cat. 63, 64). It was the first public showing of the work already announced by the Berlin Academy exhibition the previous autumn, and which Menzel characteristically, had been late finishing. An older and less complex ball scene had been on view in Paris shortly before in the 1878 exhibition, next to *The Iron Rolling Mill*[1]. As member of staff

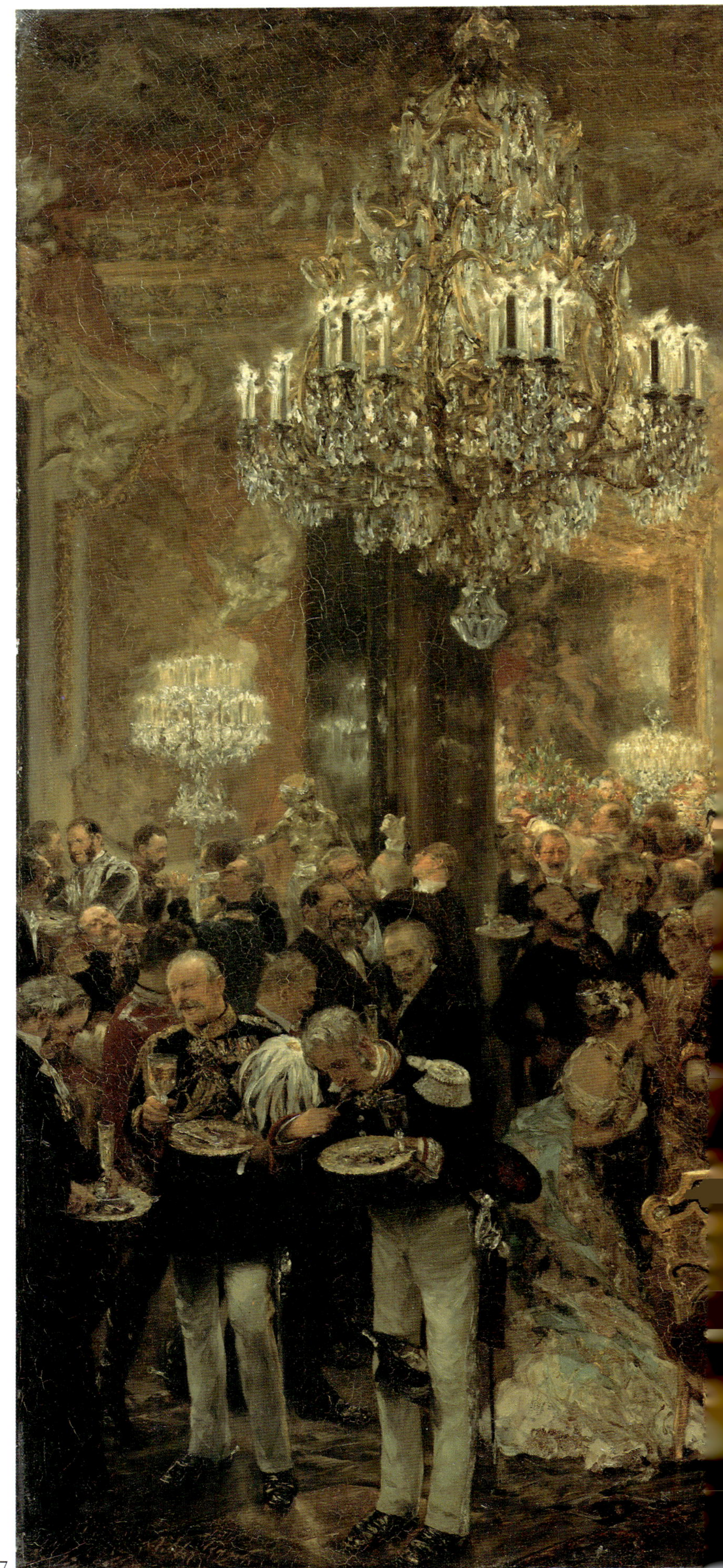

167

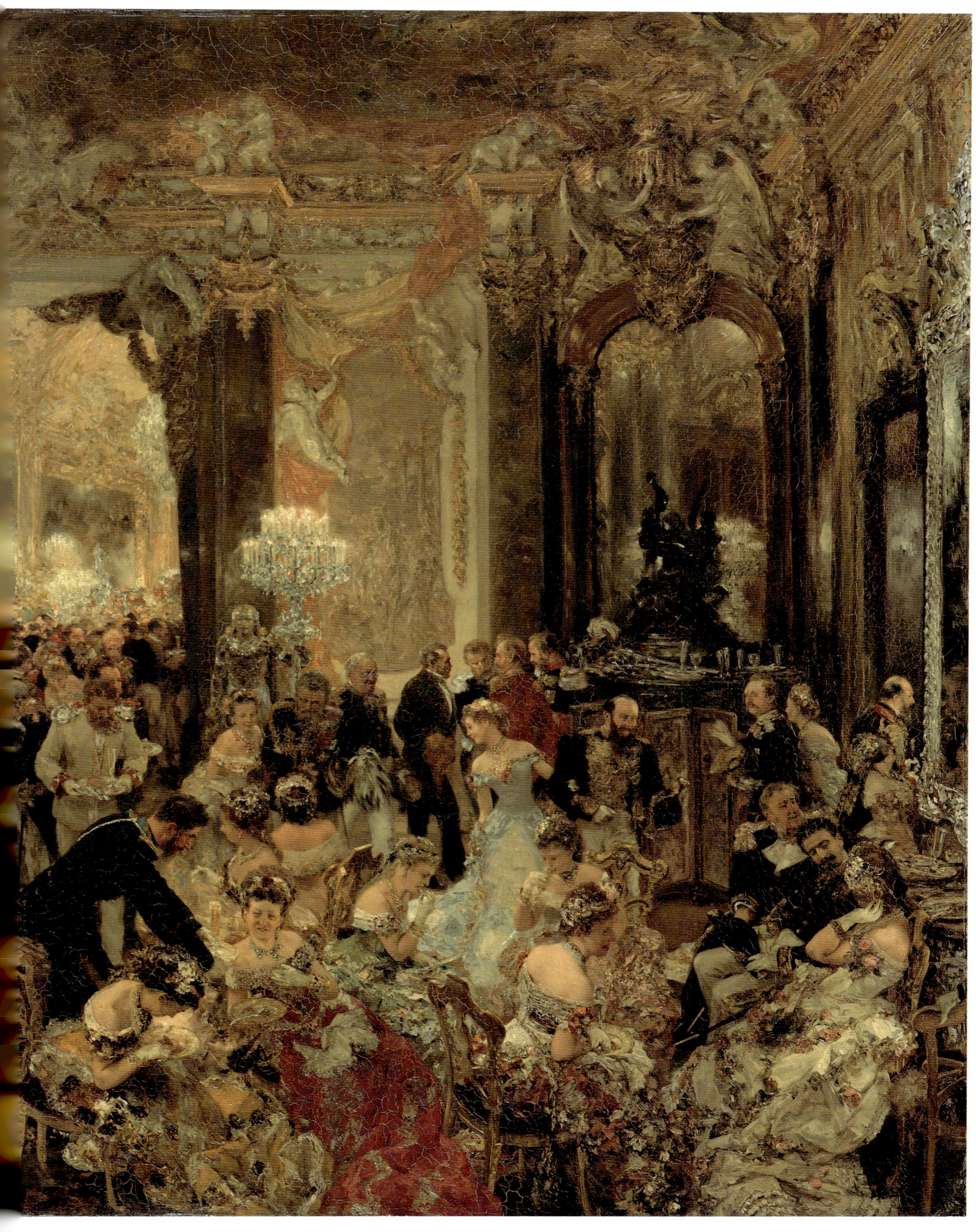

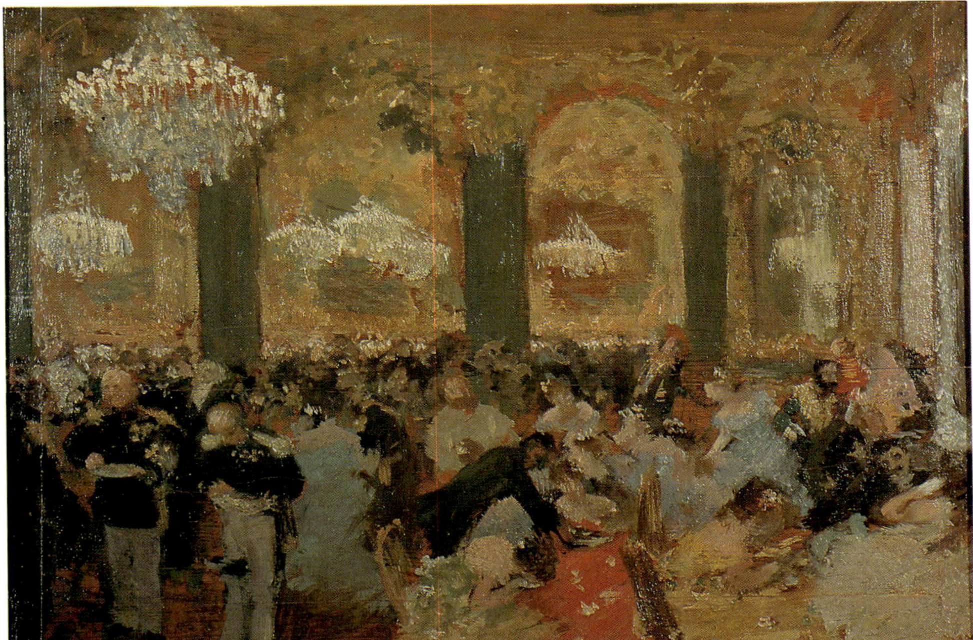

168

certainly well executed, but lacking in taste and finesse . . . . When we returned we were amazed at the superiority of Degas' sketch, although its true that a sketch has more charm, all the same'[8].

C.K.

1. *Lull at the ball*, *cf.* cat. 167, note 4.
2. Sketchbook 31 (Paris, National library, sketchbook 23), p. 47; Reff, 1976, p. 136.
3. Sketchbook 24 (Paris, National library, sketchbook 22), p. 116; Reff, 1976, p. 119; Loyrette, 1991, p. 725, note 156.
4. Elias, 1917.
5. Meier-Graefe, 1920, p. 32–6.
6. Meier-Graefe, 1920, p. 32 and ff.
7. *Le Figaro*, 10 November 1883. This was an exhibition organized by the Fritz Gurlitt gallery, at which the centrepieces were the Impressionist works collected by Carl and Felicie Bernstein.
8. Letter of Camille Pissarro to his son Lucien, 10 November 1883, Bailly-Herzberg, 1986, vol. 2, p. 249.

of the *Chronique des Arts*, Degas noticed the work. A quick sketch[2], probably from memory, shows what had struck him about the painting – the feeling of space, the archways (Degas was wrong, as Menzel portrayed rectangular openings whose angles are concealed by ornaments), the lights, some of the foreground figures and their connection with the crowd going into the background. The oblique depth of the original, with its uncertainties, seems already reduced, and Degas continued simplifying the work when he transcribed his impression of colour, still from memory, showing quickly but accurately a limited number of figures, bringing them into the foreground, making the levels parallel, reducing the space by omitting ceiling and lights. The seething crowd so well described by his friend the critic, and the delicate tones disappear in a chromatic composition dominated by flat, juxtaposed touches. Harald Keller stressed the significance of this elimination of the gold used so generously by Menzel.

Not content in his youth to copy the works of Italian Renaissance painters and those of his master Ingres, Degas occasionally continued this kind of dialogue with Delacroix, Daumier or even Whistler and Meissonier. He had known Menzel's name for a long time. In 1867 or more probably 1868, Degas met his German colleague, probably through Alfred Stevens, or at least intended to do so, as he had made a note of his address in Paris at 15 Rue Lemercier[3]. Later, in his early days as a collector, he bought a drawing which had belonged to Duranty (reprod. fig. 5). Several years before his death, according to a German art critic who was a friend of Max Liebermann, Degas spoke enthusiastically about Menzel, recalling his 1885 exhibition and other showings in Paris[4]. Julius Meier-Graefe, who wrote a subtle comparison between the two painters[5], heard from 'one of the inner circle of Degas friends', who wisely preferred to remain anonymous that 'Degas felt the German painter had had a very significant influence on his work'[6].

Not everyone shared his keen interest. In 1883, when *Le Figaro* reported some unflattering remarks made by the German painter about the Impressionist works on view in Berlin[7], Pissarro recalled Menzel's painting and found it 'heavy and devilishly bourgeois. Degas was infatuated with it at the time'. Upon viewing it, 'we found a muddy canvas

169

Concert in the White Room

1879

Pencil
36.5 × 27.1cm
Signed at the top left and the bottom right: *A.M.*
Berlin, Kupferstichkabinett (SZ Menzel N 4485)

Provenance: Painter's studio; 1905 Emilie Krigar-Menzel; acquired by the museum in 1906.
Exhibitions: Berlin, 1905, no. 6650; Berlin, 1980, no. 350.
Bibliography: Hütt, 1981, p. 106, fig. 86.

Menzel was able to capture the first impression of an event, in this case a concert, in all its freshness in sketches like this one. The moving mass of the public contrasts with the sculptural effect of the architecture. Between these two poles, the conductor and orchestra, the real actors of the evening, are given a small space in the middle ground, on the fold of the paper. (To have something firm to draw on, the artist folded the programme before he sketched on it.) The vagueness with which Menzel drew the musicians was doubtless in keeping with the degree

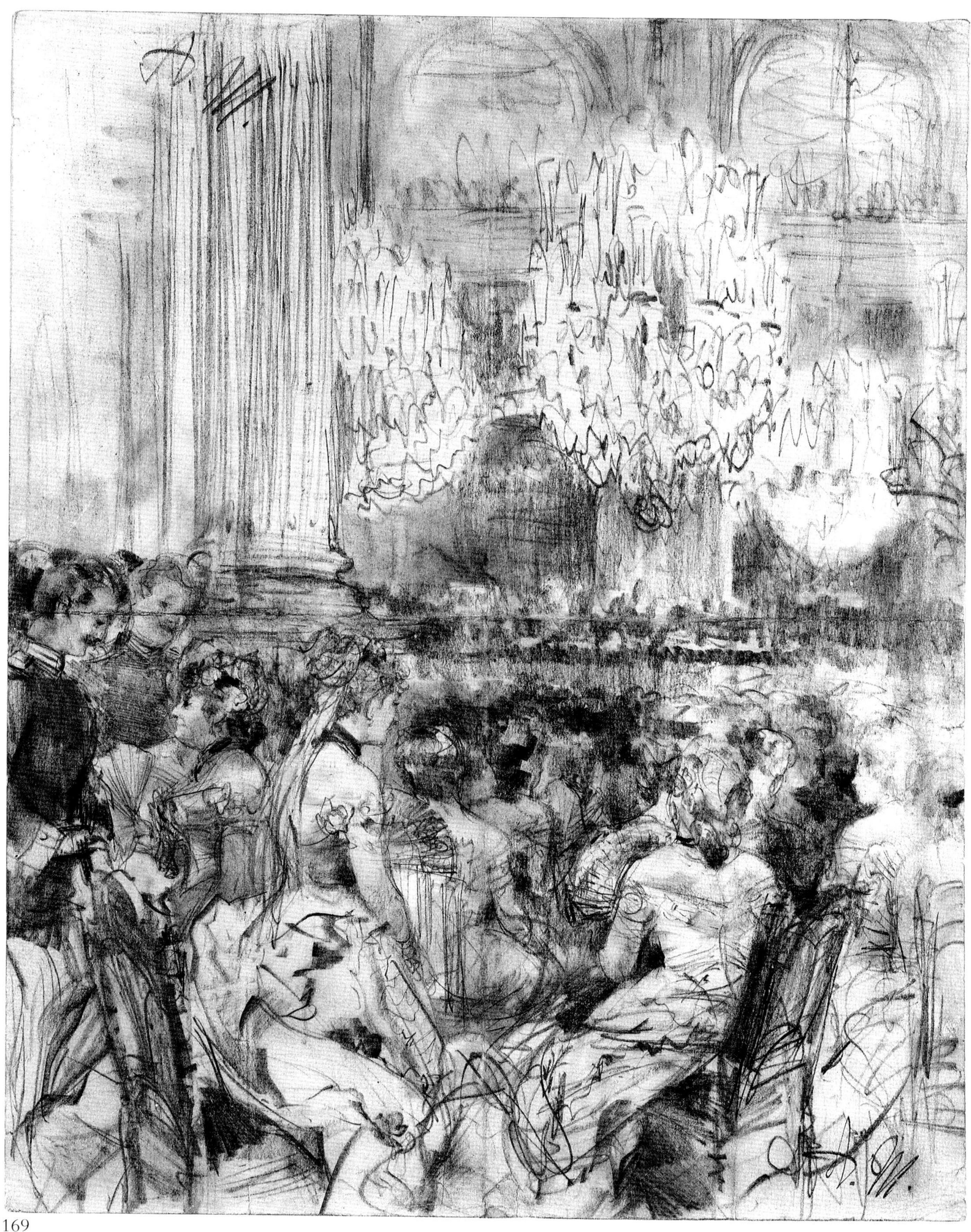

169

of importance the audience attached to this concert, which they attended like any other society event, which they used to make conversation. Two officers are talking to a woman in the left foreground, without paying the least attention to the music, and their portrayal is striking. They 'disrupt' the progress of the evening, which is translated in plastic terms by their heads, which break up the ordered rows of the drawing. Close by, a woman with long ribbons hanging from her hair is about to sit down. Drawings like these formed part of the artist's store, richer as the years went by, of court scenes experienced by him, some of which conceal the idea for a future picture. The study of the woman with ribbons in her hair was used in the same year in *William I's Circle*[1], even though the preparatory studies were carried out afterwards using a studio model.

Each of the two halves of the drawing, upper and lower, separated by the fold, bear the artist's signature. Menzel was once again underlining the contrast in their form and content. A.H.

1. 1897, Tschudi, 1905 A, no. 147; Euerbach, Georg Schäfer collection.

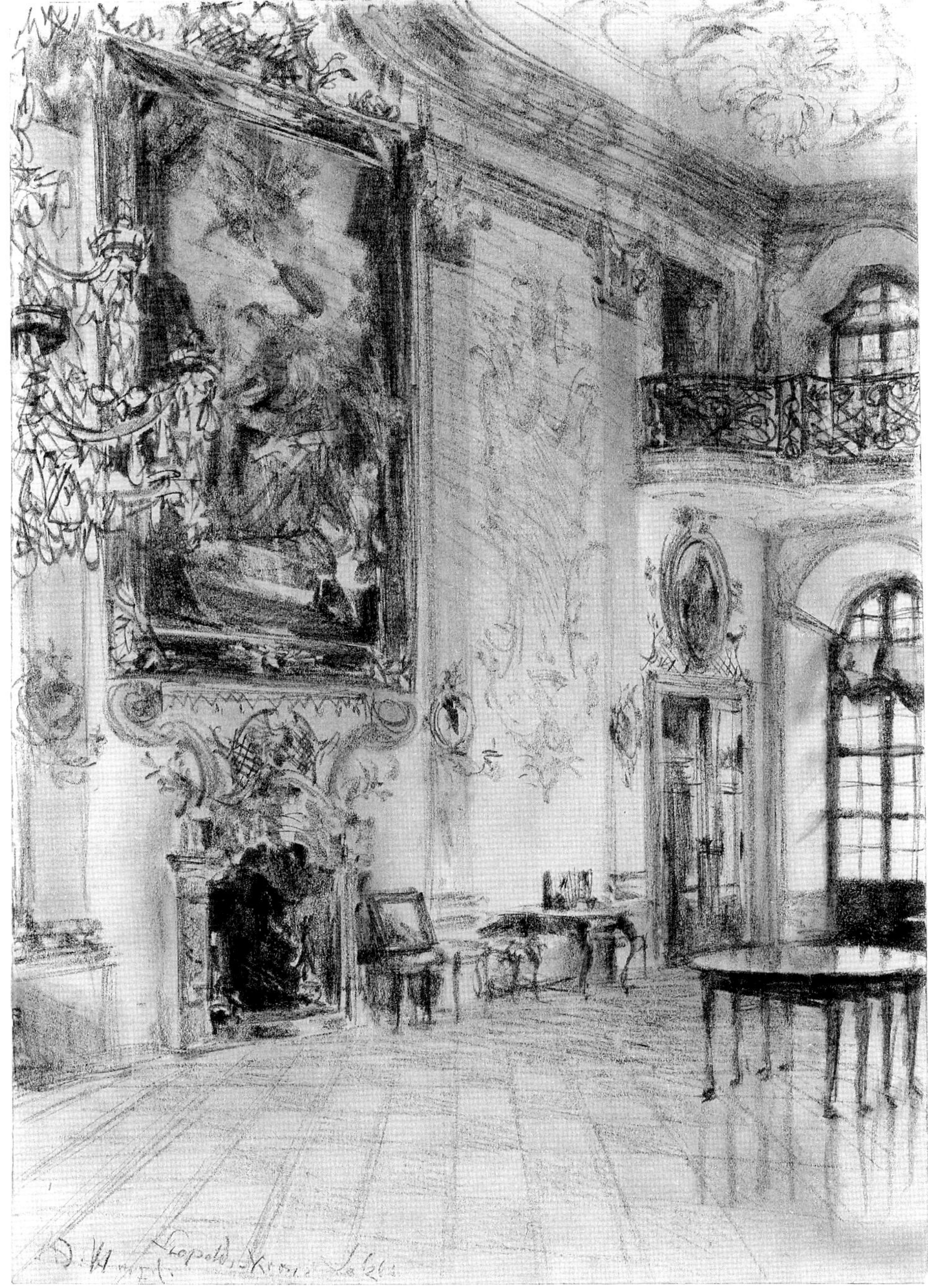

170

170

Room at Leopoldskron Castle, near Salzburg

c. 1875–80

Pencil
37.9 × 25cm
Signed at the bottom left: *Ad.Menzel.* – Annotated: *Leopolds-Kron.Salzb:*
Berlin, Kupferstichkabinett (SZ Menzel N 171)
Exhibited in Paris and Washington only

Provenance: Painter's studio; 1905 Emilie Krigar-Menzel; acquired by the museum in 1906.
Exhibitions: Berlin, 1905, no. 2247; Vienna, 1985, no. 59.
Bibliography: Kirstein, 1919, fig. p. 109; Wirth, 1974, p. 116–17.

After his first visit to Salzburg in 1852, Menzel returned there several times on his many summer trips. The drawings he brought back chart a progression, reflecting his artistic development in their variety. In 1852 he drew the famous panorama of the old town, with the Hohensalzburg fortress beyond the River Salzach, a general view unique in Menzel's work. After that, he sketched unusual views of famous baroque buildings, sculptures, objets d'art or landscapes (*cf.* cat. 189, 190). Within Salzburg he drew the interior of the pilgrimage church, Maria Plain, in the north of the town, and also Helbrunn Park in the south. The depiction of this tall, elegant function room, two storeys high, in the small castle of Leopoldskron, which was also in the south of

Salzburg, is reminiscent of Menzel's first studies of the chateau of Sanssouci at Potsdam in its clear rococo atmosphere flooded with light, although the lines of his drawing have become more powerful and elaborate. This is not one of the subjects with a complex structure and the multiple variations of light, which he so much enjoyed drawing, like his representations of the cherubs' staircase (by Lukas von Hildebrandt, from the same period), at Mirabell castle. Yet he has managed to give an overall impression of this room with its beautiful decor sanctioned by Archbishop Firmian in 1736[1] by merely portraying one corner of it. M.R.-R.

1. All the drawings quoted in the text are at the Kupferstichkabinett in Berlin.

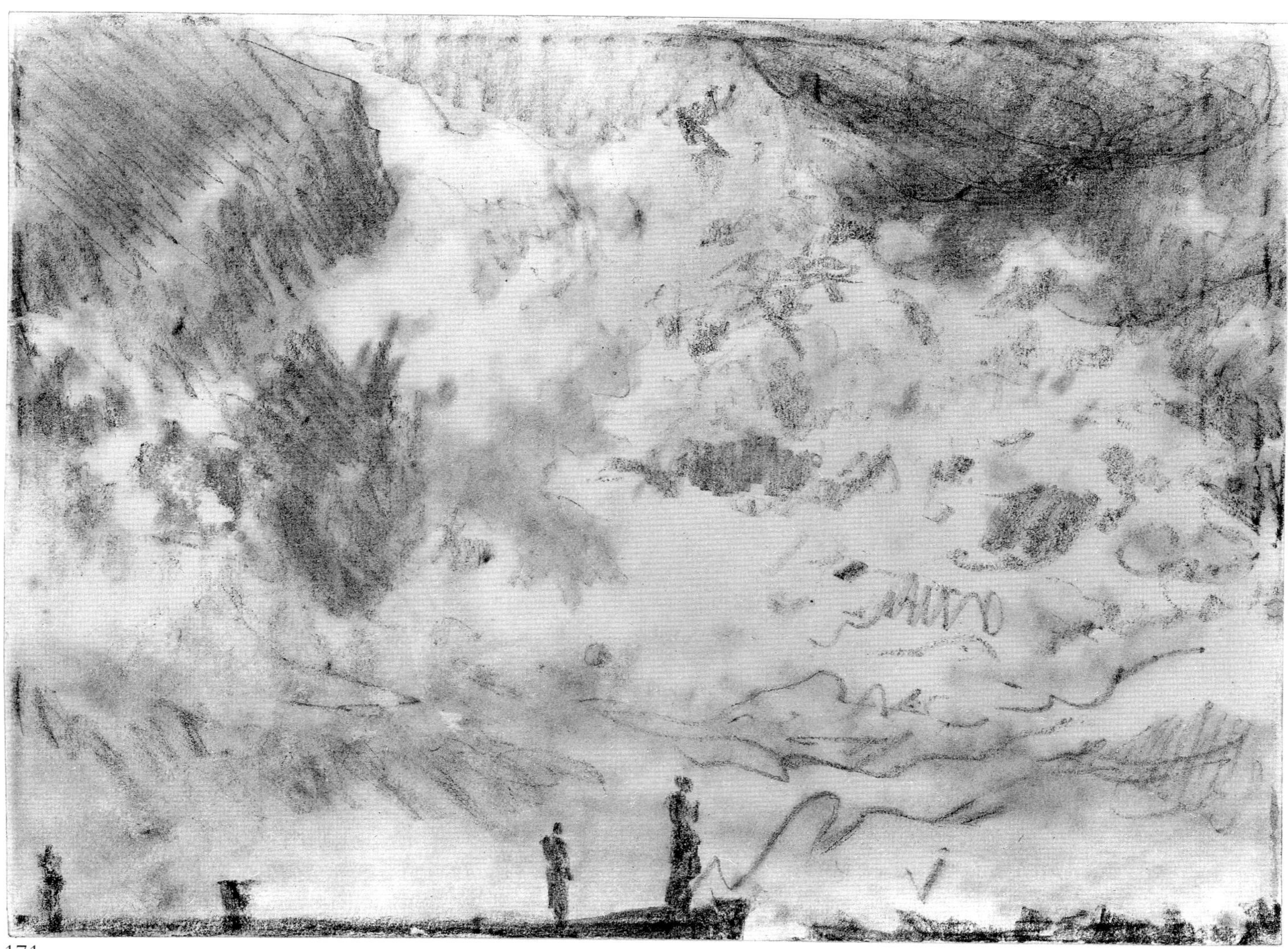
171

171
Cloudy Sky
c. 1880
Pencil and stump
23.8 × 33cm
Berlin, Kupferstichkabinett (SZ Menzel N 1168)
Exhibited in Paris and Washington only
Provenance: Painter's studio; 1905 Emilie Krigar-Menzel; acquired by the museum in 1906.

Exhibitions: Berlin, 1905, no. 3175; Berlin, 1980 A, no. 287, reprod.; Vienna, 1985, no. 120, reprod; New York, 1990, no. 63.
Bibliography: Liebermann/Kern, 1921, p. 7, col. pl. 29.

In the 1840s, and more frequently after that (*cf.* cat. 23, 59), Menzel uses an unusual perspective in both paintings and drawings which sets the tiny dimensions of an earthly form in the lower part of the work against a view of the sky. This might be the top of a tower or mountain, a tree-top or, as in this case, the sculptures on a palace roof-top. These 'dolls' as the Berliners called them, frequently adorned the roofs of prestigious baroque buildings in Berlin and Potsdam. The condensed image drawn with virtuosity, which is a feature of Menzel's later style, precludes any possibility of identifying the exact spot. The atmospheric consistency of the cloudy sky, tousled by a light wind, has such a powerful effect that the compact density of the stone figures dissolves into aerial forms, constituting a step towards abstraction. M.R.-R.

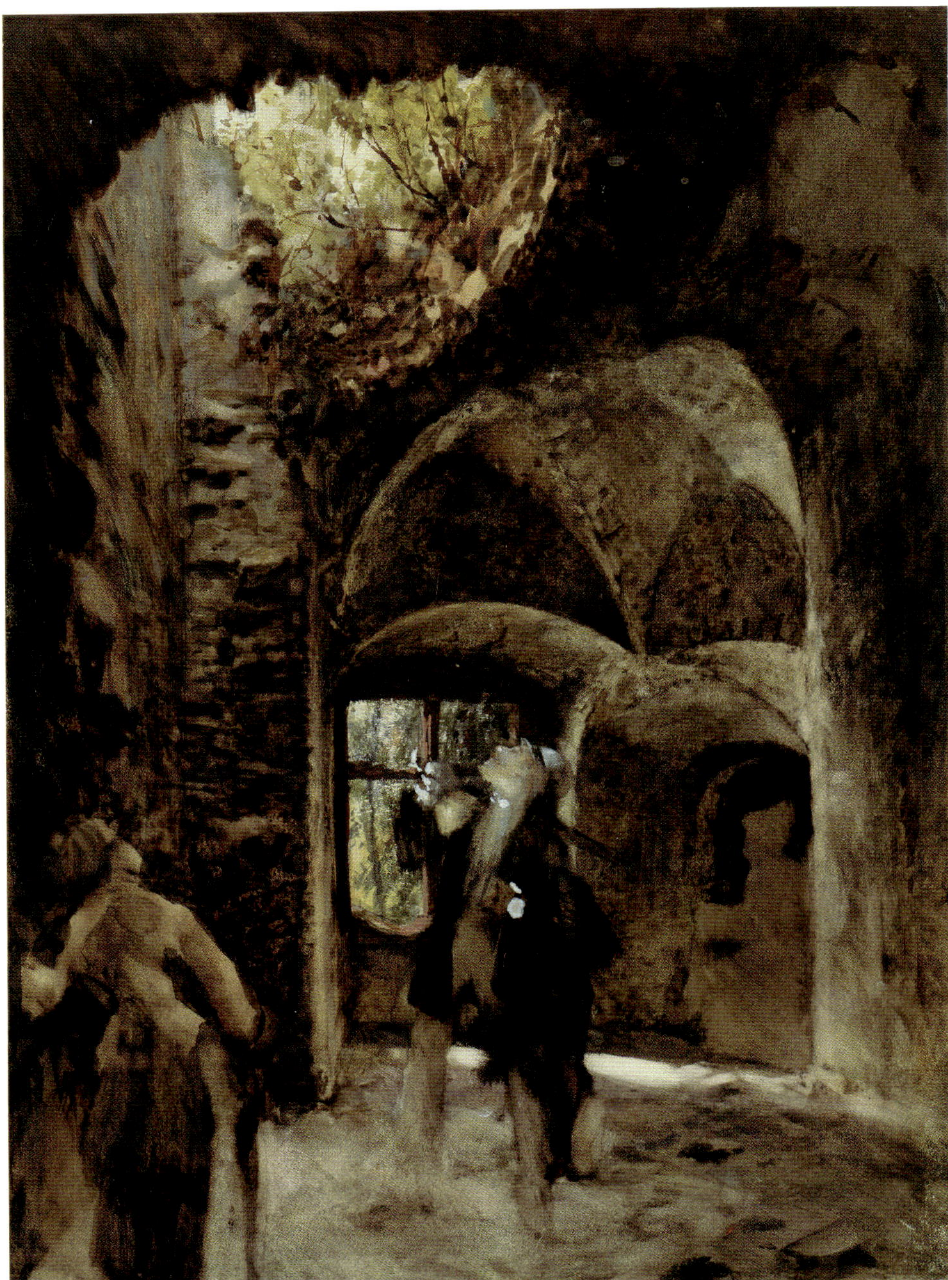

172

Fig. 213. *Tourist Looking up,* 1880, pencil, Warsaw, Narodowe Museum

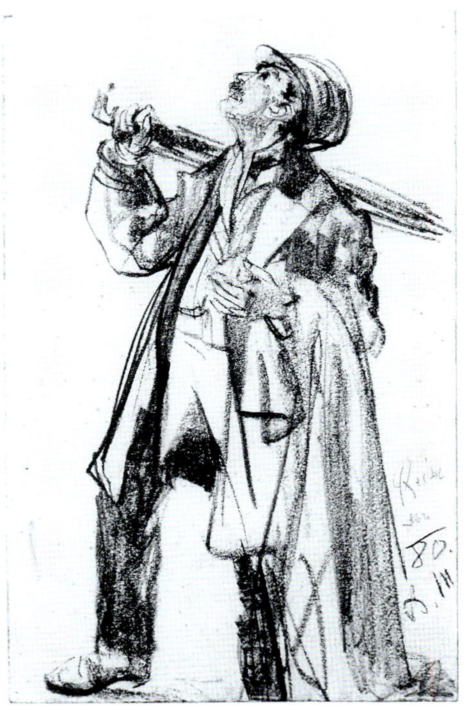

172

In the Ruin

After 1880

Gouache
37.1 × 26.5cm
Berlin, Kupferstichkabinett (SZ Menzel N 4469)
Exhibited in Washington only

Provenance: Painter's studio; 1905 Emilie Krigar-Menzel; acquired by the museum in 1906.
Exhibitions: Berlin, 1905, no. 341; Copenhagen, 1985, no. 35.
Bibliography: Tschudi, 1905 A, no. 276; exhib. cat. Vienna, 1985, col. reprod. p. 60 (erroneously illustrating the exhibited work *Ruins of Saint-Goar*).

A pencil study of a man looking up, with an umbrella over his shoulder and a rug or coat over his arm has the note 'Trip in '80'[1] written on it (fig. 213). This figure was used for the watercolour described here showing the interior space of an unknown ruin. It is supposedly a memoir of Menzel's summer trip of 1880. At the beginning of August he first went to Dresden, and from there continued to the Elbsandsteingebirge (sandstone mountains flanking the Elbe) in Swiss Saxony, where he visited a small village called Herrnskretschen, a departure point for Swiss Bohemia. But he may also have studied the figure among some ruins on another journey. The charm of this watercolour lies in the fact that it is unfinished, which renders the space vague and slightly mysterious. From beneath the lunette vaults a woman visitor emerges, a vague figure, while two other figures at the front look up at an opening in the ceiling, through which the outside world appears, as it does through a window further back. The whole picture is painted with generous, supple brushstrokes, and certain elements are only suggested.

Menzel drew and painted ruins on more than one occasion, and all ruined objects attracted him. The freedom of touch and deliberate imprecision make *In the Ruin* an unconventional work, comparable to the watercolours *Transporting Prisoners* and *Painters Preparing a Transparent Panel* (cat. 132). The much earlier watercolour, *The Ruins of Rheinfels*[2] (1855) clearly shows the strong contrast between the interior chiaroscuro and the open air. The behaviour of the tourists is not only suggested but developed to an extent which borders on the comic. Yet this anecdotal aspect of the colourful group of tourists is not present in the gouache *Aura Ruin at Kissingen* of 1884[3].

M.R.-R.

1. Varsovia, Narodowe Museum.
2. Tschudi, 1905 A, no. 334; Berlin, Kupferstichkabinett (SZ Menzel Nr 1722).
3. Tschudi, 1905 A, no. 644; location unknown.

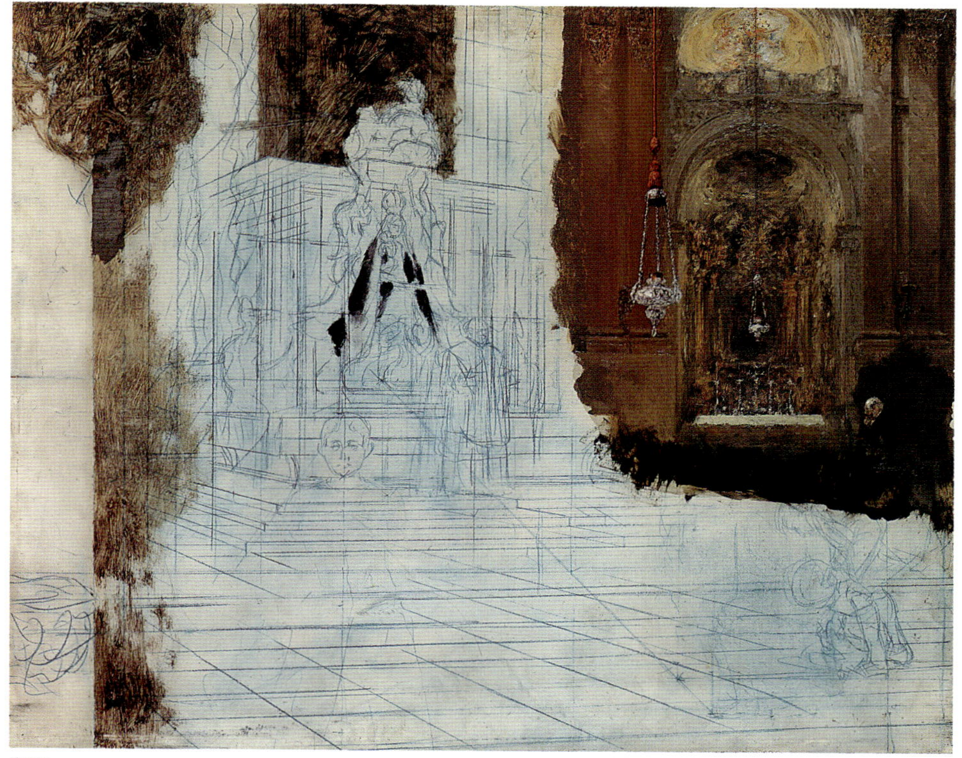

173

173

Altar in a Baroque Church

c. 1880–90

Oil and blue pencil on wood
50 × 61 cm
Berlin, Nationalgalerie (A III 508)
Exhibited in Berlin only

Provenance: Painters studio; 1905 Emilie Krigar-Menzel; acquired by the museum in 1906.
Exhibitions: Berlin, 1905, no. 101; Berlin, 1980 A, no. XXIII, fig. p. 212.
Bibliography: Tschudi, 1905 A, no. 18; cat. NG, 1986, no pag.; Gronau, 1987, p. 284, fig. 3.

None of Menzel's other unfinished paintings so clearly reveals the techniques he used in his later years as this one does. After *Address at Leuthen*, he had adopted the habit of working *alla prima* section by section, 'like a mosaic in pure colour, without additives or oils'[1], until the background was entirely covered, as well as the initial outline. This was done in blue pencil, with a surprising minuteness of detail in the construction of perspective. The ornamentation and figures, indicated more vaguely, are less imperative, because, on the right, the painter goes over the sketch of the man bending to pick something up – a rather disrespectful and basely anecdotic detail close to the altar – because it no longer fitted into his plan. It is hard to imagine how the woman who is to the left of centre would have finally appeared, with the abstract front view whose axis is marked with surprising accuracy by a long vertical line. This figure is cut off at knee-level by the edge of the picture, which seems to anticipate the compositions of Edvard Munch.

Menzel's friend Paul Meyerheim recounts his unorthodox method: 'For some pictures, like *The Iron Rolling Mill*, for example, he had marked construction plans on the canvas for periods of weeks, which were totally incomprehensible to anyone but himself, until he began to paint. He knew the exact size of each object, head or figure in the painting . . .'[2] The initial outline, in all its abstraction, may have helped him to gauge the measurements of the final format[3] and to experience the actual dimensions of the canvas. This was particularly useful since he was accustomed to prepare only his large historical compositions with an oil sketch, a method which was ultimately rejected completely. We must imagine him setting even the most infinitely complicated compositions of urban crowds directly on to the canvas. In this way he had the complete work before him as he laid on the colour (made up of painted sections and drawn sections). Once he got to the place he wanted to work on, he covered the background with a brown toned wash which almost obliterated the outline and allowed free rein to improvisation, as can be seen in the left side of *Altar in a Baroque Church*.

It is difficult to say whether this kind of pencil preparation is used often under Menzel's paintings[4]. The groups of figures in *The Coronation* were drawn 'with brush and ink', and he also took remarkable liberties with what he had drawn when he came to paint it, as photography shows[5]. For *Address at Leuthen* (cat. 90), he was content with a brief sketch in white chalk.

He regularly started by painting the background, in other words the area in which the atmosphere is created. He described this himself when talking about the *The Coronation*, and the technique is clearly visible in *Address at Leuthen*. It corresponds on a practical level to his general approach, consisting of creating the definite from the indefinite (*cf. Night in the Forest*; cat. 58).

Such a fragmentary painting would be disconcerting for those wishing to situate it within Menzel's work overall[6] without the help of a drawing[7]. The drawing in this picture unmistakably shows a man bending down. Was it a study from a model done specially for this painting? Or a chance observation drawn from memory? It is impossible to decide. The fact remains that this undated work resembles those of the 1880s in its style. Since the figure, drawn in the preliminary outline for the composition then rejected, formed part of the initial idea, it can be situated at this late period. Menzel's interest in baroque churches remained constant, but in general he painted them latterly in gouache. There is another way in which *Altar in a Baroque Church* is an exception, as works painted on wood are very rare in Menzel's overall artistic oeuvre.

The easel with the artist posing in front of it, and this work, are both recognizable in two photographs taken in 1905 in Menzel's Sigismundstrasse studio[8]. The scene is definitely posed, as the ostentatiously held palette has not been used for a long time. However, although he made public his decision never to paint in anything except gouache in 1887[9], he does not seem to have been totally resigned to this[10], as the photographs show. Moreover, the unfinished state of this picture tormented him. A painstakingly prepared drawing (1890), with a symbolic meaning, entitled *His Studio*[11], shows an assistant cleaning the painter's palette (for the last time?). In the background his abandoned masterpiece *Address at Leuthen* can be seen. It is probably *Altar in a Baroque Church* on the easel, unfinished but already framed. Even the outline of its composition is reproduced. C.K.

1. Meyerheim, (1906) 1992, p. 163.
2. Meyerheim, (1906) 1992, p. 127. Max Liebermann also saw him preparing *The Iron Rolling Mill* and *Marketplace in Verona*, describing the network of lines drawn in red or blue pencil. Liebermann, (1921) 1922, p. 200.
3. On the other hand, in the case of Constable, the sketches done before the main painting were often of the same size.
4. Minimal traces show the use of the same blue pencil for the preparation of *Marketplace in Verona* (cat. 179).
5. Exhib. cat. Berlin, 1980 A, reprod. p. 51.
6. Tschudi, 1905 A, dated it from the 1840s. Exhib. cat. Berlin 1980 dated it from the late 1850s.
7. Berlin, Kupferstichkabinett (SZ Menzel Nr 2451). Published in exhib. cat. Hamburg, 1982, no. 148, reprod. and exhib. cat. Berlin, 1984, no. 113, reprod., without reference to the picture.
8. Lammel, 1993, fig. 118–19.
9. *Cf.* cat. 201–202, note 1.
10. Delmar, (1903) 1992, p. 114 and ff. (*cf.* cat. 31).
11. Private collection. Exhib. cat. Hamburg, 1982, no. 174, reprod.

174
Corpus Christi Procession at Hofgastein
1880

Oil on canvas
51.3 × 70.2cm
Signed and dated at the bottom left: *Ad.Menzel 1880.*
Munich, Bayerische Staatsgemäldesammlungen, Neue Pinakothek (gift of the Federal Republic of Germany, L 817)
Exhibited in Berlin only

Provenance: 1885 banker Julius Schiff, Berlin; 1905 Olga Schiff, Berlin; Leo Lewin, Breslau; 1941 Th. Fischer Gallery, Lucerne; 1941 'property of the Reich'; after 1966 gift of the Federal Republic to the Neue Pinakothek in Munich.
Exhibitions: Berlin, 1880, no. 471, reprod. (detail, after a drawing by Menzel); Paris, 1882; Berlin, 1885, no. 21; Berlin, 1886, no. 2462; Vienna, 1888, no. 994; Munich, 1891, no. 1016, reprod.; Berlin, 1892, no. 785; Berlin,

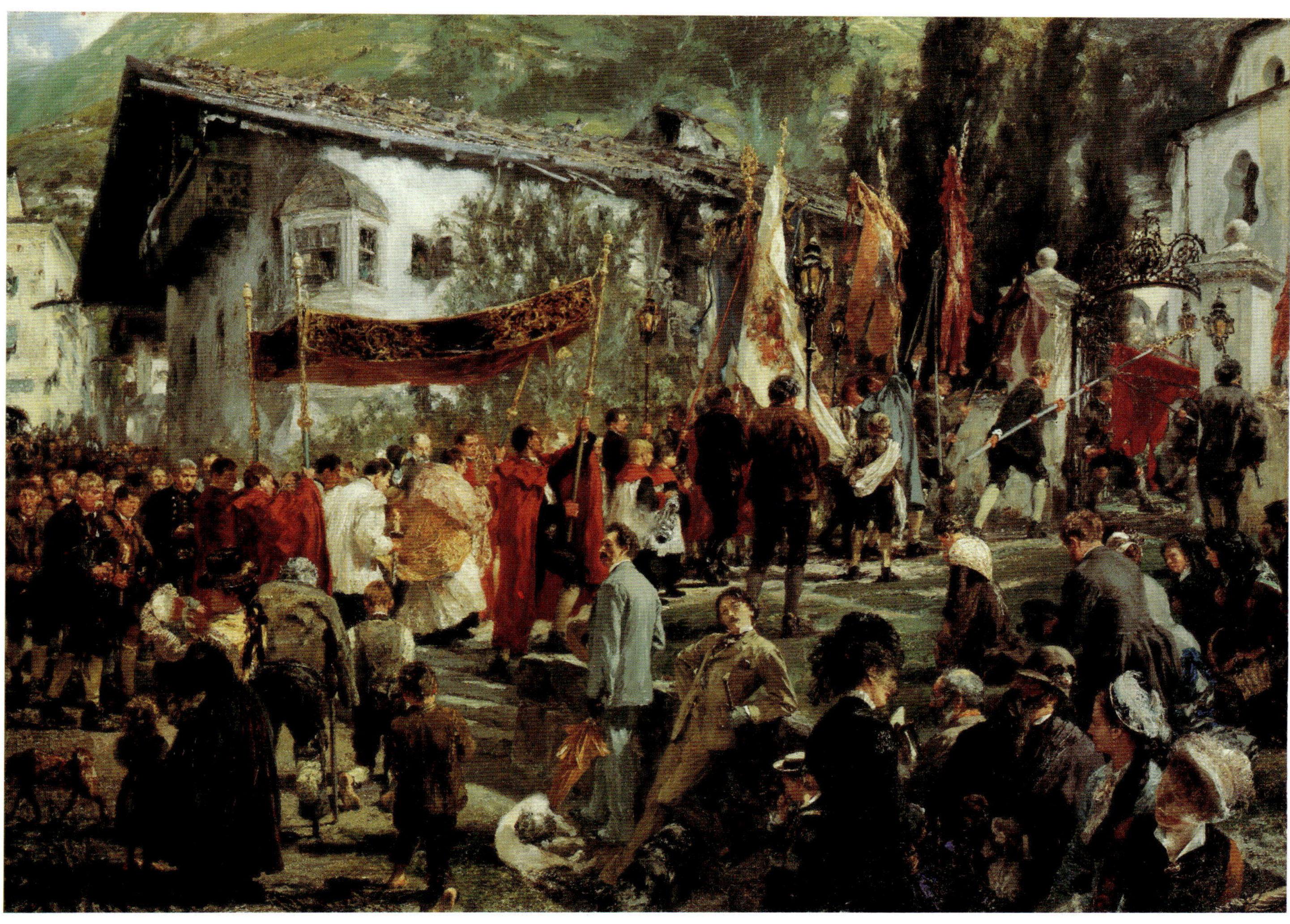

174

1895, no. 57; Hamburg, 1896, no. 18; Düsseldorf, 1904, no. 20, reprod.; Berlin, 1905, no. 90; Berlin, 1913, no. 375; Berlin, 1926, no. 45; Berlin, 1928, no. 45; Berlin, 1955 B, no. 129, fig. 59; Kiel, 1956, no. 62, reprod.; Wolfsburg, 1956, no. 129, col. pl. 9 (detail); Erlangen, 1971, no. 104, col. reprod.

Bibliography: Lostalot, 1882, p. 603 *et seq*.; Pecht, 1885–6 A, p. 3; Pecht, 1885–6 B, p. 68 and 70; Jordan, 1890, p. 74; Jordan, 1895, no. 27, p. 56, p. 71; Jordan, 1905, p. 85 *et seq*., pl. facing p. 82; Tschudi, 1905 A, no. 151; Herrmann, (1905) 1992, p. 251; Wirth, 1974, p. 122 *et seq*., p. 128, col. pl. V, VI; Hütt, 1981, fig. 98–9; Eschenburg, 1984, p. 299 *et seq*. reprod.; Wirth, 1990,p. 295 *et seq*., fig. 371; Lammel, 1993 B, p. 79 *et seq*., col. pl. 14.

Menzel had a close friendship with the Berlin banker Magnus Herrmann (*cf*. cat. 134), in contrast to a lot of his other relationships. Their friendship lasted for years, during which they shared musical evenings and New Year revelry. During the 1870s the painter stayed with his sister, brother-in-law, niece and nephew at the 'Villa Carolina' in Hofgastein, which belonged to the Herrmanns. Their daughter Agatha described their communal life and the long excursions the painter made in order to draw[1]. The gardener's house had been placed at his disposal as well as a studio (Pyrkerstrasse 14), which later became the 'Pension Menzel'. Numerous drawings depict the surrounding landscape and rural architecture, and the *Corpus Christi Procession at Hofgastein* is also one of these 'memoirs', an 'urban landscape' in appearance, even though situated in a small country town – Irmgard Wirth identified the church at Böckstein in the Gastein valley.

The Munich critic Friedrich Pecht reflected on the relationship in *Corpus Christi Procession at Hofgastein* between the immediacy and naturalism, which had such appeal for him, and the small format, which allows a greater formal freedom. This freedom totally lacks style if exercised in larger dimensions[2]. Pecht also relates that he and Carl Spitzweg carefully examined the costumes worn by the peasants in the picture, and that they identified them as coming from the region of Pingzau: '. . . in the same way that we recognize the Berlin student, the Austrian noble, or the pretentious Berliner, and certain women from Vienna, the Jewish journalist, etc.'[3]. He is speaking of human types, not individuals.

In Menzel's last years, ethnological painting of customs flourished round about him, which swung almost always between sentimentality and humour (notably Franz Defregger, Ludwig Knaus), yet this proximity is only apparent. The teeming small world in this picture, rich in happenings, and bright in the sunshine, remains confused and unfathomable. The casual perspective Menzel favoured fills the picture with subjects from one side to the other (the slope of the mountain behind the houses reveals only a small piece of sky which is barely perceptible). The space in the picture is unequally occupied by objects and groups of people who are in conflict, coming from all sides at once. The white, lop-sided house is like a ship pitching and tossing, and is skirted by the human procession. The most dignified part of the procession, the priests under the canopy, is also the most chaotic. People come straight into the picture from the left foreground and, in the right corner, boldly cut off by the edge of the picture, half-figures assail the visual field. A young whippersnapper, casually leaning against the wall, is the only person to look out of the painting straight at the painter. All the well-dressed citizens are impassive spectators, strangers in all senses of the word. The pious reverence of the peasants is also about to dissipate too. As the procession ends, banners are lowered as they enter the church courtyard.

The true celebration lies in the sunlight, which shines resplendently on the white walls, the festival costumes, the church banners stitched in gold, the red coats, and lights up a narrow road to an alley on the left. The movement from the definite to the vague in the background is technically very similar to *Marketplace in Verona*[4]. C.K.

1. Herrmann, (1905) 1992.
2. Pecht, 1885-6, p. 3.
3. Pecht, 1885, p. 70.
4. Studies of people: Berlin, Kupferstichkabinett (SZ Menzel Kat 4093–1097, N 3778); three others: exhib. cat. Hamburg, 1982, no. 119–21) (two of which are at the Hamburg Kunsthalle).

175

Knife-grinder's Workshop in the Hofgastein Smithy

1881

Oil on canvas
31.4 × 41.5cm
Signed and dated at the bottom right: Ad. Menzel 81.
Hamburg, Hamburger Kunsthalle (1272)
Exhibited in Berlin only

Provenance: 1890 Charles Deschamps, London; acquired by the museum in 1910 (Baron Johann Heinrich von Schröder Foundation).
Exhibitions: Berlin, 1955 B, no.130; Wiesbaden, 1960, no. 214; Duisburg, 1969, no. 58; Erlangen, 1971, no. 106; Hamburg, 1982, no. 127, col. reprod.; Hamburg, 1984, p. 71 *et seq.*, col. reprod.; Berlin, 1987 A, no. H 13.
Bibliography: Pecht, 1885–6 B, pl. facing p. 70; Jordan, 1890, p. 67, p. 96; Jordan, 1895, p. 50, p. 71; Jordan, 1905, p. 74; Tschudi, 1905 A, no. 152; Herrmann, (1905) 1992, p. 251; Scheffler, 1938, p. 116; Waldmann, 1941, p. 37; Krafft/Schümann, 1969, p. 220, reprod.; Wirth, 1974, p. 129, fig. 119; Hütt, 1981, fig. 112; Jensen, 1982, p. 112 *et seq.*, pl. 38; Howoldt, 1993, p. 46, reprod. p. 47.

A contrasting symmetry in choice of subjects orders all Menzel's work. However rich and dense a composition, he immediately adds the antithesis. Thus, the great picture of a modern rolling mill is succeeded by a small format painting depicting a village smithy.

'He was often in the smithy, drawing workers, tools, effects of the light'[1]. The preparatory works are like those for *The Iron Rolling Mill* in some ways[2]. But while the latter shows aspects of modern production, Menzel observed at Hofgastein the survival of ancient ways of doing things. It is not only working techniques which are traditional there, but also the relationships created between men. The workshop is like a shop, where everyone knows each other. While the large painting reveals the complexity of the subject at a distance which allows the onlooker to take in the whole, the small picture creates problems with the foreground limits of the work with the same resolve as in *Corpus Christi Procession*. This occurs because two central figures are placed so that they are moving forwards, so close that they emphasize the difference in size of the young blacksmiths on the left. The peasant smoking a pipe with his jacket over his shoulder is playing the same role as Maurice of Dessau in *Address at Leuthen*. He is waiting for the scythe blade being sharpened on the grinding wheel by the apprentice blacksmith. The woman servant checks the blade of a meat cleaver at his side, turning away abruptly.

In order to correct an art critic who had been unable to give an accurate description of the technical process, Menzel wrote: '. . . as regards the group around the anvil, the piece of white-hot iron on top of it is not a bar but a plate which has to be divided in two. What the blacksmith has in his hand is a kind of axe called a hacking knife. His left hand is holding tongs. I could not paint it more clearly because of the distance, firstly, but also to emphasize the dazzling effect. The lad will hit the hacking knife with a heavy hammer, which is what I wanted to express here. He stops for a moment so the noise does not drown what he is saying to the apprentice. I wanted the apprentice to be sharpening a scythe blade (the person waiting is a peasant, close-shaven as they are in those parts, and he is holding the shaft), but his action would have forced me to make him use different arm and hand movements which would not have fitted in so well. So I left the blade in question on the ground with some others waiting to be sharpened. It was not possible to clarify the kind of blade simply because the horizon line does not allow a plan view, which has to be imagined by the onlooker'[3].

The spectator also has to seek the picturesqueness of the workshop plunged in half-light, where daylight enters not only from behind, through the door and through an opening made in the raised partition of wooden planks on the left of the grinder (exactly on the central axis of the painting), but also through the window, which has to be imagined out of the field of vision on the right, casting a strong light upon the partition. The face and chest of the man sitting between the

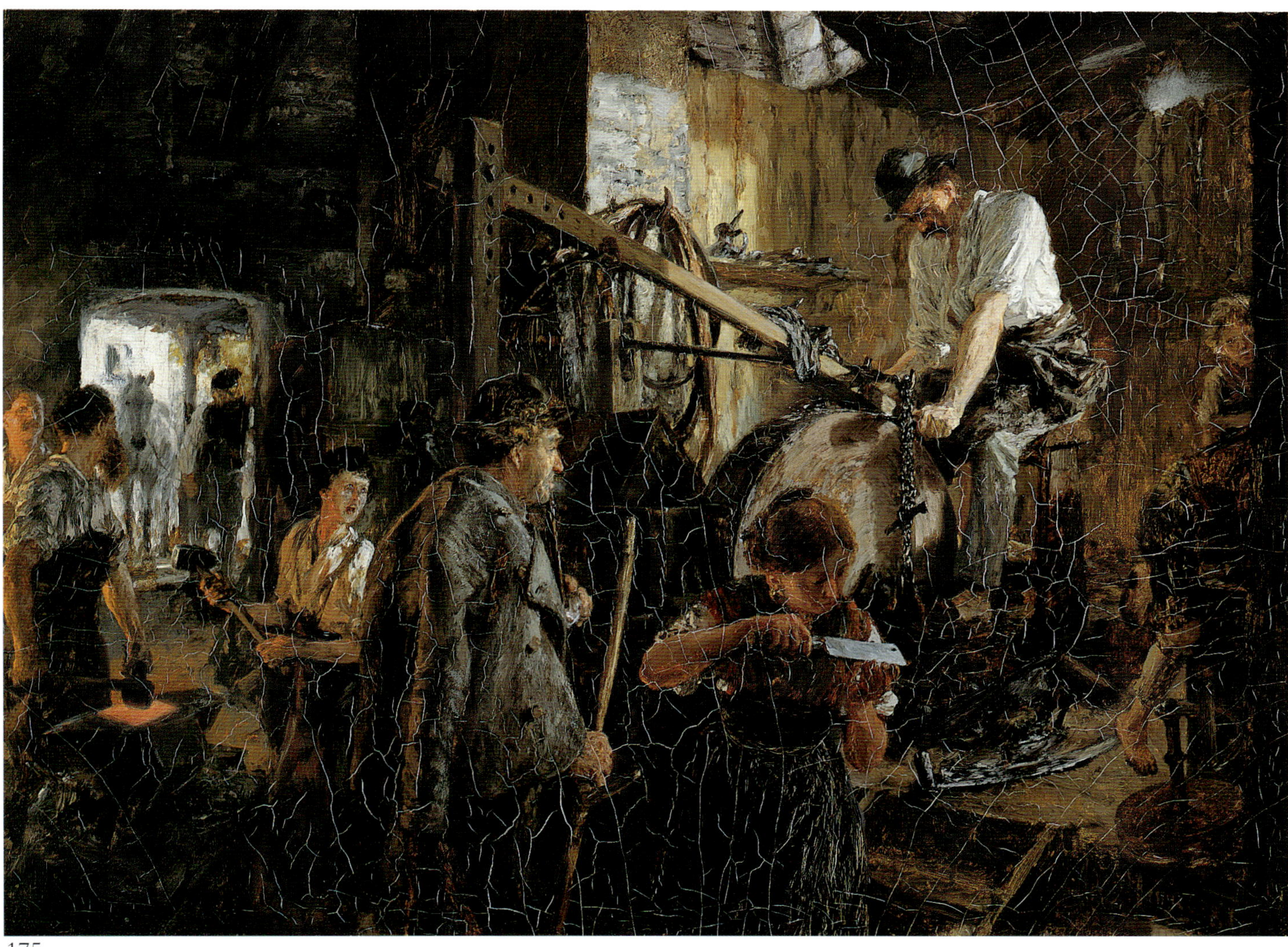

175

two sources of light remain in shadow. In addition to the natural light, there is also the firelight of the forge on the left. The white-hot iron is visible, but the firelight, which is stronger, is outside the picture, and is only recognizable from the red reflections on the skin of the blacksmiths. This link between daylight and firelight is characteristic of *The Iron Rolling Mill*.

The gouache *Blacksmiths at Hofgastein*[4] (1879) undoubtedly portrays this workshop, which still existed in the 1970s, with a single main figure, who appears small and hesitant in comparison with the wooden beams of the workshop. C.K.

1. Herrmann, (1905) 1992, p. 251.
2. Berlin, Kupferstichkabinett (SZ Menzel Kat 1099 and 1100). The last, a sketch of a blacksmith near the grinding wheel, dated 1879, was exhibited in Paris in 1885 and reproduced in the catalogue. Other studies: *cf.* exhib. cat. Hamburg, 1982, no. 128 and 129 and fig. 76 and 77. The attitude of the woman who passes her finger over the knife to check the sharpness of the blade was studied from several models, and once using a male model.
3. Letter to Ludwig Pietsch, no date, Staatsbibliothek Preussischer Kulturbesitz (1935.43, no. 1) (now in Cracow, Biblioteka Jagiellonska).
4. Gouache, 1879, Tschudi, 1905 A, no. 621; location unknown. Other gouaches of Gastein: Tschudi, 1905 A, no. 601–3.

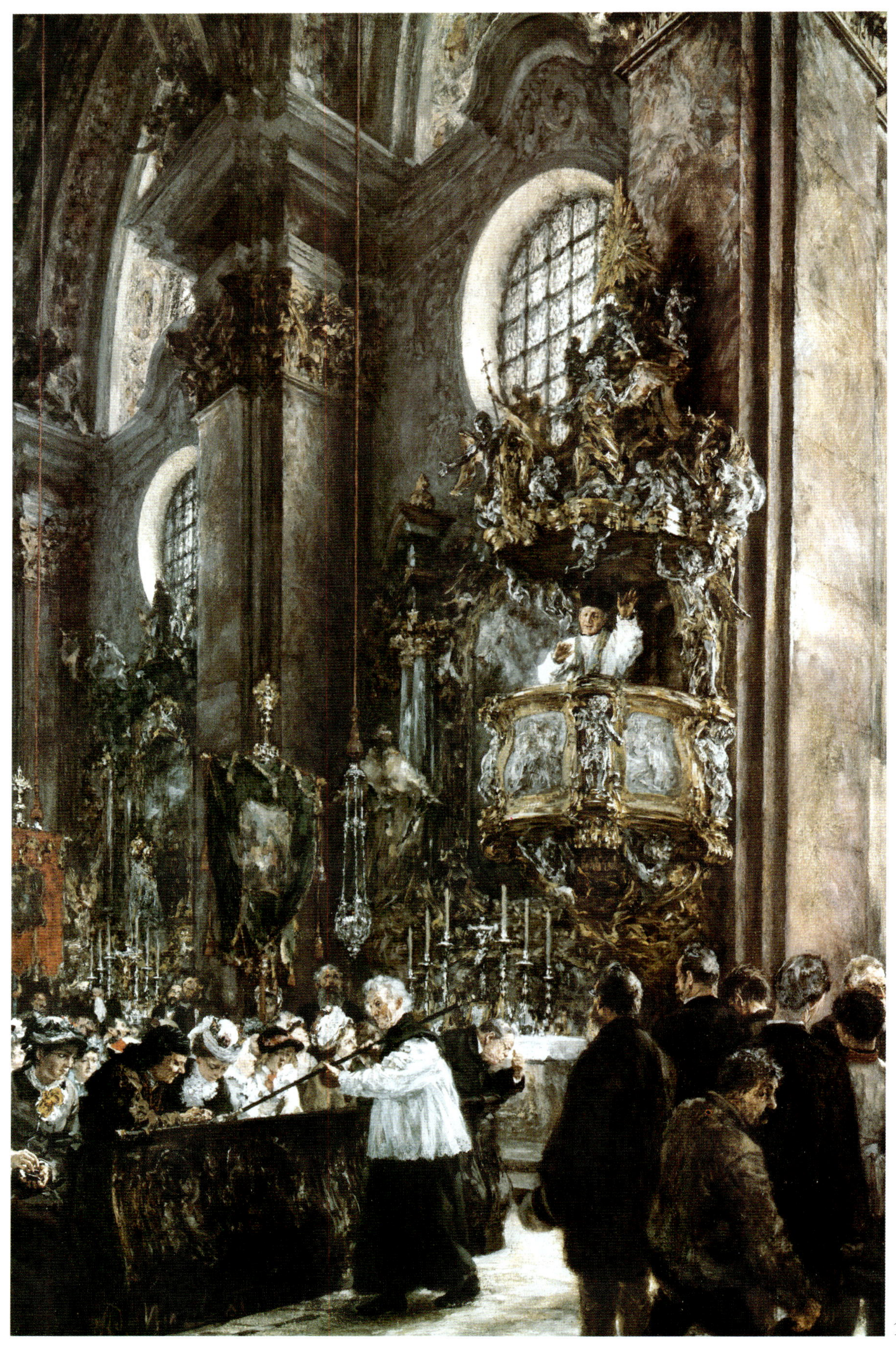

176

176

Sermon in the Parish Church in Innsbruck

1881

Gouache
42 × 28.6cm
Signed and dated at the bottom left: Ad. Menzel 81
Pal (Andorra), Heinrich Merz collection
Exhibited in Washington and Berlin only

Provenance: Hermann Frenkel, trade counsellor, Berlin; acquired by the Nationalgalerie, Berlin in 1907; exchanged in 1924 with Doctor Wendland for a work by Hans von Marées; Hugo Fischer, Bühl.
Exhibitions: Berlin, 1885, no. 81; Berlin, 1895 A, no. 109; Vienna, 1896, no. 241; Düsseldorf, 1904, no. 70; Berlin, 1905, no. 239; Tyrol and Innsbruck, 1992, no. 73.
Bibliography: Jordan, 1895, p. 71; Jordan, 1905, p. 74, reprod. p. 84; Tschudi, 1905 A, no. 628; Wirth, 1974, p. 100.

In the summer of 1859 Menzel went to the Tyrol for the first time, and revisited the capital of that province on several future occasions. Each time he was attracted by the splendour of the baroque churches, whose interiors appear repeatedly in his gouaches of the 1870s. Menzel had painted and drawn church interiors before. In the 1830s he painted the convent church in Berlin and, later, other Gothic and Romanesque churches. No other style appealed to him like the Catholic style and the theatrical pomp of its celebrations, expressed stunningly in the 1880 *Procession at Hofgastein* (cat. 174). In 1881 Menzel went on a long summer tour which took him first to Switzerland, then to the southern Tyrol and northern Italy, finishing with a stop-off in Innsbruck on the way back. It was here that he had the idea for this small painting. From the altar of the then parish church of St Jacques (a 'sacred episcopal church' since 1964) the eye moves to the pulpit and occupied pews. But Menzel creates an impression rather than a replica of reality. Not content with modifying the pulpit by Nicholas Moll, the Tyrolean sculptor, he heightens the imposing church pillars, both here and in the drawings, pillars which date from the end of the baroque period for which the Asan brothers created the stucco in 1722. With a few exceptions (*cf.* cat. 145) Menzel's church interiors are peopled by congregations and vergers, and appear as places of urban communication. From the hand of the priest in the pulpit, raised in blessing, the eye moves downwards to where the congregation is only partly paying attention as a server moves the purse and bell in front of them on the end of a long pole. There are several pencil studies of the women seated in the pews, dressed in bright colours, as there are for other figures. In contrast, a group of men viewed from behind and wearing dark colours is in the foreground, on the right edge of the composition. In the gigantic area of the parish church (made a sacred episcopal church in 1964), only the two pillars and a small part of the wall between is visible. The pillars, which are depicted much larger than their actual size, alone create the impression of a colossal church of resplendent colour. Another interior of the same church painted also only shows an oblique section of the nave[1]. This time the gaze falls upon the south oratory which overhangs the tomb of the Tyrolean prince Maximilian III, which Menzel also modified in terms of shape and position. The main altar appears half truncated on the left edge of the picture. In the same way the congregation, which is on a line parallel to the lower edge of the image, is cut off at shoulder height. The onlooker seems to be looking from a perspective at knee level up to the top of a space which Menzel created 'in his own way' without denying the undisputed character of the building in this and the later composition. M.R.-R.

1. Tschudi, 1905 A, no. 598; location unknown.

177

Self-portrait

1882

Pencil
28.2 × 22.3cm
Signed and dated at the centre left: *Adolph Menzel 30 Dezember 82*
Berlin, Kupferstichkabinett (SZ Menzel Kat 5)
Exhibited in Paris and Washington only

Provenance: Hermann Pächter (R. Wagner Gallery, Berlin); acquired by the museum in 1889.
Exhibitions: Berlin, 1905, no. 355; Berlin, 1955 A, no. 38; Berlin, 1980 A, no. 416; Vienna, 1985, no. 122; Copenhagen, 1985, no. 109; New York, 1990, no. 71.
Bibliography: Donop, 1902, no. 5; Kaiser, 1956, reprod. frontispiece; Hütt, 1981, fig. 119; Lammel, 1993 A, p. 202, fig. 154.

Menzel's self-portraits show a dualism which characterizes his entire work. The paintings created for official occasions are clearly distinguished from much more personal pictures. In the 1882 self-portrait, the artist, shortly before his sixty-seventh birthday, depicts himself frontally in a manner which belongs to that tradition of frontal portraits of which the Munich self-portrait of Dürer with long hair and wearing a fur is undoubtedly the most striking example. The seriousness of Menzel, aware of his own worth, is underlined by his gaze, which is directed straight at the observer. This gaze at first seems to be reinforced by the oval frame, but the frame alters the contours of the eyes, and softens their severity. Menzel never kept a personal diary nor wrote an autobiography. On the other hand he was an assiduous and witty correspondent, as his numerous letters show. Most of his self-portraits show moments of spontaneous self-analysis and are like fragmentary pieces. The more exteriorized self-portrait is the exception. In addition to this one, only three others are known. Since lost, the only painting among them dating from 1848 showed the young artist in profile, standing in front of his easel and turning towards his brother and sister on a sofa[1]. To this can be added an engraving using the 'black technique', dating from the 1850s, a

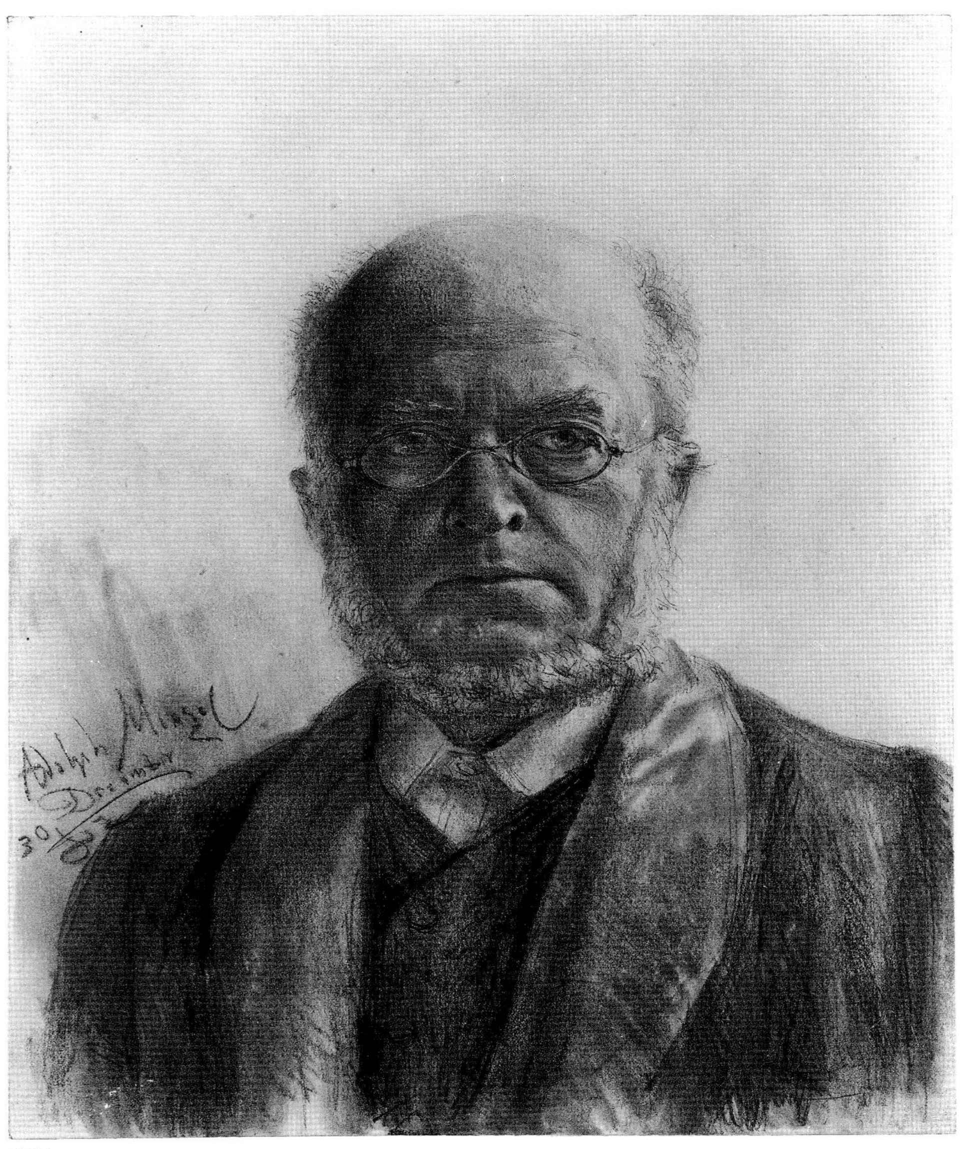

177

'hybrid in which the role of antiquary scarcely hides the artist (fig. 83) , and a drawing from 1851 in which he is standing in a position which suits him, behind his nearest and dearest gathered round an upright piano (*cf.* cat. 61). The other portraits of himself in ink, and especially in pencil, have the feel of casual jottings or strictly personal studies[2].

When Menzel drew this self-portrait he was on the verge of old age. A year later he was appointed vice-chancellor of the civil section of the Order of Merit. The completion of *The Iron Rolling Mill* undoubtedly marked the turning point towards maturity. In the middle of the 1870s Menzel thought seriously of assessing his life as an artist. On 22 February 1874 he began to write an autobiography in a simple exercise book, entitled 'Me', describing his admission forty years earlier to the Association of Young Berlin Artists. But after writing one page he stopped, only to take it up again two years later, on 8 September 1876, with the same idea. He then abandoned it two pages further on, this time for good[3]. On the other hand, on 10 October 1876, before leaving for Holland to gain first-hand experience before he illustrated Heinrich von Kleist's *Der zerbrochene Krug* (The Broken Jug; fig. 90), he began a new sketchbook which he used again in Berlin in 1877 and which could be looked on as a personal diary. He drew the most surprising self-portraits in it[4]. Only half of his face is shown, but it covers two pages deliberately and is perfectly conceived aesthetically. 'The single eye' seems to want to transfix the observer through the oval glasses in a magical way and is the subjective expression of self-knowledge. The motif of the single eye, a traditional symbolic sign, is linked here to a conception of art which is close to reality. It was not until the twentieth century that this motif became a purely artistic metaphor. Werner Schmidt's statement describing the drawing as 'detail, a single eye and yet a self-portrait' is revealing[5]. In comparison with this searching, secret study of Menzel, the 1882 portrait, created five years later in an official context, arouses less aesthetic interest. Later self-portraits show how much Menzel had aligned himself with the fragmentary, which enabled him to express fragility and the finiteness of the real more convincingly[6].

In 1889, when the 1882 portrait was to be published, Menzel wrote: 'When speaking of my portrait, are you thinking of the front-view drawing which I did several years ago for a particular occasion and which is now with Herr Pächter? If so, I would not be happy – the drawing is already old, and hardly looks like me'[7]. And he added that he preferred a recent photograph instead of the self-portrait.

Fig. 214. *Self-portrait*, 1899, pencil, Berlin, Kupferstichkabinett (sketchbook 71, pp. 4–5)

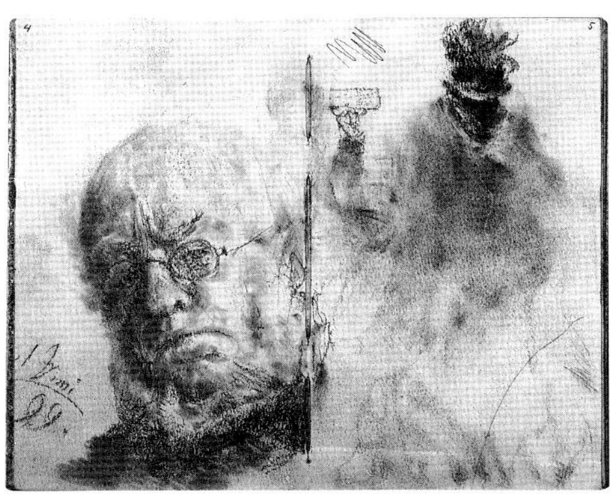

Had photography acquired greater authenticity in his eyes, as he often had his photograph taken? Yet, was authenticity always the goal of his art?

M.R.-R.

1. Missing picture, reprod. in Kirstein, 1919 (frontispiece).
2. Self-portrait as an antique dealer, about 1852-60, Bock, 1923, no. 405. He is seen from behind not only in the picture *Intimate soirée* of 1847 (cat. 28) but also in two drawings inspired by meetings of the Rütli circle of the 1850s (Marbach, Deutsches Literaturarchiv); *cf.* Lammel, 1992 A, fig. 56 and 58. For self-portraits of an unofficial kind, *cf.* for example Berlin, Kupferstichkabinett (SZ Menzel Kat 2, 3, N 955, 513–15).
3. Berlin, Stadtmuseum (formerly Märkisches Museum), quoted in Kirstein, 1919, p. 1 and ff.
4. Berlin, Kupferstichkabinett, sketchbook 51 (1976-7), p. 69-70.
5. Schmidt, 1958, p. 97-119.
6. Compare the self-portraits in the Berlin Kupferstichkabinett of 1892, sketchbook 67, p. 12-13 and of 1899, sketchbook 71, p. 4-5. In sketchbook 7 (1839-46), vigorous reworking makes the self-portrait a fragment. *Cf.* also the fragment of a self-portrait in a mirror, quoted by Eggers, 1854 (Berlin, Kupferstichkabinett, SZ Menzel kat 3); *cf.* also Korte, 1973-4, p. 8.
7. The letter is probably from 9 December 1889 (Nuremberg, Germanisches Nationalmuseum, Br. II/XII 89); it is addressed to Bruckmann, Dohme or Jordan, as it definitely relates to a work by Jordan and Dohme *Das Werk Adolph Menzels* (Munich, 1890-95), in which the portrait was to appear. The particular occasion for the 1882 self-portrait was probably the project, which seemed to come to nothing, to illustrate his biography for the 13th edition of the Brockhaus Konversationslexikon (1882-87).

178

Study of Worker for Piazza d'Erbe in Verona

1883

Pencil
30 × 23cm
Signed and dated at the bottom left: *A.M. 83.*–
Annotated: *Studie f.d. "Piazza d'Erbe" (nachher nicht verwendet)*
Zurich, Arturo Cuéllar collection
Exhibited in Berlin only

Provenance: Hermann Reemtsma, Hamburg; acquired in 1992.
Exhibitions: Berlin, 1905, no. 5444; Berlin, 1955 B, no. 213.
Bibliography: Karl and Faber, 1992, 183rd sale, no. 391, pl. 9.

This generous, accurate study from a model, drawn in carpenter's pencil, for one of the three paviours in the foreground of the painting *Piazza d'Erbe in Verona* (cat. 179) was not used, as Menzel noted on the drawing[1]. He had done a lot of preparatory studies for this group of three paviours, from the sketches on site in the sketchbook of the Verona trip in 1881 to the studies from a model of the following years[2]. In 1879 Menzel had already drawn a group of three paviours. He had called the drawing *The Artists' Break*, in which two men break off from their exhausting work to snort a pinch of tobacco[3]. The drawing shown here was on a page where Menzel did nineteen small sketches in proportional order of size, which are identifiable from the studies for *Piazza d'Erbe*[4]. Menzel did drawings of this kind on several occa-

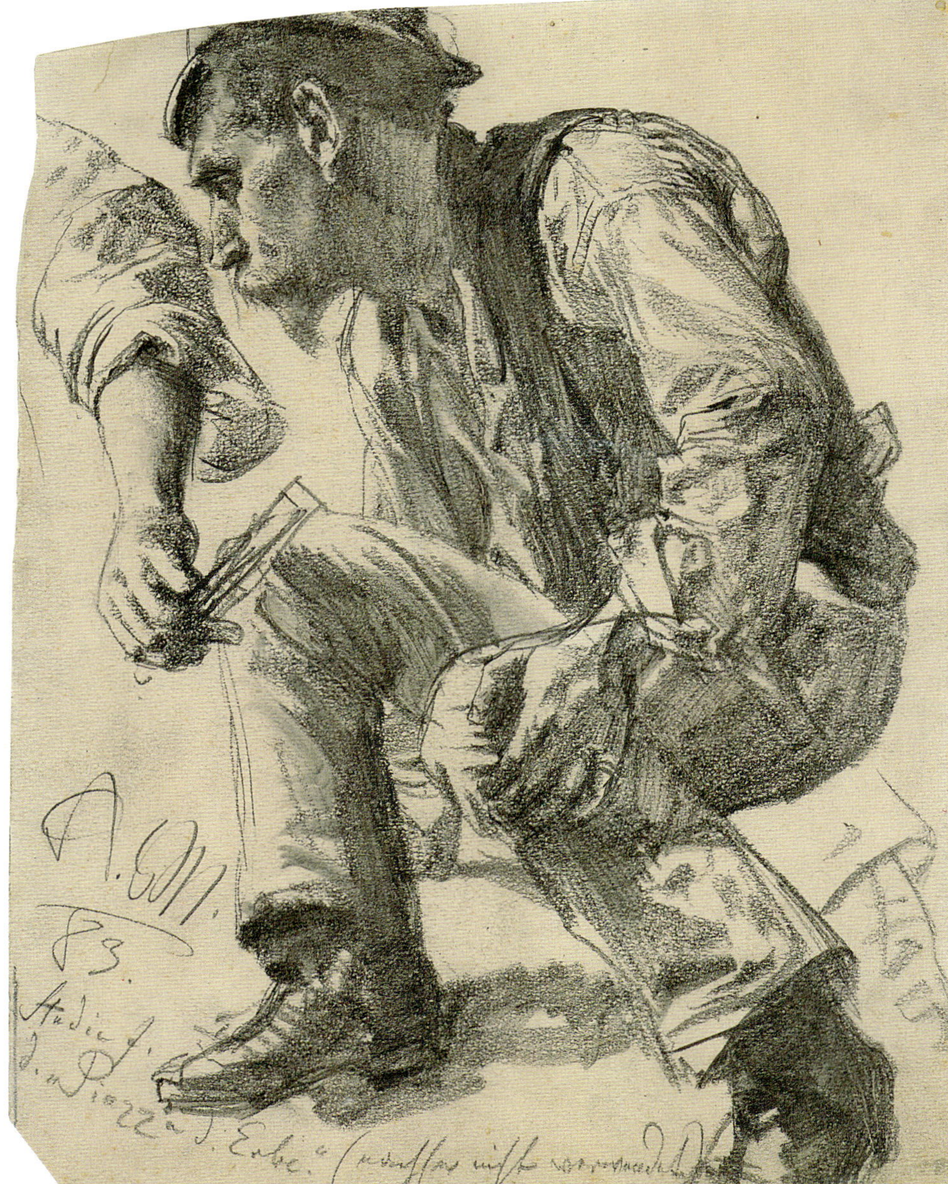

178

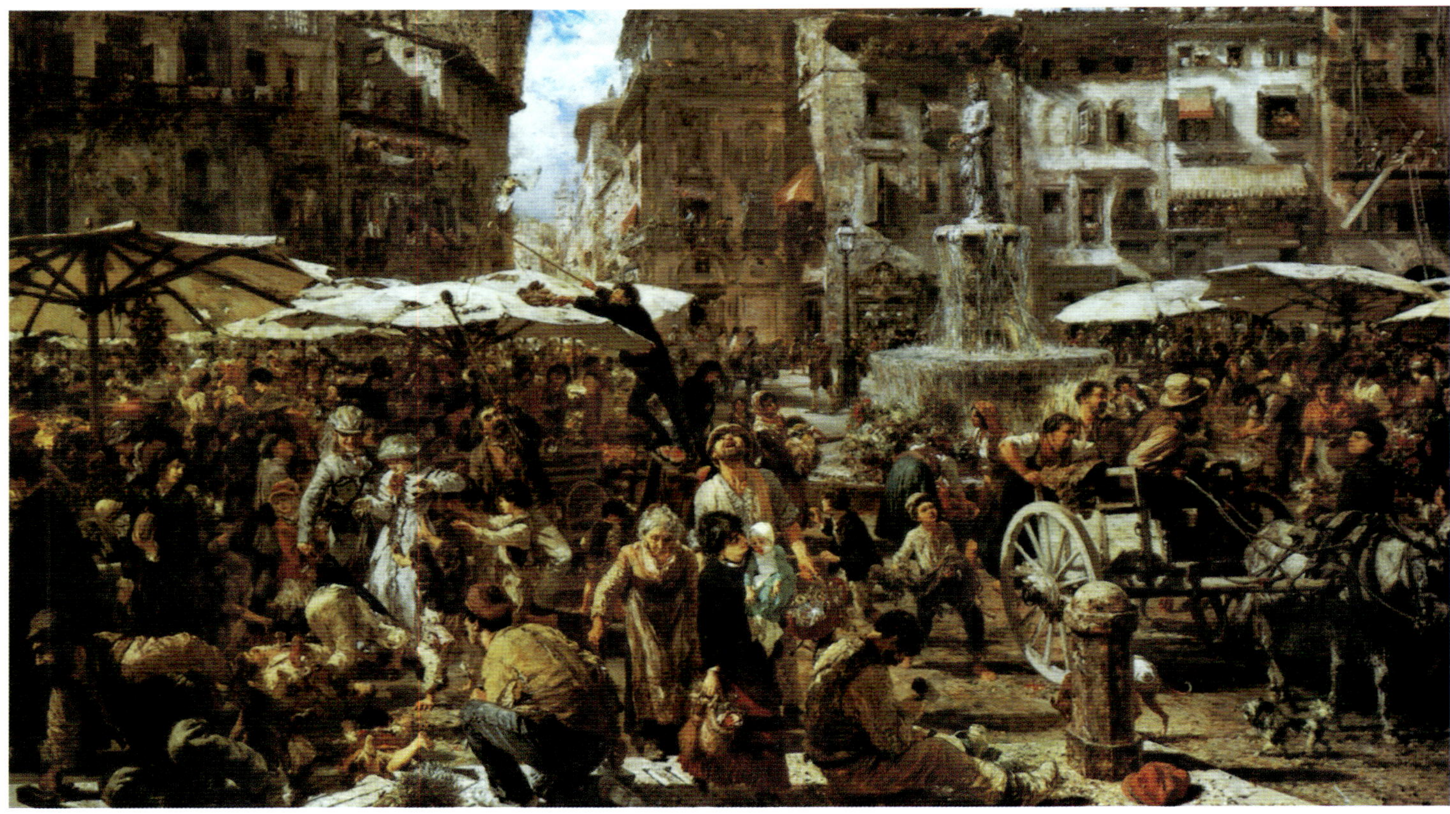

179

sions. They served as notes when drawings left his studio, either for exhibitions, for reproduction or for sale by his agent Hermann Pächter[5]. M.R.-R.

1. For the importance of this group in the composition, *cf.* Sven Kuhrau, *Adolph Menzel's Piazza d'Erbe zu Verona*, note from the Faculty of Historical Sciences at Freie Universität in Berlin (1995), p. 52.
2. Berlin, Kupferstichkabinett, sketchbook 59 (1881), p. 7 and 9. Other drawings at the Kupferstichkabinett in Berlin and previously at the one in Dresden (*cf.* Christian Dittrich, *Lost drawings from the Prints Room in Dresden*, Dresden, 1987).
3. Ink drawing for *The arbour* (location unknown), 49, 1885, reprod. before p. 810.
4. Nuremberg, Städtisches Museum, Graphische Sammlung (166/1928). Menzel noted on the page that [he had] loaned the study drawings relating to the oil painting *Marketplace in Verona* to Mr Pächter. 30 June 84. There is a second page (167/1928).
5. Other pages of this kind at Berlin in the Kupferstichkabinett (SZ Menzel Nr 1782). – Bremen, Kunsthalle (58/409).

179
Piazza d'Erbe in Verona (Marketplace in Verona)
1884

Oil on canvas
74 × 127cm
Signed and dated at the bottom right: *Adolph Menzel 1884*
Dresden, Staatliche Kunstsammlungen, Gemäldegalerie, Neue Meister
Exhibited in Berlin only

Provenance: 1885 Hermann Pächter, Berlin, who made an unsuccessful offer to the Hamburg Kunsthalle; before 1898 Henneberg gallery, Zurich; 1903 Helbing sale, Munich; 1903 Eduard L. Behrens, Hamburg; Emil Meiner, Leipzig; acquired by the museum in 1905.
Exhibitions: Berlin, 1884; Paris, 1885, no. 234; Berlin, 1885, no. 22; Vienna, 1886; Berlin, 1886, no. 2467 and 3256 (entered under both numbers); London, 1903; Dresden, 1903 B; Berlin, 1980 A, no. XXXI, reprod. p. 154.
Bibliography: Pietsch, 1884; Lichtwark, (1884) 1897, p. 186–93; Dumas, 1885, p. 9 *et seq.*; Gonse, 1885, p. 518 *et seq.*; Jordan, 1890, p. 75, pl. 111; Heilbut, 1891, p. 99; Tschudi, 1905 A, no. 153; Meier-Graefe, 1906, p. 254; Liebermann, (1921) 1922, p. 200 *et seq.*; Fechner, (1927) 1992, p. 247 *et seq.*; Waldmann, 1941, pp. 33–4, pp. 36–7, p. 40, p. 49, figs 78–9; Hütt, 1981, fig. 113 (col.); Jensen, 1982, p. 124, p. 126, col. pl. 39–40; Wirth, 1990, p. 296 *et seq.*, col. pl. 44; Zangs, 1982, p. 257–60; Lammel, 1993 B, p. 82 *et seq.*; Kuhrau, 1995.

The growing penchant for an implosion of the image by stressing and exacerbating the dissonances and incoherence is nowhere so obvious as in the last large-format painting, whose preparation covered quite a long period. Menzel was approaching seventy by the time it was finished, and he exhibited it at the Association of Berlin Artists with the preparatory drawings. Once more, a work was presented in the context of its creation (*cf.* introduction to cat. 94–9), elsewhere an unusual approach which continues today in the idea of 'work in progress'. Menzel had never been to Italy until 1881, and even in that year and also 1882 and 1883, he only skimmed the surface, stopping off at Verona. He seems to have had the idea for this composition on the second trip, and the different elements appear in two sketchbooks[1] and about twenty-four drawings[2]. A number of model studies were made in Berlin from unknown Italian models.

In contrast with *Weekday in Paris*, whose topography is imaginary, all the elements of the popular market in the famous Piazza di Erbe can be identified – the fountain of the Verona Madonna, the end of the Via Pallicciana, at the end of which the Torre del Gardello can be seen. Only the dimensions and spatial relations have been modified slightly[3].

A large opening cuts through the space, from the empty corner on the right, marked by a single bollard, as far as the road which stretches away palely in the light, and gives a unique narrow perspective on a very blue sky. All the rest is barred by the row of varied, picturesque façades, among which workers on a scaffold can be distinguished, an eternal leitmotiv. The upper part of the houses is cut off by the edge of the picture (with one almost imperceptible but essential exception).

The painter exaggerates the already known principle (*cf.* cat. 127, 174 and 203) of 'assembling' elements (figures, groups, areas of space) so that each retains an autonomous existence. Max Jordan spoke of 'mosaics' and, according to the interpretation generally accepted by Françoise Forster-Hahn, this method expresses 'the impossibility of capturing the world as a harmonious unity'. She adds, 'The totality of the world can only be lived or fixed in fragments'[4]. All the little everyday catastrophes to which Menzel has accustomed us in his paintings are multiplied here, the most noticeable being the misfortune of the couple of well-off foreign travellers frightened by the rough acrobatics of some boys. The movement is general but lacks centre or radiation.

Curiously, a group of five figures is arranged in a pyramid in the near foreground and exactly on the central axis, like an academic demonstration. This principle of composition inherited from the Renaissance is distorted and leads to an absurd result, as the figures gathered there have no relation to each other and their isolated actions diverge systematically. Menzel distanced himself from the Academies, and the order of thinking is the same here! On the other hand an allusion to Courbet's *Stone-breakers* has been detected in the paviours in the foreground; this was a painting that Menzel must have seen in Paris[5], yet Christiane Zang's idea that the 'exaggerated representation' of the crowd is a 'caricature of realism' should be borne in mind. Whatever the case, the old painter knew very well that the painting of customs had come to an end, and his work is a discordant swan-song, magnificent and ultimately sad.

Contemporaries were amazed at 'the principle of having absolutely no central focus of attention[6]. If German critics were reserved in their reactions, the French loved it, and François Guillaume Dumas spoke of 'the splendid work Menzel produced in this genre'. It would be hard not to admire this excess of chaotic life, breathless, in a panic, carried away by an unconscious gaiety which fills the space, together with small, dispersed patches of light, dry and contrasting in the foreground, and enveloping the background in a mist of dusty colour. It would also be hard not to acknowledge that the desire for a tour de force makes the painting overworked. When an admirer clumsily remarked to Menzel: 'Its magnificent – so sunny!, he replied, 'slowly, and emphasizing each word: "No, that's exactly what it is not!"'[7]

C.K.

1. Berlin, Kupferstichkabinett (sketchbooks 58 and 59).
2. Kuhrau, 1995.
3. Kuhrau shows this in his excellent monograph on this work (not yet out).
4. Forster-Hahn, 1980, p. 42.
5. Zangs, 1992. The 1849 work went later to the gallery in Dresden. It was destroyed in 1945.
6. *Deutsches Kunstblatt*, 3, 1883-4, p. 143.
7. Fechner, (1927) 1992, p. 248. Two years after this painting, a gouache depicts the stall of a poultry dealer, but in a quite different manner. *Verona market scene*, 1886, Tschudi, 1905 A, no. 655; location unknown.

180

Camel Driver at Partenkirchen

1884

Gouache
32 × 40cm
Signed and dated at the bottom right: *Ad. Menzel. 84*
Moscow, Pushkin State Museum of Fine Art
Exhibited in Paris only

Provenance: Serguei Tretiakov collection, Moscow; 1892 Tretiakov gallery, Moscow; 1925 State Fine Art Museum (the current Pushkin Museum), Moscow; 1948 Pushkin State Museum of Fine Art, Moscow.
Exhibitions: Moscow, 1930, no. 120; Moscow, 1963, p. 50 (unnumb); Moscow, 1994 (no cat.).
Bibliography: Tschudi, 1905 A, no. 641; Wirth, 1974, p. 80, col. pl. 80 (with the title *Wanderzirkus* [Touring circus]).

In his later gouaches Menzel obstinately insisted on substituting the artistically and evenly woven surface of the painting for an impression of space. His innovatory playfulness needs to be acknowledged in this respect. Menzel was more than a painter, he was a narrator[1]. In this gouache the stylistic means which create its flat surface served to retain both the fabulous and the authentic in the scene – the astonishing irruption of people walking with their strange animals in this intermediary world, like a scene in the

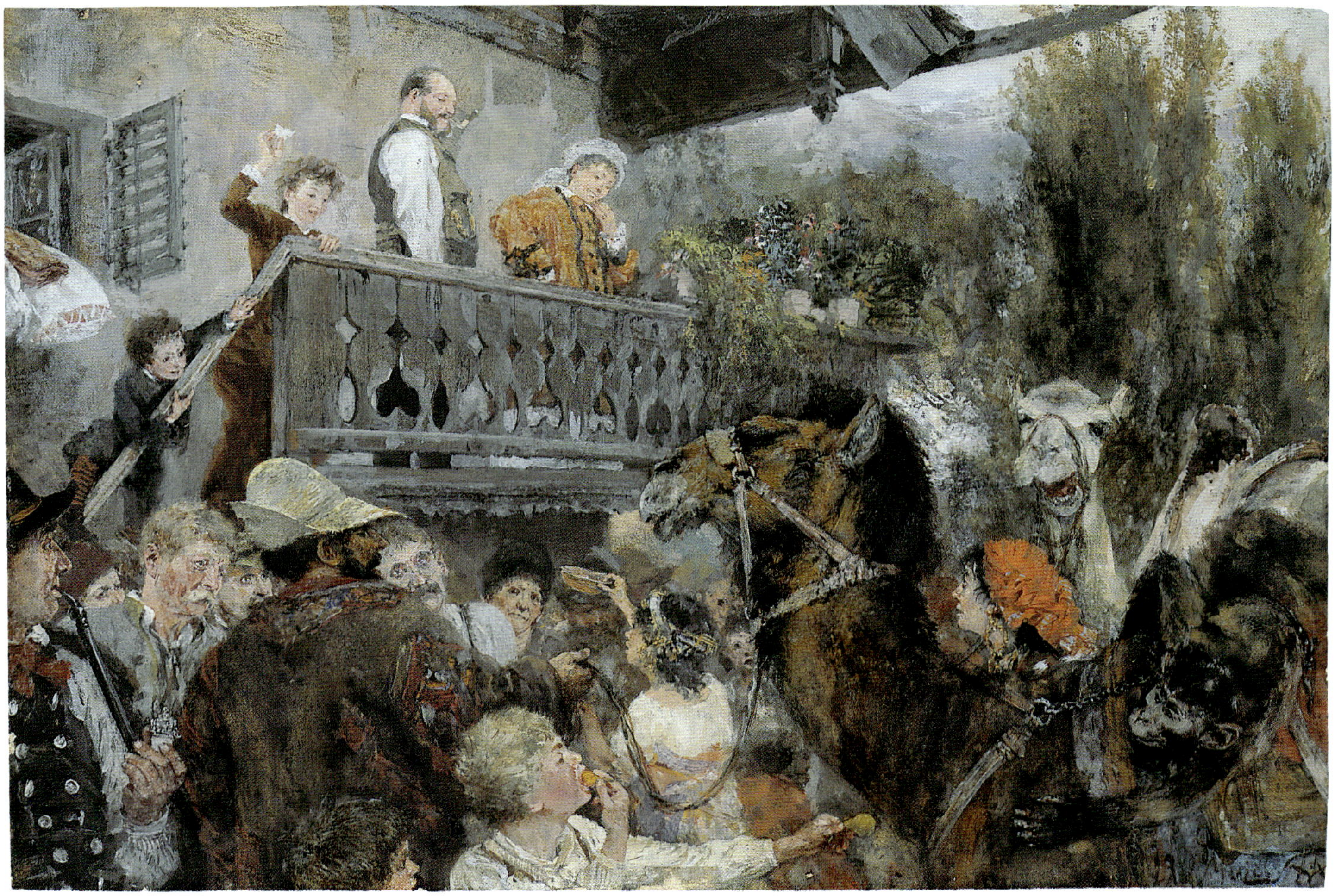

180

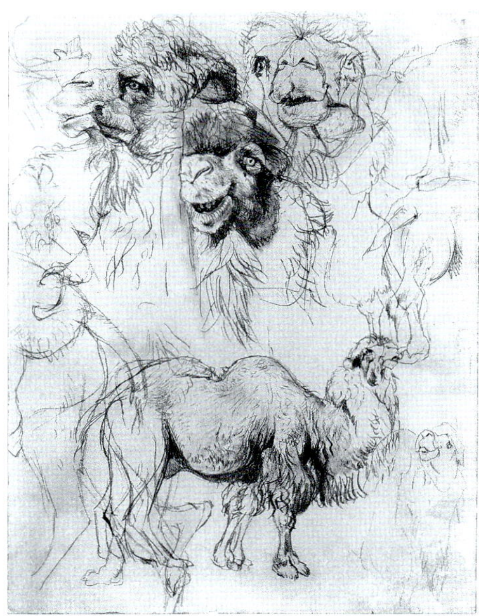

Fig. 215. *Studies of Dromedaries*, 1884, pencil, Berlin, Kupferstichkabinett

theatre. The tiny vista of the snow-capped peaks beyond the tree-tops is more a view than a perception of depth. No space is offered the eye to wander in the distance, for it is directed towards the mêlée and clash of curious villagers and gypsies, camels and monkeys. Sceptical, reserved spectators, summer visitors, appear on the balcony or gallery, their children bursting with curiosity. Bold incisions which unhesitatingly cut the head of a child in two are the stylistic means used by Menzel, like newspaper illustrations. They create the illusion of time – and therefore reality – through movement. An event actually experienced is clearly the source of this gouache[2]. Certain studies involving camels (fig. 215) show that Menzel extended to the animals his interest in the psychology of his figures, which is reflected in the fine nuances in all the faces. Like the detailed studies of human faces, those of the camels seek a characteristic expression[3]. Paul Meyerheim, who also painted animals, wrote a very instructive description of Menzel's love of them[4]. The painting *In the Animal Shed*, richly ornamented like a genre painting, shows, in a long format, the reactions of the visitors at the sight of a chained elephant. There is also a camel among the other animals[5]. In his portrayal of animals, Menzel sought to find their individuality, their essential being rather than their appearance. 'Far ahead of any Japanese, he brilliantly expresses his knowledge of the poetry of children and animals in his paintings', wrote Albert Hertel[6]. M.R.-R.

1. *Cf.* Meyerheim, (1906) 1992, p. 234.
2. The Hertel family can perhaps be recognized among the spectators on the balcony (*cf.* cat. 163). The youngest boy, Fritz, was Menzel's godson. Menzel's visits to the Hertels in Hofgastein increased during the 1870s. This is perhaps proved by the study of a woman at a balcony in the 1874 sketchbook (Berlin, Kupferstichkabinett, sketchbook 44, p. 5). Menzel marked it with a cross, showing that he used the study.
3. Berlin, Kupferstichkabinett (SZ Menzel N 264, 2202, 2203, 4488).
4. *Cf.* Meyerheim, (1906) 1992, p. 186–7. *Cf.* also Hertel on this subject (1911–12), 1992, p. 92.
5. *In the animal shedi,* oil on canvas, 86 × 217cm; formerly Nationalgalerie, Berlin, lost in the Second World War.
6. Hertel, (1911–12) 1992, p. 92–3.

181
Vault with Lunettes, by Lamplight
1884

Pencil
13 × 20.9cm
Signed and dated at the top right: *A.M.84*
Berlin, Kupferstichkabinett (SZ Menzel N 25)
Exhibited in Paris and Washington only

Provenance: painter's studio; 1905 Emilie Krigar-Menzel; acquired by the museum in 1906.
Exhibitions: Berlin, 1905, no. 2007; Berlin, 1955 A, no. 502; Berlin, 1980 A, no. 378, reprod. p. 401; Vienna, 1985, no. 125, reprod. p. 91.

A source of illumination from the right, outside the space depicted, casts its light, through the upper part of a semicircular archway, over a tunnel vault, punctuated by lunettes. The space curves before our eyes as if distorted by a capricious lens. The semicircular opening faces the onlooker, and its support is a kind of slightly projecting cornice. The eye travels to the top part of a carriage entrance, which it crosses. Outside are two gas lamps, a façade of roughly hewn round stones with blind windows in it, and at the side, a fragment of another well-lit house as well as an indistinct mass, probably of trees. But the draughtsman concentrates mainly on describing the inside of the vault. With the help of the light, he builds a rhythmic system of geometrical shapes in the fluidity of the space. The subject is portrayed in a rather ascetic way, but a narrative element appears outside – a town, the night – disturbing the pure geometry of the composition. When Menzel draws the night he places the most varied objects and figures in a bizarre perspective[1]. This vault drawn under a hard light and the view through the archway bring to mind Piranesi's engravings, his *Views of Rome* and his *Carceri*. A.H.

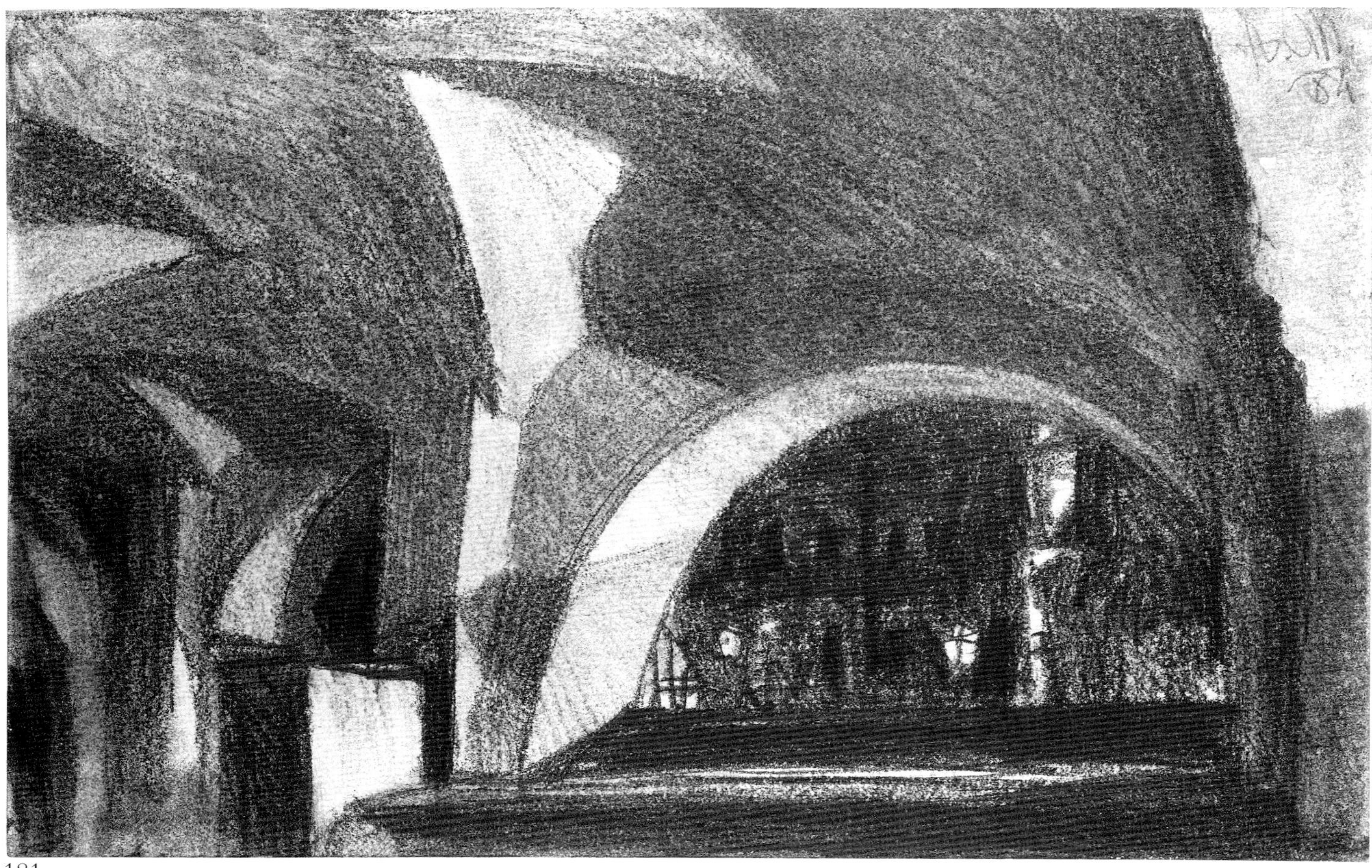

181

Exhibition: Berlin, 1905, no. 5444.
Bibliography: Ketterer, 1951, 14th sale, no. 1134; Karl & Faber, 1992, 183rd sale, no. 391, pl. 9.

This portrait of a bearded man wearing a small straw hat represents a peasant from the Bernese Oberland, whom Menzel drew at Interlaken during a summer trip to Switzerland. Sceptical, reserved features characterize the expression of this mountain peasant. His taut vitality seems to be entirely concentrated in the expression in his eyes, which is partly hidden behind half-closed eyelids. The virtuosity of this pencil drawing recalls the studies of peasants from Aiblingen made by Leibl at about the same time. Both artists use the same bold lines, the same studied play of light and shadow. While Liebl's figures are usually shown in their statuesque relationship to the internal space, here the calm dynamic of the raised head of this peasant, moulded by the natural forces of his mountain environment, literally shatters the space in Menzel's drawing, which is only constrained by the limits of the sheet of paper. M.R.-R

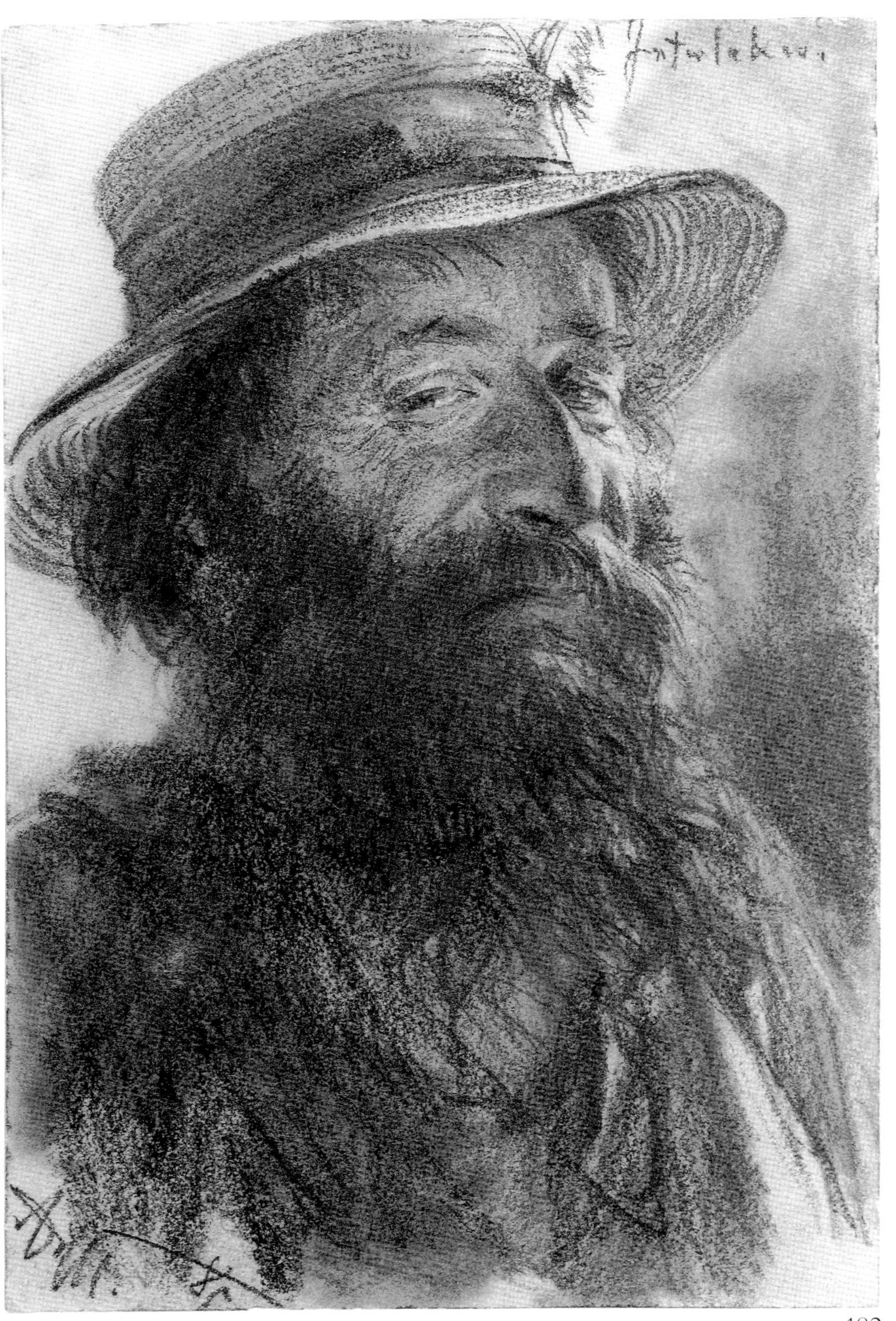

182

182

Peasant from Interlaken

1885

Pencil
18 × 11.8cm
Signed and dated at the bottom left: *A.M.85* –
Annotated at the top right: *Interlaken.*
Zurich, Arturo Cuéllar collection

183

Japanese Painter (At the Japanese Exhibition)

1885

Gouache
18 × 14cm
Signed and dated at the top, on the paper lanterns: *Menzel 1885*
Pal (Andorra), Heinrich Merz collection
Exhibited in Washington and Berlin only

Provenance: Eduard Arnhold, industrialist and collector, Berlin; Frau E. Nelke, Berlin; Hauswedell & Nolte, Hamburg, sale on 28 May 1980.
Exhibitions: Berlin, 1895 A, no.112; Hamburg, 1896, no. 71; Vienna, 1896, no. 260; Berlin, 1905, no. 5812; Berlin, 1993, no. 14.60, fig. 450.
Bibliography: Tschudi, 1905 A, no. 662; Jordan, 1895, p. 72.

1. *Cf.* in particular two drawings in Berlin which complement this one in terms of subject and date: *The courtyard side of the pavilion of the Zwinger enclosure in Dresden* (1871, SZ Menzel N 329) and *Night stroller under an archway* (1888, SZ Menzel N 23).

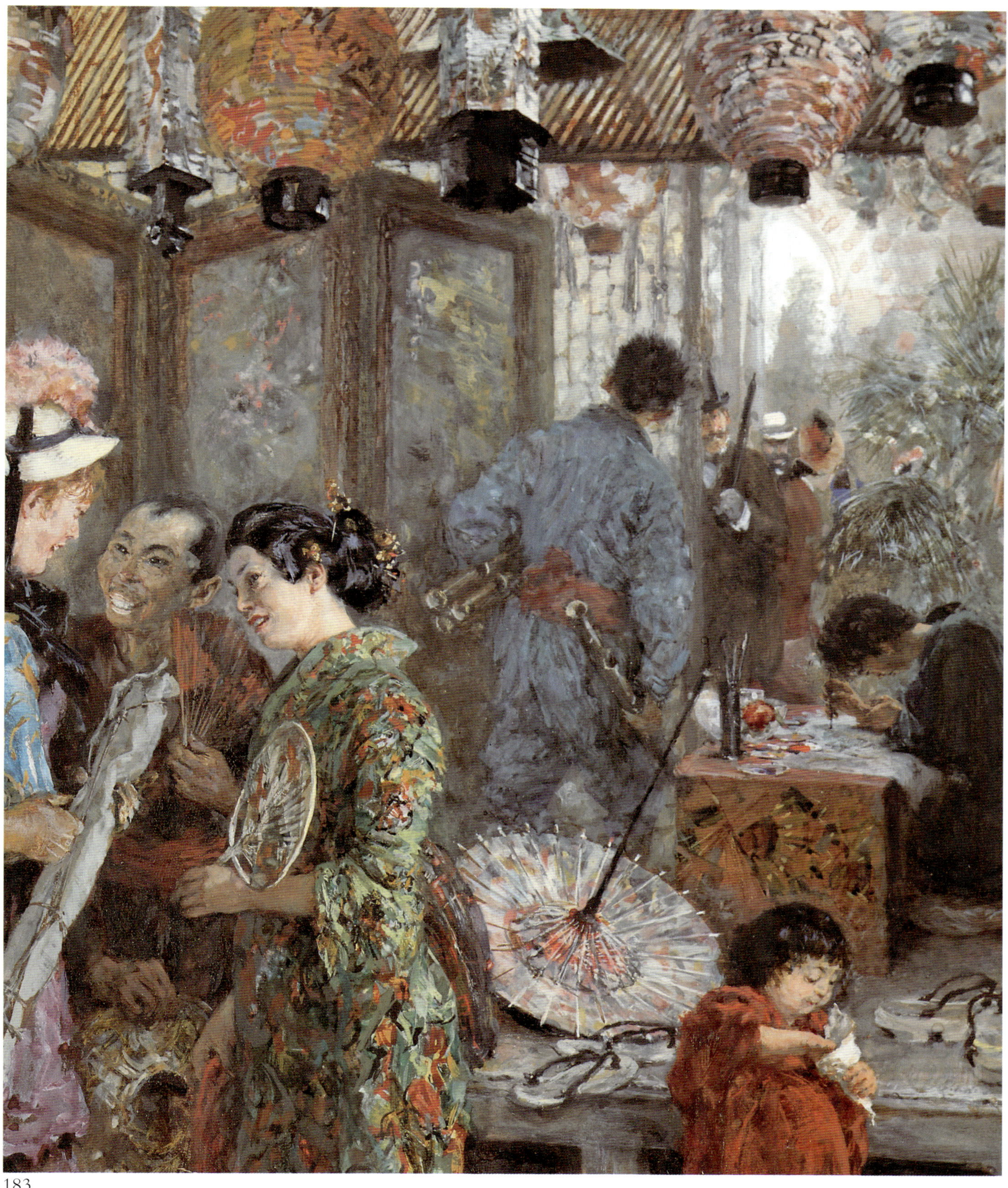

183

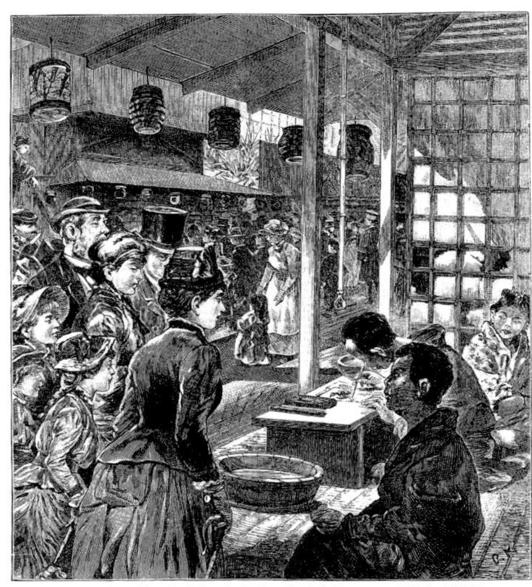

Aus der Japanischen Ausstellung in Berlin. Originalzeichnung von C. Koch. (S. 60.)

Fig. 216. After Carl Koch, *In the Japanese exhibition,* wood engraving, published by the *Leipziger Illustrierte Zeitung,* 18 July 1885

Although Germany became enthusiastic over Japan later than France and England, Menzel was definitely interested in contemporary Japanese engraving at the Universal Exhibitions in Paris in 1867 and Vienna in 1873. He had encountered Japanese art with its popular engravings (*ukiyo-e*), which showed city life or landscapes, as well as its great artists, on several occasions before he painted two gouaches on the theme of Japanese exoticism. In 1883 Louis Gonse, the director of the *Gazette des Beaux-Arts*, held a sensational exhibition of Japanese art and at the same time published two volumes entitled *Japanese Art*. He had published a critique of the Paris exhibition of the *Works of Frederick the Great* re-edited by Pächter, also in French. However, it is likely that the two men met before this. In Berlin, Pächter had become Menzel's dealer in the 1870s, after buying the R. Wagner gallery at 2 Dessauer Strasse, and he was one of the first to import Japanese articles of all kinds. He was an eccentric businessman, and had been a well-known brewer in Hamburg and long-time friend of Siegfried Bing, the famous Japanese specialist who lived in Paris. He had Menzel's complete confidence[2].

According to Jordan, it was the great Japanese exhibition at the Hygienepark in Berlin in the summer of 1885 which led Menzel to paint these pictures. 'A Japanese village with houses, streets, shops, temples, theatres, workshops, tea houses and several hundred people working, it all seems to have been brought from the depths of Asia as if by magic'. This description appeared in the *Leipziger Illustrierte Zeitung* in its article on the exhibition, which then went to Munich and Paris in 1886[2]. A wood engraving after a drawing by Carl Koch (1827–1905) was published with the article (fig. 216) and underlines, in contrast, the liveliness Menzel injected into the exotic atmosphere.

In Menzel's later work it is possible to detect stylistic elements that reflect the influence, conscious or not, of the Japanese style, such as the division of the space into layers parallel with the frame, the absence of depth reminiscent of a carpet, the surprising framing of motifs, the off-centre composition, and the plunging perspective which obliterates the horizon (*cf.* cat. 184, 192). Also, the desire shown in popular Japanese prints not to copy nature, but to interpret it, must have been close to Menzel's heart.

The two gouaches of 1885 and 1887, making a pair, one of which was exhibited, are linked by a common theme, the encounter with the world of exoticism, in the form of the pavilions selling Japanese products, with European or, more accurately, German visitors from Munich and Berlin. The same accessories are used in both works – paper lanterns hung parallel with the frame of the picture from an invisible ceiling, the Japanese screen, which if folded differently would give the impression of looking at the same single interior from different perspectives. In the 1887 gouache, *Japanese Dressmaker*, Japanese people appear, either busy or idle, as well as children and even cats, with a Bavarian in the background accompanied by a woman[3]. The exhibited gouache shows a painter at work, leaning over a very small desk. In the left foreground there are two Japanese people in front of the raised floor of the pavilion, a man and a woman engaged in animated conversation with a purchaser who already has a packet in her hands. She is cut off by the frame, like the child eating sweets from a small bag. Other visitors stroll in the background. There are numerous studies of the figures in the two gouaches and, in a pencil drawing of 1886, *Japanese embroiderers at work*[4]. This is executed very thoroughly, and the pencil lines cover the entire page with a fine, richly nuanced embroidery. It shows a Japanese room in the middle of which two drawings are hanging from an invisible ceiling, and the embroiderer, a smiling Japanese girl holding vases of flowers. A small child is between the two and there are other people behind the screens[5]. This drawing is one of the first in a series in pencil which are a good illustration of Menzel's late style.

M.R.-R.

1. Meier-Graefe, 1987, p. 230.
2. *Illustrierte Zeitung*, no. 2194 of 18 July 1885, p. 60, reprod. p. 70; Jordan, 1905, p. 88, reprod. p. 84; *Paris illustré*, special number Japan, 1 May 1886 (reprod.).
3. Euerbach, Georg Schäfer collection.
4. *Washington, National Gallery of Art; the studies: Berlin, Kupferstichkabinett.*
5. Jordan, 1895, reprod. p. 55.

184

Lady Walking by a Fountain in the Kissingen Spa Garden

1885

Gouache
18 × 11.8cm
Signed and dated at the bottom right: *Menzel 85 Kissingen*

Warsaw, Muzeum Narodowe (1361)
Exhibited in Berlin only

Provenance: 1885 and 1905 Dr von Korn, Breslau; Schlesisches Museum der bildenden Künste, Breslau; since 1946 at the national museum in Warsaw.
Exhibitions: Berlin, 1885, no. 89; Paris, 1885, no. 215; Berlin, 1895 A, no. 113; Hamburg, 1896, no. 72; Vienna, 1896, no. 255; Berlin, 1905, no. 275; Warsaw, 1991, no. 62.
Bibliography: Jordan, 1895, p. 72; Tschudi, 1905 A, no. 649.

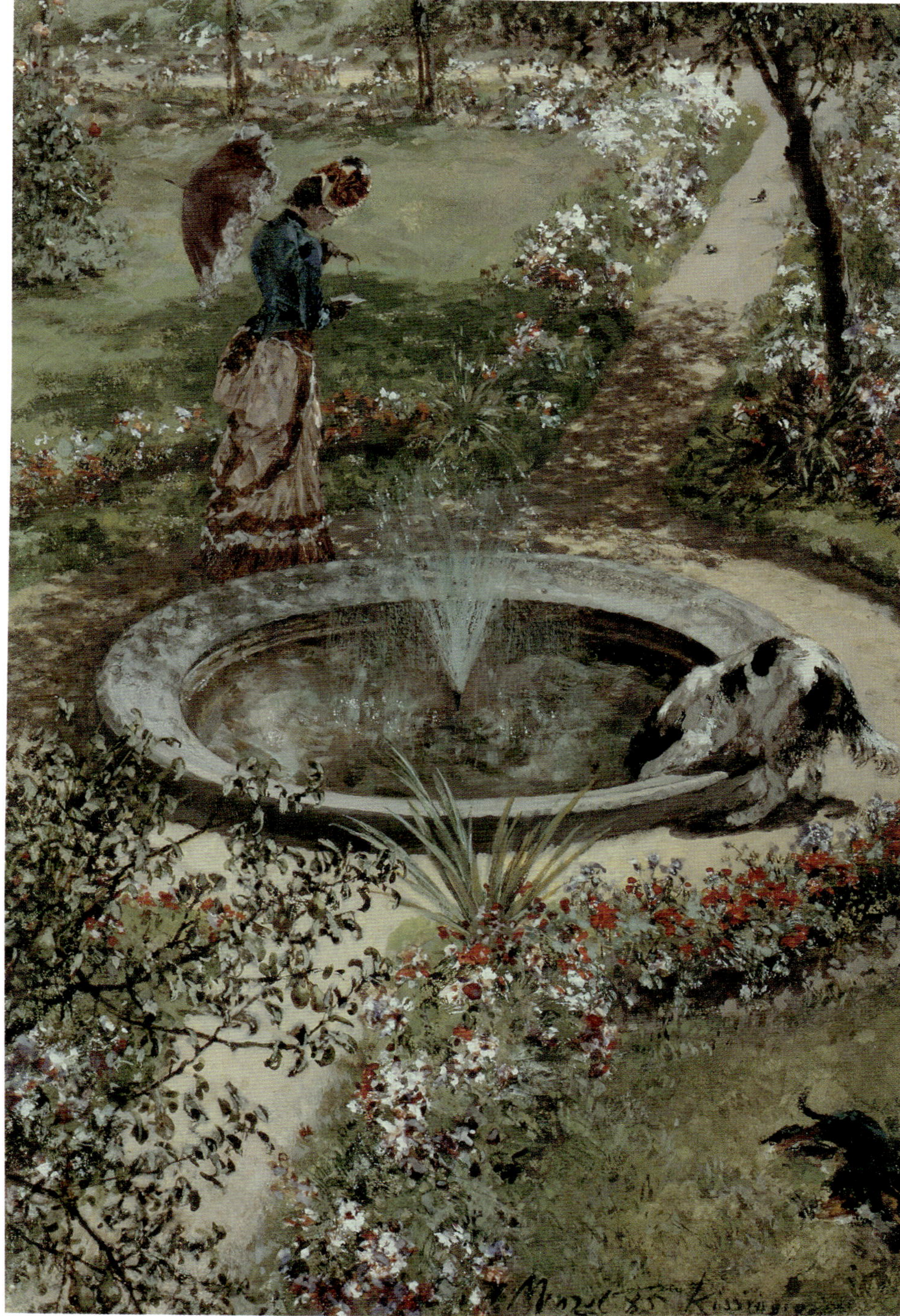

184

From the early 1870s Menzel stayed several times at Kissingen, a spa not far from Würzburg in Franconia. He prided himself on not needing the baths nor the waters, but he travelled with his sister's family and, after his brother-in-law's death in 1880, he accompanied her more or less regularly. On a curious page in 'The golden book' of Kissingen, he declared in 1889 that he was 'not taking the waters', writing 'In poculis in balneis salus' under his watercolour. A ravishing water sprite has left Bacchus' group of followers and is dancing with a faun while stirring some spring water and a glass of wine[1]. A well-known photograph from 31 July 1904 shows Menzel asleep under his umbrella on a park bench in Kissingen. In his old age he seems to have appreciated the bourgeois tranquillity of the spa and a number of drawings as well as numerous gouaches (cat. 203) show that the place provided a constant stream of subjects. Looking out of the window is a frequent motif. Menzel must have liked these strange perspectives because they showed events happening as if they were part of a carpet, without horizon, and comparable in that respect to Japanese wood block prints. Only the garden is retained in this picture, which covers the entire sheet. It is traversed diagonally by a narrow path which goes round the small pond in the centre. At the top, we realize that the path continues along the horizon, hidden by trees and bushes. The shadow theatre created by the foliage sugests a sunny day, and the climbing plants and flowers are given the lightest of touches in a way which brings the French Impressionists to mind. However, the woman walking is less a part of nature than someone with her own personal history, so that the surrounding nature is a kind of decor. Like a modern short story, Menzel shows no more than a pretty woman reading a note and smiling, with a little dog near the fountain and a cat in the immediate foreground.

M.R.-R.

1. Not mentioned by Tschudi. Reprod. in *Moderne Kunst*, XX, 1906, p. 101.

185
Spa Garden at Kissingen
1886

Pencil
41.9 × 28.8cm
Signed and dated at the top left: *Ad.Menzel Aug.86.*
Berlin, Kupferstichkabinett (SZ Menzel N 194)

Provenance: Painter's studio; 1905 Emilie Krigar-Menzel; acquired by the museum in 1906.
Exhibitions: Berlin, 1905, no. 4311; Berlin, 1980 A, no. 379, reprod. p. 282.

186
Spa Garden at Kissingen, at Night
1886

Pencil
42 × 29cm
Signed and dated at the top right: *Ad. M. Aug. 86.*
Berlin, Kupferstichkabinett (SZ Menzel N 273)

Provenance: Painter's studio; 1905 Emilie Krigar-Menzel; acquired by the museum in 1906.
Exhibition: Berlin, 1905, no. 6618.

Although it is a good excuse for a charming, anecdotal picture, the portrayal of the garden at Kissingen could also be interpreted quite differently. Menzel turned to chiaroscuro with fervour in the drawings of his later years. It was not uncommon for him to draw the same subject at different times of the day and night. In 1886 he drew three versions of the spa garden in large format, each under a different light, with several large hotels in the background whose windows look out on the small fountain. In addition to the drawings shown here there is another which, from its lighting, must have been done at a time of day between these two[1]. Menzel used a thick, broad-leaded pencil, which could equally well be used on the thin edge, to capture modifications to shape and substance created by changes in light. Short, hatched lines set one against the other in the last and darkest of the three drawings emphasize the dying light and ever-increasing darkness. A few thin light areas are done in stump or with an eraser. Often Menzel would scratch the paper violently to enhance the expressiveness of the drawing. M.R.-R.

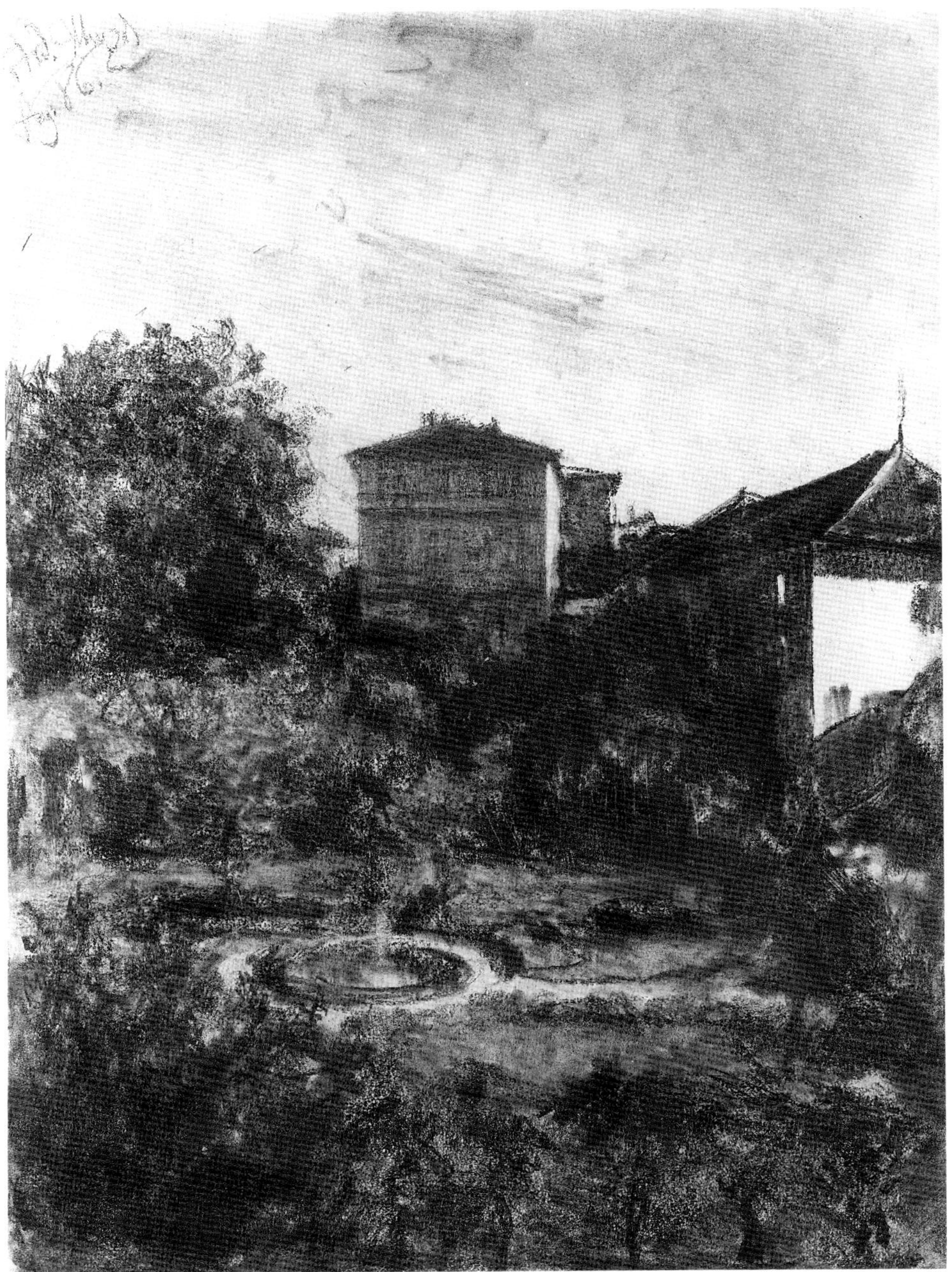
185

1. Berlin, Kupferstichkabinett, (SZ Menzel N 274).

187
Honorary Citizen's Diploma from Hamburg City Council to G.C. Schwabe
1887

Watercolour and gouache on parchment
60.5 × 46cm
Signed and dated at the bottom right: *Adolph Menzel Berlin 1887.*
Hamburg, Hamburger Kunsthalle, Kupferstichkabinett (1972/84)
Exhibited in Berlin only

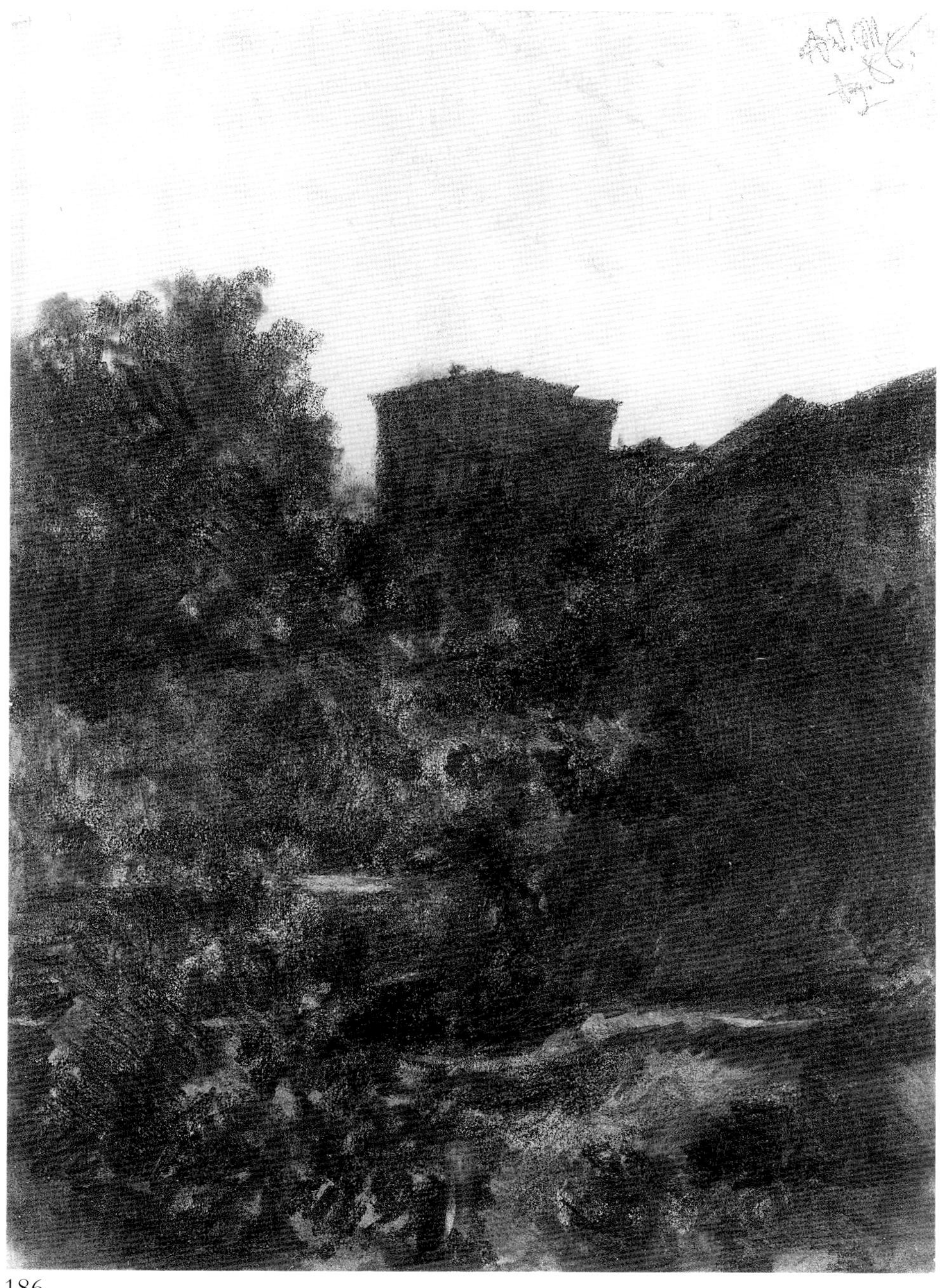

186

Provenance: Gustav Christian Schwabe, London; Captain H.B.T. Schwabe, London; acquired by the museum in 1972.
Exhibitions: Hamburg, 1896, reprod. p. 35; Hamburg, 1970, pp. 17–23, reprod. p. 18; Hamburg, 1982, no. 238.
Bibliography: Jordan, 1895, p. 52; Tschudi, 1905 A, no. 663; Lammel, 1993 A, p. 138.

Gustav Christian Schwabe was a wool merchant born in 1813 in Hamburg-Eppendorf. He lived later in Yewden near London and died in London in 1889. In 1883 he decided to bequeath his collection of paintings to the town of Hamburg for the Kunsthalle. One of the conditions of the bequest was that the collection was to be shown in five separate rooms. By the time the collection went on view in 1886, the number of paintings had increased to 128. It was basically made up of English paintings, and showed very conventional good taste. Upon the death of the Hamburg councillor who had been involved in the negotiations, Alfred Lichtwark, who was director of the Kunsthalle from 1886, tried to handle relations between the donor and the Hamburg city council when things became complicated. He suggested that Menzel should create the honorary citizen's certificate for Schwabe in 1886. It is questionable as to whether the choice was to the merchant's taste, and in fact shortly after Lichtwark had sent him the certificate in London on 30 July 1887, he informed the Kunsthalle's president and administrative committee that Schwabe wanted to donate the document to the museum. However, Schwabe changed his decision out of politeness. Alfred Lichtwark had made arrangements with Menzel, whom he admired greatly, regarding the execution of the work, and its progress can be followed in their correspondence. When he accepted the commission in December 1886, Menzel had proposed 3000 marks for a vignette but he soon announced that the work 'went beyond the simple basic idea of a "vignette"', using this to justify the delay in finishing it[1]. At the start of July 1887, Menzel 'was getting his breath back after the hectic activity of the last few weeks' and 'hoping for a favourable reception', and announced that his fees were now 18,000 marks. He also demanded the following: 'I must also make a charge for another job, cleaning all the little marks off at the start, using a sponge and water, and obliterating brushmarks over the edges'. 'Time for this was short', as it was to take a photograph[2].

As for the city council, he stressed 'that if time had not been so short, . . . an even more subtle harmony would have been achieved in several details, which would have improved the whole'. What he called 'a certain hastiness' 'which was not always avoidable in this piece of work' is in fact one of its charms today. Menzel added some recommendations on lighting, preferably from above or, if side-lighting were chosen, then 'light from the right would be most advantageous, as this was how it was painted, in other words with the left hand, like everything

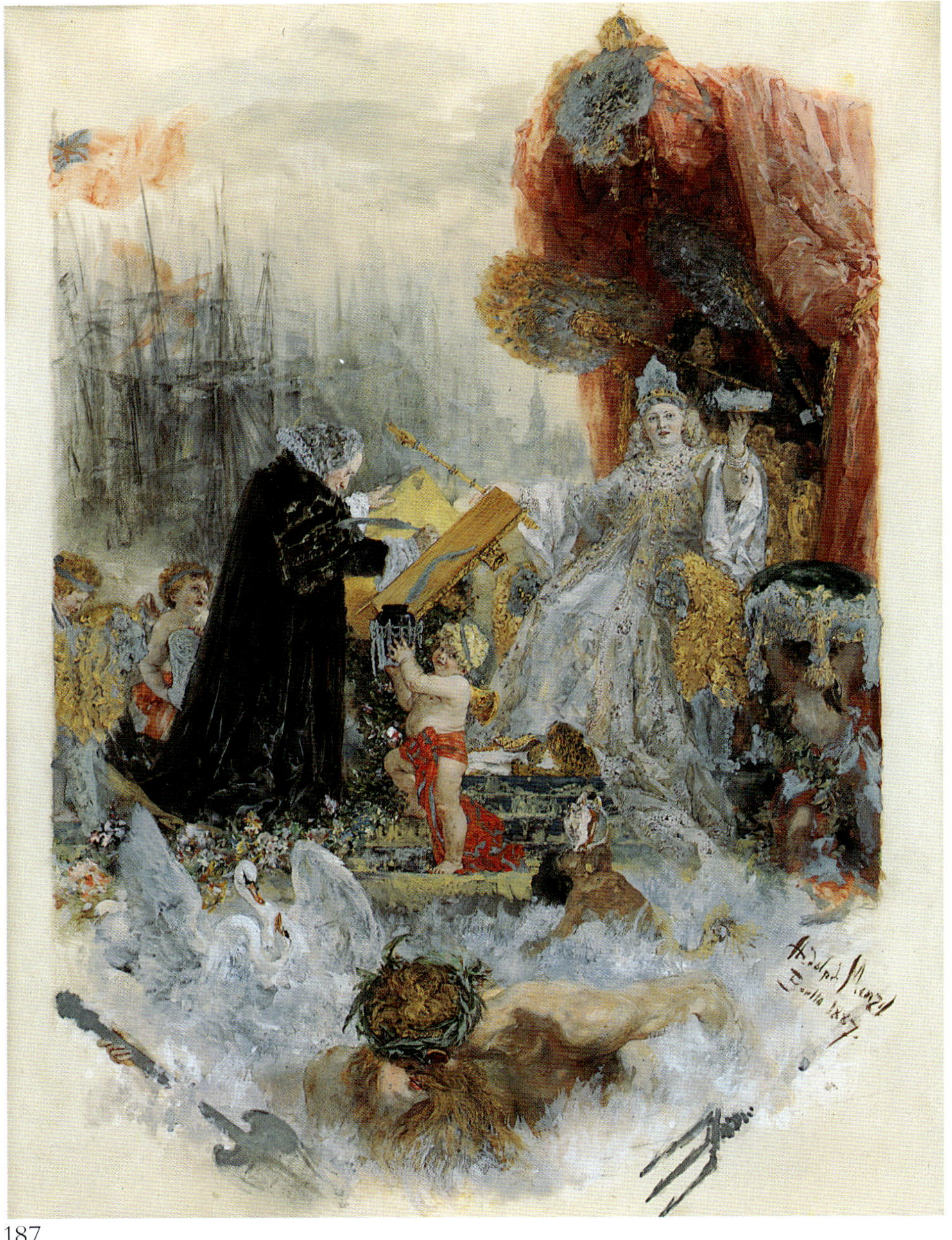

187

I paint in watercolour, and draw'. He felt this was an 'aspect not without interest'[3].

When the work was exhibited at the Kunsthalle in July 1887, the reception was very favourable. Not only had the city council agreed to pay the increased amount without haggling, but Lichtwark gave an enthusiastic description of the watercolour in the *Hamburgischer Korrespondent*, which was soon followed by that of J.Th. Schultz, less inspired but also impassioned[4]. Menzel's creation has a quite unique charm. There was nothing else like it among comparable works, of which there were many during this period. (In 1888 he also painted a diploma of honour from the Royal Berlin Academy for Gustav von Gossler, church minister[5].)

Hammonia, the divinity of the town of Hamburg, is seated on her throne mounted on a red dais, riding on the waves as if she were on some great gondola. The whole composition breathes vigour and gaiety, even humour, down to the smallest details. The goddess's dress glides with a rustling sound towards the waves at her feet which are of the same colour. Here the sea god Neptune and the Elbe join in a kiss. The silver lions with golden manes on either side of the throne caress Hammonia's knees. Lichtwark praised the inventiveness of the silver crown formed from the three towers of the town. The citizens crown she holds in her hand is also silver. The leopard at her feet, the dark-skinned servants, a small Triton, everything evokes Hamburg's commercial dealings with the rest of the world, and the background of the port of the town is formed of a sea of masts. The swans of the Alster frolic lovingly at the feet of the mayor who is wearing his black gown and is flanked by amusing little angels carrying a dragnet and a box containing sand and an inkwell, while he writes an inscription in the great golden book. On the subject of Hammonia, Menzel wrote to Lichtwark: 'At the start I conceived of her as an old woman[6], but gradually gave it up in favour of the general idea of the famous "eternal youth" of the goddesses. However, I couldn't quite create a porcelain beauty out of a woman who had already lived a bit, in the best sense of the word! A woman in her twenties is still fairly young. The imperial eagle in the medallion couldn't be used. To make it recognizable it would have had to be so big that it would have obstructed all the work on her chest. Its rightful place is above'[7]. (Menzel had been supplied with important documentation, a portrait of Hammonia with the imperial eagle on her breast, as 'sign of her affiliation'. Menzel gave her a sceptre, the sign of authority, and set the eagle on the dais.)

M.R.-R.

1. Letter to senator Möring, 30 May 1887, Hamburg, Kunsthalle, archives.
2. Letter to Alfred Lichtwark, 9 July 1887, Hamburg, Kunsthalle, archives.
3. Letter to senator Möring, 7 August 1887, Hamburg, Kunsthalle, archives.
4. Text reproduced in exhib, cat. Hamburg, 1970. *Cf.* here also details on the Schwabe collection.
5. Tschudi, 1905 A, no. 664; location unknown.
6. As can be seen in some preliminary studies (Hamburg, Kunsthalle, Berlin, Kupferstichkabinett and Moscow, Pushkin museum).
7. Letter to Alfred Lichtwark, 22 July 1887, Hamburg, Kunsthalle, archives.

188
Coming out of church
1887

Gouache
15 × 11cm
Signed and dated on the right of the staircase: *Ad. Menzel 87*
Pal (Andorra), Heinrich Merz collection
Exhibited in Washington and Berlin only

Provenance: 1895, Herr Ed. Cohen, Frankfurt am Main; private collections.
Exhibitions: Düsseldorf, 1904, no. 69; Berlin, 1905, no. 225.
Bibliography: Jordan, 1895, p. 72; Jordan, 1905, p. 88; Tschudi, 1905 A, no. 657.

Throughout his long career, Menzel also paid tribute to various areas of genre painting, the most characteristic and widespread mode of expression in nineteenth-century bourgeois art. This aspect has not been examined in great detail, nor has a comparison been made with those done at the time to analyse Menzel's originality and quality within this strongly criticized area of painting. Commissions for great historical works were never given to Menzel. However, he keenly perceived the changes taking place in his time, and gave the portraits of Frederick the Great undertaken at his own initiative psychological characteristics in the manner of genre painters, which brought them closer to the bourgeois sphere. It is all the more remarkable to see how Menzel manages to avoid his last historicized genre paintings, full of freely invented motifs, from falling into the sentimental transformation of reality, through the light, masked irony of his realistic mode of observation. His buyers were almost exclusively well-off businessmen and bankers, with some intellectuals among them. As a sacrifice to the nostalgic conventions of the art of the 'Gründerjahre', Menzel preferred the framework of Dutch baroque painting, whose tradition still kept the radiance of its origins intact. There was a strange residue of baroque style in the Neobaroque period which was felt to be out of date, even in the small 'jewels' of historicized and highly appreciated genre paintings. However, they satisfied the need for representation and identity of a large part of the bourgeoisie.

Menzel's literary leaning, together with his gift for keen observation of

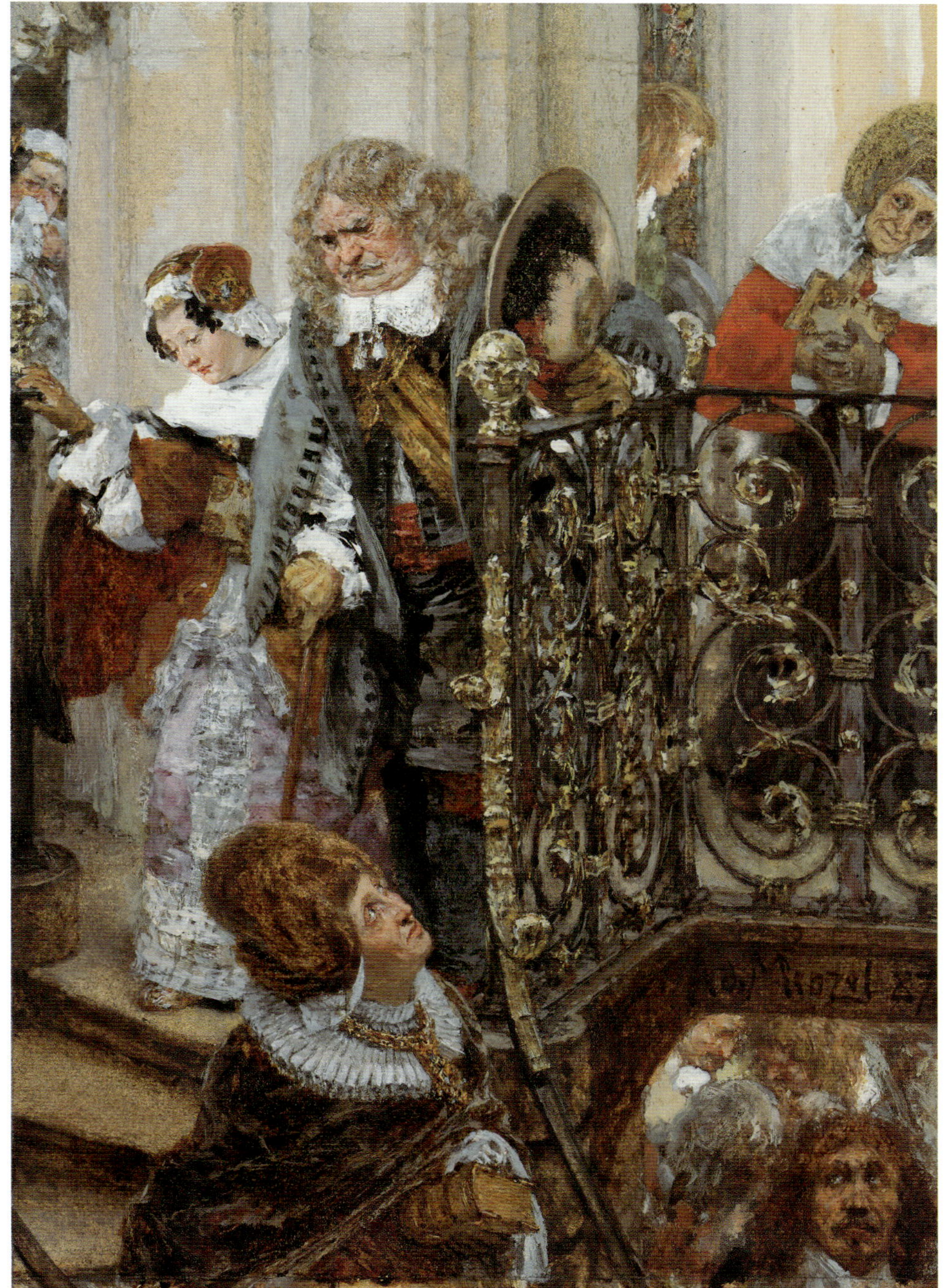

188

people and situations, enabled him to invent small scenes which he always painted with virtuosity and pleasure. In this picture an ill-assorted couple are going home after Mass. Or are they on the way to church, for the wedding of the young girl with a pitiful expression and a rich old stick-in-the-mud? Menzel never failed to create a broad scenario for the onlooker's imagination through a game of insinuation, thus increasing the 'entertainment value' of the work. Judging by its format, this small picture belongs to a series which also contains *Carelessness* and *The Letter*[1]. These works are nearly always prepared from real studies. Menzel was familiar with historical costumes and accessories because he did a number of studies of them in his youth. He never afterwards abandoned this activity[2].

M.R.-R.

1. Both date from 1866; Tschudi, 1905 A, no. 656 and 658; location unknown.
2. Berlin, Kupferstichkabinett; these studies fill a great number of boxes.

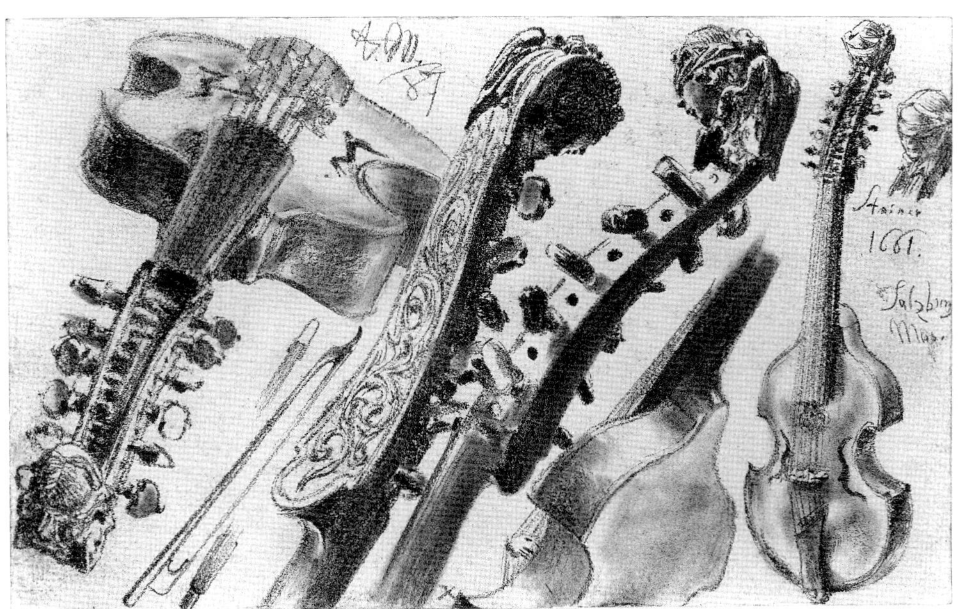

189

189

Viola d'Amore at Salzburg Museum

1887

Pencil
13 × 20.8cm
Signed and dated at the centre top: *A.M.87* – Annotated: *Stainer 1661. Salzburg Mus.*
Berlin, Kupferstichkabinett (SZ Menzel N 4482)
Exhibited in Paris and Washington only

Provenance: Painter's studio; 1905 Emilie Krigar-Menzel; acquired by the museum in 1906.
Exhibitions: Berlin, 1905, no. 2246; Vienna, 1985, no. 62, reprod. p. 131; Copenhagen, 1985, no. 54.
Bibliography: Wirth, 1974, p. 112 *et seq.*

During his numerous stays in Salzburg, Menzel drew a viola d'amore at the Museum Carolino Augusteum from various angles. After the end of the seventeenth century this very fashionable instrument was associated in particular with love, and musicians like Telemann, Quantz, Vivaldi and Benda dedicated compositions to it. It had a particularly soft tone as, in addition to the six or seven gut strings there were as many metal strings. Johann Schorn (born *c.* 1658, died 1718 in Salzburg) is sometimes quoted as the inventor of the classic viola d'amore. His two sons also worked in his workshop, and what they produced are considered today to be on a par with those of Jacob Stainer and Matthias Alban, from the Tyrol[1]. Among numerous other copies, Salzburg museum has a particularly beautiful piece in this viola d'amore, which is acknowledged today as the work of Schorn, although a false label was stuck on it bearing the information 'Jacobus Stainer 1661', which may imply dubious mercantile practices. Menzel must have admitted the attribution of the instrument to Stainer, as the inscription on his drawing shows. What is striking is the beauty of this viola, in particular the elegant dynamism of the scroll with the fine sculpted head of Love, whose eyes are blindfolded, representing the bedazzlement of love which, like the metal strings, blindly follows the tone of what has made it vibrate. As if he had the instrument in his hands, the artist turns round the box, the neck and the scroll from all angles before drawing a final overall view on the right edge of the paper, like a fine silhouette. M.R.-R.

1. *Cf.* Birsack, 1990.

190

Skeleton of a Celtic Woman and Detail of a Statue in Salzburg Museum

c. 1887

Pencil
12.5 × 20.2cm
Signed at the centre bottom: *A.M.* – Annotated: *Ant: Bronze. Mus:Salzb:Keltin*
Berlin, Kupferstichkabinett (SZ Menzel N 3976)
Exhibited in Paris and Washington

Provenance: Painters studio; 1905 Emilie Krigar-Menzel; acquired by the museum in 1906.
Exhibitions: Berlin, 1905, no. 4529; Vienna, 1985, no. 63, reprod. p. 131.

Menzel was accustomed to historical research from his youth onwards, when he acquired the habit as he studied the works of Frederick the Great's time. He rarely missed the opportunity to visit museums. Later he found inspiration for the small genre paintings in Renaissance or baroque costume that he painted to follow fashion. At Salzburg museum he drew the most diverse objects several times, for a number of years. It is like the tourist's passion for collecting curios, or like endless photographs trying to capture a 'far-off beauty', which with growing industrialization had degenerated into an exotic bourgeois adventure. Menzel's drawings appeared to retain undiscerningly everything which passed before his eyes. In this sea of signs, the relationship between form and object became uncertain. It was the start of a search for the wreckage of a lost beauty which continues in art today. In a strangely suggestive configuration, the stretched out skeleton of a Celtic woman, as the annotation tells us, meets the lower half of an antique bronze depicting a young boy. Menzel's powerful pencil was less intent on capturing the material qualities of the bronze and the old bones than in seizing the impression of living flesh next to dead matter. Other drawings done in the same museum transform the interior of the 'small Rococo room' into an orgy of the fragmentary[2]. M.R.-R.

2. Berlin, Kupferstichkabinett, (SZ Menzel N 1323, 3472).

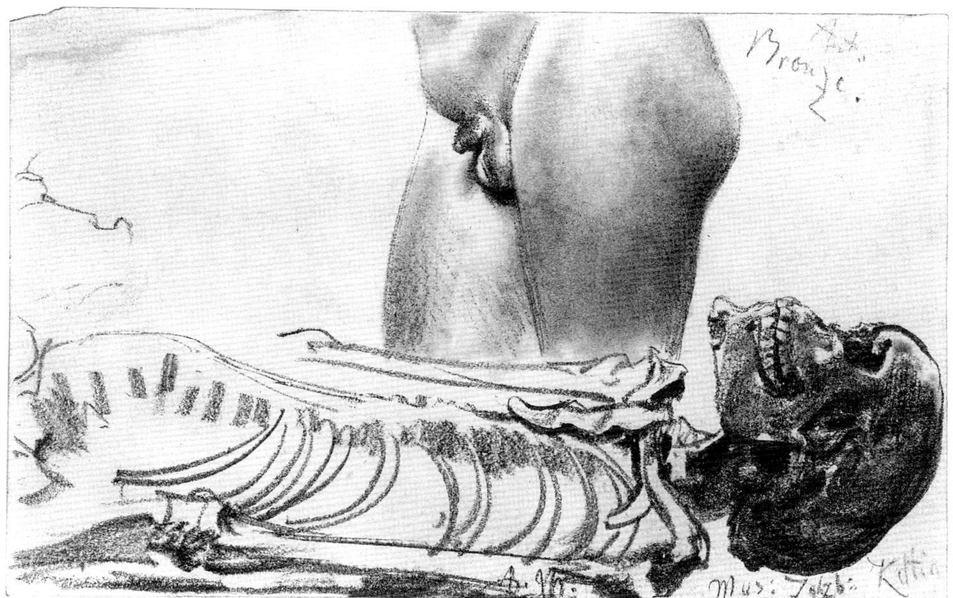

190

191

The Great Staircase at the Chateau of Pommersfelden

1888

Pencil and stump
31.2 × 22.9cm
Signed and dated at the bottom left: *Pommersfelden 11. Sept. 88 A. M.* – Annotated on the back: *Schloss Pommersfelden bei Bamberg. 88.*
Berlin, Kupferstichkabinett (SZ Menzel N 4437)
Exhibited in Washington only

Provenance: Painter's studio; 1905 Emilie Krigar-Menzel; acquired by the museum in 1906.
Exhibitions: Berlin, 1905, no. 2031; Berlin, 1955 A, no. 503.
Bibliography: Wirth, 1974, p. 47, fig. 45.

Menzel appears to have seen the Weissenstein château at Pommersfelden only once. It still belongs to the Schönborn family. At the beginning of September 1888, he was returning from his summer trip to Interlaken and Munich, when he stopped briefly at Pommersfelden, perhaps during an excursion from Bamberg.

The Schönborn's château was built very quickly between 1711 and 1718 from plans by Johann Dientzenhofer, assisted by Maximilian von Welsch and Johann Lukas von Hildebrandt. The great staircase contributes to its homogeneity and the whole is a real milestone in German baroque architecture, in its structure, decoration and painting. It had to be restored one hundred and seventy years later, and the original decoration by Johann Rudolf Byss, now recreated, disappeared under a coat of paint.

One can imagine Menzel at the famous staircase during its restoration. His gaze falls on the central axis half camouflaged by ropes and planks, and on the right part of the staircase whose top and bottom are marked by groups of small angels and vases, temporarily protected by sheets and straw. These attracted him most, so that another sketch was made of *Vases Covered up during Restoration*[1] (fig. 218). The chance situation underlines the playful nature of the decoration even more. Drawing either to memorize or file away, Menzel concentrated on the essential though not necessarily most representative motif, and on determining detail. If any detail appealed enough to his imagination, he put it on a separate page.

Although the drawings today appear somewhat abstract and surreal, Menzel was nonetheless faithful to the spectacle before him, and only the angle and frame are unconventional. A.H.

1. Berlin, Kupferstichkabinett, (SZ Menzel N 46).

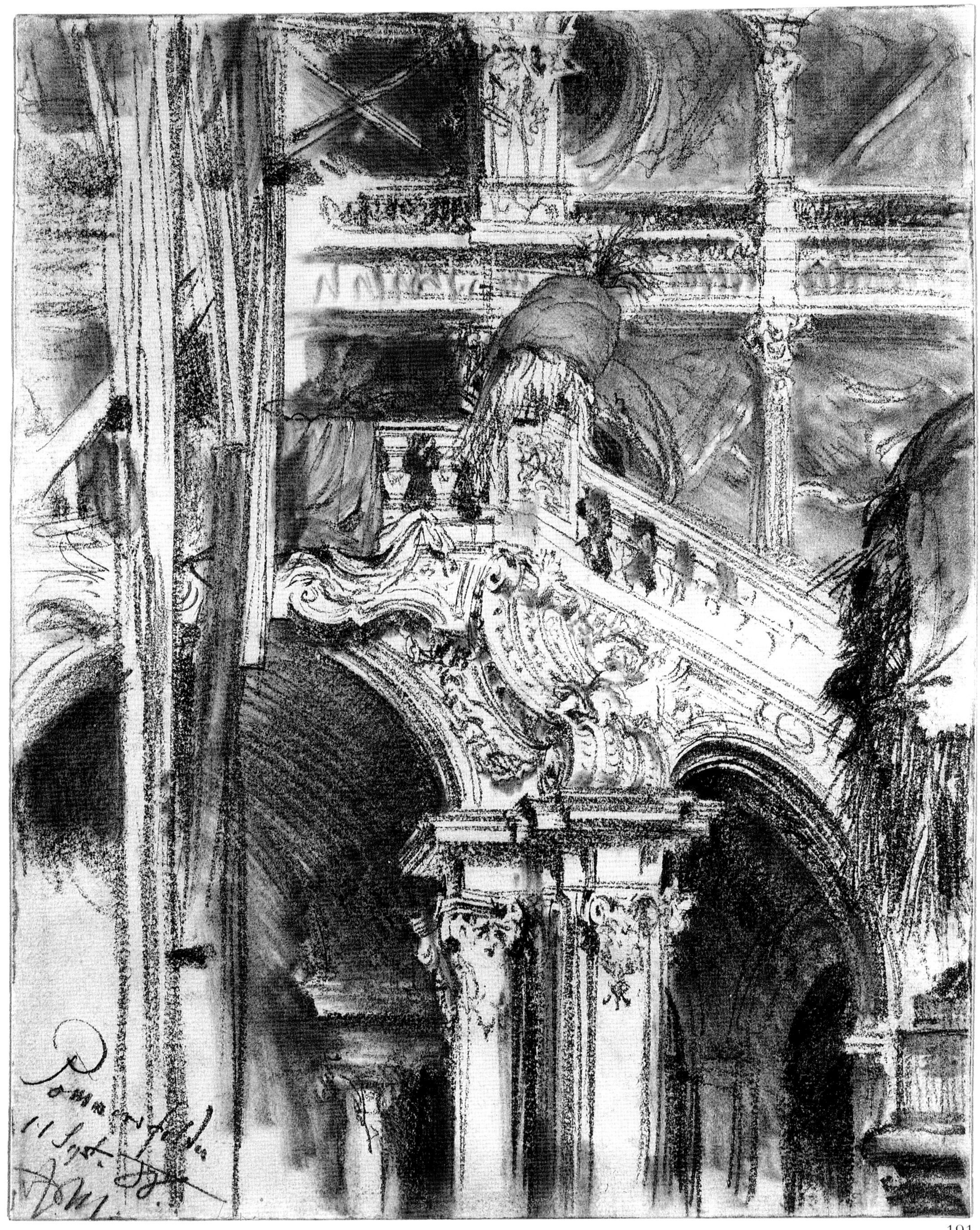

191

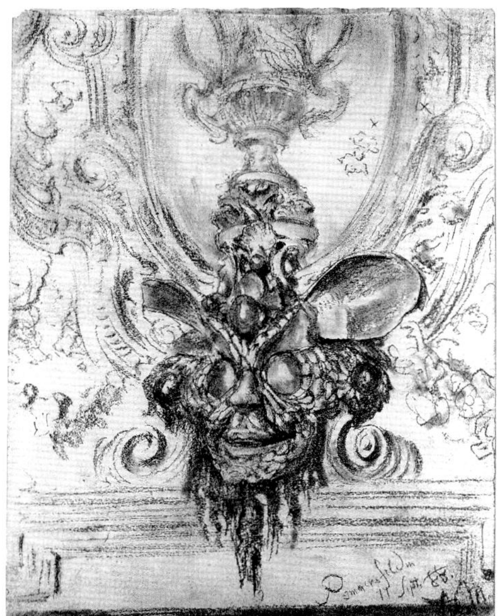

Fig. 217. *Cartouche in Château at Pommersfelden*, 1888, pencil, Berlin, Kupferstichkabinett (N 1)

Fig. 218. *Château at Pommersfelden, stairwell. Vases protected during restoration*, 1888, pencil, Berlin, Kupferstichkabinett (N 46)

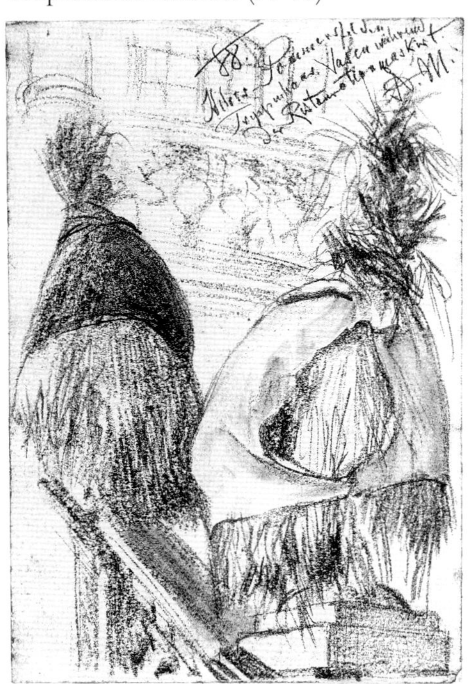

192

Kurhausstrasse at Kissingen after a Storm

1889

Pencil
18.1 × 11.7cm
Signed and dated at the centre bottom: *A.M.89.*
Berlin, Kupferstichkabinett (SZ Menzel N 2558)

Provenance: Painter's studio; 1905 Emilie Krigar-Menzel; acquired by the museum in 1906.
Exhibitions: Berlin, 1905, no. 6090; Berlin, 1980 A, no. 387, reprod. p. 403; Vienna, 1985, no. 136, reprod. p. 198; Copenhagen, 1985, no. 115, reprod.; New York, 1990, no. 65, reprod. p. 70.

Menzel drew street scenes from a window in his youth[1]. Originally he undoubtedly wanted to get to know his subjects by drawing them from varied angles[2]. Later, perhaps under Japanese influence, he used a bird's-eye view in some of his gouaches. In *Ash Wednesday Morning*[3] (1885) and in *Lady Walking by a Fountain in the Kissingen Spa Garden* (cat. 184), the composition is dominated by a road or path crossing the image diagonally, as in the drawing shown here, from top right to bottom left. The horizon, which does not appear here, recedes in the gouaches to the upper edge of the paper. In the same year as *Kurhausstrasse in Kissingen*, Menzel painted the *Road along the Schöneberg Quay*, whose horizontal format is intersected along the same diagonal by a road[4]. The same applies to the colour study of 1890, *Dinner for the Painter Carl Becker*, with its long table covered in white and viewed from above[5].

These unusual, unorthodox perspectives and layouts of figures and objects link Menzel to Caillebotte and Degas. Much later, when drawing had become his main means of expression, abstraction is more common. The object as such is lost in the amorphous and equivocal. In the drawing shown here, which depicts a street transformed into a torrent by a storm[6], the perspective only serves to emphasize the flow of water. It seems all the more dynamic since, in contrast, there are branches on the right, arranged in an almost decorative way. As if he had foreseen a time which turned away from objectivity, in his old age Menzel often saw the destructive nature of phenomena, everything which decomposes and deteriorates, and he describes the threat of this intermediate world. Here the signature corresponds to the door frame sketched diagonally facing, and facilitates orientation. The aesthetics of this drawing bring to mind Japanese calligraphy, and it could be that Menzel was aware of that particular aspect in this work. M.R.-R.

1. Berlin, Kupferstichkabinett, (SZ Menzel N 46).
1. Berlin, Kupferstichkabinett, sketchbook 7 (1839-46), p. 72 and 78.
2. *Cf.* the wax figurines at Monbijou palace, later Hohenzollernmuseum (Berlin, Kupferstichkabinett, SZ Menzel Kat 376).
3. Tschudi, 1905 A, no. 653; location unknown (before 1945, Berlin, Nationalgalerie).
4. Signed and dated: *23 Aug. 89, A.M.;* Switzerland, private collection. Reprod. in sale catalogue of a Berlin collection at Hans W. Lange, Berlin, 1939, no. 13.
5. Berlin, Kupferstichkabinett, (SZ Menzel N 1487).
6. 'Kissingen, the Kurhausstrasse after a storm' is written on the back of the drawing, probably by the heirs.

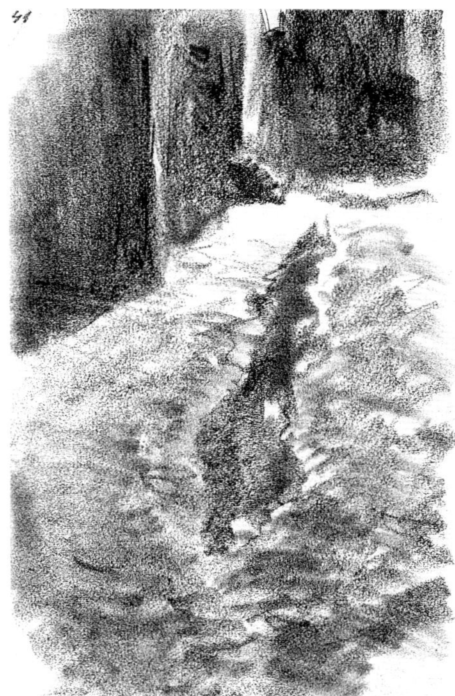

Fig. 219. *Puddles in a Street*, 1890, pencil, Berlin, Kupferstichkabinett (sketchbook 66, p. 41)

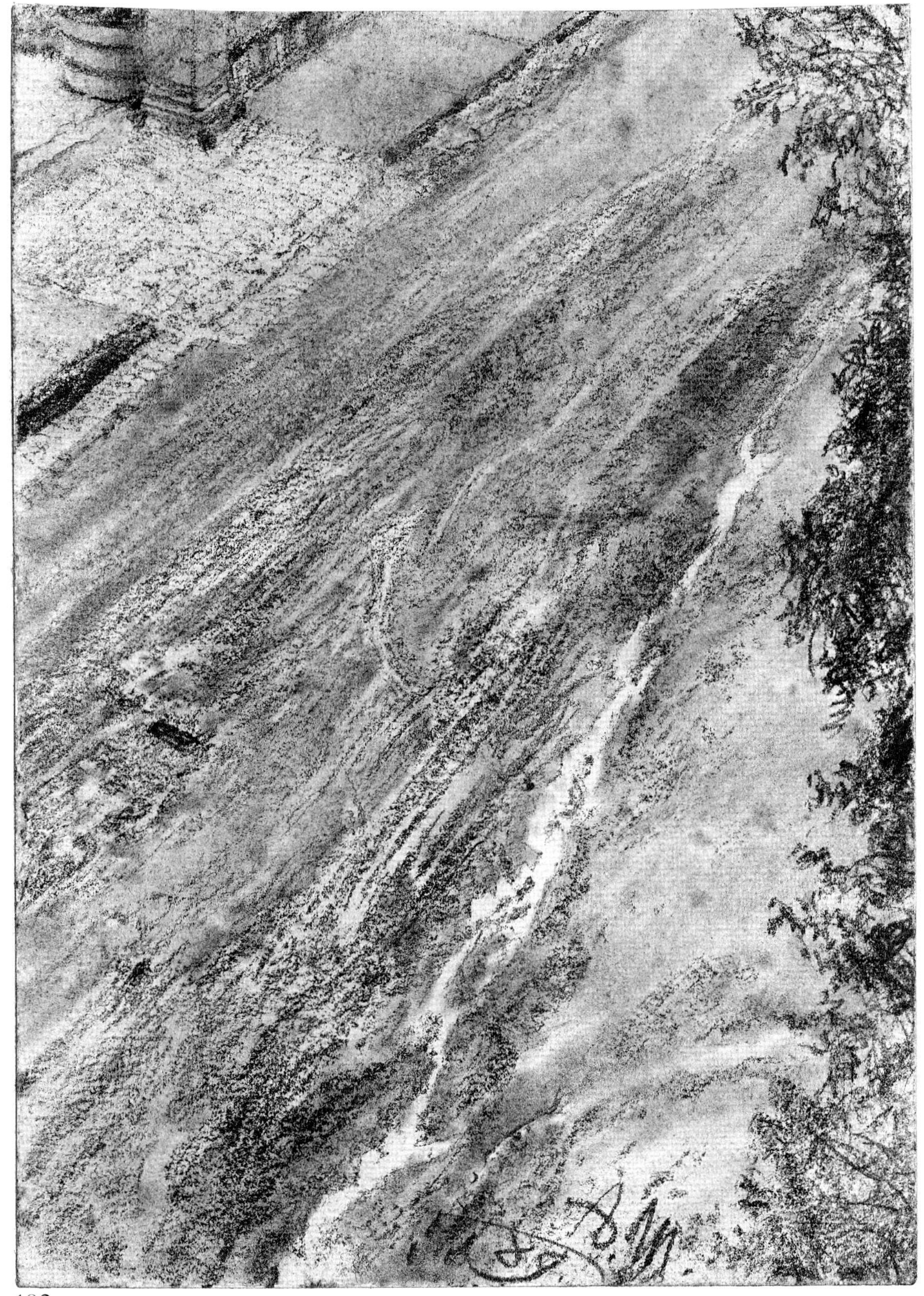

192

193

Old Documents in a Chest

c. 1880–90

Pencil
20.9 × 12.8cm
Berlin, Kupferstichkabinett (SZ Menzel N 1278)

Provenance: Painter's studio; 1905 Emilie Krigar-Menzel; acquired by the museum in 1906.
Exhibition: Berlin, 1905, no. 2317.

It is reported that, during his stay in the spa town of Kissingen, Menzel climbed the stairs of the town hall several times to admire the two old chests belonging to the town's merchant guilds and to look at 'the magnificent ironwork of the time'[1]. The drawing shown here probably portrays one of these chests. Objects in disorder never ceased to haunt Menzel, and marked his work as a draughtsman as well as a painter. The late dating of *Old Documents in a Chest* is indicated by the vigorous use of a carpenter's pencil, where the thick line is laid on top of the clouds of grey left previously by the stump. The plunging view shows the object at an angle and creates a refined effect, worthy of the ageing painter (*cf.* cat. 192). The ornamentation on the front of the chest is scarcely noticeable, and it is not the beautiful Renaissance decoration of the chest that attracts the attention, but the disorder of its contents, the old papers, letters and seals, and documents tied up with string. Faced with the absurdity of the real, Menzel seeks the symbolic. M.R.-R.

1. Vollmar, (1905-6) 1992, p. 255.

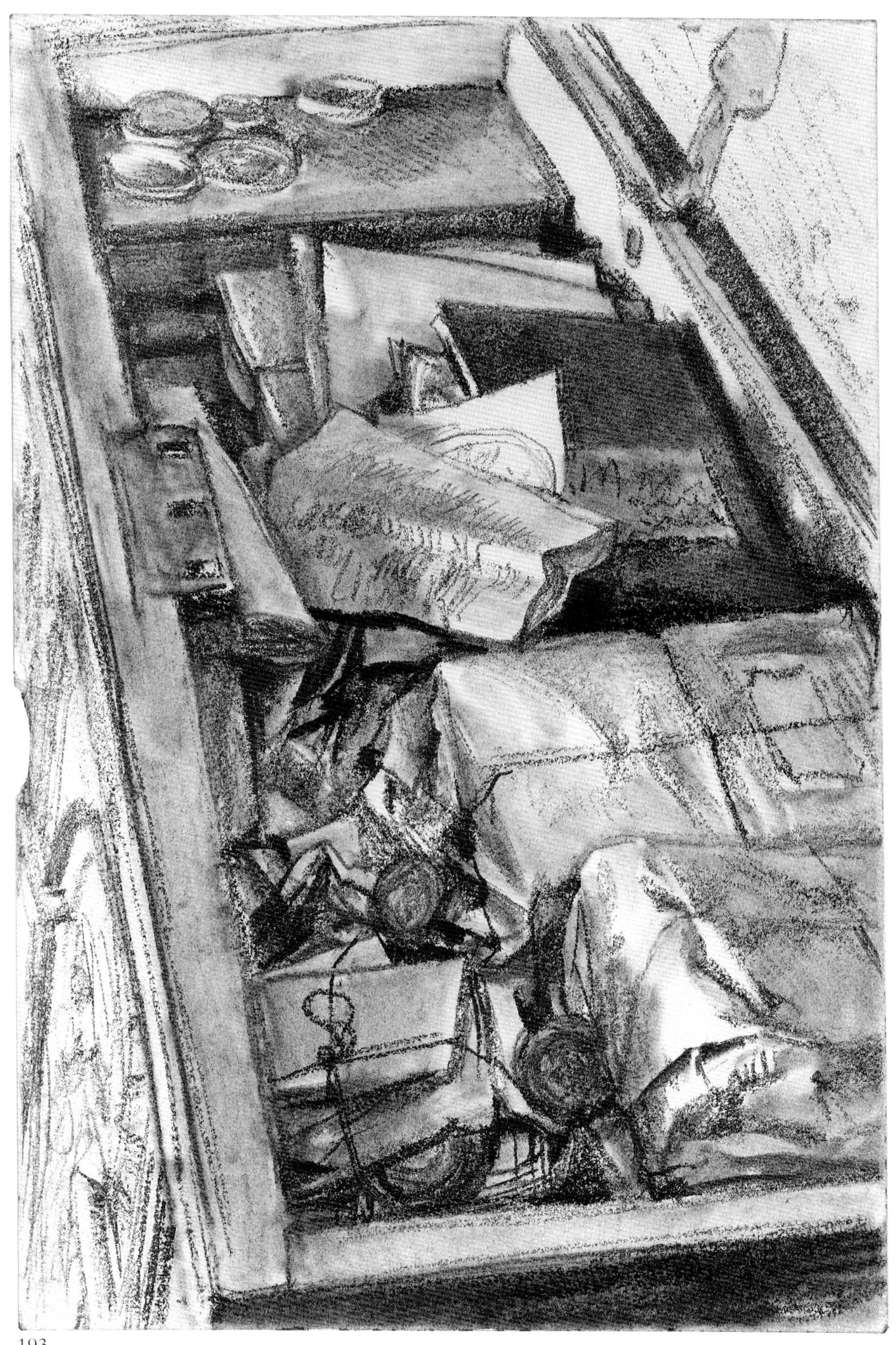

193

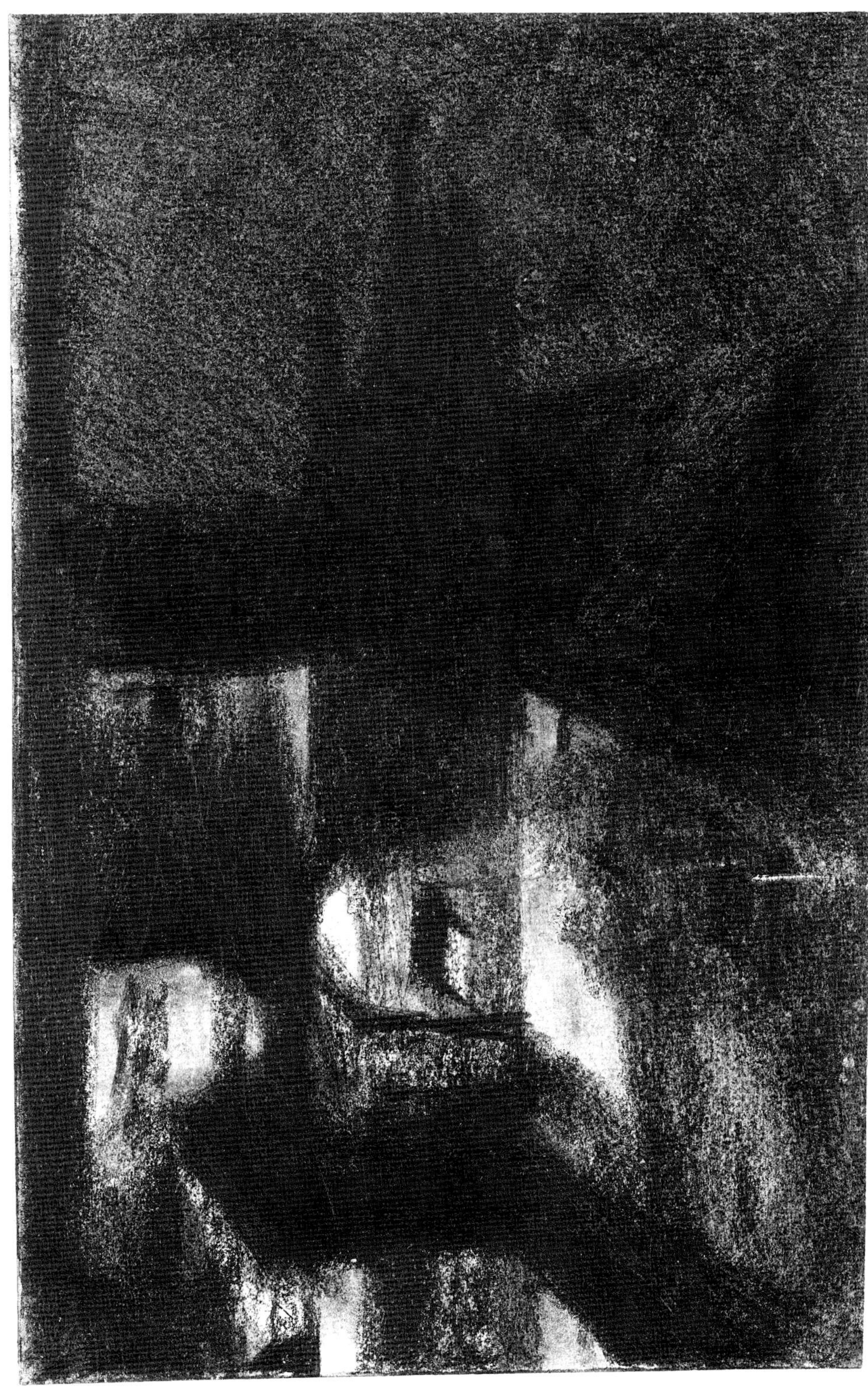

194

194

Tower of a Renaissance Chateau at Night

c. 1880–90

Pencil
20.8 × 12.1cm
Berlin, Kupferstichkabinett (SZ Menzel N 2920)
Exhibited in Washington only

Provenance: Painter's studio; 1905 Emilie Krigar-Menzel; acquired by the museum in 1906.
Exhibitions: Berlin, 1905, no. 4307; Berlin, 1955 A, no. 527; Vienna, 1985, no. 130, reprod. p. 194.

A corner of the courtyard of a Renaissance château can be seen from a high window, a tower with a pointed roof in the middle of the drawing. On the left the window-frame looks dark, kindling the onlooker's curiosity to know what is near the light. The gaze runs along the walls with their vague shapes, and the roof blends into the darkened sky. Once more Menzel's view of reality veers towards the abstract. The angle chosen is significant, and a diagonal broken twice marks the composition (*cf.* cat. 192). These types of drawing were probably done in the late 1880s. On the heavy grained paper, the broad surfaces are covered by a single tone without nuances, and flanked by a generous black. The wood of the pencil has scratched off a fine layer of graphite so as to reveal in places areas of white paper. A.H.

195

Detail of the Tomb of the Prince von Thurn und Taxis at St Emmeram in Regensburg

c. 1890

Pencil
20.2 × 12.9cm
Berlin, Kupferstichkabinett (SZ Menzel N 87)
On view only in Berlin

Provenance: Painter's studio; 1905 Emilie Krigar-Menzel; acquired by the museum in 1906.
Exhibition: Berlin, 1905, no. 2071.

The ancient conventual church of the Benedictines, St Emmeram's, at Regensburg contains the tomb of Prince Alexander Ferdinand von Thurn und Taxis (1704–73). Between 1731 and 1733 this Romanesque basilica was given new interior decoration by the Asam brothers, under the direction of Johann Michael Prunner of Linz. In the west transverse nave, near the Romanesque crypt of Saint Wolfgang, the court sculptor Simon Sorg between 1774 and 1777 raised the magnificent baroque memorial that was drawn by the visitor from Berlin, though at a time that cannot be pinpointed as he visited Regensburg on several occasions.

Menzal ignored the structure of this monumental edifice, its precious materials in varied colours, the figures of Justice and the Pietà, cherubs carrying the attributes of Hope and Love, and Fides crowning it all, and focused only on the base of the tomb, which from the side looked to him like a block covered in scrolls, raised up on some steps, on the last rounded one of which rests the robe of Death. The angle chosen makes the figure, with its scythe, stand out from the tomb and from the drapery, its skull and thorax exposed to view.

A study of the same tomb is devoted to the skull wrapped in the drapery[1]. Death apparently preoccupied Menzel increasingly as he reached seventy. The drawing *End of the Game* dated 1895 (missing since 1945) showed that these thoughts continued to haunt him. This striking *memento mori* shows Menzel's deserted studio, from where a small model elephant is trying to escape. The composition shown in *Detail of the Tomb* indicates that strange and profoundly expressive situations stimulated him to take out his pencil and sketchbook. His acute sensitivity to shape always led him to create works of an extraordinary quality. A.H.

1. Berlin, Kupferstichkabinett, (SZ Menzel N 88).

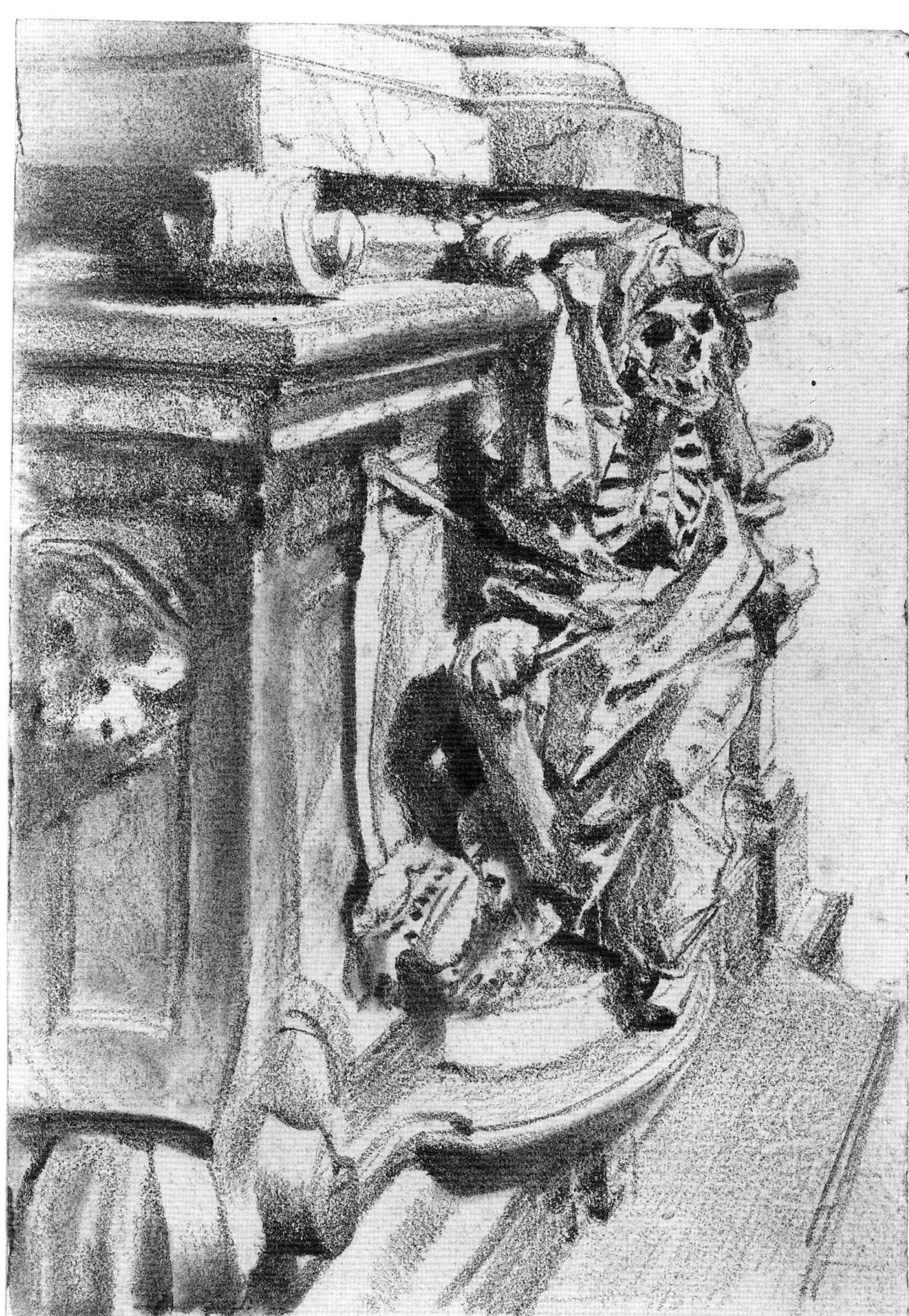

195

196

Pulpit of the Augustinian Church in Würzburg

1890

Pencil
31.3 × 23cm
Signed and dated at the bottom left: *A.M. 90. Würzburg. Augustiner-Kirche.*
Berlin, Kupferstichkabinett (SZ Menzel N 163)

Provenance: Painter's studio; 1905 Emilie Krigar-Menzel; acquired by the museum in 1906.
Exhibitions: Berlin, 1905, no. 3606; Copenhagen, 1985, no. 57.
Bibliography: Exhib. cat. Hamburg, 1982, p. 273, fig. 98.

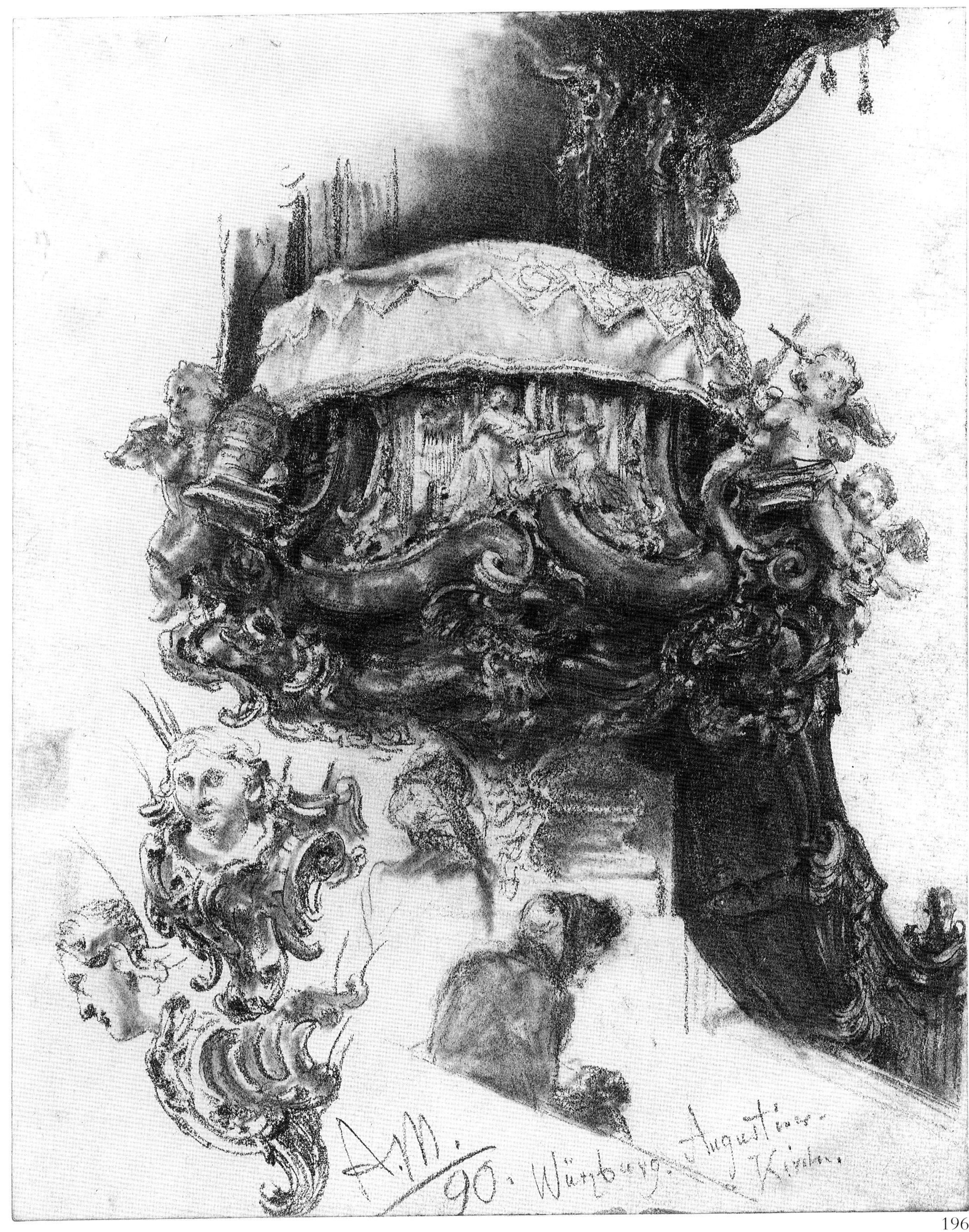

196

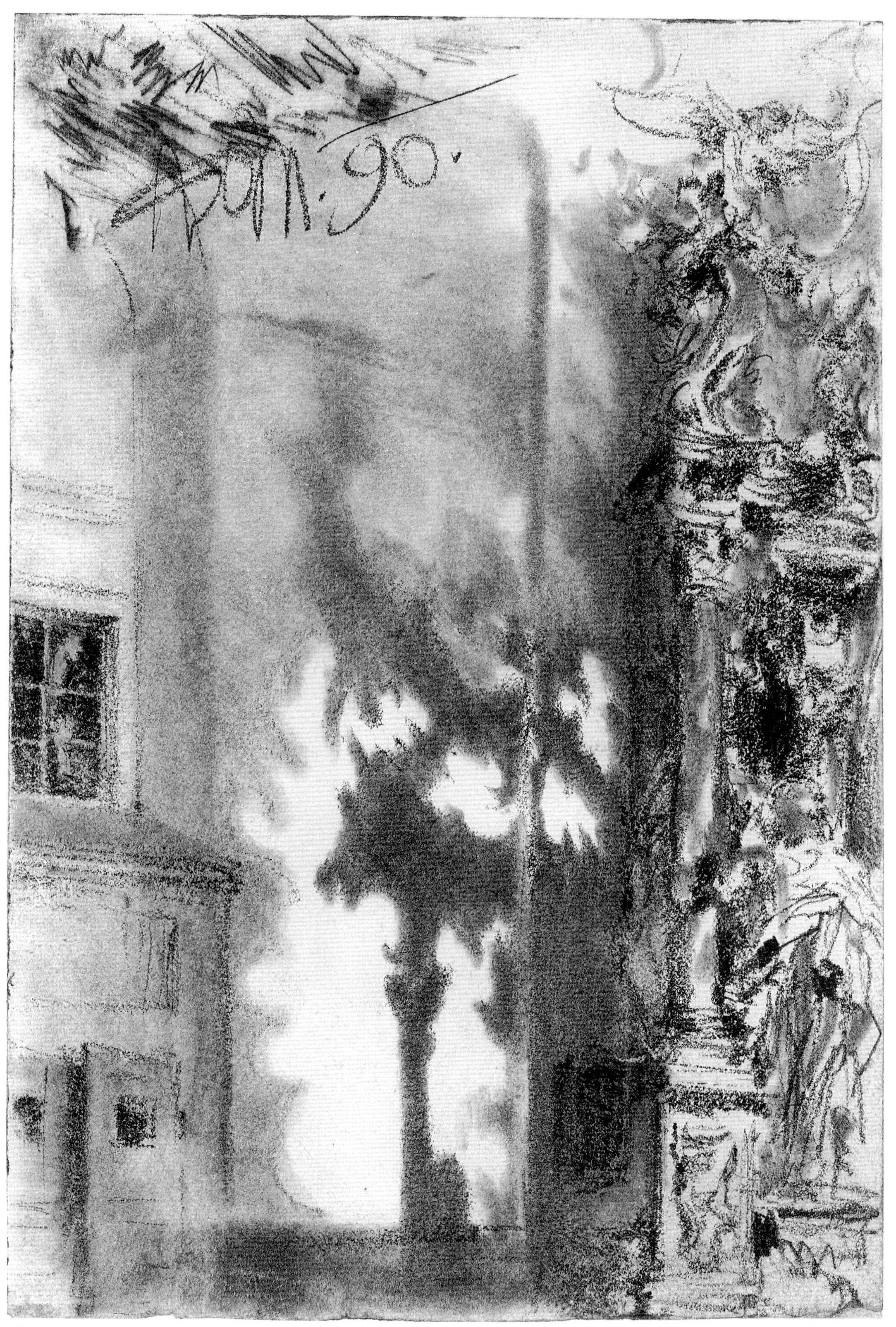

197

During his summer trip in 1890, Menzel once more sought out the Baroque. Both on the way to and from Kissingen, he stopped to draw at Veitshöchheim and, especially, at Würzburg. He made numerous drawings of the Augustinian church, one of the most famous buildings in the town. In the eighteenth century Balthasar Neumann had used all his skill to match the style of the new main nave to the early Gothic choirstalls. Two years later Menzel would focus on the sober stucco decoration on the ribs of the vault by Antonio Bossi, and in the same church would draw a baroque Pietà, which was destroyed during World War II[1]. In 1890 he drew part of one of the rococo altars and the shadow it cast on the wall (cat. 197). He also drew the pulpit with its bell and opulent wooden carvings, which like the altars, forms part of the sumptuous interior decoration created by the workshops of the court sculptor Johann Wolfgang von der Auvera (1708–56). Using the old woman sitting on a pew under the pulpit, Menzel did another sketch catching her as she stands up. There is similar duplication on the left, with detailed studies of the angel's head console from two different perspectives. A separate drawing[2] depicts the sounding-board of the pulpit and the lavish sculpture surmounting it. M.R-R.

1. Berlin, Kupferstichkabinett (SZ Menzel N 60).
2. Karlsruhe, Kunsthalle.

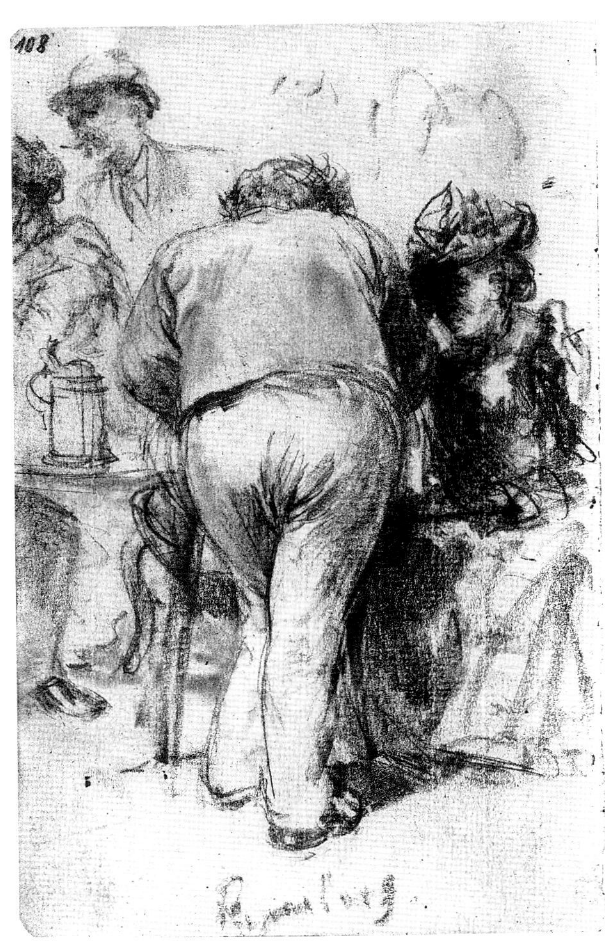

Fig. 220. *At the Open-air Café*, 1892–3, pencil, Berlin, Kupferstichkabinett (sketchbook 68, p. 100)

197
Shadow Cast by the Altar Decoration in the Augustinian Church in Würzburg
1890

Pencil and stump
20.6 × 12.8cm
Signed and dated at the top left: *A.M. 90*
Berlin, Kupferstichkabinett (SZ Menzel N 60)

Provenance: Painter's studio; 1905 Emilie Krigar-Menzel; acquired by the museum in 1906.

Exhibitions: Berlin, 1905, no. 2048; Vienna, 1985, no. 137, reprod. p. 199; Copenhagen, 1985, no. 117, reprod. p. 72; New York, 1990, no. 67, reprod. p. 198.

When Menzel was a young man of twenty he described a High Mass held on the day of Pentecost at the Catholic church in Berlin[1]. Later, during his summer journeys to southern Germany he was to stop endless times at its Baroque churches. When he stayed in Kissingen in Franconia (*cf.*cat. 184–6, 192, 203), he visited the bishop's residence at Würzburg with its magnificent, heavily baroque churches on several occasions. The overall view drawn in 1895 from a rapid glance over the houses at the foot of the heights above the River Main[2] was of less interest to him than the profusion of details in church interiors. He not only drew Riemenschneider's episcopal tombs, but also the beautiful decoration of the Augustinian church, built by Balthasar Neumann at the end of the Baroque period (*cf.* cat. 196), and that in other churches in Würzburg[3]. He was fascinated by the play of ghostly shadows cast on a church wall by the shapes on one of the altars made at the von der Auvera workshop. He caught the play of light and shadow nuanced from palest grey to the deepest black, using pencil and stump. Numerous drawings bear witness to Menzel's liking for the amorphous and even grotesque appearance of cloudy skies, a dirty wall or even a road flooded with rainwater (*cf.* cat. 192). M.R.-R.

1. Letter to Carl Heinrich Arnold, 5 May 1836, Wolff, 1914, p. 7 [dated March instead of May].
2. Berlin, Kupferstichkabinett (SZ Menzel N 52).
3. Berlin, Kupferstichkabinett; Hamburg, Kunsthalle; Karlsruhe, Kunsthalle.

198

Study of Bicycle

1890

Pencil
18.5 × 11.5cm
Signed and dated at the top left: *A.M./90.*
Berlin, Kupferstichkabinett (SZ Menzel N 2490)

Provenance: Painter's studio; 1905 Emilie Krigar-Menzel; acquired by the museum in 1906.
Exhibitions: Berlin, 1905, no. 4105e; Berlin, n.d., no. 148.

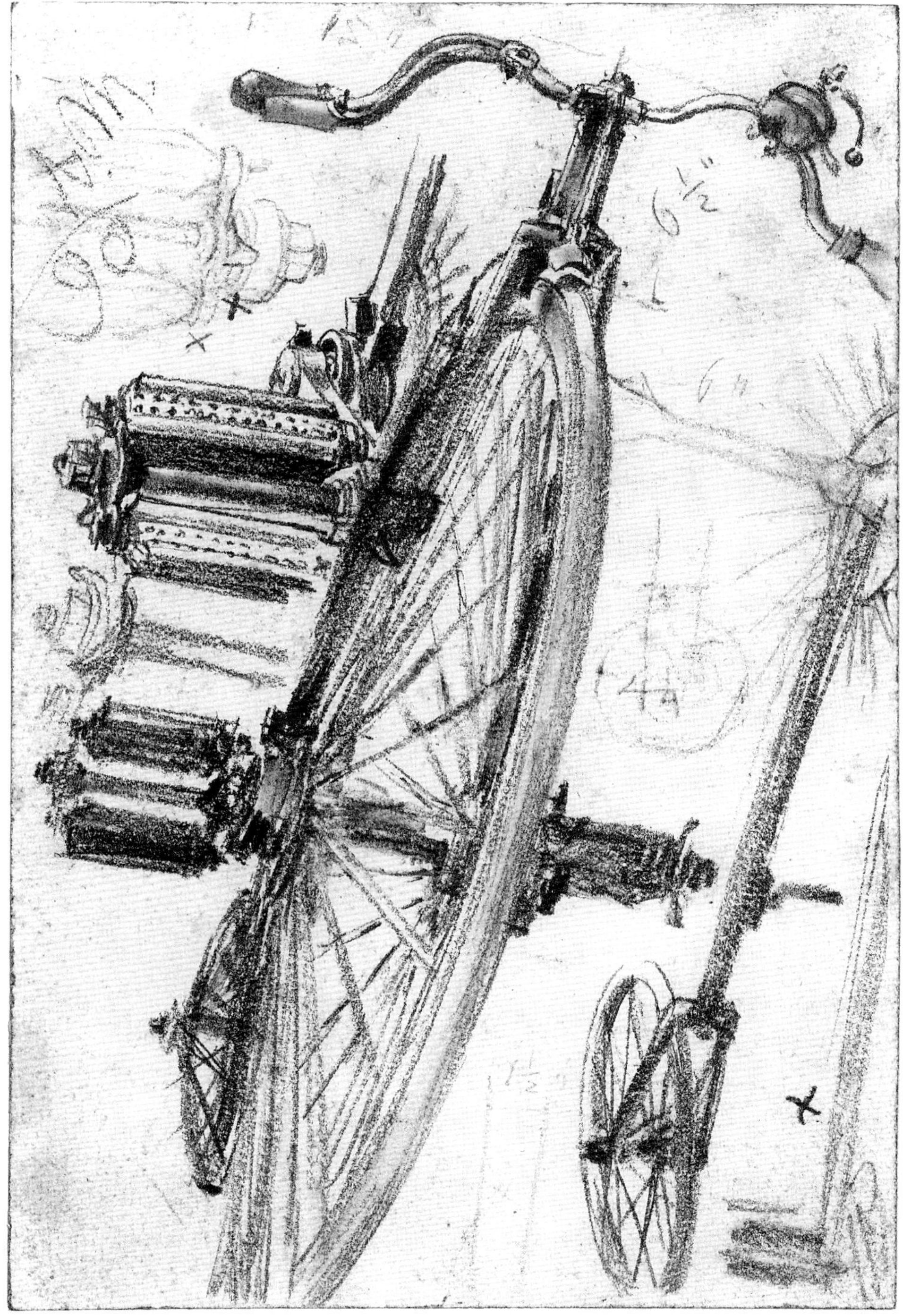

198

'Some time ago a small man went into a Berlin bicycle shop . . . and asked if he could make some sketches. He came every evening for a week and did one sketch after another until he was satisfied. It was the master Adolph Menzel who had a painting on his easel in which one of the figures was a cyclist'[1]. These studies were in preparation for the small gouache *Open-air Café at Kissingen* of 1891[2]. Three days before his death, on 6 February 1905, this gouache was purchased by the Gemäldegalerie in Dresden through the Pröll-Heuer foundation, which supported living artists by buying their works. This was Menzel's second work to join the Dresden collection, by chance to a certain extent. The price of 35,000 Reichsmarks for a 14 × 17cm format gouache was exceptional. In 1923 the work was exchanged for the picture *The Women Friends* by Lovis Corinth (1904) in the hands of the Berlin art dealer Nicolai. Then we lose trace of it. However, the pencil sketches of the bicycle went to the Nationalgalerie from the Menzel estate. Of the six sketches preserved, he used something from each for the gouache. The few drawings remaining after so many hours spent in the shop may be explained because Menzel sorted out of his drawings rigorously and only kept those he needed for his work. When he had seen them, Paul Meyerheim remarked that: '. . . it was as if he worked in a bicycle factory'[3]. This was because Menzel noted down measurements and proportions in great detail, so that we have an exact idea of the bicycle of his day. Nevertheless, the 'last style' of Menzel was not a technical exercise but one of great subtlety which stimulates the imagination and creates the aesthetic dimension of his drawings.

A.H.

1. *Die Kunst für Alle,* 1893, p. 12.
2. Tschudi, 1905 A, no. 673.
3. Meyerheim, (1906) 1992, p. 185.

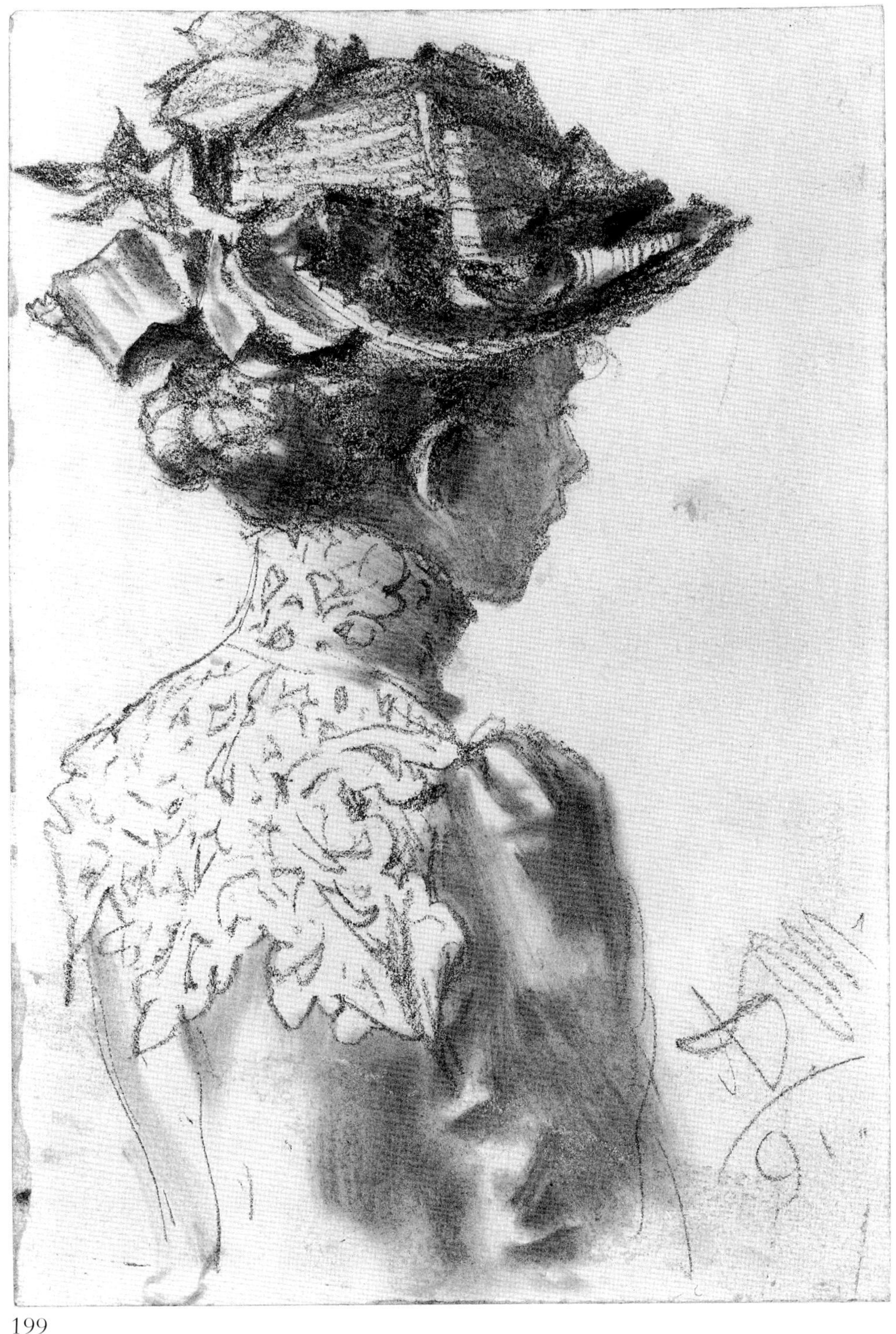

199

199

Young Woman Wearing a Hat, Half-Profile

1891

Pencil
20.6 × 2.9cm
Signed and dated at the bottom right: *A.M. 91*
Berlin, Kupferstichkabinett (SZ Menzel N 2049)
Exhibited in Washington only

Provenance: Painter's studio; 1905 Emilie Krigar-Menzel; acquired by the museum in 1906.
Exhibition: Berlin, 1905, no. 3897.

A young woman seated and elegantly attired, in a high-collared dress lavishly trimmed with lace and topped with a hat decorated with ribbons, posed for this study. The delicate contours of her face are lost in the shadow. For Menzel, this type of half-length drawing of models is very common from the 1890s onwards, although there are only a few drawings of young girls as he felt their faces lacked narrative elements. Here the model's head leans slightly to one side, with her mouth slightly open, and her eyelashes hide her expression, though her clothing seeks to dominate. At first glance it certainly seems as if her dress is the most important element, as a representation of external signs. On closer inspection, a hidden story is condensed in the face in profile, revealing the inner being. The drawings of Menzel's later years are characterized by this duality.

The drawing is executed in very minute detail, and there is no reason to think it was done on the spot. Menzel did not use it afterwards; it formed part of his stock, although it could have found a place among the Kissingen gouaches[1]. The recourse to a shaft of light falling as it does in this drawing is more accentuated in the drawing technique Menzel developed in his last years. A clear black on the stumped grey surrounds touches of light. The whole acquires a pictorial value which could not have been achieved any better using colour. A.H.

1. *Walk to Kissingen fountain*, 1890; Tschudi, 1905 A, no. 674; Euerbach, Georg Schäfer collection. – *Open-air café at Kissingen*, 1891; Tschudi, 1905 A, no. 673; location unknown. *Breakfast buffet given by a high-class bakery in Kissingen*, 1893, (cat. 203).

200

Altar of Salzburg Collegiate Church against the Light

1892

Pencil
17.9 × 11.9cm
Berlin, Kupferstichkabinett (SZ Menzel N 3456)
On view only in Berlin

Provenance: Painter's studio; 1905 Emilie Krigar-Menzel; acquired by the museum in 1906.
Exhibitions: Berlin, 1905, no. 5907; Vienna, 1985, no. 64, reprod. p. 132.

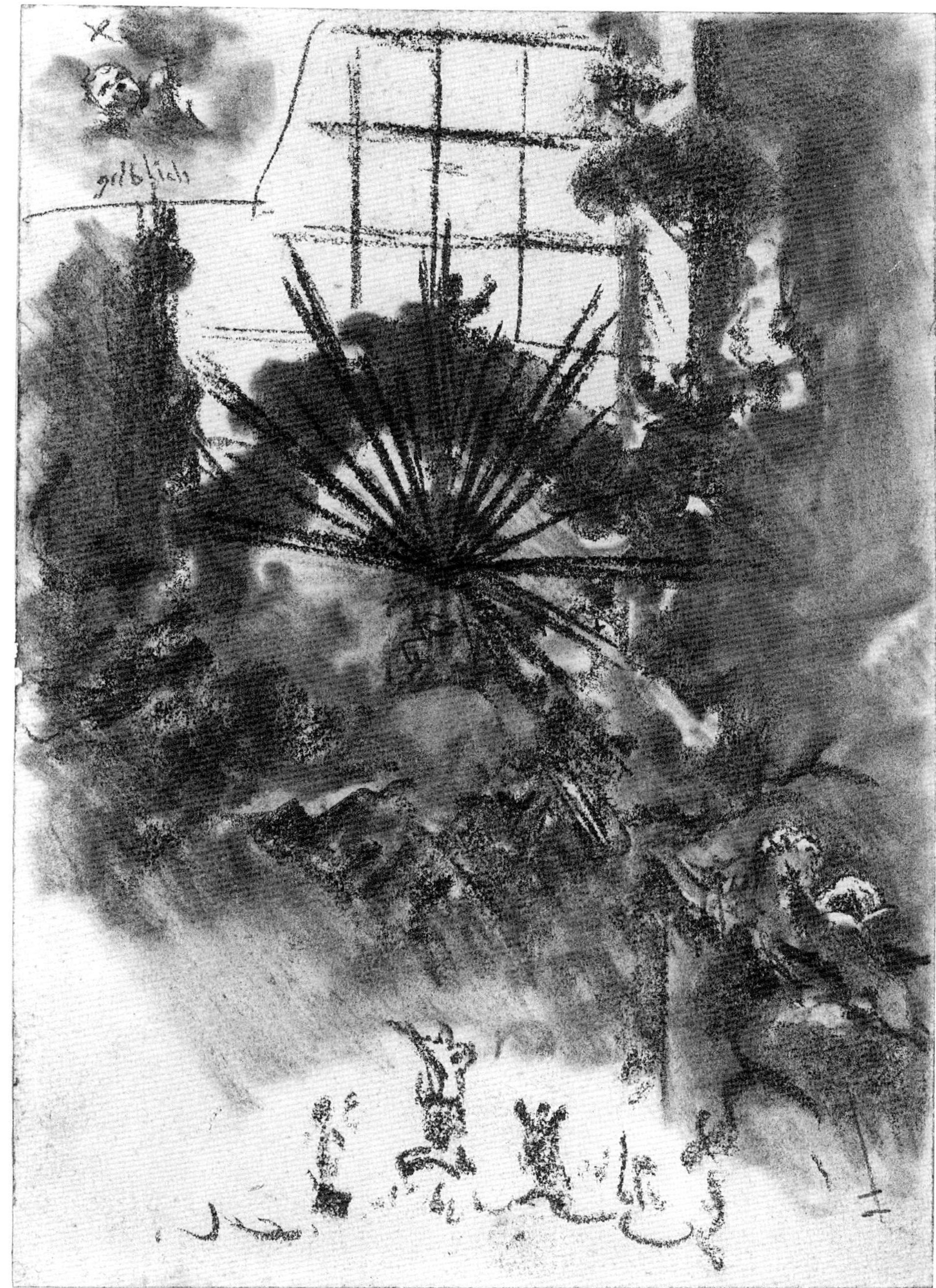

200

The exceptional unity of the baroque style of the bishop's residence in Salzburg captivated Menzel to such a degree that in his later years he returned fifteen times during different summer trips. Most of the main baroque buildings appear in drawings and coloured works, as well as other typical features of this town (cat. 170, 189, 190). At night he walked through the streets looking for subjects, and the magnificent drawing in his 1871 sketchbook of a group of horse trainers sculpted by Michael Mandl, which rises up in front of the palace marshal's watering trough has a hallucinatory chiaroscuro effect[1], yet it is just one composition among many. His pencil immortalized one of the narrow streets dominated by the moonlit façade of the collegiate church, the masterpiece of the baroque art of Fischer von Erlach. By day he drew interior views of the church, austere and vertical, particularly the area around the altar, clearly delimited by two monumental, isolated columns[2]. The Immaculate Conception soars above the Earth, surrounded by angels and putti, and clouds both large and small. Below, a colonnade crowned by a St Michael and angels surrounds the tabernacle flanked by Hope and Love on the main altar dating from 1740, and the Holy Spirit hovers over the central figure in the form of a dove. While the 1871 sketchbook gives an overall view of this complex work, the later drawing shown here (from 1892, according to the date on a detailed drawing made in the same church[3]) directs the gaze to the aureole. Here Menzel is seeking only the expressiveness and picturesque effect of this celestial illusion produced by the union of decorative forms and the dazzling light which comes through the windows. Two years before, a comparable drawing was inspired by the Augustinian church in Würzburg. Its phantasmagorical effect stems from the play of light on the opulent decoration of the altar (cat. 197). M.R.-R.

1. Berlin, Kupferstichkabinett, sketchbook 36 (1871), p. 109–10.
2. Berlin, Kupferstichkabinett, sketchbook 36 (1871), p. 121, p. 131–2, p. 139.
3. Berlin, Kupferstichkabinett (SZ Menzel N 779); *cf.* also SZ Menzel N 481.

201
Quiet Corner (Corner of an Old Park, with Two Cats)
1892

Oil on canvas, wood backing
37.5 × 22.5cm
Signed and dated at the bottom left: *Ad. Menzel 92*
Frankfurt am Main, Städelsches Kunstinstitut (1935)
Exhibited in Berlin only

Provenance: Eduard Behrens, Hamburg; Probst collection, Mannheim; acquired by the museum in 1938.
Exhibitions: Berlin, 1895 A, no. 60; Hamburg, 1896, no. 21; Düsseldorf, 1904, no. 15; Berlin, 1905, no. 45; Berlin, 1928, no. 51.
Bibliography: Jordan, 1890, p. 73; Heilbut, 1898, p. 22, pl. facing p. 22; Jordan, 1895, p. 4, p. 10, reprod.; Jordan, 1905, p. 96; Tschudi, 1905 A, no. 157; Scheffler, 1922, p. 208, reprod. p. 209; Waldmann, 1941, p. 40; Ziemke, 1972, p. 219, picture 85; exhib. cat. Hamburg, 1982, quoted in no. 191.

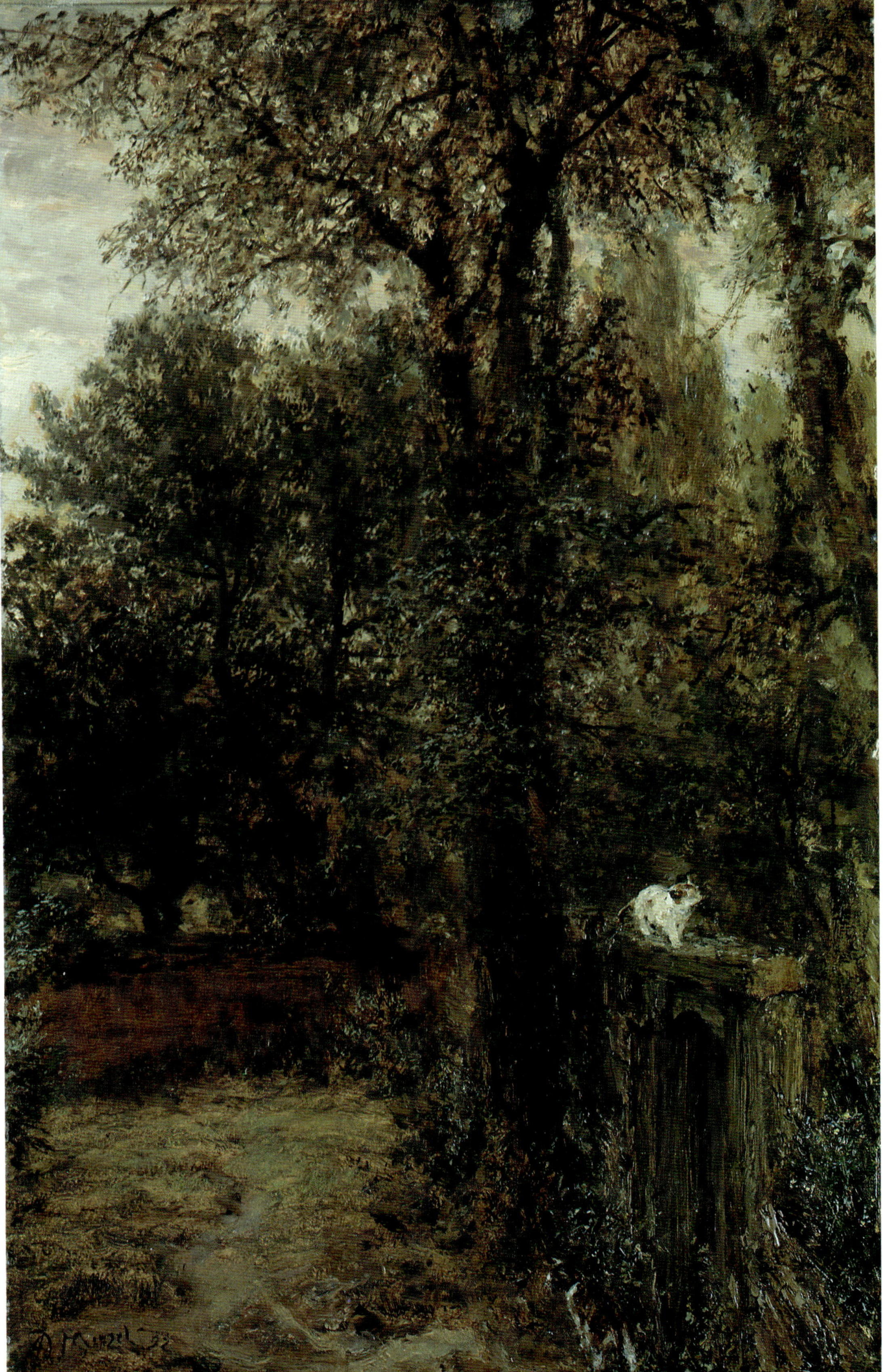
201

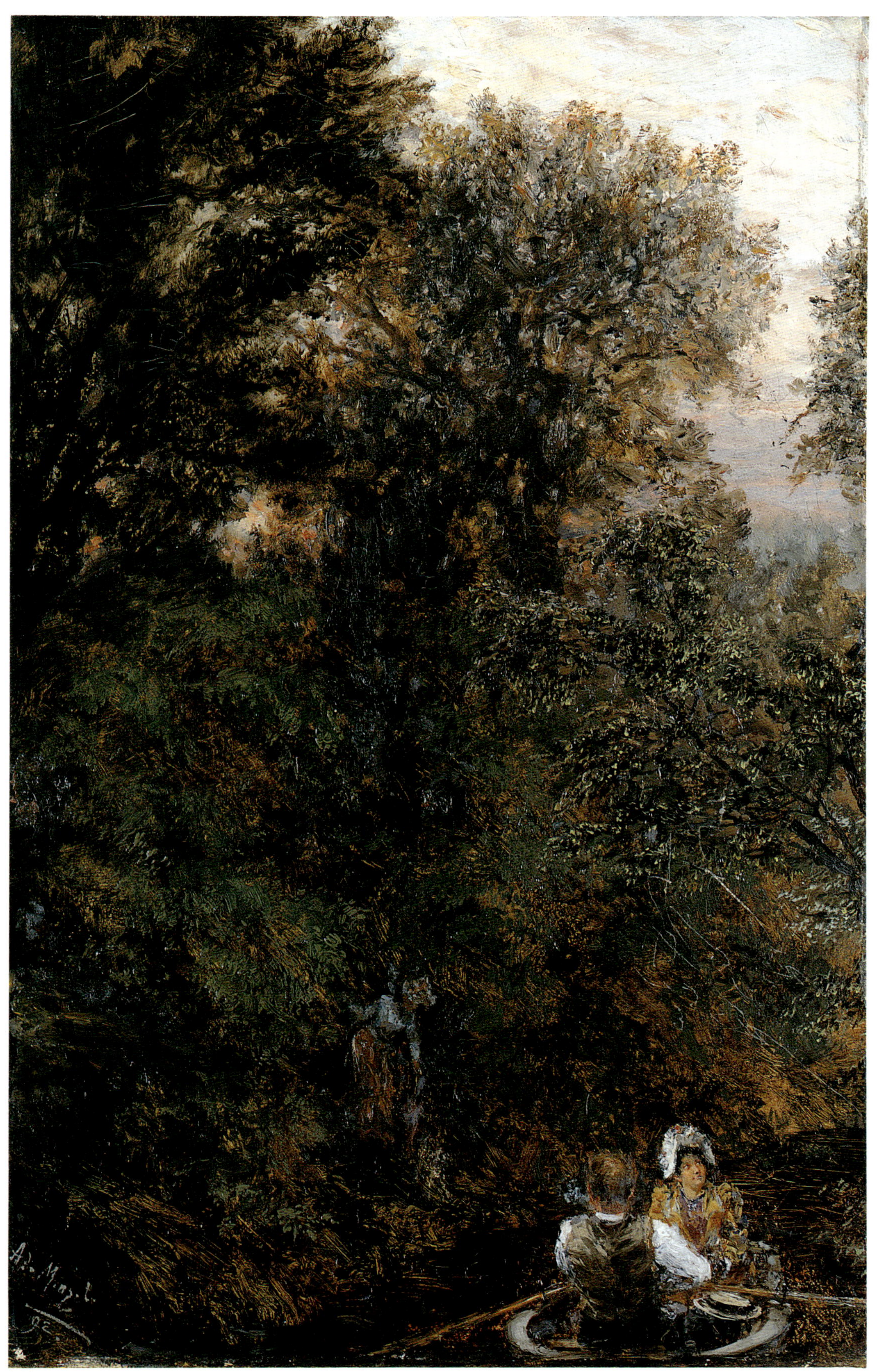
202

202

Outing in a Dinghy

1892

Oil on canvas
38 × 23.5cm
Signed and dated at the bottom left: *Ad. Menzel. /92.*
Hamburg, Hamburger Kunsthalle (2459)
Exhibited in Berlin only

Provenance: 1895 Erdwin Amsinck, Hamburg; acquired by the museum in 1921 (bequest of Erdwin Amsinck and his wife Antonie, née Lattmann, Hamburg).
Exhibitions: Berlin, 1895, no. 238; Hamburg, 1896, no. 22; Berlin, 1905, no. 38; Erlangen, 1971, no. 129, reprod.; Hamburg, 1982, no. 191, col. reprod.
Bibliography: Jordan, 1895, p. 62; Tschudi, 1905 A, no. 156; Jordan, 1905, p. 96; Waldmann, 1941, p. 40; Krafft/Schümann, 1969, p. 220, reprod.; Hütt, 1981, col. pl. 114; Howoldt, 1993, p. 48, reprod. p. 49.

'During an interview, Professor Adolph Menzel expressed his firm intention to abandon the technique of oil painting definitively from now on and work only in gouache and watercolour'. This report added that 'he had just started a series of ten watercolours, three of which are intended, if one can believe rumours, to stimulate writers to create a poetic transposition of the subjects of the pictures'[1]. This was in 1887. In fact, a series of gouaches of identical format were painted in the following years, while a few isolated works were painted in oils. These were two paintings of ball scenes the size of a sheet of writing paper[2] (1888, 1889) and finally two others scarcely any larger, *Outing in a Dinghy* and *Quiet Corner* (cat. 201). In the case described here, the dimensions were bound to be different because initially only one canvas was to be painted, which was undoubtedly fairly well advanced before it was cut in half. A thin segment in the middle was removed, evidently to correct the proportions, and the sky of *Outing in a Dinghy* was repainted. The canvas was originally to be horizontal, but it became two vertical works, finished, signed and sold separately. When the painter said his public goodbye to oil painting in 1887, the work may well have already been started. The basic reworking consists of the cutting up (an unusual procedure for Menzel) and is explained better if one assumes the works were painted over a fairly long period of time[3].

If one considers the disparate, scattered nature of Menzel's last colour works, which generally involve numerous figures and subjects, it is surprising to see a return to landscapes after a period of about ten years (except for the special case of *Garden of Prince Albert's Palace*, cat. 164). At this time, his landscapes belonged to drawing, and some dark studies are like these two paintings[4]. Was the couple in the dinghy part of the original plan or added later?[5] (A comparison with the boaters beloved of the French Impressionists indicates the difference in artistic conceptions!) Menzel's pictorial world is dualist: the people on an outing are strangers in the landscape, and are shunted to the edge of the foreground. They bring an anecdotic element (in the woman in the white hat who glances keenly upwards). The rest is suggestion, possibility, presentiment, and the woman coming out of the bushes blends into the shadow. The impression of pictorial unity and vagueness give a sensation of the fragmentary. The brushstrokes are not broad, but little touches are added without defining forms precisely, and in several places the brown scumble is almost skimped. Forty years on, Menzel returns to *Night in the Forest* (cat. 58).

In *Quiet Corner*, the garden gate with its two cats, also off-centre, has the same function as the boaters. This time the subject is even more mobile and fleeting – the cats will soon disappear. The foreshortening of the wooden gate, like that of the dinghy, suggests 'flight'. The rest is suspended in an absence of contours and material substance, as if the ailing eye could not grasp the world, as if it despaired of conveying the reciprocal nature of the single and the multiple, as if the painter, in a final perfectionist surge, tried to express the renunciation of, and progressive separation from, the visible.

C.K.

1. Die Kunst für Alle 2, 1886/7, Heft 22 vom 15.8.1887, S. 350 (Rubrik Personal und Ateliernachrichten).
2. Tschudi, 1905 A, no. 154; Euerbach, Georg Schäfer collection. – Tschudi, 1905 A, no. 155; Poznán, Narodowe Muzeum.
3. This is not invalidated by the use of drawings dated 1892. It was almost the rule that studies were drawn *ad hoc* to clarify details when the work of painting was in progress.
4. For example *A spot in the forest*, Berlin, Kupferstichkabinett (SZ Menzel N 2830); *cf.* exhib. cat. Copenhagen, 1985, no. 99, reprod. p. 62.
5. Preparatory drawings for boaters: Berlin, Kupferstichkabinett (SZ Menzel N 857-860). Three are dated 1892.

203

Breakfast Buffet given by a High-Class Bakery in Kissingen

1893

Gouache
17 × 25cm
Signed and dated at the bottom left: *Adolph Menzel. 1893*
Private collection
Exhibited in Berlin only

Provenance: 1905 Eduard Arnhold (industrialist and great collector), Berlin; private collections.
Exhibitions: Chicago, 1893; Berlin, 1895 A, no. 117; Hamburg, 1896, no. 77; Vienna, 1896, no. 234; Berlin, 1905, no. 13; Münster, 1987, no. 43, col. reprod.
Bibliography: Pietsch, 1861 B; *Kunstchronik*, 1893, col. 346; Jordan, 1895, p. 62; Peschkau, 1895, col. reprod. p. 804; *Kunstchronik*, 1900, col. 184; Jordan, 1905, p. 94–5, reprod. p. 100; Tschudi, 1905 A, no. 676.

After his last great composition involving numerous figures, *Marketplace in Verona* (cat. 179), Menzel only painted a few small-format pictures. After 1892 he finally abandoned oil painting in favour of gouache. The later gouaches, however, are prepared by a more significant number of pencil studies, another sign of the growing importance of this technique in the view of the ageing painter. The *High-Class Bakery at Kissingen* is the last of his paintings of a large number of figures. Among subjects taken from everyday life, in *Weekday in Paris* (1869, cat. 127), the bustle of a large town was tackled as a theme for the first time. The seven gouaches inspired by Kissingen which preceded the *High-Class Bakery* in 1874 and 1891 were variations on this theme. The particular quality of the individual, often scrutinized carefully and captured in preliminary studies, only becomes evident in the painting as an authentic description of the everyday. In some canvasses, the typical aspects of life in a spa town are portrayed by a group of people, as in the gouaches entitled *Near the Boiler* and *Aura Ruin*[1], or even by a single person, as in *Lady Walking by a Fountain in the Kissingen Spa Garden* (cat. 184). Others, like the two gouaches entitled *Open-air café at Kissingen* dated 1874 and 1891[2], or *A Walk by the Fountain*[3] and

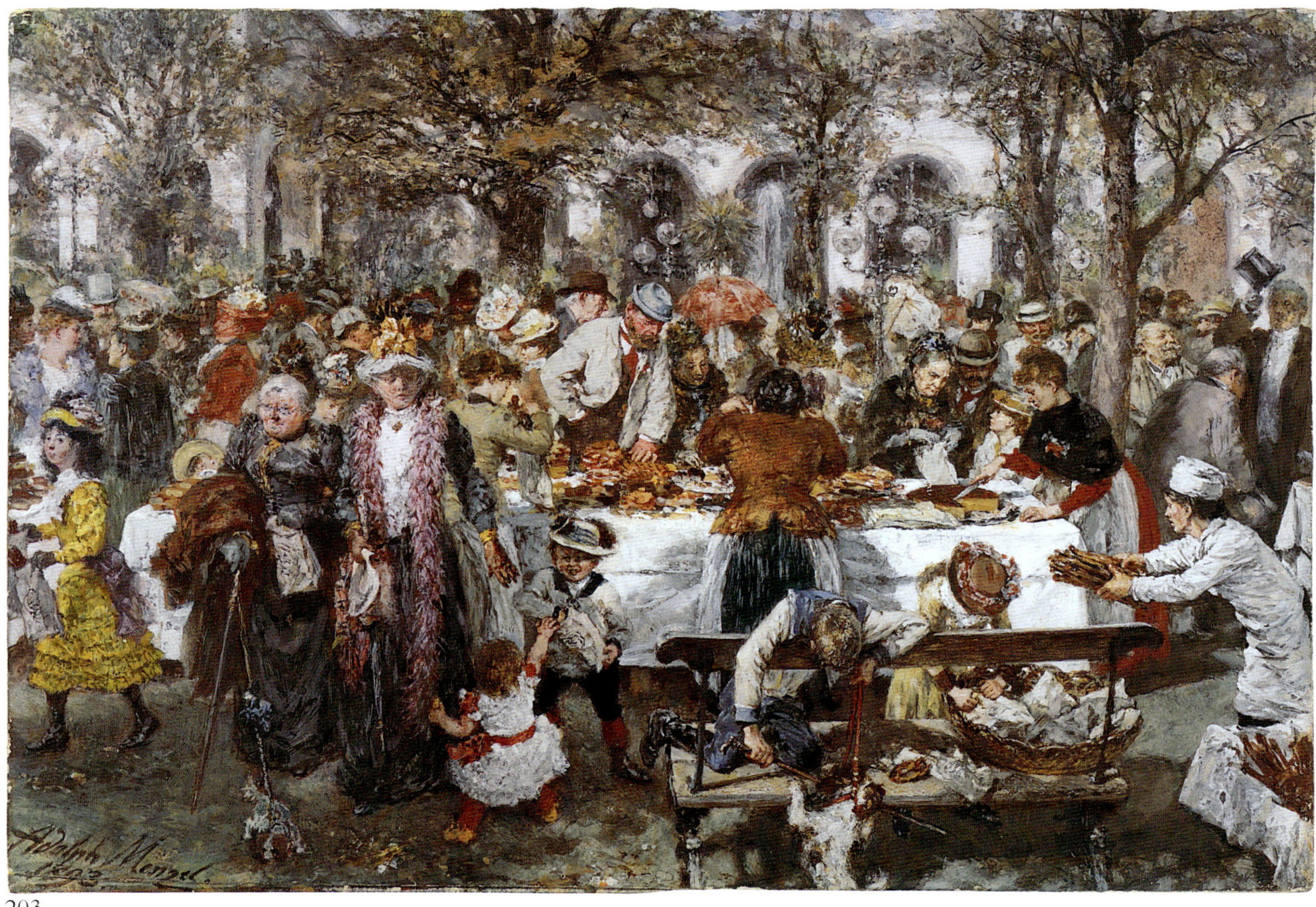

203

Coffee Time[4], suggest more or less comic behaviour, in a convincing image of bourgeois life in the spa town. Menzel is rarely ironic but, rather, his eye is sharpened by a critical faculty of differentiation which has no wish to judge, but to find the characteristic trait which makes the result so eloquent. In this search for objectivity, the *High-Class Bakery* is comparable to *Marketplace in Verona*.

In compositions after 1885, the spatial construction gives way to a surface order ruled by colour, with a horizon pushed back to the edge of the picture and almost invisible. It is hard to assess distances between figures and to measure the space. This subjective perspective reinforces the narrative aspect of these last paintings. The addition of a large number of different elements is often accompanied by less homogenous colour, benefiting brighter tones, sometimes multi-coloured and dissonant. These techniques emphasize the isolation of the individual within the crowd. Colour is synonymous with fashion and suggests personality for example, in women dressed in red and in blue.

At Kissingen Menzel observed more often than he took the waters himself. (He notes in his sketchbook in 1890, 'salt water bath at 26/27° for ten to twelve minutes'[5].) In the painting shown here he turns his attention to the cake buffet provided each morning on the promenade for breakfast. After he had been to the Weinberg bookshop, he went regularly every morning to 'choose cakes at beautiful Frau Dorothea Messerschmidt's cake stall'[6]. The colourful crowd throngs around the long table covered with a white cloth at which three women are serving cakes. Behind them dense groups of people stroll along the promenade, half-hidden by trees. A spa building can only be guessed at through the archways. Children play about in the foreground, and an apprentice baker, cut off by the right side of the picture, hurries up with some more cakes. On the left, also cut off, a little girl is carrying full bags of cakes. They all seem to revolve like a richly painted merry-go-round. The era of crowds became the age of mass entertainment, which in turn supplied pictorial subjects. In 1884 Liebermann painted a *Munich Café*. About forty sketches relating to *The High-Class Bakery* are catalogued, some of which date from 1892. Menzels studies of numerous figures

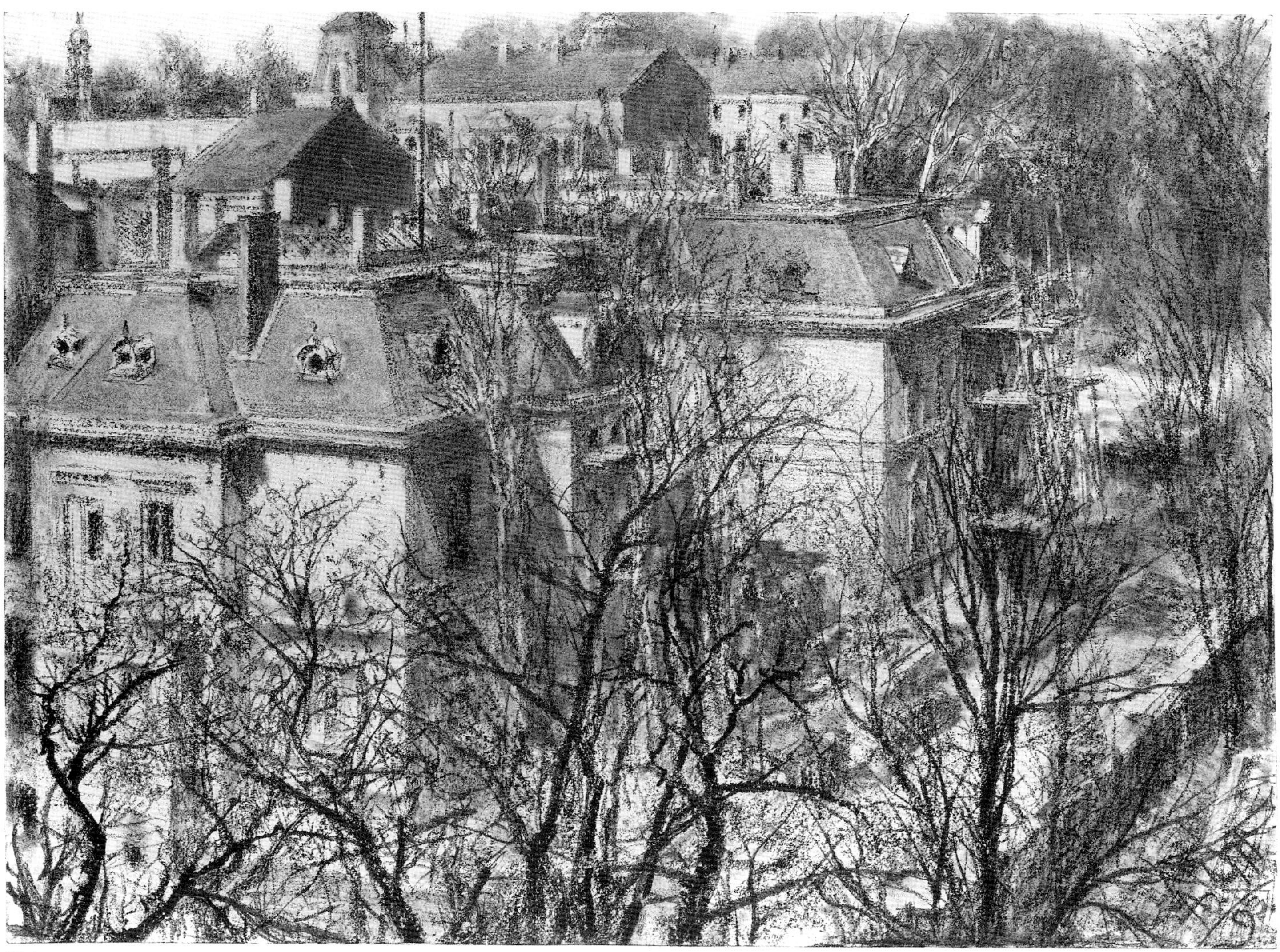

204

were extremely detailed, as in the case of the ladies' hats, whose style and colour were noted with accuracy. He even counted the buttons on the ladies' boots, yet did not give them any special importance on the actual canvas[7]. If Menzel's poetic mode of expression changed over the years, his method of elaborating a subject remained the same. To achieve maximum authenticity, he always 'forgot' his detailed documentation at the time of painting, all of which he had perceived and interiorized. M.R.-R.

1. Both dated 1884, Tschudi, 1905 A, no. 645 and 644; location unknown.
2. Tschudi, 1905 A, no. 609; Euerbach, Georg Schäfer; Tschudi, 1905 A, no. 673, *cf.* cat. 198.
3. 1890, Tschudi, 1905 A, no. 674; location unknown.
4. 1886, Tschudi, 1905 A, no. 660; private collection.
5. Berlin, Kupferstichkabinett, sketchbook 62, p. 2.
6. Vollmar, (1905-6) 1992, p. 255.
7. Berlin, Kupferstichkabinett; Leipzig, Museum der bildenden Künste, and anonymous owner.

204

Houses Behind Leafless Trees

1893

Pencil and stump
22.9 × 31.2cm
Signed and dated at the bottom right: *A.M. 93*
Berlin, Kupferstichkabinett (SZ Menzel N 967)

Provenance: Painter's studio; 1905 Emilie Krigar-Menzel; acquired by the museum in 1906.
Exhibitions: Berlin, 1905, no. 4211; Berlin, 1980 A, no. 395, reprod. p. 405; Vienna, 1985, no. 142, reprod. p. 203; Copenhagen, 1985, no. 122, reprod. p. 74; New York, 1990, no. 70, reprod. p. 204.
Bibliography: Wirth, 1965, p. 31 and text accompanying fig. 16.

From 1885 onwards Menzel increasingly

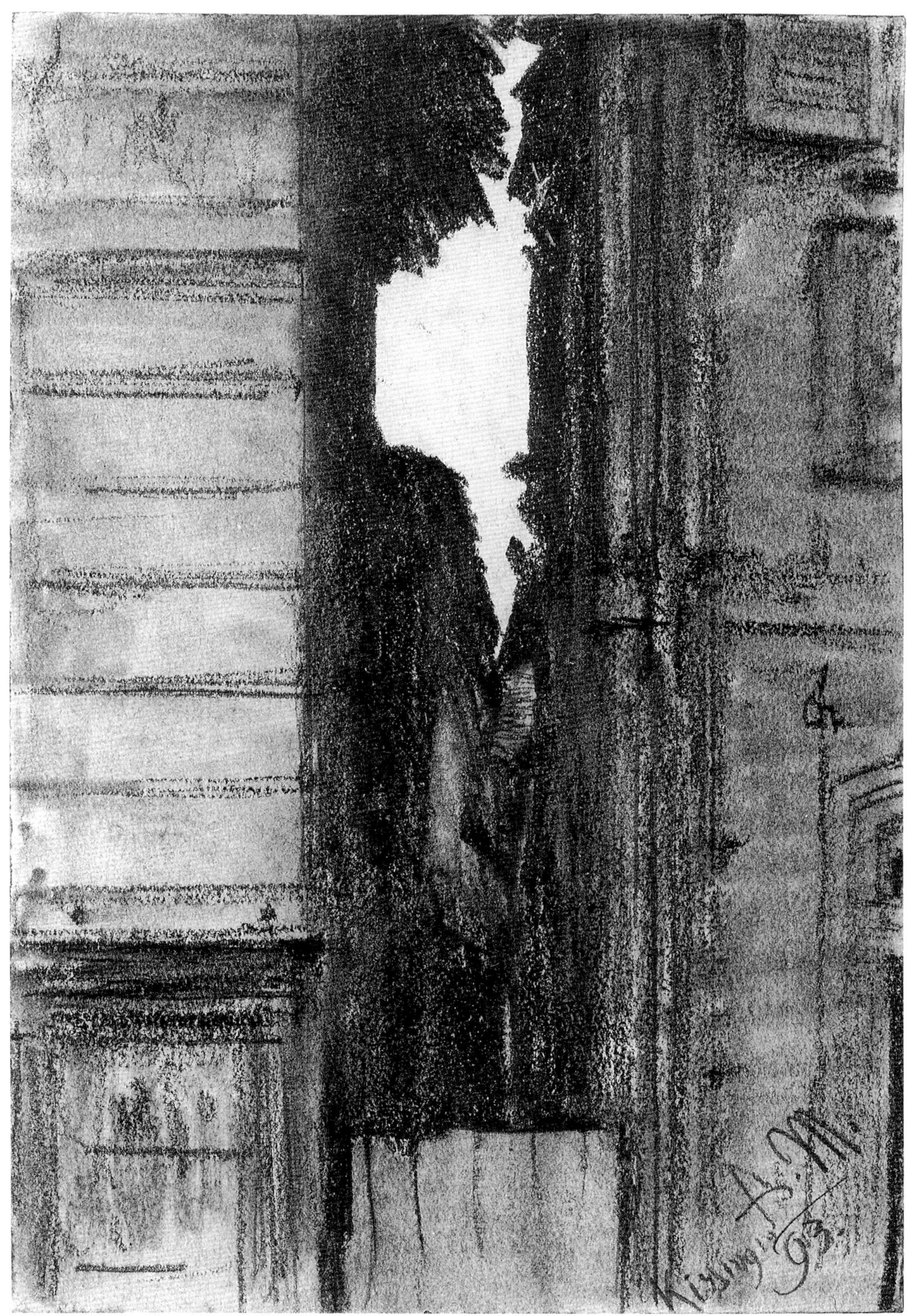

205

used pencil and stump for highly elaborate compositions. Stumping the pencil work, which replaced the chromatic range, covers every nuance from light grey to deepest black. The stumped areas give an impression like colour, and the wavy marks of the pencil on the paper are like sparkling lights with a deep black beside them. Menzel used watercolour exclusively for his paintings at this time. It is tempting to think that, after mastering all modes of expression, he discovered in the pencil a tool which offered as many possibilities as colour.

This drawing may be related to the gouache *Ash Wednesday*[1] (1885), and may be a view of the same spot. Eight years later than the gouache, the drawing takes in a wider section of the road. The view through the branches, a common technique, lends a slight vagueness to the scene, by virtue of which the object in the background attracts our interest. In not using figures – in other words, the anecdotal – Menzel is creating an urban panorama. This kind of view from above is common in his work.

A sketch dated 10 February 1893 shows the house in the foreground being built. The carpenters are in the middle of making the roof[2]. The drawing shown here must have been done in the spring or autumn of the same year. The remains of scaffolding can be seen on the villa in the background, but it is not really possible to identify the place. It could have been drawn in the district of Tiergarten or in Potsdam, from a friends house. A.H.

1. Tschudi, 1905 A, no. 653; previously at the Nationalgalerie in Berlin,currently in Kaunas Museum of Art.
2. Berlin, Kupferstichkabinett (SZ Menzel N 845).

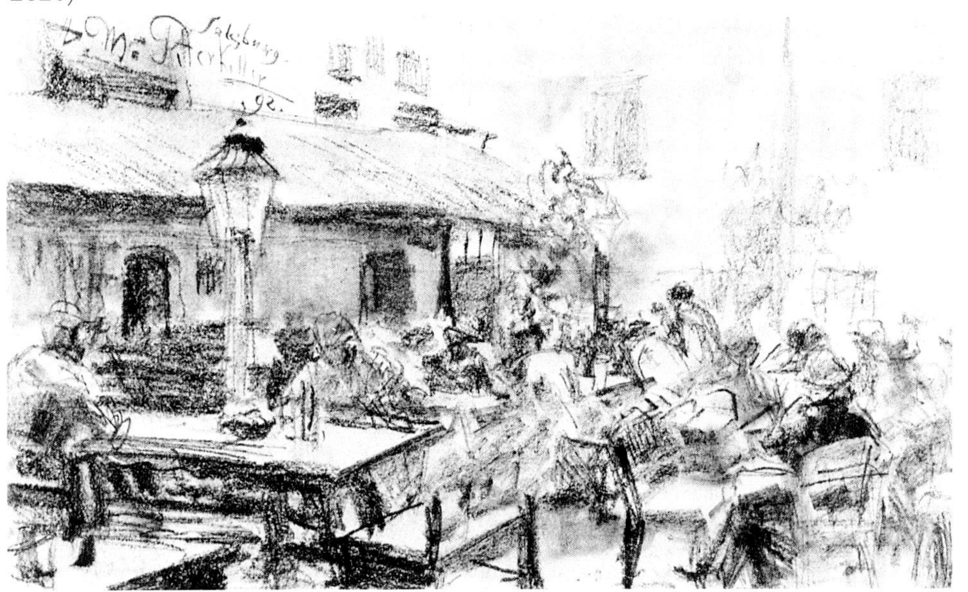

Fig. 221. *The Peterskeller in Salzburg*, 1892, pencil, Berlin, Kupferstichkabinett (N 2620)

205

Narrow View between Two Houses

1894

Pencil
18.4 × 11.7cm
Signed and dated at the bottom right: *Kissingen A.M.93.*
Berlin, Kupferstichkabinett (SZ Menzel N 2066)
Exhibited in Berlin only

Provenance: Painters studio; 1905 Emilie Krigar-Menzel; acquired by the museum in 1906.
Exhibition: Berlin, 1905, no. 6087.

The search for abstract form, as it appears, for example, in no end of drawings of cloud formations, seems to have guided Menzel on his walks as he became older, or more accurately, on his 'working excursions'. Does this search for new, entirely subjective motifs suggest a liberation from convention? In the same year he finished such contradictory compositions as *The High-Class Bakery at Kissingen* (cat. 203), with its numerous figures, and this unusual view, from above, of the walls between two houses. It is not the buildings themselves which interest Menzel, but the empty space, the nothingness which separates them. A year later he drew a similar composition, a rift in some walls and roofs in close proximity in the yard of a farm building[1].

M.R.-R.

1. Berlin, Kupferstichkabinett (SZ Menzel N 2069).

206

The Graben in Vienna

1894

Pencil
31 × 22.7cm
Signed and dated at the bottom right: *Ad. Menzel 94*
Hamburg, Hamburger Kunsthalle, Kupferstichkabinett (1937/25)
Exhibited in Paris and Berlin only

Provenance: Acquired by the museum in 1937.
Exhibitions: Hamburg, 1896, no. 238; Berlin, 1905, no. 5257; Berlin, 1955 B, no. 264; Bremen, 1963, no. 189; Berlin, 1965, no. 97; London, 1965, no. 102; Hamburg, 1982, no. 204.
Bibliography: Wirth, 1974, p. 139–40, fig. p. 128.

'The Graben, and the area around it, is still the place where everyone is seen. If an ice-cream fires your imagination, you could act in a kind of boulevard play for a moment. And as for the invigorating influence of the fair sex, the Linz women make a tourist feel he has already penetrated into the circles of influence of the Madle[1]. . . .' In Vienna Menzel felt like a tourist and, stimulated by these paradoxical ideas, he was reminded of Paris when he wrote these lines in 1871, twenty years after his first stay in Vienna.

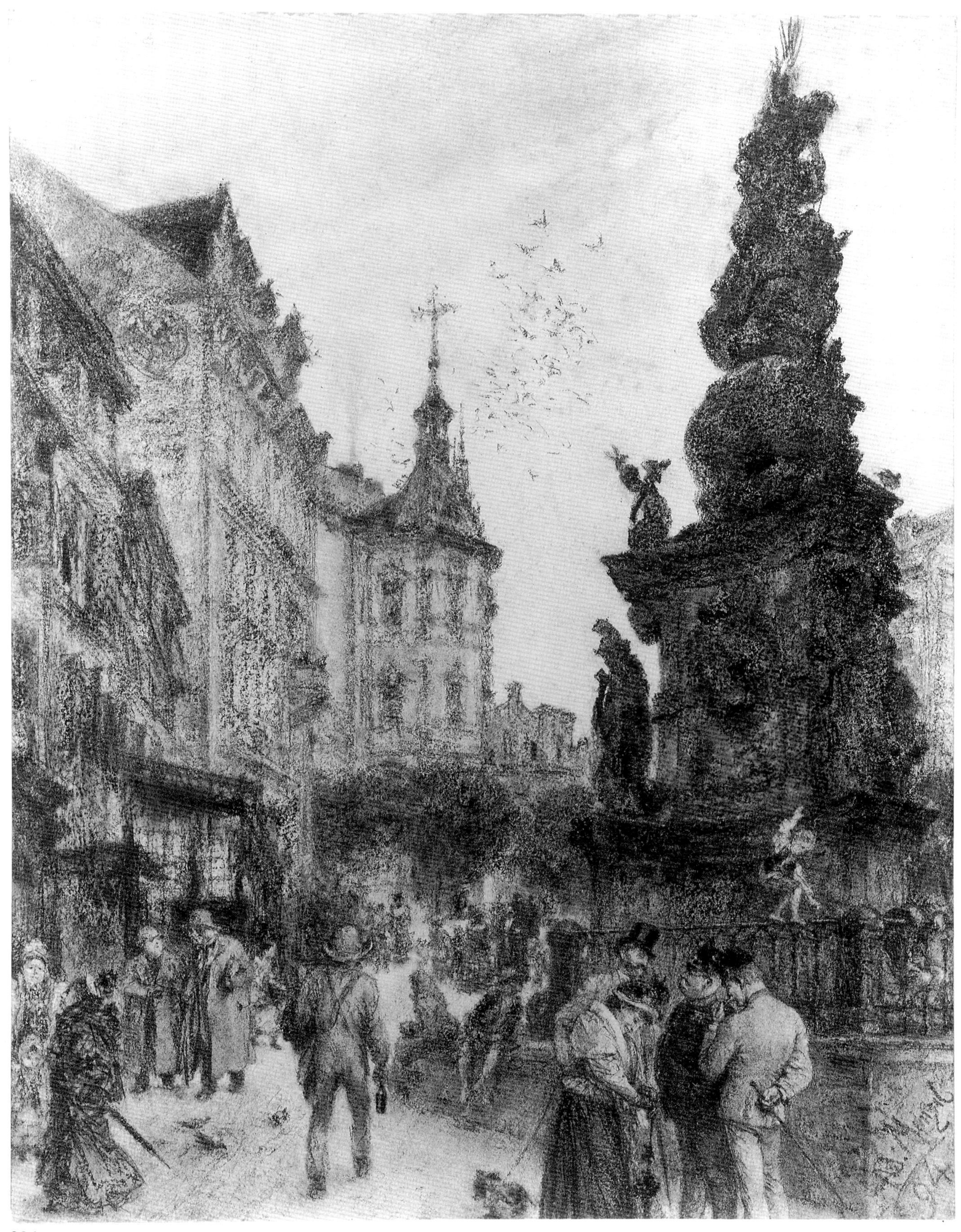

206

Twenty years later still, when he was nearly eighty, and the pencil had become the only means of expression for his pictorial ideas, he drew one of the rare pictures containing a many figures which came after *Marketplace in Verona* (cat. 179). Once more his attention focuses on a baroque work. In the drawing here the column of the Trinity, over twenty metres high and erected in 1679, after the plague, with the collaboration of Fischer von Erlach, melts into a dark tower in the shape of a cypress, only hinting at the richness of its sculptural ornamentation. Because of the very narrow angle Menzel chooses, the column and facing buildings appear to tower above, so that the people walking below seem to be crammed into a narrow alleyway. His pictorial composition exceeds the actual topography of the place. There is a study of the two gentlemen in overcoats walking side by side, deeply absorbed in their conversation[2]. The figures in the distance are picked out by a few stumped lines. Menzel depicts the four figures in the foreground as types but they are so different in their attitudes that it is possible to imagine the story which unites them from the gestures and expressions. If this drawing is compared with the view of the fountain with tritons in front of Salzburg cathedral, dated 1901, it seems that Menzel felt increasingly that the invasion of tourists was a calamity, a feeling expressed in his representation of human beings as a small crowd of swarming creatures, hurrying, walking, cycling around the grandiose monument, to which they are indifferent. M. R.-R.

1. Letter to Hermann Krigar, Vienna, 8 August 1871, Wolff, 1914, p. 216.
2. The pencil study is in the National Museum of Varsovia. *Cf.* Bredt, 1920, reprod. p. 68.

207

View of the Collegiate Church 'Unser Lieben Frau zur Alten Kapelle' in Regensburg

1894

Gouache
40.2 × 26.2cm
Berlin, Kupferstichkabinett (SZ Menzel N 4471)

Provenance: Painters studio; 1905 Emilie Krigar-Menzel; acquired by the museum in 1906.
Exhibitions: Berlin, 1905, no. 5822; Vienna, 1985, no. 139, col. reprod. p. 72; Copenhagen, 1985, no. 119; New York, 1990, no. 68, col. reprod. p. 201.
Bibliography: Tschudi, 1905 A, no. 626; Liebermann/Kern, 1921, p. 11, col. pl. 45; Kaiser, 1956, p. 110, fig. 76; Berlin, 1994, no. VII.38.

Menzel's first long trip, in summer 1852, which lasted for two months and took him to southern Germany and Austria, led him to Regensburg. A liking for baroque and rococo art, nurtured by his childhood memories of Breslau and his research on the life and work of Frederick the Great, always took him where that style flourished. Twenty years before Jacob Burckhardt drew attention to this long-disdained style and, before it had begun to have a higher profile, Menzel drew and painted monuments of baroque architecture not only in Berlin and Potsdam, but also in Dresden. In 1840, after a brief stay, he declared: 'Dresden in itself was disappointing. What makes the town interesting (the old elegant buildings and the gallery) is partly in ruins[1] . . . .'

Drawings of baroque architecture and sculpture form a large part of his late work. Menzel could not resist the splendour of baroque churches and their theatrical effects created by light and forms of an intangible yet material quality, verging on the supernatural. His impressions pour out colour and form, like the *View of the Collegiate Church at Regensburg*, which he went back to see in the summer trip of 1894. The Mass is over and the restless congregation is about to leave the church amid the sparkle of the splendid rococo decor (the church was built after 1747) and under a light falling from above. The composition seems unfinished, as the white of the paper can be seen in places. After the interiors of the Benedictine church in Salzburg[2] (1871, with about the same dimensions), the parish church in Innsbruck[3] (1872 and 1881), St Peter's church in Vienna, the ladies' collegiate church in Munich[4] (1873) and finally the convent church at Ettal[5] (1875), this drawing may have been done in 1894. Other drawings show the rich ornamentation of the church, the strange shapes of the north oratory, for example, which spread in golden flower along both sides of the nave. A sketch showing an oratory from a different angle dates from 1894, and another of the south galleries with part of the altar leads the eye inside the church, as in the gouache. It also dates from 1894 and has the following annotation: 'Grey for all the marble on the cornices of the columns, yellowish for the columns'. On the edge of the paper the marks of violent brushstrokes show that the drawing was on the table when the painter was working on the gouache[6]. Menzel's interiors of baroque churches show a highly subjective perception of space, which in general exaggerates the actual dimensions, heightening their grandeur. M.R.-R.

1. Letter to Carl Heinrich Arnold, 6 September 1840, Wolff, 1914, p. 49.
2. Tschudi, 1905 A, no. 594; location unknown.
3. Tschudi, 1905 A, no. 598; location unknown.
4. Not mentioned by Tschudi, 1905 A; Tschudi, 1905 A, no. 604; Euerbach, Georg Schäfer collection.
5. Tschudi, 1905 A, no. 619; location unknown.
6. All reference drawings are kept at the Berlin Kupferstichkabinett (SZ Menzel N 66, 365, 1172).

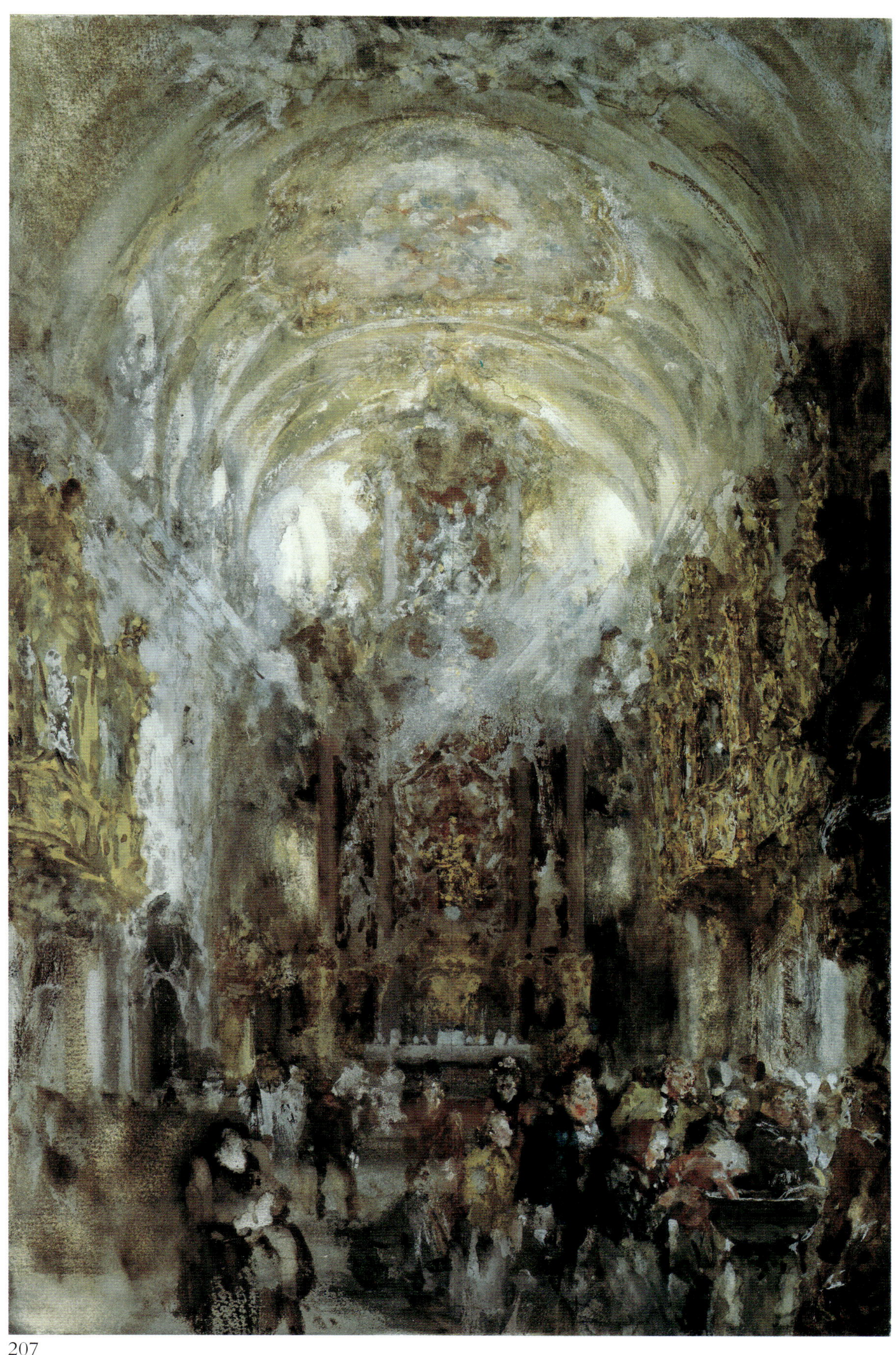

207

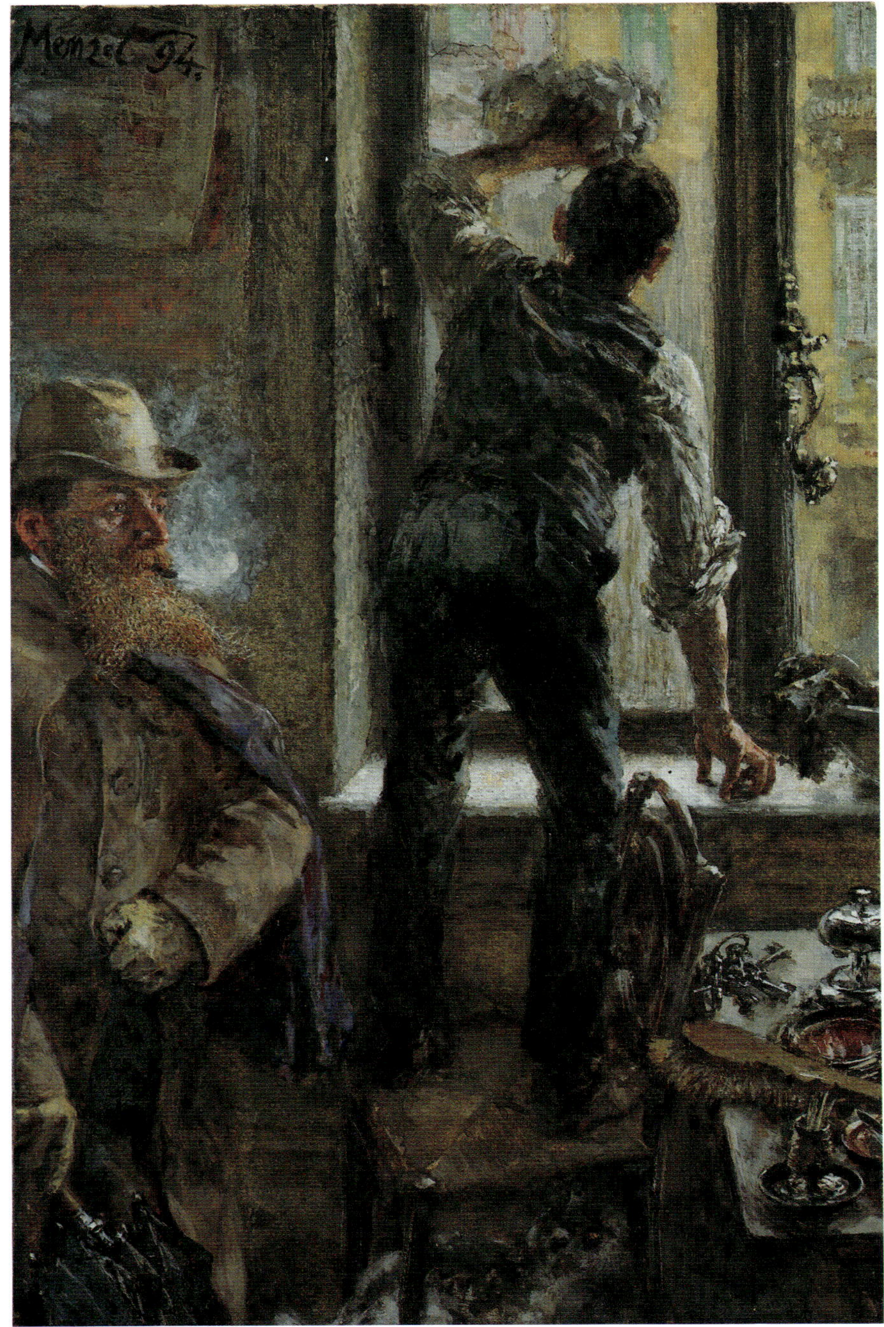

208

208
Early Morning in the Café
1894

Gouache
18.3 × 11.7cm
Signed and dated at the top left: *Menzel 94*
Hamburg, Hamburger Kunsthalle (2460)
Exhibited in Washington and Berlin only

Provenance: Baron August von der Heydt, Elberfeld; 1905 Frau L.E. Amsinck, Hamburg; acquired by the museum in 1921 in the legacy of Erdwin and A. Amsinck.
Exhibitions: Berlin, 1905, no. 207; Berlin, 1955 B, no. 139; Hamburg, 1982, no. 200.
Bibliography: Tschudi, 1905 A, no. 677; Krafft/Schümann, 1969, p. 220; Trost, 1980, pl. 27.

This gouache brings together two aspects of Menzel's late work. On the one hand we see the instantaneous seizing of a simple situation and the partly fortuitous motif of the person standing against the light on the other. This second aspect, which is singularly charming, should have encouraged Menzel to devote his time to the phenomenon of light earlier, at a time when the black of a pencil, by virtue of the range of nuances it could create on paper, was tending to be the dominant mode of expression in his drawing. There are numerous drawings of figures standing in front of a window or coming out of the darkness into the light of an open door. A similar inspiration must have produced this drawing. In two sketchbooks from 1892–3 and 1893–4, sketches of a window-cleaner[1], where only the silhouette against the background light can really be distinguished, confirm Menzel's interest in this subject. His scenes were composed by bringing these 'accessories' together. He liked to frequent the cafés and restaurants of Berlin, and those he encountered on his travels, and he often stayed until late at night. He could well have witnessed such an early morning scene. The restricted range of colours he used, red, blue, brown, a little white, even less light green – which he left as brushmarks on the edge of the page – were enough to reproduce the rather grey atmosphere of the room, in which the light only penetrates through the recently cleaned pane of glass. The still life of various objects laid randomly on the table gave him the opportunity to elevate the ordinary things he often drew to the dignity of models. A small cat hides underneath the table as someone comes in, bringing with him the rain and cold of the external world. The pictorial treatment of the animal is generous and curiously expressive. *Early Morning in the Café* is the last of the colour compositions, and in it Menzel seeks a harmonious effect. Soon, in 1897, amid the dissonance of the small gouaches, he would forsake colour entirely and use only pencil. M.R.-R.

1. Berlin, Kupferstichkabinett; there are also other studies of details used for this work.

209
Woman Combing her Hair
c. 1894

Pencil
31 × 22.9cm
Berlin, Kupferstichkabinett (SZ Menzel N 4433)
Exhibited in Paris and Washington only

Provenance: Painter's studio; 1905 Emilie Krigar-Menzel; acquired by the museum in 1906.
Exhibition: Berlin, 1905, no. 3487.

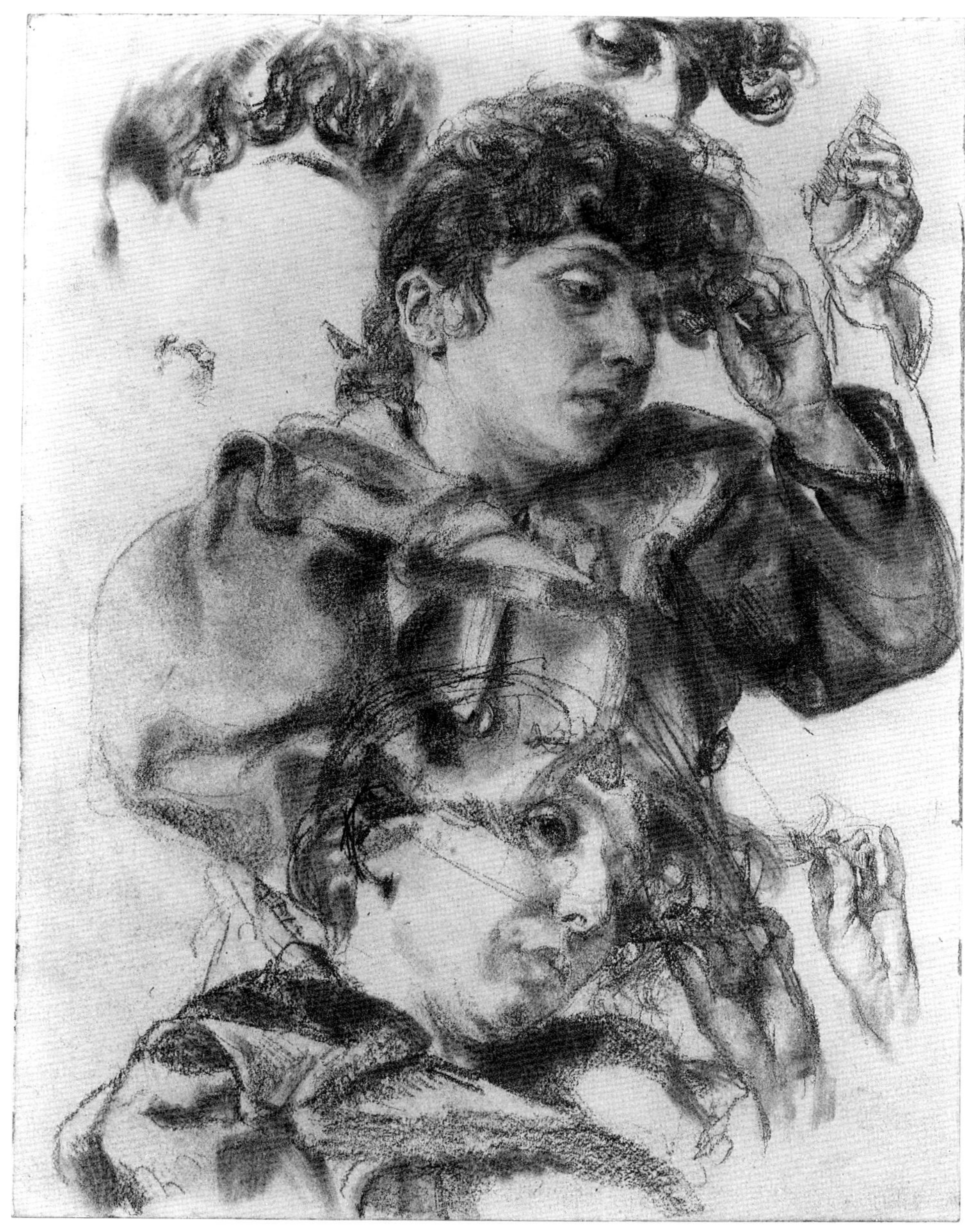
209

This study illustrates the progressive development of a movement, a pose that changes while the artist is at work. It is immaterial whether the study was conceived independently or in relation to the composition of a picture. In his last years, Menzel considered his drawings as independent works, sufficiently representative of his output to be exhibited. A drawing of this kind shows Menzel's method of work, open up to the last moment to any possible modification, until the final phase of the pictorial process, when he is painting one of his later compositions involving a lot of figures. These pages of drawings seek constantly to find what is authentic in a facial expression, a type, a detail, like a kind of optical device allowing multiple lighting. In general the painting contained no more than a condensation of what had been established by an abundance of detail in preparatory studies, in accord with the highest reality of the artistic form. It is this type of material that guarantees the astounding vivacity of Menzel's pictorial compositions. Many similar studies were made for *Marketplace in Verona* (cat. 179), in particular. In addition to the page shown here, there is another drawing dated 1894 which depicts the model more in the manner of a portrait[1]. There is no known use for these studies, and so they may be related in style and expression to the many heads, conceived of autonomously, which are a facet of the graphic work of the artists later years. M.R.-R.

1. Cambridge, Ma., Fogg Art Museum, Harvard University.

210 211 215–18

Last Drawings: Heads

Fontane's description of Menzel, then aged seventy, was characteristic of the last years of his life: 'Some rare people, I must admit, need the big city to exercise their skill, but they are lost all the same, and lost to their skill in particular, if they do not understand the difficult art of living, yet not living, in the big city. Ad. Menzel, for example, is a past master at this art, as he is at his own. Berlin has undoubtedly always been necessary to him (fifty years at Filehne and Menzel wouldn't be Menzel), but what is his life like in Berlin? He works like a hermit in his studio from nine to nine, and then at the time when other people are going to bed, he goes to Huth's'[1].

Fontane's words identify Menzel's isolation, as little by little he concentrated totally on his work. He lived an increasingly solitary life. The honours bestowed on him by the empire began to disguise the basic nature of his art, to the point that, when he was still alive, he had the feeling that he had been forgotten. In 1896 he had to sweep aside the critical analysis of his work by Hugo von Tschudi, who attributed greater artistic value to Böcklin's work in his comparative study. Menzel clearly felt the scorn of the young generation and sometimes violently pushed away his own circle[2]. He recovered from the fall he had at the end of 1895 after his eightieth birthday, but he left painting aside increasingly in favour of the pencil and stump. His last oil paintings date from 1892 (*cf.* cat. 201, 202).

Menzel finished a large number of pencil drawings in his last years, right up to his death. Once more, this work represents something new in his art. He began to draw faces in close proximity to each other, sometimes half-silhouettes, of numerous anonymous men and women he came across here and there in the streets of Berlin or in the restaurants he went to, but also on the trips he undertook. In the 1893 sketchbook, which he probably used at Karlsbad, the subject of heads began to take a hold and totally dominates the last sketchbook of his journey there in 1903[3].

The heads were sometimes brought together in small, apparently spontaneous scenes. They evoke a cinema-like panorama or compel a comparison with photographs in their fragmentary framing. From a technical point of view Menzel shows a total mastery of his art in these picturesque drawings. Working with both subtlety and boldness, he achieved the most skilled art in terms of nuances of grey and black. Pencil is used in the most diverse manifestations in these exercises, from the finest and most delicate line to rough assaults which tear the surface of the paper. The resulting rough surfaces obtained are a deliberately calculated means to express Menzel's will. As the anecdotic aspect lessens, what relates to the subject also disappears in the artists imaginary world. What is striking in the compositions of people is the stubborn perspective which often differentiates size, but not gradations of brightness. Brutally opposing movements or intense, equivocal exchanges of looks are also typical. Menzel often drew the paid models who waited at his studio. It was not individual destiny that he portrayed in these faces, but rather something universally human which he tried to grasp in fascination, like feelings which translated both the image and its reflection, disappointment perhaps, doubt, astonishment, seriousness, joy, indifference or sorrow. His encounters with these people, mostly elderly and of modest means, was one of Menzels last essential human experiences. These drawings are impressions that have taken on form, and portray variations on the theme of alienation by showing the fragile, fortuitous ways in which these people coexist or oppose each other. Previously Menzel tried to retain the essentials of peoples faces, unsuccessfully in *Address at Leuthen*. This time he attacked the task with success, in a new way. Starting from immediate reality, he created a world of the most diverse spiritual aspirations in his last drawings, shot through with the irrational, a whole silent dialogue between the master and his models with their richness of character. The human face interested him, with its appearance, 'as different as it is random', as he said to Max Jordan[4]. Fontane quoted Schopenhauer when he wrote: 'The best thing we possess is compassion'[5], and this thought could equally well be applied to the creative impulse that guided Menzel in his last pencil works. M.R.-R.

1. Theodor Fontane to Georg Friedländer, 21 December 1884, Fontane, 1980, vol. 2, p. 130. Filehne is a village in the march of Brandenburg. Huth was a restaurant near Potsdamer Platz, not far from Menzel's last apartment in the Sigismundstrasse.
2. *Cf.* Riemann on this subject, 1992, p. 188 and ff., and note 90.
3. Berlin, Kupferstichkabinett.
4. Jordan, 1905.
5. Letter from Fontane to his daughter, 24 August 1893, Fontane, 1980, p. 305.

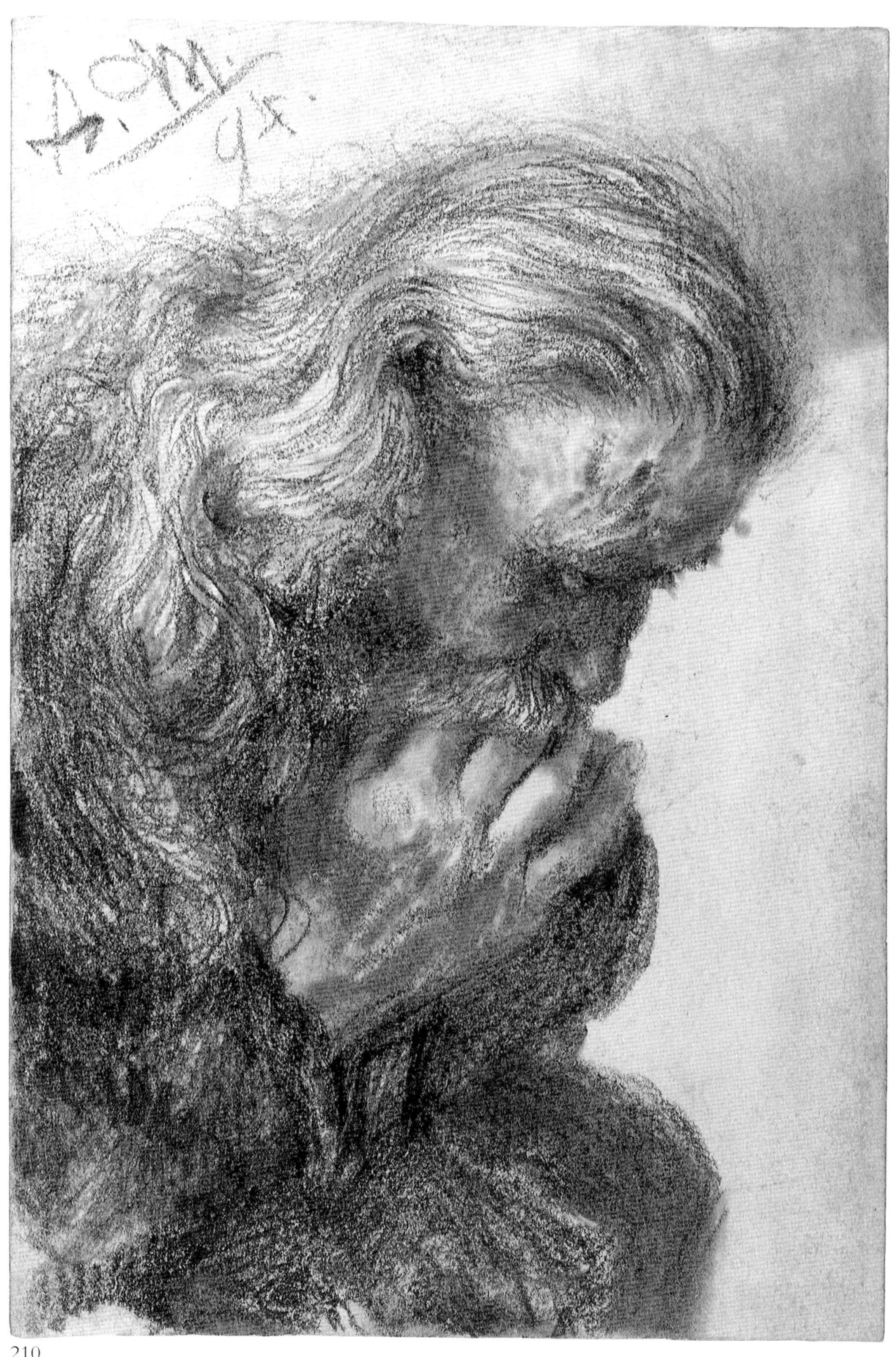

210

210

Old Man with Long Hair

1894

Pencil
18.5 × 11.8cm
Signed and dated at the top left: *A.M.94*
Zurich, Arturo Cuéllar collection

Provenance: 1905 Dr A. Wolffsohn, Hamburg.
Exhibition: Berlin, 1905, no. 5419.

There is a study in the 1894–7 sketchbook for this old man leaning his head on his raised right hand, on which Menzel noted 'v. altem Holze' (of the old school)[1] M.R.-R.

1. Berlin, Kupferstichkabinett, sketchbook 70, p. 82.

Fig. 222. *Head of a Woman with a Bun, Wearing a Bonnet, Viewed from Behind*, *c.* 1896–9, Berlin, Kupferstichkabinett (sketchbook 71, p. 23)

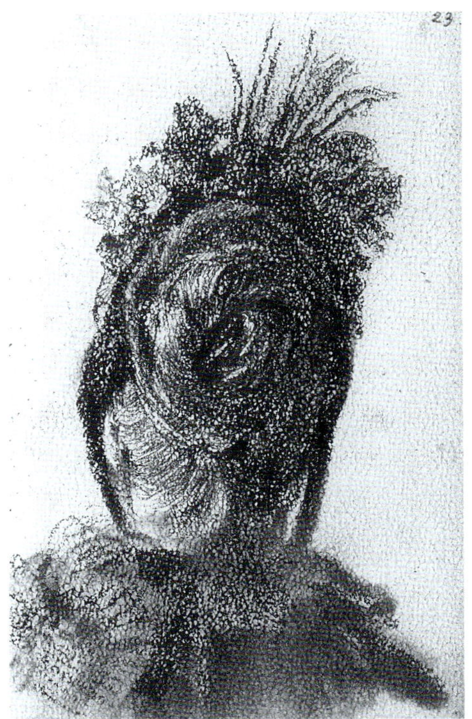

211

Head of an Old Woman

1894

Pencil
31 × 22.5cm
Signed and dated at the bottom right: *A.M.94.*
Zurich, collection of Dr Peter Nathan and Barbara Nathan

Provenance: private collection, Munich; acquired by the Arnoldi-Livie Gallery, Munich.
Bibliography: Illustrierte Zeitung, 16.2.1905, reprod. p. 26.

Menzel never ceased drawing the faces of old women. Here he captures the macabre and tragic feel[1], as well as the melancholy, of this old woman whose face reflects an entire lifetime. M.R.-R.

1. *Cf. Head of an old woman* exhib. cat. Vienna 1985, no. 143, reprod., and the same in the 1899 sketchbook, Berlin, Kupferstichkabinett.

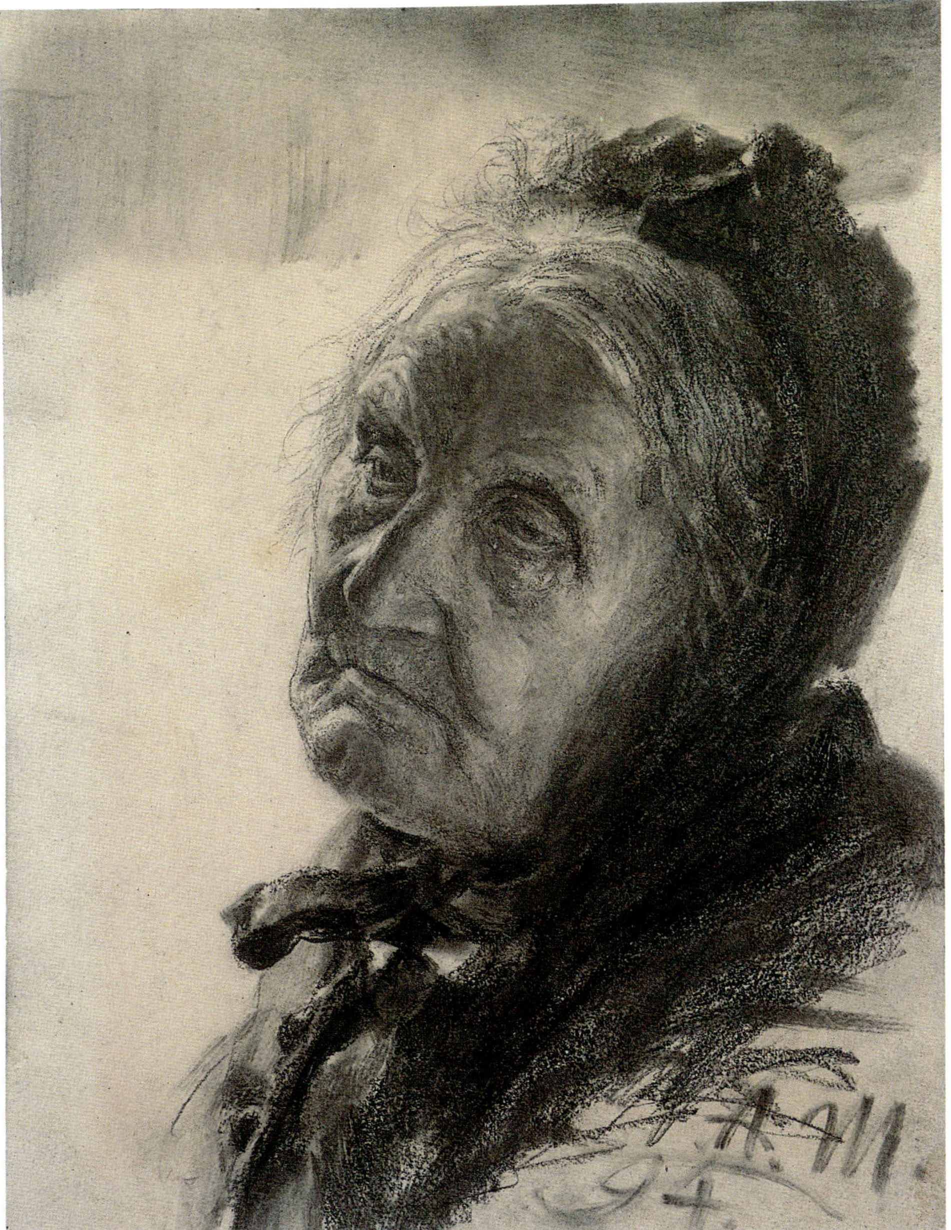

211

212

Two Men in a Window against the Light

1895

Pencil
21 × 13cm
Signed and dated at the bottom right: *A.M.95*
Berlin, Kupferstichkabinett (SZ Menzel N 2772)
Exhibited in Washington and Berlin

Provenance: Painter's studio; 1905 Emilie Krigar-Menzel; acquired by the museum in 1906.
Exhibitions: Berlin, 1905, no. 3378; Berlin, 1955 A, no. 552; Berlin, 1980 A, no. 399, reprod. p. 288; exhib. cat. Hamburg, 1982, no. 200.
Bibliography: Hütt, 1981, p. 142, fig. 125.

In front of an open window, the silhouettes of two men are manipulating a heavy object which probably goes on the cupboard on the right. The intense light entering the room obliterates details like an overexposure. There are some drawings similar to this one in the sketchbooks of the preceding years, showing scenes in front of a window[1]. Menzel used them for the gouache *Early Morning in the Café* (cat. 208). Situations near a window always interested him. Much earlier, he placed the classic figure of a man reading in front of a window in his bedroom (*cf.* cat. 34). A variation on this theme appeared in 1843 in an engraving of his sister Emilie asleep near a window[2]. Menzel joined the venerable tradition, of which Rembrandt is the most famous example, and the German knew his engravings in the Kupferstichkabinett in Berlin. He also knew Dutch paintings, and Vermeer in particular, who had opened the way for this type of representation. At the age of eighty, Menzel the subtle, experienced observer dynamizes the traditional motionless scene by introducing figures in action. He tells a story, as in the 1894 gouache. But this drawing is different in another way – the interest in the scene is structured essentially by the light. A.H.

1. Berlin, Kupferstichkabinett, sketchbook 68, 1892-3, p. 110–11 and sketchbook 69 (1893-4), p. 73.
2. *Seamstress asleep* 1843, Bock, 1923, no. 1134; *cf.* also the drawing of Emilie sitting down, in sketchbook 7 (1839-46), p. 10 and p. 56.

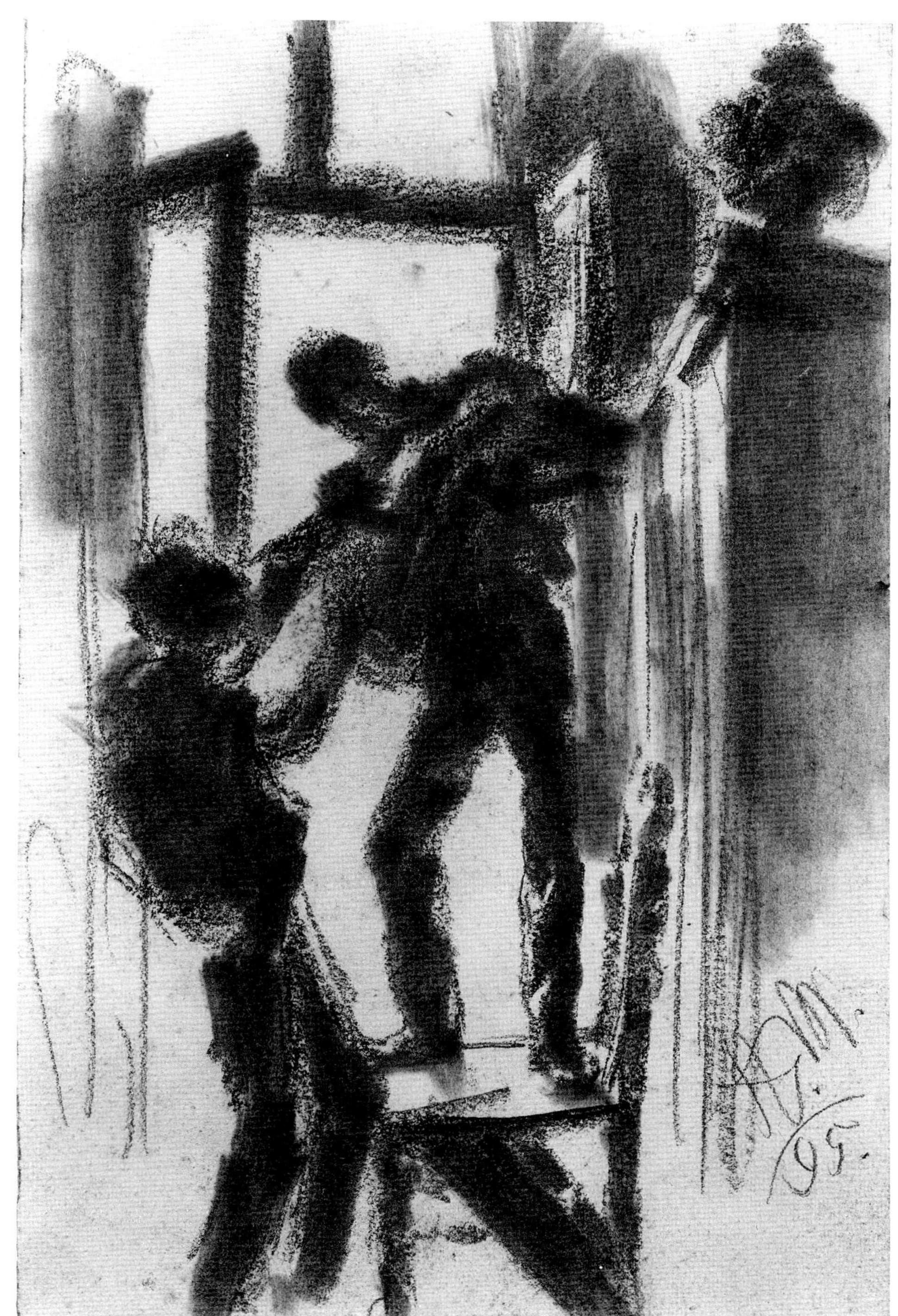

212

213
Jean (Giovanni) Boldini

Born at Ferrara in 1842, died in Paris in 1931
Portrait of Adolph Menzel
1895

Oil on canvas
41 × 54.5cm
Signed and dated in the centre right: *21 October 1895 Berlin Boldini*
Berlin, Nationalgalerie (A I 561)
Exhibited in Paris and Berlin only

Provenance: Acquired by the museum in 1897.
Exhibitions: Berlin, 1896 A, no. 274, fig. 4; Berlin, 1896 B, no. 9; Paris, 1931, no. 2; Venice, 1932, no. 231.
Bibliography: Springer, 1896, p. 310; Vollmar, 1895–6 B, p. III; cat. NG, 1897, no. 701; Vollmar, 1904–5 B, p. 184; Mauclair, 1906, p. 115; Cardona, 1931, p. 6; Ragghianti and Camescara, 1970, no. 41, fig. (truncated); Doria, 1982, p. 22, p. 140; exhib. cat. Boldini, Milan, 1989, p. 290 (not exhib.).

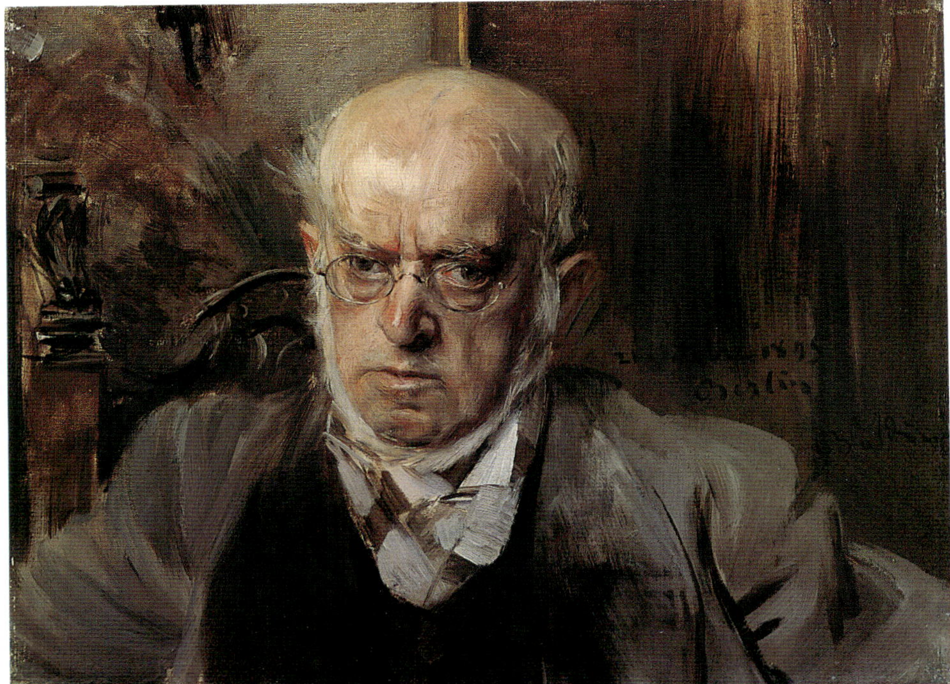

213

The signature suffices to correct the date of 1876 often suggested in works on Boldini, which seem to be unaware of the painter's stay in Berlin. In 1895 and 1896 the *fapresto* painter of society elegance, who had chosen to live in Paris, successfully took part in the Berlin salon (Grosse Berliner Kunstausstellung). Like Menzel, who had just celebrated his eightieth birthday with full honours, Boldini, younger by thirty years, was at the height of his fame. In 1892, the Uffizi Gallery in Florence requested his self-portrait in accordance with tradition (as it did later for Max Liebermann, but not for Menzel). It is said that in Berlin Boldini contemplated *The Flute Concert* and *The Iron Rolling Mill* 'for hours'[1]. A lady friend of the novelist Theodor Fontane encouraged him to paint a portrait of his colleague, interceding in his favour[2].

In contrast to the official portrait of Menzel painted by Max Koner at the same time on commission[3], Boldini's picture, which was completed in two short sittings, underlines the private aspect of the person and the spontaneity of the rapport between them. He does not spare the grumpy manner and acrimony of his model. The unusual horizontal format suggests an interior scene rather than a portrait, as does the view from above, a device which Boldini, who was also short, like Menzel, used willingly. Several of his portraits, like that of the painter Edouard Detaille[4] or of the Marquis Antonio di Rudini[5], have a comparable setting.

The work was a success in both Paris and Berlin, where people saw a 'clearly French view of Menzel'. Although only his head was painted, 'you could imagine the gnome'[6], wrote a critic rather indelicately (although, in the first half of his life, no one made any allusion to Menzel's stature, this finally entered the public domain). Camille Mauclair spoke of a 'prestigious head', perceiving both spiritual virtuosity and absence of emotion in Boldings painting.

An undated dry-point faithfully reproduces Boldini's portrait of Menzel, whom he counted throughout his life as one of his great models, although some critics drew comparisons between the two artists. When he showed his visitors the photograph of his German colleague tucked in a mirror frame, he would exclaim: 'Ah, what a painter! I am only a dauber in comparison'[7]. C.K.

1. *Cf.* Vollmar, 1904-5 B.
2. *Ibid.*
3. Berlin, Nationalgalerie.
4. 1896, private collection.
5. 1898, private collection.
6. Springer, 1896.
7. Doria, 1982, p. 22, p. 140.

214
Interior of a Barn, in Shadow
1897

Pencil
21 × 13cm
Signed and dated at the top left: *A.M.97*
Berlin, Kupferstichkabinett (SZ Menzel N 2512)
Exhibited in Washington and Berlin only

Provenance: Painters studio; 1905 Emilie Krigar-Menzel;
acquired by the museum in 1906.
Exhibition: Berlin, 1905, no. 4282.

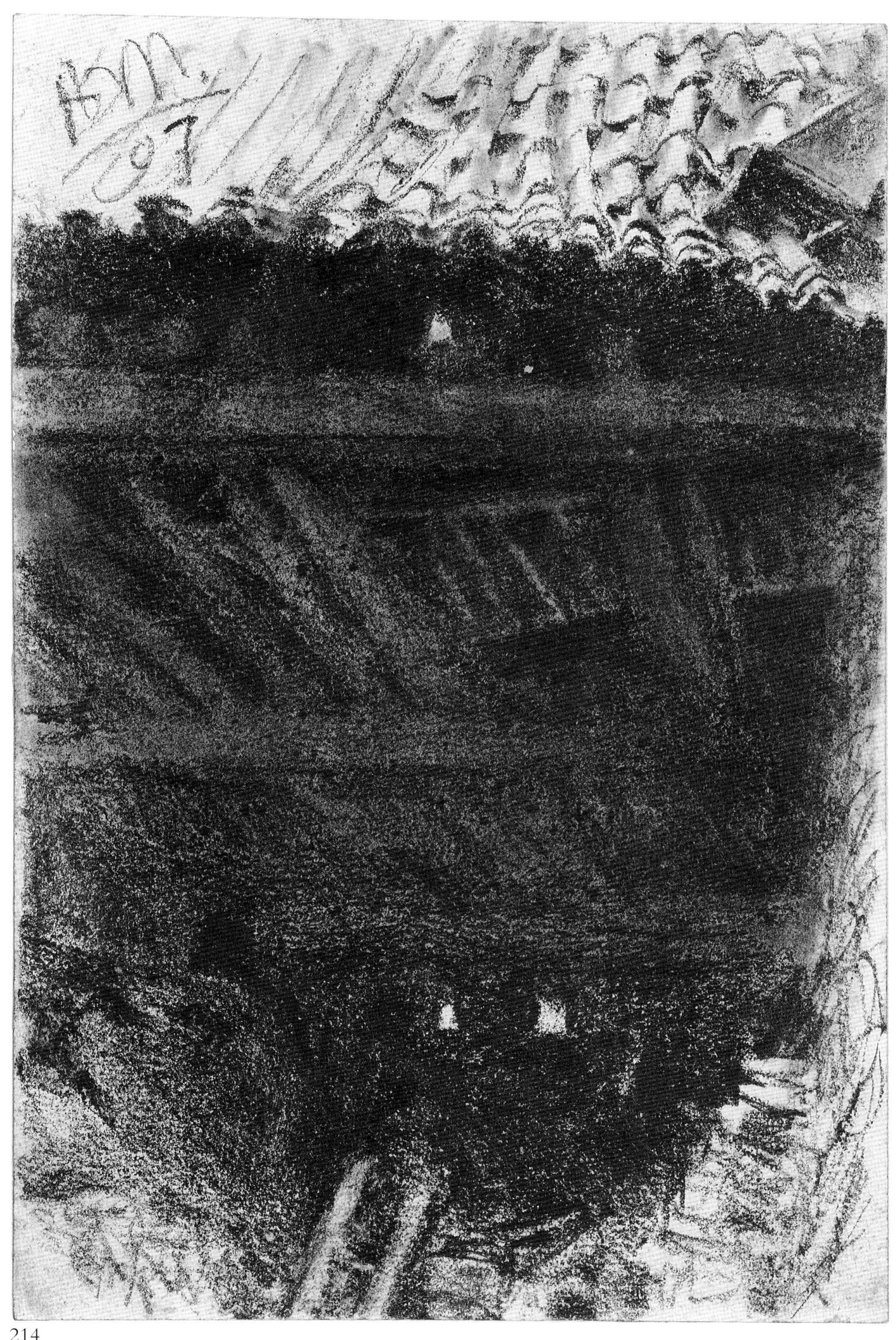

214

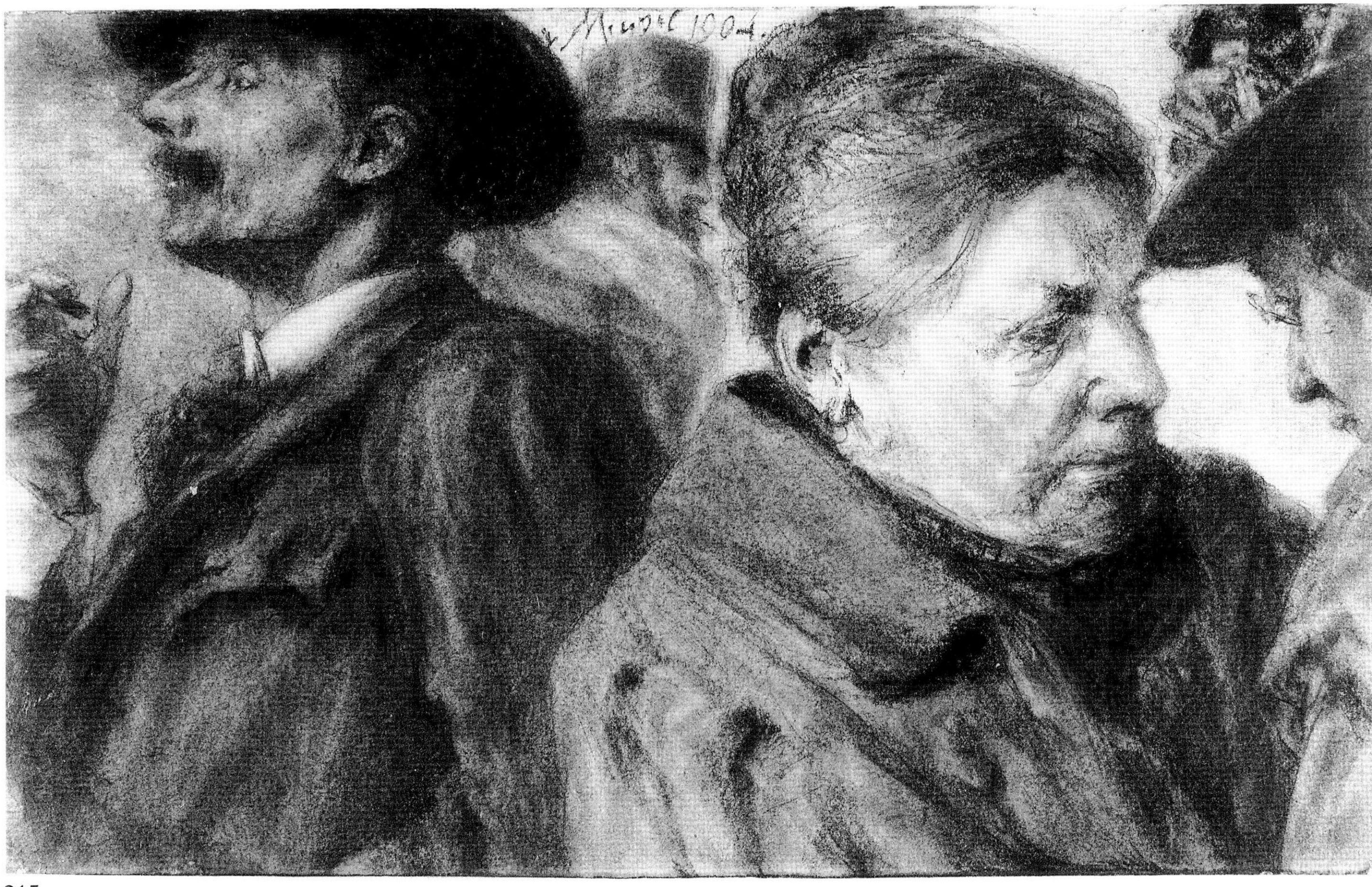

215

This drawing from the last few years of Menzel's life belongs to those works in which an insignificant subject from the inanimate world seems to offer the opportunity for a distanced representation with its own pictorial value (*cf.* cat. 192). The drawing lives in the discreet play of chiaroscuro between the white of the paper and the black of the coarse carpenters pencil. The view from above an old farm roof becomes a flat construction of horizontal and oblique strata. Space is not clearly distinguished. At the top of the picture, the edge of a tiled roof in ruins appears. The ornamental beauty of its irregular line is broken on the left to allow room for Menzels signature, which is integrated into the composition, as a kind of signal of abstraction[1]. These drawings move further and further away from the object and its well-defined data by virtue of their irrationality.

M.R.-R.

1. Menzel's fascination with Japanese wood block prints comes over in this kind of work. *Cf.* on this subject the two letters from Lichtwark to his family, 1881 and 1884, Schellenberg, 1972, p. 140 and p. 561. *Cf.* also cat. 183.

215
Four Heads
1904

Pencil
13.3 21cm
Signed and dated at the top centre: *v Menzel 1904.*
Berlin, Kupferstichkabinett (SZ Menzel N 1733)
Provenance: painter's studio; 1905 Emilie Krigar-Menzel; acquired by the museum in 1906.
Exhibitions: Berlin, 1905, no. 5223; Vienna, 1985, no. 145.
Bibliography: Riemann, 1990, p. 49, fig. 13; Berlin, 1994, no. VII.40.

Two men back to back stand beside two women facing each other. The movement and execution of the figures seem fortuitous yet are full of skill, like the fragment of a photograph taken with a wide-angle lens which would not only portray the silhouettes vaguely, but would also bring the figures in the foreground together. They are almost sketched like silhouettes and are isolated from each other. There is a special refinement in this close juxtaposition of figures. But there is no doubt – they are not touching. In his last drawings Menzel seems to have formally abandoned himself to the pleasure of an 'absence of perspective' already present in earlier works, but particularly emphasized here by the black and white technique. Degas used an analogous idea.

M.R.-R.

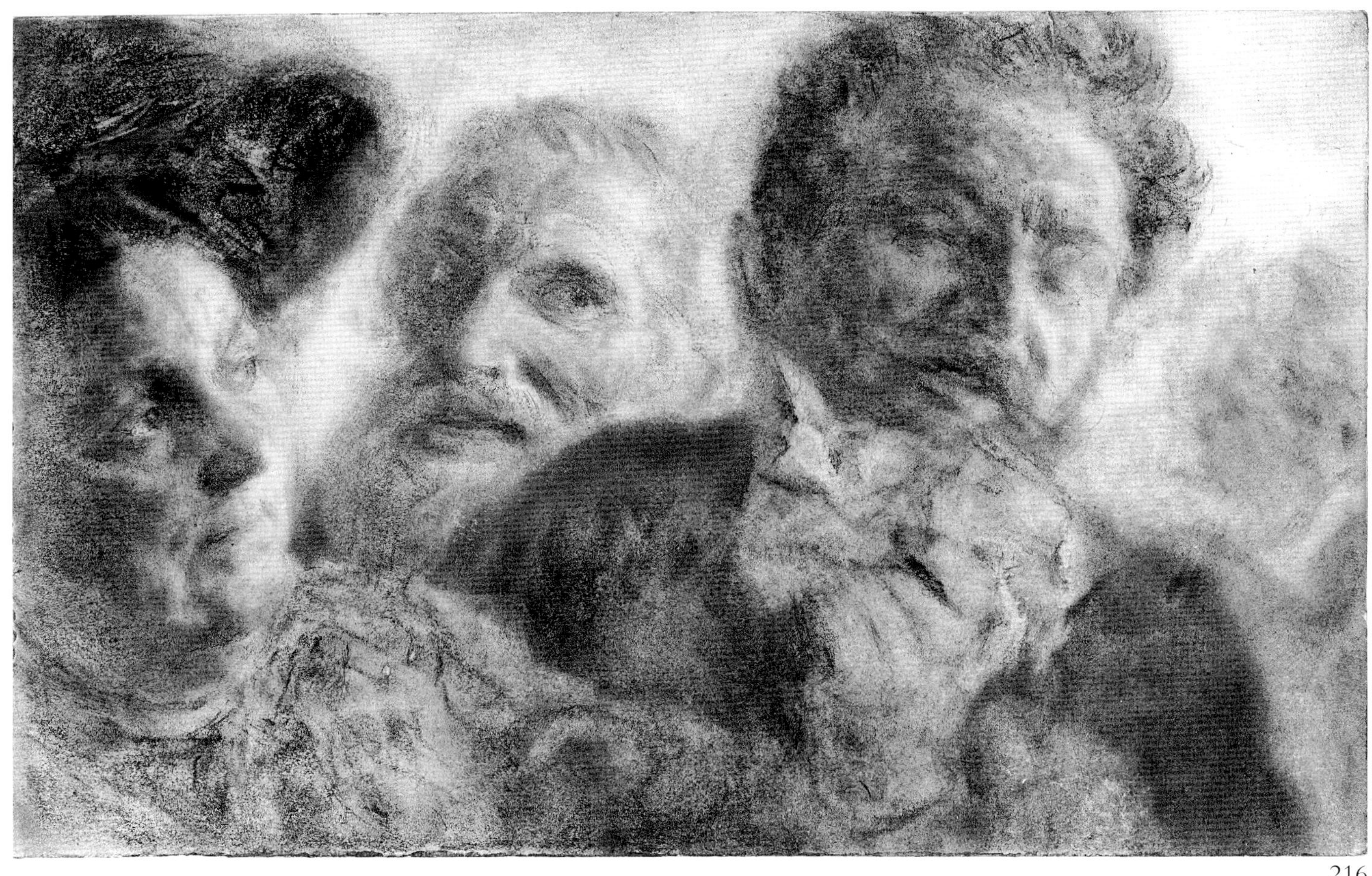

216

216

Four Heads

c. 1904

13.2 × 21.1cm
Berlin, Kupferstichkabinett (SZ Menzel N 1734)

Provenance: Painters studio; 1905 Emilie Krigar-Menzel; acquired by the museum in 1906.
Exhibitions: Berlin, 1905, no. 5229a; Copenhagen, 1985, no. 129.

217

Old Man Looking up and Four Faces

c. 1904-5

Pencil
30.9 × 22.9cm
Berlin, Kupferstichkabinett (SZ Menzel N 246)

Provenance: Painter's studio; 1905 Emilie Krigar-Menzel; acquired by the museum in 1906.
Exhibitions: Berlin, 1905, no. 5228b; Cambridge, 1984, no. 104; Berlin, 1984, no. 125.

At the time when Menzel painted the heads of elderly Jews in the 1850s, his interest in faces was already evident. A thousand miles from the genre painting or anecdote, Menzel tries to create a monumental grand manner by 'painting' with pencil and stump. This subject seems to be an extension of a drawing representing two old men in conversation[1]. M.R.-R.

1. Berlin, Kupferstichkabinett (SZ Menzel N 4435); exhib.cat. Vienna, 1985, no. 146, reprod.

218

Woman Wearing a Hat and Man Applauding

1905

Pencil
21 × 13.3cm
Signed and dated at the top right: *Ad.Menzel. 1905.*
Berlin, Kupferstichkabinett, (SZ Menzel N 1736).

Provenance: Painter's studio; 1905 Emilie Krigar-Menzel; acquired by the museum in 1906.
Exhibitions: Berlin, 1905, no. 5229b; Berlin, 1980 A, no. 404; Vienna, 1985, no. 148; New York, 1990, no. 78.

This may have been Menzel's last drawing, and it seems that the artist is taking up an old subject, that of spectators or listeners, here undoubtedly related to the memory of a journey, suggested by the folkloric hat the man is wearing. But through the souvenir, reality dissipates in a vague dreaminess. The clapping hands could also be hands in prayer, belonging to a third person whom we cannot see. They have a life as autonomous as the hat worn by the woman, which is monstrously tall, occupying nearly half the space. M.R.-R.

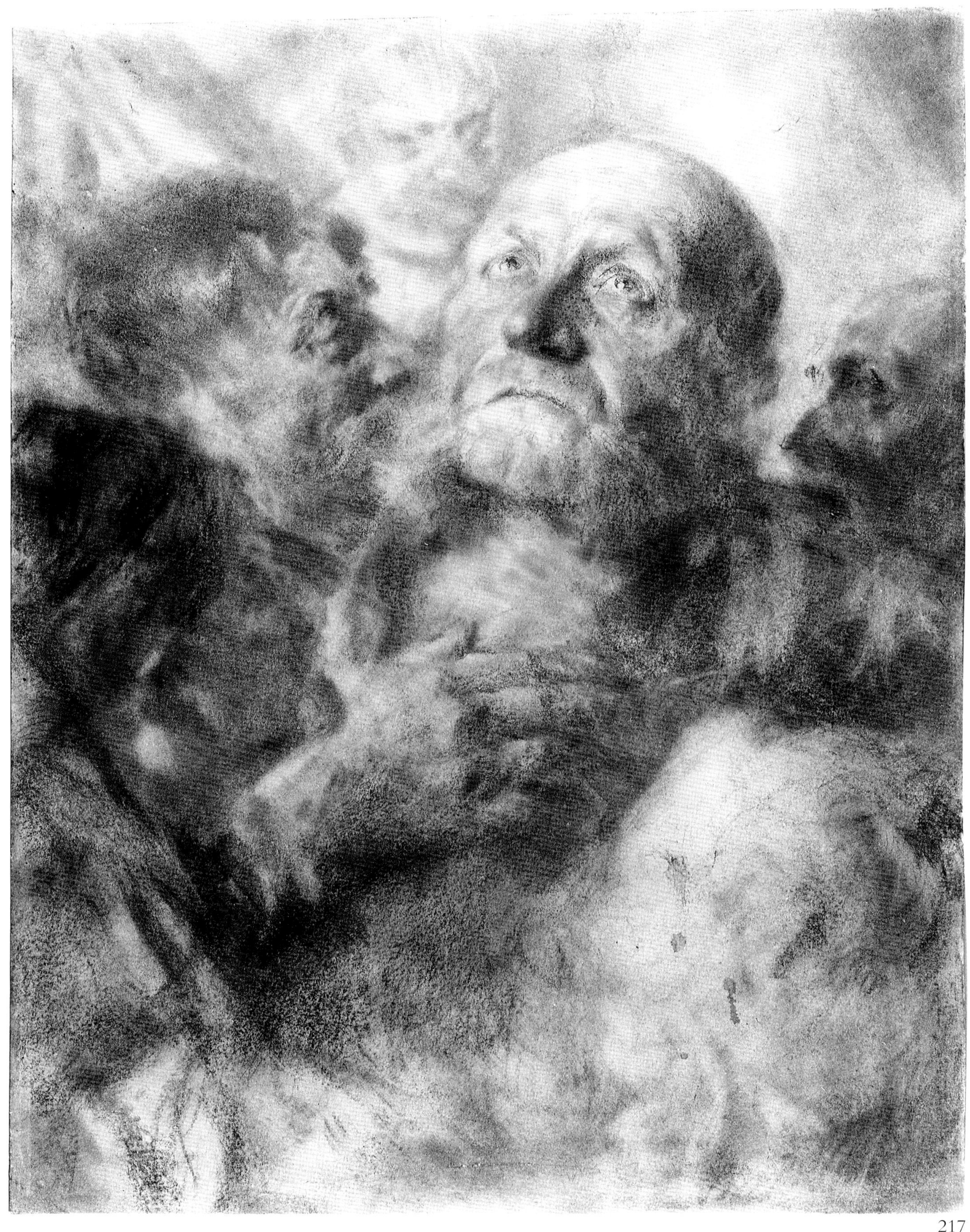

217

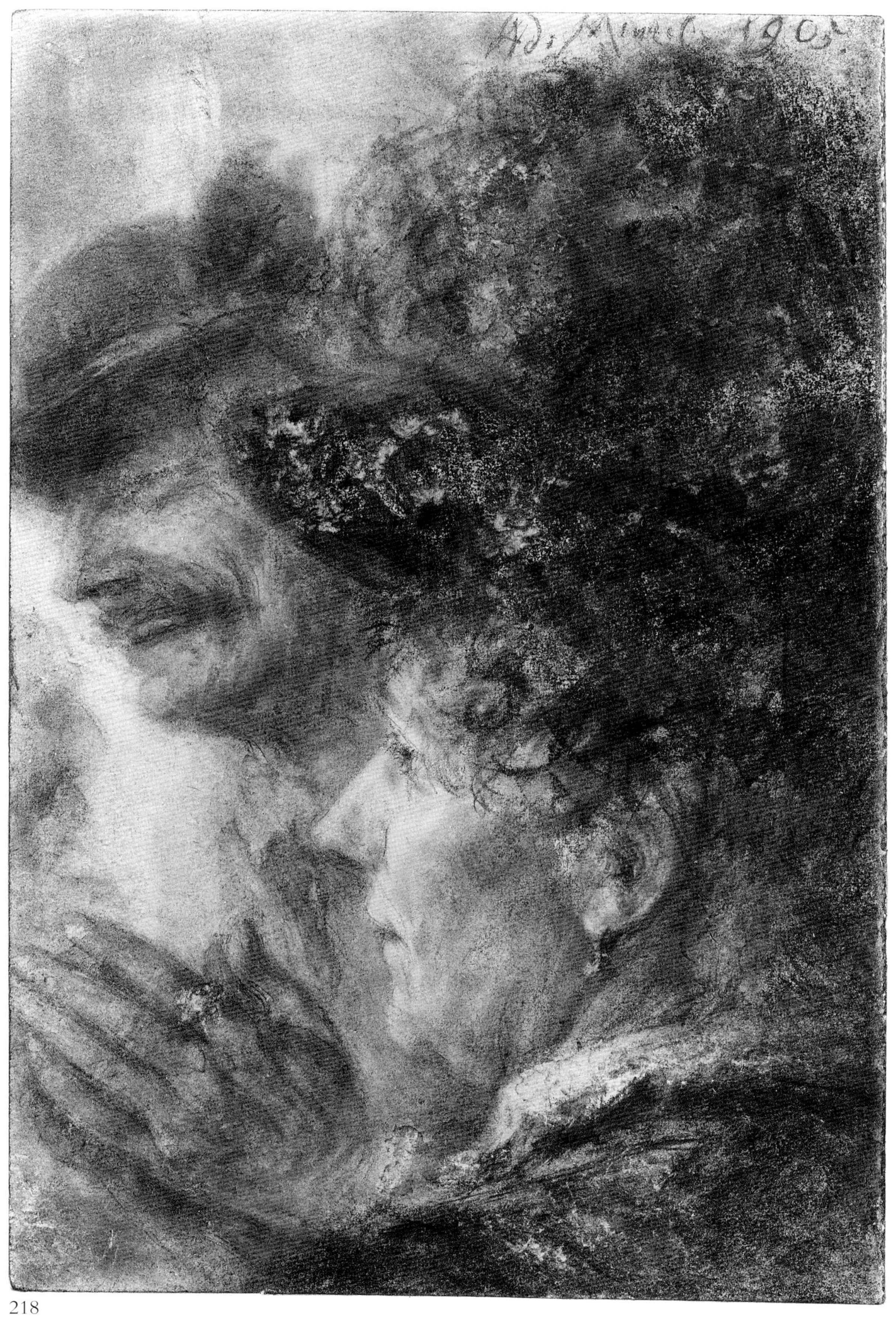

218

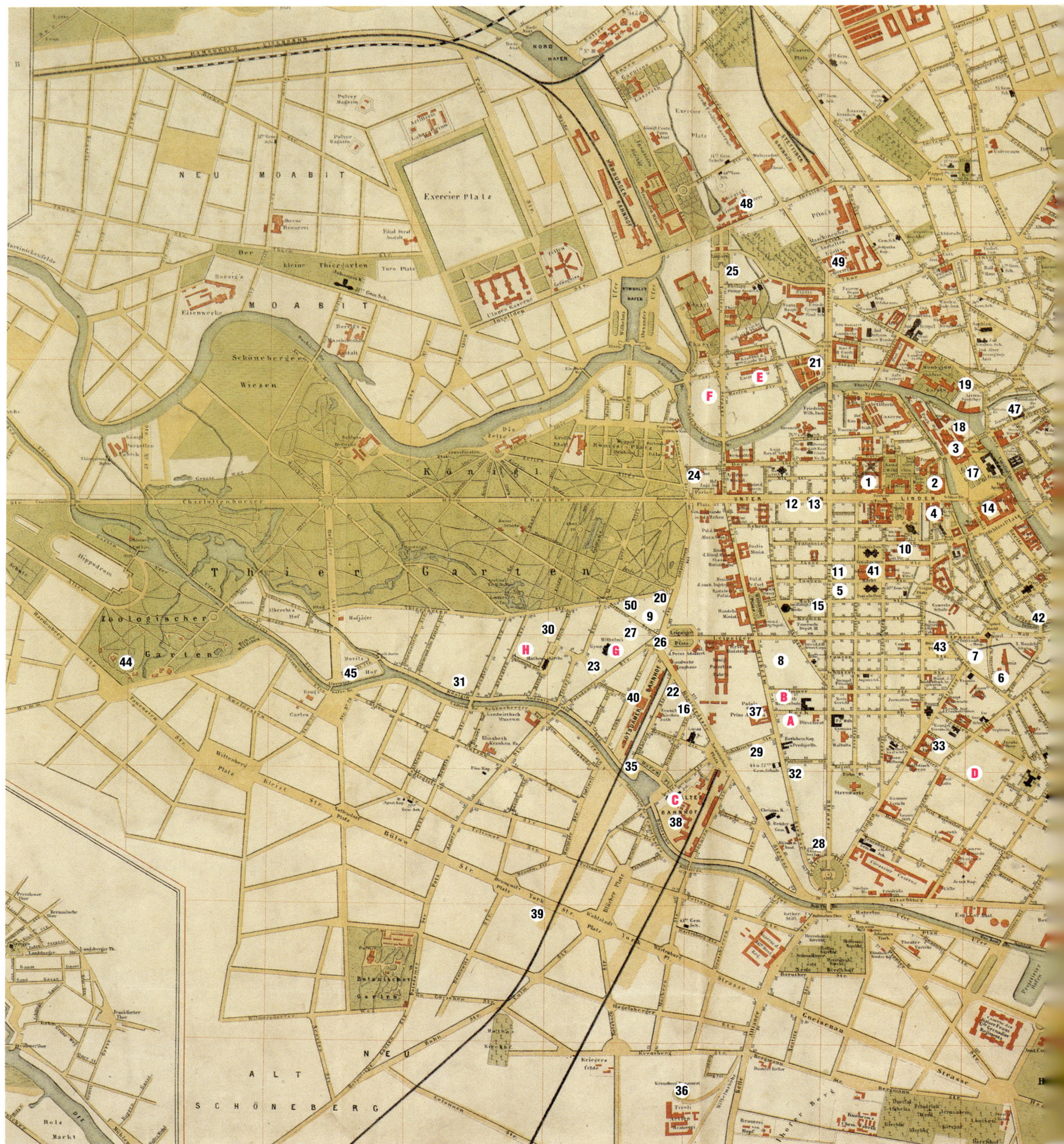

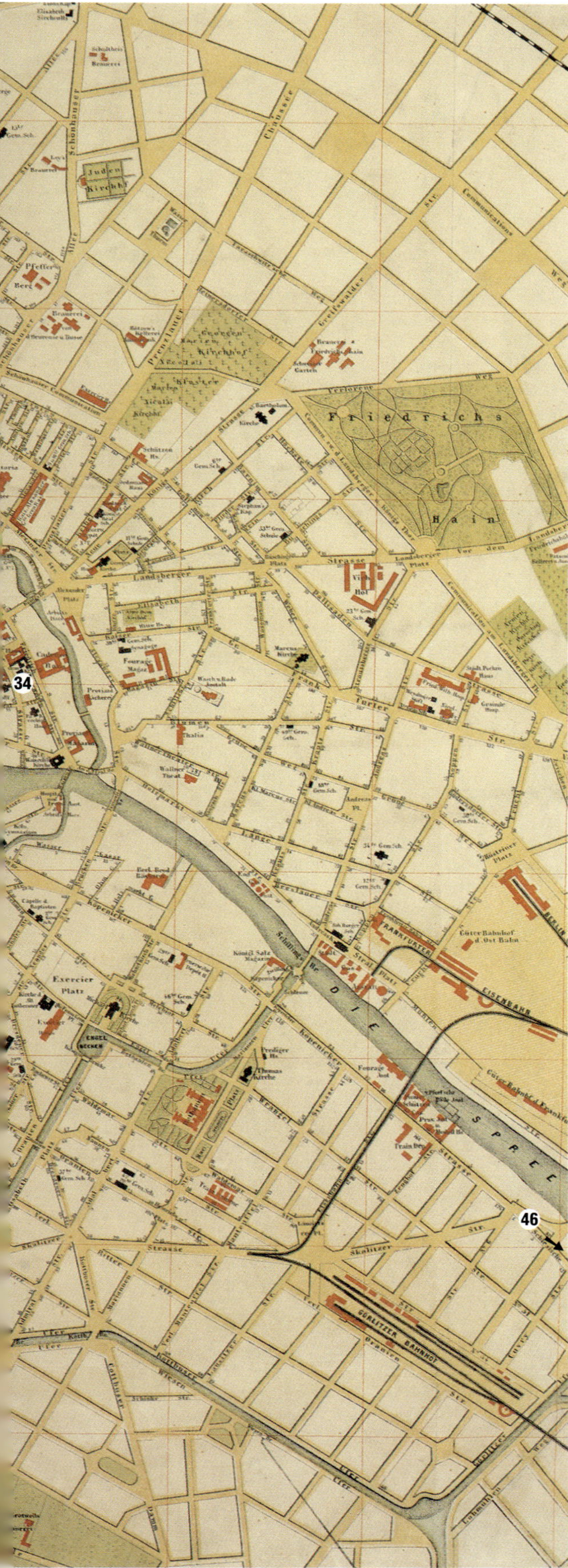

Berlin and Charlottenburg, 1869 (detail). Plan by C. Delius. Berlin, Staatsbibliothek, Maps Department

Where Menzel lived:

A Wilhelmstrasse 39 (1836 to 1839)
B Zimmerstrasse 4 (1839 to end of March 1845)
C Schöneberger Strasse 18 (later became no. 32; April 1845 to March 1847)
D Ritterstrasse 43 (April 1847 to beginning of 1862)
E Marienstrasse 22 (1862 to 1865)
F Luisenstrasse 24 (1865 to November 1870)
G Potsdamer Strasse (November 1870 to 1875)
H Sigismundstrasse 3 (1875 to 1905)

Places of study and exhibition venues:

1 Academy of Arts (Akademie der Künste)
2 The Arsenal (Zeughaus)
3 Neues Museum (with Print Room)
4 Hôtel de Russie, Niederlagstrasse: two pictures by Constable exhibited there in 1839
5 Englisches Haus, Mohrenstrasse 49: first address of the Association of Young Berlin Artists (Verein der jüngeren Künstler); also headquarters of group of intellectuals known as 'Tunnel über der Spree' ('Tunnel over the Spree')
6 Urania assembly room, Kommandantenstrasse 73: later on, headquarters of Association of Young Berlin Artists
7 Kommandantenstrasse 77-79: from 1870 to 1886 headquarters of the Association of Berlin Artists (Verein Berliner Künstler); permanent exhibition from December 1869. Party in Menzel's honour on 19 April 1884
8 Architektenhaus, Wilhelmstrasse 92-93; headquarters of the Association of Berlin Artists from 1887 to 1898
9 Bellevuestrasse 3: headquarters of the Association of Berlin Artists from 1898
10 Galerie Louis Sachse, Jägerstrasse 27; permanent exhibition from 1853 to 1874. The Sachse lithography publishing firm was located at no. 30-31
11 Galerie Louis Sachse, Taubenstrasse 34: from 1874 until it went bankrupt in 1875 shortly after exhibiting Menzel's *The Forge*
12 Galerie Lepke, Unter den Linden 17
13 Unter den Linden 22: an important exhibition of Menzel's work was held here in September 1861 in a building overlooking a courtyard; the 'private' works he showed did not meet with public approbation
14 Royal palace: Guards' room (cat. 94-9, 102, 117-19)
15 Gustav Schauer, Photographic Publications Institute, Friedrichstrasse 188, later Anhaltstrasse 14. Menzel's work was included in some of these publications
16 R. Wagner & Co. (Hermann Pächter, Menzel's dealer), Dessauer Strasse 2
17 Altes Museum (gallery of paintings and Antiquities; Menzel's funeral service held in the rotunda)
18 Nationalgalerie

Notable people and private life:

19 Carl Heinrich Arnold (home and wallpaper workshop, until 1835), Monbijouplatz 10
20 Friedrich Drake, sculptor, Schulgartenstrasse 8; his studio was 'in the Tiergarten' (cf. p. 357)
21 Friedrich Eggers, art critic, editor of the *Deutsches Kunstblatt* review, Friedrichstrasse 135A (later Hirschelstrasse 9; *cf.* p. 357, 383)
22 Theodor Fontane, Hirschelstrasse 14 (= Königgrätzer Strasse)
23 Restaurant Frederich, Potsdamer Strasse 12
24 Magnus Herrmann, Pariser Platz 6 (*cf.* p. 354)
25 Theodor Hosemann, painter friend of Menzel as a young man, Luisenstrasse 67
26 Restaurant Huth, Potsdamer Platz
27 Café Josty, Bellevuestrasse 21-22
28 Franz Kugler, Friedrichstrasse 242 (*cf.* p. 166ff)
29 Eduard Meyerheim, painter, Anhaltische Strasse 20 (cat. 3)
30 Paul Meyerheim, painter, Matthäikirchstrasse 3 (*cf.* p. 313, 383)
31 Ludwig Pietsch, art critic, Bendlerstrasse 16 (later Schöneberger Ufer 34)
32 Max Schasler, art critic, editor of the *Die Dioskuren* review, Wilhelmstrasse 25
33 Fritz Werner, painter, engraver, Menzel's friend and collaborator, Feilnerstrasse 1-2 (cat. 94-9)

Motifs:

34 Former Franciscan church (Klosterkirche), depicted by Menzel several times from 1838 on
35 Schafgraben (cat. 8, 22)
36 Kreuzberg (cat. 21, 30, 31)
37 Palace of Prinz Albrecht (cat. 23, 164)
38 Anhalt railway station (Anhalter Bahnhof; cat. 24)
39 Berlin-Potsdam railway (cat. 35)
40 Potsdam railway station (Potsdamer Bahnhof; Menzel left from here to visit the palaces of Frederick II and his friend Wilhelm Puhlmann)
41 Gendarmenmarkt (where the victims of March 1848 were placed in coffins)
42 Friedrichsgracht (cat. 76)
43 Dönhoffplatz (cat. 85)
44 Zoo (cat. 105-14)
45 Moritzhof (cat. 108); nearby, Albrechtshof (cat. 105-14)
46 Heckmann metal foundry, Schlesische Strasse (cat. 129)
47 Garnisonkirche (cat. 138-42)
48 Royal iron foundry (Königliche Eisengiesserei; wound up in 1874), Invalidenstrasse 36-38 (cat. 147-60)
49 Borsig factory and villa, Chausseestrasse 1 (later Alt-Moabit)
50 Villa Jacoby, Bellevuestrasse 6 (cat. 162)

Bibliography

In the titles of the works devoted to Menzel, the variable spelling of his first name (Adolph – Adolf, the first form being the one he always used himself) has been preserved. The same applies to the optional use of 'von' before his name designating noble status, an honour accorded to the artist late in life.

A bibliography has been devoted to Menzel: Renate Weinhold, *Menzelbibliographie*, Leipzig, 1959. *Cf.* also Trost, 1980, Zangs, 1992 and Kohle, 1993.

Achenbach, 1984 = Sigrid Achenbach, 'Die Graphik Adolph Menzels', exhib. cat. Berlin, 1984, pp. 35-40.

Amersdorffer, 1924 = *Adolph Menzel. Personalie*, facsimile edition after the manuscript held in the archives of the Berlin Academy of Arts, edited and introduced by Alexander Amersdorffer, Leipzig, 1924.

Anderson, 1983 = Benedict Anderson, *Imagined Communities. Reflections on the Origin and Spread of Nationalism*, London, 1983.

Andree, 1964 = *Katalog der Gemälde des 19. Jahrhunderts im Walraff-Richartz-Museum*, edited by Rolf Andree, Cologne, 1964.

Anon., 1852 = Anonymous, *Deutsches Kunstblatt*, III, 1852.

Anon., 1855 = Anonymous, 'Aus dem Pariser Ausstellungspalast', *Deutsches Kunstblatt*, year 6, no. 32, 9 August 1855.

Anon., 1896 = Anonymous, *Berlin und seine Eisenbahnen*, Berlin, 1896.

Anon., 1904-5 = Anonymous, 'Wie Adolph Menzel arbeitete', *Moderne Kunst in Meisterholzschnitten*, 19, 1904-5, book 7, pp. 186-7.

Anon., 1905 = Anonymous, 'Menzel-Erinnerungen', *Vossische Zeitung*, no. 71, 11.2.1905.

Arndt, 1994 = Karl Arndt, '"Orbis pictus": Zu Lichtenbergs Hogarth. Erklärungen', *Niederdeutsche Beiträge zur Kunst*, 1994, p. 113f.

Arnold, (1905) 1992 = Carl Johann Arnold, *Erinnerungen aus meinem Zusammenleben mit Adolph Menzel*, Weimar, 1905. Quoted after Lammel, 1992, pp. 127-47.

Bailly-Herzberg, 1986 = *Correspondance de Camille Pissarro*, edited by Janine Bailly-Herzberg, Paris, 1986.

Bartoschek, 1980 = Gerd Bartoschek, 'Zur Entstehung des Krönungsbildes', exhib. cat. Berlin, 1980 A, pp. 49-60.

Becker, 1922 = Robert Becker, *Adolph Menzel und seine schlesische Verwandtschaft*, Strasbourg, 1922.

Becker, 1984 A = Ingeborg Becker, 'Allegorie und Hieroglyphe – Festkarten, Diplome, Einladungen und Titelblätter', exhib. cat. Berlin, 1984, pp. 41-3.

Becker, 1984 B = Ingeborg Becker, '"Friedrich über alles" – Menzel und die Buchillustration', exhib. cat. Berlin, 1984, p. 44-51.

Beenken, 1944 = Hermann Beenken, *Das 19. Jahrhundert in der deutschen Kunst, Aufgaben und Gehalte, Versuch einer Rechenschaft*, Munich, 1944.

Beneke/Gramlich, 1994 = Sabine Beneke and Sybille Gramlich, *Berlin Museum, Märkisches Museum. Gemälde I, 1, 16.-19. Jahrhundert. Verzeichnis der Bestände des künftigen Stadtmuseums Berlin*, Berlin, 1994.

Berckenhagen, 1958 = Ekhart Berckenhagen, *Antoine Pesne*, Berlin, 1958.

Berger, n.d. = Joachim Berger, *Kreuzberger Wanderbuch*, Berlin, n.d.

Bergsträsser, 1969 = Gisela Bergsträsser, 'Menzels Zeichnungen zum Rahmen des Flötenkonzerts', *Berliner Museen*, n.s. 19, Berlin, 1969, pp. 42-5.

Berlin, 1994 = *Das Berliner Kupferstichkabinett. Ein Handbuch zur Sammlung*, edited by Alexander Dückers, Berlin, 1994.

Beta, (1898) 1992 = Ottomar Beta, 'Gespräche mit Adolf Menzel', *Deutsche Revue*, year 23, vol. 2, pp. 45-58 and vol. 3, pp. 102-18, Stuttgart and Leipzig, 1898. Quoted after Lammel, 1992, pp. 5-53.

Beta, (1899) 1992 = Ottomar Beta, 'Neue Gespräche mit A. v. Menzel', *Deutsche Revue*, year 24, vol. 3, pp. 166-79, Stuttgart and Leipzig, 1899. Quoted after Lammel, 1992, pp. 53-72.

Birsak, 1990 = Kurt Birsak, 'Die Salzburger Musikinstrumenten-Familie Schorn und ihre Viole d'amore im SMCA', *Salzburger Museum C.A. Das Kunstwerk des Monats*, January 1990, Salzburg, 1990.

Bluhm/Nitsche, 1993 = Detlef Bluhm and Rainer Nitsche (ed.), *Berlin ist das Allerletzte. Absagen in höchsten Tönen*, Berlin, 1993.

Boas, 1941 = George Boas, 'Il faut être de son temps', *Journal of Aesthetics and Art Criticism*, 1, 1941, p. 52ff.

Bock, 1923 = Elfried Bock, *Adolph Menzel. Verzeichnis seines graphischen Werkes*, Berlin, 1923.

Boime, 1980 = Albert Boime, *Thomas Couture and the Eclectic Vision*, New Haven/London, 1980.

Boime, 1990 = Albert Boime, 'Social Identity and Political Authority in the Response of two Prussian Painters to the Revolution of 1848', *Art History*, 3, 1990, pp. 344-87.

Bonhommé, 1976 = *Catalogue de l'exposition François Bonhommé dit Le Forgeron*, City of Nancy, musée de l'Histoire du fer, Jarville, 1976.

Boockmann, 1982 A = Hartmut Boockmann, *Die Marienburg im 19. Jahrhundert*, Frankfurt-am-Main/Berlin/Vienna, 1982.

Boockmann, 1982 B = Hartmut Boockmann, 'Das ehemalige Deutschordensschloß Marienburg 1772 bis 1945. Die Geschichte eines politischen Denkmals', *Geschichtswissenschaft und Vereinswesen im 19. Jahrhundert*, Göttingen, 1982 (= *Veröffentlichungen des Max-Planck-Instituts für Geschichte*, I), pp. 99-162.

Börsch-Supan, 1973 = Helmut Börsch-Supan and Karl-Wilhelm Jähnig, *Caspar David Friedrich. Gemälde, Druckgraphik und bildmäßige Zeichnungen*, Berlin, 1973.

Börsch-Supan, 1988 = Helmut Börsch-Supan, *Die deutsche Malerei von Anton Graff bis Hans von Marées*, Munich, 1988.

Brandt, 1928 = Paul Brandt, *Schaffende Arbeit und bildende Kunst*, Leipzig, 1928.

Bredt, 1920 = Ernst Wilhelm Bredt, *Adolph Menzel, Wanderbuch*, Munich, 1920.

Brinkmann, 1967 = Richard Brinkmann, *Theodor Fontane. über die Verbindlichkeit des Unverbindlichen*, Munich, 1967.

Brockerhoff, 1937 = Kurt Brockerhoff, 'Eine unbekannte Gebrauchsgraphik Adolph Menzels', *Zeitschrift des Vereins für die Geschichte Berlins*, year 54, issue 3, Berlin, 1937, pp. 86-90.

Burckhardt, 1955 = Jakob Burckhardt, *Briefe*, edited by Max Burckhardt, vol. III, Basle, 1955.

Busch, 1981 A = Günter Busch, 'Menzels Grenzen': exhib. cat. Kiel, 1981, pp. 11-12.

Busch, 1981 B = Günter Busch, 'Menzel der Zeichner', exhib. cat. Kiel, 1981, pp. 22-5.

Busch, 1985 = Werner Busch, *Die notwendige Arabeske. Wirklichkeitsaneignung und Stilisierung in der deutschen Kunst des 19. Jahrhunderts*, Berlin, 1985.

Busch, 1991 = Werner Busch, 'Adolph Menzels "Begegnung Friedrichs II. mit Kaiser Joseph II. in Neisse im Jahre 1769" und Moritz von Schwinds, "Kaiser Rudolfs Ritt zum Grabe"', *Jahrbuch der Berliner Museen*, 33, Berlin, 1991, pp. 173-84.

Cardona, 1931 = Emilia Cardona, *Vie de Jean Boldini*, n.p., 1931.

Cassirer, 1923 = Else Cassirer (ed.), *Künstlerbriefe aus dem neunzehnten Jahrhundert*, Berlin, 1923, pp. 329-50.

Cat. NG, 1876-1907 = *Verzeichnis der Gemälde und Bildwerke in der Nationalgalerie zu Berlin*, edited by Max Jordan (nos 1-16).

Cat. NG, 1908 = *Verzeichnis der Gemälde und Bildwerke in der Nationalgalerie zu Berlin*, edited by Hugo von Tschudi.

Cat. NG, 1911-18 = *Verzeichnis der Gemälde und Bildwerke in der Nationalgalerie zu Berlin*, edited by Ludwig Justi.

Cat. NG, 1913-29 = *Verzeichnis der Bildnissammlung zu Berlin*, edited by Hans

Mackowsky.
Cat. NG, 1933-5 = *Verzeichnis der Gemälde und Bildwerke im Kronprinzenpalais zu Berlin*, edited by Ludwig Justi.
Cat. NG, 1976 = *Verzeichnis der vereinigten Kunstsammlungen Nationalgalerie (Preußischer Kulturbesitz), Galerie des 20. Jahrhunderts (Land Berlin)*, vol. 1: *Nineteenth century*, edited by Dieter Honisch.
Cat. NG, 1986 = *Die Gemälde der Nationalgalerie. Verzeichnis. Deutsche Malerei vom Klassizismus bis zum Impressionismus. Ausländische Malerei von 1800 bis 1930*, Staatliche Museen zu Berlin, Nationalgalerie, Berlin, 1986.
Chapeaurouge, 1960 = Donat de Chapeaurouge, 'Das Milieu als Porträt', *Wallraf-Richartz-Jahrbuch*, XXII, Cologne, 1960, pp. 137-58.
Chapeaurouge, 1990 = Donat de Chapeaurouge, 'Menzels Friedrichbilder im "Historischen Genre"', Ekkehard Mai (ed.), *Historienmalerei in Europa*, Mainz, 1990, pp. 213-27.
Cologne, 1986 = Anonymous, *Bestandskatalog der Gemäldesammlung des Wallraf-Richartz-Museums*, 2 vols, Cologne, 1986.

Deetjen, 1934 = Werner Deetjen, 'Adolph Menzel und Adolf Schöll. Ungedruckte Briefe Menzels', *Jahrbuch der preußischen Kunstsammlungen*, vol. 55, supplement, Berlin, 1934, pp. 30-40.
Delmar, (1905) 1992 = Axel Delmar, '"Die kleine Exzellenz"', *Die Woche*, year 7, Berlin, 1905, pp. 242b-d and 277-80d. Quoted after Lammel, 1992, pp. 99-126.
Dittmar, 1987 = Peter Dittmar, 'Der zwölfjährige Christus im Tempel von Adolf Menzel: ein Beispiel für den Antijudaismus im 19. Jahrhundert', *Idea. Jahrbuch der Hamburger Kunsthalle*, 6, Hamburg, 1987, pp. 81-96.
Donop, 1902 = Lionel von Donop, *Katalog der Handzeichnungen, Aquarelle und Ölstudien in der National-Galerie*, Berlin, 1902.
Donop, 1908 = *Handzeichnungen Adolph von Menzels*. Introduction by Lionel von Donop, Neue Photographische Gesellschaft zu Berlin, 1908.
Dorgerloh, 1896 = A. Dorgerloh, *Verzeichnis der durch Kunstdruck vervielfältigten Arbeiten Adolph Menzels*, Leipzig, 1896.
Doria, 1982 = Vito Doria, *Boldini, Inedito/Inédit/Unpublished Works*, Bologna, 1982.
Dörr, 1988 = Cornelia Dörr, 'Adolph Menzel und der Kasseler Kunstverein', *Kasseler Heimat*, 38, Kassel, 1988, pp. 90-8.
Drescher/Kroll, 1981 = Renate Kroll and Horst Drescher, *Potsdam. Ansichten aus drei Jahrhunderten. Bestandskatalog des Kupferstichkabinetts und der Sammlung der Zeichnungen der Staatlichen Museen zu Berlin*, Weimar, 1981.
Dülberg, 1906 = Franz Dülberg, 'Die deutsche Jahrhundertausstellung Berlin 1906', *Zeitschrift für bildende Kunst*, XVII, Leipzig, 1906.
Dumas, 1885 = *Exposition des oeuvres d'Adolphe Menzel. Catalogue illustré*, preface by François-Guillaume Dumas, Paris, 1885. (Taken from *Etude sur Menzel* by F.-G. Dumas, Maîtres modernes, Paris, 1885).
Duranty, 1880 = Edmond Duranty, 'Adolphe Menzel', [I:] *Gazette des Beaux-Arts*, 2nd per., year 22, vol. XXI, 1880, pp. 201-17; [II:] vol. XXII, 1880, pp. 105-24.

Ebertshäuser, 1976 = Heidi Ebertshäuser (ed.), *Adolph von Menzel: Das graphische Werk*, 2 vols, Munich, 1976.
Eckardt, 1987 = Götz Eckardt, 'Der junge Menzel in Sanssouci', *Forschungen und Berichte, Staatliche Museen zu Berlin*, vol. 26, Berlin, 1987, pp. 251-8.
Eckardt, 1989 = Götz Eckardt, 'Johann Gottfried Schadow und Adolf Menzel – Zur Kontroverse von 1840 und ihren Ursachen', *Zeitschrift des Deutschen Vereins für Kunstwissenschaft*, 43, vol. 2, 1989, pp. 36-46.
Eggers, 1852 = Friedrich Eggers, 'Über Stoffe für Genre- und Landschaftsmaler', *Deutsches Kunstblatt*, vol. 3, 1852, pp. 107-8.
Eggers, 1854 = Friedrich Eggers, 'Künstler und Werkstätten: Adolph Menzel', *Deutsches Kunstblatt*, vol. 5, 1854, pp. 2-3, pp. 10-12 and pp. 18-20. Repr. Berlin, 1925.
Ellwart, 1985 = Ursula Ellwart, *Menzels Friedrichsbilder (1849-1860). Untersuchungen zu ihrer zeitgenössischen Rezeption*, thesis memoir, Tübingen, 1985.
Ellwart, 1988 = Ursula Ellwart, 'Menzels Friedrichsbilder in der zeitgenössischen Kunstkritik ', *Pantheon*, vol. XLVI, 1988, pp. 121-30.
Elvers, 1983 = Rudolf Elvers, 'Über das Berlinische Zwitterwesen: Felix Mendelssohn Bartholdy in Briefen über Berlin', exhib. cat. *Die Mendelssohns in Berlin*, Bonn/Düsseldorf/Berlin, 1983.
Engel, 1906 = Julius Engel, 'Adolph Menzel als Glasmaler', *Kunst und Künstler*, year 4, 1906, pp. 277-80.
Engels, 1848 = Friedrich Engels, 'The *Zeitungs-Halle* on the Rhine Province', *Neue Rheinische Zeitung*, no. 87, 27 August 1848.
Entrup, 1995 = Dorothee Entrup, *Adolph Menzels Illustrationen zu Franz Kuglers 'Geschichte Friedrichs des Großen'. Ein Beitrag zur historischen Bewertung der Kunst des jungen Menzel*, (thesis memoir, Göttingen, 1994) Weimar, 1995.
Erbe, 1987 = Michael Erbe, 'Berlin im Kaiserreich (1871-1918)', *Geschichte Berlins*, edited by Wolfgang Ribbe, vol. II, Munich, 1987.
Eschenburg, 1984 = Barbara Eschenburg (ed.), *Spätromantik und Realismus, Bayerische Staatsgemäldesammlungen, Neue Pinakothek, Gemäldekataloge*, vol. V, Munich, 1984.
Esner, 1996 = Rachel Esner, 'Un Prussien à Paris: l'exposition Menzel en 1885', *48/14 La revue du Musée d'Orsay*, 2, February 1996, pp. 54-61.
Essen, 1971 = Jutta Held (ed.), *Katalog der Gemälde 19. Jahrhundert*, Folkwang Museum, Essen, 1971.
Evers-Milner, (1940) 1992 = Helge Evers-Milner, 'Ein Besuch bei Adolf Menzel', *Ein Frauenbild aus der Menzelzeit*, Berlin, 1940. Quoted after Lammel, 1992, pp. 151-2.

Falkenhausen, 1984 = Susanne von Falkenhausen, 'Historie und Politik – Beliebigkeit und Sinngebung: Menzel und der Historismus', exhib. cat. Berlin, 1984, pp. 22-34.
Fechner, (1927) 1992 = Hanns Fechner, 'Meine Erinnerungen an Adolf Menzel', *Deutsche Monatshefte*, year 3, vol. 1, 1927, pp. 233-42. Quoted after Lammel, 1992, pp. 243-8.
Feist, 1980 = Peter H. Feist, 'Adolph Menzel und der Realismus', exhib. cat. Berlin, 1980 A, pp. 17-25.
Fischer, 1989 = Erik Fischer, 'Exkurs. Zwei Analysen der Arbeitsmethode Eckersbergs', exhib. cat. *Zeichnungen aus Dänemark*, Staatliche Museen zu Berlin, Nationalgalerie, Berlin, 1989, pp. 11-17.
Fontane, 1872 = Theodor Fontane, 'Dr. Friedrich Eggers. Bericht über Trauerfeier und Überführung', *Erste Beilage zur Königlich Privilegierten Berlinischen Zeitung*, no. 191, Saturday 17 August 1872.
Fontane, 1968-1971 = Theodor Fontane, *Briefe*, edited by Kurt Schreinert and Charlotte Jolles, 4 vols, Berlin, 1968-71 (Propyläen pub.).
Fontane, 1969 = Theodor Fontane, *Sämtliche Werke*, edited by Charlotte Jolles, vol. XIX, Munich, 1969.
Fontane, 1970 = Theodor Fontane, *Aufsätze zur bildenden Kunst*, vol. 23 of complete works, edited by Edgar Groß, 2 vols, Munich, 1970.
Fontane, 1972 = Theodor Fontane, *Sämtliche Werke*, edited by Kurt Schreiner and Herman Kunisch, vol. XVIII, Munich, 1972 ('Berliner Ton', written between 1876 and 1882; 'Die Märker und die Berliner', 1889).
Fontane, 1979 = Theodor Fontane, *Briefe (Werke, Schriften und Briefe, Abteilung IV)*, edited by Otto Drude and Helmuth Nürnberger, vol. II, Munich, 1979.
Fontane, 1980 = *Fontanes Briefe*, edited by Gotthard Erler, Berlin/Weimar, 1980.
Fontane, 1981 = *Theodor Fontane. Ein Leben in Briefen*, edited by Otto Drude, Frankfurt-am-Main, 1981.
Fontane, 1982 A = Theodor Fontane, *Autobiographische Schriften*, edited by Gotthard Erler, Peter Goldammer, Joachim Krüger, Berlin/Weimar, 1982.
Fontane, 1982 B = Theodor Fontane, *Briefe (Werke, Schriften und Briefe, Abteilung IV)*, edited by Otto Drude and Helmuth Nürnberger, vol. IV, Munich, 1982.
Fontane, 1994 A = Theodor Fontane, *Tagebücher 1852, 1855-1858*, edited by Charlotte Jolles in collaboration with Rudolf Muhs, Berlin, 1994.
Fontane, 1994 B = Theodor Fontane, *Tagebücher 1866-1882, 1884-1898*, edited by Gotthard Erler in collaboration with Charlotte Erler, Berlin, 1994.
Forster-Hahn, 1977 = Françoise Forster-Hahn, 'Adolf Menzel's "Daguerrotypical" Image of Frederick the Great: A Liberal Bourgeois Interpretation of German History', *Art Bulletin*, 59, 1977, pp. 242-61.
Forster-Hahn, 1978 = Françoise Forster-Hahn, 'Authenticity into Ambivalence: The Evolution of Menzel's Drawings', *Master Drawings*, vol. 16, 1978, pp. 255-83.
Forster-Hahn, 1980 = Françoise Forster-Hahn, 'Menzels Realismus im Spiegel der französischen Kritik', exhib. cat. Berlin, 1980 A, pp. 27-47.
Forster-Hahn, 1981 = Françoise Forster-Hahn, 'A. Menzels Eisenwalzwerk. Kunst im Konflikt zwischen Tradition und Wirklichkeit',

Buddensieg/Rogge (ed.), *Die nützlichen Künste*, exhibition in Berlin, 1981, pp. 122-9.
Forster-Hahn, 1988 = Françoise Forster-Hahn, '"Die Aufbahrung der Märzgefallenen". Menzel's Unfinished Painting as a Parable of the Aborted Revolution of 1848', Christian Beutler, Peter-Klaus Schuster and Martin Warnke (ed.), *Kunst um 1800 und die Folgen. Werner Hofmann zu Ehren*, Munich, 1988, pp. 221-32.
Forster-Hahn, 1991 = Françoise Forster-Hahn, '"No Day without a Line": Menzel's Construction of Authenticity', *Drawing*, XIII, 1991, pp. 49-54.
Forster-Hahn, 1993 = Françoise Forster-Hahn, 'Die "formende Kraft" historischer Bilder. Adolph Menzels und Anton von Werners Darstellungen deutscher Geschichte', exhib. cat. by Anton von Werner, *Geschichte in Bildern*, Berlin Museum and Deutsches Historisches Museum, Berlin, 1993, pp. 80-9.
Forster-Hahn, 1995 = Françoise Forster-Hahn, 'The Politics of Display or the Display of Politics?', *Art Bulletin*, vol. LXXVII, June 1995.
Forster-Hahn, 1996 = Françoise Forster-Hahn, 'Constructing New Histories: Displays of Art as Forces of Nationalism and Modernity', *Imagining Modern German Culture, 1889-1910, Studies in the History of Art*, National Gallery of Art, Washington, D.C., 1996.
Forstreuter, 1967 = Kurt Forstreuter, 'Bildnisse von Hochmeistern des Deutschen Ordens im Mittelalter', *Acht Jahrhunderte Deutscher Orden in Einzeldarstellungen*, edited by R. Klemens Wieser (in homage to Marian Tumler on her 80th birthday), Bad Godesberg, 1967, pp. 1-14.
Frank, 1994-5 = Hilmar Frank, 'Goethe, Schadow und das Formgesetz der Plastik, exhib. cat. *Johann Gottfried Schadow und die Kunst seiner Zeit*, Kunsthalle, Düsseldorf, Germanisches Nationalmuseum, Nuremberg and Nationalgalerie, Berlin, 1994-5, pp. 141-7.
Friedlaender, (1905) 1992 = Georg Friedlaender, 'Menzels Erinnerungen', *Vossische Zeitung*, 18 February 1905. Quoted after Lammel, 1992, pp. 236-40.
Frisch, n.d. = *Kaffe-Klexbilder. Humoristische Handzeichnungen von Wilh. von Kaulbach, Echter und Muhr*, edited by W. Frisch, Leipzig, n.d. [1880].

G., 1904-5 = G. [Walther Gensel?], 'Menzels Begräbnis', *Kunstchronik*, n.s., year XVl, Leipzig, 1904-5, 24 February.
Gaehtgens, 1985 = Thomas W. Gaehtgens, *Versailles als Nationaldenkmal*, Antwerp/Berlin, 1985.
Gaehtgens/Fleckner, 1995 = Thomas W. Gaehtgens and Uwe Fleckner, *Historienmalerei, eine Geschichte der klassischen Bildgattungen in Quellentexten und Kommentaren*, Berlin, 1995.
Gensel, 1904-5 = Walther Gensel, 'Die Menzel-Ausstellung in der Berliner National-Galerie', *Kunstchronik,* year XVI, no. 21, 1904-5.
Gillet, 1905 A = Louis Gillet, 'Menzel', 1st article, *Revue de l'art ancien et moderne*, vol. 17, 1905.
Gillet, 1905 B = Louis Gillet, 'Menzel', 2nd article, *Revue de l'art ancien et moderne*, vol. 17, 1905.
Glatzer, 1993 = Ruth Glatzer, *Berlin wird Kaiserstadt. Panorama einer Metropole 1871-1890*, Berlin, 1993.
Gonse, 1885 = Louis Gonse, 'Exposition d'Adolph Menzel', *Gazette des Beaux-Arts*, 1885, vol. 31, pp. 519-20.
Gréard, 1897 = M. O. Gréard, *Jean-Louis-Ernest Meissonier. Ses souvenirs – ses entretiens. Précédés d'une étude sur sa vie et son oeuvre*, Paris, 1897.
Grisebach, 1984 = Lucius Grisebach, 'Moltkes Fernglas, der Köchin Lenas Kamm und das Tintenfaß auf dem Tisch der Akademie: Menzels Blick für das Konkrete', exhib. cat. Berlin, 1984, pp. 18-20.
Grohn, 1976 = Hans Werner Grohn, *Menzel. Die Krönung König Wilhelms I. zu Königsberg. Blickpunkt 1*, Niedersächsische Landesgalerie, Hanover, 1976.
Gronau, 1987 = Hans-Joachim Gronau, 'Maltechnische Beobachtungen am unvollendeten Gemälde "Ansprache Friedrichs des Großen an seine Generale vor der Schlacht bei Leuthen" von Adolph Menzel', *Forschungen und Berichte, Staatliche Museen zu Berlin*, vol. 26, 1987, pp. 283-90.
Grossmann, 1994 = Joachim Grossmann, *Künstler, Hof und Bürgertum*, Berlin, 1994.
Günther, 1981 = Sonja Günther, 'Die Luisenstadt. "Bürgerliches Gewimmel" und "sanfte Gartenlust"', exhib. cat. Berlin, 1981, pp. 385-417.

Hagen, 1857 = August Hagen, *Die Deutsche Kunst in unserem Jahrhundert*, vol. 1, Berlin, 1857.
Hamann, 1906 = Richard Hamann, *Ein Gang durch die Jahrhundert-Ausstellung. 1775-1875*, Berlin, 1906.
Hamann, 1914 = Richard Hamann, *Die deutsche Malerei im 19. Jahrhundert*, Leipzig/Berlin, 1914.
Hamburg, 1896 = *Jahresbericht der Kunsthalle zu Hamburg für 1896*, Hamburger Kunsthalle, Hamburg, 1897.
Hamburg, 1898 = *Jahresbericht der Kunsthalle zu Hamburg für 1898*, Hamburger Kunsthalle, Hamburg, 1899.
Harden, 1910 = Maximilian Harden, 'Menzel', Maximilian Harden, *Köpfe*, Berlin, 1910, pp. 341-64.
Hartau, 1984 = Johannes Hartau, 'Don Quijotes ästhetische Feldzüge: das Erinnerungsblatt von Menzel und Hosemann aus dem Jahre 1834', *Idea. Jahrbuch der Hamburger Kunsthalle*, 3, pp. 97-120, Hamburg, 1984.
Hasselberg, 1930 = Felix Hasselberg, 'Gottfried Schadow und Adolph Menzel', *Mitteilungen des Vereins für die Geschichte Berlins*, year 47, pp. 30-2, Berlin, 1930.
Hasselberg, 1935 = Felix Hasselberg, 'Adolph Menzel als Schriftsteller. Drei unbekannte Beiträge zur "Vossischen Zeitung"', *Berliner Blätter für Geschichte und Heimatkunde*, year 2, no. 1, January, pp. 3-9, Berlin, 1935.
Hauptmann, 1985 = Gerhart Hauptmann, *Tagebuch 1892-1894*, edited by Martin Machatzke, Frankfurt/Berlin, 1985.
Heilbut, 1891 = Emil Heilbut, *Die Sammlung Eduard L. Behrens zu Hamburg*, cat., 2 vols, Munich, 1891.
Heilbut, 1898 = Emil Heilbut, *Die Sammlung Eduard L. Behrens zu Hamburg*, cat., supplement, Munich, 1898.
Heilbut, 1902-3 = Emil Heilbut, 'Chronik Berlin', *Kunst und Künstler*, vol. 1, 1902-3, p. 320.
Heise, 1980 = Wolfgang Heise, 'Adolph-Menzel-Ausstellung in Berlin ', *Bildende Kunst*, year 28, issue 10, pp. 470-2, 1980.
Hentzen, 1969 = Alfred Hentzen (ed.), *Hamburger Kunsthalle, Meisterwerke der Gemälde-Galerie*, Hamburg, 1969.
Herding, 1928 = Klaus Herding, 'Kiel, Kunsthalle, Menzel Revisited', *Burlington Magazine*, 129, pp. 188-91, 1928.
Hermand, 1986 = Jost Hermand, *Adolf Menzel in Selbstzeugnissen und Bilddokumenten*, Reinbek, 1986.
Hermand, 1988 = Jost Hermand, *Adolph Menzel. Das Flötenkonzert in Sanssouci: Ein realistisch geträumtes Preußenbild*, Frankfurt-am-Main, 1988 (= *Kunststück*, Klaus Herding ed.).
Herrmann, (1905) 1992 = Agathe Herrmann, 'Wie ich Menzel kannte', *Moderne Kunst in Meisterholzschnitten*, vol. XX, Berlin, n.d. [1905], pp. 99-101. Quoted after Lammel, 1992, pp. 249-54.
Hertel, (1911-12) 1992 A = Albert Hertel, 'Gespräche mit Menzel', *Süddeutsche Monatshefte*, 9, vol. 1, pp. 680-3. Quoted after Lammel, 1992, pp. 84-7.
Hertel, (1911-12) 1992 B = Albert Hertel, 'Erinnerungen an Menzel', *Süddeutsche Monatshefte, 9*, vol. 1, pp. 786-93. Quoted after Lammel, 1992, pp. 88-98.
Heyse, (1912) 1992 = Paul Heyse, *Jugenderinnerungen und Bekenntnisse*, Stuttgart/Berlin, 1912. Ch. on Menzel: vol. 1, p. 208ff. Quoted after Lammel, 1992, pp. 148-52.
Hobsbawm, 1990 = E.J. Hobsbawm, *Nations and Nationalism since 1780. Programme, Myth, Reality*, Cambridge, 1990.
Hochhuth, 1991 = Rolf Hochhuth, *Menzel. Maler des Lichts*, Frankfurt-am-Main/Leipzig, 1991.
Hoffmann, 1850 = A. Hoffmann, [Congratulatory address from the magistrate of Berlin to Crown Prince Frederick-William, by Menzel], *Deutsches Kunstblatt*, no. 1, 1850, p. 239.
Hoffmeister, 1985 = Christine Hoffmeister, 'Industriebild und Ideologierelevanz am Beispiel von Werken Adolf Menzels', *Wissenschaftliche Zeitschrift der Humboldt Universität zu Berlin, Gesellschaftswissenschaftliche Reihe*, 34, pp. 115-20, Berlin, 1985.
Hofmann, 1977 A = Werner Hofmann, 'D'une aliénation à l'autre. L'artiste allemand et son public au XlXe siècle', *Gazette des Beaux-Arts*, October, pp. 124-36, 1977. German version: 'Entfremdungen', *Bruchlinien. Aufsätze zur Kunst des 19. Jahrhunderts*, Munich, 1979, pp. 214-31.
Hofmann, 1977 B = Werner Hofmann, 'Menzels verschlüsseltes Manifest', *Beiträge zum Problem des Stilpluralismus*, Munich, 1977, pp. 141-8.
Hofmann, 1979 = Werner Hofmann, 'Über Menzels "Atelierwand" in der Hamburger Kunsthalle', Werner Hofmann, *Bruchlinien. Aufsätze zur Kunst des 19. Jahrhunderts*, Munich, 1979, pp. 201-13.
Hofmann, 1982 = Werner Hofmann, 'Menzels verschlüsseltes Manifest', exhib. cat. Hamburg, 1982, pp. 31-40.
Hofmann, 1995 = Werner Hofmann, *Une époque en rupture 1750-1830*, Paris, 1995

('L'univers des formes'). German edn: *Das entzweite Jahrhundert. Kunst zwischen 1750 und 1830*, Munich, 1995 (= *Universum der Kunst*, 40).
Honisch, 1979 = Dieter Honisch, *Die Nationalgalerie Berlin*, Recklinghausen, 1979.
Howoldt, 1993 = *Die Gemälde des 19. Jahrhunderts in der Hamburger Kunsthalle*, edited by Jenns Eric Howoldt and Andreas Baur, Hamburg, 1993.
Hügelshofer, 1945 = W. Hügelshofer, 'Über Adolph Menzel', *Du*, July 1945, p. 6, reprod. p. 10.
Hungerford, 1980 = Contance Cain Hungerford, 'Ernest Meissonier's First Military Paintings: II: *1814, The Campaign of France*', *Arts Magazine*, January 1980.
Hütt, 1965 = *Adolph Menzel*, Leipzig, 1965.
Hütt, 1981 = Wolfgang Hütt, *Adolph Menzel*, Leipzig, 1981.

Ihlenfeld, 1969 = Kurt Ihlenfeld, 'Kameraden der Realität: Fontane und Menzel. Ein Berliner Beitrag zur Fontanefeier', *Neue Deutsche Hefte*, 16, issue 4, 1969, p. 108ff.

Jahn, 1955 = Johannes Jahn, *Das Kinderalbum von Adolph Menzel*, Leipzig, 1955.
Janke/Wagner, 1976 = Karl Janke and Monika Wagner, 'Das Verhältnis von Arbeiter und Maschine im Industriebild', *Kritische Berichte*, IV, issue 5/6, 1976, p. 5ff.
Jensen, 1976 = Jens Christian Jensen, 'Über Adolph Menzel', Ebertshäuser, 1976, vol. 1, pp. 1-24.
Jensen, 1981 = Jens Christian Jensen, 'Adolph Menzel. Realist – Historist – Maler des Hofes', exhib. cat. Kiel, 1981, pp. 8-10.
Jensen, 1982 = Jens Christian Jensen, *Adolf Menzel*, Cologne, 1982.
Jensen, 1994 = Robert Jensen, 'Der Fall Meier-Graefe', *Marketing Modernism in Fin-de-Siècle Europe*, Princeton, 1994.
Jordan, (1905) 1992 = Max Jordan, 'Menzel und die Nationalgalerie', *Moderne Kunst in Meisterholzschnitten*, vol. XX, Berlin, n.d. [1905], pp. 97-9. Quoted after Lammel, 1992, pp. 265-71.
Jordan, 1895 = Max Jordan, *Das Werk Adolph Menzels. Eine Festgabe zum achtzigsten Geburtstage des Künstlers*, Munich, 1895 [slightly abridged version of the 1890 text].
Jordan, 1904-5 = Max Jordan, 'Adolf Menzel', *Die Kunst für Alle*, vol. XX, 1904-5, pp. 265-71.
Jordan, 1905 = Max Jordan, *Das Werk Adolph Menzels 1815-1905*, Munich, 1905 [revised and amended version of Jordan/Dohme, 1890].
Jordan/Dohme, 1890 = Max Jordan and Robert Dohme, *Das Werk Adolph Menzels. Vom Künstler autorisierte Ausgabe*, 3 vols, Munich, 1890.
Justi, 1919 = Ludwig Justi, 'Menzel', *Deutsche Zeichenkunst im 19. Jahrhundert. Ein Führer zur Sammlung der Handzeichnungen in der Nationalgalerie*, Berlin, 1919, abridged edn: pp. 65-9, complete edn: pp. 85-93.
Justi, 1920 = Ludwig Justi, *Deutsche Malkunst im 19. Jahrhundert, ein Führer durch die Nationalgalerie*, Berlin, 1920.
Justi, 1921 = Ludwig Justi, *Verzeichnis der Gemälde und Bildwerke in der Nationalgalerie zu Berlin*, Berlin, 1921.
Justi, 1926 = *200 Bilder der Nationalgalerie. Erworben 1910-1925 von Ludwig Justi*. Preface by Paul Rave and Ludwig Thormaehlen, Berlin, 1926.
Justi, 1932 = *Von Runge bis Thoma. Deutsche Malkunst im 19. und 20. Jahrhundert*, Berlin, 1932.

Kaemmerer, 1899 = Ludwig Kaemmerer, 'Adolph von Menzel, Ritter des Schwarzen Adlerordens', *Hohenzollern Jahrbuch*, 3, 1899, pp. 173-7.
Kaiser, 1953 = Konrad Kaiser, *Adolph Menzels Eisenwalzwerk*, Berlin, 1953.
Kaiser, 1956 = Konrad Kaiser, *Adolph Menzel. 1815-1905*, Berlin, 1956.
Kaiser, 1965 = Konrad Kaiser, *Adolph Menzel. Der Maler*, Stuttgart, 1965.
Kaiser, 1969 = Konrad Kaiser, *Adolph Menzel. Gemälde, Aquarelle, Guaschen, Pastelle, Handzeichnungen*, Schweinfurt, 1969.
Karlsruhe, 1973 = Anonymous, 'Staatliche Kunsthalle Karlsruhe, Neuerwerbungen', *Jahrbuch der Staatlichen Kunstsammlungen in Baden-Württemberg*, 10, Karlsruhe, 1973.
Karlsruhe, 1984 = Anonymous, 'Staatliche Kunsthalle Karlsruhe. Neuerwerbungen für die Gemäldegalerie 1972-1984', Karlsruhe, 1984.
Karlsruhe, 1988 = *Ausgewählte Werke der Staatlichen Kunsthalle Karlsruhe*, vol. 1: *150 Gemälde vom Mittelalter bis zur Gegenwart*, Karlsruhe, 1988.
Keisch, 1987 = Claude Keisch, 'Adolph Menzels "Ansprache Friedrichs des Großen an seine Generale vor der Schlacht bei Leuthen". Vermutungen über ein unvollendetes Meisterwerk', *Forschungen und Berichte, Staatliche Museen zu Berlin*, 26, Berlin, 1987, pp. 259-82.
Keisch, 1988 = Claude Keisch, 'Von Kassel bis Leuthen. Mehrdimensionalität des Augenblicks in Menzels Geschichtsmalerei', *Kunstverhältnisse. Ein Paradigma kunstwissenschaftlicher Forschung*, published by the Institut für Ästhetik und Kunstwissenschaften der Akademie der Wissenschaften der DDR, Berlin, 1988, pp. 74-9.
Keller, 1979 = Harald Keller, 'Degas-Studien', *Städel-Jahrbuch*, n.s. 7, 1979, pp. 271-95.
Kemp, 1983 = Wolfgang Kemp, 'Der "Bärenzwinger" von Adolph Menzel', *Der Anteil des Betrachters. Rezeptionsästhetische Studien zur Malerei des 19. Jahrhunderts*, Munich, 1983, pp. 56-66.
Kern, 1915 = Guido Josef Kern, 'Aus Menzels Jugend. Zur hundertsten Wiederkehr seines Geburtstages am 8. Dezember 1915', *Die Kunst für Alle*, year 31, 5/6, 1 December 1915, pp. 81-104.
Kern, 1915-16 = Guido Josef Kern, *Aus Menzels Jugend*, Munich, 1915-16.
Kern, 1920 = Guido Josef Kern, 'Ein neuer Menzel', *Zeitschrift für bildende Kunst*, n.s. 31, 1920, p. 132 and Pl. opp. p. 132.
Kern, 1932 = Guido Josef Kern, 'Zur Menzelausstellung in München 1932', *Die Weltkunst*, vol. 6, 1932, p. 38.
Kerner, 1857 = Justinus Kerner, *Kleksographien*, Stuttgart/Leipzig/Berlin/Vienna, 1857.
Kesser, 1902-3 = Hermann Kesser, 'Die Galerie Henneberg in Zürich', *Kunstchronik*, n.s. 14, 1902-3, col. 249-54, col. 315-20.
Kirstein, 1919 = Gustav Kirstein, *Das Leben Adolph Menzels*, Leipzig, 1919.
Kleburger, 1981 = Ilse Kleburger, *Preusse, Bürger, Genie: Adolph Menzel*, Berlin, 1981.
Klemm, 1995 = David Klemm, *Von Napoleon zu Bismarck. Geschichte in der deutschen Druckgraphik*, Museum für Kunst und Gewerbe, Hamburg, 1995.
Knackfuß, 1895 = Hermann Knackfuß, *Adolph Menzel*, Bielefeld/Berlin, 1895.
Kohle, 1993 = Hubert Kohle, 'Zur Menzel-Literatur der letzten 15 Jahre', *Kunstchronik*, 46, 1993, pp. 192-202.
Köhn, 1940 = H. Köhn, 'Neuerwerbungen des Folkwang Museums Essen', *Die Weltkunst*, 14 (34/35), 1940, pp. 1-4, reprod.
Koja, 1992 = Stephan Koja, *Von der Romantik zum Impressionismus. Meisterwerke deutscher Malerei des 19. Jahrhunderts aus dem Bestand der österreichischen Galerie*, österreichische Galerie Belvedere, Vienna, 1992.
Korte, 1973-4 = Claus Korte, 'Riskante Selbstspiegelungen Adolph Menzels', *Sitzungsberichte der Kunstgeschichtlichen Gesellschaft Berlin*, n.s. 22, Berlin, 1973-4, pp. 7-10.
Krafft/Schümann, 1969 = Eva Maria Krafft and Wolfgang Schümann, *Katalog der Meister des 19. Jahrhunderts in der Hamburger Kunsthalle*, Hamburg, 1969.
Kugler, 1837 = Franz Kugler, 'Neuere Gemälde. Berlin', *Museum, Blätter für bildende Kunst*, year V, Berlin, 4 September 1837, pp. 281-3.
Kugler, 1854 = Franz Kugler, *Kleine Schriften zur Kunstgeschichte*, vol. III, Stuttgart, 1854.
Kugler, 1911 = Franz Kugler, 'Briefe über die Geschichte Friedrichs des Großen', *Die neue Rundschau*, 22, Berlin, December 1911, pp. 1723-39.
Kuhrau, 1995 = Sven Kuhrau, *Adolph Menzels "Piazza del Erbe zu Verona"*, memoir for master's degree, Berlin, 1995.
Kürenberg, 1935 = Joachim von Kürenberg, *Menzel, die kleine Exzellenz*, Berlin, 1935.
Kurth, 1905 = Julius Kurth, *Adolph Menzel und sein Vaterunser. Studie auf Grund eines unveröffentlichten Schreibens des Meisters*, Berlin, 1905.
Kurth, 1941 = Willy Kurth, *Berliner Zeichner*, Berlin, 1941.

Laban, 1906 = Ferdinand Laban, 'Die deutsche Jahrhundert-Ausstellung', *Die Kunst für Alle*, XXI, 1906.
Laforgue, 1884 = Jules Laforgue, 'Correspondance de Berlin. Exposition de M. Ad. Menzel à la National-Galerie', *Gazette des Beaux-Arts*, July 1884, pp. 77-84.
Laforgue, 1886 = Jules Laforgue, 'Correspondance de Berlin. Exposition du centenaire de Menzel à Berlin', *Chronique des arts et de la curiosité*, 9 January 1886, pp. 13-14.
Laforgue, 1990 = Jules Laforgue, *Berlin. Der Hof und die Stadt. 1887*, Frankfurt-am-Main, 1990.
Lammel, 1987 = Gisold Lammel, *Adolph Menzel. Blätter mit Esprit, Humor und Satire*, Hanau, 1987.
Lammel, 1988 = Gisold Lammel, *Adolph Menzel. Fredericiana und Wilhelmiana*, Dresden, 1988.
Lammel, 1989 = Gisold Lammel, 'Der Auftraggeber ist im Bild – Anmerkungen zu Menzels Kasseler Karton', *Kunstverhältnisse. Ein*

Paradigma kunstwissenschaftlicher Forschung, Berlin, 1989, pp. 69-74.
Lammel, 1992 = Gisold Lammel (ed.), *Exzellenz lassen bitten. Erinnerungen an Adolph Menzel*, Leipzig, 1992.
Lammel, 1993 A = Gisold Lammel, *Adolph Menzel. Bildwelt und Bildregie*, Dresden/Basle, 1993.
Lammel, 1993 B = Gisold Lammel, *Adolph Menzel und seine Kreise*, Dresden/Basle, 1993.
Leistner, 1992 = Gerhard Leistner, 'Adolph Menzel: "Im Rohbau", "Mann beim Mantelanziehen und Porträtstudien". Zwei Neuerwerbungen des Museums Ostdeutsche Galerie', *Regensburger Almanach 1992*, pp. 162-7.
Leistner, 1993 = Bernd Leistner, *Gang durch die Sammlung. Gemälde, Skulpturen und Objekte. Museum Ostdeutsche Galerie*, Regensburg, 1993.
Lemoisne, 1946 = P. A. Lemoisne, *Degas et son oeuvre*, 4 vols, Paris, 1949.
Lichtwark, (1924) 1992 = Alfred Lichtwark, *Briefe an die Kommission für die Verwaltung der Kunsthalle*, Hamburg, 1924, vol. 1, pp. 184-5, pp. 226-7, pp. 237-41 and vol. 2, pp. 29-33. Quoted after Lammel, 1992, pp. 294-307.
Lichtwark, 1972 = Carl Schellenberg (ed.), *Alfred Lichtwark, Briefe an seine Familie 1875-1913*, Hamburg, 1972.
Liebermann, (1921) 1922 = Max Liebermann, 'Menzel', *Gesammelte Schriften*, Berlin, 1922, pp. 186-212. 1st edn: foreword to *Adolf Menzel. 50 Zeichnungen, Pastelle und Aquarelle aus dem Besitz der Nationalgalerie*, Berlin, 1921.
Liebermann, 1978/83 = Günter Busch (ed.), *Die Phantasie in der Malerei. Schriften und Reden*, Frankfurt-am-Main, 1978 (repr. Berlin, 1983).
Liebermann/Kern, 1921 = Max Liebermann (introd.) and G[uido] J[osef] Kern (cat.), *Adolph Menzel. Fünfzig Zeichnungen -Pastelle – Aquarelle aus dem Besitz der Nationalgalerie*, Berlin, 1921.
Lippincott, 1992 = Louise Lippincott, 'Adolph Menzel's Departure after the Party', *Carnegie Magazine*, July/August 1992, pp. 15-18.
Lorck, 1905 = Carl Berend Lorck, *Adolph von Menzel und die 'Geschichte Friedrichs des Großen'*, Leipzig, 1905 (manuscript, Berlin, Nationalgalerie, archives).
Lostalot, 1882 = Alfred de Lostalot, 'Exposition internationale de peinture, galerie Georges Petit', *Gazette des Beaux-Arts*, 2nd per., vol. 25, 1882/I, pp. 602-7.
Loyrette, 1991 = Henri Loyrette, *Degas*, Paris, 1991.

Mackowsky, 1918 = Hans Mackowsky, 'Menzels Impressionen aus Alt-Berlin', *Die Kunst für Alle*, 33, 1918, pp. 97-103.
Mantz, 1867 = Paul Mantz, 'Les Beaux-Arts à l'Exposition universelle', *Gazette des Beaux-Arts*, vol. XXIII, 1867.
Marguillier, 1905 = Auguste Marguillier, 'Adolf von Menzel (1815-1905)', *Les Arts*, no. 41, May 1905.
Marguillier, 1906 = Auguste Marguillier, 'Ouvrages récents sur Menzel', *Gazette des Beaux-Arts*, 3rd per., XXXVI, 1906/II, pp. 82-8.
Mauclair, 1906 = Camille Mauclair, 'Un factice: J. Boldini', *Trois crises de l'art actuel*, Paris, 1906, pp. 107-16.
Maue, 1982 = Hermann Maue, 'Briefe der Familie Menzel aus dem Jahre 1829. Eine Quelle zum Frühwerk Adolph Menzels', *Anzeiger des Germanischen Nationalmuseums*, Nuremberg, 1982, pp. 83-91.
Mazelière, 1990 = De la Mazelière, *La Peinture allemande du XIXe siècle*, Paris, 1990.
Mehnert, 1990 = Karl-Heinz Mehnert and Dieter Gleisberg, *Meisterzeichnungen. Museum der bildenden Künste*, Leipzig, 1990.
Meier-Graefe, 1906 = Julius Meier-Graefe, *Der junge Menzel. Ein Problem der Kunstökonomie Deutschlands*, Leipzig, 1906.
Meier-Graefe, 1987 = Julius Meier-Graefe, *Kunstschreiberei, Essays und Kunstkritik*, edited by Henry Schumann, Leipzig/Weimar, 1987.
Meissner, 1902 = Franz Hermann Meissner, *Adolph von Menzel*, Berlin/Leipzig, 1902.
Meyer, 1876 = Bruno Meyer, 'Adolph Menzel. Eine Skizze. Mit Illustrationen', *Zeitschrift für bildende Kunst*, vol. 11, 1876, pp. 1-10.
Meyerheim, (1906) 1992 = Paul Meyerheim, *Adolph von Menzel. Erinnerungen*, Berlin, 1906. Quoted after Lammel, 1992, pp. 157-235.
Moser, 1910 = Andreas Moser, *Joseph Joachim. Ein Lebensbild*, Berlin, 1910.
Müller, 1935 = Adrian Lukas Müller, 'Unbekanntes von Adolph Menzel', *Westermanns Illustrierte Deutsche Monatshefte*, vol. 159, 1935, pp. 354-77.
Munich, 1989 = *Neue Pinakothek. Erläuterungen zu den ausgestellten Werken*, 5th edn, Munich, 1989.
Münster, 1987 = *Einblicke und Anblicke des 19. Jahrhunderts*, Westfälisches Landesmuseum, Münster, 1987.
Muther, 1914 = Richard Muther, 'Wilhelm II. und die Kunst', *Aufsätze über bildende Kunst*, vol. II, Berlin, 1914.

Nalli-Ruthenberg, n.d. = Agathe Nalli-Ruthenberg, *Das alte Berlin. Erinnerungen von Agathe Nalli-Ruthenberg*, Berlin, n.d. [1912].
Nicolai, 1786 = Christoph Friedrich Nicolai, *Nachricht von den Baumeistern, Bildhauern, Kupferstechern, Malern, Stukkateuren und anderen Künstlern, welche in und um Berlin sich aufgehalten haben*, Berlin/Stettin, 1786.
Norden, (1900) 1992 = Julius Norden, 'Bei Adolf von Menzel', *Die Gegenwart*, year 29, vol. 58, 1900 (13), pp. 260-3. Quoted after Lammel, 1992, pp. 73-83.
Novotny, 1960 = Fritz Novotny, *Painting and Sculpture in Europe 1780-1880*, London, 1960.

Oettingen, 1908 = Wolfgang von Oettingen, 'Autobiographische Notizen von Menzel', *Aus stiller Werkstatt*, Leipzig, 1908.
Osborn, 1904 = Max Osborn, 'Die Düsseldorfer Ausstellung [von 1904]', *Kunst und Künstler*, II, (1903-4) (pp. 429-45).

Paret, 1980 = Peter Paret, *The Berlin Secession*, Cambridge, Mass., 1980.
Paret, 1988 = Peter Paret, *Kunst als Geschichte. Kultur und Politik von Menzel bis Fontane*, Munich, 1990. Translation of *Art as History*, Princeton, 1988.
Pauli, 1924 = Gustav Pauli, *Führer durch die Galerie der Kunsthalle zu Hamburg*, 1: *Die Neueren Meister*, Hamburg, 1924.
Pecht, 1879 = Friedrich Pecht, *Deutsche Künstler des neunzehnten Jahrhunderts. Studien und Erinnerungen*, Nördlingen, 1879, pp. 305-39.
Pecht, 1881-2 = Friedrich Pecht, 'Die Wiener internationale Kunstausstellung (III)', *Deutsches Kunstblatt*, 1, 1881-2, p. 109.
Pecht, 1885 = Friedrich Pecht, 'Zum 70. Geburtstage Adolf Menzels', *Die Kunst für Alle*, year 1, issue 5, 1 December 1885, pp. 61-71.
Pecht, 1885-6 = Friedrich Pecht, 'Über die deutsche Malerei der Gegenwart', *Die Kunst für Alle*, year 1, 1885-6, pp. 1-5.
Pecht, 1887 = Friedrich Pecht, *Deutsche Künstler*, 2nd edn (repr. of Pecht, 1879), 1887.
Peschkau, 1895 = Emil Peschkau, 'Das Morgenbüffett der Feinbäckerei in Bad Kissingen', *Die Gartenlaube*, 1895, p. 804.
Pietsch, (1905) 1992 = Ludwig Pietsch, 'Persönliche Erinnerungen an Adolf v. Menzel', *Velhagen und Klasings Monatshefte*, year 19, 1905, vol. 2, issue 8, pp. 193-208. Quoted after Lammel, 1992, pp. 319-49.
Pietsch, 1861 = L[udwig] P[ietsch], 'Die Ausstellung von Oelgemälden, Aquarellen und Handzeichnungen von Prof. Adolf [*sic*] Menzel', *Berlinische Nachrichten von Staats- und gelehrten Sachen (Haude- und Spenersche Zeitung)*, Berlin, 1861, supplement to no. 260 of 6 November.
Pietsch, 1877 = L[udwig] P[ietsch], 'Menzel-Photographien, II', *Schlesische Zeitung*, no. 89 of 23 February 1877.
Pietsch, 1879 = L[udwig] P[ietsch], 'Adolf Menzel', *Nord und Süd*, vol. 11, Breslau, 1879, pp. 439-69.
Pietsch, 1893/8 = Ludwig Pietsch, *Wie ich Schriftsteller geworden bin. Erinnerungen aus den fünfziger und sechziger Jahren*, 2 vols, Berlin, 1893-4 (new edn Berlin, 1898).
Pietsch, 1895 = L[udwig] P[ietsch], 'Adolf Menzel', *Die Gartenlaube*, vol. 47, 1895, pp. 794-8.
Pinakothek, 1908 = *Katalog der Gemälde der Königlichen Neuen Pinakothek in München. Vollständige Amtliche Ausgabe*, Munich, 1908.
Pniower, 1924 = Otto Pniower, 'Eine Autobiographie Adolph Menzels', *Kunst und Künstler*, year 22, 1924, pp. 124-31.

R., 1906 = M.R., 'Ein Menzel-Bild aus früherer Zeit. Falke, auf Taube stoßend', *Illustrirte Zeitung*, vol. 126, no. 3275, Leipzig, 5 April 1906, p. 517.
Radziewsky, 1982 = Elke von Radziewsky, 'Menzel – ein Realist?', exhib. cat. Hamburg, 1982, pp. 17-30.
Ragghianti/Camescara, 1970 = Carlo Ragghianti (introd.) and Ettore Camescara (cat.), *L'opera completa di Giovanni Boldini*, Milan, 1970.
Rave, 1940 = Paul Ortwin Rave, *Karl Blechen, Leben – Würdigungen – Werk*, Berlin, 1940.
Reff, 1982 = Theodore Reff, 'Manet and the Paris of Haussmann and Baudelaire', exhib. cat. *Manet and Modern Paris*, National Gallery of Art, Washington, D.C., 1982.
Reff, 1985 = Theodore Reff, *The Notebooks of Edgar Degas*, New York, 1985.
Reuter, 1968 = Hans-Heinrich Reuter, *Fontane*, Berlin, 1968.
Riedrich/Weiglein, 1923 = Otto Riedrich and Paul Weiglein, *Menzel auf Reisen, 58 fast durchweg unveröffentlichte Zeichnungen, ausgewählt und*

herausgegeben von O. Riedrich. Mit einem Geleitwort von Paul Weiglein, Berlin, 1923.
Riegel, 1868 = Herman Riegel, 'Eine moderne Kunstausstellung (Berlin 1866)', *Deutsche Kunststudien*, Hanover, 1868, pp. 437-54 (no information available on 1st edn).
Riemann, 1990 = Ursula Riemann, '"Courage of Vision". Traces of Alienation and Loneliness in Menzels's Work', exhib. cat. New York, 1990, pp. 41-52.
Riemann-Reyher, 1992 = Ursula Riemann-Reyher (ed.), *Adolph von Menzel. Reiseskizzen aus Preußen*, Berlin, 1992.
Ring, 1883 = Max Ring, *Die deutsche Kaiserstadt Berlin und ihre Umgebung*, vol. 1, Leipzig, 1883.
Rosenberg, 1875 = Adolf Rosenberg, 'Ein Neues Bild von Adolf Menzel', *Kunstchronik*, X, 1875, col. 372-5.
Rosenberg, 1877 = Adolf Rosenberg, 'Die akademische Kunstausstellung in Berlin', *Kunstchronik*, XII, 1876-7, col. 97-102.
Rosenberg, 1878 = Adolf Rosenberg, 'Die akademische Kunstausstellung in Berlin', *Kunstchronik*, XIII, 1878, col. 100-4.
Rosenberg, 1879 A = Adolf Rosenberg, 'Ein neues Bild von Adolf Menzel', *Kunstchronik*, XIV, no. 17, 1879, col. 265-70.
Rosenberg, 1879 B = Adolf Rosenberg, *Die Berliner Malerschule 1819 bis 1879*, Berlin, 1879.
Rosenberg, 1885-6 = Adolf Rosenberg, 'Die Menzel-Ausstellung in Berlin', *Zeitschrift für Bildende Kunst*, XXI, 1885-6, *Kunstchronik*, col. 227-31.
H.R., 1905 = H.R. [Hans Rosenhagen?], 'Die Menzel-Ausstellung in der K. Nationalgalerie zu Berlin', *Die Kunst. Monatshefte für freie und angewandte Kunst*, vol. XI, Munich, 1905.
Rosenhagen, 1903 = Hans Rosenhagen, 'Die Neuerwerbungen der Berliner Nationalgalerie', *Die Kunst. Monatshefte für freie und angewandte Kunst*, vol. VII, Munich, 1903.
Rosenhagen, 1905 = Hans Rosenhagen, 'Adolph v. Menzel', *Die Gartenlaube*, no. 10, 1905, pp. 182-5.
Rosenthal, 1988 = M. Rosenthal, 'Max Liebermann und der Antisemitismus. Ein Bild und der soziale Konflikt', *Bildende Kunst*, 36, 1988, pp. 243-6.
Roth, 1905 = Herrmann Roth, 'Münchner Menzel-Erinnerungen', *Münchner Neueste Nachrichten*, no. 72, Munich, 14 February 1905.
Rotteck/Welcker, 1847 = Carl von Rotteck and Carl Welcker, *Das Staats-Lexikon*, new edn, vol. IV, Altona, 1847.

Schaar, 1982 = Eckhard Schaar, 'Über Menzel, den Zeichner', exhib. cat. Hamburg, 1982, pp. 9-16.
Schadendorf, 1981 = Wulf Schadendorf, 'Bemerkungen zu einigen späten Bildern Menzels', exhib. cat. Kiel, 1981, pp. 17-19.
Schadow, 1849 = Johann Gottfried Schadow, *Kunstwerke und Kunstansichten*, Berlin, 1849.
Schasler, 1856 = Max Schasler, '1. Historienmalerei', *Die Dioskuren*, I, 1856.
Schasler, 1857 = Max Schasler, 'Kunst-Kritik. I. Permanente Gemäldeausstellung von Sachse', *Die Dioskuren*, II, 1857, pp. 62-4.
Schasler, 1858 = Max Schasler, 'Ueber Idealismus und Realismus in der Historienmalerei', *Die Dioskuren*, III, 1858.
Schasler, 1861 = Max Schasler, 'Kunst-Kritik. Die Ausstellung im Lokal des Kunstvereins', *Die Dioskuren*, no. 44, 1861, p. 375ff.
Schasler, 1871 = M[ax Schasle]r, 'Kunstkritik. Berliner Kunstschau', *Die Dioskuren*, 1871, p. 230.
Schasler, 1879 = Max Schasler, *Über materialistische und idealistische Weltanschauung*, Berlin, 1879 (= *Deutsche Zeit- und Streitfragen, Flugschriften zur Kenntnis der Gegenwart*, issue 113).
Scheffler, 1912 = Karl Scheffler, *Die Nationalgalerie*, Berlin, 1912.
Scheffler, 1915 = Karl Scheffler, *Adolph Menzel, der Mensch, das Werk*, Berlin, 1915.
Scheffler, 1922 = Karl Scheffler, *Adolph Menzel*, Berlin, 1922.
Scheffler, 1938 = Karl Scheffler, *Adolph Menzel*, Berlin/Leipzig, 1938.
Scheffler, 1955 = Karl Scheffler, *Adolph Menzel, der Mensch, das Werk*, new edn by Carl Georg Heise, Munich, 1955.
Schlagenhauff, 1991 = Annette Schlagenhauff, *Adolph Menzel. Works in Harvard Collections. Busch-Reisinger-Museum*, Harvard University, Boston, 1991.
Schlick, 1981 = Johann Schlick, 'Menzels Friderizìana', exhib. cat. Kiel, 1981, pp. 13-16.
Schlözer, 1856 = Kurd von Schlözer, *Chasot. Zur Geschichte Friedrichs des Großen und seiner Zeit*, Berlin, 1856 (2nd edn 1878).
Schmid-Aachen, 1896 = Max Schmid-Aachen, 'Adolf Menzel', *Zeitschrift für bildende Kunst*, 31, n.s. I, 1896, pp. 49-69.
Schmidt, 1957 = Werner Schmidt, 'Menzel und Watteau', *Festschrift Johannes Jahn*, Leipzig, 1957.
Schmidt, 1958 = Werner Schmidt, 'Das Selbstbildnis von Adolph Menzel im Skizzenbuch aus den Jahren 1876-1877. Seine Bedeutung als Ausschnitt, Einzelauge und als Selbstdarstellung', *Forschungen und Berichte, Staatliche Museen zu Berlin*, vol. 2, Berlin, 1958, pp. 97-119.
Schmoll, 1970 = J.A. Schmoll known as Eisenwerth, 'Fensterbilder. Motivketten in der europäischen Malerei', *Beiträge zur Motivkunde des 19. Jahrhunderts*, Munich, 1970 (*Studien zur Kunst des 19. Jahrhunderts*, 6), pp. 13-165.
Schneider, 1852 = Louis Schneider, *Geschichte der Oper und des Königlichen Opernhauses in Berlin*, Berlin, 1852.
Schnerb, 1913 = J.F. Schnerb, 'François Bonhommé', *Gazette des Beaux-Arts*, 4th per., vol. IX, 1913/I, pp. 11-25 and pp. 132-42.
Schoebel, 1895 = Agnes Schoebel, 'Wie Meister Menzel lebt', *Die Gartenlaube*, vol. 47, 1895, pp. 798-9.
Schrenk, 1975 = Klaus Schrenk, 'Industriedarstellungen der Mitte des 19. Jahrhunderts', *Kritische Berichte*, issue 5/6, 1975, p. 13ff.
Schultze, 1981 = Jürgen Schultze, 'Wie es eigentlich gewesen ist', exhib. cat. Kiel, 1981, pp. 20-21.
Schulz, 1981 = Walter Schulz, 'Die problematische Stellung der Kunst in Schopenhauers Philosophie', *Literaturwissenschaft und Geistesgeschichte. Festschrift für Richard Brinkmann*, Tübingen, 1981, p. 403ff.
Schwedeler-Meyer, 1929 = E. Schwedeler-Meyer, *Die Gemäldesammlung der Stadt Reichenberg. Die sud. Selbstverwaltungskörper*, vol. 1: *Reichenberg*, Berlin, 1929.
Séailles, 1910 = Gabriel Séailles, *Alfred Dehodencq. L'homme et l'artiste*, Paris, 1910 (2nd edn).
Seidel, 1914 = Paul Seidel, *Führer durch das Hohenzollernmuseum im Schlosse Monbijou*, (new edn), Berlin, 1914.
Seidlitz, n.d. = Waldemar von Seidlitz, *Führer durch die deutsche Jahrhundert-Ausstellung 1906*, Munich, n.d.
Siefart, 1908 = Major von Siefart, 'Ein Erlebnis im Grabgewölbe der Garnisonkirche', *Mitteilungen für die Geschichte Berlins*, 1, Berlin, 1908, pp. 134-6.
Simson, 1986 = Otto von Simson, *Der Blick nach innen. Vier Beiträge zur deutschen Malerei des 19. Jahrhunderts*, Berlin, 1986.
Soiné, 1990 = Knut Soiné, *Johann Peter Hasenclever. Ein Maler im Vormärz*, Neustadt/Aisch, 1990 (= *Bergische Forschungen*, XXI).
Sondermann, 1895 = Fritz Sondermann, *Adolph Menzel*, Magdeburg, 1895.
Springer, 1896 = Jaro Springer, 'Die Internationale Jubiläums-Kunstausstellung in Berlin 1896', III, *Die Kunst für Alle*, vol. 11, 1895-6, pp. 309-12.
Steinhauser, 1994 = Monika Steinhauser, 'Der inszenierte Blick des Flaneurs. Manet und Baudelaire', *Konstruktionen der Moderne, Im Blickfeld, Jahrbuch der Hamburger Kunsthalle*, 1, 1994, pp. 9-15.
Sternberg, 1852 = Alexander von Sternberg, *Ein Carneval in Berlin*, Leipzig, 1852. The passages on Menzel quoted after: Anonymous, 'Adolph Menzel als Mensch und Künstler. Urteile und Erinnerungen von Zeitgenossen (1)', *Berlinische Blätter für Geschichte und Heimatkunde*, 2, (1935). pp. 2-5.
Storm/Pietsch, 1939 = Volquart Pauls (ed.), *Correspondance entre Th. Storm et L. Pietsch*, Heide, 1939.

Teeuwisse, 1986 = Nicolaas Teeuwisse, *Vom Salon zur Secession. Berliner Kunstleben zwischen Tradition und Aufbruch zur Moderne 1871-1900*, Berlin, 1986.
Timm, 1974 = Ingo Timm, 'Adolph Menzels Gemälde "Am Kreuzberg bei Berlin"', *Das Märkische Museum und seine Sammlungen. Festgabe zum 100jährigen Bestehen*, Berlin, 1974, pp. 100-2.
Trost, 1980 = Edit Trost, 'Nachrichten über Adolph Menzel in den Berliner Kunstzeitschriften des 19. Jahrhunderts', exhib. cat. Berlin, 1980 A, pp. 83-107.
Tschudi, 1896 = Hugo von Tschudi, 'Adolf Menzel', *Pan*, year 2, vol. 1, 1896, pp. 41-4.
Tschudi, 1905 A = Hugo von Tschudi, *Adolph von Menzel. Abbildungen seiner Gemälde und Studien*, Munich, 1905.
Tschudi, 1905 B = Hugo von Tschudi, 'Aus Menzels jungen Jahren', *Jahrbuch der Kgl. Preußischen Kunstsammlungen*, vol. 26, Berlin, 1905, pp. 215-314 (partly repaginated impression, Berlin, 1906: page nos. given in brackets).
Tschudi, 1912 = *Gesammelte Schriften zur neuen Kunst*, Munich, 1912.

Uebel, 1986 = Lothar Uebel (ed.), *Die Tempelhofer Berge nebst ihrer höchsten Erhebung, dem Kreuzberge, anno 1286 bis 1986*, Berlin,

1986.
Unverricht, 1952 = Hubert Unverricht, 'Benjamin Bilse. Der Gründer der Berliner Philharmonie – wider Willen', *Zeitschrift für Musik*, no. 113, Regensburg, 1952, pp. 400-1.

Varnedoe, 1989 = Kirk Varnedoe, *Gustave Caillebotte*, New Haven/London, 1989.
Veth, (1904) 1992 = Jan Veth, 'Adolph Menzel', *Streifzüge eines holländischen Malers in Deutschland*, Berlin, 1904, pp. 41-52. Quoted after Lammel, 1992, pp. 308-18.
Vignau-Wilberg, 1979/81 = Peter Vignau-Wilberg, *Stiftung Oskar Reinhart Winterthur*, vol. II: *Deutsche und österreichische Maler des 19. Jahrhunderts*, Zurich, 1979 (2nd edn, revised and corrected, Zurich, 1981).
Vinter, 1964 = Vlastimil Vinter, *Poklady Liberecké Galerie, Nêmecké a Rakowské Malirstvi 19. Stoleti*, Liberec, 1964.
Vogl, 1984 = Elisabeth Vogl, *Die Eisenbahn als Bildmotiv in der Malerei Adolph von Menzels*, memoir for master's degree, Regensburg, 1984.
Vollmar, (1905) 1992 = Helene Vollmar, 'Menzel in Kissingen', *Moderne Kunst in Meisterholzschnitten*, vol. 20, Berlin, n.d. [1905], p. 101. Quoted after Lammel, 1992, pp. 255-7.
Vollmar, 1895-6 A = H[elene] Vollmar, 'Adolph Menzel. Zum achtzigsten Geburtstag', *Moderne Kunst in Meisterholzschnitten*, vol. 10, 1895-6, pp. 54-60.
Vollmar, 1895-6 B = H[elene] V[ollmar], 'Menzel-Bildnisse', *Moderne Kunst in Meisterholzschnitten*, vol. 10, 1895-6, supplement to no. 5, p. III.
Vollmar, 1904-5 A = H[elene] Vollmar, 'Adolph Menzel', *Moderne Kunst in Meisterholzschnitten*, vol. 19, 1904-5, issue 7, pp. 177-81.
Vollmar, 1904-5 B = H[elene] Vollmar, 'Menzeliana', *Moderne Kunst in Meisterholzschnitten*, vol. 19, 1904-5, pp. 182-4.
Voss, 1885-6 = Georg Voss, 'Die Berliner Menzel-Feste', *Die Kunst für Alle*, year 1, 1885-6, pp. 101-3.

Waldmann, 1922 = Emil Waldmann, *Menzel, Werke und Dokumente*, Munich, 1922.
Waldmann, 1941 = Emil Waldmann, *Der Maler Adolph Menzel*, Vienna, 1941.
Weber, 1973 = Rolf Weber (ed.), *Revolutionsbriefe 1848/49*, Leipzig, 1973.
Weinhold, 1956 = Renate Weinhold, 'Menzel und die Eisenbahn', *Wissenschaftliche Zeitschrift der Karl-Marx-Universität*, p. 195, Leipzig, 1956.
Weisberg, 1980 = Gabriel P. Weisberg, *The Realist Tradition. French Painting and Drawing 1830-1900*, Cleveland (Ohio), 1980, pp. 51-2 and p. 71ff.
Weiss, 1983 = Peter Weiss, *Die Ästhetik des Widerstands*, 2 vols, Frankfurt-am-Main, 1983 (new edn 1987).
Werner, 1905 = Anton von Werner, *Rede bei der Trauerfeier der Königl. Akademie der Künste für Adolph von Menzel am 6. März 1905 gehalten von Anton von Werner*, Berlin, 1905.
Werner, 1913 = *Erlebnisse und Eindrücke. 1870-1890. Von Anton von Werner*, Berlin, 1913.
Werner, 1993 = *Anton von Werner: Jugenderinnerungen (1843-1870)*. Edited by Dominik Bartmann. Commentated by Karin Schrader, Berlin, 1993 (*Quellen zur deutschen Kunstgeschichte vom Klassizismus bis zur Gegenwart*, vol. 3).
Wessely, 1873 = Joseph Eduard Wessely, *Adolph Menzel. Sein Leben und seine Werke*, Leipzig, 1873.
Wiegmann, 1855 = R. Wiegmann, 'Die illusorische Wirkung bei Gemälden, mit besonderer Beziehung auf die Portraitmalerei', *Deutsches Kunstblatt*, vol. 6, 1855, pp. 197-200.
Winkler, 1936 = Friedrich Winkler, 'Das Ausstellungsprogramm des Kupferstichkabinetts Berlin', *Berliner Museen. Berichte der Preußischen Kunstsammlungen*, no. 56, Berlin, 1936.
Wirth, 1965 = Irmgard Wirth, *Mit Adolph Menzel in Berlin*, Munich, 1965.
Wirth, 1974 = Irmgard Wirth, *Mit Menzel in Bayern und Österreich*, Munich, 1974.
Wirth, 1990 = Irmgard Wirth, *Berliner Malerei im 19. Jahrhundert: Von der Zeit Friedrichs des Großen bis zum 1. Weltkrieg*, Berlin, 1990.
With, 1975 = Christopher Becker With, *Adolph von Menzel. A Study in the Relationship between Art and Politics in Nineteenth Century Germany*, thesis, University of California, Los Angeles, 1975.
With, 1979 = Christopher Becker With, 'Adolf von Menzel and the German Revolution of 1848', *Zeitschrift für Kunstgeschichte*, vol. 42, 1979, pp. 195-214.
Wolff, 1914 = Hans Wolff (ed.), *Adolph von Menzels Briefe*, Berlin, 1914.

Zangs, 1992 = Christiane Zangs, *Die künstlerische Entwicklung und das Werk Menzels im Spiegel der zeitgenössischen Kritik* (thesis memoir, Aachen, 1987), Aachen/Mainz, 1992.
Zedlitz, 1834 = Leopold Freiherr von Zedlitz (ed.), *Neuestes Conversations-Handbuch für Berlin und Potsdam zum täglichen Gebrauch der einheimischen und Fremden aller Stände*, Berlin, 1834.
Zelger, 1977 = Franz Zelger: *Stiftung Oskar Reinhart, Sammlungskatalog, Band 1, Schweizer Maler des 18 und 19 Jahrhunderts*, Zurich, 1977.
Ziemke, 1972 = Ernst Holzinger (ed.) and Hans-Joachim Ziemke (rev. and corr.), *Die Gemälde des 19. Jahrhunderts. Katalog der Gemälde im Städelschen Kunstinstitut*, 2 vols, Frankfurt-am-Main, 1972.
Zimmermann, 1953 = Hans Zimmermann, *Ein neuerworbener Menzel. Berliner Museum, Berichte aus den ehemaligen preußischen Kunstsammlungen*, Berlin, 1953.
Zweite, 1991 = Armin Zweite, 'Vom "dernier espace" zum "Palazzo Regule". Die letzten Räume des Joseph Beuys', exhib. cat. *Joseph Beuys. Natur – Materie – Form*, Kunstsammlungen Nordrhein-Westfalen, Düsseldorf, 1991.

Exhibition catalogues

Bamberg, 1968 = [Exhibition at Bamberg Staatsbibliothek, July 1968].
Basle, 1932 = *Deutsche und Schweizer Maler des 19. Jahrhunderts aus der Sammlung Oskar Reinhart*, Kunsthalle Basel, 1932.
Berlin, 1836, 1846, 1870, 1876 A, 1877, 1880 A, 1883 = [Academy Exhibition], Royal Academy of Arts, Berlin.
Berlin, 1837 = [Galerie Louis Sachse], Berlin, 1837.
Berlin, 1849 = [Charity exhibition], Academy of Arts, Berlin, 1849.
Berlin, 1855 = [Galerie Louis Sachse], Berlin, 1855.
Berlin, 1857 = [Permanent exhibition of paintings at Louis Sachse gallery], Berlin, 1857.
Berlin, 1861 = *Ausstellung von Oelgemälden, Aquarellen und Handzeichnungen von Professor Adolph Menzel im Lokale des Kunstvereins*, Berlin, November 1861.
Berlin, 1863 = [Menzel's Frederican cycle], Academy of Arts, Berlin, 1863.
Berlin, 1869 = [Galerie Lepke], Berlin, 1869.
Berlin, 1871 = [Association of Berlin Artists], July 1871.
Berlin, 1876 B = [Menzel exhibition], Rudolph Lepke gallery, Berlin, 1876.
Berlin, 1880 = *Ausstellung der Werke von Eduard Meyerheim, Ernst Fries, Friedrich Nerly*, Königliche National-Galerie, Berlin, 1880.
Berlin, 1885 = *Ausstellung von Werken Adolph Menzels in der Kgl. Akademie der Künste zur Feier seines siebzigsten Geburtstages am 8. Dezember 1885*, Berlin, 1885.
Berlin, 1886 = *Jubiläumsausstellung der Kgl. Akademie der Künste im Landesausstellungsgebäude zu Berlin*, May-October 1886.
Berlin, 1891 = *Internationale Kunstausstellung*, Academy of Arts, Berlin, 1891.
Berlin, 1895 A = *Kunst-Ausstellung zur Ehrung der achtzigjährigen Mitglieder Andreas Achenbach, Adolph Menzel, Julius Schrader*, Royal Academy of Arts, Berlin, November 1895.
Berlin, 1895 B = *Ausstellung von Werken Adolph Menzels in der Kgl. National-Galerie*, presented by Lionel von Donop, Berlin, 1895.
Berlin, 1896 A = *Große Berliner Kunstausstellung*, Berlin, 1896.
Berlin, 1896 B = *Ausstellung der neuen Erwerbungen*, Königliche Museen zu Berlin, National-Galerie, December 1896.
Berlin, 1903 A = *Adolph von Menzel*, Artists' Association, Berlin, 1903.
Berlin, 1903 B = *Ausstellung von Werken Adolph von Menzels im Künstlerhause Berlin*, Berlin, 1903.
Berlin, 1905 = *Ausstellung von Werken Adolph von Menzels*, Königliche National-Galerie, Berlin, 1905.
Berlin, 1906 = *Die Deutsche Jahrhundertausstellung*, Königliche National-Galerie, Berlin, 1906.
Berlin, 1910 = *Die Sammlung Eduard L. Behrens zu Hamburg*, Paul Cassirer gallery, Berlin, 1910.
Berlin, n.d. = [Travelling Menzel exhibition], [*c*.1910].
Berlin, 1912 = *Friedrich der Große in der Kunst*, Royal Academy of Arts, Berlin, 1912 (the page numbers given are from the 'big' catalogue, the numbers for the 'little' catalogue are given in brackets).
Berlin, 1926 A = *Ausstellung älterer Berliner Kunst*, Nationalgalerie, Berlin, 1926.
Berlin, 1926 B = *75 Jahre klassische deutsche Malerei*, Berlin, 1926.
Berlin, 1928 = *Adolph von Menzel 1815-1905*, Thannhauser gallery, Berlin, 1928.
Berlin, 1929 = *100 Jahre Berliner Kunst*, Association of Berlin Artists, Berlin, 1929.
Berlin, 1935 = *Adolph von Menzel*, Academy of

Arts, Berlin, 1935.
Berlin, 1950-1 = *Deutsche Malerei des 19. Jahrhunderts*, Schloß Charlottenburg, Berlin, 1950-1.
Berlin, 1955 A = *Adolph Menzel, Zeichnungen*, Nationalgalerie, Berlin [Museumsinsel], 1955.
Berlin, 1955 B = *Adolph v. Menzel*, Gemäldegalerie Dahlem, Berlin, 1955.
Berlin, 1956 = *Deutsche Gemälde des 19. Jahrhunderts aus tschechoslowakischen Museen*, Nationalgalerie, Berlin, 1956.
Berlin, 1960 = *Berlin – Ort der Freiheit für die Kunst*, Nationalgalerie Berlin, exhibition at Recklinghausen, Vienna, Berlin, 1960.
Berlin, 1961 = *Künstlertradition in Berlin-Tiergarten*, Haus am Lützowplatz, Berlin, 1961.
Berlin, 1965 = *Adolph Menzel*, Haus am Tiergarten, Berlin, 1965.
Berlin, 1966 = *Berlin im Bild Berliner Maler. Ölbilder, Pastelle, Aquarelle. 20 Jahre Kunstamt Berlin-Charlottenburg*, Charlottenburg town hall, Berlin, 1966.
Berlin, 1970 = *Berliner Innenräume der Vergangenheit*, Berlin Museum, Berlin, 1970.
Berlin, 1976 = Ursula Riemann-Reyher (ed.), *Moderne Cyclopen. 100 Jahre 'Eisenwalzwerk' von Adolph Menzel*, Nationalgalerie, Berlin, 1976.
Berlin, 1979 = *Max Liebermann in seiner Zeit*, Nationalgalerie, Berlin, exhibition in Berlin and Munich, 1979-80.
Berlin, 1980 A = *Adolph Menzel. Gemälde, Zeichnungen*, Nationalgalerie, East Berlin, 1980.
Berlin, 1980 B = *Adolph von Menzel. Max Liebermann. Eine Berliner Kunstepoche, Ausgewählte Handzeichnungen und Graphiken der Jahre 1848 bis 1926*, Gerda Bassenge gallery, Berlin, 1980.
Berlin, 1981 = *Berlin zwischen 1789 und 1848. Facetten einer Epoche*, Academy of Arts, Berlin, 1981.
Berlin, 1984 = *Adolph Menzel. Zeichnungen, Druckgraphik und illustrierte Bücher. Bestandskatalog der Nationalgalerie*, West Berlin, 1984, exhibition in Berlin and Bonn-Bad Godesberg.
Berlin, 1986 = *Friedrich der Große, Ausstellung des Geheimen Staatsarchivs Preußischer Kulturbesitz anläßlich des 200. Todestages König Friedrich des II. von Preußen*, Berlin, 1986.
Berlin, 1987 A = *Kunst in Berlin. 1648-1987*, Staatliche Museen, Altes Museum, Berlin, 1987.
Berlin, 1987 B = *Stadtbilder. Berlin in der Malerei vom 17. Jahrhundert bis zur Gegenwart*, Berlin Museum, Berlin, 1987.
Berlin, 1990 = *Von Chodowiecki bis Liebermann*, Berlin Museum, Berlin, 1990.
Berlin, 1990 B = *Bismarck – Preußen, Deutschland und Europa*, Deutsches Historisches Museum in the Martin-Gropius-Bau, Berlin, 1990.
Berlin, 1991 = *Orangerie '91*, International Arts Fair at the Martin-Gropius-Bau, Berlin, 1991.
Berlin, 1993 = *Von Caspar David Friedrich bis Ferdinand Hodler. Meisterwerke aus dem Museum Stiftung Oskar Reinhart Winterthur*, Nationalgalerie, Berlin, 1993, exhibition in Los Angeles, 1993-4, New York/London, 1994, Geneva, 1994-5.
Berlin/Vienna, 1873 = *Wiener Weltausstellung, Amtlicher Katalog der Ausstellung des Deutschen Reiches*, Berlin, 1873.
Berne, 1936 = *Deutsche Malerei im 19. Jahrhundert*, Kunsthalle, Berne, 1936.
Berne, 1940 = *Sammlung Oskar Reinhart Winterthur*, Kunstmuseum, Berne, 1940.
Boston, 1909 = *Exhibition of Contemporary German Art*, The Copley Society of Boston, Boston, 1909.
Bremen, 1963 = *Adolph Menzel. Handzeichnungen*, Kunsthalle, Bremen, 1963.
Bremen, 1976 = *Berliner Biedermeier von Blechen bis Menzel*, Kunsthalle, Bremen, 1976.
Brussels, 1878 = *18th Exposition de la Société belge des Aquarellistes*, Brussels, 1878.

Cambridge, 1984 = *Prints and Drawings by Adolph Menzel. A Selection from the Collections of the Museums of West Berlin*, The Fitzwilliam Museum, Cambridge, 1984.
Kassel, 1964 = *700 Jahre Stadt Kassel*, Städtische Kunstsammlung, Kassel, 1964.
Celle, 1949-50 = *Adolph Menzel und seine Zeit. Gemälde der Berliner Nationalgalerie aus der 2. Hälfte des 19. Jahrhunderts*, Schloß Celle, 1949-50.
Cleveland, 1980 = *The Realist Tradition, French Painting and Drawing 1830-1900*, edited by Gabriel P. Weisberg, Cleveland, The Cleveland Museum of Art, 1980.
Cologne, 1922 = *Eröffnungsausstellung der Gemäldegalerie des Kölnischen Kunstvereins*, Kunstverein, Cologne, 1922.
Cologne, 1953-4 = *Begegnungen von Kunstwerken verschiedener Jahrhunderte*, Wallraf-Richartz-Museum, Cologne, 1953-4.
Cologne, 1971 = *Deutsche Malerei des 19. Jahrhunderts*, Kunsthalle, Cologne, exhibition in New Haven, Chicago, Cologne, 1970-1971.
Cologne, 1978 = *Meisterwerke deutscher und russischer Malerei aus sowjetischen Museen*, exhibition in Cologne and Bonn, 1978.
Copenhagen, 1985 = *Adolph von Menzel. Tegninger – akvareller – gouacher. Den Kgl. Kobberstiksamling*, Statens Museum for Kunst, Copenhagen, 1985.

Danzig, 1855 = [Exhibition of the Society of Artists], Danzig, 1855.
Dresden, 1887 = *Große Kunstausstellung*, Dresden, 1887.
Dresden, 1903 A = [Menzel Exhibition in the Emil Richter gallery], Dresden, 1903.
Dresden, 1903 B = [Menzel Exhibition in the Ernst Arnold gallery], Dresden, 1903.
Dresden, 1904 = *Große Kunstausstellung*, Dresden, 1904
Duisburg, 1969 = *Industrie und Technik in der deutschen Malerei von der Romantik bis zur Gegenwart*, Wilhelm-Lehmbruck-Museum, Duisburg, 1969.
Düsseldorf, 1904 = *Internationale Kunstausstellung*, Düsseldorf, 1904.
Düsseldorf, 1967 = *Preußischer Kulturbesitz*, Städtische Kunsthalle, Düsseldorf, 1967.
Düsseldorf, 1979 = *Die Düsseldorfer Malerschule*, Kunstmuseum, Düsseldorf, exhibition in Düsseldorf and Darmstadt, 1979.

Erlangen, 1971 = *Adolph Menzel, Gemälde und Zeichnungen*, Altes Rathaus, Erlangen, 1971.

Frankfurt, 1975 = *Deutsche Malerei im 19. Jahrh. – Eine Ausstellung für Moskau und Leningrad*, Städelsches Kunstinstitut, Frankfurt-am-Main, 1975.
Frankfurt/Paris, 1990 = *Le corps en morceaux*, edited by Anne Pingeot, musée d'Orsay, Paris, 1990.

Gerresheim, 1959 = [Exhibition of the collections of the Düsseldorf Kunstmuseum], Gerresheim, 1959.

Hamburg, 1887 = *Frühjahrsausstellung*, Hamburg, 1887.
Hamburg, 1888 = *Zum Besten der Überschwemmten*, Hamburg, 1888.
Hamburg, 1894 = *Große Kunstausstellung*, Hamburg, 1888.
Hamburg, 1896 = *Menzelausstellung, Veranstaltet vom Kunstverein und der Kunsthalle Hamburg*, Hamburg, 1896.
Hamburg, 1921 = *Jubiläumsausstellung zur Feier des hundertjährigen Bestehens der Galerie Commeter*, Galerie Commeter, Hamburg, 1921.
Hamburg, 1971 = *Ein Geschmack wird untersucht. Die G. C. Schwabe Stiftung*, Hamburger Kunsthalle, Hamburg, 1971.
Hamburg, 1976 = *William Turner und die Landschaft seiner Zeit*, Hamburger Kunsthalle, Hamburg, 1976.
Hamburg, 1978-9 = *Courbet und Deutschland*, Hamburger Kunsthalle, Hamburg, 1978-9.
Hamburg, 1982 = *Menzel – der Beobachter*, Hamburger Kunsthalle, Hamburg, 1982.
Hamburg, 1983-4 = *Luther und die Folgen für die Kunst*, edited by Werner Hofmann, Hamburger Kunsthalle, Hamburg, 1983-4.
Hamburg, 1984 = *Ein Hamburger sammelt in London. Die Freiherr J. H. von Schröder-Stiftung 1910*, Hamburger Kunsthalle, Hamburg, 1984.

Kampen, 1995 = *Deutsche Landschaften und Stadtansichten von Menzel bis Antes*, Pels-Leusden gallery, Berlin and Kampen on Sylt, 1995.
Kiel, 1956 = *Meisterwerke deutscher und österreichischer Malerei 1800-1900*, Kunsthalle zu Kiel, Kiel, 1956.
Kiel, 1981 = *Adolph Menzel. Realist, Historist, Maler des Hofes*, Kunsthalle zu Kiel, exhibition in Kiel, Bremen, Lübeck, Schweinfurt and Augsburg, 1981-2.

Leipzig, 1905 = *Adolph Menzel. Sonderausstellung zum Gedächtnis des Meisters*, Leipziger Kunstverein, Museum der bildenden Künste, Leipzig, 1905.
London, 1903 = [Menzel Exhibition], French Gallery, Pall Mall, London, 1903.
London, 1956 = *Hundred Years of German Painting 1850-1950*, Tate Gallery, London, 1956.
London, 1965 = *Drawings and Watercolours by Adolph Menzel 1815-1905*, edited by Irmgard Wirth, Arts Council Gallery, London, 1965.
London, 1991 = Leslie Parris and Ian Fleming-Williams, *Constable*, Tate Gallery, London, 1991.
Lyons, 1993 = *Ernest Meissonier. Rétrospective*, Paris, 1993.

Marburg, 1946 = *Meisterwerke der europäischen Malerei des 19. und frühen 20. Jahrhunderts*, Jubiläumsbau Marburg, Marburg, 1946.
Milan, 1989 = *Boldini*, Palazzo della

Permanente, Milan, 1989.
Moscow, 1930 = [*German painting from the 17th to the 19th century*], State Museum of Fine Art, Moscow, 1930.
Moscow, 1963 = [*German and Austrian paintings and drawings from the 15th to the 19th century*], State Museum of Fine Art, Moscow, 1963.
Moscow, 1994 = [West European painting from the Sergei Tretiakov collection], State Museum of Fine Art, Moscow, 1994.
Moscow/Leningrad, 1974 = [*German 19th-century Realists*], The Hermitage, Leningrad, Pushkin Museum, Moscow, 1974-5.
Munich, 1883 = *Illustrierter Katalog der internationalen Kunstausstellung im Königlichen Glaspalaste*, Munich, 1883.
Munich, 1891 = [International Exhibition], Munich, 1891.
Munich, 1896 = *Münchener Jahres-Ausstellung von Kunstwerken aller Nationen im Königl. Glaspalaste*, Munich, 1896.
Munich, 1908 = *Münchner Jahresausstellung im Kgl. Glaspalast*, Munich, 1908.
Munich, 1932 = *Adolph von Menzel, Ölgemälde, Gouachen, Aquarelle und Zeichnungen*, with an introduction by G. J. Kern, Caspari gallery, Munich, August/September 1932.
Munich, 1962 = *Berliner Bildnisse aus drei Jahrhunderten*, Städtische Galerie, Munich, 1962.
Munich, 1992 = *Sammlung Graf Raczynski. Malerei der Spätromantik aus dem Nationalmuseum Poznan*, Neue Pinakothek, Munich, 1992, exhibition in Munich, 1992, Berlin, 1992-3, Kiel, 1993.
Münster, 1980 = *Industriebilder aus Westfalen. Gemälde, Aquarelle, Handzeichnungen, Druckgraphik 1800-1960*, Westfälisches Landesmuseum für Kunst und Kulturgeschichte, Münster, 1979-80.
Münster, 1987 = *Einblicke und Anblicke des 19. Jahrhunderts*, Westfälisches Landesmuseum, Münster, 1987.

New York, 1981 = *German masters of the 19th century. Paintings and Drawings from the Federal Republic of Germany*, The Metropolitan Museum of Art, New York, exhibition in New York and Ontario, 1981.
New York, 1988 = *The Romantic Spirit. German Drawings, 1780-1850 from the Nationalgalerie (Staatliche Museen, Berlin) and the Kupferstichkabinett (Staatliche Kunstsammlungen, Dresden)*, The Pierpont Morgan Library, New York, 1988.
New York, 1990 = *Adolph Menzel 1815–1905. Master Drawings from East Berlin*, Art Services International, Alexandria, Virginia, exhibition in New York, Houston, Pittsburgh, Cambridge, 1990-1.
Nuremberg, 1990 = *800 Jahre Deutscher Orden, Ausstellung des Germanischen Nationalmuseums Nürnberg in Zusammenarbeit mit der Internationalen Historischen Kommission zur Erforschung des Deutschen Ordens*, Nuremberg, 1990.

Paris, 1878 = Universal Exhibition, Paris, 1878.
Paris, 1882 = *Exposition internationale de peinture*, galerie Georges Petit, Paris.
Paris, 1885 = *Exposition des oeuvres d'Adolphe Menzel*, Pavillon de la Ville de Paris, Paris, 1885.
Paris, 1931 = [Boldini Exhibition], galerie Jean Charpentier, Paris, 1931.
Paris, 1961 = *Panorama berlinois*, galerie Creuze, Paris, 1961.
Paris, 1976-7 = *La Peinture allemande à l'époque du romantisme*, Orangerie des Tuileries, Paris, 1976-7.
Paris, 1984-5 = *Symboles et Réalités. La peinture allemande 1848–1905*, musée du Petit Palais, Paris, 1984-5.
Paris, 1994 = *Voltaire et l'Europe*, Bibliothèque Nationale de France and Monnaie de Paris, Paris, 1994.
Prague, 1955 = [*Exhibition of German masters of the 19th and 20th centuries*], National Gallery, Prague, 1955.

Sofia, 1918 = [*4th Exhibition by the Society for the promotion of German art abroad*], Sofia, 1918.

Tyrol/Innsbruck, 1992 = *Malerische Reise durch Tirol. Von der Romantik bis zum Impressionismus*, Südtiroler Landesmuseum, exhibition in Tyrol and Innsbruck, 1992.

Venice, 1932 = *XVIII. Esposizione Biennale Internazionale d'Arte di Venezia*, Venice, 1932.
Vienna, 1873 = *Officieller Kunst-Catalog der Weltausstellung in Wien*, Vienna, 1873.
Vienna, 1876-7 = *Richard-Wagner-Ausstellung*, österreichischer Kunstverein, Vienna, 1876-7.
Vienna, 1882 = *Illustrierter Katalog der ersten Internationalen Kunst-Ausstellung im Künstlerhause*, Vienna, 1882.
Vienna, 1886= [Exhibition by the Association of Austrian Artists], Vienna, March 1886.
Vienna, 1888 = *Internationale Jubiläumsausstellung im Künstlerhaus*, Vienna, 1888.
Vienna, 1896 = *A. Menzel – Ausstellung der Genossenschaft der bildenden Künstler Wiens*, Künstlerhaus, Vienna, 1896.
Vienna, 1940 = *XXIX. Ausstellung im Oberen Belvedere*, Vienna, 1940.
Vienna, 1951 = *Europäische Malerei im XIX. Jahrhundert*, Hofburg, Vienna, 1951.
Vienna, 1985 = *Adolph von Menzel 1815-1905*, Staatliche Graphische Sammlung Albertina, Vienna, 1985.
Vienna, 1989 = *Wunderblock*, Messepalast, Reithalle in den ehemaligen Hofstallungen, Vienna, 1989.
Vienna, 1990 = *Von Caspar David Friedrich bis Adolph Menzel. Aquarelle und Zeichnungen der Romantik, Aus der Nationalgalerie, Berlin/DDR*, Kunstforum Länderbank, Vienna, 1990.
Vienna, 1992 = *Lovis Corinth*, edited by Klaus Albrecht Schröder, Kunstforum der Bank Austria, Vienna, 1992.

Warsaw, 1991 = *Mistrzowie rysunku niemieckiego od konca XVIII do poczatku XX wieku*, Ze zbiorów Muzeum Narodowego w Warszawie, Warsaw, 1991.
Washington, 1982 = *Manet and Modern Paris*, National Gallery of Art, Washington D.C., 1982.
Washington, San Francisco, 1986 = *The New Painting, Impressionism 1874-1886*, Washington/San Francisco, 1986.
Wiesbaden, 1947 = *Deutsche Malerei des 19. Jahrhunderts*, Landesmuseum, Wiesbaden, 1947.
Wiesbaden, 1952 = *Ein Jahrtausend deutscher Kunst*, Landesmuseum, Wiesbaden, 1952.
Winterthur, 1933 = *Deutsche und Schweizer Maler des XIX. Jahrhunderts aus der Sammlung Oskar Reinhart*, Kunstmuseum, Winterthur, 1933.
Winterthur, 1942 = *Der unbekannte Winterthurer Privatbesitz*, Kunsthaus, Winterthur, 1942.
Winterthur, 1947 = *Große Maler des 19. Jahrhunderts aus den Münchner Museen*, Kunstmuseum, Winterthur, 1947.
Winterthur, 1955 = *Die Privatsammlung Oskar Reinhart*, Kunstmuseum, Winterthur, 1955.
Wolfsburg, 1956 = *Deutsche Malerei. Ausgewählte Meister seit Caspar David Friedrich*, Oberschule Wolfsburg, Wolfsburg, 1956.
Würzburg, 1966 = *Eine Ausstellung des Kulturwerks Schlesien (Würzburg) und der Künstlergilde (Esslingen). Ausgesuchte Werke des Zeichners und Grafikers Adolph Menzel*, Haus zum Falken, Würzburg, 1966.

Zurich, 1917 = *Ausstellung deutscher Malerei. XIX. und XX. Jahrhundert*, Kunsthaus, Zurich, 1917.
Zurich, 1959 = *Berliner Panorama*, Kunsthaus, Zurich, 1959.

Index of Names

Names mentioned in the biography have not been included in the index.

Index of Place Names

Photographic Acknowledgments

Bamberg, Ingeborg Limmer: cat. 1
Berlin, Bildarchiv Preussischer Kulturbesitz: p. 59, 70, 142
Berlin, Landesbildstelle: p. 47
Berlin, Staatliche Museen: p. 17, 37, 43, 97a, 101,103, 104a, 104b, 105, 109, 112, 119, 131, 207, 294b, 376; cat. 23, 90, 160, 173
Berlin, Staatsbibliothek Preussischer Kulturbesitz: p. 21a, 22b, 24, 28, 48
Berlin, Stadtmuseum: p. 20a, 20b, 20c, 21b, 22a, 23, 25, 27, 29, 30, 34, 35a, 35b, 36, 53, 56, 60, 66, 67, 196, 200a, 252c, 374; cat. 31, 101, 124
Berlin, Stiftung Archiv der Akademie der Künste: p. 45, 62a, 62b
Berlin, Ullstein Bildarchiv: p. 2, 19, 40, 44, 46, 63
Berlin, Jörg P. Anders: p. 15, 26, 31, 32, 33, 38-9, 41, 43, 45, 50, 52, 54a, 55, 71, 79a, 79b, 80b, 83, 84b, 85, 88b, 89a, 92, 93, 94a, 94b, 95, 102a, 102b, 106a-f, 107a-f, 110, 115, 127a, 127b, 127c, 128a, 128b, 129, 132, 133, 135, 136, 139, 140, 145, 146, 151, 162, 167, 175, 181b, 190b, 192a, 192b, 194a, 194b, 200b, 241, 242, 248, 252a, 252b, 257, 270, 294a, 308, 313, 316a, 316b, 320, 322, 328, 329, 334, 337, 339a, 345a, 347, 358, 391a, 391b, 394, 412, 416, 420, 429a, 429b, 436, 446, 454; cat. 4-9, 10, 13-17, 25, 26, 28, 30, 55, 58, 59, 45, 46, 54-6, 59, 61, 62, 65-9, 80, 85, 86-8, 94, 96-9, 105, 105-14, 117, 119-21, 129-33, 135, 138-44, 146-51, 153-9, 161, 164, 169-72, 177, 181, 185, 186, 189-200, 204, 205, 207, 209, 212, 214-18
Berlin, Hans-Joachim Bartsch: cat. 50, 84
Berlin, Klaus Göken: cat. 48
Berlin, Dietmar Katz: p. 42, 51, 73, 75a, 156, 184a, 345b
Berlin, Bernd Kuhnert: p. 12; cat. 2, 3, 11, 12, 18, 20, 22, 27, 33, 34, 43, 44, 49, 51, 57, 40, 71, 75, 76, 79, 82, 85, 93, 95, 115, 116, 134, 167, 213
Berlin, Roman März: p. 86, 141, 184b
Berlin, Anne Schmedding: p. 69a, 69b, 72a, 72b
Budapest, Szépmüvészeti Múzeum: cat. 125

Cambridge (Mass.), Fogg Art Museum, Harvard University: p. 390
Chicago, The Art Institute of Chicago, Worcester Fund: p. 137
Cologne, archives of DuMont publishers: p. 152
Cologne, Wallraf-Richartz-Museum: cat. 21

Dresden, Deutsche Fotothek: p. 87b; cat. 123, 179
Düsseldorf, Kunstmuseum Düsseldorf im Ehrenhof: p. 84a, 177, 190a; cat. 127

Essen, Color Studio 27: cat. 162
Essen, Museum Folkwang: cat. 42, 163
Euerbach, Georg Schäfer collection: p. 155, 331

Frankfurt-am-Main, Peter Fichter: cat. 63
Frankfurt-am-Main, Ursula Edelmann: cat. 201

Hamburg, Elke Walford / Hamburger Kunsthalle: p. 77, 97b, 143, 144; cat. 47, 78, 100, 104, 122, 137, 175, 187, 202, 206, 208
Hanover, Niedersächsisches Landesmuseum: p. 291

Karlsruhe, Staatliche Kunsthalle: cat. 19

Leipzig, Museum der bildenden Künste: cat. 37, 152
Liberec, Oblastní Gallery: cat. 145
Locarno, Foto Video Garbani SA: cat. 60
London, Courtesy of Her Majesty The Queen: p. 303
London, The Trustees of the National Gallery: p. 88a

Mainz, Landesmuseum Mainz: cat. 128
Manchester, City Art Gallery: p. 87a, 375
Moscow, Pushkin State Museum of Fine Art: cat. 136, 180
Munich, Artothek: cat. 36, 72, 89, 102, 174

Nuremberg, MAN-Archiv: p. 99

Oslo, Universitetsbiblioteket: p. 75b

Pal, Heinrich Merz: cat. 176, 183, 188
Paris, Bibliothèque nationale: p. 14a, 14b
Paris, Réunion des musées nationaux: p. 114, 118, 123, 339b; cat. 168
Pittsburgh, The Carnegie Museum of Art: cat. 91
Potsdam, Stiftung Preussische Schlösser und Gärten Berlin-Brandenburg: p. 122, 232; cat. 53
Poznan, Muzeum Narodowe: cat. 64

Regensburg, Museum Ostdeutsche Galerie Regensburg: cat. 92
Rome, Dr Peter Griebert: cat. 77

San Francisco, The Fine Arts Museum: cat. 126
Stanford, Stanford University Museum of Art: p. 181a
Stockholm, Nationalmuseum: p. 54b, 225

Vienna, Graphische Sammlung Albertina: cat. 118
Vienna, österreichische Galerie: cat. 73

Warsaw, Muzeum Narodowe w Warszawie: p. 134, 404; cat. 184
Winterthur, Museum Stiftung Oskar Reinhart: cat. 24, 29, 32

Zurich, Kunsthaus Zürich: cat. 58
Zurich, Arturo Cuéllar: cat. 40, 178, 182, 210
Zurich, Dr Peter Nathan: cat. 41, 74, 211